PENGUIN HANDBOOKS

The Penguin Guide to Compact Discs and Cassettes Yearbook 1991/2

EDWARD GREENFIELD has been Record Critic of the *Guardian* since 1954, and from 1964 Music Critic too. At the end of 1960 he joined the reviewing panel of *Gramophone*, specializing in operatic and orchestral issues. He is a frequent broadcaster on music and records for the BBC and has a regular record programme on the BBC World Service. In 1958 he published a monograph on the operas of Puccini. More recently he has written studies on the recorded work of Dame Joan Sutherland and André Previn. He has been a regular juror on International Record awards and has appeared with such artists as Elisabeth Schwarzkopf and Joan Sutherland in public interviews.

ROBERT LAYTON studied at Oxford with Edmund Rubbra for composition and with Egon Wellesz for the history of music. He spent two years in Sweden at the universities of Uppsala and Stockholm. He joined the BBC Music Division in 1959 and has been responsible for such programmes as *Interpretations on Record*. He has contributed 'A Quarterly Retrospect' to *Gramophone* for a number of years and he has written books on Berwald and Sibelius and has specialized in Scandinavian music. His recent publications include a monograph on the Dvořák symphonies and concertos for the BBC Music Guides, of which he is General Editor, and the first two volumes of his translation of Erik Tawastsjerna's definitive study of Sibelius. In 1987 he was awarded the Sibelius Medal and in the following year was made a Knight of the Order of the White Rose of Finland for his services to Finnish music.

IVAN MARCH is a former professional musician and a regular contributor to *Gramophone*. He studied at Trinity College of Music, London, and at the Royal Manchester College. After service in the RAF Central Band, he played the horn professionally for the BBC and travelled with the Carl Rosa and D'Oyly Carte opera companies. Now director of the Long Playing Record Library, the largest commercial lending library for classical music on compact discs in the British Isles, he is a well-known lecturer, journalist and personality in the world of recorded music.

The Penguin Guide to Compact Discs and Cassettes

Yearbook 1991/2

Edward Greenfield, Robert Layton and Ivan March

Edited by Ivan March

Penguin Books

PENGUIN BOOKS

Published by the Penguin Group
27 Wrights Lane, London W8 5TZ, England
Penguin Books USA Inc., 375 Hudson Street, New York, New York 10014, USA
Penguin Books Australia Ltd, Ringwood, Victoria, Australia
Penguin Books Canada Ltd, 10 Alcorn Avenue, Toronto, Ontario, Canada M4V 3B2
Penguin Books (NZ) Ltd, 182–190 Wairau Road, Auckland 10, New Zealand

Penguin Books Ltd, Registered Offices: Harmondsworth, Middlesex, England

First published 1991
10 9 8 7 6 5 4 3 2 1

Made and printed in Great Britain by Clays Ltd, St Ives plc

Typeset in 8 on 9½ pt Times by Barbers Ltd, Wrotham, Kent

Contents

Preface

The present extraordinary flood of new recordings is unique in the history of the gramophone; it has continued unabated since our main 1990 volume went to print. It is as if the unrestrained response of the record industry to the Mozart Bicentenary has not only unleashed a deluge of Mozartiana but has also stimulated a renewed awareness of the whole repertoire.

Our record year has also brought celebrations of the music of Frank Martin, Martinů and Prokofiev, all born 100 years ago. Of the three, Martinů's representation in the catalogue has been all but doubled by the recordings listed in our current survey. Martin has been remembered rather less lavishly, but we have nevertheless discovered several recordings of major interest. The Prokofiev discography has also been renewed, especially by the Chandos label; even so, one might have expected a more generous response to his music outside the major ballets, concertos and symphonies. Vivaldi died 250 years ago, and this has produced a modest Vivaldi Edition from Philips. But Stravinsky left us only twenty years back – yet Sony have paid him a handsome tribute in bringing out an impressive re-presentation of his own recorded performances of all his important music, skilfully transferred on to 22 compact discs, often with marked improvement in the sound.

Not surprisingly, after the huge success of the film *Amadeus*, it is Mozart who has dominated the output of the record manufacturers, with Philips in particular determined to offer us everything he ever wrote. This company's Complete Mozart Edition of 26 fat volumes of CDs will eventually stretch along a whole wall; at the time of our going to print, about half of it has arrived, and the rest is promised before the year's end. This achievement is remarkable, but other companies, climbing aboard the Mozartian bandwagon, have also produced some very impressive records, not least EMI, who have found in their vaults treasurable recordings by artists of the calibre of Beecham and Edwin Fischer. Even the relatively new super-bargain label, Naxos – drawing on an apparently inexhaustible well of talent from Eastern Europe – has presented us with a first-class, digital, five-CD set of fifteen of the last and greatest Mozart symphonies. These splendid performances and recordings, by the Capella Istropolitana directed by Barry Wordsworth, compare favourably with the finest available, yet are offered at an unbelievably low cost.

The multitude of reissues from all labels is now almost matching in volume and scope the output of new recordings. These reissues all involve the process described as digital remastering, which is, alas, not always completely beneficial. For the most part there is an increase in vividness, clarity and presence, and quite often the improvement can be seemingly miraculous. Yet on occasion the transferring process adds a sharpness of focus to the upper range of the sound which is not wholly natural. String tone becomes disturbingly acidic, natural ambience is starved and the bass response dried out, even while it becomes firmer. This continues to trouble us, as we know it does our readers, and it can apply particularly to historical recordings, which sometimes sounded sweeter and fuller in their original, 78-r.p.m. format.

However, there are many honourable exceptions, when obviously much care has been taken with the remastering, and this gives much hope for the future. One thinks of the piano records of Dinu Lipatti, the best of which have remarkable realism and beauty on CD, and of the mono set of the complete Beethoven *String Quartets* (also from EMI) played with such conviction by the Hungarian Quartet. From Decca have come more recent analogue recordings, which have changed media very successfully, notably Bach's organ music, brilliantly registered by Peter Hurford, and the amazing achievement of the complete Haydn symphonies. Played with consistent freshness by the Philharmonia Hungarica under Antal Dorati, the CDs have sound-quality to match their musical excellence.

DG have had considerable success in transferring their earlier orchestral recordings, made in the Berlin Jesus-Christus Kirche (although even here there has been some loss in the bass response), while Sony have brought a distinct improvement to the best of the famous Szell sessions of the 1960s in Severance Hall in Cleveland. Most striking of all are the reissues on the Philips label, deriving from recordings which were always naturally balanced and which are now given greater clarity and immediacy on CD, with little or no loss of ambient warmth, as the Complete Mozart Edition readily demonstrates.

Another serious complaint concerns the non-provision of accompanying notes about the music by the major companies, on bargain labels. Naxos have shown that adequate back-up documentation can be provided economically, and their CDs are least expensive of all! Yet the Polygram group (Decca, DG and Philips) and BMG/RCA continue a disgraceful practice, which began on cassettes, of offering just the musical titles plus limited performance details, and no information about the music whatsoever.

The cries of anguish from loyal readers, when in our main volume we no longer provided information about cassettes, shows that this medium of reproduction still has many adherents, particularly for use in the car. So we now make amends by restoring cassette catalogue numbers for all new and reissued recordings, and adding them to our suggested 'Best Buys' drawn from our main volume. We have also restored reviews of the famous DG 'Walkman' series, the market leader in double-length classical bargain tapes, which are technically impressive and usually offer outstanding value for money. They are now renamed 'Compact Classics', as DG have relinquished the use of the Sony 'Walkman' trademark. In relaunching the series under its new logo, CD equivalents are also being provided. As the (approximately) ninety minutes of music included on a double-length tape exceeds the playing time possible on a single CD, DG's solution has been to provide a CD duo (ingeniously packaged in an adapted single- CD jewel case), priced at about £10, with an increase in the playing time to about two hours. This is not as generous as it might have been, and we must also register slight disappointment that – with a few obvious exceptions – the additional music is not especially interesting either. Apart from the appeal of the clearer remastered sound on disc, the tape (still derived from the original analogue masters, but offered at rather less than half the cost of the pair of CDs) remains the better value.

We have also included the cream of EMI's 'Miles of Music' cassettes, recently reissued on chrome stock. These are often very attractively compiled for their purpose of background entertainment on the motorway, and the performances are distinguished. They reproduce very well in the car but, used on wide-ranging domestic equipment, the ear often notices an imbalance in the treble response, which is very mellow and somewhat restricted, by current cassette standards.

Turning back to CDs, there is also cause for celebration with the reappearance of the Mercury label, now owned by Philips but reasserting its distinct individuality under the auspices of an amazing lady called Wilma Cozart Fine. During the 1950s and early 1960s this small independent label made an astonishing series of records, many of them first recordings and including a high proportion of twentieth-century masterpieces. These LPs, using fine orchestras resident in Chicago, Detroit, Minneapolis, Rochester, London and even Moscow, and carrying the ambient hallmarks of their recording venues, set standards of clarity and realism which caused the Music Critic of the *New York Times*, Howard Taubman, to coin the phrase, 'like being in the living presence of the orchestra'. The recordings were made by a remarkably gifted team comprising C. Robert Fine (engineer), David Hall and, later, Wilma Cozart Fine (producers) and Harold Lawrence (editor). Wilma came to be a kind of Diaghilevian catalyst for the whole operation, and it is she who came out of retirement to supervise the remastering of these remarkable recordings for CD with the dedicated care of a perfectionist. The complete Mercury/Dorati/LSO version of Stravinsky's *Firebird ballet* remains to this day one of the clearest, most transparent orchestral recordings ever made: one can sit in front of the loudspeakers and 'place' almost every orchestral soloist in the overall spectrum, believably balanced within a natural concert-hall illusion.

Clinging to our CD players and bobbing about on the turbulent deluge of CDs – new and reissued – that have flooded in upon us, at times we have felt close to being overwhelmed. By a continuing process of selectivity, we believe we have managed to include in the present *Yearbook* virtually everything of prime importance, and much on the edge of the repertoire that is stimulating. To those who complain about specific omissions, we can only quote Brahms's famous retort, when a critic drew his attention to the resemblance of the big tune in the finale of his *First Symphony* to the main theme of the finale of Beethoven's *Ninth*: 'Anyone can see that!'

But there is always a next time, and our plans to cope with the sheer volume of material provide for the publication of two separate volumes in 1992. The first, scheduled for the spring, will be *The Penguin Guide to Bargain CDs*, to be followed in the autumn by a *Penguin Guide* to CD excellence, dealing primarily with premium-priced repertoire but including also the cream of the budget issues, where they compete, quite irrespective of their cost.

Edward Greenfield, Robert Layton, Ivan March

August 1991

Introduction

The object of *The Penguin Guide to Compact Discs and Cassettes Yearbook* is to give the serious collector a comprehensive survey of the finest recordings of permanent music, primarily on compact discs, but also on cassettes. The present publication covers all the important records and tapes issued since our main volume went into print. It is best used in conjunction with that 1990 complete survey. However, it can also be used independently. We have included 'best buy' recommendations for virtually all the major repertoire works, taking into account previous issues as well as the latest arrivals. As most CDs are issued almost simultaneously on both sides of the Atlantic and use identical international catalogue numbers, this *Yearbook* should be found to be equally useful in Great Britain and the USA. The internationalization of repertoire and numbers is increasingly applying to cassettes and CDs (though, notably in regard to cassettes, EMI/Angel remains an exception to this practice). The major European labels are imported in their original formats.

The sheer number available of records of artistic merit causes considerable problems in any assessment of overall and individual excellence. While in the case of a single popular repertoire work it might be ideal for the discussion to be conducted by a single reviewer, it has not always been possible for one person to have access to every version, and division of reviewing responsibility inevitably leads to some clashes of opinion. Also there are certain works and certain recorded performances towards which one or another of our team has a special affinity. Such a personal identification can often carry with it a special perception too. We feel that it is a strength of our basic style to let such conveyed pleasure or admiration for the merits of an individual recording come over directly to the reader, even if this produces a certain ambivalence in the matter of choice between competing recordings. Where disagreement is profound (and this has rarely happened), then readers will find an indication of this difference in the text.

We have considered and rejected the use of initials against individual reviews, since this is essentially a team project. The occasions for disagreement generally concern matters of aesthetics, for instance in the manner of recording balance, where a contrived effect may trouble some ears more than others, or in the matter of style, where the difference between robustness and refinement of approach produces controversy, rather than any question of artistic integrity.

EVALUATION

Most recordings issued today by the major companies, whether on compact disc or cassette, are of a high technical standard and offer performances of a quality at least as high as is heard in the average concert hall. In adopting a starring system for the evaluation of records, we have decided to make use of from one to three stars. Brackets round one or more of the stars indicate some reservations about its inclusion and readers are advised to refer to the text. Brackets round all the stars usually indicate a basic qualification: for instance, a mono recording of a performance of artistic interest, where considerable allowances have to be made for the sound quality, even though the recording may have been digitally remastered.

Our evaluation system may be summarized as follows:

*** An outstanding performance and recording in every way.
** A good performance and recording of today's normal high standard.
* A fair performance, reasonably well or well recorded.

Our evaluation is normally applied to the record as a whole, unless there are two main works, or groups of works, and by different composers. In this case each is dealt with separately in its appropriate place. In the case of a collection of shorter works, we feel that there is little point in giving a separate starring to each item, even if their merits are uneven, since the record has to be purchased as a complete programme.

ROSETTES

To a very few records and cassettes we have awarded a rosette: ❁.

Unlike our general evaluation, in which we have tried to be consistent, a rosette is a quite arbitrary compliment by a member of the reviewing team to a recorded performance which, he finds, shows special illumination, magic, or a spiritual quality that places it in a very special class. The choice is essentially a personal one (although often it represents a shared view), and in some cases it is applied to an issue where certain reservations must also be mentioned in the text of the review. The rosette symbol is placed immediately before the usual evaluation and the record number. It is quite small – we do not mean to imply an 'Academy Award' but a personal token of appreciation for something uniquely valuable. We hope that, once the reader has discovered and perhaps acquired a 'rosette' CD or tape, its special qualities will soon become apparent.

DIGITAL RECORDINGS

All new compact discs are recorded digitally, but an increasing number of digitally remastered, reissued analogue recordings are now appearing, and we think it important to include a clear indication of the difference:

Dig. This indicates that the master recording was digitally encoded.

BARGAIN AND SUPER-BARGAIN ISSUES

Since the publication of our last volume we have seen a continuing expansion of the mid- and bargain-price labels from all the major companies. These are usually standard-repertoire works in excellent analogue recordings, digitally remastered. Often these reissue CDs are generous in playing time, increasing their value to the collector. Certain labels, notably Naxos, are now also offering even cheaper classical CDs at super-bargain price, usually featuring performances by artists whose names are not internationally familiar. Most of these recordings dervive from Eastern Europe, where recording costs are currently much lower than in the West. Many of them are digitally encoded and some offer outstanding value, both technically and musically. Thus the collector has plenty of scope in deciding how much to pay for a recorded performance, with a CD range from about £4.50 up to three times that amount and more.

Our listing of each recording first indicates if it is not in fact in the premium-price category, as follows:

(M) Medium-priced label, with the CD costing between £6 and £9.

(B) Bargain-priced label, with the CD costing £5–£6.

(BB) Super-bargain label, with the CD costing under £5.

It is possible that, in the current inflationary times, prices may rise during the lifetime of this volume so that the above price ranges become out of date, but the major manufacturers generally maintain the price ratios between labels when an overall increase is made.

LAYOUT OF TEXT

We have aimed to make our style as simple as possible, even though the catalogue numbers of recordings are no longer as straightforward as they once were. So, immediately after the evaluation and before the catalogue number, the record make is given, usually in abbreviated form (a key to the abbreviations is provided on pages xvi–xvii). In the case of a set of two or more CDs, the number of units involved is given in brackets after the catalogue number.

CASSETTES

Where a cassette is available, its catalogue number follows that for the CD, but in *italics*.

AMERICAN CATALOGUE NUMBERS

The numbers which follow in square brackets are US catalogue numbers, while the abbreviation [id.] indicates that the American number is identical to the European, which is increasingly the case.

There are certain small differences to be remembered by American readers. For instance, a CBS number could have a completely different catalogue number on either side of the Atlantic, or use the same digits with different alphabetical prefixes. Both will be clearly indicated. EMI/Angel use extra digits for their British compact discs; thus the US number CDC 47001 becomes CDC7 47001-2 in Britain (the -2 is the European indication that this is a compact disc). We have taken care to check catalogue information as far as is possible, but as all the editorial work has been done in England there is always the possibility of error; American readers are therefore invited, when ordering records locally, to take the precaution of giving their dealer the fullest information about the music and recordings they want.

The indications (M), (B) and (BB) immediately before the starring of a disc refer only to the British record, as pricing systems are not always identical on both sides of the Atlantic.

Where no American catalogue number is given, this does not necessarily mean that a record is not available in the USA; the transatlantic issue may not have been made at the time of the publication of this *Guide*. Readers are advised to check the current *Schwann* catalogue and to consult their local record store.

ABBREVIATIONS

To save space we have adopted a number of standard abbreviations in listing orchestras and performing groups (a list is provided below), and the titles of works are often shortened, especially where they are listed several times. Artists' forenames are sometimes omitted if they are not absolutely necessary for identification purposes. Also we have not usually listed the contents of operatic highlights and collections; these can be found in *The Classical Catalogue*, published by *Gramophone* magazine (177–179, Kenton Road, Kenton, Harrow, Middlesex, England, HA3 0HA).

We have followed common practice in the use of the original language for titles where it seems sensible. In most cases, English is used for orchestral and instrumental music and the original language for vocal music and opera. There are exceptions, however; for instance, the Johann Strauss discography uses the German language in the interests of consistency.

ORDER OF MUSIC

The order of music under each composer's name broadly follows that adopted by *The Classical Catalogue*: orchestral music, including concertos and symphonies; chamber music; solo instrumental music (in some cases with keyboard and organ music separated); vocal and choral music; opera; vocal collections; miscellaneous collections.

The Classical Catalogue now usually includes stage works alongside opera; in the main we have not followed this practice, preferring to list, say, ballet music and incidental music (where no vocal items are involved) in the general orchestral group. Within each group our listing follows an alphabetical sequence, and couplings within a single composer's output are *usually* discussed together instead of separately with cross-references. Occasionally and inevitably because of this alphabetical approach, different recordings of a given work can become separated when a record is listed and discussed under the first work of its alphabetical sequence. The editor feels that alphabetical consistency is essential if the reader is to learn to find his or her way about.

CONCERTS AND RECITALS

Most collections of music intended to be regarded as concerts or recitals involve many composers, and it is quite impractical to deal with them within the alphabetical composer index. They are grouped separately, at the end of the book, in three sections. In each section, recordings are usually arranged in alphabetical order of the performers' names: concerts of orchestral and concertante music under the name of the orchestra, ensemble or, if more important, conductor or soloist; instrumental recitals under the name of the instrumentalist; operatic and vocal recitals under the principal singer or vocal group, as seems appropriate.

In certain cases where the compilation features many different performers, it is listed alphabetically under its collective title, or the key word in that title (thus *Favourite operatic duets* is listed under 'Operatic duets'). Sometimes, for complicated collections, and especially compilations of favourite operatic arias, only brief details of contents and performers are given; fuller information can usually be found in *The Classical Catalogue*.

CATALOGUE NUMBERS

Enormous care has gone into the checking of CD catalogue numbers and contents to ensure that all details are correct, but the editor and publishers cannot be held responsible for any mistakes that may have crept in despite all our zealous checking. When ordering CDs, readers are urged to provide their record-dealer with full details of the music and performers, as well as the catalogue number.

DELETIONS

Compact discs are now steadily succumbing to the deletions axe, and more are likely to disappear during the lifetime of this book. Moreover, cassettes are sometimes withdrawn before their CD equivalents are deleted. Sometimes copies may still be found in specialist shops, and there remains the compensatory fact that most really important and desirable recordings are eventually reissued, usually costing less!

COVERAGE

As the output of major and minor labels continues to expand, it will obviously be impossible for us to mention *every* CD that is available, within the covers of a single book; this is recognized as a practical limitation if we are to update our survey regularly. We have to be carefully selective in choosing the discs to be included (although on rare occasions a recording has been omitted simply because a review copy was not available); anything which eludes us can always be included next time. However, we do welcome suggestions from readers about such omissions if they seem to be of special interest, and particularly if they are inexpensive. But borderline music on specialist labels that are not readily and reliably obtainable on both sides of the Atlantic cannot be given any kind of priority.

ACKNOWLEDGEMENTS

Our thanks are, as ever, due to Roger Wells, our Copy Editor, who has worked closely alongside us throughout the preparation of this book. He even burned the midnight oil alongside the Editor in the final stages, when everything had to be brought together to make a balanced survey. Barbara Menard, too, contributed to the titling, not always an easy task when the record manufacturers themselves do not always seem to be sure what music they are offering. Once again, Kathleen March zealously checked the proofs for errors and reminded us when the text proved ambiguous or plain contradictory, while Winifred Greenwood scrupulously checked all possible sources to try and ensure that there were no mistakes among the catalogue numbers and no omissions of cassette references. Finally, our grateful thanks go to all those readers who wrote to us, pointing out factual errors and reminding us about recordings which escaped our notice at the time of publication of our main volume. The great majority of these are now included.

An International Mail-Order Source for Recordings

Readers are urged to support a local dealer if he is prepared and able to give a proper service, and to remember that obtaining many CDs and tapes involves perseverance. If, however, difficulty is experienced locally, we suggest the following mail-order alternative, which operates world-wide:

Squires Gate Music Centre
Squires Gate Station Approach
Blackpool
Lancashire FY8 2SP
England

This organization (which is operated under the direction of the Editor of *The Penguin Guide to Compact Discs and Cassettes Yearbook*) patiently extends compact disc orders until they finally come to hand. A full guarantee of safe delivery is made on any order undertaken. Please write for further details, enclosing a stamped and self-addressed envelope if within the UK.

American readers seeking a domestic mail-order source may write to the following address where a comparable supply service is in operation (for both American and imported European labels). Please write for further details (enclosing a stamped, self-addressed envelope if within the USA) or send your order to:

PG Dept
Serenade Records
1713 G St, N.W.
Washington DC 20006
USA

Abbreviations

Ac.	Academy, Academic
AAM	Academy of Ancient Music
Amb. S.	Ambrosian Singers
Ang.	Angel
arr.	arranged
ASMF	Academy of St Martin-in-the-Fields
ASV	Academy Sound and Vision
Bar.	Baroque
Bav.	Bavarian
BPO	Berlin Philharmonic Orchestra
Cal.	Calliope
Cap.	Caprice
CBSO	City of Birmingham Symphony Orchestra
CfP	Classics for Pleasure
Ch.	Choir; Chorale; Chorus
Chan.	Chandos
CO	Chamber Orchestra
COE	Chamber Orchestra of Europe
Col. Mus. Ant.	Musica Antiqua, Cologne
Coll.	Collegium
Coll. Aur.	Collegium Aureum
Coll. Mus.	Collegium Musicum
Concg. O	Royal Concertgebouw Orchestra of Amsterdam
cond.	conductor, conducted
Cons.	Consort
CRD	Continental Record Distributors
DG	Deutsche Grammophon
Dig.	digital recording
E.	England, English
ECO	English Chamber Orchestra
EMI	Electrical and Mechanical Industries
Ens.	Ensemble
Fr.	French
GO	Gewandhaus Orchestra
HM	Harmonia Mundi France
HM/BMG	Deutsche Harmonia Mundi
Hung.	Hungaroton
Hyp.	Hyperion
L.	London
LAPO	Los Angeles Philharmonic Orchestra
LCO	London Chamber Orchestra

LMP	London Mozart Players
LOP	Lamoureux Orchestra of Paris
LPO	London Philharmonic Orchestra
LSO	London Symphony Orchestra
Mer.	Meridian
Met.	Metropolitan
MoC	Ministry of Culture
movt	movement
N.	North, Northern
nar.	narrated
Nat.	National
NY	New York
O	Orchestra, Orchestre
O-L	Oiseau-Lyre
Op.	Opera (in performance listings); opus (in music titles)
orch.	orchestrated
ORTF	L'Orchestre de la radio et télévision française
Ph.	Philips
Phd.	Philadelphia
Philh.	Philharmonia
PO	Philharmonic Orchestra
Qt	Quartet
R.	Radio
ROHCG	Royal Opera House, Covent Garden
RPO	Royal Philharmonic Orchestra
RSO	Radio Symphony Orchestra
S.	South
SCO	Scottish Chamber Orchestra
Sinf.	Sinfonietta
SNO	Royal Scottish National Orchestra
SO	Symphony Orchestra
Soc.	Society
Sol. Ven.	I Solisti Veneti
SRO	Suisse Romande Orchestra
Sup.	Supraphon
trans.	transcription, transcribed
Unicorn	Unicorn Kanchana
V.	Vienna
Van.	Vanguard
VCM	Vienna Concentus Musicus
VPO	Vienna Philharmonic Orchestra
VSO	Vienna Symphony Orchestra
W.	West

Adam, Adolphe (1803–56)

Giselle (ballet): complete.
(M) *** Decca Dig. 433 007-2 (2) [id.]. ROHCG O, Richard Bonynge.

Bonynge's superb performance is absolutely complete, even including interpolations by Burgmüller and Minkus. The recording, too, is richly coloured and sumptuous, and this is one of the most satisfying of Bonynge's many fine ballet recordings, made for Decca over the years. It is very welcome indeed at mid-price.

Giselle (ballet): *suite.*
(M) ** Sony SBK 46341 [id.]; *40-46341.* Phd. O, Ormandy – MEYERBEER: *Les Patineurs*; TCHAIKOVSKY: *Swan Lake.***

Ormandy's eleven-minute suite concentrates mostly on the robust music of Adam's score and thus fails to give a complete picture of the ballet's charm. Characteristically polished playing, with Philadelphian vitality and sumptuously resonant mid-1970s sound. The finest single-disc and -tape selection from Adam's ballet is by Karajan and the VPO on Decca (417 738-2; *417 738-4*).

Adams, John (born 1947)

Fearful symmetries; (i) *The wound dresser.*
*** Nonesuch/Warner Dig. 7559 79218-2; *7559 79218-4* [id.]. (i) Sanford Sylvan; St Luke's O, composer.

In *The wound dresser* Adams rises well above the limitations of minimalism in one of his most moving works. It is an extended setting of a Walt Whitman poem, inspired by the American Civil War, telling of the poet's experiences with the wounded and dying. The words have enhanced relevance in the age of AIDS, and Adams's response to them has a simple gravity and depth of feeling comparable to Britten at his finest. The piece also reflects the composer's emotions over his dying father. Sanford Sylvan is an ideal soloist, bringing out the work's intensity with natural expressiveness, helped by the composer's own unforced but understanding direction. *Fearful symmetries* is the totally contrasted work for orchestra alone that Adams wrote almost simultaneously with the cantata as a kind of counterblast. It is a characteristically strong, energetic piece, more varied in its tonal contrasts than many examples of minimalism. The quotation from Blake's *The Tyger* in the title is misleading: it simply refers to the rhythmic interplay of machinery which inspired the composer. Excellent, well-balanced sound.

Shaker loops.
❀ *** Virgin VC7 91168-2; *VC7 91168-4* [id.]. LCO, Warren-Green – GLASS: *Company* etc.; REICH: *8 Lines*; HEATH: *Frontier.****

This inspired performance by Christopher Warren-Green and his London Concert Orchestra is full of imaginative intensity, and understandably it received the composer's imprimatur. It is part of a well-conceived programme of minimalist music, almost all of which is worth returning to. Adams's four-part *Shaker loops* works within its minimalist 'straitjacket' with the utmost imagination and emotional resource. The title refers both to the weird practices of the religious group of that persuasion and to the musical devices of trills and shakes; the loops are its melodic basis. The outer movements are highly animated and strong in dynamic graduation; the inner movements are haunting, from the 'slow languid glissandi' of the *Hymning slews* to the more tangible *Loops and verses.* Outstandingly vivid recording.

Harmonium (for large orchestra and chorus).
*** ECM 821 465-2 [id.]. San Francisco SO & Ch., Edo de Waart.

Harmonium must be the most powerful of all minimalist works; indeed, there is nothing minimal about its conception, which is on the largest possible scale, nor about its realization, which is here spectacular in the extreme. It is a setting of three poems. John Donne's curiously oblique 'Negative love' ('I never stoop'd so low, as they, which on a eye, cheek, lip, can prey') opens the piece, with the orchestra lapping gently around the chorus and retaining its surface texture in a musical structure which emerges from the mists and, in the composer's words, 'builds continuously and inexorably to a harmonic culmination point some ten minutes later'. The other two poems are by Emily Dickinson. 'Because I could not stop for death' is a dream-like sequence musing on the arrest of time. Then, after a sombre, ominous preparation in the lower reaches of the orchestra, the third poem, 'Wild nights', breaks into the reverie, engulfing the listener in its violent erotic passion, until at the end, with the imagery of 'Rowing in Eden – Ah, the sea! Might I but moor – Tonight in thee!', we are serenely returned to the gentle calm of the opening. The work was commissioned by the San Francisco Symphony Orchestra and dedicated to Edo de Waart, who gives it the performance of a lifetime: the disembodied continuum of the opening and closing evocation is as hypnotically compelling as the wild fury of the choral response at the beginning of the third poem. The magnificent, resonantly expansive 1984 analogue recording is certainly worthy of the performance; one might complain that the words need projecting with greater clarity; but for the most part one feels that they are of secondary importance and act merely as a catalyst to the rippling waves of orchestral and choral texture. A remarkable work. Seekers after playing time must note that this CD plays for only just over 32 minutes, yet for some ears it may seem longer.

Alain, Jehan (1911–40)

3 Danses; Fantasmagorie; Fantaisies 1–2; Le jardin suspendu (chaconne); Litanies; Suite; Variations on a theme of Jannequin.
** Argo Dig. 430 833-2; *430 833-4* [id.]. Thomas Trotter (organ of Niewwe Kerk, Katwijk aan Zee, Netherlands).

We needed a good digital collection of Alain's splendid organ music, but this one is disappointing, and we must now wait for the return to the catalogue of the Erato recordings made by the composer's sister, Marie-Claire. The Argo recording is strong on atmosphere and its dynamic range is certainly wide. Thomas Trotter often creates some evocative sounds; he is at his best in the almost minimalist *Fantasmagorie*, which is as deliciously coloured as a box of fondant creams, while the opening of the *Première fantaisie* shines forth like a sudden beam of light. But often his articulation of the gentler music fails to register cleanly, and at times these performances lack a strong rhythmic profile; even the quirky main theme of the *Litanies* is blurred by the resonance.

Albéniz, Isaac (1860–1909)

Iberia (complete).
(M) *(*) EMI CDZ7 62889-2 (2). Aldo Ciccolini – GRANADOS: *Goyescas.**(*)

Aldo Ciccolini's recording of *Iberia* comes in harness with the *Goyescas* of Granados and on the face of it offers good value at mid-price. Book One, comprising the *Evocation*, *El Puerto* and *Fête-Dieu à Séville*, comes after the Granados on the first CD, the remaining three Books being accommodated on the second disc. The recordings were made in the Paris Salle Wagram and date from 1966. Unfortunately the sound is unappealing: a bit clattery and shallow in timbre; although Aldo Ciccolini has no lack of fire, readers will do better with Alicia de Larrocha's more poetic and idiomatic account on Decca (417 887-2 – see our main volume, p. 3).

Iberia (suite; orch. Arbós).
*** Chan. Dig. CHAN 8904; *ABTD 1513* [id.]. Philh. O, Yan Pascal Tortelier – FALLA: *Three-cornered Hat.****

The transcriptions of five of the twelve piano pieces which make up *Iberia* were made by Albéniz's contemporary and friend, Enrique Arbós. As conductor of the Madrid Symphony Orchestra he chose and orchestrated with instinctive skill, to provide an evocative suite reflecting the colours of the Spanish landscape, bright and subtly iridescent. The music itself glows and flickers with the nuances of Spanish dance-rhythms, and Yan Pascal Tortelier brings out all the sultry languor of its atmospheric pictorialism. The gaudy spectacle of the climaxes of *Fête-Dieu à Séville* is dramatically handled, yet the closing section of this piece brings a haunting, sustained pianissimo, while the kaleidoscopic changes of mood and colour of the closing *El Albaicín* – much admired by Debussy – are handled with considerable subtlety. The Philharmonia's response brings glowing woodwind colours and seductive string phrasing, well projected by the warmly resonant recording which blurs only a little at the height of the Corpus Christi festivities.

Albinoni, Tommaso (1671–1750)

Concerti a cinque, Op. 7/3, 6, 9, 12; Op. 9/2, 5, 8 & 11.
** RCA/BMG RD 60207 [60207-2-RC]. Michala Petri, I Solisti Veneti, Claudio Scimone.

While the interchange of instrumentation was standard practice in the baroque era, there seems more loss than gain in playing these oboe concertos on the recorder, whether descant, sopranino or alto. Ms Petri's piping generates charm and vitality but less depth than, for instance, Sara Francis's oboe. The latter has recorded the same programme with great distinction, and that collection gives considerably more satisfaction (Unicorn DKPCD 9088). Michala Petri is well if forwardly recorded, but Scimone's accompaniments are heavier and less resilient than those provided by the London Harpsichord Ensemble on the Unicorn disc.

Alfvén, Hugo (1872–1960)

Swedish rhapsody No. 1 (Midsummer watch), Op. 19; King Gustav II suite: Elegy.
(M) **(*) EMI CD-EMX 2176; *TC-EMX 2176* [id.]. Bournemouth SO, Berglund – GRIEG: *Peer Gynt* **(*); JÄRNEFELT: *Praeludium.****

Alfvén's *Rhapsody* has a justly famous principal theme – once made famous by Mantovani. But there is more to the piece than that, and it is all put together with imagination and skill. It is well played here, with plenty of spirit, although rather less charm. Nevertheless the remastered recording from 1974 sounds vivid, with plenty of colour; the engaging *Elegy* is affectionately done, and this makes an attractive compilation overall.

Alkan, Charles (1813–88)

7 Études from Op. 39: Nos. 1 (Comme le vent); 2 En rhythm mollosique; 4–7 (Symphony); No. 11 (Overture).
*(*) Marco Polo Dig. 8.223245 [id.]. Bernard Ringeissen.

There is currently no alternative version of the *Symphony* for piano though doubtless EMI will one day restore to circulation Ronald Smith's dazzling account from the 1970s. The French pianist Bernard Ringeissen is curiously lacking in the outsize dash and flair that this music calls for, though it is obvious that he is an artist of sensitivity and fine musicianship. His virtuosity in the extraordinary *Comme le vent* is not sufficiently effortless, but he is handicapped by being recorded in the small acoustic of the Tonstudio van Geest in Heidelberg; the sound, particularly in the upper register, is somewhat desiccated and wanting in bloom.

25 Preludes, Op. 31.
** Marco Polo Dig. 8.223284 [id.]. Laurent Martin.

Like Bernard Ringeissen, Laurent Martin is recorded in a small acoustic in the Tonstudio van Geest in Heidelberg (and with the same producer). He adapts to its limitations rather more successfully than his countryman and succeeds in getting more colour and variety of tone out the piano. True, the Op. 31 *Preludes* are more poetic than barnstorming; they date from 1847 and go through all the major and minor keys, returning to C major in No. 25, and are designed for piano or organ or the pedalier (a piano with pedal-board), the instrument for which Alkan had a special affection. Some of the pieces, such as No. 16 (*Assez lentement*) and No. 17 (*Rêve d'amour*), are affecting in their simplicity. Laurent Martin has specialized in the music of Onslow and Alexis de Castillon, so he brings a strong sense of period feeling to this repertoire and shows real lightness of touch. However, when the dynamics rise to fortissimo, the limitations of the acoustic and of the instrument (but not of the pianist) show. The finesse and sensitivity of the playing and the interest of the music make this a desirable issue, but the recommendation must, alas, be qualified.

Arnold, Malcolm (born 1921)

(i) *Clarinet concerto No. 1;* (ii) *Flute concertos Nos. 1–2;* (iii) *Horn concerto No. 2;* (iv) *Oboe concerto;* (v) *Trumpet concerto.*
(M) *** EMI CDM7 63491-2 [id.]. (i) Janet Hilton; (ii) Richard Adeney; (iii) Alan Civil; (iv) Gordon Hunt; (v) John Wallace; Bournemouth Sinf., (i; iii–v) Del Mar; (ii) Ronald Thomas.

We must here offer an apology to Richard Adeney for attributing his admirable performances of Malcolm Arnold's two *Flute concertos* to John Solum in our last volume. Adeney both commissioned and premièred them, in 1954 and 1973 respectively, and he recorded both works in 1979. His playing of the cool cantilena which forms the *Andante* of the *First Concerto* is particularly beautiful, the ending quite ethereal; while the exhilarating finale, marked *con fuoco*, has superb dash. Even so, it is the engaging *Allegretto* finale of No. 2 which lingers in the memory, one of the composer's most engaging ideas: its gentle rhythmic inflexion is perfectly caught by the soloist.

Guitar concerto.
*** Decca Dig. 430 233-2; *430 233-4* [id.]. Eduardo Fernández, ECO, Barry Wordsworth – BROUWER: *Retrats Catalans*; CHAPPELL: *Guitar concerto No. 1*.***

There are few guitar concertos to match the effectiveness of this jazz-inflected piece, written in 1959 for Julian Bream. This brilliant version by Eduardo Fernández, superbly recorded, brings glowing sound from the ECO in a fizzing performance, spikily incisive in bringing out the jazz overtones. Fernández makes the haunting melody of the second subject warm and not sentimental, and the full depth of the blues-inspired slow movement is movingly conveyed. With the unusual Brouwer pieces and Chappell's colourful concerto for couplings, this can be warmly recommended.

Cornish dances, Op. 91; English dances, Set 1, Op. 27; Set 2, Op. 33; Irish dances, Op. 126; Scottish dances, Op. 59; Solitaire (ballet): *Sarabande; Polka.*
*** Lyrita SRCD 201 [id.]. LPO, composer.
*** Chan. Dig. CHAN 8867; *ABTD 1482* [id.]. Philh. O, Bryden Thomson.

Arnold's four sets of British national dances not only make a wonderfully varied and colourful musical entertainment but, when listened to in sequence, admirably survey the stylistic changes of his composing career, from the exuberant and immensely successful *English dances*, which firmly established his reputation in 1950–51, through to the much darker, even valedictory *Irish dances* of 1986. In between come the *Scottish dances* of 1957 and the relatively sombre *Cornish dances* of a decade later. The Scottish set, besides evoking bagpipes and the snapping rhythms of strathspeys and reels, includes a wonderful slow movement, picturing the glorious Highland countryside; while the central movements of the *Cornish dances*, for all their brevity, have remarkable musical substance and powerful atmosphere. Here Arnold as interpreter is at his very finest, both in capturing the 'strange and sad beauty' of the deserted tin and copper mines and in the solemn Sankey and Moody processional which ends with a dramatic ouburst from the tambourine. (Thomson is less dramatic and more genial here.) The two numbers specially written for *Solitaire* in 1956 augmented the eight *English dances*, to form the ballet of this name. The *Sarabande* has a wistful charm (touchingly brought out by Arnold himself, who offers a version somewhat more extended than Thomson's), and the *Polka* brings chararacteristically witty orchestral colouring.

Bryden Thomson has the advantage of the extra definition superb digital sound brings, with no loss of ambient feeling. The strings are brightly lit, but the rich brass sonorities and horn whoops are vividly and excitingly defined. The composer's tempi are usually fractionally slower than Thomson's, underlining contrasts, yet Arnold's strong rhythmic pointing, as in the *Giubiloso* final *English dance* and the *Pesante* opening *Scottish dance*, brings even greater bite and thrust. Both these sets of performances are admirable in different ways, and those who choose the Chandos disc for its digital spectacle will not be disappointed. The layout here is chronological, with the *Solitaire* items treated as an appendix, whereas Arnold's own CD places the curiously haunting *Irish dances* with the *Solitaire* excerpts as a central interlude.

The Sound Barrier (rhapsody) after film score, *Op. 38*.
(M) *** ASV Dig. CDWHL 2058; *ZCWHL 2058* [id.]. RPO, Kenneth Alwyn – BAX: *Malta G.C.* etc.***

Malcolm Arnold's *Rhapsody*, adapted in 1952 from his film score, shows the composer at his most characteristically inventive. It has five tiny subdivisions but makes a satisfying whole, not a note too long, and is kaleidoscopically orchestrated. Kenneth

Alwyn and the RPO clearly relish the virtuosity demanded of them, and the recording is equally brilliant.

(i) *Symphony No. 1;* (ii) *Concerto for 2 pianos* (3 hands), *Op. 104;* (i) *Beckus the Dandipratt overture;* (iii) *English dances Nos. 3 & 5;* (i) *Solitaire: Sarabande; Polka.*
(M) *** EMI CDM7 64044-2 [id.]; *EG 764044-4.* (i) Bournemouth SO; (ii) Phyllis Sellick and Cyril Smith, CBSO; (iii) Philh. O; composer.

Arnold in his late twenties, already successful as a film composer and about to write some of the most approachable and colourful pieces since the Second World War, here made his first symphonic statement, one of total bitterness, a mood he was to find again much later in his life. But even here the idiom is direct and immediately recognizable. This is a strong performance under the composer. Malcolm Arnold wrote his three-handed concerto especially for Phyllis Sellick and Cyril Smith (who had, sadly, lost the use of one hand but continued in a duo with his wife). The first movement starts with Stravinskian bell sounds, which lead to a gently lyrical middle section. The central *Andante con moto* is a cool chaconne with an elaborate descant for the second piano. The finale is an outrageous send-up of the pop music of the 1920s, banjo-strumming and all. A delightful, undemanding work, superbly played by the dedicatees, which makes a good foil for the *Symphony* alongside the rumbustious overture, *Beckus the Dandipratt* (here rather more measured than usual), the two pieces Arnold added to his *English dances* for the ballet *Solitaire*, and two of the most attractive of the *Dances.*

Symphony No. 4, Op. 71.
*** Lyrita Dig. SRCD 200 [id.]. LPO, composer.

Arnold's *Fourth Symphony* was commissioned by the BBC and, after its broadcast first performance in 1960, Andrew Porter described it as 'a symphony for fun . . . exuberant, melodious, unabashed, likeable'. It is certainly that – and more than that, too. The scoring liberally includes Latin-American percussion instruments to create original and exotic orchestral effects, and the first movement is dominated by one of those entirely winning Arnoldian lyrical tunes, which overcomes the jagged dissonance of the central episode. The slow movement brings a long-breathed, almost Mahlerian melodic flow, and the relatively gentle scherzo is catchily rhythmic and ingeniously constructed. The finale, complete with fugue, has its bizarre moments, yet in the end almost resolves the work's contradictions. Arnold's performance brings a vital and spontaneous response from his old orchestra, the LPO, and much superb playing. The recording has the remarkable naturalness of balance and feeling of realism which has always distinguished issues on the Lyrita label, but now with the subtle extra definition of digital techniques.

Symphonies Nos. 7, Op. 113; 8, Op. 124.
*** Conifer CDCF 177; *MCFC 177* [id.]. RPO, Vernon Handley.

Arnold's *Seventh* and *Eighth Symphonies* were written in 1973 and 1978 respectively, and the music they contain is a world apart from the optimistic exuberance of the *English dances.* The bitterness in the *Seventh* is inescapable. Dedicated to the composer's three children, the writing is most strongly influenced by his son Edward, tragically autistic. Even the characteristic Arnoldian whooping horn figures of the first movement are robbed of any sense of joy, and the *Andante*, dominated by a darkly sombre trombone cantilena, becomes an obsessive soliloquy of despair. In the finale there is a bizarre, even unnerving, change of mood, when the composer introduces a piping, folksy Irish theme which appears and disappears like a fleeting spectre, and the work ends without the clouds lifting. The *Eighth* is emotionally hardly less pungent, even if some of the pessimism seems to have lifted when the first movement brings another whimsically piquant Irish marching tune. Derived from a film score, it is developed with great orchestral imagination and resourcefulness. Bleakness dominates the *Andante*, but the finale brings, at last, a return of the irrepressible vitality which we associate with Arnold's music; and the work closes in exuberance. Handley's performances of both symphonies generate great power and depth of feeling, with the most eloquent response from the RPO players, and the recording is outstandingly real and vivid. However, neither work offers an easy listening experience.

Auber, Daniel (1782–1871)

Crown Diamonds: Overture.
(M) *** Mercury 432 014-2 [id.]. Detroit SO, Paray (with Concert: *'French opera highlights'* ***).

A splendidly polished account of one of Auber's very best overtures, given a genuine French accent in Detroit by Paul Paray. The 1960 Mercury recording is well up to standard. The rest of Paray's programme is equally enticing.

Bacarisse, Salvator (1898–1963)

Concertino in A min. for guitar and orchestra, Op. 72.
(B) *(*) DG Compact Classics 413 156-2 (2) [id.]. Yepes, Spanish R. & TV O, Alonso – CASTELNUOVO-TEDESCO: *Guitar concerto* ***; FALLA: *Nights in the gardens of Spain* **(*); DRIGO: *Concertos.***

This is the least attractive component in DG's two-CD bargain compilation of concertante works for guitar, harp and piano. Bacarisse, director of the Spanish Radio in Republican days, was on this showing an uninspired composer. His *Concertino* is an unpretentious but dull little work, brilliantly played by Yepes.

Bach, Carl Philipp Emanuel (1714–88)

Flute concertos: in A, Wq.169; in G, Wq.169; in D min. (from *Harpsichord concerto*).
*** BMG/RCA Dig. RD 60244 [60244-2-RC]. James Galway, Württemberg CO, Joerg Faerber.

James Galways plays these three works with his customary musicianship, virtuosity and polish; any stylistic doubts about his vibrato and the the warm espressivo of slow movements – from soloist and orchestra alike – are silenced by the beauty of the line and the elegance of the phrasing. Decoration is nicely judged. Galway is very nimble in finales and finds great dash for the closing *Allegro di molto* of the *D minor Concerto*; indeed his articulation is breathtaking so that all thoughts of the original keyboard work are banished, and it sounds admirably suited to the flute. Faerber and his Württemberg orchestra accompany persuasively, with no attempt made to create 'authentic' textures. Excellent recording. Recommended, except to authenticists.

Harpsichord concerto in D min., Wq.22.
(B) ** CfP CD-CFP 4571; *TC-CFP 4571.* Malcolm, Bath Festival O, Y. Menuhin – J. S. BACH: *Harpsichord concerto No. 6* etc.**

C. P. E. Bach composed about four dozen harpsichord concertos, this one being written in Potsdam in 1748. Its most striking movement is the finale, which gives off plenty of sparks and here is relished with zest. The other movements are thematically less memorable: the *Poco andante* is rather conventional from a melodic point of view. Malcolm plays a modern harpsichord, balanced within the orchestra, to counterbalance the strings which have greater tonal impact than would have been likely in the composer's day. Menuhin does not seem to have solved the problem of the work's very abrupt ending. The CD transfer is fresh and clean.

(i) *Harpsichord concerto in D min., Wq.23;* (i–ii) *Double harpsichord concerto in F, Wq.46;* (iii) *Oboe concerto in E flat, Wq.165.*
(M) **(*) HM/BMG GD77061 [77061-RG-2]. (i) Leonhardt, (ii) Curtis, (iii) Hucke; Coll. Aur., Maier.

The *F major concerto* for two harpsichords and strings with the addition of two horns and continuo, Wq.46, comes from Bach's Berlin years (its probable date is 1740) and it is thoroughly representative of this extraordinary composer. The better-known *D minor concerto*, Wq.23 (1748), could almost be said to look forward to the *Sturm und Drang*, and it receives a dashing and fiery performance from Gustav Leonhardt and the Collegium Aureum. The *Oboe concerto* is much later (1765) and is notable for its forward-looking and expressive slow movement. So far as baroque oboe playing is concerned, things have moved on since this record was made; however, the performances have a spirit and expressive vitality that are sometimes missing from more modern ensembles; the excellent recordings were made in the resonant acoustic of Schloss Kirchheim in 1965 (Wq.46) and 1968 (Wq.23 and 165), when the cellos, incidentally, were led by Anner Bylsma. By the side of modern-day period ensembles, the Collegium Aureum sound positively big-band, an impression no doubt reinforced by the acoustic; for those who are worried by such matters, they play at present-day pitch.

Harpsichord concerto in G min., Wq.6.
*** Capriccio Dig. 10 283 [id.]. Gerald Hambitzer, Concerto Köln – J. C. BACH: *Sinfonia*; J. C. F. BACH: *Sinfonias*; W. F. BACH: *Sinfonia* etc.***

The *G minor Concerto*, Wq.6 (1740), is one of the most remarkable of C. P. E. Bach's early works and looks forward to the solo concerto repertoire that was to emerge later in the century. It moves away from the baroque concerto principles of Vivaldi and Handel to a more clearly defined dialogue between soloist and ensemble. Gerald Hambitzer is an expert and persuasive soloist, and the performance has abundant vitality and imagination. The recording is very naturally balanced, with the harpsichord neither too upfront nor too recessed.

Trio sonatas: in B min., Wq.76 (H.512); in A, Wq.146 (H.570); in D, H.585.
*** HM/BMG Dig. RD 77250 [77050-2-RC]. Les Adieux – J. C. BACH: *Quintets*; J. C. F. BACH: *Quartet*.***

These three sonatas span three decades: the *A major* (Wq.146) comes from 1731 but was revised in 1747, the *D major* dates from the mid-1750s and the *B minor* from 1763; between them, they give a good idea of the composer's artistic development. They are played with admirable style and no mean virtuosity by Les Adieux; their members include Mary Utiger, who makes a consistently beautiful sound, as does the flautist Wilbert Hazelzet in the *A major sonata*. Excellent recording.

Bach, Johann Christian (1735–82)

Sinfonia in G min. Op. 6/6.
*** Capriccio Dig. 10 283 [id.]. Concerto Köln – C. P. E. BACH: *Harpsichord concerto*; J. C. F. BACH: *Sinfonias*; W. F. BACH: *Sinfonia* etc.***

This remarkable symphony, written in 1770 when Johann Christian was at the height of his fame, is altogether darker than is usual with this most gracious and genial of composers, and the Concerto Köln discover greater dramatic intensity in it than do most ensembles. (Perhaps the lower pitch helps to lend it additional poignancy.) It comes at the end of a particularly valuable collection devoted to the sons of Johann Sebastian Bach and is recorded as excellently as it is played.

Quintets (for flute, oboe, violin, viola & continuo) in G & F, Op. 11/2–3.
*** HM/BMG Dig. RD 77250 [77050-2-RC]. Les Adieux – C. P. E. BACH: *Trio sonatas*; J. C. F. BACH: *Quartet*.***

The *Quintets* both come from 1774, when the composer was spending some time at the Mannheim court, and find Johann Christian at his most delightful. Their charm has a freshness and innocence that it is difficult to resist; there are moments of considerable expressive poignancy, which these imaginative and elegant players make the most of. This is one of the best records devoted to the sons of Bach and the sound-quality is first class.

Bach, Johann Christoph Friedrich (1732–95)

Sinfonias: in D min.; E flat, Wfv 1/3 & 10.
*** Capriccio Dig. 10 283 [id.]. Concerto Köln – C. P. E. BACH: *Harpsichord concerto*; J. C. BACH: *Sinfonia*; W. F. BACH: *Sinfonia* etc.***

Johann Christoph Friedrich spent the greater part of his life in relative isolation at the court of Bückenburg, to which he was appointed when he was eighteen, emerging from this provincial backwater only once, to visit his younger brother, Johann Christian, in London. Much of his work was lost during the Second World War (only two of the fifteen symphonies he wrote in his mature years survive). The rather Italianate *D minor Symphony* recorded here was copied by the German organist Johan Friedrich Peter in 1768 before he emigrated to America; it turned up recently in the Archives of the Moravian Church in North Carolina. The other and later symphony (*c.* 1770), which came to light in the collection of a Belgian antiquarian dealer in the mid-1960s, is far more indebted to Carl Philipp Emanuel. Both works recorded here are elegantly written and are well worth investigating, even if Johann Christoph Friedrich does not have the strong musical personality of his brothers. The playing of the Concerto Köln is enthusiastic, sprightly and sensitive, and they are excellently recorded.

Flute quartet No. 3 in C.
*** HM/BMG Dig. RD 77250 [77050-2-RC]. Les Adieux – C. P. E. BACH: *Trio sonatas*; J. C. BACH: *Quintets*.***

There are six *Flute quartets* from 1768 and this is the first recording of the delightful *C major*. Johann Christoph Friedrich's music is untroubled by any depths but has a genuine charm that is beautifully communicated by these accomplished players. Excellent recording.

Musikalisches Vielerley: Cello sonata in A.
*** Sony Dig. SK 45945 [id.]. Anner Bylsma, Bob van Asperen – J. S. BACH: *Viola da gamba sonatas Nos 1–3.*

This *Sonata* first appeared in 1770, when it was published in a music periodical, *Musikalisches Vielerley*, edited by Carl Philipp Emanuel Bach. It is a work of slight but not negligible musical interest, and it is here played imaginatively by Anner Bylsma, using a piccolo cello, and by Bob van Asperen on a 'trunk' or chamber organ. Excellently recorded.

Bach, Johann Sebastian (1685–1750)

The Art of fugue, BWV 1080.
(M) ** DG Dig. 431 704-2; *431 704-4* [id.]. Col. Mus. Ant., Reinhard Goebel.

Goebel's *Art of fugue* (see our main volume, p. 22) now reappears at mid-price on a single disc (76 minutes). It has genuine vitality, but the bite on the string-tone, and also the expressive bulges which are at times exaggerated, will pose a listening problem for some readers. The digital sound is faithful.

Brandenburg concertos Nos. 1–6, BWV 1046/51.
**(*) DG Dig. 431 660-2 (2) [id.]. COE.
(M) **(*) Decca 425 725-2; *425 725-4* (*Nos. 1–3*); 425 726-2; *425 726-4* (*Nos. 4–6*) [id.]. ECO, Britten.
(B) * Ph. 426 970-2 (*Nos. 1–3*); 426 971-2 (*Nos.4–6*) [id.]. I Musici.

Brandenburg concertos Nos. 3–5, BWV 1048/50.
(M) **(*) Ph. Dig. 432 037-2 [id.]. I Musici.

A spirit of fun infects the COE version. Using modern instruments, these are among the happiest performances ever, marked by easily bouncing rhythms and warmly affectionate – but never sentimental – slow movements. Some may want more severity but the joyful exuberance of Bach's inspiration is inescapable. Unfortunately, the first movement of No. 1 – the movement which many will sample first – takes relaxation too far, becoming almost ragged; conversely, the first movement of No. 6 is uncharacteristically rigid. Otherwise these performances, well recorded, give pure joy.

Britten made his recordings in the Maltings concert-hall in 1968, not long before the serious fire there. The engineers had not quite accustomed themselves to the reverberant acoustic and, to compensate, they put the microphones rather close to the players. The result is a fairly ample sound that in its way goes well with Britten's interpretations. The disappointing element is the lack of delicacy, partly textural, in the slow movements of Nos. 1, 2, 4 and 6; but the bubbling high spirits of the outer movements are hard to resist, and the harspsichordist, Philip Ledger, follows the pattern he had set in live Britten performances, with Britten-inspired extra elaborations a continual delight. The CD transfer is very successful, the sound both full and bright, and the effect of these performances is joyfully life-enhancing.

I Musici's 1984 digital set of *Brandenburgs* is already at mid-price. These are sunny performances, very realistically recorded, lacking something in imagination in slow movements but not without energy in fast ones: witness the zestfully brisk finale of No. 3. The sound is first class, with a striking presence. Disgracefully for a major mid-priced series, there are no musical notes, only a list of the other records on the Laser Line label.

Philips have also reissued I Musici's earlier (1965) analogue set at bargain price (also without documentation). Although famous soloists are featured, including Maurice André, Heinz Holliger, and Frans Brüggen, the performances are much less attractive. The approach is rather solid, generally slow of tempo and unresilient of rhythm. The CD transfer is good, but the sound is less realistically focused than on the digital recording. First choice for the *Brandenburgs* at full price remains with the English Concert under Pinnock (DG 410 500/1-2) or, if original instruments are not essential, Ledger's Pickwick set with the ECO is a fine bargain recommendation (PCD 830 & 835 [MCAD 25956/7]).

Brandenburg concertos Nos. 1–6, BWV 1046/51; Overture in B flat (from *Cantata No. 194*); *Viola da gamba sonata in C, BWV 1027* (orch. Druce).
**(*) EMI Dig. CDS7 49806-2 (2) [Ang. CDCB 49806]. Taverner Players, Parrott.

With light textures and generally fast speeds, Parrott's set of the *Brandenburgs* is one of the more individual of the period-performance versions. It also brings a valuable supplement in works using comparable forces, the *Overture* from the *Cantata No. 194* and Duncan Druce's transcription of the *C major Gamba sonata,* for the same forces as Bach adopts in the *Brandenburg No. 6*. Sometimes Parrott's speeds are so fast that resilience is lost and, with recording slightly distanced and not very sharply focused, the result at times is muddled. Parrott is also more severe than is a rival such as Pinnock and the English Concert over the question of vibrato. The squeezed style of playing sustained notes in slow movements is not easy on the ear, and the viola melody in the slow movement of No. 6 is very sour. Yet anyone who wants a radical period performance which does not go to the extremes of Goebel's Musica Antiqua of Cologne will be well pleased.

Brandenburg concertos Nos. 1–3; Orchestral suite No. 1, BWV 1066.
(M) * DG Dig. 431 701-2; *431 701-4* [id.]. Col. Mus. Ant., Goebel.

Brandenburg concertos Nos. 4–6; Orchestral suite No. 4, BWV 1069.
(M) * DG Dig. 431 702-2; *431 702-4* [id.]. Col. Mus. Ant., Goebel.

Goebel's allegros are so fast and hectic in the *Brandenburg concertos* that they have you disbelieving your ears. It is hard not to laugh out loud at the speeds for both movements of No. 3 (the second more than the first), and even more at the sketchy strumming which purports to be the first movement of No. 6. At Goebel's headlong speed, the semiquaver arpeggios are hardly audible and even the repeated quavers sound rushed. It is a tribute to the virtuosity of the Cologne ensemble that they otherwise cope so well, usually playing with a good rhythmic spring. Slow movements, by contrast, are taken relatively conservatively, though Goebel's squeezy phrasing is often uncomfortable, with the ensemble characteristically edgy in its light, clear style. The speeds mean that there is room to fit one of the *Orchestral suites* on each of the two discs. With abrasive, choppy phrasing and again using squeeze techniques on sustained notes, they present a clear, lively view of what Goebel feels constitutes authentic performance, using a normal baroque-sized orchestral group with four first and four second violins. Fine recording, but this issue is mainly of curiosity interest.

Flute concertos: in C (from *BWV 1055*); *in E min.* (from movements of *Cantata No. 35*); *in G min.* (from *BWV 1056*); *Sinfonia* from *Cantata No. 209.*
(M) **(*) Sony Dig. MDK 46510 [id.]. Rampal, Ars Redivivia, Munclinger.

If you enjoy transcriptions of Bach for the flute – and they are easy to enjoy here – it is difficult to imagine them being played better than by Jean-Pierre Rampal. The *C major* and *G minor Concertos* derive respectively from the *A major* and *F minor Harpsichord concertos.* Rampal is wonderfully nimble in the opening allegro of BWV 1055 and gives a radiantly beautiful account of the slow-movement cantilena of BWV 1056. Munclinger, who made the arrangements, provides sympathetic accompaniments, although rhythmically he does not quite display Rampal's lightness of touch. Nevertheless, this is an attractive concert, made the more welcome by the inclusion of the *Sinfonia* from *Cantata No. 209.* The digital recording is very good indeed – and well balanced, too. However, those who count minutes will note that there are only 42½ of them here.

Clavier concertos Nos. 1–7, BWV 1052/8.
*** Decca Dig. 425 676-2; *425 676-4* (2) [id.]. András Schiff (piano), COE.

András Schiff has already given us three concertos, BWV 1052 and 1055–6 on Denon, but they are now superseded by this complete set for Decca, most naturally recorded, with a well-nigh perfect balance and greater transparency and realism in the orchestral sound. As in his solo Bach records, Schiff's control of colour and articulation never seeks to present merely a harpsichord imitation, and his shaping of Bach's lovely slow movements brings fine sustained lines and a subtle variey of touch, notably the *Siciliana* of BWV 1053 and the famous *Largo* of BWV 1056 which have a pleasing simplicity and natural eloquence. He directs the Chamber Orchestra of Europe from the keyboard and chooses spirited, uncontroversial tempi for allegros, at the same time providing decoration that always adds to the joy and sparkle of the music-making. This makes a clear first choice for those who, like us, enjoy Bach on the piano and is altogether preferable to Gavrilov's competing EMI set (CDC7 47629-8), although Gavrilov has his own insights to offer.

Harpsichord concertos Nos. 1 in D min., BWV 1052; 6 in F, BWV 1057; 8 in D min., BWV 1059.
** Erato/Warner Dig. 2292 45545-2 [id.]. Koopman, Amsterdam Bar. O.

Harpsichord concertos Nos. 2 in E, BWV 1053; 3 in D, BWV 1054;, 5 in F min., BWV 1056; 7 in G min., BWV 1058.
** Erato/Warner Dig. 2292 45644-2 [id.]. Koopman, Amsterdam Bar. O.

Harpsichord concerto No. 4 in A, BWV 1055; Triple concerto for flute, violin & harpsichord in A min., BWV 1044; Triple harpsichord concertos Nos. 1 in D min.; 2 in C BWV 1063/4.
** Erato/Warner Dig. 2292 45646-2 [id.]. Koopman & soloists, Amsterdam Baroque O.

Double harpsichord concertos Nos. 1 in D min.; 2 in C; 3 in C min., BWV 1060/1062; Quadruple harpsichord concerto in A min., BWV 1065.
** Erato/Warner Dig. 2292 45649-2 [id.]. Koopman & soloists, Amsterdam Bar. O.

Koopman is a fine player and director who in the past has recorded Bach with great success. The set is valuable for offering such curiosities as the keyboard transcription of the *Double violin concerto* – with the central slow movement sounding more natural as a *siciliana* than on violins – but the performances and recording are a disappointment. The harpsichords are made to sound unpleasantly jangly, with mechanical noises intruding, while the orchestra sounds too heavy, lacking the transparency of period performance, with Koopman often failing to lift rhythms. Though Trevor Pinnock's series covers fewer works, his performances on DG Archiv (415 991/2-2, 415 131-2 and 400 041-2) are far more recommendable (see our main volume).

Harpsichord concerto No. 6 in F, BWV 1057; (i) *Triple concerto in A min., for flute, violin and harpsichord, BWV 1044.*
(B) ** CfP CD-CFP 4571; *TC-CFP 4571.* Malcolm; (i) Bennett, Y. Menuhin; Bath Fest. O, Menuhin – C. P. E. BACH: *Harpsichord concerto in D min.*

The *F major Concerto*, BWV 1057, is a transcription of the *Brandenburg concerto No. 4*, with recorder parts superbly played here by David Munrow and John Turner. George Malcolm is at his finest and Menuhin provides a sparkling accompaniment. There are good things, too, in the performance of the *Triple concerto*, especially the flute playing of William Bennett; but here the balance is slightly less well contrived and the performance has a shade less vitality. Bright and lively CD transfers.

Double clavier concerto in C, BWV 1061.
(**(*)) (M) Pearl mono GEMMCD 9399 [id.]. Artur & Karl-Ulrich Schnabel (pianos), LSO, Boult – BRAHMS: *Piano concerto No. 2.*(*)

Schnabel and his son, Karl-Ulrich, recorded the *C major Concerto* in 1936. Their performance offers fine musicianship and a spontaneity far removed from the unrelenting metronomic momentum of the present day. This is playing very much of the old school, with plenty of tonal finesse and rhythmic freedom; although the recordings reveal their age, there is a good deal of pleasure to be gained from this distinguished partnership.

Oboe concertos: in A (from *BWV 1055*); in D min. (from *BWV 1059*); *in F* (from *BWV 1053*).
*** DG Dig. 429 225-2 [id.]. Douglas Boyd, COE.

Douglas Boyd, the brilliant principal oboe of COE from its foundation, as soloist directs his colleagues in delectable performances of concertos reconstructed from keyboard concertos and cantata movements. Boyd's resilient and imaginative playing goes with well-sprung rhythms, bringing an infectious sense of fun. On the whole this may be preferred to Holliger (Philips 415 851-2 – see our main volume, p. 26), who at times leans towards Romantic expressiveness in slow movements. First-rate sound.

Organ concertos (reconstructed and ed. Schureck): *Nos. 1 in D min.* (from *BWV 146* & *BWV 1052*); *2 in D* (from *BWV 49, BWV 169* & *BWV 1053*); *3 in D min.* (from *BWV 35* and *BWV 1059*); *Sinfonia in D, BWV 1045; Canatata No. 29: Sinfonia.*
*** Argo Dig. 425 479-2 [id.]. Peter Hurford (organ of Lyons Concert Hall, York University), N. Sinfonia, Richard Hickox.

These works have nothing to do with Bach's solo organ concertos but are reconstructions from cantata sinfonias, scored for organ, wind and strings. Bach also used these allegros for the outer movements of his harpsichord concertos, and the remaining music is taken from this same source. R. J. Schureck argues that the originals may have been conceived with the organ in mind, as recent research suggests that the cantatas predate the works for harpsichord. Whatever the truth of the matter, these arrangements are highly effective and, given Peter Hurford's bright registrations on this eminently suitable York organ and the light, clean orchestral textures, this lively music-making is very enjoyable. Two extra sinfonias are thrown in for good measure: the *Sinfonia in D* is Bach's spectacular transcription of the *Prelude* from the *Unaccompanied Violin partita No. 3 in E*, BWV 1006.

Violin concertos Nos. 1 in A min.; 2 in E; (i) *Double violin concerto in D, BWV 1043.*
(M) *** HM/BMG GD 77006; *GK 77006* [77006-2-RG; *77006-4-RG*]. Sigiswald Kuijken; (i) Lucy van Dael; La Petite Bande.

As we know from his admirable recordings of the Bach *Sonatas for violin and harpsichord* (BMG/RCA GD 77170; [77170-2-RG]) Kuijken is a fine Bach player, and these performances of the *Violin concertos* go to the top of the list for those wanting period performances on original instruments. The slight edge on the solo timbre is painless and La Petite Bande provide lively, resilient allegros, the playing both polished and alert. There are touches of individuality too, especially in slow movements, and the way Kuijken's solo melisma floats freely over the rather grave accompaniment in the *A minor concerto* is particularly appealing. In the *Largo* of the *Double concerto*, both soloists phrase their beautiful imitative line with gently separated notes, the expressive feeling enhanced without a hint of romantic overlay. Excellent, well-balanced, 1981 digital recording. Those seeking the concertos on modern instruments will find Arthur Grumiaux incomparable; moreover his mid-price Philips recording (420 700-2; *420 700-4*), to which we awarded a Rosette in our main volume, also includes the *Concerto for violin and oboe*, BWV 1060.

The Musical offering, BWV 1079; (i) *Suite No. 2 in B min, BWV 1067.*
(M) **(*) Decca 430 266-2; *420 266-4* [id.]. Stuttgart CO, Münchinger, (i) with Rampal.

Münchinger's 1976 version of the *Musical offering* is strikingly well recorded: it has fullness, presence and good detail. Moreover it offers playing of genuine breadth and eloquence, particularly in the *Trio sonata*. There is some fine dark colouring from Hans-Peter Weber's cor anglais, and the string textures often bring a sombre nobility which is very affecting. The canons are grouped together and come off well. Münchinger can be heavy-handed in Bach, but the performance here has many fine qualities and its cost is reasonable. For the reissue, the 1962 recording of the *B minor Suite* for flute and strings has been added, the best of the set, with some first-class playing from Jean-Pierre Rampal whose timbre and lightness of touch are most appealing.

Orchestral suites Nos. 1–4, BWV 1066/9.
(M) *** Decca 430 378-2; *430 378-4* [id.]. ASMF, Marriner.
**(*) HM/BMG Dig. RD 77864; *RK 77864* (2) [7864-2-RC; *7864-4-RC*]. Amsterdam Bar. O, Koopman.
**(*) Erato/WEA Dig. 2292 45192-2 (*Nos. 1–2*); 2292 45193-2 (*Nos. 3–4*) [id.]. E. Bar. Soloists, John Eliot Gardiner.

We have always greatly enjoyed Marriner's 1970 recording of the Bach *Suites* with the ASMF. Now all four arrive on a single CD (77 minutes 48 seconds) and the remastering of the fine (originally Argo) recording is fresh and vivid, but without that over-lit quality and thinning of violin timbre which affected Decca's earlier reissue of the *Second* and *Third suites* (417 715-2). Thurston Dart, who plays the continuo, had a great deal to do with the preparation of these performances, and the exuberance of the music-making makes a fitting tribute to his scholarship which always sought to enhance the music's spirit, never to deaden it. The playing throughout is expressive without being romantic (the famous *Air* in the *Third Suite* is particularly successful) and always buoyant and vigorous. Perhaps the CD transfer loses a little of the weight of the originals but not their musical strength. William Bennett is the agile and sensitive flute soloist in the *Second Suite*; his decoration, never overdone, is particularly well judged in the closing *Badinerie*, played with nimble bravura. A fine bargain for those not insisting on original instruments; there is nothing remotely unstylish here.

Winner of one of the *Gramophone* Awards in 1990, Koopman's set of the Bach *Suites* brings warmly recorded performances with little of the abrasiveness that marked many earlier versions on period instruments. Slow introductions at relatively broad speeds have traditional grandeur, helped by the reverberant recording, and such a movement as the celebrated *Air* from the *Suite No. 3* is also allowed expressive breadth. Allegros are well sprung, both strong and elegant, and the *Suite No. 2* is crowned by the superb playing of the flautist, Wilbert Hazelzet, delectably light and clean at high speed in the final *Badinerie*. The snag is the extravagant layout: two full-price discs, with less than 80 minutes of music altogether, are very poor value.

Gardiner's set of the Bach *Orchestral suites*, also using period instruments, returns to the catalogue, still at full price, like the Koopman set. However, it costs three times as much as the Marriner CD, and we do feel it should have been reissued at mid-price. In his characteristic manner Gardiner's allegros tend to be fast and lightly sprung, with slower movements elegantly pointed. Though the edginess of baroque violins using a squeeze technique on sustained notes makes for some abrasiveness, Gardiner avoids the extremes which mark even Pinnock's English Concert version. Thanks to full and immediate recording, textures are fresh and clear, with trumpet and timpani biting through, but not excessively.

CHAMBER MUSIC

Viola da gamba sonatas Nos. 1–3, BWV 1027/9.
*** Sony Dig. SK 45945 [id.]. Anner Bylsma, Bob van Asperen – J. C. F. BACH: *Cello sonata in A.*
(M) *** HM/BMG GD 77044 [77044-2-RG]. Wieland Kuijken, Gustav Leonhardt.
(M) (**) Sony mono MPK 46445 [id.]. Pablo Casals, Paul Baumgartner (piano).

The three *Sonatas for viola da gamba and harpsichord* come from from Bach's Cöthen period, and the *G minor* is arguably the highest peak in this particular literature. On Sony/Vivarte comes an account with a difference: Anner Bylsma uses a piccolo cello and Bob van Asperen plays a 'trunk' organ, a small chamber organ. Bylsma argues the case for using these instruments in a persuasive (if not totally convincing) sleeve-note, and readers who wish to hear these marvellous pieces on a gamba and harpsichord should look elsewhere. The cello piccolo produces an almost viola-like tone quality in the upper register, and aurally the two instruments match beautifully. The sound is much less austere than, say, Kuijken and Leonhardt, and the brighter sonorities are undoubtedly appealing. The recording is extremely clean and well balanced.

Kuijken and Leonhardt's set is now reissued on BMG/RCA at mid-price. They are both sensitive and scholarly musicians, their tempi well judged and their artistry in good evidence. Their phrasing is finely shaped and natural, and there is no sense of the relentless flow that can so often impair the faster movements. The slow movement of the *G minor* is very slow, but the tempo obviously springs from musical conviction and as a result *feels* right. This is the most authentic account to have appeared on the market in recent years and is among the most rewarding. The recorded sound is faithful: it may be too immediate for some ears, but adjustment of the controls gives a satisfactory result.

Although there are some fine moments on this mono recording, such as Casals' phrasing of the opening Adagio of the *D major Sonata*, BWV 1028, at times the playing seems curiously deliberate. The recording, made at the Prades Festival in 1950, is acceptable but somewhat lacklustre.

(i) *Viola da gamba sonatas Nos. 1–3, BWV 1027/9*; (ii) *Violin sonatas Nos. 1–6, BWV 1014/19.*
(M) ** Sony M2K 42414 (2) [id.]. (i) Leonard Rose or (ii) Jaime Laredo, Glenn Gould (piano).

Leonard Rose does not project a larger-than-life instrumental personality like Rostropovich, but his tone is subtly coloured and beautifully focused, his playing shows a fine sensibility, and his slightly introvert style is admirably suited to the *Viola da gamba sonatas* of Bach. Moreover, he and Glenn Gould achieve a very close partnership indeed, although some of Gould's ornamentation is questionable. The cello is well forward with the piano behind, but the matching is nigh perfect, and the playing throughout is live and spontaneous. At times Glenn Gould's clean, staccato articulation in outlining the rhythm of slow movements (usually taken very slowly) seems a shade eccentric but when both artists do it together, as in the *Andante* of BWV 1027, the effect is both individual and pleasing. In allegros, the music-making has splendid vitality, and altogether these performances are rewarding, if highly idiosyncratic. In the *Violin sonatas* Jaime Laredo is also brought forward by the close balance, and this brings a degree of edge to his timbre, though the effect is not unpleasing; indeed it has an 'authentic' feel. But the close microphones do not spoil the dynamic range and there is some lovely quiet lyrical playing from Laredo. Again Gould's unforced staccato style is very apparent in slow movements, but the violin line floats serenely above (try the *Andante un poco* of BWV 1015), and again faster movements are enjoyably spirited. There is undoubtedly pleasure to be had from this pair of discs, for all the unconventionality of Gould's contribution.

(Unaccompanied) *Violin sonatas Nos. 1–3, BWV 1001, 1003 & 1005; Violin partitas Nos. 1–3, BWV 1002, 1004 & 1006.*
(M) (**) Sony mono MP2K 46721 (2) [id.]. Henryk Szeryng.

Szeryng, recorded in 1953 (although the liner notes give the date as 1965!), plays with superb confidence and absolute technical security. There is no doubt that the famous *Chaconne* which concludes the *D minor Partita* is very commanding. Yet these readings, with their bold, purposeful manner, at times seem unrelenting, and Szeryng too seldom plays really quietly. The mono sound is very faithful and real, but he is placed very near the microphone and, although this gives a realistic presence, it reduces the dynamic range still further. We remain very happy with Perlman (EMI CDS7 49483-2), where the power of the performances brings not only the widest range of tone but also, in the slow movements, hushed playing of great refinement. Milstein's mid-priced set from the mid-1970s is also most satisfying, his timbre leaner than Perlman's and very distinctive, the performances penetrating, with an aristocratic feeling for line. Like Perlman, he is given very vivid and realistic recording (DG 423 294-2).

Violin sonatas (for violin and harpsichord) *Nos. 4 in C min., BWV 1017; 5 in F min., BWV 1018; 6 in G, BWV 1019*; (i) *Violin sonata* (for violin and continuo) *in G, BWV 1021.*
**(*) RCA Dig. RD 60180 [60180-2-RC]. Joseph Swensen, John Gibbons, (i) with Elizabeth Anderson.

Joseph Swensen's performances are more robust than those from Grumiaux. John Gibbons plays a 1976 Rubio harpsichord; it makes a stronger impression than the instrument used on the Philips recording, and the balance is better. These vibrant performances on RCA are very attractive in their way: they have plenty of finesse and Swensen's lyrical playing has a full, warm profile, yet in slow movements Grumiaux's special, very pure timbre seems just right for the music (Philips 426 452-2).

KEYBOARD MUSIC

'Bach and Tureck at home' (A birthday offering): (i) *Adagio in G, BWV 968; Aria and 10 variations in the Italian style, BWV 989; Capriccio on the departure of a beloved brother, BWV 992; Chromatic fantasia and fugue, BWV 903; Fantasia, adagio and fugue in D, BWV 912; The Well-tempered clavier, Book 1: Prelude & fugue in B flat, BWV 866.* (ii) *English suite No. 3 in G min., BWV 808; Italian concerto, BWV 971; Sonata in D min.,*

BWV 964 (trans. from Unaccompanied *Violin sonata No. 2 in A min., BWV 1003*); *Well-tempered clavier, Book 1: Preludes & fugues: in C min; in C, BWV 847/8; Book 2: Preludes & fugues in C sharp, BWV 872; in G, BWV 884.* (iii) *Goldberg variations, BWV 988;* (iv) *Partitas Nos. 1 in B flat, BWV 825; 2 in C min., BWV 826; 6 in E min., BWV 830.*
❀ *** (i) Troy 010; (ii) TROY 009; (iii) TROY 007; (iv) TROY 008 (available separately). Rosalyn Tureck (piano).

These recordings originated in the home of William F. Buckley at Wallach's Point, Stamford, Connecticut, situated on a promontory with a breathtaking view overlooking Long Island Sound. They were planned as an inspired birthday present by his wife, but the initial event expanded to five evenings, the first on 24 November 1979 and the last in May 1984. Mr Buckley's resourceful partner planned the first concert in secret, invited two dozen guests, and also a professional recording engineer to ensure that her husband could repeat his listening experiences at leisure. The acoustic of the large sitting-room at Wallach's Point was ideal for home music-making, and the admirable analogue recording gives an intimate impression without being too dry; the piano has a vivid presence. Such was the balancing skill of the recording engineer, Ed Sidlawski, however, that the effect is very real without being too close for comfort. The audience makes its presence felt only by discreet applause at the end of each work. The result is a series of Bach programmes that have all the advantages of live music-making – notably a wonderfully spontaneous feeling of music taking wing as one listens – and none of the disadvantages.

Rosalyn Tureck's Bach playing is legendary, and the performances here show that her keyboard command and fluent sense of Bach style are as remarkable as ever. The variety of articulation and colour in the *Variations in the Italian style* offer endless stimulation, while the *Chromatic fantasia* is dazzling and its companion fugue opens very gently and builds to a superb climax. Later in this first CD recital, the *Adagio in D major* (which Mr Buckley tells us was the opening work of his first concert) is wonderfully dark in colouring, and the closing fugue of BWV 912 is unforgettably buoyant and life-enhancing. The second programme is hardly less successful, including as it does excerpts from *The Well-tempered clavier*, the work for which Miss Tureck is justly famous; while the *Andante* of the *Sonata in D minor*, BWV 964, is sustained at a very relaxed tempo with raptly intense concentration. Her thoughtful presentation of the *Aria* on which the *Goldberg variations* is based is also (like its final reprise) quite magical. What comes in between provides very great musical variety and satisfaction. The *Partitas*, too, show Miss Tureck at her most imaginative, with an infinite variety of touch: the opening *Sinfonia* of *No. 2 in C minor* is made to seem almost orchestral, while the *Toccata* which begins *No. 6 in E minor* is hardly less commanding. Miss Tureck uses a wide dynamic and expressive range with consummate artistry, her decoration always adds to the musical effect, and she makes us feel that Bach's keyboard music could be played in no other way than this – the hallmark of a great artist. All but one of these four discs plays for over 70 minutes (and the odd one for 66) and we must express gratitude to Mrs Buckley for her forethought in planning such bounty.

Chromatic fantasia and fugue in D min., BWV 903; Fantasy, BWV 906; Toccatas, BWV 912/4, 916.
*** DG Dig. 431 659-2 [id.]. Kenneth Gilbert (harpsichord).

Kenneth Gilbert plays a harpsichord of 1671 by the Flemish maker, Jan Couchet, enlarged by Taskin in 1778 and restored by Hubert Bédard ten years ago, and it sounds admirably rich and full-bodied. The usual grumble applies – the instrument sounds thunderous played at a normal level-setting, and readers will have to replay it at a lower setting if they are to get anywhere near a natural sound-picture. The playing is scholarly and yet by no means didactic; only in the fugue of the *Chromatic fantasia and fugue* does one feel that Gilbert is a touch heavy-handed. The four *Toccatas* are played with great spirit, though with perhaps less spontaneity than Bob van Asperen achieves on EMI (see below).

English suites Nos. 1–6, BWV 806/11.
(M) **(*) DG 427 146-2 (2) [id.]. Huguette Dreyfus (harpsichord).

Huguette Dreyfus recorded the *English suites* in 1972 but the recording does not sound dated. She plays very musically on an unnamed modern harpsichord and has plenty of rhythmic spirit. Readers who do not insist on a digital master might well consider this set, particularly given its competitive price. It does not displace either of the three-star recommendations in our main volume (Leonhardt on EMI CDS7 49000-8 and András Schiff, piano, on Decca 421 640-2) but still has a great deal to recommend it.

Goldberg variations, BWV 988.
(M) *** HM/BMG GD 77149 [77149-2-RG]. Gustav Leonhardt (harpsichord).
**(*) ECM Dig. 839 622-2 [id.]. Keith Jarrett (harpsichord).
(M) ** Sony MYK 44868 [id.]. Glen Gould (piano).

Gustav Leonhardt's third (1978) version of the *Goldberg* is most beautifully recorded. His instrument is a Dowd copy of a Blanchet; the sound is altogether mellower and more appealing than in his 1967 record for Teldec. This is an introvert and searching performance, at times rhythmically very free and with the *Black Pearl* variation a case in point; but the reading is so thoughtful that no one can fail to draw illumination from it: this account is altogether fresher and more personal than his earlier one. The CD transfer is wholly convincing.

Keith Jarrett's acount of the *Goldberg variations* is among the finest of modern digital versions. There is a thoughtful integrity here that is consistently impressive and, if at times (the *Adagio* of Variation 25, for instance) his approach seems a little introverted and literal, at other moments he can bring a keen concentration or produce an attractively spontaneous burst of vitality. He plays a Takahashi double-manual harpsichord, and he is naturally recorded within an intimate but not airless acoustic: the effect is realistic and pleasing. However, no notes are included about the music.

The Sony reissue represents Glenn Gould's recording début and is an early stereo recording from 1955 which is a little dry but quite truthful. As in his much later digital account, there are remarkable feats of prestidigitation and the clarity of the part-writing and the crispness of articulation are very impressive. No repeats are observed, and Gould's approach and style are highly individual, but he projects strong feelings about how this music should be played, and his reading is impressive in its own right.

Partitas Nos. 1–6, BWV 825/30.
(M) *** HM/BMG GD 77215 (2) [77215-2-RG]. Gustav Leonhardt (harpsichord).

Leonhardt's earlier set was not conceived as an entity but was recorded over a longish period (1963–70) in the Cerdernsaal at Schloss Kirchheim. The *Second Partita* is heard at today's pitch, while the others are recorded a semitone lower. The sound of the CD transfer is admirable, with the instrument – a 1962 Martin Skrowroneck copy of a 1745 Dulcken – set slightly back in an acoustic which provides ample space for the music to breathe, yet which is not too resonant. Variations of quality in the recordings of different partitas are minimal, and these are searching and often profound readings. There are occasional exaggerations (the *Allemande* of the *First Suite*, for example) and some of the dotted rhythms are overemphatic. Yet this still remains an impressive achievement, for the thoughts of this scholar-musician are always illuminating and his artistry compels admiration. An excellent mid-priced recommendation although, at full price, Trevor Pinnock has great spirit and panache (DG 415 493-2) and András Schiff is most persuasive if a piano version is preferred (Decca 411 732-2).

Partitas Nos. 3 in A min., 4 in D; 5 in G, BWV 827/9.
(BB) ** Naxos Dig. 8.550312 [id.]. Wolf Harden (piano).

These are crisply articulated, thoughtful performances, well recorded. Wolf Harden does not emerge as a very individual player, but he catches the character of the *Courantes, Sarabandes* and *Gigues* rather well, although the *Overture* of the *D major Partita* could do with more flair. Alongside the playing of Rosalyn Tureck, this seems rather monochrome, but many will enjoy its clean purity of style.

Toccatas: in F sharp min.; C min.; D; D min.; E min.; G min.; G; BWV 910/16.
*** EMI Dig. CDC7 54081-2 [id.]. Bob van Asperen (harpsichord).

Bob van Asperen plays an instrument of 1728 by the Hamburg maker, Christian Zell, and, as is all too often the case with the harpsichord, is recorded at a high level. However, a lower than usual volume-setting will produce eminently satisfactory results. The *Toccatas* are very varied and this distinguished Dutch player conveys their improvisatory character with great flair. This is one of the most enjoyable Bach keyboard issues of the year and can be recommended with confidence; where they overlap (in BWV 912–14 and 916), they score very slightly in terms of spontaneity over Kenneth Gilbert's excellent disc on DG Archiv (see above).

The Well-tempered Clavier (48 Preludes & fugues), BWV 846/893.
(M) (**(*)) DG mono 429 929-2 (3) [id.]. Walter Gieseking (piano).
** Hyp. Dig. CDA 66351/4 (4) [id.]. Colin Tilney (clavichord and harpsichord).

Gieseking's vintage performance on the piano, recorded for Saar Radio in 1950, is strikingly different from the historic recording made even earlier for EMI by Edwin Fischer. Gieseking is straighter and heavier; where Fischer took three years over recording the cycle, Gieseking worked quickly, and that seems to have spurred him on. From his heavy start he rises masterfully to the full challenge of the great fugues of Book Two. Though transfers are good, one has to use a creative ear to cope with the boxy sound.

It is a pity that Colin Tilney did not stick to the clavichord for both books, instead of transferring to the bigger instrument for Book Two. The feeling of a player musing his way through one prelude and fugue after another is well conveyed, but his speeds on both instruments are consistently slow, often eccentrically so. Unlike others, he plays them not in numerical order, but with keys rising by fifths in Book One and downwards by fifths in Book Two, so making the key-changes between each smooth and natural. Kenneth Gilbert on DG remains our primary recommendation for this work played on the harpsichord (413 439-2).

The Well-tempered Clavier, Book I, Preludes and fugues Nos. 1–24, BWV 846/69.
** ECM Dig. 835246-2 (2) [id.]. Keith Jarrett (piano).

Keith Jarrett's playing has great musical integrity; there is no attempt to downplay the sensibility or intelligence of the listener by investing his playing with seductive, out-of-period pianistic colour. Indeed some listeners may find it a little too monochrome, yet the cumulative effect is musically all the more satisfying for being so totally dedicated. And yet, for all the absence of surface colour, the effect, curiously enough, is not austere. The rather unglamorous piano (which at times has almost a hint of the timbre of a fortepiano) sounds as if it is recorded in an intimate domestic environment. Although sonically not the most alluring, it is a very satisfying, straightforward and carefully considered version. But those seeking this work played on the piano will find András Schiff's Decca recording even more persuasive and much more attractively recorded (414 388-2 (Book I) and 417 326-2 (Book II) – see our main volume, pp. 43/44).

Complete organ music

Volume 5: *Allabreve in D, BWV 589; Aria in F, BWV 587; Canzona in D min., BWV 588; Fantasias, BWV 563 & BWV 571; Fugues, BWV 574, BWV 578 & BWV 580; Musical offering, BWV 1079: Ricercar. Pastorale, BWV 590; Preludes, BWV 567/569; Preludes & fugues, BWV 534, 535a* (incomplete), *BWV 536, BWV 539, BWV 541, BWV 543/547; 8 Short Preludes & fugues, BWV 553/560; Prelude, trio & fugue, BWV 545b; Toccata & fugue in E, BWV 566; Trios, BWV 584, BWV 586 & BWV 1027a.*
(M) *** Decca 425 631-2 (3). Peter Hurford (organs of the Church of Our Lady of Sorrows, Toronto; Ratzeburg Cathedral; Eton College, Windsor; St Catharine's College Chapel, Cambridge; New College, Oxford; Domkirche, St Pölten, Austria; Stiftskirche, Melk, Austria; Knox Grammar School, Sydney).

Volume 6: *Chorale preludes Nos. 1–46 (Orgelbüchlein), BWV 599/644. Chorale preludes, BWV 620a, BWV 741/748, BWV 751/2, BWV 754/5, BWV 757/763, BWV 765, BWV Anh. 55; Fugue in G min., BWV 131a.*
(M) *** Decca 425 635-2 (2) [id.]. Peter Hurford (organs of the Church of Our Lady of Sorrows, Toronto; St Catharine's College Chapel, Cambridge; Eton College, Windsor).

These two volumes complete Peter Hurford's unique survey of Bach's organ music, originally recorded for the Argo label between 1974 and 1982. Volume 5 concludes the set of *Preludes and fugues* begun in Volume 1. It opens with the eight short works, BWV 553/560, now considered to be inauthentic – indeed they are dated from around the time of Bach's death; but they are attractively individual pieces, here presented genially and spontaneously. In the mature *Preludes and fugues* Hurford's tempi tend to be rather steady. His approach is particularly effective in the C minor work, BWV 546, given a spacious gravitas, and in the well-known *Fugue in G minor*, BWV 578, made famous by Stokowski's orchestral transcription, in which Hurford's simplicity is an antidote to Stokowski's flamboyance. The various shorter pieces are used to diversify the programme. The *Trio in G major*, BWV 1027a, for instance, is based on a string sonata and the arrangement is not Bach's, but it makes an entertaining interlude. Like the more complex four-movement *Pastorale*, it is most engagingly registered. The *Toccata in E*, BWV 566, looks back to Buxtehude in style and has two following fugues. Throughout, the various organs are recorded splendidly and the CD transfers are excellently managed.
The 46 *Chorales* from the *Orgelbüchlein* first appeared towards the end of the project (1981/2); they not only show Peter Hurford at his most imaginative in terms of registration and colour, but they also demonstrate the clarity with which the *cantus firmus* always emerges in his hands, however florid the texture. These are all played on the Toronto organ, which is beautifully recorded and seems ideal for this repertoire. Of the remaining twenty-three miscellaneous chorales, many are now known not to be authentic: BWV 749, 750 and 756 are omitted because they have no connection with Bach at all, and BWV 753 and 764 because they are not complete. Of the rest, some are now definitely attributed to other composers but are nevertheless included for their general musical interest. Hurford makes a good case for them.

(i) *Allabreve, BWV 589; Canzona, BWV 588; Fantasia in G, BWV 572; Prelude in A min., BWV 569;* (ii) *Trio sonatas: Nos. 1 in E flat, BWV 525; 2 in C min., BWV 526; 5 in C, BWV 529.*
(M) *** DG Dig. 431 705-2; *431 705-4* [id.]. Ton Koopman (organs of (i) Grote Kerk, Massluis; (ii) Waalse Kerk, Amsterdam).

An excellent recital, with both organs beautifully recorded, with the single proviso that it was a pity to place the *Canzona* immediately after the *Allebreve*, as they are both slow pieces in rather similar style. But it is the *Trio sonatas* here which give the most pleasure; they are full of life and colour, and Koopman's buoyant playing of the allegros confirms the fact that their character is essentially that of music for chamber ensemble rather than the keyboard.

35 Arnstadt chorale preludes, BWV 714, 719, 742, 957 & 1090/1120. Chorale prelude, BWV 639; Preludes and fugues: in C, BWV 531; in D min., BWV 549a; in G min., BWV 535; in E, BWV 566.
*** ASV Gaudeamus Dig. CD GAU 120/121 (available separately). Graham Barber (organ of St Peter Mancroft, Norwich).

This recording of the early, so-called *Neumeister chorales*, only recently discovered in the Music Library of Yale University, introduces a brilliant young organist, Graham Barber, and a fine new (1984) organ at Norwich, built with an ear to simulating the North German organs of the seventeenth century by Arp Schnitger and his contemporaries. In Graham Barber's hands it seems ideally suited for this early Bach repertoire, with the *Preludes and fugues* used to frame two separate recitals of the *Chorales*. Barber plays these opening and closing pieces with splendid vitality and structural grip, and presents the chorale variants simply and effectively, constantly changing colours and sound-weighting. The recording is very much in the demonstration class.

Concertos (for solo organ) *Nos. 1–6, BWV 592/7.*
(B) *** Vanguard VECD 7515; *VETC 6515* [VBD 35; *CHM 35* (1, 2, 3 & 5 only)]. Anton Heiler (organ of Maria Kyrka, Hälsingborg, Sweden).
(M) ** DG 431 119-2; *431 119-4* [id.]. Karl Richter (Silbermann organ, Arlesheim).

Bach's solo *Organ concertos*, based on the music of others, notably Nos. 2, 3 and 5, deriving from three string concertos by Vivaldi, require a more extrovert approach than is provided by Karl Richter, though his peal-like flourishes in the finale of No. 2 show him making a very firm response to this highly spontaneous music. But elsewhere, at times, his approach seems excessively scholarly. The Arlesheim organ is beautifully recorded, and his registration often finds some very attractive colouring, but in the last resort this playing is rather sober for music which is so often genial and outgiving. Nevertheless Richter includes all six *Concertos*, including the E flat major transcription, BWV 597, which is not now attributed to Bach. The source of its two movements is uncertain, but they are rather attractive, especially the second, a *Gigue*.

Anton Heiler offers the four best-known concertos, including the *First*, with music by Prince Johann Ernst, which has a gay opening movement, an expressive central section and a catchy finale. Throughout his performances, Heiler captures perfectly the extrovert quality of Bach enjoying himself, revelling in the music of others. Of the Vivaldi transcriptions, the one in C major, BWV 594, is irresistible with its joyous and colourful opening *Toccata* (suggesting for a fleeting moment Handel's *Hallelujah chorus*). The recording is vivid and clear and Heiler's registration in the slow movements draws some most engaging sounds from his characterful Swedish organ.

Chorales: Herr Jesu Christ, BWV 655; Liebster Jesu, wir sind hier, BWV 730/731; Chorale variations: O Lamm Gottes, BWV 656; Chorale: Wir glauben all' an einen Gott, Vater, BWV 740; Fugue in G min., BWV 578; Pastorale in F, BWV 590; Passacaglia in C min., BWV 582; Prelude and fugue in G, BWV 541.
**(*) ASV Novalis Dig. 150 052-2; *150 052-4* [id.]. Ton Koopman (Trinity organ of Ottobeuren Basilica).

Characteristically strong performances here from Ton Koopman, who also revels in the delightful sounds from the 'woodwind' stops on this fine eighteenth-century organ, especially in the *Pastorale*, the *Chorale, Wir glauben all' an einen Gott, Vater* and the fairly simple but extended choral variants on *O Lamm Gottes*. The recital opens with the *Prelude and fugue in G* which Koopman presents with plenty of flair. However, here the plangent sounds of the reeds, observed fairly closely, bring a degree of harshness which may not appeal to all tastes, while the closing *Passacaglia and fugue in C minor* is enormously portentous and weighty, with the pedals grinding out the recurring bass motif relentlessly. The effect is certainly powerful but is also a shade oppressive, when the balance is so immediate. You will either like this recital a great deal or find it at times too insistent.

8 Little Preludes and fugues, BWV 553/560; Prelude and fugue in D, BWV 532; Toccata, adagio & fugue in C, BWV 564; Trio sonata No. 1 in E flat, BWV 525.
*** ASV Novalis Dig. 150 066-2; *150 066-4* [id.]. Ton Koopman (organ of Grote Kerk, Maassluis).

Ton Koopman's continuing series never fails to stimulate, and this is one of the very finest of his recitals, demonstrating a magnificent instrument, highly suitable for Bach, of which he is completely the master. He brings the eight *Little Preludes and fugues* splendidly to life and is even more commanding in the excitingly intricate *Prelude and fugue in D minor* and the superb *Toccata, adagio and fugue*, which demands comparable bravura. Both works come from the composer's early Weimar period. The *Trio sonata* makes an effective contrast after the latter work. The digital recording is first rate: Bach organ records don't come any better than this.

VOCAL MUSIC

Volume 4: *Cantatas Nos. 12: Weinen, klagen, sorgen, zagen; 13: Meine Seufzer, meine Tränen; 14: Wär Gott nicht mit uns diese Zeit; 16: Herr Gott, dich loben wir.*
(M) *** Teldec/WEA 2292 42500-2 (2) [id.]. Gampert, Hinterreiter, Esswood, Equiluz, Van Altena, Van Egmond, Tölz Boys' Ch., King's Coll. Ch., Leonhardt Cons., Leonhardt.

It is good to welcome back to the catalogue the missing volumes of the distinguished Teldec series of Bach cantatas, which as a set deservedly won the 1990 *Gramophone* award for 'Special Achievement'. There is much wonderful music in all four works here; performances and recordings are first class. In Cantata No. 12, *Weinen, klagen, sorgen, zagen* ('Weeping, lamenting, worrying, fearing') the alto aria is particularly fine (*Kreuz und Krone sind verbunden*) and the oboe obbligato is beautifully done. No. 14, *Wär Gott nicht mit uns diese Zeit*, has a splendid extended opening chorus, of considerable complexity and striking power.

Volume 5: *Cantatas Nos. 17: Wer Dank opfert, der preiset mich; 18: Gleichwie der Regen und Schnee vom Himmel; 19: Es erhub sich ein Streit; 20: O Ewigkeit, du Donnerwort.*
(M) *** Teldec/WEA 2292 42501-2 (2) [id.]. Treble soloists from V. Boys' Ch., Esswood, Equiluz, Van Egmond, V. Boys' Ch., Ch. Viennensis, VCM, Harnoncourt.

Cantata No. 17 has a long sinfonia and opening chorus combined; and in No. 19 the introductory fugal chorus is magnificent in its tumultuous polyphony. The closing chorus is simpler, but trumpets add a touch of ceremonial splendour. No. 20 also includes a memorable alto/tenor duet, *O Menschenkind, hör auf geschwind.* The sound is first class, fresh, vivid and clear.

Volume 6: *Cantatas Nos.* (i) *21: Ich hatte viel Bekümmernis;* (ii) *22: Jesus nahm zu sich die Zwölfe; 23: Du wahrer Gott und Davids Sohn.*
(M) **(*) Teldec/WEA 2292 42502-2 (2) [id.]. Esswood, Equiluz; (i) Walker, Wyatt, V. Boys' Ch., Ch. Viennensis, VCM, Harnoncourt; (ii) Gampert, Van Altena, Van Egmond, King's College Ch., Leonhardt Cons., Leonhardt.

The magnificent *Ich hatte viel Bekümmernis* lacks something in flair and Leonhardt is a little rigid in No. 22, *Jesus nahm zu sich die Zwölfe.* Harnoncourt tends in general to be freer; but a constant source of irritation through the series is the tendency to accentuate all main beats. This was the final appearance of the King's College Choir, which made a worthwhile contribution to many of the early performances in the series.

Volume 7: *Cantatas Nos. 24: Ein ungefärbt Gemüte; 25: Es ist nicht Gesundes an meinem Leibe; 26: Ach wie flüchtig, ach wie nichtig; 27: Wer weiss, wie nahe mir mein Ende!.*
(M) *** Teldec/WEA 2292 42503-2 (2). Esswood, Equiluz, Van Egmond, Nimsgern, V. Boys' Ch., Ch. Viennensis, VCM, Harnoncourt.

This volume is worth having in particular for the sake of the magnificent *Es ist nicht Gesundes,* a cantata of exceptional richness of expression and resource. No. 27, *Wer weiss, wie nahe mir mein Ende!,* is altogether magnificent too, and the performances are some of the finest to appear in this ambitious and often impressive survey. Certainly for those dipping into rather than collecting all this series, Volume 1 (comprising Cantatas Nos. 1–4: 2292 42497-2) and Volume 7 would be good starting points, even though in the case of the latter all the cantatas are exceptionally short.

Volume 8: *Cantatas Nos. 28: Gottlob! nun geht das Jahr zu Ende; 29: Wir danken dir, Gott; 30: Freue dich, erlöste Schar.*
(M) *** Teldec/WEA 2292 42504-2 (2). Esswood, Equiluz, Van Egmond, Nimsgern, V. Boys' Ch., Ch. Viennensis, VCM, Harnoncourt.

Volume 9: *Cantatas Nos.* (i) *31: Der Himmel lacht! die Erde jubilieret;* (ii) *32: Liebster Jesu, mein Verlangen; 33: Allein zu dir, Herr Jesu Christ;* (i) *34: O ewiges Feuer, O Ursprung der Liebe.*
(M) *** Teldec/WEA 2292 42505-2 (2). (i) Esswood, Equiluz, Nimsgern, V. Boys' Ch., Ch. Viennensis, VCM, Harnoncourt; (ii) Gampert, Jacobs, Van Altena, Van Egmond, Hanover Boys' Ch., Leonhardt Cons., Leonhardt.

Volume 10: *Cantatas Nos. 35: Geist und Seele wird verwirret; 36: Schwingt freudig euch empor; 37: Wer da gläubet und getauft wird; 38: Aus tiefer Not schrei ich zu dir.*
(M) *** Teldec/WEA 2292 42506-2 (2). Esswood, Equiluz, Van der Meer, V. Boys' Ch., Ch. Viennensis, VCM, Harnoncourt.

These three boxes continue the high standard that has distinguished this enterprise. Of the new names in the roster of soloists one must mention the stylish singing of René Jacobs; Walter Gampert is the excellent treble soloist in *Liebster Jesu.* No. 34 is an especially attractive cantata; here, as throughout, one notes the liveliness as well as the authenticity of the performances, although the expressive writing is sensitively handled, too: the alto aria, *Wohl euch, ihr auser-wahlten, Seelen* ('Blessed ye hearts whom God has chosen'), with its atmospheric obbligato flutes is particularly memorable. No. 35 features an outstanding concertante organ solo; No. 36 uses a pair of oboi d'amore, and there are oboes in duet in No. 38. Most enjoyable, with excellent solo singing, and vividly clear, well-balanced sound.

Volume 11: *Cantatas Nos.* (i) *39: Brich dem Hungrigen dein Brot;* (i; ii) *40: Dazu ist erschienen der Sohn Gottes;* (iii) *41: Jesu, nun sei gepreiset; 42: Am Abend aber desselbigen Sabbats.*
(M) ** Teldec/WEA 2292 42556-2 (2). (i) Jacobs, Van Egmond, Hanover Boys' Ch., Leonhardt Cons., Leonhardt; (ii) Van Altena; (iii) Esswood, Equiluz, Van der Meer, V. Boys' Ch., Ch. Viennensis, VCM, Harnoncourt.

This is one of the less distinguished sets in this long and successful project. No. 41 probably fares best: one admires the light tone of the baroque brass instruments and the general sense of style that informs the proceedings, even if intonation, as inevitably seems to happen with authentic instruments, is not always true. The music is quite magnificent. So, too, is Cantata 42, but these artists do little to convey the feeling of the opening sinfonia, the oboe melody losing much of its expressive fervour. There is a loss of breadth also in No. 39, not altogether offset by the authenticity to which these performers are dedicated. No. 40 has some lively choruses, well sung, and there is also some excellent obbligato horn playing: here the music-making is undoubtedly spirited. But these performances sometimes radiate greater concern with historical rectitude (as these artists conceive it) than with communicating their pleasure in the music. The recordings are exemplary.

Volume 12: *Cantatas Nos.* (i) *43: Gott fähret auf mit Jauchzen; 44: Sie werden euch in die Bann tun;* (ii) *45: Es ist dir gesagt, Mensch, was gut ist; 46: Schauet doch und sehet.*
(M) *** Teldec/WEA 2292 42559-2 (2) [id.]. (i) Jelosits, Esswood, Equiluz, Van der Meer, V. Boys' Ch., Ch. Viennensis, VCM, Harnoncourt; (ii) Jacobs, Equiluz, Kunz, Hanover Boys' Ch., Leonhardt Cons., Leonhardt.

Cantata No. 46 is the one that includes the original *Qui tollis peccata* of the *B minor Mass.* This and No. 43 are not otherwise available; though the texture could be laid out more revealingly in No. 46, this is the only technical blemish in a very fine recording. All four performances are of the highest standard, and young Peter Jelosits, the boy treble, copes staunchly with the very considerable demands of Bach's writing. He really is astonishingly fine, and his companions in these records are no less accomplished. Leonhardt takes the chorale in No. 46 a little on the fast side; but enough of quibbles – this is a truly first-class box.

Volume 13: *Cantatas Nos. 47: Wer sich selbst erhöhet; 48: Ich elender Mensch, wer wird mich erlösen; 49: Ich geh' und suche mit Verlangen; 50: Nun ist das Heil und die Kraft.*
(M) *** Teldec/WEA 2292 42560-2 (2) [id.]. Jelosits, Esswood, Equiluz, Van der Meer, V. Boys' Ch., Ch. Viennensis, VCM, Harnoncourt.

The treble soloist in No. 49, *Ich geh' und suche mit Verlangen*, Peter Jelosits, really is remarkable. Perhaps the chorus in No. 50, *Nun ist das Heil und die Kraft*, is a shade overdriven; but by and large this is one of the best of the series, and the riches the music unfolds do not fail to surprise and reward the listener.

Volume 14: *Cantatas Nos. 51: Jauchzet Gott im allen Landen; 52: Falsche Welt, dir trau ihr nicht; 54: Widerstehe doch der Sünde; 55: Ich armer Mensch, ich Sündenknecht; 56: Ich will den Kreuzstab gerne tragen.*
(M) *** Teldec/WEA 2292 42422-2 (2) [id.]. Kweksilber, Kronwitter, Eswood, Equiluz, Schopper, Hanover Boys' Ch., Leonhardt Cons., Leonhardt.

A stunning set, arguably the most remarkable in the series so far. *Jauchzet Gott*, the most familiar, has an altogether superb soprano soloist in Marianne Kweksilber and Don Smithers' playing of the trumpet obbligato is no less impressive. There have been some splendid records of No. 51 in the past, but this eclipses them all; and the remaining cantatas in this box are all done with great distinction.

Volume 15: *Cantatas Nos. 57: Selig ist der Mann; 58: Ach Gott, wie manches Herzeleid; 59: Wer mich liebet, der wird mein Wort halten; 60: O Ewigkeit, du Donnerwort.*
(M) **(*) Teldec/WEA 2292 42423-2 [id.]. Jelosits, Kronwitter, Esswood, Equiluz, Van der Meer, Tölz Boys' Ch., VCM, Harnoncourt.

Volume 16: *Cantatas Nos. 61: Nun komm, der Heiden Heiland; 62: Nun komm, der Heiden Heiland; 63: Christen, ätzet diesen Tag; 64: Sehet, welch eine Liebe.*
(M) **(*) Teldec/WEA 2292 42565-2 (2) [id.]. Jelosits, Kronwitter, Esswood, Equiluz, Van der Meer, Tölz Boys' Ch., VCM, Harnoncourt.

These volumes maintain their high standards, even if their style is unlikely to appeal to all tastes. Nos. 57–60 are all short but the music is consistently fine, and they are now fitted on to a single CD. The boy soloist in No. 61 is not the equal of Peter Jelosits and he sounds short-breathed, while the vibratoless strings at the opening invite unfavourable comparisons with the Richter recording. Still, these slight inadequacies are a small price to pay for the general excellence and scholarship here.

Volume 17: *Cantatas Nos.* (i) *65: Sie werden aus Saba alle kommen*; (ii) *66: Erfreut euch, ihr Herzen; 67: Halt' im Gedächtnis Jesum Christ*; (i) *68: Also hat Gott die Welt geliebt.*
(M) ** Teldec/WEA 2292 42571-2 (2) [id.]. (i) Jelosits, Equiluz, Van der Meer, Tölz Boys' Ch., VCM, Harnoncourt; (ii) Esswood, Equiluz, Van Egmond, Hanover Boys' Ch., Ghent Coll. Vocale, Leonhardt Cons., Leonhardt.

The best thing in this volume is Leonhardt's broad and spacious account of No. 66, which also offers some stunning playing on the natural trumpet. Harnoncourt's versions of Nos. 65 and 68 are a little wanting in charm and poetry (the dialogue between the voice of Christ and the chorus in No. 67 is also prosaic). But there is fine solo singing, and that and the instrumental playing outweigh other considerations.

Volume 18: *Cantatas Nos. 69 & 69a: Lobe den Herrn, meine Seele; 70: Wachet! betet! betet! wachet!; 71: Gott ist mein König; 72: Alles nur nach Gottes Willen.*
(M) *** Teldec/WEA 2292 42572-2 (2) [id.]. Esswood, Equiluz, Van der Meer, Visser, Tölz Boys' Ch., VCM, Harnoncourt.

No. 71 is an enchanting piece, full of invention and variety. This set also includes both versions of Cantata No. 69; only the numbers which differ, or are new in its adaptation in 1730, are re-recorded. No. 72 employs more modest forces than the others. Wilhelm Wiedl (from the Tölz Choir) is the excellent treble soloist throughout, and the other soloists and instrumentalists cannot be praised too highly. The choral singing is not above crtiticism but remains more than acceptable. Excellent sound.

Volume 19: *Cantatas Nos. 73: Herr, wie du willt, so schicks mit mir; 74: Wer mich liebet, der wird mein Wort halten; 75: Die Elenden sollen essen.*
(M) ** Teldec 2292 42573-2 [id.]. Erler, Klein, Esswood, Equiluz, Kraus, Van Egmond, Hanover Boys' Ch., Ghent Coll. Vocale, Leonhardt Cons., Leonhardt.

All three cantatas offered on this single CD come from 1723–5 and none is otherwise available. The music is certainly worth getting to know. However, some of the weaknesses of the Teldec series emerge here: some sedate and really rather weak choral work and a reluctance to permit 'expressive' singing deprive the music of some of its eloquence, and the boy trebles, though possessed of musical and pleasing voices, are not fully equal to Bach's taxing writing.

Volume 20: *Cantatas Nos.* (i) *76: Die Himmel erzählen die Ehre Gottes*; (ii) *77: Du sollt Gott, deinen Herren, lieben; 78: Jesu, der du meine Seele*; (ii) *79: Gott der Herr ist Sonn' und Schild.*
(M) **(*) Teldec 2292 42576-2 (2) [id.]. Esswood, (i) Wiedl, Equiluz, Van der Meer, Tölz Boys' Ch., VCM, Harnoncourt; (ii) Bratschke, Kraus, Van Egmond, Hanover Boys' Ch., Ghent Coll. Vocale, Leonhardt Cons., Leonhardt.

Two of the cantatas in this volume are not otherwise recorded at present, and all four are of outstanding interest. As almost always in these performances, one is aware of restraints and the ear longs for bolder colours and the greater power of modern instruments. However, there is too much good music here for such reservations to worry us for long.

Volume 21: *Cantatas Nos. 80: Ein' feste Burg; 81: Jesus schläft, was soll ich hoffen?; 82: Ich habe genug; 83: Erfreute Zeit im neuen Bunde.*
(M) *(*) Teldec/WEA 2292 42577-2 (2) [id.]. Esswood, Equiluz, Van der Meer, Huttenlocher, Van Egmond, Tölz Boys' Ch., V. Boys' Ch., Ch. Viennensis, VCM, Harnoncourt.

This is one of the less successful issues in the Teldec series. *Ich habe genug* has been performed more impressively on other recordings, and Philippe Huttenlocher, though intelligent and thoughtful, is not always secure. Some of the choral singing could also do with more polish and incisiveness.

Cantatas Nos. (i; ii) *82: Ich habe genug;* (i; iii; iv) *159: Sehet, wir gehn hinauf gen Jerusalem;* (iii) *170: Vergnügte Ruh', beliebte Seelenlust.*
❀ (M) *** Decca 430 260-2; *430 260-4* [id.]. (i) Shirley-Quirk; (ii) Lord; (iii) J. Baker; (iv) Tear, St Anthony Singers; ASMF, Marriner.

John Shirley-Quirk's performance of *Ich habe genug* is much to be admired, not only for the sensitive solo singing, but also for the lovely oboe obbligato of Roger Lord. The mid-1960s sound is also remarkably fresh and present. But this reissue is to be prized even more for the other two cantatas. *Sehet, wir gehn hinauf gen Jerusalem* is one of Bach's most inspired and surely ranks high on the shortlist of essential Bach. Particularly glorious is the penultimate meditation, *Es is vollbracht* (It is finished), again with a poignant oboe obbligato. Both Dame Janet Baker and Shirley-Quirk are in marvellous voice, and *Vergnügte Ruh'* makes a worthy companion. These are also from the mid-1960s and both are performed superbly and recorded very naturally; the CD transfer retains all the warmth and refinement of the original master. This is among the half-dozen or so cantata records that ought to be in every collection.

Volume 22: *Cantatas Nos.* (i) *84: Ich bin vergnügt mit meinem Glücke; 85: Ich bin ein guter Hirt; 86: Wahrlich, wahrlich, ich sage euch; 87: Bisher habt ihr nichts gebeten;* (ii) *88: Siehe, ich will viel Fischer aussenden; 89: Was soll ich aus dir machen, Ephraim?; 90: Es reisset euch ein schrecklich Ende.*
(M) ** Teldec/WEA 2292 42578-2 (2) [id.]. Esswood, Equiluz, (i) Wiedl, Van der Meer, Tölz Boys' Ch., VCM, Harnoncourt; (ii) Klein, Van Egmond, Hanover Boys' Ch., Ghent Coll. Vocale, Leonhardt Cons., Leonhardt.

If the performances here are of variable quality, the musical inspiration is not, and the set is worth acquiring for the sake of this neglected music, much of which is otherwise unobtainable.

Volume 23: *Cantatas Nos.* (i) *91: Gelobet seist du, Jesus Christ; 92: Ich hab' in Gottes Herz und Sinn;* (ii) *93: Wer nur den lieben Gott lässt walten; 94: Was frag' ich nach der Welt.*
(M) *** Teldec/WEA 2292 42582-2 (2) [id.]. Esswood, Equiluz, (i) Bratschke, Van Egmond, Hanover Boys' Ch., Ghent Coll. Vocale, Leonhardt Cons. Leonhardt; (ii) Wiedl, Van der Meer, Huttenlocher, Tölz Boys' Ch., VCM, Harnoncourt.

One of the most desirable of these Bach sets, with assured and confident playing and singing from all concerned.

Volume 24: *Cantatas Nos.* (i) *95: Christus, der ist mein Leben; 96: Herr Christ, der ein'ge Gottesohn; 97: In allen meinen Taten;* (ii) *98: Was Gott tut, das ist wohlgetan.*
(M) **(*) Teldec/WEA 2292 42583-2 [id.]. Esswood, Equiluz, (i) Wiedl, Huttenlocher, Van der Meer, Tölz Boys' Ch., VCM, Harnoncourt; (ii) Lengert, Van Egmond, Hanover Boys' Ch., Ghent Coll. Vocale, Leonhardt Cons., Leonhardt.

There are occasional weaknesses here (Philippe Huttenlocher is not altogether happy in No. 96), but this CD is still well worth having.

Volume 25: *Cantatas Nos.* (i) *99: Was Gott tut, das ist wohlgetan;* (ii) *100: Was Gott tut, das ist wohlgetan;* (i) *101: Nimm von uns, Herr, du treuer Gott; 102: Herr, deine Augen sehen nach dem Glauben.*
(M) **(*) Teldec/WEA 2292 42584-2 (2) [id.]. Esswood, Equiluz, (i) Wiedl, Huttenlocher, Tölz Boys' Ch., VCM, Harnoncourt; (ii) Bratschke, Van Egmond, Hanover Boys' Ch., Ghent Coll. Vocale, Leonhardt Cons., Leonhardt.

With this box Teldec pass the century and, although there have been unevenesses in the series, it is no mean achievement. Cantata 99 fares less well than the others; but it would be curmudgeonly to dwell on the shortcomings of this box, given the interest of its contents.

Volume 26: *Cantatas Nos.* (i; ii) *103: Ihr werdet weinen und heulen;* (iii; iv) *104: Du Hirte Israel, höre;* (v; iv) *105: Herr, gehe nicht ins Gericht;* (vi; ii) *106: Gottes Zeit ist die allerbeste Zeit (Actus tragicus).*
(M) *** Teldec/WEA 2292 42602-2 [id.]. (i) Esswood, Equiluz, Van Egmond; (ii) Hanover Boys' Ch., Ghent Coll. Vocale, Leonhardt Cons., Leonhardt; (iii) Esswood, Huttenlocher; (iv) Tölz Boys' Ch., VCM, Harnoncourt; (v) Wiedl, Equiluz, Van der Meer; (vi) Klein, Harten, Van Altena, Van Egmond.

The best-known and most deeply moving cantata here is the *Actus tragicus.* No. 103, too, is a poignant and expressive piece that repays study. Both these performances are among the very finest to have reached us in this series. No. 105 is arguably one of the very deepest of all Bach cantatas; Harnoncourt is perhaps wanting in expressive weight here;

but neither this fact nor the reservations one might feel about his account of No. 104 diminish the value of this excellent single-CD collection.

Cantatas Nos. 106: Gottes Zeit ist die allerbeste Zeit; 118: O Jesu Christ, mein Lebens Licht (2nd version); *198: Lass, Fürstin, lass noch einen Strahl.*
*** DG Dig. 429 782-2 [id.]. Argenta, Chance, Rolfe Johnson, Varcoe, Monteverdi Ch., E. Bar. Soloists, Eliot Gardiner.

Gardiner directs dedicated, intense performances of three of Bach's finest cantatas, all valedictory works. A youthful inspiration, written when Bach was only 22, the *Actus tragicus*, BWV 106, comes with the much later and more elaborate mourning ode, BWV 198. The third item – which Gardiner also recorded earlier for Erato along with his set of the motets – is the magnificent chorale-based motet, *O Jesu Christ, mein Lebens Licht.* The new account of that motet is more intimate than the 1980 version, less grandly dramatic, more devotional; the whole record suggests a scale of performance apt for a small chapel. That allows the elaborate instrumentation to come out clearly, with the two longer works giving the lie to the idea of mourning music necessarily sounding sombre. Well-balanced sound.

Volume 27: *Cantatas Nos.* (i) *107: Wass willst du dich betrüben*; (ii) *108: Es ist euch gut, dass ich hingehe; 109: Ich glaube, lieber Herr, hilf meinem Unglauben!; 110: Unser Mund sei voll Lachens.*
(M) *** Teldec/WEA 2292 42603-2 (2) [id.]. Equiluz, (i) Klein, Van Egmond, Hanover Boys' Ch., Ghent Coll. Vocale, Leonhardt Cons., Leonhardt; (ii) Wiedl, Frangoulis, Stumpf, Lorenz, Esswood, Van der Meer, Tölz Boys' Ch., VCM, Harnoncourt.

The highest standards of this series are maintained throughout this volume, and that applies to performance, recording, CD transfer and presentation.

Volume 28: *Cantatas Nos.* (i) *111: Was mein Gott will, das gescheh' allzeit; 112: Der Herr ist mein getreuer Hirt*; (ii) *113: Herr Jesu Christ, du höchstes Gut; 114: Ach, lieben Christen, seid getrost.*
(M) *** Teldec/WEA 2292 42606-2 (2) [id.]. Equiluz, (i) Huber, Esswood, Van der Meer, Tölz Boys' Ch., VCM, Harnoncourt; (ii) Hennig, Jacobs, Van Egmond, Hanover Boys' Ch., Ghent Coll. Vocale, Leonhardt Cons., Leonhardt.

The opening chorus of No. 112 is among the most beautiful of Bach's choral fantasias, and it must be said that Harnoncourt does it justice. Leonhardt's accounts of Cantatas Nos. 113 and 114 are free from pedantry, well shaped and unaffected. This is one of the sets that lovers of the Bach cantatas should acquire, even if they have ambivalent feelings about the series as a whole.

Volume 29: *Cantatas Nos.* (i; iii; iv) *115: Mache dich, mein Geist, bereit; 116: Du Friedefürst, Herr Jesu Christ*; (ii; v; vi) *117: Sei Lob und Erh dem höchsten Gut*; (i; iii; vii) *119: Preise, Jerusalem, den Herrn.*
(M) *** Teldec/WEA 2292 42608-2 (2) [id.]. (i) Tölz Boys' Ch., VCM, Harnoncourt; (ii) Equiluz, Hanover Boys' Ch., Ghent Coll. Vocale, Leonhardt Cons., Leonhardt; with (iii) Huber, Esswood; (iv) Huttenlocher; (v) Jacobs; (vi) Van Egmond; (vii) Holl.

No. 115 is rich in melodic invention. Particularly felicitous is the aria for soprano, flute and violoncello piccolo which, despite a moment of uncertainty from the treble, Markus Huber, is most affectingly done. Its companion, No. 116, opens with a lively A major chorus and that is given with plenty of vigour and spirit. There is a demanding trio for treble, tenor and bass, which taxes the soloists but rewards the listener with invention of great contrapuntal refinement. The imposing *Sei Lob und Ehr dem höchsten Gut* is the only cantata here conducted by Leonhardt; his tempi are excellently judged, although one grumble is the detached delivery of the chorale, which sounds unnecessarily jerky. In No. 119, the tenor aria, *Wohl dir*, with its accompaniment of two oboi de caccia with organ and bassoon continuo, is rudely interrupted by a recitative with four trumpets and timpani, to provide just one of the contrasts of texture that make this so fascinating a piece. Harnoncourt is in good form and the recording is excellently balanced and splendidly truthful.

Volume 31: *Cantatas Nos.* (i) *124: Meinen Jesum lass ich nicht; 125: Mit Fried und Freud ich fahr dahin; 126: Erhalt uns, Herr, bei deinem Wort*; (ii) *127: Herr Jesu Christ wahr' Mensch und Gott.*
(M) *** Teldec/WEA 2292 42615-2 [id.]. (i) Bergius, Rampf, Esswood, Equiluz, Thomaschke, Tölz Boys' Ch., VCM, Harnoncourt; (ii) Hennig, Van Egmond, Hanover Boys' Ch., Ghent Coll. Vocale, Leonhardt Cons., Leonhardt.

No. 124 is a piece of strong melodic vitality and is full of colour too. Apart from the almost romantic tenor aria with its inspired oboe d'amore part, there is also a glorious duet for treble and alto, charmingly sung by Alan Bergius and Stefan Rampf, which also haunts the memory. No. 125 is even finer, a grave, elevated work that is most affecting. The opening chorus is inspired and the alto solo which follows is wonderfully expressive and receives eloquent treatment from Paul Esswood. No. 126 is based on a Lutheran hymn and the bellicose spirit of the first verse inspires Bach to write real battle music, with a demanding trumpet part. No. 127 is another cantata of striking richness and inspiration and includes an extraordinarily beautiful soprano aria (the plucked strings are heard against a lyrical figure, a texture comprising oboe and two recorders). It is an altogether marvellous piece and very well performed. This is another CD that collectors who are not automatically acquiring the whole series should not overlook.

Volume 33: *Cantatas Nos. 132: Bereitet die Wege, bereitet die Bahn; 133: Ich freue mich in dir; 134: Ein Herz, das seinen Jesum lebend weiss; 135: Ach Herr, mich armen Sünder.*
(M) **(*) Teldec/WEA 2292 42618-2 (2) [id.]. Hennig, Jacobs, Van Altena, Van Egmond, Hanover Boys' Ch., Ghent Coll. Vocale, Leonhardt Cons., Leonhardt

No. 132 is probably the best performance here: its young treble, Sebastian Hennig, is both secure and in tune, and the cantata itself has grandeur. As there is no final chorale, Leonhardt substitutes a chorale setting from Cantata No. 164. No. 133 comes off less well, thanks to an indifferent contribution from the Ghent Collegium Vocale, just as in its companion, No. 134, the tenor's intonation is not absolutely firm. But there is much to admire in his singing in the final cantata in the box (No. 135) and much in Leonhardt's performance that gives pleasure.

Volume 34: *Cantatas Nos. 136: Erforsche mich, Gott, und erfahre mein Herz; 137: Lobe den Herren, den mächtigen König der Ehren; 138: Warum betrübst du dich, mein Herz?; 139: Wohl dem, der sich auf seinen Gott.*
(M) ** Teldec/WEA 2292 42619-2 [id.]. Bergius, Rampf, Esswood, Equiluz, Holl, Heldwein, Hartinger, Tölz Boys' Ch., VCM, Harnoncourt.

Some relatively routine playing emerges straight away in the first of the four cantatas in this volume, all of them fitting on to a single CD. The solo singing is another matter: Paul Esswood's performance of the aria, *Es kömmt ein Tag*, is very distinguished indeed, as is Robert Holl's contribution. No. 137 is probably the best-known cantata here and it prompts some lovely singing from Alan Bergius. No. 138 is a particularly beautiful cantata; it opens with a strikingly poignant chorus which makes less effect than it might, thanks to some undistinguished singing and direction. Here the treble, Stefan Rampf, sounds distinctly insecure in the third section, *Er kann und will lasse nicht*. Nor can one say that the performance given to No. 139 is really worthy of it, with the two oboi d'amore sounding a little fragile at one point in the opening chorus. Still, the music is all very much worth having.

Volume 35: *Cantatas Nos.* (i) *140: Wachet auf, ruft uns die Stimme;* (ii) *143: Lobe den Herrn, meine Seele; 144: Nimm, was dein ist, und gehe hin;* (i) *145: Ich lebe, mein Herze, zu deinem Ergötzen; 146: Wir müssen durch viel Trübsal.*
(M) *** Teldec/Warner Dig. 2292 42630-2 (2) [id.]. Esswood, Equiluz, (i) Bergius, Hampson, Tölz Boys' Ch., VCM, Harnoncourt; (ii) Cericius, Pfeiffer, Van Egmond, Hanover Boys' Ch., Ghent Coll. Vocale, Leonhardt Cons., Leonhardt.

This two-CD set offers plenty of interest. The best known is No. 140, *Wachet auf, ruft uns die Stimme*, and, though the opening chorale is rather pedestrian, there is some felicitous singing elsewhere – the duet *Mein Freund ist mein, und ich bin sein* between Alan Bergius and Thomas Hampson is particularly fine. Cantata No. 141 is by Telemann and 142 by an unknown hand; both are omitted. Leonhardt is in charge in No. 143, *Lobe den Herrn, meine Seele*, which is unusual in having three horns. There is a particularly fine treble contribution from Roger Cericius in the working of the chorale, *Du Friedefürst, Herr Jesu Christ* and Leonhardt directs with vitality. Neither 144, *Nimm, was dein ist, und gehe hin*, nor 146, *Wir müssen durch viel Trübsal* is otherwise available – the latter opens with the first movement of the *Harpsichord concerto in D minor* (BWV 1052) as its sinfonia with the organ as soloist, and the opening duet of 145, *Ich lebe, mein Herze, zu deinem Ergötzen*, between Jesus and the Soul (Equiluz and Bergius) is beautifully done. As always in this venture, not everything is perfect, but this is one of the more satisfying of the series.

Volume 36: *Cantatas Nos.* (i) *147: Herz und Mund und Tat und Leben; 148: Bringet dem Herrn Ehre seines Namens;* (ii) *149: Man singet mit Freuden vom Sieg; 150: Nach dir, Herr, verlanget mich; 151: Süsser Trost, mein Jesus kömmt.*
(M) *** Teldec/WEA Dig. 2292 42631-2 (2) [id.]. Bergius, Hennig, Esswood, Equiluz, Hampson, Van Egmond; (i) Tölz Boys' Ch., VCM, Harnoncourt; (ii) Ghent Coll. Vocale, Leonhardt Cons., Leonhardt.

The best-known cantata here is the festive No. 147; No. 148, however, is relatively little heard and it proves an inventive and rewarding score. Paul Esswood's aria, *Mund und Herz steht dir offen*, scored for two oboi d'amore and oboe di caccia, is a delight and is beautifully played (much better than in No. 154 in Volume 37). No. 149 is another festive cantata whose opening chorus draws on No. 208, *Was mir behagt*. Generally good playing here and some fine singing, particularly from the young treble, Sebastian Hennig. No. 150 is not assigned to any specific Sunday or feast-day; if doubt has been cast on its authenticity, surely there can be none as to its merit. There is a marvellous bassoon obbligato in the bass aria, *Kraft und Starke sei gesungen Gott*, which is expertly played. (Not all the instrumental playing is flawless or tidy.) No. 151 is a Christmas cantata, and a delightful one, too.

Volume 37: *Cantatas Nos. 152: Tritt auf die Glaubensbahn; 153: Schau, lieber Gott, wie meine Feind; 154: Mein liebster Jesus ist verloren; 155: Mein Gott, wie lang, ach lange; 156: Ich steh' mit einem Fuss im Grabe.*

(M) **(*) Teldec/WEA Dig. 2292 42632-2 (2) [id.]. Wegmann, Bergius, Rampf, Esswood, Equiluz, Hampson, Tölz Boys' Ch., VCM, Harnoncourt.

Unlike the majority of these boxes, all five cantatas here are given to the Vienna Concentus Musicus under Nikolaus Harnoncourt. No. 152 has some particularly felicitous instrumental invention: the *Sinfonia* is a delight. The playing of the Concentus Musicus is eloquent and the performance as a whole very enjoyable. Unfortunately, the young Christoph Wegmann is obviously beset by nerves, though the voice, if unsteady, is admirably pure. No. 153 is a rarity and is unusual in that it discards the usual opening chorus in favour of a simple chorale: indeed, the cantata has three chorales in all. No. 154 is a powerful and emotional piece. The oboi d'amore suffer from imperfect intonation in the fourth number, *Jesu, lass dich finden*. Generally speaking, however, this is an acceptable performance. The recording is very clean indeed, but perhaps a trifle dry, with relatively little ambience.

Volume 38: *Cantatas Nos.* (i) *157: Ich lasse dich nicht, du segnest mich denn; 158: Der Friede sei mit dir; 159: Sehet, wir geh'n hinauf gen Jerusalem;* (ii) *161: Komm, du süsse Todesstunde; 162: Ach! ich sehe, jetzt, da ich zur Hochzeit gehe; 163: Nur jedem das Seine.*
(M) ** Teldec/WEA Dig. 2292 42633-2 (2) [id.]. Eiwanger, Esswood, Equiluz, Van Egmond, Tölz Boys' Ch., (i) Wegmann, Ghent Coll. Vocale, Leonhardt; (ii) Iconomou, Holl, VCM, Harnoncourt.

Of the cantatas recorded here, the finest and most familiar is undoubtedly No. 159, with its moving combination of chorale and aria, *Ich folge dir nach*, and the highly expressive aria for bass and oboe. Hardly less impressive is No. 161 for two treble recorders, strings, organ and continuo, a much earlier work from Weimar. So, too, are its companions. No. 157 is a chamber cantata for tenor, bass, strings, flute and oboe d'amore. The autograph does not survive, and the score used here is not the copy made in 1755 but a conjectural reconstruction made by Klaus Hofmann. To be frank, it is less than inspired. Its companion, No. 158, though incomplete is far from routine Bach. Although the performances are touched by moments of inspiration and are beautifully recorded, they fall short of distinction. Wind intonation at times is less than ideal.

Volume 39: *Cantatas Nos.* (i) *164: Ihr, die ihr euch von Christo nennet; 165: O heil'ges Geist und Wasserbad; 166: Wo gehest du hin?;* (ii) *167: Ihr Menschen, rühmet Gottes Liebe; 168: Tue, Rechnung! Donnerwort; 169: Gott soll allein mein Herze haben.*
(M) ** Teldec/WEA Dig. 2292 42634-2 (2) [id.]. Esswood, Equiluz, Tölz Boys' Ch.; (i) Wegmann, Eiwanger, Van Egmond, Ghent Coll. Vocale, Leonhardt Cons., Leonhardt; (ii) Iconomou, Immler, Holl, VCM, Harnoncourt.

In No. 164 at the beginning of the aria, *Nur durch Lieb und durch Erbarmen*, the intonation of the two flauto traverso and Paul Esswood is excruciating, and the direction here, under Leonhardt, laboured. Elsewhere things are much better and the aria, *Händen, die sich nicht verschliessen*, is spirited though the boy treble is rather swamped by Van Egmond. In No. 165 the treble copes well with the opening solo, which is fugal in character though a rondo in form. Though one of the more rarely performed cantatas, this is both inventive and varied, as indeed is its successor on this disc, *Wo gehest du hin?* It has an inspired tenor aria – well sung, too. No. 169 draws on material from the *E major Concerto*, BWV 1053, and No. 167 is more pastoral in character. No. 168 opens with a very spirited aria that evokes a superb response from the Vienna Concentus Musicus and finds the bass soloist in excellent form. Elsewhere there are moments when the performances sound as if they would have benefited from more rehearsal, though those under Harnoncourt are generally more lively. As usual, excellent recording and infinitely rewarding music.

Volume 40: *Cantatas Nos.* (i) *170: Vergnügte Ruh', beliebte Seelenlust;* (ii) *171: Gott, wie dein Name, so ist auch dein Ruhm;* (i) *172: Erschallet, ihr Lieder;* (ii) *173: Erhöhtes Fleisch und Blut; 174: Ich liebe den Höchsten von ganzem Gemüte.*
(M) **(*) Teldec/WEA Dig. 2292 42635-2 (2) [id.]. (i) Esswood, Van Altena, Van Egmond, Hanover Boys' Ch., Ghent Coll. Vocale, Leonhardt Cons., Leonhardt; (ii) Equiluz, Holl, Tölz Boys' Ch., VCM, Harnoncourt.

No. 170 is for alto and instruments and is without chorus or chorale. There is a moving alto aria, eloquently sung by Paul Esswood who copes with the demanding role very impressively. Leonhardt makes heavy weather of the aria, *Die Welt das Sundenhaus.* No. 171 falls to Harnoncourt. It was written for the New Year of 1729 in Leipzig and is festive in character – the aria will be familiar, since Bach borrows it from *Der zufriedengestellte Äolus* (BWV 205), while the closing chorale comes from Cantata No. 41. The boy treble Helmut Wittek is quite remarkable in the aria, *Jesus soll mein erstes Wort.* No. 172 receives a rather laboured performance from Leonhardt; 173 is a reworking of an earlier secular cantata from Cöthen. No. 174 opens with the first movement of *Brandenburg No. 3*, scored for oboes, oboe di caccia, horns and strings, plus bassoon continuo. Excellent sound and eminently serviceable performances.

Volume 41: *Cantatas Nos.* (i) *175: Er rufet seinen Schafen mit Namen; 176: Es ist ein trotzig und verzagt Ding*; (ii) *177: Ich ruf zu dir, Herr Jesu Christ; 178: Wo Gott der Herr nicht bei uns hält; 179: Siehe zu, dass deine Gottesfurcht.*
(M) ** Teldec/Warner Dig. 2292 42428-2 (2) [id.]. (i) Echternach, Esswood, Van Altena, Van Egmond, Hanover Boys' Ch., Coll. Vocale, Leonhardt Cons., Leonhardt; (ii) Wittek, Iconomou, Equiluz, Holl, Tölz Boys' Ch., VCM, Harnoncourt.

For some reason this set slipped through the net in our last edition. It is recommended to those who have followed the whole series and who will know what to expect, rather than to collectors freshly embarking on a Bach cantata collection. The first of the cantatas, No. 175, *Er rufet seinen Schafen mit Namen* for Whit Tuesday, is pastoral in mood (it is based on the parable of the Good Shepherd) and has some lovely things in it though the aria, *Es düncket mich, ich seh' dich kommen*, which Bach adapted from a secular cantata composed in honour of the birthday of Prince Leopold of Anhalt-Cöthen, is by general consent the least happy of them. Some of the playing under Gustav Leonhardt sounds a little tentative, and the performance of No. 176, *Es ist ein trotzig und verzagt Ding* (The heart is wicked and deceitful), with its powerful opening fugal chorus sounds a bit pedestrian. Paul Esswood is in excellent form, though the boy soprano Matthias Echternach is not wholly at ease in his solo contribution. No. 177, *Ich ruf zu dir, Herr Jesu Christ* (I cry to thee, Lord Jesus Christ), falls to Harnoncourt and receives a solid rather than an inspired performance, with the heavily accented first beats in the opening chorus producing an earthbound effect, though the boy alto Panito Iconomou has a distinctive vocal personality. By far the most successful on all counts is No. 178, *Wo Gott der Herr nicht bei uns hält* (Were God the Lord not on our side), which has considerable vigour and power in Harnoncourt's hands. The chorus in 179, *Siehe zu, dass deine Gottesfurcht*, make heavy weather of their powerful opening number, but there is some eloquent singing later from Kurt Equiluz and Robert Holl. Excellent recorded sound, with excellent balance between the singers and instrumentalists.

Cantata No. 205: Der zufriedengestellte Äolus.
(M) *** Teldec/Warner Dig. 2292 42957-2 [id.]. Kenny, Lipovšek, Equiluz, Holl, Arnold-Schönberg Ch., VCM, Harnoncourt.

Bach describes this cantata as '*Dramma per musica*', and some of its invention comes as close to opera as anything he wrote. It is a long piece of fifteen numbers and is written for ambitious forces, all of whom serenade the learned scholar. Picander's libretto is slight, as for that matter is the plot. Aeolus plans to release the autumn gales, and resists the pleas of Zephyrus and Pomona to desist; however, Pallas finally persuades him that to do so will spoil the festivities she plans for August Müller. The performance is very good indeed, though the heavy accents in the opening chorus of the winds and the wooden orchestral tutti in the second number must be noted. Alice Harnoncourt's obbligato in *Angenehmer Zephyrus* ('Delightful Zephyr') is a model of good style and is beautifully articulated. The singers, particularly Yvonne Kenny's Pallas and Kurt Equiluz's Zephyrus, are good; the recording has a decently spacious acoustic and no lack of detail. Recommended.

Christmas oratorio, BWV 248.
(M) **(*) Teldec/Warner 2292 42495-2 (3) [id.]. Treble soloists from V. Boys' Ch., Esswood, Equiluz, Nimsgern, V. Boys' Ch., Ch. Viennensis, VCM, Harnoncourt.
(M) ** RCA GD 77046; *GK 77046* (2) [77046-2-RG; *77046-4-RG*]. Bucchereil, Stein, Altmeyer, McDaniel, Tölz Boys' Ch., Coll. Aur., Schmidt-Gaden.

In his search for authenticity in Bach performance Harnoncourt has rarely been more successful than here. It will not be to everyone's taste to have a boy treble and male counter-tenor instead of women soloists, but the purity of sound of these singers is most affecting. Above all Harnoncourt in this instance never allows his pursuit of authentic sound to weigh the performance down; it has a lightness of touch which should please everyone. The sound, as usual from this source, is excellent and has transferred to CD with conspicuous success, but the use of three discs, even at mid-price, is disadvantageous.

The Collegium Aureum were pioneers in the period-performance movement, a less abrasive group than Nikolaus Harnoncourt's Concentus Musicus. Their recording of the *Christmas oratorio* was made in 1973 and, by latterday standards, it sounds too heavy and smooth for a period performance. Speeds are often surprisingly slow, not just for arias but also for recitatives. The all-male team of soloists includes not just a boy treble but a boy alto, who makes heavy weather of the cradle song in Cantata No. 2. Yet even with slow speeds, genuine joy is conveyed in the choruses, again with boys singing the upper parts. However, Gardiner's set is clearly preferable for those wanting an authentic performance. The freshness of the singing and playing is a constant pleasure, with Gardiner's often brisk speeds sounding bright and eager, not breathless (DG 423 232-2; *423 232-4*).

Mass in B min., BWV 232.
(M) (***) EMI mono CHS7 63505-2 (2) [Ang. CDHB 63505]. Schwarzkopf, Hoffgen, Gedda, Rehfuss, Ch. & O of V. Gesellschaft der Musikfreunde, Karajan.
(M) ** Ph. 426 657-2 (2) [id.]. Stich-Randall, Reynolds, Haefliger, Shirley-Quirk, Berlin RIAS Chamber Ch., Berlin RSO, Maazel.
** Decca Dig. 430 353-2; *430 353-4* (2) [id.]. Lott, Von Otter, Blochwitz, Shimell, Howell, Chicago SO and Ch., Solti.
** Telarc Dig. CD 80233 (2) [id.]. McNair, Ziegler, Simpson, Aler, Stone, Paul, Atlanta Chamber Ch. & SO, Shaw.

Recorded in 1952 with obbligato solos taken by the then principals of the Philharmonia in London, Karajan's historic recording combines the weight of a traditional performance with a freshness missing from most of the later and plushier Bach recordings he made in Berlin. This was one of Karajan's early collaborations with the producer, Walter Legge, and the casting of four clean-toned soloists reflects that, notably Legge's wife, Elisabeth Schwarzkopf. Though the opening *Kyrie* and the great *Sanctus* are slow and portentous in a traditional way, Karajan's intensity sustains them, with sweet rather than bright choral tone. Frequently Karajan's speeds are far faster and more resilient than was common in Bach performances at that time. This is a set full of delights to make you forget the limited mono sound, which is well transferred to CD. Dennis Brain's horn obbligato for *Qui sedes* is a wonder.

Maazel's is a thoughtful and sensitive interpretation, with the changing moods of music and text faithfully caught. Nothing sounds exaggerated and the recording is tonally beautiful and remarkably homogeneous. This suits the soloists, whose attitude to phrasing and melodic lines seems unusually consistent and admirable. The singing of the Berlin RIAS Chorus also flows smoothly and effortlessly, the upper voices soaring through Bach's expansive polyphony without strain. Indeed the contours are rounded a shade too self-consciously for the work's inherent drama to make its full effect, although there is no absence of majesty and breadth. Despite the fine solo contributions, there is an element of blandness here, even if the music's spiritual dimension is not lost.

Solti follows up his purposeful accounts of the *St Matthew Passion* and of Handel's *Messiah* with this other choral offering. With fine singing and playing and with an outstanding quartet of soloists, the result nevertheless fails to take off in the same way. It is not just that the sound is less cleanly focused, but that the performance is often laboured in a style very different from those earlier examples, which were equally on a relatively large scale but were not too heavy. The second *Kyrie* brings a return to romantic manners, hushed and slow, while the great *Sanctus* in its weight brings unwanted fierceness.

Shaw directs a plain and fresh reading with clean and immediate choral sound, offering the luxury of six soloists, all fine singers, thus eliminating the problems of tessitura that Bach presents if only four are used. The oddity is that fugal entries, as in the opening *Kyrie*, are sung by solo voices and not the chorus. For many that will be a fatal bar, and rhythmically this performance lacks the resilience and imagination of such rivals on modern instruments as Marriner (on Philips 416 415-2) and Schreier (on Eurodisc 610 089). But for those willing to accept original instruments, John Gardiner gives a magnificent account, one which attempts to stay within an authentic scale but which also triumphantly encompasses the work's grandeur (DG 415 514-2; *415 514-4*).

Motets: *Lobet den Herrn, alle Heiden, BWV 230; Sei Lob und Preis mit Ehren, BWV 231. Ich lasse dich nicht, du segnest mich denn, BWV Anh./App.159* (attrib. – probably by J. C. Bach).
(M) *** DG 427 142-2 [id.]. Regensburg Domspätzen, V. Capella Academica, Schneidt – VIVALDI: *Gloria; Kyrie.****

These motets, including one probably written by Johann Christian, are admirably fresh and feature accompaniments with period instruments. They make a fine bonus for the two Vivaldi choral works.

St John Passion, BWV 245.
**(*) EMI Dig. CDS7 54083-2 (2) [Ang. CDCB 54083]. Taverner Cons. & Players, Andrew Parrott.

(M) ** Ph. 426 645-2 (2) [id.]. Giebel, Höffgen, Haefliger, Young, Berry, Crass, Netherlands R. Ch., Concg. O, Jochum.

Andrew Parrott, using only eleven voices in all, directs an intimate, thoughtful reading of the *St John Passion*, which aims to re-create Bach's final text of this masterpiece, modified even as late as 1749. Soloists come from the choir, with Rogers Covey-Crump as the Evangelist and David Thomas as Christus also singing the tenor and bass arias respectively. There are more dramatic readings than this, and many will miss choral weight in the big outer choruses. With good authority on Bach's own usage, Parrott includes a harpsichord continuo but, as recorded, it is clangy. Though instrumental textures are commendably clear, the choral sound is not as cleanly detailed as on many versions, such as Gardiner's, using larger forces, thanks largely to the recording acoustic. Though Parrott's set is a very strong contender, the Gardiner still provides the more intense experience (DG 419 324-2; *419 324-4*).

The Concertgebouw under Jochum offer a relatively conventional interpretation of this work. The performance has some quite outstanding contributions from the soloists, particularly from Giebel and Haefliger, and some eloquent instrumental playing. As one would expect from Jochum, there is a splendid warmth and musical spontaneity about the set, which was recorded in a spacious acoustic and has considerable breadth of tone. It is not, however, particularly concerned with authenticity; the forces are of traditional size and the continuo role is divided between harpsichord and organ. Nevertherless there is much to enjoy and admire here, for the transfer to CD has improved both the immediacy of the sound and the projection of the performance.

St Matthew Passion, BWV 244.
**(*) HM/BMG Dig. RD 77848 (3) [7848-2-RC]. Prégardien, Van Egmond, Fliegner, Kiener, Jacobs, Cordier, Schäfer, Elwes, Mertens, Lika, Tölz Boys' Ch., La Petite Bande (male) Ch. & O, Leonhardt.

Leonhardt directs a spacious reading of the *St Matthew Passion* using period instruments, an all-male choir and a fine team of soloists. Christoph Prégardien makes an outstanding Evangelist and, with slow speeds and restrained manner, Leonhardt brings out the work's devotional qualities rather than the dramatic. On a satisfying scale, the performance has the necessary weight while keeping textures clean, with period instruments sounding sweet rather than abrasive. What mars the result is Leonhardt's tendency to underline rhythms too heavily, with first-beats-in-bars emphasized and with chorales becoming heavy. Well-balanced recording. As with the other major Bach choral works, our choice remains with Gardiner. The culminating issue in his series of recordings brings an intense, dramatic reading, which now makes a clear primary recommendation, not just for period-performance devotees but for anyone not dead set against the new authenticity (DG 427 648-2; *427 648-4*).

Vocal collections

Arias and choruses from: *Christmas oratorio; Mass in B min.; St John Passion; St Matthew Passion.*
(M) **(*) DG 431 703-2; *431 703-4* [id.]. Argenta, Kwella, Nichols, Von Otter, Chance, Blochwitz, Bär, Hauptmann, Monteverdi Ch., E. Bar. Soloists, Gardiner.

Although it is hardly possible to sample Bach's four masterpieces properly in 62 minutes, the excerpts here are well laid out to provide a reasonable balance of contrast. Beginning, understandably, with the joyful opening chorus from the *Christmas oratorio,* the programme then moves to the *Agnus Dei* from the *Mass in B minor*, with Michael Chance movingly expressive, and back to the *Christmas oratorio* again, before Anne Sofie von Otter's *Buss und Reu* from the *St Matthew Passion*. Patrizia Kwella and Mary Nichols then join together for the duet, *Et in unum Dominum*, from the *Mass in B minor*, followed by the double chorus, *Osanna in excelsis*, and so on. Such distinguished music-making is undoubtedly rewarding when the sound is excellent too.

Transcriptions

Transcriptions: arr. BUSONI: *Chaconne* (from *Violin Partita No. 2*); *Chorales: Ich ruf zu dir; Nun freut euch, lieben Christen; Nun komm der Heiden Heiland; Wachet auf; Toccata & fugue in D min.* arr. LISZT: *Prelude & fugue in A min.* arr. LORD BERNERS: *In dolci jubilo.* arr. MYRA HESS: *Jesu, joy of man's desiring.* arr. KEMPFF: *Siciliano.* arr. LE FLEMING: *Sheep may safely graze.* arr. RACHMANINOV: *Suite from Partita No. 3 in E.*
*** ASV Dig. CDDCA 759; *ZCDCA 759* [id.]. Gordon Fergus-Thompson (piano).

A highly entertaining collection, played with much flair and, in the case of the lyrical pieces at the centre of the recital (notably Wilhelm Kempff's delightful *Siciliano* and Dame Myra Hess's famous arrangement of *Jesu, joy of man's desiring*), stylish charm. Busoni arranged Bach flamboyantly but with authority, Liszt was unashamedly romantic and Lord Berners engagingly eccentric. (His boisterously prolix piece, with its mis-spelt title, is more composed than arranged.) But the most enjoyably characterful of all is Rachmaninov's triptych (*Preludio, Gavotte* and *Gigue*) from the *Violin partita in E major* which, pianistically, he makes very much his own. Gordon Fergus-Thompson plays this *Suite* with obvious relish and fine rhythmic sparkle. He is equally commanding in the famous opening *Chaconne* and turns the closing *Toccata and fugue in D minor*, BWV 565, into an exciting *tour de force* of bravura.

Bach, Wilhelm Friedemann (1710–84)

Sinfonia in D, F64; Adagio & fugue in D min., F65.
*** Capriccio Dig. 10 283 [id.]. Concerto Köln – J. C. F. BACH: *Sinfonia*; C. P. E. BACH: *Harpsichord concerto*; J. C. BACH: *Sinfonia.****

Wilhelm Friedemann's three-movement *Sinfonia in D major*, composed in the mid-1740s, was intended for use as an introduction to the Whitsun cantata, *Dies ist der Tag*, though it was also played in its own right as an independent piece. The better-known *Adagio and fugue in D minor* is possibly the last two movements of a symphony, though for some time it was thought to have been an introduction to a birthday cantata for Frederick the Great, written in 1758. It is a very extraordinary and expressive piece and makes one wonder whether Wilhelm Friedemann did not possess the most powerful imagination of all the sons. It is played by this period group with great expressive vitality and is well recorded.

Balakirev, Mily (1837–1910)

Chopin suite; In Bohemia; King Lear; Overture on Spanish themes.
** Marco Polo Dig. 8.220324 [id.]. Singapore SO, Choo Hooey.

An issue of exceptional interest (in that it fills in a number of gaps in the catalogue) even if ambition outstrips achievement. *In Bohemia*, or the *Overture on Czech themes*, was composed in 1866–7 after Balakirev had visited Prague to conduct performances of

Glinka's *Russlan* and *A Life for the Tsar*; like his tone-poem, *Russia*, it is based on three folk themes. But the best piece on the record is the inventive and imaginative *Overture to King Lear* (1859), which ought to be every bit as well known as *Tamara* or the popular works of Balakirev's more celebrated contemporaries. The little-known *Overture on Spanish themes* is also attractive. The *Chopin suite* comes from Balakirev's last years, and his transcription of the *C sharp minor Scherzo* (transposed into D minor) is altogether hilarious; on the other hand, the equally bizarre transcription of the *E flat minor Study* (Op. 10, No. 6) is curiously touching. The Singapore orchestra has certain weaknesses in terms of sonority and blend (the strings are meagre and intonation is not exactly spot-on), but these less-than-spectacular performances are well recorded and give pleasure.

Islamey.
(M) (**(*)) Decca mono 425 961-2 [id.]. Julius Katchen – LISZT: *Funérailles* etc; MUSSORGSKY: *Pictures.*(**(*))

Recorded in more than tolerable sound in 1954, Julius Katchen offers some pretty dazzling playing in Balakirev's remarkable display-piece. He was a notable musician and still only in his twenties when he made this recording; but his *Islamey* is still no match for the celebrated high-voltage Barere recording (CDAPR 7001 – see Recitals).

Piano sonata in B flat min.
(*) Olympia OCD 354 [id.]; Archduke *MARC 2.* Donna Amato – DUTILLEUX: *Sonata.*(*)

Donna Amato's well-paced and musicianly account of Balakirev's *Piano sonata* has now been transferred to the Olympia label.

Bantock, Granville (1868–1946)

Celtic Symphony; Hebridean Symphony; The Sea reivers; The Witch of Atlas.
*** Hyp. Dig. CDA 66450; *KA 66450* [id.]. RPO, Handley.

Hebridean symphony; Russian scenes; Old English suite.
* Marco Polo Dig. 8.223274 [id.]. Czech State PO, Adrian Leaper.

Vernon Handley conducts warmly atmospheric performances of four of Bantock's Hebridean inspirations. Most ambitious is the *Hebridean Symphony* of 1913, with nature music echoing Wagner and Delius as well as Sibelius, whose music Bantock introduced into Britain. The two tone-poems are attractive too, but best of all is the *Celtic Symphony*, a late work written in 1940, which uses strings and six harps. This is in the grand string tradition of Vaughan Williams's *Tallis fantasia* and Elgar's *Introduction and allegro*, a beautiful, colourful work that deserves to be far better known. With warm, atmospheric recording to match, Handley draws committed performances from the RPO.

Leaper's performance of the *Hebridean Symphony* with the Czech State Philharmonic of Kosice cannot compare with Handley's. It is lusty but rough, with howling East European horns and with its atmospheric nature music not helped by a dry studio acoustic. Unlike the Hyperion issue, there are no individual tracks for the different sections in this work of over half an hour. The genre pieces in the two suites are similarly given lusty performances, made to sound rougher by the recording.

Barber, Samuel (1910–81)

Adagio for strings.
(M) *** DG Dig. 431 048-2; *431 048-4* [id.]. LAPO, Bernstein – COPLAND: *Appalachian spring* ***; GERSHWIN: *Rhapsody in blue.***(*)

Bernstein's powerfully expressive and deeply felt reading of Barber's *Adagio* was (appropriately) reissued just before his death.

Cave of the heart (original version of *Medea*).
*** Koch Dig. 3-7019-2; *2-7019-4* [id.]. Atlantic Sinf., Schenck – COPLAND: *Appalachian spring.****

This disc makes a logical coupling and brings together two scores written for Martha Graham. The original version of *Medea* was called *Serpent heart* when it first appeared in 1946 and was retitled *Cave of the heart* the following year. Although it shares much of the same material as the concert suite Barber fashioned from the ballet, in places it sounds very different. It was first described as brilliant, bitter and full of amazing energy; in this original form it sounds much darker in feeling and harder-edged, and it has stronger Stravinskian overtones. The scoring is for a small group of fifteen players, yet the effect in this full-blooded, vividly present recording is, if anything, brawnier than the more sumptuous revision. A most interesting and stimulating score.

Essay for orchestra No. 3, Op. 47; Fadograph of a Yestern Scene, Op. 44; Medea: suite, Op. 23.
*** Koch Dig. 3-7010-2; *2-7010-4* [id.]. New Zealand SO, Andrew Schenck.

A welcome recording of two Barber rarities from the 1970s in sympathetic performances by the New Zealand orchestra under Andrew Schenck. The *Fadograph of a Yestern Scene* was inspired by a passage in James Joyce's *Finnegan's Wake* and is not otherwise available in Europe. It is a lyrical piece, reflective in mood and full of warmth; the *Third Essay* is a rarity in the concert hall – though there are two rival recordings – and is powerfully argued and concentrated in atmosphere. The more familiar *Medea suite*, dating from the period of the *Second Symphony* and composed for Martha Graham, is well played. The recording has outstanding clarity and definition, but the acoustic has the very slightly dry quality of a studio rather than the expansiveness of a concert hall.

Medea (ballet): suite.
(M) *** Mercury 462 016-2 [id.]. Eastman-Rochester O, Howard Hanson – GOULD: *Fall River legend* etc.***

Although the composer made a mono LP of the score, this was the first stereo recording of the *Medea suite*, which the composer said 'follows roughly the form of a Greek tragedy'. The influence of Stravinsky is clear and the work contains some of Barber's most intensely serious music, as well as some of the most expressive. As with all good ballets, however, the rhythmic element is vital. Hanson's performance is both polished and dramatic, and the brilliant 1959 Mercury recording has astonishing clarity and vivid presence.

Symphony No. 1, Op. 9; The school for scandal: overture, Op. 5.
*** Chan. Dig. CHAN 8958; *ABTD 1550* [id.]. Detroit SO, Järvi – BEACH: *Symphony in E min.****

Neeme Järvi's account of Barber's *First Symphony* is broader than usual and gains enormously in symphonic coherence. He manages its rapid shifts of mood and tempi far more convincingly than most other versions, including even Bruno Walter in his pioneering set of 78 r.p.m. records. Readers who have been looking for an ideal account of this full-hearted piece need look no further. Barber's youthful *Overture* to *The School for Scandal* with its marvellously fresh and lyrical second theme is equally well served. The *Second Symphony* would no doubt have made a more logical coupling, but the *Symphony* of Mrs Beach is well worth having instead. Good playing from the Detroit orchestra and very good recorded sound.

Summer music, Op. 31 (for woodwind quintet).
(M) **(*) Sony SMK 46250 [id.]. Members of the Marlboro Festival – NIELSEN: *Woodwind quintet*; HINDEMITH: *Octet.***

Barber's delightful *Summer music* is sensitively played by these artists who capture its air of tenderness and melancholy very well. Those who admire the sound produced by John de Lancie will enjoy the oboe playing here. The balance could perhaps have placed them a little more distantly and given a little more space round them, but the 1981 sound-quality is very acceptable and the coupling valuable.

Piano sonata, Op. 26.
(M) **(*) BMG/RCA GD 60415; *GK 60415* [60415-2-RG; *60415-4-RG*]. Van Cliburn – DEBUSSY: *Estampes* etc.**; MOZART: *Piano sonata No. 10.***

Barber's *Sonata* was an almost mandatory repertoire piece for pianists in the 1960s and '70s. Van Cliburn's recording of it is pretty masterly and, although the sound could be more ingratiating and have a warmer ambience, it is still acceptable. It has greater sonority though not more virtuosity than the 1951 Horowitz account. Van Cliburn has refinement and intelligence to commend him, and readers with a special interest in the work should make a point of hearing him.

Souvenirs.
*** Koch Dig. 3-7005-2; *2-7005-4* [id.]. New Zealand SO, Schenck – MENOTTI: *Amahl* etc.***

Souvenirs dates from the early 1950s and began life as a series of piano duets. It is an absolutely enchanting score which was first recorded by Efrem Kurtz (on a 10-inch mono LP) and was then consigned to oblivion. It has bags of charm and, unlike the delightful Menotti with which it is coupled, every idea is so memorable that it instantly replaces the one that came before. It is puzzling that such good music with all its wit, elegance and charm has languished, unloved, for so long. It is very well played here by the New Zealand Symphony Orchestra under Andrew Schenck and is eminently well recorded too. Strongly recommended.

(i) *Andromache's farewell;* (ii) *Dover Beach;* (iii) *Hermit songs;* (iv) *Knoxville: summer of 1915.*
(M) (***) Sony mono/stereo MPK 46727 [id.]. (i) Arroyo, NYPO, Schippers; (ii) Fischer-Dieskau, Juilliard Qt; (iii) Leontyne Price, composer; (iv) Eleanor Steber, Dumbarton Oaks O, William Strickland.

This collection of vintage recordings makes a splendid mid-priced Barber compendium, representing four of his finest vocal works, all in superb performances. The two older recordings – of *Knoxville* and the *Hermit songs* – are in mono, dating from the early 1950s; but the sound, limited in range, vividly captures the voices, with the composer a most persuasive piano accompanist for the young Leontyne Price. Eleanor

Steber in *Knoxville* may not quite match the wonderfully atmospheric sound that Price received for her RCA record, but it is still hauntingly evocative. Fischer-Dieskau's recording of the early *Dover Beach* is better known, a fine reading; but most vivid of all is the ripely romantic scena, *Adromache's farewell*, with text taken from Euripides' *The Trojan Women*, a superb vehicle for Martina Arroyo at her finest. Excellent CD transfers. No texts are provided but words are exceptionally clear.

Bargiel, Woldemar (1828–97)

Octet in C min. for strings, Op. 15a.
*** Hyp. Dig. CDA 66356; *KA 66356* [id.]. Divertimenti – MENDELSSOHN: *Octet.****

Woldemar Bargiel was the step-brother of Clara Schumann (née Wieck). Schumann (his step-brother-in-law) encouraged Woldemar to study in Leipzig, where his teachers were Moscheles and Gade. While still at Leipzig, he scored a considerable success with this three-movement *Octet for strings*. Wilhelm Altmann speaks of him in the 1928 *Cobbett's Encyclopaedia* as 'an adherent of Schumann'; but what strikes one about this music is its independence of outlook and dignity. It is far more individual than, say, Gade and throughout is well schooled, cultivated and inventive, the extended first movement of over 18 minutes being well sustained and well shaped. Indeed it is something of a discovery; the delightful scherzo-like section embedded in the slow movement is particularly felicitous. Divertimenti play it with real feeling and conviction and are excellently recorded.

Bartók, Béla (1881–1945)

Concerto for orchestra; (i) *The Miraculous Mandarin* (complete ballet).
**(*) Virgin Dig. VC7 91106-2; *VC7 91106-4* [id.]. (i) Dumont Singers; Melbourne SO, Iwaki.

Concerto for orchestra; The Miraculous Mandarin (ballet): *suite.*
** Nimbus Dig. NI 5229 [id.]. Hungarian State SO, Adám Fischer.

Iwaki and the Melbourne orchestra have an obvious advantage over their direct rivals in presenting the complete *Miraculous Mandarin* ballet, not just the suite, as coupling for the *Concerto for orchestra.* The recording is excellent, spacious and full, though transferred at a rather low level. The playing is finely pointed but is often too well-mannered for Bartók, lacking something in fierceness and excitement. The ballet is generously indexed with tracks.

Fischer's Nimbus disc is the first of a promised series aiming to illustrate the special traditions of Hungarian orchestral performance, which the conductor feels are in danger of being lost. The results here are positive if surprising. These are warm, heavily expressive and generally comfortable readings of both works at relaxed speeds. They are not at all biting or barbaric, and so represent an opposite extreme from the Bartók readings of the most distinguished of today's Hungarian-born conductors, Sir Georg Solti, whose fine Chicago digital version is now available at mid-price, generously coupled with a comparably brilliant account of Mussorgsky's *Pictures at an exhibition* (Decca 417 754-2).

Concerto for orchestra; Music for strings, percussion and celesta.
*** EMI Dig. CDC7 54070-2; *EL 754070-4* [id.]. Oslo PO, Jansons.

Jansons and the Oslo Philharmonic give outstanding performances of both works, making this by a small margin a first recommendation in this now-favourite coupling of two Bartók masterpieces. Reflecting his Russian training, Jansons points rhythms with flair and resilience, setting the fun in the second and fourth movements against the power and intensity of the rest. The Oslo orchestra plays with unfailingly crisp ensemble, and the sound is excellent too, full and open, with the EMI engineers mastering the difficult Oslo Konzerthus acoustic.

Piano concertos Nos. 1 – 3.
(M) *** Ph. 426 660-2 [id.]. Stephen Bishop-Kovacevich, LSO or BBC SO, C. Davis.
** Sony Dig. SK 45835 [id.]. György Sandór, Hungarian State O, Adám Fischer.

Bishop-Kovacevich's direct, concentrated readings of the three *Piano concertos* come at mid-price in this generous coupling on a Philips Silver Line reissue. Though No. 2 was recorded (with the BBC SO) in 1968, and the other two in 1975, the sound is bright and clear, giving extra bite to the performances, although the effect of the original resonance remains. Sir Colin Davis accompanies sensitively and vigorously, with lifted folk-rhythms in No. 1 sharply pressed home and the violent finale exhilarating, with its many unexpected changes of tempo expertly controlled. After the fierceness of the first two, Bishop-Kovacevich seems intent on countering the idea that No. 3 is a facile work, with the central *Adagio religioso* played with hushed dedication between spiky outer movements, giving concentrated intensity to compare with late Beethoven. The thrust of the scherzando passages in the first movement has a lively wit, and the finale, at a relatively fast and exuberant tempo, registers the 3/8 marking far more clearly than usual. At mid-price, this disc is hard to beat.

Though the Sony coupling of the three *Concertos* has modern digital sound, the distancing and ambient acoustic take away some necessary bite. Sandór – the original interpreter of No. 3 – with Hungarian colleagues brings out both the expressive warmth and the Hungarian wit of the writing rather than the fierceness, with hushed slow movements treated atmospherically.

Viola concerto; Hungarian peasant songs; 3 Rondos on Slovak folk tunes.
* Conifer Dig. CDCF 189; *MCFC 189* [id.]. Rivka Golani, Budapest SO, András Ligeti – SERLY: *Viola concerto; Rhapsody for viola and orchestra.***

An intelligent and useful coupling. Bartók left the *Viola concerto* unfinished on his death and it fell to Tibor Serly to impose order on the sketches. Although Bartók spoke of them as 'ready in draft so that only the score has to be written out, a purely mechanical work', the piece survived only on loose sheets whose sequence was not always easy to establish, any more than his corrections and afterthoughts were easy to decipher. Thus the work remains to some extent conjectural. A CD version is overdue, but Rivka Golani's intonation is far too erratic to give much pleasure, despite the obvious warmth of her playing. The orchestra understandably sounds dispirited. Both the other Bartók works on the disc, crisp and colourful, are orchestrations of piano pieces, the first done by Bartók himself, the second by Antal Dorati. The sound is open and full-bodied, with the soloist well forward.

Violin concertos Nos. 1 and 2.
(M) *** Decca Dig./Analogue 425 015-2; *425 015-4* [id.]. Kyung Wha Chung, Chicago SO or LPO, Solti.
** Sony Dig. CD 45941; *40-45941* [id.]. Midori, BPO, Mehta.

Decca's mid-price issue in the Ovation series brings a generous and apt coupling of two earlier recordings, No. 1 in digital sound done in Chicago in 1983, No. 2 done in London in 1976 with first-rate analogue sound, well transferred. Though the soloist is rather forwardly balanced, the hushed intensity of the writing, as well as bitingly Hungarian flavours, is caught superbly, thanks to the conductor as well as to the soloist. Though the expressive warmth behind Bartók's writing is fully brought out, there is no sentimental lingering. This leads the field in both works.

Midori's warmth of temperament comes out in both concertos, which are given spacious readings, with slow movements far more expansive than is usual and with the soloist often producing ravishing half-tones, helped by a natural balance with the orchestra. The Berlin recording is warmly atmospheric but grows confused and lacking in bite in tuttis, underlining the romantic approach of both conductor and orchestra, as well as that of the soloist.

Dance suite; Music for strings, percussion and celesta.
(M) ** Ph. 426 661-2 [id.]. Philharmonia Hungarica, Dorati.

Dorati gives surprisingly relaxed performances of both works. The opening of the *Dance suite* is positively charming, and a persuasive case is made throughout for a smiling view of a work which usually belies its lightweight title. The expressive warmth of the opening slow fugue of the *Music for strings, percussion and celesta* is also most convincing, but the second and fourth movements ideally need more bite and brilliance, due in part to the recording, although the impact is sharpened by the CD transfer.

Hungarian sketches; Roumanian folk dances.
(M) *** Mercury 432 005-2 [id.]. Minneapolis SO, Dorati – KODÁLY: *Dances; Háry János.****

Dorati, himself a Hungarian, provided the pioneer stereo recording of these works, yet the 1956 sound is vivid and full and wears its years very lightly indeed. The Minneapolis orchestra, on top form, provides plenty of ethnic feeling and colour. This is Bartók at his most winningly approachable, and the style of the music-making has an agreeable air of authenticity.

The Miraculous Mandarin (complete ballet).
(M) ** Decca 425 026-2; *425 026-4* [id.]. VPO, Dohnányi – STRAVINSKY: *Petrushka.***

Dohnányi's direction of *The Miraculous Mandarin*, long regarded as an unusually barbaric score, is clean, precise and often beautiful. It is far less violent and weighty than usual, and not everyone will respond to what could almost be described as an unsuspected neo-classical element in the score. The playing of the VPO is very fine, helped by spacious recording, not very analytical in detail, and a faithful transfer, but Abbado's DG version remains first choice for this ballet (410 598-2).

The Wooden prince (ballet), *Op. 13* (complete); *Hungarian pictures.*
*** Chan. Dig. CHAN 8895; *ABTD 1506* [id.]. Philh. O, Järvi.

By contrast with Bartók's other two dramatic works, also one-Acters – the ballet *The Miraculous Mandarin* and the opera *Bluebeard's Castle* – this other ballet, first performed in 1917, presents the composer at his most euphonious and least barbaric. Unlike the other two, it was an instant success in Budapest, but latterly has often seemed lacking in flavour, even to Bartók devotees. Järvi's red-blooded performance relates the work to romantic sources, even to Wagner's *Rheingold* at the very start. The drama of the fairy story is told in glowing colours and, unlike most rivals, Järvi ignores the many little cuts that the composer sanctioned, reluctantly or not, over the years. The opulent playing of the Philharmonia is greatly enhanced by the full, vivid Chandos recording. The suite, *Hungarian pictures*, drawn from various folk-based piano pieces, provides a colourful if trivial makeweight. The extra richness both in the recording and in the performance makes this far preferable to Boulez's Sony disc of the ballet.

String quartets Nos. 1–6.
*** DG Dig. 423 657-2 (2) [id.]. Emerson Qt.

The Emerson Quartet are completely at home in the world of Bartók, and these concentrated and brilliant performances, very well recorded, make a clear first choice.

Violin sonata No. 1.
*** DG Dig. 427 351-2 [id.]. Gidon Kremer, Martha Argerich – JANÁČEK: *Sonata* **(*); MESSIAEN: *Theme and variations.****

The *First Violin sonata* (1921) is one of Bartók's most uncompromising pieces and a work of enormous originality; there are moments when one is reminded of the world of the Szymanowski *Mythes*. It is played with great expressive intensity, enormous range of colour and effortless virtuosity by Gidon Kremer and Martha Argerich; indeed it would be difficult to improve on their performance or the excellent DG recording.

Bax, Arnold (1883–1953)

Malta G.C. (complete); *Oliver Twist: suite* (film-scores).
(M) *** ASV Dig. CDWHL 2058; *ZCWHL 2058* [id.]. RPO, Kenneth Alwyn – ARNOLD: *The Sound Barrier.****

Both these film-scores are in the form of a series of miniatures; on the whole, *Oliver Twist* stands up more effectively without the visual imagery. The use of concertante piano is effective in a brief nocturnal portrayal of Oliver and later in a sequence called *Oliver and Brownlow*. *Oliver and the Artful Dodger* and *Fagin's romp* both give rise to effective and inventive scherzando writing, and the finale brings a resplendent Waltonian jubilation. In *Malta G.C.* much of the score is concerned with wartime action: it is the gentler music, the *Intermezzo* and *Reconstruction* and again the final apotheosis, that brings the most memorable writing. Kenneth Alwyn conducts the RPO with fine flair and commitment, Eric Parkin is the brief soloist and the recording is brilliantly colourful and vivid, if at times a little lacking in the richest sonority. Originally issued by Cloud Nine, this is welcome back in the catalogue at mid-price, with Arnold's *Rhapsody* as a bonus.

Symphonies 1–7.
*** Chan. Dig. CHAN 8906/10 [id.]. LPO or Ulster O, Bryden Thomson.

Chandos have repackaged the cycle of seven symphonies on five CDs. Nos. 3 and 7 have discs to themselves, while Nos. 1 and 6 share a disc. Only the *Fourth* is split between two discs: the first two movements are placed after the *Fifth Symphony* and the finale precedes the *Second Symphony*. Inevitably, the fill-ups that accompanied the symphonies first time around are sacrificed, notably *Tintagel*, originally coupled with the *Fourth Symphony*, and *Christmas Eve*. But, of course, it makes better sense for those primarily interested in these richly imaginative symphonies to pay for five rather than seven CDs, and the recordings continue to make a strong impression. They are all discussed individually in our main volume.

The Truth about the Russian dancers (incidental music); *From dusk till dawn* (ballet).
*** Chan. Dig. CHAN 8863; *ABTD 1478* [id.]. LPO, Bryden Thomson.

Bax was a frequent visitor to Diaghilev's 1911 season at Covent Garden and, inspired by its brilliance, worked throughout the year on a ballet called *Tamara*, only to find in the following season that Balakirev's tone-poem of the same name was being danced. Its main theme is quoted in the second movement of *The Truth about the Russian dancers.* Bax abandoned the ballet, but some of its music found its way into the later ballet, *From dusk till dawn* (1917) and the music to J. M. Barrie's whimsical play, *The Truth about the Russian dancers* (1920), in which Karsavina danced. The latter is vintage Bax, full of characteristic writing decked out in attractive orchestral colours. *From dusk till dawn* has many evocative ideas with some impressionistic orchestral touches, but each of its twenty movements is very short, the whole work lasting as many minutes. Not top-drawer Bax but often delightful, and very well played by the London Philharmonic under Bryden Thomson, and splendidly recorded.

(i) *Piano quintet in G min.; String quartet No. 2.*
**(*) Chan. Dig. CHAN 8795 [id.]. Mistry Qt; (i) with David Owen Norris.

The *Piano quintet* comes from 1914–15, before Bax had completed *The Garden of Fand.* It is symphonic in scale and almost as long as the *Third Symphony.* Its first movement alone lasts for twenty minutes and is marked 'passionate and rebellious'. At times its expansive gestures and ambitious proportions cry out for the orchestra; the only real disappointment is the rather folksy and discursive finale, though this has imaginative moments too. The playing of the Mistry Quartet is dedicated and David Owen Norris is the excellent and sensitive pianist. The *Second Quartet* (1925) is dedicated to Vaughan Williams and is tauter and more powerful, though its chromatic part-writing poses occasional problems for the players, who do not seem quite as comfortable here as they are in the *Quintet.* The leader is not dead in tune at the opening of the slow movement, and the tone could at times be more firmly focused. However, the performance has plenty of feeling and gives little cause for real complaint; the recording is excellent, and mention should be made of the useful and informative notes that Lewis Foreman has contributed throughout the Chandos Bax cycle.

Beach, Amy (1867–1944)

Symphony in E min. (Gaelic).
*** Chan. Dig. CHAN 8958; *ABTD 1550* [id.]. Detroit SO, Järvi – BARBER: *Symphony No. 1* etc.***

Amy Beach is a rather more remarkable figure than she is given credit for outside (or even in) the United States. She did not study in Europe and, apart from lessons with Junius Hill and Karl Baermann in Boston, she was largely self-taught. Her orchestration she learnt from Berlioz's treatise which she translated. Her *Symphony in E minor,* her only essay in the form, was performed with great success in Boston in 1896. It begins with a slightly Lisztian flourish, and Dvořák was obviously a major influence, but it was the 'simple, rugged and unpretentious beauty' of a collection of old Irish melodies she came across that provided its main inspiration. There is nothing 'new' or profoundly original in this music, but it operates at a high level of accomplishment and has a winning charm, particularly its delightful and inventive second movement. Once heard, this haunting movement is difficult to exorcize from one's memory. A very persuasive performance by the Detroit orchestra under Neeme Järvi, and good recorded sound.

Becker, John (1886–1961)

Symphonia brevis.
** Albany TROY 027-2 [id.]. Louisville O, Mester – HARRIS: *Epilogue to profiles in courage* etc.**; SCHUMAN: *Symphony No. 4* etc.**

John Becker is little known outside the United States but he is associated with Ives, Carl Ruggles, Henry Cowell and Wallingford Riegger – though this short symphony, his *Third*, composed in 1933, does not make quite as individual an impression as do they. Written as a 'protest against a world civilization that starves its millions in peacetime and murders those same millions in wartime', it remains anonymous, particularly in comparison with such strong musical personalities as Roy Harris and William Schuman. The recording dates from the early 1970s.

Beethoven, Ludwig van (1770–1827)

Piano concertos Nos. 1–5; Choral fantasy.
*** EMI Dig. CDC7 54063-2 (3) [Ang. CDCC 54063]. Melvyn Tan, L. Classical Players, Norrington.

We awarded Melvyn Tan's *Emperor* and *Choral fantasy* a Rosette in our last *Guide* (not least for the latter, which is a stunning performance) and those wanting a complete set of the Beethoven *Concertos* on period instruments need look no further than this fine three-CD set. The rival version on Decca from Steven Lubin and the Academy of Ancient Music has many merits, too, and should not lightly be passed over, but the Tan–Norrington partnership has greater spontaneity and Melvyn Tan has a flair and poetic feeling that is rather special. Collectors understandably happy with a mid-priced box of the five concertos played on modern instruments could well choose Perahia (Sony M3K 44575) although Kempff's accounts are at bargain price and the DG box includes the *C minor Piano sonata*, Op. 111 (427 237-2).

Piano concerto No. 1 in C, Op. 15; Rondo in B flat, WoO 6.
(BB) **(*) Naxos Dig. 8.550190 [id.]. Stefan Vladar, Capella Istropolitana, Wordsworth.

Stefan Vladar's performance of Beethoven's *C major Concerto* is among the finest in his Naxos super-bargain series. The first movement has striking freshness and spontaneity, and the spacious *Largo* makes an eloquent contrast with the sparkle of the joyful finale. Excellent accompaniments from Wordsworth and the Capella Istropolitana, alert and sympathetic and full of spirit. The coupling, however, is not generous, although here too the playing is strong in personality. Throughout, the digital recording is fresh, full and clean; but one remembers that the outstanding Bishop-Kovacevich analogue recordings of both the *First* and *Second Concertos* are available, coupled together, on the Philips bargain label (422 968-2).

Piano concertos Nos. (i) *1 in C, Op. 15;* (ii) *3 in C min., Op. 37.*
(M) *(**) Sony MK 42259 [id.]. Rudolf Serkin, (i) Phd. O, Ormandy; (ii) NYPO, Bernstein.

Rudolf Serkin in the mid-1960s was a very impressive Beethovenian indeed, and in the slow movements of both these concertos his aristocratic phrasing is very commanding. In

No. 1 he has the advantage of Ormandy as accompanist and this is a very positive reading. The first movement is brisk but the performance clearly looks forward to the great works of the composer's maturity, and the poetic *Largo* (realized with considerable intensity) lends itself to a broad conception. The recording is forward but has fine, bold piano timbre. Unfortunately, in the first movement of the *C minor Concerto* (recorded in 1964, a year before the *C major*) Bernstein brutalizes the tuttis of the first movement, and both outer movements are made to seem super-brilliant, not helped by a degree of coarseness in the recorded sound.

Piano concerto Nos. 1 in C, Op. 15; 4 in G, Op. 58.
*** EMI Dig. CDC7 54058-2; *EL 754058-4* [id.]. Maria Tipo, LSO, Hans Graf.

While Maria Tipo is relatively little known to the wider musical public in this country (there is a fine Bach recital record), she is much admired among pianists. She studied first with her mother, who was a Busoni pupil, and then with the composer-pianist, Casella and Guido Agosti. Although it is unlikely that collectors will gravitate towards a little-known name in preference to Perahia and Bishop-Kovacevich, those who do will not be disappointed by these beautifully recorded performances, which are unfailingly sensitive and intelligent. There is perhaps a certain want of tension in the slow movement of the *C major Concerto* but the finale has tremendous sparkle. Maria Tipo made her breakthrough with the *G major Concerto* when she was sixteen (the first time she had played with an orchestra, with Ansermet conducting) and with which she won the Geneva competition. Hers is a completely relaxed and inward account of the kind one recalls from Myra Hess. These are not 'high-voltage' performances – and are all the better for that, though at times one would welcome a stronger sense of direction from the conductor. But generally both readings are selfless, musical and often illuminating. Tipo belongs to that genre of pianist who can give the illusion that the piano has no hammers. Not necessarily a first choice, but a very satisfying one.

Piano concertos Nos. 3 in C min., Op. 37; 4 in G, Op. 58.
(BB) **(*) Naxos Dig. 8.550122 [id.]. Stefan Vladar, Capella Istropolitana, Barry Wordsworth.
(M) *(**) Tuxedo TUXCD 1016 [id.]. Brendel, V. Pro Musica O or V. State Op. O, Wallberg.
(BB) ** Pickwick PWK 1153. Julius Katchen, LSO, Piero Gamba.

Vladar's cycle of Beethoven concertos for Naxos is apparently recorded using a Bösendorfer piano, and the bright, rather dry sound in the instrument's higher tessitura stems from the character of this particular instrument, which has the flavour of a fortepiano. It adds classical bite to performances which are dramatic and fresh, with the slow movement of No. 3 strongly contrasted in its expressive feeling. The brightness in the piano's upper range seems less obvious in the *G major Concerto* – in all other respects the sound is very good in both works – and its essential lyricism is well understood by soloist and conductor alike. At super-bargain price, this is certainly very recommendable – though, by paying a little more, one can get these works on the Philips bargain label in a superb coupling by Steven Bishop-Kovacevich and the BBC Symphony Orchestra under Sir Colin Davis (426 062-2), as fine an interpretation as any available. (The companion Bishop-Kovacevich disc, including *Concertos 1* and *2*, is on Philips 422 968-2.)

Brendel's 1959 Vox performances (originally issued on Turnabout in the UK) are very welcome back to the catalogue. Both interpretations are deeply satisfying, with the most delicate tonal and rhythmic control married to intellectual strength. The slow movement of No. 3 combines depth with poetry, and the finale is engagingly jaunty. In No. 4 the orchestral accompaniment is unimaginative: the first-movement tutti, for example, is rhythmically stodgy; but Brendel's control of phrase and colour is such that his reading rides over this impediment and the contrasts of the slow movement are strongly and poetically made. It is noteworthy that he uses the second of the cadenzas written for the work, one not generally heard. In spite of the shrill, thin orchestral strings (cleanly remastered), many will count these among the finest Beethoven concerto recordings Brendel has committed to disc.

Julius Katchen's account of the *C minor Concerto* dates from 1959, the *G major* from five years later. Both were very well recorded (by Decca), though the remastering reveals their early dates by the sound of the fortissimo violins; the piano image, however, is most real, and there is a good balance and plenty of ambient warmth. The first movement of No. 3 takes a little while to warm up but, when Katchen enters, the performance springs splendidly to life. The slow movement is sustained with considerable tension, its beauty readily conveyed, and there is plenty of vigour and sparkle in the finale. Katchen is less penetrating in No. 4. His virtuosity is remarkable and the performance is by no means without feeling, but Kempff and Bishop-Kovacevich find more expressive depth in this work than he does. Nevertheless, this is an enjoyable coupling and undoubtedly good value in the lowest price-range.

(i) *Piano concertos Nos. 3–4; Piano sonata No. 21 in C (Waldstein), Op. 53.*
(B) *** DG Compact Classics *419 086-4* [id.]. Wilhelm Kempff, (i) with BPO, Leitner.

This bargain-price Compact Classics tape is made the more attractive by the addition of Kempff's cool, fresh version of the *Waldstein Sonata* to the usual coupling of the *Third* and *Fourth Piano concertos*. In the *C minor Concerto* Kempff's approach is relatively measured, somewhat serious in mood; but in its unforced way, happily lyrical, brightly sparkling in articulation, it is refreshingly spontaneous. Kempff may characteristically adopt a flowing speed for the slow movement, but this natural thoughtfulness gives it the necessary gravity and intensity. Again, in the *Fourth Concerto* Kempff's delicacy of fingerwork and his shading of tone colour are as effervescent as ever, and the fine control of the conductor ensures the unity of the reading. In both concertos the recording of the orchestra is bright and resonant, the piano tone warm as well as clear.

Piano concerto No. 4 in G, Op. 58.
(M) *** Sony MYK 44832 [id.]; *40-44832*. Leon Fleisher, Cleveland O, Szell – MOZART: *Piano concerto No. 25.****
(M) (*) Decca mono 425 968-2 [id.]. Clara Haskil, LPO, Carlo Zecchi – SCHUMANN: *Concerto.*(*)

Fleisher's is a magical performance, memorable in every bar, to rival even Kempff's version. Starting with the genuine tension of a live performance and displaying throughout a commanding control of argument from soloist and conductor alike – the orchestral playing is superb – this is among the finest recordings of the work ever committed to disc. Fleisher's half-tones are most beautiful and his fingerwork is dazzling without ever giving the slightest impression of mere slickness. In some ways this scores over Kempff's more idiosyncratic approach, although the 1959 CBS recording is rather less agreeable than the DG balance. It has, however, been skilfully remastered for CD and can be made to sound well.

Clara Haskil's account of the *Fourth Piano concerto* with Carlo Zecchi and the LPO comes from 1947 and, although it has its insights, is not Haskil at her most impressive. The recording is very monaural and monochrome, and her playing surely had a greater tonal and dynamic range than emerges here. Nor does the Lipatti coupling do him full justice.

(i) *Piano concertos No. 4 in G, Op. 58;* (ii) *5 in E flat (Emperor), Op. 73.*
(M) **(*) Decca Dig. 430 704-2; *430 704-4* [id.]. Vladimir Ashkenazy, VPO, Mehta.
(M) *(**) Sony MK 42260 [id.]. Rudolf Serkin, (i) Phd. O, Ormandy; (ii) NYPO, Bernstein.

The relaxation and sense of spontaneity which mark Ashkenazy's Vienna cycle bring a performance of the *Fourth Piano concerto* which may lack something in heroic drive but which, in its relative lightness, never loses concentration and brings a captivating sparkle to the finale. Though this may not be as powerful as Ashkenazy's earlier, Chicago recording with Solti, and Mehta is a less individual accompanist, it is fresher and more natural, with fewer expressive hesitations. The spaciousness of the first movement of the *Emperor*, combined with clarity of texture, is most persuasive, and so is the unusually gentle account of the slow movement. Only in the finale does Ashkenazy's easy and relaxed approach bring a slackening of tension to reduce the impact of the reading. Excellent recording, full and brilliant; if this disc does not represent a first choice, the coupling remains enjoyable and rewarding.

If again it is Serkin's partnership with Ormandy rather than with the highly charged Bernstein that is the more successful, here the difference is less striking when the *Emperor* clearly suits Bernstein's temperament. The performance of the *Fourth* is on a grand scale, yet is full of tenderness and delicacy when those qualities are needed. Ormandy matches Serkin's individuality with an understanding born of long association, but in the slow movement he goes too far. Normally the soloist allows himself full, free rubato in his hushed, expressive solos, and then the conductor punctuates them at a steadier, necessarily faster-sounding speed with the dramatic orchestral interjections. Ormandy, however, allows himself similar expansiveness to Serkin's and the result is heavy. Nevertheless, anyone wanting a sample of Serkin at his most compelling will not be disappointed here. He is also characteristically noble and commanding in the *Emperor* – the slow movement again is superbly poised and the finale quite brilliant. Bernstein gives sympathetic support on the whole; but it is not just the somewhat coarse orchestral recording which prevents this from being among the most refined and powerful versions: both soloist and orchestra fall a little short on occasion.

Piano concerto No. 5 in E flat (Emperor), Op. 73.
(M) **(*) EMI Dig. CDD7 63892-2 [id.]; *ET 763892-4*. Yuri Egorov, Philh. O, Sawallisch – MOZART: *Piano concerto No. 20.***
(B) **(*) Pickwick PWK 1146. Friedrich Gulda, VPO, Horst Stein.

(i) *Piano concerto No. 5 in E flat (Emperor)*; (ii) *Choral fantasia, Op. 80.*
(M) *(**) Tuxedo TUXCD 1038 [id.]. (i) Brendel, V. Pro Musica O, Mehta; (ii) (mono) Wührer, Ac. Chamber Ch., VSO, Clemens Krauss.

(i) *Piano concerto No. 5 in E flat (Emperor). 2 Rondos, Op. 51/1–2; Piano sonatas Nos. 19 in G min.; 20 in G, Op. 49/1–2.*
(M) **(*) Decca Dig. 425 025-2; *425 025-4* [id.]. Radu Lupu, (i) Israel PO, Mehta.

Radu Lupu's *Emperor* was the first version to be issued on compact disc. Lupu gives a performance which, while not lacking strength, brings thoughtfulness and poetry even to the magnificence of the first movement, with classical proportions made clear. The slow movement has delicacy and fantasy, the finale easy exhilaration, though neither conductor nor orchestra quite matches the soloist's distinction. The upper range has the characteristically bright sound of Decca's early digital recordings, but there is plenty of weight and the orchestral layout is convincing; if the piano image seems a trifle near, it gives a commanding presence to the solo playing. The encores are generous and are played most beautifully: the two *Rondos* are immaculately done and are full of charm; the *Sonatas* are persuasive in their sense of scale, while still showing Lupu's characteristic sensibility. They are all very pleasingly recorded; though the *Sonatas* have an analogue source, their sound is truthful in both balance and colour.

This was Yuri Egorov's first concerto recording, made in 1982; it gives a refreshingly direct but still individual account of the opening allegro, helped by authoritative conducting from Sawallisch. The finale too has splendid drive and attack, with full digital sound. The slow movement, however, is the controversial point: it is taken at a very measured *Adagio* which might have flowed better had Egorov adopted a more affectionate style of phrasing. For its reissue it has been generously coupled with a good but less distinctive version of Mozart's *D minor Concerto.*

With its dramatically recorded opening (the tone of the Bösendorfer piano extremely vivid), Gulda's account of the first movement does not lack a robust quality, yet the passages in his reading that re-echo in the memory are the gentle and poetic ones, whether the half-tones of the second subject in the first movement or the serene phrases of the *Adagio*, given here with real *Innigkeit*. After this, the lively joy of the finale is the more telling. The Decca recording has been remastered brightly, and the orchestral sound may need just a little smoothing; although there are more individual performances available, this Pickwick bargain reissue will not disappoint the impulse-purchaser.

On Tuxedo, Brendel gives a splendidly bold and vigorous reading and he is well suppported (in 1959) by Zubin Mehta and the Vienna Pro Musica Orchestra. As for the (originally Vox/Turnabout) recording, the orchestral sound leaves much to be desired although, as in the coupling of Nos. 3 and 4, the piano image is convincing. But the performance generates a spontaneity which is less apparent in his later versions for Philips; it may be a reading without idiosyncrasy, but it is strong in style and personality. The beginning of the finale is prepared beautifully and the main rondo theme merges vividly and with great character. As a coupling, we are given the famous Vox pioneering mono recording of the *Choral fantasia*, with enthusiastic if rough-and-ready vocal contributions from the Vienna Academy Chamber Choir, but with Friedrich Wührer undoubtedly powerful in the opening section. Fair recording. Our first choice for the *Emperor* rests with the late Claudio Arrau (Philips 416 215-2; *416 215-4*) – and there could be no better memento of his artistry.

(i) *Piano concerto No. 5 (Emperor);* (ii) *Violin concerto, Op. 61;* (iii) *Fidelio: overture, Op. 72b* (CD only: (iv) *Leonora overture No. 2, Op. 72a;* (iii) *Leonora overture No. 3, Op. 72b*).
(B) *** DG Compact Classics 413 145-2 (2); *413 145-4* [id.]. (i) Eschenbach, Boston SO, Ozawa; (ii) Schneiderhan, BPO, Jochum; (iii) Dresden State O, Boehm. (CD only: (iv) BPO, Jochum).

Eschenbach gives a deeply satisfying interpretation of the *Emperor*, helped by the equally youthful urgency of his accompanist, Ozawa. With thoughtfulness, power and bravura nicely balanced, this interpretation is very impressive. On tape the high-level transfer conquers the reverberant acoustic; although detail is not as sharp as in some versions, the sound has fine weight and richness, with the piano timbre appropriately firm and bold. The recording dates from 1974, whereas the coupling – sounding hardly less full-bodied – is from 1962. Schneiderhan's stereo version of the *Violin concerto* is among the greatest recordings of this work: the serene spiritual beauty of the slow movement, and the playing of the second subject in particular, have never been surpassed on record; the orchestra under Jochum provides a background tapestry of breadth and dignity. It is a noble reading with an innate sense of classicism, yet the first movement offers wonderful lyrical intensity. As an added point of interest, Schneiderhan uses cadenzas that were provided for the transcription of the work for piano and orchestra. The first-movement cadenza is impressive in scale and adds a solo part for the timpani. This makes a very real bargain for tape collectors. The pair of CDs are digitally remastered, and offer a sharper sonic profile: the extra pair of overtures are well worth having, partricularly Jochum's *Leonora No. 2.*

(i) *Piano concerto No. 5 in E flat (Emperor)*; (ii) *Triple concerto for violin, cello and piano in C, Op. 56.*
(M) *** Sony SBK 46549 [id.]. (i) Leon Fleisher, Cleveland O, Szell; (ii) Stern, Rose, Istomin, Phd. O, Ormandy.

A unique coupling, and in this case an indispensable one – for this is one of Sony's 'Essential Classics' that is justly named. Leon Fleisher is a pianist who worked with special understanding in the Szell regime at Cleveland, and by any count his reading of the *Emperor* is impressive for its youthful, dramatic vigour. Fleisher has a considerable personality as an interpreter, but one suspects that here he projects Szell's view of Beethoven, so the advantages of youth and experience are combined with exceptional intensity. Like Szell himself, Fleisher sometimes finds it hard to relax naturally – as in the espressivo passages in the finale (which has a marvellously buoyant rhythmic spring). Yet in one important detail this version relaxes more than its rivals. Szell has noted that at the very end of the slow movement Beethoven's autograph asks for pizzicato strings half a bar after the point where the indication appears in printed scores. With Szell, after a lyrical span of poised beauty, the first indication of the magical key-change comes gently on a sustained bowed note, instead of with the usual 'plonk', quite an important point. The 1961 recording is very bright, but the Severance Hall ambience ensures fullness too, and the bold presence given to the piano produces a riveting moment when Fleisher plays Beethoven's commanding octave passage in the first movement. For the coupling we move to Philadelphia and a recording made in the Town Hall there, three years later. Stern, Rose and Istomin – three friends who invariably reveal their personal joy in making music together – make a wonderful trio of soloists. There is no apology whatever in the performance. Though Stern is undoubtedly the leader of the group, the dominance over his colleagues is benevolent and the individual expressiveness of each soloist keeps the attention riveted. Ormandy, too, proves to be a marvellous accompanist: his very opening pianissimo is full of tension and he begins the slow movement equally atmospherically, preparing the way for Leonard Rose's magical solo; indeed, the cello solos are so superbly expressive and the concentration of his colleagues so rapt that the movement acquires a depth beyond its spare proportions. The finale brings some wonderfully springy Polacca rhythms that take Beethoven very close to Eastern Europe. Unfortunately the CBS balance, as usual, favours the soloists so that the contrast of their soft playing is endangered; but the performance as a whole is so compelling that it would take a much more serious recording fault to undermine the concentration.

(i) *Violin concerto in D, Op. 61;* (ii) *Overtures: Coriolan; Creatures of Prometheus.*
(M) **(*) Chan. Analogue/Dig. CHAN 6521 [id.]. (i) Erich Gruenberg, New Philh. O, Horenstein; (ii) CBSO, Weller.

Horenstein provides a firm classical backing for Erich Gruenberg, who gives a refined and direct reading of the first movement. His timbre, already small, is thinned down a little by the recording, but the *Larghetto* brings beautiful pianissimo tone, especially at the ethereal reprise, and in the finale the lightness of the solo articulation adds to the spirit of the dance. The analogue orchestral recording has a slight tendency to harshness but the balance is good. Weller's accounts of the two overtures offer fine, modern, digital sound. First choice for the *Violin concerto* remains with Perlman, and his latest recording with Barenboim and the BPO includes also the two *Romances* (EMI CDC7 49567-2; *EL 749567-4*).

Konzertsatz (Concerto movement) in C, WoO 5; Romance No. 1 in G, Op.40.
(M) *** DG 431 168-2; *431 168-4* [id.]. Kremer, LSO, Tchakarov – SCHUBERT: *Konzertstück* etc.***

The early *Concerto movement in C* reveals Beethoven at twenty writing on an ambitious scale but rarely, if ever, achieving the touches of individuality which mark his mature concertos. The piece is performed in a completion by Wilfried Fischer that is effective enough; and the mixed bag of Schubert which acts as coupling is certainly apt. All the music is played beautifully by Kremer and the 1978 recording, made in the London Sir Henry Wood Hall, has transferred splendidly to CD.

Triple concerto for violin, cello and piano in C, Op. 56.
(B) ** DG 429 934-2 [id.]. Schneiderhan, Fournier, Anda, Berlin RSO, Fricsay – BRAHMS: *Double concerto.***
(B) ** DG Compact Classics *415 332-4* [id.]. Schneiderhan, Starker, Anda, Berlin RSO, Fricsay – BRAHMS: *Double concerto*; MOZART: *Violin concerto No. 3.***
(M) *(*) Ph. 426 631-2; *426 631-4* [id.]. Szeryng, Starker, Arrau, New Philh. O, Inbal – BRAHMS: *Double concerto.*(*)*

(i) *Triple concerto for violin, cello & piano, Op. 56;* (ii) *Symphony No. 10: First movement* (realized & completed by Barry Cooper).
(M) *** Chan. Dig. CHAN 6501; *MBTD 6501* [id.]. (i) Kalichstein–Laredo–Robinson Trio, ECO, Gibson; (ii) CBSO, Weller.

The 1984 Chandos version of the *Triple concerto* with three young American soloists is exceptionally well recorded, with problems of balance resolved better than on any other version. The playing is immaculate, and Sharon Robinson, the cellist, takes the lead with pure tone and fine intonation, though both her partners are by nature more forceful artists. A clean-cut, often refreshing view of the work, it is now reissued – as part of the first release in the Chandos Collect series – coupled with Weller's strong version of Barry Cooper's completion of the first movement of Beethoven's projected *Tenth Symphony*, also very well recorded. This mid-priced disc becomes much more competitive than the original CD, which was uncoupled.

The 1960 recording by Anda, Schneiderhan and Fournier was recorded in the Berlin Jesus-Christus Kirche, which means that there is plenty of atmosphere; but the balance is artificial, with the solo players (clearly separated) well forward and with their contribution dynamically nearly matching that of the orchestra, reducing the natural contrast. This gives the solo playing much more presence than that of the competing team on Philips, but Fricsay's vibrant orchestral tuttis have plenty of impact on the remastered CD. The performance has breadth and a genuine grasp of structure, with an eloquent contribution from each of the distinguished soloists. Only in the first movement does one sense a slight want of spontaneity, but the reading undoubtedly has more grip than the Philips/Inbal account. This version is also offered on a DG Compact Classics tape. Coupled with Brahms's *Double concerto* and Mozart's *Violin concerto No. 3*, this is generous value.

The Philips issue has spendidly full and spacious orchestral recording (dating from a decade later), but Arrau and his colleagues are less strongly projected and, by adopting very unhurried tempi, they run the risk of losing concentration. The central brief *Largo* is exquisitely done, and Starker's dedicated and spacious reading of the great cello solo has rarely been matched; but the outer movements, with the solo playing almost on a chamber scale, lack the bite and bravura of the finest rivals. First bargain choice for this coupling with Brahms remains with the David Oistrakh/Knushevitzky/Oborin recording on EMI Laser (CDZ7 62854-2), although the DG disc is by no means to be ignored.

Overtures: The Consecration of the House, Op. 124; Coriolan, Op. 62; The Creatures of Prometheus, Op. 43; Egmont, Op. 84; Fidelio, Op. 72c; King Stephen, Op. 117; Leonora No. 3, Op. 72b; The Ruins of Athens, Op. 113; Zur Namensfeier, Op. 115.
(B) *** Ph. 426 630-2; *426 630-4* [id.]. Leipzig GO, Kurt Masur.

This collection shows Kurt Masur and his Leipzig players at their very finest. These performances are more direct than those of Karajan and are wholly satisfying in their strong motivation and lack of mannerism. This is not to suggest they are without individuality: they have a combination of breadth and excitement that communicates readily – *Leonora No. 3* is every bit as gripping as Karajan's version. The Philips recording, from the early 1970s, is of high quality, and the remastering has enhanced its vividness and impact. This generous reissue (71 minutes) acts as a bargain sampler for the Silverline catalogue; but this means that its liner carries details of other records rather than notes about the music.

Romances for violin and orchestra Nos. 1 in G, Op. 40; 2 in F, Op. 50.
(B) *** DG Compact Classics 413 844-2 (2); *413 844-4* [id.]. D. Oistrakh, RPO, Goossens – BRAHMS: *Violin concerto* **(*); BRUCH: *Concerto No. 1* ** (CD only: DVOŘÁK: *Concerto* **(*)).

David Oistrakh's performances of the Beethoven *Romances* are of high quality and are well recorded. If the other works on this DG Compact Classics tape are attractive, this is good value. The pair of digitally remastered CDs also includes an attractive account of the Dvořák *Concerto*.

Symphonies Nos. 1–9.
(M) (**(*)) EMI mono CHS7 63606-2 (5). VPO or Stockholm PO, Furtwängler, (with soloists & Ch. in No. 9).
** Decca Dig. 430 400-2 (6) [id.]. Chicago SO, Solti (with soloists & Ch. in No. 9).

Symphonies Nos. 1 in C, Op. 21; 3 in E flat (Eroica), Op. 55.
(M) (***) BMG/RCA mono GD 60252 [60252-2-RG]. NBC O, Toscanini.

Symphonies Nos. 2 in D, Op. 36; 7 in A, Op. 92.
(M) (***) BMG/RCA mono GD 60253; [60253-2-RG]. NBC O, Toscanini.

Symphonies Nos. 4 in B flat, Op. 60; 6 in F (Pastoral), Op. 68.
(M) (**(*)) BMG/RCA mono GD 60254; [60254-2-RG]. NBC O, Toscanini.

Symphonies Nos. 5 in C min., Op. 67; 8 in F, Op. 93; Leonora No. 3.
(M) (**(*)) BMG/RCA mono GD 60255; [60255-2-RG]. NBC O, Toscanini.

Symphony No. 9 in D min., Op. 125 (Choral).
(M) (**(*)) BMG/RCA mono GD 60256; [60256-2-RG]. Farrell, Merriman, Peerce, Scott, Shaw Ch., NBC O, Toscanini.

It is welcome to have the individual issues in Toscanini's Beethoven cycle available separately. The transfers are the same as in the Toscanini Edition boxed set, carefully remastered with the original hum almost eliminated but with the sound still inevitably dry and harsh and with excessive treble emphasis in the *Ninth*. Nevertheless these are performances which convey breathtaking power, notably the magnificent accounts of the *Eroica* and the *Ninth*, never comfortable but far from rigid or unloving. The *Fourth* and *Fifth* sound less well than the others, taken from live, rather than studio, performances. *Leonore No. 3* dates from earlier than the rest, taken from a 1939 broadcast.

By unearthing a live recording of No. 2, made in the Royal Albert Hall in 1948, and borrowing a radio recording of No. 8 made in Stockholm, EMI managed to put together a complete Furtwängler cycle, and very impressive it is interpretatively. The sound of those two ad hoc recordings may be very rough indeed, with heavy background noise, but the performances – with one or two oddities – are electrifying. No. 9 comes in the dedicated performance given at Bayreuth in 1951, uniquely historic, but the others are EMI's studio versions, not always as inspired as Furtwängler's live performances but still magnetic and, with generally well-balanced mono sound, very well transferred.

Solti's second Beethoven cycle with the Chicago Symphony, made between 1986 and 1990, brings some surprising contrasts with his earlier set (Decca 421 673-2) recorded in the 1970s. Where earlier his speeds were generally spacious – notably in the *Eroica* and the *Ninth* – the later performances are much brisker, but not as a rule more resilient. The more ample digital recording is often a help, but the extra tensions, particularly in the even-numbered symphonies, make these performances generally less sympathetic. Karajan's first stereo recording of the nine Beethoven symphonies, made with the BPO in 1971–2, makes an outstanding recommendation on five CDs at bargain price (429 036-2).

Symphonies Nos. 1–9 (arr. Liszt).
**(*) Teldec/WEA Dig. 9031 71619-2 (6) [id.]. Cyprien Katsaris (piano).

We have greeted most (though not all) of the individual issues in Cyprien Katsaris's cycle of the Liszt/Beethoven transcriptions. He uses a Bechstein in Nos. 1–3, a Steinway in No. 5 and an instrument by Mark Allen in the rest. The sound generally speaking is a bit synthetic; but in the *Eroica*, the *Eighth* and the *Choral*, the playing is really quite astonishing, not only in purely pianistic terms and in a feeling for texture but also for architecture. The *Fifth* is the only real let-down.

Symphonies Nos. 1 in C, Op. 21; 2 in D, Op. 36.
(M) *** Ph. 432 274-2; *432 274-4* [id.]. ASMF, Sir Neville Marriner.
*(*) Decca Dig. 430 320-2; *430 320-4* [id.]. Chicago SO, Solti.

Marriner presents the first two symphonies on modern instruments but on an authentic scale with a Mozart-sized orchestra, and the result is fresh and lithe, with plenty of character but with few, if any, quirks and mannerisms. Nor are the dramatic contrasts underplayed, for the chamber scale is most realistically captured in the excellent 1970 recording, admirably remastered.

The first two symphonies in Solti's later cycle both bring taut *Allegros* that are so fast that rhythms fail to spring. The flowing speeds for the slow movements are lighter and more apt for early Beethoven; but there are many better versions of this regular coupling, notably Jochum's sparkling accounts on a bargain Philips disc (422 966-2) or the comparably priced Sony/CBS recordings by Bruno Walter, which achieve a happy medium between the music's eighteenth-century ancestry and its forward-looking qualities (MBK 44775).

Symphonies Nos. 1 in C, Op. 21; 6 in F, Op. 68 (Pastoral).
(M) **(*) Sony SMK 45891 [id.]. Marlboro Festival O, Pablo Casals.

Symphonies Nos. 1 in C, Op. 21; 6 in F (Pastoral), Op. 68; Overture Egmont, Op. 84.
(M) ** Sony SBK 46532 [id.]. Cleveland O, Szell.

Sony do not give the actual date of these Marlboro performances, which must come from the late 1960s or early 1970s, but they do publish a list of the orchestra's personnel, which includes some pretty distinguished names: Shmuel Ashkenazi, Jaime Laredo, Pina Carmirelli, Miklos Perenyi, Richard Stoltzman and many others. The *Pastoral* radiates integrity and warmth. It is totally free from any expressive exaggeration and tempi are well judged. These are performances of a vital sensitivity and, paradoxically, although everything is kept on a pretty tight rein it all seems relaxed and unhurried. The recording quality is dryish but eminently acceptable.

In the *First Symphony*, the characteristic 1964 Cleveland sound with its absence of real pianissimo, very bright and rather fierce on CD, may prove disconcerting for some listeners; but the clarity, the polish, the dynamism, the unfailing alertness of Szell's performance make up for any absence of charm. In the *Pastoral*, recorded in 1962, where the quality is smoother and warmer, Szell is subtle in his control of phrasing, for all the firmness of his style. However, it is a pity that the close-up sound robs the slow movement of much of its gentleness and delicacy of atmosphere. The finale, by contrast, is attractively relaxed. The fill-up, a version of the *Egmont overture* recorded in 1966, is excellently performed in Szell's intense way.

Symphony No. 2 in D, Op. 36; Overture Egmont, Op. 84.
(M) ** Sony CD 46247 [id.]. Marlboro Festival O, Casals – BRAHMS: *Variations on a theme by Haydn.***

Casals' performance of the *Second Symphony* was recorded at Marlboro in 1969 and the *Egmont Overture* the following year. The orchestra includes such players as Shmuel Ashkenazi, Pina Carmirelli, Felix Galimir and Masuko Ushioda in the violins with Arnold Steinhardt leading, while the cellists include Herman Busch and Miklos Perényi among the back desks! The *Second Symphony* is a performance of some stature and great integrity, with no whipped-up excitement or playing to the gallery. The recording is a bit dry and the balance not always perfect, but this is live music-making that is well worth hearing, despite the dated sound. Neither the symphony nor the overture has appeared before.

Symphonies Nos. 2 in D; 4 in B flat, Op. 60.
(M) (**) EMI mono CDH7 63192-2 [id.]. BPO, Furtwängler.

This disc brings the most marked discrepancy in sound between the two symphonies, with the scrunching background for No. 2 very distracting, though the live performance, given in the Royal Albert Hall, is electrifying. No. 4 comes in one of Furtwängler's finest studio recordings; though it is heavier and not quite as freely expressive as his live performances, its individuality is most compelling.

Symphony No. 3 in E flat (Eroica).
(M) (*) Decca mono 425 971-2 [id.]. LPO, Victor de Sabata (with: BERLIOZ: *Le carnaval romain overture*; SIBELIUS: *Valse triste*; WAGNER: *Ride of the Valkyries.*(*))

Victor de Sabata's 1946 *Eroica* with the LPO is not free from eccentricity; the very first edition of Edward Sackville-West and Desmond Shawe-Taylor's *The Record Guide* thought its first movement sluggish. Tempo fluctuations are far more obtrusive than in his glowing and celebrated account of the *Pastoral*, made with the Santa Cecilia Orchestra at about the same time. The Berlioz overture and *Valse triste* have great sensitivity to texture. The remastered recording, however, is not flattering.

Symphonies Nos. 3 in E flat (Eroica); 8 in F, Op. 93.
(M) **(*) Sony SBK 46328; *40-46328* [id.]. Cleveland O, Szell.

Szell's is a fine performance in the Toscanini tradition, hard-driven and dramatic. The speed of the first movement is almost the same as Toscanini's, the reading more rugged than with Karajan, but with more changes of tempo. The slow movement is most impressive; the prominence of the trumpet in the great climax may strike some listeners as vulgar but it cannot be denied that this is an exciting performance, and the final subdued disintegration of the theme is most deeply felt. The digital remastering of the recording (from the late 1950s) is very successful: the sound is firm, full and brilliant. The performance of the *Eighth* is also a compelling one. The first-movement repeat is taken and the performance is not over-driven; indeed, the finale is slower than usual, with plenty of consideration for the players' comfort. The 1962 recording is full and well detailed. There are plenty of alternative choices of distinction for the *Eroica*, notably Klemperer (EMI CDM7 63356-2; *EG 763356-4*), while Norrington's account on original instruments is among the most enjoyable of his Beethoven symphony series with the London Classical Players (EMI CDC7 49101-2; *EL 749101-4*).

Symphony No. 4 in B flat, Op. 60.
** Olympia OCD 225 [id.]. Leningrad PO, Mravinsky – SALMANOV: *Symphony No. 4 in B min.***

Mravinsky's record of the *Fourth Symphony* is a concert performance from 1973 and the sound-quality is not up to much. The audience is at times obtrusive and the upper strings are acidulated and climaxes distort. All the same, right from the opening bars one knows that this is going to be a performance of some stature; so it proves, and few will resist being drawn into its world. There is the right kind of tension and drama, and every phrase is beautifully shaped. Sonic limitations prevent this from being a first choice, or anywhere near it, but it is certainly a performance to be heard and studied.

Symphonies Nos. 4 in B flat, Op. 60; 5 in C min., Op. 67.
(M) **(*) Sony MK 42011 [id.]. Columbia SO, Bruno Walter.

Walter's coupling from 1959 has re-emerged from Sony at mid-price, with the same catalogue number as before. His reading of the *Fourth* is splendid, the finest achievement of his whole cycle. There is intensity and a feeling of natural vigour which makes itself felt in every bar. The first movement may not have quite the monumental weight that Klemperer gives it, but it is livelier. The slow movement gives Walter the perfect opportunity to coax a genuinely singing tone from his violins as only he knows how; and the finale allows the wind department its measure of brilliance. All aspects of this symphony – so much more varied than we have realized – are welded together here and show what depths it really contains. The recording is full yet clear, sweet-toned with a firm bass. Here as in the *Fifth* the sound-balance is richer and more satisfying than in many modern recordings. In Walter's reading of the *Fifth*, the first movement is taken very fast, yet it lacks the kind of nervous tension that distinguishes Carlos Kleiber's famous version. The middle two movements are contrastingly slow. In the *Andante* (more like *adagio*) there is a glowing, natural warmth, but the scherzo at this speed is too gentle. The finale, taken at a spacious, natural pace, is joyous and sympathetic, but again fails to convey the ultimate in tension. The digital remastering for CD has left behind a residue of pre-Dolby background hiss, but it is not too distracting.

Symphonies Nos. 4 in B flat, Op. 60; 8 in F, Op. 93.
** Ph. Dig. 420 539-2; *420 539-4* [id.]. Concg. O, Haitink.
** RCA Dig. RD 60362; *RK 60362* [60362-2-RC; *60362-4-RC*]. RPO, André Previn.

Symphonies Nos. 4 in B flat; 8 in F; Overtures: King Stephen, Op. 117; The Ruins of Athens, Op. 113.
**(*) Nimbus NI 5130 [id.]. Hanover Band, Roy Goodman.

Taken from the Hanover Band's fresh and alert Beethoven cycle on period instruments, this Nimbus coupling brings the substantial bonus of the two rare overtures, equally well done. The sound is reverberant in the characteristic Nimbus manner.

Haitink's performances of Nos. 4 and 8 are among the most sympathetic of his Concertgebouw cycle, generally fresh and resilient – even though the introduction to No. 4 is slack. The main snag is the recorded sound, reverberant enough to obscure detail in tuttis, and not always kind to the violins.

Previn's preference for broad speeds in Beethoven works far better in No. 4 than in No. 8. The slow movement of No. 4 is warmly affectionate, and the outer movements well sprung, but No. 8 sounds too laboured, not just a question of speed. The sound is refined but rather distanced.

Symphony No. 5 in C min., Op. 67; Overture Egmont (both arr. Frackenpohl); *Wellington's Victory* (*Battle Symphony;* arr. McNeff).
**(*) Ph. Dig. 426 487-2 [id.]. Canadian Brass, augmented by Boston SO and NYPO brass sections (members), George Tintner.

In their home country the Canadian Brass reach new audiences with their augmented concert spectaculars which feature complete performances of transcriptions of major classical works. Certainly George Tintner's reading of the *Fifth Symphony* is impressive in its own right: it has real grip and fine lyrical feeling. The *Egmont overture* is even more telling, its rich sonorities particularly suitable for this kind of transcription. But, surprisingly, *Wellington's Victory* disappoints, with poor special effects in the actual battle sequence. The recording is undoubtedly in the demonstration class and, if you are tempted by the prospect of Beethoven on brass, you will hardly do better than this.

(i) *Symphonies Nos. 5–6 (Pastoral); Overture: Egmont* (CD only: (ii) *Overtures: Consecration of the House; Namensfeier*; (iii) *The Ruins of Athens*).
(B) **(*) DG Compact Classics 413 144-2; *** *413 144-4* [id.]. (i) VPO, Boehm; (CD only: (ii) LOP, Markevitch; (iii) Bav. RSO, Jochum).

Boehm's Compact Classics coupling is generous in offering the *Egmont* overture as well as the *Fifth* and *Sixth Symphonies* on a single cassette. His account of the *Fifth* may not be the most powerful available, but the excellent playing and recording, rich and weighty in the bass as well as lively on top, make it a good version to live with. It pairs naturally with Boehm's warmly lyrical account of the *Pastoral* in its display of positive feeling and absence of neurosis. The reading of the *Pastoral* has a natural, unforced beauty, and is very well played (with strings, woodwind and horns beautifully integrated). In the first movement Boehm observes the exposition repeat (not many versions do); although the dynamic contrasts are never underplayed and the phrasing is affectionate, there is a feeling of inevitable rightness about Boehm's approach, no sense of an interpreter imposing his will. Only the slow movement with its even stressing raises any reservation, and that is very slight. The chrome-tape transfers of both works are very successful; in offering nearly 90 minutes of music, this is undoubtedly good value. The pair of CDs, digitally remastered, adds three more overtures, which many collectors will not consider an advantage. Jochum's *Ruins of Athens* is more distinguished than the other two, even if the Bavarian orchestral playing lacks the last ounce of polish. As it happens, the stylistic contrast is less distracting than one would expect, though naturally the Paris orchestra with its French vibrato does not always sound idiomatic. The recording is also more dated. Markevitch makes *The Consecration of the House* less weighty than usual, almost frivolous, but the interpretation of *Namensfeier* is clean and dramatic.

Symphonies Nos. 5 in C min., Op. 67; 7 in A, Op. 92.
(M) *** Decca Dig. 430 701-2; *430 701-4* [id.]. Philh. O, Ashkenazy.
(*) BBC mono CD 784 [id.]. RPO, Weingartner.

When these symphonies last appeared, separately and at full price, we complained that a CD comprising a single symphony plus an overture or two as fill-up offered short measure. Now they have been reissued, coupled together and at mid-price, and the extra value is obvious. Ashkenazy's reading of the *Fifth* is urgent and vivid, and is notable for its rich Kingsway Hall recording. Well-adjusted speeds here (the *Andante* on the slow side, the finale somewhat quick), with joyful exuberance a fair substitute for grandeur. The reading of the *Seventh* is equally spontaneous, a generally direct performance taken steadily at unexaggerated speeds; the result is glowingly convincing, thanks to fine playing and recording that set new standards in this work, full and spacious yet warmly co-ordinated. After a grave and simple account of the slow introduction, the allegro at first sounds deceptively relaxed in pastoral mood, until the dramatic urgency of the movement takes over, its dance rhythms nicely lifted. The finale is a shade slower than usual, but effectively so. This mid-priced CD ranks high among couplings of these two symphonies, especially for those for whom outstanding recording quality is a priority.

Weingartner's 'lean-beef' Beethoven (the phrase is Peter Stadlen's) was the yardstick by which others were judged in the 1920s and 1930s, and his authority in the classical repertoire was long uncontested except by Toscanini and Furtwängler. He recorded the *Fifth* and *Seventh Symphonies* for Columbia in 1927 at the Scala Theatre in London. The sound is rather amazing for its age and is more present than one would expect for the period. Weingartner's *Seventh* is much tauter than the more celebrated records he made with the Vienna Philharmonic in 1936. The opening has far more intensity and the scherzo is almost twice as fast. Unfortunately there are disturbing changes of pitch between 78 sides (side 2 is much sharper than its neighbours and there is an unbearable lurch in the middle of the scherzo).

Symphonies Nos. 5 in C min.; 8 in F, Op. 93.
** Ph. Dig. 422 071-2; *422 071-4* [id.]. ASMF, Marriner.

Marriner's version of No. 5 may miss some of the full biting drama but, as in the rest of the cycle, the sound is clean and refined. In the first two movements at least, Marriner's account of No. 8 is surprisingly broad, well sprung but risking the danger of heaviness, where by contrast the finale goes like the wind. Jochum continues to lead the field in this coupling, the performances unmarred by any romantic exaggeration but gripping in a totally natural, unforced way. The sound is extremely good and at bargain price this is very recommendable (Philips 422 474-2).

Symphonies Nos. 6 in F (Pastoral), Op. 68; 8 in F, Op. 93.
(M) *** EMI Dig. CDD7 63891-2 [id.]; *ET 763891-4*. LPO, Tennstedt.

(B) * DG 431 159-2; *431 159-4* [id.]. BPO, Karajan.

Tennstedt's fresh, alert and imaginative performance of the *Pastoral* comes in a generous coupling with the *Eighth*, given an equally enjoyable reading in which the second movement *Allegretto* at a fast speed is made into a scherzo while the Minuet is spaciously lyrical. In the *Pastoral*, the slow movement brings a finely moulded performance from Tennstedt, a dramatic account of the *Storm* and a radiant reading of the finale. Well-balanced recording, bright and fresh. If the coupling is suitable, this is well worth considering. This is strongly recommendable.

Karajan's 1962 version of the *Pastoral* was by far the least appealing of his first Berlin Beethoven cycle, with hectically fast tempi. Ironically, his sharply dramatic reading of the *Eighth* offers an excellently performed fill-up. The playing throughout is very refined and the sound remarkably good for its period but, even at bargain price, this does not compete with the EMI/Tennstedt mid-price coupling of the same two symphonies.

Symphony No. 7 in A, Op. 92.
(BB) ** Pickwick PWK 1156. SRO, Ansermet.

Ansermet's Beethoven has always been underestimated. His Swiss players could not rival the finest international orchestras in discipline and polish; but this conductor never made a record that was not tinglingly alive, and so it is here. He starts well, with a poised introduction (taken rather fast), building up to a fine climax; both outer movements have plenty of adrenalin, and the final coda is thrilling. There is no lack of warmth either, and the 1960 recording, made in the Vicoria Hall, Geneva, is astonishingly vivid and full. This is by no means a general recommendation, but Ansermet admirers will not be disappointed.

Symphony No. 7 in A, Op. 92; Wellington's victory (Battle Symphony), Op. 92.
**(*) Ph. Dig. 426 239-2 [id.]. ASMF, Marriner.

Marriner's crisp and well-sprung reading of No. 7 – though with a slow, rather dull *Allegretto* – comes in coupling with a delightful squib, an inspired recording of the *Battle Symphony*. This starts, not with music, but with the sounds of nature (recorded not on the battlefield of Vittoria in Spain but at Waterloo in Belgium), and then you hear the respective armies arriving, together with their anthems. Sonically, it is a *tour de force* – which is a help with a work not among Beethoven's most inspired. Marriner and the ASMF give an exemplary account of music which presents surprising difficulties in performance. Vivid sound.

Symphonies Nos. 7 in A, Op. 92; 8 in F, Op. 93.
(M) *(*) Sony SMK 45893 [id.]. Marlboro Festival O, Casals.

Symphonies Nos. 7 in A, Op. 92; 8 in F, Op. 93; The Creatures of Prometheus: Overture.
(**(*)) Music Memoria/Scott Butler mono 30269 [id.]. VPO, Weingartner.

Weingartner's 1936 record of the *Seventh* is of a less high voltage than his earlier, RPO account but has a wonderfully natural feel about it. While listening to these performances one soon comes to believe that this is the voice of Beethoven in much the same way as one does about Schnabel's late sonatas. There are sonic limitations, and side-joins are not always expert: a couple of beats are added in the middle of the first movement of No. 8. However, the insights Weingartner brought to this music were special and his selfless classical view of both symphonies still retains its allure.

These performances by Casals may well divide opinion concerning the *Eighth Symphony*, as it divided us when it first appeared on LP. The actual sound-quality is pretty dreadful (No. 8 dates from 1963 and is very scrawny), but the performance has tremendous concentration and fire. The *Seventh*, too, is a performance of some stature. The orchestral personnel span the generations and include Hermann Busch and Felix Galimir, the young Lynn Harrell and David Soyer.

Symphony No. 9 in D min. (Choral), Op. 125.
(M) *** Decca 430 438-2; *430 438-4* [id.]. Lorengar, Minton, Burrows, Talvela, Chicago Ch. & SO, Solti.
(BB) *** Pickwick (Decca) PWK 1150. Sutherland, Procter, Dermota, Arnold van Mill, Brassus Ch. & Ch. Vaudoise, SRO, Ansermet.
**(*) DG Dig. 427 655-2; *427 655-4* [id.]. Varady, Van Nes, K. Lewis, Estes, Senff Ch., BPO, Giulini.
**(*) RPO Dig. CDRPO 7001; *ZCRPO 7001* [id.]. Falcon, McKellar-Ferguson, Margison, Thomas Thomashcke, Brighton Festival Ch., RPO, Menuhin.
(M) ** EMI Dig. CDD7 63902-2 [id.]; *ET 763902-4*. Armstrong, Finnie, Tear, Tomlinson, Philh. Ch. & O, Sanderling.
(M) ** Ph. 432 039-2 [id.]. J. Price, Finnilä, Laubenthal, Rintzler, Concg. Ch. & O, Haitink.
(*) Scott Butler & Thames mono 30279 [id.]. Helletsgrüber, Anday, Maikl, Mayr, V. State Op. Ch., VPO, Weingartner.

Symphony No. 9 in D min. (Choral); (i) *Contredanses, WoO 17.*
(M) (*) Pearl mono GEMMCD 9407 [id.] Helletsgrüber, Anday, Maikl, Mayr, V. State Op. Ch., VPO, or (i) LPO, Weingartner.

Symphony No. 9 in D min. (Choral), Op. 125; Overture Fidelio, Op. 72b.
(M) **(*) Sony SBK 46533 [id.]; *40-46533*. Addison, Hobson, Lewis, Bell, Cleveland O Ch. & O, Szell.

Solti's 1972 recording of the *Ninth* is one of his outstanding gramophone achievements, long praised by us in its original LP and tape formats. If you regard the sublime slow movement as the key to this epic work, then Solti is clearly with you. With spacious, measured tempi he leads the ear on, not only with his phrasing but also with his subtle shading of dynamic down to whispered pianissimo. Here is *Innigkeit* of a concentration rarely heard on record, even in the *Ninth*. Solti in the first movement is searing in his dynamic contrasts – maybe too brutally so – while the precision of the finale, with superb choral work and solo singing, confirms this as one of the finest *Ninths* on CD. In almost every way it is preferable to his later, digital version (Decca 417 800-2 – see our main volume, p. 122), particularly in terms of choral balance. Recorded in Krannert Center at the University of Illinois, the analogue recording is full, yet clean and bright, its various elements very well co-ordinated in the CD transfer. Karajan's 1977 account, the finest of the three he made in stereo, should also be considered at mid-price (DG 415 832-2; *415 832-4*), but Solti's version should disappoint no one.

Ansermet's 1965 recording of the *Choral Symphony* was one of the first successful stereo versions to appear on a single LP. Now it makes its return to the catalogue as a super-bargain CD, still sounding vividly clear. Such clean detail (although there is atmosphere too) suits the direct style of the conductor; it seems that Ansermet was inspired beyond his usual achievement by the greatest challenge of all in Beethoven, helped by a fine group of soloists and incisive choral singing. In the first two movements he is clear-cut and rhythmically precise (though by no means inflexible), and the slow movement, if not wearing its heart on its sleeve, certainly does not lack expressive feeling. The finale is strong and exciting, with the quality of the recording telling, even if, like the first movement, it lacks some weight (as did the original LP). Ansermet demonstrates here that the Viennese tradition is not the only way with Beethoven.

Giulini's version brings a characteristically spacious reading, strong and measured, but – except in the jollity of the dancing triplets in the drum-and-fife section – the finale is less intense: amiable and relaxed rather than powerful. Apart from Simon Estes at times sounding under-the-note, the singing is first rate, both from soloists and from choir.

As bitingly dramatic as Toscanini in the first movement and electrically intense all through, Szell directs a magnetic, seemingly inevitable account of the *Ninth* which demonstrates the glories of the Cleveland Orchestra. With speeds never as extreme as Toscanini's, he yet captures a comparable fire. Though with close-up CBS recording, the slow movement never conveys anything like a pianissimo, the beauty of line in immaculate legato gives persuasive warmth and sweetness. The chorus sings with similarly knife-edged ensemble, set behind the orchestra but not too distantly. Soloists are well forward, so that words are exceptionally clear. The 1961 sound, bright and forward, has come up satisfyingly full-bodied, if with some analogue hiss. At mid-price a first-rate recommendation for those wanting a commanding reminder of a great conductor's work. The performance of the *Fidelio* overture is electrifying.

Menuhin celebrated his 75th birthday in April 1991 by conducting Beethoven's *Ninth* with the same forces as on this RPO disc, which appeared simultaneously. It is a strong, urgent reading at speeds on the fast side, similar to those preferred by Karajan. Yet Menuhin by nature is a less dictatorial Beethovenian than Karajan. Characteristically, in the slow movement he moulds phrases with natural affection, even at a fast-flowing speed. The playing throughout is powerful but lacks something in bite, largely a question of the recording, which brings odd balances for wind and brass and tends to blur detail. In the finale the chorus produces luminous tone, but the backward balance does not help its impact, and the soloists – the tenor apart – are disappointing.

Sanderling's 1984 digital performance of the *Ninth* has a rugged directness – an unvarnished honesty, as one commentator put it – which has special links with the Philharmonia versions conducted by Klemperer. Like Klemperer, Sanderling prefers slowish tempi, steadily maintained. This *Ninth* may lack mystery at the start, and the finale is dangerously slow; but the power of the work is caught splendidly. The soloists make an excellent team, but the Philharmonia Chorus is just below its best form, the singing of the sopranos not always well supported. This record undoubtedly has its rewards to offer but, except for those insisting on digital recording, there are many more distinctive mid-priced alternatives. Solti's version, for instance, is at once more vibrant and more searching, and the choral singing is much more compulsive, too.

Haitink's 1980 digital recording was made at a live concert in the Concertgebouw, but one would not know that: there are few if any signs of an audience, and – disappointingly – the performance fails to convey the excitement of a live occasion. The reading is satisfyingly unidiosyncratic, direct and honest; but with this work one needs more. The sound is good, but this reissue includes no information about the music itself.

Weingartner's celebrated 1935 account of the *Ninth* is one of the noblest ever committed to disc. Neither of these transfers quite fits the bill: the Scott Butler disc is tonally superior but is disfigured by obtrusive 78-r.p.m. side-joins, which one does not expect to encounter these days. Pearl has more surface noise but is tonally less faithful to the original sound (the upper strings are fierce and thin). It enjoys two advantages: it has the delightful *Contredanses*, WoO 17, which sound much better, and it is offered at at mid-price. All the same, the Scott Butler makes for more pleasing listening tonally, the Pearl being difficult to tame.

CHAMBER MUSIC

Cello sonatas Nos. 1–5.
*** Decca Dig. 417 628-2 (2) [id.]. Harrell, Ashkenazy.

Artistically these performances are in the first league and they have the advantage of superb recording.

Clarinet trio, Op. 11; Septet in E flat, Op. 20.
*** Virgin Dig. VC7 91137-2; *VC7 91137-4* [id.]. Nash Ens.

There is pure magic in these performances, with the members of the Nash Ensemble conveying their own enjoyment in the young Beethoven's exuberant inspiration. So the *Clarinet trio* finds each player, not just the fine clarinettist Michael Collins but also the pianist Ian Brown and the cellist Christopher van Kampen, pointing rhythms and phrases as a friendly challenge to be answered and capped by colleagues, the spontaneous interplay of the moment. It is a happy phenomenon, too rarely evident on record but delectably present here. An apt sense of fun also infects the *Septet*, though the allegros in the outer movements, exhilaratingly fast, would have been even more winning at speeds a shade more relaxed. But here too the performance brims with joy. Good, atmospheric sound.

Piano trios Nos. 1–11; Trio in E flat (from Septet), Op. 38; Trio in D (from *Symphony No. 2*); *Trio movement in E flat*
(M) **(*) Ph. Analogue/Dig. 432 381-2 (5) [id.]. Beaux Arts Trio.

Unlike their earlier set, made in the late 1960s and accommodated on four mid-price LPs (now no longer available), the present Beaux Arts box offers absolutely everything Beethoven composed (or arranged) for this grouping. Four of the recordings are digital, and everything has been economically fitted on five CDs, four of which have playing times of over 70 minutes. The transfers are well up to the usual high Philips standard and the performances are as accomplished and musical as one would expect from this celebrated team. However, it has to be said that the earlier, analogue set had a freshness and sparkle that these new accounts do not wholly match. Moreover competition is strong. On four full-priced EMI discs (CDS7 47455-8) Ashkenazy, Perlman and Harrell offer the eleven major trios plus the '*Kakadu' variations* and the early *Allegretto in E flat*. Their playing is unfailingly perceptive and the digital recordings are altogether first class. Alternatively (beside a fine, classically orientated set by Kempff, Szeryng and Fournier on DG 415 879-2), Barenboim, Zukerman and Jacqueline du Pré (by omitting Nos. 4 and 8) fit the bulk of this repertoire on to three mid-priced CDs. This set brings more idiosyncratic music-making but it has rare concentration, and any tendency to self-indulgence is counterbalanced by its urgency and intensity. The CD transfers are fresh and natural, although the remastering has brought a degree of dryness on fortissimo tuttis (EMI CDM7 63124-2).

Piano and wind quintet in E flat, Op. 16.
(B) *** Hung. White Label HRC 169 [id.]. Sándor Fálvai, Hungarian Wind Qt – MOZART: *Quintet*.***

This excellent, bargain-priced Hungaraton coupling stands up well to the distinguished competition. The three movements are admirably paced and spontaneously interrelated in mood, the woodwind playing is individually characterful yet well blended, and the pianist, Sándor Fálvai, dominates with fresh, rhythmic articulation and shapely phrasing.

The Hungaraton recording is clear and natural, and the acoustic and balance are equally felicitous. Most enjoyable – although first choice for this coupling at full price rests with Perahia and members of the ECO (Sony MK 42099).

Serenade in D, Op. 8 (arr. Matiegka).
(M) ** BMG/RCA GD 87870; *GK 87870* [7870-2-RG; *7870-4-RG*]. Heifetz, Primrose, Piatigorsky – SPOHR: *Violin concerto No. 8* etc.(***)

The Heifetz–Primrose–Piatigorsky record was made in 1960 at the same tine as the *D major Trio*, Op. 9, No. 2. The sound is dry but not unacceptably so, and the playing is immaculate. It comes with an altogether remarkable account of Spohr's so-called *Gesangsszene concerto.*

Serenade in D, Op. 8.
*** Mer. Dig. CDE 84199 [id.]. Clive Conway, Paul Silverthorne, Gerald Garcia – KREUTZER; MOLINO: *Trios.****

Beethoven's early *Serenade* for string trio was arranged for violin, viola and guitar as early as 1807 by the Bohemian composer and guitarist, Wenceslaus Matiegka. Gerald Garcia has here rearranged it for the present unusual and delightful combination, offering the violin part to the flute, and giving the guitar a more taxing contribution. As a companion-piece for the rare Kreutzer and Molino items, it makes a charming oddity in its seven brief movements, very well played and warmly recorded.

String quartets Nos. 1–16; Grosse Fuge, Op. 133.
(M) (***) EMI mono CZS7 67236-2 (7). Hungarian Quartet.

String quartets Nos. 1–16; Grosse Fuge; Quartet in F from Sonata, Op. 14/1 (transcription).
(B) ** DG Dig. 431 094-2 (9) [id.]. Melos Qt.
(M) ** Intercord/Koch INT 820 750/752 (*Quartets Nos. 1–6 & Quartet in F*); INT 820 753/5 (*Quartets Nos. 7–11*); INT 820 756/8 (*Quartets Nos. 12–16 & Grosse Fuge*) [id.]. Melos Qt.

Recorded in 1953 before the age of stereo, the Hungarian Quartet's first recorded cycle of the Beethoven *Quartets* has long been overshadowed by their later, stereo set of 1966. Yet this very welcome reissue, with the mono sound firm and full and with fine presence, brings out the palpable advantages of the earlier performances. Originally issued on the Columbia label, this was the first complete cycle made in the LP era, soon to be followed by cycles from the Budapest, Pascal and Végh quartets – their earlier mono versions. The Hungarians' matching is superb, with tonal beauty never an end in itself. The *senza vibrato* playing of the chorale in the great *Heilige Dankgesang* of Opus 132 has never been more perfectly achieved. Polished ensemble goes with a sense of spontaneity in readings fresher and more direct than those of 1966. The spacious, unhurried playing of the great slow movements here has rarely been matched. Those primarily concerned with the music as opposed to sound-quality will find little difficulty in adjusting to the recording; indeed, on first hearing, so vivid and full is the sound that it would be easy to believe one was listening to a very early stereo recording, while the layout on only seven discs (with each one offering well over 70 minutes of music) makes it a bargain too. Unlike the Amadeus's seven-disc cycle on DG, this one has exposition repeats observed, while the Italian series, in three boxes, involves ten discs. Although the Italians are to be preferred, both as performances and as recordings, the Hungarians make a very good bargain alternative.

The performances by the Melos Quartet of the early and middle-period *Quartets* offer a refined blend, impeccable intonation and superb ensemble. However, admiration rather than unalloyed pleasure is one's final reaction. Speeds are on the fast side, nor does this group convey a sufficient sense of pleasure in the courtly exchanges that take place between the instruments in the early *Quartets*, and at times their playing has an aggressive edge. There are, of course, some very good things in the set, and there is no question as to the finesse and mastery of the playing or the vividness of the recording. The players adopt a generally sound approach and eschew unnecessary interpretative eccentricities. Dynamic nuances and other markings are scrupulously observed. But far too many of the finales are too fast - the first movement in Op. 59/1 is incredibly rushed. Although they offer performances of some of the *Quartets* which are as finely played as any, the impression is of superb quartet playing rather than of great Beethoven. The Melos players seem most naturally attuned to the late *Quartets*, where they are strong and positive in fast movements, deeply expressive in slow ones, although here the playing is not as hushed as it might be. The players are particularly impressive in their powerful reading of the *Grosse Fuge*. As a novelty, they include Beethoven's own transcription of the *Sonata*, Op. 14, No. 1, which is not otherwise available. The complete set is now offered in a box, on nine bargain-priced CDs.

The alternative Melos cycle on Intercord is very competitively priced and enjoys the advantage over rival mid-priced packages in being available singly. There are, however, no notes or documentation. The recordings come from 1970 and may well attract some collectors, since the performances are more relaxed and more naturally paced than the later Melos survey on DG. However, a major snag lies in the recording quality, which is variable, at times rather dry and at others fierce; occasionally the leader sounds wiry above the stave. This is a pity, as there is much in Op. 18 to give pleasure, and the first of the *Rasumovsky quartets* is without doubt artistically more satisfying than the DG version from the mid-1980s, with more natural articulation and greater concentration. The fugal finale of Op. 59, No. 3, is taken at a much more sensible pace here. Op. 130 has more feeling and intensity than on DG. However, given the quality of the current alternatives (Quartetto Italiano, Lindsays, Végh, Talich – see our main volume), it would be a mistake to choose these in preference.

String quartets Nos. 1–6, Op. 18/1–6.
(B) ** Hung. White Label HRC 156/7. Bartók Qt.
(M) *(*) RCA GD 60456; *GK 60456* (3) [60456-2-RG]. Guarneri Qt.

The Bartók Quartet plays with great elegance and aplomb, though they rarely penetrate far below the surface. The performances first appeared in the early 1970s and the recordings are satisfactory but no more. Tempi tend to be brisk: the first-movement exposition repeat in the *F major* is not observed, but all the others are. There are good things here, but they would not add up to more than a cautious recommendation, were they not so economically priced. They are certainly good value on a pair of super-bargain discs, although the Italian Quartet on Philips bring greater musical rewards (426 046-2).

The Guarneri set dates from 1969 and is probably the best of their cycle. Three quartets are accommodated on the first CD, two on the second, and the *B flat* (No. 6) has a disc to itself. Room could surely have been found for, say, the *String quintet*, which the Guarneri recorded at about this time. The performances are very efficient, but the sound is inclined to be hard and wiry.

String quartets Nos. 1–6, Op. 18/1–6; 10 in E flat (Harp), Op. 74; 11 in F min., Op. 95.
*** ASV CDDCS 305 (3) [id.]. Lindsay Qt.

The great merit of the Lindsay Quartet in Beethoven lies in the natural expressiveness of their playing, most strikingly of all in slow movements where, even in these early works, such movements as the D minor *Adagio affetuoso* of No. 1 has a hushed inner quality too rarely caught on record. The sense of spontaneity necessarily brings the obverse quality: these performances are not as precise as those in the finest rival sets; but there are few Beethoven quartet recordings that so convincingly bring out the humanity of the writing, its power to communicate. The recording of Op. 18, set against a fairly reverberant acoustic, is warm and realistic, and the CD transfer is very successful: the 1979 sound is fuller in the treble than the quality Philips have achieved in their remastering of the Quartetto Italiano. The Lindsays are equally penetrating and unhurried in the slow movements of Op. 74 and Op. 95; elsewhere there are one or two rough edges, tonally speaking, but again the transfers reflect the fact that the recordings are more modern and rather fuller than the remastered Philips quality for the Italian group.

String quartets Nos. 3, 4 & 6; Op. 18/3, 4 & 6.
** Hyp. Dig. CDA 66402; *KA 66402* [id.]. New Budapest Qt.

This is a great improvement over the first release in the Hyperion/New Budapest series, as indeed it needs to be (see our main volume, p. 130). There is more fire and a greater sense of involvement and the players are far more attentive to dynamic nuance – though, even so, contrasts between *forte* and *piano* could with advantage be stronger. Although there are better versions of each quartet, these can still hold their own in the catalogue, and they are very well recorded.

String quartets Nos. 5 in A, Op. 18/5; 7 in F (Rasumovsky), Op. 59/1.
**(*) Hyp. Dig. CDA 66403 [id.]. New Budapest Qt.

The New Budapest players produce consistent refinement of sound and have impeccable intonation. Their account of the *A major Quartet* has no want of vitality in its outer movements, though the middle two movements suffer a little from gentility. All the more surprising, then, to find them so impressive in the first *Rasumovsky quartet.* The slow movement may not match the finest rival accounts in depth of feeling but the performance holds together remarkably well and the meticulous care taken over detail pays strong musical dividends. Very good recording.

String quartets Nos. 7–9 (Rasumovsky Nos. 1–3), Op. 59/1–3.
*** ASV Dig. CDDCS 207 (2) [id.]. Lindsay Qt.
*(*) Teldec/WEA 2292 46016-2 (2). Vermeer Qt.

String quartets Nos. 7–9 (Rasumovsky Nos. 1–3), Op. 59/1–3; 10 in E flat, Op. 74; 11 in F min., Op. 95.
(M) * RCA GD 60457; *GK 60457* (3) [60457-2-RG]. Guarneri Qt.

The Lindsays' are very considerable performances – see our main volume – and are now placed together in a box, with some saving in cost.

The *F major*, Op. 59, No. 1, is the best thing in the Guarneri set, made in the late 1960s, and it is less overdriven than the others. In general the playing here is never less than brilliant and virtuosic, which is not enough in this repertoire. The finale of Op. 59, No. 3, is horribly scrambled and the *E minor* is brash and aggressive. The recording enhances this impression: it is rather dry, airless and hard.

The Vermeer Quartet give us eminently well-proportioned and serious accounts, which are somewhat handicapped by the dryish, cramped acoustic which entails a certain loss of bloom. The playing is eminently well drilled and the choice of tempi sensible. Dynamic markings are at times a bit generalized (*mf* instead of *p*), though this may well be the fault of the close balance. These are readings to respect rather more than to warm to.

String quartets Nos. 7 in F; 8 in E min. (Rasumovsky), Op. 59/1–2.
(M) **(*) Sony SBK 46545 [id.]. Budapest Qt (Joseph Roisman; Alexander Schneider, Boris Kroyt, Mischa Schneider).

The Budapest Quartet on CBS were the first group to provide a complete stereo set of the Beethoven *Quartets*, although the Amadeus followed quickly after and, because of the greater refinement of their playing, tended to eclipse the earlier achievement. The Budapest were at their finest in the late *Quartets* and we hope these will be reissued soon on CD. The rugged masculinity of their approach (heard most strikingly here in the *Allegretto vivace* of Op. 59/1) is very suitable in such works, and it brings plenty of bite to both performances. They are closely balanced, which does not help in the provision of pianissimos, yet there is no real lack of light and shade. At times the leader's intonation is less than ideal; but this is powerfully felt playing of a kind we do not often encounter today – the *Adagio* of the *E minor*, Op. 59/2, shows this readily. Moreover the music-making is strongly communicative – the rough edges are caused by commitment to Beethoven, not by lack of rehearsal, and the ensemble playing generally has the most powereful unanimity. The sound on CD is balanced in favour of the leader, but otherwise is remarkably good, and the effect is very live.

String quartets Nos. 7 in F; 9 in C (Rasumovsky Nos. 1 & 3), Op. 59/1 & 3.
(B) ** Hung. White Label HRC 153. Bartók Qt.

These two quartets can easily be accommodated on one CD these days, even though the *F major* often takes longer than 40 minutes. The Bartók get through both in 62 minutes flat by adopting pretty fast tempi and omitting exposition repeats. The performances are good, if less than searching, and the 1970s recordings are fully acceptable, if nothing out of the ordinary. But this CD is nevertheless economically priced.

String quartets Nos. 10 in E flat (Harp), Op. 74; 11 in F min., Op. 95.
*(*) Nimbus Dig. NI 5242 [id.]. Medici Qt.

The Medici Quartet is wanting in that concentrated energy that the opening movement of Op. 95 must have. They sound curiously underpowered throughout; and their account of the *Harp*, though better, is not among the best things in the cycle. The recordings are very good, but in this particular coupling readers would be better advised to look elsewhere.

String quartets Nos. 15 in A min., Op. 132; 16 in F, Op. 135.
Nimbus Dig. NI 5285 [id.]. Medici Qt.

String quartets Nos. 12 in E flat, Op. 127; 13 in B flat, Op. 130; 14 in C sharp min., Op. 131; 15 in A min., Op. 132; 16 in F, Op. 135; Grosse Fuge in B flat, Op. 133.
(M) ** DG 431 141-2 (3) [id.]. LaSalle Qt.
(M) * RCA GD 60458; *GK 60458* (3) [60458-2-RG]. Guarneri Qt.

Technically, the LaSalle Quartet are unfailingly impressive and they bring unanimity of ensemble and fine tonal blend to these awe-inspiring scores. But there is no sense of mystery, little feeling of inwardness or depth. The recordings (made between 1973 and 1977) were of DG's best analogue quality, and they have been transferred cleanly and firmly to CD; but the Lindsays (ASV DCS 403) and Italians (Philips 426 050-2) bring us much closer to this music (see our main volume).

The Guarneri are brash and hard, and rarely penetrate below the surface. Even if they did, it would be difficult in this day and age to recommend a set that manages to split Op. 127 over two CDs and also accommodates Op. 130 and the *Grosse Fuge* on separate discs.

String quartet No. 13 in B flat, Op. 130; Grosse Fuge in B flat, Op. 133.
*(*) Nimbus NI 5254 [id.]. Medici Qt.

As with earlier issues in their cycle, the Medici have the advantage of the fine acoustic of The Maltings, Snape, which puts plenty of air round the sound. They give an honest, forthright account of Op. 130, though the *Grosse Fuge* proves to be rather a hard nut for them to crack. Of course it should sound intractable, but here it poses strains that are not completely surmounted. Incidentally, the Medici place the *Grosse Fuge* before Beethoven's definitive finale.

String quartet No. 14 in C sharp min., Op. 131; Grosse Fuge, Op. 133 (orchestral versions).
**(*) Capriccio Dig. 10 356 [id.]. International Musical Seminar Soloists, Végh.

The practice of performing this repertory for full strings dates back to the beginning of the century. (Mahler even played Schubert's *Death and the Maiden quartet* in that form.) If you are going to do it at all, these serious and dedicated performances by a group of accomplished musicians working with an artist of Végh's insights show how it should be done. There are four players to a part, and their numbers include some distinguished soloists who appear in these pages in their own right. Moreover they play with great responsiveness and understanding in both works. The sound is varied – there is none of the opulence of the Vienna Philharmonic strings who recorded this with Bernstein for DG, but the sonority is much more varied. The *Grosse Fuge* is more frequently encountered on full strings (from Furtwängler and Klemperer, among others), but this performance is as fine as any. The recording is also good, though there is a less than pleasing coldness about the upper strings that may be the product of the acoustic or the recording.

String quartets Nos. 15 in A min., Op. 132; 16 in F, Op. 135.
** Nimbus Dig. NI 5285 [id.]. Medici Qt.

The Medici have the advantage of a good recording acoustic (Nimbus use The Maltings, Snape) and there is no attempt to score interpretative points. However, the sound they produce throughout the cycle needs a little more range. Op. 135 is a bit tame and, although there are good moments in Op. 132, the sound the leader makes is somewhat wanting in tonal bloom. On the face of it, good value, since the disc offers two major works, but artistically it is not a strong contender.

String quartet No. 16 in F, Op. 135.
* DG Dig. 429 224-2 [id.]. Emerson Qt – SCHUBERT: *String quartet No. 15.**

The Emerson account of Op. 135 is unpleasantly hard-driven and aggressive. The playing is superb in terms of ensemble and precision, but understatement is foreign to their nature. Every dynamic marking is underlined and the musical argument overdramatized. Overlit, forwardly balanced recording.

(i) *String trio No. 1 in E flat, Op. 3;* (ii) *String quartet No. 11 in F min., Op. 95.*
(B) *(*) Hung. White Label HRC158. (i) Kovács, Németh, Banda; (ii) Bartók Qt.

The *E flat String trio* is an underrated and masterly work, and it is given an eminently respectable performance by these distinguished players. However, neither as a performance nor as a recording can it hold a candle to the Cummings Trio on Unicorn (DKPCD 9059, more appropriately coupled with the *Serenade in D*, Op. 8), discussed on p. 135 of our main volume. The Bartók's account of Op. 95 is of much the same vintage (the early 1970s) and is workmanlike rather than inspired. The recording is fully acceptable, but this is mainly recommendable to bargain-hunters.

String trio No. 2 in D, Op. 9/2.
(M) ** BMG/RCA GD 87873; *GK 87873* [7873-2-RG; *7873-4-RG*]. Heifetz, Primrose, Piatigorsky – BRAHMS: *Piano quartet in C min.*; SCHUBERT: *Fantaisie.***

The performance of the *D major Trio* comes from 1960 and is the earliest of the recordings on this disc. The dryish sound remains a handicap but, as one would expect from these artists, the playing is magisterial.

Violin sonatas Nos. 5 in F (Spring), Op. 24; 9 in A (Kreutzer), Op. 47.
(BB) *** Naxos Dig. 8.550283 [id.]. Takako Nishizaki, Jenö Jandó.
(B) *** DG Compact Classics *415 615-4* [id.]. Yehudi Menuhin, Wilhelm Kempff – BRAHMS: *Violin sonata No. 2.****

Violin sonatas Nos. 5 in F (Spring); 9 in A (Kreutzer); 10 in G, Op. 96.
(M) **(*) Sony SBK 46342; *40-46342* [id.]. Zino Francescatti, Robert Casadesus.

Takako Nishizaki does not produce a large sound but the balance with Jandó is expertly managed, and the result is very natural and real. The performances are delightful in their fresh spontaneity. The opening of the *Spring sonata* is disarming in its simplicity, the variations in the *Kreutzer* are splendidly flowing and alive, and the finale, lightly pointed by both artists, has an irresistibly infectious sparkle. This is a bargain.

The Compact Classics tape offers a recoupling from the Menuhin/Kempff recordings of the early 1970s. Their reading of the *Spring sonata* has the magic which characterizes the whole cycle, and the performance of the *Kreutzer* is also unique. In many ways it is not as immaculate as earlier accounts, but the spontaneous imagination of the playing, the challenge between great artists on the same wavelength, is consistently present. The recording too is admirably 'live'.

The Francescatti/Casadesus performances date from between 1959 and 1962. They are unfailingly musical and Casadesus's playing is always illuminating. Francescatti is warm-timbred, though not all ears will take to the slightly febrile quality of his vibrato. There is an occasional tendency to virtuosity at the expense of poise, although no one could fail to respond to the joyous vigour of the finale of the *Kreutzer*, following after a fine set of variations. Op. 96 is a more intimate performance and an appealing asset to the disc. Very good remastering: the piano tone is full and the overall effect is real, with good presence for both artists.

SOLO PIANO MUSIC

Piano sonatas Nos. 1–32.
❀ (M) (***) EMI mono CHS7 63765-2 (8) [Ang. CDHH 63765]. Artur Schnabel.
(B) *** DG 429 306-2 (9) [id.]. Wilhelm Kempff.

Schnabel's survey originally appeared as part of a subscription venture (the Beethoven Sonata Society) in bulky albums of 78-r.p.m. shellac records. In the 1970s they were transferred to thirteen LPs and now, some twenty years on, can be accommodated on eight well-filled CDs – one fewer than most of the competition. For many music-lovers and record collectors of an older generation, Schnabel was the voice of Beethoven;

returning to this pioneering set again, one realizes that his insights were deeper than those of almost anyone who followed him, though his pianism has been surpassed. It was Schnabel who said that this music is better than it can ever be played, but his profound understanding of it shines through almost every bar. Of course his *Hammerklavier* has its moments of inelegance (to say the least) and his pianistic mannerisms are well in evidence in some of the earlier sonatas. Anyone can hear these moments of rough-and-ready playing, but no modern masters (Gilels the possible exception) have penetrated closer to the truth than he. No one has ever made the last movement of Op. 111 mean as much or found as much depth in Op. 110 as he did. This is one of the towering classics of the gramophone and, whatever other individual Beethoven sonatas you may have (be they by Gilels, Richter, Fischer, Perahia) or sets (Kempff, Brendel or Ashkenazy), this is an indispensable reference point.

Kempff's recordings, all dating from 1964/5, are to the 1960s what Schnabel's were to the pre-war years – performances that represent a yardstick by which all others are judged. The original LPs lacked the warmth of sonority and bloom of the very finest piano records of the analogue era, but the CD transfers bring a distinct improvement: the sound is fuller and firmer now, and the sense of presence is very striking. Some slight background hiss remains, but Kempff's shading of pianistic colour is so imaginative that the ear readily accommodates any slight dryness in the upper range. The interpretations have a commanding stature, yet Kempff brings his own individuality to every bar and a clarity and sparkle that make you want to go on listening. In his relatively measured speeds for fast movements Kempff is dramatic as well as fresh, while his flowing speeds in slow movements have a repose and concentration that belie the metronome. Where he is occasionally fast (in the slow movements of Opp. 26 and 110, for example) he is invariably illuminating. There is no doubting the inner compulsion and spiritual intensity which hold all these performances together. With his lucid and refreshing style, Kempff, more than any pianist of our time, has the power to make one appreciate and understand Beethoven in a new way, and that is so, however many times one hears him. It makes a fascinating study to compare these interpretations not only with those of other pianists but with his own previous mono recordings. Above all, these magnificent records never fail to reveal his own spontaneity in the studio, his ability to rethink the reading on each occasion. The layout on nine CDs, presented in three separate jewel boxes within a slip-case, is admirably planned, and the records are offered at bargain price. Of the boxed sets of Beethoven's sonatas now before the public, this would be a first choice for many collectors, and rightly so.

Piano sonatas Nos. 1 in F min.; 2 in A; 3 in C, Op. 2/1–3.
(BB) **(*) Naxos Dig. 8.550150 [id.]. Jenö Jandó.

Jenö Jandó's complete recording of the Beethoven *Piano sonatas* offers a consistently high standard of musicianship and excellent digital recording. The piano sound is real, full and bold, and well placed within the highly suitable acoustics of the Italian Institute of Budapest, which are neither dry nor too resonant. Apart from the ten separate issues discussed here, the records are also available in two flimsy slip-cases, each comprising five CDs (8.505002 and 8.505003). This first CD (actually Volume 3) establishes Jandó's credentials as a strong, unidiosyncratic Beethovenian. In the early sonatas, slow movements have a simple, unaffected eloquence, allegros are well paced, articulation is clean and often brilliant, and the classical structures are perceptively held together. If there is not the individuality of a Kempff or a Barenboim, the playing is always direct and satisfying, and if the *grazioso* finale of the *A major* seems a shade studied, the account here of *No. 3 in C major* is particularly fresh and enjoyable.

Piano sonatas Nos. 4 in E flat, Op. 7; 13 in E flat, Op. 27/1; 19 in G min., 20 in G, Op. 49/1–2; 22 in F, Op. 54.
(BB) **(*) Naxos Dig. 8.550167 [id.]. Jenö Jandó.

Our copy of Jandó's Volume 8 is incorrectly documented: the notes (but not the listing) apply to another disc; however, we hope this will be corrected by the time we are in print. The performances of both the *E flat Sonata*, Op. 7, with its memorable slow movement, and the *Sonata quasi una fantasia*, Op. 27/1, in which Jandó is comparably responsive to Beethoven's wide expressive range, show the continuing excellence of this series, and the three shorter works are also freshly presented.

Piano sonatas Nos. 5 in C min.; 6 in F; 7 in D, Op. 10/1–3; 25 in G, Op. 79.
(BB) *** Naxos Dig. 8.550161 [id.]. Jenö Jandó.

The three splendid Op. 10 sonatas show Jandó at his most perceptive and unselfconscious. The performances are spontaneous and admirably paced, and the musical characterization is strong. Slow movements are thoughtful and have a natural expressive feeling. Op. 79 is also very appealing, and altogether Volume 5 may be regarded as one of the most successful in this excellent series.

Piano sonatas Nos. 8 (Pathétique); 14 (Moonlight); 15 (Pastoral); 23 (Appassionata); 26 (Les Adieux) (CD only: *17 in D min. (Tempest), Op. 31/2*).
(B) *** DG Compact Classics 413 435-2 (2); *413 435-4* [id.]. Wilhelm Kempff.

Kempff's masterly recordings show so well his ability to rethink Beethoven's music within the recording studio. Everything he does has his individual stamp, and above all he never fails to convey the deep intensity of a master in communion with Beethoven. The Compact Classics tape collection of five favourite named sonatas is an obvious bargain, while the digitally remastered two-CD set offers also the *Tempest*, and the piano quality has undoubtedly gained in firmness.

Piano sonatas Nos. 8 in C min. (Pathétique), Op. 13; 14 in C sharp min. (Moonlight), Op. 27/2; 23 in F min. (Appassionata), Op. 57.
(M) **(*) Sony MYK 42539 [id.]. Rudolf Serkin.
(BB) **(*) Naxos Dig. 8.550045 [id.]. Jenö Jandó.

Serkin recorded remarkably few of the Beethoven sonatas, considering how eminent a pianist he is. Instead, he has concentrated on the popular named works, and these three in particular, each recorded by him several times before. His aristocratic approach is immediately apparent at the opening of the *Moonlight Sonata*, and in the allegros he is as incisive and dramatic as ever. As with all master pianists, one finds many points of insight emerging as well as one or two points of personal mannerism. The piano recording, from the early 1960s, is firmer and more real than in its previous LP incarnation.

Jandó's grouping of the three most famous named sonatas is in fact Volume 1 in his continuing series and immediately establishes the lifelike nature of the Naxos recording. Jandó's clean, direct style and natural spontaneity are particularly admirable in the slow movements of the *Pathétique* and *Appassionata*, warmly lyrical in feeling, yet not a whit sentimental. Only in the coda of the finale of the *Appassionata* does one feel a loss of poise, when the closing *presto* becomes *prestissimo* and the exuberance of the music-making nearly gets out of control.

Piano sonatas Nos. 8 in C min. (Pathétique), Op. 13; 21 in C (Waldstein), Op. 53; 23 in F min. (Appassionata), Op. 57.
(M) **(*) Ph. 432 041-2; *432 041-4* [id.]. Claudio Arrau.

Arrau's performances are magnificently recorded. They were made at different times (1984–7) and in different places (Switzerland and New York), but the digital piano sonority is full and satisfying, the image bold and realistic. This helps to make Arrau's *Appassionata* very commanding indeed, with gloriously rich timbre in the central *Andante*. It is a distinguished performance, powerful and commanding in the same way as his *Emperor concerto*. The *Waldstein* is impressive too, though not as incandescent as Kempff's. The *Pathétique* (recorded in 1986 when Arrau was eighty-three) is just a little wanting in colour and vitality, and some listeners may feel that the *Adagio cantabile* is too measured. However, the playing throughout this record is impressive and, for all the individual mannerisms, the interpretations are authoritative and convincing. No musical notes are provided.

Piano sonatas Nos. 9 in E; 10 in G, Op. 14/1–2; 24 in F sharp, Op. 78; 27 in E min., Op. 90; 28 in A, Op. 101.
(BB) *** Naxos Dig. 8.550162 [id.]. Jenö Jandó.

Volume 6 represents Jandó's finest achivement in the series so far. The readings are freshly immediate and communicative, very like being at a live recital. Opp. 90 and 101 show this artist at full stretch. These are demanding works and he does not fall short, particularly in the slow movements, which are very eloquent indeed. The piano sound is most believable.

Piano sonatas Nos. 11 in B flat. Op. 22; 18 in E flat, Op. 31/3.
*(*) Ph. Dig. 426 297-2 [id.]. Claudio Arrau.

The great Chilean-born pianist was well into his eighties when he made this version and, for all the richness and naturalness of the Philips recording, it must be conceded that his earlier cycle with its firmer focus and fresher tone did him greater justice. (His post-war 78s of Op. 31, No. 3, should be transferred to CD.) Of course, there are lovely things here, and some of the distinctive piano timbre we associate with Arrau is still in evidence.

Piano sonatas Nos. 11 in B flat, Op. 22; 29 in B flat (Hammerklavier), Op. 106.
(BB) **(*) Naxos Dig. 8.550234 [id.]. Jenö Jandó.

Volume 9 opens with another reading which demonstrates Jandó's direct and spontaneous style at it most impressive, although the articulation in the first movement of this *B flat Sonata*, Op. 22, (as in the *Waldstein*) is almost too clear and clean in its precision; the *Adagio*, however, is played most expressively. From its very opening bars, the *Hammerklavier* is commanding; there is rapt concentration in the slow movement, and the closing fugue runs its course with a powerful inevitability. Again, most realistic recording.

Piano sonatas Nos. 12 in A flat, Op. 26; 16 in G; 18 in E flat, Op. 31/1 & 3.
(BB) **(*) Naxos Dig. 8.550166 [id.]. Jenö Jandó.

Volume 7 with its trio of middle-period sonatas can be recommended with few reservations. In No. 12 the *Andante con variazioni* is very engaging, but the *Marcia funebre* has moments when Jandó's articulation seems marginally over-forceful; at the opening of the *Adagio* of No. 16, the accompaniment is very marked in its rhythmic emphasis and some ears may find this overdone. Yet No. 18 is a considerable success, and there is much to stimulate the listener's interest here. Excellent sound.

Piano sonatas Nos. 14 (Moonlight); 21 (Waldstein); 23 (Appassionata).
(BB) **(*) Naxos Dig. 8.550294 [id.]. Jenö Jandó.
** Decca Dig. 425 838-2; *425 838-4* [id.]. Vladimir Ashkenazy.

A separate, alternative grouping of the named sonatas in Jandó's highly musical and well-recorded performances, not included in the boxed sets.

There is some good but not outstanding playing from Ashkenazy in his new, digital account of these three sonatas – and we could do without the little distortions in the flow of the first movement of the *Moonlight*. The first movement of the *Waldstein* is very measured and the movement, though held together well, is lacking in fire. The sound has splendid transparency and body, but there are other versions of all three works that go deeper.

Piano sonatas: No. 15 in D (Pastoral), Op. 28; (Kurfürstensonaten) in E flat, F min., D, WoO 47/1–3; in C (incomplete), *WoO 51; Sonatinas: in G, F, Anh. 5/1–2.*
(BB) ** Naxos Dig. 8.550255 [id.]. Jenö Jandó.

This CD, Volume 10 in Jandó's integral set, acts mainly as an appendix to the major sonatas. The playing is fresh, clean and intelligent and, if the two *Sonatinas* are not authentic, they make agreeable listening here. The *Pastoral sonata* is admirably done.

Piano sonatas Nos. 17 in D min. (Tempest), Op. 31/2; 21 in C (Waldstein), Op. 53; 26 in E flat (Les Adieux), Op. 81a.
(BB) **(*) Naxos Dig. 8.550054 [id.]. Jenö Jandó.

Volume 2 in Jandó's Naxos series contains the other three famous named sonatas, and very enjoyable they are in their direct manner, if lacking that little extra imaginative touch that Kempff, for one, can bring to the *Waldstein*, where Jandó's sharply articulated opening movement could ideally be more resilient. But *Les Adieux* has a simplicity that is disarming, and Op. 31/2 has strength and fine control of the work's emotional ebb and flow.

Piano sonatas Nos. 30 in E, Op. 109; 31 in A flat, Op. 110.
❀ (***) EMI mono CDH7 63787-2 [id.]. Myra Hess (with BACH: *Jesu, joy of man's desiring* and music by BEETHOVEN, BRAHMS, GRANADOS, MENDELSSOHN and D. SCARLATTI (***)).

These celebrated performances were recorded in mono in 1953, and to say that the sound is greatly improved is something of an understatement: it is much firmer at both ends of the register and is altogether more cleanly focused. Myra Hess was in her mid-sixties at this time and her playing is every bit as masterly and seraphic as one had remembered; Desmond Shawe-Taylor and Edward Sackville-West in *The Record Guide* said that her Beethoven performances could 'safely be held up as models of style'. At times, some might feel the need for a more firmly etched line (in the final movement of Op. 110, for instance), but most collectors will wonder at her great plasticity of touch and sheer tonal beauty. The record comes with a generous recital of encore pieces, ranging from her famous arrangement of Bach's *Jesu, joy of man's desiring*, Brahms, Beethoven (*Für Elise*), two Scarlatti sonatas, Granados (*The Maiden and the nightingale*) and a Mendelssohn *Song without words*, all recorded in the late 1950s. But it is for the Beethoven collector that these thoughtful and deeply musical performances will be essential.

Piano sonatas Nos. 30 in E, Op. 109; 31 in A flat, Op. 110; 32 in C min., Op. 111.
(BB) *** Naxos Dig. 8.550151 [id.]. Jenö Jandó.

The last three sonatas of Beethoven, offered in Volume 4, are very imposing indeed in Jandó's hands. Moreoever they are given very realistic recording, with great presence. There is serenity and gravitas in these readings and a powerful control of structure. The thoughtful concentration of the closing *Arietta* of No. 32 puts the seal on a cycle which can receive the strongest advocacy, even without taking into consideration the super-bargain status of the set.

Miscellaneous piano music

7 Bagatelles, Op. 33; 11 Bagatelles, Op. 119; 6 Bagatelles, Op. 126.
(B) *** Ph. 426 976-2; *426 976-4* [id.]. Stephen Bishop-Kovacevich.

Beethoven's *Bagatelles*, particularly those from Opp. 119 and 126, have often been described as chips from the master's workbench; but rarely if ever has that description seemed so apt as in these searchingly simple and completely spontaneous readings by Bishop-Kovacevich. The memorability and sparkle of each idea comes over with astonishing freshness and the crisp, clear recording projects the music-making admirably, with CD giving a real presence, yet bringing a natural warmth of colour to Beethoven's engaging *Andante* and *Allegretto* movements.

6 Variations in F, Op. 34; 15 Variations and fugue on a theme from Prometheus in E flat (Eroica variations), Op. 35; 2 Rondos, Op. 51; Bagatelle: Für Elise, WoO 59.
*** Chan. Dig. CHAN 8616; *ABTD 1305* [id.]. Louis Lortie.

The Canadian pianist Louis Lortie is an artist of distinction, and his performances of both the *Eroica* and the *F major variations*, Op. 34, deserve the highest accolade. His readings have both grandeur and authority, and his pianism has an elegance and sensitivity that are always put to musical ends. The Chandos recording, made at The Maltings, Snape, does full justice to the wide range of colour and dynamic nuance he commands. This account of the *Eroica variations* belongs in exalted company and can be recommended alongside such magisterial accounts as that of Gilels.

VOCAL MUSIC

Ah! perfido (concert aria), *Op. 65.*
(M) ** EMI CMS7 63625-2 (2) [Ang. CDMB 63625]. Callas, Paris Conservatoire O, Rescigno – CHERUBINI: *Medea.***

Recorded in 1964 at what proved to be the very end of her recording career, this Beethoven scena exposes the flaws that sadly emerged in the great Callas voice, but her fire-eating manner is irresistible. A welcome fill-up for the Cherubini opera.

Egmont: Overture and incidental music: (2 Entr'actes, Die Trommel gerühret, Freudvoll und Leidvoll, Victory symphony), Op. 84.
(M) *** Decca 425 972-2 [id.]. Lorengar, VPO, Szell – TCHAIKOVSKY: *Symphony No. 4.****

Szell's splendid 1970 version of the *Egmont Overture and incidental music* comes as an odd but attractive fill-up to his searingly intense account of Tchaikovsky's *Fourth Symphony*. The Beethoven pieces are very well played and were recorded in the Sofiensaal in Vienna. For the reissue, the spoken dialogue included on the original LP has been excised, although the songs, movingly sung by Pilar Lorengar, remain, plus the two entr'actes, and the final brief *Victory Symphony.*

Missa solemnis in D, Op. 123.

❀ *** DG Dig. 429 779-2; *429 779-4* [id.]. Margiono, Robbin, Kendall, Miles, Monteverdi Ch., E. Bar. Soloists, Eliot Gardiner.

(M) *** Ph. 426 648-2; *426 648-4* (2) [id.]. Giebel, Höffgen, Haefliger, Ridderbusch, Netherlands R. Ch., Concg. O, Jochum.

(M) (**(*)) BMG/RCA mono GD 60272; *GK 60272* (2) [60272-RG-2; *60272-RG-4*]. Marshall, Merriman, Conley, Hines, Robert Shaw Ch., NBC SO, Toscanini – CHERUBINI: *Requiem.*(**(*))

This superb issue from DG marks a breakthrough in period performance of Beethoven. Gardiner's inspired reading matches even the greatest of traditional performances on record in dramatic weight and spiritual depth, while bringing out the white heat of Beethoven's inspiration with new intensity. The sense of a superman creator wrestling with the deepest meaning of the liturgy comes over more acutely than ever. Speeds tend to be on the fast side, but they quickly come to seem right, establishing a symphonic tautness. Even in the hushed dedication of the *Sanctus* Gardiner rivals such masters as Karajan and Jochum in their much slower readings; while the rhythmic swing of the compound time in the *Dona nobis pacem* has a joy in it that no traditional performance can quite match. Though the performers are fewer in number than in traditional accounts, the gain in sharpness of focus makes the results even more dramatic, with the period instrument players stretched to the limit. The Monteverdi Choir sings with bright, luminous tone, and the four soloists are excellent – two strong, sensitive and clear-toned newcomers, the soprano Charlotte Margiono and the bass Alastair Miles, joined by the mezzo Catherine Robbin and the tenor William Kendall. The recording is vivid too, and it comes on a single disc instead of the more usual two. Even those who normally resist period performance will find this very compelling.

Jochum's 1970 recording with the Netherlands Radio Chorus is among the most inspired readings of the *Missa solemnis* yet issued, especially in the way it conveys the hushed inner intensity of the work. The soloists not only make a splendid team, they are individually finer than we had remembered. The CD transfer is excellent too, more vivid than the LPs were, heightening the incandescence of a performance which comes over with the sort of glow one experiences only rarely, even in the concert hall. To cap a superb reissue, the obbligato violin playing of Hermann Krebbers is movingly pure and beautiful. The performance, at 81 minutes, is just too long for a single CD and, maddeningly, Philips have reissued it on two mid-priced discs (instead of choosing a bargain format). In the same price-range, Karajan's outstanding 1966 set for DG, which has comparable intensity and concentration (and superb soloists, too: Janowitz, Ludwig, Wunderlich and Berry), is offered with the generous bonus of an outstanding performance of Mozart's *Coronation Mass* (DG 423 913-2).

Toscanini's tensely dramatic account of the *Missa solemnis* leaves you in no doubt as to the work's magisterial power, even if the absence of a true pianissimo makes it less meditative than usual. The supreme revelation comes at the end of the *Dona nobis pacem*, in which – after the menacing sounds of war – the final coda brings a sense of culmination such as few other conductors have achieved. Fine singing from choir and soloists alike, though the typical harshness of the recording is unappealing. It is a pity that RCA did not offer the whole performance on a single CD, instead of breaking before the final movement and putting the Cherubini on the second disc.

Fidelio (complete).
*** Ph. Dig. 426 308-2; *426 308-4* (2) [id.]. Jessye Norman, Goldberg, Moll, Wlaschiha, Coburn, Blochwitz, Dresden State Op. Ch. & O, Haitink.
(M) *(*) BMG/Eurodisc GD 69030; *GK 69030* (2). Altmeyer, Jerusalem, Adam, Nimsgern, Meven, Nossek, Wohlers, Leipzig R. Ch. & GO, Masur.

The unsurpassed nobility of Jessye Norman's voice is perfectly matched to this noblest of operas. In detail of characterization she may not outshine Christa Ludwig, Klemperer's firm and incisive Leonore, or Helga Dernesch, Karajan's warmly emotional heroine, but her reading is consistently rich and beautiful, like those rivals bringing a new revelation. That is so, not just in her singing but in her speaking of the dialogue, with the personality beaming out in individuality even before she starts singing. The Canon quartet of Act I is then taken dangerously slowly, but it is superbly sustained by Haitink at a steady tempo, with Pamela Coburn and Hans Peter Blochwitz well matched as Marzelline and Jaquino, and the resonant Kurt Moll as the jailer, Rocco. The great test of the *Abscheulicher* then finds Norman at her peak, not as animated as Dernesch but rich and varied. Reiner Goldberg, strained at times and no match for Jon Vickers on both the Klemperer and Karajan sets, is still an impressive Florestan by latterday standards, and Ekkehard Wlaschiha, best known for his portrayal of Alberich in various *Ring* cycles, is a superb Pizarro, strong and sinister. With excellent digital sound and with strong, forthright conducting from Haitink, this is the finest of modern versions, even if it does not replace Klemperer or Karajan.

Fitted now on to two mid-priced CDs, instead of three full-priced discs as originally, Masur's version is offered in well-balanced, modern, analogue sound. It is played very well by the Leipzig orchestra, but this is a surprisingly small-scale view, lacking the full dramatic bite needed in this towering masterpiece. Neither Jeannine Altmeyer nor Siegfried Jerusalem had achieved their peak when they made the recording in 1982 and, though there is fine singing from the male members of the cast, the Marzelline of Carola Nossek is thin and unsteady. The whole performance has the feeling of a well-behaved run-through. Among mid-priced issues, both Klemperer (❀ EMI CMS7 69324-2) and Karajan (EMI CMS7 69290-2) are far more inspired, with older recording still sounding well. Both of these are also offered on a pair of CDs – see our main volume, pp. 153–4.

Fidelio: highlights.
(B) **(*) Pickwick IMPX 9021. Rysanek, Haefliger, Fischer-Dieskau, Frick, Seefried, Engen, Bav. State Op. Ch. & O, Fricsay.
(B) *(*) DG Compact Classics *427 713-4* [id.] (from complete recording, with Gwyneth Jones, James King, Talvela, Crass, Leipzig R. Ch., Dresden State Op. O, Boehm – MOZART: *Die Zauberflöte: highlights.**(*)*

The Fricsay set dates from 1958, but the recording has responded well to the CD remastering and has both vividness and atmosphere. Fricsay's direction – from the Overture onwards – has the excitement and genuine tension of a Toscanini performance. Ernst Haefliger is a fine Florestan, and Frick and Fischer-Dieskau offer strong characterizations. Rysanek's Leonore is also impressive and her *Abscheulicher* is very dramatic, helped by splendid Bavarian horn playing. By including snippets of dialogue the selection succeeds in linking the story from beginning to end in an hour of music (rather as happened during the mono LP era, with Fricsay's earlier highlights from Mozart's *Die Zauberflöte*, an ideal example of the genre). The snag with this CD is that here, unlike the original LP from which it is taken, there is no text with translation, only a brief synopsis.

Boehm's selection comes from his flawed 1969 Dresden recording, where none of the principals is shown in a flattering light. The sound is rather middle- and bass-orientated.

Bennett, Robert Russell (1894–1981)

Symphonic songs for band.
(M) *** Mercury 432 009-2 [id.]. Eastman Wind Ens., Fennell – HOLST: *Hammersmith*; JACOB: *William Byrd suite*; WALTON: *Crown Imperial.****

Bennett's triptych, not surprisingly, relies more on colouristic manipulation and sonority than on content, although the opening *Serenade* is catchily rhythmic and the final *Celebration* is certainly rumbustious (if empty). Marvellous playing and Mercury's best recording. The disc also includes a *Fanfare and allegro* by Clifton Williams, which is self-descriptive and equally well presented.

Berg, Alban (1885–1935)

Chamber concerto for piano, violin & 13 wind.
*** Teldec/WEA Dig. 2292 46019-2; *2292 46019-4* [id.]. Maisenberg, COE, Holliger – SCHOENBERG: *Chamber symphony.****

(i) *Chamber concerto*; (ii) *Violin concerto.*
(M) *** Decca Analogue/Dig. 430 349-2 [id.]. (i) Pauk, Crossley, L. Sinf., Atherton; (ii) Kyung Wha Chung, Chicago SO, Solti.

As a birthday tribute to Schoenberg, his friend and teacher, Berg wrote the *Chamber concerto*, his most concentratedly formalized work, a piece that can very easily seem cold and unexpressive. Atherton rightly takes the opposite view: that, for all its complexity, it is romantic at heart so that one hears it as a melodic work, full of humour, and the waltz rhythms are given a genuine Viennese flavour. György Pauk and Paul Crossley are outstanding soloists, the Sinfonietta plays with precision as well as commitment, and the 1980 analogue recording is excellent, cleanly detailed yet not too dry. The appropriate coupling is Kyung Wha Chung's fine 1983 version of the *Violin concerto*. Chung may not be as powerful as Perlman, but her tenderness and poetry bring an added dimension to the music. The violin is placed well in front of the orchestra, but not aggressively so, and the brilliant Chicago digital recording is more spacious than some from this source.

Despite rather reticent soloists, the Teldec version of the *Chamber concerto* also brings out all the necessary warmth, with superb playing from the COE. Those wanting a modern digital recording and for whom the coupling with Schoenberg is suitable will find this gives every satisfaction. Unlike Atherton on Decca and the rival analogue Boulez issue (DG 423 237-2, which is coupled with the *Clarinet pieces* and *Piano sonata*), this one observes the long repeat in the finale, which radically affects the balance of movements. Excellent recording.

Violin concerto.
(M) *** DG 431 740-2 [id.]. Szeryng, Bav. RSO, Kubelik – SCHOENBERG: *Concertos.***(*)*

An outstanding version of Berg's *Violin concerto* from Henryk Szeryng, who gives a persuasive, perceptive and sympathetic account of this fine work, and is well accompanied by the Bavarian orchestra under Kubelik. Given such superb playing, and a recording that has transferred well to CD, this makes an attractive supplement to the two Schoenberg concertos with which it is coupled.

(i) Violin concerto; (ii) *Lyric suite.*
(**) Symposium/HM mono SBT 1004 [id.]. (i) Louis Krasner, BBC SO, Webern; (ii) Galimir Qt.

Louis Krasner commissioned the Berg *Violin concerto* and gave its first performance with Scherchen in Barcelona in April 1936 just as the Spanish Civil War was breaking out. He subsequently recorded it on 78s with the Cleveland Orchestra under Artur Rodzinski. This recording, however, is even earlier and derives from acetate discs made at its second performance in the Concert Hall of Broadcasting House in London under Webern on 1 May 1936. It is a historical document of great value, and the playing of the then relatively new BBC Symphony Orchestra has an extraordinary glowing intensity. Berg's death, four months earlier, and the death of Manon Gropius (the composer's granddaughter) which inspired the piece lent an altogether special poignancy to the occasion. The sound is very naturally balanced; though the surface noise and, in the opening bars, audience noises must be noted, they in no way detract from the impact this performance makes. The first commercial recording of the *Lyric suite* was also made in 1936 on four gold-label Decca-Polydor records. This was an expert ensemble and they play with dedication and accuracy, but the dry sound favoured in chamber-music recordings of this period is rather unpleasing.

3 Pieces for orchestra, Op. 6; (i) *Lulu: symphonic suite.*
(M) *** Mercury 432 006-2 [id.]. (i) Helga Pilarczyk; LSO, Dorati – SCHOENBERG; WEBERN: *Orchestral pieces.****

In his pioneering 1962 Mercury coupling Dorati set the pattern for later recordings of this twentieth-century orchestral triptych, none recorded more clearly or vividly. Schoenberg's *Five Pieces*, Op. 16, are the parent work and Berg has taken and developed the emotional basis of his mentor's inspiration and treated it expansively – at least by the standard of the Schoenberg school – and to this Dorati readily responds. There is brilliance, even self-indulgence, which contrasts strongly with Webern's spare, introspective thought, revealed at its purest in his *Five Pieces*, Op. 10. The LSO plays fluently and warmly. For the CD reissue, the recording of the *Lulu suite*, recorded a year earlier, has generously been added. Its big emotions are underlined, at the expense of Berg's markings if necessary; but no one hearing this could possibly miss the fearsome power that erupted in the creation of this opera. Helen Pilarczyk, in her first recording, is most impressive: the murder produces the most blood-curdling scream.

Berio, Luciano (born 1925)

Differences; 2 Pieces; (i) *Sequenza III;* (ii) *Sequenza VII;* (i) *Chamber music.*
(M) *** Ph. 426 662-2 [id.]. (i) Cathy Berberian; (ii) Heinz Holliger; Juilliard Ens. (members), composer.

This is an excellent mid-price compilation of recordings made in the late 1960s with the composer himself in charge. The biggest work is *Differences* for five instruments and tape; but the two virtuoso solos – *Sequenza III* for voice (Cathy Berberian) and *Sequenza VII* for oboe (Heinz Holliger) – are if anything even more striking in their extensions of technique and expressive range. The *Two Pieces* and *Chamber music* are both collections of brief inspirations, the latter with voice as well as instrumental trio. First-rate sound, well transferred.

Eindrucke; Sinfonia.
*** Erato/WEA Dig. 2292 45228-2 [id.]. Pasquier, New Swingle Singers, O Nat. de France, Boulez.

It was in 1969 that Berio's *Sinfonia*, written for the New York Philharmonic, made a far wider impact on the music world than is common with an avant-garde composer. The colour and energy of his writing, his wit (not least in the vocal commentary for the Swingle – now the New Swingle – Singers) make for a piece that is both memorable and attractive. His own CBS recording, made in New York at the time, enjoyed a deserved success, but it omitted the fifth movement, which he had added within months to the original four. Boulez records the complete work for the first time in this fine Erato version, and that substantial finale proves essential to an appreciation of the whole piece when, with its reminiscences, it sums up what has gone before. *Eindrucke*, written between 1973 and 1974, is another powerful work, much more compressed, bare and uncompromising in its layering of strings and wind. Boulez draws vivid performances of both from his French players, and the recording is colourful to match, though vocal balances sometimes sound contrived.

Berlioz, Hector (1803–69)

Harold in Italy, Op. 16.
(BB) ** Pickwick PWK 1152. Daniel Benyamini, Israel PO, Mehta.

(i) *Harold in Italy, Op. 16;* (ii) Romance: *Rêverie et caprice, Op. 8.*
(M) ** EMI CDM7 63530-2; *EG 763530-4.* Y. Menuhin, Philh. O, (i) C. Davis; (ii) Pritchard.

Mehta draws sonorous playing from the Israel Philharmonic and the 1975 (Decca) recording has the sort of brilliance and separation that one used to associate with Mehta's Los Angeles analogue recordings, while there is also plenty of warmth and sense of spectacle. It is very effectively remastered; though the solo viola is balanced too close and some of Berlioz's subtlety is missing, this is certainly an enjoyable and often exciting account, worth its modest cost.

Menuhin asserts his personality strongly, even over that of Sir Colin Davis, and the 1963 recording of the Philharmonia openly treats the work as a concerto, with the soloist often dictating the rhythm, which the orchestra has to follow. Nevertheless this makes an enjoyable version, although the recording could ideally have greater warmth and bloom. It is now made slightly more competitive by including the *Rêverie et caprice*, made in 1965. With Menuhin placed rather too close to the microphone for comfort, this is less appealing than the Perlman/Barenboim version. For *Harold in Italy* first choice rests with Sir Colin Davis and the LSO (Philips 416 431-2). Nobuho Imai, his violist, is on top form, and this CD also has several rare and attractive bonuses.

Overtures: *Benvenuto Cellini; Le carnaval romain, Op. 9; Le Corsaire, Op. 21; Le Roi Lear, Op. 4; Damnation de Faust: Marche hongroise; Menuet des follets. Roméo et Juliette: Scène d'amour.*
(BB) *(*) Naxos 8.550231 [id.]. Polish State PO (Katowice), Kenneth Jean.

The Polish orchestra generally plays very well and the recording has a spectacular concert-hall acoustic. There is plenty of enthusiasm here – especially from the brass – and there is excitement too, notably in the *Hungarian march*, which opens the programme vividly, and in the closing *Le Corsaire*, which goes swingingly. But one ideally needs more sophistication and Gallic flair. Kenneth Jean is rather heavy-handed in his lyrical phrasing, especially in the introduction to *Le Roi Lear*, and his *Scène d'amour* from *Roméo et Juliette* is no match for Ozawa's in subtlety of line and dynamic control. Incidentally, the listing and sleeve notes indicate that the *Danse des Sylphes* is included in the programme, but it turns out to be the *Minuet of the Will o'the Wisps*.

Roméo et Juliette: Queen Mab scherzo.
(M) (**) BMG/RCA GD 60328; *GK 60328* (4) [60328-2-RG; *60328-4-RG*]. Phd. O, Toscanini – Concert.(**(*))

Toscanini's quicksilver reading of this fairy scherzo has much in common with his fine Philadelphia recording of Mendelssohn's fairy music. The 1941 recording is clear but lacking in dynamic subtlety.

Symphonie fantastique, Op. 14.
*** Denon Dig. DC 8097 [id.]. Tokyo Metropolitan SO, Jean Fournet – SAINT-SAËNS: *Danse macabre.****
(B) **(*) Pickwick PWK 1147. Paris Conservatoire O, Argenta.
(M) ** Sony SBK 46329; *40-46329* [id.]. Phd. O, Ormandy – DUKAS: *L'apprenti sorcier*; MUSSORGSKY: *Night.****
(BB) * Naxos Dig. 8.550093 [id.]. CSR (Slovak) RSO, Bratislava, Pinchas Steinberg.

Symphonie fantastique, Op. 14; La damnation de Faust, Op. 21: Danse des sylphes; Marche hongroise; Menuet des follets; Overture: Le carnaval romain, Op. 9.
(M) **(*) EMI CDM7 63762-2 [id.]; *EG 763762-4*. Hallé O, Barbirolli.

(i) *Symphonie fantastique, Op. 14*; (ii) *Overtures: Le carnaval romain, Op. 9; Le Corsaire, Op. 31.*
*** EMI Dig. CDC7 54010-2 [id.]. Capitole de Toulouse O, Plasson.
(B) **(*) RCA VD 60478; *VK 60478* [60478-2-RV; *60478-4-RV*]. Boston SO, (i) Prêtre; (ii) Munch.

Symphonie fantastique, Op. 14; (i) *Roméo et Juliette, Op. 17: Scène d'amour.*
(M) **(*) DG 431 169-2; *431 169-4* [id.]. (i) New England Conservatory Ch.; Boston SO, Ozawa.

Even in a competitive market, Michel Plasson's recording deserves to rank among the best. He finds new things to say about this familiar score and brings to it a keen and vital sensitivity. The Toulouse orchestra respond with both enthusiasm and discipline and the recording, though reverberant, is eminently detailed. The first movement has fire and a notable sense of purpose. Sir Colin Davis remains first choice for this work (Philips 411 425-2) but Plasson's is a performance of character, and it has the advantage of fine digital sound.

Jean Fournet draws thoroughly idiomatic playing and an appropriately Gallic sonority from his fine Tokyo orchestra. There is no point-making in this completely unaffected and well-recorded interpretation, and nowhere does this much underrated conductor interpose himself between us and Berlioz. Although the *Marche au supplice* could perhaps have higher voltage, this 1983 recording has much to commend it. Among the many recommendable versions of the *Symphonie fantastique*, this has a place of honour, though it does not necessarily displace Martinon, which comes in harness with *Lélio* at mid-price on two discs (EMI CZS7 62739-2), or Inbal, also on Denon (CO 73208), which is given the most spectacular modern digital recording.

It is good to welcome back to the catalogue Ataulfo Argenta's (originally Decca) recording from the earliest days of stereo. Argenta's career was tragically cut short by his sudden death in 1958, but he left a number of records in which he was served uniformly well by the Decca engineers. His *Symphonie fantastique* won the *News Chronicle* award for the best classical disc of the year in its mono form. It was considered to be of demonstration standard in its day, and the overall balance is still very impressive, with the French brass full of character yet not sounding too blatant. The reading is individual and distinguished. The balance between reflection and neurosis in the first movement is admirable: the *Allegro agitato* is impetuous, yet never gets out of control. The *Waltz* is very poised and the *Adagio* is a thing of sheer beauty: the spirit of Beethoven is felt in the closing pages. Argenta observes the repeat in the *March to the scaffold* – for the first time on disc – and the finale is strong on atmosphere as well as drive.

Barbirolli provides a reading of the *Symphonie fantastique* which is not only impulsively exciting but also possesses a breadth of imagination that is missing in many other performances. A lyrical spaciousness is felt in the slow movement, which is played most beautifully, yet the thunder at the end, on the timpani, bursts into the room and anticipates the mood of the *March to the scaffold*. This is full of energy and fire; and in the finale there is a demonic impulse, with the detailed realization of Berlioz's orchestration vividly projected, not least the plangent bell-toll. The overture is full of adrenalin too, but most striking of all are the three pieces from *La damnation de Faust*, vividly characterized and presented with great flair and spontaneity, with the *Danse des sylphes* given a gossamer delicacy. Unfortunately the (originally Pye) recording, dating from 1959, has been remastered fiercely and, although the original ambience remains to give fullness and atmosphere, the upper range needs a great deal of control to sound comfortable at fortissimo levels.

Prêtre's excitingly chimerical account – discussed in our main volume – has now reappeared on RCA's bargain Silver Seal label. It was recorded at about the same time as Argenta's, but the upper range is less full. Munch's famous accounts of the two *Overtures* make a thrilling bonus, but here the sound tends to shrillness. With the treble cut back, however, this CD makes a very strong impression.

Ozawa's 1973 recording has come up splendidly in its CD transfer with the recording full, atmospheric and vivid. The reading, characteristically flexible in expressiveness and rhythmically resilient (the *March to the scaffold* – taken fast – has an almost balletic, jaunty rhythmic bite) does not lack excitement and is beautifully played; even if the last degree of demonic force is missing from the finale, this is enjoyable in its fresh, spontaneous feeling. The *Love scene* from *Roméo et Juliette*, which provides a considerable bonus, has all the warmth and glow required to sustain its span.

Ormandy's 1961 account, with the Philadelphia Orchestra playing brilliantly, is certainly gripping. There are one or two mannered touches in the first movement, and the very fast opening of the allegro rather overdoes the neurotic aspect of the music, but the *Waltz* has panache and the last two movements have plenty of pungency and spectacle; there is no doubting the Satanic feeling in the finale. The very brilliantly lit recording does not lack fullness, but tends to emphasize the hyperbole of the reading.

Pinchas Steinberg's Naxos version is well played and recorded, but the reading is too comfortable to be really convincing: it is never really gripping, and the finale needs more Satanic feeling.

Solti's Chicago version – reissued on a mid-priced CD in the 'Solti Collection', coupled with *Les Francs-juges overture* – is no more successful, despite extremely vivid sound. Hardly a semiquaver is out of place, but the spirit of the music eludes the conductor (Decca 430 441-2; *430 441-4*).

L'enfance du Christ, Op. 25.
*** Erato/Warner Dig. 2292 45275-2 (2) [id.]. Von Otter, Rolfe-Johnson, Van Dam, Cachemaille, Bastin, Monteverdi Ch., Lyons Op. O, Gardiner.
**(*) EMI Dig. CDS7 49935-2 (2); *EX 749935-4.* Ann Murray, Thomas Allen, Wilson Johnson, Finley, King's College Ch., RPO, Cleobury.
** Denon Dig. CO 76863/64 [id.]. Zimmermann, Schulte, Dean, Aler, Kang, N. German & Cologne R. Ch., Frankfurt RSO, Inbal.

John Eliot Gardiner has the advantage of fine modern recording, made in the Church of Sainte-Madeleine, Pérouges, very well balanced but with the resonance bringing warm atmosphere rather than great clarity. He has some fine soloists, too; some will prefer Anthony Rolfe-Johnson's mellow narration to Eric Tappy's rather more characterful but less melliflous contribution on the Davis set. Anne Sophie von Otter's Mary is outstanding, by far the best currently on record, sung with rapt simplicity; Van Dam's Herod is also debatably the best we have at present. The others are more mixed in appeal, although Giles Cachemaille is a very impressive Joseph. Gardiner often – though not always – adopts brisker tempi than Davis, and his vibrancy brings a new dimension to some of the music. This is a very vivid reading, marred only by two questionable speeds. Generally, however, Davis's choice of pacing is even more apt – he has a special feeling for this work, born of long experience, notably so in the *Shepherds' chorus*, where he moves the music on more firmly than Gardiner.

Stephen Cleobury directs a brisk, dramatically taut reading, atmospherically recorded against the reverberant acoustic of King's College Chapel. The freshness is enhanced by the singing of King's College Choir with its trebles, and the soloists are a characterful team, if not as sweet-toned as some. David Wilson Johnson is a powerful Herod, though the voice as recorded has a rather rough edge. Ann Murray as Mary sings movingly, but ideally one would look for a firmer tone. Thomas Allen as Joseph is warmer than he was in Colin Davis's Philips version and Robert Tear is at his most expressive, helped by the acoustic. Cleobury, though occasionally fussy with detail, as in the *Shepherds' farewell*, has a fine feeling for dramatic timing and tension.

Recorded in warm, immediate sound, with John Aler making an instant impact as the narrator, Inbal's Frankfurt performance is well paced, with fine dramatic tension and feeling for atmosphere, but with some disappointing solo singing. The fruity tones of Margarita Zimmermann are hardly apt for the role of Mary, and Eike Wilm Schulte is rough and unimaginative as Joseph. Stafford Dean – his name misspelt on the label – is a superb Herod, dark and intense, and Aler amply lives up to the promise of his first entry. Though in many ways a good set, this is no match for the finest.

Davis's 1961 recording, originally made for L'Oiseau-Lyre, remains a marginal first choice, fresh and urgent and admirably cast. Not only does it have the advantage of economy, but the two-disc set also includes a major grouping of off-beat vocal works (*Méditation religieuse, La mort d'Orphée, Sara la baigneuse* and *La mort de Cléopâtre*, all very well performed: Decca 425 445-2).

(i) *Requiem Mass (Grande messe des morts), Op. 5;* (ii) *Te Deum, Op. 22.*
(M) **(*) Sony M2YK 46461 (2) [id.]. (i) Stuart Burrows, Ch. of R. France, O Nat. de France, O Philharmonique, Bernstein; (ii) Jean Dupory, Jean Guillov, Ch. d'Enfants de Paris, Maîtrise de la Resurrection, Paris Ch. & O, Barenboim.

In a characteristically powerful and vibrant reading, Bernstein adopts a moulded, consciously persuasive style, and the result is atmospheric and dramatic. In *Rex tremendae*, for example, his expansiveness is well in scale with the music. In the

Lacrymosa he is faster and more urgent, with an irresistible, wave-like rhythm; and he is notable for warmth and expressiveness. The acoustic is reasonably ample, and this allows the chorus to sound larger than some. The remastering improves the effect enormously – indeed the impact of drums and brass in the *Dies irae* is almost overwhelming. At lower dynamic levels textures are fresh and appealing, the flutes especially radiant. Stuart Burrows's headily ardent solo in the *Sanctus* is tellingly projected, and altogether the performance communicates vividly. The coupling is hardly less exciting. However, first choice for the *Requiem* still rests with Sir Colin Davis's account, which also includes the *Symphonie funèbre et triomphale* (Philips 416 283-2).

Recorded in 1977 during the quadraphonic era, Barenboim's Paris version of the *Te Deum* brings a strong and characterful performance, occasionally exaggerated, with fine choral singing and a stylish tenor soloist. The recording is not as sharply focused as it should be, although it is made much more immediate on CD; overall, this is hardly less compelling than the *Requiem*, to make this reissue a real bargain. Strongly recommended.

Mélodies: *Aubade; La belle voyageuse; La captive; Le chasseur danois; Le jeune pâtre breton; La mort d'Ophélie; Les nuits d'été; Zaïde.*
*** Erato/Warner Dig. 2292 045517-2 [id.]. Montague, Robbin, Fournier, Crook, Cachemaille, Lyon Op. O, Gardiner.

Mélodies: *La belle voyageuse; La captive; Les nuits d'été, Op. 7; Zaïde.*
*** Virgin Dig. VC7 91164-2; *VC7 91164-4* [id.]. Dame Janet Baker, City of L. Sinf., Hickox – RESPIGHI: *La sensitiva.****

John Eliot Gardiner, like Sir Colin Davis on a disappointing Philips issue, here divides the six keenly atmospheric songs of *Les nuits d'été* between four singers, in some ways an ideal solution when each song demands such different timbre and different tessitura. His choice of singers is inspired. Catherine Robbin, with clear echoes of Dame Janet Baker, gives a rich and moving account of *La spectre de la rose* (as she does also of the final item from among the miscellaneous orchestral songs, *La mort d'Ophélie*), and Diana Montague is full and bright in her two songs, coping splendidly with Gardiner's very fast speed for the final *L'île inconnue*, which brings a delightful pay-off. Pierre Cachemaille gives a thrilling bite to *Sur les lagunes*, and Howard Crook, with his rather thin, reedy tenor, is well suited to *Au cimetière* but is even more striking in the extraordinary *Aubade*, the rarest of the miscellaneous songs, with its accompaniment for two cornets and four horns. Above all, the presiding genius of the conductor makes this a memorable Berlioz disc and the Lyon Opera Orchestra is helpfully recorded, not in the dry acoustic of the opera house, but atmospherically in a Lyon church.

Like Gardiner's Erato issue, Dame Janet's new recording of *Les nuits d'été* also includes extra orchestral songs. Helped by full, rich recording and a warmly sympathetic accompaniment from Hickox, the interpretation, if anything, glows even more warmly than in Dame Janet's classic EMI reading with Barbirolli (coupled with *La mort de Cléopâtre* and excerpts from *Les Troyens* – CDM7 69544-2), and the voice shows next to no sign of the passing years. Respighi's sensitive setting of Shelley in Italian translation, *La sensitiva*, makes a generous fill-up, equally well recorded.

Bernstein, Leonard (1918–90)

Candide: overture; Facsimile (choreographic essay); *Fancy free* (ballet); *On the town (3 Dance episodes).*
(M) **(*) EMI Dig. CDD7 63905-2 [id.]; *ET 763905-4*. St Louis SO, Slatkin.

Though Slatkin cannot quite match Bernstein himself in the flair he brings to his jazzier inspirations, this is an attractive and generous collection. Next to Bernstein, Slatkin sounds a little metrical at times, but it is a marginal shortcoming, and he directs a beautiful, refined reading of the extended choreographic essay, *Facsimile*. As a gimmick, the song 'Big Stuff' before *Fancy Free* is recorded in simulation of a juke-box, complete with 78-r.p.m. surface-hiss and a blues singer with very heavy vibrato. The sound otherwise is full rather than brilliant, set in a helpful, believable acoustic.

Candide overture; On the Town: 3 Dance episodes. On the Waterfront (symphonic suite); West Side story: Symphonic dances.
(M) **(*) Sony MYK 44773 [id.]. NYPO, composer.

Bernstein's dazzling performance of the *Candide overture* with the NYPO is the most brilliant on record. He did not quite match its zest himself in his later performance for DG. Both the *Symphonic dances* from *West Side story* and the film score, *On the Waterfront*, are comparably vibrant and are played superbly, but it is a pity about the element of harshness in the CBS sound (especially when compared with his later DG versions).

(i) *3 Meditations* (for cello and orchestra) *from Mass; On the Waterfront* (symphonic suite); (ii) *Symphony No. 1 (Jeremiah).*
(M) *** DG Dig./Analogue 431 028-2; *431 028-4* [id.]. (i) Rostropovich; (ii) Christa Ludwig; Israel PO, composer.

This assembly of three works representing different sides of Bernstein's musical personality was put together for the mid-priced DG Bernstein Edition, and it works well. The recordings are all discussed in their original formats in our main volume.

West Side story: Symphonic dances.
(B) **(*) DG Compact Classics 413 851-2 (2); *** *413 851-4* [id.]. San Francisco SO, Ozawa – GERSHWIN: *American in Paris* etc.**(*) (CD only: RUSSO: *3 Pieces for Blues band & orchestra, Op. 50* – with the Siegel-Schwall Band).

Ozawa's performance is highly seductive, with an approach that is both vivid and warm, yet conceals any sentimentality. The 1973 recording sounds excellent in its tape format but has also responded well to its digital remastering for CD: the rich ambience remains and the focus is almost always clean. However, the additional item on the pair of CDs by William Russo is no great asset, not very convincingly inhabiting that curiously indeterminate middle ground between popular and concert-hall music. Bernstein's own complete recording of *West Side story* (DG 415 253-2; *415 253-4*) will serve alongside the new recording of *Candide* to remind us of his special genius in the world of popular music.

Candide (final, revised version).
❀ *** DG Dig. 429 734-2; *429 734-4* (2) [id.]. Hadley, Anderson, Green, Ludwig, Gedda, Della Jones, Ollmann, LSO Ch., LSO, composer.

With the loss of Leonard Bernstein, one of the greatest of Americans and a musician with an almost unbelievable range of talents, it was unthinkable to omit from our current survey the new DG recording of the (inevitably) final revised score of *Candide*. The musical has had a chequered career. In its original 1956/7 New York presentation, with a book by Lillian Hellman, based on Voltaire's picaresquely cynical moral tale, the piece ran for only 229 performances, a flop by Broadway standards. But the score was too good to be abandoned (as the peppy original Broadway cast CD – Sony MK 38732 – readily demonstrates), and over the following years various attempts were made to revive it, each time with musical and textural revisions. An essentially frivolous one-Act version, abandoning the Hellman libretto and cutting half the score, was an off-Broadway success in 1973. In 1982 this was expanded by John Mauceri into a longer, two-Act 'opera' (which was recorded with great success on New World NWCD 340/1 – see our main volume, p. 174). But Mauceri was dissatisfied with the results and undertook yet a further revision in the mid-1980s, this time with Bernstein's collaboration. The original order of the music was restored, as were several musical numbers not heard since the original production. Perhaps most importantly, the spirit of the original was recaptured, and two of the finest songs are placed where the composer wanted them and *Candide's lament* (so movingly sung by Jerry Hadley) is again heard near the beginning of the show. This version was first performed by Scottish Opera in 1988, and it forms the basis for the new recording. Bernstein saw his work – written in the wake of McCarthyism during the chilliest days of the Cold War, when the American government even withdrew the composer's own passport – as essentially serious. Its humour, satirically reflecting Voltaire's rubbishing of enforced establishment values, at one point draws a ready parallel between the Spanish Inquisition and Bernstein's own experience during America's darkest political era.

This is one occasion when we have been able to review a new issue only by sampling excerpts from the complete studio recording, as well as having had the opportunity of watching a screening of the video of the exhilaratingly inspired complete live performance, conducted by Bernstein at the Barbican in 1989, at which E. G. was fortunate enough to be present. With the soloists in evening dress, but not missing a trick in the dramatic and humorous presentation of their numbers, the whole thing is made into a superb entertainment on film. Costumes and scenery are rendered unnecessary by Adolf Green's infectiously delivered narration, specially prepared by Bernstein and John Wells, which in every way speeds up the pace of the show. The narrative is understandably omitted from the studio recording, but Green also takes the role of Dr Pangloss, a part he was surely born to play. June Anderson, too, makes an the ideal personification of the heroine, Cunegonde; the richness of her voice combines with amazingly precise and sparkling coloratura to provide an unforgettable account of the famous *Glitter and be gay*; while Christa Ludwig proves to be an equally inspired choice, cast as the Old Lady. She turns *I am easily assimilated* and the delicious following Parisian waltz, *What's the use?*, into a show-stopper; it has a tune that refuses to budge from the memory. Jerry Hadley has never given a finer performance on record than as the long-suffering but eternally optimistic hero. We hope to discuss this electrifying music-making in more detail in our next volume; what is already clear, however, is that this new recording readily demonstrates what riches the score contains, not just in the most fizzing of all American overtures, but in one dazzlingly inventive number after another.

Berwald, Franz (1797–1868)

(i) *Piano quintet No. 1 in C min.;* (ii) *Piano trios Nos. 1 in E flat; 3 in D min.*
*** MS Dig. MSCD 521 [id.]. (i) Stefan Lindgren, Berwald Qt; (ii) Bernt Lysell, Ola Karlsson, Lucia Negro.

The performances of the *Trios* are very good indeed, though not necessarily superior to those of the Prunyi–Kiss–Onczay team on Marco Polo. One minor quibble: a little more space round and distance from the instruments would have shown these fine players to even greater advantage. They are too closely observed, as for that matter are Stefan Lindgren and the eponymous Berwald Quartet in the *C minor Quintet*, though this is not a fatal handicap. Their performance is every bit a match for the Vienna Philharmonia

Quintet and vastly superior to the old Benthien. The sleeve notes by Hans Epstein are a model of their kind, thorough and scholarly. Recommended.

Piano trios Nos. 1 in E flat; 2 in F min., 3 in D min.
*** Marco Polo Dig. 8.223170 [id.]. Prunyi, Kiss, Onczay.

Although he is best known for the four symphonies, written in the 1840s, Berwald composed a considerable amount of chamber music, most notably in the 1850s when he was again living in Sweden. There are several piano trios – there is a *C major Trio* from 1845 and a fragmentary work in the same key from about the same time – before the *First Trio* (1849) included on this CD. Berwald started another trio in the same key (E flat) that same year, but it remained incomplete. The *F minor* and *D minor Trios* both come from 1851 (and there is an even later trio in C major which was published in Copenhagen in 1896). These Hungarian players give spirited accounts of all three recorded here and make out a persuasive case for this music which has so often been idly dismissed as Mendelssohnian. The string players (András Kiss and Czaba Onczay) are both highly accomplished; perhaps the most demanding writing is for the piano and it is a pity that Ilona Prunyi proves at times to be a little less imaginative than her companions. The recording, made at the Italian Institute in Budapest, is very good indeed, fresh and present. A valuable issue, which conveniently fills a gap in the catalogue.

Biber, Heinrich (1644–1704)

Sonata à 3; Sonata VII à 5 (Sonatae Tam Aris quam Aulis Servientes); Sonata à 6; Sonata à 7; Sonata I à 8; Sonata pro tabula; Sonata Sancti Polycarpi à 9.
*** O-L Dig. 425 834-2 [id.]. New L. Cons., Philip Pickett – SCHMELZER: *Ballets & Sonatas.****

Heinrich Ignaz Franz von Biber wrote his instrumental music for the Prince-Archbishops of Salzburg. Twelve of his sonatas were published in 1676, which suggests they were widely in use at the time. Collectors picking up this disc in a shop will see the simple description 'Trumpet Music' on the cover. But Biber's sonatas are much more than that. Although they were often heard in Salzburg Cathedral, in this concert the acoustic, though not lacking space and resonance, generally gives a more intimate effect. The *Sonata à 7* for trumpets and timpani, which begins the programme, also includes an organ continuo, and the opening is imposingly sonorous, while the closing *Sonata Sancti Polycarpi* uses the eight brass instruments in two antiphonal groups. The style is simpler than the Renaissance writing of the Gabrielis, and the effect is grand without being overwhelming. The *Sonata pro tabula* alternates recorders, violins and violins with considerable charm, and the *Sonatae Tam Aris* offers a comparable interplay between trumpet duo, violin and viols; both these pieces also use a continuo of organ, theorbo and lute to piquant effect. The *Sonata à 3* features sackbut and strings with comparable ingenuity, and throughout these pieces there is an agreeable feeling of a chamber group. The artists contributing are all experts, with Crispian Steele-Perkins and Michael Laird among the trumpeters, Anneke Boecke leading the recorder consort and Paul Nieman on sackbut. Original instruments are played to impressive effect (the ear soon adjusts to the curiously 'split' production of the early trumpets) and the engineers have managed an almost perfect balance so that all the polyphonic lines are clear yet pleasingly matched.

Rosenkranz sonatas Nos. 1–16.
*** Virgin Dig. VCD7 9038-2; *VCD7 9038-4* (2). John Holloway, Davitt Moroney, Tragicomedia.

(M) ** HM/BMG Dig. GD 77102 (2) [77102-RG]. Franzjosef Maier, Franz Lehrndorfer, Max Engel, Konrad Junghänel.

Biber's *Sonatas*, based on the Mysteries of the rosary, for violin and basso continuo are unique in a number of respects. They represent the first attempt to introduce a programmatic content into the instrumental sonata and the first at a connected sequence of pieces (the Kuhlau *Biblical sonatas*, for keyboard instruments, are of later provenance). Each of the 15 *Sonatas* calls for a different tuning of the strings (*scordatura*) so that, instead of the strings being tuned in fifths, they can be at fourths, thirds or even seconds, thus producing an unusual timbre. Each of the *Sonatas* is prefaced by a small copperplate depicting one of the Mysteries and these are reproduced in both booklets. The *Sonatas* include music of great poetic feeling and sensibility, and these two new versions have much to commend them.

Franzjosef Maier and his colleagues enjoy a price advantage over their Virgin rivals. Their set, made in 1981, appeared two years ago, when EMI distributed the Deutsche Harmonia Mundi label, but slipped through our net when this arrangement expired. It reappears in immediate competition with a brand-new Virgin set which, as a recording, can boast much finer definition, clarity and a more detailed ambience. John Holloway is a highly intelligent player and this shines through each of those *Sonatas* we sampled. His white, cool vibrato-less tone is not to all tastes and will no doubt present an obstacle for some collectors, despite his undoubted sensitivity and imagination. However, if his timbre presents no problems, this is the set to have. Davitt Moroney and the continuo team are inventive and more varied in sonority than their rivals, and there is no question as to the artistry of all concerned nor the superiority of the Virgin recording.

When Archiv reissue their admirable set from 1967 by Eduard Melkus, Huguette Dreyfus, Lionel Rogg and Karl Scheit at mid-price, this will provide a useful alternative. If you actively like the sound Holloway makes, he brings many insights and great sympathy to this repertoire. Otherwise the Harmonia Mundi set should be considered, for it has considerable merits.

Birtwistle, Harrison (born 1934)

Endless parade.
*** Ph. Dig. 432 075-2 [id.]. Hardenberger, BBC PO, Howarth (with Concert of 20th century trumpet concertos ***).

Harrison Birtwistle's new piece for trumpet and orchestra moves solo instrument and accompaniment through a kaleidoscopic processional of constantly changing aural images of great imaginative diversity. Its language is far from easily assimilable, but there is no question that it is a major piece, nor that both performance and recording are outstandingly fine.

Bizet, Georges (1838–75)

L'Arlésienne (original scoring): *suite.*
*** Decca Dig. 430 231-2; *430 231-4* [id.]. Saint Paul CO, Hogwood: GOUNOD: *Symphonies.****

Because of the limited resources available to the impresario, Léon Carvalho, who produced Alphonse Daudet's play, *L'Arlésienne*, Bizet's orchestra for the incidental music was limited to 26 players. Hogwood uses a chamber orchestra for his suite to good effect, and the reduced strings are particularly telling in the famous *Adagietto*, while the combination of hand horn plus a valved horn adds to the wind colour, notably in the *Entr'acte.* Excellent playing of about 20 minutes of the music, always fresh if just a little short on charm. But the interest of the original score more than compensates, and the sound is excellent.

L'Arlésienne (incidental music): *suite No. 1.*
(M) ** Sony Dig. MDK 46504 [id.]. Toronto SO, Andrew Davis – DVOŘÁK: *Slavonic dances, Op. 46.***

L'Arlésienne (incidental music): *suite No. 2; Jeux d'enfants.*
(M) **(*) Sony MDK 46508 [id.]. Toronto SO, Andrew Davis – ROSSINI/RESPIGHI: *La boutique fantasque.**** ❀

Andrew Davis gives an alert, quite stylish performance of the *First suite* with the excellent Toronto Symphony Orchestra. The *Adagietto*, opening with a real pianissimo, is beautifully done and the digital recording is excellent. But it is a pity that the suites have been split up for reissue. Davis's *Second suite* is also well played and recorded (neither has the distinction or individuality of Stokowski), and the charming *Jeux d'enfants* has both sparkle and affection. This latter is more than acceptable as a bonus for the outstanding Rossini/Respighi coupling.

L'Arlésienne (incidental music): *suites Nos. 1–2; Carmen: suite No. 1.*
(B) *** DG 431 160-2; *431 160-4* [id.]. BPO, Karajan (with OFFENBACH: *Contes d'Hoffmann: Barcarolle; Orpheus in the Underworld: overture* **(*)).

L'Arlésienne (incidental music): *suites Nos. 1–2; Carmen: suites Nos. 1–2.*
(M) *** CBS MBK 44808 [MYK 37260]. Nat. PO, Stokowski.

L'Arlésienne: suites Nos. 1–2; Carmen: suite No. 1; suite No. 2: excerpts.
(B) *** DG Compact Classics 413 422-2 (2); *413 422-4* [id.]. LSO, Abbado (with CHABRIER: *España*; DUKAS: *L'apprenti sorcier*; RIMSKY-KORSAKOV: *Capriccio espagnol* **(*) and on CD only: FALLA: *Three cornered hat*: dances).

Stokowski's outstanding CBS record, made in 1977 during the great conductor's Indian summer in the recording studios not long before he died, equals and almost out-Beechams Beecham in excitement and sheer panache. The polish and vitality of the playing are electrifying from the opening bars of the *Carmen Prélude*, taken at a cracking pace but never sounding rushed. Stokowski's affectionately romantic approach is helped by the most refined solo wind playing, yet he never sentimentalizes; and in both scores his vitality is often breathtaking. The CD transfer brings just a touch of brashness to the upper range, but the hall resonance gives an attractive bloom to Bizet's colourful scoring. A winner, even if there is no proper documentation.

The metallic clash of the cymbals for the opening *Carmen Prélude* on Karajan's 1971 disc sets the seal on the brilliance of both the orchestral playing and the recording. Yet the acoustic is attractively resonant, allowing plenty of orchestral bloom. There is some marvellously crisp and stylish woodwind playing, and the characterization of the music is dramatic and vivid. This version is undoubtedly fresher than Karajan's later, digital recording with the same forces, in which the conductor sounds at times too languid. The two Offenbach encores, polished and vivacious, are welcome, although in the *Overture* the 1981 digital recording sounds rather dry.

Among other analogue couplings of *L'Arlésienne* and *Carmen suites*, Abbado's 1981 recording also stands out. The orchestral playing is characteristically refined, the wind solos cultured and eloquent, especially in *L'Arlésienne*, where the pacing of the music is nicely judged. A vibrant accelerando at the end of the *Farandole* only serves to emphasize the obvious spontaneity of the music-making. There is warmth too, of course, and in the opening *Prélude* of the *Carmen suite* plenty of spirit. With vivid and truthful recording, this is very attractive if the couplings are suitable, for the tape transfers are well managed. The CD transfer sounds even better. Abbado's selection from the *Carmen* suite is supplemented with two extra items, well played by the Hague Philharmonic Orchestra under Willem van Otterloo. The other highlight of this collection is Lorin Maazel's famous (1960) recording of Rimsky-Korsakov's *Capriccio espagnol*, lustrously played by the Berlin Philharmonic Orchestra in sparkling form; and there are also lively accounts of *L'apprenti sorcier* (Fiedler and the Boston Pops) and Chabrier's *España*, in a spirited performance by the Warsaw Philharmonic Orchestra under Jerzy Semkow. On the pair of digitally remastered CDs, four dances from Falla's *Three-cornered Hat*, brilliantly done by Maazel and the Berlin Radio Symphony Orchestra make a lively, if none too generous bonus.

Symphony in C.
(B) *** Sony MBK 44894 [id.]. Nat. PO, Stokowski – MENDELSSOHN: *Symphony No. 4 (Italian).****

Stokowski's exhilaratingly polished account of the Bizet *Symphony* is yet another example of his last vintage recording period with CBS in London at the end of the 1970s. David Theodore's oboe solo in the *Adagio* is very elegantly done and the *moto perpetuo* finale is wonderfully light and sparkling. A fine bargain coupling, ranking alongside the top recommendations, by Marriner and Beecham. The remastered recording sounds well, fresh and bright.

Symphony in C; Carmen: suites Nos. 1–2; Jeux d'enfants; Patrie: overture.
(M) ** EMI Dig. CDD7 63898-2 [id.]; *ET 763898-4*. O Nat. de France, Seiji Ozawa.

Eminently good performances from the Orchestre National de France and Ozawa, with the exception of the *Carmen* extended suite. Here, the music-making sounds too much like a rehearsal and refuses to spring fully to life; Ozawa's direction is lacking in flair. There are, of course, even finer versions of the *Symphony* (apart from Stokowski, above, Beecham, Haitink and, at mid-price, Marriner all spring to mind, but none of these is digital). The EMI recording is vivid and clear, and this is certainly an attractive programme.

Clovis et Clotilde (cantata); *Roma* (suite).
** Erato/WEA Dig. 2292 45016-2; *2292 45016-4* [id.]. Caballé, Garino, Martinovic, Lille Nat. O, Jean-Claude Casadesus.

Clovis et Clotilde was the cantata which won for Bizet the Prix de Rome. After a single performance in 1857, it was buried until the present performers revived it in 1988. It is conservative in idiom – to please the judges, perhaps – but attractive in a Gounod-esque way. Except in the free lyricism, it shows few distinctive marks of the later Bizet. Caballé's French is imperfect, but she and the tenor Gerard Garino both sing well; the one snag is the unsteadiness of the bass, Boris Martinovic. *Roma* – inspired by Bizet's stay in Italy as a consequence of winning the prize – is relatively well known, an uneven score but with plenty of fresh, characteristic ideas. With the Lille orchestra oddly balanced, this is not the finest version, but it makes an apt coupling for the rare cantata.

Carmen (opera; complete).
(B) *** DG 427 440-2 (3) [id.]. Horne, McCracken, Krause, Maliponte, Manhattan Op. Ch., Met. Op. O, Bernstein.
(M) ** EMI CMS7 63643-2 (2) [CDMB 63643]. Bumbry, Vickers, Freni, Paskalis, Les Petits Chanteurs à la Croix de Bois, Paris Op. Ch. & O, Frühbeck de Burgos.
(M) *(*) BMG/Eurodisc GD 69147 (2). Moffo, Corelli, Cappuccilli, Donath, Schönberg Boys' Ch., German Op. Ch. & O, Berlin, Maazel.
(M) * Decca 411 630-2 (2) [id.]. Resnik, Del Monaco, Sutherland, Krause, Geneva Grand Theatre Ch., SRO, Schippers.
(B) * Naxos Dig. 8.660005/7 [id.]. Alperyn, Lamberti, Titus, Palade, Schaechter, Liebeck, Slovak Philharmonic Ch., Bratislava Children's Ch., Slovak RSO (Bratislava), Alexander Rahbari.

Bernstein's 1973 *Carmen* was recorded at the New York Metropolitan Opera, the first recording undertaken there for many years. It was based on the Met.'s spectacular production with the same cast and conductor as on record, and the sessions plainly gained from being interleaved with live performances: Bernstein adopted the original version of 1875, with spoken dialogue but with variations designed to suit a stage production. Some of his slow tempi will be questioned, too; but what really matters is the authentic tingle of dramatic tension which permeates the whole entertainment. Never before, not even in Beecham's classic set, had the full theatrical flavour of Bizet's score been conveyed, and Marilyn Horne – occasionally coarse in expression – gives a most fully satisfying reading of the heroine's role, a great vivid characterization, warts and all. The rest of the cast similarly works to Bernstein's consistent overall plan. The singing is not all perfect, but it is always vigorous and colourful, and so (despite often questionable French accents) is the spoken dialogue. It is very well transferred and comes on three bargain CDs. At full price, Karajan's digital set with Baltsa, Carreras and Van Dam, also on three discs, still makes a clear first choice (DG 410 088-2).

Frühbeck uses the original 1875 version of Bizet's score without the cuts that were made after experience in the theatre, and with spoken dialogue instead of the recitatives which Guiraud composed after Bizet's early death. Quite apart from that, Grace Bumbry makes a disappointing, generally unimaginative Carmen, singing with good tone but with few of the individual touches that bring the words or musical phrases to life. Vickers makes a strong, heroic Don José, but he rarely sounds idiomatic; and, surprisingly, Frühbeck's conducting lacks sparkle. Paskalis makes a gloriously rich-toned Escamillo and Freni an exquisite Micaela.

At mid-price on only two discs, Maazel's 1979 Eurodisc version of *Carmen*, using the expanded Fritz Oeser edition, makes a doubtful bargain. The casting is starry – with such celebrated singers as Arleen Augér and Jane Berbié in the small roles of Frasquita and Mercedes – but almost totally non-French and not always apt. Anna Moffo, lacking mezzo weight, is hardly an ideal Carmen, and she makes up for that by underlining her characterization too heavily. Franco Corelli too is heavy-handed as Don José, not as effective as he was for Karajan in his earlier recording (BMG/RCA GD 86199 [6199-2-RG]). Helen Donath makes a charming Micaela, light and sweet, while Piero Cappuccilli as Escamillo produces a stream of strong, firm tone, even if – like others in the cast – his French is not his strong point. Maazel as in his later, Erato version (the one used in Franco Rosi's film) directs a bright and forceful performance, dramatically tense, exaggerated by the fierceness of the recorded sound in tuttis. Otherwise the recording (not digital) is reasonably atmospheric.

One cannot imagine why Decca chose to reissue this early stereo *Carmen* (despite brilliant engineering). Resnik has a fruitier tone than her many rivals, but her aim is wild compared with Baltsa, Price and de los Angeles. Del Monaco sings coarsely and, though Sutherland sings beautifully as Micaela, it sounds as though Lucia had strayed into the wrong opera. Schippers drives very hard indeed.

The Naxos version on three discs at budget price brings refined playing from the Czecho-Slovak Radio Symphony Orchestra but low tensions and little feeling of atmosphere. As Carmen, Graciela Alperyn sings with rich, firm tone and secure control but lacks all dramatic weight, making a colourless figure. Giorgio Lamberti is a coarse Don José and Doina Palade a fluttery Micaela, though Alan Titus is a good, virile Escamillo.

Carmen: highlights.
(B) **(*) Pickwick (Decca) IMPX 9016. Marilyn Horne, Michael Molese, Soloists, RPO Ch., RPO, Henry Lewis.
(B) ** DG Compact Classics *427 719-4* [id.] (from above complete set with Horne, MacCracken, cond. Bernstein) – PUCCINI: *Tosca*: highlights.**(*)

This (originally Decca Phase 4) selection of *Carmen* excerpts dates from 1970, some years before Marilyn Horne made her complete New York recording. She it was who provided the ghost voice behind Dorothy Dandridge in the film *Carmen Jones*; here, with a further decade of experience, she is even more searingly compelling as the fire-eating heroine. Not only is there dramatic presence but musical control too, and the voice is at its ripest. Henry Lewis's conducting has no lack of flair – although the 37-minute selection (after the *Prelude*) concentrates entirely on solos, duets and the quintet featuring the heroine, while Escamillo fails to appear at all! Yet the vivid projection of Horne's vocal personality on this excellently transferred bargain CD is well worth sampling.

Highlights from Bernstein's recording are offered on a bargain Compact Classics tape, coupled with a matching *Tosca* selection. The compilation is well made to demonstrate Marilyn Horne's seductively vibrant assumption of the title-role, although Bernstein's sometimes leisurely tempi are not helped by a preponderance of bass in the sound balance, noticeable immediately in the opening *Prelude*.

Blake, Howard (born 1938)

(i) *Piano concerto (In honour of the 30th birthday of the Princess of Wales)*; (ii; iii) *Diversions for cello and orchestra;* (iii) *Toccata*.
*** Sony Dig. HB 3; *HBC 3* [id.]. (i) composer, Philh. O, Willcocks; (ii) Cohen, (iii) Philh. O, composer.

Howard Blake, brilliantly successful as a composer of light music (notably with *The Snowman*), here attempts more demanding repertory. The *Piano concerto*, written for the Princess of Wales on her thirtieth birthday, owes much to the example of the Ravel *Piano concerto* in its amiable neo-classical figuration for the piano, its jazzy rhythms and its colourful orchestration. Elegant and undemanding, if with fewer tunes than such a piece should ideally have, it makes an attractive addition to the surprisingly limited list of modern British piano concertos. The *Diversions* started out as seven genre pieces for cello and piano, but the composer's orchestrations add greatly to their point and charm, each sharply characterized in brilliant, rich-toned playing from Robert Cohen. The orchestral *Toccata* comes closer to Blake's regular idiom, an agreeable 'celebration of the orchestra' which concentrates on lyricism rather than on brilliance. Excellent performances and recording, with the composer impressive both as pianist and conductor.

Bliss, Arthur (1891–1975)

Checkmate (ballet): *suite.*
*** Hyp. Dig. CDA 66436; *KA 66436* [id.]. E. N. Philh. O, Lloyd-Jones – LAMBERT: *Horoscope* *** ❀; WALTON: *Façade.****

David Lloyd-Jones is a highly sympathetic advocate of Bliss's ballet suite; the recording, while warm enough to convey the score's lyricism, has a touch more bite for the lively *Red Knight's mazurka.* This is very enjoyable, but it is the superb couplings that make this triptych distinctive.

Morning heroes.
(M) **(*) EMI CDM7 63906-2 [id.]; *EG 763906-4.* Westbrook (nar.), Royal Liverpool PO Ch. & O, Groves.

Morning heroes is an elegiac work, written as a tribute to the composer's brother and to all who fell in the First World War. The sincerity of the writing is never in doubt but there is less contrast here than in comparable war-inspired works by Vaughan Williams and Britten. One misses both the anger of those other composers and their passages of total simplicity; but it is good that one of Bliss's most ambitious works should be available in so strong a performance. Fine recording and an excellent transfer.

Music for strings; (i) *Lie strewn the white flocks (Pastoral).*
*** Chan. Dig. CHAN 8886; *ABTD 1497* [id.]. (i) Della Jones, N. Sinfonia Ch.; N. Sinfonia, Richard Hickox.

This record would make a good starting point for anyone beginning to explore Bliss's music. Richard Hickox and the Northern Sinfonia give a most persuasive account of the *Music for strings*, the finest since Boult's pioneering records with the BBC Symphony Orchestra. The strings of the Northern Sinfonia produce a sumptuous quality and make the most of Bliss's plangent and sensuous harmonies; they are recorded in a flattering acoustic. The slightly earlier *Pastoral* (*Lie strewn the white flocks*) was the outcome of a visit to Sicily where, as he put it in his autobiography, 'the southern light, the goatherds, the sound of a pipe all evoked the image of some classical pastoral scene' and prompted him to assemble a short anthology of poems, ranging from Theocritus and Ben Jonson to Robert Nichols and depicting a Sicilian day from dawn to evening. The work is scored for flute, chorus, strings and timpani; one of the numbers includes a solo for mezzo soprano, beautifully sung by Della Jones. Richard Hickox produces a most sensitive reading which does justice to its rich vein of lyricism. There is one instance of less than spot-on intonation from the flautist, but otherwise these are excellent performances and the recording is very good indeed.

Bloch, Ernest (1880–1959)

Concerti grossi Nos. 1 & 2; (i) *Schelomo.*
(M) *** Mercury 432 718-2 [id.]. Eastman-Rochester O, Hanson, (i) with Miquelle.

Bloch's two *Concerti grossi* were written in 1925 and 1952 respectively. Although separated by more than a quarter of a uniquely fast-moving century, they are surprisingly similar in style. They may not be among Bloch's most deeply personal works but they are thoroughly enjoyable. The neo-classical style brings a piano continuo in the Baroque manner in No. 1; the second, for strings alone, is more intense in feeling. The performances here are admirable, lively and sympathetic, and the slightly spiky tinge to the otherwise full Mercury sound is like an attractive condiment. *Schelomo*, with Georges Miquelle its soloist, makes a useful bonus for this mid-priced reissue.

Violin sonatas Nos. 1; 2 (Poème mystique); Baal Shem.
*** ASV Dig. CDDCA 714; *ZCDCA 714* [id.]. Leonard Friedman, Allan Schiller.

Bloch has yet to come in from the cold: at the time of writing, only *Schelomo* enjoys decent representation in the catalogue. The two *Violin sonatas* come from the 1920s and contain some fine music, notably in the quieter, more inward-looking slow movements. The declamatory writing of the first movement of No. 1 is pretty unremitting and hectoring in tone, though Leonard Friedman and Allan Schiller do their best to put it across persuasively. The *Second Sonata* is the stronger of the two and is eloquently played and well recorded.

Blow, John (1649–1708)

Venus and Adonis.
(M) *** HM/BMG GD 77117 (2). Kirkby, Tubb, King, Wistreich, Bonner, Holden, Cass, Nichols, Cornwell, Müller, Consort of Musicke, Rooley – GIBBONS: *Cupid and Death.****

Venus and Adonis, 'a masque for the entertainment of the king' dating from around 1682, was the first through-composed opera in English. *Dido and Aeneas* by Blow's pupil, Purcell, followed it before the end of the decade, and it is sad that so promising a start never led to the development of a school of English opera. In form, this is like a Lully opera in miniature. Its length makes it more likely to suit twentieth-century taste, with the Prologue and three brief Acts presenting a fast-moving sequence of choruses, dances and 'act-tunes' as well as arias, often with chorus. Rooley directs an elegant, lightly sprung performance, very well sung, recorded in good analogue sound (1984) in a warm acoustic. It takes up only part of the first disc of the two-disc set, now reissued by BMG at mid-price.

Boccherini, Luigi (1743–1805)

Cello concerto No. 2 in D, G. 479.
(B) *** DG Compact Classics *415 330-4* [id.]. Rostropovich, Zurich Coll. Mus., Sacher – HAYDN **, DVOŘÁK: *Cello concertos.****

Rostropovich in Boccherini offers a highly individual musical experience. Although essentially a performance in the grand manner (with Rostropovich providing his own cadenzas), the music-making has tremendous vitality, with extremely lively outer movements to balance the eloquence of the *Adagio*. The forceful nature of the performance is short on charm and so perhaps a little out of character for an essentially elegant composer like Boccherini; but Rostropovich is so compelling that reservations are swept aside. He is given an alert accompaniment by Sacher, and the recording has fine body and presence. This is among the most worthwhile of DG's series of bargain-price double-length Compact Classics tapes, for it includes a very fine account of the Dvořák *Cello concerto* partnering Fournier and Szell. The chrome-tape transfer has excellent range and detail.

Piano quintets: in A min., Op. 56/2, G.412; in E flat, Op. 56/3, G.410; in E min., Op. 57/3, G.415; in C, Op. 57/6, G.418.

(M) *** BMG/RCA Dig. GD 77053 [77053-2-RG]. Les Adieux.

Two of the six Op. 56 *Quintets* (1797), the last work Boccherini composed in his capacity as court composer to Friedrich Wilhelm II of Prussia, are included, together with two from Op. 57 (1799) dedicated to the whole French nation, no less. The most haunting of them are the lovely *E minor* (Op. 57/3), which starts the disc, and the *A minor* (Op. 56/2); both have those hints of beguiling, almost sultry melancholy that makes this composer's musical language so distinctive. This accomplished period-instrument group turn in performances of great finesse and charm, though the recording balance places the listener very much in the front row of the salon. But this music has much more to it than it is given credit for.

Boieldieu, François (1775–1834)

Harp concerto in 3 tempi in C.

❀ (M) *** Decca 425 723-2; *425 723-4* [id.]. Marisa Robles, ASMF, Iona Brown – DITTERSDORF; HANDEL: *Harp concertos* etc.*** ❀

Boieldieu's *Harp concerto* has been recorded elsewhere but never more attractively. Iona Brown and the Academy set the scene with an alert, vigorous introduction and Miss Robles provides contrasting delicacy. Much play is made with the possibilities of light and shade, the harp bringing gentle echo effects in repeated phrases. The slow movement is delightful and the lilt of the finale irresistible. The (originally Argo) recording is still in the demonstration class and very sweet on the ear. To make the reissue even more attractive, three beguiling sets of *Variations* have been added, derived from a separate solo LP, including music by Handel, Beethoven's *6 Variations on a Swiss song* and a *Theme, variations and Rondo pastorale* attributed to Mozart.

Boito, Arrigo (1842–1918)

Mefistofele (opera): *Prologue.*

(M) (***) BMG/RCA mono GD 60276; *GK 60276* [60276-2-RG; *60276-4-RG*]. Moscona, Robert Shaw Ch., Columbus Boychoir, NBC SO, Toscanini – VERDI: *I Lombardi; Rigoletto*: excerpts.(**)

(M) **(*) DG 431 171-2; *431 171-4* [id.]. Ghiaurov, V. State Op. Ch., VPO, Bernstein – R. STRAUSS: *Salome* etc.**(*)

Whatever the limitations of the sound, the hair-raising intensity of Toscanini's performance gives Boito's multi-layered *Prologue* a cogency never matched since on record. The dryness of sound even seems to help, when off-stage choruses are accurately focused, and the singing of the Robert Shaw Chorale has thrillingly dramatic bite. This was taken from one of the very last broadcasts Toscanini ever made, and with the Verdi items it makes a magnetically involving historic document.

The DG recording was made in Vienna in 1977 and finds Ghiaurov in excellent form. Bernstein, too, conducts this highly imaginative piece vividly and atmospherically. The CD transfer has greatly improved the focus and now the offstage choruses register impressively. This does not quite have the electricity of Toscanini but, for those wanting a modern version, it will serve admirably.

Borodin, Alexander (1833–87)

Prince Igor: Overture and Polovtsian dances.
*** Virgin Dig. VC7 91174-2; *VC7 91174-4* [id.]. Royal Liverpool PO Ch. & O, Mackerras – MUSSORGSKY: *Night* etc.**

A splendid account of the *Prince Igor overture*, with the brilliant, jaggedly thrusting imitation in the allegro given plenty of bite and the lyrical secondary melody glowingly phrased by principal horn and strings alike. The *Polovtsian dances* proceed with comparable brilliance and fervour, with the Royal Liverpool Philharmonic Choir producing expansive lyrical tone and joining in the frenzy of the closing section with infectious zest. Excellent recording too, vivid and full; if only the Mussorgsky coupling had produced comparable electricity, this record would have been a world-beater.

(i) *Symphonies Nos. 1–3; Prince Igor:* (i; ii) *Overture and Polovtsian dances;* (iii) *In the steppes of Central Asia; Nocturne for string orchestra* (arr. Sargent).
(M) *(**) Sony M2YK 46459 (2) [id.]. (i) Toronto SO, Andrew Davis, (ii) with Ch.; (iii) Phd. O, Eugene Ormandy.

Symphonies Nos. 1 in E flat; 2 in B min.
** Ph. Dig. 422 996-2 [id.]. Rotterdam PO, Valéry Gergiev.

Symphonies Nos. 1–2; 3 in A min. (completed & orch. Glazunov).
(BB) ** Naxos Dig. 8.550238 [id.]. Bratislava RSO, Stephen Gunzenhauser.

Though the *Second* is by far the best known of the Borodin symphonies, both its companions deserve greater popularity, especially the *First* which, in Andrew Davis's hands, sounds a fully mature work in its own right and not just a preparation for the well-known *Symphony in E flat*. It is colourful and ebullient, with a particularly appealing scherzo. The *Third* brings some most engaging playing from the Toronto woodwind. It is a pastoral two-movement torso, completed by Glazunov from sketches, and here it sounds delightfully spontaneous. In the *Second Symphony* Davis's tempi are admirably judged: the bold rhythmic figure of the first movement has both Russian power and bite, and the performance overall has striking colour and vitality, with a superb horn solo in the *Andante*. In short, these are easily the finest performances available and the Toronto orchestra find plenty of zest and romantic feeling for the *Prince Igor Overture*, provided as a bonus, while the *Polovtsian dances*, complete with unnamed chorus, bring a thrilling Beechamesque excitement and flair. Unfortunately the Toronto orchestra is not flattered by the 1977 CBS recording which, although fully acceptable, is lacking in natural ambience and bloom, its two-dimensional sound-picture all the more apparent on CD. The two encores from the Philadelphia Orchestra under Ormandy, recorded nearly two decades earlier, must be written off. The rich sounds which obviously emanate from the Philadelphia strings in their opulent account of the *Nocturne* are rendered sterile in the CD transfer by a piercingly thin sound for the violins above the stave, and *In the steppes of Central Asia* is even more disagreeable, with discoloration of the upper harmonics of the woodwind immediately noticeable at the opening.

The Naxos disc is an undoubted bargain in offering good recordings of all three symphonies (76 minutes) at a very modest price indeed. One ideally needs a more sumptuous body of sound for this music than the Bratislava Radio Symphony Orchestra can provide, but Gunzenhauser brings more buoyant vitality to the first movement of the *Second Symphony* than Gergiev who, at a slower tempo, is broader and rhythmically heavier. Altogether these are fresh, pleasing performances but not distinctive.

Helped by the warmly resonant acoustics of their concert hall, the Rotterdam orchestra create richer, more expansive textures in the *Andantes* of both the *E flat* and *B minor* works, with a fine horn solo in the latter (though not as memorable as that by the Toronto player), and it is a pity that the conductor does not move the music on more. He is also rhythmically less invigorating in outer movements, though by no means dull; the scherzos of both symphonies are very colourful in his hands, and here the warm ambience adds a good deal. Yet the Slovaks play this music with enthusiasm and colour, and the unfinished *A minor* work – completed by Glazunov, partly from memory – is appealingly fresh; its inclusion on Naxos, at a third of the cost, rather puts the less generous (full-priced) Philips offering out of court.

Boulez, Pierre (born 1926)

Messagesquisse; Notations Nos. 1–4; Rituel: In memoriam Bruno Maderna.
*** Erato/WEA Dig. 2292 45493-2 [id.]. O de Paris, Barenboim.

Barenboim here couples the movingly elegiac *Rituel*, written in memory of Boulez's friend, Bruno Maderna, with two other shorter works which Boulez also composed in the 1970s. In *Rituel* Barenboim cannot quite match the biting intensity of the composer himself in this music – the latter's fine recording is issued on CD by Sony at mid-price – but, in its softer-grained way, the warmth of expressiveness compellingly holds together this massive ceremonial in its clearly defined sections. Where Barenboim gains is in the warmth and spaciousness of the recording, important when the orchestra, like the work itself, is sharply sectionalized. Barenboim is similarly persuasive in the four *Notations*, pieces of Webernian brevity, and in *Messagesquisse* for seven cellos, an elaborately constructed tribute to Paul Sacher.

Brade, William (1560–1630)

Hamburger Ratsmusik: Allemandes, Canzonas, Courantes, Galliards, Intradas (1609, 1614 & 1617 collections).
(M) *** HM/BMG Dig. GD 77168 (2) [77168-2-RG]. Hespèrion XX, Jordi Savall.

William Brade spent most of his life on the Continent, serving at the Court of Christian IV of Denmark in the 1590s, and subsequently at the Brandenburg Court in Berlin and in Bückenburg, Halle and in Hamburg, where he died in 1630. Count Ernst III of Holstein-Schaumburg in Bückenburg described Brade as 'a wanton, outrageous fellow' who, spurred on by his ambitious wife, openly threatened to strike, to secure a 150 per cent rise to 1,000 Thalers per annum! At this period Hamburg employed eight town musicians who were paid by the city and were attached to the Wedde, or police department of the Republic of Hamburg. This collection of dances is based on the three main prints which appeared in 1609, 1614 and 1617 in Hamburg and Lübeck, and embraces all the contemporary forms, Allmand, Paduana, Galliard and a variety of descriptive pieces. The titles mention that they contain choice new dances and that they 'may be pleasingly executed on all kinds of musical instruments, particularly on viols' – as indeed is certainly the case here. Their realization is absolutely delightful, varied in both content and instrumental colour, and excellently played by Hespèrion XX under Jordi Savall, while the recording, from 1981, is very good indeed.

Brahms, Johannes (1833–97)

Piano concerto No. 1 in D min., Op. 15.
(M) **(*) Sony MK 42261 [id.]. Rudolf Serkin, Cleveland O, Szell – R. STRAUSS: *Burleske.***

(i) *Piano concerto No. 1 in D min., Op. 15;* (ii) *Variations on a theme of Haydn, Op. 56a.*
(M) *** EMI CDM7 63536-2; *EG 763536-4* [id.]. (i) Barenboim, Philh. O; (ii) VPO; Barbirolli.

(i) *Piano concerto No. 1 in D min., Op. 15. 4 Ballades, Op. 10.*
(M) *** DG 431 595-2; *431 595-4* [id.]. Gilels, (i) BPO, Jochum.

(i) *Piano concerto No.1 in D min., Op. 15; 6 Pieces, Op. 118.*
** EMI Dig. CDC7 49934-2 [id.]; *EL 749934-4.* Peter Donohoe; (i) Philh. O, Svetlanov.

It is good to have Gilels's 1972 version of the *D minor Concerto* available again, separately, and now at mid-price. This reading is to the 1970s what Curzon was to the 1960s; it has a magisterial strength blended with a warmth, humanity and depth that are altogether inspiring. Jochum is a superb accompanist and the remastered recording has a better focus on CD, if slightly less glowing warmth than the original LP. The *Ballades*, recorded three years later, make a considerable bonus. They have never been played so marvellously on record, and the recording is very believable.

Barenboim recorded the two Brahms *Piano concertos* with Barbirolli in 1968, at almost exactly the same time as the conductor was doing his Vienna cycle of the *Symphonies*. It was by the choice of the pianist that tempi were so unusually slow, but it was a decision with which Barbirolli wholly sympathized, drawing even more loving playing from the Philharmonia than he had done from the Vienna Philharmonic in the orchestral works. Their performance of the *First Concerto* is among the most inspired ever committed to disc. If at first the opening tempo seems disconcertingly measured, it falls into place on a second hearing. The playing is heroic and marvellously spacious, and the performance is sustained by the intensity of concentration, especially in the pianissimo passages of the slow movement; the joyous finale uplifts the spirit and communicates a life-enhancing confidence. The *Variations*, laid out for the listener in affectionate detail, again show the conductor at his finest; the late-1960s recordings have transferred splendidly to CD, with plenty of body and the upper range brighter but without edginess.

Serkin's late-1960s account with Szell, his third on LP, brought tremendous command and grandeur. This is undoubtedly a memorable performance and the support from Szell and the Cleveland Orchestra has great power. Were the CBS/Sony recording as fine as that offered by EMI to Barenboim or by Decca to Curzon, this would be a formidable issue. The balance lacks a natural perspective and needs more opulence and depth, although the CD remastering makes the very most of the sound-quality, and the hall's ambience prevents brashness. Admirers of Serkin will find the overall effect is far from unacceptable.

Peter Donohoe is an artist of intelligence, and he is well served both by the Philharmonia Orchestra under Svetlanov and by the EMI engineers. If one heard this musicianly performance in the concert hall, one would join in the applause but neither the *Concerto* nor the *Six Pieces*, Op. 118, evoke a sufficiently individual response to prompt one to return to the disc very often.

Piano concerto No. 2 in B flat, Op. 83.
** Virgin Dig. VC7 91138-2; *VC7 91138-4* [id.]. Stephen Hough, BBC SO, Andrew Davis.

(M) (*) Pearl mono GEMMCD 9399 [id.]. Schnabel, BBC SO, Boult – BACH: *Double concerto.*(**(*))

(i) *Piano concerto No. 2 in B flat, Op. 83;* (ii) *Academic festival overture; Tragic overture.*
(M) *** EMI CDM7 63537-2; *EG 763537-4* [id.]. (i) Barenboim, Philh. O; (ii) VPO, Barbirolli.

(i) *Piano concerto No. 2 in B flat, Op. 83. Intermezzi, Op. 119/1–3; Rhapsody, Op. 119/4.*
(M) **(*) Sony MK 42262 [id.]. Rudolf Serkin, (i) Cleveland O, Szell.

(i) *Piano concerto No. 2 in B flat, Op. 83;* (ii) *6 Piano pieces, Op. 118.*
(B) **(*) DG 431 162-2; *431 162-4* [id.]. (i) Géza Anda, BPO, Karajan; (ii) Wilhelm Kempff.

While Barenboim's reading with Barbirolli remains an individual view, the tendency to slow tempi brings the advantage that the lyrical passages merge spontaneously into the whole. The first two movements remain grandly heroic and the slow movement has something of the awed intensity you find in the middle movement of the *First Concerto*, while the finale erupts gracefully into rib-tickling humour. Barenboim's touch here reminds one of Rubinstein's famous version. This is a performance to love in its glowing spontaneity; the first-rate 1968 recording has splendid Brahmsian body and breadth, and no lack of brilliance. Of the fill-ups, the *Tragic overture* is a performance of considerable subtlety in matters of mood and style, and has no lack of impulse; but many will feel that the measured account of the *Academic festival overture*, attractively affectionate as it is, could do with more sparkle.

As with the *First Concerto*, Serkin's recording with Szell was his third on LP, and on balance it is the finest. There is a strength and purposefulness about all the playing; with the help of Szell, Serkin achieves an ideal balance between straightforwardness and expressiveness. In the opening cadenza, for example, he has all the weight one could ask for, but he still manages to point the dotted rhythm very winningly and achieves remarkable clarity. In the scherzo he is again strong but manages to convey more lilt than many rivals, while the slow movement has a genuine 'inner' intensity, with some wonderfully expressive playing by the Cleveland principal cellist. Serkin chooses a comparatively slow speed for the finale, but the flow and energy of the music are not impaired and the Hungarian motifs of the second subject sparkle with point and wit. Unfortunately the piano tone is not as full as one would ideally like but, as with the *First Concerto*, the remastering produces a firm orchestral image and the hall ambience contributes to a Brahmsian sonority. The solo items have a patrician command rather than any desire to charm, but this is undoubtedly fine playing.

The 1968 partnership of Anda with the BPO provides much fine playing from soloist and orchestra alike. The performance opens slowly and is rhapsodically free; it has plenty of impulse, but Anda is wayward at times, although he is always commanding. But there is poetry here, and undoubted power. The slow movement is often richly eloquent, and the finale has a persuasive, lyrical charm. There is much to enjoy, not least the glorious orchestral response. The recording is appropriately bold and full, and the balance is good; it sounds brighter now than originally, and internal detail is much clearer. As sound, this makes satisfying listening. In the six *Klavierstücke*, Op. 118, Kempff shines in exactly those pieces where many modern pianists fall short, emphasizing poetry rather than brilliance, subtle timbres rather than virtuosity, the gentle fancies of Brahms's last period, evocative and meaningful beyond the mere notes. The first piece, in A minor, sounds a little shallow as recorded here, but after that the piano timbre is full of colour.

Hough's is an easy, clean-cut, often surprisingly gentle view of this warhorse of a virtuoso concerto. It is a pity that the distancing of sound in this Virgin recording softens the focus further and that the orchestral playing is not tense enough. The kernel of the reading lies in the slow movement, which Hough makes as poetic as Chopin, while giving it genuinely Brahmsian dedication. The lightness of the finale is attractive too.

Schnabel's performance with the BBC Symphony Orchestra comes from 1935. On this occasion, however, he was distinctly below par and, although there are characteristic insights, there is some pretty rough pianism, with plenty of splashes. The BBC orchestra under Boult give generally impressive support, and the transfers, though not ideal, are eminently acceptable.

Violin concerto in D, Op. 77.
*** ASV CDDCA 748; *ZCDCA 748* [id.]. Xue-Wei, LPO, Ivor Bolton – MENDELSSOHN: *Violin concerto.****
*** Chan. Dig. CHAN 8974; *ABTD 1563* [id.]. Hideko Udagawa, LSO, Mackerras – BRUCH: *Concerto No. 1.****
(B) **(*) RCA VD 60479; *VK 60479* [60479-2-RV; *60479-4-RV*]. Ughi, Philh. O, Sawallisch – BRUCH: *Concerto No. 1.***(*)
**(*) EMI Dig. CDC7 54187-2; *EL 754187-4* [id.]. Nigel Kennedy, LPO, Klaus Tennstedt.
(B) **(*) DG Compact Classics 413 844-2 (2); *413 844-4* [id.]. Ferras, BPO, Karajan – BEETHOVEN: *Romances* ***; BRUCH: *Violin concerto No. 1* **; (on CD only:) DVOŘÁK: *Violin concerto.***(*)
(BB) * Naxos Dig. 8.550195 [id.]. Nishizaki, Slovak PO, Gunzenhauser – BRUCH: *Concerto No. 1.**(*)

Violin concerto in D, Op. 77; Academic festival overture.
** Teldec/Warner Dig. 2292 46944-2; *2292 46944-4* [id.]. Thomas Zehetmair, Cleveland O, Dohnányi.

(i) *Violin concerto in D;* (ii) *Violin sonata No. 2 in A, Op. 100.*
(M) **(*) DG 415 838-2; *415 838-4* [id.]. Zukerman; (i) O de Paris, Barenboim; (ii) Barenboim (piano).

Xue-Wei's version of the Brahms, fresh and well-mannered, is particularly attractive when it is so generously coupled with the Mendelssohn *Concerto*, equally well done. There is a degree of emotional reticence here compared with more flamboyant performers but, with Ivor Bolton drawing first-rate playing from the LPO, it is a performance to live with and can be warmly recommended. The sound is first rate too.

Hideko Udagawa gives a powerful, persuasively spontaneous-sounding reading. Her daring in virtuosity, her biting attack on the most taxing passages, is often thrilling, even if her violin sound is not always the sweetest. The personality of the player, her magnetic temperament submerges reservations on detail, particularly when Mackerras draws comparably powerful playing from the LSO, with the opening tutti building tension strongly. Warm, full and well-balanced recording.

Ughi's account has the advantage of a strong and passionate orchestral backing from Sawallisch and first-rate (1983) digital sound, with a good balance. As with the Bruch coupling, this is a fresh, direct reading, not as charismatic as some, but with moments of considerable lyrical intensity and by no means unimaginative in the control of light and shade. At bargain price, it is well worth considering.

Kennedy's much-advertised version of the Brahms is by a fair margin the slowest ever put on disc. Not only are the basic speeds slow – notably in the first two movements – he allows himself extra slowings and tenutos at the least excuse. In principle the result may be intolerably self-indulgent, but Kennedy's musical personality (as opposed to his media image) and his devotion to the work (as he claims, his desert-island concerto) give an intensity to sustain all the eccentricities. The finale, less eccentric, is relatively small-scale and wild at times but conveys a winning sense of fun. This is a version to hear as a one-off experience rather than to live with; if through being a best-seller it brings new listeners to a supreme violin masterpiece, then it will have served its purpose. Tennstedt draws concentrated playing from the LPO, the whole richly recorded.

Zuckerman's is a well-conceived reading that has finish and facility and is sweet-toned, but his general approach can often seem a little bland by comparison with some other versions. He is exposed to a close balance, but this does not mask the Orchestre de Paris under Barenboim, who give excellent support and receive a well-detailed recording, in spite of the unrealistic perspective. For the reissue the *A major Violin sonata* has been added, but this is also available, more appropriately coupled, with the other two sonatas – see below.

Much depends on one's attitude to Ferras's tone-colour whether the Ferras/Karajan Compact Classics version is a good recommendation or not. DG have placed him close to the microphone so that the smallness of tone that in the concert hall is disappointing is certainly not evident here. Moreover, there is a jewelled accuracy about the playing that is most appealing, and Karajan conducts vividly. The recording is of good quality and the high-level transfer is of striking liveliness. The digitally remastered pair of CDs offer an enjoyable account of the Dvořák *Violin concerto* as a bonus.

Zehetmair's is a warm and thoroughly musical account: his timbre is sweet, and both he and Dohnányi, who accompanies sympathetically, offer a good response to Brahmsian lyricism. The Cleveland orchestral playing is beyond criticism and the Teldec sound-balance impressively natural. But other versions of this work have a much stronger profile and this performance fails to resonate in the memory.

Takako Nishizaki seems somehow not quite comfortable in this concerto, as if straining to make a bigger, more ardent reading than is natural to her. Some of the upper tessitura, so pressured, is not very sweet, and she makes Kreisler's first-movement cadenza sound laboured. The coupled Bruch suits her better, but this is not one of her recommendable records.

(i) *Violin concerto in D, Op. 77;* (ii) *Double concerto for violin, cello and orchestra, Op. 102.*
(M) (***) EMI mono CDH7 63496-2 [id.]. (i) Y. Menuhin, Lucerne O; (ii) Boskovsky, Emanuel Brabec, VPO; Furtwängler.
(M) **(*) Sony SBK 46335 [id.]; *40-46335*. Stern, (ii) with Rose; Phd. O, Ormandy.

Menuhin's 1949 recording of the Brahms *Violin concerto*, like his earliest version of the Beethoven which he made with the same forces, brings a towering performance. The unlikely and, at the time, controversial partnership brought a dedication that has rarely been matched, with each responding to the challenge of the other's highly individual artistry. As Menuhin himself said, it was 'an experience of almost religious intensity'. Even in the opening tutti, the playing of the orchestra is incandescent and, contrary to what one might expect, there is little self-indulgence in the reading, with the second movement pure and flowing and the finale given a persuasive Hungarian lilt at a relatively easy speed. The feeling of co-ordination is intensified by the natural, un-spotlit balance of the violin. Even with the Cedar noise-reduction process, the 78 surfaces are heavier than usual; but with such magnetic playing one can easily listen through the interference. The *Double concerto* brings a live performance of comparable warmth, recorded in 1952. With the distinguished concertmaster and the principal cello of the Vienna Philharmonic, Furtwängler was prepared to allow his soloists the fullest freedom.

The cellist in particular – for much of the time the senior partner – is ripely expansive. The result is again magnetic, not perfect in detail but a historic reading to cherish.

Stern's splendid 1959 account of the *Violin concerto* with Ormandy now returns to the catalogue satisfactorily remastered and, although the balance still spotlights the solo violin, the overall impression is of a better integration than in previous CD incarnations. For the first time we are also offered a coupling that is both generous and suitable, the mid-1960s collaboration with Leonard Rose in the *Double concerto*. In the most naturally expressive way, relaxed yet commanding, the two soloists unfailingly match each other's playing. Each has a creative ear in pointing a comment so that the response is made to sound like an unfolding conversation, with Ormandy always an understanding accompanist. Both in the detailed pointing of phrasing (the opening of the finale has a most engagingly light touch), in the bite of bravura passages, and in the rich expansiveness of the slow movement, as a performance this compares very favourably with the Oistrakh/Fournier account. The forward balance of the soloists brings glorious tone, even if this means that there are no pianissimos (although one can tell when they are playing quietly from the tone-colour). The CD transfer is well managed; though light in bass, the sound overall is full and clear.

Double concerto for violin, cello and orchestra in A min., Op. 102.
(B) ** DG 429 934-2 [id.]. Schneiderhan, Starker, Berlin RSO, Fricsay – BEETHOVEN: *Triple concerto.***
(B) ** DG Compact Classics *415 332-4* [id.]. Schneiderhan, Starker, Berlin RSO, Fricsay – BEETHOVEN: *Triple concerto*; MOZART: *Violin concerto No. 3.***
(M) *(*) Ph. 426 631-2; *426 631-4* [id.]. Szeryng, Starker, Concg. O, Haitink – BEETHOVEN: *Triple concerto.**(*)

We have always enjoyed the Schneiderhan/Starker/Fricsay version of the *Double concerto* ever since it first came out on a ten-inch LP in 1961. The remastering for CD may have brightened the upper range, but the acoustic of the Berlin Jesus-Christus Kirche provides warmth, even though the two soloists are very forwardly balanced. Fricsay shapes the work splendidly and there is plenty of impetus. The Schneiderhan/Starker/Fricsay version of the *Double concerto*, coupled with Beethoven's *Triple concerto*, makes a fair bargain on a DG Compact Classics cassette which also includes Mozart.

The Szeryng/Starker version, recorded in 1970 in the Concertgebouw, has a richer orchestral tapestry; indeed the Philips sound is first class. However, although the engineers also balance the soloists fairly closely, their account makes far less of an impact musically. This version remains obstinately unmemorable and is ultimately disappointing, though it is not easy to fault any individual detail and the *Andante* is songful.

Hungarian dances Nos. 1–21.
❀ (BB) *** Naxos Dig. 8.550110 (*Nos. 1–2; 4–21*) Budapest SO, István Bogár.
**(*) Chan. Dig CHAN 8885; *ABT 1496* [id.]. LSO, Järvi.

(i) *Hungarian dances Nos. 1–21;* (ii) *Variations on a theme of Haydn, Op. 56a.*
(M) *** DG Dig./Analogue 431 594-2; *431 594-4* [id.]. (i) VPO; (ii) Dresden State O; Abbado.

The Budapest recording of the Brahms *Hungarian dances* is sheer delight from beginning to end. The playing has warmth and sparkle, and the natural way the music unfolds brings a refreshing feeling of rhythmic freedom. Yet there are also many delightful individual touches from the conductor, with the woodwind joyfully producing some most engaging colours. Bogár's rubato is wholly spontaneous; the strings bring plenty of temperament to their phrasing of the more sultry tunes, while their lighter articulation is infectious. The recording is warm and full, yet transparent, with just the right brilliance on top. This is an outright winner among available versions, but there is a small snag with the layout and documentation. The *Third dance* (a charming *Allegretto in F major*, led by the woodwind) has inadvertently been added to track 2 and follows on immediately after the *Second dance*. The listing on the CD anticipates the presence of all 21 dances, separately banded and, from No. 3 (actually No. 4) onwards, gives the wrong timings, with each applying to the previous number. Even with this minor problem, which is primarily one of access, one would far rather have this set of dances (particularly on such an inexpensive disc), than any of the other alternative versions.

Järvi's complete set is brilliantly played and given spectacular recording, vivid and wide-ranging.There is much to enjoy here and, had one not experienced the Budapest music-making, this would have been rated even more highly. But in the moulded, lyrical tunes on the strings, Järvi's style is that bit more self-conscious; even though the LSO playing is polished and lively, at times exhilarating, the effect is less chimerical. If one compares, for instance, the *Allegretto grazioso* of *No. 15 in B flat*, one finds Järvi slower, less incandescent, while the Budapest playing has a lighter rhythmic feeling and greater vivacity and sparkle; and there are many other dances in which a direct comparison reveals the Budapest performances as sunnier and more infectious.

Abbado's fine complete digital set of the *Hungarian dances* – see our main volume, pp. 201–2 – now reappears at mid-price, coupled with his excellent 1972 Dresden account of the *Haydn variations*, a work he always did well. This, together with the reduced price, now gives it the edge over Masur's Leipzig alternative (Philips 411 426-2).

Hungarian dances Nos. 1, 3, 5, 6 18–19.
(M) **(*) Ph. 432 046-2; *432 046-4* [id.]. Leipzig GO, Masur – DVOŘÁK: *Slavonic dances.***(*)

Those wanting just a selection from Masur's complete set of the *Hungarian dances* will find these performances are very sympathetic and well recorded. However, the coupling of Dvořák, with only twelve of the sixteen *Slavonic dances* included, does not seem very sensible planning, and no information about the music is included.

Piano quartet in G min. (orch. Schoenberg).
*** Collins Dig. 1175-2; *1175-4* [id.]. LPO, Rozhdestvensky – RACHMANINOV: *Études-tableaux.****

Piano quartet in G min. (orch. Schoenberg); *Variations and fugue on a theme by Handel, Op. 24* (orch. Rubbra).
*** Chan. Dig. CHAN 8825; *ABTD 1450* [id.]. LSO, Järvi.

The current craze for Schoenberg's transcription of the Brahms *Piano quartet in G minor* is puzzling, and even more so is Schoenberg's recourse to glockenspiel and xylophone, which could be compared – if it hasn't already – to painting a moustache on the Mona Lisa. When one recalls the relative neglect of the marvellous orchestral *Serenades*, it seems a pity that Schoenberg's essay should be so often duplicated. Brahms knew a thing or two about the orchestra and, had he wanted to score this quartet, he would doubtless have done so. If you want to hear it in this form, however, Neeme Järvi's new version with the LSO is as good as any. It is performed with some enthusiasm and well recorded.

So too, for that matter is Gennady Rozhdestvensky's account with the London Philharmonic, which makes out every bit as good a case for Schoenberg's often masterly scoring. Choice will probably depend on the coupling. Edmund Rubbra's transcription of the *Variations and fugue on a theme by Handel* is the more logical, though not all of it comes off equally well. Respighi was a greater man of the orchestra – though not perhaps so deep a composer – and his celebrated version of Rachmaninov's *Études-tableaux* sounds splendidly idiomatic.

Serenade No. 1 in D, Op. 11; Academic festival overture; Tragic overture.
*** Sony Dig. SK 45932 [id.]; *40-45932.* LSO, Michael Tilson Thomas.

It is a pity that Sony have missed the opportunity of giving us both *Serenades* on one CD. The catalogue is not really in need of either another *Academic festival overture* or *Tragic overture*, even in such good performances as the LSO give under Michael Tilson Thomas. All the same, this new version of the glorious *D major Serenade* has a sunny geniality and a youthful radiance that are most persuasive. Tilson Thomas's version has both vitality and sensitivity in its favour, and the recording is very natural and well detailed. Neither Slatkin (RCA) nor Abbado offers a fill-up, nor are as well recorded, though Kertész's very accepable bargain reissue from the 1960s (Decca 421 628-2; *421 628-4*) offers both *Serenades* together, as does Bertini's Orfeo disc (C 008101A – also analogue but at full price). But if the *D major Serenade* is your priority, the new Sony version must take precedence.

Serenade No. 2 in A, Op. 16; Academic festival overture; Variations on a theme by Haydn.
**(*) BMG/RCA Dig. RD 87920; *RK 87920* [7920-2-RC; *7920-4-RC*]. St Louis SO, Slatkin.

Leonard Slatkin gets very musical results from the excellent St Louis orchestra in the *Serenade No. 2*, and there is nothing slick about this sensitive, unforced performance. The recording is just a little two-dimensional and wanting in bloom. There was sufficient room to have given us the *D major Serenade* instead of yet another account of the *Academic festival overture* and the *St Antoni chorale variations*, which Michael Tilson Thomas also chooses for his Sony disc.

Symphonies Nos. 1–4.
(M) **(*) HM/BMG Dig. GD 60085; *GK 60085* (3) [60085-2-RG; *60085-4-RG*]. N. German RSO, Wand.

Symphonies Nos. 1–4; Academic festival overture; Tragic overture; Variations on a theme of Haydn.
(M) **(*) Sony/CBS SM3K 45823 (3) [id.]. Cleveland O, George Szell.

Szell's powerful view of Brahms is consistently revealed in this masterful series of performances, recorded in the 1960s when he had made the Cleveland Orchestra America's finest. His approach is generally plain and direct, crisp and detached rather than smooth and moulded. Speeds are broad, but only in the first movement of No. 4 does that undermine the electric tension of conductor and orchestra. In the manner of the time, no exposition repeats are observed, not even in No. 3. Though the sound, as transferred, is not as full as on the original LPs (when EMI had the CBS-Epic concession), it is clear and bright, with superb detail. Complete with all the shorter pieces on three discs, it makes an excellent bargain.

Wand's complete cycle, originally on EMI and now reissued on three mid-priced Deutsche Harmonia Mundi discs, has the advantage of digital recording, although the sound brings a degree of fierceness on violin tone in all but No. 2. Wand's is a consistently direct view of Brahms, yet the reading of each symphony has its own individuality. In the opening movement of the *First*, like Toscanini he brings great intensity to the slow introduction by choosing an unusually fast speed, then leading naturally by modular pacing into the main allegro. The extra unity is clear. There is a comparable dramatic intensity in the finale, although his choice of a tempo for the main marching melody, far slower than the rest, brings uncomfortable changes of gear. Yet the performance is made convincing by its spontaneity.

Even though he does not observe the exposition repeat, Wand's reading of the *Second* is the pick of his Brahms series, a characteristically glowing but steady reading, recorded with a fullness and bloom that are missing in the companion issues. His unsensational approach exactly matches this sunniest of symphonies. Its lyricism is made to flow freely, and the slow movement is robust, its melancholy underplayed. The third movement is light and fresh, the finale warm and exhilarating. In the *Third Symphony* Wand does observe the exposition repeat and his wise way with Brahms, strong and easy and steadily paced, works beautifully here, bringing out the autumnal moods, ending with a sober view of the finale. The bright sound underlines the reedy twang of the Hamburg woodwind – rather rough in the slow movement – while the horn could be more secure in his solo in the third movement. By contrast, the reading of No. 4 initially seems understated. At a fastish speed, the first movement is melancholy rather than tragic, while the slow movement, similarly steady and flowing, makes no great expansion for the big melody of the counter-subject. The third movement in jollity has plenty of light and shade, and the finale is rather brisk and tough, with the great flute passage in the passacaglia tender but not drawn out. It is quite a strong reading, but marred by recording that is less than ideally clear, with edgy violins as in Nos. 1 and 3.

Symphonies Nos. 1–4; Academic festival overture; (i) *Double concerto in A min., Op. 102. Hungarian dances Nos. 1, 17, 20 & 21; Tragic overture; Variations on a theme of Haydn;* (ii) *Liebeslieder-Walzer, Op. 52;* (iii) *Song of the Fates (Gesang der Parzen). Op. 89.*
(M) (***) RCA mono GD 60325 *GK 60325* (4) [60325-2-RG; *60325-4-RG*]. NBC SO, Toscanini, with (i) Mischakoff; Miller; (ii) Ch., Artur Balsam, Joseph Kahn; (iii) (without O) Robert Shaw Ch.

Though Toscanini's direction of the delightful *Liebeslieder waltzes* is impossibly regimented and lacking in lilt (he hardly needed to conduct with only two pianos), the rest of this set reveals the maestro as a much warmer and more spacious Brahmsian than has often been thought. The *First Symphony* starts very fast and intensely; but often speeds are surprisingly broad, and the *Fourth symphony*, Toscanini's favourite, brings a magnificent performance. The soloists in the *Double concerto* were principals in the NBC orchestra, Mischa Mischakoff and Frank Miller, both very fine artists, even though Toscanini allowed them less expressive freedom than they really needed. The CD transfers do everything possible for the dry and limited original sound. The extra items date mainly from 1948, recorded several years earlier than the symphonies.

Symphony No. 1 in C min., Op. 68.
(B) *** DG 431 161-2; *431 161-4* [id.]. BPO, Karajan – SCHUMANN: *Overture, Scherzo and Finale.****
(*) Chesky CD 19. LSO, Jascha Horenstein (with WAGNER: *Tannhäuser: Venusburg Bacchanale* *).
(M) ** DG Dig. 431 591-2; *431 591-4* [id.]. LAPO, Giulini.

Symphony No. 1 in C min.; Academic festival overture; Tragic overture.
(M) *** Ph. 432 275-2; *432 275-4* [id.]. Concg. O, Haitink.

Symphony No. 1 in C min.; Tragic overture.
** ASV Dig. CDDCA 729; *ZCDCA 729* [id.]. Philh. O, d'Avalos.

Symphony No. 1 in C min.; Variations on a theme by Haydn, Op. 56a.
*(*) Ph. Dig. 426 299-2; *426 299-4* [id.]. Phd. O, Muti.

(i) *Symphony No. 1 in C min.; Variations on a theme of Haydn;* (ii) *Hungarian dances Nos. 17–21.*
(M) **(*) Sony SBK 46534 [id.]. (i) Cleveland O, Szell; (ii) Phd. O, Ormandy.

Haitink's 1972 recording of the *First Symphony* emerges splendidly in its remastered CD format. It is a strong, well-argued reading of considerable power, and superbly played. Haitink does not observe the first-movement exposition repeat but, that apart, it remains among the very finest versions, with recording that is full and spacious and well balanced. The *Tragic overture* is also a particularly arresting account, and the *Academic festival overture* has plenty of vitality.

Karajan's 1977 analogue recording – his fourth – is still highly recommendable (especially at bargain price and now with its present Schumann coupling), and the sound is still remarkably good. The superbly committed response of the Berlin Philharmonic players, in repertoire to which they are completely attuned, is a joy in itself.

Szell's account of No. 1 is one of the most impressive of his set. His bold, direct thrust gives the outer movements plenty of power and impetus, and the inner movements bring relaxation and a fair degree of warmth. The *Variations* are strongly characterized, too, and have plenty of finesse in the matter of light and shade. But, as in the symphony, Szell does not seek to charm. The sound is remarkably good, bright and vivid, certainly, but not without the body so necessary in Brahms. For an encore Ormandy chooses the last five *Hungarian dances*, as orchestrated by Dvořák, and plays them with characteristic flair. They are enjoyable, but it is a pity that the recorded sound of the violins is not sweeter and more opulent above the stave.

The refinement of Horenstein's reading comes out incomparably at the start of the *Andante*, wonderfully delicate in lyricism at a really hushed pianissimo. Horenstein is a Brahmsian who, with a broadly expressive style from phrase to phrase, yet prefers to keep a basically steady pulse through a movement. The LSO was at its peak when this record was made, at Walthamstow Town Hall, for *Reader's Digest* magazine in the 1960s (the horn playing is magnificent) and, with well-balanced recording, this can be strongly recommended to Horenstein admirers, although the fact that it is a premium-price reissue will make it less attractive for the general collector. The curious coupling of the *Venusberg* sequence from *Tannhäuser* makes an attractive bonus, with spacious direction and fine singing from the Beecham Choral Society.

Francesco d'Avalos conducts a positive, well-played performance which yet lacks detail and suffers from a curious inconsistency. Where in the first three movements his speeds are on the brisk side – notably in the main allegro of the first movement, in which he allows little relaxing – the finale is slow to the point of sluggishness both in the introduction and in the main theme. D'Avalos then changes gear rapidly for the main allegro. The *Tragic overture* is more satisfyingly consistent. The recording is full and warm, but reverberation tends to cloud tuttis.

Giulini's spacious 1982 Los Angeles recording – see our main volume, pp. 203–5 –

has reappeared in DG's Brahms Edition. It is still at mid-price but is now without the coupling of Schumann's *Manfred overture.*

Muti is more in tune with this first of the Brahms symphonies than with the other three, and the first two movements bring strong, sympathetic, well-paced performances. The recessive mood characteristic of this Brahms series then takes over for the other two movements, though the ensemble remains excellent. The *Variations* bring back the alert Muti; but what undermines this as a contender is the mushy recording, with tuttis sounding woolly and unfocused and violin tone surprisingly thin.

(i) *Symphonies Nos. 1;* (ii) *4 in E min., Op. 98;* (CD only: (iii) *Tragic overture;* (iv) *Variations on a theme of Haydn*).
(B) *** DG Compact Classics 413 424-2 (2); *413 424-4* [id.]. (i) BPO; (ii) VPO, Boehm (CD only: (iii) BPO, Maazel; (iv) LSO, Jochum).

Anyone learning their Brahms from Boehm's performances cannot go far wrong. His Berlin Philharmonic version of the *First* comes from the early 1960s (he recorded it again later, rather less successfully, with the VPO). It is a centrally recommendable version, with tempi that are steady rather than volatile; but with polished playing from the Berliners, the performance is undoubtedly effective, and the well-balanced recording emerges here to excellent effect. Boehm's account of the *Fourth* was the most successful performance in his Vienna cycle, with a spacious and noble reading of the first movement and a finely contrasted view of the final passacaglia, lyrical and dramatic elements sharply defined. There is heavy underlining in the great string melody of the slow movement, but this and other idosyncrasies never interfere with the consistency of the reading. The tape transfer has plenty of life and warmth. For the pair of digitally remastered CDs, Maazel's self-consciously brilliant account of the *Tragic overture* has been added plus Jochum's LSO version of the *St Anthony Variations.* Jochum proves as naturally a Brahmsian as he is a Brucknerian, and this performance has a natural freshness which disguises the subtlety of detail.

Symphony No. 2 in D, Op. 73.
*** Decca Dig. 430 324-2; *430 324-4* [id.]. Concg. O, Chailly – WEBERN: *Im Sommerwind.****
(M) **(*) Unicorn UKCD 2036 [id.]. Danish RSO, Horenstein (with recorded interview between Jascha Horenstein and Alan Blyth).

Symphony No. 2 in D; Academic festival overture.
*(*) RCA Dig. RD 87980; *RK 87980* [7980-2-RC]. Bav. RSO, Sir Colin Davis.

Symphony No. 2 in D; Academic festival overture; Tragic overture.
(M) **(*) DG Dig. 431 592-2; *431 592-4* [id.]. VPO, Bernstein.

Symphony No. 2 in D; Variations on a theme of Haydn.
** EMI Dig. CDC7 54059-2; *EL 754059-4* [id.]. LPO, Wolfgang Sawallisch.

Anyone who fancies a nature tone-poem as lusciously evocative as any Delius to accompany their Brahms will find the Chailly version the perfect answer. The Webern makes the perfect 'Guess what?' item, and the Brahms performance is attractively fresh and direct, superbly played and recorded in full, bright, Decca sound, with plenty of detail. Chailly prefers a relatively plain and detached Brahms style with generally steady tempi, but there is no lack of warmth either. Only in an account of the third movement that is rather short on charm does the directness obtrude at all. However, among modern versions Abbado's account with the BPO now stands as an easy first choice, particularly when, with Marjana Lipovšek a radiant soloist, it also contains a gravely beautiful account of the *Alto rhapsody* (DG 427 643-2; *427 643-4*).

Bernstein's live 1982 recording is here reissued in DG's Brahms Edition, with the *Tragic overture* added to the original coupling. It is a warm, expansive account, notably less free and idiosyncratic than the others in Bernstein's Vienna cycle, yet comparably rhythmic and equally spontaneous-sounding. With good recording, considering the limitations of a live concert, this is worth considering at mid-price.

In course of rescuing as many Horenstein performances as possible from oblivion, Unicorn Kanchana lighted on this highly characterful account of the *Second Symphony*, recorded live in Copenhagen in March 1972. The reading – which includes the first-movement exposition repeat – is marked by spaciousness and lyricism, and only in the finale, which avoids any suspicion of whipping up excitement, will some listeners feel that the result is a shade reserved, though the performance does not lack spontaneous feeling. Well-balanced radio recording, which has transferred well to CD. The effect is not too studio-ish and has plenty of warmth; even if the Danish violins do not have the body of tone of, say, the Berlin Philharmonic, they play with fine ensemble and considerable ardour, and there is no shrillness. The recording includes a 20-minute BBC interview, with the conductor talking to Alan Blyth. This will be of interest to admirers of the conductor, although it has no connection with the present record; he talks about other composers, Mahler and Berg included.

Sawallisch's live performances of Brahms have consistently revealed his warm understanding, and there is much to enjoy in his reading of No. 2. Yet this performance is less bitingly dramatic than it might be, thanks to a recording balance which sets the orchestra at a slight distance and fails to register the full impact of sforzandos. There is no exposition repeat in the first movement, but the fill-up is more generous than most, a generally expansive reading of the *Variations on a theme of Haydn* that only occasionally reveals Sawallisch at his tautest.

Sir Colin Davis and the Bavarian Radio Orchestra give a refined reading, very plain in its Brahmsian manners, but the distancing of sound blunts the impact, undermining the freshness and making the result sound too cautious. As with Sawallisch, there is no exposition repeat in the first movement. The *Overture* is similarly slow and well-mannered.

(i) *Symphonies Nos. 2–3;* (ii) *Academic festival overture.*
(B) **(*) DG Compact Classics *415 334-4*. (i) VPO, Boehm; (ii) BPO, Abbado.

Boehm's readings of the two middle symphonies will seem to most Brahmsians more idiosyncratic than those of Nos. 1 and 4, though the conductor himself might have pointed out that he learned his Brahms interpretations from the composer's friend, Eusebius Mandyczewski. His approach to the *Second Symphony* is certainly volatile in the first movement, with the *Adagio* very expansive indeed. But here the conductor's moulded style rivets the attention and one quickly accepts the extra spaciousness. After a gracefully phrased *Allegretto*, the finale is strong. The *Third Symphony* is very broadly conceived, the reins held comparatively slackly throughout until the finale, where the increased momentum creates a sense of apotheosis. The recordings date from 1976 and sound well, with the Vienna strings given more body than in the original LP issue of No. 2. The excellent account of the *Academic festival overture* by Abbado makes a good bonus for a chrome cassette already offered at bargain price.

Symphony No. 3 in F, Op. 98; Serenade No. 1 in D, Op. 11.
**(*) ASV Dig. CDDCA 745; *ZCDCA 745* [id.]. Philh. O, d'Avalos.

Symphony No. 3 in F; Tragic overture; (i) *Song of Destiny (Schicksalslied), Op. 54.*
*** DG Dig. 429 765-2; *429 765-4* [id.]. BPO, Abbado; (i) with Ernest-Senff Ch.

Symphony No. 3 in F; Variations on a theme of Haydn, Op. 56a.
(B) *** Sony CD 42022 [id.]. Columbia SO, Bruno Walter.

Symphony No. 3 in F; (i) *Alto rhapsody, Op. 53.*
* Ph. Dig. 426 253-2; *426 253-4* [id.]. (i) J. Norman, Choral Arts Soc., Phd. O, Muti.

As in his earlier recording of No. 2 with the Berlin Philharmonic, Abbado directs a glowing, affectionate performance of No. 3, adopting generally spacious speeds and finely moulded phrasing but never sounding self-conscious, thanks to the natural tension which gives the illusion of live, spontaneous music-making. The rich, well-balanced, clean-textured recording underlines the big dramatic contrasts, and the playing matches the finest achieved by this great orchestra in the Karajan period, smooth still but with more emphasis on clarity. This now heads the list of modern digital recordings of this symphony. The *Tragic overture* brings a brisk, keenly dramatic performance, and the rare cantata makes a very welcome extra, given a warm, intense performance, beautifully sung.

Bruno Walter's *Third* is highly recommendable, both as a performance and as a recording. His pacing is admirable and the vigour and sense of joy which imbues the opening of the first movement (exposition repeat included) dominates throughout, with the second subject eased in with wonderful naturalness. The central movements provide contrast, though with an intense middle section in II. There is beautifully phrased string and horn playing in the *Poco Allegretto.* The finale goes splendidly, the secondary theme given characteristic breadth and dignity and the softening of mood for the coda sounding structurally inevitable. The CD transfer brings soaring upper strings, excellent detail with glowing woodwind, and a supporting weight. The account of the *Variations* is relaxed and smiling, with deft and affectionate detail, moving forward to a majestic restatement of the chorale. The recording is clear and spacious.

The ASV version brings a fresh, thrustful account of the *Third Symphony* from d'Avalos and the Philharmonia, well played and warmly recorded, though with some clouding through reverberation. What distinguishes the disc is the winningly genial account of the *Serenade* that comes as a generous fill-up, with rustic overtones brought out and rhythms delectably sprung.

The low tension of Muti's account of the *Third Symphony* is emphasized when, with the arrival of Jessye Norman as soloist in the *Alto rhapsody*, the whole atmosphere is transformed. It is sad that so glorious a performance of that autumnal masterpiece should be linked to a surprisingly dull account of the symphony, which is also marred by the muzzy sound that is characteristic of this series.

Symphonies Nos. 3 in F, Op. 90; 4 in E min., Op. 98.
(M) *** DG 431 593-2; *431 593-4* [id.]. BPO, Karajan.

In his 1978 recording Karajan gives superb grandeur to the opening of the *Third Symphony* but then characteristically refuses to observe the exposition repeat which, in this of all Brahms's first movements, is necessary as a balance to the others. Comparing this reading with Karajan's earlier, 1964 version (available, coupled with No. 2, on DG 429 153-2; *429 153-4*), one finds him more direct, noticeably less mannered in his treatment of the third movement and strikingly more dynamic and compelling. Though one may criticize the recording balance, the result is powerful and immediate. In the *Fourth Symphony* Karajan refuses to overstate the first movement, starting with deceptive reticence. His easy lyrical style, less moulded in this 1978 reading than in his

1964 account, is fresh and unaffected and highly persuasive. The scherzo, fierce and strong, leads to a clean, weighty account of the finale. The overall performance is very satisfying. The recording is vivid but, as with the *F major Symphony*, balances are not quite natural.

Symphony No. 4 in E min., Op. 98.
**(*) Chesky CD 6 [id.]. RPO, Fritz Reiner (with BEETHOVEN: *Egmont overture*, cond. René Leibowitz).
*(*) RCA Dig. RD 60383 [60383-2-RC]. Bav. RSO, Sir Colin Davis.

Symphony No. 4 in E min., Op. 98; Academic festival overture.
(B) ** Sony MBK 44959 [id.]. Cleveland O, Szell.

Symphony No. 4 in E min.; Academic festival overture; Tragic overture.
(M) ** Sony SBK 46330; *40-46330* [id.]. Cleveland O, Szell.

Symphony No. 4 in E min.; Hungarian dances Nos. 5 & 6.
**(*) Ph. Dig. 426 391-2 [id.]. Saito Kinen O, Ozawa.

Symphony No. 4 in E min.; Tragic overture.
*** DG Dig. 429 403-2; *429 403-4* [id.]. VPO, Giulini.
** EMI Dig. CDC7 54060-2; *EL 754060-4* [id.]. LPO, Wolfgang Sawallisch.

Symphony No. 4; Variations on a theme by Haydn (St Anthony chorale), Op. 56a.
(M) *** Decca 430 440-2; *430 440-4* [id.]. Chicago SO, Solti.

Very characteristically, Giulini takes the most spacious view in his live recording with the Vienna Philharmonic, and though in principle the speeds are too slow, the result has a radiance and luminosity that magnetically set it apart. As the delicate opening demonstrates, Giulini's affectionate control of line completely disguises any slowness, and in the development the big, dramatic fortissimo contrasts bring a rugged manner, equally compelling. The great melody of the slow movement is rapt and refined as well as warm, and the last two movements bring satisfyingly extreme contrasts of tension and dynamic, helped by the rich and refined recording. The *Tragic overture* is given a similarly spacious and affectionate reading, with slow speeds again masterfully sustained. There is no applause at the end of either work, suggesting that there was an editing session after the live concert.

Solti's *Fourth*, the finest of his cycle, returns to the catalogue at mid-price with a comparably fine account of the *Variations* as coupling. The reading shows him at his most vibrantly individual when, after a very direct, strongly motivated first movement, his view of the *Andante moderato* second movement is more an *Adagio*, unfailingly pure and eloquent. The scherzo has ebullience and the finale undoubted power. The playing of the Chicago orchestra is magnificent and the recording, full and precise, has been remastered for this latest CD appearance and the bass (previously boomily resonant) made firm.

Reiner's *Fourth*, one of his rare recordings with the RPO, was made for *Reader's Digest* in the early 1960s. It is one of the tautest readings available, without any loss of warmth. The RPO made this record with Beecham personnel still present, and the incisive playing brings strength as well as warmth and polish. The first movement may strike some readers as too fast and its opening not sufficiently spacious, but few would question its sense of flow and urgency. The excellent recording was made in Walthamstow Town Hall. Leibowitz provides a vibrant filler in a strong account of the *Egmont overture*. However, the attractions of this reissue are diminished by its no longer being in the mid-price range, as it once was on LP.

The Saito Kinen Orchestra, formed in 1984 to commemorate the work of the great Japanese cellist, conductor and teacher, Hideo Saito, gives a superb demonstration of its playing here under its co-founder, Seiji Ozawa. Balance and ensemble are immaculate, and the sound – on the reverberant side but not too seriously – allows the freshness of a generally brisk, plain reading to come over well. Only in the passacaglia finale does the performance lose some of its bite.

As ever, Sawallisch reveals himself to be a sympathetic Brahmsian, and he starts amiably at the most relaxed speed, and then he effectively tautens the argument at a much faster basic tempo for the movement. Unfortunately, the distancing in the sound prevents dynamic contrasts from having their full effect, most seriously so in the last two movements. The slow movement is beautifully done, though there the great cello melody is too recessed to come over clearly. There is much more bite in Sawallisch's account of the *Tragic overture*, which comes as fill-up.

Szell's account of Brahms's *Fourth* is unexpectedly relaxed: his tempi for all four movements are slower than Karajan's. In spite of fine orchestral playing and plenty of lyrical feeling, he does not exert his usual grip, although the finale knits together impressively in the closing pages. The *Academic festival overture* is also comparatively mellow. The remastered sound, from the mid-1960s, is both clear and full. This is available at either bargain or mid-price with, in the latter case, the *Tragic overture* also included.

Davis's light, easy manner at the start immediately reveals his sympathy. As in his other Brahms recordings with the Bavarian orchestra, his approach is rather plain and detached, but there are signs of affection too. What undermines a recommendation is the distancing of sound, which blunts the impact of the last two movements. The absence of coupling also makes the disc uncompetitive.

Variations on a theme by Haydn, Op. 56a.
(M) ** Sony CD 46247 [id.]. Marlboro Festival O, Casals – BEETHOVEN: *Symphony No. 2* etc.**

The Casals account is a concert performance recorded at the Marlboro Festival, Vermont, in 1969 and is broad, spacious and eminently straightforward, an account that well deserves to be heard. The sound is of course somewhat dated, and the string-tone needs more bloom, but nothing Casals did was without stature or interest.

CHAMBER MUSIC

Cello sonatas Nos. 1 in E min., Op. 38; 2 in F, Op. 99.
(M) (**) Decca mono 425 973-2 [id.]. Fournier, Backhaus (with BACH: *Viola da gamba sonata in G, BWV 1027*, partnered by Ernest Lush).
*(*) BMG/RCA Dig. RD 71255; *RK 71255*. Ofra Hornay, William Aide.

That aristocrat of cellists, Pierre Fournier, recorded the two Brahms *Sonatas* with Backhaus in 1955 in Victoria Hall, Geneva. The sound is surprisingly – though not unacceptably – dry and the frequency range is constricted. These fine performances are a welcome reminder of Fournier's art and it is worth making allowances for the sonic limitations.

We felt the need for a stronger interpretative profile and a bigger sound when we first heard the 1983 Ofra Hornay/ William Aide reecord. That verdict stands, for the playing, though undoubtedly sensitive, lacks the strong personality this music requires and the balance rather favours the piano. There are no liner notes. Rostropovich and Serkin (DG

410 510-2) are much to be preferred. Harrell and Ashkenazy on Decca (414 558-2) give almost ideal performances; however, their recording is a little diffuse in focus.

(i) *Clarinet quintet in B min., Op. 115;* (ii) *Clarinet sonata No. 2 in E flat, Op. 120/2.*
(M) *** Chan. CHAN 6522 [id.]. Janet Hilton, (i) Lindsay Qt; (ii) Peter Frankl.

Janet Hilton's essentially mellow performance of the *Clarinet quintet*, with the Lindsay Quartet playing with pleasing warmth and refinement, has a distinct individuality. She creates quite a strong solo profile and her boldness is especially striking in the *Zigeuner* interlude at the centre of the *Adagio*, where she provides an exciting burst of bravura. Her lilting syncopations in the third movement are delightful and the theme and variations of the finale are full of character. The 1980 analogue recording has a natural presence without being obtrusively close. Hilton's partnership with Peter Frankl in the *E flat Clarinet sonata* is rather less idiosyncratic and individual; nevertheless, this performance offers considerable artistic rewards, even if the resonance means that the aural focus is a little diffuse. The balance is otherwise natural and makes this a good mid-priced recommendation.

Clarinet trio in A min., Op. 114; Piano quintet in F min., Op. 34.
*** Decca Dig. 425 839-2; *425 839-4* [id.]. Ashkenazy, Cleveland O Qt.

Vladimir Ashkenazy and musicians from the Cleveland Orchestra give impressive accounts of both the *A minor Clarinet trio*, that Brahms wrote towards the end of his life for Richard Mühlfeld, and the *F minor Piano quintet*, which had given him so many problems thirty years earlier. In the *Quintet* the playing has fire and authority, and there is plenty of warmth. The Decca recording is excellent and in the best traditions of the house. This issue more than holds its own with the best of the current opposition (Previn and the Musikverein Quartet on Telarc, and Pollini and the Quartetto Italiano on DG); indeed many collectors will be happier with it.

(i) *Horn trio in E flat, Op. 40;* (ii) *String sextet No. 2 in G, Op. 36.*
❀ (M) **(*) Sony SMK 46249 [id.]. (i) Myron Bloom, Michael Tree, Rudolph Serkin; (ii) Pina Carmirelli, Toth, Naegele, Caroline Levine, Arico, Reichenberger.

(i) *Horn trio in E flat, Op. 40;* (ii) *Liebeslieder waltzes, Op. 52.*
(M) *(**) Sony stereo/mono MPK 46448 [id.]. Rudolph Serkin, with (i) Myron Bloom, Michael Tree; (ii) Fleisher, Valente, Kleinman, Conner, Singer.

The performance of the *Horn trio*, recorded at the Marlboro Festival in 1960, is quite splendid, the warmly romantic feeling of the first movement matched by subtlety of colour in the *Adagio* and the wonderful bite and rhythmic exhilaration of the scherzo and finale. Myron Bloom's horn playing is superb, and Michael Tree matches his lyrical feeling, while Serkin holds the performance together so that, when the fervour of the music-making brings a few slips in rhythmic precision, the listener is carried along by the exhilaration of the moment.

The *Trio* comes paired with another Marlboro performance, of the *G major String sextet*, by a string group led by Pina Carmirelli. Recorded in 1967, is at an altogether lower voltage. But even if the playing is not in any way memorable, its direct response to one of Brahms's most lyrical string works is not unappealing. The sound is quite well matched and balanced, if a little thin on top (though not edgy). But the *Horn trio* is unforgettable and earns our Rosette: one all too rarely experiences this kind of inspiration and fire in music-making on a record, and the sound is remarkably vivid.

The alternative coupling offering the *Liebeslieder waltzes* is much less successful. The voice of the soprano, Benita Valente, does not seem tailor-made for this work and it is the gentler numbers that come off best; elsewhere, the presentation has more vigour than subtlety. The recording is fully acceptable.

Piano quartet No. 3 in C min., Op. 60.
(M) ** BMG/RCA GD 87873; *GK 87873* [7873-2-RG; *7873-4-RG*]. Lateiner, Heifetz, Schonbach, Piatigorsky – BEETHOVEN: *Trio*; SCHUBERT: *Fantaisie.***

This is a powerful, big-boned performance of the *C minor Piano quartet* (at times perhaps a bit too high-powered, but let that pass). However, the dry, boxed-in acoustic diminishes the pleasure these players give.

Piano quintet in F min., Op. 34.
(BB) *** Naxos Dig. 8.550406 [id.]. Jenö Jandó, Kodály Qt – SCHUMANN: *Piano quintet.****

(i) *Piano quintet in F min., Op. 34. Ballade, Op. 10/4; 3 Fantaisies, Op. 116/3, 4 & 7.*
** RCA Dig. RD 86673 [6673-2-RC]. Barry Douglas, (i) with Tokyo Qt.

Although not quite as refined, either as a performance or as a recording, as the Ashkenazy Decca version, above (coupled with the *Clarinet trio*), this fine Naxos account has a great deal going for it, even though (unlike the Decca Cleveland version) it does not include the first-movement exposition repeat. The playing is boldly spontaneous and has plenty of fire and expressive feeling. The opening of the finale has mystery too and, overall, with full-bodied recording and plenty of presence, this makes a strong impression. It is certainly a bargain.

The Douglas version of the Brahms *Quintet* first appeared in 1987 and was discussed in our 1988 volume. Listening again, we found it rather more enjoyable this time, though it does not really have quite the urgency or tension this music requires. The Tokyo Quartet is not ideal in Brahms, producing a cultured but slightly sweet sonority that does not wholly harmonize with the bigger sound the pianist provides. The piano fill-ups are thoughtfully and sensitively played.

String quartets Nos. 1 in C min.; 2 in A min., Op. 51/1–2.
*** Decca Dig. 425 526-2; *425 526-4* [id.]. Takács Qt.

The Takács Quartet coupling of the *C minor* and *A minor Quartets* has vitality and sensitivity, and their accounts of both works are eminently well shaped. The recording is not as reverberant as their Haydn Op. 76 of some years ago and in most respects they are to be preferred to the Melos on DG and may be recommended alongside the Gabrielis on Chandos (CHAN 8562; *ABTD 1264*).

String quartet No. 1 in C min., Op. 51/1.
** DG Dig. 431 650-2 [id.]. Emerson Qt – SCHUMANN: *String quartet No. 3.**

The Emerson Quartet's account of the *C minor Quartet* is pretty high-powered, but the work can survive the chromium-plated sonority and thrusting rhythmic accents more successfully than the Schumann with which it is coupled. It is all brightly lit, played with dazzling virtuosity and precise ensemble, but in the slow movement there is little sense of repose.

String sextets Nos. 1 in B flat, Op. 18; 2 in G, Op. 36.
(M) **(*) EMI CDM7 63531-2 [id.]. Y. Menuhin, Masters, Aronowitz, E. Wallfisch, Gendron, Simpson.

Menuhin's group of star players integrate well together and transmit their enjoyment of these warmly lyrical works. The performances are relaxed and often agreeably affectionate, with the last two movements of the G major work particularly beguiling. Perhaps both opening movements could have more grip, but the spirit of the music is well projected; the mid-1960s recording has retained its original warmth and it now has greater freshness and is better defined, without edginess.

String sextet No. 2 in G, Op. 36.
* EMI Dig. CDC7 54140-2 [id.]. Vienna String Sextet – SCHOENBERG: *Verklaerte Nacht.**

Rather surprisingly, given their provenance, the Vienna String Sextet do not make a particularly beautiful sound and their leader is rather too dominant. There is little real sense of forward movement or vitality. This comes with a somewhat unmagical account of Schoenberg's *Verklaerte Nacht.* No challenge here to the Raphael (see our main volume, p. 216), who couple both *Sextets* together (Hyperion CDA 66276), or, for that matter, Menuhin's mid-price reissue (see above).

Violin sonatas Nos. 1 in G, Op. 78; 2 in A, Op. 100; 3 in D min., Op. 108.
*** Sony Dig. SK 45819 [id.]. Itzhak Perlman, Daniel Barenboim.
(M) *** DG 431 599-2; *431 599-4* [id.]. Pinchas Zukerman, Daniel Barenboim.

Both Perlman and Barenboim already have versions of the three Brahms *Violin sonatas* in the CD catalogue, but with different partners. This Sony recording, made at a live recital in Chicago, finds Perlman in far more volatile form, more urgently persuasive with naturally flowing speeds and more spontaneous rubato than he adopts in his spacious readings with Ashkenazy on EMI. Barenboim too is less aggressive and more fanciful than he was with Zukerman on DG. The sound is more limited in dynamic range than the earlier, studio recordings but is still very acceptable, and this makes a very enjoyable concert.

Zukerman and Barenboim, recorded in 1975, re-emerge as strong contenders for this triptych, now that DG have reissued their performances at mid-price – see our main volume, p. 217.

Violin sonata No. 2 in A, Op. 100.
(B) *** DG Compact Classics *415 615-4* [id.]. Christian Ferras, Pierre Barbizet – BEETHOVEN: *Violin sonatas 5 & 9.****

This intimately lyrical performance of the *A major Sonata* is most enjoyable. It is placed on side one of the Compact Classics cassette, immediately following the Menuhin/Kempff version of Beethoven's *Spring sonata*, and acts as an excellent foil to it. The recording is truthful and the transfers excellent.

PIANO MUSIC

4 Ballades, Op. 10; 7 Fantasias, Op. 116; Hungarian dances Nos. 1–10; (i) *Nos. 11–21. 3 Intermezzi, Op. 117; 8 Piano pieces, Op. 76; 6 Piano pieces, Op. 118; 4 Piano pieces, Op. 119; Piano sonata Nos.1 in C, Op. 1; 2 in F sharp min., Op. 2; 3 in F min., Op. 5; 2 Rhapsodies, Op. 79; Variations on a Hungarian song, Op. 21/2; Variations on a theme by Paganini, Op. 35; Variations and fugue on a theme by Handel, Op. 24; Variations on a theme by Schumann, Op. 9; Variations on an original theme, Op. 21/1; Waltzes, Op. 39.*
(M) **(*) Decca mono/stereo 430 053-2 (6) [id.]. Julius Katchen, (i) with Marty.

Brahms often brought out the best in Katchen, and he is particularly good in the impulsive early music. If at times one could make small criticisms, the spontaneity and understanding are always there, and of course the excitement that comes when bravura is controlled by a sensitive and musical mind. Katchen's style in Brahms is distinctive: there is a boldness about it that suits some works better than others. In general the bigger, tougher pieces come off better than the gentle *Intermezzi* of Opp. 116 and 117, which lack the sort of inner tension that Bishop-Kovacevich can convey. Yet even so there is much beautiful playing here, especially in Op. 117/1 and 2, while Katchen's free, musing rubato in Op. 119/1 is most appealing, and Op. 119/4 shows him at his most masterful. Such pieces as the two *Rhapsodies*, Op. 79, are splendidly done, and so are the *Ballades*. The *Waltzes*, brief trivial ideas but on the whole extrovert, come somewhere in between. Katchen's playing in the first two *Sonatas* hardly achieves the compelling intensity of some of his rivals, but the result is always exciting. The playing is extremely brilliant and assured, and a certain lack of resilience in the style scarcely mars the performances, rather giving them a tough individuality; and his account of Op. 5 is similarly commanding. The lesser-known *Variations on a Hungarian song* and *On an original theme*, plus those *On a theme by Schumann* are particularly successful. They are played with the utmost persuasiveness and artistry. On the other hand, the *Handel* and *Paganini* sets, Opp. 24 and 35, are very extrovert in style and, for all their pyrotechnical display, lack a degree of spontaneity, though not excitement. Katchen plays Book One of the *Hungarian dances*, usually given in their chamber version as piano duets, in Brahms's later arrangement for piano solo; the remaining dances are offered in the more traditional form with Jean-Pierre Marty as Katchen's partner. On CD the recordings, made between 1962 and 1966, are remarkably realistic, full in timbre and with good presence. The four *Ballades* are mono. A fine set which will give much satisfaction. But it is a pity that the cueing is so ungenerous in the *Variations* and (especially) the *Waltzes*.

4 Ballades, Op. 10.
*** Ph. Dig. 426 439-2; *426 439-4* [id.]. Alfred Brendel – WEBER: *Piano sonata No. 2.****

A thoughtful (and at times self-aware) account of the Op. 10 *Ballades* in a wonderfully clear, digital recording. There is some highlighting of subsidiary part-writing that may strike some as just a little self-conscious but much else that will delight the listener. This is playing of stature that should be heard by all the great pianist's admirers. The Gilels set, now available with his Brahms *D minor concerto* (see above), or the Bishop-Kovacevich are no less masterly and authoritative, yet are a shade more spontaneous in feeling.

4 Ballades, Op. 10; 6 Pieces, Op. 118; Variations on an original theme; Variations on a Hungarian song, Op. 21/1–2.
*(*) RCA/Eurodisc Dig. RD 69247 [in 69245-2-RG (5)]. Gerhard Oppitz.

Gerhard Oppitz is much admired in Germany; he was a pupil of Kempff whose mantle he appears to have inherited. There is a long essay on him in the notes (at least as long as that on the music) which shows the esteem in which he is held in his native country. It is obvious from his five-disc Brahms set (all of them available separately in the UK, and as a box set in both the UK and the USA) that he is a dedicated and intelligent Brahmsian, though he is not always subtle in his use of colour or dynamics and, in that respect, cannot match his mentor. He has a commanding technique and is thoroughly inside this composer's mind. He plays a Bösendorfer Imperial which might have sounded better in a more appropriate acoustic. As it is, it is dryish and clattery in certain registers, twangy in others. It sounds as if the artist is in a small domestic environment but projecting as though he were in a large concert hall; the closely balanced recording does not give his pianissimo playing space in which to register, and the effect is curiously unpleasing. This is true of all five CDs.

7 Fantasias, Op. 116; 2 Rhapsodies, Op. 79; Scherzo in E flat min., Op. 4; Variations on a theme by Paganini, Op. 35.
*(*) RCA/Eurodisc Dig. RD 69249 [in 69245-2-RG (5)]. Gerhard Oppitz.

In fairness we would urge readers to investigate Gerhard Oppitz's Brahms records for themselves, since matters of sound-quality can be very personal. The longer we hear this set, the uglier the sound seems; the twangy octaves of the very opening *B minor Rhapsody* may not worry you so much as they did us, for we soon succumbed to aural fatigue. No quarrels with Oppitz's Brahmsian instincts, and much admiration for his technical command. In the Op. 116 *Pieces*, readers will find Gilels (DG) or Stephen Bishop-Kovacevich infinitely more satisfying on all counts.

Intermezzi, Op. 117; 6 Pieces, Op. 118; Variations on a theme by Paganini, Op. 35.
*** DG Dig. 431 123-2 [id.]. Lilya Zilberstein.

Lilya Zilberstein made an impressive début with a Rachmaninov/Shostakovich disc and her Brahms is hardly less striking, even if it would not necessarily be a first choice. She has flawless technique and keen musical instincts. The instrument is in perfect condition and sounds excellent, and the recording is marvellously present and clear (one can almost see one's own reflection in the high black polish of the grand piano). In Opp. 116 and 118 Lupu and Bishop-Kovacevich have the greater maturity and wisdom and, in the former, Gilels is also to be preferred. In the *Paganini variations* she can hold her own in the present catalogue.

Piano sonata No. 1 in C, Op. 1; 4 Pieces, Op. 119; Variations & fugue on a theme by Handel, Op 24.
*(*) RCA/Eurodisc Dig. RD 69246 [in 69245-2-RG (5)]. Gerhard Oppitz.

Gerhard Oppitz is handicapped throughout his series by the sound-quality. His is big-boned, no-nonsense Brahms and he is obviously a thoughtful player. In the *C major Sonata* the reader is infinitely better served, both artistically and technically, by Krystian Zimerman (DG) and, in the *Handel variations* by Osorio (ASV), Bolet and Katchen (both Decca).

Piano sonata No. 2 in F sharp min., Op. 2; 3 Intermezzi, Op. 117; 8 Pieces, Op. 76.
* RCA/Eurodisc Dig. RD 69248 [in 69245-2-RG (5)]. Gerhard Oppitz.

There is little real pianissimo here, though the fault is not entirely that of Gerhard Oppitz. He is recorded relatively closely in an unflattering acoustic on his Imperial Bösendorfer. He is not always the most poetic of pianists, but he has a keen musical intelligence and makes a stronger impression in the flesh than he does here. Readers wanting the *Intermezzi* should look to Lupu (Decca) or Stephen Bishop-Kovacevic (Philips) and, as far as the *F sharp minor Sonata* is concerned, Zimerman (DG), Katchen (Decca) or Jorge-Federico Osorio (ASV) are more competitive.

Piano sonata No. 3 in F min., Op. 5; Variations on a theme by Schumann, Op. 9; 16 Waltzes, Op. 39.
*(*) RCA/Eurodisc Dig. RD 69250 [in 69245-2-RG (5)]. Gerhard Oppitz.

Gerhard Oppitz's account of the *F minor Sonata* is a strong one, but the oppressive recording (and the tonal limitations of his Imperial Bösendorfer) induces aural fatigue. Be that as it may (and some readers may not be so troubled by the actual sound-quality), this set presents no challenge to Lupu (Decca), Zimerman (DG) or Kocsis (Hungaroton).

Piano sonata No. 3 in F min., Op. 5; 3 Intermezzi, Op. 117.
**(*) Sony Dig. SK 45933 [id.]. Emanuel Ax.

After RCA's Oppitz recordings, the ear takes very readily to the quality Sony provide for Emanuel Ax. He gives an appropriately massive performance, but the fortissimo he produces is never ugly and his pianissimo tone is always most refined and of great beauty. The slow movement in particular is played with great tenderness and poetic feeling. There is plenty of space round the aural image, and the sound is a joy in itself. Although he is an artist of the highest intelligence, Ax is at times prone to moments of expressive exaggeration and phrases are sometimes self-consciously moulded, almost cosseted, as if he did not quite trust the music to speak for itself. This disc has much going for it, but, for all its many beauties and the excellence of the recorded sound, it does not displace Zimerman or Lupu, who are equally thoughtful and polished but straighter.

VOCAL MUSIC

Lieder: *Ach, wende diesen Blick; Die Mainacht; Heimweh; Mädchenlied; Meine Liebe ist grün; O kühler Wald; Ständchen; Unbewegte laue Luft; Von ewiger Liebe; Wie rafft' ich mich auf; Wiegenlied.* (i) *2 Songs with viola: (Gestille Sehnsucht & Geistliches Wiegenlied) Op. 91.* 3 Volkslieder: *Dort in den Weiden; Sonntag; Vergebliches Ständchen. 8 Zigeunerlieder Op. 103/1–7 & 11.*
*** DG Dig. 429 727-2 [id.]. Anne Sofie von Otter, Bengt Forsberg, (i) with Nils-Erik Sparf.

Anne Sofie von Otter gives these Brahms Lieder the natural freshness of folksong, which so often they resemble, or even quote, as in the radiant melody of *Sonntag*. Aptly, the collection begins with eight of the often rumbustious *Gypsy songs* of Opus 103 and embraces songs from the early *Wie rafft' ich mich auf*, written when Brahms was thirty, through the Daumer settings, Op. 57, to the later songs of Opp. 106 and 107. Von Otter's open, easy style conceals high art in the poise and control of her exceptionally beautiful and even mezzo voice. She phrases unerringly, holding and changing tension and mood as in a live recital. Compared with some, there is still a degree of expressive restraint – as in *Von ewiger Liebe* – but there are few Brahms song-recital discs to match this one, and her accompanist is the strongly supportive Bengt Forsberg, who plays with intelligence and sensitivity. In the Op. 91 settings they are joined by Nils-Erik Sparf, who plays with admirable taste. A varied, well-chosen and beautifully recorded programme that will give pleasure to this artist's admirers.

(i) *Alto rhapsody, Op. 53. 4 Gesänge, Op. 17.*
*** Virgin Dig. VC7 91123-2; *VC7 91123-4* [id.]. (i) J. Baker; LSO Ch., L. Sinf., Hickox – MENDELSSOHN: *Infelice* etc.***

Alto rhapsody, Op. 53; Song of destiny (Schicksalslied), Op. 54.
(M) ** Sony MYK 45503 [id.]; *40-45503*. Mildred Miller, Occidental College Concert Ch., Columbia SO, Bruno Walter – MAHLER: *Lieder eines fahrenden Gesellen.***

Though the Virgin recording of the *Alto rhapsody* was recorded after Dame Janet's retirement from the concert platform, the voice is in glorious condition, superbly controlled. This is a more openly expressive and spacious reading than her earlier, EMI one with Boult, matching her performances in the two Mendelssohn items. The four early

Brahms songs, Opus 17, for women's chorus with two horns and harp accompaniment, are delightfully done.

Mildred Miller is a fresh rather than an inspirational soloist in the *Alto rhapsody* and, despite coaching from Walter (who had decided views on the interpretation of this fine work), she gives a somewhat strait-laced account of the opening pages. The *Song of destiny* is very satisfactory, however, and displays the capability of the chorus to good effect. The CD transfers are well managed, with the orchestral detail in the *Rhapsody*, and the fine choral singing in both works, showing that Walter's directing hand has a special contribution to make.

Lieder: *An Die Nachtigall; Bottschaft; Dein blaues Auge hält so still; Feldeinsamkeit; Der Gang zum Liebchen; Geheimnis; Im Waldeseinsamkeit; Komm bald; Die Kränze; Die Mainacht; Meine Liebe ist grün; Minnelied; Nachtigall; O wüsst ich doch den Weg zurück; Sah dem edlen Bildnis; Salamander; Die Schale der Vergessenheit; Serenade; Sonntag; Ständchen; Von ewiger Liebe; Von waldbekränzter Höhe; Wie bist du, Meine Königin; Wiegenlied; Wir Wandelten.*
*** Virgin Dig. VC7 91130-2 [id.]. Thomas Allen, Geoffrey Parsons.

Thomas Allen, in one of his most successful Lieder records yet, gives fresh, virile performances of a particularly attractive collection of Brahms songs. There is less underlining of words than in Brahms sung by Fischer-Dieskau or Bär but still a keen and detailed feeling for meaning as well as mood. If one generally associates the great song *Von ewiger Liebe* with a woman's voice, Allen triumphantly shows what benefits there are from having a baritone, hushed and intimately confidential at the start and bitingly powerful at the climax in heightened contrast. There are many such felicities here, with Geoffrey Parsons an ever-sympathetic accompanist and with sound more cleanly focused than in earlier Lieder issues from this source.

Ave Maria, Op. 12; 3 Fest- und Gedensprüche, Op. 109; Geistliche Chöre, Op. 37; Geistliches Lied, Op. 30; 2 Motets, Op. 29; 2 Motets, Op. 74; 3 Motets, Op. 110; Psalm 13, Op. 27.
** Hyp. Dig. CDA 66389; *KA 66389* [id.]. Corydon Singers, Matthew Best.

This exactly duplicates the sixteen items included on the outstanding Conifer issue from the Trinity College Choir (CDCF 178 – see our main volume, p. 223). The singing here is also first rate, but the recording is far too washy, diluting the effect of the singing. The Conifer issue remains a clear first choice.

Lieder: *Dein blaues Auge hält; Dort in den Weiden; Immer leiser wird mein Schlummer; Klage I & II; Liebestreu; Des Liebsten Schwur; Das Mädchen; Das Mädchen spricht; Regenlied; Romanzen und Lieder, Op. 84; Salome; Sapphische Ode, Op. 94/4; Der Schmied;* (i) *2 Songs with viola, Op. 91; Therese; Vom Strande; Wie Melodien zieht es; Zigeunerlieder, Op. 103.*
(M) *** DG Dig. 431 600-2; *431 600-4* [id.]. Jessye Norman, Daniel Barenboim; (i) Wolfram Christ.

Jessye Norman's glorious Lieder recital with Barenboim, recorded in 1981/2, is one of the reissued mid-priced bargains in DG's Brahms Edition - see our main volume, pp. 220–1.

German requiem, Op. 45.
❀ *** Ph. Dig. 432 140-2; *432 140-4* [id.]. Margiono, Gilfry, Monteverdi Ch., O Révolutionaire et Romantique, Eliot Gardiner.

(M) *** DG Dig. 431 598-2; *431 598-4* [id.]. Popp, Wolfgang Brendel, Prague Philharmonic Ch., Czech PO, Sinopoli.
**(*) Chan. Dig. CHAN 8942; *ABTD 1506* [id.]. Lott, Wilson-Johnson, LSO Ch. & LSO, Hickox.
**(*) DG Dig. 431 651-2 [id.]. Hendricks, Van Dam, V. Singverein, VPO, Karajan.

Gardiner's 'revolutionary' account of the *German requiem* was recorded in the studio immediately after the orchestra's very first public appearances at Queen Elizabeth Hall, and the range of choral sound is even more thrilling than in the concert hall. With period instruments and following Viennese practice of the time, speeds tend to be faster than usual, but not rigid and not by much, and the result is tough, muscular and very dramatic. With relatively thin violins set against warm choral sound, the contrasts of dynamic and timbre are heightened, making this anything but small-scale. *Denn alles Fleisch* ('Then all flesh is grass') has rarely sounded so thrilling and the sixth movement ('Death is swallowed up in victory') rarely so taut, though the speed for the big fugue is surprisingly relaxed. Charlotte Margiono makes an ethereal soprano soloist, while the American baritone, Rodney Gilfry, despite a rapid vibrato, is aptly fresh and young-sounding. One could not ask for a more complete renovation of a masterpiece often made to sound stodgy and square.

The Sinopoli version of Brahms's *German requiem*, discussed and praised by us on pp. 221–2 of our main volume and already available at mid-price, is also to be had as part of DG's Brahms Edition.

With opulent Chandos recording giving weight to the choral fortissimos, Hickox directs a smoothly moulded performance at broad, slow speeds. The soprano solo, *Ich habt nun Traurigkeit*, brings one of the very slowest performances on record, yet, with Felicity Lott caught at her purest and sweetest, the tempo is well sustained. David Wilson-Johnson too is better focused than often on record. This is a warm, amiable reading, lacking the dramatic bite of the finest rivals.

The last of Karajan's four recordings of the *German requiem*, originally issued on two discs with fill-up, is here reissued on a single CD. The chorus sounds disappointingly opaque, but otherwise it is a warmly persuasive reading, not quite as polished as his previous versions but with a keener sense of spontaneity. For all her sweetness of tone, however, Barbara Hendricks does not sound innocent enough for *Ich habt nun Traurigkeit*, thanks to her rapid vibrato.

Brian, Havergal (1876–1972)

Symphony No. 1 (Gothic).
*** Marco Polo Dig. 8.223280/1; *4.223280/1* [id.]. Jenisová, Pecková, Dolezal, Mikulás, Slovak Philharmonic Ch., Slovak Nat. Theatre Op. Ch., Slovak Folk Ens. Ch., Lucnica Ch., Bratislava Chamber Ch. & Children's Ch., Youth Echo Ch., Czech RSO (Bratislava), Slovak PO, Ondrej Lenárd.

Was Havergal Brian, composer of 32 symphonies, 20 of them written after he was eighty, a genius or just an obsessed megalomaniac? Whatever the answer, this first of the symphonies, 1 hour 50 minutes long and involving performers by the hundred, here receives a passionately committed performance from Slovak forces. Despite a few incidental flaws, it conveys surging excitement from first to last, helped by a rich recording which gives a thrilling impression of massed forces. On one level this is music for wallowing in; yet on repetition it is a work which firmly establishes its landmarks in the memory, starting with such simple, direct effects as the timpani outbursts at the very start and the still horn-chords that keep echoing Wagner's *Rheingold*. The final *Te Deum*, alone lasting 72 minutes, brings fervent choral writing of formidable complexity, with the challenge superbly taken up by the Czech musicians.

Bridge, Frank (1879–1941)

Oration (Concerto elegiaco) for cello and orchestra.
(M) *** EMI Dig. CDM7 63909-2 [id.]; *EG 763909-4*. Isserlis, City of L. Sinfonia, Hickox – BRITTEN: *Symphony for cello & orchestra.****

Completed in 1930, *Oration* is in effect a massive cello concerto in nine linked sections lasting a full half-hour. It is an elegiac work which, like Bridge's ambitious *Piano sonata* of 1924, reflects the composer's continuing desolation over the deaths of so many of his friends in the First World War. As in the *Sonata*, Bridge's idea of writing an elegiac work made for the opposite of comfortable consolation. In its often gritty textures and dark concentration it is fundamentally angry music, stylistically amazing – like other late Bridge – for a British composer to have been writing at the time. Though Isserlis is not always as passionate as Julian Lloyd Webber was on the earlier, Lyrita version, his focus is sharper, and with Hickox he brings out the originality of the writing all the more cleanly. It is fascinating to find some passages anticipating the more abrasive side of Britten, and specifically the *Cello symphony* with which this is coupled.

3 Idylls for string quartet.
*** Conifer Dig. CDCF 196; *MCFC 196*. Brindisi Qt – BRITTEN: *String quartet No. 2*; Imogen HOLST: *String quartet No. 1.****

The *Three Idylls* are an early work, dating from 1906 and following close on the heels of the *First Quartet*. It was on the *Second Idyll* that Benjamin Britten based his celebrated *Variations*. They are currently unrepresented in the catalogue except by this CD, and are well served by the Brindisi Quartet.

Phantasie trio in C min.
*** Gamut Dig. GAMCD 518 [id.]. Hartley Trio – CLARKE: *Piano trio*; IRELAND: *Phantasie.****

Bridge was the most successful of the composers who took up the challenge of W. W. Cobbett to develop the idea of one-movement chamber works, incorporating various sections like the Elizabethan Fantasies. Bridge's *Phantasie trio*, just over 15 minutes long, is an urgent and passionate piece which richly deserves this revival, along with trios by other pupils of Stanford. Warmly persuasive playing, well recorded. Admirers of Frank Bridge may care to be reminded that there is an equally fine performance of the *Phantasie trio* by the Dartington Trio, superbly recorded on Hyperion (CDA 66279) and coupled with the *Phantasie quartet* and *Second piano trio* (see our main volume, p. 226).

String quartet No. 3.
*** Virgin Dig. VC7 91196-2 [id.]. Endellion Qt – WALTON: *String quartet.****

Bridge's keenly imaginative string quartets have, surprisingly, been neglected on CD, but this superb performance of what is arguably the finest of the four helps to fill a serious gap. Like the *Piano sonata*, this was a work profoundly influenced by the composer's response to the First World War and the deaths of many friends, bringing a rejection of his earlier English-based idiom. Often bald in expression, bitter and abrasive, the three large-scale movements no longer seem disturbing in their idiom, though they are still disturbing in their emotions. This is the deeply felt and original expression of a composer whose achievement lay in his own music, not just in discovering and drawing out the talents of Benjamin Britten. The Endellion Quartet, one of our very finest, plays with polish, purpose and passion, and is very well recorded.

PIANO MUSIC

Arabesque; Capriccios Nos. 1–2; Dedication; Fairy tale suite; Gargoyle; Hidden fires; In autumn; 3 Miniatures; Pastorals, Sets 1–2; Sea idyll; 3 Improvisations for the left hand; Winter pastoral.
*** Continuum Dig. CCD 1016 [id.]. Peter Jacobs.

Berceuse; Canzonetta; 4 Characteristic pieces; Dramatic fantasia; Étude rhapsodic; Lament; Pensées fugitives; 3 Pieces; 4 Pieces; 3 Poems; Scherzettino.
*** Continuum Dig. CCD 1018 [id.]. Peter Jacobs.

Piano sonata; Graziella; The Hour-glass; 3 Lyrics; Miniature pastorals, Set 3; Miniature suite (ed Hindmarsh); *3 Sketches.* arr. of BACH: *Chorale: Komm, süsser Tod, BWV 478.*
*** Continuum Dig. CCD 1019 [id.]. Peter Jacobs.

Peter Jacobs has been a consistent champion of neglected piano music, including the sonatas of Harold Truscott. Here he provides a complete survey of the piano music of Frank Bridge, and it proves an invaluable enterprise. What an intelligent and sensitive player this artist is, and how pleasing to hear an instrument in such good condition! The recorded sound is very good indeed: clean, well defined and present, and the acoustic lively. Bridge has a much larger body of keyboard music to his credit than is generally supposed, and the present set covers almost three decades of creative activity, from the *Capriccio No. 1 in A minor*, written in 1903 and entered for a competition sponsored by Mark Hambourg, through to the *Gargoyle* (1928). The *Sonata*, written in memory of his friend and fellow composer, Ernest Farrar, who was a casualty of the war in 1917, is outstanding by any standards; but many of the shorter pieces are highly imaginative, and almost everything is very rewarding. Calum MacDonald's excellent notes tracing his development over these years are worth a mention too.

Piano sonata; Capriccios Nos. 1 & 2; Ecstasy; The Hour-glass; Sea Idyll; Vignettes de Marseille.
*** Conifer Dig. CDCF 186; *MCFC 186* [id.]. Kathryn Stott.

Kathryn Stott provides a formidable and illuminating single-disc and -tape selection from the piano music of Frank Bridge, for those who are unable or unwilling to stretch to Peter Jacobs's indispensable complete survey. Kathryn Stott's recital culminates in the masterly large-scale *Sonata* that Bridge wrote in disillusion in the years after the First World War, and she gives it a powerfully concentrated account. That darkly elegiac piece marked a breakthrough in Bridge's work, when he cast aside conventional English attitudes and produced a piece which took note of the then avant garde in Europe. It is arguably the greatest piano sonata ever written by a British composer. The short early pieces, brilliantly and imaginatively written, give little inkling of such a development. The *Vignettes de Marseille* were inspired by a holiday the Bridges spent with his patron, Elizabeth Sprague Coolidge, in 1925 and are highly colourful and atmospheric display pieces which owe more to Ravel than to Schoenberg; but the three thoughtful little vignettes which make up *The Hour-glass* have a depth and originality that belie their scale, while *The Dusk* in the *The Hour-glass* almost calls to mind the Debussy of the

Études. Kathryn Stott is responsive to every changing mood, and these are outstanding performances, very well recorded.

Britten, Benjamin (1913–76)

(i) *Piano concerto in D, Op. 13; Paul Bunyan overture.*
*** Collins Dig. 1102-2; *1102-4* [id.]. (i) Joanna MacGregor; ECO, Bedford – SAXTON: *Music to celebrate the resurrection of Christ.****

When still only 26, Britten wrote his formidable *Piano concerto* for a Prom in 1938. He later rejected the slow movement, a quirky *Recitative and aria* with tongue-in-cheek hints of blues, a polka and even Rachmaninov. He replaced it in 1945 with an *Impromptu*, simpler and more obviously apt. The sparkiness of the young Britten makes the original well worth hearing too; the characterful young Joanna MacGregor gets the best of both worlds by recording both slow movements, so that you can take your pick. She may not quite match the command of Sviatoslav Richter in his classic recording of the later version with the composer conducting (now on CD, coupled with the *Violin concerto*: Decca 417 308-2), but with Steuart Bedford a deeply understanding conductor, this is a ripe and refreshing performance, well recorded. The brassy *Paul Bunyan overture*, never used with the operetta, has been orchestrated by Colin Matthews.

(i) *Violin concerto, Op. 15; Canadian carnival overture, Op. 19; Mont Juic* (written with Lennox Berkeley).
❀ *** Collins Dig. 1123-2; *1123-4* [id.]. (i) Lorraine McAslan, ECO, Steuart Bedford.

Lorraine McAslan studied with the celebrated Dorothy Delay, whose pupils included Itzhak Perlman and Cho-Liang Lin, and hers is a performance of consummate and commanding artistry. The virtuosity is effortless and always subservient to musical ends; her artistic insights are unusually keen and she brings to the *Concerto* a subtle imagination and great emotional intensity. There is a demonic fire to the scherzo which is even more effective than the composer's own version with Mark Lubotsky. Steuart Bedford gets first-class playing from the English Chamber Orchestra and underlines the pain and poignancy underlying much of this music. The recording is remarkably well balanced: those who dislike the upfront larger-than-life aural image found in so many *Concerto* recordings (Perlman's for example) will welcome this truthful and exceptionally wide-ranging and vivid recording. *Mont Juic*, written in collaboration with Lennox Berkeley, is a less rewarding score, but both this and the *Canadian carnival overture* are eminently well served by these splendid musicians and the engineers.

Matinées musicales; Soirées musicales; (i) *The Young person's guide to the orchestra, Op. 34; Peter Grimes: 4 Sea interludes & Passacaglia.*
(M) (**) EMI mono CDM7 63777-2 [id.]; *EG 763777-4*. LPO, Boult, (i) nar. Boult.

Although Boult gave many early performances of Britten's music, he never disguised the fact that he did not find an affinity with the composer's output to match the striking sympathy that he so obviously had with the music of Elgar. Neverthless he conducts Britten's Rossini arrangements with evident relish, and the LPO plays them with gusto. The *Peter Grimes interludes*, however, are a disappointment. To get the full salty flavour of Britten's music you need crisper, more biting playing than this, and an overall control which, besides being sensitive to atmosphere, has a firm emotional grip. *The Young person's guide*, however, is admirably spirited and is made something of a collector's item in including here (for the first time) Boult's own narration of Eric Crozier's script, which he does with characteristic disarming and gentlemanly simplicity. The early stereo is vividly unrefined, but quite acceptable.

Mont Juic (suite, written in conjunction with Lennox Berkeley).
(*) Collins Dig. 1031-2; *1031-4* [id.]. ECO, Steuart Bedford – WALTON: *Symphony No. 1.*

This first CD recording of the *Mont Juic suite* of Catalan dances makes an odd, ungenerous coupling for Frémaux's Walton. This joint composition by Lennox Berkeley and the young Benjamin Britten, his junior by ten years, is an appealing, colourful work, even if Berkeley's first movement – the least distinctive of the four – sounds very tame after the electricity of the Walton. The suite receives a first-rate performance from the ECO under Steuart Bedford.

Suite on English folk tunes; A time there was; The Young person's guide to the orchestra, Op. 34; Gloriana: courtly dances (suite); Peter Grimes: 4 Sea interludes & Passacaglia, Op. 34.
** Nimbus Dig. NI 5295 [id.]. English SO, William Boughton.

This is claimed as the 'première recording in Symphony Hall, Birmingham', made in April 1991 even before the hall was officially opened. Whatever the reasons, the recorded sound is disappointingly lacking in inner detail, with rapid passage-work in the *Young person's guide* disappearing in a fuzz. Nor is the orchestra's ensemble sharp enough to match that of the finest rivals. What the disc does present is an attractive collection of shorter Britten pieces; and it is valuable for including potential new favourites like the folksong suite, *A time there was*, and the *Gloriana dances*, as well as the well-known *Sea interludes* from *Peter Grimes*.

(i) *Spring Symphony, Op. 44;* (ii) *Welcome ode, Op. 95;* (iii) *Psalm 150, Op. 67.*
**(*) Chan. Dig. CHAN 8855; *ABTD 1472* [id.]. (i) Gale, Hodgson, Hill, Southend Boys' Ch., LSO; (ii) City of London Schools' Ch., LSO; (iii) City of London Schools' Ch. and O; Richard Hickox.

Richard Hickox's version brings the advantage not only of warm and refined digital sound but also of a first recording of Britten's last completed work, the *Welcome ode*, an unpretentious little suite of five movements, three of them choral, written for children only three months before he died. It makes an apt fill-up when its mood of optimism so closely reflects the exhilarating close of the *Spring Symphony*, with its descant of *Sumer is icumen in*. The third work, equally apt, is the boisterous setting of Psalm 150, which Britten wrote for the preparatory school he had attended as a boy in Lowestoft. With more variable soloists – the tenor Martyn Hill outstandingly fine, the soprano Elizabeth Gale often too edgy – Hickox's version of the *Spring Symphony* does not quite match the composer's own in gutsy urgency, even in the final ensemble, but there is compensation in the refinement of detail and of sound.

Symphony for cello and orchestra, Op. 68.
(M) *** EMI Dig. CDM7 63909-2 [id.]; *EG 763909-4*. Stephen Isserlis, City of L. Sinfonia, Hickox – BRIDGE: *Oration.****

Stephen Isserlis provides a valuable mid-priced alternative both to Rostropovich (Decca 425 100-2), inspirer of the *Cello symphony* and soloist in the first recording, and to Wallfisch on Chandos (CHAN 8363). With speeds generally a little slower, Isserlis is not quite as taut and electric as his rivals, partly because the recording does not present the solo instrument so cleanly. It remains a powerful, dramatic performance and makes excellent value, if the Bridge coupling is suitable.

The Young person's guide to the orchestra (Variations and fugue on a theme by Purcell), Op. 34.
(M) *** EMI Dig. CD-EMX 2165; *TC-EMX 2165*. LPO, Sian Edwards – PROKOFIEV: *Peter and the wolf* **(*); RAVEL: *Ma Mère l'Oye.* **

Sian Edwards, always impressive in the recording studio, provides an excellent mid-priced digital version of Britten's orchestral showpiece. She does not press the earlier variations too hard, revelling in the colour of her wind soloists, yet the violins enter zestfully and the violas make a touching contrast. The brass bring fine bite and sonority. The fugue has plenty of vitality and the climax is spectacularly expansive in the resonant acoustics of Watford Town Hall.

CHAMBER MUSIC

String quartet No. 2 in C.
*** Conifer Dig. CDCF 196; *MCFC 196*. Brindisi Qt – BRIDGE: *3 Idylls*; Imogen HOLST: *String quartet No. 1.****

The Brindisi on Conifer give an excellent account of the *Second Quartet* which can hold its own with the best and comes with interesting couplings. They are an accomplished body and are well (if a shade too forwardly) recorded.

Music for 2 pianos: (i) *2 Lullabies; Mazurca elegiaca; Introduction and Rondo alla burlesca.* (Piano): *3 Character Pieces; Holiday Diary; Notturno; Sonatina romantica; 12 Variations; Five Walztes.*
*** Virgin Dig. VC7 91203-2 [id.]. Stephen Hough, (i) with Ronan O'Hora.

Though he was a brilliant pianist himself, Britten wrote relatively little piano music. This superb disc, with Stephen Hough an inspired interpreter, generously collects it all, including early pieces revived since the composer's death. The earliest music is the charming set of *Walztes* (his original boyhood mis-spelling) that he wrote between the ages of ten and twelve, published in 1970 with only minor modification. In the *Notturno*, written for the first Leeds Piano Competition, Hough's love of keyboard sonorities masterfully overcomes the awkwardness of the writing. Hough is joined by a most sympathetic partner for the items for two pianos, the early *Lullabies* and the larger-scale wartime pieces, the *Mazurka* and the *Rondo*, both grittily demanding. Excellent sound.

Folk-song arrangements: *The ash grove; Avenging and bright; La belle est au jardin d'amour; The bonny Earl o'Moray; The brisk young widow; Ca' the yowes, Come you not from Newcastle; Early one morning; The foggy, foggy dew; How sweet the answer; The last rose of summer; The Lincolnshire poacher; The miller of Dee; The minstrel boy; Oft in the stilly night; O Waly Waly; The plough boy; Le roi s'en va-t'en chasse; Sally in our alley; Sweet Polly Oliver; Tom Bowling.*
(M) *** Decca 430 063-2 [id.]. Peter Pears, Benjamin Britten.

It is good to have the definitive Pears/Britten collaboration in the folksong arrangements back in the catalogue on CD. To the main LP recital, made in the Kingsway Hall in 1961, Decca have added four earlier recordings from 1959, including the most famous, *The foggy, foggy dew* and *The Lincolnshire poacher*, with its witty obbligato to match the whistle of *The plough boy*. Pears's voice was at its freshest, as can be heard in

Early one morning and *The ash grove*, while the French song about the king going hunting is sheer delight. Excellent, faithful recording, well transferred to CD.

A Ceremony of carols, Op. 28; Festival Te Deum; Hymn to St Colomba; Hymn to St Peter; Hymn to the Virgin; Jubilate Deo; Missa brevis; Rejoice in the Lamb, Op. 30.
(M) *** Decca 430 097-2; *430 097-4* [id.]. Tear, Forbes Robinson, St John's College Ch., Guest; Robles; Runnett.

An exceptionally attractive and generous compilation of St John's recordings, derived from the old Argo catalogue. Guest's account of the delightful *Ceremony of carols* has tingling vitality, spacious sound and a superb contribution from Marisa Robles who plays with masterly sensitivity, especially in her solo *Interlude*. The performance of *Rejoice in the Lamb* is very similar to Britten's own, but much better recorded, and the *Missa brevis* has the same striking excellence of style. Of the other items added for the CD reissue, the *Hymn to the Virgin* is an engaging early work written in 1930. All these shorter pieces show the choir in superb form and the Argo analogue engineering at its most impressive.

(i) *St Nicholas, Op. 42;* (ii) *Rejoice in the Lamb, Op. 30.*
(M) (***) Decca mono 425 714-2 [id.]. (i) Hemmings, Pears, St John Leman School, Beccles, Girls' Ch., Ipswich School Boys' Ch., Aldeburgh Festival Ch. & O; R. Downes; (ii) Hartnett, Steele, Todd, Francke, Purcell Singers, G. Malcolm; composer.

With rare exceptions, Britten's own first recordings of his own works have a freshness and vigour unsurpassed since. Here are two fine examples which vividly draw on the brightness of boys' voices – not least that of the future film star, David Hemmings, as the youthful St Nicholas. The expression may be direct but the emotions behind both these works are more complex than one might at first appreciate. Britten's performances capture the element of vulnerability, not least in the touching setting of words by the deranged poet, Christopher Smart, *Rejoice in the Lamb*.

Serenade for tenor, horn and strings.
*** ASV Dig. CDRPO 8023; *ZCRPO 8023* [id.]. Martyn Hill, Bryant, RPO, Ashkenazy – KNUSSEN: *Symphony No. 3*; WALTON: *Symphony No. 2*.***

If it seems strange that Martyn Hill has made a second recording of this masterpiece so soon after the Virgin Classics one with Hickox, the choice of Jeffrey Bryant for the horn part brings ample justification, quite apart from Ashkenazy's red-blooded direction. For many years Bryant has been an outstanding principal in the orchestra, and here at last he gets his due recognition on record in a superb performance, ripe-toned and expressive. Though, unlike the two symphonies with which it is coupled, this was recorded in the studio, Ashkenazy's reading has the expansiveness and warmth of a live performance. The oddly balanced recording – with tenor and horn set behind the strings – hardly interferes with the compulsion of the performance.

OPERA

Peter Grimes (complete).
(M) *** Ph. 432 578-2 (2) [id.]. Vickers, Harper, Summers, Bainbridge, Cahill, Robinson, Allen, ROHCG Ch. & O, C. Davis.

Sir Colin Davis takes a fundamentally darker, tougher view of *Peter Grimes* than the composer himself (whose Decca recording – 414 577-2 – received a Rosette in our main volume). In some ways the result on Davis's set is even more powerful, if less varied and atmospheric, with the Borough turned into a dark place, full of Strindbergian tensions, and Grimes himself, powerful physically (not a misplaced intellectual), turned into a Hardy-like figure. It was Jon Vickers's heroic interpretation in the Met. production in New York which first prompted Davis to press for this recording, and the result sheds keen new illumination on what arguably remains the greatest of Britten's operas, even if it cannot be said to supplant the composer's own version. Plainly close in frame and spirit to Crabbe's rough fisherman, Vickers, slow-spoken and weighty, is frighteningly intense. Heather Harper as Ellen Orford is very moving, and there are fine contributions from Jonathan Summers as Captain Balstrode and Thomas Allen as Ned Keene. The lack of atmospheric effects in this set reinforces Davis's contention that the actual notes need no outside aid. The recording is full and vivid, with fine balancing.

(i) *Noye's fludde;* (ii) *Serenade for tenor, horn & strings, Op. 31.*
**(*) Virgin Dig. VC7 91129-2; *VC7 91129-4* [id.]. (i) Maxwell, Ormiston, Pasco, Salisbury & Chester Schools Ch. & O, Coull Qt, Alley, Watson, Harwood, Endymion Ens. (members); (ii) Martyn Hill, Frank Lloyd, City of L. Sinf., Hickox.

A modern digital recording of Britten's vividly atmospheric setting of the Chester Miracle Play is timely, when the Decca version, with the original team of performers conducted by Norman Del Mar, is 30 years old. The sound for this fine Hickox performance is clearer, fuller and richer, and the performance generally has cleaner attack and discipline, yet in one important way it does not match its predecessor. On the Virgin disc the instrumental forces, including a schools' orchestra as well as professional soloists, are relatively recessed. Compare the storm sequence here with the Decca account (425 161-2, coupled with *The Golden Vanity*), and the distancing undermines any feeling of threat so that the entry of the hymn, *Eternal father*, instantly submerges the orchestral sound, instead of battling against it. There the Del Mar performance remains far more exciting, and not even Donald Maxwell as Noah, strong and virile, can efface memories of the incomparable Owen Brannigan. The entry of the animals and birds is also caught less dramatically, though it is much more precise on detail. Taken on its own, this is a splendid issue, made the more attractive by the inclusion of Martyn Hill's account of the *Serenade*. This is alternatively available in coupling with the *Nocturne* and *Les illuminations* (VC7 90792-2; *VC7 90792-4*).

The Turn of the Screw.
(M) (***) Decca mono 425 672-2 (2) [id.]. Pears, Vyvyan, Hemmings, Dyer, Cross, Mandikian, E. Op. Group O, composer.

Though the recording is in mono only, the very dryness and the sharpness of focus give an extra intensity to the composer's own incomparable reading of his most compressed opera. With such sound, the claustrophobic quality of this weird ghost story is intensified, along with the musical cogency of this sequence of fifteen closely knit scenes. Peter Pears as Peter Quint is superbly matched by Jennifer Vyvyan as the governess and by Joan Cross as the housekeeper, Mrs Grose. It is fascinating too to hear the film-star-to-be, David Hemmings, as a boy treble, already a confident actor. Excellent CD transfer.

Brouwer, Leo (born 1939)

Retrats Catalans.
*** Decca Dig. 430 233-2; *430 233-4* [id.]. Eduardo Fernández, ECO, Barry Wordsworth – ARNOLD: *Guitar concerto*; CHAPPELL: *Guitar concerto No. 1.****

An unusual coupling for two superb guitar concertos, Chappell's as well as Arnold's.

With the solo instrument well integrated in Brouwer's pieces, textures go in search of a theme in the first, and turn into a dance in the second. Both were inspired by great Catalonian figures, the composer Mompou and the architect Gaudi.

Bruch, Max (1838–1920)

Violin concertos Nos. 1 in G min.; 2 in D min., Op. 44; 3 in D min., Op. 58; Adagio appassionato, Op. 57; In Memoriam, Op. 65; Konzertstücke, Op. 84; Romanze, Op. 42; Serenade, Op. 75.
(M) *** Ph. 432 282-2 (3) [id.]. Salvatore Accardo, Leipzig GO, Kurt Masur.

This is an immensely valuable set of great distinction; it gathers together all Bruch's major works for violin and orchestra. Although no other piece quite matches the famous *G minor Concerto* in inventive concentration, the delightful *Scottish fantasia*, with its profusion of good tunes, comes near to doing so, and the first movement of the *Second Concerto* has two themes of soaring lyrical ardour. Even if the rest of the work has a lower level of inspiration, it is still richly enjoyable. The *Third Concerto* brings another striking lyrical idea in the first movement and has an endearing *Adagio* and a jolly finale. The engagingly insubstantial *Serenade*, a four-movement piece dating from the turn of the century, was originally intended to be a fourth violin concerto. Its nostalgic opening *Andante* is highly characteristic, then comes a balletic little march, a dreamy *Notturno* and a gay, Spanish-influenced finale, full of sparkling bravura. The two-movement *Konzertstück* dates from 1911 and is one of Bruch's last works. As in the case of the *Serenade*, Bruch had toyed with the idea of calling it a violin concerto, but he finally decided on *Konzertstück* since the piece has only two movements. The second, an *Adagio*, is really very touching. *In Memoriam* is finer still (Bruch himself thought highly of it); it has genuine depth and nobility. The *Adagio appassionato* and *Romanze* are strongly characterized pieces and their eloquence is striking in performances of this calibre. Throughout the set Accardo's playing is so persuasive in its restrained passion that even the less inspired moments bring pleasure, and there are many pages of music that show the composer nearing his finest form. When this set was first issued on LP in 1978, we thought it difficult to imagine it being surpassed for many years to come. This applies equally today – with the caveat that, because of the resonant Leipzig acoustics, the Philips engineers put their microphones rather too close to the soloist. With the sharpening of focus which comes with the CD remastering, his image is balanced very forwardly, almost out of the hall acoustic, and there is at times a degree of shrillness on his upper range. This is most noticeable on the first disc, containing the *G minor Concerto*, but the ear adjusts; throughout the rest of the collection one's pleasure is hardly diminished, for the orchestral recording is full and spacious.

Violin concerto No. 1 in G min., Op. 26.
(M) *** Sony/CBS Dig. MDK 44902; *40-44902* [id.]. Cho-Liang Lin, Chicago SO, Slatkin – MENDELSSOHN: *Concerto* *** (with Sandra Rivers (piano): SARASATE: *Introduction and Tarantella* ***; KREISLER: *Liebesfreud* ***).
*** Chan. Dig. CHAN 8974; *ABTD 1563* [id.]. Hideko Udagawa, LSO, Mackerras – BRAHMS: *Concerto.****
(M) **(*) Sony/CBS CD 45555 [MYK 37811]; *40-45555*. Stern, Phd. O, Ormandy – LALO: *Symphonie espagnole.***(*)
(B) **(*) RCA VD 60479; *VK 60479* [60479-2-RV; *60479-4-RV*]. Ughi, LSO, Prêtre – BRAHMS: *Concerto.***(*)

(M) (***) Ph. 426 639-2; *426 639-4* [id.]. Accardo, Leipzig GO, Masur – MENDELSSOHN: *Concerto.****

(B) ** DG Compact Classics 413 844-2 (2); *413 844-4* [id.]. Yong Uck Kim, Bamberg SO, Kamu – BEETHOVEN: *Romances* ***; BRAHMS: *Violin concerto* **((*) (CD only: DVORAK: *Violin concerto* **(*)).

(BB) ** LaserLight Dig. 15 615 [id.]. Szenthelýi, Budapest PO, Sándor – MENDELSSOHN: *Concerto.***

(BB) *(*) Naxos Dig. 8.550195 [id.]. Nishizaki, Slovak PO, Gunzenhauser – BRAHMS: *Concerto.**

(BB) *(*) Pickwick PWK 1151 [id.]. Ion Voicou, LSO, Frühbeck de Burgos – MENDELSSOHN: *Concerto.**(*)

Sony, taking note of the competition, have now issued Cho-Liang Lin's radiantly beautiful 1986 account of the *G minor Concerto*, recoupled with the Mendelssohn, to make an outstanding mid-priced digital recommendation. There have been few accounts on record of Bruch's slow movement that begin to match the raptness of Lin. He is accompanied most sensitively by Slatkin and the Chicago orchestra, and this reading is totally compelling in its combination of passsion and purity, strength and dark, hushed intensity. The Kreisler and Sarasate bonuses, recorded three years earlier, are also presented with great flair. The recording is excellent.

Full of temperament, Hideko Udegawa gives a persuasively passionate performance of the Bruch, very well recorded, and with strong, colourful playing from the orchestra too. Her violin sound is not always of the sweetest, but it is always true and clear, and the hushed opening of the slow movement is caught beautifully. A generous coupling for her strong, daring performance of the Brahms.

It is good to welcome back to the catalogue Stern's 1967-vintage recording with Ormandy. Although the balance is totally unrealistic, this is one of the great classic recordings of the work, gloriously warm-hearted and with a very involving account of the slow movement, which sustains the greatest possible intensity. The finale, too, has wonderful fire and spirit. Ormandy's accompaniment is first class and triumphs over the unrealistic balance and a less than refined orchestral image.

Those looking for a bargain coupling with the Brahms *Concerto* and very good (1982) digital recording might well choose Uto Ughi on RCA. His is a fresh, direct reading. It may not have the individuality of Lin or the extrovert ardour of Stern, but it is still a fine performance, and good value too.

Accardo's playing is very persuasive is its restrained eloquence. This is also outstanding in its way, and the slow movement generates considerable intensity; but the snag is the 1977 recording. The violin is forwardly balanced and, under pressure, the timbre catches the microphone and becomes edgy.

Miklós Szenthelýi's performance has an appealing lyrical ardour. His tone is full, and his account of the *Adagio* combines passionate feeling with tenderness, while the outer movements have plenty of eager momentum. There is certainly no lack of spontaneity here; although the forward balance, for both soloist and orchestra, brings an element of rawness to the string timbre, this is easily smoothed, and otherwise the digital sound is vivid, with plenty of ambience. Good value in the lowest price-range.

Yong Uck Kim's performance impresses by its purity of style and understated feeling. But such an approach is not entirely successful in this ripely romantic concerto which does not always respond to such delicacy of feeling. Unfortunately the orchestral response, though good, does not match the solo playing in finesse, but the recording is full and well balanced and the Compact Classics tape is well transferred. The digitally remastered pair of CDs also include a freshly enjoyable account of the Dvořák *Concerto*.

Takako Nishizaki plays the slow movement gently and sweetly, and the first movement goes quite well. But the finale lacks sparkle, and altogether this is not one of her recommendable couplings.

The Voicou/Frühbeck de Burgos performance (recorded by Decca in the mid-1960s) has some really fine moments. The opening sections of the first and second movements have expressive magic and the closing tutti of the latter brings great ardour, while the soloist often phrases with subtlety. The pity is that his timbre, as recorded, is somewhat febrile and (like the upper strings of the orchestra) made to sound wiry, and this spoils an otherwise impressive reading.

Kol Nidrei, Op.47.
(M) *** Decca Dig. 425 020-2; *425 020-4* [id.]. Harrell, Philh. O, Ashkenazy – DVOŘÁK: *Cello concerto* **; TCHAIKOVSKY: *Rococo variations.****
(M) ** Mercury 432 001-2 [id.]. Starker, LSO, Dorati – DVOŘÁK: *Cello concerto*; TCHAIKOVSKY: *Rococo variations.***

Bruch's withdrawn, prayerful piece finds a natural response in Lynn Harrell, whose musical personality is often comparatively reticent; his account with Ashkenazy is both eloquent and atmospheric, and is certainly well recorded.

Although beginning rather solemnly, Starker's reading of Bruch's serene cantilena is very sympathetic, without wearing its heart on its sleeve, and is accompanied most sympathetically. Indeed, Dorati opens and closes the piece with a striking feeling for the work's colour and atmosphere.

Bruckner, Anton (1824–96)

Symphonies Nos. 1–9.
(M) *** EMI CZS7 62935-2 (9) [Ang. CDZI 62935]. Dresden State O, Jochum.
(M) ** BMG/RCA GD 69227 (10) [id.]. Leipzig GO, Kurt Masur.

Like Jochum's earlier set for DG (429 079-2), made between 1957 and 1967 with either the Berlin Philharmonic (in Nos. 1, 4 and 7–9) or the Bavarian Radio Symphony Orchestra (2, 3, 5 and 6), this accommodates all the symphonies, one to a disc. (Incidentally we were in error in our main volume in saying that DG had taken the opportunity of spacing the Karajan, which still remains our primary recommendation – 429 648-2 – in similar fashion.) The EMI set, made with the Staatskapelle Dresden between 1975 and 1980, has the advantage of more modern recorded sound (though readers will be surprised how well the 1957 stereo recording of the *Fifth Symphony* on DG actually sounds). Jochum's allegiance to the Novak editions remains unchanged and, apart from various odd details, so does his overall approach. His readings have a spirituality and nobility that remain rather special, notwithstanding the claims of his many distinguished rivals. Either the DG or the EMI set will give great satisfacton.

Kurt Masur's survey comes from much the same period and some, though by no means all, of the symphonies appeared on LP during the late 1970s. Generally speaking, it is what one might call a sound rather than an inspired cycle. He is a dedicated Brucknerian and the Leipzig Gewandhaus is a responsive body, but for those who (rightly) attach importance to continuity, it occupies ten as opposed to nine discs – like Wand's set with the Cologne Radio Orchestra.

Symphony No. 2 in C min.
*** DG Dig. 415 988-2 [id.]. BPO, Karajan.

Karajan's reading is not only powerful and polished, it is distinctive on matters both of tempi and text. The digital recording is of good quality, although rather brightly lit.

Symphony No. 3 in D min. (original, 1873 version).
**(*) Teldec/Warner Dig. 2292 42961-2 [id.]. Frankfurt RSO, Inbal.

There are in all three versions of the *Third Symphony*: the first completed on the last day of 1873, a second which Bruckner undertook immediately after the completion of the *Fifth Symphony* in 1877, and then, after that proved unsuccessful, a third which he made in 1889. The 1873 is by far the longest version, running to nearly 66 minutes (the first movement alone lasts 24 minutes), and for those who have either of the others it will make far more than a fascinating appendix. The playing of the Frankfurt Radio Orchestra under Eliahu Inbal is very respectable indeed, with a sensitive feeling for atmosphere and refined dynamic contrasts; the recording in its CD format is most acceptable without being top-drawer. This edition has never been recorded before, and the symphony can at last be heard in the form in which it was presented to Wagner.

Symphony No. 3 in D min. (1877 version).
*** Ph. Dig. 422 411-2 [id.]. VPO, Bernard Haitink.

At the time of writing, Bernard Haitink is the only conductor to have given us a digital version of the 1877 edition of the *Third Symphony*. (He also recorded it on LP with the Concertgebouw in the 1960s.) Karajan, Jochum and Wand all opt for the 1889 revision. Bruckner embarked on this after Hermann Levi had rejected the *Eighth Symphony*, making a number of cuts suggested by the Schalk brothers. Haitink gives us the version favoured by many Bruckner scholars. Questions of edition apart, this is a performance of enormous breadth and majesty, and Philips give it a recording to match. The playing of the Vienna Philharmonic is glorious throughout, and even collectors who have alternative versions should acquire this magnificent issue.

Symphony No. 3 in D min.
(M) ** Sony MPK 45880 [id.]. Cleveland O, George Szell.

Szell's way with Bruckner is reserved, almost severe. He opens atmospherically, but he does not indulge the listener in a gentle, moulded style. All the same, the reading has undoubted strength, and it is a pity that Szell uses the controversial 1890 edition, in which Bruckner was persuaded by Franz Schalk to cut large sections of the finale. It makes the piece much tauter, but many Brucknerians will resist the truncation. The orchestral playing is outstanding and the recording on CD is given a fairly wide dynamic range, in spite of the relatively close balance which does bring a degree of harshness.

Symphony No. 4 in E flat (Romantic) (1874, original version).
* Telarc Dig. CD 80188 [id.]. Cincinnati SO, Lopez-Cobos.

The Cincinnati orchestra and Jésus Lopez-Cobos on Telarc offer the only current challenge to Inbal and the Frankfurt Radio Orchestra in the early version of the *Fourth Symphony* with its completely different scherzo. The latter, however, scores over it in terms of orchestral playing. Not to beat about the bush, this is pretty ordinary.

Symphony No. 4 in E flat (Romantic) (1878/80 version).
(M) **(*) EMI Dig. CDD7 63895-2 [id.]; *ET 763895-4*. BPO, Tennstedt.
*(*) DG Dig. 431 719-2 [id.]. VPO, Abbado.

There are now some two dozen accounts of Bruckner's *Fourth Symphony* – and probably Jochum's bargain DG version is as fine as any (427 200-2) – a far cry from the days just after the war when there was only one 78-r.p.m. set, and that available only to special order! In Tennstedt's 1982 version the breadth of the recording is admirable, if with a degree of fierceness on fortissimos. This is a reading that combines concentration and a degree of ruggedness; plainness goes with pure beauty and natural strength in the first two movements. The scherzo is urgent, the finale resplendent. With one or two modifications, the Haas edition is used. Not a first choice, but nevertheless compelling.

Claudio Abbado's account with the Vienna Philharmonic has the advantage of cultured orchestral playing and a well-shaped and finely paced architecture. The recording is good without being particularly distinguished and does not match the front runners in the field; and the performance as a whole possesses the sense of neither the innocence nor mystery that must be present if the music is to move the listener and which conductors like Blomstedt, Karajan, Jochum and Walter have brought to this work.

Symphony No. 5 in B flat.
(M) **(*) Decca Dig. 425 008-2 (2) [id.]. Chicago SO, Solti – SCHOENBERG: *Variations.***(*)
(M) **(*) EMI CDM7 63612-2; *EG 763612-4* [id.]. New Philh. O, Klemperer.
** BMG/RCA Dig. RD 60361; *RK 60361* [60361-2-RC; *60361-4-RC*]. N. German RSO, Wand.

Solti's conducting undoubtedly gives off electric sparks and his precise control of this performance underlines dramatic contrasts, helped by the clarity and brilliance of the digital recording, with its extremely wide dynamic range, so striking on CD. The slow movement finds the necessary warmth with Solti in what, for him, may be called Elgarian mood; but it is the intensity and sharpness of profile that give the special character to this reading.

Klemperer's account is certainly expansive, though some may find it heavy-handed. Without doubt the conception is massive; this results in rich, powerful brass sonorities, with a cathedral-like breadth, but at times there is a suspicion of bombast, and this is heightened by the somewhat drier and sharper focus of the CD sound-picture. In the beautiful slow movement, where others are more lyrical, the second C major theme makes a stirring impact as presented by Klemperer; taking the reading overall, one has the impression that lyricism has been subordinated to architectural strength.

Günter Wand's first recording of the *Fifth Symphony* was perhaps one of the less successful in his earlier cycle. This newcomer has better sound than its predecessor and better also than its recently issued companions, Nos. 8 and 9, having been recorded in the Hamburg Musikhalle rather than in the more resonant acoustic of Lübeck Cathedral. His new account is also accommodated on one disc, whereas both the Karajan and Haitink versions involve two. The Karajan offers also the *First Symphony* (DG 415 985-2); Haitink provides the *Te Deum* (Philips 422 342-2). There are pros and cons about both these alternatives and we can only refer readers back to our main volume, pp. 247 and 251. Wand is never kapellmeister-ish but, at the same time, never inspired either. He tends to move things on just a little too awkwardly at times – the lead into the allegro of the first movement – and the slow movement is not really *sehr langsam*; Karajan takes five minutes longer over it and Jochum four. Wand communicates a sense of awe only intermittently.

Symphonies Nos. (i) *5 in B flat;* (ii) *7 in E.*
(M) *(*) Sony MY2K 45669 (2) [id.]. (i) Phd. O, Ormandy; (ii) Columbia SO, Walter.

An unfortunate and unnecessary coupling, as each symphony is complete on a single

CD. Ormandy's *Fifth* with the Philadelphia Orchestra lacks atmosphere and mystery, and the recording is two-dimensional with little lustre to the strings. Walter is infinitely better recorded, but his reading of the *Seventh* suffers from the fault of concentrating on detail at the expense of structure. The outer movements bring many illuminating touches and the final climax of the first is imposingly built, but overall the tension is held loosely. In the *Adagio*, which is kept moving fairly convincingly, the climax is disappointing, made the more so by the absence of the famous cymbal clash, as Walter uses the original text. The 1963 recording has been opened up in its remastering for CD and sounds fuller and more spacious than the original LPs.

Symphony No. 6 in A.
**(*) BMG/RCA Dig. RD 60061; *RK 60061* [60061-2-RC; *60061-4-RC*]. N. German RSO, Wand.

Wand's account of the *Sixth* gets off to a rather heavy-handed start but turns into something really rather imposing. The sense of awe, missing from his *Fifth*, is present here and the architecture of the work unfolds with impressive logic. Haitink has yet to reach this symphony in his second cycle, and it may be worth waiting for. Generally speaking, the *Sixth* has fared unpredictably and been something of a problem child in Brucknerian circles. This is undoubtedly one of the better ones; the playing of the Hamburg orchestra is very fine indeed, and so is the sound. However, the best buy for this work is probably the Sawallisch Orfeo account with the Bavarian State Orchestra, beautifully shaped, spacious, yet never portentous or inflated. The recording is excellent too (C 024821).

Symphony No. 7 in E.
Telarc Dig. CD 80188 [id.]. Cincinnati SO, Lopez-Cobos.

The Cincinnati version under Jésus Lopez-Cobos has the merit of decent recorded sound; but in every other respect, in terms of both orchestral playing and interpretation, it is pretty uncompetitive. No stars. While Karajan (DG 419 195-2) and Haitink (Philips 420 805-2) both give of their finest in this work, Chailly's account with its superb Decca digital recording seems to be a front runner (414 290-2). At mid-price, Karajan's earlier EMI recording can be strongly recommended (CDM7 69923-2; *EG 769923-4*).

Symphony No. 8 in C min. (original, 1887 version).
**(*) Teldec/Warner Dig. 2292 43791-2 (2) [id.]. Frankfurt RSO, Inbal.

Eliahu Inbal has strong Brucknerian instincts and, although the Frankfurt Radio Orchestra is not thought of as being in the first bracket, it produces more than acceptable results. There are considerable divergences here from the versions we know, and readers will undoubtedly derive much fascination from comparing them. The recording is very good and, like its companion, No. 3, this is mandatory listening for all Brucknerians.

Symphony No. 8 in C min.
**(*) BMG/RCA Dig. RD 60364 [60364-2-RC]. N. German RSO, Wand.
(B) **(*) DG 431 163-2; *431 163-4* [id.]. BPO, Jochum.
** EMI Dig. CDS7 49990-2 (2) [id.]. BPO, Maazel.
(M) ** EMI CMS7 63835-2 (2). New Philh. O, Klemperer – HINDEMITH: *Nobilissima visione*: suite (**); WAGNER: *Die Walküre: Wotan's farewell.* **(*)

Günter Wand has become something of a cult figure in recent years and, if he is admittedly far more than a Kappellmeister, he falls short in some of the classical repertoire of real stature. However, his Bruckner is another matter and both enjoys and deserves its wide following. Here he has exchanged the plainer studio acoustic of his earlier set for the reverberance of Lübeck Cathedral, and his Cologne Radio Orchestra for that of the excellent Hamburg Nord Deutscher Rundfunks. This record is assembled from performances given at the 1987 Schleswig-Holstein Festival and first appeared briefly on EMI before migrating to RCA. There is great breadth and a sense of space here, imposed no doubt by the acoustic, and considerable majesty. However, in climaxes there is an overhanging resonance that might pose problems for some collectors and which prevents this occupying a premier position in what is a highly competitive field.

When Jochum's recording of Bruckner's *Eighth* was first issued on LP, we had some doubts concerning his somewhat wayward inspirational style. It is a work which needs a performance of the utmost grip (of the kind that Karajan can exert) if it is not to seem to ramble on, stopping and starting here and there. Indeed Richard Osborne, writing in *Gramophone* about Jochum's integral recording of all nine symphonies, suggested that 'in some ways it [the *Eighth*] is the set's Achilles heel'. Jochum uses the Nowak Edition, which involves cuts in the slow movement and finale, and in addition he often presses the music on impulsively in both the outer movements and especially in his account of the *Adagio*, where the climax has great passion and thrust. One is undoubtedly caught up with this, and there is also some marvellously serene playing from the Berlin Philharmonic strings, with a noble contribution from the brass. The use of the Philharmonie instead of the Jesus-Christus Kirche for the 1964 recording brought a certain forceful and sometimes piercing brightness to the trumpets, and the recording needs to be reproduced at a high level for its breadth and fullness to be properly experienced; but there can be no doubting the skill of its remastering. The combination of the Nowak cuts and Jochum's accelerandos means that the overall playing time is just over 74 minutes, and the symphony fits on to a single bargain-priced CD – which is worth any Brucknerian's money.

Lorin Maazel, like Jochum, parts company from Wand in using the Nowak edition and he has the inestimable advantage of having the Berlin Philharmonic and very good recording quality. All the same, there is more to this music than this well-prepared and finely executed performance gives us. One remains on the outside admiring what is going on, rather than confronting the real majesty of Bruckner's vision. As playing and recording, this really should have a three-star rating, but as a musical experience it does not rate much more than one. The superb version that Karajan recorded in Vienna some months before his death, to which we awarded a Rosette in our last edition, remains unchallenged (DG 427 611-2).

Klemperer's version was impressively recorded in the Kingsway Hall in 1970, but the performance does little credit to his memory. It was one of his last records, and funereal tempi make it seem one of the longest. The performance also suffers from untidiness here and there and, although many details inspire respect and even moments of admiration, the set must regretfully be passed over.

Symphony No. 9 in D min.

(M) *** DG 429 904-2; *429 904-4* [id.]. BPO, Karajan.

**(*) HM/BMG Dig. RD 60365; *RK 60365* [60365-2-RC; *60365-4-RC*]. N. German RSO, Wand.

(M) *(*) EMI CDM7 63916-2 [id.]; *EG 763916-4*. New Philh. O, Klemperer.

This DG Galleria reissue offers a glorious performance of Bruckner's last and uncompleted symphony, moulded in a way that is characteristic of Karajan and displaying a simple, direct nobility that is sometimes missing in this work. Here he seems to find it unnecessary to underline but, with glowing playing from the Berlin

Philharmonic and spectacular recording, he gives the illusion of letting the music speak for itself. Yet no Bruckner interpreter has a clearer idea of the composer's architecture and, as one appreciates the subtle gradation towards the climax in the concluding slow movement, one knows how firmly Karajan's sights have been set on this goal all along. The differences between this superlative 1966 version and Karajan's later one (DG 419 083-2), recorded with the same orchestra eight years later, are relatively small. The clue lies principally in the recording quality. Whereas the digital remastering of the mid-1960s version has brought a brighter, more boldly focused sound, the acoustics of the Jesus-Christus Kirche still provide a basically mellow ambience; the later, 1977 recording-balance is sharper and closer, to suggest that Karajan wanted to convey a tougher impression. Where the present, earlier version brings natural gravity and profound contemplation in greater measure, with manners a degree more affectionate, the later one concentrated on strength and impact. Even in a competitive field, this 1966 disc stands out at mid-price, to rank alongside Bruno Walter's noble 1959 version (Sony MYK 44825) and, among modern digital recordings, Giulini's VPO *Ninth* (DG 427 345-2), a performance of comparable stature, and the product of deep thought.

Günter Wand's account of the *Ninth Symphony*, made with the Hamburg North German Radio Orchestra, is far more expansive than his earlier version. The Hamburg strings are more sumptuous than their Cologne colleagues, though the generous acoustic of Lübeck Cathedral no doubt helped to enrich them. Given the greater length of reverberation, Wand naturally adapts his pace to the acoustic and adds about five minutes overall to his earlier account. Consideration of these matters is inevitably personal, and for many collectors the acoustic may not pose problems; but the overhang, particularly in tuttis, does muddy the texture at times. Moreover one is not quite sure where one is actually sitting: the brass seem much nearer than the strings and wind. The generous pacing and obvious warmth that Wand secures from his Hamburg forces is impressive, but the performance as a whole does not strike the same note of awe and concentration (particularly in the *Adagio*) that marked his earlier, Cologne reading. Now that the first Karajan version is restored to circulation at mid-price and there is such stiff competition from Giulini, Jochum and others, this does not warrant a full three-star rating.

Klemperer's performance is slow and deliberate but far from unimpressive; it is more effectively held together than his *Eighth*, and the fine 1970 Kingsway Hall recording has transferred effectively to CD. Devotees of this conductor may feel this well worth pursuing, but for most collectors it will not seriously challenge the finest alternative versions.

Te Deum.
(M) * DG 429 980-2; *429 980-4* [id.]. Perry, Müller-Molinari, Winbergh, Malta, V. Singverein, VPO, Karajan – MOZART: *Coronation Mass.***(*)

Karajan's digital version of Bruckner's *Te Deum* is not made any more attractive by being reissued at mid-price – see our main volume.

Brumel, Antoine (*c.* 1460– *c.* 1520)

Missa, Et ecce terrae motus (in twelve parts); *Sequentia, Dies irae Dies illa.*
❀ *** Sony Dig. SK 46348 [id.]. Huelgas Ens., Paul van Nevel.

Brumel belongs to the same period as Josquin, Isaac, Pierre de la Rue and Obrecht, and was spoken of with veneration by such contemporaries as Rabelais and Glareanus. Born in Chartres, he served at Notre-Dame and at Chambéry in Savoy, before settling in Italy where he succeeded Josquin as *maestro di cappella* at Ferrara. Morley in his *Plaine and Easie Introduction to Practicall Musicke* wrote that 'only Josquin des Pres and Brumel were able to teach one everything about older canonic techniques'. Lassus himself prepared and took part in a performance of the 12-part *Mass, Et ecce terrae motus* in Munich in the 1570s, and this recording was made from the manuscript he used – the only copy of the work that survives. It is not just the contrapuntal ingenuity of his music that impresses but the sheer beauty of sound with which we are presented. Not only was Brumel one of the first composers to write a polyphonic *Requiem* but the very first to make a polyphonic setting of the sequence, *Dies irae Dies illa.* This is a more severe work than the glorious 12-part Mass which occupies the bulk of this CD, and is written in a more medieval tonal language. The performances by the Huelgas Ensemble under its founder-director, Paul van Nevel, are fervent and eloquent and vividly bring this music back to life (this is its first recording). The recording, made in the ample acoustic of the Irish Chapel in Liège, is resplendent. This will be something of a revelation to those for whom Brumel has been only a name in the history books.

Bush, Geoffrey (born 1920)

Farewell, earth's bliss; 4 Hesperides songs; A Menagerie; (i) *A Summer serenade.*
*** Chan. Dig. CHAN 8864; *ABTD 1479* [id.]. Varcoe, Thompson, Westminster Singers, City of London Sinfonia, Hickox, (i) with Eric Parkin.

Few living composers can match Geoffrey Bush in responding to the rhythms and cadences of English words. His writing for voice regularly combines a Britten-like flexibility of line with the snappy pointing of Walton – like both of them, creating ideas that instantly catch in the mind. This collection of Bush's vocal works has an open freshness stemming from the easy inevitability of the settings, firmly tonal in idiom but not merely derivative. The delightful *Summer serenade* of seven song-settings, written in 1948, five years after Britten's very comparable *Serenade*, has long been his most frequently performed work – a favourite with small choral groups – and this first recording glowingly brings out the sharp contrasts of mood within and between the songs. Bush even manages to give a new slant to words memorably set by Britten in his *Serenade*, Blake's *O rose thou art sick*, making it a funeral procession with chorus. The instrumentation is just as felicitous as the choral writing, with a spiky concertante part for piano played by Eric Parkin. That 20-minute piece is well coupled with a solo song-cycle of comparable length, *Farewell, earth's bliss*, with Stephen Varcoe the baritone soloist; four songs from Herrick's *Hesperides*, also for baritone and strings; and three for unaccompanied voices, including an insistently menacing setting of Blake's *Tyger*. The tenor, Adrian Thompson, not ideally pure-toned, contributes to only two of the *Serenade* songs; otherwise these are near-ideal performances in warm, open sound. Readers unfamiliar with this repertoire should explore it for, quite apart from the vocal line, Bush's string writing is a pleasure in itself.

Busoni, Ferruccio (1866–1924)

Piano concerto, Op. 39.
*** EMI Dig. CDC7 49996-2 [id.]; *EL 749996-4*. Peter Donohoe, BBC SO & Singers, Mark Elder.
**(*) CPO CPO 999 017-2 [id.]. Volker Banfield, Bav. RSO, Herbig.

Piano concerto, Op. 39; Fantasia contrappunistica.
** Erato/Warner Dig. 2292 45478-2 [id.]. Viktoria Postnikova, French R. Ch. & Nat. O, Rozhdestvensky.

Peter Donohoe's formidable version was recorded live at the Proms in August 1988. The snag is that the sound, thanks to the acoustic of the Royal Albert Hall, is a little diffuse, reducing the dramatic impact. The chorus in the final movement is rather distant and, inevitably, orchestral ensemble is less clean than in a studio performance. Where it gains is in the surge of excitement that Donohoe builds up from one vast movement to the next, as when his sparklingly volatile account of the scherzo leads into the longest of the five movements, the *Pezzo serioso.* Helpfully, EMI have given separate tracks to the four different sections in that extended third movement. Though this does not replace John Ogdon's classic first-ever recording, which remains our primary recommendation – now on EMI Studio at mid-price: CDM7 69850-2 – it makes an attractive, freely expressive alternative.

Volker Banfield on CPO gives an extraordinary performance, thrilling in its virtuosity. Speeds in the first two movements are far faster than on any current rival, with the scherzo wild in its urgency. The *Pezzo serioso* is then exceptionally spacious, beautifully controlled. The finale too is slow, but there the result is sluggish. This is a personal reading which will attract many by its very daring. The Bavarian Radio recording of 1986, in analogue sound only, is generally well balanced.

Postnikova's version with her husband conducting is a curiosity. Her characteristic magic and that of Rozhdestvensky keep tension sustained for much of the time, despite speeds that by most standards are grotesquely slow, but the result is eccentric. The *Fantasia contrappuntistica* makes a valuable fill-up, but all other CD versions fit the whole of the concerto on to a single disc. Recording is good, but the choir in the finale sounds dim.

Buxtehude, Diderik (*c.* 1637–1707)

Canzonetta in A min., BuxWV 225; Chorales: Ach Herr, mich armen Sünder, BuxWV 178; Es ist das Heil uns kommen her, BuxWV 186; Gelobet seist du, Jesu Christ, BuxWV 189; In dulci jubilo, BuxWV 197; Kommt her zu mir, spricht Gottes Sohn, BuxWV 201; Mensch, willt du leben seliglich, BuxWV 204; Nun bitten wir den Heiligen Geist, BuxWV 208; Nun komm, der Heilden Heiland, BuxWV 211; Puer natus in Bethlehem, BuxWV 217; Von Gott will ich nicht lassen, BuxWV 220; Passacaglia in D min., BuxWV 161; Preludes and fugues: in C, BuxWV 138; in D, BuxWV 139; in G min., BuxWV 148; in A min., BuxWV 153. Toccatas: in F, BuxWV 156; in G, BuxWV 164.
** Virgin Dig. VC7 91139-2 [id.]. Nicholas Danby (organ of St Laurents, Alkmaar).

Canzona in G, BuxWV 170. Chorales: *Ach Herr, mich armen Sünder, BuxWV 178; Erhalt uns, Herr, BuxWV 185; Es ist das Heil, BuxWV 186; Gott der Vater, BuxWV 190; Herr Jesu Christ, BuxWV 193; In dulci jubilo, BuxWV 197; Jesus Christus unser Heiland, BuxWV 198; Kommt her zu mir, BuxWV 201; Lobt Gott, ihr Christen allzugleich, BuxWV 202. Fugue in C (Gigue), BuxWV 174; Passacaglia in D min., BuxWV 161; Preludes & fugues: in D, BuxWV 139; in E, BuxWV 141; in F sharp, BuxWV 146.*
(M) *** Decca Dig. 430 262-2; *430 262-4* [id.]. Peter Hurford (organ of the Church of Our Lady of Sorrows, Toronto).

Turning to survey a wider Baroque field, Peter Hurford here alights on Buxtehude whom, the story goes, Bach walked 200 miles to visit. Hurford's recital subdivides into two sections, each opening with an impressively structured *Prelude and fugue* and the first ending with the *D minor Passacaglia*; the *E major Prelude and fugue* rounds off the second half. In between comes a series of agreeable and mellifluous chorales, obviously a model for Bach, but not imaginatively on a par with the latter's inspired embroidery. What catches the ear most strikingly here are the delightful *Canzona in G* and the captivating *'Gigue' Fugue in C*, uncannily like Bach's *Fugue à la gigue in G*, BWV 577. Hurford's registration here is agreeably apt, giving both pieces a piquant bite to offset the blander sounds he creates for the amiable chorale preludes. A distinguished recital, played with characteristic spontaneity on a splendid organ that is highly suitable for this repertoire.

Nicholas Danby's collection is very similar to Peter Hurford's less expensive Decca collection, but in the event is much less attractive, and not only on price. Danby's performances – especially of the chorales – are blander, and the Alkmaar organ is rather resonantly recorded, so that the focus of the articulation is much less clean than with Hurford's Canadian recital.

Cantatas: *An Filius non est Dei, BuxWV 6; Cantata Domino, BuxWV 12; Frohlocket mit Händen, BuxWV 29; Gott fähret auf mit Jauchzen, BuxWV 33; Herr, wenn ich nur Dich habe, BuxWV 39; Heut triumphieret Gottes Sohn, BuxWV 43; Ich bin die Auferstehung, BuxWV 44; Ich habe Lust abzuscheiden, BuxWV 46; Ihr lieben Christen, BuxWV 51; In dulci jubilo, BuxWV 52; Jesus dulcis memoria, BuxWV 56; Jesu meines Lebens Leben, BuxWV 62; Jubilate Deo, BuxWV 64; Mein Gemüt erfreuet sich, BuxWV 72; Nichts soll uns scheiden, BuxWV 77; Nun danket alle Gott, BuxWV 79; Wie wird erneuet, wie wird er freuet, BuxWV 110.*
*** Erato/Warner Dig. 2292 45294-2 (3) [id.]. Schlick, Frimmer, Chance, Jacobs, Prégardien, Kooy, Hannover Knabenchor, Amsterdam Bar. O, Koopman.

It seems possible that Ton Koopman may be planning to do for Buxtehude's cantatas what Harnoncourt and Leonhardt have achieved with Bach on Teldec. There are well over a hundred of them to be explored, and on the evidence of this box they contain much fine music, even if they are not as inspired as Bach's cantatas. All the works here are of a pietist religious character, although the music readily expands into joyously extrovert expressions of praise. Some attractively combine the form of a *concerto grosso*, with alternating solos and tuttis, and a few are more ambitious, including chorus, trumpets and cornetts, and even trombones, and drums too. The brass writing is inevitably primitive, but highly effective in its stylized way. The work which ends the first disc, *Heut triumphieret Gottes Sohn*, is worthy of Bach and is quite spectacular with its closing *Victoria* and *Allelujah*, and a similar mood prevails at the end of *Jesu meines Lebens Leben*, which opens the second disc. The solo singing is excellent, and the soloists match pleasingly when they sing in duet or trio. René Jacobs has *Jubilate Dominum* effectively to himself, Peter Kooy brings appropriate darkness of timbre to *Ich bin die Auferstehung*, and Barbara Schlick, whose contribution gives much pleasure throughout, has a fine extended solo in *Herr, wenn ich nur Dich habe. Nichts soll uns scheiden von der Liebes Gottes* ('Nought shall take God's love from us') has a delightful opening trio, with the opening *Nichts* repeated twice, to give an attractively light rhythmic touch. There is plenty to discover here for any collector who enjoys the pre-Bach era. Accompaniments are alive, textures transparent, and the recording balance is altogether excellent.

Byrd, William (1543–1623)

Cantiones sacrae, Book 1: 9 motets.
*** CRD Dig. CRD 3420 [id.]. New College, Oxford, Ch., Higginbottom.

This appears to be a straight reissue of CRD 3408, discussed on p. 262 of our main volume alongside its companion, CRD 3439, which contains excerpts from Book 2, and where a full listing of the contents of both CDs will be found. The recording is rich and firm and the acoustic admirably handled. The fresh, spontaneous style of the New College, Oxford, choristers in this repertoire is very moving, and this would seem an excellent point at which to start an exploration of Byrd's Latin vocal music, once the the great Masses have been encountered.

Mass for 3 voices; Mass for 4 voices; Mass for 5 voices.
*** Argo Dig. 430 164-2; *430 164-4* [id.]. Winchester Cathedral Ch., David Hill.

David Hill and the Choir of Winchester Cathedral are the latest to offer all three Byrd *Masses* on one CD, and their version can be confidently recommended for those wanting the convenience of all three together on disc. Fine performances that can rate alongside the Tallis Scholars (Gimell CDGIM 345; *ZCBYRD 345*) without displacing it. (The Gimell CD includes also the *Ave verum corpus*; the equivalent cassette offers additionally the motets, *Deficit in dolore* and *Infelix ego*, and so is the best value of all.) The standard of both singing and recording in this particular repertory remains high.

Mass for 4 voices with *Propers for the Feast of Saints Peter and Paul (Gradualia 1607);* Motets: *Hodie Simon Petrus; Quodcunque ligaveris; Quomodo cantabimus?; Tu es pastor omnium.*
*** Virgin Dig. VC7 91133-2 *VC7 91133-4* [id.]. The Sixteen, Harry Christophers.

Mass for 5 voices with *Propers for the Feast of All Saints (Gradualia 1605);* Motets: *Ad dominum cum tribularer; Diliges dominum.*
*** Virgin Dig. VC7 90802-2; *VC7 90802-4* [id.]. The Sixteen, Harry Christophers (with: MONTE: *Super flumina Babylonis* ***).

The Byrd *Masses for 3, 4 and 5 voices* can now be (and have been) accommodated on one CD, but the advantage of the two Virgin discs by The Sixteen and Harry Christophers is that the Masses are placed in a wider musical context; the *Mass for 4 voices* is contrasted with some of the richer six-part motets from the 1607 *Gradualia*, including *Quomodo cantabimus?* Suitably appended is Philippe de Monte's *Super flumina Babylonis* which the composer had sent Byrd in 1583 and to which the *Quomodo cantabimus?* is a response.

The *Mass for 5 voices* similarly comes with the *Propers for the Feast of All Saints*, which come from the *Gradualia* of 1605 and includes the 8-part motet *Ad dominum cum tribularer*, notable for its rich-textured, poignant false relations. The singing is very impressive, the recording excellently focused and the acoustic appropriately spacious.

Canteloube, Marie-Joseph (1879–1957)

Chants d'Auvergne: Series 1–5.
(M) *** EMI CDM7 63178-2 [id.]. Victoria de los Angeles, LOP, Jacquillat.
(M) **(*) CBS Dig. MDK 46509 [id.]. Frederica von Stade, RPO, Antonio de Almeida.

It is good to have Victoria de los Angeles' pioneering set of the *Chants d'Auvergne* (recorded in Paris in 1969 and 1974) now available at mid-price. There is some 70 minutes of music here, and the recording seems more vivid than ever.

Frederica von Stade is no less generous, offering 25 of the 30 songs. She has the advantage of 1982 digital sound, clean and immediate, if not as evocative as the EMI analogue recording for de los Angeles, or as vividly atmospheric as Jill Gomez's alternative (shorter) digital selection on EMI Eminence (CD-EMX 9500 [CDM 62010]), also at offered mid-price. Fine as von Stade's singing is, she is stylistically and temperamentally not always as completely at home in Canteloube's lovely folksong settings as her colleagues. However, certain songs have more charm and obvious personal identification than others, and admirers of this artist will still find a good deal to admire here. Full texts and translations are provided.

Carver, Robert (*c.* 1484–*c.* 1568)

10-part Mass, 'Dum sacrum mysterium'; Motets: *Gaude flore Virginali; O bone Jesu.*
*** Gaudeamus Dig. CDGAU 124; *ZCGAU 124* [id.]. Cappella Nova, Alan Tavener.

There is relatively little biographical information to be had about the Scottish composer, Robert Carver – even his dates are uncertain: Kenneth Elliott, the author of his entry in *Grove*, gave *c.* 1490–1546, but in his authoritative notes to this disc he tells us that Carver's life was more extended and that he is now known still to have been alive in 1568. This CD and tape, the first in a series of Scottish Renaissance Polyphony, offers three works. The opening piece, the motet *O bone Jesu*, dating from the 1520s, is in 19 parts and is of exceptional luminosity and richness. The 10-part Mass, *Dum sacrum mysterium*, was written at the beginning of the sixteenth century: various dates between 1506 and 1513 are suggested and it is thought that in its final form it was performed at the coronation of the infant James V at Stirling. As the note puts it, among Carver's Masses this is 'undoubtedly the grandest in scope, the most extended in development and the richest in detail'. The motet, *Gaude flore Virginali*, for five voices is of slightly later provenance, perhaps dating from about 1515; though less sumptuous, it has some adventurous modulations. The Cappella Nova under Alan Tavener give a thoroughly dedicated account of all three pieces, though the pitch drops very slightly in the *Gaude flore Virginali*. The recording is very good indeed.

Casken, John (born 1949)

Golem (chamber opera in 2 parts).
*** Virgin Dig. VC7 91204-2 [id.]. Clarke, Hall, Robson, Music Projects London, Richard Bernas.

Golem is based on the well-known Jewish legend of the rabbi, the Maharal, who creates a saviour figure, a Golem, from lifeless clay. The Maharal's altruistic aims are thwarted when the Golem, developing human feelings, refuses to be controlled. It was this score which in 1990 won for Casken the first Britten Award for Composition, with this recording as part of the prize. It is a curious piece but a memorable and atmospheric one, with this splendid performance taken from a brilliantly re-edited version of BBC tapes. The piece is the more involving for the often sinister atmospheric writing, as when at the start of the story, after the flashback opening scene, the orchestra simulates the beating of the wings of a great bird, a frightening sound. Though through the Prelude and five continuous scenes the Maharal's monologues take up a disproportionate share of the whole, that matters little in a recording, particularly when the role is so confidently taken by Adrian Clarke. John Hall as the Golem is equally convincing, and most striking of all is Christopher Robson in the counter-tenor role of Ometh, 'a Promethean figure of hope and conscience'. The meeting between the Golem and Ometh in the final scene brings a tender resolution, when in their halting way they realize that, but for the Maharal's obstruction, their partnership could have brought success, not tragedy.

Castelnuovo-Tedesco, Mario (1895–1968)

Guitar concerto in D, Op. 99.
(B) *** DG Compact Classics 413 156-2 (2) Yepes, LSO, Navarra – BARCARISSE: *Concertino* *(*); FALLA: *Nights in the gardens of Spain* **(*); RODRIGO: *Concertos.***

Castelnuovo-Tedesco's *Guitar concerto* is a work of considerable charm, with its gently lyrical first movement and Andantino with a 'lollipop' tune that reminds one of something else. It is very well played by Yepes who is attentively accompanied by Navarro and the LSO, and the DG sound is fresh.

Violin concerto No. 2 (I Profeti).
(M) (**) BMG/RCA mono GD 87872; *GK 87872* [7872-2-RG; *7872-4-RG*]. Heifetz, LAPO, Wallenstein – FERGUSON: *Sonata No. 1* **; FRANÇAIX: *Trio* ***; K. KHACHATURIAN: *Sonata.***

Castelnuovo-Tedesco is virtually a one-work composer, known almost exclusively for the *Guitar concerto*, first recorded by Segovia. His collaboration with Heifetz began in 1930 when the latter commissioned a work for violin and piano. The following year, Heifetz played the *First violin concerto* of 1924 in New York, and in due course presented the *Second* (1931) at a concert conducted by Toscanini. It is subtitled *The Prophets* and, though free of programme associations, the composer sought to represent the fiery eloquence of the ancient prophets among the surrounding voices of the people and the voices of nature. It is a neo-romantic piece whose opening suggests Bloch or Vaughan Williams; but the idiom is predominantly sunny, though the thematic substance is thin. Heifetz plays with glorious, full-throated tone and the Los Angeles orchestra under Wallenstein give excellent support. The 1954 recording places the soloist far forward but is otherwise quite spacious and, despite some distortion in climaxes, is generally acceptable.

Catalani, Alfredo (1854–93)

La Wally (opera): complete.
(M) *** Decca 425 417-2 (2). Tebaldi, Del Monaco, Diaz, Cappuccilli, Marimpietri, Turin Lyric Ch., Monte Carlo Op. O, Fausto Cleva.
** BMG/Eurodisc Dig. RD 69073 (2) [69073-2-RC]. Eva Marton, Araiza, D'Artegna, Titus, Kaufmann, Bav. R. Ch., Munich R. O, Pinchas Steinberg.

This unashamed piece of hokum was much loved by Toscanini, who named his children after characters in it. The title-role prompts Renata Tebaldi to give one of her most tenderly affecting performances on record, a glorious example of her singing late in her career. Her poise and control of line in the celebrated aria, *Ebben? Ne andro lontana*, provide a model for any generation. The work's mixture of sweetness and melodrama has its attractions despite the absurdity of the story. The last Act leads to a concluding love-duet, set in the Swiss mountains, when the warbling of hero and heroine is curtailed by an avalanche. The hero is swept away, and the heroine distractedly throws herself after him.

Tebaldi is well matched by a strong cast. Mario del Monaco begins coarsely, but the heroic power and intensity of his singing are formidable, and it is good to have the young Cappuccilli in the baritone role of Gellner. The sound in this late-1960s recording is superbly focused and vividly real, a fine example of Decca recording at a vintage period, with only a touch of over-brightness in the CD transfer. At mid-price on two discs only (two Acts per disc) with libretto and translation, it will not easily be displaced.

The Eurodisc version fails to match its Decca predecessor, even in recorded sound. The voices are set a little fuzzily at a slight distance, with the recording tending to exaggerate the vocal unevennesses of all three principals. Eva Marton makes a powerful but erratic heroine, and though Francisco Araiza is more subtle than most Italian tenors would be, the heroic Italianate timbre is missing. Alan Titus in the principal baritone role is disappointing too. The orchestral playing under Pinchas Steinberg is a degree more polished than on the Decca version, but the performance is nowhere near so warmly expressive.

Chabrier, Emmanuel (1841–94)

España (rhapsody).
(M) **(*) EMI Dig. CDM7 63572-2; *EG 763572-4* [id.]. Phd. O, Muti – FALLA: *Three-cornered hat*; RAVEL: *Rapsodie espagnole.***(*)

España (rhapsody); *Suite pastorale.*
*** Chan. Dig. CHAN 8852; *ABTD 1469* [id.]. Ulster O, Yan Pascal Tortelier – DUKAS: *L'apprenti sorcier; La Péri.***(*)

Yan Pascal Tortelier and the excellent Ulster Orchestra give an altogether first-rate account of Chabrier's delightful *Suite pastorale*, distinguished by an appealing charm and lightness of touch. The third movement, *Sous bois*, which was rushed off its feet in the old Decca set, is suitably atmospheric and enchanting. There is a spirited account of *España*, too.

Muti's manner is brisk but lilting in Chabrier's dance rhythms, an apt makeweight for two other works inspired by the Spanish sun. The brilliant (1980) digital recording has a touch of glare, but is one of the best from this source. However, with only 44 minutes of music, this is not remarkable value, even at mid-price.

(i; ii) *A la musique; Habanera;* (iii) *Larghetto for French horn; Valses romantiques;* (ii; iv) *La Sulamite. Gwendoline: Overture;* (i) *Aria: Ne riez pas.*
**(*) EMI Dig. CDC7 54004-2 [id.]. (i) Hendricks; (ii) Choeurs de Toulouse-midi-Pyrénées; (iii) Vescovo; (iv) Mentzer; O de Capitole Toulouse, Michel Plasson.

This is a most useful addition to the catalogue, for it introduces some Chabrier that is new to CD. Indeed *A la musique* will come as a revelation to most music-lovers acquainted only with the popular pieces such as *España* and the *Suite pastorale. A la musique* sings the praises of music 'which cradles the child and charms the old' and is a lovely piece, full of voluptuous harmonies. The solo part is beautifully sung, but the Choeurs de Toulouse-midi-Pyrénées are less than first class and are not perfectly in tune. If the rest of *Gwendoline* is like the charming aria (from Act I, scene ii) that Barbara Hendricks gives us, it should be worth hearing complete. Beecham used to champion the rather Wagnerian *Overture* and Plasson shows himself no less responsive to its dramatic fire. Another delightful discovery is *La Sulamite* ('The Shulamite Woman') a scène lyrique for mezzo-soprano, women's voices and orchestra whose sensuous atmosphere exerted an influence on the young Debussy. (Roger Delage's note points to the mysterious opening chordal sequence in *La demoiselle élue.*) The recording, made in the warm, reverberant-acoustic Salle-aux-grains, Toulouse, is eminently acceptable, and the playing of the Orchestre du Capitole de Toulouse is very persuasive.

Chadwick, George (1854–1931)

Serenade for strings.
*** Albany Dig. TROY 033-2 [id.]. V. American Music Ens., Hobart Earle – GILBERT: *Suite.****

Chadwick's *Serenade,* written in 1890, is here given its European première. It is a delightful work which ought to be much better known. The lyrical feeling of the first movement and the haunting nostalgia of the *Andante* are matched by the expressive warmth of the Minuet which has a genial, Dvořákian intensity and variety of rhythmic style. The finale is hardly less striking in its dancing melodic appeal, and altogether this very well-crafted piece by the so-called 'Boston classicist' gives much pleasure. It is quite beautifully played by this excellent Viennese group, drawn from younger members of the Vienna Symphony Orchestra, who clearly relish its fresh melodic appeal and provide a Viennese lilt in the finale. The sound too is first rate, a successful example of a 'live recording' bringing no loss in realism and a gain in spontaneity.

Chappell, Herbert (born 1934)

Guitar concerto No. 1 (Caribbean concerto).
*** Decca Dig. 430 233-2; *430 233-4* [id.]. Eduardo Fernández, ECO, Barry Wordsworth – ARNOLD: *Guitar concerto*; BROUWER: *Retrats Catalans.****

Chappell's warm and vigorous concerto makes a splendid coupling for the Arnold work. Like Arnold a skilled film composer, Chappell has here written a Caribbean-inspired piece which, with few pretensions, vies with the ubiquitous *Concierto de Aranjuez* in immediate colourfulness and with Arthur Benjamin's Caribbean pieces in energy. Unlike most guitar concertos, which keep stopping and starting, this one builds consistently. The slow movement hinges on a simple surging melody not too distant from Khachaturian's *Spartacus Adagio* (*Onedin Line*), and is followed by a riotous finale on Cuban dance rhythms. A winner, brilliantly played and colourfully recorded.

Charpentier, Gustave (1860–1956)

Louise (opera): complete.
(M) *** Sony S3K 46429 (3) [id.]. Cotrubas, Berbié, Domingo, Sénéchal, Bacquier, Amb. Op. Ch., New Philh. O, Prêtre.

Even more than Mascagni and Leoncavallo, Gustave Charpentier is a one-work composer, and one might be forgiven for thinking that that work, the opera *Louise*, is a one-aria opera. No other melody in the piece may quite match the soaring lyricism of the heroine's *Depuis le jour*, but this fine, atmospheric recording, the first in stereo, certainly explains why *Louise* has long been a favourite opera in Paris. It cocoons the listener in the atmosphere of Montmartre in the 1890s, with Bohemians more obviously proletarian than Puccini's, a whole factory of seamstresses and an assorted range of ragmen, junkmen, pea-sellers and the like making up a highly individual cast-list. Only four characters actually matter in a plot that remains essentially simple, even though the music (not counting intervals) lasts close on three hours. Louise is torn between loyalty to her parents and her love for the Bohemian, Julien. The opera starts with a love duet and from there meanders along happily, enlivened mainly by the superb crowd scenes. One of them, normally omitted but included here, proves as fine as any, with Louise's fellow seamstresses in their workhouse (cue for sewing-machines in the percussion department) teasing her for being in love, much as Carmen is teased in Bizet's quintet. The love duets too are enchanting and, although the confrontations with the boring parents are far less appealing, the atmosphere carries one over. Ileana Cotrubas makes a delightful heroine, not always flawless technically but charmingly girlish. Placido Domingo is a relatively heavyweight Julien and Jane Berbié and Gabriel Bacquier are excellent as the parents. Under Georges Prêtre, far warmer than usual on record, the ensemble is rich and clear, with refined recording every bit as atmospheric as one could want. A set which splendidly fills an obvious gap in the catalogue.

Charpentier, Marc-Antoine (1634–1704)

Le malade imaginaire (incidental music).
*** HM Dig. HMC 90-1336; *40-1336* [id.]. Zanetti, Rime, Brua, Visse, Crook, Gardeil, Les Arts Florissants, Christie.

Even next to the outstanding first recording made a little earlier for Erato by Marc Minkowski (2292 45002-2), this issue brings important advantages, not least the practical ones of a rather more extended treatment and more cueing points. It was recorded after a live stage production, and the acting is somewhat more uninhibited than on the Erato issue, perhaps too much so. With rather less forward and more refined sound, Christie – though he uses percussion just as dramatically as his rival – is lighter in his textures and rhythms, often opting for faster speeds. Whichever version is preferred, this is a masterly example of writing for the stage and, in the vigour and speed of its comic-opera interludes, it makes one wish Charpentier had had more chance to rival Lully. The format is cumbersome, with a single disc contained in a double jewel-case, but the libretto is far more readable.

Chausson, Ernest (1855–99)

Symphony in B flat, Op. 20.
*** Denon Dig. CO 73675 [id.]. Netherlands R. PO, Jean Fournet – FAURÉ: *Pelléas et Mélisande.****
* ASV Dig. CDDCA 708; *ZCDCA 708* [id.]. Philh. O, D'Avalos – FRANCK: *Symphony.**

Symphony in B flat, Op. 20; Vivianne (symphonic poem), *Op. 9.*
**(*) Erato/WEA 2292 45554-2; *2292 45554-4* [id.]. Basle SO, Jordan.

Jean Fournet's new account of the *Symphony in B flat* is arguably the finest now on the market. Not only is it very well shaped, but the texture in the voluptuous slow movement is heard in excellent focus. Fournet paces all three movements well and gets sensitive results from his players. It is to be preferred to Plasson's account (currently out of the catalogue), though that is more logically coupled with other Chausson pieces, *Soir de Fête* and *Viviane.* So is the Chandos version by Serebrier and the Belgian Radio Orchestra, which again offers *Soir de Fête*, plus two scenes from the incidental music for *The Tempest.* Serebrier's account of the *Symphony* has real conviction and receives good recording (CHAN 8369; *ABTD 1135*), but on balance Fournet is first choice.

Armin Jordan and the Basle orchestra give a well-shaped account of the *Symphony* and are thoroughly atmospheric in the Wagnerian slow movement. The orchestral playing is responsive and the recording has an agreeable warmth, with plenty of space round the sound. Jordan is a fine (and much underrated) conductor with an obvious sympathy for this work, and he is thoroughly convincing in both the symphony and *Viviane*. This issue did not deserve its generally cool press reception and can be recommended alongside (but not in preference to) the Serebrier on Chandos.

Francesco D'Avalos has the advantage of the Philharmonia Orchestra but, despite many incidental beauties, the playing has little of the personality one knows this orchestra to possess. Not a strong contender.

Concert in D for piano, violin & string quartet, Op. 21.
(*) Decca Dig. 425 860-2; *425 860-4* [id.]. Thibaudet, Bell, Takács Qt – RAVEL: *Piano trio.*(*)

Chausson's *Concert* has come in from the cold; it languished, unrepresented in the catalogues, for some years during the 1970s. Decca's team comprises Joshua Bell, Jean-Yves Thibaudet and the Takács Quartet, and they give a good account of themselves. Joshua Bell is perhaps a little too forceful and thrustful in tone in the main theme of the first movement, and they are rather on the fast side in the finale and wanting in breadth. These artists do not convey much period feeling or atmosphere and are less inside its sensibility than Collard, Dumay and the Muir Quartet, who remain a first choice. The recording is bright and well focused. Choice of couplings will inevitably affect choice, but readers primarily wanting the Chausson will find the Collard (see our main volume, p. 273) more satisfying.

Chanson perpétuelle, Op. 37.
❀ (M) *** Decca 425 948-2 [id.]. Dame Janet Baket, Melos Ens. (with *French song recital* *** ❀).

Dame Janet Baker's magical performance of Chausson's setting of the Charles Cros poem – a declaration of passion to a departed lover, with the words inspiring continuous music – is part of a collection of French songs of the greatest distinction. It was originally issued on Oiseau-Lyre in 1967, recorded with the combination of atmosphere and presence for which that label was famous.

Le roi Arthus (opera): complete.
(M) *** Erato/Warner Dig. 2292 45407 (3) [id.]. Zylis-Gara, Quilico, Winbergh, Massis, Fr. R. Ch. & New PO, Jordan.

This first ever recording of *Le roi Arthus* reveals it as a powerful piece, full of overt Wagnerian echoes; it places Arthur, Guinevere and Lancelot in a sequence of situations closely akin to those of King Mark, Isolde and Tristan. The musical parallels are often bare-faced and the result could easily have emerged as just a big Wagnerian pastiche, but the energy and exuberant lyricism of the piece give it a positive life of its own. The vigour and panache of the opening suggest *Tannhäuser* and *Walküre* rather than *Tristan*, while the forthright side of *Parsifal* lies behind the noble music for Arthur himself, a more virile figure than King Mark. The love-duets in Tristan-style, of which there are several, have a way of growing ever more lusciously lyrical to bring them close to Massenet and Puccini. Armin Jordan directs a warmly committed performance which brings out the full stature of the work, far more than just a radio recording translated. Gino Quilico in the name-part sings magnificently, and the freshness and freedom of Gösta Winbergh's tone are very apt for Lancelot's music. Teresa Zylis-Gara, though not always ideally sweet-toned, is an appealing Guinevere; the recorded sound is generally full and well balanced. This makes a valuable addition to the catalogue and is guaranteed to delight many more than specialists in French opera.

Cherubini, Luigi (1760–1842)

Medea (complete).
(M) ** EMI CMS7 63625-2 (2) [Ang. CDMB 63625]. Callas, Scotto, Pirazzini, Picchi, La Scala Ch. & O, Serafin – BEETHOVEN: *Ah! perfido.***

Callas's 1957 studio recording of *Medea* may not bring out the full expressiveness of her historic reading of a long-neglected opera – live recordings reveal it better – but it is still a magnificent example of the fire-eating Callas. She completely outshines any rival. A cut text is used and Italian instead of the original French, with Serafin less imaginative than he usually was; but, with a cast more than competent – including the young Renata Scotto – it is an enjoyable set. Callas's recording of the Beethoven scena, *Ah perfido*, makes a powerful fill-up, even though in this late recording (1963/4) vocal flaws emerge the more.

Requiem.
(M) (**(*)) BMG/RCA mono GD 60272; *GK 60272* (2) [60272-RG-2; *60272-RG-4*]. Marshall, Merriman, Conley, Hines, Robert Shaw Ch., NBC SO, Toscanini – BEETHOVEN: *Missa solemnis.*(**(*))

Toscanini, like his latterday disciple, Riccardo Muti, was an admirer of Cherubini's choral music, and though the start of this live performance of 1950 lacks the full Toscanini electricity, the Shaw Chorale, superbly disciplined, quickly responds to the maestro, to produce searingly incisive singing in such movements as the *Dies irae*. It makes a fair coupling for Toscanini's keenly dramatic account of Beethoven's *Missa solemnis*; but it would have been better to have had them separated, as could easily have been arranged. Characteristically dry recording.

Chopin, Frédéric (1810–49)

Chopiniana (ballet, arr. Glazunov).
(BB) ** Naxos Dig. 8.550324/5 [id.]. Slovak RSO (Bratislava), Lenárd – TCHAIKOVSKY: *Nutcracker.***

The presentation and titling of the Naxos CDs (though not the documentation inside) suggest that *Chopiniana* is the same as *Les Sylphides*, which it is not. It opens robustly rather than evocatively, with the *Polonaise in A major*, and closes with the *Tarantella*, Op. 43. Glazunov's scoring for the most part has bright primary colours, effective in context, but the moonlit atmosphere of Roy Douglas's magical arrangement is only sporadic. This is not the fault of the excellent Slovak playing, which is bright and lively and vividly recorded. But this work fails to convince the listener that orchestral transcriptions of Chopin's piano music add anything new, whereas the Douglas *Les Sylphides* has quite the opposite effect.

Piano concertos Nos. (i) *1 in E min., Op. 11;* (ii) *2 in F min., Op. 21.*
(M) ** CBS SBK 46336; *40-46336* [id.]. (i) Gilels, Phd. O, Ormandy; (ii) Watts, NYPO, Schippers.
*(*) Decca Dig. 425 859-2; *425 859-4* [id.]. Jorge Bolet, Montreal SO, Dutoit.

Gilels's account of the *E minor Concerto* is one of the most thoughtful and dramatic currently available. He does not match the youthful fire of Pollini or Zimerman, but the lambent quality and the sensitivity of his playing, with every phrase breathing naturally, make the most poetic impression. Ormandy gives good support and the recording seems fuller and more pleasing in its CD format. However, André Watts's version of the *F minor Concerto*, although dreamily persuasive in the *Larghetto* and with plenty of life in the finale, is less distinctive overall, and this coupling cannot be recommended in preference to Székely, digitally recorded on Naxos (8.550123), or Vásáry on DG (429 515-2), both of whom are even more competitively priced. However, Zimerman's premium-priced DG record (415 970-2) still leads the field.

Jorge Bolet made this CD of the concertos with the Montreal orchestra and Dutoit in the last year of his life. As always with this artist, there is some fine pianism and refined tonal colouring, but the finales of both concertos need far more sparkle and vivacity. The Decca sound is excellent and Dutoit and his fine Montreal orchestra are admirably supportive but, given the competition presently available, these accounts are unlikely to win favour.

(i) *Piano concerto No. 1. Andante spianato et Grande polonaise brillante, Op. 22; Piano sonata No. 3 in B min., Op. 58; Mazurka in F sharp min., Op. 59/3; Prelude in C sharp min., Op. 45.*
(B) **(*) DG Compact Classics *419 089-4* [id.]. Argerich; (i) LSO, Abbado.

Martha Argerich's recording dates from 1969 and helped to establish her international reputation. The distinction of this partnership is immediately apparent in the opening orchestral ritornello with Abbado's flexible approach. Martha Argerich follows his lead and her affectionate phrasing provides some lovely playing, especially in the slow movement. Perhaps in the passage-work she is sometimes rather too intense, but this is far preferable to the rambling style we are sometimes offered. With excellent recording, this is one of the most satisfactory versions available of this elusive concerto. This Compact Classics tape also offers fine performances of the *B minor Sonata* and the *Andante spianato* plus two other pieces, all given excellent sound.

(i) *Piano concerto No. 1 in E min., Op. 11. Ballade No. 2 in F, Op. 38; Scherzo No. 4 in E, Op. 54.*
(M) *** DG Analogue/Dig. 431 580-2; *431 580-4* [id.]. Krystian Zimerman, (i) with Concg. O, Kondrashin.

Zimerman's 1979 live performance of Chopin's *E minor Concerto* is admirable in all respects, not least for his sympathetic rapport with Kondrashin. It is very well recorded too and is here reissued with his more recent, digital recording of the *F major Ballade* (see below) and the *Scherzo in E major* (which has some breathtaking passages), taken from his début recital, recorded rather dryly by Polskie Nagrania.

Piano concerto No. 2 in F min., Op. 21.
(B) ** Sony MBK 44803 [id.]. Charles Rosen, New Philh. O, Pritchard – LISZT: *Piano concerto No. 1.***(*)

(i) *Piano concerto No. 2 in F min.;* (ii) *Andante spianato & Grande polonaise brillante, Op. 22;* (i) *Fantasia on Polish airs, Op. 13.*
(M) * RCA/BMG GD 60404; *GK 60404* [60404-2-RG; *60404-4-RG*]. Artur Rubinstein, (i) Phd. O, Ormandy; (ii) Symphony of the Air, Wallenstein.

(i; ii) *Piano concerto No. 2 in E min.;* (iii) *3 Mazurkas, Op. 59;* (i) *Nocturnes Nos. 1 in B flat min., Op. 9/1; 9 in B; 10 in A flat, Op. 32/1–2; in C sharp min., Op. posth.;* (iv) *Waltzes Nos. 2, 4, 8–10, 11, 13–14.*
(B) *** DG Compact Classics *413 425-4* [id.]. (i) Vásáry; (ii) BPO, Kulka; (iii) Argerich; (iv) Zimerman.

Tamás Vásáry's performance of the *Concerto* is one of his finest Chopin recordings and the 1964 sound remains first class. The balance is exceptionally convincing. The slow movement is played most beautifully, and in the other movements Kulka's direction of the orchestra has striking character and vigour. Side one is completed by four *Nocturnes* and side two includes a generous selection from Zimerman's distinguished set of the *Waltzes*, with performances as fine as any in the catalogue. It ends with Martha Argerich characteristically volatile in three *Mazurkas*. The transfers to chrome tape are first class throughout.

Pritchard makes an impressive opening tutti and Rosen undoubtedly finds the music's poetry but, in relaxing for the first movement's passagework, he loosens the overall structure. The finale has brilliance and the recording is good, but the competition is formidable in this work.

Rubinstein's 1968 recording of Chopin's *F minor Piano concerto* was one of his rare failures in the recording studio. He and Ormandy – normally such a sympathetic accompanist – failed to find an artistic rapport, and Rubinstein's playing is curiously unmelting. The recording isn't very special either. The *Fantasia on Polish airs* also fails to take off, and the closing *Kujawiak* is unspontaneous. The *Andante spianato*, recorded a decade earlier with Wallenstein, is a different matter, and Rubinstein gives an interpretation to the manner born, at once showy and emotional, yet sensitive. Incidentally, Chopin added the slow introduction to the more obvious showpiece when the work was published. The curious marking *spianato* underlines the steady pulse of the accompaniment, over which Rubinstein's right hand, in typical Chopin fashion, weaves florid decorations with the utmost magic.

Les Sylphides (arr. Roy Douglas).
(M) *** Sony SBK 46550 [id.]. Phd. O, Ormandy – DELIBES: *Coppélia; Sylvia:* suites ***; TCHAIKOVSKY: *Nutcracker suite.***(*)

We have long praised Karajan's performance of Roy Douglas's inspired orchestration of *Les Sylphides* as being ideal. It is still available at bargain price, coupled with a truncated suite from *Coppélia* and an extended set of racy excerpts from the Offenbach/Rosenthal *Gaîté parisienne* (DG 429 163-2; *429 163-4*). But Ormandy's 1961 recording is by no means outclassed. The Philadelphia strings are perfectly cast in this score and, although the CBS sound is less svelte than the DG quality for Karajan, it is still very good. Ormandy begins gently and persuasively but with the rhythmic moulding more positive in the opening *Prelude* and *Nocturne* than with Karajan, but not lacking in charm. Later the lively sections are played with irrepressible brilliance, and some might feel that this extrovert approach is almost overdone in the first *Waltz*, where Ormandy gives the upper strings their head. But later the playing has that rich, expansive excitement for which this orchestra is famous. Ormandy's couplings are more generous than the DG alternative, with nearly 76 minutes of ballet music, all equally charismatic.

(i) *Cello sonata in G min., Op. 65; Introduction and polonaise brillante in C, Op. 3;* (ii) *Ballades Nos. 3 in A flat, Op. 47; 4 in F min., Op. 52.*
(M) *** DG 431 583-2; *431 583-4* [id.]. (i) Rostropovich, Argerich; (ii) Sviatoslav Richter.

With such characterful artists as Rostropovich and Argerich challenging each other, this is a memorably warm and convincing account of the *Cello sonata*, Chopin's last published work, a piece which clicks into focus in such a performance. The contrasts of character between expressive cello and brilliant piano are also richly caught in the *Introduction and polonaise*, and the recording is warm to match. The digital remastering for this reissue as part of DG's Chopin Edition is most successful; the sound always refined, with a good balance, is now firmer and clearer. Richter's 1961/62 accounts of the two *Ballades* have a commanding individuality, and the recording is remarkably good: No. 4 comes from a live recital.

PIANO MUSIC

Andante spianato and grand polonaise brillante in E flat, Op. 22; Ballades Nos. 1–4; Berceuse, Op. 57; Nocturne in C sharp min., Op. posth.; Tarantelle in A flat, Op. 43.
*(*) Nimbus Dig. NI 5249 [id.]. Bernard d'Ascoli.

Bernard d'Ascoli fares better than many pianists who have recorded on this label and the sound, though far from ideally balanced, is acceptable. He is a highly musical player, but for the most part these readings do not displace rival issues. He makes heavy weather of the passage leading into the second group of the *G minor Ballade* and elsewhere pulls other details out of shape.

Ballades Nos. 1–4; Barcarolle, Op. 60; Fantaisie in F min., Op. 49.
*** DG Dig. 423 090-2; *423 090-4* [id.]. Krystian Zimerman.

Krystian Zimerman's impressive set of the *Ballades* appeared as long ago as the autumn of 1988, at the same time as his aristocratic account of the Liszt concertos, and they seem unaccountably to have been overlooked in the flood of new issues. Both they and the other two works on this disc are touched by distinction throughout and have spontaneity as well as tremendous concentration to commend them. Indeed readers who elect to have only one set of the *Ballades* would find this an eminently satisfying first choice.

Ballades Nos. 1–4; Piano sonata No. 3 in B min., Op. 58.
**(*) EMI Dig. CDC7 54006-2 [id.]. Jean Philippe Collard.

Jean Philippe Collard plays with an impressive mastery throughout and is decently enough recorded. The *Ballades* are strongly characterized and have the authority and elegance one associates with this artist. Were his recording really first class, this might rate a stronger recommendation.

Études, Op. 10/1–12; Op. 25/1–12.
(***) Nimbus Dig. NI 5223 [id.]. Ronald Smith.

Ronald Smith is a grievously underrated artist whose musicianship and artistry excite wide admiration and respect among connoisseurs: his playing has tenderness and spontaneity, a fine sense of line and good poetic feeling. If only he were better served by the recording engineers, this would be strongly competitive. However, the piano sound is not quite in focus and the instrument sounds as if it is at the end of a very reverberant studio. Artistically, however, there are few complaints: indeed the playing rates three stars – but one cannot escape from the distinctly unpleasing recorded sound.

Études, Op. 10/1–12; Op. 25/1–12; 24 Préludes, Op. 28; Polonaises 1–7.
(B) *** DG 431 221-2 (3) [id.]. Maurizio Pollini.

The reissue of these works on three CDs at bargain price makes a most attractive package. Pollini offers playing of outstanding mastery, and the DG engineers have accomplished the remastering with splendid freshness. The three individual records are discussed in our main volume, pp. 281–4.

Mazurkas Nos. 1–51.
*** BMG/RCA RD 85171 (2) [5614-2-RC]. Artur Rubinstein.

The *Mazurkas* contain some of Chopin's most characteristic music and in Rubinstein's hands these 51 pieces are endlessly fascinating.

Nocturnes Nos. 1–11.
(B) * Ph. 426 979-2; *426 979-4* [id.]. Nikita Magaloff.

Magaloff's *Nocturnes* do not command a strong recommendation, even at bargain price. The recording is good, though not quite as sonorous as on LP, but the playing is curiously measured and deliberate; one needs more incandescence and poetic feeling in this repertoire.

Nocturnes Nos. 1–4; 7–10; 12–13; 15; 18–19.
(M) **(*) DG 431 586-2; *431 586-4* [id.]. Daniel Barenboim.

Barenboim's selection has been generously expanded for this reissue (72 minutes). The performances, taken from his complete set, are intense, thoughtful and poetic, the phrasing lovingly moulded, following rather in the mid-European tradition. Compared with Rubinstein, whose complete set is available on BMG/RCA (RD 89563 [5613-2-RC]), they lack a mercurial dimension. The recording is first class.

Polonaises Nos. 1–7.
*** BMG/RCA RD 89814 [5615-2-RC]. Artur Rubinstein.

Rubinstein's easy majesty and natural sense of spontaneous phrasing give this collection a special place in the catalogue.

24 Preludes, Op. 28; Prelude No. 25 in C sharp min., Op. 26; Barcarolle, Op. 60; Berceuse, Op. 57; Impromptus Nos. 1–4; Fantaisie-impromptu.
(M) (**(*)) EMI mono CDH7 61050-2 [id.]. Alfred Cortot.

Cortot's celebrated recording of the *Preludes* was made in 1933–4, as were the *Impromptus* and the *Barcarolle*. The *Prelude*, Op. 26, and the *Berceuse* come from a visit he made to England in 1949, when he had lost some of his technique but none of his poetry. (We remember hearing him in Oxford that year.) He was a stylist of the first order, a master of characterization and, as Jeremy Siepmann puts it in his notes, 'in his hands, phrases never really followed one another, they grew, in a continuous organic chain of cause and effect'. The sound of the 1930s' recordings is inevitably frail and papery, and the digital mastering does not seem a great improvement on the analogue LP that appeared in France some years ago.

24 Preludes, Op. 28; Preludes Nos. 25–26; Impromptus Nos. 1–3; 4 (Fantaisie-impromptu).
(M) **(*) Ph. 426 634-2; *426 634-4* [id.]. Claudio Arrau.

Arrau's *Preludes* date from the mid-1970s and are much admired. He certainly receives a full-bodied recording which does justice to his subtle nuances of tone; every *Prelude* bears the imprint of a strong personality. Arrau can sometimes sound a shade calculating (his rubato seeming arbitrary and contrived), but there is little evidence of this here. His *Preludes* appear to spring from an inner conviction, even if the outward results will not have universal appeal. The same thoughts might be applied to the *Impromptus*. Arrau's Chopin is seldom mercurial, but it is never inflexible and has its own special insights. The *Fantaisie-impromptu*, with its nobly contoured central melody, is a highlight here, with the richly coloured piano timbre contributing a good deal to the character of its presentation.

24 Preludes, Op. 28; Preludes Nos. 25–26; 3 Mazurkas, Op. 59; Scherzo No. 3 in C sharp min., Op. 39.
(M) *** DG 431 584-2; *431 584-4* [id.]. Martha Argerich.

The *Preludes* show Martha Argerich at her finest, spontaneous and impetuous in her fiery way when the music demands an impulsive response. Her instinct here is sure and there are many poetic touches. The *Mazurkas* are similarly volatile, and the *Scherzo* brings some glitteringly delicate articulation to make one catch one's breath. The recording of the *Preludes*, made in Watford Town Hall in 1977, was among the best she received from DG.

Piano sonata No. 2 in B flat min. (Funeral march), Op. 35; Barcarolle in F sharp, Op. 60; Polonaise No. 6 in A flat (Heroic), Op. 53; Polonaise-fantaisie in A flat, Op. 61.
(M) **(*) DG 431 582-2; *431 582-4* [id.]. Martha Argerich.

Martha Argerich's playing has a highly strung quality that will not be to all tastes. Her *B flat minor Sonata* was recorded in 1975 and its combination of impetuosity and poetic feeling is distinctly individual. Her brilliance is admirably suited to the two *Polonaises*, and the *Barcarolle* (the earliest recording here) is also charismatic. The recording still sounds fresh and the CD transfer gives her plenty of presence. Our main recommendations for the *Second* and *Third Sonatas* coupled together remain with Rubinstein (BMG/RCA RD 89812 [5616-2-RC]) and Pollini (DG 415 362-2).

(i) *Piano sonata No. 3 in B min., Op. 58;* (ii) *Polonaises Nos. 1 in C sharp min.; 2 in E flat min., Op. 26/1–2;* (i) *3 in A (Military); 4 in C min., Op. 40/1–2.*
(M) **(*) DG 431 587-2; *431 587-4* [id.]. (i) Emil Gilels; (ii) Lazar Berman.

Gilels's account of the *B minor Sonata* is thoughtful and ruminative, seen through a powerful mind and wholly individual fingers. There are some highly personal touches, for example the gentle undulating accompaniment, like quietly tolling bells, caressing the second group of the first movement, and a beautifully pensive and delicately coloured slow movement. The first movement is expansive and warmly lyrical, and there is not a bar that does not have one thinking anew about this music. An altogether haunting reading and an obligatory acquisition, even if it does not prompt one to discard Lipatti, Rubinstein or Perahia. The two *Polonaises* are also superb: they have majesty, grandeur and poetry, and the 1978 recording, made in the Berlin Jesus-Christus Kirche, is very satisfactory. For the reissue, DG have added the two Op. 26 *Polonaises*, recorded in Munich by Lazar Berman a year later. These readings possess a certain magisterial command and are also well recorded; but Berman does not invest each phrase with the intensity of Pollini or the sheer poetry of Gilels, and they have less character and colour than either of these artists provide.

Piano sonata No. 3 in B min., Op. 58; Waltzes Nos. 1–14.
(M) *(*) Sony SBK 46346 [id.]. Alexander Brailowsky.

Brailowsky's recordings date from the mid-1970s and, despite a certain character in the shaping of the *Waltzes*, do not show him at his best, either technically or artistically. There is a curious lack of flair, and the recording too is rather lacklustre.

Waltzes Nos. 1–17.
** DG Dig. 431 779-2 [id.]. Jean-Marc Luisada.

Jean-Marc Luisada was born in Bizerta, Tunisia, and studied at the Menuhin School in England and, later, in Paris. There is an engaging quality about his playing, and something of the winning platform personality he possesses comes over in his performances here. He made a pleasing impression at the 1985 Warsaw Competition, where he was among the finalists. There is a certain freshness about these performances, which are eminently musical, though ultimately Luisada's readings lack a strong profile, and as yet he does not convey the kind of authority that persuades the listener that this is the only way this music can be played: one feels that on another occasion he could take a completely different view of the individual waltzes. He is very well recorded. Lipatti's classic performances, which are uniquely perceptive, are now available in a boxed set with his other major recordings, an indispensable acquisition for any serious collector (see our Concerts section, below). For a modern, single-disc recommendation, we would suggest Ashkenazy (Decca 414 600-2; *414 600-4*).

RECITAL COLLECTIONS

Andante spianato and grande polonaise brillante, Op. 22; Ballade No. 1 in G min., Op. 23; Fantaisie in F min., Op. 49; Mazurkas: in G min.; in C; in B flat min., Op. 24/1, 2 & 4; Waltz in A flat, Op. 34/1.
(M) **(*) Analogue/Dig. DG 431 589-2; *431 589-4* [id.]. Krystian Zimerman.

Much of this programme derives from Zimerman's 1977 initial recital, recorded by Polskie Nagrania, when we commented: 'A remarkably promising début. This first recital leaves no doubts as to the astonishing security of Zimerman's technique (there are some breathtaking passages in the *Andante spianato*), nor the individual quality of his artistic personality. Here is an artist to watch.' And so it proved, as his later, mercurial, digital recordings of the *Fantaisie in F minor* and the *First Ballade* so readily demonstrate. The earlier recordings are dry and close, but the CD transfer makes them sound firmer than in their original LP format.

'Favourite Chopin': Ballade No. 3 in A flat, Op. 47; Études: in G flat, Op. 10/5; A flat; G flat, Op. 25/1 & 9; Nocturnes Nos. 10 in A flat, Op. 32/1; 15 in F min., Op. 55/1; Polonaise No. 6 in A flat, Op. 53; Preludes, Op. 28, Nos. 6 in B min.; 20 in C min.; Scherzo No. 3 in C sharp min., Op. 39; Waltzes Nos. l (Grande valse brillante), Op. 18; 11 in G flat, Op. 70/1.
(M) *** CD-EMX 2045. Daniel Adni.

This collection was recorded in 1951 to provide a brilliant début for a young and talented artist who was only nineteen at the time, and who has made all too few recordings since. His sensibility in this repertoire is matched by the kind of effortless technique that is essential to give Chopin's music its line and flow. From the glitter and brilliance of the opening *Grande valse brillante* to the evocative reading of the famous *'Sylphides' Nocturne in A flat*, the tonal shading is matched by the spontaneity of the rubato, and the closing *Polonaise* is arresting. The programme is beautifully balanced to make one of the freshest and most enjoyable Chopin collections available at any price. Adni is given most natural recorded sound and a real sense of presence on CD.

Berceuse in D flat, Op. 57; Études, Op. 10/1–4, 6–7; Op. 255/1, 4, 6 & 7; Nocturnes: in G min., Op. 37/1; in B, Op. 62/1; Scherzo No. 1 in B min., Op. 20; Waltzes: in E flat (Grand valse brillante), Op. 18; in A min., Op. 34/2; in C sharp min., Op. 64/2.
(M) **(*) DG 431 588-2; *431 588-4* [id.]. Tamás Vásáry.

An excellent recital compiled from Vásáry's mid-1960s recordings, showing this artist at his most impressive in this repertoire. The opening *Scherzo* is brilliantly and flexibly done and the *Études* are authoritative and commanding, the famous *E major*, Op. 10, No. 3, beautifully done. Perhaps the *Berceuse* is a shade deliberate; but both the *Nocturnes* and *Waltzes* have plenty of colour and their rubato is generally convincing. The layout is satisfyingly conceived, and the recital ends dashingly with the *Grand valse brillante*. The sound is generally very believable, with only a hint of brittleness in the opening *Scherzo*.

Études: in C min. (Revolutionary), Op. 10/12; in D flat, Op. 25/8; Impromptus Nos. 1 in A flat, Op. 29; 2 in F sharp, Op. 36; 3 in G flat, Op. 51; Fantaisie-impromptu, Op. 6; Mazurkas: in D; in C, Op. 33/2–3; in C sharp min., Op. 41/4; in C sharp min., Op. 63/3; in C, Op. 67/3; Nocturne in F sharp, Op. 15/2; Waltzes: in G, Op. 34/3; in E; in E flat; in A flat, Op. posth.
(M) ** DG Dig. 431 585-2; *431 585-4* [id.]. Stanislav Bunin.

Stanislav Bunin won the 1983 Marguerite Long Competition in Paris when he was only sixteen and the Warsaw Chopin Competition two years later. Still in his early twenties, he is a player of some fire and temperament, and these recordings (made during the course of the Warsaw Competition) show his remarkable technical address and musicianship – but also his idiosyncratic manner. His fingers are more than equal to this repertoire and he has a strong sense of style, but he is rather self-aware too. His rubato sometimes sounds studied, but his *Écossaises* have much rhythmic charm. The *Fantaisie-impromptu* and the *Revolutionary study* show him at his most brilliant, and the *A flat Impromptu* is impressively individual; but the *Grande valse brillante* is gabbled (though it evokes much applause at the close of the recital). The sound is realistic.

Cilea, Francesco (1866–1950)

Adriana Lecouvreur (complete).
*** Decca Dig. 425 815-2; *425 815-4* (2) [id.]. Sutherland, Bergonzi, Nucci, d'Artegna, Ciurca, Welsh Nat. Op. Ch. & O, Bonynge.
(M) **(*) Decca 430 256-2 (2) [id.]. Tebaldi, Simionato, Del Monaco, Fioravanti, St Cecilia, Rome, Ac. Ch. & O, Capuana.

Sutherland's performance in the role of a great tragic actress could not be warmer-hearted. The generosity of Sutherland as an artist, her ability to magnetize as well as to thrill the ear with her distinctive timbre, still full and rich, make this an essential set for all devotees, a recording made right at the end of her career. There are others on record with a more natural feeling for the role – Renata Scotto for one on the rival Sony/CBS set (CD 79310 [M2K 34588]), much happier as an Italian in the passages of spoken dialogue – but, despite the beat in her voice, Sutherland outshines Scotto in richness and opulence in the biggest test, the aria, *Io son l'umile ancella*, an actress's credo. Sutherland's formidable performance is warmly backed up by the other principals, and equally by Richard Bonynge's conducting, not just warmly expressive amid the wealth of rich tunes, but light and sparkling where needed, easily idiomatic. Carlo Bergonzi, like Sutherland, is a veteran acting a young character, but his feeling for words and his legato line never fail him. Among the others, Cleopatra Ciurca makes a sympathetic, warm-toned Princess. Full, warm recording. A clear first choice.

Tebaldi's consistently rich singing misses some of the flamboyance of Adriana's personality and in her characterization both *Io son l'umile ancella* and *Poveri fiori* are lyrically very beautiful. But then, this is an opera that relies very largely on its vocal line for its effect. One wishes that Del Monaco had been as reliable as Tebaldi but, alas, there are some coarse moments among the fine, plangent top notes. Simionato is a little more variable than usual but a tower of strength nevertheless. The recording is outstanding for its time (early 1960s), brilliant and atmospheric.

Clarke, Rebecca (1886–1979)

Piano trio.
*** Gamut Dig. GAMCD 518 [id.]. Hartley Trio – BRIDGE: *Phantasie trio*; IRELAND: *Phantasie.****

Rebecca Clarke, British-born, a viola-player as well as a composer (pupil of Stanford in his later years) had great success in the United States after the First World War. Her superb *Viola sonata* vied with Bloch's *Viola suite* in a major competition, and she followed that up with this equally striking *Piano trio*, which similarly shows influences from Bloch and Bartók much more than from English sources. The vehemence of the first movement gives way to mystery and melancholy in the slow movement, with the finale drawing on both those contrasting moods. The Hartley Trio gives a passionate, warmly persuasive performance, and if the cello-line is not as strongly projected as the rest, that is largely a question of the recording which otherwise is full and forward. The *Phantasie trios* of Bridge and Ireland make a valuable if not very generous fill-up.

Coates, Eric (1886–1958)

Ballad; By the sleepy lagoon; London suite; The Three Elizabeths suite; The three bears (phantasy).
(M) *** ASV CDWHL 2053; *ZCWHL 2053* [id.]. East of England O, Malcolm Nabarro.

This is the first recording by the East of England Orchestra, formed in 1982 by Malcolm Nabarro, and it is appropriate that they should make their début with music by the East-Midlander, Eric Coates – 'the man who writes tunes', as Dame Ethel Smyth described him. There are plenty of them here and one of the most memorable comes in the central movement of *The Three Elizabeths. Elizabeth of Glamis* celebrates the Queen Mother (who is charmingly pictured on the front of the disc) and draws a springtime evocation of Glamis Castle, not missing out the cuckoo. Its delightful main theme, complete with Scottish snap, is given to the oboe, and Gareth Hulse presents it simply but not too ripely, as is suitable for the Scottish climate. Nabarro has the full measure of Coates's leaping allegros: the first movement of the same suite – famous as the TV signature-tune of *The Forsyte Saga* – has admirable rhythmic spirit, and he plays the famous marches with crisp buoyancy. *The Three Bears* sparkles humorously, as it should; only in *By the sleepy lagoon* does one really miss a richer, more languorous string-texture. Excellent, bright recording, and the price is right.

Coleridge-Taylor, Samuel (1875–1912)

Scenes from The Song of Hiawatha (complete).
*** Argo Dig. 430 356-2; *430 356-4* (2) [id.]. Helen Field, Arthur Davies, Bryn Terfel, Welsh Nat. Op. Ch. & O, Kenneth Alwyn.

Coleridge Taylor's choral trilogy based on Longfellow's epic poem had its first performance under the composer in the Royal Albert Hall in 1900. It took a while to catch on, but every year from 1924 until the outbreak of war in 1939 it was given a staged presentation at the same venue. Often nearly a thousand costumed 'Red Indian' performers came to enjoy themselves hugely, singing under the baton of their tribal chief, Sir Malcolm Sargent. His splendid record of Part One, *Hiawatha's wedding feast* (EMI CDM7 68689-2), remains unsurpassed by the present, complete version, and its ambience is more convincing too. Part One is still regularly performed by choral societies in the north of England, and one wondered about the neglect of Parts Two and Three, *The Death of Minnehaha* and *Hiawatha's departure*. Alas, the reason is made clear: there is a distinct falling-off in the composer's inspiration, so fresh and spontaneously tuneful in Part One; when the main theme of *Hiawatha's wedding feast* returns in Part Three (band 12), with the words *From his place rose Hiawatha,* one realizes how memorable it is, compared with what surrounds it. Of course the choral writing is always pleasingly lyrical and makes enjoyable listening. Part Two has plenty of drama, and towards the end Helen Field has a memorably beautiful solo passage, which she sings radiantly, echoed by the chorus, *Wahonomin! Wahonomin! Would that I had perished for you.* There is also an almost Wagnerian apotheosis at the actual moment of the Farewell (band 14), which is sung and played here with compelling grandiloquence. Indeed Kenneth Alwyn is completely at home in this music. (By coincidence, he attended the same school in Croydon as the composer – although not, of course, at the same time!) He directs a freshly spontaneous account and has the advantage of excellent soloists, though the Welsh Opera Choir seem less naturally at home in the idiom than Sargent's own Royal Choral Society. The recording was made in the rather intractable Brangwyn Hall, Swansea, and the engineers have put their microphones fairly close to the performers. The result, while vivid, lacks the glowing ambient effect of the Royal Albert Hall, which would have been a much better venue.

Copland, Aaron (1900–90)

Appalachian spring (ballet; complete original version)
*** Koch Dig. 3-7019-2; *2-7019-4* [id.]. Atlantic Sinf., Schenck – BARBER: *Cave of the heart.****

This Koch International issue offers a welcome chance to hear a modern digital recording of *Appalachian spring* in its original form for thirteen instruments. In this it makes a logical coupling to the original Barber *Medea*, also composed for Martha Graham. It sounds very different from the more familiar version and, as in the case of the Barber coupling, a spikier, more Stravinskian character emerges. There are a few differences of text and of sonority but more of character between the two, and the playing of the Atlantic Sinfonietta and the bright, upfront recording present the chamber version in the best possible light. This is a most interesting and stimulating issue.

Appalachian spring: ballet suite.
(M) *** DG 431 048-2; *431 048-4* [id.]. LAPO, Bernstein – BARBER: *Adagio* ***; GERSHWIN: *Rhapsody in blue.***(*)

Bernstein's digital recording of *Appalachian spring* now comes at mid-price, recoupled with his rather less recommendable second recording of Gershwin's *Rhapsody in blue.*

(i) *Appalachian spring: ballet suite; Billy the Kid: ballet suite;* (ii) *Clarinet concerto;* (i) *Danzón Cubano;* (iii) *El Salón México;* (i) *Fanfare for the common man; John Henry; Letter from home;* (i; iv) *Lincoln portrait;* (iii) *Music for movies;* (i) *Our Town; An Outdoor overture; Quiet city; Rodeo (4 Dance episodes);* (i) *Symphony No. 3;* (i) *Las agachadas.*
(M) *** Sony SM3K 46559 (3) [id.]. (i) LSO; (ii) Benny Goodman, Columbia Symphony

Strings; (iii) New Philh. O; (iv) with Henry Fonda; (v) New England Conservatory Ch., composer.

There are already available, from this same source, three separate mid-priced discs covering the two major ballet suites (plus the original, full chamber score of *Appalachian spring*), a number of Copland's shorter orchestral pieces, and the *Old American songs* (MK 42429/30/31 – see our main volume, pp. 293–4). Now Sony have gone one better and offer a comprehensive anthology of the major orchestral works, ballet suites and film scores dating from Copland's vintage period: 1936–48. The composer again directs with unrivalled insight throughout. Alongside the many familiar scores there are three novelties: *John Henry*, the railroad ballad about the black folk hero who was regarded as the finest rail-layer and rock-crusher of his time; the engaging *Letter from home* ('It's very sentimental,' said Copland, 'but it *modulates*!'); and a vocal vignette which, as such, doesn't properly belong here but is very welcome neverthless, *Las agachadas* ('The shake-down song'), an unaccompanied choral piece, sung spiritedly in Spanish. Benny Goodman's instinctively idiomatic account of the *Clarinet concerto*, which he commissioned, is indispensable in such a collection, as is the *Third Symphony*. By the side of Bernstein's vibrant account, the composer's approach seems comparatively mellow – even gentle at times, as in the scherzo. But the natural authority is commanding, and the work's freshness of inspiration communicates anew. Any listener who responds to the famous *Fanfare for the common man* will be delighted to find it in use here as a launching-pad for the finale: in the composer's hands, the way it steals in is sheer magic. As before, the remastering for CD is done most skilfully, retaining the ambience of the originals, while achieving more refined detail. With 226 minutes of consistently inspired music offered on three CDs, this is a bargain of the utmost distinction. But Bernstein's disc, below, makes an essential appendix.

Appalachian spring: ballet suite. Billy the Kid: ballet suite. Rodeo: 4 dance spisodes. Symphony No. 3: Fanfare for the common man.
❀ (M) *** Sony MK 42265 [id.]. NYPO, Leonard Bernstein.

Bernstein recorded the three Copland ballet suites in the early 1960s when he was at the peak of his creative tenure with the NYPO. No one – not even the composer – has approached these performances for racy rhythmic exuberance or for the tenderness and depth of nostalgia in the lyrical music, especially in the opening sequence of *Appalachian spring* and the *Corral Nocturne* from *Rodeo*. The opening *Buckaroo holiday* and the final *Hoedown* from the latter ballet, taken at a tremendous pace, have an unforgettable rhythmic bite and zest, with amazing precision of ensemble from the New York players, whose adrenalin is obviously running at unprecedented levels. The evocation of *The open prairie* in *Billy the Kid* is magical and the picture of a *Street in a frontier town* has a piquant charm, while the projection of the score's more strident moments brings a characteristic pungency. The *Fanfare for the common man* is not the original, commissioned in 1942 by Eugene Goossens for the Cincinnati Orchestra, but the composer's reworking, when he introduced it as a springboard for the finale of his *Third Symphony*. There could be no finer memorial to Copland's genius or Bernstein's interpretative flair than this ballet triptych, and we are fortunate that the recordings are so good, vivid, spacious and atmospheric. *Appalachian spring* (1961) and *Rodeo* (1960) were made at the Manhattan Center (once again put to use by DG for their recordings by the Orpheus Chamber Orchestra) and *Billy the Kid* in Symphony Hall, Boston, in 1959.

Appalachian spring: ballet suite; Dance Symphony; El salón México; Fanfare for the common man; Rodeo: 4 dance episodes.

(M) *** Decca Dig. 430 705-2; *430 705-4* [id.]. Detroit SO, Dorati.

Dorati has the full measure of Copland's masterly *Appalachian spring* score, creating a marvellous evocation at the opening and a feeling of serene acceptance at the close, while the affectionately witty portrayal of *The revivalist and his flock* is presented with sparklingly precise rhythms and splendid string and woodwind detail. The *Solo dance of the bride* is equally characterful; throughout, Dorati finds a balance between the nicely observed interplay of the human characters and the spacious and lonely grandeur of the Appalachian backcloth. The 1984 Decca digital recording is impressive in its range and beauty of texture, and again confirms the excellence of the acoustic of the Old Orchestral Hall, Detroit. The other works on this mid-priced CD were all digitally recorded in the United Artists Auditorium in 1981. They are notable for their bright, extrovert brilliance, having evidently been chosen for their immediate, cheerful, wide-open-spaces qualities. The playing demonstrates very clearly the degree of orchestral virtuosity available in Detroit, and the recording has a clarity and impact that suit the music. The only reservation is that, rather surprisingly, Dorati's treatment of jazzy syncopations – an essential element in Copland of this vintage – is very literal, lacking the lift we think of as idiomatic. Nevertheless, as sound this is very impressive and the performances have much vitality.

Appalachian spring (original version); *Fanfare for the common man; Nonet for strings; Quiet city; Rodeo* (4 dance episodes).
**(*) Nimbus Dig. NI 5246 [id.]. English SO, William Boughton.

Copland, played with sensitivity and, in the case of *Rodeo*, with much gusto by an English orchestra, and recorded in the Great Hall of Birmingham University, offers an unusual listening experience. The nostalgic *Corral nocturne* from *Rodeo* and the opening of *Appalachian spring* have an affectingly warm evocation although, at the end of the latter, Boughton overdoes his broadening of the climax of the variations on *The gift to be simple*. (He uses the original chamber score, but the strings are augmented.) *Hoe-down*, the barn-dance sequence from *Rodeo*, sounds almost as if it is taking place in Blackpool's Tower Ballroom; while in *Quiet city* the wide reverberation inflates the trumpet solo. Important though this instrument is, the work is not a trumpet concerto. The highlight of the very generous programme (75 minutes) is the *Nonet for strings*, a spare and at times austere neo-baroque masterpiece, written in 1960, which shows the composer at his most searchingly powerful. The opening and closing sections are hauntingly beautiful in their dark nostalgia. The work is played with great sympathy and concentration, and the ambience seems exactly right for the music.

American songs; 4 Piano blues; Rodeo; Variations.
(***) Nimbus Dig. NI 5267 [id.]. Alan Marks.

Alan Marks's superbly alert and idiomatic playing rates three stars. He has real feeling for the style, and all the expertise and energy in the world; he has also made effective transcriptions of the delightful *American songs*. But the recording is terrible: the piano is at the other end of a very reverberant studio.

Old American songs (1st & 2nd sets).
*** Decca Dig. 433 027-2; *433 027-4* [id.]. Samuel Ramey, Warren Jones – IVES: *Songs.****

Ramey's magnificent voice is splendidly suited to these memorable songs, the colourful and often boisterous American equivalents of Britten's folksong settings. They are ideally coupled with a particularly attractive collection of ten Ives songs. Lively, pointed accompaniment and warm, atmospheric recording.

Corelli, Arcangelo (1653–1713)

Concerti grossi, Op. 6/1, 3, 7, 8 (Christmas), 11 & 12.
(M) *** DG Dig. 431 706-2; *431 706-4* [id.]. E. Concert, Trevor Pinnock.

We have given high praise to the complete set, from which these performances come. The English Concert are entirely inside the sensibility of this music and the playing of the continuo group is wonderfully fresh. At mid-price, with the *Christmas concerto* included, this will admirably suit those collectors who want an original-instrument version and who are content with a single-disc selection.

Concerti grossi, Op. 6/5–8 (Christmas concerto).
(M) ** Erato/Warner Dig. 2292 45215-2 [id.]. Sol. Ven., Scimone.

I Solisti Veneti offer polished accounts of the set and are well enough recorded by the Erato engineers. They bring a robust vitality to some of the quicker movements – but are heavy-handed on occasion. On CD, the sound is fresh and full-bodied and the recorded image is very realistic; however, more transparency of texture and a lighter touch are needed in this repertoire, if modern stringed instruments are to be used.

Corigliano, John (born 1938)

(i) *Oboe concerto;* (ii; iii) *3 Irish folk song settings: The Sally Gardens; The foggy dew; She moved thro' the fair;* (ii; iv) *Poem in October.*
(M) *** BMG Analogue/Dig. GD 60395 [60395-2-RG]. (i) Humbert Lucarelli, American SO, Kazuyoshi Akiyama; (ii) Robert White; (iii) Ransom Wilson; (iv) Nyfenger, Lucarelli, Rabbai, American Qt, Peress (cond. from harpishcord).

John Corigliano's highly imaginative *Oboe concerto* (written in 1975 and given this superb première recording a year later) is an ambitious four-movement piece (26 minutes), requiring great flexibility and virtuosity from its soloist as well as the ability to provide beautiful tone and a sustained line in the haunting *Song*, the first of the two slow movements. The work opens ingeniously with the orchestra tuning up, and the music springs fairly naturally from this familiar aleatory pattern of sound. The composer calls his first movement *Tuning game*, and the soloist engages in a not entirely friendly interplay with each of the orchestra's instrumental groups as his 'A' is proffered seductively to each in turn. Later, the scherzo interrupts the end of the *Song* with what the composer describes as 'a polyrhythmic episode for oboe multiphonics and percussion, with harp and piano'. At a concert this crossover intervention might be fun, but on record a little of it goes a long way. The *Aria* has the style of a concerto grosso, with a string quartet concertino heard against orchestral tutti, the oboe providing a bravura cadenza, and the rondo finale is based on a ferocious Moroccan dance. Here the soloist is called on to imitate the rheita (or rhaita), an Arabic double-reed cousin of his own instrument, by playing 'without using his lips and tongue against the reeds'. Later the Moroccan timbre is contrasted with the Western oboe sound when the soloist plays a duet with the orchestra's principal oboe. The performance here is outstanding, expert and spontaneous and very well recorded. The three *Folksong settings* are for tenor and flute; the latter's embroidery is effective, without adding anything very significant, but Robert White's headily distinctive light tenor gives much pleasure, as he does in the Dylan Thomas setting, *Poem in October*. Essentially lyrical, the music is in a rondo format with the instrumental interludes imaginatively separating the seven verses, and the composer's response, not just to the poem's imagery but to the richness of words and metaphor, is full of individuality and communicates readily. White's performance is most beautiful, especially in the poignant closing section. His diction is remarkably clear, but even so the omission of the texts in the accompanying leaflet is unforgivable.

Symphony No. 1.
*** Erato/Warner Dig. 2292 45601-2 [id.]. Stephen Hough, John Sharp, Chicago SO, Barenboim.

This fine, deeply felt work is an elegy for friends of the composer, three in particular who have died of AIDS. The *Symphony* opens with an expression of rage, subsiding to a pianissimo, when from afar you hear Hough on the piano playing Godowsky's arrangement of the Albéniz *Tango*, quoted at length. It is a haunting effect, potentially sentimental but saved from being so by the sharpness of the composer's response: the friend commemorated was a pianist and this is the piece specially associated with him. The *tarantella* of the second movement is a nightmare development of a trivial piano piece that Corigliano wrote for the second friend; and the third movement, a chaconne, has as a central motif a solo cello theme improvised by the third friend when he recorded a tape with Corigliano years earlier. That third movement develops a web of interweaving themes – each representing a friend who died – first contrapuntally and finally into a funeral march. The brief fourth movement is an epilogue quoting all three movements. Barenboim and the Chicago orchestra bring out the full passionate intensity of the inspiration in this live recording. The sound is immediate and full-bodied, giving full scope to the colourful and often spectacular orchestral writing. This is well worth exploring and very rewarding.

Couperin, François (1668–1733)

L'Art de toucher le clavecin: Preludes in A, C, B flat, D min., E flat, F, & G min. L'Arlequine; Les Baricades mistérieuses; Suites in C min., Ordre 3; B min., Ordre 8; Suite in A.
❀ *** HM/BMG Dig. RD77219 [77219-2-RC]. Skip Sempé (harpsichord).

Skip Sempé has become something of a cult figure in the last year or two, but don't let that put you off. This is playing of real insight and flair, by far the best Couperin recital to have appeared in recent years and one of the most imaginative. Skip Sempé plays the 3rd and 8th *Ordres*, interspersing them with half a dozen of the preludes from the *Art de toucher le clavecin* and a handful of other pieces from the 6th (*Les Barricades mistérieuses*), 15th, 23rd (*L'Arlequine*) and 24th *Ordres*. There is expressive freedom about this playing and a poetic vitality that will persuade those who have hitherto found it difficult to come to terms with eighteenth-century French keyboard music. Sempé plays a modern copy by Bruce Kennedy of a Ruckers–Taskin and is very well recorded, though readers will find they will get better results by listening at a slightly lower-level setting than usual. An altogether outstanding issue and an ideal starting point for any collector embarking on Couperin.

Les Nations (Ordres 1–4) complete.
(M) * DG Dig. 427 164-2 (2). Col. Mus. Ant.

This account by the Cologne Musica Antiqua has the benefit of recent scholarship which suggests that many of the dance movements were faster than had been believed previously. They certainly seem faster – yet, paradoxically, each of these suites feels longer; perhaps this is due to the want of tonal variety and generosity. This group is greatly respected in Early Music circles but, to be frank, their playing conveys little sense of the nobility and grandeur of this music, nor does it bring any sense of pleasure. The recording is satisfactory without being top-drawer. Recommended only to admirers of this ensemble.

Couperin, Louis (c. 1626–61)

Harpsichord suites: in A min.; in C; in F; Pavane in F sharp min.
(M) *** HM/BMG GD 77058 [77058-2-RG]. Gustav Leonhardt (harpsichord).

Gustav Leonhardt plays a copy by Skrowroneck of a 1680 French harpsichord, and the sound is altogether vivid and appealing; the quality of the recording is completely natural and lifelike. Louis Couperin's invention is not always as rich in character as that of his nephew, and it needs playing of this order to show it to best advantage. Leonhardt's playing has such subtlety and panache that he makes the most of the grandeur and refinement of this music to whose sensibility he seems wholly attuned. This is the best introduction to Louis Couperin's keyboard suites now before the public.

Cowen, Frederick (1852–1935)

Symphony No. 3 in C min. (Scandinavian); The Butterfly's ball: concert overture; Indian rhapsody.
** Marco Polo Dig. 8.220308 [id.]. Czechoslovak State PO (Košice), Adrian Leaper.

As a child Frederick Cowen studied with two Mozart pupils, Attwood and Hummel, before enrolling at the Leipzig Conservatoire where his teachers included Reinecke and Moscheles. He composed six symphonies and some 300 or so songs, and was for a time conductor of the Hallé and the Liverpool Philharmonic. The *Symphony No. 3* (1880) was inspired by a tour he made of the Scandinavian countries as accompanist to the French contralto, Zélia Trebelli. It shows (to borrow Hanslick's judgement) 'good schooling, a lively sense of tone painting and much skill in orchestration, if not striking originality'. But what Cowen lacks in individuality he makes up for in natural musicianship and charm. His best-known work is the *Concert overture*, *The Butterfly's ball* (1901), which is scored with Mendelssohnian delicacy and skill. The *Indian rhapsody* (1903) with its naïve orientalisms carries a good deal less conviction. The performances are eminently lively, though the upper strings sound a little undernourished. The recording is pleasingly reverberant but somewhat lacking in body.

Creston, Paul (born 1906)

Symphony No. 2, Op. 35; Corinthians XIII, Op. 82; Walt Whitman, Op. 53.
*** Koch Dig. 37036-2 or KI 7036 [id.]. Krakow PO, David Amos.

It is good that the American symphonists of the 1940s and 1950s are coming back into their own. Paul Creston's music is still neglected outside the United States, though an LP of his *Second* and *Third Symphonies* was once available on this side of the Atlantic. He was self-taught and originally planned a literary career, but in his twenties he decided on music. His musical language is strongly influenced by French music – one passage from *Walt Whitman* (1952) sounds as if it has migrated from *Daphnis et Chloé*, and the harmonic language of the first part of *Corinthians* (1963) is also Ravel-derived. Creston's orchestration is both opulent and expert, though some climaxes are overblown. (This is not the sort of music that would appeal to admirers of Elliott Carter.) Creston was championed by such conductors as Ormandy, Monteux and Stokowski and, like Walter Piston and David Diamond, found serial and post-serial techniques foreign to his nature. The *Second Symphony* (1944) opens rather like a Roy Harris symphony but subsequently becomes highly exotic in the manner of a Roussel or a Villa-Lobos, with infectiously vital rhythms and lush textures. It is played with real enthusiasm and affection by these Polish forces and is well very recorded, even though the sound could do with greater transparency in the upper range. This should enjoy wide appeal.

(Editor's note: For many years R. L. was puzzled by a piece of tape – at 3¾ inches per second – a Swedish friend had produced, asking him to identify the music it contained. He relates: 'We both liked it very much – I was absolutely convinced it was Roussel or Villa-Lobos or someone like Ginastera – and spent a long time poring over scores and listening to records. I discovered in the '60s, rather to my astonishment, that it was a bit of the last movement of this Creston symphony'.)

Crusell, Bernhard (1775–1838)

Concertino for bassoon and orchestra in B flat; Introduction et air suédois for clarinet and orchestra, Op. 12; Sinfonia concertante for clarinet, horn, bassoon and orchestra, Op. 3.
*** BIS Dig. BIS CD 495 [id.]. Hara, Korsimaa-Hursti, Lanzki Otto, Tapiola Sinf., Vänskä.

The most substantial piece here is the *Sinfonia concertante*, for clarinet, horn, bassoon and orchestra (1808), which was Crusell's most frequently performed work in nineteenth-century Stockholm. It was composed for himself and two of his colleagues – the horn player, Hirschfeltdt, and Conrad Preumayr, bassoon – to play, and the latter subsequently became his son-in-law! The finale is a set of variations on a chorus from Cherubini's opera, *Les deux journées*. The much later *Concertino for bassoon and orchestra*, written for a European tour Preumayr made in 1829–30, is an altogether delightful piece, which quotes at one point from Boieldieu. It is played with appropriate freshness and virtuosity by László Hara. The best-known and most recorded work on the CD is the *Introduction et air suédois* for clarinet and orchestra (1804) which is nicely done by Anna-Maija Korsimaa-Hursti. The Tapiola Sinfonietta, the orchestra of Esspoo, play with enthusiasm and spirit for Osmo Vänskä, and the BIS recording has lightness, presence and body. This is by no manner of means great music, but it has distinct charm.

Da Ponte, Lorenzo (1749–1838)

L'ape musicale.
**(*) Nuova Era Dig. 6845/6 (2). Scarabelli, Matteuzzi, Dara, Comencini, Teatro la Fenice Ch. & O, Vittorio Parisi.

This greatest of librettists was no composer, but he was musical enough to devise a pasticcio like *L'ape musicale* ('The musical bee') from the works of others, notably Rossini and Mozart. His first pasticcio under this title was given in 1791 before Mozart died, and Da Ponte went on to use the theme three times more, last of all when he had emigrated to New York. It is that final version which has been reconstructed here by Giovanni Piazza, and it makes a delightful, if offbeat entertainment, generally well sung in a lively performance. The first Act – full of Rossinian passages one keeps recognizing

– leads up to a complete performance of Tamino's aria, *Dies Bildnis*, sung in German at the end of the Act. Similarly, Act II culminates in an adapted version of the final cabaletta from Rossini's *Cenerentola.* Documentation is copious but, in translation, not always very explicit, though the various sources of musical material are identified in a classified table (Italian only). The libretto is given in Italian and English texts, the latter (presumably) in the free translation which Da Ponte himself made. The sound is dry, with the voices slightly distanced. The stage and audience noises hardly detract from the fun of the performance.

Debussy, Claude (1862–1918)

2 Arabesques; Clair de lune (arr. Caplet); *Estampes: Pagodes* (arr. Grainger); *La Mer; Petite suite; Prélude: La cathédrale engloutie* (arr. Stokowski); (i) *Rhapsody for clarinet and orchestra.*
*** Cala Dig. CACD 1001 [id.]. (i) James Campbell, Philh. O, Geoffrey Simon.

Geoffrey Simon's warm, urgent reading of *La Mer*, very well recorded, comes in coupling with six items originally involving piano. Debussy did his own arrangement of the *Clarinet rhapsody* and approved André Caplet's arrangement of *Clair de lune* as well as Henri Büsser's of the *Petite suite*. Stokowski's freely imagined orchestral version of *La cathédrale engloutie* is effectively opulent, and the most fascinating instrumentation of all comes in Percy Grainger's transcription of *Pagodes*, with an elaborate percussion section simulating a Balinese gamelan.

Children's corner; Danse: Tarantelle styrienne (arr. Ravel); *Estampes: La soirée dans Grenade* (arr. Stokowski). *L'isle joyeuse; Nocturnes; Préludes: Bruyères; La fille aux cheveux de lin.*
*** Cala CACD 1002 [id.]. Philh. O, Geoffrey Simon.

Geoffrey Simon's version of the three *Nocturnes*, colourful and atmospheric, with nothing vague in *Fêtes*, follows the formula of the companion record. The orchestrations of piano music include Stokowski's vivid realization of *La soirée dans Grenade*, as well as Ravel's magical re-interpretation of *Danse*. Debussy himself approved André Caplet's sensitive orchestration of *Children's corner* ('so gorgeously apparelled', he said), with its reference to *Tristan* in the final *Golliwog's cakewalk* underlined by the orchestration. Full, vivid recorded sound. This is a most stimulating pair of discs.

Children's corner; Petite suite.
*** Chan. Dig. CHAN 8756; *ABTD 1395* [id.]. Ulster O, Yan Pascal Tortelier – RAVEL: *Le tombeau de Couperin; Valses nobles et sentimentales.****

Like Ravel's *Le tombeau de Couperin* and the *Valses nobles*, with which they are coupled, these pieces are for the piano but, unlike them, they were transcribed by other hands, the *Children's corner* by André Caplet and the enchanting *Petite suite* by Henri Büsser. The Ulster Orchestra certainly play very well for Yan Pascal Tortelier and the recording is every bit as good as predecessors in this series. Doubtless choice will rest on the matter of coupling, but no one investing in the present disc will be disappointed.

(i) *Danses sacrée et profane;* (ii) *La Mer;* (iii) *Prélude à l'après-midi d'un faune.*
(B) *** DG Compact Classics 413 154-2 (2); *413 154-4* [id.]. (i) Zabaleta, Paul Kuentz CO, Kuentz; (ii) BPO, Karajan; (iii) Boston SO, Tilson Thomas – RAVEL: *Alborada; Boléro; Pavane; Rapsodie espagnole* (CD only: *Tombeau de Couperin; Valses nobles.***(*)*)

Three fine performances. Zabaleta's *Danses sacrée et profane* come from the late 1960s and are beautifully played; Karajan's analogue *La Mer* is very much in a class of its own and Tilson Thomas's *Prélude* is refined and atmospheric, with excellent recording from the early 1970s. Ozawa's Ravel couplings have a less striking profile, though they again show the Boston orchestra on top form and offer very impressive sound in both formats. The pair of digitally remastered CDs includes two extra Ravel works.

La Mer.
(M) **(*) EMI/Phoenixa CDM7 63763-2; *EG 763763-4* [id.]. Hallé O, Barbirolli – RAVEL: *Daphnis et Chloé* etc.**(*)

La Mer; Images: Ibéria (only).
(M) (*) BMG/RCA mono GD 60328; *GK 60328* (4) [60328-2-RG; *60328-4-RG*]. Phd. O, Toscanini – Concert.(**(*))

La Mer; (i) *Nocturnes.*
(M) **(*) EMI CZS7 62669-2 (2) [id.]. O de Paris, Barbirolli; (i) with female Ch. (with Concert: *French music* ***).

(i) *La Mer; Nocturnes;* (ii) *Prélude à l'après-midi d'un faune.*
(M) *(*) Ph. 426 635-2; *426 635-4* [id.]. Concg. O, (i) with Netherlands R. Ch., Inbal; (ii) Fournet.
(M) * Decca Dig. 430 732-2; *430 732-4* [id.]. Cleveland O, Ashkenazy, with women's Ch. in *Nocturnes.*

La Mer: Prélude à l'après-midi d'un faune.
(M) ** Decca 430 444-2; *430 444-4* [id.]. Chicago SO, Solti – RAVEL: *Boléro* etc.*(*)

Barbirolli's 1959 Hallé version of *La Mer* readily demonstrates his special feeling for the atmosphere and rhapsodical freedom of Debussy's masterly score. The performance has remarkable grip and becomes increasingly exciting in its closing section. The remastering for CD of the (originally PRT) recording is a great success, cutting down background noise without losing vividness, and simultaneously improving the focus.

The later, French account, recorded in Paris in 1968, is also very sympathetic and certainly does not lack sensuous, evocative feeling. Barbirolli and the Orchestre de Paris are helped by the more modern sound; moreover the CD brings better-defined detail than the original LP, without losing the warmth of texture provided by the ambience of the Salle Wagram. There is some lack of inner tension about the playing, both here and in the *Nocturnes*, where the close balance of the female chorus in *Sirènes* reduces the ethereal effect, but, as in the earlier, Hallé recording, there is plenty of adrenalin flowing in the closing *Dialogue du vent et de la mer* of the former piece.

Whether or not influenced by the character of the Ravel coupling, Solti treats the evocative Debussy works as virtuoso showpieces. That works very well in the two fast movements of *La Mer* (helped by brightly analytical recording), but much of the poetry is lost in the opening movement, not to mention *L'après-midi.* The CD transfer brings vivid, clean sound without added edge.

Inbal's accounts do little to make the pulse beat faster. His tempi are brisk; however, though the orchestral playing is of a high standard, both *La Mer* and the *Nocturnes* sound prosaic and rarely rise above the routine.

Although Ashkenazy's Cleveland versions of these works have the advantage of superb 1987 digital sound, Ashkenazy seems unable to get inside the music, tempi are often unconvincing and the beautiful *Prélude à l'après-midi d'un faune* lacks shape without a really strong central climax.

Toscanini's Debussy and Respighi are the least successful of his Philadelphia recordings made in the winter season of 1941–2. The sound is poorer than on the other Philadelphia discs, with the Debussy spoiled by heavy surface noise. The performances too are less sympathetic, more regimented, than those Toscanini recorded with the NBC and BBC Symphony Orchestras. Karajan's famous 1964 recording of *La Mer* for DG remains pre-eminent, and no collector should be without it (427 250-2).

CHAMBER MUSIC

Cello sonata in D min.; Minstrels; La plus que lente (both arr. Maisky).
(M) *** EMI Dig. CDM7 63577-2 [id.]. Maisky, Argerich – FRANCK: *Sonata.****

Mischa Maisky brings such ravishing warmth of tone and finesse of colour to the *Cello sonata* that one is almost persuaded to forgive him the coupling he has chosen (an arrangement of the Franck *Violin sonata*). Taken on its merits, this performance and recording are as good as any, but Debussians will probably want something other than the Franck.

Cello sonata; Sonata for flute, viola and harp; Syrinx; Violin sonata in G min; (i) *Chansons de Bilitis* (song-cycle).
** Virgin Dig. VC7 91148-2; *VC7 91148-4* [id.]. (i) Delphine Seyrig; Nash Ens.

Sonata for flute, viola and harp; Syrinx; (i) *Chansons de Bilitis* (complete version).
** DG Dig. 429 738-2 [id.]. (i) Catherine Deneuve, Vienna/Berlin Ens. – RAVEL: *Introduction and allegro* etc.**

From the Nash Ensemble, there is a little too much of a halo of resonance round Marcia Crayford in the *Violin sonata* and the piano looms too large both here and in the *Cello sonata*, exquisitely played by Christopher van Kampen. Nor is the *Trio sonata* ideally balanced: there is too much flute, though again there are no grumbles about the playing. The *Chansons de Bilitis* are excellently done, though the resonant acoustic serves to produce a slightly plummy sound for the ensemble which is too overpowering for Delphine Seyrig's intimate, almost whispered delivery. This is an agreeable programme but it is not as successful sonically as it is artistically.

On DG, the *Trio sonata* is better balanced than in the Nash version, though the performance is a good deal less intimate in feeling. In the complete *Chansons de Bilitis* for speaker, two flutes, two harps and celeste (not to be confused with the songs), every word spoken by Catherine Deneuve is clearly heard and an excellent balance is struck between speaker and instruments. There is perhaps too much '*schlagobers*' from the flutes (the sound is not quite ethereal enough) and that also goes for the Ravel *Introduction and allegro*; but otherwise there is much to admire here, and the recording has admirable clarity despite a resonant acoustic.

Sonata for flute, viola and harp.
*** Koch Dig. 3-7016-2 [id.]. Atlantic Sinf. – JOLIVET: *Chant de Linos*; JONGEN: *Concert.****

The three members of the Atlantic Sinfonietta (Bradley Garner, Lois Martin and Gillian Benet) are better balanced than either the members of the Nash (Virgin) or the Ensemble Wien-Berlin (DG) and achieve a feeling of repose and mystery. This is the best of the recent recordings of this enormously civilized and ethereal music, though readers are reminded that Ossian Ellis and the Melos (Decca 421 154-2 – see our main volume, pp. 315–16) are still peerless. The present version comes with a multi-composer coupling, and the Jongen is an amiable rather than an outstanding piece.

String quartet in G min.
(*) Pickwick Dig. MCD 17; *MCC 17.* New World Qt – RAVEL: *Quartet* **(*); DUTILLEUX: *Ainsi la nuit.**

The Debussy is very well played but a bit overprojected. The New World Quartet is Harvard-based and their playing gives undoubted pleasure, even if it is not as memorable as the best recommendations listed in our main volume. The expressive rubato of the leader may pose problems for those with austere tastes. However, most rivals offer only the Ravel *Quartet* whereas these artists add an interesting Dutilleux piece. They are very well recorded. The disc is priced at around £10. Our premier recommendation for the coupling of the Debussy and Ravel *Quartets* remains with the Melos (DG 419 750-2), although at mid-price the Chilingirian Quartet are in every way competitive (EMI CD-EMX 2156; *TC-EMX 2156*).

Violin sonata in G min.
*** Collins Dig. 1112-2; *1112-4* [id.]. Lorraine McAslan, John Blakely – RAVEL; SAINT-SAËNS: *Sonatas.****

Violin sonata in G min.; Prélude (La fille aux cheveux de lin) arr. Arthur Hartmann.
(M) (**) BMG/RCA mono GD 87871; *GK 87871* [7871-2-RG; *7871-4-RG*]. Heifetz, Bay – MARTINŮ: *Duo* ***; RAVEL: *Trio* etc.(**); RESPIGHI: *Sonata.*(***)

Lorraine McAslan gives a very fine account of the Debussy *Sonata*, perhaps not quite as outstanding as the Ravel, where she could well be a first choice, but impressive enough in all conscience. She is well partnered by John Blakely, and the recording is very good indeed, well balanced and truthful.

Heifetz's immaculately played account of the *Violin sonata* was recorded in the 1950s and, although the golden tone is glorious, allowances have to be made for the dryish piano timbre – though not, of course, for Emanuel Bay's playing. Perhaps David Oistrakh and Frida Bauer achieved a more ethereal effect in the closing pages of the slow movement (Philips 420 777-2).

PIANO DUET

Danses sacrée et profane; En blanc et noir; Lindaraja; Nocturnes (trans. Ravel); *Prélude à l'après-midi d'un faune.*
*** Hyp. Dig. CDA 66468 [id.]. Stephen Coombs and Christopher Scott.

Stephen Coombs and Christopher Scott made an outstanding début with this fine recording, which leads the field in this repertoire (see our main volume, p. 316). It now reappears on Hyperion, who seem to have taken over recordings made on the LDR label.

En blanc et noir; Marche écossaise; Petite suite; Prélude à l'après-midi d'un faune; Fêtes (from *Nocturnes*, arr. Ravel).
** CRD CRD 3425 [id.]. Bracha Eden and Alexander Tamir (2 pianos).

For the CD issue, CRD have added more music and the recording has enhanced presence. However, the reverberant acoustic is still noticeable and, although the playing is sympathetic, it is not really distinctive. The *Petite suite* does not sparkle as it might, and the middle section of *Fêtes* (arranged by Ravel) lacks incandescence.

PIANO MUSIC

Ballade; Berceuse héroïque; Danse; Danse bohémienne; D'un cahier d'esquisses; Élégie; Hommage à Haydn; L'isle joyeuse; Masques; Mazurka; Morceau de concours; Nocturne; Page d'album; Le petit nègre; La plus que lente; Valse romantique.
*** ASV Dig. CDDCA 711; *ZCDCA 711* [id.]. Gordon Fergus-Thompson.

Children's corner; Estampes; Images, I & II.
*** ASV Dig. CDDCA 695; *ZCDCA 695* [id.]. Gordon Fergus-Thompson.

Études, Books 1–2; Pour le piano.
*** ASV Dig. CDDCA 703; *ZCDCA 703* [id.]. Gordon Fergus-Thompson.

Préludes, Book 1; 2 Arabesques; Images oubliées.
*** ASV Dig. CDDCA 720; *ZCDCA 720* [id.]. Gordon Fergus-Thompson.

Préludes. Book 2; Suite bergamasque.
*** ASV Dig. CDDCA 723; *ZCDCA 723* [id.]. Gordon Fergus-Thompson.

Gordon Fergus-Thompson's set of the Debussy *Études* is altogether excellent, both artistically and so far as recording is concerned and, purely on its own merits, can be recommended. Unfortunately it has thc misfortune to appear not long after Mitsuko Uchida's remarkable account on Philips (422 412-2), which is not only one of the best Debussy piano records in the catalogue and arguably her finest recording, but also one of the best ever recordings of the instrument. (We now feel inclined, on reflection, to award this a retrospective Rosette.) However, readers who are collecting Fergus-Thompson's ASV cycle will not be in the least disappointed with the present issue, which certainly deserves a three-star rating. It also includes *Pour le piano*, whereas the Uchida CD is uncoupled. As far as the remainder of Fergus-Thompson's survey is concerned, he maintains a consistently high standard of artistry. If one places his sets of *Préludes* alongside recordings by Arrau or Gieseking, then they are clearly less individually distinctive, but overall this playing shows a genuine feeling for the Debussy palette and, with fine modern digital sound, these records will give considerable satisfaction. The collection of shorter pieces is particularly successful.

Estampes; Images, Books 1–2; Préludes, Books 1–2.
(M) *** Ph. 432 304-2 (2) [id.]. Claudio Arrau.

Claudio Arrau's versions of these solo piano works by Debussy, praised in our main volume in their full-price format, have been re-released by Philips at mid-price as part of their Arrau Edition, commemorating the death of the great pianist. The piano timbre in these 1978/9 analogue recordings has a consistent body and realism typical of this company's finest work.

Estampes: La soirée dans Grenade; Jardins sous la pluie. Étude No. 5 pour les octaves. Images, Book 1: Reflets dans l'eau. Préludes, Book 2: La terrasse des audiences du clair de lune; Feux d'artifice.
(M) ** BMG/RCA GD 60415; *GK 60445* [60415-2-RG; *60415-4-RG*]. Van Cliburn – BARBER: *Sonata* **(*); MOZART: *Sonata No. 10.***

Van Cliburn shows that he is no mean interpreter of Debussy in these sensitive performances, but he is handicapped a little by the lustreless recording. Nevertheless the disc is well worth having for the Barber *Sonata*.

Images, Book 1; L'isle joyeuse; Préludes, Book 1.
*** Hyp. Dig. CDA 66416 [id.]. Lívia Rév.

Lívia Rév's complete Debussy was one of the splendours of the LP catalogue and held its own against many rivals that were priced above their station. On this Hyperion CD, she gives us one book of the *Préludes*, the first of the *Images* and *L'isle joyeuse*. While it is a pity that Hyperion did not see fit to couple both books of *Préludes* together, Rév's sensitivity to atmosphere, her clarity of articulation and beauty of sound give much pleasure. She is very well recorded, with plenty of space round the sound. At one point – the sforzandi in *Le vent dans la plaine* – one almost feels there is too much ambience. However, this is very distinguished playing indeed and must be strongly recommended to those for whom the programme is suitable.

Préludes, Books 1 & 2.
*** Pickwick Dig. MCD 16. Martino Tirimo.

No grumbles about value for money or about quality from Martino Tirimo on Pickwick. He accommodates both Books on the same disc, which is very competitive in the £10 price range. His playing is very fine indeed and can withstand comparison with most of his rivals – and, apart from the sensitivity of the playing, the recording is most realistic and natural. This is first choice for those wanting a modern digital record offering the complete set.

OPERA

Pelléas et Mélisande (complete).
*** Decca Dig. 430 502-2 (2) [id.]. Alliot-Lugaz, Henry, Cachemaille, Thau, Carlson, Golfier, Montreal Ch. & SO, Dutoit.

In the first complete opera recording made in the warm ambience of St Eustache, Charles Dutoit brings out the magic of Debussy's score with an involving richness typical of that venue which has played so important a part in the emergence of the Montreal orchestra into the world of international recording. This is not the dreamy reading which some Debussians might prefer, but one which sets the characters very specifically before us as creatures of flesh and blood, not mistily at one remove. The first inspiration was to choose Colette Alliot-Lugaz as Mélisande, already well known from her commanding performances in Lyon Opera recordings, notably under John Eliot Gardiner. She presents, not the fey, elfin figure often portrayed, but a bright, characterful heroine, full of girlish fun. With Dutoit choosing his singers most carefully, much is gained from having an entirely French-speaking cast, with Alliot-Lugaz well matched by Didier Henry as Pelléas, light and young-sounding. Gilles Cachemaille, strong and incisive, is young-sounding too as Golaud, not as sinister or sumptuous-toned as some but much more a potential lover, no mere villain. Apart from Pierre Thau, wobbly at times as the aged Arkel, the rest are first rate, and the aural staging adds realism discreetly without being intrusive. The clinching point in Dutoit's favour over the lavishly Wagnerian Karajan on EMI is that all five Acts are squeezed on to only two CDs instead of three.

Delibes, Leo (1836–91)

Coppélia: suite; *Sylvia*: suite.
(M) *** Sony SBK 46550 [id.]. Phd. O, Ormandy – CHOPIN: *Les Sylphides* ***; TCHAIKOVSKY: *Nutcracker suite.* **(*)

Ormandy and the Philadelphia Orchestra are on top form here. The playing sparkles and has a fine sense of style. *Sylvia* is particularly successful: the gusto of the opening and closing sections is infectious, with its life-assertive geniality; the more delicate numbers, including the famous *Pizzicato*, are played with affection and polish. The selection of items from *Coppélia* is generous, each strongly characterized. Both suites are done in a continuous presentation but are, unfortunately, not banded. The recording is notably full and brilliant in the CBS manner. There are excellent mid-price Decca recommendations conducted by Richard Bonynge of the complete scores of Delibes's two major ballets. *Coppélia* is played by the Suisse Romande Orchestra (425 472-2) and *Sylvia* by the New Philharmonia Orchestra (425 475-2). Both have attractive Massenet ballets as encores.

Delius, Frederick (1862–1934)

2 Aquarelles (arr. Fenby); *Fennimore and Gerda: Intermezzo. Hassan: Intermezzo & Serenade* (all arr. Beecham); *Irmelin: Prelude. Late swallows* (arr. Fenby); *On hearing the first cuckoo in spring; Song before sunrise; Summer night on the river.*
(M) *** Chan. CHAN 6502 [id.]. Bournemouth Sinf., Norman Del Mar.

There are few finer interpreters of Delius today than Del Mar, once a protégé of Beecham; and this nicely balanced collcction of miniatures, now reissued at mid-price, is among the most broadly recommendable of the Delius collections available. The 49-minute concert creates a mood of serene, atmospheric evocation – into which Eric Fenby's arrangement of *Late Swallows* from the *String quartet* fits admirably – and the beauty of the 1977 analogue recording has been transferred admirably to CD, with all its warmth and bloom retained to make a highlight in the Chandos budget Collect series, although the autumnal sleeve design seems hardly appropriate.

Brigg Fair; In a summer garden.
(BB) ** Naxos Dig. 8.550229 [id.]. CSR SO (Bratislava), Adrian Leaper – ELGAR: *Pomp and circumstance marches* etc.**

Entitled *'English Festival'*, this generous (70 minutes) Naxos collection, digitally recorded in the Concert Hall of Slovak Radio, is undoubtedly good value, for the acoustic is expansive and the playing (especially of the woodwind and the solo horn in *Brigg Fair*) is sensitive. Adrian Leaper's readings are sympathetic and well judged, although *In a summer garden* sounds rather episodic.

Brigg Fair; In a summer garden; North country sketches; A Village Romeo and Juliet: Walk to the Paradise Garden.
**(*) Argo Dig. 430 202-2; *430 202-4* [id.]. Welsh Nat. Op. O, Mackerras.

Mackerras is just as warmly sympathetic in these Delius orchestral pieces as in his complete opera recording, also for Argo. The contrast between the two performances of the interlude, the *Walk to the Paradise Garden*, reflects the contrast between the orchestras, the Welsh more direct and passionate. The woodwind playing in particular is excellent, but the recording, made in Brangwyn Hall, Swansea, is less spacious, less sensuous than the Austrian-made one, lacking Delian mystery. The massed strings in particular have too much brightness; one requires more lambent textures in this music. Beecham's RPO set, containing many of the most famous orchestral works of Delius, still remains indispensable for serious collectors of this repertoire (EMI CDS7 47509-8).

OPERA

A Village Romeo and Juliet (complete).
*** Argo Dig. 430 275-2; *430 275-4* (2) [id.]. Field, Davies, Hampson, Mora, Dean, Schoenberg Ch., Austrian RSO, Mackerras.

This is one of Delius's most beautiful and heart-warming scores, and Sir Charles Mackerras, even more than Sir Charles Groves on the earlier LP recording from EMI, brings that out lovingly. His approach is rather broader and more affectionate, with each scene timed to convey its emotional thrust, however flimsy the story-line. The Argo cast is even finer than the EMI one, with Helen Field and Arthur Davies very sympathetic as the lovers and with the rich-toned Thomas Hampson adding international glamour. Drawing sensuous, refined playing from the Austrian Radio Orchestra, Mackerras brings out the ecstasy of the piece. The spacious, atmospheric recording has the voices cleanly focused, with offstage effects beautifully caught.

Diepenbrock, Alphons (1862–1921)

(i) *Hymne an die Nacht;* (ii) *Hymne;* (i) *Die Nacht;* (iii) *Im grossen Schweigen.*
*** Chan. Dig. CHAN 8878; *ABTD 1491* [id.]. (i) Linda Finnie; (ii) Christoph Homberger; (iii) Robert Holl; Hague Residentie O, Hans Vonk.

If, for most people outside the Netherlands, Diepenbrock is little more than a name, the release last year of a CD of his best-known (or, rather, least unfamiliar) works, *Marsyas* and *Elektra*, came as something of a revelation. This second volume brings four symphonic songs, all of great beauty and with an almost Straussian melancholy. There are touches of Reger and Debussy as well as Strauss, and all four pieces are expertly and delicately scored. Diepenbrock was something of a polymath and was a musician of great culture; this music has languished in neglect far too long and deserves to come in from the cold. Those who tried and liked the first disc (see our main volume, p. 329) will naturally want this, but others should start here, for it will kindle even greater enthusiasm. Good performances from all three soloists and the Residentie Orchestra under Hans Vonk, and very good recording indeed.

Dittersdorf, Carl Ditters von (1739–99)

(i) *Double-bass concerto in E;* (ii) *Flute concerto in E min.;* (iii) *Symphonies in C & D.*
** Olympia OCD 405 [id.]. (i) Stefan Thomas, Arad PO, Boboc; (ii) Gavril Costea, Cluj-Napoca PO, Cristescu; (iii) Oradea Philharmonic CO, Ratiu.

Dittersdorf spent the years 1765–9 in Oradea, augmenting the bishop's orchestra with imported Viennese instrumentalists and organizing regular concerts. It seems appropriate that the present orchestra of that Transylvanian town should take an interest in his music, and they give lively performances of two of his symphonies. The *C major* is an agreeably conventional three-movement piece; but the *D major* is more elaborate, with an infectious opening movement, an engaging *Chanson populaire d'Elsass* for its Andante, a minuet with two trios and a set of variations for its modestly paced finale. The other works are also played by Transylvanian musicians. Both the concertos are attractive and require considerable bravura from their soloists. The double-bass soloist is especially impressive; even if – by the very nature of his instrument – he cannot help sounding lugubrious in the *Adagio*, Stefan Thomas is able to impress us by his easy command in the work's outer movements, especially during the jolly finale. The recorded sound varies somewhat but is always fully acceptable and quite well balanced.

Harp concerto in A (arr. Pilley).
❀ (M) *** Decca 425 723-2; *425 723-4* [id.]. Marisa Robles, ASMF, Iona Brown – BOIELDIEU; HANDEL: *Harp concertos* etc.*** ❀

Dittersdorf's *Harp concerto* is a transcription of an unfinished keyboard concerto with additional wind parts. It is an elegant piece, thematically not quite as memorable as the Boieldieu coupling, but captivating when played with such style. The recording too is from the old Argo catalogue's top drawer. With its additional solo items (see under Boieldieu for details), this collection makes one of the most rewarding anthologies for harp ever issued.

Dohnányi, Ernst von (1877–1960)

(i) *Variations on a nursery tune, Op. 25; Capriccio in F min., Op. 28.*
*** Chesky CD-13 [id.]. Earl Wild, (i) New Philh. O, Christoph von Dohnányi – TCHAIKOVSKY: *Piano concerto No. 1.****

A scintillating account of the piano part from Earl Wild is matched by a witty accompaniment directed by the composer's grandson, who doesn't miss a thing. The New Philharmonia Orchestra plays superbly and obviously relishes the humour: the pompous introduction is not overdone, and the chimerical and eclectic changes of style in the variations are beautifully managed. Splendid vintage analogue recording from the early 1960s, fresh, natural, very well balanced and immaculately transferred to CD. The *Capriccio*, brilliantly played, acts as an encore (before the Tchaikovsky coupling), but the recording is rather recessed.

Donizetti, Gaetano (1797–1848)

Alina (complete).
(*) Nuova Era Dig. 033.6701 [id.]. Dessi, Tabiadon, Blake, Coni, Martin, Bertocchi, Ch. of Regional Theatre of Parma, Arturo Toscanini SO, Antonello Allemandi.

This Nuova Era issue is taken from the first ever live performances this century of an opera which Donizetti wrote in 1828 and which then surfaced intermittently in Italy until 1891. It tells the improbable story of Alina, a country girl in Provence who is captured by pirates and taken to Golconda, where she becomes queen – an amiable piece with Rossinian manners and some pretty tunes. Sadly, both the performance and the presentation here are inadequate. After the slackest possible start the orchestra perks up in allegros, but much of the singing is poor. Fortunately the two principals, Daniela Dessi and Rockwell Blake, are vocally more distinguished, but with only a summary of the plot in English to explain the Italian libretto, and with totally inadequate background information, only those determined to hear rare Donizetti need bother.

L'elisir d'amore (complete).
(M) **(*) Decca 411 699-2 (2). Gueden, Di Stefano, Corena, Capecchi, Mandelli, Maggio Musicale Fiorentino Ch. & O, Molinari-Pradelli.
** DG Dig. 429 744-2; *429 744-4* (2) [id.]. Battle, Pavarotti, Nucci, Dara, Upshaw, Metropolitan Op. Ch. & O, James Levine.

Decca's first stereo set of this opera dates from the mid-1950s but still sounds fresh.

Giuseppe di Stefano was at his most headily sweet-toned and Hilde Gueden at her most seductive. Capecchi as Belcore and Corena as Dulcamara are both splendidly comic, and the performance overall admirably conveys the sparkle and charm of Donizetti's inspiration. Though without the sophistication of the later Decca version with Sutherland and Pavarotti, this makes a fine alternative, mid-priced recommendation.

It is a welcome development that opera recordings are again being made with the company of the Met. in New York, but Levine's conducting proves too heavy-handed for this frothy, comic piece. Speeds tend to be on the slow side, and with Pavarotti – who can be incomparable in the role of Nemorino – that brings an element of coarseness. He sang much better when he took this role in the Decca recording opposite Joan Sutherland (414 461-2 – still our primary recommendation for this opera). Kathleen Battle makes a delightfully minx-like Adina, and Leon Nucci as Belcore and Enzo Dara as Dulcamara are both characterful, but necessary lightness is missing.

La Favorita (complete).
(M) **(*) Decca 430 038-2 (3). Cossotto, Pavarotti, Bacquier, Ghiaurov, Cotrubas, Teatro Comunale Bologna Ch. & O, Bonynge.

No opera of Donizetti shows more clearly than *La Favorita* just how deeply he influenced the development of Verdi. Almost every scene brings anticipations, not just of early Verdi but of the middle operas and even of such mature masterpieces as *Don Carlos* and *La forza del destino*. *La Favorita* may not have as many memorable tunes as the finest Donizetti operas, but red-blooded drama provides ample compensation. Set in Spain in the early fourteenth century, the story revolves around the predicament of Fernando – strongly and imaginatively sung here by Pavarotti – torn between religious devotion and love for the beautiful Leonora, who (unknown to him) is the mistress of the king. The recording, made in Bologna, is not ideal – showing signs that the sessions were not easy – but the colour and vigour of the writing are never in doubt. The mezzo role of the heroine is taken by Fiorenza Cossotto, formidably powerful if not quite at her finest, while Ileana Cotrubas is comparably imaginative as her confidante Ines, but not quite at her peak. Bacquier and Ghiaurov make up a team which should have been even better but which will still give much satisfaction. Bright recording, vividly transferred, but the effect is not quite out of Decca's top drawer.

Lucia di Lammermoor (complete).
(M) (***) EMI mono CMS7 63631-2 (2) [Ang. CDMB 63631]. Callas, Di Stefano, Panerai, Zaccaria, La Scala Ch. & O, Karajan.
(M) **(*) Ph. 426 563-2 (2) [id.]. Caballé, Carreras, Sardinero, Ahnsjö, Murray, Ramey, Amb. S., New Philh. O, Lopez-Cobos.

Recorded live in 1955, when Karajan took the company of La Scala to Berlin, for years this finest of Callas's recordings of *Lucia* was available only on pirate issues. Callas was an artist who responded vividly to an audience and an occasion, particularly with a great conductor in charge. Karajan's insight gives a new dimension to the work, even though the usual, much-cut text is used. Despite the limited sound, Callas's voice is caught with fine immediacy. Her singing is less steely than in the 1953 studio recording, and far firmer than in the 1959 one.

The idea behind the set with Caballé is fascinating, a return to what the conductor, Jésus Lopez-Cobos, believes is Donizetti's original concept, an opera for a dramatic soprano, not a light coloratura. Compared with the text we know, transpositions paradoxically are for the most part upwards (made possible when no stratospheric coloratura additions are needed); but Cobos's direction hardly compensates for the lack of brilliance and, José Carreras apart, the singing, even that of Caballé, is not especially persuasive. Good, refined recording. Our primary recommendation is the Sutherland – Pavarotti recording under Richard Bonynge (Decca 410 193-2).

Dowland, John (1563 – 1626)

Second Booke of Songes (1600): *I saw my lady weep; Flow my tears; Sorrow, stay; Die not before thy day; Mourn day is with darkness fled; Time's eldest son; Then sit thee down; When others say Venite; Praise blindness eyes; O sweet words; If floods of tears; Fine knacks for ladies; Now cease my wond'ring eyes; Come, ye heavy states of night; White as lilies was her face; Woeful heart; A shepherd in a shade; Faction that ever dwells; Shall I sue; Toss not my soul; Clear or cloudy; Humour say what mak'st thou here.*
*** Decca 425 889-2 [id.]. Kirkby, York Skinner, Hill, D. Thomas, Cons. of Musicke, Rooley.

The *Second Booke* contains many of Dowland's best-known songs, such as *Fine knacks for ladies, I saw my lady weep* and *Flow my tears*. Incidentally, the latter are performed on lute and two voices, the bass line being sung by David Thomas; this is quite authentic, though many listeners will retain an affection for its solo treatment. The solo songs are given with great restraint (sometimes perhaps rather too great) and good musical judgement, while the consort pieces receive expressive treatment. Emma Kirkby gives an excellent account of *Come, ye heavy states of night* and *Clear or cloudy*. Perhaps it is invidious to single her out, as the standard of performance throughout is distinguished. Refined intelligence is shown by all taking part. This will inevitably be the most sought after of all the *Bookes of Songes* since it contains so many of Dowland's finest and most inspired pieces. The recording is of the highest quality.

Dukas, Paul (1865 – 1935)

L'apprenti sorcier (The sorcerer's apprentice).
(M) *** Sony SBK 46329; *40-46329* [id.]. Phd. O, Ormandy – BERLIOZ: *Symphonie fantastique* **; MUSSORGSKY: *Night*.***
*** EMI Dig. CDC7 49964-2 [id.]. Oslo PO, Mariss Jansons – RAVEL: *Daphnis* **(*); RESPIGHI: *Feste romane*.***
(M) **(*) Chan. CHAN 6503 [id.]. SNO, Gibson – ROSSINI/RESPIGHI: *La boutique fantasque*; SAINT-SAENS: *Danse macabre*.**(*)

L'apprenti sorcier; La Péri.
(*) Chan. Dig. CHAN 8852; *ABTD 1469* [id.]. Ulster O, Yan Pascal Tortelier – CHABRIER: *España* etc.*

Ormandy's 1963 recording of Dukas's famous orchestral narrative, played with great orchestral bravura, is very exciting at the calamitous climax, yet it does not miss the underlying humour of the apprentice's predicament. The pacing is just right, and the imagery of Walt Disney's *Fantasia* springs readily to mind. Spectacular sound too.

Although there is just an occasional hint of the self-consciousness affecting *Daphnis et Chloé*, Jansons' account of *L'apprenti sorcier* is brilliant and exhilarating. There is a strong sense of atmosphere, and the playing of the Oslo orchestra in all departments reminds us that it is now among the very finest in Europe. All the same, among recent *Sorcerers* the Tortelier account with the Ulster Orchestra, though not so well played, conveys a more narrative feel.

It is puzzling that so attractive, colourful and potentionally popular a score as *La Péri* is neglected. It seldom figures in the concert hall and this is its only recent recording. Yan Pascal Tortelier takes the opening fanfare much quicker than did Ansermet and Dervaux, and the begining of the ballet proper is oddly balanced: the horn and woodwind interpolations (marked *pp*) are a bit too close by comparison with the strings (also marked *pp*, but almost *ppp* on this disc), and the string line could afford to be more prominent throughout. It is, however, a very good performance indeed with plenty of atmosphere and feeling. The wind and strings are much more naturally proportioned in *L'apprenti sorcier*, which is equally successful as a performance.

Gibson secures excellent playing from the SNO, if without the sheer panache of his Philadelphia competitors. His basic tempo is apt and there is fine momentum and zest. The recording (made in City Hall, Glasgow, in 1972) is less overtly brilliant than Ormandy's but has plenty of atmosphere. The Chandos disc, however, is ungenerous in playing time (37 minutes).

Ariane et Barbe-bleue (opera): complete.
(M) *** Erato/Warner Dig. 2292 45663-2 (2) [id.]. Ciesinski, Bacquier, Paunova, Schauer, Blanzat, Chamonin, Command, Fr. R. Ch. & O, Jordan.

Ariane et Barbe-bleue is a rarity and this is its first appearance on CD. It is rich in invention and atmosphere, as one would expect from the composer of *La Péri* and *L'apprenti sorcier*, and its vivid colours should ensure its wide appeal. Dukas was enormously self-critical and consigned an earlier opera, *Horn and Rimenhild*, to oblivion, along with much other music. *Ariane* is, like Debussy's *Pelléas*, set to a Maeterlinck text but there is none of the half-lights and the dream-like atmosphere of the latter. The performance derives from a French Radio production and is, with one exception, well cast; its direction under the baton of Armin Jordan is sensitive and often powerful; the recording is eminently acceptable. The complete libretto is included, and this most enterprising and valuable reissue is strongly recommended.

Dutilleux, Henri (born 1916)

Ainsi la nuit.
*** Pickwick Dig. MCD 17; *MCC 17* [id.]. New World String Qt – DEBUSSY: *String quartet*; RAVEL: *String quartet*.**(*)

Dutilleux's score dates from the mid-1970s but, despite its title, the music is not intended to be programmatic in any depictive sense; instead it is meant to conjure up the moods and impressions surrounding the idea of Night – not night itself so much as its aura. As so often with this composer, the writing is highly imaginative, and the New World Quartet convey its sense of mystery and its scurrying whispers most effectively. Excellent recording too.

Piano sonata.
(*) Olympia Dig. OCD 354 [id.]; Archduke *MARC 2*. Donna Amato – BALAKIREV: *Sonata*.(*)

Donna Amato's committed and persuasive account of the large-scale *Piano sonata* now reappears on the Olympia label coupled, as before, with Balakirev.

Dvořák, Antonin (1841–1904)

Cello concerto in B min., Op. 104.
(B) *** DG Compact Classics *415 330-4* [id.]. Fournier, BPO, Szell – BOCCHERINI ***; HAYDN: *Cello concertos.***
(M) (***) EMI CDH7 63498-2 [id.]. Casals, Czech PO, Szell – ELGAR: *Concerto* (**(*)) (with BRUCH: *Kol Nidrei* (***)).
(M) ** Decca 425 020-2; *425 020-4* [id.]. Harrell, Philh. O, Ashkenazy – BRUCH: *Kol Nidrei*; TCHAIKOVSKY: *Rococo variations.****
(M) ** Mercury 432 001-2 [id.]. Starker, LSO, Dorati – BRUCH: *Kol Nidrei*; TCHAIKOVSKY: *Rococo variations.***

Fournier's reading has a sweep of conception and richness of tone and phrasing which carry the melodic lines along with exactly the mixture of nobility and tension that the work demands. Fournier can relax and beguile the ear in the lyrical passages and yet catch the listener up in his exuberance in the exciting finale. The phrasing in the slow movement is ravishing, and the interpretation as a whole balances beautifully. DG's recording is forward and vivid, with a broad, warm tone for the soloist. It dates from 1962 and sounds newly minted on this Compact Classics chrome-tape transfer. With couplings of Haydn (Fournier stylish but less impressively accompanied) and Rostropovich's larger-than-life version of Boccherini, this is another fine DG tape bargain.

Casals' celebrated account was recorded in Prague with George Szell, the year before the Nazi invasion. Casals plays with astonishing fire and the performance seems to spring to life in a way that eludes many modern artists; the rather dry acoustic of the Deutsches Haus, Prague, and the limitations of the 1937 recording are of little consequence. This disc is one of the classics of the gramophone – and when you recall that this CD accommodates nine old 78-r.p.m. discs which at the end of the war would have cost about £4.50 altogether, the present asking price is hardly inflationary!

Lynn Harrell's 1982 digital version of the Dvořák *Cello concerto* for Decca, while brilliantly recorded, is relatively disappointing compared with his fervent earlier, analogue version with James Levine for RCA, which remains a strong medium-price recommendation (GD 86531; *GK 86531*).

Starker and Dorati, Hungarians both, bring a partnership of contrasts to Dvořák's *Cello concerto.* The exciting orchestral introduction immediately establishes the electricity of Dorati's contribution, but Starker is a less extrovert artist. Although the latter plays with consistent eloquence and much beauty of phrase, he is not helped by a recording which produces a balance of cello timbre in which the upper partials predominate over the lower, without a balancing resonance in the bass. The orchestral recording is extremely vivid – some ears may find the upper focus a shade too brilliant – but the warm acoustics of Watford Town Hall add depth to the sound-image, and the solo cello is very naturally balanced. Not a first choice but, with generous couplings, worth considering by admirers of Starker. Others will turn to the justly famous Rostropovich/Karajan version (DG 413 819-2) or, among modern digital recordings, the splendid account by Rafael Wallfisch with the LSO under Mackerras (Chandos CHAN 8662; *ABTD 1348*).

(i) *Cello concerto in B min., Op. 104*; (ii) *Violin concerto in A min., Op. 53.*
(M) ** Sony CD 46337; *40-46337* [id.]. (i) Leonard Rose; (ii) Isaac Stern; Phd. O, Ormandy.

Leonard Rose's reading of the *Cello concerto* is one of the utmost simplicity; its heart lies in the slow movement, which flows onward with an unruffled lyrical impulse. Other versions may have more extrovert feeling and greater imagination in matters of detail – but if you feel that this work is normally spoilt by too much ripe romanticism, this version provides a healthy antidote. Ormandy accompanies with his usual warmth and the recording is full and realistically balanced. Stern's performance of the *Violin concerto* has plenty of power and eloquence, although it is less natural in feeling than some more recent versions. The violin is forwardly balanced, though not as spotlit as on some of his records; and Ormandy's accompaniment is well in the picture.

Violin concerto in A min., Op. 53.
(B) **(*) DG Compact Classics 413 844-2 (2) [id.]. Edith Peinemann, Czech PO, Peter Maag – BEETHOVEN: *Romances* ***; BRAHMS: *Violin concerto* **(*); BRUCH: *Violin concerto No. 1.***

Edith Peinemann's poetic and pleasingly natural account of Dvořák's *Violin concerto* is the bonus item provided to fill out this pair of CDs, which otherwise match the equivalent DG Compact Classics cassette. She is well partnered by Peter Maag, and the Czech Philharmonic provide a vividly idiomatic accompaniment, especially in the very winning finale. The recording, although somewhat reverberant, can be made to yield satisfactory results.

Violin concerto in A min.; Romance in F min., Op. 11.
** Teldec/Warner Dig. 2292 46328-2 [id.]. Zehetmair, Philh. O, Inbal.

(i) *Violin concerto; Romance, Op. 11;* (ii) *4 Romantic pieces, Op. 75.*
**(*) BMG/RCA Dig. RD 60431 [60431-2-RC]. Ughi, (i) Philh. O, Slatkin; (ii) Slatkin (piano).

Neither of these new discs matches in magic the Chung (EMI CDC7 49858-2) or Midori (Sony MK 44943) versions of this same coupling, but both are very well played and recorded. Thomas Zehetmair plays with brilliance and precision and is satisfyingly clean in attack, but this is an undercharacterized performance with little sense of fantasy or feeling for the Slavonic idiom. Dvořák is brought firmly into the central Viennese tradition, with Czech flavours played down. Even in the Slavonic dance of the finale there is next to no lilt.

Ughi on the RCA disc is just as fast in the finale, but he characterizes far more positively, playing throughout with panache, and he is helped by brighter, fuller sound. Thanks to the rather close balance of the soloist, there are moments – particularly in the slow movement and in the *Romance* – when Ughi with his heavy vibrato sounds too coarse, but he shows how gently he can play in the middle section of the slow movement, when his pianissimos are breathtaking. The advantage of his disc is that, in addition to the concerto and *Romance*, he has an extra fill-up. In the four charming and lyrical *Romantic pieces* he is accompanied by Slatkin at the piano, playing crisply and sympathetically.

Serenade for strings, Op. 22.
(*) Virgin Dig. VC7 91165-2; *VC 791165-4*. LCO, Warren-Green – SUK: *Serenade* *; TCHAIKOVSKY: *Serenade.***(*)

Warren-Green and his excellent London Chamber Orchestra bring their characteristically fresh, spontaneous approach to the Dvořák *Serenade*, with the opening nostalgia not over-indulged and with agreeably light articulation in allegros: the scherzo and finale are exhilarating. If without the winning individuality of the outstanding COE version under Schneider (coupled with the *Wind serenade* on ASV CDCOE 801; *ZCCOE 801*), this is still very enjoyable, and the Suk coupling is outstanding. Excellent sound: the recording was made in All Saints', Petersham, but enjoys acoustic bloom without ecclesiastical blurring.

Slavonic dances Nos. 1–8, Op. 46; 9–16, Op. 72.
❀ *** Decca Dig. 430 171-2 [id.]. Cleveland O, Christoph von Dohnányi.
(M) **(*) Decca Dig. 430 735-2; *430 735-4* [id.]. RPO, Dorati.
(M) **(*) CBS/Sony MBK 44802. Cleveland O, Szell.
(BB) ** Naxos Dig. 8.551043 [id.]. Slovak PO, Košler.
(M) ** Sony Dig. MDK 46504 [id.] (Nos. 1-8 only). Philh. O, Andrew Davis – BIZET: *L'Arlésienne suite No. 1.***

Christoph von Dohnányi has already provided outstanding CDs of the late Dvořák symphonies. Now he gives us a splendid set of the *Slavonic dances*, superbly played by the Clevelanders, matching the polish of their earlier versions with Szell, but now offering even more obvious affectionate warmth. Dohnányi's rhythmic flexibility and the ebb and flow of his rubato are a constant delight. The changing moods of Nos. 2 and 3 of Op. 46 are winningly handled, and the woodwind delicacy of No. 4 is no less engaging; No. 5 is irresistibly infectious, and the string articulation in No. 6 is deliciously refined, followed by some equally delicate woodwind playing in No. 7. The bustling energy of Nos. 1 and 8 and the opening dance of Op. 72 have plenty of impetus, yet never bring a feeling that the music is pressed too hard; the panache of the playing is simply exilharating. The sweep of the violins in the languorous E minor dance, Op. 72, No. 2, is thrilling, while the gentle melancholy of the D flat major dance (Op. 72/4) and the wistful introduction to the last of this second set are equally well caught. This final dance is done most imaginatively with a musing, improvisatory freedom, almost valedictory in feeling. The recording is superb, very much in the demonstration bracket, with the warm acoustics of the Cleveland Hall ideal in providing rich textures and brilliance without edge.

Dorati's complete set with the RPO has reappeared from Decca with a new catalogue number, still at mid-price. It has the advantage of modern digital recording, but otherwise is a second choice in this price-range to Kubelik's analogue alternative on DG (419 056-2; *419 056-4* – see our main volume, p. 349).

Szell's exuberant and marvellously played accounts of the complete *Slavonic dances* at last reappear on a single budget-priced CD. For orchestral elegance they are hard to beat, and there is much affection and delicate colouristic detail to enjoy, alongside the sheer zest of the presentation. The recording on CD is brightly lit, but is also full and not fierce.

Zdeněk Košler's performance have the advantage of Slovak orchestral playing, which brings an obvious idiomatic flavour, and clean, bright, digital sound. But the performances are less exhilarating than Szell's; in almost all cases the timings are longer, sometimes by nearly a minute. This brings a more laid-back effect, and although the vigorous dances are still lively they have less panache.

Andrew Davis's set of Op. 46, with the Philharmonia Orchestra, is lively and stylish, and very well played and recorded. But who wants Op. 46 without Op. 72 or, for that matter, Bizet's *L'Arlésienne suite No. 1* alone?

Slavonic dances, Op. 46/1–5.
(B) *** DG Compact Classics *413 159-4* [id.]. Bav. RSO, Kubelik – LISZT: *Hungarian rhapsodies* etc.; SMETANA: *Má Vlast* excerpts.***

The performances on the Compact Classics cassette are part of an attractive compilation of popular Slavonic music (with Kubelik again conducting Smetana, and

Karajan in Liszt). Kubelik's accounts of the five *Slavonic dances* from Op. 46 offer polished, sparkling orchestral playing and very good sound.

Slavonic dances Nos. 1–8, Op. 46; 9–10, 12 & 15, Op. 72/1, 2, 4 & 7.
(M) **(*) Ph. Dig. 432 046-2; *432 046-4* [id.]. Leipzig GO, Masur – BRAHMS: *Hungarian dances.***(*)

Masur's performances are highly sympathetic and very well played. Although the Leipzig auditorium brings some clouding of focus, the sound is otherwise ripe and pleasing. However, it seems perverse to omit just four dances from the complete set, in order to accommodate a Brahms coupling. There is no accompanying information about the music, apart from the titles.

Symphonies Nos. 1–9; Overtures: Carnaval; Hussite; My home; Othello.
(M) ** Ph. 432 602-2 (6) [id.]. LSO, Rowicki.

When it first appeared on separate LPs, Rowicki's Dvořák cycle was rather overshadowed by the Kertész series with the same orchestra. Heard as a whole in this mid-price box, Rowicki's readings present a consistent and fairly satisfying view of Dvořák, slightly understating the expressiveness of slow movements and often in fast movements adding a touch of fierceness. The opening of No. 6, for example, with the syncopated accompaniment very clearly defined, sounds unusually fresh and individual, even if one would not always want to hear it interpreted in that way. The recordings, made between 1965 and 1972, are generally refined, warm and full-bodied in the Philips manner. The CD transfer has opened up the sound; although it is still resonantly weighty, the effect is more vivid than on LP. This is certainly enjoyable listening. However, bearing in mind that the Kubelik set is also available at mid-price, also on six CDs, if with slightly different fill-ups and less fulsome sound-quality (DG 423 120-2), this set would have been more attractive at bargain price. But overall Järvi's complete cycle remains the primary recommendation, with each record available separately with various makeweights, as follows: No. 1: CHAN 8597; *ABTD 1271.* No. 2: CHAN 8589; *ABTD 1283.* No. 3: CHAN 8575; *ABTD 1270.* No. 4: CHAN 8608; *ABTD 1251.* No. 5: CHAN 8552; *ABTD 1258.* No. 6: CHAN 8530; *ABTD 1240.* No. 7: CHAN 8501; *ABTD 1211.* No. 8: CHAN 8666; *ABTD 1352.* No. 9: CHAN 8510; *ABTD 1220.*

Symphonies Nos. 3 in E flat, Op. 10; 6 in D, Op. 60.
(BB) *** Naxos Dig. 8.550268 [id.]. Slovak PO, Stephen Gunzenhauser.

These exhilarating performances of the *Third* and *Sixth Symphonies* are well up to the standard of earlier records in this splendid Naxos series. Gunzenhauser and his Bratislava orchestra sail off with fine lyrical impetus into the first movement of the E flat work, and in the slow movement the Dvořákian freshness triumphs readily over the Wagnerian influences, when Gunzenhauser keeps the music moving onwards. The vivace finale has great zest. Similarly in No. 6 the lyrical flow of the opening movement is matched by a serene *Adagio*, sustained by the eloquence of the orchestral response, with lovely wind and string playing. The scherzo/furiant has all the sparkle of a Slavonic dance and the lightest rhythmic touch, and the finale makes a joyous conclusion, again with the woodwind providing all the colour one could want. Gunzenhauser's pacing is admirably judged through both works, and rhythms are always lifted. Excellent, vivid recording in the warm acoustics of the Bratislava Concert Hall.

Symphony No. 5 in F, Op. 76; Othello overture, Op. 93; Scherzo capriccioso, Op.66.
❀ *** EMI Dig. CDC7 49995-2 [id.]; *EL 749995-4.* Oslo PO, Jansons.

Jansons directs a radiant account of this delectable symphony and the EMI engineers put a fine bloom on the Oslo sound. With its splendid encores, equally exuberant in performance, this is one of the finest Dvořák records in the catalogue.

Symphony No. 6 in D, Op. 60.
*** Decca Dig. 430 204-2; *430 204-4* [id.]. Cleveland O, Dohnányi – JANÁČEK: *Taras Bulba.****

Dohnányi continues his Dvořák series in Cleveland with a superb account of No. 6, coupling it unexpectedly but pointfully with another Czech masterpiece, the Janáček rhapsody. With its obvious echoes of Brahms's *Symphony No. 2* (also in D major), this is a work which gains from the refinement of the playing, with the violin melody at the start of the slow movement given ethereal beauty. Dohnányi even underlines the likeness with the Brahms *Second* at the start of the finale, with the opening given a hushed expectancy before blazing out. But nor does Dohnányi in his warmth and freshness miss the earthy qualities of the writing either; and the impact of the performance is greatly enhanced by the fullness and weight of the recording, one of Decca's most vivid. This easily takes precedence over the Järvi version on Chandos, though some will still prefer the latter's rare Dvořák coupling, *The Noonday witch.*

Symphonies Nos. 7 in D min., Op. 70; 8 in G, Op. 88.
(M) ** DG Dig. 429 976-2; *429 976-4* [id.]. VPO, Maazel.
** BIS Dig. CD 452 [id.]. Gothenburg SO, Myung Whun Chung.

Maazel's reluctance to relax in Dvořákian happiness and innocence produces a powerful, incisive performance of No. 7, with the slow movement spacious and refined, though the bright DG recording fails to place the orchestra against any defined acoustic, making fortissimos somewhat aggressive. The performance of the *Eighth* is a fierce one, lacking the glow or warmth one associates with this work. Despite excellent playing, the hardness of the reading is underlined by the recording balance which favours a bright treble against a rather light bass. Though the trumpet fanfare heralding the start of the finale is wonderfully vivid, the sound lacks something in body. First mid-priced choice for this coupling is Sir Colin Davis's outstanding analogue Philips CD and tape with the Concertgebouw Orchestra (420 890-2; *420 890-4*).

Chung directs civilized, thoughtful performances of Nos. 7 and 8 which, next to the finest, sound small-scale. The lightness of the playing is often attractive but, particularly in No. 7, one wants the darker side of this most tragic of the Dvořák symphonies to be brought out more bitingly. Not only are power and drama missing, the opening lacks mystery. In this generous and apt coupling, Pešek's Virgin disc (VC7 90756-2) is far preferable.

(i) *Symphonies Nos. 7 in D min., Op. 70; 8 in G, Op. 88;* (ii) *Slavonic dances Nos. 9, 10 and 15, Op. 72/1, 2 and 7.*
(B) *** DG Compact Classics *419 088-4* [id.]. (i) BPO; (ii) Bav. RSO; Kubelik.

Kubelik gives a glowing performance of the *Seventh*, one of Dvořák's richest inspirations. His approach is essentially expressive, but his romanticism never obscures the overall structural plan and there is no lack of vitality and sparkle. The account of the *Eighth* is a shade straighter, without personal idiosyncrasy except for a minor indulgence for the phrasing of the lovely string theme in the trio of the scherzo. Throughout both works the playing of the Berlin Philharmonic Orchestra is most responsive, with the polish of the playing adding refinement. The orchestral balance in the *G major Symphony* is particularly well judged. The recordings come from 1971 and 1966 respectively and sound admirably fresh, full yet well detailed, the ambience attractive. They hardly sound dated; nor do the beguilingly shaped *Slavonic dances*, from 1975, with the Bavarian orchestra on top form. They are used as encores following the close of each symphony.

Symphonies Nos. 7 in D min., Op. 70; 9 (New World).
(M) **(*) EMI/Phoenixa CDM7 63774-2; *EG 763774-4* [id.]. Hallé O, Sir John Barbirolli.

Barbirolli's recordings derive from the Pye/Nixa label and date from 1957 and 1959. The remastering has successfully cleaned up the fizzy upper focus of the LP originals, and the sound, though a little limited on top, is now full and vivid. Indeed the *Seventh* emerges totally renewed. Its first movement has fine exhilaration and a superb burst of adrenalin in the closing pages; the *poco adagio* has an engaging Dvořákian lyrical flow, and the scherzo is contagiously buoyant, after its gently seductive opening. The finale opens powerfully and gathers further momentum to reach a thrilling dénouement. In the *New World* Barbirolli achieves memorability by the utmost simplicity of his approach. The first movement unfolds dramatically after a presentation of the second subject which achieves lyrical contrast with very little relaxation of tempo. There is an electrifying tightening of tension towards the end of the movement (an effect which is repeated with equal compulsion in the finale). The *Largo* is sustained with unaffected beauty, and the scherzo is notable for its woodwind colour and especially the delightful trills in the trio. The finale gathers the music's threads together before the exciting close, with a real sense of apotheosis. Altogether this is Barbirolli at his revelatory finest.

Symphony No. 8 in G, Op. 88.
** DG Dig. 431 095-2; *431 095-4* [id.]. VPO, Karajan – SCHUMANN: *Symphony No. 4.***

Symphony No. 8 in G, Op. 88; Serenade for strings.
*(*) RCA Dig. RD 60234 [60234-2-RC]. RPO, Flor.

Karajan's 1985 DG recording of the *Eighth* is here reissued, coupled with a disappointing new version of Schumann's *Fourth*. The Dvořák is a characteristically big-scale reading, well detailed but – like the Schumann – lacking a little in spontaneity. The recording, with its close-up spotlighting of individual solos, does not help.

Flor's performance of the *Symphony* is disappointingly sluggish, rhythmically heavy, generally at speeds slower than usual, though the RPO ensemble is crisp enough. It is much the same in the *Serenade for strings*, which again tends to be sluggish, sounding cautious rather than tense. The dullish recorded sound does not help.

Symphony No. 9 (From the New World).
(B) *** Sony MBK 44887 [id.]. Columbia SO, Bruno Walter.
(M) **(*) EMI Dig. CDD7 63900-2 [id.]; *ET 763900-4*. BPO, Tennstedt – KODÁLY: *Háry János.****
(M) (***) BMG/RCA mono GD 60279; *GK 60279* [60279-2-RG; *60279-4-RG*]. NBC SO, Toscanini – KODÁLY: *Háry János*: suite (***); SMETANA: *Má Vlast: Vltava.*(**)
(M) ** EMI CDM7 63869-2 [id.]; *EG 763869-4*. Philh. O, Klemperer – SCHUBERT: *Symphony No. 5.****

(i) *Symphony No. 9 in E min. (From the New World);* (ii) *American suite, Op. 98b.*
(M) *** Decca Dig. 430 702-2; *430 702-4* [id.]. (i) VPO, Kondrashin; (ii) RPO, Dorati.

Symphony No. 9 (From the New World); Carnaval overture.
** Telarc Dig. CD 80238 [id.]. LAPO, Previn.

(i) *Symphony No. 9 (From the New World);* (ii) *Scherzo capriccioso, Op. 66;* (iii) *Serenade for strings in E, Op. 22.*
(B) *** DG Compact Classics *413 147-4*. (i) BPO; (ii) Bav. RSO; (iii) ECO; Kubelik.

(i) *Symphony No. 9 (New World)*; (ii) *Serenade for strings in E, Op. 22.*
(M) **(*) Sony SBK 46331; *40-46331* [id.]. (i) LSO, Ormandy; (ii) Munich PO, Kempe.

Kondrashin's Vienna performance of the *New World Symphony* was one of Decca's first demonstration CDs, and its impact remains quite remarkable. Recorded in the Sofiensaal, the range of the sound is equalled by its depth. The ambience of the hall prevents a clinical effect, yet every detail of Dvořák's orchestration is revealed within a highly convincing perspective. Other performances may exhibit a higher level of tension, but there is a natural spontaneity here, with the first-movement exposition repeat fitting naturally into the scheme of things. The cor anglais solo in the *Largo* is easy and songful, and the finale is especially satisfying, with the wide dynamic range adding drama and the refinement and transparency of the texture noticeably effective as the composer recalls ideas from earlier movements. This splendid disc now returns to the top of the list of recommedations as a superb mid-priced bargain, enhanced by the inclusion of Dorati's RPO version of the engaging *American suite*, which also has clear influences from the New World. It was written first (in 1894) in a piano version, but was turned into an orchestral piece the following year. The Kingsway Hall recording balance seems to suit the scoring rather well; the music is slight but, given Dorati's characteristic brio, sounds very fresh. The orchestral response is warmly lyrical when appropriate, and the woodwind playing gives much pleasure.

Bruno Walter's version dates from 1960 and was originally one of the first completely successful stereo recordings of this work. However, the CBS engineers have resisted the temptation to 'enhance' the sound, which has a warm ambient resonance without clouding of detail, and the violins are fresh and sweet. There is some remaining background hiss but it is not troublesome. Walter's is not a conventional reading, but it is one to fall in love with. Its recognizably Viennese roots lead to a more relaxed view of the outer movements than usual. Nevertheless, as so often with Walter, there is underlying tension to knit the structure together; the *Largo* is radiant and the scherzo lilting. The spacious finale finds dignity without pomposity and the result is more involving and satisfying than some other rivals which have more surface excitement.

Kubelik's marvellously fresh account of the *New World*, recorded in the early 1970s, is certainly among the top versions. The hushed opening immediately creates a tension which is to be sustained throughout, and the *Largo* has a compelling lyrical beauty, with playing of great radiance from the Berlin Philharmonic. After a scherzo of striking character and a finale of comparable urgency, Kubelik then relaxes magically, when the composer recalls earlier themes as in a reverie. Kubelik's accounts of the *Scherzo capriccioso* and *String serenade* have a comparable freshness. The *Scherzo* is attractively spirited and colourful, while the account of the *Serenade* is beautifully lyrical yet strong in impulse. The playing of the ECO here is attractively polished as well as resilient. The recording is brightly lit and, like the *Symphony*, somewhat dry in the bass, but the chrome-tape transfers are of DG's finest quality. The *Symphony* is offered without a break.

Tennstedt's is a warm, romantic reading, freely expressive at generally spacious speeds, very much in the German rather than the Czech tradition. Though he fails to observe the important exposition repeat in the first movement, the symphonic weight of the work is powerfully conveyed with full, forward recording and outstanding playing from the Berlin Philharmonic, not least the soloists. The natural, easy warmth of the famous cor anglais solo at the start of the slow movement has a pure felicity that it would be hard to match. The CD adds clarity to the rich, full recording; however, it also adds a degree of shrillness on the treble in fortissimos. The addition of the *Háry János* suite to Tennstedt's *New World* adds greatly to the attractiveness of this budget-price CD.

With speeds consistently fast and the manner clipped, Toscanini's reading of the *New World* is anything but idiomatic, but it still tells us something unique about Dvořák and his perennial masterpiece, presenting a fiery, thrilling experience. The sound is fuller than most from this source and the transfer brings that out, despite the usual dryness. With equally electric performances of Smetana and Kodály for coupling, it is a most valuable reissue in the Toscanini series.

Ormandy rarely made records outside the USA; his 1969 London recording of the *New World Symphony*, besides offering plenty of excitement, shows unusual care in preparation, even though the first-movement exposition is not repeated. The playing of the LSO has life and spontaneity, and the rhythmic freshness of the scherzo (achieved by unforced precision) is matched by the lyrical beauty of the *Largo* and the breadth and vigour of the finale. Perhaps the reading has not the individuality of the finest versions; but the sound is full and firm in the bass to support the upper range's brilliance: the opening of the finale has a striking lower sonority, which indicates immediately that the CBS engineers were working on the European side of the Atlantic. For coupling, we are offered an essentially mellow account of the *String serenade*, with sound to match. It is directed by Kempe with affectionate warmth, but has no lack of brilliance in the finale.

Klemperer is given very good EMI recording, dating from 1963, and fine playing from the Philharmonia Orchestra. The *Largo* is very beautiful but, although the conductor's deliberation in the first movement brings a well-detailed account of the score, the scherzo and finale are too solid to be totally convincing. Admirers of this conductor's style will probably not be disappointed.

When Previn and the Los Angeles Philharmonic consistently convey joy and exhilaration in their recording of No. 8 (Telarc CD 80206), it is disappointing to find their account of No. 9 less electrifying, a relaxed rather than a dramatic reading. It is a fresh, unmannered performance, and the hushed playing in the slow movement is most beautiful, but the ungenerous coupling does not help to make it competitive in an overcrowded field. Even now, there is no version of the *New World* more attractive and more vividly and warmly recorded than Kondrashin's at mid-price on Decca Ovation (see above), or fresher than Macal's, at bargain price on CFP (CD-CFP 9006; *TC-CFP 4382*).

CHAMBER MUSIC

Piano quartets Nos. 1 in D, Op. 23; 2 in E flat, Op. 87; Piano quintet in A, Op. 81; Bagatelles, Op. 47.

(M) **(*) Sony M2YK 45672 (2) [id.]. Rudolph Firkusny, Juilliard Qt.

Firkusny is a fine Dvořákian, and the Juilliards play sympathetically throughout and with plenty of character too. Pacing is well judged, and undoubtedly these performances are tinged with distinction. One has only to sample the *Theme and variations* second movement of the *D major Piano quartet* or the engaging interplay between piano and cello (the unnamed cellist makes a memorable contribution throughout) at the beginning of the *Lento* of Op. 87, to find that this playing is warmly imaginative. It has brio and spirit too, and the *Piano quintet* has plenty of life. The snag is the forward balance, particularly in the latter work and in the *Bagatelles*, where the harmonium is presumably played by Firkusny, though no credit is given. Here the acoustic dryness is unsympathetic to this unusual but effective combination; more ambience would have produced a better blend with the strings. There is more space for the *Piano quartets*; here the sound is undistracting, and undoubtedly these performances make a very strong impression. However, the Hyperion coupling by Domus of these two *Quartets* is one of the finest chamber-music records available, and we gave it a Rosette in our main volume (CDA 66287; *KA 66287*).

Piano quintet in A, Op. 81.
(B) ** Van. VCD 72028. Peter Serkin, Schneider Ens. – MOZART: *Piano quartet No. 1.***

A strongly expressive account of Dvořák's lovely *Piano quintet* from Peter Serkin and the accomplished Schneider group. They are well recorded, too; but the warmth of their approach at times lends itself to a shade too much affectionate languishing. Clifford Curzon's performance of the *Piano quintet* with the VPO Quartet is a classic record and is now available at mid-price on Decca, coupled with the Franck *Quintet* (421 153-2; *421 153-4*).

String quartets Nos. 8 in E, Op. 80; 9 in D min., Op. 34.
**(*) Chan. Dig. CHAN 8755; *ABTD 1394* [id.]. Chilingirian Qt.

String quartets Nos. 10 in E flat, Op. 51; 11 in C, Op. 61.
**(*) Chan. Dig. CHAN 8837; *ABTD 1458* [id.]. Chilingirian Qt.

Recordings of the Dvořák quartets are not so thick on the ground that one can afford to be ungrateful for good new versions. Chandos provide very fine recorded sound for the Chilingirians, who play with sensitivity in all four *Quartets*, though in terms of sonority they are not as full-blooded as, say, the Endellion (Virgin) listed below. These are straightforward, well-paced readings that are eminently serviceable. Some collectors may feel, perhaps, that they fall short of the very highest distinction, but they are unfailingly musicianly and vital.

String quartet No. 12 in F (American), Op. 96.
(*) Virgin Dig. VC7 90807-2; *VC7 90807-4* [id.]. Endellion Qt – SMETANA: *Quartet No. 1.*(*)
** DG Dig. 429 723-2 [id.]. Emerson Qt – SMETANA: *Quartet No. 1.***

The Endellion Quartet give probably the best of recent accounts of this beautiful *Quartet* which, alas, has for so many music-lovers overshadowed its equally fine or finer companions. Mind you, one is pulled up with a start at the second theme of the first movement, which Andrew Watkinson overcharacterizes (a euphemism for 'pulls out of shape'). However, these players are robust in style, their music-making has conviction and they are eminently well recorded. Good though this is, it does not displace existing recommendations in our main volume, of which first choice must be the bargain Pickwick CD by the Delmé Quartet, coupled with the Brahms *Clarinet quintet* (PCD 883; *CIMPC 883* [MCA MCAD 25214]).

As a quartet, the Emersons are technically in a class of their own. They produce the sonority of a full orchestra and their virtuosity, in terms of ensemble and attack, is matchless. But many will find their performances overprojected and slick, and their Op. 96, though not as superficial as their Beethoven Op. 135, certainly excites more admiration than it gives musical pleasure. The DG recording is very vivid and present.

Te Deum, Op. 103.
(*) Telarc Dig. CD 80287 [id.]. Atlanta Ch. & SO, Robert Shaw – JANÁČEK: *Glagolitic Mass.*(*)

Dvořák's vigorous, grandly ceremonial setting of the *Te Deum*, written for his very first concert in New York in 1892, is surprisingly neglected on record. Shaw conducts a glowing performance, very well played and sung, though the relatively backward balance of the chorus – a fault of the Janáček recording too – takes away some of the dramatic impact. The orchestral sound is vivid and forward.

Egk, Werner (1901–83)

The Temptation of St Anthony (cantata).
(M) *** DG 429 858-2 [id.]. J. Baker, Koekert Qt, Bav. RSO (strings), composer – MARTIN: *Everyman; The Tempest.**** ❀

Werner Egk's song-cycle *The Temptation of St Anthony* comes from 1945 and is a setting for contralto, string quartet and string orchestra of some eighteenth-century verses. It has a certain folk-like simplicity; as a modest makeweight for the Martin *Everyman* songs it is not of comparable distinction. Dame Janet Baker was in particularly good voice at this period in her career and the recording, which dates from the mid-1960s, is very good.

Einem, Gottfried von (born 1918)

(i) *Violin concerto*. arr. of MUSSORGSKY: *Night on a bare mountain*. arr. of SCHUBERT: *Kuppelwieser waltzes*.
** Marco Polo Dig. 8.223334 [id.]. (i) Christiane Edinger, N. German R. O, Hannover, Alfred Walter.

The Austrian composer Gottfried von Einem came into prominence after the Second World War with his operas, *Dantons Tod* (1947) and *Der Prozess* (1953) based on Kafka and possibly his own interrogation at the hands of the Gestapo in 1944. The *Violin concerto* was composed during the 1960s at the behest of Nathan Milstein. Its structure is unusual in that the first and last of the four movements are slow: the first begins with a cadenza from the soloist which seems even longer than its three minutes. In fact none of its ideas are particularly individual or memorable; there is no strongly distinctive profile but rather a generous indulgence in note-spinning. Christiane Edinger gives an excellent account of this unrewarding piece, which comes as a disappointment after *Dantons Tod* in which the composer's creative fires burned more brightly. The record is completed by von Einem's effective orchestrations of Mussorgsky's *Night on a bare mountain* and the Schubert *Kuppelwieser waltzes*. Good playing and decent recording.

Elgar, Edward (1857–1934)

Caractacus: Interlude. Carissima; Chanson de matin; Chanson de nuit, Op. 15/1–2; Contrasts (The Gavotte, AD 1700–AD 1900), Op. 10/3; Dream children, Op. 43/1–2; Falstaff: 2 Interludes. May song; Mazurka, Op. 10/1; Mina; Rosemary (That's for remembrance); Salut d'amour, Op. 12; Serenade lyrique; Serenade mauresque, Op. 10/2.
*** EMI Dig. CDC7 47672-2 [id.]. N. Sinf., Richard Hickox.

Although much of this programme is slight, it has great charm, and Richard Hickox's performances are both affectionate and sensitive, helped by fine recording. The *Falstaff* interlude and the *Caractacus* excerpt slot nicely in among the regular pieces. The silent background of a CD is ideal for these often gently scored pieces.

Caractacus: Triumphal march; Cockaigne overture, Op. 40; Coronation march (1911); *Empire march* (1924); *Imperial march, Op. 32; Pomp and circumstance marches Nos. 1–5.*
**(*) Virgin Dig. VC7 91175-2; *VC7 91175-4* [id.]. RPO, Menuhin.

Menuhin brings out the *nobilmente* in this patriotic programme (released, opportunely, to coincide with the ending of the Gulf War), but there is certainly no lack of spirit. Tempi are at times extreme; thus the *First* and *Second Pomp and circumstance marches* are pressed on with such gusto that the orchestral ensemble is less crisp than it might be, while the *Coronation march* is very slow and grandiloquent, sustained by its rich sonority and expansive organ pedals. *Cockaigne* (which comes last in a generous programme) has plenty of life and colour, but Menuhin's lyrical broadening at the end may strike some ears as being not wholly spontaneous. The recording, made at EMI's Abbey Road Studio, has a convincing concert-hall effect without too much resonance, and the brass are resplendent, especially in the *Triumphal march* from *Caractacus.*

Cockaigne overture, Op. 40; Crown of India suite, Op. 66; Enigma variations, Op. 36; Falstaff, Op. 68; Imperial march, Op. 32; Pomp and circumstance marches Nos. 1–5, Op. 39; Serenade for strings, Op. 20.
(M) **(*) Sony M2YK 46465 (2) [id.]. LPO or ECO, Barenboim.

Barenboim's habit in Elgar of moulding the music in flexible tempi, of underlining romantic expressiveness, has never on record been so convincing as here in *Falstaff*, where the big contrasts of texture, dynamic and mood are played for all they are worth. Rarely, even under the composer, has the story-telling element in Elgar's symphonic study been so captivatingly presented. The Gadshill episode with its ambush is so vivid one can see the picture in one's mind's eye. *Cockaigne* is also given a colourful reading, though the recording is not ideally balanced. Barenboim's view of *Enigma* is full of fantasy. Its most distinctive point is its concern for the miniature element. Without belittling the delicate variations, Barenboim both makes them sparkle and gives them emotional point, while the big variations have full weight, and the finale brings extra fierceness at a fast tempo. Barenboim's readings of the ceremonial music are never less than interesting, but his judgement is not infallible. Tempi are surprisingly fast in the *Pomp and circumstance marches* (though Elgar's tended to be fast too), and not all Elgarians will approve of his updating of Edwardian majesty. The sound is clear and firm; ideally, one wants rather more opulence (especially in *Pomp and circumstance*), but the transfers are sophisticated and well balanced, with *Cockaigne*, the *Crown of India* and the *Serenade* notably fresh and clear.

Cello concerto in E min., Op. 85.
(M) (**(*)) EMI mono CDH7 63498-2 [id.]. Casals, BBC SO, Boult – DVOŘÁK: *Concerto* (***) (with BRUCH: *Kol Nidrei* (***)).

Casals recorded the Elgar *Cello concerto* in London in 1946, and the fervour of his playing caused some raised eyebrows. In the first edition of *The Record Guide* (1951), Edward Sackville-West and Desmond Shawe-Taylor found that 'the great cellist's idiosyncrasies take us too far away from the composer's intentions'; the autumnal episode in the finale prompted their thoughts to turn to *Amfortas*! But if it is less than Elgarian in its reticence, the same also must be said of many later versions. A powerful account, not least for Sir Adrian's contribution, even though its eloquence would have been even more telling were the emotion recollected in greater tranquillity. A landmark of the gramophone all the same, and the strongly characterized Max Bruch *Kol Nidrei* makes a fine encore. The Jacqueline du Pré performance with Barbirolli, which has never been surpassed, is another such landmark. Coupled with Dame Janet Baker's *Sea Pictures*, this is one of those records which is so innately self-recommending that it is only necessary for us to give the catalogue number (EMI CDC7 47329-2; *TC-ASD 655*).

(i) *Cello concerto in E min., Op. 85. Elegy, Op. 58; Enigma variations, Op. 36; Introduction and allegro, Op. 47.*
❀ (M) *** EMI CDM7 63955-2 [id.]; *EG 763955-4*. (i) Navarra, Hallé O, Barbirolli.

This is the most fascinating and desirable of all the Barbirolli reissues on the EMI Phoenixa label. The documentation reveals that, astonishingly, this Hallé version of the *Enigma variations* was recorded in the Manchester Free Trade Hall in 1956 by the Mercury team, Wilma Cozart and Harold Lawrence. In its new CD transfer the sound is extraordinarily good, and the performance is revealed as Barbirolli's finest account ever on record. There is a naturally spontaneous flow and marvellous detail, both affectionate and perceptive; *Nimrod* has never sounded as nobly resonant as here, and the finale is the most exciting of any performance in the catalogue. In the finale Barbirolli generates powerful fervour and an irresistible momentum: at the very end, the organ entry brings an unforgettable, tummy-wobbling effect which engulfs the listener thrillingly. The *Introduction and allegro*, though not quite so impressively recorded, has comparable pasion – the recapitulation of the big striding tune in the middle strings has superb thrust and warmth. The concert closes with a moving account of the *Elegy*, simple and affectionate. In between comes Navarra's strong and firm view of the *Cello concerto*. With his control of phrasing and wide range of tone-colour this 1957 perfomance culminates in a most moving account of the Epilogue. Only the scherzo falls slightly short – slower than usual, but Navarra manages some beautifully light bowing, and the virtuoso passages of the finale are played with reliable intonation. Again, the recording is firmer and fuller on CD than it ever was on LP.

Violin concerto in B min., Op. 61.
❀ (M) *** EMI Dig. EMX 2058 [CDM7 63795-2]; *TC-EMX 2058*. Nigel Kennedy, LPO, Handley.

Recorded before Nigel Kennedy had become a popular evangelist for the classics and changed his hair-style and manner of apparel to suit his new audience, this remains his finest achievement on record, arguably even finer than the long line of versions with star international soloists either from outside or within Britain. With Vernon Handley as guide it is a truly inspired and inspiring performance and the recording is outstandingly faithful and atmospheric. At mid-price it is a supreme Elgarian bargain.

Enigma variations (Variations on an original theme), Op. 36.
(M) ** Ph. 432 276-2; *432 276-4* [id.]. Concg. O, Haitink – STRAUSS: *Ein Heldenleben*.***

Haitink's reading of the *Enigma variations*, while thoughtfully direct and beautifully played, nevertheless lacks the dynamism to weld the separate variations into a unity. The blood never tingles, as it does in the Strauss coupling of *Ein Heldenleben*. Excellent, refined analogue recording.

Enigma variations (Variations on an original theme), Op. 36; Falstaff, Op. 68.
**(*) Decca Dig. 430 241-2; *430 241-4* [id.]. Montreal SO, Charles Dutoit.

Dutoit and the Montreal Symphony may not be as naturally attuned to Elgar as they were to Holst in their recording of *The Planets*, but these are strong and urgent versions of both works, superbly played. At generally brisk speeds, Dutoit is particularly successful with *Falstaff*: it may at times lack a degree of delicacy and tenderness but in its complexity it is held strongly and purposefully together, with an acute feeling for the story-telling. *Enigma* is comparably clean-cut – though, for all the power of the playing, there is a slight lack of emotional commitment, and this may disconcert Elgar devotees. Warm, full recording, though rather more distanced than is usual in the Montreal venue. Except for those who must have a modern digital recording, Barbirolli's mid-priced EMI record (CDM7 69185-2) remains first choice for this coupling – see our main volume, pp. 373–4.

Enigma variations (Variations on an original theme), Op. 36; Pomp and circumstance marches Nos. 1–5, Op. 39.
(M) *** Chan. CHAN 6504 [id.]. SNO, Sir Alexander Gibson.

Enigma variations (Variations on an original theme); Pomp and circumstance marches Nos. 1 & 4; Salut d'amour.
(BB) ** Naxos Dig. 8.550229 [id.]. CSR SO (Bratislava), Adrian Leaper – DELIUS: *Brigg Fair* etc.**

Sir Alexander Gibson's reading of *Enigma* has stood the test of time and remains very satisfying, warm and spontaneous in feeling, with a memorable climax in *Nimrod.* The 1978 recording, made in Glasgow's City Hall, remains outstanding, with the organ sonorously filling out the bass in the finale, which has real splendour. The *Pomp and circumstance marches,* too, have fine nobilmente and swagger. The CD transfers retain all the character and bloom of the original recordings, and this makes another highlight in Chandos's mid-priced Collect series, in spite of the unappealing picture of the composer on the cover.

The Naxos CD has excellent modern digital recording, made in the Concert Hall of Slovak Radio. Adrian Leaper's reading of *Enigma* is pleasingly fresh and idiomatic, and the orchestra responds with warmth to his understanding direction. The direct, naturally paced performance is not unlike Gibson's, with only marginally less character overall. The encores are vigorous, and *Salut d'amour* is not sentimentalized. Good value in the bargain basement.

(i) *Enigma variations;* (ii) *Pomp and circumstance marches Nos. 1 and 3* (CD only: (iii) *Cello concerto in E min.*).
(B) *** DG Compact Classics 413 852-2 (2); *413 852-4* [id.]. (i) LSO, Jochum; (ii) RPO, Del Mar (CD only: (iii) Fournier, BPO, Wallenstein) – HOLST: *Planets.***(*)

The Compact Classics cassette is a fine bargain in combining Steinberg's exciting and sumptuously recorded complete set of the Holst *Planets* with Eugen Jochum's inspirational reading of *Enigma*, and bringing as a bonus two of Del Mar's extremely spirited *Pomp and circumstance marches.* The equivalent pair of digitally remastered CDs adds Fournier's moving and eloquent account of the *Cello concerto* which, by reason of the forward balance of the soloist, is made to sound more extrovert than usual. It has undoubted fervour and conviction, even if the close microphone placing, besides reducing the dynamic contrast of the solo playing, also obscures some of the orchestral detail. When Jochum recorded *Enigma* in 1975, he had not conducted it for several decades, but his thoughtful insight, in fresh study, produced an outstanding reading, consistently satisfying. The key to the whole work, as Jochum sees it, is *Nimrod.* Like others – including Elgar himself – Jochum sets a very slow *adagio* at the start, slower than the metronome marking in the score; unlike others, he maintains that measured tempo and, with the subtlest gradations, builds an even bigger, nobler climax than you find in *accelerando* readings. It is like a Bruckner slow movement in microcosm, around which revolve the other variations, all of them delicately detailed, with a natural feeling for Elgarian rubato. The finale has a degree of restraint in its nobility, no vulgarity whatsoever. The playing of the LSO and the recording match the strength and refinement of the performance. The chrome-tape transfer is not made at the highest level, but the sound does not seem to suffer.

Enigma variations (Variations on an original theme), Op. 36; In the South (Alassio): concert overture, Op. 50; Froissart overture.
**(*) Conifer Dig. CDCF 187; *MCFC 187* [id.]. BBC PO, Edward Downes.

Downes directs beautifully played, generally well-paced readings of all three works. The statement of the theme in *Enigma* is slow and self-conscious, but after that the reading is attractively fresh and direct, and very well recorded with warm, well-detailed sound. The initial restraint of *Nimrod* is particularly moving. The overtures are well done too, though there the lack of emotional weight is more serious, lacking something of the tension of live communication.

Enigma variations (Variations on an original theme), Op. 36; In the South (Alassio): concert overture, Op. 50; Serenade for strings.
*** DG Dig. 423 679-2 [id.]. Philh. O, Sinopoli.

Whatever individual quirks there are in Sinopoli's readings of Elgar, the passion behind them is highly authentic and totally convincing, harking back to the composer's own unashamedly emotional performances. Not that the quirks are as extreme here as in the *Second Symphony*, though some will feel that the *Serenade*, expansive and opulent, is presented on too large a scale. Though Sinopoli avoids the usual speeding-up at the end of *Enigma*, the thrust of that and of all the other climaxes is pressed home passionately. The warmth of *In the South* from an Italian conductor is exceptionally sympathetic. The sound is rich and forward, adding to the dramatic impact, with the Philharmonia, strings in particular, playing superbly. A splendid acquisition for collectors seeking a fresh view of these ageless masterpieces.

Symphony No. 1 in A flat, Op. 55.
** Virgin Dig. VC7 90773-2. RPO, Menuhin

Symphony No. 1 in A flat, Op. 55; Cockaigne overture.
*** Decca Dig. 430 835-2; *430 835-4* [id.]. LSO, Mackerras.

Symphony No. 1 in A flat, Op. 55; In the South (Alassio): concert overture, Op. 50.
**(*) BMG/RCA Dig. RD 60380 [60380-2-RC]. LPO, Slatkin.

It was with the LSO in 1930 that Elgar himself made his own recording of the *First Symphony*. In its passionate intensity it has never been surpassed since, and the composer at times made important modifications to the markings in the score. Since then, that oldest of London's independent orchestras has done relatively little recording of the central Elgar repertory compared with its rivals, but Mackerras's superb performance rights the balance. It is the most bitingly passionate reading since Elgar's own, brilliantly recorded with the rasp of the brass in particular echoing the sort of sound that Elgar himself plainly preferred. Signs are that Mackerras has studied that Elgar recording, both on the detailed modifications implied and on the way that the composer built and resolved climaxes, using flexible rubato allied to acute timing of the key moment of resolution. So, in the middle section of the finale when the main theme appears in augmentation, Mackerras reserves an extra surge of volume for the climactic violin phrase, and his account of the brassy final coda is the most stirring yet, a thrilling culmination. The *Cockaigne overture*, brilliantly done with high contrasts and incisive attack, makes a generous and welcome fill-up.

Slatkin's reading for RCA has an even more generous coupling with *In the South*. In his thoughtful and deeply committed readings of Elgar, Slatkin here leans towards relatively extreme speeds, fast as well as slow. The overture is pressed hard and, though it loses something in Italianate warmth, the close is thrust home superbly. In the symphony he sustains his speeds well, and in the first three movements the orchestra's ensemble is tellingly crisp, even in the headlong speed for the scherzo, which yet begins to sound rushed. Anyone specially wanting this coupling should certainly consider this, but the slight distancing of the sound takes away some of the impact, unless volume is turned high.

As in his account of No. 2, Menuhin, with his natural feeling for Elgarian phrasing and rhythm, gives a warmly understanding performance, though, unlike Mackerras, he stands by the letter of the score, rather than by what Elgar himself did on record. The Virgin sound is warm and atmospheric, if a little diffused; with the rival new issues providing a fill-up for this work, this version might be counted uncompetitive.

Symphony No. 2 in E flat, Op. 63.
** Virgin Dig. VC7 91182-2; *VC7 91182-4* [id.]. RPO, Sir Yehudi Menuhin.

Symphony No. 2 in E flat; The Crown of India (suite), *Op. 66.*
(M) *** Chan. CHAN 6523 [id.]. SNO, Gibson.

Symphony No. 2 in E flat; Imperial march, Op. 32; Sospiri, Op. 70. Dream of Gerontius: Prelude. CHOPIN, arr. Elgar: *Funeral march.*
(M) (***) EMI mono CDH7 63134-2. BBC SO, Boult.

Gibson recorded the *Second Symphony* in 1977, the year before his outstanding account of *Enigma.* It shows his partnership with the SNO at its peak, and this performance captures all the opulent nostalgia of Elgar's masterly score. The reading of the first movement is more relaxed in its grip than Handley's, but its spaciousness is appealing and, both here and in the beautifully sustained *Larghetto*, the richly resonant acoustics of Glasgow City Hall bring out the full panoply of Elgarian sound. The finale has splendid nobilmente, with a thrilling reprise, and the relaxation of tension for the closing pages is most sensitively managed. In the *Crown of India* suite Gibson is consistently imaginative in his attention to detail, and the playing of the Scottish orchestra is again warmly responsive, especially in the score's more delicate moments.

No more exhilarating account of Elgar's *Second* has ever been put on disc than this, the first of Boult's five recordings. The sessions in Bedford, where the orchestra was still evacuated, took place in the closing months of the Second World War and reflect the tense yet newly optimistic atmosphere of the time. It helped too that this was the first ever recording after the composer's own, a special event. Boult's noble reading of this work was at its very freshest here, with dramatic and emotional points thrust home unerringly. The transfer has some edge on it, not ideally rounded, but brings out the fine detail in what at the time marked a new development in hi-fi recording. The other items, all recorded in the 1930s, make welcome and generous fill-ups.

Menuhin, as one would expect of one who worked with the composer himself, is an urgently warm-hearted Elgarian, and his account of the *Second Symphony*, like the *First*, is well paced and sympathetic. But despite delicate, refined textures in pianissimos, the playing is flawed – with some thinness on exposed violin tone and with passages of rhythmic instability, notably in the finale, which comes near to being perfunctory in places. Good, if slightly distanced sound. Handley's remains the most satisfying modern version of a work which latterly has been much recorded (CfP CD-CFP 9023).

The Apostles, Op. 49.
*** Chan. Dig. CHAN 8875/6; *DBTD 2024* (2) [id.]. Hargan, Hodgson, Rendall, Roberts, Terfel, Lloyd, LSO Ch., LSO, Hickox.

Even when Sir Adrian Boult's pioneering first recording of *The Apostles* reappears on CD, this passionately committed account from Richard Hickox will still have the balance of advantage, not just because of the full, glowing sound but for the extra warmth. Where Boult's reading has four-square nobility, Hickox is far more flexible in his expressiveness, drawing singing from his chorus which far outshines that on the earlier reading. Most of his soloists are preferable too, for example Stephen Roberts as a light-toned Jesus and Robert Lloyd characterful as Judas. Only the tenor, David Rendall, falls short, with vibrato exaggerated by the microphone. By his pacing Hickox brings out the dramatic element in the music, giving many scenes an apt and welcome operatic flavour. The recording, made in St Jude's, Hampstead, is among Chandos's finest, both warm and incandescent, with plenty of detail.

COLLECTION

'The world of Elgar': (i) *Introduction & allegro, Op. 47;* (ii) *Pomp and circumstance marches Nos. 1 & 4;* (iii) *Serenade for strings, Op. 20;* (iv) *Enigma variations: Nimrod.* (v) *Salut d'amour, Op. 12;* (vi) *Dream of Gerontius: But hark! a grand mysterious harmony . . . Praise to the holiest in the height.* (vii) *Give unto the Lord;* (viii) *There is sweet music.*
(B) ** Decca 430 094-2; *430 094-4* [id.]. (i) ECO, Britten; (ii) LSO, Bliss; (iii) ASMF, Marriner; (iv) LSO, Monteux; (v) Kyung Wha Chung, Moll; (vi) Soloists, LSO Ch., King's College Ch., LSO, Britten; (vii) Canterbury Cathedral Ch., Wicks; (viii) Louis Halsey Singers, Halsey.

This collection is worth its modest cost for Britten's individually creative account of the *Introduction and allegro,* full of ardour at the climax, and for Marriner's warmly elegant account of the *Serenade,* both sounding well on CD. Bliss's rumbustious *Pomp and circumstance marches* and Monteux's famous account of *Nimrod,* with its rapt opening pianissimo are worth having, but the early recording brings a lack of amplitude in the violin timbre; and the rather brief excerpt from Britten's *Dream of Gerontius* lacks ideal clarity and bite in the choral focus. The welcome surprise is *There is sweet music,* a delightful performance by the Louis Halsey Singers.

Enescu, Georges (1881–1955)

Roumanian rhapsody No. 1.
(M) *** Mercury 432 015-2 [id.]. LSO, Dorati – LISZT: *Hungarian rhapsodies Nos. 1–6.* **(*)

Enescu's chimerical *First Roumanian rhapsody* combines a string of glowing folk-derived melodies with glittering scoring to make it the finest genre piece of its kind in laminating Eastern gypsy influences under a bourgeois orchestral veneer. Dorati finds both flair and exhilaration in the closing pages, and the Mercury sound, from the early 1960s, is well up to the standards of the house. The coupling with the Liszt *Hungarian rhapsodies* is entirely appropriate.

Oedipe (opera) complete.
*** EMI Dig. CDS7 54011-2 (2) [Ang. CDCB 54011]. Van Dam, Hendricks, Fassbaender, Lipovšek, Bacquier, Gedda, Hauptmann, Quilico, Aler, Vanaud, Albert, Taillon, Orfeon Donostiarra, Monte Carlo PO, Lawrence Foster.

This is an almost ideal recording of a rare, long-neglected masterpiece, with a breathtaking cast of stars backing up a supremely fine performance by José van Dam in the central role of Oedipus. Unlike others who have adapted Sophocles for the opera stage, in his four compressed, vividly atmospheric Acts Enescu attempts to cover the whole story, from Oedipus's birth and the baleful prophecy of his tragic fate through to his exile in Attica. So Act III alone encapsulates the story as told by Stravinsky in *Oedipus Rex*. The idiom is tough and adventurous as well as warmly exotic, with vivid choral effects, a revelation to anyone who knows Enescu only from his *Romanian rhapsody*. The only reservation is that the pace tends to be on the slow side, but the incandescence of the playing of the Monte Carlo Philharmonic under Lawrence Foster and the richness of the singing and recorded sound amply compensate for that. The veteran, Gabriel Bacquier, is a moving Tiresias, Brigitte Fassbaender characterful as Jocasta, while Maria Lipovšek's one scene as the Sphinx makes the spine tingle. With such stars as Barbara Hendricks, Nicolai Gedda, John Aler and Gino Quilico in incidental roles, this is a musical feast.

Falla, Manuel de (1876–1946)

(i) *El amor brujo* (ballet; complete); (ii) *Nights in the gardens of Spain*.
❀ (M) *** Decca Dig. 430 703-2; *430 703-4* [id.]. (i) Tourangeau, Montreal SO, Dutoit; (ii) De Larrocha, LPO, Frühbeck de Burgos – RODRIGO: *Concierto*.*** ❀

Dutoit's brilliantly played *El amor brujo* has long been praised by us. With recording in the demonstration class, the performance has characteristic flexibility over phrasing and rhythm and is hauntingly atmospheric. The sound in the coupled *Nights in the gardens of Spain* is equally superb, rich and lustrous and with vivid detail. Miss de Larrocha's lambent feeling for the work's poetic evocation is matched by her brilliance in the nocturnal dance-rhythms. There is at times a thoughtful, improvisatory quality about the reading and the closing pages are particularly beautiful. Even if it were not offered at mid-price, with its generous and outstanding Rodrigo coupling this would still be one of the most attractive compilations of Spanish music in the catalogue.

(i) *El amor brujo* (ballet; complete); (ii; iii) *Nights in the gardens of Spain*; (iii) *The Three-cornered hat: 3 dances.*
(M) **(*) Sony mono/stereo MPK 46449 [id.]. Phd. O, with (i) Shirley Verrett, cond. Stokowski; (ii) Philipe Entremont, (iii) Ormandy.

According to Oliver Daniel's discography in his biography of Stokowski, his recording of *El amor brujo* was made in 1960. (The CBS documentation would prefer the prospective purchaser to believe that it dates from 1979.) It is undoubtedly mono, yet the ear could almost be fooled for, though the treble is a bit spiky, the ambient effect is impressive. Stokowski's magnetism is undiluted: the dramatic effects are superbly strong, *El circulo magico* is drawn by a true magician of the orchestra, the seductive *Pantomime* is characteristically voluptuous, and there is a haunting, atmospheric delicacy for the ghostly *Escena* that precedes the *Canción del fuego fatuo*. This, like the other vocal interpolations, is unforgettably sung by Shirley Verrett with full-throated flamenco fire and darkly resonant timbre. The Philadelphia Orchestra, who play so vibrantly for

Stokowski, are again at their most flamboyantly expressive in the spectacular 1964 recording of *Nights in the gardens of Spain.* Philip Entremont plays with coruscating brilliance: he is forwardly balanced but the orchestra is well in the picture (the climax of *En el Generalife* is almost overwhelming). Ormandy again demonstrates his skill in a concertante work; this is a true partnership, with pianistic and orchestral colours glowing, blending and glittering in an essentially extrovert performance which generates much electricity yet which has plenty of atmosphere plus a moulded, expressive diversity that is characteristic of Ormandy when he is not making routine responses. The sound is less opulent in the three dances from *The Three-cornered hat*: the violins are a bit glassy but there is Spanish sunshine too, and the playing is strong and fiery. *The Miller's dance* has an arrestingly bold horn solo, matched by a cor anglais response that is nearly as full-throated as Miss Verrett in her first solo of *El amor brujo.* For the finest modern recording of *El amor brujo* coupled with the complete *Three-cornered hat* ballet, one turns naturally to the Montreal recording under Dutoit. Few more atmospheric records have ever been made (Decca 410 008-2).

Nights in the gardens of Spain.
(B) **(*) DG Compact Classics 413 156-2 (2); *413 156-4* [id.]. Margrit Weber, Bav. RSO, Kubelik – RODRIGO: *Concierto serenata* etc.** (CD only: BACARISSE: *Concertino* *(*); CASTELNUOVO-TEDESCO: *Concerto.****)
(M) **(*) EMI Dig. CDD7 63886-2 [id.]; *ET 763886-4.* Ciccolini, RPO, Bátiz – RODRIGO: *Concierto de Aranjuez*; TURINA: *Danzas fantásticas.***(*)

The DG recording is extremely vivid, with the performers going all out to bring the utmost grip and excitement to the score. With Margrit Weber giving a brilliant account of the solo part, particularly in the latter movements, the effect is both sparkling and exhilarating. A little of the fragrant atmosphere is lost, particularly in the opening section (where de Larrocha is gentler), but the performance, with its strong sense of drama, is certainly not without evocative qualities. This Compact Classics cassette is in the main devoted to the music of Rodrigo, and the three coupled recordings are of mixed appeal; but those wanting an inexpensive version of Rodrigo's delightful *Concierto serenata* for harp should not be disappointed with the Falla. The digitally remastered pair of CDs, which acts as an equivalent, also offers concertos by Castelnuovo-Tedesco and (less temptingly) Bacarisse.

Bátiz is given digital recording that is brilliantly clear but not lacking in ambient warmth, and Aldo Ciccolini is a very good soloist. If some of the music's atmospheric mystery is lost when the sound-picture is so brilliantly lit and detail so sharply drawn, this very positive, 1984 version makes a striking and involving impression.

The Three-cornered Hat (ballet; complete).
*** Chan. Dig. CHAN 8904; *ABTD 1513* [id.]. Jill Gomez, Philh. O, Yan Pascal Tortelier – ALBÉNIZ: *Iberia.****

Yan Pascal Tortelier is hardly less seductive than Dutoit (Decca 410 008-2) in handling Falla's beguiling dance-rhythms, and the Philharmonia respond to the rhythmic inflexions of the fandango, seguidilla, and more robust farruca as to the manner born. The fine Chandos recording is full and vivid, if rather reverberant – as the opening fanfare immediately demonstrates – and Jill Gomez's contribution floats within the resonance; but the acoustic warmth adds to the woodwind bloom and the strings are beguilingly rich. Tortelier brings out the score's humour as well as its colour and, although he is not as excitingly brilliant as Muti, the closing *Jota* is joyfully vigorous.

The Three-cornered hat: Suites Nos. 1 & 2.
(M) **(*) EMI Dig. CDM7 63572-2; *EG 763572-4* [id.]. Phd. O, Muti – CHABRIER: *España*; RAVEL: *Rapsodie espagnole.***(*)

Muti's reading of the colourful *Suites* is characteristically thrustful, lacking just a little in rhythmic subtlety but making up for that in bite. They incorporate the greater part of the ballet – although, with only 44 minutes' music on the disc, there would easily have been room for the complete score. The 1980 sound, typically reverberant and somewhat brash, is characteristic of early digital recordings from this source.

Fauré, Gabriel (1845–1924)

Dolly (suite, orch. Henri Rabaud), *Op. 56; Masques et bergamasques: suite; Pelléas et Mélisande: suite, Op. 80.*
(M) *** EMI CZS7 62669-2 (2) [Ang. CDMB 62669]. O de Paris, Serge Baudo (with Concert: *French music* ***).

Serge Baudo is at his most sympathetic and perceptive here. All three performances are well observed and are distinguished by eloquent string-playing that can be both passionate and tender. *Dolly* is Beechamesque in its gentle detail. The *Ouverture* of *Masques et bergamasques* has an engaging rhythmic spring and the closing *Pastorale* is quite lovely. The performance of *Pelléas et Mélisande* is dignified and the beautiful *Prélude* is given with much feeling. The Orchestre de Paris is a fine ensemble, and the warmth of the 1968/69 recording, made in the kindly acoustics of the Salle Wagram, has not been lost, while detail has been refined. This is part of a highly recommendable two-disc concert.

Élégie in C min. (for cello and orchestra).
(B) *** DG 431 166-2; *431 166-4* [id.]. Heinrich Schiff, New Philh. O, Mackerras – LALO: *Cello concerto*; SAINT-SAËNS: *Cello concerto No. 1.****
** Ph. Dig. 432 084-2; *432 084-4* [id.]. Julian Lloyd Webber, ECO, Yan Pascal Tortelier – D'INDY: *Lied*; HONEGGER: *Concerto*; SAINT-SAENS: *Concerto* etc.**(*)

Heinrich Schiff gives an eloquent account of the *Élégie*, and he is finely accompanied and superbly recorded. This 1977 performance, coupled with equally enjoyable versions of the Saint-Saëns and Lalo *Cello concertos*, makes an outstanding bargain.

Julian Lloyd Webber plays Faure's *Élégie* sensitively enough, yet does not command quite the eloquence or sonority to match the rival accounts listed in our main volume. His account comes, however, on a disc of much interest in that it includes rarities by Honegger and Vincent d'Indy.

Pelléas et Mélisande (suite), *Op. 80.*
*** Denon Dig. CO 73675 [id.]. Netherlands R. PO, Fournet – CHAUSSON: *Symphony.****
*(*) Sony Dig. CD 45870 [id.]. Israel PO, Mehta – SCHOENBERG: *Pelléas* **; SIBELIUS: *Pelléas.**(*)

The Prelude to *Pelléas* must be one of the most beautiful things in all music. Jean Fournet's account has a charm that is essential in this repertoire, and the Netherlands Radio Orchestra plays most sensitively throughout. They are also very well recorded.

Mehta on Sony (like David Zinman's Philips LP set in the 1980s) offers the Sibelius incidental music and Schoenberg's tone-poem on the same theme. He is short on delicacy and grace here but is more impressive in the Schoenberg.

Piano music (complete).
* Erato/WEA Dig. 2292 45023-2 (4) [id.]. Jean Hubeau.

Jean Hubeau is now in his early seventies, a distinguished teacher, composer and pianist. His earlier survey of Fauré's piano music appeared some twenty years ago in a five-LP box. It was subsequently superseded in the late 1970s/early 1980s both artistically and technically by younger artists such as Jean-Philippe Collard, Pascal Rogé and Paul Crossley. The new digital version has much the same character of reliability and taste but, to be frank, Hubeau is not the most imaginative or poetic of players. His range of keyboard colour is distinctly limited and he fails to make the most of this music's expressive eloquence.

(i) *Requiem, Op. 48;* (ii) *Messe basse.*
(M) ** EMI Dig. CD-EMX 2166; *TC-EMX 2166.* (i) Augér, Luxon; (ii) Paul Smy; King's College Ch., ECO, Ledger.

Ledger presents the *Requiem* on a small scale with more restraint than usual. The singing is refreshingly direct; but anyone who warms to the touch of sensuousness in the work, its Gallic quality, may be disappointed, in spite of the full, yet clear digital recording. It is not nearly as beautiful a performance as the earlier one from King's Choir under Sir David Willcocks. The *Messe basse*, also sweetly melodic, makes an apt coupling. John Rutter's inspired reconstruction of Fauré's original 1893 score of the *Requiem* is as fine as any available version of this lovely work (Collegium COLCD 109; *COLC 109*), although there are plenty to choose from and readers will need to consult our main volume for an analysis of their pros and cons.

Ferguson, Howard (born 1908)

(i) *Octet, Op. 4;* (ii; iii) *Violin sonata No. 2, Op. 10;* (iii) *5 Bagatelles.*
*** Hyp. Dig. CDA 66192; *KA 66192* [id.]. (i) Nash Ensemble; (ii) Levon Chilingirian; (iii) Clifford Benson. – FINZI: *Elegy.****

This richly satisfying collection is headed by an ensemble piece with few rivals. Ferguson's *Octet* is written for the same instruments as Schubert's masterpiece, a delightful counterpart. From the first seductive clarinet motif onwards, its clean-cut arguments, based on sharply memorable material, emerge naturally and freshly. With echoes of Walton in the idiom, the four compact movements are finely balanced, with a hornpipe scherzo leading to a broadly lyrical slow movement and a jolly jig finale. The other works on the disc display the same gift of easy, warm communication, not just the *Bagatelles* for piano solo but also the darker *Violin sonata No. 2*, written after the Second World War. Finzi's haunting *Elegy for violin and piano*, also played by Levon Chilingirian and Clifford Benson, is an attractive makeweight.

(i) *Partita for 2 pianos, Op. 56; Piano sonata in F min., Op. 8.*
*** Hyp. CDA 66130 [id.]. Howard Shelley, (i) Hilary Macnamara.

Written in memory of his teacher, Harold Samuel, Ferguson's *Sonata* is a dark, formidable piece in three substantial movements, here given a powerful and intense performance. Though Ferguson with rare restraint decided later in life that he would write no more, here his creative urge is never less than purposeful in a romantic sonata that is well constructed with a style which, for all its echoes of Rachmaninov, is quite individual. The *Partita* is set in a neo-classical mould of four movements – overture, courante, sarabande and gigue – but is in no sense shallow in its expression, a large-scale piece, full of good ideas, in which Howard Shelley is joined for this two-piano version by his wife, Hilary Macnamara. Excellent, committed performances and first-rate recording, vividly transferred to CD.

Violin sonata No. 1, Op. 2.
(M) ** RCA GD 87872; *GK 87872* [7872-2-RG; *7872-4-RG*]. Heifetz, Steuber – CASTELNUOVO-TEDESCO: *Concerto No. 2* (**); FRANÇAIX: *Trio* ***; K. KHACHATURIAN: *Sonata.***

Howard Ferguson's *First Violin sonata* was written in 1931 when the composer was in his early twenties. It is beautifully crafted and, though not strongly individual (it springs from the tradition of Brahms and Elgar), is a satisfying musical experience, the product of a fastidious intelligence. The finale, which is the longest of the three movements, is particularly impressive. It was recorded in stereo in 1966, but in a dryish acoustic which does not flatter the bottom-heavy and closely balanced piano of Lillian Steuber. However, it comes in a particularly enterprising compilation and is not otherwise available.

Finzi, Gerald (1901–56)

The Fall of the leaf, Op. 20 (ed. Ferguson); *New Year music, Op. 7.*
*** EMI Dig. CDC7 49912-2; *EL 749912-4* [id.]. N. Sinf., Hickox – MOERAN: *Serenade* etc.**(*)

The Fall of the leaf was left by Finzi with its scoring incomplete but Howard Ferguson finished it with such skill that one would never guess. This and the even more touching *New Year music* have a gentle, elegiac quality which is well caught by the lovely playing here. The warm acoustics of All Saints', Newcastle-upon-Tyne, increase the feeling of evocation.

Elegy for violin and piano.
*** Hyp. Dig. CDA 66192; *KA 66192* [id.]. Chilingirian, Benson – FERGUSON: *Octet* etc.***

Finzi's moving little *Elegy for violin and piano* makes an apt fill-up for the record of chamber music by his friend, Howard Ferguson.

(i) *Dies natalis; For St Cecilia;* (ii) *In terra pax; Magnificat.*
(M) *** Decca 425 660-2; *425 660-4* [id.]. (i) Langridge, LSO Ch., LSO; (ii) Burrowes, Shirley-Quirk, Hickox Singers, City of L. Sinfonia; Hickox.

Dies natalis is one of Finzi's most sensitive and deeply felt works, using meditative texts by the seventeenth-century writer, Thomas Traherne, on the theme of Christ's nativity. Finzi's profound response to the words inspires five intensely beautiful songs; only the central *Rapture*, subtitled *Danza*, provides vigorous contrast to the mood of contemplation. *In terra pax* is another Christmas work, this time more direct, opening atmospherically with the baritone's musing evocation of the pastoral nativity scene. Then comes a burst of choral splendour at the appearance of the Angel of the Lord, and after her gentle declaration of the birth of Christ comes another, even more resplendent depiction of the 'multitude of the heavenly host', and the music returns to the thoughtful, recessed mood of the opening. The cantata commissioned for the St Cecilia's Day celebration in 1947 has an opening full of pageantry in the Elgarian tradition; although the mood softens in the second section, this is an altogether more external work. Even so, Finzi was able to respond individually to the text which was specially written by his contemporary, Edmund Blunden. The concert ends with the fine *Magnificat* setting from 1951, an American commission. All the performances here are both strong and convincing in their contrasting moods; if the earlier EMI recording of *Dies natalis* under the composer with the late Wilfred Brown as soloist (CDM7 63372-2) was even more searching, overall this generous Decca anthology, taken from vintage Argo recordings made in 1978/9, remains highly recommendable.

Françaix, Jean (born 1912)

String trio in C.
(M) *** RCA GD 87872; *GK 87872* [7872-2-RG; *7872-4-RG*]. Heifetz, De Pasquale, Piatigorsky – CASTELNUOVO-TEDESCO: *Concerto No. 2* (**); FERGUSON: *Sonata No. 1* **; K. KHACHATURIAN: *Sonata.***

Jean Françaix's debonair *String trio* of 1933 is a delight, full of sophistication and tenderness. All four movements are far too short. Marvellously played by Heifetz, Joseph de Pasquale and Piatigorsky, recorded in 1964 – and, as if to remind us that they are human, there is even some tuning between the third and fourth movements that we don't recall from the LP!

Franck, César (1822–90)

Le chasseur maudit; Les Éolides; Psyché (orchestral sections only).
**(*) Erato/WEA Dig. 2292 45552-2; *2292 45552-4* [id.]. Basle SO, Armin Jordan.

These three underrated works by Franck receive excellent performances from Armin Jordan. There is much fine musicianship in evidence in *Psyché*, and the playing of the Basle orchestra has delicacy and sensitivity. Jordan generates considerable excitement in *Le chasseur maudit*, one of Beecham's favourites; this is a worthy successor to his celebrated account, and both *Les Éolides* and the orchestral movements we are given from *Psyché* show real *tendresse*. The only thing lacking is real weight of sonority in the lower strings, but the intelligence of the playing makes up for this. Recommended.

Le chasseur maudit; (i) *Symphonic variations for piano and orchestra. Symphony in D min.*
** Collins Dig. 1158-2; *1158-4* [id.]. (i) Seta Tanyel; Philh. O, Kaspszyk.

This Collins disc generously offers César Franck's three most famous and successful orchestral works, and the recording, made at St John's, Smith Square, gives a powerful and full-bodied impression, vivid and spacious. *Le chassuer maudit* opens the programme boldly, and no one could complain that it lacks drive or excitement. A similarly direct approach to the *Symphony* is less successful, however. Kaspszyk often moulds the lines convincingly, but he fails to find the necessary balance between the spontaneous flare-up of extrovert passion and the underlying intensity, sombre and simmering, to which the composer often returns and which is the hallmark of this work. Moreover the *Allegretto* does not make a strong impression as an essential period of lyrical repose between the neurosis of the first movement and the blazing energy of the finale. The *Symphonic variations*, too, are inclined to be over-assertive in the orchestra, although Seta Tanyel is a sensitive soloist, and the closing section goes with a swing.

(i) *Les Djinns. Psyché* (orchestral sections only); *Symphony in D min.*
**(*) Decca Dig. 425 432-2; *425 432-4* [id.]. (i) Vladimir Ashkenazy (piano/cond.), Berlin RSO.

It is good to have a fine modern recording of *Les Djinns*, Franck's symphonic poem for piano and orchestra. Inspired by Hugo's poem, *Les Orientales*, it is structured as a long crescendo and decrescendo, with the piano in a redemptive role, constrasting with the orchestral demonry. The performance is first class, and Ashkenazy is equally at home in the balmy eroticism of *Psyché*. The Decca recording is suitably alluring and more transparent than Barenboim's DG version. Ashkenazy is less idiomatic in the *Symphony*, playing it with considerable fervour, in the manner of a work in the Russian tradition. With a vivid response from the Berlin Radio Orchestra, he thrusts forward throughout the piece (keeping up a fair momentum in the *Allegretto* while still maintaining its textural delicacy). The orchestral textures do not smooth out the plangent quality of Franck's scoring, and the music-making is undoubtedly exciting; but the reading overall does not resonate in the memory afterwards, as does Monteux's or even Plasson's (see below).

Psyché (symphonic poem); *Symphony in D min.*
(M) *(*) DG 431 468-2; *431 468-4* [id.]. O de Paris, Daniel Barenboim.

In *Psyché* Barenboim limits himself to the purely orchestral passages of this extended work, leaving plenty of room for the *Symphony*. In the symphonic poem he draws rich, refined playing from the Paris orchestra, a little sleepy at times but suitably sensuous. But in the first movement of the *Symphony* he adopts a surprisingly plodding main tempo, the first subject lacking bite. There are places too where the reading is self-indulgent (Barenboim putting on his Furtwänglerian mantle) and, in an otherwise fine account of the slow movement, the cor anglais solo is disappointingly wooden. The 1976 sound, however, is firmer than the original and very acceptable.

Symphonic variations for piano and orchestra.
(B) * EMI CDZ7 62859-2; *LZ 762859-4*. John Ogdon, Philh. O, Barbirolli – GRIEG; SCHUMANN: *Piano concertos.**

John Ogdon opens in improvisatory style and the result is curiously unspontaneous; the best section is the finale, where a certain rhythmic spring catches the listener's previously flagging interest. Good 1963 recording.

Symphony in D min.
(B) * DG Compact Classics *413 423-4* [id.]. O de Paris, Barenboim – SAINT-SAËNS: *Symphony No. 3; Danse macabre.****
* ASV Dig. CDDCA 708; *ZCDCA 708* [id.]. Philh. O, D'Avalos – CHAUSSON: *Symphony.**

Although he is well recorded, Barenboim's account is disappointing (see above). However, the coupling on the chrome Compact Classics tape brings two of his finest performances on record.

Given the competition, Francesco D'Avalos doesn't stand much of a chance, but even if his were the solitary recording rather than one among a dozen, it would be difficult to work up much enthusiasm for it. The Philharmonia lacks its familiar lustre and sonority, and D'Avalos does not seem to have the strong grip on the architecture of this formidable work that is needed.

Symphony in D min.; (i) *Symphonic variations.*
(M) *** EMI Dig. CDD7 63889-2 [id.]; *ET 763889-4.* (i) Collard; Capitole Toulouse O, Plasson.

Plasson gives a straightforward and powerful account of the *Symphony* with his Orchestre du Capitole, Toulouse. His 1985 version has conviction and genuine lyrical fervour, equally strikingly in the chromatic secondary theme of the first movement and the impulsive gusto of the finale. At the same time Plasson handles the overall ebb and flow of tension convincingly. This may not seem as individual an account as those by Beecham and Monteux, but it is certainly both exciting and satisfying, and the recording is much more impressive than RCA's recording for Monteux, even if it is not quite top-drawer EMI. Fortissimos are vividly projected but the score's quieter pages, though atmospheric, are less sharply detailed, notably in the slow movement. Jean-Philippe Collard's performance of the *Symphonic variations* is characteristically sensitive and full of imaginative colours and is touched by distinction. All in all, those looking for a mid-priced digital version of this coupling should be well satisfied.

CHAMBER MUSIC

Cello sonata in A (transcription of *Violin sonata*).
(M) *** EMI Dig. CDM7 63577-2 [id.]. Maisky, Argerich – DEBUSSY: *Cello sonata* etc.***
(*) CRD CRD 3391 [id.]. Robert Cohen, Roger Vignoles (with DVOŘÁK: *Rondo*) – GRIEG: *Cello sonata.*(*)

This was Mischa Maisky's first record for EMI; it is strange that, with so much other music available, he should have turned to this transcription as a coupling for his splendid account of the Debussy *Sonata.* However, he is a remarkably fine artist and, for those who are happy with the coupling, there is no doubting his eloquence and range of colour, or the sensitivity of Argerich's contribution – this is a true partnership. Good recording too.

Cohen gives a firm and strong rendering of the Franck *Sonata* in its cello version, lacking a little in fantasy in the outer movements but splendidly incisive and dashing in the second-movement *Allegro.* The Grieg coupling is attractive and apt, but the recording is more limited than one expects from CRD, a little shallow. The addition of the Dvořák *G minor Rondo,* Op. 94, makes a pleasing bonus.

Violin sonata in A.
(M) *** DG 431 469-2; *431 469-4* [id.]. Kaja Danczowska, Krystian Zimerman – SZYMANOWSKI: *Mythes* etc.*** ❀
(*) DG Dig. 429 729-2 [id.]. Gil Shaham, Gerhard Oppitz – RAVEL: *Tzigane*; SAINT-SAENS: *Sonata No. 1.*(*)

Kaja Danczowska was a pupil of Eugenia Uminska and the late David Oistrakh and, on the evidence of this 1980 début recording, she is an artist to reckon with. Her account of the Franck is distinguished by a fine sense of line and great sweetness of tone, and she is partnered superbly by Krystian Zimerman. Indeed, in terms of dramatic fire and strength of line, this version can hold its own alongside the finest, and it is perhaps marginally better-balanced than the Kyung Wha Chung and Radu Lupu recording (Decca 421 154-2). This DG issue has a particularly valuable and interesting coupling and would be worth acquiring for that alone. Certainly the sound is very immediate and present, and the acoustic is naturally resonant in a most attractive way.

The young American violinist Gil Shaham is obviously a major talent: he was only eighteen when this disc was made. He is still studying at the Juilliard with Dorothy DeLay. He produces a big and varied range of tone and has no lack of temperament. There is great intensity here (at times, one feels it is almost unrelieved) and Gerhard Oppitz partners him with much dexterity. The pianism is perhaps a little too muscular at times, though Oppitz accompanies the opening movement with great sensitivity. Others (Danczowska/Zimerman on DG and Chung/Lupu on Decca, both at mid-price) have moments of greater repose and poetry, but there is no doubt that this is a remarkable début.

VOCAL AND CHORAL MUSIC

Les Béatitudes.
**(*) Erato/WEA Dig. 2292 45553-2 [id.]. Lebrun, Berbié, Stutzmann, Randall, Jeffes, Vanaud, Loup, Ottevaere, Fr. R. Ch. & Nouvel PO, Armin Jordan.

Les Béatitudes occupied Franck through the 1870s but, despite the revival of interest in his work in recent years, it has never really established itself. There is much writing of quality – as one would expect – but also much that is pedestrian by the standards of the *Symphony*, the *Sonata* or *Psyché*. Also on such a canvas (the score runs to two hours) the invention is curiously deficient in character and in rhythmic variety. The recording was made at a live performance in Paris in 1985 and is sensitively shaped under the baton of Armin Jordan. The solo singers are more than adequate; the choral and orchestral contributions are also admirable, and the sound-picture is very natural.

Frescobaldi, Girolamo (1583–1643)

Keyboard music: *Ancidetemi pur d'Archadelt passaggiato; Canzona quarta; Capriccio di Durezze; Capriccio sopra la Bassa Fiamenga; Cento partite sopra passacagli; Corrrenti Nos. 1–4; Corrente & ciaccona; Gagliarde Nos. 1–5; Partite sopra l'aria della Romanesca; Partite sopra ciaccona; Partita sopra passacagli; Toccata prima; Toccata nona.*
** Dorian Dig. DOR 90124 [id.]. Colin Tilney (harpsichord).

Colin Tilney's survey of Frescobaldi's keyboard music begins and ends with two keyboard elaborations of the vocal style found in the monodic continuo songs of Peri and Caccini and in the madrigals of Monteverdi. Between these two *Toccatas* come a variety of pieces, drawn mostly from the 1620s. in the free style he developed. There is what we would call a transcription of the madrigal *Ancidetemi pur* of 1539 by Arcadelt, and various canzone and passacaglias. Colin Tilney plays an eighteenth-century instrument of unknown derivation and has a persuasive way with him in this repertoire. The only snag is the recording, which is rather closely balanced and needs to be played at a much lower-level setting than usual.

Capricci, Book 1.
(M) ** HM/BMG GD 77071 [77071-2-RG]. Gustav Leonhardt, Harry Van Der Kamp.

Frescobaldi was one of the greatest keyboard masters of his day and, as organist of St Peter's, Rome, enjoyed a legendary reputation during his lifetime. The *Capricci* (the word means 'moods') were published in 1624 with a dedication to Prince Alfonso of Modena and were written for those interested in 'seriousness of style, a difficult and learned perfection', and were intended not only with didactic ends in mind but as intellectual relaxation for performers and audience. Gustav Leonhardt's analogue recording dates from 1979 and has splendid clarity and warmth. It first appeared briefly on EMI/Deutsche Harmonia Mundi, with almost 80 minutes' playing time, but did not stay in circulation long enough to be listed by us. It now reappears from RCA, albeit with one of the pieces, the *Capriccio cromatico con ligature*, omitted. Nevertheless, at 73 minutes and at mid-price, this is still good value for money, and the music is certainly rewarding. The recording is far too close and wanting in tonal variety; the effect can be improved somewhat by playing at a lower than usual level-setting.

Froberger, Johann (1616–67)

Canzon No. 2; Capriccio No. 10; Fantasia No. 4 sopra sollare; Lamentation faîte sur la mort très douloureuse de Sa Majesté Imperiale, Ferdinand le troisième; Ricercar No. 5; Suites Nos. 2 & 30; Suite No. 14: Lamentation sur ce que j'ay été volé. Toccatas Nos. 9, 10 & 114; Tombeau faict à Paris sur la mort de M. Blancrocher.
*** HM/BMG Dig. RD 77923 [7913-2-RC]. Gustav Leonhardt (harpsichord).

Froberger's contemporaries regarded him as the most important German keyboard composer of the seventeenth century, and his fame extended well into the eighteenth; Bach himself knew and admired his music. He was also one of the most cosmopolitan of north German musicians; his father had introduced him to the music of Josquin and of contemporary German, English and Italian masters, and he also studied for a time in Rome with Frescobaldi, where he met Carissimi. Froberger's music is highly exploratory in idiom and, in works such as the *Tombeau faict à Paris sur la mort de M. Blancrocher* and the *Plainte faite à Londres pour passer la Melancholie*, from the *Suite No. 3*, he reveals great expressive poignancy. There is a searching, thoughtful quality about this music and its composer obviously possessed a strong vein of melancholy. There is rather more space round the instrument than in Leonhardt's Frescobaldi recital and, heard at a low level-setting, it produces very good results. Recommended with enthusiasm.

Fuchs, Robert (1847–1927)

Clarinet quintet, Op. 102.
*** Marco Polo Dig. 8.223282 [id.]. Rodenhäuser, Ens. Villa Musica – LACHNER: *Septet.****

Robert Fuchs is probably best known as a teacher: he was a professor at the Vienna Conservatory where his pupils included Mahler, Sibelius, Schreker and Zemlinsky. He was quite a prolific composer, as a glance at the opus number of his *Clarinet quintet* shows; it was composed in 1914, though it could have been written fifty years earlier. It is beautifully crafted and speaks with the accents of Schubert and Brahms rather than with any strong individuality. It is nicely played by the Mainz-based Ensemble Villa Musica whose excellent clarinettist, Ulf Rodenhäuser, is worth a mention. (His name is buried in small print on the inner sleeve.) A curiosity rather than a revelation then, but eminently well recorded.

Furtwängler, Wilhelm (1886–1954)

Symphony No. 3 in C sharp min.
*(*) Marco Polo Dig. 8.223105 [id.]. RTBF SO, Alfred Walter.

Like his colleagues, Weingartner and Klemperer, Furtwängler was a composer of considerable ambitions. He recorded his *Second Symphony* (a work much admired by Honegger, among others) for DG in the days of mono LPs. His *Third Symphony* is conceived on a grand scale: each of its four movements, including the scherzo, lasts about

17 minutes. It comes from the last years of his life and Furtwängler had intended to revise the finale but did not live to do so. In scale and idiom it has the seriousness and breadth of Bruckner or Strauss; and if there is no strong individuality, there is an obvious depth and sense of movement. The overall effect is quite moving and would be even more so, were the recording better. As it is, the orchestral textures are ill ventilated, the frequency-range is a bit constricted and climaxes cramped. The Belgian Radio and Television Orchestra play conscientiously for Alfred Walter, and the disc is certainly worth hearing.

Gabrieli, Andrea (1520–86)

Laudate dominum.
(M) **(*) Decca 430 359-2; *430 359-4* [id.]. Magdalen College, Oxford, Ch., Wren O, Rose – G. GABRIELI: *Motets* **(*); PERGOLESI: *Miserere II* *** (with BASSANO: *Ave Regina* **(*)).

In modern times the name Gabrieli has usually suggested Giovanni, nephew of Andrea, but in their day they were both held in equal esteem; this fine setting of *Laudate dominum* for two five-part choirs helps to explain why. Also included is a splendid *Ave Regina* by Andrea's contemporary, Giovanni Bassano, which is laid out for three four-part choirs and brass in a similar polychoral style. Both are are well performed, if without strong individuality, and the recording is magnificently expansive.

Gabrieli, Giovanni (1557–1612)

Hodie Christus natus est; Plaudite; Virtute magna.
(M) **(*) Decca 430 359-2; *430 359-4* [id.]. Magdalen College, Oxford, Ch., Gowman (organ), Wren O, Rose – A. GABRIELI: *Laudate dominum* **(*); PERGOLESI: *Miserere II.****

This coupling of three comparatively rare pieces by Giovanni Gabrieli, as well as an item by his uncle Andrea, is welcome and apt. The Christmas motet, *Hodie Christus natus est*, is justly the most celebrated; but the other pieces too are most beautiful, notably *Plaudite* for three separate choirs. With the *Ave Regina* of the Gabrielis' contemporary, Giovanni Bassano, as makeweight, this make a valuable bonus for the Pergolesi *Miserere*. The performances, though finely controlled, could be more positive and dramatic, but they are very well recorded.

Gade, Niels (1817–90)

Korsfarerne (The Crusaders), Op. 50.
*** BIS Dig. CD 465 [id.]. Rorholm, Westi, Cold, Canzone Ch., Da Camera, Kor 72, Music Students' Chamber Ch., Aarhus SO, Frans Rasmussen.

Gade's *Korsfarerne* was composed in 1866, a year after the *Seventh Symphony*. It is in three sections, *In the desert*, *Armida*, and *Towards Jerusalem*, and lasts the best part of an hour. The Danish forces assembled here do it proud, as do the BIS recording team, but it is difficult to summon up much enthusiasm for the music itself. It is impeccably crafted, ideas are well paced, and there are moments of real freshness, but the debt to Mendelssohn, say in the *Chorus of the Spirits of Darkness* which opens the second section, overwhelms any feeling of originality.

Gay, John (1685–1732)

The Beggar's Opera (arr. Bonynge and Gamley).
*** Decca Dig. 430 066-2 (2) [id.]. Kanawa, Sutherland, Morris, Dean, Mitchell, Hordern, Marks, Lansbury, Resnik, Rolfe Johnson, London Voices, Nat. PO, Bonynge.

This entertaining digital version of *The Beggar's Opera* creates the atmosphere of a stage musical. The spoken prologue comes before the overture (rather in the way some films complete their opening sequence before the main titles appear). With Warren Mitchell and Sir Michael Hordern immediately taking the stage, the listener's attention is caught before the music begins. The musical arrangements are free – including an unashamedly jazzy sequence in Act II, complete with saxophones – but the basic musical material is of vintage quality and responds readily to a modern treatment which is always sparkling and often imaginative. The casting is imaginative too. With Alfred Marks and Angela Lansbury as Mr and Mrs Peacham a touch of humour is assured; if James Morris is not an entirely convincing Macheath, he sings nicely, and Joan Sutherland makes a spirited Lucy. The rest of the participants show themselves to be equally at home with singing and speaking, an essential if the piece is to spring fully to life. Kiri Te Kanawa as Polly undoubtedly steals the show, as well she should, for it is a peach of a part. She sings deliciously and her delivery of the dialogue is hardly less memorable. The whole show is done with gusto, and the digital recording is splendid, as spacious as it is clear.

Geminiani, Francesco (1687–1762)

Concerti grossi, Op. 2/5–6; Op. 3/3; Op. 7/2; in G min. (after Corelli, *Op. 5/5*); *in D min.*(after Corelli, *Op. 5/12*); *Theme & variations (La Follia).*
(M) *** BMG/RCA Dig. GD 77010 [77010-2-RG]. La Petite Bande, Sigiswald Kuijken.

A more considerable and innovative figure than is generally supposed, the quality of invention in the Geminiani concertos recorded here rises high above the routine. There is considerable expressive depth in some of the slow movements too. La Petite Bande is incomparably superior to many of the period-instrument ensembles; their string-tone is light and feathery, accents are never overemphatic, and there is a splendid sense of movement. Those who are normally allergic to the vinegary offerings of some rivals will find this record a joy. It is beautifully recorded too, and makes an admirable and economical introduction to this underrated and genial composer.

Gershwin, George (1898–1937)

(i) *An American in Paris;* (ii) *Piano concerto in F; Rhapsody in blue.*
(B) **(*) DG Compact Classics 413 851-2 (2); *413 851-4* [id.]. (i) San Francisco SO, Ozawa; (ii) Szidon, LPO, Downes; (iii) Siegfried Stöckigt, Leipzig GO, Masur – BERNSTEIN: *West Side story: Symphonic dances.**** (CD only: (i) RUSSO: *3 Pieces for Blues band and orchestra* – with Siegel-Schwall Band).
(BB) * Naxos Dig. 8.550295 [id.]. (ii) Kathryn Selby; (i) CSR SO (Bratislava); (ii) Slovak PO; Richard Hayman.

An American in Paris; Porgy and Bess: Symphonic picture (arr. Robert Russell Bennett).
(M) **(*) Sony MBK 44812 [id.]. Phd. O, Ormandy.

(i) *An American in Paris; Porgy and Bess: Symphonic picture* (arr. Robert Russell Bennett); (i; ii) *Rhapsody in blue;* (ii) *3 Preludes.*
(M) ** EMI CDM7 63736-2. (i) Hollywood Bowl SO, Felix Slatkin; (ii) Leonard Pennario.

(i) *An American in Paris;* (ii) *Rhapsody in blue.*
(M) *** Sony MYK 42611 [id.]. (i) NYPO, Bernstein; (ii) Bernstein with Columbia SO.

Piano concerto in F.
(M) ** Sony SBK 46338; *40-46338* [id.]. Entremont, Phd. O, Ormandy – RAVEL: *Concertos.***

Rhapsody in blue.
(M) **(*) DG 431 048-2; *431 048-4* [id.]. Bernstein with LAPO – BARBER: *Adagio;* COPLAND: *Appalachian spring.****

Bernstein's famous 1959 CBS (now Sony) coupling returns at mid-price and newly remastered, the sound slightly brighter and brasher, which brings both gains and losses. Fortunately, the piano timbre remains unscathed in the *Rhapsody*. This remains a uniquely desirable coupling – see our main volume, p. 412.

Ormandy's imaginative approach to the symphonic picture from *Porgy and Bess* (with superb orchestral playing throughout) makes this piece sound uncommonly fresh, especially the atmospheric opening section. *An American in Paris* is played with great panache, the blues tune is marvellous, and the CD transfers bring out the sumptuousness of the Philadelphian sound. But this is short measure at only 43 minutes.

The DG Compact Classics tape provides a mid-European slant on Gershwin, although the performance of the *Rhapsody* comes from further east, with the Leipzig Gewandhaus Orchestra under Masur providing a cultured accompaniment to the extremely lively account of the piano part by Siegfried Stöckigt. The jazzy flavour is enhanced by the blend of saxophone and string timbre in the big tune, which has an air of pre-1939 Berlin. The performance of the *Concerto* is even finer, with Robert Szidon treating the work as he would any other Romantic concerto; with rhythms superbly lithe and subtle tonal colouring, the result has both freshness and stature. The jazz idiom is seen here as an essential, but not overwhelmingly dominant, element. Downes and the LPO match the soloist in understanding and virtuosity. The softness of focus of Ozawa's account of *An American in Paris* fits in well with this more restrained approach to Gershwin's genius, especially as the sound throughout this chrome tape is full as well as vivid. The Bernstein coupling is no less attractive, but the Russo bonus item, which is included on the pair of digitally remastered CDs only, is far from indispensable.

Spirited, rumbustious performances on EMI, with the forward balance bringing a vividly brash sound-picture which serves to emphasize the episodic nature of Slatkin's readings of *An American in Paris* and the *Symphonic picture*, *Porgy and Bess*, in which the orchestral playing is superb. Pennario makes a distingushed contribution to an essentially jazzy version of the *Rhapsody* and is no less at home in the *Three Preludes*. A lively and enjoyable collection, but there are better versions of all three major works.

Entremont plays well enough in the *Concerto*, which has the appropriate transatlantic rhythmic verve, and Ormandy again directs the proceedings with flair. But the recording is not distinguished: piano tone is rather shallow, the strings have a tendency to edginess and the drum resonance at the opening is not cleanly caught.

The Naxos collection is totally unidiomatic. Everything is well played, even refined (especially the slow movement of the *Concerto*), but the rhythmic feeling of this music eludes these players: the *Rhapsody* is unmemorable and the blues tune in *An American in*

Paris is square. Good modern recording, but the jazzy element is too diluted for this music-making to be fully convincing.

Bernstein's later digital recording of the *Rhapsody in blue*, reissued again, differently coupled, has all the immediacy of live music-making, but it does not match his inspired, earlier, CBS version.

Overtures: Funny Face; Let 'em Eat Cake; Oh Kay!. Girl Crazy: suite. Of Thee I Sing: Wintergreen for President (orch. Paul). *3 Preludes* (orch. Stone); (i) *Second Rhapsody* (for piano and orchestra).
(B) **(*) Pickwick (Decca) IMPX 9013. Boston Pops O, Fiedler; (i) with Ralph Votapek.

This (1979, Decca Phase 4) Gershwin concert has transferred splendidly to CD: the sound has warmth, sparkle and colour. There are plenty of good tunes hidden here (not least *'S Wonderful* from *Funny Face*) and the orchestrations sound authentic. *Wintergreen for President* quotes exuberantly from a number of sources (including a snippet from *The Pirates of Penzance*) and Fiedler, always lively, catches its roisterous ambience. The *Second Rhapsody*, one of Gershwin's near-misses, is given with considerable fervour, with Ralph Votapek sparking off a good orchestral response. The three piano *Preludes* do not readily transcribe for orchestra, but Fiedler makes the most of them.

Porgy and Bess: Symphonic picture (arr. Bennett).
(M) *** Decca 430 712-2; *430 712-4* [id.]. Detroit SO, Dorati – GROFÉ: *Grand Canyon suite*.***

Robert Russell Bennett's famous arrangement of Gershwin melodies has been recorded many times, but never more beautifully than on this Decca digital version from Detroit. The performance is totally memorable, the opening evocatively nostalgic, and each one of these wonderful tunes is phrased with a warmly affectionate feeling for its character, yet is never vulgarized. The sound is quite superb: on CD the strings have a ravishing, lustrous radiance that stems from the refinement of the playing itself, captured with remarkable naturalness. Readers should not forget that EMI's gloriously rich and colourful recording of Gershwin's opera, conducted by Simon Rattle, remains the single most desirable acquisition in the whole Gershwin discography (EMI CDS7 49568-2 [Ang. CDDC 49568]; *EX 749568-4*).

Girl crazy (musical).
*** Elektra-Nonesuch/Warner Dig. 7559 79250-2; *7559 79250-4*. Judy Blazer, Lorna Luft, David Carroll, Eddie Korbich, O, John Mauceri.

Girl crazy, despite its hit numbers – *Embraceable you, I got rhythm* and *Bidin' my time* – has always been counted a failure; but this lively recording, with an ensemble of distinguished New York musicians conducted by John Mauceri, gives the lie to that. It is an escapist piece, typical of the early 1930s, about a New Yorker, exiled by his rich father to the Wild West, who sets up a dude ranch in an outpost previously bereft of women. The story of love and misunderstanding is largely irrelevant, but the score has point and imagination from beginning to end, all the brighter for having removed the sugar-coating which Hollywood introduced in the much-mangled film version of 1943. The casting is excellent. Judy Blazer takes the Ginger Rogers role of Kate, the post-girl, while Judy Garland's less well-known daughter, Lorna Luft, is delightful in the Ethel Merman part of the gambler's wife hired to sing in the saloon. David Carroll is the New Yorker hero, and Frank Gorshin takes the comic role of the cab-driver, Gieber Goldfarb. The whole score, 73 minutes long, is squeezed on to a single disc, packaged with libretto and excellent notes, the first of a projected Gershwin series. The only serious reservation is that the recording is dry and brassy, aggressively so – but that could be counted typical of the period too.

Gibbons, Christopher (1615–1676)

Cupid and Death (with Matthew Locke).
(M) *** HM/BMG GD 77117 (2). Kirkby, Tubb, King, Wistreich, Thomas, Holden, Cass, Nichols, Cornwell, King, Consort of Musicke, Rooley – BLOW: *Venus and Adonis.****

Cupid and Death, 'a masque in four entries', dates from 1653, or nearly 30 years before the better-known Blow work with which it is coupled. Gibbons, the son of Orlando Gibbons and the teacher of Blow, seems to have been the lesser partner in the project, with Matthew Locke providing the bulk of the music for this rustic fantasy on an ancient fable. Each of the five 'entries' or Acts is formally laid out in a set sequence of items – a suite of dances, a dialogue, a song and a chorus – and Rooley's team consistently brings out the fresh charm of the music. For repeated listening, the spoken sections, up to ten minutes long, can easily be programmed out on CD. A welcome reissue at mid-price.

Gibbons, Orlando (1583–1625)

Anthems & Verse anthems: *Almighty and Everlasting God; Hosanna to the Son of David; Lift up your heads; O Thou the central orb; See, see the word is incarnate; This is the record of John.* Canticles: *Short service: Magnificat and Nunc dimittis. 2nd Service; Magnificat and Nunc dimittis.* Hymnes & Songs of the church: *Come kiss with me those lips of thine; Now shall the praises of the Lord be sung; A song of joy unto the Lord. Organ fantasia: Fantasia for double organ; Voluntary.*
*** ASV Gaudeamus CDGAU 123; *ZCGAU 123* [id.]. King's College Ch., L. Early Music Group, Ledger; John Butt.

This invaluable anthology was the first serious survey of Gibbons's music to appear on CD. The disc has now reverted to the Gaudeamus label. It contains many of his greatest pieces and accommodates seventeen items in all, including superlative accounts of such masterpieces of the English repertoire as *This is the record of John* and *Almighty and Everlasting God.* Not only are the performances touched with distinction, the recording too is in the highest flight and the analogue sound has been transferred to CD with complete naturalness. Strongly recommended.

Gilbert, Henry (1868–1928)

Suite for chamber orchestra.
*** Albany Dig. TROY 033-2 [id.]. V. American Music Ens., Hobart Earle – CHADWICK: *Serenade for strings.****

Henry Gilbert was born in Somerville, Massachusetts, and studied under MacDowell at the New England Conservatory. He belonged to a time when almost all musical influences came from Europe and the American public did not value the output of its indigenous composers. This recorded live performance represents the European première of the *Suite*, which harmonically is innocuous but which has an agreeable nostalgic languor, while its central movement, *Spiritual*, makes an early attempt to incorporate local idiomatic influences, without direct quotation. The flavour has something in common with Delius's *Florida suite*, although Gilbert's invention is less indelible. An excellent performance here from members of the Vienna Symphony Orchestra, who are completely at home in the music, as well they might be. The recording is excellent.

Glass, Philip (born 1937)

Company; Façades.
*** Virgin Dig. VC7 91168-2; *VC7 91168-4* [id.]. LCO, Warren-Green – ADAMS: *Shaker loops* *** ❀; REICH: *8 Lines* ***; HEATH: *Frontier.****

These two works show Philip Glass at his most approachable and rewarding. *Company* consists of four brief but sharply memorable movements for strings, derived from the same basic material but strongly contrasted in mood, dynamic and atmosphere. *Façades* offers a haunting cantilena for two soprano saxophones suspended over atmospherically undulating strings. It was conceived in the composer's mind with a montage of Wall Street skyscrapers. The performances are full of intensity and are expertly played, and the recording is excellent.

Glazunov, Alexander (1865–1936)

Chant du ménestrel (for cello and orchestra), *Op. 71.*
(M) *** DG 431 475-2; *431 475-4* [id.]. Rostropovich, Boston SO, Ozawa – SHOSTAKOVICH: *Cello concerto No. 2*; TCHAIKOVSKY: *Andante cantabile.****

Glazunov's *Chant du ménestrel*, which dates from 1900, is an amiable four-minute piece which serves as an excellent encore for the Shostakovich and Tchaikovsky works which it follows on Rostropovich's CD. It is played with simple eloquence and is admirably recorded.

Violin concerto in A min., Op. 82.
(*) Collins Dig. 1128-2; *1128-4* [id.]. Kurt Nikannen, LPO, Simonov – TCHAIKOVSKY: *Concerto.*

Kurt Nikannen, now in his mid-twenties, studied with Roman Totenberg and at the Juilliard School with Dorothy DeLay. He produces a particularly sweet sound and has an agreeably wide tonal and dynamic palette. His account of the Glazunov is both musical and intelligent, but the Tchaikovksy *Concerto* with which it is coupled is not flawless and would not be among the strongest recommendations in spite of many excellent qualities. As is the case with the Tchaikovsky coupling, the LPO under Yuri Simonov accompany sensitively, the recording is excellent and the balance between soloist and orchestra is very natural indeed.

The Seasons (complete ballet), *Op. 67; Concert waltzes Nos. 1 in D, Op. 47; 2 in F, Op. 51; Stenka Razin, Op. 13.*
(M) ** Decca 430 348-2 [id.]. SRO, Ernest Ansermet.

Ansermet, after his Diaghliev experience, had a very special way with ballet music. His meticulous feeling for detail and colour immediately catches the ear at the opening of Glazunov's *Seasons*, and every bar is tinglingly alive. The big string-tune at the opening of *Summer* is impressively spacious and the vibrantly rhythmic *Autumn* theme – one of the composer's most memorable ideas – has enormous zest and gusto. One wishes that the remastered 1967 recording had a little more amplitude at these moments, but the Geneva acoustics have plenty of atmosphere and Ansermet's vivid woodwind colours gleam and glitter. The two slight *Concert waltzes* are played with affectionate delicacy and charm;

the Suisse Romande is not one of the world's most opulent-sounding orchestras but, with Ansermet at the helm, their playing always has much character. *Stenka Razin* is a melodramatic, descriptive piece which uses the *Volga boat song* at the very opening and again at its Lisztian climax. The performance here is certainly dramatic enough, and Ansermet winningly catches the sinuous, oriental flavour of the secondary theme. The early (1954) stereo is somewhat primitive, but acceptable.

Glière, Reinhold (1875–1956)

(i) *Concerto for coloratura soprano, Op. 82;* (ii) *Harp concerto, Op. 74.*
(M) *** Decca 430 006-2 [id.]. (i) Sutherland; (ii) Ellis, LSO, Bonynge – with Recital.**(*)

Glière's brilliant *Coloratura concerto* inspires Joan Sutherland to some dreamily beautiful singing. The first movement sounds like a Russian version of Villa-Lobos's famous *Bachianas brasileiras No. 5*, and the second movement has echoes of Johann Strauss, but with a Russian accent. The *Harp concerto* is as easy, unpretentious and tuneful as the vocal concerto, with Osian Ellis performing brilliantly. Excellent 1968 Kingsway Hall recording. For the rest of the collection, see under 'Sutherland' in the Vocal Recitals.

Gluck, Christophe (1714–87)

Le Cinesi (The Chinese woman).
(M) *** HM/BMG Dig. GD 77174 [77174-2-RG]. Poulenard, Von Otter, Banditelli, De Mey, Schola Cantorum Basiliensis O, Jacobs.

Gluck's hour-long opera-serenade, written in 1754 for a palace entertainment given by Prince Joseph Friedrich of Saxe-Hildburghausen, provides a fascinating view of the composer's lighter side. In the comedy here one can even detect anticipations of Mozart, though with recitative taking up an undue proportion of the whole – including one solid span, near the beginning, of over ten minutes – Gluck's timing hardly compares. The chinoiserie of the story was reflected at that first performance in elaborate Chinese costumes, a novelty at the time; more importantly for us, Gluck, rather like Mozart in *Entführung*, uses jangling and tinkling percussion instruments in the overture to indicate an exotic setting. Otherwise the formal attitudes in Metastasio's libretto – written some twenty years before Gluck set it – are pure eighteenth century.

René Jacobs, a distinguished singer himself, directs a fresh, lively and understanding performance, marked by good singing from all four soloists, notably Anne Sophie von Otter and Guy de Mey. There is an aria for each of the soloists and, typical of the genre, they come together for a final quartet. First-rate playing and excellent sound. This is most welcome in its mid-price reissue.

Orfeo ed Euridice (complete).
(M) ** EMI Dig. CMS7 63637-2 (2) [Ang. CDMB 63637]. Baltsa, Marshall, Gruberová, Amb. Op. Ch., Philh. O, Muti.

Muti chose to record the relatively severe 1762 version of *Orfeo ed Euridice* which eliminates some much-loved passages added later, but then opted for a most unstylish approach, sleek and smooth but full of romantic exaggerations. The pity is that the trio of principals was one of the strongest on record. Sadly, even Agnes Baltsa cannot make *Che farò* sound stylish when the speed is so leaden. The recording is warm and rounded and the sound generally first class.

La rencontre imprévue (opéra-comique).
*** Erato/Warner Dig. 2292 45516-2 (2) [id.]. Lynne Dawson, Le Coz, Flechter, Dubosc, Marin-Degor, Guy de Mey, Viala, Lafont, Cachemaille, Dudziak, Lyon Op. O, Gardiner.

This is another of the revelatory recordings of Gluck that John Eliot Gardiner has made with the Lyon Opera. Here he demonstrates that one of Gluck's comic operas – a genre long disparaged for bad timing and poor invention – can come up as freshly as the great reform operas like the two *Iphigénie* works he previously recorded. It is true that *Les pèlerins de la Mecque* – as Gardiner prefers to call it, rather than using its duller, more usual title, given above – has nothing like the comic timing of Mozart. Yet the brief 'Turkish' overture with its jingles has a breeziness that rivals that of *Entführung*, and all through the brisk sequence of arias and ensembles Gardiner gives the lie to the idea of the score being banal. The story may be disjointed but, with dialogue neatly edited and with some excellent singing, these three 35-minute Acts make delightful entertainment on record. The sweet-toned Lynne Dawson is charming as the heroine, Rezia, and Guy de Mey as the hero, Ali, is one of the few tenors who could cope effortlessly with the high tessitura, even though the voice does not sound quite young enough. Pierre Cachemaille sings powerfully in an incidental role, and other excellent members of the Lyon team include the tenor, Jean-Luc Viala, and the baritone, Francis Dudziak. The Lyon acoustic, as usual, is on the dry side, as recorded, but that has many advantages in comic opera.

Goehr, Alexander (born 1932)

Metamorphosis/Dance, Op. 36; (i) *Romanza for cello and orchestra, Op. 24.*
(M) *** Unicorn Dig. UKCD 2039 [id.]. (i) Moray Welsh; Royal Liverpool PO, Atherton.

Originally recorded in 1981 in first-rate digital sound, this invaluable issue, now on mid-price CD, offers two of the most representative works of a fine composer who has tended to be outshone by his younger colleagues from the New Manchester School, Peter Maxwell Davies and Harrison Birtwistle. Goehr wrote the *Romanza*, one of his most lyrical works, with Jacqueline du Pré in mind. Moray Welsh plays warmly and stylishly, but it is a pity that the dedicatee never recorded this piece which, in its serial argument, still requires persuasiveness, with its rhapsodic layout of *Aria* incorporating scherzo and cadenza. *Metamorphosis/Dance* was inspired by the Circe episode in the *Odyssey*, a sequence of elaborate variations, full of strong rhythmic interest. Not for nothing did the composer describe the piece as an 'imaginary ballet', though he would have done better to have chosen a less daunting title. The performance is excellent.

Gould, Morton (born 1913)

Fall River legend (ballet; complete).
*** Albany Dig. TROY 035 [id.]. Brock Peters, National PO, Milton Rosenstock (with recorded conversation between Agnes de Mille and Morton Gould).

Fall River legend: suite; Spirituals for string choir and orchestra.
(M) *** Mercury 432 016-2 [id.]. Eastman-Rochester SO, Howard Hanson – BARBER: *Medea*: suite.***

This complete recording of *Fall River legend* was associated with the Dance Theatre of Harlem's 1983 production of the ballet. The grim narrative concerns Lizzie Borden, a respectable American spinster of thirty-three who – according to the ballet, though not the decision of the court, which sympathetically pronounced her not guilty – murdered both her father and the malignant stepmother who had destroyed her hopes of happiness. It inspired an attractive sub-Copland score. The work opens dramatically with the Speaker for the Jury reading out the Indictment at the trial, and then the ballet tells the story in flashback. Gould's music has a good deal in common with the folksy writing in *Appalachian spring*, and it is given a splendidly atmospheric performance and recording by the New York orchestra under Rosenstock, the Harlem Dance Theatre's Musical Director. There is also a 26-minute discussion on the creation of the ballet between Agnes de Mille and the composer.

On Mercury comes the composer's orchestral suite from the ballet, vividly played by the Eastman-Rochester Orchestra under the highly sympathetic Howard Hanson, who also gives an outstandingly vibrant account of the *Spirituals*, which resourcefully and wittily uses the massed string choir as an autonomous body in concertante with the rest of the orchestra. The 1959/60 recording has astonishing clarity, range and presence and makes one realize why Mercury engineering established such a high reputation early in the stereo era. However, the Albany complete recording has more atmosphere.

Gounod, Charles (1818–93)

Faust: ballet music (suite).
(M) **(*) Decca Dig. 430 718-2; *430 718-4* [id.]. Montreal SO, Dutoit – OFFENBACH: *Gaîté parisienne.***(*)

Gounod's attractive suite is warmly and elegantly played by the Montreal orchestra under Dutoit, although the conductor's touch is not as light as one would have expected. The CD sounds first rate. However, there is a splendidly 'French' performance conducted by Paul Paray on Mercury in a collection called 'French Opera Highlights' (Philips/Mercury 432 014-2) – see under Detroit Symphony Orchestra in our Concerts section, below.

Symphonies Nos. 1 in D; 2 in B flat.
(M) **(*) EMI CDM7 63949-2 [id.]. Toulouse Capitole O, Plasson.

Symphony No. 1 in D; Petite symphonie in B flat for wind instruments.
*** Decca Dig. 430 231-2; *430 231-4* [id.]. Saint Paul CO, Hogwood – BIZET: *L'Arlésienne.****

Gounod's two *Symphonies* sound astonishingly youthful, though they were composed in quick succession in his mid-thirties. Listening to No. 1 – especially in Hogwood's sparklingly fresh performance, with its fizzing finale – the Bizet *Symphony* springs to mind. The effortless flow of first-rate ideas and the mastery, both of the orchestra, which is handled with the greatest expertise, and of symphonic form, are very striking. The *Second Symphony* is very like the *First*, and both receive decent performance from Michael Plasson. He is thoroughly in sympathy with the composer's infectious style, as is the Orchestra of the Capitole Toulouse, although the playing is not quite as finished or as accomplished as the music deserves. The EMI engineers have produced good if not outstanding sound, which is fresh enough in its CD transfer.

Instead of the *Second Symphony*, Hogwood offers the *Petite symphonie for wind*, which dates from Gounod's later years: he was nearly seventy when he wrote it for one of the celebrated Parisian wind ensembles of the day. The work has impeccable craftsmanship and is engagingly witty and civilized. Hogwood has its full measure and, with his 'authentic' ear for colour, makes the most of its scoring, even noting the composer's fondness for the lowest bassoon note, B flat. The work's lovely *Andante cantabile*, with its memorable flute solo, is played most beautifully, and the outer movements are infectious in their sprung rhythms. The Saint Paul Chamber Orchestra plays on modern instruments, but their crisp, athletic style brings clean textures, and the trumpets in the finale of *Symphony No. 1* are attractively bright and well focused. In the *Petite symphonie* the matching wind timbres have lots of character and the bright horn articulation at the opening of the scherzo is typical of the zest of the playing. Excellent recording and an interesting Bizet coupling.

Grainger, Percy (1882–1961)

(i) *Air from County Derry (Londonderry air); Country gardens;* (ii) *Danish folk music suite;* (i) *Handel in the Strand;* (ii) *The immovable 'Do'; In a nutshell suite;* (i) *Mock morris; Molly on the shore; Shepherd's hey;* (Piano) *Knight and shepherd's daughter; Walking tune.* Arrangements: FAURÉ: *Nell, Op. 18/1.* GERSHWIN: *Love walked in; The man I love.*
(M) *** EMI CDM7 63520-2; *EG 763520-4* [id.]. (i) Light Music Soc. O, Dunn; (ii) E. Sinfonia, Dilkes; (iii) Daniel Adni.

A useful and very generous Grainger anthology (79 minutes long). The performances under Sir Vivian Dunn are particularly spontaneous and the recording is bright and fresh, perhaps not as sumptuous in the *Londonderry air* as might be ideal. Of the Dilkes items, *In a nutshell* is an early work, a collection of original tunes colourfully set, with exotic percussion effects, while the *Danish folk music suite* is equally attractive and unpretentious, if less distinctive. *The immovable 'Do'* is a piece inspired by a time when Grainger had a 'cipher' on his harmonium and the note C went on sounding through everything. The inclusion of the piano pieces is particularly welcome. Daniel Adni plays them with a combination of sound musical instinct and good taste that gives unfailing pleasure, and he is very well recorded. The curiosities here are the Fauré and Gershwin arrangements, models of their kind.

'Dished up for piano', Volume 1: *Andante con moto; Arrival platform humlet; Bridal lullaby; Children's march; Colonial song; English waltz; Gay but wistful; The Gum-suckers' march; Handel in the Strand; Harvest hymn; The Immovable 'Do'; In a Nutshell (suite); In Dahomey; Mock morris; Pastoral; Peace; Sailor's song; Saxon twi-play; To a Nordic princess; Walking tune.*
*** Nimbus Dig. NI 5220 [id.]. Martin Jones.

'Dished up for piano', Volume 2: Arrangements: BACH: *Blithe bells.* BRAHMS: *Cradle song.* Chinese TRAD.: *Beautiful fresh flower.* DOWLAND: *Now, o now, I needs must part.* ELGAR: *Enigma variations: Nimrod.* Stephen FOSTER: *Lullaby; The rag-time girl.* GERSHWIN: *Love walked in; The man I love.* RACHMANINOV: *Piano concerto No. 2: Finale* (abridged). R. STRAUSS: *Der Rosenkavalier. Ramble on the last love-duet.* TCHAIKOVSKY: *Piano concerto No. 1* (opening); *Paraphrase on the Flower waltz.*
**(*) Nimbus Dig. NI 5232 [id.]. Martin Jones.

'Dished up for piano', Volume 3: Folksong arrangements: *The brisk young sailor; Bristol Town; Country gardens; Died for love; Hard-hearted Barb'ra Helen; The hunter in his career; Irish tune from County Derry; Jutish medley; Knight and shepherd's daughter; Lisbon (Dublin Bay); The merry king; Mo Ninghean Dhu; Molly on the shore; My Robin is to Greenwood gone; One more day my John* (2 versions, easy and complex); *Near Woodstock Town; The nightingale and the two sisters; O gin I were where Gowrie rins; Rimmer and goldcastle; The rival brothers; Scotch Strathspey; Shepherd's hey; Spoon*

River; Stalt vesselil; Sussex mummer's Christmas carol; The widow's party; Will ye gang to the Hielands, Lizzie Lindsay.
*** Nimbus Dig. NI 5244 [id.]. Martin Jones.

Martin Jones's survey of Grainger's piano music is refreshingly lively and spontaneous. Volume 1 is particularly attractive, and that is the place to start, for there is not a dull item here. The jolly pieces come off engagingly, but Jones often finds hidden depths in a composer best known for his boisterous and whimsical frivolousness. *The Bridal lullaby* (a delightful miniature), the charming *Colonial song* and the broodingly evocative *Pastoral*, the surprisingly extended, almost profound, last movement of the *In a Nutshell suite*, all show Jones at his most penetratingly thoughtful. This is lovely playing. There is plenty of dash in the folksong arrangements, and charm too, and they display a much greater range than one might have expected. Not all are equally memorable but, with a programme of 68 minutes to choose from, that hardly matters. The transcriptions are the most fascinating of all. The opening of the Tchaikovsky *Piano concerto* – some would say the 'best bit' – is transcribed straightforwardly, with a flamboyant flourish to finish it off, and the purple patch at the end of the Rachmaninov No. 2 cannot fail to make an impact in a performance as brilliant as this. Martin Jones then plays the Gershwin pieces in a beguilingly sultry manner, and he is equally good in the freely composed pastiche on Bach's *Sheep may safely graze* (*Blithe bells*). But he plays *Nimrod* and the *Der Rosenkavalier* excerpts too slowly; such a degree of languor might come off with the orchestra, but on the piano the effect is enervating. In all other respects the collection of transcriptions is most entertaining. The piano is recorded reverberantly in the Nimbus manner – but it rather suits this repertoire, and the image is absolutely truthful.

Granados, Enrique (1867–1916)

12 Danzas españolas, Op. 5.
* Telarc Dig. CD 80216 [id.]. Angel and Celedonio Romero.

These performances are amiable and not without colour, but are curiously lacking in Spanish temperament. The opening *Minueto* is bland, and the delicious *Oriental* – more famous in its orchestral format – is hardly sultry; while the famous *Andaluza* has nothing like the magic which Julian Bream imparts to it (BMG/RCA RCD 14378). Livelier numbers, like the *Zarabanda* and Jota (*Rondalla aragonesa*) bring a curious feeling of deliberation. At best this is pleasant, wallpaper-music-making.

Allegro de concierto; Danza lenta; El Pelele; Goyescas.
*** BMG/RCA Dig. RD 60408; *RK 60408* [60408-2-RC]. Alicia de Larrocha.

Alicia de Larrocha recorded the *Goyescas* for Decca plus *El Pelele* in 1976 and the *Allegro de concierto* in the early days of digital recording. There is really rather little to choose between the older Decca account (411 958-2 – see our main volume, p. 437) and her excellently recorded newcomer on RCA. Her view of these pieces has not changed substantially, though her responses in the earlier recording are perhaps marginally fresher and more poetic. The RCA sound is very present and vivid, though the listener is closer to the instrument than in the earlier record, where there is a shade more space round the aural image. Recommended, though it should not displace the earlier version.

Goyescas (complete).
(M) *(*) EMI CZS7 62889-2 (2). Aldo Ciccolini – ALBÉNIZ: *Iberia*.*(*)

Aldo Ciccolini's recording of the *Goyescas* looks like good value at mid-price, particularly with *Iberia* thrown in for good measure. But the recordings, made in the Salle Wagram in Paris in 1966, are a bit subfusc. The piano-tone is clattery and shallow in timbre and does not show the admirable Ciccolini in the best light. Readers will do better with Alicia de Larrocha, who is more realistically recorded and both more poetic and idiomatic.

Graun, Johann Gottlieb (1703–71)

Oboe concerto in C min.
(M) *** DG 431 120-2; *431 120-4* [id.]. Holliger, Camerata Bern, Van Wijnkoop – KREBS: *Double concerto* **(*); TELEMANN: *Concerto.****

This Graun was the brother of the better-known composer of the opera *Montezuma*, and the *C minor Concerto* is delectable in its originality. All three movements are highly inventive, and the only pity is that this CD reissue omits the companion *G minor concerto*, included on the original LP. There would have been plenty of room for it, with a playing time here of only 55 minutes. Nevertheless this is a valuable reissue and, with Holliger at his most sparkling and with excellent sound, is well worth exploring.

Gregorian Chant

Alleluia; Antiphon: Montes Gilboe; Antiphonal Psalmody; Antiphons; Ave verum; Communions; Flores apparuerunt; Gospel tone; Gradual; Hymns; Laudes seu Acclamationes; Marian antiphons; Responsories.
(M) *** Decca 425 729-2; *425 729-4* [id.]. Edgar Fleet, L. Carmelite Priory Ch., John McCarthy.

Planned by the late Alec Robertson, who also provided fascinating background information, this beautifully sung and excellently recorded anthology is the finest possible introduction to plainsong. Extra variety of tone is given by the use of female voices as well as male; but care is taken to ensure that their vibratoless vocal line blends successfully. Edgar Fleet acts as cantor and John McCarthy directs the singing with dedication and authority. The sound (with a Oiseau Lyre source) is very fine.

Grieg, Edvard (1843–1907)

Piano concerto in A min., Op. 16.
(B) *** CfP Dig. CD-CFP 4574 [id.]; *TC-CFP 4574*. Pascal Devoyon, LPO, Maksymiuk – SCHUMANN: *Piano concerto.****
(M) **(*) EMI Dig. CDD7 63903-2 [id.]; *ET 763903-4*. Cécile Ousset, LSO, Marriner – RACHMANINOV: *Piano concerto No. 2.****
(M) **(*) Sony SBK 46543 [id.]. Philippe Entremont, Phd. O, Ormandy – SCHUMANN: *Piano concerto* etc.*
(M) **(*) Sony/CBS CD 44849; *40-44849*. Fleisher, Cleveland O, Szell – SCHUMANN: *Concerto.***(*)
(B) * EMI CDZ7 62859-2; *LZ 762859-4*. Ogdon, New Philh. O, Berglund – FRANCK: *Symphonic variations*; SCHUMANN: *Concerto.**
(M) * Decca Dig. 430 719-2; *430 719-4* [id.]. George Bolet, Berlin RSO, Chailly – SCHUMANN: *Concerto.**(*)

(i) *Piano concerto in A min., Op. 16; 6 Lyric pieces, Op. 65.*
*** Virgin Dig. VC7 91198-2; *VC7 91198-4* [id.]. Leif Ove Andsnes, (i) Bergen PO, Dmitri Kitaenko – LISZT: *Piano concerto No. 2.****

Piano concerto in A min.; Lyric pieces, Op. 12/1; Op. 43/1, 3 & 6; Op. 47/1 & 3; Op. 57/2; Op. 65/6; Op. 71/7.
(M) **(*) EMI/Phoenixa stereo/mono CDM7 63778-2; *EG 763778-4* [id.]. Richard Farrell, Hallé O, Weldon – LISZT: *Piano concerto No. 1.****

(i) *Piano concerto in A min.;* (ii) *Peer Gynt suites Nos. 1 – 2.*
(B) ** DG Compact Classics 413 158-2 (2); *413 158-4* [id.]. (i) Anda, BPO, Kubelik; (ii) Bamberg SO, Richard Kraus – SIBELIUS: *Finlandia; Karelia; Valse triste* *** (CD only: *En Saga; Legend: The Swan of Tuonela* ***).

Leif Ove Andsnes was still in his teens when he recorded the Grieg and Liszt *Concertos* in Grieg's home town with the Bergen Philharmonic. Youthful virtuosi are almost two-a-penny nowadays, but Andsnes wears his brilliance lightly. There is no lack of display and bravura here, but no ostentation. Indeed he has great poetic feeling and delicacy of colour, and Grieg's familiar warhorse comes up with great freshness. His piano is in perfect condition (not always the case on records) and is excellently balanced in relation to the orchestra. This is one of the best modern accounts and ranks alongside Perahia (Sony MK 44899; *40-44899*) and Bishop-Kovacevich (Philips 412 923-2). These two performances are, of course, coupled with the Schumann *Concerto*, so, being paired with Liszt, this makes a genuine alternative.

The French pianist Pascal Devoyon is now in his thirties and has never enjoyed the recognition he so richly deserves on record. His account of the Grieg *Concerto* is characteristic of him: aristocratic without being aloof, pensive without being self-conscious, and brilliant without being flashy. He is a poetic artist whose natural musicianship shines through. At bargain price this excellent account is competitive, though the piano itself, while very good, is not perhaps in such top condition as Andsnes's Steinway on Virgin Classics. Yet this remains a very fine issue, with excellent playing from the LPO under Jerzy Maksymiuk.

Ousset's is a strong, dramatic reading, not lacking in warmth and poetry but, paradoxically, bringing out what we would generally think of as the masculine qualities of power and drive. The result, with excellent accompaniment recorded in very full sound, is always fresh and convincing. A good choice for anyone wanting this unusual coupling with the Rachmaninov *Concerto No. 2.*

The outstanding New Zealand pianist, Richard Farrell, had his career tragically terminated at the age of thirty-two by a car accident in Sussex in 1958, not long after he had recorded this poetic account of an elusive romantic concerto of which he has the full measure. There is no lack of brilliance here, yet it is the gentle moments which one best remembers, with the most subtle tonal shading. George Weldon accompanies most sympathetically, and the recording is excellent: it does not sound its age in the least. The generous selection of *Lyric pieces* also shows Farrell's winning understanding of Grieg; if here the musical characterization is at times a shade less strong, this is still fine playing.

Entremont's, too, is a fresh, vital performance, with Ormandy as well as the soloist on top form. The orchestral opening of the slow movement is beautifully played and the piano entry is a moment of magic, while the finale is splendidly sprited. Characteristically lavish CBS/Philadelphia sound, brightly lit. Unfortunately, the Serkin Schumann coupling is very unenticing.

Fleisher is another outstanding artist, and his recordings are too little known in Europe.

His performance of the Grieg ranks with the finest, combining strength with poetry in a satisfying balance. The Cleveland Orchestra gives a very positive accompaniment under Szell, with deeply expressive playing in the *Adagio*. There is plenty of sparkle in the outer movements. The recording is bold and clear – bordering on the fierce so far as the upfront orchestral presence is concerned – and tape-hiss seems more obtrusive than usual in the CD transfer.

Anda's account of the *Concerto*, offered on the DG Compact Classics issue, is more wayward than some, but it is strong in personality and has plenty of life. Kubelik's accompaniment is very good too and the early 1960s recording sounds well. A rather fuller selection from the *Peer Gynt suite No. 2* is offered on the digitally remastered pair of CDs. Grieg's perennially fresh incidental music is vividly played in Bamberg, but the early stereo recording here sounds a bit thin in the strings (in both formats). The Sibelius couplings, however, are first rate, with two of the performances conducted by Karajan, and excellent accounts under Okko Kamu of *En Saga* and *The Swan of Tuonela* added to the CD programme.

John Ogdon's version is disappointing. Clearly the partnership with Berglund did not work well and the end result is dull, in spite of an often bold solo contribution and fine recording from the early 1970s, most effectively remastered.

Bolet shows little affinity with Grieg's delightful concerto. He seeks to give a spacious reading and the result is merely lethargic and heavy; even the first-movement cadenza drags. The recording is the best part of the affair – it is of Decca's finest quality.

(i) *Piano concerto in A min.; Lyric suite, Op. 54, Peer Gynt suite No. 2, Op. 55.*
**(*) Chan. Dig. CHAN 8723; *ABTD 1363* [id.]. (i) Margaret Fingerhut; Ulster O, Vernon Handley.

Margaret Fingerhut is the young British pianist who has so eloquently championed Bax on the Chandos label and has put us in her debt with other keyboard rarities. With the Grieg *Concerto* she enters a more competitive field and gives a thoughtful and musicianly reading that holds a fine balance between the virtuosic and poetic elements in the concerto. Her first-movement cadenza shows tenderness as well as brilliance, as indeed does the slow movement. Only in the finale does she fall short of distinction if we compare her to Bishop-Kovacevich, Lipatti and other classic accounts (and, even so, the slow middle section has many felicitous touches). Not perhaps the very first choice, given the abundance of rivals, but a far from negligible account. Vernon Handley makes a little too much of the *Peer Gynt suite*, which is occasionally somewhat overblown, but he gets generally sympathetic and responsive playing from the Ulster Orchestra and is well recorded.

Holberg suite, Op. 40; Lyric suite, Op. 54; Sigurd Jorsalfar (suite), *Op. 56.*
(M) **(*) Ph. 432 277-2; *432 277-4* [id.]. ECO, Raymond Leppard.

Grieg's delightful *Lyric suite* is the finest of the performances here; very freshly played, it has warm, transparent string textures and the closing *March of the dwarfs* is earthily malignant. *Sigurd Jorsalfar* goes well, too: the remastering has made the recording sound more vivid and the opening *Prelude* is nicely paced. The relative disappointment here is the *Holberg suite*, in which the playing has an element of routine that is unexpected from this conductor. But the 1979 sound is very good indeed.

Holberg suite, Op. 40; 2 Norwegian melodies, Op. 63.
(*) RCA Dig. RD 60368; *RK 60368* [60368-2-RC; *60368-4-RC*]. Moscow Soloists, Yuri Bashmet – TCHAIKOVSKY: *Serenade for strings*.(*)

Bracing, almost astringent allegros, with brilliant playing from the Moscow Soloists and an elegiac feeling in slow movements. The contrasts are emphasized by the very brightly lit recording with its wide dynamic range. There is no lack of ambience, yet the overall effect is rather cool. The *Norwegian dances* are rhythmically strong and the second, the *Cowkeeper's tune and country dance*, has an infectious exuberance. But otherwise there is a certain lack of charm here.

Lyric suite, Op. 54; Sigurd Jorsalfar (suite), *Op. 56; Symphonic dances, Op. 64.*
**(*) ASV Dig. CDDCA 722; *ZCDCA 722* [id.]. RPO, Yondani Butt.

The *Symphonic dances* are particularly successful here. They are not easy to bring off, yet Butt and the RPO capture their charm and energy without succumbing to melodrama in No. 4. The *Lyric suite*, too, is fresh and the trolls in the finale have an earthy pungency. However, the outer movements of *Sigurd Jorsalfar* are less successful, with an element of ponderousness. One can too easily overdo the homage in the *Homage march*. Excellent, vivid recording with a nice degree of resonance.

Cello sonata in A min., Op. 36.
(*) CRD CRD 3391 [id.]. Robert Cohen, Roger Vignoles – FRANCK: *Cello sonata.*(*)

With his clean, incisive style Cohen gives a strong performance of the rarely heard Grieg *Sonata*, sensitively accompanied by Roger Vignoles. In the folk element Cohen might have adopted a more persuasive style, bringing out the charm of the music more, but certainly he sustains the sonata structures well. The last movement is one of Grieg's most expansive. The recording lacks a little in range at both ends of the spectrum but presents the cello very convincingly. It has been most naturally transferred to CD.

String quartet in G min., Op. 27.
** Ph. Dig. 426 286-2 [id.]. Guarneri Qt – SIBELIUS: *Quartet.***

Grieg's only *Quartet* (apart from a later, unfinished work in two movements) comes from 1878, two years after the first production of *Peer Gynt*, and gave him much trouble. It is cyclic. A theme from his Op. 25 Ibsen setting of *Spillemaend* ('Fiddlers') serves as a unifying motive and also provided a model for Debussy's *Quartet* in the same key. The Guarneri play with splendid ensemble and unanimity but without the fresh innocence and charm this composer ideally calls for. At present there is no CD alternative, and there can be no quarrels with the recording; but it is probably wiser to wait until a more enjoyable performance comes along.

Violin sonata No. 3 in C min. Op. 45.
** Audiofon Dig. CD 72026 [id.]. Aaron Rosand, Seymour Lipkin – STRAUSS; SAINT-SAENS: *Violin sonatas.***

Older collectors may recall Aaron Rosand's LP of the Sibelius *Humoresques*, way back in the 1960s, and the purity of intonation and breathtaking virtuosity that distinguished his playing. He never enjoyed the exposure to which his gifts entitled him. Now he has a rather wider vibrato than he had then, but no less personality. The expressive vibrato may be too sweet for some tastes, particularly in the slow movement of the Grieg *Sonata*. But there is something of the grand manner about his playing that is likeable, and the recording is vivid, though the studio is on the small side.

Lyric pieces, Books 1–10 (complete).
(M) **(*) Unicorn Dig. UKCD 2033, *UKC 2033* (1–4); UKCD 2034, *UKC 2034* (5–7); UKCD 2035, *UKC 2035* (8–10) [id.]. Peter Katin.

Peter Katin is a persuasive and sensitive exponent of this repertoire, and he has the benefit of a recording of exceptional presence and clarity (though very occasionally it seems to harden in climaxes, when one notices that the microphone is perhaps a shade close). Katin has the measure of Grieg's sensibility and characterizes these pieces with real poetic feeling. His performances do not displace the famous Gilels anthology, but they are by far the most sensitive and idiomatic survey of the complete set at present on offer.

Peer Gynt (incidental music), *Op. 23.*
**(*) EMI Dig. CDC7 54119-2 [id.]; *EL 754119-4*. Salomaa, McNair, Borg, Ernest Senff Ch., BPO, Tate.

There is some beautiful and at times thrilling playing here from the Berlin Philharmonic under Jeffrey Tate, even though it does not always sound fully idiomatic. The new EMI compilation offers the best part of 70 minutes' music, four minutes less than Blomstedt's Decca CD (425 448-2). Like Blomstedt, Tate also offers some of the Norwegian dialogue, though his soloists are not quite as persuasive as those on rival versions. The EMI disc is excellently recorded. However, more of the atmosphere of *Peer Gynt* comes across in the Järvi (DG 427 325-2; *427 325-4*) or Blomstedt performances.

Peer Gynt suites Nos. 1, Op. 46; 2, Op. 55.
(M) **(*) EMI CD-EMX 2176; *TC-EMX 2176*. Bournemouth SO, Berglund – ALFVÉN: *Swedish rhapsody* **(*); JÄRNEFELT: *Praeludium*.***

Berglund's performances are strongly characterized. *Morning* is undoubtedly fresh and *Ingrid's lament* is notably sombre. Although the orchestral playing is persuasive, there is some lack of charm here; the upper strings are made to sound unnaturally brilliant and fierce at the climax of the *Death of Aase* (something which derives from the balance of the original recording rather than the CD transfer).

Songs: *Den Saerde; En Drøm; Eros; En svane; Fra Monte Pincio; Guten; Med en primulaveris; Med en vandlilje; Millom Rosor; Modersorg; Og jeg vil ha mig en Hjertenskjaer; Prinsessen; Tak for dit Räd; Våren; Ved Rundarne. Peer Gynt: Solveigs song*
(M) (***) EMI mono CDH7 63305-2 [id.] (with songs by Hurum; Lie; Alnaes; Bull; Grøndahl; Sinding). Kirsten Flagstad, Philh. O, Braithwaite; Susskind; Moore McArthur; Alnaes.

What an extraordinary and glorious sound Flagstad produced! These inimitable performances come from 1948, when her voice was in its prime, and remain unsurpassed. (Her later Grieg recitals, recorded for Decca in the 1950s, wonderful though they were, found the voice past its peak.) Her masterly pacing, sense of vocal colour and command of atmosphere in this repertoire are flawless. The recital includes sixteen of Grieg's best-known songs and a handful of other Norwegian songs recorded in Oslo in 1929 (the earliest are songs by Sinding and Backer-Grøndahl, recorded in 1923). No collector of Grieg's music or of fine singing should overlook this compilation.

Grofé, Ferde (1892–1972)

Grand Canyon suite.
(M) *** Decca 430 712-2; *430 712-4* [id.]. Detroit SO, Dorati – GERSHWIN: *Porgy and Bess*.***

Antal Dorati has the advantage of superlative Decca recording, very much in the demonstration class, with stereophonically vivid detail. Yet the performance combines subtlety with spectacle, and on CD the naturalness of the orchestral sound-picture adds to the sense of spaciousness and tangibility. With its outstanding coupling, and its price advantage, this version is very much in a class of its own, even though we have a very soft spot for the recording on Telarc (CD 80086) by the Cincinnati Pops Orchestra under Kunzel, which optionally interpolates a real-life thunderstorm, to spectacular effect (see our main volume).

Halvorsen, Johan (1864–1935)

Air Norvégien, Op. 7; Danses Norvégiennes.
(BB) *** Naxos Dig. 8.550329 [id.]. Dong-Suk Kang, Slovak (Bratislava) RSO, Adrian Leaper – SIBELIUS: *Violin concerto*; SINDING: *Légende*; SVENDSEN: *Romance.****

Dong-Suk Kang plays the attractive *Danses Norvégiennes* with great panache, character and effortless virtuosity, and delivers an equally impeccable performance of the earlier *Air Norvégien.*

Handel, George Frideric (1685–1759)

Ballet music: *Alcina: overture; Acts I & III: suites. Il pastor fido: suite. Terpsichore: suite.*
(M) *** Erato/Warner Dig. 2292 45378-2 [id.]. E. Bar. Soloists, Gardiner.

As so often in the history of staged dance music, Handel wrote his ballet music for a specific dancer, in this case Marie Sallé, and her special skills demanded a high proportion of lyrical music. Handel rose to the challenge: the expressive writing here is very appealing; so is the scoring with its felicitous use of recorders. John Eliot Gardiner is just the man for such a programme. He is not afraid to charm the ear, yet allegros are vigorous and rhythmically infectious. The bright and clean recorded sound adds to the sparkle, and the quality is first class. A delightful collection, and very tuneful too.

12 Concerti grossi, Op. 6/1–12.
** Denon Dig. CO 76305/7 [id.]. I Solisti Italiani.

I Solisti Italiani are given a realistic recording, with the solo group balanced forwardly. But the engineers have not succeeded in creating enough depth of perspective and the *ripieno* seldom really separates from the *concertino.* When the larger group takes up a passage from the smaller this works well, but overall the element of contrast is minimized. The playing can be rhythmically crisp (as at the opening *Larghetto e spiccato* of No. 5) and the fugues are cleanly and brightly enunciated. Slow movements are expressive without being fulsome: the opening *Andante larghetto* of *No. 2 in F major* comes off rather well, but there is often the feeling that the music is undercharacterized. Handel's famous *Larghetto e piano* in No. 12 is presented with agreeable simplicity, but other performances reveal the nobility of Handel's melodic line more readily. Slow introductions are strong but there also is a certain heaviness at times, as at the *Largo* opening of No. 9. All in all, and especially at full price, this would not head the list of recommendations for this great work. Our first choice remains with the splendid ASMF set, directed by Iona Brown, which earned a Rosette in our main volume (Philips 410 048-2).

Concerti grossi, Op. 6/4–6; Concerto grosso, Op. 3/3.
(BB) * Naxos Dig. 8.550157 [id.]. Capella Istropolitana, Jozef Kopelman.

Concerti grossi, Op. 6/8, 10 & 12; in C (Alexander's Feast).
(BB) * Naxos Dig. 8.550158 [id.]. Capella Istropolitana, Jozef Kopelman.

As we know from their recordings of Bach, Haydn and Mozart, the Capella Istropolitana is an excellent group; their playing here is warm and polished, and the Naxos recording is flattering. But Jozef Kopelman's rhythmic manner is too easy-going – one needs more bite at the opening of Op. 6/5, and slow movements are often rather lazily expressive and almost bland.

(i) *Harp concerto, Op. 4/6. Variations for harp.*
❀ (M) *** Decca 425 723-2; *425 723-4* [id.]. Marisa Robles, (i) ASMF, Iona Brown – BOIELDIEU; DITTERSDORF: *Harp concertos* etc.*** ❀

Handel's Op. 4/6 is well known in both organ and harp versions. Marisa Robles and Iona Brown make an unforgettable case for the latter by creating the most delightful textures, while never letting the work sound insubstantial. The ASMF accompaniment, so stylish and beautifully balanced, is a treat in itself, and the recording is well-nigh perfect. This collection (which also includes solo harp variations by Beethoven and a set attributed to Mozart) amounts to a good deal more than the sum of its parts.

Organ concertos, Op. 4/1–6; Op.7/1–6; Second set: Nos. 1 in F; 2 in A; Arnold edition: Nos. 1 in D; 2 in F.
❀ *** Erato/Warner Dig. 2292 45394-2 (3) [id.]. Ton Koopman, Amsterdam Bar. O.

It is good to have Ton Koopman's complete set of Handel's *Organ concertos* back in the catalogue. They take precedence over all the competition, both as performances and as recordings. The playing has wonderful life and warmth, tempi are always aptly judged and, although original instruments are used, this is authenticity with a kindly presence, for the warm acoustic ambience of St Bartholomew's Church, Beek-Ubbergen, Holland, gives the orchestra a glowingly vivid coloration, and the string timbre is particularly attractive. So is the organ itself, which is just right for the music. Ton Koopman plays imaginatively throughout and he is obviously enjoying himself: no single movement sounds tired and the orchestral fugues emerge with genial clarity. Koopman directs the accompanying group from the keyboard, as Handel would have done, and the interplay between soloist and ripieno is a delight. The sound is first class and the balance could hardly be better.

Organ concertos, Op. 4/1 & 5; in F (Cuckoo and the nightingale); in A, HWV 296.
(M) ** EMI CD-EMX 2115 [CDM7 63579-2]. Simon Preston, Bath Fest. O, Y. Menuhin.

In this EMI reissue from the late 1960s, Simon Preston uses the organ in Merchant Taylors Hall, London, and is partnered by Menuhin. They use the Neville Boyling edition and, though there are minor criticisms to be made of tempi and phrasing, on the whole these are enjoyably lively accounts. The CD transfer is very brightly lit.

Organ concertos, Op. 4/2; Op. 7/3, 4 & 5; in F (Cuckoo and the nightingale).
(M) *** DG Dig. 431 708-2; *431 708-4* [id.]. Simon Preston, E. Concert, Pinnock.

This is more generous than the previous sampler from Preston's series with Pinnock; all the Op. 7 works plus the *Cuckoo and the nightingale* are recorded on the organ at St John's, Armitage, in Staffordshire, which seems particularly well suited to this repertoire. Both performances and sound are admirably fresh.

Music for the Royal Fireworks; Concerto grosso in C (Alexander's Feast); Concerti grossi, Op. 6/1 & 6.
(M) *** DG 431 707-2; *431 707-4* [id.]. E. Concert, Trevor Pinnock.

Pinnock's performance of the *Fireworks music* has tremendous zest; this is not only the safest but the best recommendation for those wanting a period-instrument version. The DG recording is outstanding in its combination of brightness and colour, and it certainly does not lack weight. The account of the *Alexander's Feast concerto* has both vitality and imagination and is no less recommendable; for those who already have a complete set of Op. 6, yet who want to experience Pinnock's way with this music, the disc makes a useful sampler. The performances have admirable lightness and an infectious spirit but have less of a sense of grandeur. Excellently balanced and truthful recording.

Music for the Royal Fireworks; Water music (complete).
(M) ** Decca 430 717-2; *430 717-4* [id.]. Concg. CO, Simon Preston.

Although the very opening of the *Water music* could have a stronger rhythmic profile, on the whole both of Handel's great sets of occasional pieces are given alert performances by Simon Preston and the Concertgebouw Chamber Orchestra, while the boisterous horns and the bright, clean string textures readily show influences from the authentic school. So, too, does the performance of the famous *Air*, which lacks charm. In the last resort the effect here is too briskly stylish; there is no sense of glee in Handel's profusion of colourful melody. Excellent, modern, digital sound, and no doubt many will find the energy of the music-making stimulating. But for a sparkling performance on modern instruments that conveys warmth too, one readily turns back to Marriner and the ASMF on Decca (414 596-2; *414 596-4*). This is still at premium price; bargain-hunters will find Szell's splendidly alive performances of the old Handel–Harty suites no less vivid or expressively appealing; with the outstandingly crisp and polished LSO playing, they make one relish Harty's colourful additions to Handel's original scoring (Decca 417 694-2; *417 694-4*).

(i) *Music for the Royal Fireworks; Water music* (both complete); (ii) *Harp concerto, Op. 4/6;* (iii) *Messiah: Sinfonia* (CD only: (iv) *Organ concerto in F, Op. 4/4*).
(B) ** DG Compact Classics 413 148-2 (2); *413 148-4*. (i) BPO, Kubelik; (ii) Zabaleta, Kuentz CO, Kuentz; (iii) LPO, Karl Richter (CD only: (iv) Michael Schneider, Bav. RSO, Jochum).

Kubelik's well-upholstered, full-orchestral version of the complete *Water music* has been freshly remastered and, if not especially individual, combines a sense of grandeur with liveliness. It is splendidly played, as is the *Fireworks music*, where the focus of the sound is slightly less clean. Zabaleta's approach to the *Harp concerto* is as cool as a spring stream and eminently musical, while the sound-balance is excellent. At bargain price this Compact Classics tape is fair value. The pair of digitally remastered CDs includes also a lively account of the *Organ concerto in F*, Op. 4/4, not a particularly substantial bonus.

Harpsichord suites Nos. 1–8.
(M) *** DG 427 170-2 (2) [id.]. Colin Tilney (harpsichord).

Colin Tilney plays two fine period instruments from Hamburg (both pictured in the accompanying booklet). The 1728 Zell (used for *Suites 1, 3, 6* and *7*) has two manuals and is gloriously decorated with nature paintings and subjects from ancient mythology. It must be one of the most beautiful restored harpsichords in existence. The 1710 Fleischer – the oldest surviving harpsichord known to have been made in Hamburg – is played in

Suites 2, 4, 5 (with its famous *Harmonious blacksmith* variations) and *8*; it has only one manual and its elegant design follows English models. Both suit this repertoire extremely well and there are subtle and occasionally striking differences in colour and resonance between the two instruments. One has to be a little careful with the volume control but both instruments are recorded within a proper ambience, and a most vivid and truthful image can be obtained. Tilney has a fine technique and a firm rhythmic grip and he shows awareness of stylistic problems (he plays the *Allemande* in the *A major Suite* in the French way), even if there are inconsistencies with double-dotting. His approach is direct and thoughtful, not inflexible, and at times has almost a rhapsodic element, as at the improvisatory flourish which forms the *Prelude* of the *Third Suite in D minor*. Altogether this playing has much to commend it in its vitality and consistency of style.

COLLECTIONS

(i) *Oboe concerto No. 1 in B flat;* (ii) *Organ concerto, Op. 7/1. Rodrigo: suite;* (iii) *Xerxes (Serse): suite.*
(M) ** EMI CDM7 63956-2 [id.]; *EG 763956-4.* (i) Rothwell; (ii) Chadwick; (iii) Lewis, Hallé O, Barbirolli (with PURCELL: *Suite for strings* **).

This collection is well recorded and Barbirolli's directing hand ensures that all the music is alive. The snag is the question of style, over which Barbirolli seems to have managed a not entirely happy compromise. He uses a fairly large modern orchestral group and includes a harpsichord to be on the safe side. *Ombra mai fù* therefore opens gorgeously, with a richly phrased orchestral ritornello, and, when Richard Lewis begins to sing, his purity of style is a little disconcerting. But Sir John plays both the orchestral suites with vigour, and some of this music is the kind that enjoys enthusiasm and warmth every bit as much as scholarship. Lady Barbirolli's playing is, as ever, delightful; if the effect of the *Organ concerto* is somewhat pontificatory, the grandeur of the piece comes over too. Sir John makes a good deal of the ground bass (a little like the last movement of the *Eroica Symphony*) which links and permeates the work's first two movements. With all one's reservations, this disc is full of personality. The sound is good, with an exciting dynamic range in the *Organ concerto*. The additional Purcell suite is also very welcome, arranged by Barbirolli from movements derived from various stage works. Incidentally, although described as being for strings, there is a demure flute solo in the Minuet from *The Virtuous Wife*.

VOCAL AND CHORAL MUSIC

Dixit dominus; Nisi dominus; Silete venti.
*** Chan. Dig. CHAN 0517; *EBTD 0517* [id.]. Dawson, Russell, Brett, Partridge, George, The Sixteen Choir & O, Harry Christophers.

Harry Christophers directs lively performances of Handel's two great Psalm-settings using period instruments and a fine team of soloists. In both *Dixit dominus* and *Nisi dominus* his readings come into rivalry with Trevor Pinnock's outstanding DG Archiv disc. Christophers' speeds tend to be more extreme, slow as well as fast, and the recorded sound, though full and well detailed, is less immediate. On balance Pinnock with his rather more bouncy rhythms remains the first choice, but the Chandos issue gains significantly from a much more generous third item. The motet *Silete venti*, with soprano solo, is a substantial piece of nearly half an hour which allows the silver-toned Lynne Dawson to shine even more than in the other items, ending with a brilliant *Alleluia* in galloping compound time.

Jephtha.
** Teldec/Warner 2292 42592-2 (3) [id.]. Hollweg, Gale, Linos, Esswood, Thomaschke, Sima, Mozart Boys' Ch., Schönberg Ch., VCM, Harnoncourt.

Jephtha, the last oratorio that Handel completed, is a strange and not always very moral tale. With the threat of blindness on him, the composer was forced to break off from writing for several months, but that threat seems only to have added to the urgency of inspiration. Harnoncourt's pursuit of extra authenticity, with an orchestra using original instruments, will make his version an automatic choice for many; for the general listener, however, it has its snags, and not just in the acid timbres of the strings. Harnoncourt takes an operatic view of the work, but he mars the impact of that by too frequently adopting a mannered style of phrasing. The soloists too are on balance far less impressive than those on the Gardiner/Philips version. The recording acoustic, typically clean, is less helpful in its relative dryness next to the rival set. With a very full text this makes a long haul, and Gardiner's set is preferable in almost every way (Philips 422 351-2).

Joshua (complete).
❀ *** Hyp. Dig. CDA 66461/2; *KA 66461/2* [id.]. Kirkby, Bowman, Ainsley, George, Oliver, New College, Oxford, Ch., King's Consort, King.

It is astonishing that Handel's oratorio, *Joshua*, one of his most popular during his lifetime and regularly performed until this century, has been so neglected on record. Though a rival is promised almost simultaneously, this first recording will not easily be surpassed. Written in 1747, five years after *Messiah* first appeared, *Joshua*'s popularity owed much to two numbers which at once gained currency outside the opera house, the chorus *See, the conqu'ring hero comes* and the brilliant soprano aria *O, had I Jubal's lyre*. In the context of the whole oratorio, heard in quick succession in the triumphant third Act, their magnetism is enhanced, with the patriotic chorus atmospherically bringing louder, grander repetitions, and with Emma Kirkby here ideally sparkling and light in the solo. Her Act I aria too is a delight, *Hark, 'tis the linnet*, full of delightful bird noises. She has the role of Achsa, daughter of the patriarchal leader, Caleb (taken here by the bass, Michael George). Her love for Othniel, superbly sung by James Bowman, provides the romantic interest in what is otherwise a grandly military oratorio, based on the Book of Joshua. The brisk sequence of generally brief arias is punctuated by splendid choruses, with solo numbers often inspiring choral comment. The call to arms in Act I is particularly effective, with the brass silent until that moment. Act II then tells the story of the siege of Jericho, leading up to Joshua's stopping of the sun in the astonishingly original *O thou bright orb*. In that final number of the Act for tenor and chorus, first high violins and then the rest of the strings are eerily stilled to represent the miracle, with the chorus finally fading away at the end of the Act. The sounds of victory are then left for Act III. The singing is consistently strong and stylish, with the clear, precise tenor, John Mark Ainsley, in the title-role giving his finest performance on record yet. Robert King and his Consort crown their achievement in other Hyperion issues, notably their Purcell series, with polished, resilient playing, and the choir of New College, Oxford, sings with ideal freshness. Warm, full sound. On two well-packed discs, it makes an exceptionally attractive Handel issue.

Messiah (complete).
(M) *** EMI CZS7 62748-2 (2) [Ang. CDMB 62748]. Harwood, J. Baker, Esswood, Tear, Herincx, Amb. S., ECO, Mackerras.

(M) *** Erato/Warner 2292 45447-2 (2) [id.]. Palmer, Watts, Davies, Shirley-Quirk, ECO Ch., ECO, Leppard.
**(*) Decca 430 488-2; *430 488-4* (2) [id.]. Nelson, Kirkby, Watkinson, Elliott, D. Thomas, Christ Church Cathedral, Oxford, Ch., Hogwood.
(B) **(*) CfP CD-CFPD 4718; *TC-CFPD 4718* (2) [id.]. Morison, Thomas, Lewis, Milligan, Huddersfield Ch. Soc., Royal Liverpool PO, Sargent.
(M) *(*) EMI CMS7 63621-2 (3) [id.]. Schwarzkopf, Hoffman, Gedda, Hines, Philh. Ch. & O, Klemperer.
(M) * Eurodisc/BMG GD 69088; *GK 69088* (2). (Sung in German) Bjoner, Töpper, Traxel, Engen, St Hedwig's Cathedral Ch., Berlin SO, Karl Forster.

The EMI/Mackerras set was first issued in 1967, just a few months after Sir Colin Davis's first LSO recording for Philips. It provided a comparable new look, but also a clear alternative in its approach. The choruses on EMI have not quite the same zest as on Philips, but they have a compensating breadth and body. More than Davis, Mackerras adopted Handel's alternative versions, so the soprano aria *Rejoice greatly* is given in its optional 12/8 version, with compound time adding a skip to the rhythm. A male alto is also included – Paul Esswood, who was already making his mark in the Teldec series of Bach cantatas – and he is given some of the bass arias as well as some of the regular alto passages. Among the soloists, Dame Janet Baker is outstanding. Her intense, slow account of *He was despised* – with decorations on the reprise – is sung with profound feeling. Like Davis, Mackerras includes all the numbers traditionally omitted. The recording is warm and full in ambience and, with the added brightness of CD, sounds extremely vivid.

Raymond Leppard presents a fine, enjoyable account of *Messiah*, which lies somewhere between Sir Colin Davis's earlier Philips set (420 865-2) and the Mackerras EMI version. His tempi, unlike Davis's, are never exaggeratedly fast and his ornamentation is less fancy than Mackerras's on EMI. The closest Leppard comes to eccentricity is in his tempo for *The trumpet shall sound*, very fast indeed, like Davis's with the same baritone; *All we like sheep*, preceded by a delightful flourish from the organ, is even jauntier than Davis's account. Leppard has the same contralto, Helen Watts, as well as the same bass and, if anything, both are in finer form. Felicity Palmer is fresher-toned than she sometimes is on record, while Ryland Davies sings brightly and cleanly. The chorus is admirably resilient and luminous; although the acoustics of St Giles, Cripplegate, prevent an absolutely sharp focus, the fine 1976 Erato recording is obviously fuller and more modern than either the Davis/Philips or Mackerras/EMI sets.

By aiming at re-creating an authentic version – based meticulously on material from the Foundling Hospital, reproducing a performance of 1754 – Christopher Hogwood has managed to have the best of both worlds, punctilious but consistently vigorous and refreshing and never falling into dull routine. The trebles of Christ Church are superb, and though the soloists cannot match the tonal beauty of the finest of their rivals on other sets, the consistency of the whole conception makes for most satisfying results. As to the text, it generally follows what we are used to, but there are such oddities as *But who may abide* transposed for a soprano and a shortened version of the *Pastoral Symphony*. The recording is superb, clear and free to match the performance, and the CD transfer is exceptionally successful, adding to the presence and immediacy within the resonant Christ Church acoustics. This version is now reissued on two CDs only. However, first choice still rests with Pinnock on DG who, with Arleen Augér, Anne Sofie von Otter and the counter-tenor Michael Chance among his outstanding soloists, presents a performance using authentically scaled forces which rise to a grandeur and magnificence that Handel himself would have relished (423 630-2; *423 630-4*).

It is good to have Sir Malcolm Sargent's 1959 recording now restored to the catalogue in full for, apart from the pleasure given by a performance that brings out the breadth of Handel's inspiration, it provides an important corrective to misconceptions about pre-authentic practice. Sargent writes a forthright note in which he is quite scathing about scholarly authenticity: he has no time for keyboard recitatives, and he is quite sure that Handel would have preferred to use large forces had he been able to get them. Sargent unashamedly fills out the orchestration (favouring Mozart's scoring where possible). By the side of Davis, his tempi are measured, but his pacing is sure and spontaneous and, with a hundred-strong Huddersfield group, no one will be disappointed with the weight or vigour of the choruses. There is some splendid singing from all four soloists, and Marjorie Thomas's *He was despised* is memorable in its moving simplicity. The success of the CD transfer is remarkable: the old analogue LPs never sounded as clear as this. At bargain price – though with traditional cuts – this is well worth sampling.

The glory of the Klemperer set lies in the singing of the chorus. There is a freshness, clarity and edge to it that shows up many of the rival performances on record. Nor is Klemperer's direction dull, despite his characteristic determination to underline the solidity of the music and, like Sargent, to pay no heed to scholarly ideas on the text. So far so good . . . but the soloists' contribution is far more questionable. Schwarzkopf sings beautifully in her way, and in the recitatives she is undoubtedly imaginative. But in the arias her line is not always impeccable: *I know that my Redeemer liveth*, for example, with its combined elements of Lieder and opera, sounds curiously unsympathetic. Even so, she is unfailingly stimulating – which is more than can be said for Grace Hoffman. *O thou that tellest* is sung badly, though *He was despised* is far better. Gedda is interesting but not always comfortable in the part; Jerome Hines, despite a big, dark voice, also seems out of his element and is scarcely imaginative. Both chorus and orchestra make some lovely sounds and, with the Kingsway Hall providing a fine ambient glow, the clarity of detail and natural balance of the CD transfer are most impressive. But EMI's use of three CDs for this set makes it highly uncompetitive.

The Eurodisc/BMG set, directed by Karl Forster, is sung straightforwardly in German. It is not absolutely complete. The soloists are good, particularly the soprano and bass. But the orchestral sound is as richly upholstered as the choral sound is solidly weighty and the St Hedwig's *Hallelujah* must be one of the longest on record. The documentation offers only a German text, without translation. Those wanting *Messiah* sung in German would do far better to consider Mackerras's Austrian DG performance of Mozart's version – see below.

Der Messias (sung in German, arr. Mozart).
(M) **(*) DG 427 173-2 (2) [id.]. Mathis, Finnilä, Schreier, Adam, Austrian R. Ch. & O, Vienna, Mackerras.
**(*) Erato/Warner Dig. 2292 45497-2 (2). Michael, Dami, Van Nes, Blochwitz, Fink, Lausanne Vocal & Instrumetal Ens., Corboz.

Mozart's arrangement of *Messiah* has a special fascination. It is not simply a question of trombones being added but of elaborate woodwind parts too – most engaging in a number such as *All we like sheep*, which even has a touch of humour. *Rejoice greatly* is given to the tenor (Peter Schreier sounding too heavy) and *The trumpet shall sound* is considerably modified and shortened. To avoid the use of a baroque instrument, Mozart shares the obbligato between trumpet and horn. Mackerras leads his fine team through a performance that is vital, not academic in the heavy sense. The remastered recording is excellent and a translation is provided.

The Erato set offers modern digital sound of high quality, but has few other advantages compared with the Mackerras set. Moreover the translation does not offer the English words we know, so that we are told 'Behold a Virgin becomes pregnant' and 'Oh you, the bliss promised in Zion, get on your way, beam happily around you'. A treble is introduced to take the Angel's role and Magali Dami's *There were shepherds abiding in the fields* is delightful. The other soloists are all appealing, highly musical and pleasingly flexible. The choruses, not lacking boldness or weight, yet have a light touch and plenty of rhythmic resilience, and the stylish orchestral playing also gives much pleasure.

Messiah: highlights.
(M) ** Ph. Dig. 432 047-2; *432 047-4* [id.]. M. Price, Schwarz, Burrows, Estes, Bav. R. Ch. & SO, C. Davis.

Messiah: choruses.
(M) *** Decca Dig. 430 734-2; *430 734-4* [id.]. Chicago Ch. & SO, Solti.

Sir Colin Davis's 1984 digital set is disappointing, compared with his earlier, LSO version. Hanna Schwarz lets the side down among the otherwise excellent soloists; the chorus is lively, but the Bavarian Radio Orchestra is a degree too smooth. The selection plays for only a few seconds over an hour, so there would have been room for more, the notable omission being *The trumpet shall sound*. There are no notes about the music, just a list of the excerpts.

The choruses were a strong feature of Solti's fine complete set on Decca, and they are now available separately at mid-price.

La Resurrezione.
*** Erato/Warner Dig. 2292 45617-2 [id.]. Argenta, Schlick, Laurens, De Mey, Mertens, Amsterdam Bar. O, Ton Koopman.

Koopman's recording of this oratorio – a work seriously under-appreciated because of the absence of a chorus – provides a valuable alternative to the fine Hogwood version on Oiseau-Lyre (421 132-2 – see our main volume, pp. 465–6). Koopman's cast of soloists is just as strong, with Barbara Schlick as the Angel outstandingly fine and Klaus Mertens as Lucifer weightier and stronger than his oppposite number. Koopman's approach is lighter and more resilient, allowing more relaxation, though the recording is less well focused, with voices less full and immediate.

Saul.
** Teldec/Warner 2292 42651-2 (2) [id.]. Fischer-Dieskau, Rolfe Johnson, Esswood, Varady, V. State Op. Ch., VCM, Harnoncourt.

Harnoncourt's version was recorded live at the Handel Tercentenary celebrations in Vienna in 1985 and, whatever the advantages of period performance, the extraneous noises of coughs and creaks, together with the odd slip in execution, seriously reduce its merits. Dietrich Fischer-Dieskau in the name-part is most characterful, but his expressive style is very heavy for Handel, particularly in the recitatives. It is still for the most part a rich and noble performance, however, and Julia Varady, though not quite idiomatic, is also individual, with tone cleanly focused. The English members of the cast sing stylishly, notably Anthony Rolfe Johnson as Jonathan and Paul Esswood as David. Elizabeth Gale's bright soprano is not always caught sweetly by the microphones, but it is a sympathetic performance. Harnoncourt's direction is lively, but he misses much of the grandeur of the work, and some of the cuts he makes are damaging. The Vienna State Opera Concert Choir are responsive, but they never quite sound at home coping with English words. This is a fair stop-gap, at a period when there is no competition; but as an alternative, even with modern instruments and a large amateur chorus, Sir Charles

Mackerras's 1973 version for DG Archiv is preferable on almost every count, and we hope this will shortly reappear on CD.

Susanna (oratorio): complete.
**(*) HM Dig. HMU 907030/2 [id.]. Hunt, Minter, Feldman, Parker, J & D. Thomas, U. C. Berkeley Chamber Ch., Philh. Bar. O, McGegan.

This is the first ever recording of a superb oratorio, written right at the end of Handel's composing career. The richness of inspiration comes very near to matching that of the other biblical piece he wrote earlier in the summer of 1748, *Solomon*. It is a much more intimate piece and, if it has failed to achieve the impact it deserves, that is largely because choruses are very few, making it unappealing to choral societies. Yet the wealth of arias and the refreshing treatment of the Apocrypha story of Susanna and the Elders make it ideal for records. McGegan's performance does not quite match those of his earlier Handel recordings, made in Budapest. This one was done live with a talented period group from Los Angeles. The main snag is that the dry acoustic brings an abrasive edge to the instrumental sound and takes away bloom from the voices. It also underlines a certain squareness in the rhythmic treatment, with tension often low, even in such a magnificent number as the chromatic chorus which follows the overture. Yet with fine soloists including Lorraine Hunt (Susanna), Drew Minter (Joacim) and Jill Feldman (Daniel), this is far more than a mere stop-gap.

Theodora (complete).
**(*) Teldec/Warner Dig. 2292 46447-2; *2292 46447-4* (2) [id.]. Alexander, Blochwitz, Kowalski, Van Nes, Scharinger, Schönberg Ch., VCM, Harnoncourt.

Theodora, first heard in 1750, was one of the very last of Handel's oratorios, with only *Jephtha* of the major works to come. It badly needed a CD recording, and there is much to enjoy in this lively account, with fresh, clean textures typical of the Concentus Musicus, and with Harnoncourt thrusting in manner, occasionally to the point of being heavy-handed. The Schönberg Choir sings with apt weight and freshness. The jollity of the choruses of heathens is nicely distinguished from the far more solemn choruses for Christians, though words are often unclear. The solo casting is strong, though this team of international singers does not always sound at home, either stylistically or in singing English. Roberta Alexander sings with characteristic warmth in the title-role of the noble Christian, in this story of self-sacrifice in Antioch during the period of persecution under the Romans. Though a purer voice would have been even more apt, she is the finest of the soloists, with the counter-tenor Jochen Kowalski exceptionally warm of tone but hardly sounding Handelian in the role of Didymus, the centurion converted to Christianity. Jard van Nes is warm and fruity as Irene and Hans Peter Blochwitz is light and fresh as Septimius. Bright, full recording.

OPERA

Alessandro (complete).
(M) **(*) HM/BMG GD 77110 (3) [77110-2-RG]. Jacobs, Boulin, Poulenard, Nirouët, Varcoe, Guy de Mey, La Petite Bande, Kuijken.

Sigiswald Kuijken directs his team of period-performance specialists in an urgently refreshing, at times sharply abrasive reading of one of Handel's key operas, the first in which he wrote roles for the rival prima donnas, Faustina and Cuzzoni, not to mention the celebrated castrato, Senesino. As a high counter-tenor, René Jacobs copes brilliantly with the taxing Senesino role of Alexander himself. His singing is astonishingly free and agile, if too heavily aspirated. Among the others, Isabelle Poulenard at her best sounds a little like a French Emma Kirkby, though the production is not quite so pure and at times comes over more edgily. The others make a fine, consistent team, the more effective when the recording so vividly conveys a sense of presence with sharply defined directional focus. Even though reissued at mid-price, the set is well documented and with full translation: the printing apparently uses period-style fonts. The three CDs have 70 separate points of access.

Amadigi.
*** Erato/Warner Dig. 2292-45490-2 [id.]. Stutzmann, Smith, Harrhy, Fink, Musiciens du Louvre, Minkowski.

Written in 1715, *Amadigi* was the fifth of the Italian operas that Handel wrote for London, following up the success of the first, *Rinaldo*, and rounding off his early period of operatic experimentation. Much of its initial success was owed to the lavishness (by the standards of the time) of the staging but, perhaps surprisingly, it involves only five high voices, with no tenor or bass among the soloists. That hardly limits the variety or vigour of Handel's inspiration, with brilliant arias for Prince Dardano of Thrace in particular, superbly sung by Bernarda Fink. Nathalie Stutzmann sings Amadigi's gentle arias most affectingly, notably the lovely *Sussurate, onde vezzose*, and the two women characters, Amadigi's lover Melissa and Princess Oriana, are well taken by Eiddwen Harrhy and Jennifer Smith. As in his splendid recording of Charpentier's music for *Le malade imaginaire*, Marc Minkowski directs an electrifying performance, which is given greater impact by the closeness of the recording. That also brings an abrasiveness to the period strings, but not disagreeably so; rather, the impression is of a performance on an intimate scale, and the more involving for that.

Orlando (complete).
*** O-L Dig. 430 845-2 (3) [id.]. Bowman, Augér, Robbin, Kirkby, D. Thomas, AAM, Hogwood.

Hogwood and his fine team made this recording immediately after taking this opera on tour in the United States, giving semi-staged performances. Based on Ariosto's *Orlando furioso* and, more closely, on a libretto earlier used by Domenico Scarlatti, Handel's *Orlando* was radically modified to provide suitable material for individual singers, as for example the bass role of the magician, Zoroastro, specially created for a member of Handel's company. Even so, the title-role seems to have failed to please the celebrated castrato, Senesino, for whom it was intended, probably because of Handel's breaks with tradition, notably in the magnificent mad scene which ends Act II on the aria, *Vaghe pupille*, with the simple ritornello leading to amazing inspirations. That number, superbly done here by James Bowman, with appropriate sound effects, is only one of the virtuoso vehicles for the counter-tenor. This was written in 1732, after Handel had begun to compose English oratorios, and that experience evidently encouraged him to be more adventurous in his handling of operatic form. For the jewelled sequences of arias and duets, Hogwood has assembled a near-ideal cast, with Arleen Aug-e1r at her most radiant as the queen, Angelica, and Emma Kirkby characteristically bright and fresh in the lighter, semi-comic role of the shepherdess, Dorinda. Catherine Robbin assumes the role of Prince Medoro strongly, though the recording sometimes catches an unevenness in the voice. Though a weightier bass would be preferable, David Thomas sings stylishly as Zoroastro. Acclaimed as Hogwood's first complete opera set, this is one of his finest achievements on record, taut, dramatic and rhythmically resilient. Vivid, open sound.

The three Acts might just have been squeezed on to two discs, but the three-disc layout allows each Act to occupy a single disc, if at considerable extra expense.

Partenope (complete).
(M) *** HM/BMG GD 77109 (3) [77109-2-RG]. Laki, Jacobs, York, Skinner, Varcoe, Müller-Molinari, Hill, La Petite Bande, Kuijken.

By the time he wrote *Partenope* in 1730 Handel was having to cut his cloth rather more modestly than earlier in his career. In its limited scale this opera has few heroic overtones, yet a performance as fresh and alert as this amply demonstrates that the result can be even more invigorating. One problem for Handel was that at this time his company could call on only one each of soprano, tenor and bass; with an excellent team of counter-tenors and contralto, however, this performance makes light of that limitation. With the exception of René Jacobs, rather too mannered for Handel, the roster of soloists is outstanding, with Krisztina Laki and Helga Müller-Molinari welcome additions to the team. Though ornamentation is sparse, the direction of Sigiswald Kuijken is consistently invigorating, as is immediately apparent in the *Overture*. The 1979 recording sounds quite marvellous in its CD format, and the only irritation is that the English translation is printed separately – in an old-style font – from the Italian original. Each is cued, however – there are 74 points of access – so it is fairly easy to link the two.

Rinaldo (complete).
* Nuova Era Dig. 6813/4 (2). Horne, Gasdia, Palacio, Weidinger, La Fenice O, John Fisher.

This was the first opera that Handel wrote after settling in London, a piece full of memorable numbers and with four starring roles. This vigorous Venice performance of June 1989, recorded live, provides the star names, but it is very much an adaptation to modern stage conditions, with plentiful cuts and a performing style leaning towards the romantic, such as one might more normally have encountered 30 years ago. Marilyn Horne remains a formidable Handelian, with voice strong and flexible, though not so fresh as before. Cecilia Gasdia sings warmly and affectingly as Almirena, but attack is not always clean enough, as in the bird-song aria, *Augelletti*, or the lovely *Lascia ch'io piango*. Christine Weidinger makes a powerful Armida, strong in coloratura, but the voice is edgy, and Ernesto Palacio has his coarse moments. Particularly with its stage-noises, this cannot compare with the excellent 1977 CBS set with a first-rate cast under Jean-Claude Malgloire, which Sony should certainly reissue on CD.

Tamerlano (complete).
(M) *** Erato/Warner Dig. 2292 45408-2 (3) [id.]. Ragin, Robson, Argenta, Chance, Findlay, Schirrer, E. Bar. Soloists, Gardiner.

Recorded at a live concert performance for West German Radio immediately after a staging in Lyons and Göttingen, John Eliot Gardiner's set of *Tamerlano* presents a strikingly dramatic and immediate experience. One has no doubt whatever that this is one of Handel's most masterly operas. The pacing of numbers and of the recitative is beautifully thought out and, with a cast notable for clean, precise voices, the result is electrifying, the more so when, more than usual, in this opera Handel wrote ensemble numbers as well as solo arias, most of them crisp and compact. Leading the cast are two outstanding counter-tenors, whose encounters provide some of the most exciting moments: Michael Chance as Andronicus, firm and clear, Derek Ragin in the name-part equally agile and more distinctive of timbre, with a rich, warm tone that avoids womanliness. Nigel Robson in the tenor role of Bajazet conveys the necessary gravity, not least in the difficult, highly original G minor aria before the character's suicide; and Nancy Argenta sings with starry purity as Asteria. The only serious snag is the dryness of the sound, which makes voices and instruments sound more aggressive on CD than they usually do in Gardiner's recordings with the English Baroque Soloists. However, even that flaw might be thought to add to the dramatic impact.

'Great choruses': Coronation anthem: Zadok the Priest; Excerpts from: *Israel in Egypt; Jephtha; Judas Maccabaeus; Messiah; Saul; Solomon.*
(B) ** Pickwick IMPX 9011. Handel Opera Soc. Ch. & O, Charles Farncombe.

Enjoyably fresh and vigorous singing. The concert opens with a buoyant account of *Hallelujah* and an equally enthusiastic account of *See the conquering hero comes* from *Judas Maccabaeus* (with fine horn playing). Of the lesser-known choruses one highlight is *May no rash intruder* from *Solomon*, with its evocative pastoral scene. The small orchestral group is well balanced with the amateur choir, and the conveyed enjoyment and spontaneity here make up for any lack of polish. The recording is bright and forward. Not a generous concert (only 44 minutes long), but an invigorating one.

Hanson, Howard (1896–1981)

Symphonies Nos. 1 in E min. (Nordic), Op. 21; 2 (Romantic), Op. 30; (i) *Song of democracy.*
(M) *** Mercury 432 008-2 [id.]. Eastman-Rochester O, composer; (i) with Eastman School of Music Ch.

Hanson's own pioneering stereo recordings of his two best-known symphonies have a unique thrust and ardour, with the sense of the orchestral musicians being stimulated, both by the composer's direction and by the music's emotional force. The recordings date from 1958 and 1960 respectively and, while not having quite the fullness of records made three decades later, still sound astonishingly vivid. The *Song of democracy*, an effective occasional piece setting words by Walt Whitman, has plenty of dramatic impact and is also very well recorded.

Harbison, John (born 1938)

(i) *Concerto for double brass choir and orchestra;* (ii) *The Flight into Egypt;* (iii) *The Natural world.*
*** New World Dig. 80395-2 [id.]. (i) LAPO, Previn; (ii) Roberta Anderson, Sanford Sylvan, Cantata Singers & Ens., David Hoose; (iii) Janice Felty, Los Angeles Philharmonic New Music Group, Harbison.

These three fine works provide an illuminating survey of the recent work of one of the most communicative of American composers today. The most striking and vigorous is the concerto he wrote as resident composer for Previn and the Los Angeles Philharmonic, and for the orchestra's brass section in particular. The very opening may promise minimalism, nagging and very loud, but that quickly gives way to colourful and energetic writing with plenty of cross-rhythms of the kind loved by Previn. The other two works reveal the more thoughtful Harbison, the one a collection of three songs to nature poems by Wallace Stevens, Robert Bly and James Wright. The text for *The Flight into Egypt* is taken from the St Matthew Gospel in the King James Bible version, a measured and easily lyrical setting of the story of the Holy Family fleeing from King Herod. Sanford

Sylvan and the choir sing the main text, with Roberta Anderson interjecting as the Angel. Excellent performances and recording.

Harris, Roy (1898–1979)

Epilogue to profiles in courage; When Johnny comes marching home (An American overture).
** Albany TROY 027-2 [id.]. Louisville O, Jorge Mester – BECKER: *Symphonia brevis*; SCHUMAN: *Symphony No. 4* etc.**

Roy Harris's overture, *When Johnny comes marching home*, dates from 1934, and thus precedes the famous *Third Symphony*. It was composed in two clear sections of just under four minutes each with the side-lengths of a 78-r.p.m. record in mind and was one of his first works to be put on record (by Ormandy and the Minneapolis orchestra). It is a fresh and attractive piece and, like most of Harris's music of the 1930s, has a vital impulse which by 1964, when he composed the *Epilogue to profiles in courage*, had slackened into self-imitation. Good performances and rather good recording too (the overture comes from 1978 and the *Epilogue* from 1966).

Hartmann, Karl Amadeus (1905–63)

Concerto funèbre.
** Thorofon Capella Dig. CTH 2057 [id.]. Edinger, Katowice RSO, Penderecki – SZYMANOWSKI: *Violin concerto No. 1.***

Karl Amadeus Hartmann's *Concerto funèbre* for violin and string orchestra was written (but, of course, not performed) at the time of the Nazi annexation of much of Czechoslovakia as a result of the Munich agreement. It strikes a note of lamentation and quotes from the Hussite chorale ('Ye who are warriors of God') also quoted by Smetana in *Mà Vlast*. It was taken up by the Czechs after the war and was recorded with André Gertler as soloist, but has remained on the fringes of the repertoire. It is a bleak but strangely impressive work. Christiane Edinger plays with some eloquence, but the disc is short in playing time and the performance of the Szymanowski *Concerto* is not an unqualified success. Vladimir Spivakov has recorded this work too (see Recitals, below).

Haydn, Josef (1732–1809)

Cello concertos in C and D, Hob VIIb/1–2.
** BMG/RCA Dig. RD 77757 [7757-2-RC]. Anner Bylsma, Tafelmusik O, Jean Lamon – KRAFT: *Cello concerto.***

Recordings of both Haydn *Concertos* abound, but Anner Bylsma and the Canadian period-music group, Tafelmusik, under Jean Lamon come into direct competition with Christophe Coin and the Academy of Ancient Music (O-L 414 615-2). The present version has the advantage of excellent, well-balanced recording and a pleasantly warm but not excessively resonant acoustic. The accomplished players have plenty of spirit, though they are not always agreed in matters of intonation. An example can be found from 5 minutes 50 seconds through to about 6 minutes 30 seconds in track 4 (the first movement of the *D major concerto*). Anner Bylsma himself is not totally flawless, inclining towards the flat side of the note, and there are some occasional (and unimportant) blemishes in the double-stopping; but Tafelmusik too are not always true. This will disturb some collectors more than others, and there is no doubt about the excellence or sense of style of these performances.

(i) *Cello concerto in C, Hob VIIb/1;* (ii) *Horn concertos Nos. 1–2 in D, Hob VIId/3–4;* (iii) *Trumpet concerto in E flat.*
(M) *** Ph. Dig. 432 060-2; *432 060-4* [id.]. (i) Heinrich Schiff; (ii) Baumann; (iii) Hardenberger, ASMF, Marriner or I. Brown.

A self-recommending collection. All the solo playing is first class: Schiff is superbly stylish in the *C major Cello concerto*, Baumann's warm tone and fine sense of line in the works for horn are most appealing, and Hardenberger's famous account of the *Trumpet concerto* is unsurpassed. The accompaniments are admirable and the recording is of Philips's best, if rather resonant. There is no more enticing collection of Haydn concertos than this; the only snag is the total absence of information about the music.

Cello concerto in D, Hob VIIb/2.
(B) ** DG Compact Classics *415 330-4* [id.]. Fournier, Lucerne Festival O, Baumgartner – DVOŘÁK; BOCCHERINI: *Concertos.****

Fournier plays with style and polish; if Baumgartner's accompaniment is relatively unimaginative, the 1968 recording sounds better here than it has on some previous presentations. The Boccherini and Dvořák couplings are very attractive, and this Compact Classics chrome tape certainly offers value for money.

Violin concertos: in C, Hob VIIa/1; in G, Hob VIIa/4.
(B) *** Ph. 426 977-2; *426 977-4* [id.]. Grumiaux, ECO or New Philh. O, Leppard – MOZART: *Adagio; Rondo*; SCHUBERT: *Rondo.****

Haydn's *Violin concertos* are early works; the *C major*, with its winding, serenade-like melody in the slow movement, is probably the finer, but the *G major* too has an eloquent *Adagio* and a bustling finale. They make perfect vehicles for Grumiaux's refined classicism; he shows a real feeling for the music's simple lines, and the central movement of No. 1 soars gently and engagingly. Grumiaux plays his own cadenzas. Good mid-1960s sound and alert, gracious support from Leppard. A pity there are no insert notes about the music.

SYMPHONIES

Symphonies Nos 1–104; A; B.
❀ (M) *** Decca 430 100-2 (32) [id.]. Philharmonia Hungarica, Antal Dorati.

Antal Dorati was ahead of his time as a Haydn interpreter when, in the early 1970s, he made his pioneering recording of the complete Haydn symphonies. Superbly transferred to CD in full, bright and immediate sound, the performances are a consistent delight, with brisk allegros and fast-flowing andantes, with textures remarkably clean. The slow rustic-sounding accounts of Minuets are more controversial, but the rhythmic bounce makes them very attractive too. The packaging is excellent, available either in eight separate boxes or as a complete set, with the sequence kept helpfully in numerical order. The time-length is generous, but it is a pity that no way was found of including the extra and alternative movements which Dorati originally recorded along with the complete cycle. That would make a valuable supplementary disc and could have been given free with the complete set.

Symphonies Nos. 1 in D; 2 in C; 3 in G; 4 in D; 5 in A; 6 in D (Le Matin); 7 in C (Le Midi); 8 in G (Le Soir); 9 in C; 10 in D; 11 in E flat; 12 in E; 13 in D; 14 in A; 15 in D; 16 in B flat.

(M) *** Decca 425 900-2 (4) [id.]. Philharmonia Hungarica, Antal Dorati.

By his own calculation Haydn did not start writing symphonies until he was twenty-five and, though his earliest symphonies make a long list, there is not an immature one among them. The urgent crescendo which opens *Symphony No. 1* at once establishes the high voltage of inspiration, and from then on there is no suspicion of a power failure. These works – antedated by one or two symphonies that are later in the Breitkopf numbering – came from the early Esterhazy period (1759–63) and show the young, formidably gifted composer working at full stretch, above all in the fairly well-known trilogy of symphonies, *Le Matin*, *Le Midi* and *Le Soir* (also available separately on Decca 421 627-2), with their marvellous solos for members of the Esterhazy orchestra. Dorati left these symphonies until well on in his great pioneering recording project, and the combination of exhilaration and stylishness is irrresistible.

Symphonies Nos. 17 in F; 18 in G; 19 in D; 20 in C; 21 in A; 22 in E flat (Philosopher) (1st version); *23 in G; 24 in D; 25 in C; 26 in D min. (Lamentatione); 27 in G; 28 in A; 29 in E; 30 in C (Alleluja); 31 in D (Hornsignal); 32 in C; 33 in C.*
(M) *** Decca 425 905-2 (4) [id.]. Philharmonia Hungarica, Antal Dorati.

Because of the idiosyncrasies of the Breitkopf numbering, this sequence of symphonies includes one, *Lamentatione*, that is later than the rest, a transitional work leading into the dark, intense manner of Haydn's middle period. It gives marvellous perspective to the rest, all of them fascinating and many of them masterly. Even with familiarity, the sound Haydn creates, using two cors anglais in the opening chorale of the *Philosopher*, continues to tweak the ear, almost like an anticipation of *Zauberflöte*, and there are many other imaginative touches of colour in these works. The early festive symphonies, like Nos. 32 and 33, both in C major, with trumpets and timpani, have their individual marks of inspiration, for example in the C minor slow movement of No. 33. As in the rest of the cycle, Dorati's performances, helped by vivid recording, have you listening on from one symphony to the next, compulsively following the composer's career.

Symphonies Nos. 21 in A; 22 in E flat (Philosopher); 23 in G; 24 in D; 28 in A ; 29 in E; 30 in C (Alleluja); 31 in D (Horn Signal); 34 in D min.
**(*) O-L Dig. 430 082-2; *430 082-4* (3) [id.]. AAM, Christopher Hogwood.

This first box of Hogwood's projected Haydn cycle on period instruments brings fresh and lively allegros and outstandingly vivid and immediate sound. The classical style of Hogwood and the AAM has perceptibly mellowed since they recorded their Mozart symphony cycle, and the playing itself is even more refined, but there is still a degree of stiffness in slow movements.

Symphonies Nos. 34 in D min.; 35 in B flat; 36 in E flat; 37 in C; 38 in C (Echo); 39 in G min.; 40 in F; 41 in C; 42 in D; 43 in E flat (Mercury); 44 in E min. (Trauer); 45 in F sharp min. (Farewell); 46 in B; 47 in G.
(M) *** Decca 425 910-2 (4) [id.]. Philharmonia Hungarica, Antal Dorati.

Despite the numbering, this set of symphonies arguably includes the very first symphony of all, *No. 37 in C*, revealing, as H. C. Robbins Landon points out in his absorbing commentary, 'impeccable craftsmanship and enormous energy'. The 3/8 finale is exhilarating – but then all of these works, as played by Dorati and the Philharmonia Hungarica, reflect the composer's unquenchable genius. This particular sequence brings us to the frontier in Dorati's interpretations between those using and not using harpsichord continuo. He switches over in the middle of *No. 40 in F* – not illogically, when the finale is a fugue in which continuo would only be muddling. The two named symphonies towards the end of the box (*Trauer* and *Farewell*) lead into the darker intensity of Haydn's so-called *Sturm und Drang* period. Unfailingly lively performances and abiding, brightly vivid sound.

Symphonies Nos. 44 in E min. (Trauer); 88 in G; 104 in D (London).
(BB) *** Naxos Dig. 8.550287 [id.]. Capella Istropolitana, Barry Wordsworth.

Symphonies Nos. 45 in F sharp min. (Farewell); 48 in C (Maria Theresia); 102 in B flat.
(BB) *** Naxos Dig. 8.550382 [id.]. Capella Istropolitana, Barry Wordsworth.

Symphonies Nos. 82 in C (The Bear); 96 in D (Miracle); 100 in G (Military).
(BB) *** Naxos Dig. 8.550139 [id.]. Capella Istropolitana, Barry Wordsworth.

Symphonies Nos. 83 in G min. (The Hen); 94 in G (Surprise); 101 in D (The Clock).
(BB) *** Naxos Dig. 8.550114 [id.]. Capella Istropolitana, Barry Wordsworth.

Symphonies Nos. 85 in B flat (La Reine); 92 in G (Oxford); 103 in E flat (Drum Roll).
(BB) *** Naxos Dig. 8.550387 [id.]. Capella Istropolitana, Barry Wordsworth.

Like Barry Wordsworth's recordings of Mozart symphonies, also with the Capella Istropolitana on the Naxos label, this Haydn collection provides a series of outstanding bargains at the lowest budget price. The sound is not quite as clean and immediate as in the Mozart series, a little boomy at times in fact, and Wordsworth's preference for relatively relaxed speeds is a little more marked here than in Mozart, but the varied choice of works on each disc is most attractive. It is good that, in addition to named symphonies, Wordsworth includes two of the supreme masterpieces among those unnamed, both with supremely beautiful slow movements, *No. 88 in G* and *No. 102 in B flat*. At their modest cost, these are well worth collecting alongside Dorati's Philharmonia Hungarica boxes.

Symphonies Nos. 45 in F sharp min. (Farewell); 48 in C (Maria Theresia).
(M) *** Sony Dig. MDK 46507 [id.]. L'Estro Armonico, Derek Solomons.

The warmest of welcomes for a single CD from Derek Solomons' outstanding series of Haydn symphonies on CD. His plan, to record the complete set in chronological order, has apparently been stymied for the moment, but the results so far are very impressive indeed. No better sampler could be devised than this remarkable coupling from Haydn's *Sturm und Drang* period. The musical marvel of No. 45 in the rare key (for Haydn's time) of F sharp minor brings one of Solomons' finest performances. The picturesque story of the departing players in the finale tends to obscure the work's status as one of the most powerful of this rare, dark series of symphonies, not to mention the sheer originality (practical motives apart) of that amazing close. Solomons keeps his ensemble of period instruments very small, with six violins but only one each of the other stringed instruments, a scale Haydn himself employed at Esterháza, and in the slow movement of the *Farewell* the effect is touchingly graceful, almost ethereal in texture. The robust Minuet which follows makes a striking contrast. Special mention must be made of the brilliant horn playing of Anthony Halstead (no concessions here to any technical problems) not only in this work but also in the slow movement of No. 48, again hauntingly beautiful. The invigorating opening movement of that same work, bursting with exuberance and with the first horn, crooked in C alto, shining out over the strings, brings thrilling sound, and the Minuet is no less impressive. Recorded in the pleasingly atmospheric acoustic of St Barnabas Church, Woodside Park, the sense of vibrant yet intimate music-making is most stimulating. Repeats are generously observed, which is why these two symphonies have a combined playing time of 66 minutes.

Symphonies Nos. 48 in C (Maria Theresia); 49 in F min. (La Passione); 50 in C; 51 in B flat; 52 in C min.; 53 in D (L'Impériale); 54 in G; 55 in E flat (Schoolmaster); 56 in C; 57 in D; 58 in F; 59 in A (Fire).
(M) *** Decca 425 915-2 (4) [id.]. Philharmonia Hungarica, Antal Dorati.

The nine symphonies which comprise the bulk of this box, from *Maria Theresia* onwards, show Haydn in the full flight of his *Sturm und Drang* period: tense, exhilarating music, full of anguished minor-key arguments that belie the idea of jolly 'Papa' Haydn working patiently for his princely master. Their emotional basis clearly points forward to the Romantic movement which, within decades, was to overtake music. Indeed the literary movement which gives the appellation *Sturm und Drang* itself marks the first stirrings of Romanticism. While individual performances of some of these symphonies have already appeared on CD, the special value of Dorati's box is that it enables the listener to hear the ongoing sequence of nine works and to experience their historical impact in the same way as Prince Esterhazy and his court must have. The impact is the more powerful because of the splendid notes written by Profesor Robbins Landon, whose comments are fascinating at every level, whether for the specialist or the beginner. Such symphonies as *La Passione* and *Maria Theresia* are already quite well known, but the others without sobriquets are no less compelling; and it is impossible to become bored for a moment by the vigorous, committed performances given by Dorati and his orchestra of Hungarian exiles, especially as the last symphonies in this collection are already moving towards the stylistic changes which came in Haydn's middle period. The CD transfers continue to be outstandingly vivid.

Symphonies Nos. 60 in C (Il Distratto); 61 in D; 62 in D; 63 in C (La Roxolane); 64 in A; 65 in A; 66 in B flat; 67 in F; 68 in B flat; 69 in C (Laudon); 70 in D; 71 in B flat.
(M) *** Decca 425 920-2 (4) [id.]. Philharmonia Hungarica, Antal Dorati.

Even Robbins Landon underestimates the mastery of these middle-period symphonies. All in major keys, they represent the comparatively extrovert period immediately after Haydn had worked through the bitterest tensions of his *Sturm und Drang* era but before he expanded into the international world of music-making with the *Paris* and *London Symphonies*. Even if they are not quite as fascinating as the surrounding works, these maintain an amazing standard of invention, with such movements as the Adagio and 6/8 finale of No. 61 endlessly interesting. With the exception of an occasional movement (No. 69/II or No. 70/III), this music is riveting, and even where the actual material is conventional, as in the theatrical first movement of No. 69 (nicknamed Laudon after a field marshal), the treatment is sparkling, with many surprising turns. The only serious flaw in Dorati's interpretations – and it is something to note in a few of the symphonies in other boxes too – is his tendency to take minuets rather slowly. In many of them Haydn had already moved half-way towards a scherzo. But the Philharmonia Hungarica maintains its alertness with amazing consistency, never giving the suspicion of merely running through the music. As in the other boxes, Professor Robbins Landon's notes provide an ideal preparation for listening with a historical ear, and even his tendency to understate the merits of the lesser-known works makes one tend to enjoy them the more in sheer defiance of his authority. Nos. 65 to 71 were included in the very first album of symphonies to be issued on LP in September 1970 in Decca's integral series, and the dynamic tone of the whole project was at once established with works that had previously been not just neglected but absurdly underrated. The continuing vividness of the playing is matched by the bright CD transfers.

Symphonies Nos. 72 in D; 73 in D (La chasse); 74 in E flat; 75 in D; 76 in E flat; 77 in B flat; 78 in C min.; 79 in F; 80 in D min.; 81 in G; 82 in C (L'Ours); 83 in G min. (La Poule).
(M) *** Decca 425 925-2 (2) [id.]. Philharmonia Hungarica, Antal Dorati.

This collection – apart from No. 72, which is an earlier work, and the two *Paris Symphonies* tacked on at the end – centres on nine symphonies written more or less consecutively over a compact period of just four years (1780–84). Robbins Landon emphasizes that these are much more courtly works than their *Sturm und Drang* predecessors and that at this time Haydn was regarding the symphony as a side concern, being mainly concerned with opera. Even so, what will strike the non-specialist listener is that, whatever the courtly manners of the expositions (and even there moods vary, particularly in the two minor-key symphonies), the development sections give a flashing reminder of Haydn's tensest manner, with kaleidoscopic sequences of minor keys whirling the argument in unexpected directions. On this showing, even when he was not really trying Haydn was incapable of being boring, and some of these works are in every way remarkable in their forward-looking reminders, often of Mozart's most visionary works. At that time Haydn had just made contact with Mozart and though, on chronological evidence, the direct similarities can only be accidental the influence is already clear. The performances achieve an amazing degree of intensity, with alertness maintained throughout.

Symphonies Nos. 73 in D (La chasse); 74 in E flat; 75 in D.
*** Hyp. Dig. CDA 66250; *KA 66250* [id.]. Hanover Band, Roy Goodman.

In his projected Haydn cycle for Hyperion, Goodman chose for one of his first discs not only the spectacular *La chasse* (very exciting with its braying natural horns in the hunt finale) but the two surprisingly neglected symphonies adjacent to it. It makes a promising start, with sound warm yet well focused. Unlike Hogwood in his rival series, Goodman uses a harpsichord continuo, prominently placed. Most enjoyable.

Symphonies Nos. 84 in E flat; 85 in B flat (La Reine); 86 in D; 87 in A (Paris Symphonies); 88 in G; 89 in F; 90 in C; 91 in E flat; 92 in G (Oxford); 93 in D; 94 in G (Surprise); 95 in C min.
(M) *** Decca 425 930-2 (4) [id.]. Philharmonia Hungarica, Antal Dorati.

It is a pity that Decca's layout in four-CD groups, and employing a consistent numerical sequence, has meant that Dorati's sets of both the six *Paris* and the first six *London Symphonies* have each had to be split over two separate CD boxes. However, here we have not only the last four of the main *Paris* set (Nos. 84–7) but also the other Paris-based works, all given fresh and stylish performances. Even the least-known of the *Paris* set, No. 84, has a first movement of the most delicate fantasy, while No. 89 is rounded off with an extraordinarily witty movement that looks directly forward to the fun of Johann Strauss's polkas, with a delicious *portamento* in each reprise down to the main theme. Of the three *London Symphonies* included here, No. 93 brings one of the most delightful performances of Dorati's cycle, with a delectable, Ländler-like first movement; No. 94 is one of the more controversial, with a fast trotting slow movement (less of a 'surprise') and a fraction less delicacy in the playing. No. 95 is the only work in the set which lacks a slow opening section. Its compactness and the C minor tensions, however, recall the *Sturm und Drang* period.

Symphonies Nos. 90 in C; 91 in E flat.
** Virgin Dig. VC7 91141-2 [id.]. La Petite Bande, Kuijken.

Symphonies Nos. 90 in C; 91 in E flat; 92 in G (Oxford).
*** Hyp. Dig. CDA 66521; *KA 66521* [id.]. Hanover Band, Roy Goodman.

Goodman and Kuijken are in direct rivalry over the surprisingly neglected Nos. 90 and 91, two symphonies that come between the *Paris* set and the final *London Symphonies*. On every count Goodman and the Hanover Band are preferable, with their brisker speeds and more resilient rhythms, and their disc also includes the *Oxford Symphony*. Kuijken, so masterly with the Orchestra of the Age of Enlightenment in the *Paris Symphonies*, also on Virgin, is here less lively with La Petite Bande, regularly taking *Andantes* slower than such a traditional rival as Dorati. The recording for Goodman is preferable, pleasantly atmospheric and more cleanly focused than in his earlier recordings for Nimbus.

Symphonies Nos. 92 in G (Oxford); 94 in G (Surprise); 96 in D (Miracle).
(M) *** Sony SBK 46332 [id.]; *40-46332*. Cleveland O, Szell.

Symphonies Nos. 93 in D; 94 in G (Surprise); 95 in C min.; 96 in D (Miracle); 97 in C; 98 in B flat (London Symphonies).
(M) *** Sony MY2K 45673 (2) [id.]. Cleveland O, Szell.

With superb polish in the playing and precise phrasing it would be easy for such performances as these to sound superficial, but Haydn's music obviously struck a deep chord in Szell's sensibility and there is humanity underlying the technical perfection. Indeed there are many little musical touches from Szell to show that his perfectionist approach is a dedicated and affectionate one. There is also the most delectable pointing and a fine judgement of the inner balance. Szell's minuets have a greater rhythmic spring than Bernstein's, and his account of No. 96 compares favourably with Beecham's mono version, with Szell having the additional advantage of using modern editions of these scores. The finale is particularly felicitous, the orchestral articulation a delight. The recordings have been splendidly remastered and the sound is fuller and firmer than it ever was on LP, with the Cleveland ambience well caught. The underlying aggressiveness in the recording still produces a thinness in the violins in No. 95 and, to a far lesser extent, in No. 97. Both Nos. 97 and 98 are strong performances. Szell brings out the forceful maturity of first movements – the slow introduction of No. 98 is most arresting – and the beauty of the *Adagios*, both among Haydn's finest. These are most distinguished reissues, and all collectors should try the disc offering the three named symphonies.

Symphonies Nos. (i) *92 in G (Oxford);* (ii) *100 in G (Military); 101 in D (Clock).*
(B) **(*) DG Compact Classics *415 329-4* [id.]. (i) VPO, Boehm; (ii) LPO, Jochum.

On this Compact Classics tape Boehm conducts the *Oxford Symphony* and he secures finely disciplined playing from the VPO. The recording too is excellent, but the weightiness of the approach may not please all tastes, even if the phrasing has much finesse, and the finale is agreeably vivacious. Jochum's performances are another matter. He too is well recorded and inspires the LPO to fresh, polished performances that do not miss the genial side of Haydn. The performance of the finale of the *Military Symphony* is very good indeed and, throughout, the *Clock* is alert and sparkling. The sound, from the early 1970s, is naturally balanced and has transferred admirably in its tape format.

Symphonies Nos. 94 in G (Surprise); 103 in E flat (Drum Roll); 104 in D (London).
(B) *** DG Compact Classics *413 426-4* [id.]. LPO, Jochum.

Like Jochum's companion Compact Classics coupling (see above), these performances derive from the complete set of *London Symphonies* DG released in 1973, the *Surprise* having appeared the previous year as a trailer. The playing is elegant yet fresh, allegros marvellously crisp, slow movements warm and humane. This is among the musically most satisfying accounts of No. 104 in the catalogue; throughout, the recording is of DG's best analogue quality. A bargain.

Symphonies Nos. 96 in D (Miracle); 97 in C; 98 in B flat; 99 in E flat; 100 in G (Military); 101 in D (Clock); 102 in B flat; 103 in E flat (Drum Roll); 104 in D (London). Symphonies A in B flat; B in B flat; Sinfonia concertante in B flat (for oboe, bassoon, violin, cello & orchestra).
(M) *** Decca 425 935-2 (4) [id.]. Philharmonia Hungarica, Antal Dorati.

Dorati and the Philharmonia Hungarica, working in comparative isolation in Marl in (what was) West Germany, completed their monumental project of recording the entire Haydn symphonic *oeuvre* with not a suspicion of routine. These final masterpieces are performed with a glowing sense of commitment, and Dorati, no doubt taking his cue from the editor, H. C. Robbins Landon, generally chooses rather relaxed tempi for the first movements. In slow movements his tempi are on the fast side and, though an extra desk of strings has been added to each section, the results are authentically in scale, with individual solos emerging naturally against the glowing acoustic, and with intimacy comes extra dramatic force in sforzandos. The sound has immediacy and range, the bass is firmly defined and detail is clean. The playing is vital and sensitive and there is a splendid sense of style. Other versions of these late masterpieces may have a degree more refinement and polish, but the Philharmonia Hungarica provide a robust, spontaneous approach that is invigorating. As an appendix we are given the *Sinfonia concertante* and *Symphonies A* and *B*, which were not included in the numerical list simply because originally they were not thought to be symphonies at all. They are presented with characteristic vitality. Dorati's account of the *Sinfonia concertante* is a performance of few extremes, one which – not surprisingly, given the context – presents the work as a further symphony with unusual scoring, rather than as a concerto-styled work.

Symphonies Nos. 103 in E flat (Drum Roll); 104 in D (London).
(**) Teldec/Warner Dig. 2292 43526-2 [id.]. Concg. O, Harnoncourt.

Harnoncourt's record has some bizarre eccentricities. He opens the *Drum Roll* not with a roll but with a timpani fanfare – no explanation is given for this in the accompanying notes. The performances are undoubtedly forward-looking. Pacing is fast and the minuet of No. 104, strongly accented, almost becomes a scherzo. This is music-making of a powerful persuasion, very well played and recorded, but it cannot receive a general recommendation.

CHAMBER MUSIC

Piano trios (complete).
❀ (M) *** Ph. 432 061-2 (9) [id.]. Beaux Arts Trio.

The original Beaux Arts set of the complete *Piano trios* was not only awarded a Rosette by us but was also named 1979 Record of the Year by *Gramophone* and went on in 1980 to win the 'Grand Prix International du Disque de l'Académie Charles Cros'. It is not often possible to hail one set of records as a 'classic' in quite the way that Schnabel's Beethoven sonatas can be so described; all too few performances attain that level of artistic insight and, such is the sheer proliferation of material today, that records have an increasing struggle for attention. Yet this set can be described in those terms, for the playing of the Beaux Arts Trio is of the very highest musical distinction. The contribution of the pianist, Menahem Pressler, is little short of inspired, and the recorded sound on CD is astonishingly lifelike. The performances follow the Critical Edition of H. C. Robbins Landon, whose indefatigable researches have increased the number of *Trios* we know in the standard edition from 31 to 43. This is the kind of inflation one welcomes! Most collectors will find something new in this box, and its riches will stand us in good stead for many decades. Here is music that is sane and intelligent, balm to the soul in a troubled world, and the recording is wonderfully natural. The CD transfer has enhanced detail without losing the warmth of ambience or sense of intimacy.

String quartets Nos. 34 in D, Op. 20/4; 47 in C sharp min., Op. 50/4; 77 in C (Emperor), Op. 76/3.
*** ASV Dig. CDDCA 731; *ZCDCA 731* [id.]. Lindsay Qt.

The Lindsay performances were recorded, as were other issues in this series, at public performances, on this occasion in London's Wigmore Hall. The advantages this brings are twofold: higher spontaneity and a greater propensity to take risks. The disadvantages can be the absence of the last ounce of polish, and a tendency to overproject in the concert hall, with a resultant loss of intimacy and, in slower movements, repose. In all three performances the gains outweigh any loss, though the balance tends to cause some coarse-sounding tone in fortissimo passages. An excellent disc and tape, all the same.

String quartets Nos. 50–56 (The Seven Last Words of Christ); 63–68, Op. 64 1–6 (Tost quartets).
(M) **(*) DG 431 145-2 (3) [id.]. Amadeus Qt.

It is perhaps a pity that the Amadeus version of *The Seven Last Words of Christ* is linked on CD with Op. 64, for the immaculate Amadeus style, though not lacking in drama, does tend to smooth over the darker side of Haydn. The last six of the twelve *Tost quartets* are another matter. Dedicated to a rich, self-made patron, Johann Tost, they include a number of masterpieces, not least the *Lark*, Op. 64/5. Here the superb ensemble and cultivated playing are always easy on the ear when the recording is so well balanced and natural. There is no lack of life in allegros, for all their neat, spick-and-span precision; if other performances of some the great slow movements have more intensity, the playing here is still certainly felt, as well as being assured and beautiful, with tempi aptly chosen and well sustained. Indeed, overall these performances give much pleasure. On Naxos (8.500346) the Kodály Quartet give an outstanding performance, strongly characterized and beautifully played. This not only has the advantage of economy but includes also Haydn's last, unfinished string quartet, Op. 103.

String quartets Nos. 57 in G; 58 in C; 59 in E, Op. 54/1-3.
(BB) *** Naxos Dig. 8.550395 [id.]. Kodály Qt.

The Op. 56 *Quartets* were the first of six dedicated to Johann Tost, a violinist who led the second violins of Haydn's Esterháza orchestra for five years from 1783; he then departed for Paris to become a musical entrepreneur and had chamber music dedicated to him by Mozart as well as by Haydn. The present works show Haydn at his most inventive; all have fine first movements, and Op. 54/1 has a particularly witty and zestful finale. Op. 54/2 contrasts a profound C minor *Adagio* with a catchy Minuet, leading to a highly original finale, beginning and ending *Adagio*, yet with a central *Presto* featuring unexpected pauses. The Kodály players enter animatedly into the spirit of the music and give a fine, direct account of Op. 54/1; the leader, Attila Falvay, shows himself fully equal to Haydn's bravura embellishments in the demanding first violin writing, both here and in Op. 54/3. Perhaps the Lindsays (ASV CDDCA 582; *ZCDCA 582*) are even finer, being especially compelling in the slow movement of Op. 54/2 – which is not to say that the Kodály players miss its restrained intensity. The Naxos sound, too, is fresh and truthful, well up to the standard of this excellent super-bargain series.

String quartets Nos. 69–74, Op. 71/1–3; Op. 74/1–3 (Apponyi quartets).
(BB) *** Naxos Dig. 8.550394 & 8.550396 [id.]. Kodály Qt.

These Naxos recordings by the Kodály Quartet are outstanding in every way and would be highly recommendable even without their considerable price advantage.

String quartet No. 77 in C (Emperor), Op. 76/3.
(M) *** Teldec/Warner 2292 42440-2 [id.]. Alban Berg Qt – MOZART: *Quartet No. 17.****

Back in the 1970s the Alban Berg displayed admirable polish, but the end-result was without that hint of glossy perfection which poses a problem with some of their more recent recordings. This performance of Haydn's *Emperor quartet*, dating from 1975, has playing of striking resilience and sparkle. The famous slow movement has seldom been put on on record with such warmth and eloquence. The sound is bright, clear and well balanced, and the Mozart coupling is even finer.

String quartets Nos. 81 in G; 82 in F, Op. 77/1–2; 83 in D min., Op. 103.
*** Decca Dig. 430 199-2; *430 199-4* [id.]. Takács Qt.
*** Hyp. Dig. CDA 66348 [id.]. Salomon Qt.
(M) **(*) HM/BMG Dig. GD 77106 [77106-2-RG]. Smithson Qt.

The Takács Quartet play with warmth, expressive refinement and vitality. The excessive reverberation which marred their Op. 76/1–3 set (421 360-2; *421 360-4*) is not present here; the sound is clean and well focused, with just the right amount of resonance. Those who prefer the usual modern string quartet approach need not hesitate and cassette collectors, who in any event have no choice, need not worry unduly on that count.

The Smithson Quartet is led by Jaap Schröder and is one of the pre-eminent period-instrument ensembles in America. They are recorded in the generous acoustic of the Evangelical Church of Blumenstein near Berne, which helps to enrich the sonority. Readers who prefer their Haydn quartets with this purer timbre rather than with the traditional greater warmth of the modern string quartet will find much to admire here.

The Salomon, recorded in a less ample acoustic, produce an altogether leaner sound but one that is thoroughly responsive to every shift in Haydn's thought. Of the two period-instrument groups they seem to have the greater inner vitality and feeling.

Piano sonatas Nos. 33 in C min., Hob XVI/20; 59 in E flat, Hob XVI/49.
(M) *** Ph. 426 815-2 [id.]. Alfred Brendel.

This is the first of the four Haydn discs Brendel made for Philips (see our main volume, p. 492) and was recorded in 1979 in very clean, warm, analogue sound. In some ways it is one of his very best: there is no trace of the excessively brittle staccato which has troubled some of his recent Mozart and, although it is obvious that the performances are the product of much thought, there is still a sense of spontaneity. At its new competitive price this is well worth acquiring.

Piano sonatas Nos. 58 in C; 59 in E flat; 60 in C; 61 in D; 62 in E flat, Hob XVI/48–52.
*** RCA Dig. RD 77160 [77160-2-RC]. Andreas Staier (fortepiano).

Andreas Staier's recital of late sonatas is one of the best Haydn discs on the market. He plays a recent copy by Christopher Clarke of a fortepiano from around 1790 by the Viennese maker, Anton Walter, and proves a highly sensitive and imaginative interpreter. He brings a surprisingly wide dynamic range as well as a diversity of keyboard colour to these pieces and holds the listener throughout. He is very well recorded indeed.

VOCAL MUSIC

The Creation (complete; in English).
*** EMI Dig. CDS7 54159-2 [Ang. CDCB 54159]; *EX 754159-4* (2). Augér, Langridge, David Thomas, CBSO & Ch., Simon Rattle.
*** Decca Dig. 430 397-2; *430 397-4* (2) [id.]. Kirkby, Rolfe Johnson, George, AAM Ch. & O, Hogwood.

Both Rattle and Hogwood use the English text, which Haydn himself recognized as having equal validity with the German. In 1800 it made publishing history when the score was printed with dual text and a bilingual title-page. That was only fitting when it was an English source – a libretto based on Milton, said to have been written for Handel – that provided the original inspiration. The English version may have its oddities – like the 'flexible tiger' leaping – but it is above all colourful, and Rattle brings out that illustrative colour with exceptional vividness: birdsong, lion-roars and the like. The subtlety of his control of rhythm and phrase gives extra point and more light and shade than the other versions, even Hogwood's using period instruments. Rattle consistently brings out the fun in the writing, as well as the serious purpose, with the grandest of themes given sparkle, thanks to a composer who, more than any, recognized how vital humour can be in music. Rattle has plainly learnt from period performance, not only concerning speeds – often surprisingly brisk, as in the great soprano aria, *With verdure clad* – but as regards style too. The male soloists sound none too sweet as recorded, but they characterize positively; and there is no finer account of the soprano's music than that of Arleen Augér. Fast or not, *With verdure clad* brings heavenly sweetness and purity, with Augér soaring up effortlessly. The weight of the Birmingham chorus is impressive, achieved without loss of clarity or detail in a full, well-balanced recording.

Hogwood defies what has become the custom in period performance and opts for large forces such as Haydn – who during his trips to London was much impressed by large-scale performances of Handel oratorios – would have welcomed. The result, for all its weight, retains fine clarity of detail and an attractive freshness, as in the television performance which used substantially the same numbers. The choir of New College, Oxford, with its trebles adds to the brightness of choral sound, and the trio of soloists is admirably consistent – Emma Kirkby brightly distinctive, and Anthony Rolfe Johnson sweet-toned. Michael George is wonderfully intense in the hushed opening recitative before the blazing outburst on the creation of light, even if later the voice emerges less beautifully. Hogwood may lack some of the flair and imagination of Rattle, but it would be hard to find a period performance to match this. The sound has fine presence and immediacy.

The Creation (*Die Schöpfung;* in German).
(M) *** DG 435 077-2 (2) [id.]. Janowitz, Ludwig, Wunderlich, Krenn, Fischer-Dieskau, Berry, V. Singverein, BPO, Karajan.
**(*) Erato/Warner Dig. 2292-45449-2 (2) [id.]. Margaret Marshall, Branisteanu, Tappy, Rydl, Huttenlocher, Suisse Romande R. Ch., Pro Arte of Lausanne, Lausanne CO, Jordan.
** Teldec/Warner Dig. 2292 42682-2 (2) [id.]. Gruberová, Protschka, Holl, Schönberg Ch., VSO, Harnoncourt.

** DG Dig. 427 629-2 (2) [id.]. Battle, Winbergh, Moll, Stockholm R. Ch. & Chamber Ch., BPO, Levine.

Among versions of *The Creation* sung in German, Karajan's 1969 set remains unsurpassed and, at mid-price, is a clear first choice despite two small cuts (in Nos. 30 and 32). Here Karajan produces one of his most rapt choral performances; his concentration on refinement and polish might in principle seem out of place in a work which tells of religious faith in the most direct of terms, but in fact the result is outstanding. The combination of the Berlin Philharmonic at its most intense and the great Viennese choir makes for a performance that is not only polished but warm and dramatically strong too. The soloists are an extraordinarily fine team, more consistent in quality than those on almost any rival version. This was one of the last recordings made by the incomparable Fritz Wunderlich, and fortunately his magnificent contribution extended to all the arias, leaving Werner Krenn to fill in the gaps of recitative left unrecorded. The recording quality is both atmospheric and lively in its CD transfer.

Exceptionally among recent versions, Armin Jordan's recording with the Lausanne Chamber Orchestra uses separate soloists for Adam and Eve in the final part, both lighter-toned than their counterparts earlier. With immediate recording which brings soloists and orchestra close together, the impression is of an intimate chamber performance with a substantial chorus set slightly back. With Jordan pointing rhythms lightly and naturally, the joy of the writing is well caught. Though never sluggish, speeds are generally traditional, usually slower than with Rattle, notably in *With verdure clad* (*Nun beut die Flur*). Margaret Marshall is warmly caught but the balance prevents a genuine pianissimo. Eric Tappy is rather tight-toned and Kurt Rydl is a weighty bass soloist.

Harnoncourt's version with the Vienna Symphony Orchestra was recorded live. It follows the first printed edition of 1800, using the same size of forces as in performances of that date, with a gentle fortepiano replacing harpsichord in recitatives. Compared with the finest versions, the ensemble is on the rough side and the singing of the male soloists is often rough, too. The tenor, Josef Protschka, shouts Uriel's first entry but settles down after that; while by far the most distinguished singing of the set comes from Edita Gruberová, dazzling and imaginative, with slightly backward balance helping to eliminate the touch of hardness that the microphone often brings out in her voice. The sound otherwise is full and clear.

Levine's is an unashamedly big-scale reading which exaggerates contrasts – a point evident at the very start in the funereally slow account of the opening prelude with its picture of Chaos. The style is far smoother as well as weightier than in the other versions, with cruder detail. (For a traditional approach, the two earlier DG sets, both of live performances, are preferable, Karajan's from the 1982 Salzburg Festival and Bernstein's from Munich.) Though two fine Swedish choirs were assembled in Berlin, the recording makes them sound thick and heavy, with sound recessed too far back. Among the soloists Kurt Moll has authentic weight, but Kathleen Battle, for all her richness of tone, lacks innocence, and Gösta Winbergh sounds strained.

Masses Nos. (i) *7 in B flat: Missa brevis Sancti Joannis de Deo (Little organ mass), Hob XXII/7;* (ii) *8 in C (Mariazellermesse): Missa Cellensis, Hob XXII/8;* (iii) *Organ concerto No. 1 in C, Hob XVIII/1.*

(M) *** Decca 430 160-2; *430 160-4* [id.]. (i) J. Smith; Scott; (ii) J. Smith, Watts, Tear, Luxon; (i; ii) St John's College, Cambridge, Ch., Guest; (i–iii) ASMF; (iii) Preston, Marriner.

The *Little organ mass* dates from 1775 and fares even better here than in the earlier

Decca version under Münchinger, coupled with *The Creation*, good though that is. There is some fine invention in this piece, though it is not by any means the equal of the *Mariazellermesse* of 1782, which H. C. Robbins Landon called 'the most perfect large-scale work Haydn achieved' in this particular period. With excellent singing and fine orchestral playing, this is a very desirable issue in the splendid Guest series, and was originally recorded by Argo in 1977. The CD transfers are admirably fresh and well focused, and for a bonus we are given Simon Preston's persuasive account of an early organ concerto, written about 1756. Preston's vivid registration and Marriner's spirited accompaniment ensure the listener's pleasure, and the fine 1966 recording, sounding cleaner in the bass than in its original LP format, was also made at St John's.

Mass No. 9 in B flat (Heiligmesse): Missa Sancti Bernardi von Offida, Hob XXII/10.
(M) *** Decca 430 158-2; *430 158-4* [id.]. Cantelo, Minty, Partridge, Keyte, St John's College, Cambridge, Ch., ASMF, Guest – MOZART: *Litaniae de venerabili.****

Of all Haydn's Masses the *Heiligmesse* is one of the most human and direct in its appeal. Its combination of symphonic means and simple vocal style underlines its effectiveness. Haydn started writing this Mass in the first year after his return from London, at about the same time that he wrote the *Paukenmesse*; but it was not completed until later, and was finally dedicated to the memory of St Bernard of Offida, newly canonized by Pope Pius VI barely a century after his death. The name *Heiligmesse* derives from the church song on which Haydn based the *Sanctus*. Among the special points of interest in the work are the slow introduction to the *Kyrie*, very like the introductions to Haydn's late symphonies, and the subdued *Agnus Dei* in the (for the time) extraordinary key of B flat minor. Like the other records in this series, this is a splendid performance, and the vintage Argo sound is transferred very successfully to CD. The solo singing is good, if not always equally distinguished, and the choral response is excellent. For its reissue, the Mass is generously joined with Mozart's *Litaniae de venerabili altaris sacramento*, recorded over a decade later.

Mass No. 10 in C: Missa in tempore belli (Paukenmesse), Hob XXII/9.
(M) *** Decca 430 157-2; *430 157-4* [id.]. Cantelo, Watts, Tear, McDaniel, St John's College, Cambridge, Ch., ASMF, Guest – MOZART: *Vesperae sollennes.****

This was the last of the six Haydn late Masses to be recorded by Guest and his St John's forces for Argo, in 1969, and it is well up to the standard previously set. Guest provides a clean, brightly recorded account with good soloists – although Heather Harper (in the earlier, EMI recording from King's College – not yet available on CD) was markedly sweeter-toned than April Cantelo here. That said, the Argo performance is every bit the equal of the earlier one and sounds very fresh in its remastered format. It is now generously coupled with a fine Mozart recording, made a decade later.

Mass No. 12 in B flat (Theresienmesse), Hob XXII/12.
(M) *** Decca 430 159-2; *430 159-4* [id.]. Spoorenberg, Greevy, Mitchinson, Krause, St John's College, Cambridge, Ch., Guest – M. HAYDN: *Ave Regina*; MOZART: *Ave verum corpus.****

The *Theresa Mass* followed on a year after the *Nelson Mass*. It may be less famous but the inspiration is hardly less memorable, and Haydn's balancing of chorus against soloists, contrapuntal writing set against chordal passages, was never more masterly than here. Argo had started recording these late Masses with the other great Cambridge choir, at King's College; but after the *Nelson Mass* (Decca 421 146-2) Argo moved down the road to St John's. George Guest injects tremendous vigour into the music (as in the

Harmoniemesse, there is a 'military' conclusion in the *Donna nobis pacem*) and the St John's Choir, in splendid form, makes the very most of this fine work. Good solo singing and brilliant, vivid, 1965 recording.

Mass No. 13 in B flat (Schöpfungsmesse).
(M) *** Decca 430 161-2; *430 161-4* [id.]. Cantelo,, Watts, Tear, Forbes Robinson, St John's College, Cambridge, Ch., ASMF, Guest – MOZART: *Mass No. 12 (Spaur).****

The *Schöpfungsmesse* or 'Creation Mass' was the last but one of the magnificent series that Haydn wrote yearly in his retirement for his patron, Prince Esterházy. Guest again draws an outstanding performance from his own St John's College Choir and an excellent band of professionals, a fresh and direct reading to match the others of his highly successful Argo series. The very opening has superb weight and vigour matched by the *Gloria*, rich with brass, and the exuberant *Credo*; while in the introduction to the *Benedictus* Haydn uses the horns to create a most forward-looking warmth of colour, before the richly-textured vocal entry.

Mass No. 14 in B flat (Harmoniemesse), Hob XXII/14.
(M) *** Decca 430 162-2; *430 162-4* [id.]. Spoorenberg, Watts, Young, Rouleau, St John's College, Cambridge, Ch., Guest – MOZART: *Vesperae de Dominica.****

The *Harmoniemesse* was the last of the six Masses, all of them masterpieces, that Haydn wrote after his return from London. He had just completed *The Seasons* and, in 1802 when he wrote the Mass, the Esterházy orchestra was at its most expansive; typically, Haydn took advantage of the extra instruments available: his colourful scoring for a full range of wind and brass led to the German sobriquet. Haydn was over seventy when he started writing this Mass, but his freshness and originality are as striking as in any of the earlier works. In particular the last section of the Mass brings a wonderfully memorable passage when, after the genial, life-enhancing *Benedictus*, comes the contrast of a gentle setting of the *Agnus Dei*, with the spirit of Mozart hovering in the background. Then Haydn bursts out with fanfares into a vigorous, even aggressive *Donna nobis pacem*. The fine performance caps the others in this outstanding series. The quartet of soloists is strong, with Helen Watts in particular singing magnificently. The brilliant and well-balanced 1966 recording has been transferred splendidly to CD, which now offers a substantial bonus in the Mozart *Vespers*, recorded at St John's over a decade later.

The Seasons (in German).
**(*) Teldec/Warner Dig. 2292 42699-2 (2) [id.]. Blasi, Protschka, Holl, Schönberg Ch., VSO, Harnoncourt.

Harnoncourt's version is characteristically vibrant and his dramatization of the elements strong, with Robert Holl making a memorable contribution in *Winter*. On the other hand, Protschka's style is lighter than that of Siegfried Jerusalem with his honeyed elegance and heroic ring. Angela Maria Blasi has a sweet, small timbre and is consistently persuasive. The Arnold Schönberg Choir sing with fine bite and fervour and are especially invigorating in the harvest celebrations of *Autumn*. Detail is perceptively observed throughout the work, and Harnoncourt brings his usual powerful rhythmic feeling to the music-making – accents are readily stressed here and the narrative flow is vividly maintained. The Teldec recording is excellent, with good balance and realistic projection, and there is certainly no lack of drama.

Haydn, Michael (1737–1806)

(i) *Clarinet concerto in D, P. 54;* (ii) *Double concerto for harpsichord, viola and strings, P. 55;* (iii) *Violin concerto in B flat, P. 53.*
** Olympia OCD 406 [id.]. (i) Popa, Quodlibet CO; (ii) Botár, Thurzo; (iii) Ille; Oradeo PO, Acél.

Haydn divided his time between Vienna and Salzburg, where he was a colleague and friend of Mozart; but for five years (1757–62) he was Kapellmeister of the Oredea Cathedral in Transylvania; hence that Rumanian town has embarked on a project to record much of his output. Two of the three concertos here come from this period, while the work for clarinet, originally a flute concerto, was written later in Salzburg, in 1766. It has the strongest personality of the three, and its chortling solo part in the first movement is very engaging. Aurelian Octav Popa is a good soloist, but he makes the mistake of conducting the accompanying group himself; the Adagio *moves* along without displaying its geniality, and the Minuet finale, although not without finesse, needs a bit more sparkle. The *Violin concerto*, if not melodically memorable, has an appealing simplicity of line and is rather attractive in its plain classicism. The *Double concerto* is busily inventive, somewhat after the way of a concerto grosso, and the balance reflects that, with both soloists interchanging ideas in the forefront and the orchestra just behind. It is a lively and inventive work and completes an interesting, well-recorded and generous (74 minute) triptych.

Symphonies: in C, P. 10; in D, P. 11/21; in D min., P. 20.
(*) Olympia OCD 407 [id.]. Oredeo PO, Ervin Acél or Miron Ratu.

The 1784 *Symphony in D minor* has only three movements, after the style of an Italian overture, and draws on folk music for its melodic style, using its oboes, bassoons, horns and trumpets to colourful effect. The *C major*, P. 10, is from a decade earlier, yet is already anticipating this folk style; it is in four movements, however, including a Minuet between *Andante* and finale. The *D major* work, however, is an amalgam, organized by the Hungarian scholar, Pál Gombos, using an introductory *Adagio* and *Allegro spiritoso* from the 1785 *D major Symphony*, P. 21, then moving via a bridge passage to the second theme of the opening allegro of P. 11 of 1774, followed by the *Adagio*, Minuet and finale of that earlier symphony. The reasons for this procedure are not given, but it works well enough. Unfortunately, as in the companion disc, the orchestral playing, although lively, is unattractively sour and poorly balanced.

Symphonies: in E flat, P.26; in B flat, P.28; in D, P.29; in D, P.42; in B flat, P.52; Pastorello in C, P.91.
(*) Olympia OCD 404 [id.]. Oredea PO, Ervin Acél.

Haydn's younger brother divided his time between Vienna and Salzburg where he was a colleague and friend of Mozart, but for five years (1757–62) he was Kapellmeister of the Oredea Cathedral in Transylvania; hence the Rumanian town has embarked on a project to record much of his output. The symphonies recorded here do not come from this period: the *D major*, P.29, comes from 1778 but the remainder from 1788; the *Pastorello in C major* and the *B flat Symphony*, P.52, are Salzburg works from 1766. (The 'P' stands for the scholar, Louis Perger, who published a thematic catalogue of his instrumental works early this century.) The music is far from unpleasing or uninventive, though there are few memorable ideas. The recordings come from 1971 and 1984 respectively and are made in a somewhat resonant acoustic. The playing of the Oredea Philharmonic for Ervin

Acél is a shade characterless, and the rather thin, top-heavy, bottom-light string-sound proves tiring, even in small doses.

Duo sonata for violin and viola No. 1 in C.
(M) *** Ph. 426 098-2 [id.]. Mark Lubotsky, Nobuko Imai – MOZART: *Duos*.***

Michael Haydn's *Duo sonata* is not quite as ambitious as the two by Mozart, with which it is associated, but it has a rather fine central *Adagio* and the outer movements certainly do not lack vitality. It is vividly played and recorded here, but there would have been room for another from the set to be included on this disc.

Ave Regina.
(M) *** Ph. 430 159-2; *430 159-4* [id.]. St John's College, Cambridge, Ch., Guest – J. HAYDN: *Theresienmesse*; MOZART: *Ave verum corpus*.***

This lovely antiphon, scored for eight-part double choir, looks back to Palestrina and the Venetian school of the Gabrielis and the young Monteverdi. It is beautifully sung and recorded, and makes an unexpected yet welcome fill-up for the fine Guest version of the *Theresienmesse*.

Heath, Dave (born 1956)

The Frontier.
*** Virgin VC7 91168-2; *VC7 91168-4* [id.]. LCO, Warren- Green – ADAMS: *Shaker loops* *** ❀; GLASS: *Company* etc.***; REICH: *8 Lines*.***

Most minimalist composers are American and, although Dave Heath was born in Manchester, the influences on his music are transatlantic, not only from jazz (which he acknowledges) but also with Copland-like whiffs of the barn dance. In *The Frontier* the incisive rhythmic astringency is tempered by an attractive, winding lyrical theme which finally asserts itself just before the spiky close. The work was written for members of the LCO, and their performance, full of vitality and feeling, is admirably recorded.

Henze, Hans Werner (born 1926)

(i) *Compases para preguntas ensimismadas* (music for viola & 22 players); (ii) *Violin concerto No. 2* (for solo violin, tape voices & 33 instrumentalists, using Hans Magnus Enzensberger's poem, 'Homage à Gödel'); (iii) *Apollo et Hyazinthus.*
(M) *** Decca 430 347-2 [id.]. (i) Hirofumi Fukai; (ii) Brenton Langbein; (iii) Anna Reynolds, John Constable; (i–iii) L. Sinf., composer.

An important reissue from the early 1970s. *Compases* is a relatively gentle work, with the solo instrument supported by a shimmering orchestral texture, a piece than can easily seem flat and uneventful until you have a chance to hear it repeatedly on record. Of the *Violin concerto No. 2* Henze said that 'it is very nearly a stage piece but not quite' and, with a poem by Enzenberger sung and recited during its course, the drama of the music is strongly presented, with the violin as prime actor. *Apollo et Hyazinthus* is at one and the same time a miniature tone-poem and a harpsichord concerto. Its sonorities are admirably calculated and attractive. All these works are expertly performed and recorded under the composer's authoritative direction, and are of unfailing concern to all who are interested in his development. The music is all transferred brightly to CD, with the sharpest detail.

Symphonies Nos. (i) *1–5*; (ii) *6.*
(M) *** DG 429 854-2 (2) [id.]. (i) BPO, (ii) LSO, composer.

The Henze *Symphonies* are remarkable pieces which inhabit a strongly distinctive sound-world. The *First* with its cool, Stravinskyan slow movement is a remarkable achievement for a 21-year-old, though we hear it in a revision Henze made in early 1963. There is a dance-like feel to the *Third* (1950), written while Henze was attached to the Wiesbaden Ballet. It is rich in fantasy – the titles of its three movements, *Apollo*, *Dithyramb* and *Conjuring dance*, show its involvement in the dance. The *Fourth* was originally intended for the opera *König Hirsch* and was meant to connote 'an evocation of the living, breathing forest and the passing of the seasons'. It is among the most concentrated and atmospheric of his works; there is at times an overwhelming sense of melancholy and a strongly Mediterranean atmosphere to its invention. The *Fifth Symphony* comes from the period of the *Elegy for young lovers* and quotes from one of its arias; the language is strongly post-expressionist. One wonders, however, what its first audience, 'soldiers of the Cuban revolutionary army, sons of workers and students', must have made of the *Sixth Symphony*, composed while Henze was living in Havana! The performances, dating from 1966 and 1972, are excellent and the recorded sound amazingly vivid, even if a comparison between the CD transfer of No. 3 and the original LP reveals some compression – not in terms of dynamic or frequency range, quite the contrary – but in the sense of space occupied by the orchestra. An important and indispensable set, recommended with enthusiasm. Let us hope that DG will soon add the *Seventh Symphony* to their catalogue.

Hérold, Ferdinand (1791–1833)

Zampa: Overture.
(M) *** Mercury 432 014-2 [id.]. Detroit SO, Paray (with Concert: *'French opera highlights'* ***).

It is good to have this old warhorse of the bandstand, a favourite demonstration record of the era of 78s, back in the catalogue in a performance as exhilarating as it is colourful. Marvellous playing and top-class Mercury sound from 1960. The rest of the programme is pretty good too.

Herrmann, Bernard (1911–75)

North by Northwest (film score).
(M) **(*) Unicorn Dig. UKCD 2040. London Studio SO, Laurie Johnson.

Although inventive and scored with Herrmann's usual feeling for atmosphere, this selection of incidental music runs for only 38 minutes. It has a distinctively attractive romantic theme, a simple phrase which becomes quite haunting, introduced first in a section called *Conversation piece* and reprised later in *Duo*. The rest of the score is a series of vignettes, representing various incidents in the screenplay; but one would have to know the film very well to link up much of the music with the narrative. Moreover, the most famous scene in the film – which is illustrated on the front of the CD – Cary Grant's eluding the menacing crop-dusting aircraft, is accompanied by silence! The playing is excellent and the digital recording of high quality.

Hindemith, Paul (1895–1963)

Mathis der Maler (Symphony); *Concert music, Op. 50; Symphonic metamorphoses on themes by Weber.*
*** DG Dig. 429 404-2; *429 404-4* [id.]. Israel PO, Bernstein.

High-voltage Hindemith from Bernstein and the Israel Philharmonic; it was recorded live in the Robert Mann Auditorium in Tel Aviv whose dry acoustic is a handicap. However, accepting this limitation, the DG engineers have produced sound of great clarity and presence that reveals every strand in the orchestral texture. Judging from this record, the Israel orchestra is in much better shape than it was some years ago, with first-class strings rich in sonority, and good brass ensemble. In both the *Concert music for brass and strings* and the *Weber metamorphoses* the playing is exhilarating and, though some may find Bernstein a shade too intense at the opening of the *Mathis Symphony*, the performance is thrilling. In the *Symphony* Blomstedt has the best recording of all (Decca 421 523-2) and both he and Karajan (EMI CDM7 69242-2) have the advantage of a better acoustic; while, in the *Concert music*, Hindemith's own performance from the 1950s – not quite so well played – remains very competitive (EMI CDH7 63373-2). But these Bernstein performances have a lot going for them all the same.

Nobilissima visione: suite.
(M) (**) EMI mono CMS7 63835-2 (2). Philh. O, Klemperer – BRUCKNER: *Symphony No. 8* **; WAGNER: *Die Walküre: Wotan's farewell.* **(*)

Klemperer recorded only the three-movement suite from *Nobilissima visione*, but the three movements incorporate music from all five numbers of the ballet. The Philharmonia plays gravely and nobly (especially in the final *Passacaglia*) and Klemperer's rather austere style suits the music. The 1954 mono Kingsway Hall recording is remarkably good.

Symphonic metamorphosis on themes by Weber.
*** Ph. Dig. 422 347-2 [id.]. Bav. RSO, C. Davis – REGER: *Mozart variations.* *** ❀

Sir Colin Davis's account of the *Symphonic metamorphosis on themes by Weber*, which must now be Hindemith's most popular work, is first class, though not perhaps as gutsy as Bernstein (DG). However, the cultured sound produced by the Bavarian Radio Symphony Orchestra is a joy in itself and the reading has plenty of character and enormous finesse. It comes with an altogether masterly reading of Reger's glorious *Variations and fugue on a theme by Mozart* and is given state-of-the art Philips recording. Recommended with enthusiasm.

Octet (for wind and strings).
(M) ** Sony SMK 46250 [id.]. Members of the Marlboro Festival – BARBER: *Summer music* **(*); NIELSEN: *Woodwind quintet.* **

Those unsympathetic to the composer will find Hindemith at his ugliest and most manufactured in the *Octet* (1957–8). It is a divertimento-like piece of about 28 minutes, and even those who like his music may find it hard going at times. The artists recorded here play it more persuasively than most predecessors on disc, and the recording balance places slightly more air round the sound than in the Nielsen. The disc as a whole is well worth investigating.

(i) *Viola sonatas* (for viola and piano) *Op. 11/4; Op. 25/4;* (Unaccompanied) *Viola sonatas: Op. 11/5; Op. 25/1; Op. 31/4.*
*** ECM Dig. 833 309-2 (2) [id.]. Kim Kashkashian, (i) Robert Levin.

Hindemith was himself a distinguished violist and gave the first performance of the Walton *Concerto*. In all, he composed seven sonatas for the viola, four for solo instrument and three for viola and piano. The solo *Sonatas* are all accommodated on the first CD; they are played with superb panache and flair – and, even more importantly, with remarkable variety of colour – by Kim Kashkashian, who has an enormous dynamic range. Although listening to all four straight off is not advised, the listener will be surprised at how interesting an experience this artist makes of what are normally thought of as severe scores. The performances of the sonatas with piano are hardly less imaginative. Robert Levin is a marvellously sensitive accompanist who is inspired to similarly imaginative heights by his partner; though the piano sound is not absolutely ideal (nor, for that matter, is the instrument itself – there are one or two twangy notes and a slightly tubby bottom end – but too much should not be made of this), the recording is generally good. The prospect of seven *Viola sonatas* by anyone, let alone Hindemith, may seem uninviting, but this set proves a great and welcome surprise.

Berceuse; In einer Nacht, Op. 15; Kleines Klavierstück; Lied; 1922 Suite, Op. 26; Tanzstücke, Op. 19.
**(*) Marco Polo Dig. 8.223335 [id.]. Hans Petermandl.

Exercise in three pieces, Op. 31/I; Klaviermusik, Op. 37; Series of little pieces, Op. 37/II; Sonata, Op. 17; Two little piano pieces.
** Marco Polo Dig. 8.223336 [id.]. Hans Petermandl.

Ludus Tonalis; Kleine Klaviermusik, Op. 45/4.
** Marco Polo Dig. 8.223338 [id.]. Hans Petermandl.

Piano sonatas Nos 1–3; Variations.
** Marco Polo Dig. 8.223337 [id.]. Hans Petermandl.

This first CD survey of Hindemith's keyboard music by the Austrian pianist, Hans Petermandl, begins with the pieces composed in the 1920s, his window-breaking period. The *Dance suite*, which he later disowned, could be compared with the Stravinsky of the little *Suites for orchestra* though the Hindemith pieces have less elegance and flair. They have what Hans Petermandl calls 'a provocative delight in dissonance and the borrowing of vulgar contemporary dance forms'; they are very much of the period but do not quite transcend it. Hindemith prefaced the *Ragtime* of the *1922 Suite* by saying, 'Don't worry whether you should play D sharp with the fourth or the sixth finger, play this piece ferociously but always very strict in rhythm like a machine.' Hans Petermandl is an expert guide in this repertoire and presents it with real sympathy for, and understanding of, the idiom; his performances of some of these smaller pieces, like the beautiful *Lied* (1921), are very persuasive. The three *Sonatas for piano* come from 1936, shortly after Hindemith had established himself firmly with the wider musical public with *Mathis der Maler*. The *First* is an unusual five-movement structure with a powerful march as the second movement replacing a set of variations, which is included as an appendix. Hindemith never published them, though it seems that he thought well of them. The short sonatina-like *Second Sonata* has a charm that this admirable pianist does not wholly communicate. The textures in Hindemith's piano music are often unbeautiful and less than transparent and, although neither the piano nor the acoustic of the Concert Hall of Slovak Radio is outstanding, the sound is perfectly acceptable.

When lilacs last in the dooryard bloom'd (Requiem).
(M) **(*) Sony/CBS CD 45881. Louise Parker, George London, NY Schola Cantorum, NYPO, composer.

Hindemith's *When lilacs last in the dooryard bloom'd* was written at the end of the Second World War as the result of a commission from the Robert Shaw Chorale, who have made an outstanding Telarc recording of it, discussed in our main volume (CD 80132). However, here Hindemith himself is at the helm, so the performance carries a special authority. The music has surpassing beauty and eloquence, and the work must be numbered among his most impressive achievements, from the dignified and noble prelude right through to the imposing finale. Why it is not performed more often is a mystery indeed. Louise Parker and George London are committed soloists and, though they are too forward in relation to the orchestra, the recording has a full and realistic acoustic and is perfectly acceptable in its CD format, given the interest of the composer's own interpretation.

Holst, Gustav (1874–1934)

Hammersmith: Prelude and scherzo, Op. 52.
(M) *** Mercury 432 009-2 [id.]. Eastman Wind Ens., Fennell – BENNETT: *Symphonic songs*; JACOB: *William Byrd suite*; WALTON: *Crown Imperial.****

Holst's highly original and characteristically individual piece was commissioned in 1930 by the BBC, but the planned first performance never took place, and Holst never heard the piece in its original form. It is scored for 25 individual wind instruments (there is no doubling of parts in this recording). Holst insisted that *Hammersmith* is not programme music, yet he admitted that the ever-flowing Thames nearby was part of his inspiration. The work has an indelible principal theme, its effects are colourful and imaginative, and its range of mood wide, from introspection to rather jolly folk-dance rhythms. Fennell's pioneering stereo recording is superbly played by these expert students from the Eastman School, and the effect is totally spontaneous. The recording remains demonstration-worthy, though it dates from 1958!

The Planets (suite), *Op. 32.*
(M) **(*) Decca 430 447-2; *430 447-4* [id.]. LPO & Ch., Solti (with ELGAR: *Pomp and circumstance marches Nos. 1, 4 & 5.***(*))
(B) **(*) DG Compact Classics 413 852-2 (2); *413 852-4* [id.]. Boston Ch. & SO, Steinberg – ELGAR: *Enigma variations; Pomp and circumstance* *** (CD only: *Cello concerto* ***).
**(*) DG Dig. 429 730-2; *429 730-4* [id.]. Chicago SO & Ch., James Levine.
(**) Koch mono 3-7018-2; *2-7018-4* [id.]. LSO, composer – VAUGHAN WILLIAMS: *Symphony No. 4.*(**)

The Planets (suite), *Op. 32; Suite de ballet in E flat, Op. 10.*
(B) ** Naxos Dig. 8.550193 [id.]. CRS SO, Bratislava, Adrian Leaper.

Solti's set of *Planets* is full of adrenalin, and the brilliantly colourful, analogue recording is more vivid than many digital CDs. The performance is discussed more fully (on p. 506 of our main volume) under its earlier reissue, offered by Decca at the same price in their British Music series. This has more generous and more appropriate couplings: Boult's fine performances of Holst's *Egdon Heath* and *Perfect Fool suite* (Decca

425 152-2; *425 152-4*). Solti's accounts of the *Pomp and circumstance marches* are vigorous and polished and equally brilliantly recorded – but why only three from the set of five, when the disc has a playing time of only 67 minutes?

Steinberg's fine performance is available in its original analogue format played uninterrupted on one side of a double-length chrome tape, and coupled with Jochum's inspirational account of *Enigma*, plus a dash of *Pomp and circumstance* to balance out the side-lengths. Steinberg draws sumptuous playing from the Boston Symphony, and he is helped by reverberant recording that makes this a feast of sound. Anyone who wants to wallow in the opulence and colour of this extrovert work will certainly be delighted – the more so, one suspects, when Steinberg departs in certain respects from British convention. *Mars* in particular is intensely exciting. At his fast tempo he may get to his fortissimos a little early, but rarely has the piece sounded so menacing on record. The testing point for most will no doubt be *Jupiter*, and here Steinberg the excellent Elgarian comes to the fore, giving a wonderful nobilmente swagger. The tape transfer faithfully captures the richly vivid qualities of the recording, even though the resonance has brought a lower than usual level. The pair of digitally remastered CDs offers a brighter, slightly less opulent sound-image and includes Fournier's ardent reading of Elgar's *Cello concerto* as a substantial bonus.

On DG, the sumptuous acoustics of Orchestra Hall, Chicago, make a resonantly atmospheric setting for the ferocity of the orchestral attack in Levine's exciting account of *Mars* and add bloom to the transluscent purity of *Venus*, while bringing a glowing palette of colour to *Mercury*, played with graceful virtuosity and exuberance. *Jupiter*, with rollicking horns and a richly sonorous statement of the famous central melody, is also appropriately sumptuous, but the textural amplitude means that *Saturn* and *Uranus*, both weightily expansive, are less contrasted than usual. The Chicago Chorus make a bleakly atmospheric contribution to *Neptune*. An enjoyable performance, then, with plenty of impact, but in the last resort not really distinctive.

Gustav Holst made this recording of *The Planets* in 1926 (there was an earlier acoustic version in 1923, which Pearl have announced) and it sounds amazingly good, bearing in mind the cramped conditions under which it was made. It does not quite have the range or warmth of the EMI LP transfer but this is of academic interest, comparatively speaking, for it is still very good and an enormously valuable document. Holst kept a very strong grip on proceedings and, as his daughter put it, never allowed the rhythm to sag. *Mars* is particularly menacing and, despite the unfaded chorus, *Neptune* has plenty of atmosphere. *Venus* is probably faster than he would ideally have liked it; the 1923 version is almost a minute longer (early electric records reduced the number of grooves per inch to encompass the wider frequency-range); and, indeed, all the others are also fractionally shorter in the later version. All the same, one can get a pretty good idea of the composer's intentions here.

On Naxos, the Slovak Radio Orchestra under an English conductor give a direct, straightforward reading, without much subtlety of detail, but strong in effect, helped by excellent, full-bodied, digital recording. The big tune in *Jupiter*, taken spaciously, is sonorously eloquent. The novelty is the inclusion of Holst's early four-movement *Suite de ballet*, written in 1899 and revised in 1912. The invention is attractively robust, apart from the winningly fragile *Valse*, and the work is presented enthusiastially. Good orchestral playing throughout. However, easily the finest modern version of the *Planets*, both from the point of view of performance and recording, is Charles Dutoit's with the Montreal Symphony Orchestra (Decca 417 553-2; *417 553-4*).

The Cloud messenger, Op. 30; The Hymn of Jesus, Op. 37.
*** Chan. Dig. CHAN 8901; *ABTD 1510* [id.]. Della Jones, LSO Ch. & O, Richard Hickox.

Hickox's account of Holst's choral masterpiece, *The Hymn of Jesus,* dramatic and highly atmospheric, easily outshines even Sir Adrian Boult's vintage version for Decca – now on CD in coupling with Britten's reading of Elgar's *Dream of Gerontius* (Decca 421 381-2). Not only does modern digital sound make an enormous difference in a work where the choral sounds are terraced so tellingly, but Hickox secures tauter and crisper ensemble, as well as treating the sections based on plainchant with an aptly expressive freedom. The coupling is ideal. Inspired by Sanskrit literature, the long-neglected choral piece, *The Cloud messenger,* may lack the concentration of *The Hymn of Jesus* but it brings similarly incandescent choral writing. If the measured opening seems rather bland, the atmosphere is transformed when the chorus enters at full force in a thrilling sunburst. Holst's early Wagnerian sympathies bring some echoes of *Parsifal* – apt for a mystic journey with visions of the Himalayas – even if some of the oriental effects are unsubtle. Warmly and positively realized by Hickox and his powerful forces, with Della Jones a fine soloist, it makes a major discovery, whatever its incidental shortcomings. Hickox proves abundantly that it has never deserved the dismissal which followed its unfortunate first performance in 1913. Rich and ample Chandos recording adds to the involvement.

OPERA

(i; ii) *Sávitri* (chamber opera; complete). (iii) *Choral hymns from the Rig Veda* (3rd group) *H.99. The Evening watch, H.159;* (ii) *7 Partsongs, H.162.*
(M) *** Decca 430 062-2 [id.]. Purcell Singers with (i) J. Baker, Tear, Hemsley; (ii) ECO; (iii) Osian Ellis; Imogen Holst.

There are few chamber operas as beautifully scaled as *Sávitri.* With light texture and many slow tempi, it is a work which can fall apart in an uncommitted performance, but the interpreters on this reissued 1965 Decca (originally Argo) version could hardly be more imaginative. Dame Janet Baker produces some of her most intense and expressive singing. There is no mistaking that the piece is one of Holst's most perfectly conceived works. Aptly, the *Rig Veda hymns,* which follow the opera on this record, are also from a Sanskrit source, and the composer himself suggested that the last of them could, if necessary, be used as a postlude to *Sávitri* (something one can easily arrange with the facilities of CD). The opening *Hymn to the dawn* brings echoes of *Neptune* from *The Planets* and the fast, rhythmically fascinating *Hymn to the waters* is even more attractive. To fill up the disc, the no less imaginative *Partsongs* and the magical *Evening watch* have been added. Beautifully atmospheric Kingsway Hall recording, admirably remastered to match intense and sensitive performances.

Holst, Imogen (1907–84)

String quartet No. 1.
*** Conifer Dig. CDCF 196; *MCFC 196.* Brindisi Qt – BRIDGE: *3 Idylls*; BRITTEN: *String quartet No. 2.****

Imogen Holst is best known as the author of a study of her father and a book on Byrd, and for her work for Benjamin Britten. She directed the Purcell Singers and collaborated with Britten on his edition of *Dido and Aeneas.* Her two-movement *Quartet* is a shortish work, written in Cornwall in 1946; although not strongly personal, it is full of interest.

There is a scurrying scherzo which leaves an impression of Britten's own *Second Quartet*, and there are faint traces of Bartók, Hindemith and Shostakovich – and, in the first movement, a whiff of her own father's late music, such as *Hammersmith* or *Egdon Heath*. Both performance and recording are of high quality.

Honegger, Arthur (1892–1955)

Cello concerto.
(*) Ph. Dig. 432 084-2; *432 084-4* [id.]. Julian Lloyd Webber, ECO, Yan Pascal Tortelier – FAURÉ: *Élégie* **; D'INDY: *Lied* **(*); SAINT-SAENS: *Concerto* etc.(*)

Honegger's pastoral *Concerto* (1929–30) has been neglected: it last appeared on record in the 1960s on Miloš Sadlo's Supraphon LP. Julian Lloyd Webber deserves thanks for his enterprise in restoring it to circulation (though as we go to press Erato have announced a recording by Rostropovich). Dedicated to Maurice Maréchal, who recorded it with the composer in the days of 78s, it is a work of immense charm. Although, as recorded, he does not produce a big (or well-focused) tone, Lloyd Webber plays with refined musicianship and conveys the charm and character of this piece very effectively. He is well supported by Yan Pascal Tortelier, and the Philips recording is eminently natural and well balanced.

Film music: *Mermoz: suites 1 & 2. Les Misérables: suite. Napoléon (suite; original version). La Roue: Overture.*
** Marco Polo Dig. 8.223134 [id.]. Slovak RSO, Adriano.

Honegger composed music for some forty films, as well as incidental music for the theatre. The first surviving score is the *Overture* to Abel Gance's melodrama of 1922, a rather episodic piece which makes passing reference to one idea of *Pacific 231*. Gance's most celebrated film was *Napoléon* (1927), which has only recently come into its own. In anticipation of Cinemascope, three screens are employed; at its Paris première in 1927, the final triptych was tinted into the Tricolour and the film ran to four hours, with a full symphony orchestra in the pit. Much of the musical invention is predictably episodic and not always worth hearing in concert form, out of context; but what is surprising is how good much of it is. Adriano (who does not appear to have another name) has devoted his energies to film music and provides very thorough documentation. The playing is decent and the recording adequate (the studio acoustic is somewhat unglamorous) rather than distinguished.

Film music: *Les Misérables* (complete).
*(*) Marco Polo Dig. 8.223181 [id.]. Slovak RSO, Adriano.

Honegger's score for Raymond Bernard's 1934 black-and-white film of Victor Hugo's novel comprises 23 movements or 'cues' of which 17, lasting about an hour, are presented here (the omissions comprise three dance pieces by another hand and some inconsequential bars elsewhere; other passages, cut from the film for editing reasons, are restored). The music is of considerable interest, for Honegger was a highly imaginative composer, though not all of it merits rehearing out of context. (The scoring is interesting: no double-basses but saxophone, piano and harp.) Not essential Honegger, but worth having all the same – Koechlin, who was a keen *cinéaste*, thought it 'undoubtedly one of the best film-scores hitherto created'. The playing of the Bratislava orchestra is very acceptable, but the studio acoustic is wanting in bloom.

Symphony No. 2 for string orchestra and trumpet.
(*) Koch Multisonic 31 0022-2 [id.]. Czech PO, Münch – MILHAUD: *Music for Prague.*(**)

Charles Münch made the pioneering set of 78s of Honegger's bleak wartime *Second Symphony* and a subsequent stereo account with the Orchestre de Paris, which EMI briefly made available in 1988 in a three-CD set and which also included his *Symphonie fantastique* and some Ravel. The present electrifying performance was recorded at the 1957 Prague Spring Festival, and it must be the most intense and awe-inspiring of them all. No performance on disc is of higher voltage but, alas, the Czech Radio recording is execrable and cannot be recommended.

Symphonies Nos. 2; 4 (Deliciae Basiliensis).
**(*) Erato/Warner Dig. 2292 45247-2 [id.]. Bav. RSO, Dutoit.

Symphonies Nos. 2; 4 (Deliciae Basiliensis); (i) *Christmas cantata.*
(M) ** Decca 430 350-2 [id.]. SRO, Ansermet, (i) with Pierre Mollet, R. Lausanne Ch. & children's Ch.

Dutoit has the advantage of excellent recording. The perspective is completely natural and there is plenty of air around the various instruments, while detail is clean and well focused. He draws very cultured string playing from the Bavarian Radio orchestra in the dark, introspective *Symphony for strings* and his performance is thoroughly meticulous in its observance of detail, but it is just a shade deficient in vitality and drive. The *Deliciae Basiliensis* also has rather measured tempi. In expressive intensity it does not match Karajan's account on DG, coupled with No. 3 (423 242-2, given a Rosette in our main volume). However, Dutoit's beautifully recorded performance of No. 4 serves to rekindle enthusiasm for a much-underrated work whose sunny countenance and keen nostalgia unfailingly bring delight.

Ansermet's performance of the *Second Symphony* is vigorous and spirited, and is well recorded for its time (1961). The *Fourth* is also presented characterfully, but the playing does not really do justice to its lightness and wit, although the 1968 sound remains impressive. The *Christmas cantata* is an effective and often moving work and Ansermet's performance is committed; though problems of intonation crop up from time to time, they do not detract too much from the impact of the music-making. However, there are preferable modern versions of all these works available now, so this disc will be mainly of interest to Ansermet devotees.

Symphonies Nos. 3 (Symphonie liturgique); 5 (Di tre re).
** Erato/Warner 2292 45208-2 [id.]. Bav. RSO, Dutoit.

The playing of the Bavarian Radio orchestra is alert and disciplined, and Dutoit gives thoroughly idiomatic accounts of both symphonies. But he fails to galvanize his orchestra into performances with the same degree of expresssive feeling as does Karajan in the *Symphonie liturgique* on DG. Of course the Erato recording is obviously more modern, but it is only marginally better than the DG and the performance is not in the same street.

Jeanne d'Arc au bûcher.
❀ *** DG Dig. 429 412-2 [id.]. Keller, Wilson, Escourrou, Lanzi, Pollet, Command, Stutzman, Aler, Courtis, R. France Ch., Fr. Nat. O, Seiji Ozawa.

As the centenary of his birth approaches, Honegger seems to be receiving greater attention from the record companies, and a new recording of *Jeanne d'Arc au bûcher* was long overdue. The work was commissioned by Ida Rubinstein, whom we have to thank for Debussy's *Le Martyre de Saint Sébastien.* This DG account is much more successful than Ozawa's 1970s recording in English for CBS. There is a strong cast of both singers and actors and this newcomer, which has the merit of being given in the original French, is currently the only version now before the public. Honegger's 1935 setting of the Claudel poem is one of his most powerful and imaginative works, full of variety of invention, colour and textures. While many of its episodes make a strong effect, the work is more than the sum of its parts. It is admirably served by these forces, and in particular by the Joan of Marthe Keller. The singers, too, are all excellent and the Choir and the six soloists of the Maîtrise of Radio France are as top-drawer as the orchestra. The DG engineers cope excellently with the large forces and the acoustic of the Basilique de Saint-Denis. There is an excellent perspective, with plenty of detail and presence, as well as a wide dynamic range. In short, a powerful and important work, performed with dedicated artistry and recorded with splendid realism.

Howells, Herbert (1892–1983)

(Organ): *Psalm prelude, Set 1/1; Paen; Prelude: Sine nomine.* (Vocal): *Behold, O God our defender; Here is the door; Missa Aedi Christi: Kyrie; Credo; Sanctus; Benedictus; Agnus Dei; Gloria. Sing lullaby; A spotless rose; Where wast thou?.*
*** CRD Dig. CRD 3455 [id.]. New College, Oxford, Ch., Edward Higginbottom (organ).

A further collection of the music of Herbert Howells, splendidly sung by Edward Higginbottom's fine choir, while he provides the organ interludes in addition. The opening *Behold, O God our defender* expands gloriously, and the excerpts from the *Missa Aedis Christi* (heard in two groups) are almost equally impressive. Among the shorter pieces, the carol-anthem, *Sing lullaby*, is especially delightful, and the programme ends with the motet, *Where wast thou?*, essentially affirmative, in spite of the question posed at the opening. Beautifully spacious sound makes this a highly rewarding collection.

Humperdinck, Engelbert (1854–1921)

Hänsel und Gretel (complete).
*** EMI Dig. CDS7 54022-2 (2) [Ang. CDCB 54022]; *EX 754022-2.* Von Otter, Bonney, Lipovšek, Schwarz, Schmidt, Hendricks, Lind, Tölz Boys' Ch, Bav. RSO, Tate.

Tate brings a Brucknerian glow to the *Overture*, and then launches into a reading of exceptional warmth and sympathy at speeds generally faster than those in rival versions. Karajan in his vintage EMI recording may be more rapt, finding more mystery in the *Evening hymn* and *Dream pantomime*, but the freshness of Tate avoids any hint of sentimentality, giving the *Evening hymn* the touching simplicity of a children's prayer. He relates the opera to the Wagner of Act II of *Die Meistersinger*, rather than to anything weightier. The Witch of Marjana Lipovšek is the finest of all, firm and fierce, using the widest range of expression and tone without any of the embarrassing exaggerations that mar, for example, Elisabeth Söderström's strong but controversial reading for Pritchard on Sony, and without any of the fruitiness of the conventional readings provided on the other sets. The chill that Lipovšek conveys down to a mere whisper makes one regret, more than usual, that the part is not longer. All the casting matches that in finesse, with no weak link. Barbara Bonney as Gretel and Anne Sofie von Otter as Hänsel are no less fine than the exceptionally strong duos on the rival sets, notably Schwarzkopf and Grümmer on the splendid mid-priced Karajan set (EMI CMS7 69293-2) and Cotrubas and von Stade on the excellent alternative from Pritchard (Sony M2K 79217 [M2K 35898]). The main difference is that Bonney and von Otter have younger, fresher voices. The casting of the parents reflects that young approach too: Hanna Schwarz and Andreas Schmidt. There is only a slight question mark over the use of the Tölzer Boys' Choir for the gingerbread children at the end. Inevitably they sound what they are, a beautifully matched team of trebles, and curiously the heart-tug is not quite so intense as with the more childish-sounding voices in the rival choirs. That is a minimal reservation, however, when the breadth and warmth of the recording add to the compulsion of the performance, giving extra perspectives in focus and dynamic, compared with any other version.

Ibert, Jacques (1890–1962)

Escales (Ports of call).
(M) **(*) Mercury 432 003-2 [id.]. Detroit SO, Paray – RAVEL: *Alborada* etc.***

Paray's 1962 recording catches the Mediterranean exoticism of *Escales* admirably, and the 1962 Mercury recording has plenty of atmosphere as well as glittering detail. The diaphanous strings in the opening *Palermo* are particularly impressive, and only in the loudest tuttis does the sound seem over-brilliant. The Ravel couplings are very impressive too.

d'Indy, Vincent (1851–1931)

Diptyque méditerranéan; Poème des rivages (symphonic suite).
(M) **(*) EMI Dig. CDM7 63954-2 [id.]. Monte Carlo PO, Prêtre.

Neither work represents d'Indy at his most consistently inspired, but there are still good things. The *Soleil matinal* of the *Diptyque* has that blend of the Wagner of *Parsifal* and a quality of conservative impressionism that d'Indy made so much his own after the turn of the century. There are considerable beauties in this piece and in the *Poème*, and though the recording is not top-drawer this is still worth investigating, despite some unequalness of inspiration.

Lied, Op. 19.
(*) Ph. Dig. 432 084-2; *432 084-4* [id.]. Julian Lloyd Webber, ECO, Yan Pascal Tortelier – FAURÉ: *Élégie* **; HONEGGER: *Concerto* **(*); SAINT-SAENS: *Concerto* etc.(*)

There is no alternative recording of Vincent d'Indy's *Lied for cello and orchestra*, and all credit to Julian Lloyd Webber for returning it to currency. It has something of the nobility that always distinguished this composer, and it comes with an interesting coupling in the shape of the Honegger *Concerto*.

(i) *Symphonie sur un chant montagnard français (Symphonie cévenole);* (ii) *Symphony No. 2 in B flat, Op. 57.*
(M) *** EMI CDM7 63952-2 [id.]. (i) Ciccolini, O de Paris, Baudo; (ii) Toulouse Capitole O, Plasson.

The *Symphonie sur un chant montagnard français* is the work by which Vincent d'Indy is best known in this country, though the *Second Symphony* is occasionally heard. So the present coupling in EMI's '*L'esprit français*' reissue series is propitious. Aldo Ciccolini gives a good account of himself in the demanding solo part of the former, and the Orchestre de Paris under Serge Baudo give sympathetic support. The music is charming and resourceful and the recording, if not outstanding, is pleasing and with a convincing piano image. The *Second Symphony* (1902–3) is as impressive as it is neglected. Although its cyclic organization betrays its francophilia, there is intellectual vigour, charm (as in the modal, folk-like *Modéré* of the third movement) and nobility in the arching lines of the fugue in the finale. Michel Plasson proves a sympathetic and committed advocate, and his orchestra, though not in the luxury bracket, responds with enthusiasm and sensitivity to his direction. The recording too is very good: spacious, full and well focused. Those who complain about repeated duplications of the Franck *Symphony* should investigate this disc and discover one of the composer's most powerful works.

Ippolitov-Ivanov, Mikhail (1859–1935)

Caucasian sketches, Op. 10.
(B) ** Van. VCD 72019 [id.]. Utah SO, Abravanel – RIMSKY-KORSAKOV: *Symphony No. 2 (Antar).***

Abravanel's treatment of Ippolitov-Ivanov's picaresque suite is sophisticated, helped by a recording of wide dynamic range and some excellent solo wind-playing from the orchestra. The most famous number, the *Procession of the Sardar*, is vividly done. As a bonus, Abravanel offers a lively account of Glière's *Russian sailor's dance* from *The Red Poppy*, and to fill out the CD the *Waltz* and *Finale* from Tchaikovsky's *Swan Lake*.

Ireland, John (1879–1962)

A London overture; Epic march; (i) *The Holy Boy; Greater love hath no man; These things shall be; Vexilla regis.*
*** Chan. Dig. CHAN 8879; *ABTD 1492* [id.]. (i) Bryn Terfel, LSO Ch., LSO, Richard Hickox.

This CD forms as good an introduction as any to John Ireland's music, which has not enjoyed the same revival of interest as his contemporary, Arnold Bax (although, of course, Ireland's splendid *Piano concerto* should also be part of any representative collection: Chandos CDCF 175, *MCFC 175*; Unicorn DKPCD 9056, *DKPC 9056*; or Chandos CHAN 8461, *ABTD 1174*, according to choice of coupling – see our main volume, pp. 516–17). Richard Hickox is a sympathetic interpreter of the composer and obtains sensitive results (and good singing) in *The Holy Boy* and *These things shall be* (surprisingly, the latter is not otherwise available on silver disc). He does make heavy weather of the opening of *A London overture* but more than compensates for that in his sensitive phrasing of the second group. The disc is of particular interest in that it brings a rarity, *Vexilla Regis* for chorus, brass and organ, composed when Ireland was nineteen and still a student of Stanford. First-class recorded sound.

Phantasie (trio) in A min.
*** Gamut Dig. GAM CD 518 [id.]. Hartley Trio – BRIDGE; CLARKE: *Trios.****

Built on striking material, energetically argued, the Ireland *Phantasie* is one of the finest of the one-movement works prompted by the sponsorship of W. W. Cobbett. One ideally should have a whole disc devoted to the *Piano trios* of Ireland, but this fine work, well played and recorded, makes an excellent fill-up for the similar Bridge *Phantasie* and the splendid *Piano trio* of Rebecca Clarke.

Ives, Charles (1874–1954)

Calcium light night; Country band march; Largo cantabile: Hymn; 3 Places in New England; Postlude in F; 4 Ragtime dances; Set for theatre orchestra; Yale–Princeton football game.
*** Koch Dig. 37025-2; *37025-4* [id.]. O New England, Sinclair.

This selection of shorter Ives pieces makes an ideal introduction for anyone wanting just to sample the work of this wild, often maddening, but always intriguing composer. Some of these pieces, like the evocations of college life in the Yale–Princeton football game and *Calcium light night*, encapsulate the kind of raw material Ives developed in bigger works like *Three places in New England*, one of his most colourfully attractive works. Excellent performances and recording.

Symphonies Nos. 1; 4.
**(*) Sony Dig. SK 44939 [id.]. Chicago SO, Michael Tilson Thomas.

Tilson Thomas's strong and brilliant Chicago performances make a generous and apt coupling, the more valuable for providing first recordings of the revised editions of the composer's tangled scores. These may not be the warmest or most concentrated of performances but, with bright, well-detailed sound and superb playing, they can be strongly recommended to those wanting the generous and apt coupling.

Symphonies Nos. 2; 3 (The camp meeting).
**(*) Sony Dig. SK 46440 [id.]; *40-46440*. Concg. O, Michael Tilson Thomas.

This recoupling is welcome when it so neatly provides a counterpart to Tilson Thomas's Chicago recordings of the other two Ives symphonies. The performances may not have the fervour of a Bernstein in this music – perhaps reflecting the fact that this is not an American orchestra – but they are strong and direct, and in No. 3 the revised edition is used on record for the first time. The recording, though not ideally sharp in its focus, is warm and atmospheric.

Symphonies Nos. 3 (The Camp Meeting); (i) *4; Set for theatre, Circus band march.*
(B) **(*) Van. VCD 72030 [id.]. (i) Amb. Ch.; New Philh. O or RPO, Faberman.

Bargain hunters looking for a characteristic Ives collection could hardly do better than Faberman's 1967 Vanguard concert. Besides excellent accounts of the folksy *Third Symphony* and the more spectacular *Fourth*, with its riotously exhilarating scherzo, there is the exuberant *Circus march*, as unpredictable in its flashes of dissonance as it is striking in its melodic outline. The rarer *Set for theatre* moves from an impression of a caged animal, through a topsy-turvy nightclub sequence to a haunting landscape of the night. The performances are powerfully sympathetic, and the recording, brilliant but not edgy, is transferred effectively to CD. There are adequate notes.

(i) *Symphony No. 4; Robert Browning Overture;* (ii) Songs: *An Election, Lincoln the great commoner; Majority, They are There!*
(M) *** Sony MPK 46726 [id.]. (i) NY Schola Cantorum; (ii) Gregg Smith Singers; American SO, Stokowski

This reissue of three vintage Stokowski recordings of Ives makes a welcome addition to the Masterworks Portrait series, well transferred to CD. The originally 1965 recording of the *Fourth Symphony*, made at the same period as the belated première of the work, brings a stunning performance, with sound that is still amazingly full and vivid.

Stokowski also brings out the often aggressive vigour of the *Robert Browning Overture*. The choral songs with orchestra provide an attractive makeweight.

Songs: *At the river; Charlie Rutledge; The children's hour; The circus band; He is there; In the alley; A night song; An old flame; Romanza di Central Park; Slow march.*
*** Decca Dig. 433 027-2; *433 027-4* [id.]. Samuel Ramey, Warren Jones – COPLAND: *Old American songs.****

With some characteristically vigorous songs as well as many that might almost be Edwardian ballads (spiced Ives-style), this group of ten songs, superbly done, makes an ideal and attractive coupling for the colourful Copland settings, very well recorded. A coupling not to be missed.

Jacob, Gordon (1895–1987)

William Byrd suite.
(M) *** Mercury 432 009-2 [id.]. Eastman Wind Ens., Fennell – BENNETT: *Symphonic songs*; HOLST: *Hammersmith*; WALTON: *Crown Imperial.****

Gordon Jacob's arrangement of the music of Byrd is audaciously anachronistic, but it is very entertaining when played with such flair under that supreme maestro of the wind band, Frederick Fennell. The closing number, *The Bells* (*Variations on a ground*), is particularly successful. The recording is up to the usual high Mercury standard in this repertoire.

Janáček, Leoš (1854-1928)

Sinfonietta.
*** Chan. Dig. CHAN 8897; *ABTD 1508* [id.]. Czech PO, Bělohlávek – MARTINŮ: *Symphony No. 6*; SUK: *Scherzo.****

Jíři Bělohlávek's exultant and imaginative account of the *Sinfonietta* is one of the best currently on offer and is coupled with an outstanding version of Martinů's *Sixth Symphony*. The players, as one would expect, are entirely inside this repertoire and the recording, made in the Smetana Hall, Prague, is impressive. There are also fine versions by Abbado and Rattle, both paired with the *Glagolitic Mass* (see our main volume), so choice will depend mainly on the coupling most suitable.

Sinfonietta; Preludes: From the House of the Dead; Jealousy (original *Overture to Jenůfa*); *Katya Kabanova; The Makropulos affair.*
(M) *(**) EMI CDM7 63779-2 [id.]; *EG 763779-4*. Pro Arte O, Mackerras (with WEINBERGER: *Schwanda the Bagpiper: Polka & fugue.* SMETANA: *Bartered Bride: Overture* ***).

Sir Charles Mackerras (having studied in Prague with Václav Talich) became for the music of Janáček what Beecham before him had been for the promulgation of the works of Delius. This 1959 version of the *Sinfonietta* was the first of his many recordings and prompted Andrew Porter to write in *Gramophone*: 'His readings combine a sense of burning belief in and love of Janáček's music; they are well prepared; yet on each occasion it is as if the strangeness and beauty of the music were being revealed for the first time.' The present performance has a fire and bite that are not quite matched even by Mackerras himself in his later, Decca record. The playing of the Pro Arte Orchestra is immensely vivid; its lack of the last degree of refinement seems to increase its forceful projection. The brass sonorities (the work uses twelve trumpets) are pungent, and elsewhere the recording has striking detail and colour. The original coupling of the four operatic *Preludes* was an imaginative choice, and similar comments apply to the vibrant playing here. The only snag is that in this bright CD transfer the EMI engineers have rather gone over the top in the upper range, which is very brightly lit indeed to the point of shrillness. The two vivacious encores by Weinberger and Smetana have comparable colour and zest, plus excellent detail, and it is a pity that, even here, the upper range is a bit fierce.

Taras Bulba (rhapsody).
*** Decca Dig. 430 204-2; *430 204-4* [id.]. Cleveland O, Dohnányi – DVOŘÁK: *Symphony No. 6.****

Opulently recorded in Decca's finest Cleveland style, like the Dvořák symphony with which it is coupled, Dohnányi's version of *Taras Bulba* provides a generous makeweight on a fine disc. Quite apart from the sound, this brings a more warmly expressive reading than the brilliant rival Decca version from Mackerras and the Vienna Philharmonic. Paradoxically, the Cleveland account is the more Viennese in style, where Mackerras persuades his truly Viennese musicians to sound like Czechs, playing with a sharp attack very apt for this composer's music.

Violin sonata.
(*) DG Dig. 427 351-2 [id.]. Gidon Kremer, Martha Argerich – BARTÓK: *Sonata No. 1*; MESSIAEN: *Theme and variations.**

Like the Bartók, with which it is coupled, the Janáček *Sonata* comes from 1921 and is a powerfully impassioned and original work. It is played with great imaginative intensity and power by Gidon Kremer and Martha Argerich, though it is less selfless here than with Sitkovetsky on Virgin (see our main volume): there is some expressive exaggeration, and those who are at times disturbed by the note of hysteria and narcissism that characterizes Kremer's tone will find evidence of it here. Excellent DG recording.

Piano sonata (1.X.1905); In the mist; 3 Moravian dances; On an overgrown path: Books 1 & 2; A recollection.
*** EMI Dig. CDC7 54094-2 [id.]. Mikhail Rudy.

Piano sonata (1.X.1905); In the mist; On the overgrown path, Book 2; A recollection.
**(*) BMG/RCA Dig. RD 60147 [60147-2-RC]. Rudolf Firkušný.

Piano sonata (1.X.1905); In the mist; On the overgrown path, Book 2; A recollection; Theme & variations.
(M) *** DG 429 857-2 [id.]. Rudolf Firkušný.

Rudolf Firkušný brings a special authority and sensitivity to this repertoire. As a small boy he played many of these pieces to the composer, but it is his selfless dedication to this music that tells. His basic approach has not varied greatly since he last recorded these pieces for DG in the early 1970s, and he produces the same seamless legato lines, hammerless tone and rapt atmosphere. The three stars are for the marvellous playing; the RCA recording does not give us the best piano quality: though it is perfectly acceptable, it is a little biased towards the middle and bass registers. Given its more competitive price, many collectors will opt for his earlier anthology, which is still sounds very good and which also includes the *Zdenka Theme and variations.*

Mikhail Rudy proves a perceptive and sympathetic guide in this music. His is a fine account of the *Sonata*, and he succeeds in penetrating the world of the *Overgrown path* miniatures to perfection. He conveys their acute sense of melancholy and their improvisatory character with distinction. Rudolf Firkušný has special claims in this repertoire, and this anthology supplements rather than displaces his CD, but it is thoroughly recommendable, and the recorded sound is very natural.

Glagolitic Mass.
**(*) Telarc Dig. CD 80287 [id.]. Atlanta Ch. & SO, Robert Shaw – DVOŘÁK: *Te Deum.* **(*)

Shaw conducts an incisive, freshly dramatic reading of Janáček's colourful masterpiece, lacking only a little in idiomatic Czech flavour. Though the Telarc recording presents the orchestra (and organ) forwardly and vividly, the chorus is relatively backward, a great pity when the singing is so fine. That flaw in the recording balance need not deter anyone who fancies the unusual but apt coupling.

OPERA

(i) *From the house of the dead;* (iii) *Mládí* (for wind sextet); (ii; iii) *Říkadla* (for Chamber Ch. & 10 instruments).
*** Decca Dig. 430 375-2 (2) [id.]. (i) Jedlička, Zahradníček, Žídek, Zítek, V. State Op. Ch., VPO, Mackerras; (ii) L. Sinf. Ch.; (iii) L. Sinf., Atherton.

With fine digital recording adding to the glory of the highly distinctive instrumentation, the Decca version of Janáček's last opera outshines even the earlier recordings in Mackerras's series. By rights, this piece – based on Dostoevsky – should be intolerably depressing in operatic form, but in effect, as this magnificent performance amply demonstrates, the mosaic of sharp response, with sudden hysterical joy punctuating even the darkest, most bitter emotions, is consistently uplifting. With one exception the cast is superb, with a range of important Czech singers giving sharply characterized vignettes. The exception is the raw Slavonic singing of the one woman in the cast, Jaroslav Janska as the boy, Aljeja, but even that fails to undermine the intensity of the innocent relationship with the central figure, which provides an emotional anchor for the whole piece. The chamber-music items added for this reissue are both first rate: *Mládí*'s youthful sparkle comes across to excellent effect in the London Sinfonietta's fine version, as does *Říkadla*, a rarity for chamber choir and ten instruments.

(i) *The Makropulos affair (Věc Makropulos)*: complete; (ii) *Lachian dances.*
*** Decca 430 372-2 (2) [id.]. (i) Söderström, Dvorský, Blachut, V. State Op. Ch., VPO, Mackerras; (ii) LPO, Huybrechts.

Mackerras and his superb team provide a thrilling new perspective on an opera which is far more than the bizarre dramatic exercise it once seemed, with its weird heroine preserved by magic elixir well past her 300th birthday. In most performances the character of the still beautiful Emilia seems mean beyond any sympathy, but here the radiant Elisabeth Söderström sees it rather differently, presenting from the first a streak of vulnerability. She is not simply malevolent: irritable and impatient rather, no longer an obsessive monster. Framed by richly colourful singing and playing, Söderström amply justifies that view, and Peter Dvorský is superbly fresh and ardent as Gregor. The recording, like others in the series, is of the highest Decca analogue quality. The performance of the *Lachian dances* by the London Philharmonic under the Belgian conductor, François Huybrechts, is highly idiomatic and effective and makes a good bonus.

Järnefelt, Armas (1869–1958)

Praeludium.
(M) *** EMI CD-EMX 2176; *TC-EMX 2176.* Bournemouth SO Berglund – ALFVÉN: *Swedish rhapsody*; GRIEG: *Peer Gynt.***(*)

Järnefelt's charming miniature has been absent from the catalogues for too long (it used to be very familiar because it fitted easily on to a 78-r.p.m. side). Here it is nicely played and given bright, immediate recording. A pleasing lollipop, used as an encore for a well-planned concert of Scandinavian music.

Jolivet, André (1905–74)

Chant de Linos.
*** Koch Dig. 3-7016 [id.]. Atlantic Sinf. – JONGEN: *Concert*; DEBUSSY: *Sonata.****

The *Chant de Linos* is among the most demanding pieces for flute in the chamber-music repertoire. It was originally composed in 1944 for flute and piano as a competition piece for the Paris Conservatoire, but Jolivet subsequently made this highly effective transcription for flute, violin, viola, cello and harp. It is played with exemplary taste and effortless virtuosity by Bradley Garner and his colleagues of the Atlantic Sinfonietta and is most beautifully recorded. It comes with a poetic and thoughtful account of the Debussy *Trio sonata* and a Jongen rarity.

Jongen, Joseph (1873–1953)

Concert à cinq.
*** Koch Dig. 3-7016-2 [id.]. Atlantic Sinf. – DEBUSSY: *Sonata*; JOLIVET: *Chant de Linos.****

The Belgian composer Joseph Jongen was enormously prolific (he reached Opus 241) and self-critical (towards the end of his life he destroyed over 100 of his works). His three-movement *Concert à cinq* for flute, harp and string trio is a civilized piece very much in the post-impressionist style. It remains more pleasing than memorable, though these players do their utmost for it. The record is well worth getting, as it offers an outstandingly sensitive account of the Debussy *Trio sonata* and is beautifully balanced.

Kabalevsky, Dmitri (1904–87)

The Comedians (suite), *Op. 26.*
(M) *** EMI Dig. CDD7 63893 [id.]; *ET 763893.* Bav. State O, Sawallisch (with Concert of Russian music ***).

Kabalevsky's suite has a certain brashness in its scoring at times, but the polished playing of the Bavarian State Orchestra adds a touch of elegance and these ten charming vignettes, full of colour and vitality, are made to sound very entertaining indeed. The most famous is the exuberant *Galop*, a knockabout circus piece, complete with xylophone; but the charming *Intermezzo* and the gentle *Little lyrical scene* are just as memorable in their contrasting restraint, while the Scherzo is worthy of Prokofiev. First-class sound, with plenty of ambience, so that the music can be boisterous without vulgarity.

Violin concerto in C, Op. 48.
*** Chan. Dig. CHAN 8918; *ABTD 1519* [id.]. Lydia Mordkovitch, SNO, Järvi - KHACHATURIAN: *Violin concerto.****

Kabalevsky's *Violin concerto* comes from 1948 and is designed for a young audience. It is slight, lasting no more than a quarter of an hour, but it has a particularly attractive slow movement with a haunting, folklike idea, perhaps prompted by Zhdanov's decree from earlier that year advocating a populist style. It is most persuasively presented by these artists. Throughout, Lydia Mordkovitch plays with great flair and aplomb and is given first-class Chandos recording.

Khachaturian, Aram (1903–78)

Piano concerto in D flat.
(***) Olympia mono OCD 236 [id.]. Moura Lympany, LPO, Fistoulari – SAINT-SAENS: *Piano concerto No. 2.*(**(*))

Moura Lympany gave Khachaturian's *Piano concerto* its London première in 1940, and in 1952 she made the present mono recording for Decca with Fistoulari, who was also the conductor of the wartime London première of the *Violin concerto*. The *Piano concerto* is by no means as fine a work but, for all its moments of cheapness, it has an inherent vitality which has kept it in the record catalogues despite the initial, exotically witty summary of its merits (or lack of them) in the Desmond Shawe-Taylor/Sackville-West *Record Guide*: 'This long and tedious work sets going the entire apparatus of the late Romantic Piano Concerto. In the first movement we are ushered into a kind of Fun Land, decorated in the Oriental style. Slot-machines compete for our attention; high-spirited youths are breaking china at sixpence a go; all kinds of dubious characters lurk in the shadows. In the second movement we have our fortune told by a gypsy, mysterious in yards of voile and complete with tambourine and a dreadful instrument called the Flexatone [a kind of musical saw]. In the finale we emerge from a stuffy tent to end the evening on the swings and roundabouts.' The Lympany/Fistoulari account has a dash, sparkle and bravura which have never been matched on record since: even the Flexatone warbling in the *Andante* is made to seem convincing, and Khachaturian's melancholy Armenian melodies are given their full character. The recording, first rate in its day, now sounds curiously cavernous, though perfectly acceptable; the sheer élan of the performance soon makes one forget the aural deficiencies.

Violin concerto in D min.
*** Chan. Dig. CHAN 8918 [id.]. Lydia Mordkovitch, SNO, Järvi - KABALEVSKY: *Violin concerto.****
* Olympia OCD 135 [id.]. Valery Klimov, USSR Ac. SO, Svetlanov – SCHOENBERG: *Concerto.**

Among more recent performances of this attractively inventive concerto, Lydia Mordkovitch is probably the most competitive. She gives a thoroughly committed account of this popular score and receives sensitive support from Neeme Järvi and the Scottish National Orchestra. She plays with real abandon and fire, and Chandos balance her and the orchestra in a thoroughly realistic perspective. David Oistrakh's outstanding mono version should not be forgotten (Chant du Monde LDC 278883 – see our main volume), but this new version has far superior sound.

Olympia offer one of the most bizarre couplings to have appeared for many a year, juxtaposing one of the most demanding of modern concertos with perhaps the most immediately accessible of them all. Valery Klimov plays with plenty of spirit and with full-throated lyricism, though the 1981 analogue recording in no way does justice to the sumptuous string-tone that the USSR Academic Symphony Orchestra under Yevgeny Svetlanov produces in the flesh. The soloist is very closely balanced and the balance is a multi-mike, synthetic affair, and tuttis sound rough.

Gayaneh (ballet): suite.
(B) **(*) DG Compact Classics *413 155-4* [id.]. Leningrad PO, Rozhdestvensky – RIMSKY-KORSAKOV: *Scheherazade*; STRAVINSKY: *Firebird suite.***(*)

No one does the *Sabre dance* like the Russians, and with Rozhdestvensky it makes a sensational opening, exploding into the room at the end of Stravinsky's *Firebird suite.* The performance overall combines excitement with panache, and the original drawback of a rather fierce recording has been met here by the slight attenuation of the upper range of the chrome-tape transfer. But the sound remains vivid.

Spartacus (ballet): *suites Nos. 1–3.*
*** Chan. Dig. CHAN 8927; *ABTD 1529* [id.]. SNO, Neeme Järvi.

The ripe lushness of Khachaturian's scoring in *Spartacus* narrowly skirts vulgarity. Yet Shostakovich admired the work, and its vitality is undeniable. The most famous number, and rightly so, is the splendidly languorous tune for the *Adagio of Spartacus and Phrygia* (long famous as the theme for BBC TV's *Onedin Line* series); it is presented here with splendid opulence and ardour. The melody returns later, more delicately, in Phrygia's parting scene. Other memorable items are the jolly *Variations of of Aegina*, and there is plenty of gusto in the music for the Merchants and Pirates, while the Gaditianian maidens and the *Dance of the Egyptian girl* bring an exotically decadent, sensuous allure. Järvi and the SNO clearly enjoy the music's tunefulness and primitive vigour, while the warmly resonant acoustics of Glasgow's Henry Wood Hall bring properly sumptuous orchestral textures, smoothing over the moments of crudeness without losing the Armenian colouristic vividness.

Khachaturian, Karen (born 1920)

Violin sonata in G min., Op. 1.
(M) ** RCA GD 87872; *GK 87872* [7872-2-RG; *7872-4-RG*]. Heifetz, Steuber – CASTELNUOVO-TEDESCO: *Concerto No. 2* (**); FERGUSON: *Sonata* **; FRANÇAIX: *Trio.****

Karen is the nephew of Aram Khachaturian and studied with Miaskovsky and Shostakovich in the late 1940s. Their tutelage shows in every bar of this eminently well-fashioned but not particularly individual piece. It is well laid out for the instruments and very accomplished for an Opus 1, and it has attracted the advocacy of David Oistrakh as well as of Heifetz. The work is beautifully played by Heifetz, though Lillian Steuber is not the most poetic of pianists. Goodish 1966 recording, but with not quite an ample enough acoustic.

Knussen, Oliver (born 1952)

Symphony No. 3.
*** ASV Dig. CDRPO 8023; *ZCRPO 8023* [id.]. RPO, Ashkenazy – BRITTEN: *Serenade*; WALTON: *Symphony No. 2.****

This performance of Knussen's powerfully concentrated symphony was recorded live in concerts which took place when Ashkenazy returned to Russia after many years of exile in the West. Though, inevitably, ensemble does not always have pin-point precision in a live performance of a complex score, the warmth of communication is enhanced. Next to the Philharmonia players in Tilson Thomas's studio recording for Unicorn Kanchana, the RPO sounds liberated, bringing out the mystery of the opening far more intensely and regularly revealing the emotional thrust of Knussen's beautiful and complex writing. More expansive in manner, it is a performance to recommend to anyone who as yet does not know this young composer's formidable but deeply rewarding music. This closely argued one-movement symphony, lasting in this performance 16½ minutes, is the work which most clearly reveals his weight as a composer.

Kodály, Zoltán (1882–1967)

Dances of Galánta; Háry János: suite; Variations on a Hungarian folksong, 'The Peacock'.
(M) (**(*)) Decca 425 969-2 [id.]. LPO, Solti.

(i) *Dances of Galánta; Marosszék dances;* (ii) *Háry János: suite.*
(M) *** Mercury 432 005-2 [id.]. (i) Philharmonia Hungarica; (ii) Minneapolis SO, Dorati – BARTÓK: *Hungarian sketches* etc.***

From sneeze to finale, the Minneapolis orchestral playing in the *Háry János suite* is crisp and vigorous; the excellent 1956 Mercury stereo, while providing well-integrated tuttis, also gives simple separation for the solos and delicate highlighting of the more subtle percussion effects, especially the cimbalom. Dorati went on to record the other two sets of dances with the Philharmonia Hungarica in 1958. The playing of the woodwind soloists in the slow dances is intoxicatingly seductive, and the power and punch of the climaxes come over with real Mercury fidelity. An outstanding disc, since the Bartók couplings are equally successful.

Solti's performances have a natural idiomatic flair. *The Peacock variations* are subtle and very Hungarian in feeling, and both *Háry János* and the *Dances of Galánta* combine sophistication of detail with excitement. The recordings were made in the Kingsway Hall between 1952 and 1955 and the mono sound has a characteristic overall bloom. But the bright, very sharply etched upper string sound is fierce in fortissimos, and this inhibits unalloyed enjoyment.

Háry János: suite.
(M) *** EMI Dig. CDD7 63900-2 [id.]; *ET 763900-4*. LPO, Tennstedt – DVOŘÁK: *Symphony No. 9.***(*)
(M) (***) BMG/RCA mono GD 60279; *GK 60279* [60279-2-RG; *60279-4-RG*]. NBC SO, Toscanini – DVOŘÁK: *Symphony No. 9* (***); SMETANA: *Má Vlast: Vltava.*(**)

Tennstedt might seem an unlikely conductor for Kodály's sharply characterized folk-based score, but his performance has sympathy as well as power and brilliance, drawing out the romantic warmth of the *Intermezzo.* Digital sound of the fullest, richest EMI vintage.

There is nothing relaxed about Toscanini's view of *Háry János*. He seems not to realize that a joke is involved; but the intensity of the performance gives the music a new and bigger scale, whether appropriate or not. A valuable and rare coupling for the fine examples of Toscanini conducting Czech music.

Kokkonen, Joonas (born 1921)

The Last Temptations (opera): complete.
**(*) Finlandia FACD 104 (2) [id.]. Auvinen, Ruohonen, Lehtinen, Talvela, Savonlinna Op. Festival Ch. & O, Söderblom.

Kokkonen is now quite well represented on disc. Our main volume lists the *Fourth Symphony*, the *Symphonic sketches* and the *Cello concerto*, beautifully playd by Torleif Thedéen. Now Finlandia restore the 1977 set of his opera, *The Last Temptations*, which was previously available on three LPs from DG. The opera tells of a revivalist leader, Paavo Ruotsalainen, from the Finnish province of Savo and of his inner struggle to discover Christ. The opera is dominated by the personality of Martti Talvela, and its invention for the most part has a dignity and power that are symphonic in scale. Too much of the opera takes place in the same tonal area, but overall the work makes a strong impact. All four roles are well sung, and the performance under Ulf Söderblom is very well recorded indeed.

Korngold, Erich (1897–1957)

String sextet, Op.10.
*** Hyp. Dig. CDA 66425 [id.]. Raphael Ens. – SCHOENBERG: *Verklaerte Nacht.****

The Korngold *Sextet* is an amazing achievement for a seventeen-year-old. Not only is it crafted with musicianly assurance and maturity it is also inventive and characterful. The Raphael Ensemble play it with great commitment and the Hyperion recording is altogether first class. It comes with a very enjoyable recording of *Verklaerte Nacht.*

Kraft, Anton (1749–1820)

Cello concerto in C, Op. 4.
** BMG/RCA Dig. RD 77757 [7757-2-RC]. Anner Bylsma, Tafelmusik O, Jean Lamon – HAYDN: *Cello concertos.***

Anton Kraft came from Rokycany, near Pilsen, where his father was a brewer. He studied philosophy but eventually turned to music, joining Haydn's orchestra at Esterháza as a cellist. For a time Haydn's *D major concerto* was attributed to him and, in the interesting notes which acompany this CD, Anner Bylsma argues that Kraft had a hand in its composition. The *Concerto in C*, Op. 4, is a rather delightful piece, full of fun and delight and with some memorable ideas, even if it is bereft of any great depth. Good playing and recording, and generally more perfectly in tune than the Haydn works with which it is coupled.

Krebs, Johann Ludwig (1713–80)

Double concerto in B min. for harpsichord, oboe and strings.
(M) **(*) DG 431 120-2; *431 120-4* [id.]. Jaccottet, Holliger, Camerata Bern, Van Wijnkoop – GRAUN; TELEMANN: *Concertos.****

Krebs was a pupil of J. S. Bach; he left Leipzig with a glowing testimonial from the master. One can understand why from this delightful *Double concerto*, which makes a good coupling for the concertos of Graun and Telemann. Holliger as ever plays beautifully, but Christiane Jaccottet adopts too romantically expressive a style. However, this remains well worth hearing, and the recording is first rate.

Chorales: *Es ist gewisslich an der Zeit* (with horn); *Gott der Vater wohn uns bei* (with clarino); *Herr Jesu Christ, meins Lebens Licht* (with oboe); *Herzlich lieb hab ich dich, o Herr; In allen meinen Taten* (both with trumpet); *Jesu meine Freude, meine Seel, ermuntre dich; O Gott, du frommer Gott* (all with oboe); *Treuer Gott, ich muss dir klagen* (with oboe d'amore); *Wachet auf; Fantasia on Wachet auf* (with trumpet); *Wachet auf* (2nd version with clarino; 3rd version with trumpet). *Fantasias: Nos. 1–2 in F; in F min.* (all with oboe); *in C* (flute).
*** Argo Dig. 430 208-2; *430 208-4* [id.]. Bennett, Black, Laird, Thompson, Hurford (organ of Gloucester Cathedral).

Here is further proof, if any were needed, that Bach's favourite pupil, Johann Ludwig Krebs, was a considerable musician in his own right and a composer of some individuality. His special innovation was to extend the Bachian organ chorale to feature a solo wind or brass instrument playing the cantus firmus melody against the organ's decorative variants. These could be relatively simple, like *Trauer Gott, ich muss dir klagen*, where the oboe d'amore sings the theme demurely; or more florid, as in the lovely *Herr Jesu Christ, meins Lebens Licht* (with oboe). Sometimes the keyboard figurations might be quite exuberant, as in the opening chorale on this collection, *Gott der Vater wohn uns bei*, where the clarino (high trumpet) plays the tune regally against the organ's lively discourse. Krebs then went further, providing his wind players with freer, more complex concertante parts, as the two *Fantasias in F* (with oboe) demonstrate engagingly. The brass lines remain uncomplicated, yet the full horn timbre in *Es ist gewisslich an der Zeit* and the gleaming trumpet in *Wachet auf* bring added colour and interest to the music. Krebs's intricate invention in the keyboard writing sounds attractively spontaneous in the hands of Peter Hurford, whose registration is, as ever, a joy to the ear. The wind and brass players are all experts and their contributions are distinguished. The organ of Gloucester Cathedral seems eminently suited to this repertoire, and the recording is beautifully balanced and vivid. This is a collection with wide appeal.

Kreisler, Fritz (1875–1962)

Allegretto in the style of Boccherini; Allegretto in the style of Porpora; Caprice viennoise; Cavatina; La Chasse in the style of Cartier; La Gitana; Grave in the style of W. F. Bach; Gypsy caprice; Liebesfreud; Liebesleid; Praeludium and allegro in the style of Pugnani; Recitative and scherzo; Schön Rosmarin; Shepherd's madrigal; Sicilienne et rigaudon in the style of Francoeur; Toy soldiers' march; Viennese rhapsodic fantasia; arr. of *Austrian National Hymn.*
(B) **(*) ASV CDQS 6039; *ZCQS 6039* [id.]. Oscar Shumsky, Milton Kaye.

A generous (67 minutes) and well-varied bargain recital of Kreislerian encores. To open with the famous *Austrian Hymn* played as a violin solo was not a very good choice, but most of the programme comes off splendidly. Oscar Shumsky's combination of technical mastery and musical flair is ideal for this music; and it is a pity that the rather dry recording and forward balance – well in front of the piano – makes the violin sound almost too close.

Caprice viennois, Op. 2; La Gitana; Liebesfreud; Liebesleid; Polichinelle; La Précieuse; Recitativo and scherzo caprice, Op. 6; Rondo on a theme of Beethoven; Syncopation; Tambourin chinois; Zigeuner (Capriccio). Arrangements: ALBÉNIZ: *Tango, Op. 165/2.* WEBER: *Larghetto.* WIENIAWSKI: *Caprice in E flat.* DVOŘÁK: *Slavonic dance No. 10 in E min.* GLAZUNOV: *Sérénade espagnole.* GRANADOS: *Danse espagnole.*
(M) *** DG 423 876-2; *423 876-4* [id.]. Shlomo Mintz, Clifford Benson.

One can understand why DG chose to introduce Shlomo Mintz with this Kreisler programme in 1981 alongside his coupling of the Bruch and Mendelssohn *Concertos.* He plays with a disarmingly easy style and absolute technical command, to bring out the music's warmth as well as its sparkle. Try *La Gitana* to sample the playing at its most genially glittering. A very attractive programme, given first-class recording and splendid presence without added edge on CD.

Kreutzer, Joseph (*c.* 1820)

Grand Trio.
*** Mer. Dig. CDE 84199 [id.]. Conway, Silverthorne, Garcia – BEETHOVEN: *Serenade*; MOLINO: *Trio.****

Joseph Kreutzer, thought to be the brother of Rodolphe Kreutzer, dedicatee of Beethoven's *A major Violin sonata,* wrote many works for the guitar, of which this is a delightful example. The guitar, given at least equal prominence with the other instruments, brings an unusual tang to the textures of this charming piece, ending with a rousing *Alla Polacca.* A nicely pointed performance, very well recorded in warm, faithful sound.

Kuhlau, Friedrich (1786–1832)

(i) *Concertino for two horns, Op. 45;* (ii) *Piano concerto in C, Op. 7; Overture Elverhøj (The elf's hill), Op. 100.*
*** Unicorn Dig. DKPCD 9110; *DKPC 9110* [id.]. (i) Ib Lansky-Otto, Frøydis Ree Wekre; (ii) Michael Ponti; Odense SO, Othmar Maga.

No one would claim that any of Kuhlau's music has great depth, but there is a freshness and grace about it that engages one's sympathies. The overture *Elverhøj* or *The Elf's Hill* is probably his best-known work and is certainly the finest piece on the disc. The *Piano concerto in C*, Op. 7, is modelled on Beethoven's concerto in the same key and was composed in 1810, before the composer fled his native Germany for Copenhagen to avoid being drafted into the advancing Napoleonic armies. The *Concertino for two horns* (1821) is full of initially engaging, but eventually unmemorable, ideas. Very good performances from all concerned, and satisfactory recording.

Lachner, Franz (1803–90)

Septet in E flat.
*** Marco Polo Dig. 8.223282 [id.]. Ens. Villa Musica – FUCHS: *Clarinet quintet.****

Franz Lachner was a friend of Schubert, and his *Septet* dates from 1824, the same year as the Schubert *Octet.* After completing his studies in Vienna, in 1836 he moved to Munich where he remained until he was forced into early retirement by the arrival of

Wagner in 1864. The *Septet* is not great music but has an easy-going charm that is really quite winning, and it is nicely played and well recorded by this Mainz-based group.

Lalo, Eduard (1823–92)

Cello concerto No. 1 in D min., Op. 33.
(B) *** DG 431 166-2; *431 166-4* [id.]. Heinrich Schiff, New Philh. O, Mackerras – FAURÉ: *Élégie*; SAINT-SAENS: *Cello concerto No. 1.****

This was Heinrich Schiff's début recording in 1977, made when he was still very young. His account of the Lalo *Concerto* is fresh and enthusiastic and very well recorded for its period. With its excellent coupling it makes a real bargain.

Symphonie espagnole (for violin and orchestra), *Op. 21.*
(M) **(*) Sony/CBS 45555 [MYK 37811]; *40-45555.* Stern, Phd. O, Ormandy – BRUCH: *Concerto No. 1.***(*)

Stern's version from the late 1960s has all the rich, red-blooded qualities which have made this artist world-famous; indeed this coupling with the Bruch *G minor Concerto* is one of his very finest records. Reservations concerning the close solo balance are inevitable (although Ormandy's fine accompaniment is not diminished); nevertheless the playing makes a huge impact on the listener and, although the actual sound-quality is far from refined, the charisma of the performance is unforgettable. However, Perlman's brilliant and colourful version has the advantage of modern digital recording and is available at mid-price, coupled with Saint-Saëns's *Violin concerto No. 3* (DG 429 977-2; *429 977-4*).

Symphony in G min.; Rapsodie norvégienne; Le roi d'Ys: overture.
(M) *** Ph. 432 278-2; *432 278-4* [id.]. Monte Carlo Opera O, Antonio de Almeida.

Symphony in G min.; Rapsodie norvégienne; Le roi d'Ys: overture. Scherzo in D min.
** ASV Dig. CDDCA 709; *ZCDCA 709* [id.]. RPO, Yondani Butt.

Lalo's *G minor Symphony* is not the strongest of nineteenth-century French symphonies but, as this Philips reissue demonstrates, it is worth an occasional airing. Beecham was a keen champion of out-of-the-way French music of this period, and his recording with the French Radio Orchestra (which is due back in the catalogue soon) has maintained public awareness of the work. The Monte Carlo orchestra is not as impressive an orchestra as the French group; but Almeida's recording of the *Symphony* is every bit as competitive and is greatly preferable to the new digital version from Butt on ASV. Almeida observes the repeat in the first movement and plays the work with evident affection. He is a most convincing advocate, particularly in the *Adagio* and finale. Moreover the 1974 Philips recording is superior to both the early Beecham EMI and the digital ASV alternatives. Both the *Rapsodie norvégienne* (especially the exciting *Presto* secondary section) and *Le roi d'Ys* are also very well played. Almeida, though not dull, refuses to go over the top in the latter piece, to good effect.

The Schumannesque textures of the *Symphony* are not helped on ASV by a resonant ecclesiastical acoustic, with almost overwhelming Wagnerian brassiness at the end of the slow movement. Butt does his best within these somewhat oppressive acoustic surroundings, but the music fails to take off. The independent *Scherzo in D minor* is another matter and is played with fine zest. In Butt's hands *Le roi d'Ys* is endearingly melodramatic in a Gallic way; he makes the most of its somewhat vulgar scoring and is appropriately rumbustious. The *Rapsodie norvégienne* was planned as a work with a violin obbligato, and it shows. It is pleasant enough and, like the rest of this programme, is well played. But if you want the *Symphony*, the Philips reissue is the one to go for.

Lambert, Constant (1905–51)

Horoscope (ballet): *suite.*
⊛ *** Hyp. CDA 66436; *KA 66436* [id.]. E. N. Philh. O, Lloyd-Jones – BLISS: *Checkmate*; WALTON: *Façade.****

Constant Lambert was one of the great characters of British music. He had a major influence on Walton, whose *Façade* is also included in this splendid Hyperion triptych; but Lambert was also a considerable composer in his own right. The music for *Horoscope* is sheer delight, and it seems incredible that the only other complete recording of the suite was made in the mid-1950s by Irving for Decca. David Lloyd-Jones is equally sympathetic to its specifically English atmosphere. He wittily points the catchy rhythmic figure which comes both in the *Dance for the followers of Leo* and, later, in the *Bacchanale,* while the third-movement *Valse for the Gemini* has a delectable insouciant charm. Excellent playing and first-class sound, perhaps a shade resonant for the ballet pit, but bringing plenty of bloom.

Le Flem, Paul (1881–1984)

(i) *Piano quintet;* (ii) *3 Pieces for piano.*
*(*) Cybella Dig. CY 815 [id.]. (i) Centre Nat. de Musique de Chambre d'Aquitaine; (ii) Armand Bex.

When the Breton composer Paul Le Flem died a few years ago at the age of 103, there was an upsurge of interest in his music. He wrote a good deal for the stage and for the cinema, and also four symphonies, the last in 1977 when he was in his mid-90s. Le Flem studied with Vincent d'Indy, whose influence is strongly in evidence in this relatively early *Piano quintet* (1910), a long piece of some 40 minutes. The rather Debussian piano pieces (*Le Vieux Calvaire*, *Avril* and *Par Landes*) are not separately banded. They are sensitively played by Armand Bex but the recordings, made in the Château La Ligne (Gironde) ideally need a rather more spacious acoustic. The performance of the *Quintet* is decent – no more – and, generally speaking, readers will find the idiom sympathetic but the work overlong.

Leoncavallo, Ruggiero (1858–1919)

La Bohème (complete).
* Nuova Era Dig. 6917/19 [id.]. Praticò, Senn, Lucia Malagnini, Mario Malagnini, Summers, Pagliuca, Spagnoli, Emili, Grazioli, De Mola, Ch. & O del Teatro La Fenice, Jan Latham-Koenig.

Jan Latham-Koenig makes a persuasive case for this 'other' *Bohème*, drawing lively, sharply pointed playing from his Venice orchestra. Yet in its timing and dramatic layout – with Mimi in the mezzo role stealing the final scene from the soprano–tenor duo of Musetta and Marcello – this cannot compare with Puccini. Despite the vigour, and some good singing from the men – Bruno Praticò as Schaunard, Mario Malagnini as Marcello and Jonathan Summers as the baritone Rodolfo – this is a seriously flawed set. The stage noises in this live recording are thunderous, the prompter keeps interrupting, and the orchestra is backwardly balanced with voices dry and close. Worst of all, Martha Senn makes a shrill and fluttery Musetta, and the mezzo, Lucia Malagnini, is barely more acceptable as Mimi. The opera is extravagantly laid out on three discs, when Acts II and III could easily have been contained on a single disc.

I Pagliacci (complete).
(M) **(*) EMI CMS7 63650-2 (2). Scotto, Carreras, Nurmela, Amb. Op. Ch., Philh. O, Muti – MASCAGNI: *Cavalleria Rusticana.***(*)

Under Muti's urgent direction both *Cav.* and *Pag.* represent the music of violence. In both he has sought to use the original text, which in *Pag.* is often surprisingly different, with many top notes eliminated and Tonio instead of Canio delivering (singing, not speaking) the final *La commedia è finita.* Muti's approach represents the antithesis of smoothness, and the coarse rendering of the *Prologue* in *Pag.* by the rich-toned Kari Nurmela is disappointing. Scotto's Nedda goes raw above the stave, but the edge is in keeping with Muti's approach, with its generally brisk speeds. Carreras seems happier here than in *Cav.*, but it is the conductor and the fresh look he brings which will prompt a personal choice here. The sound is extremely vivid.

I Pagliacci: highlights.
(B) *** DG Compact Classics *427 717-4* [id.] (from complete recording with Joan Carlyle, Bergonzi, Benelli, Taddei, La Scala Milan Ch. & O, Karajan) – MASCAGNI: *Cavalleria Rusticana*: Highlights.***
(M) ** Decca 421 870-2; *421 870-4* [id.]. Freni, Pavarotti, Wixell, L. Op. Ch., Nat. PO, Patanè – MASCAGNI: *Cavalleria Rusticana*: highlights.**

Karajan's refined approach to Leoncavallo is matched by fine singing from all the principals and, with all the key items from the opera included, this is a very attractive Compact Classics tape coupling. The sound is excellent, although the choral focus is rather soft-grained.

On Decca, a reasonably generous coupling of excerpts from *Cav.* and *Pag.* with about half an hour from each opera. The sound is extremely lively and vivid, even if the performances are flawed. Pavarotti is obviously committed, though in both operas he seems reluctant to sing anything but loud. Voices are recorded rather close, and Freni is not helped by the balance, not as sweet-sounding as she usually is.

Leuning, Otto (born 1900)

(i) *Legend;* (ii) *Lyric scene.*
** ASV CDDCA 741; *ZCDCA 741* [id.]. (i) Erik Larsen; (ii) Per Oien; Oslo PO, José Serebrier – MENOTTI: *Sebastian.***

Otto Leuning is one of the leading protagonists of electronic music, which he first heard about as a student of Busoni. However, neither the *Legend*, for oboe and orchestra, nor the *Lyric scene*, for flute, composed in memory of Busoni, is in the least unconventional; even though they do not betray a strong musical personality, they are nevertheless pleasing, well-wrought compositions. The recording is decent rather than distinguished.

Liszt, Franz (1811–86)

Piano concertos Nos. 1–2; Fantasia on Hungarian folk songs (for piano & orchestra).
*** RCA Dig. RD 87916 [7916-2-RC]. Barry Douglas, LSO, Hirokami.

Piano concertos Nos. (i) *1 in E flat;* (ii) *2 in A; Années de pèlerinage: Sonetto 104 del Petrarca. Hungarian rhapsody No. 6; Valse oubliée.*
(M) *** Mercury 432 002-2 [id.]. Byron Janis, (i) Moscow PO, Kondrashin; (ii) Moscow RSO, Rozhdestvensky (also with SCHUMANN: *Romance in F sharp; Novellette in F.* FALLA: *Miller's dance.* GUION: *The harmonica player* ***).

Piano concertos Nos. 1 and 2; Étude transcendante d'après Paganini.
(B) **(*) DG Compact Classics 413 850-2 (2); *413 850-4* [id.]. Vásáry, Bamberg SO, Prohaska – RACHMANINOV: *Piano concerto No. 2* etc.** (CD only: *Piano concerto No. 1* **).

Barry Douglas gives a very creditable account of both *Concertos* and commands a wide variety of keyboard colour. He keeps the flamboyant showmanship in hand and a shows a good deal of poetic feeling; his readings are well thought out and never unimaginative. However, these performances do not have the stature of Zimerman's, which remain a first recommendation among the more recent versions (DG 423 571-2; *423 571-4*), or Brendel's (Philips 426 637-2; *426 637-4*). These artists share the same coupling, with the *Totentanz.* Richter has something very special to say about this music, too, but his record from the early 1960s now seems expensive at full price (Philips 412 006-2).

Around the time they were recording Richter's Liszt *Concertos* for Philips in London, the Mercury engineers paid a visit to Moscow to record Byron Janis in the same repertoire, and his is a comparably distinguished coupling. The partnership between the soloist and both his Russian conductors is unusually close. Janis's glittering articulation is matched by his sense of poetry and drama, and there is plenty of dash in these very compelling performances, which are afforded characteristically brilliant Mercury sound, although the piano is too close. The encores which follow the two *Concertos* are also very enjoyable.

The generously coupled Compact Classics tape offers three concertos, plus solo items, and – while Vásáry's version of the Rachmaninov *C minor* is less impressive than his Liszt – this is still good value. His recording of Liszt's *E flat Concerto* still sounds very well indeed; the performance is distinguished by considerable subtlety and refinement, yet with no loss of impact, even if there is little barnstorming. His approach to the *A major,* too, is thoughtful and sensitive. The accompaniments under Prohaska are sympathetic and the 1960 sound remains vivid, clear and full. On the digitally remastered pair of CDs another concerto is added, and the Vásáry/Ahronovitch performance of Rachmaninov's *First* is agreeably impulsive and alive.

Piano concerto No. 1 in E flat.
(M) *** EMI/Phoenixa CDM7 63778-2; *EG 763778-4.* Richard Farrell, Hallé O, Weldon – GRIEG: *Concerto* etc.**(*)
(B) **(*) Sony MBK 44803 [id.]. Charles Rosen, New Philh. O, Pritchard – CHOPIN: *Concerto No. 2.***

Even more than in the coupled Grieg, Liszt's *E flat Concerto* shows the flair and poetry of Richard Farrell's playing, and George Weldon is inspired to provide an equally charismatic accompaniment. The warm, poetic feeling of the *Poco adagio* is matched by the skittish wit of the scherzo and the dash and power of the finale. Fine recording, too. This record is a real bargain.

Rosen's performance of the *E flat major Concerto* is most impressive, dashing and poetic, and very well accompanied by Pritchard. The recording is extremely vivid, especially in the vivacious scherzo, if a shade lacking in refinement.

Piano concerto No. 2 in A.
*** Virgin Dig. VC7 91198-2; *VC7 91198-4* [id.]. Leif Ove Andsnes, Bergen PO, Dmitri Kitaenko – GRIEG: *Piano concerto* etc.***
(BB) **(*) Pickwick PWK 1154. Katchen, LSO, Gamba – MENDELSSOHN: *Piano concerto No. 1.***(*)

Leif Ove Andsnes is a gifted young Norwegian player who is far more than just another boy wonder with dazzling fingers – though he certainly has them. There is no lack of display and bravura in the Liszt but no narcissistic ostentation. Indeed he is a real musician who plays with great tenderness and poetic feeling as well as bravura. Marvellous sound, too, with a piano in perfect condition (not always the case on records) and an excellent balance. The Bergen Philharmonic under their newly appointed Soviet conductor are obviously in good shape and give eminently sympathetic support. This is as good as any version now before the collector.

Katchen's is a commanding performance of the *A major Concerto*, and Gamba provides admirable support. This is exciting music-making, showing the pianist in his best light. But Katchen is even better in the *First Concerto*, which he recorded at the same time, and one can only lament its absence here. There would have been plenty of room for it, as the CD plays for only 41 minutes! But this disc is offered at super-bargain price and the (originally Decca) recording, although dating from the very earliest days of stereo, is very good.

(i) *Fantasia on Hungarian folk tunes; Hungarian rhapsodies Nos. 2 & 5; Mephisto waltz.*
(M) *** DG 419 862-2 [id.]. (i) Shura Cherkassky; BPO, Karajan.

This Galleria mid-priced CD duplicates three of the items on the bargain disc listed in our main volume (429 156-2). The *Mephisto waltz* is now added, brilliantly played and used to introduce the rest of the programme.

A Faust Symphony.
(M) *** DG 431 470-2; *431 470-4* [id.]. Kenneth Riegel, Tanglewood Festival Ch., Boston SO, Bernstein.
(M) *** EMI Dig. CDC7 49062-2. Winberg, Westminster Ch., College Male Ch., Phd. O, Muti.

Bernstein recorded this symphony in the mid-1960s; but this 1976 version, made in Boston, is both more sensitive and more brilliant. Indeed, from the very opening its adrenalin surge is compelling – it was the first modern recording to challenge Beecham's classic account, made in 1959. The DG sound is considerably superior and many will now consider it the best buy for this work, which can be as elusive in the concert hall as in the recording studio. Bernstein seems to possess the ideal temperament for holding together grippingly the melodrama of the first movement, while the lovely *Gretchen* centrepiece is played most beautifully (the Boston woodwind are an aural delight) with finely delineated detail and refined textures. Kenneth Riegel is an impressive tenor soloist in the finale, there is an excellent, well-balanced choral contribution, and the Boston Symphony Orchestra produce playing which is both exciting and atmospheric. The vividness of the recording overall is most compelling, and listening to the CD is undoubtedly a thrilling experience.

Muti's digital recording has been reissued for his fiftieth birthday, but at full price. As an ardent Tchaikovskian, he shows a natural sympathy for a piece which can readily seem over-long, and he finds obvious affinities in the music with the style of the Russian master. Some might feel that he is too overtly melodramatic in the finale, yet his pacing of the first movement is admirable, finding tenderness as well as red-blooded excitement. In the *Gretchen* movement he conjures the most delicately atmospheric playing from the orchestra, and throughout he is helped by the ambience of the Old Met. in Philadelphia, which seems especially suitable for this score. The digital recording is brilliant yet full-bodied, and without glare.

Symphonic poems: *Hungaria; Mazeppa; Les Préludes; Tasso, lamento e trionfo.*
(M) ** Ph. 426 636-2; *426 636-4* [id.]. LPO, Haitink.

Haitink recorded all Liszt's symphonic poems with the LPO at the end of the 1960s, with variable amounts of success. The music of *Mazeppa, Les Préludes* and *Tasso* creates its scenic backgrounds with bold strokes of the brush. Haitink rather shirks the melodrama, but the LPO catches the music's idiom without self-consciousness, and *Hungaria* is effective with a limited degree of flamboyance. The added vividness of the CD transfer is certainly an advantage, and some listeners will enjoy *Les Préludes* with the rhetoric understated; but the dramatic denouement of *Mazeppa* is far more thrilling in Karajan's hands.

Hungarian rhapsodies Nos. 1–6.
(M) **(*) Mercury 432 015-2 [id.]. LSO, Dorati – ENESCU: *Roumanian rhapsody No. 1.****

Dorati's is undoubtedly the finest set of orchestral *Hungarian rhapsodies.* He brings out the gypsy flavour and, with lively playing from the LSO, there is both polish and sparkle, but the music does not become urbane. The use of the cimbalom within the orchestra brings an authentic extra colouring. The Mercury recording is characteristically vivid, if not quite as full in the upper range as we would expect today.

Hungarian rhapsody No. 2 in C sharp min.; Les Préludes.
(B) *** EMI CDZ7 62860-2; *LZ 762860 4* [id.]. Philh. O, Karajan – MUSSORGSKY: *Pictures.****

Karajan's 1958 *Les Préludes* is second to none, exciting without brashness and superbly played. The recording hardly sounds dated at all and the *Hungarian rhapsody* is very successful too.

Hungarian rhapsodies Nos. 2 and 4; Les Préludes.
(B) *** DG Compact Classics *413 159-4* [id.]. BPO, Karajan – DVOŘÁK: *Slavonic dances;* SMETANA: *Vltava* etc.***

Karajan is completely at home in this repertoire. He goes over the top in *Les Préludes,* not helped by a very brightly lit recording which manages to make even the Berlin Philharmonic sound brash; but in the rest of the music here he secures marvellous playing and fine characterization. The approach to the *Hungarian rhapsodies* is somewhat urbane, yet there is plenty of sparkle. On this excellently engineered Compact Classics tape, these three popular works are featured as part of a well-organized anthology of Slavonic music.

SOLO PIANO MUSIC

Années de pèlerinage: 2nd Year (Italy): Sonetti del Petrarca Nos. 47; 104; 123. 3 Concert studies: Il lamento; La leggierezza; Un sospiro. Liebesträume Nos. 1–3.
** Conifer Dig. CDCF 180; *MCFC 180* [id.]. Kathryn Stott.

Kathryn Stott has already given us successful popular groupings of the music of

Debussy (Conifer CDCF 148; *MCFC 148*), Fauré (CDCF 138; *MCFC 138*) and Rachmaninov (CDCF 159; *MCFC 159*); by comparison with those recitals, this Liszt collection is a little disappointing. She plays with plenty of romantic feeling, indeed rather too much, and the *Tre sonetti del Petrarca* need a firmer profile. Even the most famous of the three *Liebesträume* and *Un sospiro* seem to gush a little, although technically the performances are impressive. Fine piano-sound; if you like highly romanticized Liszt, this will undoubtedly fit the bill.

Chorales: Crux ave benedicta; Jesus Christe; Meine Seele; Nun danket alle Gott; Nun ruhen all Walder; O haupt; O Lamm Gottes; O Traurigkeit; Vexilla Regis; Was Gott tut; Wer nur den Lieben. Via Crucis; Weihnachtsbaum.
**(*) Hyp. Dig. CDA 66388 [id.]. Leslie Howard.

Concert paraphrases: Berlioz: *L'Idée fixe; Overtures: Les Francs-Juges; Roi Lear; Marche des pèlerins; Valse des Sylphes.* Chopin: *6 Chants polonais.* Saint-Saëns: *Danse macabre.*
**(*) Hyp. Dig. CDA 66346 [id.]. Leslie Howard.

Leslie Howard is currently in the process of recording Liszt's entire output for the piano, and he is doing so with some considerable success. The Hyperion series has been honoured with a *Prix du disque* in Budapest itself. Howard has impressive technical address, though he does not always command the imagination and poetry one finds in some of the great pianists who have recorded this demanding repertoire. He rarely takes one's breath away either by his virtuosity or poetic insight, yet his playing is unfailingly intelligent and offers much to admire. He is very well recorded too.

Harmonies poétiques et religieuses: Funérailles; Mephisto waltz No. 1; Hungarian rhapsody No. 12.
(M) (**(*)) Decca mono 425 961-2 [id.]. Julius Katchen – BALAKIREV: *Islamey*; MUSSORGSKY: *Pictures.*(**(*))

Julius Katchen's impressive pianistic fireworks are heard to excellent effect in this generous recital. He recorded the Liszt in 1953–4 and, though the sound is now no longer of the highest quality, Katchen's pianism and musicianship still sing loud and clear.

Piano sonata in B min; Années de pèlerinages, 2nd Year (Italy): Après une lecture de Dante (Dante sonata); Harmonies poétiques et religieuses: Invocation; La lugubre gondola, Nos. 1–2.
(M) *** Ph Dig. 432 048-2; *432 048-4* [id.]. Alfred Brendel.

Brendel's latest account of the *Sonata* has received wide acclaim. It is certainly a more subtle and concentrated account than his earlier version, made in the mid-1960s – brilliant though that was – and must be numbered among the best now available. There is a wider range of colour and tonal nuance, yet the undoubted firmness of grip does not seem achieved at the expense of any spontaneity. It is most realistically recorded.

Lloyd, George (born 1913)

Piano concertos Nos. 1 (Scapegoat); 2.
* Albany Dig. TROY 037-2; *TROY 037-4* [id.]. Martin Roscoe, BBC PO, composer.

George Lloyd's first two *Piano concertos* exist in very much their own world and are a curious amalgam of scherzando elements, lyricism and bursts of violence. But Lloyd's violence has none of the harsh asperities of the contemporary avant-garde. The *First Concerto*, nicknamed *Scapegoat*, in the composer's words 'attempts to give an impression of the feelings aroused during the period I have lived through', with obvious allusions to the Second World War. The concerto was written with the late John Ogdon in mind, and he gave its first performance. The *Second Concerto*, like the *First*, is in a single movement and has a mood of 'gleeful viciousness' with a dance-like motif (associated with an image of Hitler 'dancing a sort of jig in triumph') and running the gamut of various moods and tempo changes, 'binding together cantabile sections, a tragic and violent cadenza, a sad slow central piece, and a military evocation'. Martin Roscoe played for its première and it is he who, under the composer's direction, gives brilliant, vividly spontaneous accounts of both *Concertos*, with the BBC Philharmonic Orchestra responding splendidly. The recording is most convincingly balanced and speaks well for the acoustics of Studio 7 in Broadcasting House, Manchester, where it was made.

Piano concerto No. 3.
**(*) Albany Dig. TROY 019-2; *TROY 019-4* [id.]. Kathryn Stott, BBC PO, composer.

The *Third Piano concerto*, also inspired by events during the Second World War, is more amiable than one might expect, after the first two. It is very eclectic in style, with flavours of Prokofiev (with diluted abrasiveness) and even of Khachaturian – minus vulgarity – in outer movements which have a toccata-like brilliance and momentum. Kathryn Stott plays with a pleasing, mercurial lightness and makes the most of the music's lyrical feeling. But the slow movement – which recalls 'the knock on the door at midnight that terrorised the countries occupied by Hitler' – is too long (19½ minutes) and its passionate climax uses material which does not show Lloyd at his best. On the other hand, the wistful tune at the centre of the finale is rather appealing. The composer achieves a fine partnership with his soloist and the performance has undoubted spontaneity. But one wonders whether a virtuoso of the calibre of Kissin or Pletnev would add more force and power to the outer movements.

Symphonies Nos. 1 in A; 12.
*** Albany Dig. TROY 032-2; *TROY 032-4* [id.]. Albany SO, composer.

The pairing of George Lloyd's first and last symphonies is particularly appropriate, as both share a theme-and-variations format. The *First*, written in 1932 but recently revised, is relatively lightweight, it is based on a rhythmically catchy main theme, and the variations fall naturally into three basic sections: fast–slow–fast. The mature *Twelfth* uses the same basic layout but ends calmly with a ravishingly sustained pianissimo, semi-Mahlerian in intensity, that is among the composer's most beautiful inspirations. At the beginning of the work, the listener is soon aware of the noble lyrical theme which is the very heart of the *Symphony*. The Albany Symphony Orchestra gave the work its première and they play it with enormous conviction and eloquence. The concentration of the music-making throughout is that of a live performance, helped by the superb acoustics of the Troy Savings Bank Music Hall, which produces sound of demonstration quality, glowing in warmth and sonority and with the most vivid detail. The symphony is full of attractive orchestral effects and shows Lloyd at his very finest. This record therefore makes an admirable starting point for anyone wishing to begin an exploration of the music of a composer who communicates readily and who has already assembled a growing public of admiring music-lovers who find a great deal of contemporary writing totally inaccessible.

Symphony No. 5 in B flat.
*** Albany Dig. TROY 022-2; *TROY 022-4* [id.]. BBC PO, composer.

The *Fifth Symphony* is a large canvas, with five strong and contrasted movements, adding up to nearly an hour of music. It was written during a happy summer spent living simply on the shore of Lac Neuchâtel, during the very hot summer of 1947. The pastoral scene is well caught in the idyll of the first movement. After a Chorale second movement comes a will-o'-the-wisp Rondo (marked *Delicatamente scherzando*) and then a Lamento, march-like, with a powerful climax. In the finale the composer tells us: 'everything is brought in to make as exhilarating a sound as possible – strong rhythms, vigorous counterpoints, energetic brass and percussion'. The movement is loosely structured and is the least cogent part of a work which is strong in invention and orchestral colour. It is played with much commitment by the BBC Philharmonic under the composer, who creates a feeling of spontaneously live music-making throughout. The recording is first class.

The Vigil of Venus (Pervigilium Veneris).
*** Argo Dig. 430 329-2; *430 329-4* [id.]. Carolyn James, Thomas Booth, Welsh Nat. Op. Ch. & O, composer.

Following up the success of his recordings of his symphonies, George Lloyd here directs Welsh National Opera forces in this ambitious oratorio. Here, as in the symphonies, he thumbs his nose at fashion in a score which both pulses with energy and cocoons the ear in opulent sounds. Delian ecstasy is contrasted against the occasional echo of Carl Orff, an attractive mixture, even if – for all the incidental beauties – there is dangerously little variety of mood in the nine substantial sections. The composer was not entirely happy with what he was able to achieve in that first recording; even so, his performance certainly does not lack intensity and the recording is excellent, given the inherent problems of the recording venue in Swansea.

Lloyd Webber, Andrew (born 1948)

Variations Nos. 1–4; Requiem: Pie Jesu. Excerpts from: *Amazing Technicolor Dreamcoat; Aspects of Love; Cats; Evita; Jesus Christ Superstar; Phantom of the Opera; Starlight Express; Tell me on a Sunday* (all arr. Cullen).
**(*) Ph. 432 291-2; *432 291-4* [id.]. Julian Lloyd Webber, RPO, Wordsworth.

The idea of Julian Lloyd Webber providing a concertante collection of his brother's more famous tunes was commercially irresistible, and the credentials of the performers here are impeccable, with rhythm, guitars and synthesizers added to the main orchestral group where appropriate. But the results are rather mixed. The characterful, if rather vulgar *Variations* have plenty of impact, but otherwise the performers don't seem to have warmed up fully in the first half of the programme, and even the famous *Memory* from *Cats* produces a rather cool response from the solo cello. *Music of the night* is pleasing, if restrained; but it is from *Don't cry for me, Argentina* onwards that the music-making springs to life. Here Julian Lloyd Webber, at his most eloquent, is accompanied lusciously by the RPO strings, and they join him again very elegantly in the delightful pastiche, *The first man you remember*, an engaging hit from *Aspects of Love. All I ask of you* (from *Phantom*) is warmly romantic and *Tell me on a Sunday*, one of the composer's most indelible ideas, is equally expressive. *Close every door* (from *Joseph*) lies particularly well for the cello; after the vibrant excerpt from *Jesus Christ Superstar*, which produces both special effects and another fine lyrical idea, the programme ends with the lovely *Pie Jesu* from the *Requiem*, given with a moving simplicity. Good, vivid recording.

Lutoslawski, Witold (born 1916)

Concerto for orchestra; Funeral music for string orchestra; Venetian games.
(M) ** Ph. 426 663-2 [id.]. Warsaw Nat. PO, Rowicki.

The Lutoslawski *Concerto* is a brilliant, inventively scored work; its idiom is accessible and the ideas have character. It plumbs no great depths – but then nor do the composer's later and less accessible works. Rowicki gives it a thoroughly idiomatic performance and secures playing of real brilliance from the Warsaw orchestra. The *Funeral music* is an angular and rather empty piece whose feelings seem to reside very much on the surface. *Venetian games*, a work that contains randomly generated interpolations, is quite an attractive piece. Both are well played here. The recording is good but the strings are not ideally lustrous, and overall the sound could use a more vivid colouring.

MacDowell, Edward (1861–1908)

Piano concertos Nos. 1 in A min., Op. 15; 2 in D min., Op. 23.
❀ *** Olympia Dig. OCD 353 [id.]; Archduke *MARC 1*. Donna Amato, LPO, Paul Freeman.

Donna Amato's performances have polish and elegance as well as fire, and it is good to welcome them back to the catalogue on the Olympia label.

Magnard, Albéric (1865–1914)

Symphonies Nos. 1 in C min., Op. 4; 3 in B flat min., Op. 11.
*** EMI Dig. CDC7 54015-2 [id.]. Capitole Toulouse O, Plasson.

After a long period of neglect, Albéric Magnard is at last coming into his own. All four symphonies are now on record, though we have found copies of the *Second* hard to trace and the *Fourth* is currently awaiting reissue by EMI. Ansermet recorded the *Third* in the 1960s, but the new version by the Orchestre du Capitole de Toulouse under Michel Plasson is in every way superior. The work comes from the mid-1890s and has a sustained nobility and dignity that strike one from the very opening bars. This music has the breath and pulse of real symphonism and, of the four major French successors of César Franck (the others being Chausson, Vincent d'Indy and Dukas), Magnard is in some ways the most impressive. The music radiates integrity, a sense of purposeful movement and a strong personality that make his premature death all the more tragic (he was shot while defending his home from the invading Germans early in 1914). His *First Symphony* (1889–90) was composed in the shadow of his friend and mentor, Vincent d'Indy, and follows more strictly cyclical principles. Yet its ideas still show individuality and character, even though there is a strong post-Wagnerian aftertaste. There is a magical passage of almost Brucknerian mystery, about 7 minutes into the first movement, which is really quite inspired. Michel Plasson directs and his Toulouse orchestra play with strong sympathy and conviction; the recording, though a bit reverberant, is eminently acceptable.

Mahler, Gustav (1860–1911)

Symphony No. 1 in D min.
*** DG Dig. 429 228-2 [id.]. Philh. O, Sinopoli.

*(*) Decca Dig. 425 718-2; *425 718-4* [id.]. Cleveland O, Dohnányi.
*(*) Virgin Dig. VC7 91096-2; *VC7 91096-4* [id.]. Minnesota O, Edo de Waart.
(B) * Pickwick Dig. PCD 941; *CIMPC 941*. LSO, Yondani Butt.

Sinopoli's is a warmly satisfying reading, passionately committed, with refined playing from the Philharmonia. Unlike Dohnányi, Sinopoli in his fine control allows the fullest expressiveness, with bold, theatrical gestures thrust home purposefully. The sound is rich and refined to match, with the orchestra set at a slight distance, though not enough to lose impact.

With immaculate ensemble in brilliant, full-bodied sound, the Dohnányi version should be more convincing than it is. One admires without being moved. This is Mahler viewed from one remove instead of from the inside, too firmly controlled to let the full emotion emerge.

Edo de Waart's reading with the Minneapolis Orchestra is disappointingly matter-of-fact, lacking tension for much of the time. The finale is better, but still cannot match the finest versions.

Yondani Butt's version for IMP brings bold and brassy playing from the LSO but lacks rhythmic subtlety. Little spring is given to the Wunderhorn themes, and even the great melody in the finale is treated prosaically. The recording, made by EMI engineers at Walthamstow, is full and vivid, but the reverberation seriously obscures detail in rapid passages, notably in the first movement. However, first choice still remains with Bernstein and the Concertgebouw Orchestra, who give a wonderfully alert and imaginative performance, very well recorded (DG 431 036-2; *431 036-4*).

Symphonies Nos. 1; (i) *2.*
(M) **(*) Decca 425 005-2 (2) [id.]. (i) Harper, Watts, LSO Ch.; LSO, Solti.

We have long been admirers of Solti's 1964 LSO account of Mahler's *First Symphony* and it is high on our list of recommendations (Decca 417 701-2). Now it reappears in the Solti Edition coupled with No. 2, which was also recorded in the Kingsway Hall two years later. It remains a demonstration of the outstanding results Decca were securing with analogue techniques at that time, although on CD the sharpness of focus (especially in No. 2) and the brilliance of the fortissimos, emphasized by the wide dynamic range, may not suit all ears. Yet in the slow *Ländler* of the second movement the clarity means that Solti can bring superb refinement of detail and a precise control of dynamic; while again in the third movement he concentrates with hushed intensity on precise control of dynamic and atmosphere; the natural ambience of the Kingsway Hall recording is particularly striking here. Helen Watts is wonderfully expressive in the chorale, conveying real inner feeling, while the chorus has a rapt intensity that is the more telling when the recording perspectives are so clearly delineated.

Symphony No. 2 in C min. (Resurrection).
(M) (**) Decca mono 425 970-2 [id.]. Vincent, Ferrier, Amsterdam Toonkunstkoor, Concg. O, Klemperer.

It is fascinating to eavesdrop on Klemperer's live performance, recorded from Dutch Radio on 12 July 1951, towards the end of Kathleen Ferrier's brief career. The mono sound is limited but reasonably clear. What is disappointing is the lack of that very quality one looks for in a live performance, the drive and thrust which are often difficult to recapture in the studio. Only in the final movement with its vision of heaven does the magic quality at last emerge at full intensity; but even there the later, Philharmonia studio performance gives a more complete idea of Klemperer's genius (EMI CDM7 69662-2; *EG*

769662-4), and elsewhere there is no question of the superiority of the studio account, one of the conductor's strongest statements. The soloists are wonderfully characterful, Vincent as well as Ferrier. These are the two who appeared in the first performance of Britten's *Spring Symphony*, and they here provide the best justification for hearing the set. Klemperer's modern version is a superb bargain, being on a single, mid-priced CD or tape; but even so, first choice of the *Resurrection Symphony* rests with Simon Rattle's reading with the CBSO, among the very finest records he has yet made, superlative in the breadth and vividness of its sound and including Arleen Augér and Dame Janet Baker as its distinguished soloists (EMI CDS7 47962-8 [Angel CDCB 47962]; *EX 747962-4*).

Symphony No. 3 in D min.
*(*) DG Dig. 427 328-2; *427 328-4* (2) [id.]. Ludwig, NY Ch. Artists, Brooklyn Boys' Ch., NYPO, Bernstein.
(M) *(*) Decca 414 254-2 (2) [id.]. Helen Watts, Amb. Ch., Boys from Wandsworth School, LSO, Solti.

With sound lacking bloom and a performance less spontaneous-sounding than usual from him, Bernstein's DG version of No. 3, made in New York, is one of the less successful of his later Mahler series. Expressive gestures seem exaggerated, failing to match the weight of emotion implied. This is no match for the Abbado version on the same label (410 715-2), while Tilson Thomas on CBS/Sony provides a substantial bonus in the *Rückert Lieder*, sung by Dame Janet Baker (M2K 44553).

In Solti's earlier series of Mahler recordings for Decca with the LSO, the *Third Symphony* brought disappointment, notably in the brassy and extrovert account of the last movement, all the more apparent on CD. That movement in the digital, Chicago version (Decca 414 268-2 - see our main Volume, pp. 578–9) is transformed, hushed and intense and deeply concentrated, building up superbly, even though the hastening is a shade excessive towards the end.

Symphony No. 4 in G.
(M) *** DG 419 863-2; *419 863-4* [id.]. Edith Mathis, BPO, Karajan.
(M) **(*) Chan. Dig. CHAN 6505; *MBTD 6505* [id.]. Margaret Marshall, SNO, Gibson.
(B) ** DG 431 165-2; *431 165-4* [id.]. Elsie Morison, Bav. RSO, Rafael Kubelik.

Karajan's refined and poised, yet undoubtedly affectionate account remains among the finest versions of this lovely symphony, and Edith Mathis's sensitively composed contribution to the finale matches the conductor's meditative feeling. With glowing sound, this makes an outstanding mid-priced recommendation alongside Szell's renowned Cleveland CD with Judith Raskin (see below).

Gibson has the advantage of modern digital recording and the warm acoustic of the Henry Wood Hall in the SNO Centre, Glasgow, which conveys the breadth and clarity of the sound impressively within an attractive ambient bloom. There is some delightfully fresh and stylish playing from the Scottish orchestra and this is a characteristically unmannered reading, slightly wanting in dramatic grip but not in tenderness. The finale, however, lacks some of the repose necessary in this child-song, with Margaret Marshall sounding a little tense.

The Bavarian orchestra phrase beautifully for Kubelik, and their playing has great vitality. With generally faster tempi than is common, the effect is light and luminous, with a charming, boyish account of the final song from Elsie Morison. This is fair value at bargain price, but the bright CD transfer means that the 1968 recording, though not lacking ambient warmth, shows its age a little in the violin timbre.

(i) *Symphony No. 4 in G;* (ii) *Lieder eines fahrenden Gesellen.*
(M) *** Sony SBK 46535 [id.]; *40-46535.* (i) Judith Raskin, Cleveland O, Szell; (ii) Frederica von Stade, LPO, Andrew Davis.

Reissued on Sony's 'Essential Classics' label, for once the sobriquet is fully justified. George Szell's 1966 record of Mahler's *Fourth* represented his partnership with the Cleveland Orchestra at its highest peak. The digital remastering for CD brings out the very best of the original recording, making it sound translucently clear, yet without losing the ambient warmth. The performance remains uniquely satisfying: the interpretation has an element of coolness but the music blossoms, partly because of the marvellous attention to detail (and the immaculate ensemble) but more positively because of the committed and radiantly luminous orchestral response to the music itself. In the finale Szell found the ideal soprano to match his conception: Judith Raskin sings without artifice, and her voice has an open colouring like a child's, yet the feminine quality subtly remains. An outstanding choice in the mid-price range and comparable with the finest premium-priced versions. In contrast with most other recorded performances, Frederica von Stade insinuates a hint of youthful ardour into her highly enjoyable account of the *Wayfaring Lad* cycle. If the playing of the LPO under Andrew Davis seems at times to lack refinement, this is partly the fault of close analogue recording.

Symphony No. 5 in C sharp min.
(M) *** EMI Dig. CD-EMX 2164; *TC-EMX 2164.* Royal Liverpool PO, Mackerras.
**(*) Chan. Dig. CHAN 8829; *ABTD 1454* [id.]. SNO, Järvi.
(M) **(*) Decca 430 443-2; *430 443-4* [id.]. Chicago SO, Solti.
(M) *(*) Ph. 426 638-2; *426 638-4* [id.]. Leipzig GO, Neumann.

With brilliant, refined playing from the Liverpool orchestra, in warm, well-detailed sound, the Mackerras version at mid-price on Eminence is a match for any in the catalogue at whatever price, whether in performance or recording. Mackerras in his well-paced reading sees the work as a whole, building each movement with total concentration. There is a thrilling culmination on the great brass chorale at the end, with polish allied to purposefulness. Barbirolli in his classic reading (EMI CDM7 69186-2; *EG 769186-4*) may find more of a tear-laden quality in the great *Adagietto*; but Mackerras, with fewer controversial points of interpretation and superb modern sound, makes an excellent first choice.

Järvi directs a characteristically red-blooded, spontaneous-sounding reading with the SNO, wild at times, not always immaculate in ensemble or consistently concentrated, but with opulent sound generally satisfying.

Solti's 1971 reading (see our main volume, pp. 581–3) has been reissued at mid-price as part of the 'Solti Collection'. There is some very beautiful playing here, but this cannot be recommended in preference to Barbirolli's inspirational version with the New Philharmonia Orchestra in the same price-range.

Recorded in 1966, Neumann's version offers a polished, well-mannered reading on the Philips mid-price label, though Western ears may well find the fruity vibrato of the brass uncongenial. The CD transfer is rather edgy, with high tape-hiss.

Symphony No.6 in A min.
*** Ph. Dig. 426 257-2 [id.]. BPO, Haitink – *Lieder eines fahrenden Gesellen.****
*** Decca Dig. 430 165-2; *430 165-4* (2) [id.]. Concg. O, Chailly – ZEMLINSKY: *Maeterlinck Lieder.****

**(*) EMI Dig. CDS7 54047-2 (2) [Ang. CDCB 54047]; *EX 754047-4*. CBSO, Simon Rattle.

Haitink conducts a noble reading of this difficult symphony, underplaying the neurosis behind the inspiration, but, in his clean-cut concentration and avoidance of exaggeration, making the result the more moving in its degree of reticence. This is a far finer reading than the one he conducted earlier with the Concertgebouw, thanks largely to the playing of the Berlin Philharmonic, beautiful, polished and, above all, intensely committed. Jessye Norman's rich-toned account of *Lieder eines fahrenden Gesellen* makes a powerful bonus. Excellent sound, both full-blooded and refined.

Chailly's version with the Concertgebouw offers brilliant playing and spectacular sound in a reading remarkable for the broad, rugged approach in the outer movements. There is relentlessness in the slow speed for the first movement, with expressive warmth giving way to a square purposefulness, tense and effective. The third movement brings a comparably simple, direct approach at a genuine flowing *Andante*. In its open songfulness it rouses Wunderhorn echoes. Anyone fancying the unexpected but attractive Zemlinsky coupling need not hesitate.

At spacious speeds Rattle directs a thoughtful, finely detailed reading of what has become a favourite symphony for him. The performance yet lacks the electric tension which usually marks his work with this orchestra, with ensemble less crisp. One admires without being involved in the way Mahler demands, even in Rattle's tender and hushed account of the slow movement, which he places second in the scheme instead of third, following Mahler's last thoughts on the work rather than what is published. It was thoughtless of EMI, therefore, to divide the two-disc set between slow movement and scherzo, so preventing the listener from programming whichever order he or she prefers, as can be done on rival sets. The sound is full and warm but in its diffuseness undermines tension further compared with the finest versions.

Symphony No. 7 in E min.
*** Ph. Dig. 426 249-2; *426 249-4* (2) [id.]. Boston SO, Seiji Ozawa – *Kindertotenlieder*.***

With the sound forward and immediate, Ozawa directs a warmly persuasive account of Mahler's most problematical symphony. It may lack the purposefulness of Abbado or the rugged strength of Bernstein, but the work has never sounded more beautiful, with the two *Nachtmusik* movements played impressionistically. In the outer movements Ozawa's keen control of tension goes with well-lifted, swaggering rhythms. A powerful bonus is the live recording of *Kindertotenlieder* with Jessye Norman at her most compelling. Even so, first choice for this symphony remains with Abbado and the Chicago Symphony Orchestra. His command of Mahlerian characterization has never been more tellinglt displayed than in this most problematic of the symphonies, and the recording is one of the finest DG has made with this orchestra (417 773-2).

Symphony No.8 (Symphony of 1000).
*(*) Sony Dig. S2K 45754 (2) [id.]; *40-45754*. Sweet, Coburn, Quivar, Fassbaender, Leech, Nimsgern, Estes, Vienna Boys' Ch., Schönberg Ch., Austrian R. Ch., V. State Op. Concert Ch., VPO, Maazel.

At an unusually spacious basic speed Maazel's account of the first movement rather lacks the biting tensions needed, and there is little sense of awe in the massive second movement. Though the women soloists are excellent, low tension goes with ensemble that is slacker than one expects from Maazel and these forces. A disappointing last instalment for a cycle of mixed quality. Tennstedt's magnificent account still reigns supreme in this work and his modern, EMI recording copes superbly with even the heaviest textures (CDS7 47625-8).

Symphony No. 9 in D min.
(M) ** Decca 430 247-2 (2) [id.]. LSO, Solti – WAGNER: *Siegfried idyll.****

Solti's 1967 version of Mahler's *Ninth* was an outstandingly successful example of Decca's vintage analogue techniques: there is a fantastic range of dynamic, combined with fine detail and a natural perspective. It is a brilliant, dramatic reading, but one which finally falls just a little short of being a great performance in its extrovert approach to the spiritual beauty of the finale. In the middle two movements it would be difficult to match Solti for the point and precision of the playing; the tempo for the second-movement *Ländler* may be slow but, with such pointing, the slowness is amply justified – quite apart from following Mahler's marking. The third movement is given the most brilliant account ever, but in the outer movements one feels that Solti is not penetrating deeply enough. He allows Mahler's passionate utterances to emerge too readily. He makes Mahler wear his heart on his sleeve and, although there may be justification for that, it misses something we have come to expect. The CD transfer, like the others in this series, achieves remarkable clarity of focus. First choice remains with either Karajan, one of his supreme Mahlerian achievements (DG 410 726-2), or, as a splendid bargain, Barbirolli's fine version with the same Berlin Philharmonic Orchestra. This is an unquestionable bargain on a single CD or tape (EMI CDM7 63115-2; *EG 763115-4*).

LIEDER AND SONG-CYCLES

Kindertotenlieder.
*** Ph. Dig. 426 249-2; *426 249-4* (2) [id.]. Jessye Norman, Boston SO, Seiji Ozawa – *Symphony No. 7.****

Jessye Norman is supremely moving in Mahler's darkly elegiac cycle. This is a live recording, made in Frankfurt in 1988 when the orchestra was on tour, an intense performance with the soloist at her most spontaneously expressive. A valuable makeweight for a fine reading of the *Seventh symphony*.

Des Knaben Wunderhorn: Das irdische Leben; Wo die schönen Trompeten blasen; Urlicht. Rückert Lieder: Liebst du um Schönheit; Ich bin der Welt.
(M) **(*) Ph. 426 642-2; *426 642-4* [id.]. Jessye Norman, Irwin Gage – SCHUBERT: *Lieder.***(*)

Jessye Norman recorded these Mahler songs in 1971, near the beginning of her career, and already the voice was developing magically. There is less detail here than in more recent performances, but the magisterial sustaining of long lines at very measured speeds is impressive. Irwin Gage accompanies sensitively, though he cannot efface memories of the orchestral versions. Good recording for its period, skilfully transferred to CD.

Lieder eines fahrenden Gesellen.
*** Ph. Dig. 426 257-2 [id.]. Jessye Norman, BPO, Haitink – *Symphony No. 6.****
(M) ** Sony MYK 45503 [id.]. Mildred Miller, Columbia SO, Bruno Walter – BRAHMS: *Alto rhapsody* etc.**

Though the *Lieder eines fahrenden Gesellen* is hardly the Mahler cycle one would associate with the opulent tones of Jessye Norman, this is a joy to the ear, with Haitink, in his accompaniment for the jaunty second song, providing the necessary lightness. The stormy darkness of the third song fits the soloist more naturally, always a magnetic singer. It makes a valuable extra for Haitink's deeply satisfying version of the *Sixth Symphony*.

Mildred Miller sings well enough, although her vocal production is at times a little restricted and, instead of long, resonant phrases, the listener sometimes receives an impression of short-term musical thought. Yet Walter keeps the performance dramatically alive and there is superb orchestral detail, brought out most vividly by the excellent CD transfer, which is atmospheric and refined. The tangibility of both voice and orchestra is striking and the balance is first class.

Das Lied von der Erde.
(M) **(*) Sony MYK 45500 [id.]. Mildred Miller, Ernst Haefliger, NYPO, Bruno Walter.

Though Bruno Walter's New York version does not have the tear-laden quality in the final *Abschied* that made his earlier Vienna account (in mono) with Kathleen Ferrier unique, that is its only serious shortcoming. Haefliger sparkles with imagination and Miller is a warm and appealing mezzo soloist, lacking only the last depth of feeling you find in a Ferrier; and the maestro himself has rarely sounded so happy on record, even in Mahler. The remastered recording has been considerably improved for CD and now sounds both warm and vivid. Current first choice probably remains with Karajan, also at mid-price, with Christa Ludwig and René Kollo. Under his baton *Das Lied* becomes a most seductive sequence of atmospheric songs, with an underlying deep sense of melancholy (DG 419 058-2; *419 058-4*).

Malipiero, Gian (1882–1973)

String quartet No. 1 (Rispetti e Strambotti).
*** Denon Dig. CO 77150 [id.]. I Solisti Italiani – RESPIGHI: *Ancient airs & dances: suite No. 3*; WOLF: *Italian serenade.***

Rispetti and *Strambotti* are forms of Italian love-poetry, and Malipieri's *Quartet* – heard here in a highly effective version for string orchestra – is structured in twenty brief 'stanzas', linked by a central theme. The treatment is colourful and inventive, and the work inspires I Solisti Italiani to their best performance on this CD. They are faithfully recorded in a sympathetic acoustic.

Marais, Marin (1656–1728)

Suites for viols: in D min.; in G; Tombeau de Mr Meliton.
*** HM/BMG Dig. RD 77146 [77146-2-RC]. Kenneth Slowik, Jaap ter Linden, Konrad Junghänel.

The viol music of Marin Marais is, like certain white wines, an acquired taste; however, once acquired, it is quite addictive. The two suites recorded here come from the first of his five books of *Pièces de voile*, containing in all some 600 pieces. The music dates from 1686 when he was '*ordinaire de viole de la musique de la chambre du Roi*', and an obvious favourite of Lully, to whom there is a fulsome dedication. The present artists, Kenneth Slowik and Jaap ter Linden, alternate between bass viol and gamba in the two suites, with Konrad Junghänel on theorbo; all three belong to the Smithsonian Institute's chamber group and give vibrant, spirited performances that are most persuasive. The recording needs to be played at a lower than usual level-setting if a realistic result is required, as the balance places the listener rather nearer the players than is ideal.

Marsh, John (1752–1828)

Symphonies Nos. 1 in B flat (ed. Robins); *3 in D; 4 in F; 6 in D; A Conversation Symphony for 2 Orchestras* (all ed. Graham-Jones).
** Olympia Dig. OCD 400 [id.]. Chichester Concert, Ian Graham-Jones.

John Marsh was born in Dorking, Surrey. Trained as a lawyer, he was essentially a musical amateur (in the best sense), starting off in Salisbury, then taking on the promotion and musical direction of subscription concerts, first at Canterbury in the early 1780s then continuing at Chichester from about 1787 to 1812, when he retired from music altogether. As a composer he was largely self-taught, yet he shows a considerable facility both in organizing his musical material and in handling orchestral colour. In a sense he was innovative: because of the continuing influence of Handel, the symphony format was not fashionable in England at that time. Yet Marsh was prolific, writing over two dozen of them, of which nine have survived in published form. For the most part they each consist of three short movements and, while the tunes sometimes have a whiff of Handel, there is a strong element of the English village green. Not surprisingly, the harmonic progressions are not always very sophisticated, but they are well wrought and have a certain robust appeal. The *Conversation Symphony* does not divide into two separate ensembles but makes contrasts between higher and lower instrumental groupings. Five of his works are presented here with enthusiasm by an aptly sized authentic baroque group; they play well enough and are quite effectively recorded, but one wonders what the extra finesse and vitality of Pinnock and his English Concert could make of them.

Martin, Frank (1890–1974)

(i) *Cello concerto; The Four elements.*
(M) *** Preludio PRL 2147 [id.]. (i) Jean Decroos, Concg. O, Haitink.

The Four elements was composed in 1963/4 for Ernest Ansermet's eightieth birthday and the *Cello concerto* in 1966 for Pierre Fournier. These two excellent performances come from Dutch Radio tapes, and no apologies need be made for the quality of the sound, which compares favourably with some commercial recordings. The sound is unobtrusively natural and the balance beautifully judged, which enables Martin's subtle and expertly judged orchestral sonorities to register. The *Cello concerto* has been available in America, but it is astonishing that a work of this quality has not found more champions. Jean Decroos, from the first desk of the Concertgebouw, gives an impressive account of the piece and Haitink secures excellent playing from the Concertgebouw Orchestra. *The Four elements* is another Martin rarity, rich in invention and imaginative resource: its neglect is little short of scandalous. Both performances were recorded at public concerts in 1965 and 1970 respectively, but audience noise is minimal and the quality first rate.

Concerto for 7 wind instruments, timpani, percussion and strings; Études for strings; (i) *Petite symphonie concertante for harp, harpsichord, piano and double string orchestra.*
(M) (***) Decca mono 430 003-2 [id.]. (i) Jamet, Vauchet-Clerc, Rossiaud, SRO, Ansermet.

This CD contains the pioneering record of Frank Martin's masterpiece, the *Petite symphonie concertante*, one of the very first Decca LPs. This authoritative performance has a concentration and an atmosphere that have not really been matched since. The three excellent soloists, Pierre Jamet (harp), Germaine Vauchet-Clerc (harpsichord) and Doris Rossiaud (piano) are at no point named in the documentation, but their contribution deserves recognition. The 1951 recording does not sound as spectacular as it seemed at the time, and the string-tone shows its age. No apologies need be made for the remarkably vivid recording of the *Études for strings* and the masterly *Concerto for 7 wind instruments*. An indispensable issue.

(i) *Passacaglia for orchestra;* (ii) *Petite symphonie concertante for harp, harpsichord, piano and double string orchestra;* (iii) *Maria Triptychon.*
(*(*)) Jecklin Disco mono JD 645-2. (i) BPO; (ii; iii) SRO; composer, with (ii) Hunziker, Vauchet-Clerc, Rossiaud; (iii) Irmgard Seefried, Schneiderhan.

This CD will be of particular interest to admirers of Martin, since it gives the composer's own view of the celebrated *Petite symphonie concertante*: much more atmospheric and concentrated than any other, and gaining in eloquence by being taken a good deal more slowly. (Two of the excellent soloists are the same as in Ansermet's pioneering version – see above.) The recording is a Swiss Radio tape from 1970, but it is in mono and is wanting in richness and depth. The *Maria Triptychon* for soprano, violin and orchestra comes from the late 1960s and was written for Schneiderhan and his wife, Irmgard Seefried. Again the recording emanates from radio tapes of the first performance and calls for tolerance, but the piece is not otherwise available (though Edith Mathis's 1984 recording for Schwann/Harmonia Mundi may come into currency during the lifetime of this book). In 1952 Martin made a transcription for string orchestra of his (1944) *Passacaglia for organ* and in 1962 an arrangement for full orchestra. The latter is the most effective of the three, though the subtlety of Martin's orchestral palette is not well served by the rather subfusc mono recording. However, no other version is currently available.

Piano quintet; String quintet (Pavane couleur de temps); String trio; Trio sur des mélodies populaires irlandaises.
*** Jecklin-Disco JD 646-2 [id.]. Zurich Ch. Ens.

This excellent disc explores Martin's work composed between 1919 and 1936. The *Piano quintet* is the earliest work included here, and it inhabits much the same world as that of Ravel and late Fauré; it has an eloquence and an elegiac dignity that are impressive. Ravel's influence is strongly in evidence in the trio section of the second movement and, for that matter, in the short string quintet, subtitled *Pavane couleur de temps*, from 1920. The title is taken from a fairy story in which a young girl wishes for 'a dress the colour of time'. Like the *Piano quintet*, this is a beautiful piece. The *Piano trio on Irish popular themes* (1925) is the best known of these early chamber works. In Martin's words, 'everything is achieved through rhythm', rather than via any harmonic and contrapuntal ingenuity. It is full of imagination and rhythmic life. The more cerebral *String trio* of 1936 is a tougher nut to crack; its harmonies are more astringent and its form more concentrated. To summarize: altogether a most satisfying disc, offering very good performances. Although the recordings were made in 1989–90 they are analogue, presumably emanating from Swiss Radio, but none the worse for that.

6 Monologues from Everyman; The Tempest: 3 excerpts.
❀ (M) *** DG 429 858-2 [id.]. Fischer-Dieskau, BPO, composer – EGK: *The temptation of St Anthony.****

The *Everyman Monologues* is a masterpiece – one of the great song-cycles of the twentieth century. Composed in the wake of *Der Cornet*, it is a setting of six monologues from Hofmannsthal's play on the theme of a rich man dying, and gives expression to both the fear of death and the doctrine of resurrection through love. The music is of extraordinary vision and imaginative power, and this classic performance from Fischer-Dieskau and the composer sounds as vivid and fresh as ever. The three excerpts from *The Tempest* make one long to hear the rest of the opera, which comes from the early 1950s, the same period as the *Violin concerto* and the *Harpsichord concerto*, to which it is related. The orchestral Prelude casts a strong and powerful spell and the two arias, from Act III (*My Ariel! Hast thou, which art but air*) and the Epilogue (*Now my charms are all o'erthrown*), are hardly less magical. This music impresses when one first encounters it, yet its beauties grow with each hearing.

Mass for double choir.
*** Koch Bayer Dig. BR 100084 [id.]. Frankfurt Vocal Ens., Ralf Otto – REGER: *Geistliche Gesänge.****
(*) Nimbus Dig. NI 5197 [id.]. Christ Church Cathedral Ch., Oxford, Stephen Darlington – POULENC: *Mass in G* etc.*

The *Mass* is an early work, composed in 1922 when Martin was in his early thirties, though the *Agnus Dei* was added four years later. It has great purity and, in the hands of Ralf Otto's fine Frankfurt choir, much eloquence too. They have a great understanding of and feeling for this work, and convey its poignancy and depth. Their performance is quite a powerful and moving experience, and they produce a refined and expressive tonal blend as well as a wide dynamic range, which are well captured by the engineers. At 50 minutes it offers ungenerous playing time but it is not short on quality, for the Reger coupling is music of great simplicity and eloquence.

The Choir of Christ Church Cathedral, Oxford, under Stephen Darlington also give a good account of themselves: their tone is clean and beautifully balanced. The boys' voices are moving in a different way from that of the Frankfurt choir, but the English performance does not add up to quite as impressive or richly imaginative a musical experience. The Nimbus disc is eminently well recorded.

Martinů, Bohuslav (1890–1959)

Concerto for double string orchestra, piano and tympani; Symphony No. 1.
*** Chan. Dig. CHAN 8950; *ABTD 1544* [id.]. Czech PO, Jiří Bělohávek.

The centenary year in 1990 seems to have unleashed a flurry of activity; whereas a few years ago the *First Symphony* had only a tenuous foothold on the recorded repertory, its current representation is quite generous. Jíři Bělohlávek's dedicated and imaginative account is fine; though readers who have Järvi's impressive BIS recording coupled with the *Second Symphony* (BIS CD 362) need have no cause for concern, this new Czech version is very good indeed. Bělohávek is totally inside this music, and the recording, made in the agreeably resonant Spanish Hall of Prague Castle, is very natural. (Järvi's acoustic is only marginally less resonant and, if anything, his recording reproduces a little more detail.) The *Double concerto* is one of the most powerful works of the present century, and its intensity is well conveyed in this vital, deeply felt performance. Strongly recommended for both works.

Concerto for double string orchestra, piano and timpani; Concerto for string quartet and orchestra; Sinfonia concertante for oboe, bassoon, violin, cello and orchestra.
*** Virgin Dig. VC7 91099-2; *VC7 91099-4* [id.]. Endellion Qt, City of L. Sinf., Hickox.

The *Double concerto* has splendid vitality in Hickox's hands (he is brisker than Jiří Bělohávek and the Czech Philharmonic on Chandos), and he has obvious sympathy for this repertoire. The level of transfer throughout is low and, in the slow movement in particular, pianissimos call for a higher than usual volume setting. The *Sinfonia concertante* was written a decade later, in 1948, and was inspired by (and written for the same combination as) the famous Haydn score for which Martinů, rightly, had great affection. It is more rewarding than the neo-Baroque *Concerto for string quartet and orchestra*, written for the Pro Arte Quartet in the early 1930s, which is very manufactured. However, this is a useful addition to the growing Martinů discography, and Richard Hickox is an enthusiastic and expert guide in this terrain.

(i) *Piano concerto No. 3;* (ii) *Rhapsody-concerto for viola and orchestra.*
** Sup./Koch Dig. 110 374-2 [id.]. (i) Josef Páleníček, (ii) Josef Suk; Czech PO, Neumann.

Páleníček recorded Martinů's *Third Piano concerto* (1947–8) with Ančerl in the 1960s, but this is long deleted. This 1982 account is less subtle and not so finely shaded, an impression heightened no doubt by the somewhat closer balance. Though it does not rank among the composer's best work, the *Concerto* has many attractive ideas and a refreshing air of gaiety. The *Rhapsody-concerto* is a work of greater substance and depth, and the recording is less bottom-heavy than its companion. Josef Suk gives a thoroughly sympathetic performance, though it in no way displaces Rivka Golani and Peter Maag, who create a stronger atmosphere and find greater depths (Conifer CDFC 146 – see our main volume, p. 596).

Serenades: Nos. 1 for clarinet, horn, 3 violins and viola; 2 for 2 violins and viola; 3 for oboe, clarinet, 4 violins and cello; 4 (Divertimento) for violin, viola, oboe, piano and strings; 5 (Serenade) for chamber orchestra.
** Sup. SUP 11 098-2 [id.]. Prague CO, Oldrich Viček.

The *Serenade for chamber orchestra* (No. 5 of those listed here) was written in tribute to Roussel, with whom Martinů studied when he first came to Paris. At nearly 12 minutes, it is the longest of the five (the others are about half that length), and its opening appears to pay tribute to the French master. It is a delightful and inventive score. No. 4, written for the Société d'Études Mozartiennes in Paris, has a good deal of charm; but it must be said that some of the others are variable in quality. The performances are vital and alert but the balance is pretty synthetic. Not essential listening except perhaps for the most committed Martinů admirer and, at just under 40 minutes, not particularly good value.

Sinfonietta giocosa; Divertimento.
* Sup. Dig. 11 0373-2 [id.]. Jan Panenka, Prague CO, Bohumil Gregor.

Sinfonietta giocosa; Sinfonietta La Jolla; Toccata e due canzoni.
**(*) Chan. Dig. CHAN 8859; *ABTD 1475* [id.]. Julian Jacobson, Bournemouth Sinf., Vásáry.

Julian Jacobson and the Bournemouth Sinfonietta under Tamás Vásáry give a better idea of the *Sinfonietta giocosa* than do their Czech rivals. At least the main thematic line is not obscured, though one could wish that rhythmic accents were more lightly pointed. It is astonishing that this radiant and sunny work with its abundance of good ideas should come from the darkest time of Martinů's life when he was in Vichy France trying to escape from the Nazis. Better nourished string-tone would be welcome in the *Toccata e due canzoni* and, for that matter, in the *Sinfonietta La Jolla*, and greater lightness of touch would have been welcome throughout. However, the playing has vigour, and the affecting wind idea in the first movement of the *Sinfonietta La Jolla* is beautifully shaped. These performances may not offer the last word in subtlety, but they still have a lot going for them and are well recorded.

In the Czech recording the *Sinfonietta giocosa* starts unpropitiously; the subsidiary woodwind parts completely swamp the infectiously high-spirited string line, obviously the main theme, at the very opening. The acoustic is far too resonant and the balance totally synthetic. The actual playing of Jan Panenka and the Prague Chamber Orchestra is crisp and vital, but listeners unfamiliar with the piece would form an incomplete picture of it. The *Divertimento*, for piano left hand, is an early work, completed in Paris in 1926; it was refashioned by Oskar Holman as a concertino but is now recorded for the first time in something near its original form.

Symphonies Nos. 1–6 (Fantaisies symphoniques).
(M) *** Sup. 11 0382-2 (3) [id.]. Czech PO, Václav Neumann.

Neumann's complete set of the Martinů symphonies was recorded in the Dvořák Hall of the House of Artists, Prague, over a period between January 1976 (No. 6) and 1978 (No. 5). The transfers to CD are excellently done: the sound is full, spacious and bright, it has greater presence and better definition than the original LPs, yet with no edginess in the strings. The orchestral playing, it hardly needs saying, is first class and Neumann's readings have a spacious intensity, a relaxed grip and a natural feeling for the colour and atmosphere of these works. The *First Symphony* dates from 1942, the year after Martinů arrived in the United States; like so much good music of the period, it was written in response to a commission from Koussevitzky. What Virgil Thomson described as the work's 'singing syncopation' lends the *Symphony* a forward thrust and subtlety which Neumann catches admirably. The *Second* (1943) is the most relaxed of the six; its ideas are unforced, its mood easy-going and bucolic. Much of it is exhilarating, particularly the delightful finale, and in Neumann's hands it has much charm in its pastoral slow movement. The coupling of the *Third* and *Fourth* on the second disc brings two of the finest performances in the cycle. The *Third* is in some ways the weightiest of the set; it is without doubt the most concentrated and powerful, with the possible exception of the *Sixth*. It has something of the dark purposefulness and vision of the *Double concerto*, and its splendid central slow movement brings great intensity of feeling and real depth from the Czech players, with the finale by no means an anticlimax. Neumann gives an authoritative reading, with well-shaped phrasing, and his conception is more spacious than was Sejna's in his post-war set. The *Fourth* is perhaps the most immediately attractive and appealing of all six, and Neumann's performance is eminently recommendable. The remastered recording, too, is strikingly vivid; its resonance does not blur the bright colours of the *Allegro vivo* second movement, and there is radiance in the violins at the sustained opening of the *Largo*. The *Fifth* (written for the Prague Spring Festival in 1946) is a marvellous piece. Its opening is invitingly confident (it is full of brightness and intensity with woodwind chirping and violins gleaming), while its closing pages radiate an almost incandescent quality and a life-enhancing power quite out of tune with the bleak post-war years that gave it birth. Neumann's account does not displace Ančerl's version – see below – but it is still powerfully communicative and has the spontaneity that distinguishes all the performances offered here. The *Sixth* is much later (1953) and was introduced to the gramophone by Charles Munch and the Boston Symphony, to whom the work is dedicated. The composer said that he wrote it to give pleasure to the conductor, and his comment that 'Munch's spontaneous approach to music, in which a composition freely acquires its form and flows out unrestrainedly', so that 'a hardly perceptible rippling or acceleration brings the melody to life', might be applied to the music itself. (It is also reassuring to find in the 1950s a great composer giving prime importance to melodic flow at a time when serious music was already entering a period when major figures were no longer able to find a central role for melody in their writing, to the consternation of the musical public, if not of the ivory-towered critical fraternity.) Yet Martinů's orchestration and imaginative design for the *Sixth* are by no means conservative or backward-looking. The exotic textures still intrigue the ear (the opening sounds for all the world like a cloud of Amazonian insects) and must initially, for the composer, have outweighed the musical cogency and sweep of his score, so that he was doubtful of its symphonic status. He subtitled it *Fantaisies symphoniques*, and even briefly asked for it not to be included in his numbered symphonies. Václav Neumann's performance has an impressive spaciousness and, though there could be more urgency and fire in places, the reading has life, colour and impetus, and is thoroughly compelling when the Czech orchestra play so vividly: witness the powerful trumpet solo in the finale.

Symphonies Nos. 1–2.
**(*) BMG/RCA Dig. RD 60154 [60154-2-RC]. Berlin SO, Claus Peter Flor.

Claus Peter Flor and his Berlin forces come into direct competition with Neeme Järvi on BIS, and readers who have invested in the latter need not feel impelled to make the change. Not that these performances (or, for that matter, the recording) are greatly inferior, but Järvi offers the more detailed sound, as does Bělohávek on Chandos in No. 1.

Symphonies Nos. 1; 3; 5.
*** Multisonic 31 0023-2 (2). Czech PO, Ančerl.

This is the real thing. Whether or not you have modern versions of these Martinů symphonies, you should obtain these powerful, luminous performances. The music glows in Ančerl's hands and acquires a radiance that quite belies its date. He recorded the *Fifth* on a 10-inch Supraphon LP in mono, but this is a much later performance; they come from Czech Radio recordings made in 1963, 1966 and 1962 respectively. Two symphonies could easily be accommodated on one disc and it is maddening that the *Third* is split between the first and second CDs. Never mind – these are such superb and convincing readings that readers should not hesitate.

Symphonies Nos. 3–4.
*** Chan. Dig. CHAN 8917; *ABTD 1525* [id.]. SNO, Bryden Thomson.

The excellent Bryden Thomson gets thoroughly committed playing from his Scottish players in both symphonies – at last this hitherto underrated conductor seems to be coming into his own. These are fine performances, even if some of the sense of mystery is missing in the middle movement of the *Third* and the opening of the *Fourth* could with advantage be just a shade faster and lighter. The exhilarating scherzo could not be improved upon and the conductor's affection for this music shines throughout. The Chandos recording is first class, brighter and more detailed than is Järvi on BIS (CD 363) though, on balance, the latter remains a first recommendation.

Symphony No. 6 (Fantaisies symphoniques).
*** Chan. Dig. CHAN 8897; *ABTD 1508* [id.]. Czech PO, Bělohlávek – JANÁCEK: *Sinfonietta*; SUK: *Scherzo*.***

Jiří Bělohlávek's account of the *Fantaisies symphoniques* is probably first choice in the current catalogue. Until now, among modern recordings Neeme Järvi on BIS has led the field (CD 402), but this Chandos reading has the inestimable benefit of the Czech

Philharmonic. Moreover the interpretation has greater dramatic strength and is more fully characterized; undoubtedly these players believe in every note. This is an outstanding performance that does full justice to the composer's extraordinary imaginative vision. Furthermore, the Chandos recording is every bit as good as the BIS, though the coupling will inevitably be a factor, and readers who already have the Janáček will probably gravitate towards the BIS.

CHAMBER MUSIC

Duo for violin and cello.
(M) *** RCA GD 87871; *GK 87871* [7871-2-RG; *7871-4-RG*]. Heifetz, Piatigorsky – DEBUSSY: *Sonata* etc.(**); RESPIGHI: *Sonata* (***); RAVEL: *Trio* etc.(**)

All the other works on the Heifetz disc are mono recordings from 1950 and, although the Respighi *Sonata* has never been surpassed, the Ravel *Trio* is wanting in atmosphere. The repertoire for violin and cello is not extensive (Kodály and Ravel wrote for this partnership) and Martinů composed two *Duos*, the first in 1927. A short but powerful piece, it was recorded in 1964 and, though the acoustic is a bit dryish, the playing is fabulous.

Violin sonatas Nos. 2–3; 5 Madrigal stanzas.
** Sup. Dig. 11 0099-2 [id.]. Josef Suk, Josef Hála.

The *Second Violin sonata*, composed in 1931, comes from the Paris years and is not really Martinů at his best. There is far more to the *Third* (1944), which comes from his American years, as do the *Five Madrigal Stanzas* (1943), and both are more characteristic. Josef Suk and Josef Hála are recorded in the Dvořák Hall at the House of Artists where, oddly enough, one feels the need for more space round the sound and greater freshness of timbre. Alert playing from both artists, but greater tonal colour would have been welcome; the piano is curiously monochrome.

The Epic of Gilgamesh (oratorio).
❀ *** Marco Polo Dig. 8.223316 [id.]. Depoltová, Margita, Kusnjer, Vele, Karpílšek, Slovak Ph. Ch. & O, Zdeněk Košler.

The Epic of Gilgamesh comes from Martinů's last years and is arguably his masterpiece: it has vision, depth and power. Like Honegger's *King David*, it is for narrator, soloists, chorus and orchestra, and it similarly evokes a remote and distant world, full of colour and mystery. *Gilgamesh* is the oldest poem known to mankind: it predates the Homeric epics by 1,500 years, which places it at 7000 B.C. or earlier. The story survives in fragmentary form and tells, in the first part of Martinů's oratorio, how Gilgamesh, King of Uruk, hears of the great warrior, Enkidu, a primitive who is at home with the world of nature and of animals. The king befriends him, they quarrel and fight, before their friendship is finally sealed. The second part tells of Enkidu's death and of Gilgamesh's grief; and the third addresses the themes of death and immortality, Gilgamesh's plea to the gods and his encounter with Enkidu's spirit. The final pages are awesome, even chilling, and the work abounds with invention of the highest quality and of consistently sustained inspiration. The performance is committed and sympathetic and the recording very natural in its balance. A powerful and gripping work – indeed, one of the most imaginative choral works of the present century.

OPERA

The Greek Passion (sung in English).

*** Sup. Dig. 10 3611/2 [id.]. Mitchinson, Field, Tomlinson, Joll, Moses, Davies, Cullis, Savory, Kuhn Children's Ch., Czech PO Ch., Brno State PO, Mackerras.

Written with much mental pain in the years just before Martinů died in 1959, this opera was the work he regarded as his musical testament. Based on a novel by Nikos Kazantzakis (author of *Zorba the Greek*), it tells in an innocent, direct way of a village where a Passion play is to be presented; the individuals – tragically, as it proves – take on qualities of the New Testament figures they represent. At the very opening there is a hymn-like prelude of diatonic simplicity, and what makes the work so moving – given occasional overtones of Janáček, Mussorgsky and Britten – is Martinů's ability to simplify his message both musically and dramatically. On stage, the degree of gaucheness can be hard to present effectively, but on record it is a quite different matter. This extraordinarily vivid recording – almost stereoscopic in its clear projection of the participants – was made by a cast which had been giving stage performances for the Welsh National Opera; the singing is not just committed but accomplished too. The Czechs were happy to record the opera (in 1981, using Japanese digital equipment, which perhaps accounts for the sharpness of focus on CD) in what in effect is the original language of Martinů's libretto, English. Virtually every word is crystal clear and the directess of communication to the listener is riveting, particularly as the choral perspectives are so tellingly and realistically managed. The combination of British soloists with excellent Czech choirs and players is entirely fruitful. As a Czech specialist, Mackerras makes an ideal advocate, and the recording is both brilliant and atmospheric – for instance, the scena with the accordion in Act III is handled most evocatively. With the words so clear, the absence of an English libretto is not a serious omission, but the lack of any separate cues within the four Acts is a great annoyance. But in its simple way *The Greek Passion* makes a most moving experience, and on CD the projection really does give the listener the impression that the tragedy is bring played out 'live' in the area just behind the speakers.

Martucci, Giuseppe (1856–1909)

(i) *Piano concerto No. 1 in D min.;* (ii) *La canzone dei Ricordi.*
** ASV Dig. CDDCA 690; *ZCDCA 690* [id.]. (i) Caramiello; (ii) Yakar; Philh. O, d'Avalos.

In our main volume we greeted the appearance of Martucci's *First Symphony* (ASV CDDCA 675; *ZCDCA 675*) with some enthusiasm. He is a key figure in the renaissance of Italian instrumental music and the leading figure before the so-called 'generazione dell'Ottanta': Pizzetti, Malipiero and Casella. Although he is not so strong a musical personality, there is a parallel with Stenhammar. Both musicians were commanding pianists, famous interpreters of the Brahms concertos and excellent conductors, in the concert hall and also the opera pit (Martucci conducted the first Italian performance of *Tristan* in 1888). Both also had wide musical sympathies; Martucci introduced Italian audiences to much other contemporary music – Franck, d'Indy, Dvořák, Strauss, Debussy and our own Stanford and Parry. The *First Piano Concerto* (with Francesco Caramiello as a capable soloist) comes from 1878, when Martucci was in his early twenties, and was never performed or published in his lifetime (hence the absence of an opus number). It is inevitably derivative, and it is the song-cycle that is the chief attraction here: Rachel Yakar sings beautifully and is particularly affecting in the Duparc-like *Cantavál ruscello la gaia canzone.* The recording is generally faithful, but is a bit 'up-front' so that climaxes come close to coarseness.

(i) *Piano concerto No. 2 in B flat min., Op. 66. Canzonetta, Op. 55/1; Giga, Op. 61/3; Minuetto, Op. 57/2; Momento musicale, Op. 57/3; Serenata, Op. 57/1; Tempo di gavotta, Op. 55/2.*
** ASV Dig. CDDCA 691; *ZCDCA 691* [id.]. Francesco Caramiello; (i) Philh. O, d'Avalos.

The *Second Piano concerto* is a work of Martucci's maturity. It is a big, 40-minute work in a Brahmsian mould but is nevertheless full of individual touches. It was admired and conducted by Toscanini, Weingartner and Mahler, and soloists have included d'Albert and Horszowski. Caramiello copes very successfully with its very considerable demands, and the results all round are eminently acceptable – though, without any disrespect to these artists, it would be good to hear the work in the hands of a soloist and conductor of the very first rank. The fill-ups derive mainly from piano pieces and are wholly delightful. The recording is good, though in the *Concerto* the orchestral texture needs better ventilation and tutti do not have quite enough room in which to expand.

Symphony No. 2 in F, Op. 81; Andante in B flat, Op. 69; Colore orientale Op. 44/3.
** ASV Dig. CDDCA 689; *ZCDCA 689* [id.]. Philh. O, d'Avalos.

The *Second Symphony* is a relatively late work, coming from 1904. Toscanini, who conducted it the following year, was one of its champions. Its ideas assume greater potency and individuality the closer one comes to it. Though the performance falls short of distinction, it leaves the listener in no doubt as to Martucci's quality as a composer and the nobility of much of his invention. Let us hope that the appearance of this disc will encourage other conductors to take it up. The *Colore orientale* is an arrangement of a piano piece; the beautiful *Andante*, a work of depth, is a transcription of a piece for cello and piano and has a Fauréan dignity. The recording is a bit too closely balanced for, though it is pleasing in less heavily scored passages, there is not enough space round the sound and, as a result, tutti tend to coarsen. But there is no mistaking that this is music of some quality, which deserves wider dissemination.

Mascagni, Pietro (1863–1945)

Cavalleria Rusticana (complete).
**(*) DG Dig. 429 568-2 [id.]. Baltsa, Domingo, Baniewicz, Pons, Mentzer, ROHCG Ch., Philh. O, Sinopoli.
(M) **(*) Decca 425 985-2 [id.]. Tebaldi, Bjoerling, Bastianini, Maggio Musicale Fiorentino Ch. & O, Erede.
(M) **(*) EMI CMS7 63650-2 (2). Caballé, Carreras, Hamari, Manuguerra, Varnay, Amb. Op. Ch., Southend Boys' Ch., Philh. O, Muti – LEONCAVALLO: *I Pagliacci.* **(*)

Highly individual, passionately committed, only occasionally wilful, Sinopoli's reading is quite unlike any other. Traditionalists may well not like it, and they will be able to test that soon enough when the opening prelude, very flexible in its rubato, shows the conductor at his most extreme. This performance has the sort of high emotional tension which marks Sinopoli's readings of Elgar, and he is superbly backed by the Philharmonia, the strings in particular playing with a luminous warmth. Regularly Sinopoli brings out markings in the score that are usually neglected, and among the soloists it is Domingo, the keenest musician, who thrives on them most, giving a superb, imaginative performance, vocally as rich as ever. The characterful timbres of Baltsa's mezzo are not ideally suited to the role of Santuzza: there is little sense of vulnerability in her tough sound, even though her vehemence is apt. Juan Pons as the carter, Alfio, sings well, but there is no snarl in the voice, and Suzanne Mentzer rather lacks sparkle in Lola's solo. Yet with rich, spacious sound this single disc provides a warm and refreshing experience.

The early (1957) Decca recording with Tebaldi offers a forthright, lusty account of Mascagni's piece of blood and thunder and has the distinction of three excellent soloists. Tebaldi is most moving in *Voi lo sapete*, and the firm richness of Bastianini's baritone is beautifully caught. As always, Bjoerling shows himself the most intelligent of tenors, and it is only the chorus that gives serious cause for disappointment. They are enthusiastic and accurate enough when accompanying Bjoerling's superb account of the drinking scene (in Italy no doubt the directions for wine were taken literally), but at other times they are very undisciplined. But at mid-price this is well worth considering.

There are fewer unexpected textual points in the EMI *Cav.* than in *Pag.*, but Muti's approach is comparably biting and violent, brushing away the idea that this is a sentimental score, though running the risk of making it vulgar. The result is certainly refreshing, with Caballé – pushed faster than usual, even in her big moments – collaborating warmly. So *Voi lo sapete* is geared from the start to the final cry of *Io son dannata*, and she manages a fine snarl on *A te la mala Pasqua*. Carreras does not sound quite so much at home, though the rest of the cast is memorable, including the resonant Manuguerra as Alfio and the veteran Astrid Varnay as Mamma Lucia, wobble as she does. The recording is forward and vivid.

Cavalleria Rusticana: highlights.
(B) *** DG Compact Classics *427 717-4* [id.] (from complete recording with Cossotto, Bergonzi, Guelfi, La Scala, Milan, Ch. & O, Karajan) – LEONCAVALLO: *Pagliacci*: highlights.***
(M) ** Decca 421 870-2; *421 870-4* [id.]. Varady, Pavarotti, Cappuccilli, Gonzales, L. Op. Ch., Nat. PO, Gavazzeni – LEONCAVALLO: *I Pagliacci*: highlights.**

Karajan's set of *Cavalleria Rusticana* is still high on the recommended list, and this Compact Classics highlights tape includes the key items, with both Cossotto and Bergonzi in splendid form. There is some lack of bite in the choruses, but that is caused as much by the orginal recording balance as by the tape transfer, which is otherwise admirable.

These Decca excerpts from *Cavalleria Rusticana* include *Santuzza's Prayer* and *Voi lo sapete*, very welcome because Julia Varady is the most individual member of the cast. Pavarotti is loud and unsubtle as Turiddù, though the tone is often beautiful. The recording is brilliant, with striking presence and fine atmosphere.

Lodoletta (complete).
*** Hung. Dig. HCD 31307/8 [id.]. Maria Spacagna, Kelen, Szilágyi, Polgár, Kálmándi, Hungarian State Op. Children's Ch., Hungarian R. & TV Ch. & State O, Charles Rosekrans.

In vivid sound and with some excellent singing, this valuable first recording from Hungaroton makes a persuasive case for Mascagni's unashamed mixture of charm and sentimentality. The plot, based on *Two little wooden shoes* by Ouida, is so soft-centred that the shrewd Puccini firmly gave up his option to set it, having considered it closely. The scene-setting, as at the very start in Holland, is often delightful, although the melodies rarely stick in the mind. As the little Dutch girl, Lodoletta, Maria Spacagna sings most sensitively, even if the voice is too warm and full to suggest extreme youth. As the dissolute painter who unwittingly drives her to her death Péter Kelen proves a stylish and heady-toned lyric tenor, singing his big Act I solo, the *Song of the flowers*, very beautifully. The American, Charles Rosekrans, makes a very sympathetic conductor, in charge of a strong cast from the Hungarian State Opera.

Massenet, Jules (1842–1912)

Werther (complete).
(M) *** DG 403 304-2 (2) [id.]. Domingo, Obraztsova, Augér, Grundheber, Moll, Cologne Children's Ch. and RSO, Chailly.

With a recording that gives fine body and range to the sound of the Cologne orchestra, down to the subtlest whisper from the pianissimo strings, the DG version stands at an advantage, particularly as Chailly proves a sharply characterful conductor, one who knows how to thrust home an important climax as well as how to create evocative textures, varying tensions positively. Placido Domingo in the name-part sings with sweetness and purity as well as strength, coping superbly with the legato line of the aria *Pourquoi me réveiller?*. Elena Obraztsova is richer and firmer than she usually is on record, but it is a generalized portrait, particularly beside the charming Sophie of Arlene Augér. The others make up a very convincing team.

Maxwell Davies, Peter (born 1934)

Ave maris stella; Image, reflection, shadow; (i) *Runes from a holy island.*
*** Unicorn UKCD 2038; *UKC 2038* [id.]. Fires of London, (i) cond. composer.

This is a CD compilation of key Maxwell Davies works, more generously as well as more aptly coupled than on the original LPs. *Ave maris stella*, essentially elegiac, finds the composer at his most severe and demanding. The second piece, *Image, reflection, shadow*, is a kind of sequel; both of them are extended works for small chamber ensemble, which are played here without conductor. The one, using plainchant as its basis, suggested further exploration in the other, both ritualistic in their simple dedication yet not easy in their idiom. *Runes*, conducted by the composer, is much shorter yet just as intense in its rapt slowness. Ideal performances, well recorded, from the group for which all this music was written.

(i) *Trumpet concerto;* (ii) *Symphony No. 4.*
*** Collins Dig. 1181-2; *1181-4* [id.]. (i) John Wallace, SNO; (ii) SCO; composer.

Inspired by the dazzling and poetic playing of the Philharmonia principal, John Wallace, the soloist on the record, the *Trumpet concerto*, written in 1988, is one of the most rewarding of Maxwell Davies's later works. In three movements lasting a full half-hour, it brings a technical challenge to the soloist which makes for atmospheric poetry as well as dramatic excitement. Another source of inspiration has been St Francis, and the slow movement links with the saint's sermon to the birds, deeply meditative; the final coda in its Messiaenic jangling represents sublime glorification when St Francis receives the stigmata. The power and effectiveness of this work has already occasioned a second recorded performance, from Håkan Hardenberger, equally brilliant and evocative (Philips 432 075-2, coupled with other concertos -see our Concerts section below).

The *Fourth Symphony* of 1984 brings similarly striking landmarks. Though it uses chamber forces, this four-movement work is texturally the thorniest of the composer's symphonies, not an easy piece but one with a powerful physical impact. The playing both of the SNO in the concerto and of the SCO in the symphony (the orchestra of which Davies is the Associate Conductor) is strongly committed, with excellent recorded sound.

The Boyfriend; The Devils (film-scores): suites. (i) *Seven in nomine.*
*** Collins Dig. 1095-2; *1095-4* [id.]. (i) Mary Thomas; Aquarius, Nicholas Cleobury.

In 1971 Maxwell Davies did the sharply imagined scores for two Ken Russell films, not only the study in insanity, *The Devils*, but also Sandy Wilson's affectionate Twenties' send-up (with Twiggy as heroine), *The Boyfriend.* Davies's distorting lens works surprisingly well in both. These are the concert suites he drew from the film-scores, the one sparkling, the other creepily atmospheric. Nicholas Cleobury draws alert playing from Aquarius, though in *The Boyfriend* the distant recording takes away some of the necessary bite. From the same crisply economical period *Seven in nomine* is a series of rather severe reworkings of the *In nomine* theme of John Taverner, which somewhat obsessed Maxwell Davies while writing his opera on that Tudor composer. He wrote the piece for his own group, The Fires of London, but the members of Aquarius are just as understanding.

OPERA

The Martyrdom of St Magnus.
*** Unicorn Dig. DKPCD 9100 [id.]. Dives, Gillett, Thomson, Morris, Kelvin Thomas, Scottish Chamber Op. Ens., Michael Rafferty.

Lasting just over 70 minutes, this chamber opera in nine scenes, based on the novel *Magnus* by George Mackay Brown, fits neatly on to a single CD. The five soloists – taking multiple parts – belong to Music Theatre Wales, whose director, Michael McCarthy, was responsible for the stage production which forms the basis of this fine recording, made in the concert hall of the Royal College of Music in London. With Gregorian chant providing an underlying basis of argument, Davies has here simplified his regular idiom. The musical argument of each of the nine compact scenes is summarized in the interludes which follow. The story is baldly but movingly presented, with St Magnus translated to the present century as a concentration camp victim, finally killed by his captors. Outstanding among the soloists is the tenor, Christopher Gillett, taking among other roles that of the Prisoner (or saint).

Medtner, Nikolai (1880–1951)

Improvisation No. 2 (in the form of variations), Op. 47; Sonata-idylle, Op. 56; Vergessene Weisen (Forgotten melodies), Op. 39.
*(*) Chesky Dig. AD 1 [id.]. Earl Wild.

The *Second Improvisation in the form of variations*, Op. 47, is a big work, lasting almost half an hour, and is of some considerable importance in Medtner's output. Earl Wild is a magnificent artist who commands both virtuosity and sensibility. The performances are impressive and are well worth a three-star rating – but the recording rates barely one. It was made in a small, confining studio which dries out the timbre of the instrument in an unappealing fashion. Both the *Second Improvisation* and the *Vergessene Weisen* (*Forgotten melodies*), Op. 39, are included in Hamish Milne's excellent CRD set (see our main volume pp. 605–6).

Mendelssohn, Felix (1809–47)

Piano concerto No. 1 in G min., Op. 25.
(BB) **(*) Pickwick PWK 1154. Peter Katin, LSO, Anthony Collins – LISZT: *Concerto No. 2.***(*)

(i) *Piano concertos Nos. 1 in G min., Op. 25; 2 in D min., Op. 40;* (ii) *Capriccio brillante in B min., Op. 22.*
(M) (*) Sony MPK 45690 [id.]. Rudolf Serkin, (i) Columbia SO; (ii) Phd. O, Ormandy.

(i) *Piano concertos Nos. 1–2;* (ii) *Violin concerto in E min., Op. 64.*
(M) * Sony SBK 46542 [id.]. (i) Rudolf Serkin, Phd. O or Columbia SO, Ormandy; (ii) Stern, Phd. O, Ormandy.

Anyone wanting the more often played of the two Mendelssohn *Piano concertos* will find Katin's performance engagingly affectionate and stylish, with Anthony Collins (in one of his rare stereo appearances) providing an excellent accompaniment. It is almost impossible to believe that the date of this recording was 1955, so fresh and well balanced is the sound. But with only 41 minutes' playing time there would have been plenty of room for another concerto here, whether by Mendelssohn or Liszt. (Katin's coupling of both Mendelssohn concertos plus the *Capriccio brilliant* and *Rondo brillante* makes a stronger recommedation on Decca's own bargain label: 425 504-2; *425 504-4.*)

Serkin's performances are brilliant in the extreme, but they lack the first essential in performances of Mendelssohn's piano music: a degree of charm; while the overall style in outer movements is much too bold and heavy. The aggressive 1960 sound makes things worse and, if anything, this is exaggerated by the CD transfer: the opening of the *G minor Concerto* is grotesquely clattery. The *Capriccio brillante*, recorded a decade later, brings much the same approach and even less refined sound.

Serkin's unattractively aggressive accounts of the two *Piano concertos* are also available, coupled with the *Violin concerto* on one of Sony's very inessential 'Essential classics' reissues. Those seeking Stern's superbly eloquent account of the latter work would be far better advised to turn to its pairing with the Tchaikovsky *Concerto* on Sony CD 42537 [MYK 36724].

Violin concertos: in D min. (for violin & strings); *in E min., Op. 64.*
*** Ph. Dig. 432 077-2; *432 077-4* [id.]. Viktoria Mullova, ASMF, Marriner.

Mendelssohn's early *D minor Violin concerto* was completed when he was thirteen, after he had written the first five *Symphonies for strings.* As a structure it is amazingly accomplished; but only the finale, with its dancing main theme, is really memorable. Purity is the keynote of Mullova's fresh and enjoyable readings of both concertos, the early *D minor* as well as the great *E minor.* Whether influenced by having them in juxtaposition, she refuses to treat the *E minor* as a big warhorse work. Both her refinement and that of the Academy present it on a smaller scale than usual, tenderly expressive rather than flamboyant in the expression of emotion, yet with concentration keenly maintained. So the lovely downward phrase leading into the second subject of the first movement has rarely had more poetry in it, the central *Andante* is sweet and songful and, best of all, the finale, light and fanciful, conveys pure fun in its fireworks. The early work follows a similar pattern, with youthful emotions given full rein and with the finale turned into a headily brilliant Csardas. The Philips recording is admirably natural and beautifully balanced.

Violin concerto in E min., Op. 64.
(M) *** CBS Dig. MDK 44902; *40-44902* [id.]. Cho-Liang Lin, Philh. O, Tilson Thomas – BRUCH: *Concerto No. 1* *** (with encores by SARASATE and KREISLER ***).
*** ASV CDDCA 748; *ZCDCA 748* [id.]. Xue-Wei, LPO, Ivor Bolton – BRAHMS: *Violin concerto.****
(M) *** Ph. 426 639-2; *426 639-4* [id.]. Accardo, LPO, Dutoit – BRUCH: *Concerto No. 1.*(***)
(BB) ** LaserLight Dig. 15 615 [id.]. Verhey, Budapest SO, Joó – BRUCH: *Concerto No. 1.***
(BB) *(*) Pickwick PWK 1151. Ion Voicou, LSO, Frühbeck de Burgos – BRUCH: *Concerto No. 1.**(*)

Cho-Liang Lin's vibrantly lyrical account now reappears with the Bruch *G minor* (plus some attractive encores) to make an unbeatable mid-priced coupling. These are both immensely rewarding and poetic performances, given excellent, modern, digital sound, and Michael Tilson Thomas proves a highly sympathetic partner in the Mendelssohn *Concerto.*

Xue-Wei's version, clean and fresh if a little reticent emotionally, makes a generous and attractive coupling for his equally recommendable version of the Brahms. There are more strongly characterized readings than this but, with its pastel-shaded lyricism, this is undoubtedly satisfying, helped by first-rate recording.

Accardo's freshness of style is most appealing. Outer movements are lithe and sparkling; and the *Andante*, taken more slowly than usual, is expressive in a natural, unforced way. Some ears may find the refined phrasing a little understated here, but overall this reading is distinctive for its gentle, romantic feeling. Dutoit's accompaniment is in every way first class, and the sound here is very good, better balanced than in the Bruch coupling.

Emmy Verhey's approach has a comparable simplicity and lyrical ardour. Her playing is gently honeyed and she displays a fine sense of line in the *Andante*. Hers is a less assertive account than some, and the balance is natural and slightly recessed to suit the style of the music-making. Arpád Joó provides a most sympathetic accompaniment, and this performance will suit those who like a degree of restraint in this work; the finale has both sparkle and a pleasing lightness of touch. Excellent value in the bargain basement.

The Voicou/de Burgos combination undoubtedly has its moments: the second subject of the first movement is genuinely touching, the *Andante* has a pleasing simplicity and the finale scintillates, when the soloist's articulation is light and feathery, and nicely integrated with the accompaniment. But the 1965 Decca recording gives Voicou's timbre a febrile wiriness that is ill-suited to Mendelssohn's elegant lyricism.

(i) *Violin concerto in E min., Op. 64;* (ii) *Symphony No. 4 in A (Italian), Op. 90;* (iii) *A Midsummer Night's Dream: Overture and incidental music* (CD only: (iv) *Overtures: Fair Melusina; A Calm sea and a prosperous voyage*).
(B) *** DG Compact Classics 413 150-2 (2); *413 150-4.* (i) Milstein, VPO, Abbado; (ii) BPO, Maazel; (iii) Mathis, Boese, Bav. RSO with Ch., Kubelik (CD only: (iv) LSO, Chmura).

This is one of the most attractive compilations in DG's Compact Classics tape series. Milstein's 1973 account of the *Violin concerto* is highly distinguished. With excellent recording and balance this is worthy to rank with the best, and it is greatly enhanced by the sensitivity of Abbado's accompaniment. Maazel's *Italian* offers a fast, hard-driven but joyous and beautifully articulated performance of the first movement and equal clarity and point in the vivacious finale. The central movements are well sustained, and altogether this is highly enjoyable, the recording resonantly full-timbred. Kubelik's fairly complete version of the incidental music for *A Midsummer Night's Dream* is no less enjoyable and the sound is very good here, too. On the pair of digitally remastered CDs the *Midsummer Night's Dream* selection is extended, and performances of two of Mendelssohn's less often heard overtures are added. The collection from which these are derived is discussed below.

A Midsummer Night's Dream: Overture, Op. 21, & incidental music, Op. 61.
(M) (***) BMG/RCA mono GD 60328; *GK 60328* (4) [60328-2-RG; *60328-4-RG*]. Eustis, Kirk, University of Pennsylvania Women's Glee Club, Phd. O., Toscanini – Concert.(**(*))

Toscanini's Philadelphia recording offers the seven most popular numbers from the *Midsummer Night's Dream* music, including the song with chorus, *You spotted snakes*, and the final melodrama. In sparkling performances it offers a fine example of his more relaxed manners in his one Philadelphia season.

Overtures: A Calm sea and prosperous voyage, Op. 27; Fair Melusina, Op. 32; The Hebrides (Fingal's Cave), Op. 26; A Midsummer Night's Dream, Op. 21; Ruy Blas, Op. 95.
(B) ** DG 423 025-2; *423 025-4* [id.]. LSO, Gabriel Chmura.

When this record was published in 1977 its young conductor, Gabriel Chmura, had recently won both the Cantelli and Karajan competitions and this was his recording début. He was obviously on guard against the impetuosity of youth, and these performances tend towards the other extreme: he errs on the side of expressive caution in *The Hebrides*, where his tempo is a bit too measured. This could have more romantic feeling, and *Ruy Blas*, too, needs more zest if it is to be really exciting. Yet he pays scrupulous attention to detail and is plainly both conscientious in his approach and deeply musical. The orchestral playing is obviously well prepared and has real finish, and the result is almost to bring a Mozartian classicism to these works. The recording is clean, well focused and bright, without being over-lit, and it has transferred very freshly to CD. This is reasonably priced; but those seeking really memorable performances of these overtures would do better to pay more and investigate either Flor (BMG/RCA RD 87905), who omits the charming *Melusina*, or Abbado (DG 423 104-2), who offers all the five overtures here, plus two intriguing novelties (see our main volume, p. 610).

Symphonies Nos. 1–5.
(B) ** Ph. 432 598-2 (3) [id.]. Donath, Hansmann, Kmentt, New Philh. Ch. (in *No. 2*), New Philh. O, Sawallisch.

The well-recorded and expertly transferred Sawallisch set is the least expensive way of acquiring the Mendelssohn symphonies complete, but the Karajan/BPO series, made in 1971–2, is far superior and is excellently transferred to CD on three mid-priced discs (DG 429 664-2 – see our main volume, pp. 611–12). Sawallisch is not really a committed enough Mendelssohnian to brazen his way through the less than inspired passages of the *Hymn of Praise*, and the New Philharmonia Chorus for once sounds relatively uninvolved. The early *C minor Symphony*, however, is more successful and sounds anything but pretentious in Sawallisch's hands. The *Scottish Symphony* is a well-played but routine performance which lacks spontaneity and zest. Best of the set are the *Italian* and *Reformation Symphonies*, but these performances are already available separately (Philips 422 470-2 – see our main volume, pp. 615–16).

Symphony No. 2 in B flat (Hymn of Praise), Op. 51.
(M) *** DG 431 471-2; *431 471-4* [id.]. Mathis, Rebmann, Hollweg, German Op. Ch., BPO, Karajan.

We have already praised the 1972 Karajan recording of the *Hymn of Praise* within the context of his complete set of Mendelssohn symphonies (see our main volume). In some ways Abbado's digital version is even finer, if not more clearly recorded (DG 423 143-2), but the Karajan CD has a price advantage and, although he has a less individual team of soloists, it is a very satisfying account, with the chorus vibrantly caught within the spacious acoustics of the Berlin Jesus-Christus Kirche.

Symphonies Nos. 3 in A min. (Scottish), Op. 56; 4 in A (Italian), Op. 90.
*** EMI CDC7 54000-2 [id.]; *EL 754000-4*. L. Classical Players, Norrington.
(M) **(*) EMI CDM7 63853-2 [id.]; *EG 763853-4*. Philh. O, Klemperer.
(B) ** RCA VD 60483; *VK 60483* [60483-2-RV; *60483-4-RV*]. Boston SO, Munch.

Symphonies Nos. (i) *3 in A min. (Scottish), Op. 56;* (ii) *4 in A (Italian), Op. 90; Overture: The Hebrides, Op. 26.*
(M) **(*) Sony Dig./Analogue SBK 46536 [id.]. (i) Bav. RSO, A. Davis; (ii) Cleveland O, Szell.

There have been previous recordings of the *Italian Symphony* on period instruments, but this is the first disc to offer the *Scottish* as well. As in his Schumann, Norrington opts for unexaggerated speeds in the outer movements, relatively brisk ones for the middle movements. The reults are similarly exhilarating, particularly in the clipped and bouncy account of the first movement of the *Italian*. The *Scottish Symphony* is far lighter than usual, with no hint of excessive sweetness. The scherzo has rarely sounded happier, and the finale closes in a fast gallop for the 6/8 coda with the horns whooping gloriously. Good, warm recording, only occasionally masking detail in tuttis. Mackerras directing the Orchestra of the Age of Enlightenment is very slightly to be preferred in the *Italian Symphony*, if his coupling of the overture and incidental music to *A Midsummer Night's Dream* is suitable (Virgin VC7 90725-2).

The front of the Sony CD is misleading in implying that all three performances are by Szell, although on the back the performance details are given correctly. As it happens, the CBS digital recording of the *Scottish Symphony*, dating from 1980, is of high quality, and Andrew Davis's reading is freshly straightforward, supported by excellent playing from the Bavarian Radio Orchestra. But the score's pianissimo markings are much less strikingly contrasted here than in some other versions, and this is not just a matter of the forward balance. The scherzo is very successful (helped by the transparent detail of the sound) and the slow movement is memorable, nicely paced and beautifully shaped. The finale is alert and zestful. Szell and his Cleveland Orchestra then appear to present the rest of the programme, and are heard in bravura form in their recording of the *Italian Symphony* from 1962. This was the first stereo recording to include the first-movement exposition repeat, and Szell's approach is dramatic and often exhilarating but, as Klemperer has proved, the work's gaiety and sunlight can be readily captured with more relaxed tempi. Nevertheless the the precision of the playing is remarkable and there is never any hint of scurrying. The Cleveland sound is full as well as brilliant.

Klemperer's conception of the *Scottish Symphony* is broad and expansive, with an orchestral texture that is almost Brahmsian. There is no denying the weight and power of this reading, and the colourful Scherzo and richly played *Adagio* come off especially well. Perhaps the opening movement is a little too mannered – especially the introduction – to sound entirely spontaneous, but its closing pages are certainly gripping. In the finale Klemperer's broad treatment of the maestoso section is quite convincing in context. Originally the 1960 (Columbia) sound was appropriately warm and spacious, but the tuttis were not very clear or transparent; the CD transfer has brought added clarity, but the sound itself remains warm and beautiful. In the *Italian Symphony*, Klemperer takes the first movement substantially more slowly than usual, but this is no heavily monumental and humourless reading: the playing has sparkling incandescence. The second movement is also taken at a moderate tempo; but the way Klemperer moulds and floats the main theme over the moving bass defeats all preconceptions in its sustained beauty. A fast pacing of the Minuet, but still with wonderful phrasing; and it is the beautiful shaping of a phrase that makes the finale so fresh and memorable. There is no lack of exhilaration yet none of that feeling of being rushed off one's feet. The recording (again from 1960) is atmospheric, clearer than it was originally but still pleasingly full. This coupling is obviously not a first choice, but all admirers of the conductor will want it for his unique interpretation of the *Italian Symphony*.

Munch secures some outstanding bravura from his Boston players: the scherzo of the *Scottish* is particularly nimble, while the clean articulation means that the allegros of the outer movements of the *Italian* can be hard-driven without stress. However, some may feel that Munch's style is emotionally too fierce in the first movement of the *A minor Symphony* and that a little more relaxation in the *Italian* would not come amiss. Nevertheless the excitement of these performances cannot be denied, and both slow movements are songful. The RCA engineers have done wonders with the 1958/9 recordings, which sound fuller and smoother than they did on LP. The omission of first-movement exposition repeats is a drawback here, however, and the best bargain recommendation for these works must remain with Mark Lubbock and the Orchestra of St John's, performances of delightful lightness and point, warmly and cleanly recorded (ASV CDQS 6004). But Abbado's comparable mid-price coupling with the LSO is finer still and has the advantage of digital recording (DG 427 810-2; *427 810-4*).

Symphony No. 4 in A (Italian), Op. 90.
(B) *** Sony MBK 44894 [id.]. Nat. PO, Stokowski – BIZET: *Symphony.****
(BB) *(*) Pickwick (Decca) PWK 1149. RPO, Vonk – SCHUBERT: *Symphony No. 8.***

Stokowski's *Italian* is very distinguished indeed, ranking alongside the very finest versions, including Beecham's. Stokowski includes the essential first-movement exposition repeat and leads back simply yet with striking inevitability. His tempi throughout are quite perfectly judged, the *Andante* particularly pleasing in its combination of elegance and spirit; and there is plenty of sparkle in the outer movements without the music ever sounding rushed, always a hallmark of a first-rate performance. The recording, from the late 1970s, is vivid and fresh and has not lost its bloom.

Hans Vonk, recorded by Decca in 1975, sets a very fast tempo in the first movement, with no exposition repeat and no really gentle playing. The originally Decca Phase 4 recording is on the coarse side for this composer, though the effect on CD is vivid enough.

CHAMBER MUSIC

Octet in E flat, Op. 20.
*** Hyp. Dig. CDA 66356; *KA 66356* [id.]. Divertimenti – BARGIEL: *Octet.****
** Chan. Dig. CHAN 8790; *ABTD 1423* [id.]. ASMF Chamber Ens. – RAFF: *Octet.***

Divertimenti give a very natural and unforced account of the celebrated *Octet* which, though it may not be the most distinguished in the catalogue, still gives great pleasure.

Their disc is of special interest in offering a particularly interesting rarity in the form of Woldemar Bargiel's *Octet in C minor*. Excellent recorded sound.

The Academy of St Martin-in-the-Fields also offer a rarity in the form of Raff's *Octet*, though this is by no means as interesting as the Bargiel. Their performance, though equally unaffected, is untouched by distinction and is a good deal less successful than their earlier, three-star account (Philips 420 400-2 – see our main volume, p. 616 – coupled with the Mendelssohn *Quintet in B flat, Op. 87*).

Piano quartets Nos. 1 in C min.; 2 in F min.; 3 in B min., Op. 1–3.
*** Virgin Dig. VC7 91183-2; *VC7 91183-4* [id.]. Domus.

The *Piano quartet No. 1 in C minor* comes from 1822, when Mendelssohn was thirteen, and was the composer's first published composition and was succeeded the following year by another dedicated to 'Monsieur le Professeur Zelter par son élève Felix Mendelssohn-Bartholdy', equally fluent and accomplished. However, none of the ideas of this F minor work are as remarkable as those of its successor in B minor of 1825, dedicated to Goethe (Mendelssohn had made enormous strides in the intervening two years). In any event, all three pieces have charm, vitality and musicianship, particularly in the hands of this ensemble, who play with the taste and discernment we have come to expect from them. Excellent recording.

Piano trios Nos. 1 in D min., Op. 49; 2 in C min., Op. 66.
** CRD Dig. CRD 3459; *CRDC 4159* [id.]. Israel Piano Trio.

Very musical playing from the Israel Piano Trio, though even greater lightness of touch from the pianist would have been welcome. Neither performance is particularly strong on charm though neither is entirely without it. The acoustic of Rosslyn Hill Chapel in Hampstead is very lively and is perhaps a shade too reverberant in climaxes. All the same, there is plenty to enjoy, even though this is not as fine as the LP Beaux Arts coupling, which will surely be reissued on a Philips budget-priced CD in the fullness of time.

String quartets Nos. 1 in E flat, Op. 12; 2 in A, Op. 13.
*** Hyp. Dig. CDA 66397 [id.]. Coull Qt (with *2 Pieces, Op. 81* ***).
** Chan. Dig. CHAN 8827; *ABTD 1452* [id.]. Gabrieli Qt.

The Coull Quartet on Hyperion give fresh and unaffected accounts of both *Quartets* and have the benefit of very good recorded sound. Their performances will give real pleasure, even if they may not have the unanimity or finesse of some ensembles currently before the public. They are to be preferred to the rather more brilliant, but less feeling, Melos discussed in our main volume. Tempi are well judged and everything flows naturally. The Coull offer the additional inducement of two of the *Four pieces*, Op. 81, which were published after Mendelssohn's death.

The Gabrieli are, if anything, even better recorded on Chandos than the Coull but, moving between one and the other, the greater freshness of the younger group tells. The second movement of the *E flat Quartet* is more deliberate in tempo on Chandos than on Hyperion and is held together less well. Generally speaking, there is less enthusiasm about the playing of the Gabrielis.

String quartet No. 2 in A min., Op. 13.
** EMI Dig. CDC7 54036-2 [id.]. Cherubini Qt – SCHUMANN: *String quartet No. 3.***

The Cherubini Quartet offer probably the most accomplished and ardent performance of the *A minor Quartet* currently available, though they are guilty of being a bit self-conscious. The opening of the Menuetto is marred by very studied phrasing and accentuation, which will not be to all tastes and is not wholly to ours. Dynamic markings are rather exaggerated and the opening of the finale is overdramatized.

String quintets Nos. 1 in A, Op. 18; 2 in B flat, Op. 87.
(M) *** Sony/CBS CD 45883. Laredo, Kavafian, Ohyama, Kashkashian, Robinson.

A welcome addition to the catalogue. Laredo and his ensemble achieve good matching of timbre, and they give lively accounts of both these neglected works, lacking neither warmth nor finesse. The 1978 recording has responded well to remastering, and has body and presence.

VOCAL MUSIC

Elijah (oratorio; sung in German), *Op. 70.*
(M) ** Sony M2YK 46455 (2) [id.]. Augér, Schreckenbach, Tear, Nimsgern, Gächinger, Kantorei, Stuttgart RSO, Rilling.

There is room for a performance of *Elijah* in German, when Mendelssohn composed from a German text. However, this live recording from Stuttgart is hardly the answer, generally a rather dull performance with variable singing. Best among the soloists is the pure-toned Arlene Augér, and Robert Tear is as reliable as ever but hardly inspired. Nimsgern as Elijah himself sounds uninvolved, and Gabriele Schrekenbach is disappointingly monochrome. The CD transfer brings bright, vivid sound but (even at mid-price) this is not very recommendable. First choice rests with the splendid Richard Hickox set with the LSO Chorus on Chandos (CHAN 8774/5; *DBTD 2016*).

Infelice; Psalm 42 (As the hart pants), Op. 42.
*** Virgin Dig. VC7 91123-2; *VC7 91123-4* [id.]. J. Baker, LSO Ch., City of L. Sinf., Hickox – BRAHMS: *Alto rhapsody* etc.***

The scena, *Infelice* – a piece which harks back to an earlier tradition – and the Psalm-setting both have the solos prescribed for soprano, but they suit Dame Janet well, here making a welcome foray out of official retirement for a recording. The voice is in superb condition, with the weight of expressiveness as compelling as ever. The Psalm sounds very like an extra item from *Elijah.*

A Midsummer Night's Dream: overture, Op. 21; incidental music, Op. 61.
*** BMG/RCA Dig. RD 87764 [7764-2-RC]. Popp, Lipovšek, Bamberg SO, Flor.
*** EMI CDC7 47163-2 [id.]. Watson, Wallis, Finchley Children's Ch., LSO, Previn.

Flor's account omits the little melodramas, which is a pity; but, for those who require the major items only, this superb RCA digital CD, very beautifully recorded, could well be a first choice. However, on EMI Previn offers a wonderfully refreshing account of the complete score, with the little melodramas sounding remarkably spontaneous. His analogue recording is naturally balanced and has much refinement of detail.

St Paul, Op. 36.
(M) *** EMI CMS7 64006-2 (2) [id.]. Donath, Schwarz, Hollweg, Fischer-Dieskau, Boys' Ch., Dusseldorf Musikverein & SO, Frühbeck de Burgos.

St Paul (or, in German, *Paulus*) was for long notorious as one of the most sanctimonious of Victorian oratorios. This sympathetic performance under the conductor who helped us review our ideas on *Elijah* – the return of his outstanding EMI/Philharmonia set, with gorgeous singing from Dame Janet Baker, cannot be too far away – gives the lie to that, a piece full of ideas well worthy of the composer of the *Italian*

Symphony. Like *Elijah* ten years later, *Paulus* – completed in 1836 – was Mendelssohn's substitute for opera. In youthful zest it erupts in great Handelian choruses, and a Bachian style of story-telling is neatly updated in its choral interjections and chorales, with the soprano joining the traditional tenor in the narration. What reduces the dramatic effectiveness is that Mendelssohn, ever the optimist, comes to his happy resolution of the plot far too quickly and with too little stuggle involved. This performance glows with life. Fischer-Dieskau takes the name-part (as he did for *Elijah*), leading an excellent team of soloists and with admirable support from the Dusseldorf choir and orchestra. The recording is full and atmospheric, its vividness enhanced on CD.

Menotti, Gian-Carlo (born 1911)

Amahl and the night visitors: Introduction; March; Shepherd's dance. Sebastian (ballet): *suite*.
*** Koch Dig. 3-7005-2; *2-7005-4* [id.]. New Zealand SO, Schenck – BARBER: *Souvenirs*.***

Menotti composed *Sebastian* in 1944 for the Marquis de Cuevas, and he fashioned this seven-movement suite soon after. It is beautifully crafted and expertly scored music whose attractions are strong even if the ideas are not always as memorable as their presentation. Menotti's charming opera, *Amahl and the night visitors*, was the first opera conceived and written for television, albeit black-and-white. It was composed in 1951 and immediately assumed classic status. The three movements recorded here are the charming *Introduction*, the rather Prokofievian *March* and the *Rustic dance*, used to depict the three Shepherds' homage to the Magi, which Balanchine later choreographed. The players under Andrew Schenck, who sound as if they are enjoying themselves, are well recorded, even if the studio acoustic of Symphony House, Wellington, is very slightly dry.

Sebastian (ballet): complete.
** ASV CDDCA 741; *ZCDCA 741* [id.]. LSO, José Serebrier – LUENING: *Legend* etc.**

Menotti's one-Act ballet in three scenes is an attractive, well-written and inventive piece whose place on the musical map lies somewhere between Stravinsky, Barber and Hollywood. It is not a long work (37 minutes) but is, as so often with this composer, strong on charm. The recent (but not digital) recording is good, and gets a well-groomed performance from the LSO under José Serebrier.

Messiaen, Olivier (born 1908)

Les offrandes oubliées.
(M) *** EMI CZS7 62669-2 (2) [id.]. O de Paris, Serge Baudo (with Concert: *French music* ***).

Les offrandes oubliées (*The forgotten offerings*) is an early work, dating from 1930, when Messiaen was twenty-two, yet it is entirely characteristic. The outer sections of the triptych (*La Croix* and *L'Eucharistie*) have that magnetic mixture of sensuous mysticism and purity of spirit which makes this composer's music so haunting. In between comes the brief *Le Péché*, which is vehemently, self-evidently sinful. The work is played with great feeling for its atmosphere and power and is very well recorded. An excellent introduction to Messiaen's orchestral writing which even anticipates the *Turangalîla Symphony*.

Theme and variations.
*** DG Dig. 427 351-2 [id.]. Gidon Kremer, Martha Argerich – BARTÓK: *Sonata No. 1* ***; JANÁČEK: *Sonata.***(*)

Messiaen's *Theme and variations* is an early work, coming from 1932, and is something of a rarity on disc. The distinctive personality is already discernible and the music's fervour is well captured here. Collectors will want this disc for the Bartók, which is marvellously played and excellently recorded.

Visions de l'Amen.
*** EMI CDC7 54050-2 [id.]. Alexandre Rabinovitch, Martha Argerich.

Messiaen's *Visions de l'Amen* for two pianos was composed in 1943 for himself and his future wife, Yvonne Loriod, to play, shortly after his release from a Nazi concentration camp, where he had written the *Quatuor pour le fin du temps*. It is a long, eloquent work in seven sections with a powerful sense of mystery, and is played with uncommon conviction by the Russian pianist-composer, Alexandre Rabinovitch, with Martha Argerich at the second piano. Two pianos are notoriously difficult to balance and tune, but the recording does them justice.

Catalogue d'oiseaux, Book 7; Supplement: La fauvette des jardins.
*** Unicorn Dig. DKPCD 9090; *DKPC 9090* [id.]. Peter Hill.

We have admired earlier releases in this series, and this is every bit as good. In addition to the last book of the *Catalogue d'oiseaux* we have *La fauvette des jardins*, composed in the summer of 1970, which the sleeve annotator describes as the perfect parergon to the cycle. It lasts over half an hour and is as long as *La rousserole effarvatte*. The composer himself has spoken with great warmth of this artist and, given what we hear on this disc, he has every reason to. Peter Hill plays with total dedication and, as was the case with earlier issues in the series, he is recorded with the utmost clarity and definition.

Vingt regards sur l'Enfant-Jésus.
(M) ** Decca 430 343-2 (2) [id.]. John Ogdon.

John Ogdon is unfailingly thoughtful and conscientious, but one needs more spontaneity and a greater feeling for atmosphere than he finds in this extended work. The 1969 recording, made by Argo engineers in Decca's West Hampstead studio, is bold and clear.

Meyerbeer, Giacomo (1791–1864)

Les Patineurs (ballet suite, arr. & orch. Lambert).
(M) ** Sony SBK 46341 [id.]; *40-46341*. Phd. O, Ormandy – ADAM: *Giselle*; TCHAIKOVSKY: *Swan Lake.***

Ormandy takes the *pesante* marking in the opening number rather literally, but otherwise this playing is invigoratingly polished, and is recorded in the usual resonant Philadalphia manner. There is plenty of flair and rhythmic energy here, but less in the way of subtlety.

Miaskovsky, Nikolay (1881–1950)

Symphony No. 12 in G min., Op. 35; Silence (symphonic poem after Poe), *Op. 9*.
**(*) Marco Polo Dig. 8.223302 [id.]. Slovak RSO (Bratislava), Robert Stankovsky.

The *Twelfth Symphony* comes from 1932; it is endearingly old-fashioned and has strong appeal. (Some of it could have been written in the 1880s – though so fresh is much of its invention that it is none the worse for that!) By the early to mid-1930s the adventurous artistic policies of the new Soviet regime were succumbing to the increasing Stalinization of the arts, so that it is perhaps no accident that this symphony is subtitled *Kolkhoz* ('Collective Farm'). Although some of the big rhetorical gestures of the *Sixth Symphony* are to be found in the second movement, there are also some pre-echoes of things to come in the later symphonies. It is highly enjoyable, particularly when it is as well played as it is here by the Bratislava Radio Orchestra under their gifted young conductor, Robert Stankovsky, who was still in his early twenties when this record was made. The tone-poem *Silence* dates from 1909, the year after the *First Symphony*, when Miaskovsky was still studying with Liadov at the St Petersburg Conservatoire. It draws for its inspiration on Edgar Allan Poe's *The Raven* – which must have been enjoying a vogue at this time, for in 1911 Sibelius was also setting it (these ideas eventually found their way into the finale of the *Fourth Symphony*). *Silence* has a strongly atmospheric quality with a distinctly *fin-de-siècle* air: if you enjoy Rachmaninov's *Isle of the dead* or Glière's *Ilya Murometz Symphony*, you should investigate it. It is perhaps too long, given the strength of its melodic ideas, but is full of incidental interest. The orchestra play with enthusiasm and they are decently recorded.

Piano sonatas Nos. 6 in A flat, Op. 62/2; 7 in C, Op. 82; 8 in D min., Op. 83; 9 in F, Op. 84.
**(*) Marco Polo Dig. 8.223178 [id.]. Endre Hegedüs.

Piano sonatas Nos. 7 in C, Op. 82; 8 in D min., Op. 83; 9 in F, Op. 84; Reminiscences, Op. 29; Rondo-Sonata in B flat min., Op. 58; String quartet No. 5: Scherzo (trans. Aliawdina): *Yellowed Leaves, Op. 31.*
**(*) Olympia Dig. OCD 252 [id.]. Murray McLachlan.

The sonatas on the Olympia disc are all from 1949, and thus were written in the wake of the notorious Zhdanov Congress when, along with Shostakovich and Prokofiev, Miaskovsky underwent criticism as mindless as that suffered by the Chinese musicians at the time of the Cultural Revolution. The music is of the utmost simplicity but has an endearing warmth. We spoke with appreciation of the earlier discs Murray McLachlan made in this series and, although there are some touches of routine – almost inevitable in such an undertaking – this is so enterprising an issue that it deserves wide dissemination. As in the earlier discs McLachlan provides scholarly and intelligent notes. The recording is good though the acoustic ambience is perhaps not absolutely ideal.

No sooner had Murray McLachlan completed his cycle of the Miaskovsky sonatas than a rival was announced. A first disc, which we have not heard, offers the *Sonatas Nos. 2, 3* and *5* (Marco Polo 8.223156) while this brings the last four: *No. 6 in A flat* dates from 1944 and shares the same opus number as No. 5. The young Hungarian pianist, Endre Hegedüs, is often the more imaginative interpreter: he colours the second theme of the *Barcarolle sonatina* of the *Eighth Sonata* with greater tenderness and subtlety than Murray McLachlan on Olympia, though the latter has great freshness. Hegedüs is recorded in the Concert Hall of the Liszt Academy. The sound is a little wanting in bloom and his piano is not always in good condition; a technician should have been at hand to correct the tired notes in the second movement of the *Sixth Sonata*. On balance, then, honours are fairly even between these two artists.

Milhaud, Darius (1892–1974)

Music for Prague; Symphony No. 10.
(**) Koch Multisonic mono 31 0022-2 [id.]. Czech PO, Milhaud – HONEGGER: *Symphony No. 2.*(*)

Two Milhaud rarities from the 1960s. At this time Milhaud was in his mid-seventies but still strong enough to direct his own music, and these performances come from the 1966 Prague Spring Festival. Allowance must be made for the quality of the tape which seems to have suffered some deterioration or drying out, either through the passing of time or by the process of digital refurbishing. Milhaud recorded his *Tenth Symphony* at about this time with the BBC Symphony Orchestra, which, to judge by a recent broadcast repeat, has survived in better condition. All the same it is good to have this uneven but often imaginative music available, as Milhaud's representation on CD is lamentably meagre. The recordings appear to be monaural.

Moeran, Ernest J. (1894–1950)

Serenade in G (published score); *Sinfonietta.*
(*) EMI Dig. CDC7 49912-2 [id.]; *EL 749912-4*. N. Sinf., Hickox – FINZI: *Fall of the leaf* etc.*

Serenade in G (complete original score); (i) *Nocturne.*
*** Chan. Dig. CHAN 8808; *ABTD 1436* [id.]. Ulster O, Vernon Handley – WARLOCK: *Capriol suite* etc.***

The *Serenade in G* is a welcome addition to the catalogue, a work which has a good deal in common with Warlock's *Capriol suite* in its orchestral dress, which is the coupling on the Chandos issue. Both use dance forms from a previous age and transform them with new colours and harmonic touches. Moeran's work is more than twice the length of Warlock's and is mellower, more lyrial in style. Handley and the Ulster Orchestra present it with striking freshness and warmth in its original version. This includes the *Intermezzo* and *Forlana*, charming miniatures which were jettisoned after the first performance at the insistence of the publisher, who thought the piece otherwise too long. Handley proves otherwise. He also offers the lovely *Nocturne*, a setting of a poem by Robert Nichols for baritone solo and eight-part chorus, which inspired Moeran from its very opening line ('Exquisite stillness! What serenities of earth and air!'). It was much admired by Britten, who commented about its obvious debt to Delius, to whom it was posthumously dedicated: 'Of course the *Nocturne* owes much to the shifting harmonies of the senior master, but the twilight, nostalgic beauty of this music is Moeran's own.' It is given a wholly sympathetic performance and recording here, and the resonant acoustics of the Ulster Hall, Belfast, provide a warmly atmospheric ambient glow.

The Hickox performance of the *Serenade* is also very pleasing, if without quite such a strong profile as Handley's account; moreover, by playing just the published score, it omits the two rediscovered movements. However, the coupling of a fine account of the *Sinfonietta*, one of Moeran's very best works, almost rights the balance. The recording, made in All Saints', Newcastle-upon-Tyne, is agreeably flattering, but brings a less well-defined bass than on the Chandos disc. Even so, with its attractive Finzi couplings, this is still worth considering.

Molino, Francesco (1775–1847)

Trio, Op. 45.
*** Mer. Dig. CDE 84199 [id.]. Conway, Silverthorne, Garcia – BEETHOVEN: *Serenade*; JOSEPH KREUTZER: *Grand Trio*.***

Italian-born, Molino first settled in Spain, before going on to London and Paris, where he built a reputation as a violinist and guitarist. Unlike the other two works on the disc, this unpretentious trio brings a Spanish flavour in the guitar writing, pointedly brought out by Gerald Garcia. Undemanding music to complete a charming disc for a rare combination. First-rate playing and recording.

Monteverdi, Claudio (1567–1643)

Madrigals, Book 6 (complete).
*** Virgin Dig. VC7 91154-2; *VC7 91154-4* [id.]. Consort of Musicke, Anthony Rooley.

Il sesto libro de madrigali (1614) includes the five-part transcription of the *Lamento d'Arianna* and *Zefiro torno*, and also pieces from Monteverdi's years at Mantua. The Consort of Musicke maintain the high standards of taste and artistry with which we associate them; and collectors building a Monteverdi library are unlikely to be disappointed by this example of their sensitive response to this repertoire. Excellent recording.

Madrigals, Book 8: Madrigali amorosi.
*** Virgin Dig. VC7 91157-2; *VC7 91157-4* [id.]. Consort of Musicke, Anthony Rooley.

Monteverdi published his *Eighth Book* in 1638 after a long gap in his madrigal output. (The previous collection dates from 1619.) As Denis Arnold put it in his Master Musicians study, this collection, like its companions, is 'never purely fashionable nor artificially difficult or experimental'. One of the very greatest of the songs is *Lamento della ninfa* (which Nadia Boulanger so memorably recorded) in what Monteverdi called the *stile rappresentativo* or theatre style, and that is affectingly done here. The whole book is entitled *Madrigali guerrieri et amorosi* and there is a companion disc devoted to the warlike and other theatrical madrigals, which include *Il ballo delle ingrate* and *Il combattimento di Tancredi e Clorinda* (Virgin VC7 91158-2, *VC7 91158-4*), which we have not been able to hear and which will have to wait to be included next time. (Meanwhile collectors can rest content with Leppard's finely sung mid-priced Philips coupling of this marvellously imaginative pair of works – 426 451-2; *426 451-4*). The present Virgin CD has very good recording, slightly on the dry side, which aids clarity of texture.

Motets: *Ego flos campi; Ego sum pastor bonus; Exulta, filia Sion; Fuge, fuge anima mea, mundum; Iusti tulerunt spolia; Lapidabant Stephanum; Lauda, Jerusalem; Laudate Dominum; Nigra sum; O bone Jesu, illumina oculos meos; O bone Jesu, O piissime Jesu; O quam pulchra es; Pulchra es; Salve regina; Spuntava al dì; Sugens Jesus, Dominus noster; Surge propera, amica mea; Veni in hortum meum* (with PICCININI: *Toccata X*).
*** Virgin Dig. VC7 91145-2; *VC7 91145-4* [id.]. Brigitte Lesne, Gérard Lesne, Josep Benet, Josep Cabré, Il Seminario Musicale, Tragicomedia.

The music on this disc encompasses all periods of Monteverdi's career; the earliest comes from his first published collection, the *Sacrae Canticulicae* (1582) composed when he was only fifteen. The three-part motets are all taken from this youthful publication; the solo pieces come from the 1610 *Vespers* music, which show the increasing interest he took in monody during his time in Mantua. Other pieces, such as the *Salve Regina*, come from the *Selva Morale* (1640), while *Pulchra es* and *Nigra sum* are performed on instruments alone. The solo motet *O quam pulchra es* is preceded by a Toccata by Alessandro Piccinini about which the excellent notes are silent. Gérard Lesne has sung with various groups including Les Arts Florissants and Hespèrion XX before founding his own group, Il Seminario Musicale; the performances here are expert and totally committed. Excellent recording.

Vespro della Beata Vergine (Vespers).
❀ *** DG Dig. 429 565-2; *429 565-4* (2) [id.]. Monoyios, Pennicchi, Chance, Tucker, Robson, Naglia, Terfel, Miles, H. M. Sackbutts & Cornetts, Monteverdi Ch., London Oratory Ch., E. Bar. Soloists, Gardiner.
*** HM/BMG Dig. RD 77760; *RK 77760* (2) [7760-2-RC; *7760-4-RC*]. Zanetti, Fisher, Cordier, Elwes, Kenmdall, Van der Meel, Kooy, Cantor, Stuttgart Chamber Ch., Cologne Musica Fiata, Bernius.
** O-L Dig 425 825-2; *425 825-4* (2). Bott, Bonner, Robson, King, Ainsley, George, Grant, New L. Cons., Pickett.

Recorded in conjunction with a video performance for television, Gardiner's second recording of the *Vespers* vividly captures the spatial effects that a performance in the Basilica of St Mark's, Venice, made possible. Instead of being consistently placed close, solo voices are beautifully presented in perspective, heightening the atmosphere. Gardiner made his earlier recording for Decca in 1974 using modern instruments, but since then the art of period performance has developed out of all recognition. Here, with the English Baroque Soloists and a team of soloists less starry but more aptly scaled than in 1974, all of them firm and clear, he directs a performance even more compellingly dramatic. It would be hard to better such young soloists as the counter-tenor Michael Chance, the tenor Mark Tucker and the bass Bryn Terfel. Unlike most period performances, this one does not aim to present the *Vespers* on a small scale in a liturgical context. Unashamedly Gardiner refuses to miniaturize this most magnificent of early choral works. Without inflating the instrumental accompaniment – using six string-players only, plus elaborate continuo and six brass from His Majesties Sackbutts and Cornetts – he combines clarity and urgency with grandeur. The difference this time is less one of scale than of freedom of expression, for, even more than in 1974, he directs with panache. Some will still prefer the more intimate, liturgically based view of Parrott (EMI CDS7 47078-8) or Christophers (Hyperion CDA 66311/2; *KA 66311/2*); but Gardiner's version more than any other conveys the physical thrill which above all has established this long-neglected work as music for today, bringing it into the central repertory alongside the choral masterpieces of later centuries. Treating it in this way as a concert work, Gardiner (as before) does not include plainchant antiphons, and so has room on the two discs for the superb alternative setting of the *Magnificat*, in six voices instead of seven. Recorded back in England with most of the same forces, that supplement brings sound marginally less spacious but more sharply focused, in another dedicated performance.

With excellent soloists, choir and players, Frieder Bernius directs an outstandingly fresh reading which neatly fills the gap between the intimacy of Parrott and the dramatic grandeur of Gardiner. In his pursuit of a liturgical approach Bernius is not as comprehensive as Parrott; but in fresh and immediate sound he draws performances from his team which are at once rhythmically lively and beautifully moulded. The moments of waywardness, as in *Laudate pueri*, are few, and even then the result is characterful. It is a pity that the booklet fails to identify which soloist sings what; and the second disc brings short measure; but nevertheless for some this will be a first choice.

Like Parrott and Harry Christophers, Pickett presents the *Vespers* in a liturgical context, with plainchant antiphons between the numbers. The sound is warm and well balanced, with clarini in the Consort particularly beautiful, but there is a serious snag in the heavily aspirated style of the tenors in their florid music. In this approach, Parrott and Christophers are still preferable (see our main volume, pp. 635–6).

OPERA AND OPERA-BALLET

L'Incoronazione di Poppea (complete).
**(*) HM Dig. HMC 901330/2 [id.]. Borst, Laurens, Köhler, Larmore, Schopper, Lootens, Concerto Vocale, Jacobs.

Like the Virgin set conducted by Richard Hickox (VCT 790775-2 – see our main volume, pp. 637–8), the one directed by René Jacobs was recorded immediately after stage performances. This helps to give it fluency, though neither the characterization nor the timing of dialogue gives quite the same illusion of staging. Danielle Borst as Poppea and the Nerone of Guillemette Laurens are both fresh and stylish, if not quite as sharply distinctive as their counterparts. With the exception of a tremulous counter-tenor as Ottone, this is a strong cast, with such fine singers as Guy de Mey and Dominique Visse in subsidiary roles, and with Jennifer Larmore as the wronged Ottavia far richer and more sympathetic than her opposite number. Jacobs' restoration of instrumental ritornellos between scenes is welcome, even if Hickox's balder treatment often brings extra gravity. Excellent, clear recording, but the Virgin set, with Arleen Augér a tenderly expressive Poppea, remains first choice.

Orfeo (opera): complete.
** Teldec/Warner 2292 42494-2 (2) [id.]. Kozma, Hansmann, Katanosaka, Berberian, Rogers, Equiluz, Van Egmond, Villisech, Munich Capella Antiqua, VCM, Harnoncourt.

In Harnoncourt's version, the ritornello of the Prologue might almost be by Stravinsky, so sharply do the sounds cut. In compensation, the simple and straightforward dedication of this performance is most affecting, and the solo singing, if not generally very characterful, is clean and stylish. One exception to the general rule on characterfulness comes in the singing of Cathy Berberian as the Messenger. She is strikingly successful and, though slightly differing in style from the others, she sings as part of the team. Excellent restrained recording, as usual in Harnoncourt's remastered Telefunken CD series. The extra clarity and sharpness of focus – even in large-scale ensembles – add to the abrasiveness from the opening *Toccata* onwards, and the 1969 recording certainly sounds immediate, with voices very realistic.

Mozart, Wolfgang Amadeus (1756–91)

Adagio in E, K.261; Rondo in C, K.373 (both for violin & orchestra).
(B) *** Ph. 426 977-2; *426 977-4* [id.]. Grumiaux, New Philh. O, Leppard – HAYDN: *Violin concertos*; SCHUBERT: *Rondo*.***

These two Mozart movements are far from slight: the *Adagio* is really lovely on Arthur

Grumiaux's bow and the *Rondo* sparkles. Excellent, stylish accompaniments and very good sound. This makes a strong contribution to a splendid bargain anthology.

(i) *Adagio and fugue in C min., K.456;* (ii) *Piano concerto No. 25 in C, K.503;* (iii) *Serenade No. 12 in C, K.388.*
(M) **(*) EMI CDM7 63620-2 [id.]. (i) Philh. O; (ii) Barenboim, New Philh. O; (iii) New Philh. Wind Ens., Klemperer.

Barenboim recorded K.503 earlier for EMI in his series with the ECO, directing from the keyboard; but here, with Klemperer conducting, the manner is different, predictably weightier. It is one of the few Mozart concertos that could benefit from such a collaboration, and the other two items bring similar Klemperer revelations, rugged performances defying Mozartian convention, beautifully played.

Cassations Nos. 1 in G, K.63; 2 in B flat, K.99; 3 Divertimenti for strings, K.136/8. Divertimenti Nos. 1 in E flat, K.113; 2 in D, K.131; 7 in D, K.205; 10 in F, K.247; 11 in D, K.251; 15 in B flat, K.287; 17 in D, K.334. Serenades Nos. 1 in D, K.100; 2 in D, K.131; 3 in D, K.185; 4 in D (Colloredo), K.203; 5 in D, K.204; 6 in D (Serenata notturna), K.239; 7 in D (Haffner), K.250; 8 in D (Notturno for 4 orchestras), K.286; 9 in D (Posthorn), K.320; 13 in G (Eine kleine Nachtmusik), K.525. A Musical joke, K.522.
(M) *** Decca 430 311-2 (8) [id.]. V. Mozart Ens., Willi Boskovsky.

There are many delights in these justly famous Boskovsky performances, recorded in the 1960s and '70s. Unlike the Marriner survey, which involves two separate boxes, this single collection includes nearly all the major *Divertimenti* and *Serenades* which are not intended solely for wind instruments. The delightful *First Cassation* has two enchanting slow movements. The first is an atmospheric *Andante*, reminiscent of *Così fan tutte* in mood; the second introduces a cantilena for solo violin. The invention in the other works, too, usually finds Mozart at his most gracious and smiling. Beecham's account of the *Divertimento in D*, K.131, remains firmly in the memory but, even by Beecham's standards, these are all fine performances. Indeed the playing is so totally idiomatic and masterly that once scarcely thinks of the artists at all, only of the music. K.334, for instance, with its famous Minuet, offers sparkling, unaffected music-making of great spontaneity. The *Serenades* are hardly less distinguished. K.203, for instance, written – when Mozart was eighteen – for the name-day of Archbishop Colloredo, embraces a violin concerto, and the solo part is played here by Aldred Staar with great distinction; the *Night music* for muted strings is altogether delightful. The *Haffner* and *Posthorn Serenades* are marvellously alive with admirable phrasing and feeling for detail. *Eine kleine Nachtmusik* and *A Musical joke* (which are also available separately – see below) are as fine as any in the catalogue. The recordings were made over a decade between 1967 and 1978 in the Sofiensaal, and the remastering throughout is strikingly fresh and vivid, with the warm Viennese ambience bringing bloom to the overall sound. The violins are brightly lit and in K.203 (the earliest, made in 1967) there is a degree of fierceness in tuttis, and this appears again in the *Haffner Serenade* and, to a lesser extent, in the *Posthorn*. But generally the transfers are most impressively managed.

Complete Mozart Edition, Volume 3: *Cassations Nos. 1 in G, K.63; 2 in B flat, K.99; Divertimento No. 2 in D, K.131; Galimathias musicum, K.32; Serenades Nos. 1 in D, K.100* (with *March in D, K.62); 3 in D, K.185* (with *March in D, K.189); 4 in D (Colloredo), K.203* (with *March in D, K.237); 5 in D, K.204* (with *March in D, K.215); 6 in D (Serenata notturna), K.239; 7 in D (Haffner), K.250* (with *March in D, K.249); 8 in D*

(Notturno for 4 orchestras), K.286; 9 in D (Posthorn), K.320 (with *Marches in D, K.335/1–2); 13 in G (Eine kleine Nachtmusik), K.525.*
(M) *** Ph. Dig. 422 503-2 (7) [id.]. ASMF, Sir Neville Marriner.

Marriner and his Academy are at their very finest here and make a very persuasive case for giving these works on modern instruments. The playing has much finesse, yet its cultivated polish never brings a hint of blandness or lethargy; it is smiling, yet full of energy and sparkle. These performances of the major *Serenades* include the 'entry' marches, and their spirit carries forward into the allegros. In the concertante violin roles Iona Brown is surely an ideal soloist, her playing full of grace. The novelty is the inclusion of the amazingly mature-sounding *Galimathias musicum*, written in 1766 when the composer was ten years old. Leopold Mozart described it as 'A Quodlibet for two violins, two oboes, two horns, obbligato harpsichord, two bassoons, violas and bass. All the instruments have solos and at the end there is a fugue with all the instruments on a Dutch song called *Prince William*. The scoring and invention are delightfully fresh and the seventeen movements are engagingly varied, even interpolating a brief chorus in No. 8, presumably meant to be sung by the orchestra, but here performed with considerable refinement. Throughout this set the digital recording brings an almost ideal combination of bloom and vividness, achieving a natural balance without loss of inner definition, even though the acoustic is fairly reverberant.

CONCERTOS

Complete Mozart Edition, Volume 9: (i) *Bassoon concerto;* (ii) *Clarinet concerto;* (iii) *Flute concertos Nos. 1–2; Andante in C for flute & orchestra;* (iii; iv) *Flute and harp concerto;* (v) *Horn concertos Nos. 1–4; Concert rondo in E flat for horn and orchestra;* (vi) *Oboe concerto. Sinfonia concertante in E flat, K.297b; Sinfonia concertante in E flat, K.297b* (reconstructed R. Levin).
(M) **(*) Ph. Dig. 422 509-2 (5) [id.]. (i) Thunemann; (ii) Leister; (iii) Grafenauer; (iv) Graf; (v) Damm; (vi) Holliger; ASMF, Marriner (except (vi) Holliger).

The principal wind concertos here are recent digital versions. They are all well played and recorded, notably the works for flute (see our main volume, pp. 643–4), while Holliger does not disappoint in the *Oboe concerto* (this is his third recording). However, there is a slightly impersonal air about the accounts of the *Bassoon* and *Clarinet concertos*, well played though they are; and there are more individual sets of the works for horn. The *Sinfonia concertante* is offered both in the version we usually hear (recorded in 1972, with the performance attractively songful and elegant) and in a more modern recording of a conjectural reconstruction by Robert Levin, based on the material in the four wind parts.

(i) *Bassoon concerto in B flat, K.191;* (ii) *Horn concertos Nos. 1–4.*
(M) **(*) DG Dig. 431 284-2; *431 284-4* [id.]. (i) Frank Morelli; (ii) David Jolley (*1* & *4*), William Purvis (*2–3*); Orpheus CO.

Frank Morelli has an engagingly woody tone and plays a very nimble bassoon in the opening allegro of K.191, while his lively decoration of the gracious Minuet finale is full of imaginative use of light and shade. The *Andante*, too, is phrased most pleasingly. The appropriately named David Jolley is very personable in the *First* and *Fourth* of the *Horn concertos*; he brings a winning flair and crisp articulation to his solo role, and the slow movement of K.495 (No. 4) is particularly imaginative. In the remaining two concertos William Purvis plays fluently and agreeably, even if without quite the same strength of personality as his colleague. Accompaniments throughout are well up to Orpheus standard in matters of finesse, warmth and polish, and the recorded sound is most believable. At medium price this is worth considering by those who require modern, digital versions of these works.

(i) *Clarinet concerto;* (ii) *Flute concerto No. 1 in G, K.313;* (iii) *Flute and harp concerto* (CD only: (iv) *Oboe concerto in C, K.314*).
(B) **(*) DG Compact Classics 413 428-2 (2); *413 428-4* [id.]. (i) Prinz, VPO, Boehm; (ii) Linde, Munich CO, Stadlmair; (iii) Schulz, Zabeleta, VPO, Boehm (CD only: (iv) Holliger, Munich CO, Stadlmair).

Prinz's 1974 recording of the *Clarinet concerto* is here available on an excellent Compact Classics tape alongside Linde's impeccably played account of the *G major Flute concerto.* This has a touch of rigidity in the outer movements, but in the slow movement the playing is beautifully poised and the melody breathes in exactly the right way. Boehm's *Flute and harp concerto* comes from 1976 and the performance could hardly be bettered. The balance, as far as the relationship between soloists and orchestra is concerned, is expertly managed, and this is altogether refreshing. The sound throughout these recordings is excellent, except that Linde's 1966 *Flute concerto* shows its earlier date in the quality of the string timbre. On the digitally remastered pair of CDs Holliger's first recording of the *Oboe concerto* is added. His playing, needless to say, is first class, his tone appealing and his style and technique serving the music's grace and elegance. But Stadlmair's accompaniment is crisply straightforward rather than especially imaginative.

(i) *Clarinet concerto in A, K.622;* (ii; iii) *Flute and harp concerto in C, K.299.* (ii) *Andante for flute and orchestra in C, K.315.*
(M) *** DG Dig. 431 283-2; *431 283-4* [id.]. (i) Charles Neidlich; (ii) Susan Palma; (iii) Nancy Allen; Orpheus CO.

Susan Palma is an essentially gentle flautist and her playing in the *C major Andante* has a disarming innocence; the *Flute and harp concerto* too, in which Nancy Allen makes a sympathetic partner, is striking for its delicacy of feeling and texture. Some might feel that the orchestra leans a little strongly in formulating the opening phrase of the *Andantino*, but the flute entry dispels any doubts and the finale has the lightest possible touch. Charles Neidlich's account of the *Clarinet concerto* has an altogether stronger profile. He rightly chooses the basset clarinet and clearly relishes not only its range but also its colour. In the very spirited finale he produces some captivating lower tessitura, while in the *Adagio* he plays radiantly, after a bright, briskly paced first movement, essentially fresh and spring-like. At the reprise of the main theme in the second movement he drops to pianissimo and then decorates the lovely melody simply and affectionately; this leads to a glorious blossoming as the orchestra takes up the melody. The recording is very realistic and well balanced throughout, and this is one of the finest reissues in DG's mid-priced 3D Mozart Collection.

(i) *Clarinet concerto in A, K.622;* (ii) *Oboe concerto in C, K.314.*
(B) **(*) HM/BMG Dig. VD 77509 [Victrola 77509-2-RV]. (i) Hans Deinzer; (ii) Helmut Hucke; Coll. Aur., Franzjosef Maier.

Anyone looking for a bargain coupling of these concertos played on authentic instruments (Hans Deinzer is pictured using a basset clarinet to good effect) will find these performances characterful and spontaneous, with both soloists fluently mastering technical difficulties. Helmut Hucke's woody oboe timbre is distinctly appealing; if Deinzler gives a rather straight account of the central *Adagio* of the work for clarinet, this is otherwise an enjoyably fresh performance. The acoustics of the Cedernsaal in the Schloss Kirchheim bring a resonant mellowness to the violins: there is no acidity of timbre here, yet the digital sound has good definition. However, these German Harmonia Mundi Mozart Edition reissues have no back-up documentation.

(i) *Clarinet concerto in A;* (i; ii) *Sinfonia concertante, K. 297b.*
** EMI Dig. CDC7 54138-2 [id.]. (i) Sabine Meyer; (ii) Jonas, Schneider, Azzolini, Dresden State O, Hans Vonk.

(i) *Clarinet concerto in A;* (i; ii) *Sinfonia concertante, K.297b;* (iii) *Oboe concerto in C, K.314.*
*** ASV Dig. CDCDO 814; *ZCCDO 814* [id.]. (i) Richard Hosford; (ii) Boyd, Hosford, O'Neill, Williams; (iii) Douglas Boyd; COE, Schneider.

The COE issue is a generous and attractive recoupling of three earlier recordings from the mid-1980s. First on the disc comes the *Oboe concerto*, and it would be hard to imagine a performance that conveys more fun in the outer movements, infectiously pointed and phrased, both by the ever-imaginative Douglas Boyd and by his colleagues. The wind soloists in this live recording of the *Sinfonia concertante* are four COE artists who each know when to take centre stage and when to hold back in turn. The variations of the finale are pure delight. Richard Hosford in his reading of the *Clarinet concerto* uses a basset clarinet with its extended lower range, allowing Mozart's original intentions to be realized. At slowish speeds he leans towards the lyrical rather than the dramatic, even in the first movement, and ends with a delightfully bouncy account of the finale. Alexander Schneider, a friend and associate of these players since the orchestra's formation, ideally draws them out with well-paced speeds and well-sprung rhythms. Full, atmospheric recording.

Sabine Meyer as ever reveals herself as a naturally imaginative artist, moulding phrases with a refinement and individuality that have you listening afresh to new expressive detail. The gentleness of her pianissimo playing is a marvel, not just in the slow movement. This account of the *Sinfonia concertante* brings comparably refined playing from all four soloists, but the result has far less of the imaginative interplay and individuality of the rival COE performance. When the ASV issue also adds an extra work in the *Oboe concerto*, infectiously done, the EMI takes second place for this coupling.

(i) *Clarinet concerto in A, K.622. Symphonies Nos. 25 in G min., K.183; 29 in A, K.201.*
* DG Dig. 429 221-2 [id.]. (i) Peter Schmidl; VPO, Bernstein.

Bernstein offers an attractive coupling, but all three performances are disappointing. In No. 29 the first three movements are slack and heavy, while in No. 25 it is the finale that falls short. Peter Schmidl, very reedy of tone, sounds uncomfortably sour in the concerto, and his phrasing and rhythm are often ungainly.

Flute concertos Nos. 1 in G, K.313; 2 in D, K.314; Andante in C for flute and orchestra, K.315.
(M) ** HM/BMG GD 77054; *GK 77054.* Barthold Kuijken, La Petite Bande, Sigiswald Kuijken.

Those who seek authentic performances of Mozart's three major concertante works for flute on a mid-priced disc will find that playing and recording here are eminently satisfactory, if a little reserved. Other versions yield more individuality and colour.

(i) *Flute and harp concerto, K.299;* (ii) *Piano concerto No. 12 in A, K.414;* (iii) *Violin concerto No. 4 in D, K.218.*
(M) (***) EMI mono CDH7 63820-2 [id.]. (i) Le Roy, Laskine; (ii) Kentner; (iii) Heifetz; (i; iii) RPO; (ii) LPO; Beecham.

This CD assembles three classic performances from the 1940s conducted by Beecham. The *Concerto in C major for flute and harp*, K.299, has a cool elegance in this 1947 performance with René Le Roy and Lili Laskine; and listening to Louis Kentner's much earlier (1940) record of the *Piano concerto in A major*, K.414, which is very enjoyable indeed, makes one wish that this much-underrated musician had recorded the lot. The Heifetz is a bit high-powered – but is marvellously played, of course. If the performance does not have that sense of carefree joy that made Beecham's Mozart so peerless, it still sparkles; at mid-price, this triptych makes a splendid bargain. The transfers are much smoother than the Beecham/Mozart symphonies, and in the *Piano concerto* Louis Kentner's tone has fine naturalness and colour.

Piano concertos

Complete Mozart Edition, Volume 7: (i) *Piano concertos, K.107/1–3;* (ii) *Nos. 1–4;* (iii) *5, 6, 8, 9, 11–27; Concert rondos 1–2;* (iii; iv) *Double piano concertos, K.242 & K.365*; (v) *Triple concerto in F, K.242.*
(M) **(*) Ph. Analogue/Dig. 422 507-2 (12) [id.]. (i) Ton Koopman, Amsterdam Bar. O; (ii) Haebler, Vienna Capella Academica, Melkus; (iii) Brendel, ASMF, Marriner; (iv) Imogen Cooper; (v) Katia and Marielle Labèque, Bychkov, BPO, Bychkov.

The Philips Mozart Edition *Piano concertos* box is based on Brendel's set with the ASMF under Marriner. Throughout, his thoughts are never less than penetrating. The transfers are consistently of the very highest quality, as is the playing of the Academy of St Martin-in-the-Fields under Sir Neville Marriner. To make the set complete, Ingrid Haebler gives eminently stylish accounts of the first four *Concertos* on the fortepiano, accompanied by Melkus and his excellent Vienna Capella Academica; the sound is admirably fresh. However, on disc two the ear gets rather a shock when Ton Koopman presents the three works after J. C. Bach. The abrasive opening tutti of K.107/1 takes the listener by surprise into an entirely different sound-world. Convincing though these performances are, it seems a strange idea to offer an authentic approach to these three concertos alone, particularly as at the end of the disc we return to a delightfully cultured performance on modern instruments of the alternative version for three pianos of the so-called *Lodron Concerto*, K.242, provided by the Labèque duo plus Semyon Bychkov, with the Berlin Philharmonic Orchestra accompanying in the most sophisticated modern fashion. The Philips offering is on one CD less than the Sony/Perahia complete set, but that must inevitably still be our primary recommendation (M13K 42055).

Piano concertos Nos. 5, 6, 8, 9, 11–27; (i) *Double piano concerto, K.365;* (i; ii) *Triple piano concerto, K.242. Concert Rondos 1–2.*
(M) *** DG Dig. 431 211-2 (9) [id.]. Malcolm Bilson (fortepiano), E. Bar. Soloists, Gardiner, (i) with Robert Levin; (ii) Melvin Tan.

Malcolm Bilson's complete set of the Mozart *Piano concertos* appears on nine mid-price CDs. Bilson is an artist of excellent musical judgement and good taste, and his survey is the only one at present available on the fortepiano, though we gather that one is underway from Melvyn Tan, who features here in the *Triple concerto*. We have discussed most of the issues in our main volume and see no cause to modify our general welcome. Going back to the set, there are some occasions when one feels that Bilson could have been a little more unbuttoned and others where he is too judicious. For the most part, however, there is little to quarrel with and much to enjoy.

Piano concertos Nos. 9 in E flat (Jeunehomme), K.271; 27 in B flat, K.595.
(BB) **(*) Naxos Dig. 8.550203 [id.]. Jenö Jandó, Concentus Hungaricus, András Ligeti.

In Volume 3 of Jandó's ongoing series, the earlier concerto is the more consistently successful, refreshing in its alert vigour in outer movements, with the simple *Andantino* contrasting nicely with the exhilarating finale. K.595 does not lack strength, but this performance does not have the individuality of the finest versions. Excellent sound, the piano forward but with a realistic overall balance.

Piano concertos Nos. 11 in F, K.413; 12 in A, K.414.
**(*) Ph. Dig. 422 458-2; *422 458-4* [id.]. Mitsuko Uchida, ECO, Jeffrey Tate.

As in earlier concertos in their cycle, Mitsuko Uchida and the English Chamber Orchestra under Jeffrey Tate are given state-of-the-art recording, with ideal balance between soloist and orchestra and plenty of air round the aural image. Uchida plays with great elegance and taste but is perhaps just a shade too polite and genteel. The slow movement of the *F major*, beautiful though it is, lacks the expressive intensity or inner life of Perahia; though the two performances are full of lovely details, the chink of Dresden china can clearly be discerned.

Piano concertos Nos. 12 in A, K.414; 14 in E flat, K.449; 21 in C, K.467.
(BB) *** Naxos Dig. 8.550202 [id.]. Jenö Jandó, Concentus Hungaricus, András Ligeti.

Volume 2 in the Naxos series makes an impressive bargain triptych. In Jandó's hands the first movement of K.449 sounds properly forward-looking; the brightly vivacious K.414 also sounds very fresh here, and its *Andante* is beautifully shaped. Similarly the famous slow movement ever associated with the film, *Elvira Madigan*, is most sensitive, with a gently poignant cantilena from the strings. The resonance of the Italian Institute in Budapest, where this series of recordings is made, adds warmth and generally provides fullness and bloom without clouding detail. The excellent orchestral response distinguishes the first movement of K.467: both grace and weight are here, and some fine wind playing. An added interest in this work is provided by Jandó's use of cadenzas provided by Robert Casadesus. Jandó is at his most spontaneous throughout these performances and this is altogether an excellent disc.

Piano concertos Nos. (i) *13 in C, K.415;* (ii) *15 in B flat, K.450;* (i) *23 in A, K.488.*
(M) (*) EMI mono CDH7 63819-2 [id.]. Michelangeli, (i) O Alessandro Scarlatti, Caracciolo; (ii) Milan CO, Gracis.

The *B flat concerto*, K.450, with Ettore Gracis, recorded with the Milan Chamber Orchestra in 1951, strains the bounds of tolerance; the tape seems to have suffered much deterioration. The *C major*, K.415, and *A major*, K.488, are better, though the sound is barely passable and the strings sound pretty scrawny. Michelangeli's playing is a vast improvement over his recent DG recordings and has something of the cool distinction we associate with him. But despite some felicitous touches in the *C major concerto*, this is no match for other recordings of the period by Solomon or Gieseking.

Piano concertos Nos. 13 in A, K.415; 20 in D min., K.466.
(BB) **(*) Naxos Dig. 8.550201 [id.]. Jenö Jandó, Concentus Hungaricus, András Ligeti.

This is Volume 1 in the planned complete recording of the Mozart piano concertos by Naxos with Jenö Jandó and the excellent Concentus Hungaricus, a polished chamber group using modern instruments, here directed to stylish effect by András Ligeti. These performances set a high standard in their communicative immediacy, and if they have not quite the individuality of Perahia or Ashkenazy, they are worth a place in any collection and are very modestly priced. Here the early *A major Concerto* comes up with enticing freshness, allegros are crisp and alert and the slow movement has a disarming simplicity. Ligeti creates a sense of anticipatory tension at the opening of the coupled *D minor Concerto* and this performance has plenty of drama, with the *Romance* very appealingly shaped. Jandó uses Beethoven's cadenzas with impressive authority. The balance and recording are most believable and there is good documentation throughout this series.

(i) *Piano concertos Nos. 15 in B flat, K.450;* (ii) *23 in A, K.488; 24 in C min., K.491.*
(M) (***) EMI mono CDH7 63707-2 [id.]. Solomon, Philh. O, (i) Ackermann; (ii) Menges.

At last EMI have restored Solomon's classic Mozart concerto accounts to circulation. It is astonishing that this company has been so tardy in paying due recognition to one of the greatest pianists of the present century. These records all come from 1953–5 and have that classical purity and tonal finesse for which Solomon was so famous. They are a model of style and have an extraordinary poise and authority. The recordings come up very well, and no apologies need be made for the sound quality or the recorded balance. Essential listening for all Mozartians.

Piano concertos Nos. 17 in G, K.453; 18 in B flat, K.456.
(BB) *** Naxos Dig. 8.550205 [id.]. Jenö Jandó, Concentus Hungaricus, Mátyás Antal.

Volume 5 is one of the finest so far in Jandó's excellent super-bargain series. The orchestral response under Mátyás Antal is very persuasive, with the finesse of the string playing immediately apparent at the very opening of K.453, and the final *Allegretto* similarly stylish. Tempi are admirably judged and both slow movements are most sensitively played. The variations which form the *Andante* of K.456 are particularly appealing in their perceptive use of light and shade, while the very lively *Allegro vivace* finale of the same work is infectiously spirited. Jandó uses Mozart's original cadenzas for the first two movements of K.453 and the composer's alternative cadenzas for K.546. Excellent sound. This may not quite match Perahia's full-priced analogue coupling of the same two concertos (CBS MK 35586), but it is thoroughly worthwhile in its own right and remarkably inexpensive.

Piano concertos Nos. 17; 20; 22; 24; 25; Rondo in D, K.382. Piano sonatas Nos. 10, K.330; 11, K.331; Fantasias, K.396 & K.475; Romanze, K.Anh.205; Minuet, K.1.
(M) (***) EMI mono CHS7 63719-2 (3). Edwin Fischer, various orchs. & conductors.

Edwin Fischer's record of the *G major concerto*, K.453, directed from the keyboard, is among the classics of the gramophone; it could still serve as a model of style in 1991, for it has radiant vitality, freshness and spirit and its 1937 sound is very good indeed. The first CD couples it with an almost equally magisterial account of the *D minor*, K.466, with the *C major Sonata* as a fill-up. Fischer's pre-war recording of K.482, with Barbirolli and the LPO, on the second CD is hardly less powerful, wonderfully paced, concentrated and alive, as is his *C minor*, K.491, with Lawrance Collingwood and the Barbirolli Chamber Orchestra. The last CD brings us a post-war account of the *C major*, K.503, with the Philharmonia under Josef Krips, not quite of the same stature as K.453 and K.482 but full of illuminating touches and fine musicianship. There is much for any Mozartian to learn throughout this set: Fischer plays his own cadenzas, an object lesson in themselves. Listening to these performances, one understands why this artist is so admired by a later generations of Mozartians – pianists like Denis Matthews, Alfred Brendel and Murray

Perahia. By comparison with the French LP transfer of K.453 some years back, the sound is a little dried out but still generally very good.

Piano concertos Nos. 19–21; 24; 27; (i) *Double piano concerto in E flat, K.365. Piano sonatas Nos. 12 in F, K.332; 16 in B flat, K.570; Rondo in A min., K.511.*
(M) (***) EMI mono CHS7 63703-2 (3) [Ang. CDHC 63703]. Artur Schnabel; (i) with Karl Urich Schnabel; various orchestras & conductors.

Schnabel's Mozart is every bit as personal and impulsive as one would expect, more fiery and impetuous than Gieseking and less polished and poised. He occasionally thrusts ahead and makes much of the pre-echoes of Beethoven in the *C minor*, K.491, recorded with the Philharmonia under Walter Süsskind in 1948. His own cadenza, which serves to remind us that he was himself a composer, plunges us into an entirely different world which approaches Busoni in its wild harmonies and sudden modulations. His K.595 was much earlier (1934) and sounds extraordinarily good for the period, though allowances must be made for the very different style of string-playing of the LSO, with Barbirolli producing some period *portamenti*. The *Double concerto*, made with the LSO and Sir Adrian Boult at about the same time as the Bach *C major*, has plenty of sparkle and spontaneity. His K.467 (recorded with Sargent in 1937) also has a Schnabel cadenza which, though less celebrated than the one for the *C minor*, is engagingly out of period. There are great musical insights, particularly in the slow movement of K.595 and the *A minor Rondo*, K.511 (like the *F major Sonata*, a post-war recording). However, among the pianists of the time, if you find Gieseking too cool and well-bred and Schnabel too full of temperament, and you set greater store by sheer keyboard finesse and elegance, Edwin Fischer is a far better choice, for he brings to Mozart both the dedication and thoughtfulness of Schnabel and the perfect sense of style and mastery of colour of Gieseking.

Piano concerto No. 20 in D min., K.466.
(M) ** EMI CDD7 63892-2 [id.]; *ET 763892-4.* Yuri Egorov, Philh. O, Sawallisch – BEETHOVEN: *Piano concerto No. 5.***(*)

A generous coupling for an imaginative if slightly controversial account of the *Emperor concerto.* The Mozart performance, though well played, is less distinctive, even though Egorov is stylish and Sawallisch finds plenty of drama in the outer movements and begins the finale, the most striking of the three, with great energy and bustle. Good, bright 1985 EMI digital recording, made at Abbey Road.

(i; iii) *Piano concerto No. 20 in D min., K.466;* (iii) *3 German dances, K.605; Overtures: La clemenza di Tito; La finta giardiniera; Le nozze di Figaro; Serenade No. 13 (Eine kleine Nachtmusik), K.525; Symphonies Nos. 38 in D (Prague);* (iv) *39 in E flat, K.453;* (iii) *41 in C, K.551 (Jupiter);* (ii; iii) *Requiem Mass, K.626.*
(M) (**) EMI mono CHS7 63912-2 (3) [id.]. (i) Bruno Walter (piano); (ii) Schumann, Thorborg, Dermota, Kipnis, V. State Op. Ch., (iii) VPO; (iv) BBC SO; all cond. Walter.

Bruno Walter had originally planned to become a pianist but a visit to Bayreuth in 1891 prompted him to change course. He remained a good accompanist and continued to direct Mozart concertos from the keyboard. To judge from his 1938 recording (it sounds earlier) of the *D minor Concerto*, K.466, he was no match for Edwin Fischer: his rhythmic control is far from flawless and his playing lacks the very last ounce of finish. All the same, there is the familiar humanity and warmth, which are much in evidence in the other performances. He and Koussevitzky were among the first guests whom Boult invited to conduct his newly formed BBC Symphony Orchestra, and the 1934 account of the *E flat Symphony* has great sparkle and freshness. The *Requiem* was recorded in 1937 at the Théâtre des Champs Elysées, Paris, with a distinguished team of soloists, but Walter never approved its release (there were minor blemishes of the kind one encounters in a concert) and it did not appear until a 1986 LP. For all their sonic frailty, these performances are rewarding and well worth having.

Piano concertos Nos. 20 in D min., K.466; 21 in C, K.467.
(M) *(*) DG 431 278-2; *431 278-4* [id.]. Rudolf Serkin, LSO, Abbado.

(i) *Piano concertos Nos. 20 in D min., K.466; 21 in C, K.467;* (ii) *Don Giovanni: overture.*
(B) ** RCA VD 60484; *VK 60484*. (i) Géza Anda, VSO; (ii) Chicago SO, Reiner.

These RCA recordings were made in 1973 after Géza Anda's complete cycle for DG. The two performances offered here do not add greatly to what has been said before, although K.466 is strikingly dramatic, rather more individual than K.467. Excellent recording. Reiner's fizzing 1959 account of the *Don Giovanni overture* makes an enjoyable encore, with splendid Chicago sound.

It is sad that Serkin had to leave it until his eighties to attempt a full series of the Mozart concertos. Though his thoughtfulness as an artist is often clear, his passage-work in these performances is scrappy and, though there are flashes of authority, the ends of phrases are not beautifully turned. Refined accompaniments from Abbado and the LSO, but even there the styles clash. There are stronger and more sensitive accounts of both concertos, though few that are better recorded, even to the point of including the soloist's vocal additions.

Piano concertos Nos. 20–21; 26 in D (Coronation), K. 537 (CD only: *27 in B flat, K.595*).
(B) ** DG Compact Classics 413 427-2 (2); *(*) *413 427-4*. [id.]. Géza Anda, Salzburg Mozarteum O.

Anda's versions from the early 1960s are reasonably competitive in Compact Classics format. The recording sometimes sounds a little dated now in the matter of string timbre, but the piano is clearly focused and truthful. *No. 20 in D minor* is one of Anda's stronger performances, with solo playing that is both stylish and spontaneous; No. 21 is notable for its poised introduction to the famous slow movement. One notices a certain rhythmic rigidity, and a lighter touch in the finale would have been acceptable, but on the whole this is satisfying. The *Coronation concerto*, however, is disappointing. Anda's reading lacks the magisterial quality of the finest accounts and there is a slightly routine feeling about the accompaniment. The balance is restored, however, on the pair of digitally remastered CDs, by the addition of Mozart's last concerto. Anda's performance of K.595 is one of the finest available. His playing is authoritative, deft and lively, and the recording is clear and fresh to match the music-making.

Piano concertos Nos. 20 in D min., K.466; 23 in A, K.488.
(M) **(*) Ph. Dig. 432 049-2; *432 049-4* [id.]. Mitsuko Uchida, ECO, Jeffrey Tate.

Although Uchida's superbly recorded disc represents excellent value at mid-price and both performances are beautifully played, there is a sense of reserve about the reading of K.466 which loses some of its dramatic cohesion. About the *A major Concerto*, K.488, there can be no reservations: Uchida's gentle manner never becomes self-effacing and her restrained, lyrical feeling is very affecting when the the contribution of the ECO under Tate has a matching sensibility. The only snag is the lack of any information about the music itself.

Piano concertos Nos. (i) *21 in C, K.467;* (ii) *22 in E flat, K.482; 23 in A, K.488;* (i) *24 in C min., K.491;* (ii) *26 in D (Coronation), K.537; 27 in B, K.595;* (iii) *Double piano concerto in E flat, K.365.*
❀ (M) **(*) Sony SM3K 46519 (3) [id.]. Robert Casadesus, with (i) Cleveland O, Szell; (ii) Columbia SO, Szell; (iii) Gaby Casadesus, Phd. O, Ormandy.

A very distinguished set, effectively transferred to CD. Casadesus's Mozart may at first seem understated, but the imagination behind his readings is apparent in every phrase and the accompaniment could hardly be more stylish. Casadesus takes the finale of No. 21 at a tremendous speed, but for the most part this is exquisite Mozart playing, beautifully paced and articulated. While not scaling the heights of Casadesus's earlier accounts with Bigot and Münch, the present versions with the Cleveland Orchestra still sound pretty marvellous, for all the shortcomings of the recording balance and the sometimes over-tense precision of Szell. In fact the balance is better than we had remembered it. Although the orchestra tends to dwarf the soloist in tuttis, the placing of the piano is very pleasing, and the subtleties of the solo playing are naturally caught. In No. 22, Casadesus is second to none: he has space and proportion on the one hand and a marvellously alive sense of detail and phrasing on the other. He is first rate in the *A major* too, accompanied in this and No. 22 by Szell again but this time with the Columbia Symphony Orchestra. Mozart's last piano concertos inspire two extremely memorable performances, each of them underlining the dramatic contrast of soloist and orchestra, almost as a meeting of heroine and hero. The *Double concerto* is essentially a genial work, and this is the one quality completely missing from Casadesus's performance, which has a matching dry recording. All the solo concertos, however, were recorded in Severance Hall, Cleveland, between 1959 and 1962 (except for No. 23, which dates from 1969) and the hall ambience provides an attractive fullness to the overall sound.

(i) *Piano concertos Nos. 20; 23–25;* (ii) *Piano and wind quintet, K.452.*
(M) (***) EMI mono CHS7 63709-2 (2). Walter Gieseking, with (i) Philh. O, Karajan or Rosbaud; (ii) Philh. Wind Qt.

There is some very distinguished playing here, far more memorable and characterful than the set of complete solo keyboard music on which Gieseking embarked immediately after these recordings. The *D minor* and *C major Concertos* (K.466 and K.503) were recorded in 1953 under Hans Rosbaud, and their appearance serves as a timely reminder of what a fine conductor he was. In the *D minor* Gieseking plays the Beethoven cadenzas and in the *C major* his own. The *A major*, K.488, and *C minor*, K.491 (in which he plays the Hummel cadenza), were made with Karajan at much the same time. The *A major* unfolds in a wonderfully serene and spacious fashion, and the Philharmonia wind are in superb form. Gieseking's celebrated record of the *Piano and wind quintet* with the Philharmonia Wind Quartet, all glorious players (Sidney Sutcliffe, Bernard Walton, the legendary Dennis Brain and Cecil James), was made in 1955 and has enjoyed classic status ever since, despite the rather unexpansive acoustic. The electrical hum in K.448 and K.503, for which the sleeve apologizes, is not a real problem and should not deter Gieseking aficionados or even the non-specialist collector, for the transfers are very well managed indeed.

(i) *Piano concerto No. 21 in C, K.467;* (ii) *Violin concerto No. 5 in A (Turkish), K.219.*
(BD) * Naxos Dig. 8.550293 [id.]. Capella Istropolitana, with (i) Peter Lang, (ii) Nishizaki; (i) Erberlee; (ii) Gunzenhauser.

There is nothing at all special about this performance of the *C major Piano concerto.*

The first movement is somewhat square and the finale very fast, and even the famous *Romanza* is not particularly enticing. Takako Nishizaki's performance of the *Fifth Violin concerto* is a different matter, but this is also available coupled with No. 3, a splendid disc – see below.

Piano concertos Nos. 22 in E flat, K.482; 25 in C, K.503.
(M) *(**) Tuxedo TUXCD 1046 [id.]. Brendel, VCO or V. State Op. O, Paul Angerer.
(M) *(*) DG Dig. 429 978-2; *429 978-4* [id.]. Rudolf Serkin, LSO, Abbado.

Brendel's recordings of the Mozart concertos made for Vox/Turnabout in the early 1960s were special. Even if the string tone is thin and the orchestral focus is less than perfect, there is some fine wind playing and Angerer directs the proceedings with plenty of character. Brendel plays the first movement of K.482 with great authority, the *Andante* very beautifully and the finale quite enchantingly. He is eminently stylish, too, in K.503; his phrasing of the lyrical secondary themes of the outer movements gives much pleasure. There is a sparkle and spontaneity in these performances that emerge less strikingly in his later, better-recorded versions for Philips, fine as these are.

Serkin made some distinguished Mozart concerto records way back in the days of shellac; some of his later recordings for CBS with Szell and Ormandy are also now reappearing on Sony. At the beginning of the 1980s he embarked on a new cycle as the eightieth year of his own life was fast approaching. Unfortunately he is now no match for the current competition, and no one listening to these versions would imagine that this was the same Serkin whose playing so captivated listeners to the old Busch Chamber Players' account of the *Brandenburg No. 5*. That sparkled with delight; this is hard work, with only the occasional glimmer of past glories.

Piano concertos Nos. 23 in A, K.488; 24 in C min., K.491.
(B) **(*) Decca 430 497-2; *430 497-4* [id.]. Clifford Curzon, LSO, Kertész (with SCHUBERT: *Impromptus: in G flat & A flat, D.899/3 & 4* ***).
(B) **(*) CfP CD-CFP 4511; *TC-CFP 4511*. Ian Hobson, ECO, Sir Alexander Gibson.
(BB) **(*) Naxos Dig. 8.550204 [id.]. Jenö Jandó, Concentus Hungaricus, Mátyás Antal.
(M) *(*) DG Dig. 431 279-2; *431 279-4* [id.]. Rudolf Serkin, LSO, Abbado.

Curzon's account of these two concertos is immaculate; no connoisseur of the piano will fail to derive pleasure and refreshment from them. Curzon has the advantage of sensitive support both from Kertész and from the Decca engineers, and only the absence of the last ounce of sparkle prevents this from being very strongly recommended. Two of the Schubert Op. 90 *Impromptus*, added as an attractive fill-up, are undoubtedly distinguished and add to the attractiveness of this reissue.

Ian Hobson, the fourth-prizewinner in the 1978 Leeds Piano Competition who then came back to win that international event three years later, is generally associated with virtuoso piano music, but here shows himself a stylish Mozartian, if a somewhat reticent one. These are clean, generally refreshing performances, remarkably free of mannerism and lacking only the last degree of individuality. Speeds are unexceptionable, the accompaniment admirable and the sound first rate, making this an excellent bargain, clear and vivid. Hobson contributes his own tasteful cadenza for the first movement of K.491.

Antal's tempo in the first movement of the well-loved *A major Concerto* is bracingly brisk. The effect is undoubtedly fresh, but some ears may find the music could do with a touch more relaxation. This certainly comes in the *Adagio*, which has a simple melancholic nostalgia, and the energy returns appropriately in the vivacious closing *Allegro assai*. The operatic drama inherent in the first movement in the *C minor Concerto* is brought out well, and Jandó imaginatively and effectively chooses a cadenza by Hummel for this movement. Then, after the refined sensibility of the *Larghetto*, the finale is quite admirably paced. Recording is well up to the standard of the series.

Serkin's performances are for aficionados only. His playing is short on finish and elegance, nor is this offset on the balance sheet by the interpretative insights that distinguished his pre-war Mozart records. Well recorded as it is, the playing is just too unmelting to convey pleasure in K.588, and is insufficiently searching in the great *C minor*.

Piano concertos Nos. 23 in A, K.488; 26 in D (Coronation), K.537.
(M) *** CBS MPK 45884 [id.]. Casadesus, Cleveland O, Szell.

Here is a coupling to match that by these artists of Nos. 21 and 24 (CBS MYK 42594 – see our main volume, p. 657). K.537 inspires Casadesus and Szell to a really outstanding performance. Casadesus is marvellous in No. 23, too; though neither Kempff (DG 423 885-2) nor Pollini (DG 429 812-2) is displaced, this disc is the pick of the three records included in the box discussed above. Szell's accompaniments could hardly be more stylish. The transfers to CD are excellently managed; the sound has good ambience and fullness. This is a splendid disc.

Piano concerto No. 25 in C, K.503.
(M) *** Sony MYK 44832 [id.]; *40-44832*. Leon Fleisher, Cleveland O, Szell – BEETHOVEN: *Piano concerto No. 4*.***

Fleisher and Szell achieve a memorable partnership in this 1959 recording. The kernel of the performance is the beautiful slow movement, classically serene; Szell's accompaniment matches the soloist in poise, and the music is given a Beethovenian depth. The commanding outer movements have great vitality: Fleisher shapes the first movement's second subject most engagingly and is wonderfully nimble in the finale, while Szell's orchestral detail is a constant source of pleasure. The coupling is equally outstanding, and the recording emerges freshly on CD.

Piano concertos Nos. 25 in C, K.503; 27 in B flat, K.595.
(M) *(*) DG Dig. 431 280-2; *431 280-4* [id.]. Rudolf Serkin, LSO, Abbado.

If Rudolf Serkin's present Mozart was as good as the pre-war vintage – or, for that matter, as some of the recordings he made at Marlboro in the 1960s – this would be a most valuable re-coupling. There is much to admire, including a clear, well-focused recording and refined accompaniments from Abbado – the opening of K.595 is measured and spacious – with an excellent response from the LSO. But even there Serkin is wanting in the grace he once commanded: the insights this distinguished Mozartian brings to these concertos do not compensate for the ungainly passage-work and other infelicities. His vocal melisma is also slightly distracting.

Double piano concerto in E flat, K.365; (i) *Triple piano concerto in F (Lodron), K.242.*
(M) **(*) EMI Dig. CD-EMX 2124; *TC-EMX 2124*. Eschenbach, Frantz; Helmut Schmidt, LPO, Eschenbach.

Eschenbach's 1981 version of the *Double concerto* which he directs from the keyboard is the only one to include the clarinets, trumpets and timpani published in the orchestral material by Breitkopf & Härtel in 1881. These instruments were added for the Vienna performance of 1781, but there is some doubt as to their authenticity. Both Eschenbach and Frantz are lively and persuasive in the concerto, though comparison with the Gilels version on DG, coupled with K.595, is not to their advantage: that is a glorious record. In the *Triple concerto* the third pianist is Helmut Schmidt, at the time of the record Chancellor of West Germany, who makes a creditable showing. The digital recording is very good indeed in both formats, but the coupling does not displace Gilels in K.365.

Violin concertos

Complete Mozart Edition, Volume 8: (i) *Violin concertos Nos 1–5; 7 in D, K.271; Adagio in E, K.361; Rondo in B flat, K.269; Rondo in C, K.373.* (i; ii) *Concertone, K.190;* (iii; iv) *Double Concerto in D for violin, piano and orchestra, K.315f;* (iii; v; vi) *Sinfonia concertante in A, for violin, viola, cello and orchestra, K.320e.* (iii; v) *Sinfonia concertante in E flat, K.364.*
(M) **(*) Ph. Analogue/Dig. 422 508-2 (4). (i) Szeryng, (ii) with Poulet, Morgan, Jones; New Philh. O, Gibson; (iii) Iona Brown, with (iv) Shelley, (v) Imai, (vi) Orton; ASMF, Marriner.

Volume 8 in the Philips Complete Mozart Edition is even more interesting than most, when it contains very convincing reconstructions of works that Mozart left as fragments. Philip Wilby has not only completed the first movement of an early *Sinfonia concertante for violin, viola and cello* (Mozart's only music with concertante cello) but also, through shrewd detective work, has reconstructed a full three-movement *Double concerto* from what Mozart left as 'a magnificent torso', to use Alfred Einstein's description; it is for violin, piano and orchestra, and Wilby's premiss is that – for reasons which he gives in fair detail – the *Violin sonata in D*, K.306, was in fact a reworking of the *Double concerto* which Mozart said he was writing in 1778 and which he could well have completed. The result here is a delight, a full-scale, 25-minute work which ends with an effervescent double-variation finale, alternately in duple and compound time. That is superbly done with Iona Brown and Howard Shelley as soloists; and the other ASMF items are very good too, with Iona Brown joined by Nobuko Imai most characterfully on the viola in the great *Sinfonia concertante*, K.364. What is a shade disappointing – even in a well-filled set at mid-price – is to have Henryk Szeryng's readings of the main violin concertos from the 1960s, instead of the Grumiaux set (which fortunately are available separately at bargain price on Philips 422 938-2). Szeryng is sympathetic but a trifle reserved and not as refreshing as Grumiaux.

(i) *Violin concertos Nos. 1 in B flat, K.207;* (ii) *2 in D, K. 211;* (iii) *3 in C, K.216;* (ii) *4 in D, K.218;* (i) *5 in A (Turkish), K.219;* (ii) *Adagio in C, K.261; Rondo No. 2 in C, K.373; Haffner Serenade, K.250: Rondo* (all for violin & orchestra); (iv) *Sinfonia concertante in E flat, K.364;* (v) *Divertimento in E flat for string trio (violin, viola & cello), K.563.*
(M) **(*) Sony SM3K 46523 [id.]. Isaac Stern, with (i) Columbia SO, Szell; (ii) ECO, Schneider; (iii) Cleveland O, Szell; (iv) Zukerman, ECO, Barenboim; (v) Pinchas Zukerman, Leonard Rose.

Unlike most sets of the Mozart *Violin concertos*, Stern's recordings were made at different times and with different conductors, with somewhat variable results. It goes without saying that the solo playing is always splendid; it is simply that he is not always as sensitive on detail as his rivals, and this especially applies to No. 1 and rather less so to No. 5 where the accompaniment is provided by the Columbia Symphony Orchestra under Szell. The interpretation of No. 3, however, displays Stern's qualities of sparkling stylishness at their most intense in a very satisfying reading, with a beautifully poised and pointed accompaniment from the same conductor but now with the splendid Cleveland Orchestra. Here the beauty of Stern's contribution easily triumphs over the comparatively undistinguished sound. In Nos. 2 and 4, Stern has the benefit of rather fuller recording and his playing, as always, is full of personality. Stern recorded the great *Sinfonia concertante* for CBS at least twice before this version, which stands among the finest available and is certainly the jewel in this set, presenting as it does two soloists of equally strong musical personality. The central slow movement is taken at a very expansive *Andante* but the concentration intensifies the beauty, and the finale is sparkling and resilient – more so than on Stern's previous version which he conducted himself. Fair, if somewhat aggressive recording, with the two soloists too closely balanced. The trio of famous virtuosi, Stern, Zuckerman and Rose, brings an individually characterized performance of the *Divertimento for string trio* with hushed playing accurately conveyed and the players clearly separated within an atmospheric acoustic, even though the recording is rather close and bright. Besides the *Adagio*, K.261, beautifully played, and the *Rondo*, K.373, Stern also offers the fourth-movement *Rondo* of the *Haffner Serenade*, which has a fizzing concertante violin part.

Violin concertos Nos 1–7; Adagio, K.261; Rondos, K.269, K.373 (for violin & orchestra).
(B) ** Pickwick Dig. PCD 946-8 (3). Ernst Kovacic, SCO.

In full and vivid sound Kovacic's fresh and alert performances provide a fair recommendation for Mozart's violin concertante music. Generally urgent and direct, they lack something in individuality and Mozartian sparkle. That they remain rather straight-faced, with rhythms at times a little square, probably reflects the absence of conductor.

Violin concertos Nos 1–5; Adagio in E, K.261; Rondos in B flat, K.269 & in C, K.373; (i) *Concertone, K.190; Sinfonia concertante, K.364.*
(B) *** Hung. Dig. HCD 31030/32 (3) [id.]. Gyorgy Pauk, (i) with Rolla; Franz Liszt CO, Janos Rolla.

Pauk, silvery-toned and elegant, gives performances that reject the still-prevalent nineteenth-century idea of these works as virtuoso vehicles. With Janos Rolla drawing crisp, resilient playing from the Franz Liszt Chamber Orchestra, these are lighter, fresher readings than most on rival sets. Pauk brings out the fun and sparkle of Mozart consistently, with speeds often a shade brisker than in weightier versions. That is particularly striking in the *Concertone*, an early work that is here given an athletic reading, full of youthful high spirits. The sound is refined yet immediate, matching the elegance of the playing. Rolla acts as second soloist in both the *Concertone* and (on the viola) in the great *Sinfonia concertante*, not as individual a player as Pauk but satisfyingly full-toned. A fine digital bargain recommendation.

Violin concertos Nos. 1 in B flat, K.207; 2 in D, K.211; Rondo in B flat, K.269; Andante in F (arr. Saint-Saëns from *Piano concerto No. 21, K.467*).
(BB) **(*) Naxos Dig. 8.550414 [id.]. Takako Nishizaki, Capella Istropolitana, Johannes Wildner.

This was the last disc to be recorded (in 1990) of Takako Nishizaki's fine survey of the violin concertos. The opening movement of K.207 is brisk and fresh, with the bright, digital sound emphasizing the immediacy; although the *Adagio* is played with an agreeable, simple eloquence, this is the least individual of Nishizaki's readings. The *Second Concerto*, K.211, although still admirably direct, has rather more flair, the *Andante* touchingly phrased, and the finale has a winning lightness of touch. The *Rondo* is also an attractively spontaneous performance, and as an encore we are offered Saint-Saëns's arrangement of the famous '*Elvira Madigan*' theme from the *C major Concerto*, K.467. Obviously the French composer recognized a 'lollipop' when he heard one.

Violin concertos Nos. 1 in B flat, K.207; 2 in D, K.211; 3 in G, K.216.
(M) **(*) Sony Dig. SBK 46539 [id.]. Zukerman, St Paul CO.

Zukerman's set has the advantage of excellent digital recording and a good balance, the violin forward but not distractingly so. The playing of outer movements is agreeably simple and fresh, and in the slow movements of both the *D major* and *G major Concertos* Zukerman's sweetness of tone will appeal to many, although his tendency to languish a little in his expressiveness, particularly in the *G major*, may be counted a less attractive feature. The St Paul Chamber Orchestra is clearly in rapport with its soloist/director and accompanies with stylish warmth.

Violin concertos Nos. 1 in B flat, K.207; 2 in D, K.211; 5 in A (Turkish), K.219.
(M) ** DG Dig. 431 281-2; *431 281-4* [id.]. Gidon Kremer, VPO, Harnoncourt.

Neither Kremer nor Harnoncourt is entirely consistent in their approach to these three concertos. Kremer's playing is expert throughout but, for all his finesse, the *B flat Concerto* is curiously uninvolving and the digital recording is inclined to be fierce in the treble. Harnoncourt's opening movement of K.211 is brisk and clean, then the slow movement is purposefully moulded. With Kremer playing sweetly throughout, this is undoubtedly enjoyable, and the finale is attractively spirited. The recording, too, made in the Musikverein, is fuller, if still brightly lit. In No. 5, the last to be recorded (in 1987), Kremer's elegant vitality is again apparent, although there are individual touches in both phrasing and dynamic contrast which may not appeal to all. Harnoncourt's tuttis are strong and direct and the partnership is generally successful, with the fine VPO playing always providing an anchor for the soloist, while remaining resilient at all times. The recording is full and clear, but remains very bright.

(i) *Violin concertos Nos. 2; 5 (Turkish), K.219;* (ii) *Divertimento for string trio in E flat, K.563.*
(B) ** DG Compact Classics *423 289-4* [id.]. (i) Wolfgang Schneiderhan, BPO; (ii) Italian String Trio.

Schneiderhan's performances come from a complete set, made with the Berlin Philharmonic Orchestra at the end of the 1960s. He plays with effortless mastery and a strong sense of classical proportion. The Berlin orchestra accompany well for him, though there is a slightly unsmiling quality at times. The tape transfers are very successful, smooth and vivid. The recording of the masterly *Divertimento for string trio* also sounds well in its tape format. The performance is remarkable for its accuracy of intonation. The Italian String Trio is a wonderfully polished group – in a sense too polished, for their trim, fast speeds reveal rather too little temperament. Even so, this is very acceptable when it is so generously coupled.

Violin concertos Nos. 2 in D, K.211; 7 in D, K.271a; Rondo in C, K.373.
*** Sony Dig. SK 44913 [id.]; *40-44913*. Cho-Liang Lin, ECO, Leppard.

Lin's coupling of the early *D major concerto* and the doubtfully attributed K.271a follows the pattern of his earlier Mozart recordings in sweet, elegant playing, beautifully supported by Leppard in a traditional but uninflated style. First-rate recording.

Violin concerto No. 3 in G, K.216.
(B) ** DG Compact Classics *415 332-4* [id.]. Wolfgang Schneiderhan, BPO – BEETHOVEN: *Triple concerto*; BRAHMS: *Double concerto.***

Schneiderhan's is a finely wrought performance, strongly classical and well recorded for its period. He plays his own cadenzas and although there is a slight want of sparkle, and perhaps the atmosphere is also a shade cool, the reading is still thoroughly enjoyable. The Compact Classics tape is well engineered and offers generous couplings.

Violin concertos Nos. 3 in G, K.216; 4 in D, K.218; Rondos (for violin & orchestra) Nos. 1 in B flat, K.269; 2 in B flat, K.373.
(M) *** DG Dig. 431 282-2; *431 282-2* [id.]. Itzhak Perlman, VPO, Levine.

Perlman likes to be closely balanced, and in K.216 one is very conscious of his virtuosity. But this element of self-consciousness does not seriously detract from the Mozartian spirit, thanks to the calibre of the playing and the finesse and warmth of his phrasing. In No. 4 the artistic rapport between soloist and orchestra is particularly striking. Once again Perlman's bravura is effortless and even more charismatic, and the orchestral playing is glorious. The perspective of the recording seems rather more natural here. The two engaging *Rondos* are played with fine style.

Violin concertos Nos. 3 in G, K.216; 5 in A (Turkish), K.219.
(BB) *** Naxos Dig. 8.550063 [id.]. Takako Nishizaki, Capella Istropolitana, Stephen Gunzenhauser.

This is the finest of Nishizaki's three discs of the Mozart violin concertos. The readings are individual and possess the most engaging lyrical feeling, stemming directly from the lovely solo timbre and the natural response of the soloist to Mozartian line and phrase. In the opening movement of K.219 (which comes first on the disc), Gunzenhauser's introduction is full of life and, at the expressive violin entry, Nishizaki holds the tempo back just a little and then sails off into the allegro with great zest. The *Adagio* is tender and serene, and the contrasting episodes of the finale are sparklingly handled, with the 'Turkish' interlude full of character. A sprightly vigour also informs the outer movements of K.216 and the *Adagio* has a gentle beauty, with the light-hearted finale providing a perfect contrast. A good balance, the soloist forward, but convincingly so, and the orchestral backcloth, always polished and supportive, in natural perspective. A real bargain.

Violin concerto No. 4 in D, K.218; (i) *Sinfonia concertante in E flat, for violin, viola and orchestra, K.364.*
(BB) **(*) Naxos Dig. 8.550332 [id.]. Takako Nishizaki, (i) Ladislav Kyselak; Capella Istropolitana, Stephen Gunzenhauser.

A fine account of No. 4, with Takako Nishizaki's solo playing well up to the high standard of this series and with Stephen Gunzenhauser's perceptive pacing, especially of the tranquil *Andante cantabile* and the engaging finale with its contrasting duo-tempi, adding to our pleasure. The *Sinfonia concertante* is very enjoyable too, if perhaps slightly less distinctive. It does not lack intensity of feeling from the well-matched soloists; indeed, at their expressive entry at the end of the exposition – which has a strong orchestral tutti with some fine horn playing – there is a brief passage of affectionate indulgence. The finale is infectious in its liveliness, its rhythms buoyantly pointed. Again, a good balance and excellent sound.

Violin concertos Nos. 4 in D, K.218; 5 in A (Turkish), K.219; Adagio in E, K.261; Rondo in C, K.373 (both for violin & orchestra).
(M) **(*) Sony SBK 46540 [id.]. Zukerman, St Paul CO.

Zukerman's account of K.218 is unmannered and stylish, admirably direct in approach, though the *Andante* is taken rather slowly. The pacing of the last movement is somewhat idiosyncratic. His admirers will not be disappointed with K.219, although his sweet tone and effortless facility do not always engage one's sympathies. He languishes lovingly in the slow movement (though rather less so than in the *G major*, K.219) and is not always subtle in his expression of feeling. The shorter pieces are played with some flair, the *Adagio* most appealingly. The St Paul Chamber Orchestra obviously contains some fine players and the accompaniments, which Zukerman also directs, are polished, the recording vivid and rather brightly lit.

Dances and Marches

Complete Mozart Edition, Volume 6: *La Chasse, KA.103/K.299d; Contredanses, K.101; K.123; K.267; K.269b; K.462; (Das Donnerwetter) K.534; (La Bataille) K.535; 535a; (Der Sieg vom Helden Koburg) K.587; K.603; (Il trionfo delle donne) K.607; (Non più andrai) K.609; K.610; Gavotte, K.300; German dances, K.509; K.536; K.567; K.571; K.586; K.600; K.602; K.605; Ländler, K.606; Marches, K.214; K.363; K.408; K.461; Minuets, K.61b; K.61g/2; K.61h; K.94, 103, 104, 105; K.122; K.164; K.176; K.315g; K.568; K.585; K.599; K.601; K.604; Minuets with Contredanses, K.463; Overture & 3 Contredanses, K.106.*
❀ (M) *** Ph. 422 506-2 (6). Vienna Mozart Ens., Willi Boskovsky.

Philips have chosen to use Willi Boskovsky's famous series of recordings of the dance music, made for Decca in the mid-1960s, for Volume 6 of their Complete Mozart Edition. Much of the credit for this remarkable undertaking should go to its expert producer, Erik Smith, who, besides providing highly stylish orchestrations for numbers without Mozart's own scoring, illuminates the music with some of the most informative and economically written notes that ever graced a record. On the completion of the orginal project, H. C. Robbins Landon cabled his praises and hailed 'the most beautiful Mozart playing and most sophisticated sound I know'. The CD transfers preserve the excellence of the sound: it is a shade crisper in definition and outline but has not lost its bloom. The layout is historical, with the music grouped into five sections: Salzburg and Italy (1769–77); Paris (1778); Vienna and Salzburg (1782–4); Prague (1787); and Dances for the Redoutensaal (1788–91). The collector might feel that he or she is faced here with an *embarrsas de richesses* with more than 120 *Minuets*, nearly 50 *German dances* and some three dozen *Contredanses*, but Mozart's invention is seemingly inexhaustible, and the instrumentation is full of imaginative touches. As Erik Smith comments, 'In the late dances Mozart seems to have used the medium of dance music to experiment in. Here is instrumentation as rich as Brahms, yet utterly lucid. There is nothing quite like it in the late symphonies and only a little in *Così fan tutte* and *Die Zauberflöte*.' Of course these are records to be dipped into rather than played a whole disc at a time; but there are surprises everywhere, and much that is inspired.

Contredanses: La Bataille, K.535; Das Donerwetter, K.534; Les filles malicieuses, K.610; Der Sieg vom Helden Koburg, K.587; It trionfo delle donne, K.607. Gallimathias musicum (quodlibet), K.32; 6 German dances, K.567; 3 German dances, K.605; German dance: Die Leyerer, K.611. March in D, K.335/1. A Musical joke, K.522.
*** DG Dig. 429 783-2; *429 783-4* [id.]. Orpheus CO.

A splendid sampler of the wit and finesse, to say nothing of the high quality of entertainment, provided by Mozart's dance music, which kept people on their feet till dawn at masked balls in the 1780s and early 1790s. The little *March in D* is full of buoyant rhythmic zest, and the felicity of the characteristic *Contredanses* is a constant delight, with *Les filles malicieuses* the model of elegance and *La Bataille* picaresquely celebrated with trumpet, fife and drum. *Die Leyerer* ('The hurdy-gurdy men') are no less piquantly depicted, but the other *German dances* (of which the most famous is the *Sleigh-ride*, K.605/3) are hardly less inventive in style and colour. The playing of the Orpheus group is winningly polished, flexible and smiling, and they bring off the *Musical joke* with considerable flair, both in the gentle fun of the *Adagio cantabile*, which is exquisitely played, and in the outrageous grinding dissonance of the 'wrong notes' at the end. First-class sound, fresh, transparent and vividly immediate.

Complete Mozart Edition, Volume 4: *Divertimenti for strings Nos. 1–3, K.136/8; Divertimenti for small orchestra Nos. 1 in E flat, K.113; 7 in D, K.205* (with *March in D, K.290); 10 in F, K.247* (with *March in F, K.248); 11 in D, K.251; 15 in B flat, K.287; 17 in D, K.334* (with *March in D, K.445); A Musical joke, K.622; Serenade (Eine kleine Nachtmusik), K.525.*
(M) *** Ph. Dig. 422 504-2 (5) [id.]. ASMF CO.

This is one of the most attractive of all the boxes in the Philips Mozart Edition. The music itself is a delight, the performances are stylish, elegant and polished, while the digital recording has admirable warmth and realistic presence and definition.

Divertimenti for strings Nos. 1 in D; 2 in B flat; 3 in F, K.136–8; Serenades Nos. 6 in D (Serenata notturna); 13 in G (Eine kleine Nachtmusik).
(M) *** Ph. Dig. 432 055-2; *432 055-4* [id.]. I Musici.

I Musici's outstanding recording of the three *String divertimenti* is now joined with their remarkably fresh account of *Eine kleine Nachtmusik*, as fine as any in the catalogue and better than most. The vivid digital sound has excellent balance and striking presence throughout. A self-recommending mid-priced reissue, except for the lack of any information about the music being included.

(i) *Divertimenti for strings Nos. 1, K.136, & 3, K.138; Serenade No. 6 (Serenata Notturna);* (ii) *Serenade No. 13 (Eine kleine Nachtmusik);* (iii) *Sinfonia concertante in E flat, K.297b* (CD only: (iv) *Serenade No. 12 in C min., K.388*).
(B) **(*) DG Compact Classics 413 152-2 (2); *413 152-4* [id.]. (i) BPO, Karajan; (ii) VPO, Boehm; (iii) BPO, Boehm (CD only: (iv) VPO Wind Ens.).

Karajan's performances of the *String divertimenti* and the *Serenata notturna* are beautifully played, and as such they prompt the liveliest admiration. At the same time there is a predictably suave elegance that seems to militate against spontaneity. Cultured and effortless readings, beautifully recorded and well balanced, they somehow leave one untouched. There is too much legato and not always a balancing sparkle. Boehm's contribution to this bargain-priced Compact Classics tape is another matter. His 1976 VPO version of Mozart's *Night music* is among the finest of those played by a full complement of strings, polished and spacious, with a neat, lightly pointed finale. The account of the *Sinfonia concertante* is of superlative quality, sounding amazingly idiomatic and well blended, with the balance between soloists and orchestra nicely managed. This is altogether refreshing. The chrome-tape transfers are generally very well managed. The pair of digitally remastered CDs also include the *Wind Serenade*, K.388, and here there are some reservations about the overall matching of timbres. The Viennese oboe is thinner and reedier than one would like, though the clarinet is particularly smooth in tone. This well-recorded performance will undoubtedly give pleasure, but ideally one needs a rather more homogeneous blend in Mozart.

Complete Mozart Edition, Volume 5: *Divertimentos for wind Nos. 3 in E flat, K.166; 4 in B flat, K.186; 6 in C, K.188; 8 in F, K.213; 9 in B flat K.240; 12 in E flat, K.252; 13 in F,*

K.253; 14 in B flat, K.270; 16 in E flat, K.289; in E flat, K.Anh. 226; in B flat, K.Anh. 227; Divertimentos for 3 basset horns, K.439b/1–5; Duos for 2 horns, K.487/1–12; Serenades for wind No. 10 in B flat, K.361; 11 in E flat, K.375; 12 in C min., K.388; Adagios: in F; B flat, K.410–11.
*** Ph. Analogue/Dig. 422 505-2 [id.]. Holliger Wind Ens. (or members of); Netherlands Wind Ens., De Waart (or members of); ASMF, Marriner or Laird.

Mozart's wind music, whether in the ambitious *Serenades* or the simpler *Divertimenti*, brings a naturally felicitous blending of timbre and colour unmatched by any other composer. There is a considerable variety of instrumentation here and an unending diversity of invention. It seems that even when writing for the simplest combination of wind instruments, Mozart is incapable of being dull. The works for two horns are conjecturally allocated. The principal role involves some hair-raising bravura; thus it is suggested by some authorities that they were intended for basset horns. But given the kind of easy virtuosity they receive here, from Iman Soeteman and Jan Peeters, they get our vote in favour of horns every time. To afford maximum variety, they are presented in groups of three movements, interspersed with the other divertimentos. The playing of the more ambitious works is admirably polished and fresh, and it is interesting to note that Holliger's group provides a stylishly light touch and texture with the principal oboe dominating, while the blending of the Netherlanders is somewhat more homogeneous, though the effect is still very pleasing. It is very easy to enjoy both, when the recording is so well balanced and realistic.

Divertimenti Nos. 7 in D, K.205; 10 in F, K.247; Serenade No. 13 in G (Eine kleine Nachtmusik), K.525.
(B) *(*) HM/BMG VD 77521 [Victrola 77521-2-RV]. Coll. Aur., Fanzjosef Maier.

Polished performances of both these fine *Divertimenti*, effectively using original instruments; but the playing has a definite absence of charm, and the violin timbre is rather grainy, especially in K.247, recorded in 1964. *Eine kleine Nachtmusik* is later (1975, like K.205) and comes off much better, the playing agreeably fresh and spontaneous; here the string texture is distinctly more pleasing.

Divertimento No. 15 in B flat, K.287; Serenades Nos. 6 in D (Serenata notturna), K.239; 13 in G (Eine kleine Nachtmusik).
(M) **(*) DG Dig. 431 272-2; *431 272-4* [id.]. BPO, Karajan.

The finesse and the unforced virtuosity of the Berlin Philharmonic (featuring the full string section) in the large-scale *Divertimento*, K.287, is very easy to enjoy. So is the *Night music*, which has both vitality and elegance. This is the mid-priced reissue of a disc reviewed in our main volume (p. 668) with the elegant, if slightly bland account of the *Serenata notturna* added for good measure (in DG's 3D Mozart Collection).

Divertimento No. 17 in D, K.334; Notturno (Serenade) in D, K.286; Serenade No. 13 in G (Eine kleine Nachtmusik), K.525.
(B) *** Decca 430 496-2; *430 496-4* [id.]. ASMF, Marriner.

Mozart's innocently tricky *Notturno for four orchestras*, with its spatial interplay, is here played with superb style and is very well recorded. The *Divertimento*, equally, finds the Academy of St Martin's at its peak, relishing the technical problems of co-ordinating music which is often performed by solo strings and playing with great finesse. Versions of *Eine kleine Nachtmusik* which have such fresh, unaffected refinement are rare, but this analogue recording from the old Argo catalogue of the most popular of Mozart's serenades is delightfully played and wears its years lightly, like the others on this disc. A fine and generous bargain triptych.

3 German dances, K.605; Overtures: *Così fan tutte; Don Giovanni; Die Entfürung aus dem Serail; La finta giardinera; Idomeneo; Le nozze di Figaro; Der Schauspieldirektor; Die Zauberflöte. Serenades Nos. 6 (Serenata Notturna), K.239; 13 (Eine kleine Nachtmusik), K.525.*
(B) ** EMI CDZ7 62858-2 [id.]. RPO or Philh. O, Sir Colin Davis.

Sir Colin Davis and the Philharmonia are most successful in Mozart's two nocturnal serenades. The *Nachtmusik* is relaxed yet entirely convincing and spontaneous, and the orchestral soloists in the *Serenata notturna* are of a high order. It is a pity that the CD transfer over-brightens the violin timbre, so that one needs to soften the upper range in playback. The overtures are stylishly conceived performances with polished RPO playing, especially from the first violins and woodwind. There is no lack of drama here, though a lighter touch is given to the charming *La finta giardiniera*, and *Così fan tutte* bubbles vivaciously. Clean, bright recording, still brightly lit.

Masonic funeral music (Maurerische Trauermusik) – see below, under VOCAL MUSIC

A Musical joke, K.522; Notturno for 4 orchestras, K.286; Serenades Nos. 6 (Serenata notturna), K.239; 13 (Eine kleine Nachtmusik), K.525.
(M) *** Decca 430 259-2; *430 259-4* [id.]. V. Mozart Ens., Boskovsky.

This delightful collection shows just how good Boskovsky and his Vienna Mozart Ensemble were in their prime. The recordings were made in the Sofiensaal in 1968–9 and 1978 (K.239 and K.286); in remastered form they all sound wonderfully fresh and realistic. One wonders who would want to listen to Mozart on acerbic 'authentic' violins after experiencing the transparency and elegance of the string playing here? We have often praised this version of *Eine kleine Nachtmusik* for its grace and spontaneity – one has the impression that one is hearing the piece for the first time – and the same comment could be applied to the string playing in the *Musical joke* (especially the delectable Minuet and the neat, zestful finale which ends with spectacular dissonance). The horns are superbly po-faced in their wrong notes in the former and Boskovsky's 'misjudged' scale at the end of the *Adagio* has comparable aplomb. The *Notturno for four orchestras* is a less inspired piece, but its spatial echoes are ingeniously contrived and their perspective admirably conveyed by the recording.

Serenade No. 4 in D (Colloredo), K.203; March in D, K.237.
(B) **(*) HM/BMG Dig. VD 77536; *VK 77536* [77536-2-RV; *77536-4RV*]. Coll. Aur., Franzjosef Maier.

Serenade No. 5 in D, K.204; March in D, K.215.
(B) **(*) HM/BMG Dig. VD 77568; *VD 77568* [77568-2-RV; *77568-4-RV*]. Coll. Aur., Franzjosef Maier.

Serenade No. 7 in D (Haffner), K.250; 5 Contredanses, K.609.
(B) **(*) HM/BMG VD 77548; *VK 77548* [77548-2-RV; *77548-4-RV*]. Coll. Aur., Franzjosef Maier.

These recordings of K.203 and K.204 date from 1982/3. They were made in the kindly acoustics of the Schloss Kirchheim: the sound is resonantly warm and full, disguising astringencies, if there are any, brought about by the use of original string instruments. The phrasing, too, comes before the days of mercilessly squeezing the melodic line, so that the main aural difference is in the woodwind timbres. Both the *Serenades*, K.203 and K.204, encompass a three-movement violin concerto in their midst, played very well indeed by Franzjosef Maier. Tempi are occasionally a bit problematic. In the *Haffner Serenade* – recorded earlier, in 1970 – the effect is a shade bland, despite the neat, polished playing, and the last Minuet of K.204 is positively funereal. But there are enough good things here to make the performances enjoyable, and these reissues are inexpensive. The five *Contredanses* (recorded in 1979 and sounding very fresh) make a most attractive encore for the *Haffner Serenade*. They are played with much spirit by a chamber group (2 violins, double-bass, flute and drum) and have real Viennese flair: the first quotes directly from *Le nozze di Figaro* and the last is a hurdy-gurdy simulation. It is a great pity that this Collegeum Aureum series is not provided with adequate musical documentation.

Serenade No. 7 in D (Haffner), K.250; March in D, K.249.
** Teldec/Warner Dig. 2292 43040-2 [id.]. Zehetmair, Dresden State O, Harnoncourt.

Like the *Posthorn serenade*, the *Haffner* enfolds a miniature violin concerto within its eight movements. As in his record of the former, Harnoncourt's soloist is Thomas Zehetmair, who gives a splendid account of himself. Harnoncourt offers an eminently spacious and expressive view of the piece, at times a little idiosyncratic. (He puts the brakes on the Trio sections of the Minuets of movements 3, 5 and 7, and the phrasing is mannered.) However, though the recording is very good, this does not displace versions by Marriner (Philips 412 725-2) and Mackerras (Telarc CD 80161).

Serenade No. 9 in D (Posthorn), K.320; A Musical joke, K.522.
(B) *** HM/BMG VD 77544; *VK 77544* [77544-2-RV; *77544-4-RV*]. Coll. Aur., Franzjosef Maier.

Aficionados should certainly not overlook the Collegium Aureum version of the *Posthorn Serenade*, particularly as it is now offered at bargain price. The playing is sensitive and vital and never sounds pedantic. About twenty-five instrumentalists take part, playing period instruments or copies, and the problems of intonation are altogether minimal. Indeed the woodwind sounds in the first-movement *Allegro con spirito* are full of character and quite delightful in the concertante, *Andante grazioso*. If, in the latter and the other concertante movement, the tempos are a little leisurely, the effect is so musical that this seems of little account. The remastered recording (from 1976), made in the spacious acoustics of Schloss Kirchheim, brings a brighter sound than in the earlier *Serenades* and gives the players a striking presence. The *Musical joke* (recorded in 1979) is effectively presented on a chamber sextet. The jokes are boldly made, and if this hasn't quite the charm of Boskovsky's version (see above), the use of one instrument to each part is especially telling in the vivacious finale. This is the most successful of the Collegium Aureum *Serenades* series.

Serenade No. 9 in D (Posthorn); Symphony No. 31 in D (Paris), K.297.
(M) ** DG 431 271-2; *431 271-4* [id.]. VPO, James Levine.

Levine's account of the *Posthorn serenade* is made more competitive at mid-price. Levine's tempi are well judged and the VPO contribution is distinguished. The early digital recording (1983) is a shade clinical, though well balanced. The inclusion of the *Paris Symphony*, a lithe, alert account if a little lacking in individuality, may attract some collectors. The inadequate documentation refers mainly to the symphony.

Serenade No. 10 in B flat for 13 wind instruments, K.361.
(B) **(*) CfP CD-CFP 4579; *TC-CFP 4579*. LPO Wind. Ens.

**(*) Teldec/WEA Dig. 2292 46471-2 [id.]. Soloists of COE.
(M) **(*) DG Dig. 431 273-2; *431 273-4* [id.]. Orpheus CO.
(B) ** HM/BMG Dig. VD 77540; *VK 77540* [77540-2-RV; *77540-4-RV*]. Coll. Aur., Franzjosef Maier.
(M) ** DG Dig. 429 979-2; *429 979-4* [id.]. BPO (members).

Outstanding playing from the wind ensemble of the London Philharmonic, richly blended, warmly phrased and full of character. The articulation and rhythmic feeling of the outer movements and the *Theme and variations* are particularly spontaneous; however, in the slower sections, notably the third-movement *Adagio*, one feels the need of a conductor's directing hand: there is some loss of character both here and, occasionally, elsewhere. Even so, with modern digital recording, attractively coloured by the ambience and refined in detail, this is good value at bargain price.

Immaculate in their playing as ever, the wind soloists of the COE, without a director, here give a more anonymous account of the *Gran partita* than they did in their earlier recording with Alexander Schneider. Many will prefer the brisker speeds here, but the affectionate manner of the earlier performance is largely missing, and that ASV record still remains our first choice for this much-recorded serenade (CDCOE 804; *ZCCOE 804*).

The Orpheus version is not a first choice either, but it is enjoyable and well recorded, another mid-priced reissue in DG's 3D Mozart Collection (see our main volume, pp. 673–4).

The Collegium Aureum version, without being an obvious first choice, it is an eminently satisfactory reading and gains considerable character by the unabrasive use of original instruments, although the blend is less homegeneous than in some more modern versions. The very plain rhythmic style will not suit all ears, though the relaxed manner of the variation movement is most attractive. The recording is warm and truthful, yet vivid.

The DG digital recording by the Berlin Philharmonic Orchestra's wind players is somewhat controversial. Some ears find the balance too analytical – although it is only fair to say that the sound is robust as well as clearly detailed. The playing of the BPO wind, while in its way impeccable, is curiously bland: there is none of the feeling of fresh discovery here and many moments when the dead hand of routine seems to touch their music-making. This is not the case in the glorious variation movement, but otherwise the performance is wanting in real personality.

Serenades Nos. 11 in E flat, K.375; 12 in C min., K.388; (i) *6 Notturni for voices & woodwind, K.346, K.436–9, K.549.*
(M) *** EMI mono/stereo CDM7 63958-2 [id.]; *EG 763958-4*. (i) Emerentia Scheepers, Monica Sinclair, Sir Geraint Evans; L. Bar. Ens., Karl Haas.

Mozart's *C minor Serenade* is dark in mood and colouring and is obviously intended to be taken seriously rather than simply to divert, and this is emphasized by the lean if by no means inexpressive style of the performance here, which is distinguished by its strength of character. Mozart's genius for part-writing and for the perfect blending of wind voices ensures that a wide range of colour and expression is possible with such a combination, and this is especially apparent in the fine set of variations which closes the piece. Both this work and its companion in E flat receive wonderfully smooth yet alive playing from the London Baroque Ensemble (including such charismatic names as Jack Brymer, Bernard Walton, Dennis Brain and Alan Civil in its roster of distinguished wind virtuosi) under Karl Haas, and very well-balanced recording. The charming *Notturni*, mostly love-songs, thought to have been performed first by Mozart's wife Constanze at social gatherings, are accompanied by either two clarinets and a basset horn or three basset horns. This was their first (1953) recording, mono, but smooth and faithful.

Sinfonia concertante in E flat for oboe, clarinet, horn, bassoon and orchestra, K.297b; (i) *Horn concerto No. 3 in E flat, K.447.*
(B) ** HM/BMG VD 77505 [Victrola 77505-2-RV]. (i) Hubert Crüts; Coll. Aur., Franzjosef Maier.

A good, robust account of the *Sinfonia concertante* on original instruments, with the warm resonance of the Cedernsaal of Schloss Kirchheim as usual disguising any acerbity in the upper string range. In the concerto Hubert Crüts plays his hand-horn fluently, demonstrating that this work can be presented effectively with only minor slips in intonation, using a minimum of stopped notes. However, few collectors will crave a disc, playing for only 45 minutes, which offers only one of the four *Horn concertos.*

(i) *Sinfonia concertante in E flat for violin, viola and orchestra, K.364;* (ii) *Symphony No. 39 in E flat, K.543.*
(M) ** Chan. Dig. CHAN 6506; *MBTD 6506* [id.]. (i) Brainin, Schidlof, ECO, Gibson; (ii) LPO, Handley.

Although offered at mid-price, this is a less attractive coupling than the original, which offered the *Concertone* (see our main volume, p. 665). Brainin and Schidlof bring plenty of warmth and character to K.364, but the symphony is more of a routine affair, although the *Andante* is beautifully played. The digital sound is first class in both works.

Complete Mozart Edition, Volume 21: (i) *Sonatas for organ and orchestra (Epistle sonatas) Nos. 1–17* (complete). *Adagio & allegro in F min., K.594; Andante in F, K.616; Fantasia in F min., K.608.*
(M) **(*) Ph. 422 521-2 (2). Daniel Barenboim (organs at Stift Wilhering, Linz, Austria; Schlosspfarrkirche, Obermarchtal, Germany – K.594; K.608); (i) German Bach Soloists, Helmut Winschermann.

Brightly recorded accounts of these pleasing and lively works, with plenty of ambience. The *Epistle sonatas* are so called because they were intended to be heard between the Epistle and the Gospel during the Mass. The balance folds the organ within the strings, perhaps rather too much so, especially in the later works where the obbligato solo part is more important. The final *Sonata*, K. 263, becomes a fully fledged concerto. The set is completed with the other works by Mozart which are usually heard on the organ, and here Barenboim's registration is particularly appealing. Indeed the performances are expert and can be recommended.

SYMPHONIES

Symphonies Nos. 1–47 (including alternative versions); in C, K.35; in D, K.38; in F, K.42a; in B flat, K.45b; in D, K.46a (K.51); in D, K.62a (K.100); in B flat, K.74g (K.216); in F, K.75; in G, K.75b (K.110); in D, K.111a; in D, K.203, 204 & 196 (121); in G, K.425a (K.444); in A min. (Odense); in G (New Lambacher).
(M) *** O-L Analogue/Dig. 430 639-2 (19) [id.]. AAM, Schröder, Hogwood.

The monumental complete recording of the Mozart *Symphonies*, using authentic manners and original instruments, now arrives as a complete set on 19 mid-priced CDs. With Jaap Schröder leading the admirably proportioned string group (9.8.4.3.2) and Christopher Hogwood at the keyboard, this was a remarkably successful joint enterprise. The playing has great style, warmth and polish and, if intonation is not always absolutely refined, that is only to be expected with old instruments. The survey is complete enough to include No. 37 – in fact the work of Michael Haydn but with a slow introduction by Mozart. The *Lambacher* and *Odense Symphonies* are also here, plus alternative versions, with different scoring, of No. 40; while the *Paris Symphony* is given two complete performances with alternative slow movements. Not all ears respond favourably to the non-vibrato tang of the Academy of Ancient Music's exploratory string-sound, and in certain of the earlier symphonies textures are sometimes thinned even further by the use of solo strings in sections of the music, which seems a questionable practice. However, the vitality and resilience of allegros is consistently refreshing and, although some listeners will prefer a more relaxed and less metrical style in slow movements, this remains a remarkable achievement.

Symphonies (complete).
** Capriccio Dig. 60 021/13 [id.]. Salzburg Mozarteum O, Hans Graf.

With 51 symphonies offered on these thirteen discs, Graf's Capriccio set brings plain, undistracting readings, brightly and fully recorded in digital sound. Next to the finest versions, including a bargain series like Barry Wordsworth's on Naxos, they rather lack imagination and elegance. Interpretatively, Marriner's Philips set with the ASMF is fresher and livelier, but Graf can be recommended to those wanting a complete cycle in modern digital sound. No harpsichord continuo is used, even in the earliest works. The Capriccio Mozart edition offers in addition two three-disc selections from the series, one of 17 of the earliest boyhood symphonies (10 803) and the other of the late masterpieces, Nos 34–36 and 38–41 (10 802).

Complete Mozart Edition, Volume 1: *Symphonies Nos. 1 in E in E flat, K.16; 4 in D, K.19; in F, K.19a; 5 in B flat, K.22; 6 in F, K.43; 7 in D, K.45; in G (Neue Lambacher), G.16; in G (Alte Lambacher), K.45a; in B flat, K.45b; 8 in D, K.48; 9 in C, K.73; 10 in G, K.74; in F, K.75; in F, K.76; in D, K.81, 11 in D, K.84; in D, K.95; in C, K.96; in D, K.97; 12 in G, K.110, 13 in F, K. 112; 14 in A, K.114; 15 in G, K.124; 16 in C, K.128; 17 in G, K.129; 18 in F, K.130; 19 in E flat, K.132* (with alternative slow movement); *20 in D, K.133; in D, K.161 & 163; in D, K.111 & 120; in D, K.196 & 121; in C, K.208 & 102. Minuet in A, K.61g/1.*
(M) *** Ph. 422 501-2 (6) [id.]. ASMF, Marriner.

The reissue, in the Philips Complete Mozart Edition, of Marriner's recordings of the early symphonies confirms the Mozartian vitality of the performances and their sense of style and spontaneity. There are some important additions, recorded digitally in 1989, notably the *Symphony in F*, K.19a, written when the composer was nine. This reappeared as recently as 1981, when a set of parts was discovered in Munich. Also now included is an alternative Minuet for the Salzburg *Symphony No. 14 in A*, K.114, and another charmingly brief (56 seconds) *Minuet in A*, K.61g/1, previously associated with this work. Modern research suggests that it was written a year earlier (1770), in Italy. The layout remains on six compact discs and the ear is again struck by the naturalness and warm vividness of the transfers. Except perhaps for those who insist on original instruments, the finesse and warmth of the playing here is a constant joy.

Complete Mozart Edition, Volume 2: *Symphonies Nos. 21–36; 37: Adagio maestoso in G, K.44* (Introduction to a symphony by M. Haydn); *38–41; Minuet for a Symphony in C, K.409.*
(M) **(*) Ph. 422 502-2 [id.]. ASMF, Marriner.

As with the early works, the later symphonies in the Marriner performances, as reissued in the Philips Mozart Edition, are conveniently laid out on six mid-priced CDs, offered in numerical sequence, without a single symphony having to be divided between discs. No. 40 is now restored to its expected position, where in the earlier CD box it was out of order. However, the over-resonant bass remains in the recording of this work and also in the *Haffner* (both of which date from 1970, nearly a decade before the rest of the cycle was recorded). Otherwise the transfers are of Philips's best quality, and the performances generally give every satisfaction, even if their style does not show an awareness of the discoveries made – in terms of texture and balance – by the authentic school.

Symphonies Nos. 21 in A, K.134; 22 in C, K.162; 23 in D, K.181; 24 in B flat, K.182; 25 in G min., K.183.
(B) *** Ph. 426 973-2; *426 973-4* [id.]. Concg. O, Josef Krips.

Krips's bargain Concertgebouw sequence of Mozart symphonies leading up to the early masterpiece in G minor (which is done most persuasively) is worth any collector's money. The Dutch players bring the necessary warmth, as well as proving characteristically stylish in phrasing and execution. The *Allegro con spiritoso* movements of Nos. 23 and 24 are certainly spirited and, in the former work, Krips makes the most of the charm of the *Andantino grazioso*, if at a slower tempo than Mackerras. The 1973/4 sound is full, yet the remastering has brought improved detail and freshness. This is one of the best of the Krips series.

Symphonies Nos. 21 in A, K.134; 23 in D, K.181; 24 in B flat, K.182, 27 in G, K.199.
*** Erato/Warner Dig. 2292 45544-2 [id.]. Amsterdam Bar. O, Koopman.

Koopman's readings of these delightful early symphonies are much less severe than most on period instruments, and are sparklingly recorded. Helped by the sound-quality, Koopman consistently catches the fun of early Mozart, as in the delectable finale of No. 21. He also brings out the lightness and elegance of slow movements. This is one of the most enjoyable of recent Mozart symphony records, a welcome foretaste of Koopman's projected cycle of all the symphonies.

Symphonies Nos. 24–36; 38–41 (Jupiter); Masonic funeral music; Minuet & Trio, K.409.
(M) **(*) EMI Dig. CMS7 63856-2 (6). ASMF, Marriner.

Marriner's third set of Mozart symphony recordings is the most beautifully recorded of all. The playing, too, is graceful and elegant. With bracing rhythms and brisker pacing than in his earlier, Philips set, these readings are positive yet unidiosyncratic. Phrasing is supple and the Mozartian spirit is always alive here. There is not quite the incandescent freshness of his earliest, Argo/Decca series (see below), and there is a degree of disappointment in the *Haffner* and *Jupiter Symphonies*, which are slightly undercharacterized. For the most part, however, this music-making will give a great deal of pleasure. The six individual CDs, as discussed below and in our main volume, are offered here at mid-price, in their original jewel-boxes, within a slip-case.

Symphonies Nos. 25 in G min., K.183; 26 in E flat, K.184; 27 in G, K.199; 29 in A, K.201; 32 in G, K.318.
(M) *** Decca 430 268-2; *430 268-4* [id.]. ASMF, Marriner.

A splendidly generous reissue (70 minutes) which makes a fascinating comparison with Marriner's most recent recordings for EMI. Although the remastered Argo sound – which is brighter and with rather more edge to the violins – has something to do with it, there is no doubt that in 1969 and 1971 the Academy playing had greater rhythmic bite than it displays in the late 1980s. With an aptly sized group, very well balanced by the engineers,

Marriner secures effervescent performances of the earlier symphonies, especially the little *G minor*, the first of the sequence of really great works. The pointing of phrases is done with great vitality and a superb sense of style. The scale of No. 29 is broad and forward-looking, yet the continuing alertness is matched by lightness of touch, while the imaginative detail of any interpretative freedoms adds positively to the enjoyment. The spacious acoustic is well controlled on CD and, though textures are less glowingly rich than in the EMI series, that doesn't seem aurally disadvantageous.

Symphonies Nos. 25 in G min., K.183; 26 in E flat, K.184; 29 in A, K.201.
*** DG Dig. 431 679-2 [id.]. E. Concert, Pinnock.

Coupling the two finest (and most popular) of the teenage works, Nos. 25 and 29, with an electrifying account of the tiny No. 26, this first English Concert issue of Mozart symphonies could not be more promising, with freshness and clarity married to persuasive expressiveness and vividly immediate recording. The brief No. 26 immediately brings to mind Pinnock's highly enjoyable DG Archiv issues of Haydn symphonies from the *Sturm und Drang* period. With sharp attack and big contrasts it too becomes a *Sturm und Drang* symphony. Pinnock has you registering the often abrasive toughness that must have hit early listeners, yet he also manages to convey the genial side of Mozart, both in the rhythmic bounce which has long characterized the work of the English Concert and in his choice of speeds. These are period performances for the general listener when, as in his Bach, Pinnock is not afraid to choose relaxed speeds in slow movements, and the rhythmic lift in all movements is consistently infectious. In No. 29 his relaxed view of the *Andante* brings out its lyricism most persuasively, and the natural horns are thrillingly bright in this bouncy, ebullient account of the finale.

Symphonies Nos. 25 in G min., K.183; 29 in A, K.201; Serenade No. 6 in D (Serenata notturna), K.239.
(B) *** Decca 430 495-2; *430 495-4* [id.]. ECO, Britten.

Several years before his untimely death Benjamin Britten recorded these exhilarating performances of the two greatest of Mozart's early symphonies. Inexplicably, the record remained unissued, finally providing a superb codicil to Britten's recording career. Now it reappears on CD at bargain price. It is striking that in many movements his tempi and even his approach are very close to those of Marriner on his early, Argo recordings; but it is Britten's genius, along with his crisp articulation and sprung rhythms, to provide the occasional touch of pure individual magic. Britten's slow movements provide a clear contrast, rather weightier than Marriner's, particularly in the little *G minor*, where Britten, with a slower speed and more expressive phrasing, underlines the elegiac quality of the music. Full, well-balanced recording. The addition of the *Serenata notturna*, played most engagingly, serves only to make this analogue collection more desirable.

Symphonies Nos. 25 in G min., K.183; 32 in G, K.318; 41 in C (Jupiter), K.551.
(BB) *** Naxos Dig. 8.550113 [id.]. Capella Istropolitana, Barry Wordsworth.

Symphonies Nos. 27 in G, K.199/161b; 33 in B flat, K.319; 36 in C (Linz), K.425.
(BB) *** Naxos Dig. 8.550264 [id.]. Capella Istropolitana, Barry Wordsworth.

Symphonies Nos. 28 in C, K.200; 31 in D (Paris), K.297; 40 in G min., K.550.
(BB) *** Naxos Dig. 8.550164 [id.]. Capella Istropolitana, Barry Wordsworth.

Symphonies Nos. 29 in A, K.201; 30 in D, K.202; 38 in D (Prague), K.504.
(BB) *** Naxos Dig. 8.550119 [id.]. Capella Istropolitana, Barry Wordsworth.

Symphonies Nos. 34 in C, K.338; 35 in D (Haffner), K.385; 39 in E flat, K.543.
(BB) *** Naxos Dig. 8.550186 [id.]. Capella Istropolitana, Barry Wordsworth.

Symphonies Nos. 40 in G min., K. 550; 41 in C (Jupiter), K.551.
(BB) *** Naxos Dig. 8.550259 [id.]. Capella Istropolitana, Barry Wordsworth.

Barry Wordsworth's series of 15 symphonies on the Naxos super-bargain-priced label brings consistently refreshing and enjoyable performances. The Capella Istropolitana consists of leading members of the Slovak Philharmonic Orchestra of Bratislava; though their string-tone is thinnish, it is very much in scale with the clarity of a period performance but tonally far sweeter. The recording is outstandingly good, with a far keener sense of presence than in most rival versions and with less reverberation to obscure detail in tuttis. Very strikingly indeed, the sound here allows a genuine terracing, with the wind instruments, and the horns in particular, rising clear of the string band. Wordsworth observes exposition repeats in first movements, but in the finales only in such symphonies as Nos. 38 and 41, where the movement particularly needs extra scale. In slow movements, as is usual, he omits repeats. Consistently a principal concern with him is clarity of texture. That means he often adopts speeds that are marginally slower than we expect nowadays in chamber-scale performances; but, with exceptionally clean articulation and infectiously sprung rhythms, the results never drag, even if No. 29 is made to sound more sober than usual. In every way these are worthy rivals to the best full-priced versions, and they can be recommended with few if any reservations. Anyone wanting to sample might try the coupling of Nos. 34, 35 and 39 – with the hard-stick timpani sound at the start of No. 39 very dramatic, preferable even to the near-rival coupling from Tate (of Nos. 32, 35 and 39). The *Linz* too is outstanding. For some, the option of having the last two symphonies coupled together will be useful.

Symphonies Nos. 25 in G min., K.183; 27 in G, K.199; 31 in D, K.297.
*** EMI Dig. CDC7 49998-2 [id.]. ECO, Jeffrey Tate.

Tate's record, coupling the little *G minor* with the once-neglected but increasingly popular No. 27, as well as the *Paris Symphony*, makes an excellent addition to his successful EMI series. In No. 25 Tate is generally smoother in style than Glover, but the characterization is more marked, with fine detail and clean articulation freshening the result. He gives the symphony a bigger scale than usual by observing second-half repeats, making it a full 27 minutes long. In all three works he provides a winning combination of affectionate manners, freshness and elegance. Like Mackerras in his brighter, more thrustful account of the *Paris*, Tate provides the alternative *Andante* slow movement, an interesting curiosity, and on CD you can readily programme whichever you prefer.

Symphonies Nos. 25 in G min., K.183; 29 in A, K.201; 33 in B flat, K.319.
**(*) ASV Dig. CDDCA 717; *ZCDCA 717* [id.]. L. Mozart Players, Jane Glover.

Glover may not quite match Sir Charles Mackerras in his Prague Chamber Orchestra series for Telarc in flair or imagination, but these are very fresh and enjoyable performances of all three symphonies, with the two greatest of the boyhood works, Nos. 25 and 29, attractively coupled with the most unjustly neglected of the later symphonies, No. 33. The recording, made in Fairfield Hall, Croydon, matches the others in the series, refined and not as immediate as, say, the sound for Mackerras in Prague. Second-half repeats are omitted, but there is little disadvantage in that.

Symphonies Nos. 25 in G min., K.183; 38 in D (Prague), K. 504.
(M) ** DG Dig. 431 270-2; *431 270-4* [id.]. VPO, James Levine.

There have been more characterful and distinctive readings of No. 25 than this; but the Levine formula of fast allegros, brilliantly played, and a crisp slow movement, all marked by refined Viennese playing, works well enough. The *Prague* has rather more individuality; it certainly shows the VPO on top form in all departments. The sound is good.

Symphonies Nos. 26 in E flat, K.184; 27 in G, K.199; 28 in C, K.200; 29 in A, K.201.
(B) *** Ph. 426 974-2; *426 974-4* [id.]. Concg. O, Josef Krips.

Mozart wrote these four key works – which show his symphonic writing moving into maturity – in Salzburg during 1773 and early 1774. Krips recorded them exactly 200 years later; he secures superbly characterful playing from the Concertgebouw Orchestra: the *Molto presto* of No. 26 is bracingly vigorous, yet the work's lyrical counterpart is eminently graceful. Both the previously underrated No. 28 in C and the first great masterpiece in A major are very persuasively done, with apt pacing and almost ethereal delicacy from the strings in the beautiful *Andante* of No. 29, and the horns thrusting exuberantly in the coda of the finale. The CD transfers are exemplary, greatly improving the original LPs' sound, with extra firmness and better-focused detail, yet with no added edge in the treble. The appealing Concertgebouw acoustic adds bloom but does not blur textures. Unfortunately there is no documentation with this Philips series.

Symphonies Nos 26 in E flat, K.184; 27 in G, K.199; 28 in C, K.200; 30 in D, K.202; 32 in G, K.318.
*** ASV Dig. CDDCA 762; *ZCDCA 762* [id.]. LMP, Jane Glover.

Glover's generous coupling of five early symphonies brings typically fresh and direct readings, marked by sharp attack and resilient rhythms, at speeds on the fast side. With tuttis a little weightier than with most rivals, these are brightly enjoyable performances very much in line with the others in the series.

Symphonies Nos. 26 in G min., K.183; 28 in in C, K.200; 29 in A, K.201; 30 in D, K.202.
*** EMI Dig. CDC7 54092-2 [id.]. ECO, Jeffrey Tate.

Tate's readings of these four teenage symphonies are characteristically elegant, matching the fresh and warm qualities in his other Mozart recordings. His reading of No. 29, by far the most ambitious of the group and the most popular, begins with a typically relaxed account of the first movement, light and persuasive; but both in the slow movement and, most strikingly, in the finale he is refreshingly brisk. Warm, well-balanced sound, as in the rest of the this EMI series.

Symphonies Nos. 28 in C, K.200; 29 in A, K.201; 30 in D, K.202.
**(*) EMI Dig. CDC7 49864-2 [id.]. ASMF, Marriner

In his continuing series for EMI, Marriner secures warm and gracious playing from the Academy. The spacious acoustic of EMI's No. 1 Studio at Abbey Road adds an agreeable fullness and colour to the orchestral sound, which makes very pleasurable listening; but, with articulation that brings neat rather than sharp rhythmic incisiveness, the effect is somewhat more bland than with Marriner's earlier, Argo recordings. Slow movements are very persuasive, in both their delicacy of touch and elegant contours, and the first movement of No. 28 is admirably spirited, with the genial nature of the finale also giving much pleasure. In No. 29 Marriner observes more repeats than before and the performance has an affectionate breadth, with plenty of energy reserved for the last movement. The *Molto allegro* which opens No. 30 has energy without forcefulness, and again the dancing finale brings the most sophisticated lightness of touch.

Symphonies Nos. 28 in C, K.200; 29 in A, K.201; 34 in C, K.338.
** Ph. Dig. 426 236-2; *426 236-4* [id.]. Dresden State O, Sir Colin Davis.

As in his previous Mozart recordings with the Dresden orchestra, Davis directs refined and elegant readings of these three symphonies which are far smoother and gentler in their manners than we have come to expect from this conductor. They reflect little or no influence from period performance and will be enjoyed by Mozartians who prefer sweetness and good manners. The warm Dresden acoustic matches the performances, tending to obscure detail in tuttis.

Symphonies Nos. 29; 31 (Paris); 34; 35 (Haffner); 36 (Linz); 38 (Prague); 39–41 (Jupiter).
(M) (**(*)) EMI mono CHS7 63698-2 (3) [Ang. CDHC 63698]. LPO, Sir Thomas Beecham.

Beecham's pre-war accounts of the Mozart symphonies with the LPO on the old Columbia blue label hold a special place in the affections of older collectors – and rightly so, for, good though his post-war versions with the RPO were, these had a purity of style and a vitality of spirit that he never completely recaptured. The playing as such is marvellous and the lightness of rhythmic accent and plasticity of phrasing have few equals. The *Prague* and the *G minor Symphony* enjoy special status, even among these classic readings. It goes without saying that these performances are three star and more, but the sound does not compare favourably with the last LP reissue on World Records; it suffers just a little from what can best be described as dehydration (a too common affliction with CD transfers, which means that collectors who have stayed loyal to analogue LPs can claim with justification that they are able to achieve more realistic reproduction). The basically warm studio ambience remains, but the real problem is the sound of the violins above the stave which are piercing and shrill at peaks. Such a technical drawback is, however, not serious enough to discourage the Beecham enthusiast who has an efficient treble roll-off on his or her reproducer. But this was not how these records sounded on a normal domestic reproducer of the 1940s (especially using 'fibre' needles), which could then compare with the quality of a BBC live broadcast; it ought to have been possible to make CD transfers without this degree of shrillness in the upper range. Even so, this remains a mandatory acquisition for all Mozartians with a CD player.

Symphonies Nos. 29 in A, K.201; 39 in E flat, K.543.
(M) **(*) DG Dig. 431 268-2; *431 268-4* [id.]. BPO, Karajan.

Karajan's 1968 coupling is now reissued at mid-price in DG's 3D Mozart Collection. Although this is very much big-band Mozart with full, weighty sound, it is easy to respond to the warmth of Karajan's approach to the *A major Symphony*. There is some radiant string playing from the Berlin orchestra – the sounds produced utterly different from the textures of Hogwood's Academy – and if the *E flat Symphony* has a degree of heaviness (like the Minuet of K.201), the strength of the reading is in no doubt and the woodwind detail of the finale is perceptively illuminated.

Symphonies Nos. 29 in A, K.201; 41 in C (Jupiter), K.551; Overture: Die Zauberflöte.
(M) ** EMI CDM7 63959-2 [id.]; *EG 763959-4*. Hallé O, Barbirolli.

As with certain others of the old Pye/Barbirolli records reissued on EMI's Phoenixa label, the sound here has been immeasurably improved in the CD remastering and is strikingly firmer and better focused. The *Jupiter Symphony* is given a much stronger profile. There is still the Italianate warmth in the slow movement and the Minuet's main theme floats gracefully over its accompanying chords, but the finale now sounds more purposeful and dramatic. Some may feel that Barbirolli's warmth in No. 29 brings a degree of slackness, but this is still a charismatic reading, which the conductor's admirers will not want to be without.

Symphonies Nos. 31 in D (Paris), K.297; 33 in B flat, K.319; 34 in C, K.338; Masonic funeral music, K.477; Andantino, K.297; Minuet, K.409.
**(*) EMI Dig. CDC7 54078-2 [id.]. ASMF, Sir Neville Marriner.

The disc containing the *Paris Symphony* and Nos. 33 and 34, which completes Marriner's series, brings a generous coupling. He has the *Masonic funeral music* as an extra, as well as the alternative *Andante* slow movement for the *Paris* and the Minuet thought to be meant for No. 34. Curiously, the disc puts the rare alternative slow movement in the *Paris* as first choice, with the regular (and much more delightful) *Andantino* presented merely as a supplement after the finale, quite the wrong way round. Performances are fresh and polished, as one would expect, though the second movement of No. 34, at a slow tempo, is uncharacteristically slack.

(i) *Symphonies Nos. 31 in D (Paris); 35 in D (Haffner); 40 in G min., K.550; 41 in C (Jupiter)* (CD only: *Symphony No. 32 in G, K.318;* (ii) *Masonic funeral music, K.477*).
(B) **(*) DG Compact Classics 413 151-2 (2); *413 151-4* [id.]. (i) BPO; (ii) VPO, Karl Boehm.

These symphony recordings date from between 1960 and 1966 and come from Boehm's complete Berlin cycle. The playing is first class and the recordings sound well in their tape format. In the *G minor Symphony* Boehm's featuring of oboes in place of clarinets (he uses Mozart's earlier version of the score) is hardly noticed, so mellifluous is the playing. This is excellent value at Compact Classics price, even if the later Vienna recordings (notably of Nos. 40 and 41) have rather more character. No. 32 in G plus Boehm's VPO account of the *Masonic funeral music* are added to fill out the pair of digitally remastered CDs attractively.

Symphonies Nos. 32 in G, K.318; 35 in D (Haffner), K.385; 39 in E flat, K.543.
*** Telarc Dig. CD 80203 [id.]. Prague CO, Mackerras.

Mackerras offers the same coupling as Tate and the ECO on EMI (CDC7 47327-2 – see our main volume, p. 684), and the contrasts are characteristic of their rival series. Mackerras observes repeats more consistently and regularly chooses brisker tempi. He is fresh rather than elegant, yet with rhythms so crisply sprung that there is no sense of rush. His whirling one-in-a-bar treatment of Minuets may disconcert traditionalists, but brings exhilarating results. The third movements of both the *Haffner* and No. 39 become scherzos, not just faster but fiercer than regular minuets, and in the *Haffner* trumpets and timpani bite through textures dramatically. In the little No. 32, Mackerras is brighter and more urgent than Tate in all three sections, and generally his account of No. 39 is as commanding as his outstanding versions of the last two symphonies. The slow introduction is crisply dotted, and the 3/4 Allegro is purposeful rather than easily lyrical. The clanging attack of harpsichord continuo is sometimes disconcerting, but this music-making is very refreshing.

Symphonies Nos. 33 in B flat, K.319; 35 in D (Haffner), K.385; 36 in C (Linz), K.425.
(B) ** HM/BMG VD 77525 [77525-2-RV]. Coll. Aur., Franzjosef Maier.

The Collegium Aureum, led rather than conducted by Franzjosef Maier, was one of the earlier groups to play Mozart on original instruments; these excellent analogue recordings, made in the warm acoustics of the Cedernsaal of Schloss Kirchheim, have none of the acerbic, squeezed string timbres which characterized a later generation. Indeed the effect is very like that of a normal chamber orchestra, often quite weighty, as in the first movement of the *Haffner Symphony*. The playing is polished and well paced but the readings are in no way distinctive, although the finale of the *B flat Symphony* is very felicitous.

Symphonies Nos. 35 in D (Haffner), K.385; 36 in C (Linz), K. 425.
(M) ** DG Dig. 431 269-2; *431 269-4* [id.]. VPO, James Levine.

Levine's coupling brings characteristically brisk and athletic performances marked by superb playing from all sections of the VPO. There is more life in these readings of the better-known works than in his versions of the earlier symphonies. Repeats are observed and the sound is clean and fresh. But this is not really distinctive.

'The birth of a performance': (recorded rehearsals of *Symphony No. 36*). *Symphonies Nos. 35 (Haffner); 36 (Linz); 38 (Prague); 39 in E flat; 40 in G min.; 41 (Jupiter).*
(M) *** Sony stereo/mono SM3K 46511 (3) [id.]. Columbia SO, Bruno Walter.

Walter's set of Mozart's last symphonies, all but the *Linz* recorded in California at the beginning of the 1960s, has been reissued by Sony on three mid-priced CDs. The *Linz* was recorded earlier in mono in New York City in 1955. Also included are the famous rehearsals of the *Linz Symphony*, called 'The birth of a performance', occupying the first disc. The second disc comprises Walter's mono performance of the *Linz* together with the *Prague* and No. 40, while the third disc contains performances of the *Haffner*, No. 39 and the *Jupiter* symphonies. These stereo recordings are all discussed in detail in our main volume, p. 685.

Symphonies Nos. 35 in D (Haffner), K.365; 40 in G min., K.550; 41 in C (Jupiter), K.551.
(M) *** Sony SBK 46333 [id.]; *40-46333*. Cleveland O, Szell.

As in his companion triptych of late Haydn symphonies, Szell and his Clevelanders are shown at their finest here. The sparkling account of the *Haffner* – the first movement incisively brisk but with the daintily rhythmic secondary theme deliciously pointed – is exhilarating, and the performances of the last two symphonies are equally polished and strong. Yet there is a tranquil feeling to both *Andantes* that shows Szell as a Mozartian of striking sensibility and finesse. He is at his finest in the *Jupiter*, which has great vigour in the outer movements and a proper weight to balance the rhythmic incisiveness; in spite of the lack of repeats, the work's scale is not diminished. Here the sound is remarkable considering the early date (late 1950s), and the remastering throughout is impressively full-bodied and clean.

Symphonies Nos. 35 in D (Haffner), K.385; 41 in C (Jupiter), K.551.
** EMI Dig. CDC7 47466-2 [id.]. ASMF, Marriner.

With allegros on the brisk side, yet with rhythms well pointed and with immaculate, totally unmannered phrasing, Marriner's newest EMI digital coupling of the *Haffner* and the *Jupiter* will appeal to anyone preferring direct and unidiosyncratic Mozart. Crisp and polished as the playing is, some may find that the performances lack a little in both spontaneity and touches of individuality, next to the most magnetic readings; but, with excellent sound, forward and full but not aggressive, they make an agreeable choice in this coupling.

Symphonies Nos. 37 in G, K.444: Introduction (completed by M. Haydn); *40 in G min., K.550; 41 in C (Jupiter), K.551.*
*** ASV Dig. CDDCA 761; *ZCDCA 761* [id.]. L. Mozart Players, Jane Glover.

This is an excellent example of Jane Glover's work with the LMP. It is good that in addition to the regular coupling of the last two masterpieces the disc offers the so-called *Symphony No. 37.* Mozart's contribution to that work is limited to the slow introduction. The rest of this compact, three-movement symphony is by Mozart's friend, Michael Haydn, younger brother of Joseph. It is a bright and attractive rarity, even though Mozart's introduction is conventionally elegant rather than distinctive. Anyone who fancies this generous coupling need hardly hesitate, particularly when in the two last Mozart symphonies Glover does not skimp on repeats, as she might have done. She omits them – as most versions do – in the slow movements, but includes exposition repeats in the finales as well as in first movements, particularly important in the *Jupiter*, with its grandly sublime counterpoint. There Glover's speed is exceptionally fast, with ensemble not quite so refined or crisp as in such rival versions as Jeffrey Tate's with the ECO, Mackerras's with the Prague Chamber Orchestra or Menuhin's with the Sinfonia Varsovia, but still making for a strong and enjoyable reading.

Symphonies Nos. 38 in D (Prague), K.504; 39 in E flat, K.543; (i) *Rondo in C* (for violin & orchestra), *K.373.*
(B) **(*) HM/BMG VD 77529 [77529-2-RV]. Coll. Aur., Franzjosef Maier, (i) with Maier (violin).

This is among the most impressive of the Collegium Aureum recordings made in the Schloss Kirchheim, now reissued in the German Harmonia Mundi Mozart Edition. The weighty, rather grand effect, not at all what one expects from original instruments, suits these two symphonies and especially *No. 39 in E flat*, which is given an expansive reading, very well played. The violins are sweet but lithe, and the orchestral sound is as full as that of a modern chamber orchestra. Franzjosef Maier is the soloist in an attractive account of the *Rondo*, K.373, and here the leonine solo timbre does sound rather more 'authentic'. There is no back-up documentation with this series.

Symphonies Nos. 38 in D (Prague), K.504; 40 in G min., K.550.
(B) *** Decca 430 494-2; *430 494-4* [id.]. ECO, Britten.

In his perfomance of No. 40, Britten takes all repeats – the slow movement here is longer than that of *Eroica* – but is nevertheless almost totally convincing, with the rich Maltings sound to give added weight and resonance. In the *Prague* as in No. 40, Britten conveys a real sense of occasion, from the weighty introduction through a glowing and resilient account of the *Allegro* to a full, flowing reading of the *Andante*.

Symphonies Nos. 39 in E flat, K.543; 40 in G min., K 550.
* Erato/Warner Dig. 2292 45464-2; *2292 45464-4* [id.]. Ens. O de Paris, Armin Jordan.

Armin Jordan with his Parisian chamber group, founded in 1978 as 'a Mannheim-style permanent ensemble', brings intelligent readings which never commit any major sin but which lack the tensions of live music-making. They are run-throughs rather than real performances.

Symphonies Nos. 39 in E flat, K.543; 41 in C (Jupiter), K.551.
**(*) RCA/BMG Dig. RD 60714 [60714-2-RC]. N. German RSO, Wand.
** EMI Dig. CDC7 54090-2; *EL 754090-4* [id.]. L. Classical Players, Roger Norrington.

Wand's performances with the North German Radio Orchestra were recorded live, bringing immediate, intense communication. In many ways they are old-fashioned performances. Wand never observes exposition repeats and Minuets tend to be slow and rather heavy. But otherwise his speeds, though never hectic, are beautifully judged, with slow movements never dragging and with rhythms, phrasing and finely detailed dynamic shading always leading the ear onwards. The warm, immediate recording brings a vivid sense of presence, and the conductor's admirers will not be disappointed with this.

Even those well adjusted to period performance of Mozart are likely to raise their eyebrows at the opening of Norrington's version of No. 39. At high speed the *Adagio* introduction hits the ear abrasively with its dizzily swirling violins. The 3/4 *Allegro* is then relatively normal with well-sprung rhythms, but the *Andante con moto* is so fast it acquires a scherzando element in the crisp dotted rhythms. The Minuet becomes a scherzo, while the finale is light and transparent, bringing no sense of rush, even at high speed. In the *Jupiter*, comparable treatment underlines a military element in the brass writing, even in the *Andante cantabile.* As in No. 39, Norrington's reading is strong and characterful, but for repeated listening these performances will be too relentless for most Mozartians, eliminating tenderness and charm. Excellent sound, both clear and atmospheric.

Symphony No. 40 in G min., K.550.
(*) Linn Dig. CKD 003 [id.]. English Classical Players, Jonathan Brett – SCHUBERT: *Symphony No. 5.*(*)

The English Classical Players are a new London orchestral group, playing on modern instruments, who made their début in June 1990, when this record was made. Their playing is alive and polished, phrasing is graceful and the orchestral blend in Mozart and Schubert very appealing. Jonathan Brett's reading of the *G minor Symphony* is well paced and fresh. He is generous with repeats and only in the finale (9 minutes 25 seconds) does one question this, for just a little more unbuttoned zest would have been welcome here. But this is an impressive first recording, truthfully balanced, in London's Henry Wood Hall.

Symphonies Nos. 40 in G min., K.550; 41 in C (Jupiter), K.551.
❀ (M) *** DG Dig. 431 267-2; *431 267-4* [id.]. VPO, Leonard Bernstein.
(M) **(*) Decca Dig. 430 713-2; *430 713-4* [id.]. AAM, Hogwood.
(M) **(*) EMI Dig. CDD7 63897-2 [id.]; *ET 763897-4*. ASMF, Marriner.
(M) ** Decca Dig. 430 437-2; *430 437-4* [id.]. COE, Solti.
*(*) DG Dig. 429 731-2; *429 731-4* [id.]. VPO, James Levine.

This re-coupling represents the finest single issue from the 25 discs which make up DG's mid-priced 3D Mozart Collection, and is perhaps the most distinguished of Bernstein's Mozart records. Both recordings were made in the Musikverein Grosser Saal in January 1984 and were edited together from live performances. Bernstein's electrifying account of No. 40 is keenly dramatic, individual and stylish, with the finale delightfully airy and fresh. If anything, the *Jupiter* is even finer: it is exhilarating in its tensions and observes the repeats in both halves of the finale, making it almost as long as the massive first movement. Bernstein's electricity sustains that length, and one welcomes it for establishing the supreme power of the argument, the true crown in the whole of Mozart's symphonic output. Pacing cannot be faulted in any of the four movements and, considering the problems of making live recordings, the sound is first rate, lacking only the last degree of transparency in tuttis.

Now reissued at medium price, this separate issue of Nos. 40 and 41 from Hogwood's collected edition makes a first-rate recommendation for those wanting period performances: brisk and light, but still conveying the drama of No. 40 and the majesty of the *Jupiter*; though the lack of expressive feeling typical of slow movements will be disappointing for some. Excellent 1983 digital recording.

On EMI, Marriner is at his best in No. 40, a work he always did very sympathetically. In the last two movements he is strikingly dramatic, with crisper articulation and faster speeds than in his earlier recording for Philips, and this time in the slow movement he observes the first-half repeat. The *Jupiter* is also very well done, but the effect is less charismatic – though, as in No. 40, the recording is first rate.

The talented young players of the Chamber Orchestra of Europe respond acutely to Solti's direction with finely disciplined ensemble, paradoxically producing an interpretation which in many places is uncharacteristic of the conductor, unforced and intimate rather than fiery. The middle movements of No. 40 are disappointing for opposite reasons, the *Andante* too self-consciously pointed and the Minuet too heavy. The *Jupiter* is plainer and much more successful, brightly detailed and crisply articulated. The recording, made in Frankfurt, has plenty of bloom on the sound as well as good detail.

Levine's performances in this favourite coupling are strong and energetic, but lack the tension of live music-making. Mozartian elegance is lacking too; the results are rough in their manners (if not in their execution), next to the finest modern versions.

CHAMBER MUSIC

Complete Mozart Edition, Volume 10: (i; vi) *Clarinet quintet;* (ii) *Flute quartets Nos. 1–4;* (iii; vi) *Horn quintet;* (iv; vi) *Oboe quartet;* (v) *Sonata for bassoon and cello, K.292.* (vi) Fragments: *Allegro in F, K.App. 90/580b for clarinet, basset horn, & string trio; Allegro in B flat. K.App. 91/K.516c for a clarinet quintet; Allegro in F, K.288 for a divertimento for 2 horns & strings; String quartet movements: Allegro in B flat, K.App. 72/464a; Allegro in B flat, K.App. 80/514a; Minuet in B flat, K.68/589a; Minuet in F, K 168a; Movement in A, K.App. 72/464a. String quintet No. 1 in B flat, K.174: 2 Original movements: Trio & Finale. Allegro in A min., K.App. 79 for a string quintet. Allegro in G, K.App. 66/562e for a string trio* (completed, where necessary, by Erik Smith).
(M) *** Ph. Analogue/Dig. 422 510-2 (3) [id.]. (i) Pay; (ii) Bennett, Grumiaux Trio, (iii) Brown; (iv) Black; (v) Thunemann; Orton; (vi) ASMF Chamber Ens.

These highly praised performances of the major chamber works featuring modern wind instruments (Antony Pay uses a normal clarinet) are also available on two separate mid-priced CDs: those with solo clarinet, horn and oboe on 422 833-2, *422 833-4*; and William Bennett's superb set of *Flute quartets* on 422 835-2, *422 835-4* (see our main volume, pp. 693–4). The *Duo for bassoon and cello* is also very engaging, although the balance somewhat favours the bassoonist, Klaus Thunemann, at the expense of his partner, Stephen Orton. But it is the fragments which make this box particularly enticing. Erik Smith tells us in the notes that, with a single exception, he confined himself to 'filling in the missing instrumental parts without adding any more bars'. The exception is the *Movement in A*, K.464a, planned at the finale for the *String quartet No. 18*, K.464: 'The temptation to complete this extensive fragment and make its lovely music playable proved too strong for me,' says E. S., and he goes on to tell how he ingeniously incorporated a 12-bar sketch of a fugue in G minor, changing the key and building it into the unfinished movement with linking material from elsewhere in the movement. The result is a great success. The rest of the items are by no means inconsequential offcuts but provide music of high quality, notably the *String quartet movement*, K.514a. The *Minuet in B flat*, K.589a, in the rhythm of a polonaise and possibly the first draft for the finale of the *Hunt quartet*, is a real charmer which, had it received more exposure, might well have become a Mozartian lollipop like the famous and not dissimilar Minuet in the *D major Divertimento*, K.334. The two pieces with solo clarinet are also very winning (we have had them before, from Alan Hacker – see our main volume, p. 692). The performances here are all polished and spontaneous and beautifully recorded.

(i) *Clarinet quintet in A, K.581;* (ii) *Oboe quartet in F, K.370.*
(B) *** CfP CD-CFP 4377; *TC-CFP 4377.* (i) Andrew Marriner; (ii) Gordon Hunt, Chilingirian Qt.
On the bargain-priced CfP version, recorded in 1981, the young Andrew Marriner's persuasive account occupies the front rank, quite irrespective of price. It is coupled with an equally fine performance of the delightful *Oboe quartet* by Gordon Hunt, another young musician and principal oboe with the Philharmonia at the time of the recording. Marriner's playing in the *Quintet* is wonderfully flexible; it reaches its apex in the radiantly beautiful reading of the slow movement, although the finale is also engagingly characterized. The *Oboe quartet* is delectable too, with Hunt a highly musical and technically accomplished soloist. The Chilingirian players contribute most sympathetically to both works, and the performances are generous in repeats. The CfP issue was recorded in the Wigmore Hall and the sound-balance is most believable.

(i) *Clarinet quintet in A, K.591*; (ii) *String quintet No. 4 in G min., K.516.*
(M) **(*) DG Dig. 431 286-2; *431 286-4* [id.]. (i) Eduard Brunner, Hagen Qt; (ii) Melos Qt with Franz Beyer.

It was a happy idea to couple what are perhaps Mozart's two greatest quintets for reissue in DG's 3D Mozart Collection, even if the performances are uneven. In the *Clarinet quintet* Eduard Brunner provides a mellifluous tone-quality and blends ideally with the fine Hagens. Everything is musically turned out and tempi are unfailingly sensible, relaxed and unforced. Brunner uses a modern instrument, and those not requiring the use of the more authentic basset clarinet will find this highly musical and the DG recording excellent. The Melos Quartet with their second violist, Franz Beyer, give a finely prepared and thoughtfully conceived account of the *G minor String quintet*, with the overall structure well held together.The famous Adagio is played simply and quite eloquently; but here, as elsewhere, their dynamic range does not vary greatly, and one feels the need for more expressive intensity. Again the sound is natural and well balanced.

Complete Mozart Edition, Volume 13: (i) *Divertimento in E flat for string trio, K.563;* (ii) *Duos for violin and viola Nos. 1–2, K.423/4;* (i) *6 Preludes and fugues for string trio, K.404a;* (iii) *Sonata (String trio) in B flat, K. 266.*
(M) *** Ph. 422 513-2 (2) [id.]. (i) Grumiaux, Janzer, Szabo; (ii) Grumiaux, Pelliccia; (iii) ASMF Chamber Ens.

The *Divertimento in E flat* is one of the richest of Mozart's last-period chamber works, far too rarely heard in the concert hall. Grumiaux's 1967 recorded performance remains unsurpassed, with its combination of refined classicism and spontaneity (see our main volume, p. 694). The recording has been remastered again and the excess brightness tamed for its reissue in Philips's Complete Mozart Edition: the balance still favours Grumiaux but he also dominates the performance artistically (as he does also in the *Duos*) and the result is now fully acceptable. In the *Duos*, which are ravishingly played, the balance is excellent, and Arrigo Pelliccia proves a natural partner in these inspired and rewarding works. The *Sonata for string trio* dates from 1777 and has a somewhat bland *Adagio/Andante*, followed by a jaunty Minuet. It is no missing masterpiece but is well played by the ASMF Chamber Ensemble and it has a modern, digital recording. Of the six *Preludes and fugues*, the first three derive from Bach's *Well-tempered clavier*, the fourth combines an *Adagio* from the *Organ sonata*, BWV 527, with *Contrapunctus 8* from the *Art of fugue*, the fifth is a transcription of two movements from the *Organ sonata*, BWV 526, and the sixth uses music of W. F. Bach. Mozart made these arrangements in the early 1780s for Baron Gottfried van Swieten in Vienna, composing *Adagio* introductions for Nos. 1 – 3 and 6. The performances here are sympathetic and direct, the recorded sound bold, clear and bright.

(i) *6 Divertimenti for 2 clarinets and bassoon, K.439b; 12 Duos (Kegelduette), K.487.*
(M) **(*) DG 431 472-2 (2) [id.]. Alfred Prinz, Peter Schmidl, (i) with Dietmar Zeman.

Neither of these sets of works is in Mozart's own catalogue, nor can the *Divertimenti* be dated accurately; furthermore their intended instrumentation is uncertain, although scholars suggest that they were intended for three basset-horns. On the other hand, it seems almost certain that the *Duos*, K.487, were written for a pair of horns; even though the writing demands considerable virtuosity from the players, the layout of notes is in the range of the hand-horn, and the very first piece immediately sounds like horn-writing. Moreover the twelve individual movements are nearly all quite brief. All the *Divertimenti* consist of five movements each: they were originally published as 25 separate items but fit naturally together in groups, especially *Divertimenti Nos. 5* and *6*, which contain some of the most attractive ideas. Mozart's part-writing for wind instruments was incomparable and, whatever the intended instrumentation, the blend of two clarinets and bassoon sounds most felicitous, especially in the delightful *Adagios* of Nos. 5 and 6. Alfred Prinz, Peter Schmidl and Dietmar Zeman match their timbres elegantly and play this music in excellent style, even if at times one feels that their approach is just a little sober. Prinz and Schmidl then use basset-horns characterfully enough in the *Duos*, even if one feels that the music would sound more exciting on hand-horns. The recording (made in Vienna in 1978/9) is immaculate and the CD transfers bring a natural presence to each group. But this is music to dip into rather than to be taken a whole disc at a time.

Divertimento in E flat for string trio, K.563.
*** EMI Dig. CDC7 54009-2 [id.]. Dumay, Caussé, Hoffman.

The EMI version with Augustin Dumay, Gérard Caussé and Gary Hoffman must be numbered among the best currently available. They are tremendously spirited and full of inner life, their dynamic range is exceptionally wide (some may find it too wide), as is their command of tonal colour. Tempi are well judged and phrasing sensitive, and the recording has plenty of space round the aural image. A distinguished performance which can be recommended alongside that of Kremer, Kashkashian and Yo-Yo Ma on Sony (MK 39561).

Duos for violin and viola Nos. 1 in G; 2 in B flat, K.423/4.
(M) *** Ph. 426 098-2 [id.]. Mark Lubotsky, Nobuko Imai – M. HAYDN: *Duo.****

Mozart wrote these two *Duos* in 1783 under a pseudonym to help out his colleague and friend, Michael Haydn. Six such works had been commissioned by the Archbishop of Salzburg and Michael Haydn had completed four when he fell seriously ill. The archbishop threatened to stop his salary unless all six were delivered on time. Mozart quickly stepped in, and Haydn copied out the manuscripts so that the the archbishop never discovered the deception. They are splendid works; with the fullness of their instrumentation, their felicitous invention and inspired part-writing, the ear never feels that the textures are sparse. They are excellently played here by Lubotsky and Imai, coupled with one of the finest of Michael Haydn's own duos. The two players are truthfully recorded and the CD gives them a vivid presence; but this is a disc that sounds best with the volume level down a little to distance the music-making slightly.

Flute quartets Nos. 1 in D, K.285; 2 in G, K.285a; 3 in C, K.285b; 4 in A, K.298.
(B) ** HM/BMG VD 77517 [77517-2-RV]. Barthold Kuijken, Coll. Aur. (members), Maier.

Those wanting the *Flute quartets* played on a period flute will find the performances by Barthold Kuijken elegantly agreeable. His support from the forwardly balanced members of the Collegium Aureum, recorded within the ample acoustics of the Jagdsaal of the Schloss Schwetzingen, is warm and somewhat larger than life. As usual with this group, the string sound is much mellower than the timbre one normally expects from original instruments.

(i) *Horn quintet in E flat, K.407;* (ii) *String quartets Nos. 21 in D, K.575; 22 in B flat, K. 589 (Prussian Quartets Nos. 1–2).*
(B) **(*) Hung. White Label HRC 174 [id.]. (i) Ferenc Tarjáni, Kodály Qt; (ii) Eder Qt.

Ferenc Tarjáni is a characterful and sensitive horn player, managing a judicious degree of vibrato with finesse, yet phrasing eloquently and articulating the closing rondo with spirit. He is well partnered by the Kodály players. The Eder Quartet are only slightly less striking in the two *Prussian Quartets*; their playing is polished and sympathetic and they are smoothly recorded. Indeed the sound throughout is vivid and without edginess. Good value.

Piano quartet No. 1 in G min., K.478.
(B) ** Vanguard VCD 72028. Peter Serkin, Schneider Ens. – DVOŘÁK: *Piano quintet, Op. 81.*

Piano quartets Nos. 1 in G min., K.478; 2 in E flat, K.493.
(B) *** Hung. White Label HRC 170 [id.]. Gyula Kiss, Tátrai Trio.

Piano quartets Nos. 1 in G min., K.478; 2 in E flat, K.493; Adagio & fugue, K.546.
** EMI Dig. CDC7 54008-2 [id.]. Collard, Zazofsky, Keyes, Ansell, Reynolds.

Another fine record in Hungaroton's bargain-priced chamber music series brings a very enjoyable pairing of the two *Piano quartets.* Gyula Kiss, the pianist, is a fine and characterful Mozartian, and he dominates performances which are convincingly paced and alive, with the Tátrai string group making an excellent partnership. Both slow movements show the pianist at his most sensitive and the finales have a contrasting lightness of touch that is most appealing. Natural sound with good presence yet no edginess on the strings.

No quarrels with the EMI reading by Jean-Philippe Collard and three members of the Muir Quartet, who observe both the spirit and the letter of these marvellous scores. Collard shows himself to be a fine Mozartian; but the recording, made in the Salle Adyar, Paris, is a little dry, robbing the string-tone of some of its bloom. (The acoustic is not dissimilar to that used in the 1930s for the Pro Arte Quartet, when a slight dryness proved an aid to clarity.)

The playing of Peter Serkin and Schneider's group is enjoyably fresh and spontaneous: the effect is somewhat robust, but the recording, though forward, is truthfully balanced.

(i) *Piano quartet No. 1 in G min., K.478. String quartet No. 16 in E flat, K.428;* (ii) *String quintets Nos. 3 in C, K.515; 4 in G min., K.516; 5 in D, K.593.*
(M) (***) EMI mono CHS7 63870-2 (2) [id.]. (i) Schnabel; Pro Arte Qt, (ii) with A. Hobday.

These classic accounts from the 1930s are in some ways unsurpassed and withstand the passage of time. Schnabel was sometimes wanting in the pianistic grace we associate with later Mozartians, but these are among his best chamber music records; and the playing of the Pro Arte has a very special wisdom and humanity. The slow movement of the *E flat Quartet* will be a revelation to readers who have not encountered this ensemble before and who are used to the hard-boiled Mozart we are offered so often nowadays. The Pro Arte Quartet and Alfred Hobday find more depth and pathos in the *Adagio* fourth movement of the *G minor Quintet* than any ensemble since, and they bring us very close to the spirit of Mozart. A special issue – even in a year that has been rich in historic Mozartiana.

Piano and wind quintet in E flat, K.452.
(B) *** Hung. White Label HRC 169 [id.]. Sándor Fálvai, Hungarian Wind Quintet – BEETHOVEN: *Quintet*.***

An enjoyably fresh performance from Sándor Fálvai and these excellent Hungarian wind players, given a most natural and realistic sound-balance in a pleasing acoustic. The playing has vitality and finesse, and an attractive degree of robustness too. Yet the *Andante* is appealingly serene and gentle, to act as a foil to the infectious finale. A bargain, though not superior to the versions with Perahia (CBS MK 42099), Lupu (Decca 414 291-2) or Ashkenazy (Decca 421 151-2), all of which cost more, though the Ashkenazy is at mid-price.

Complete Mozart Edition, Volume 12: *String quartets Nos. 1–23*
(M) *** Ph. 422 512-2 (8) [id.]. Italian Qt.

Those who do not already own the survey of Mozart's *String quartets* by the Quartetto Italiano should lose no time in obtaining Volume 12 of the Philips Complete Mozart Edition. Admittedly the earliest recordings now begin to show their age (notably the six *Haydn Quartets*, which date from 1966): the violin timbre is thinner than we would expect in more modern versions. But the ambience of La Chaux-de-Fonds, Switzerland, is ideal for chamber music and this project continued into the early 1970s. The quality is generally very satisfactory, for the Philips sound-balance is admirably judged. As a set, the performances have seen off all challengers for two decades or more; one is unlikely to assemble a more consistently satisfying overview of these works, or one so beautifully played. They hold a very special place in the Mozartian discography.

String quartets Nos. 1 in G, K.80; 2 in D, K.155; 3 in G, K.156; 4 in C, K.157; 5 in F, K.158; 6 in B flat, K.159; 7 in E flat, K.160; 8 in F, K.168; 9 in A, K.169; 10 in C, K.170; 11 in E flat, K.171; 12 in B flat, K.172; 13 in D min., K.173; Divertimenti: in G, K.136; in B flat, K.137; in F, K.138.
*** DG Dig. 431 645-2 (3) [id.]. Hagen Qt.

This set of three CDs presents all of Mozart's music for string quartet up to the age of seventeen and, although (with the best will in the world) this cannot be called great music, it is played with such charm and polish that one is almost – but not quite – tempted to believe that it is. Unlike the Quartetto Italiano, the Hagens include the *Divertimenti*, K.136–8. They have already given ample evidence of their artistry and musicianship in their recordings of K.589 and K.590. In this present set they strike an excellent balance between naturalness of utterance and sophistication of tone, and the DG recording is in the very first flight.

String quartets Nos. 14–19 (Haydn Quartets).
*** Hyp. Dig. CDS 44001/3 [id.]. Salomon Qt.

Admirers of the Salomon Quartet's 'authentic' approach to Mozart will be glad to learn that their versions of the *Haydn Quartets*, discussed on p. 698 of our main volume, are now available in a three-CD boxed set at a slightly reduced price.

String quartet No. 17 in B flat (Hunt), K.458.
(M) *** Teldec/Warner 2292 42440-2 [id.]. Alban Berg Qt – HAYDN: *Quartet No. 77.****

String quartets Nos. 17 in B flat (Hunt), K.458; 19 in C (Dissonance), K.465.
❀ *** Teldec/Warner 2292 43037-2 [id.]. Alban Berg Qt.
(M) * DG Dig. 431 285-2; *431 285-4* [id.]. Emerson Qt.

The warmest possible welcome must be given to the return of this early Teldec coupling by the Alban Berg Quartet. At that period in their history these players had not yet acquired the glossy surface veneer that sometimes detracts from their more recent digital recordings. Their version of the *Hunt quartet* dates from 1979 and is still possibly the finest account on the market. It has much greater polish and freshness even than the Quartetto Italiano, the Melos or the Amadeus, and well withstands all the competition that has come since. The *Dissonance* is of similar vintage, though it never appeared in the UK at the time. It, too, is first class, with a wonderfully expressive account of the slow movement. Although dynamic gradations are steep, there is no sense of exaggeration – on the contrary, there is only a sense of total dedication about these wholly excellent performances, which are recommended with enthusiasm. No reservations about the transfers. Readers should note that the Alban Berg's 1979 version of the *Hunt quartet* is also available coupled with Haydn's *Emperor quartet.*

When issued at full price, the Emerson coupling also included Haydn's *Emperor quartet*. This latter has been removed for the mid-priced reissue in DG's 3D Mozart Edition. The Emersons are stunningly articulate performers; they are meticulous too: every 't' is crossed and every 'i' dotted. In terms of sonority and ensemble the listener is bowled over by their virtuosity. But this is eminently self-aware, over-projected playing that might possibly be appropriate in William Schuman or Elliott Carter but which is totally out of place in Mozart. They are not helped by a rather unspacious (though not unacceptable) recorded sound.

String quartets Nos. 20 in D (Hoffmeister), K.499; 21 in D, K.575; 22 in B flat, K.589; 23 in F, K.590 (Prussian Quartets Nos. 1–3).
(M) **(*) DG Dig./Analogue 431 153-2 (2). Melos Qt.

String quartets Nos. 20 in D (Hoffmeister), K.499; 21 in D, K.575.
** EMI Dig. CDC7 49583-2 [id.]. Alban Berg Qt.

String quartets Nos. 22 in B flat, K.589; 23 in F (Prussian), K.590.
** EMI Dig. CDC7 49971-2 [id.]. Alban Berg Qt.

The Melos coupling of the *Second* and *Third Prussian Quartets*, K.589/590, is the most attractive of their Mozart recordings. These works were written for the Prussian king, Friedrich Wilhelm II, who was a keen cellist, and the Melos group possesses a particularly fine cellist in Peter Buck. He has a strong personality and a positive sense of characterization. These artists bring plenty of warmth to the slow movements of both quartets, and the transfer of the 1979/80 analogue recordings is fresh and clear. The other two quartets of the set were recorded digitally in 1981 and 1983. Here there is very accomplished playing, with all the musical intelligence and expertise one expects from this ensemble. In the first movement of the *Hoffmeister* they move things along with the right feeling of musical continuity and rhythmic momentum, but do so at the cost of a certain grace – and this strikes the listener more forcibly in the wonderful Minuet. Nevetheless these performances have many virtues: fine internal balance between the players, a keen responsiveness, superb ensemble and beauty of sound. The recording is excellent. While the Chilingirians remain first choice in Mozart's last four quartets, they are at full price, though worth it (CRD 3427/28); those looking for something more economical could well be satisfied with this DG alternative.

The Alban Berg Quartet play with sumptuous tone and the greatest polish, but neither of these records is wholly satisfying. Everything sounds a bit overnourished, as if the entire Philadelphia Orchestra were playing an early Haydn symphony. As quartet playing it is beyond reproach, and it would be wrong to suggest that they do not give some degree of pleasure. All the same, they do not always bring this music to life in the way that they undoubtedly intend. Excellent recorded sound.

String quartets Nos. 20 in D (Hoffmeister), K.499; 22 in B flat, K.589.
*** Virgin Dig. VC7 90772-2; *VC7 90772-4* [id.]. Endellion Qt.

At least this sounds like music. So many present quartets play Mozart like a jet taking off: candlelight gives way to strip-lighting. This may not be impeccable quartet-playing when compared to some earlier gramophone performances, but one is undoubtely given the impression that these artists are enjoying themselves. Phrasing is freshly thought out and there is a considerable degree of spontaneity as well. Good, truthful recordings.

String quintets Nos. 1–6.
(M) *** Ph. 422 511-2 (3). Grumiaux Trio, with Gerecz, Lesueur.
(M) **(*) DG 431 149-2 (3). Amadeus Qt, with Cecil Aronowitz.

The Grumiaux recordings of the *String quintets* reappear (now at upper mid-price) as Volume 11 in the Philips Mozart Edition, while DG have now reissued their Amadeus set, recorded between 1968 (K.406, K.515) and 1970 (K.516). While the Grumiaux set is still to be preferred in terms both of interpretation and of recorded sound, the Amadeus is also distinguished by fine playing and the recordings are remarkably successful in their CD transfers, with only a slight degree of thinness on top to date the earlier sessions. The Amadeus accounts of the *C minor* (K.406) and *C major* (K.515) works are particularly searching and spontaneous, and obviously much thought and skill have gone into the matter of internal balance as well as the interpretations. Their account of the *G minor* (K.516) with its elysian slow movement has also been admired, and there is no question about the refinement and polish of the playing, both here and in the *D major* (K.593). Yet overall the Grumiaux performances are fresher and purer in utterance.

String quintets Nos. 5 in D, K.593; 6 in E flat, K.614.
*(*) DG Dig. 429 777-2 [id.]. Melos Qt with Piero Farulli.

For all their distinction, the Melos Quartet and Piero Farulli offer rather less musical satisfaction than many rivals. Their tempi incline to be a little brisk and their approach, if not brusque, is rather matter-of-fact. Ultimately these are workmanlike readings that convey little sense of grace and little variety of dynamic nuance.

Complete Mozart Edition, Volume 15: *Violin sonatas Nos. 1–34; Sonatinas in C & F, K.46d & 46e; Sonatina in F (for beginners), K.547; Sonata in C, K.403* (completed Stadler); *Adagio in C min., K.396; Allegro in B flat, K.372; Andante & allegretto in C, K.404; Andante in A & Fugue in A min., K.402* (completed Stadler); *12 Variations on 'La bergère Célimène', K.359; 6 Variations on 'Hélas, j'ai perdu mon amant', K.360.*
(M) **(*) Ph. Analogue/Dig. 422 515-2 (7). Gérard Poulet, Blandine Verlet; Arthur Grumiaux, Walter Klien; Isabelle van Keulen, Ronald Brautigan.

Two of the seven CDs in Volume 15 of Philips's Complete Mozart Edition are analogue and are from the mid-1970s. The early sonatas, from K.6 through to K.31, were recorded by Gérard Poulet with Blandine Verlet on harpsichord. The various fragments, sonatinas, sonatas (K.46d, K.46e, K.403 and K.547), and variations were recorded in 1990 by Isabelle van Keulen and Ronald Brautigan. For the remaining four CDs, Philips have turned to the set by Arthur Grumiaux and Walter Klien, recorded digitally in the early 1980s. There is a great deal of sparkle and some refined musicianship in these performances, and pleasure remains undisturbed by the balance which, in the 1981 recordings, favours the violin. The later recordings, from 1982 and 1983, are much better in this respect. It goes without saying that there is some distinguished playing here, even if the two artists are not quite so completely attuned as were Grumiaux and Haskil in their earlier, mono set (412 253-2 and 416 478-2 – see our main volume, pp.701–2).

Violin sonatas Nos. 17–34; Violin sonatina in F, K.547.
(M) *** Decca 430 306-2 (4) [id.]. Szymon Goldberg, Radu Lupu.

Both Goldberg and Lupu bring humanity and imagination to their performances of the mature sonatas, and the playing has freshness and sensitivity. There is no doubt that in these works Goldberg shows a wisdom, born of long experience, that is almost unfailingly revealing. Lupu gives instinctive musical support to his partner; and the recordings, made in the Kingsway Hall in 1975, are expertly balanced and have transferred vividly and realistically to CD. The sense of natural presence is remarkable. An outstanding set in every way.

Violin sonatas Nos. 17 in C, K.296; 18 in G, K.301; 25 in F, K.377.
(M) *** DG Dig. 431 276-2; *431 276-4* [id.]. Itzhak Perlman, Daniel Barenboim.

Violin sonatas Nos. 21 in E min., K.304; 23 in D, K.306; 24 in F, K.376.
(M) *** DG Dig. 431 277-2; *431 277-4* [id.]. Itzhak Perlman, Daniel Barenboim.

The *Sonata in C*, K.296, is the first of what Alfred Einstein described as Mozart's concertante sonatas; even here, however the piano is dominant, a point reflected in the fact that, for all Perlman's individuality, it is Barenboim who leads. This is playing of a genial spontaneity that conveys the joy of the moment with countless felicitous details. Excellent, vivid recording, with lots of presence. Neither disc offers particularly generous measure (around 50 minutes) but their reissue comes at mid-price in DG's 3D Mozart Collection.

PIANO MUSIC

Complete Mozart Edition, Volume 16: (i) *Andante with 5 variations, K.501; Fugue in C min., K.426; Sonatas for piano duet in C, K.19d; D, K.381; G, K.357; B flat, K.358; F, K.497; C, K.521; Sonata in D for two pianos, K.448;* (ii) *Larghetto and Allegro in E flat* (reconstructed Badura-Skoda).

(M) ** Ph. 422 516-2 (2) [id.]. (i) Ingrid Haebler, Ludwig Hoffman; (ii) Jörg Demus, Paul Badura-Skoda.

This two-CD set includes all the music Mozart composed for piano duet or two pianos in elegant (if at times a little too dainty) performances by Ingrid Haebler and Ludwig Hoffman in recordings dating from the mid-1970s. Also included is a Mozart fragment, the *Larghetto and Allegro in E flat*, probably written in 1782–3 and completed by Paul Badura-Skoda, who recorded it in 1971 for the Amadeo label with Jörg Demus. Despite the occasional distant clink of Dresden china, all these performances give pleasure and are very decently recorded.

Solo piano music

Complete solo piano music.
(M) (**) EMI mono CHS7 63688-2 (8) [id.]. Walter Gieseking.

Gieseking recorded his complete Mozart cycle between 1953 and 1955 for the Columbia label, possibly the first time that any company had embarked on a complete survey of this particular repertoire by a single artist. Such an ambitious survey, comprising some nine hours of music, enjoys intermittent successes and it must be conceded that the playing (like the music) is of variable quality. The 1955 edition of the *Record Guide* spent more than two pages discussing the first two LPs and, writing of the earliest pieces, was 'a little surprised that Gieseking does not accord them more charm . . . and we have heard him turn more pearly ornaments than he does here [in K.3 and 4]', but admired 'his eggshell delicacy of tone' elsewhere. Dipping into this set reaffirms the reputation enjoyed in their day by the original LPs; however, while they never fell below a certain level of artistry, they rarely rose to the greatest heights. At times, particularly in the variations, Gieseking is perfunctory; even in such masterpieces as the *C minor Fantasy*, K.475, and *Sonata No. 14 in C minor*, K.457, he is less illuminating than one might expect. Despite the occasional felicities, there are many records that do greater justice to Gieseking's memory than these. The recordings were always a trace dry, and the remastering by Paul Baily enhances the originals considerably.

Piano sonatas Nos. 1–18 (complete).
(M) *** EMI CZS7 67294-2 (5). Daniel Barenboim.

Complete Mozart Edition, Volume 17: *Piano sonatas Nos. 1–18; Fantasia in C min., K.475.*
❀ (M) *** Ph. Dig. 422 517-2 (5) [id.]. Mitsuko Uchida.
(M) *** Decca 430 333-2 (5). András Schiff.
**(*) Olympia Dig. OCD 5003 (5) [id.]. Peter Katin.

On Philips, Mitsuko Uchida's self-recommending collection, with beautiful and naturally balanced digital recording made in the Henry Wood Hall, London, has now been reissued on 5 mid-priced CDs by omitting the shorter pieces, except for the *C minor Fantasia*.

András Schiff's earlier, Decca recordings now also reappear, in a box in the same price-range, and they remain in groups, rather than being presented in Köchel-number order like the Philips set. Schiff, without exceeding the essential Mozartian sensibility, takes a somewhat more romantic and forward-looking view of the music. The piano is set just a little further back than with Philips, and the acoustic is rather more open. It is analogue sound at its best, and its realism is striking. Other differences are discussed more fully in the original reviews in our main volume (pp. 702–4).

Barenboim's distinguished set of the Mozart *Piano sonatas* is reissued not only at mid-price but now on five CDs instead of the original six. Barenboim, while keeping his playing well within scale in its crisp articulation, refuses to adopt the Dresden china approach to Mozart's *Sonatas.* Even the little *C major*, K.545, designed for a young player, has its element of toughness, minimizing its 'eighteenth-century drawing-room' associations. Though – with the exception of the two minor-key sonatas – these are relatively unambitious works, Barenboim's voyage of discovery brings out their consistent freshness, with the orchestral implications of some of the allegros strongly established. The recording, with a pleasant ambience round the piano sound, confirms the apt scale.

Peter Katin recorded his cycle in 1988–9 in the pleasing acoustic of the Ski Church Hall in Oslo and he has the benefit of the excellent engineering of Arne Akselberg. His playing has much to recommend it; he is an instinctive musician who produces consistent beauty of sound. Given the enormous number of complete cycles or single discs of Mozart sonatas, this would have to be touched with greater distinction than it is to be a first recommendation. It must be said in its favour that Dresden china is nowhere to be heard, and the *A minor Sonata*, K.310, can hold its own with the best. Elsewhere, as is perhaps inevitable with complete surveys of this kind, there is a trace of routine. The playing is selfless and unfailingly musical but perhaps a little impersonal.

Piano sonatas Nos. 3 in B flat, K.281; 10 in C, K.330; 13 in B flat, K.333.
(M) **(*) DG 431 274-2; *431 274-4* [id.]. Vladimir Horowitz.

It is sensible to have Horowitz's Mozart sonata recordings gathered together. There have to be slight reservations about the sound: the quality in K.333 is rather dry, while K.281 is the most satisfactory. But this was still just about the best recording he received, apart from his live recitals for RCA, and the playing is remarkable, quite unlike any other. It is not always free from affectation but is never less than elegant. A distinguished contribution to DG's 3D Mozart Edition.

Piano sonatas Nos. 8 in A min., K.310; 14 in C min., K.457; Fantasia in C min., K.475; Rondo: Alla turca (from *Sonata No. 11, K.331*).
(M) *** DG Dig. 431 275-2; *431 275-4* [id.]. Maria João Pires.

Maria João Pires is a stylist and a fine Mozartian, as those who have heard any of her cycle on Denon will know. Pires is always refined but is never wanting in classical feeling, and she has a vital imagination. The performance of the *C minor* is particularly fine and her *Rondo Alla turca* engagingly varied in dynamic range: it begins quite gently. Good, clear piano recording, bright but realistic.

Piano sonatas Nos. 8 in A min., K.310; 18 in D, K.576; Fantasias: in C min.; in D min., K.396/7; 12 Variations on 'Je suis Lindor', K.354.
*** EMI Dig. CDC7 54021-2 [id.]. Melvyn Tan (fortepiano).

Here is Mozart playing of temperament by Melvyn Tan which enhances this young player's growing reputation. As always, he is sure-fingered and brilliant. His rather brisk tempi in Schubert did not always convince (see our main volume), but there are no quarrels with his judgement here. Tempi allow every musical point to be made, and thoughtful musical points there are in plenty. The *A minor Sonata* is outstanding: free, fiery and impassioned, with a clear, well-defined sense of line; and there is some fine legato playing in the slow movement of the *D major*, where some of the rubato is a bit overdone, as it is in the *D minor Fantasia*, K.397. The *Variations on 'Je suis Lindor'* are done with great flair, and the whole programme is most vividly recorded.

Piano sonata No. 10 in C, K.330.
(M) ** BMG/RCA GD 60415; *GK 60415* [60415-2-RG; *60415-4* RG]. Van Cliburn – DEBUSSY: *Estampes* etc.**; BARBER: *Sonata.***(*)

Van Cliburn's record, made in the mid-1960s, offers intelligent playing but sound that is wanting in timbre and sonority. The Debussy and Barber are better in this respect but still dryish.

Piano sonatas Nos. 11 in A, K.331; 14 in C min., K.457; Fantasias: in D min., K.397; in C min., K.475.
*** DG Dig. 429 739-2 [id.]. Maria João Pires.

Maria João Pires recorded a Mozart *Sonata* cycle in Tokyo in the mid-1970s (see our main volume, p. 704) and has now embarked on a new survey of the sonatas for DG. She is a Mozartian of integrity and a stylist; her approach is very different from that of, say, Mitsuko Uchida, and she eschews excessive beautification. She favours chiaroscuro rather than rich colourings, and her directness of statement may not be to all tastes. The *C minor Fantasia* and *Sonata* are finely thought out and well held together, and the *A major Sonata* has depth as well as charm. The DG recording is very bold and well focused. However, readers will note that some of these recordings have been reissued at mid-price in DG's Mozart 3D Collection – see above.

VOCAL MUSIC

Concert arias: *Alma grande e nobil core, K.578; Ch'io mi scordi di te?, K.505; Nehmt meinen Dank, K.383; Vado, ma dove?, K.583.* Lieder: *Abendemfindung; Als Luise die Briefe; Die Alte; An Chloë; Dans un bois solitaire; Im Frühlingsanfang; Das Kinderspiel; Die kleine Spinnerin; Das Lied der Trennung; Oiseaux, si tous les ans; Ridente la calma; Sehnsucht nach dem Frühling; Das Trumbild; Das Veilchen, Der Zauberer; Die Zuhfriedenheit.*
(M) (***) EMI mono/stereo CDH7 63702-2 [id.]. Schwarzkopf, Gieseking; Brendel; LSO, Szell.

On an earlier CD (EMI CDC7 47326-2) Schwarzkopf's classic series of the Mozart songs with Gieseking was used incomplete as a fill-up for her recordings of Schubert with Edwin Fischer. In this Schwarzkopf Edition issue at mid-price the missing songs are restored – including the most famous one, *Das Veilchen.* With such inspired performances one hardly worries over mono sound. As a generous coupling, the disc also includes Schwarzkopf's much later recordings, with Szell conducting four concert arias – including the most taxing of all, *Ch'io mi scordi di te.* Though the voice is not quite so fresh in the concert arias, the artistry and imagination are supreme, and stereo recording helps to add bloom.

Ave verum corpus, K.618.
(M) *** Decca 430 159-2; *430 159-4* [id.]. St John's College, Cambridge, Ch., Guest – J. HAYDN: *Theresienmesse*; M. HAYDN: *Ave regina.****

This simple and eloquent account of Mozart's choral lollipop is beautifully recorded and, it is to be hoped, may introduce some collectors to the inspired late Haydn Mass with which it is coupled.

Litaniae de venerabili altaris sacramento, K.243.
(M) *** Decca 430 158-2; *430 158-4* [id.]. Marshall, Cable, Evans, Roberts, St John's College, Cambridge, Ch., Wren O, Guest – HAYDN: *Heiligmesse.****

Mozart made four settings of the Litany, of which this is the last, written in 1776. It is ambitiously scored for an orchestra of double wind, two horns and three trombones – used to add sonorous gravity to many of the choral passages and to bring point and drama to the choral fugue, *Pignus futurae gloriae*. The opening *Kyrie* and the later *Hostia sancta* integrate the vocal quartet with the chorus almost operatically; among the solo items is a lively, florid tenor contribution to the *Panis vivus*, while in the beautiful *Dulcissimum convivium* the solo soprano is accompanied with flutes added to the orchestra in place of the oboes. Then the trombones return to introduce the *Viaticum in Domino morientium*, sung by the choral sopranos in unison against a pizzicato accompaniment; and later, in the soprano's lovely *Agnus Dei*, both obbligato flute and oboe are used in the scoring. It is Mozart at his most imaginative and vital; the artists here rise to the occasion and give a highly responsive performance, with Margaret Marshall outstanding among the soloists. Excellent 1980 sound.

Masonic music: *Masonic funeral music (Maurerische Trauermusik), K.477; Die ihr des unermesslichen Weltals Schöpfer ehrt* (cantata), *K.619; Die ihr einen neuen Grade, K.468; Dir, Seele des Weltalls* (cantata), *K.429; Ihr unsre neuen Leiter* (song), *K.484; Lasst uns mit geschlungnen Händen, K.623a; Laut verkünde unsre Freude, K.623; O heiliges Band* (song), *K.148; Sehen, wie dem starren Forscherange, K.471; Zerfliesset heut', geliebte Brüder, K.483.*
(M) *** Decca 425 722-2; *425 722-4* [id.]. Werner Krenn, Tom Krause, Edinburgh Festival Ch., LSO, Kertesz.

This Decca reissue is among the most worthwhile of those stimulated by the Bicentenary. It contains the more important of Mozart's Masonic music in first-class performances, admirably recorded. Most striking of all is Kertesz's strongly dramatic account of the *Masonic funeral music*; the two lively songs for chorus, *Zerfliesset heut'* and *Ihr unsre neuen Leiter*, are sung with warm humanity and are also memorable. Indeed the choral contribution is most distinguished throughout, and Werner Krenn's light tenor is most appealing in the other items which he usually dominates.

Mass No. 12 in C (Spaur), K.258.
(M) *** Decca 430 161-2; *430 161-4* [id.]. Palmer, Cable, Langridge, Roberts, St John's College, Cambridge, Ch., Wren O, Guest – HAYDN: *Schöpfungsmesse.****

The *Spaur mass* is not among Mozart's most inspired, but its directness is appealing and the *Benedictus*, which offers a fine Mozartian interplay of chorus and soloists, is very appealing. In a vigorous performance like this, with trombones justifiably doubling some of the choral lines, it is most enjoyable. Excellent Argo sound, 1979 vintage.

Mass No. 16 in C (Coronation), K.317.
(M) **(*) DG Dig. 429 980-2; *429 980-4* [id.]. Battle, Schmidt, Winbergh, Furlanetto, V. Singverein, VPO, Karajan – BRUCKNER: *Te Deum.**

Karajan's 1985 recording of Mozart's *Coronation Mass* is certainly vibrant, with fine choral singing and good soloists. Kathleen Battle sings beautifully in the *Agnus Dei*, and the recording is bright, if not ideally expansive. But the Bruckner coupling is much less recommendable.

(i) *Mass No. 16 in C (Coronation), K.317;* (ii) *Requiem Mass in D min., K.626.*
(B) **(*) DG Compact Classics *419 084-4* [id.]. (i) Mathis, Procter, Grobe, Shirley-Quirk, Bav. R. Ch. and SO, Kubelik; (ii) Mathis, Hamari, Ochman, Ridderbusch, V. State Op. Ch., VPO, Boehm.

A characteristically generous Compact Classics coupling, with good sound throughout. Both recordings were made in the early 1970s. Kubelik draws a fine, mellow-toned performance of the *Coronation Mass* from his Bavarian forces, lacking something in exuberance but still alive and well sung. Boehm's account of the *Requiem* is also spacious but has more power, and the majesty of the closing *Agnus Dei* is very involving. The recording loses little in its chrome-tape transfer and is strikingly well balanced.

Mass No. 18 in C min. (Great), K.427.
(M) *** DG Dig. 431 287-2; *431 287-4* [id.]. Hendricks, Perry, Schreier, Luxon, V. Singverein, BPO, Karajan.

Karajan's 1982 digital recording of the *C minor Mass* now arrives at mid-price in DG's 3D Mozart Collection. Karajan gives Handelian splendour to this greatest of Mozart's choral works and, though the scale is large, the beauty and intensity are hard to resist. Solo singing is first rate, particularly that of Barbara Hendricks, the dreamy beauty of her voice ravishingly caught. Woodwind is rather backward, yet the sound is both rich and vivid – though, as the opening shows, the internal balance is not always completely consistent.

Requiem Mass (No. 19) in D min., K.626 (completed Eybler/Süssmayr, ed. Robbins Landon).
**(*) Nimbus Dig. NI 5241 [id.]. Janowitz, Bernheimer, M. Hill, D. Thomas, Hanover Band Ch., Hanover Band, Goodman.

Requiem Mass (No. 19) in D min., K.626.
(M) *** DG Dig. 431 288-2; *431 288-4* [id.]. Tomowa-Sintow, Müller Molinari, Cole, Burchuladze, V. Singverein, VPO, Karajan.
*(*) Sony Dig. SK 45577 [id.]. Dawson, K. Lewis, Van Ness, Philh. Ch. & O, Giulini.

(i) *Requiem Mass (No. 19) in D min., K.626 Masonic funeral music, K.477.*
**(*) ASV CDDCA 757; *ZCDCA 757* [id.]. (i) Howarth, Montague, Maldwyn Davies, Roberts, BBC Singers; LMP, Glover.

Karajan's 1987 digital version is now reissued in DG's mid-priced 3D Mozart Collection. It is a large-scale reading, but one that is white-hot with intensity and energy. The power and bite of the rhythm are consistently exciting. The solo quartet is first rate, though Helga Müller Molinari is on the fruity side for Mozart. Vinson Cole, stretched at times, yet sings very beautifully, and so does Paata Burchuladze with his tangily distinctive Slavonic bass tone. The close balance adds to the excitement, though the sound, both choral and orchestral, lacks transparency.

Often at brisk speeds, Jane Glover directs a fresh and direct reading of the *Requiem*, a version which brings a valuable and apt bonus in the *Masonic funeral music*. The playing and singing are first rate, with an exceptionally fine quartet of soloists, and the only snag is the rather backward balance of the chorus, reducing the dramatic impact of some numbers.

Roy Goodman's Nimbus CD, with the Hanover Band, has the distinction of presenting the new Robbins Landon edition on disc for the first time. As Landon explains in his notes, he 'decided to investigate the very first attempts at reconstruction, even before Süssmayr completed his'. Landon has therefore incorporated the orchestrations completed by another Mozart pupil, Joseph Eybler, where possible, in place of the usual Süssmayr ones, keeping the rest of the text in the Süssmayr edition. As he says, 'We believe that pupils of Mozart are better equipped to complete Mozart's torso than a 20th-century scholar, however knowledgeable.' The practical differences are less than might be expected. The thickness of some of Süssmayr's orchestration is avoided, though it is disappointing not to have dramatic trombones interjecting at the start of the *Rex tremendae*. The performance, using period instruments on an intimate scale, is first rate, though the reverberant recording does not allow detail consistently to come through. With Gundula Janowitz still golden-toned, it is a pity that her voice is not more sharply focused. Gardiner's version with the Monteverdi Choir and the English Baroque Soloists will probably be preferred by those seeking an authentic performance, a bitingly intense reading opting for the traditional course of using the Süssmayr completion but favouring period instruments at lower pitch. Moreover he throws in the superb *Kyrie in D minor*, K.341, for good measure (Philips 420 197-2; *420 197-4*).

Despite fine singing from soloists and chorus, Giulini's Sony version is a disappointment. His earlier, EMI recording, reissued on the Laser budget label (CZS7 62892-2), is far finer, with speeds already on the slow side, but not dragging as they tend to do in this later one, which is altogether heavier. The heavyweight recording does not help.

Vesperae de dominica, K.321.
(M) *** Decca 430 162-2; *430 162-4* [id.]. Marshall, Cable, Evans, Roberts, St John's College, Cambridge, Ch., Wren O, Guest – HAYDN: *Harmoniemesse.****

Aptly coupled with Haydn's *Harmoniemesse*, Mozart's vibrant *Vesperae de dominica* opens with a series of brilliant choral settings (with contrasting solo quartet), accompanied by trumpets and strings, without violas – *Dixit Dominus . . . Confitebor . . . Beatus vir* – followed by a *Laudate pueri* 'in the learned style'. Margaret Marshall is appropriately agile in the lively soprano solo of the *Laudate Dominum*, and the work closes with an ambitious *Magnificat* in which all the participants are joined satisfyingly together. The St John's performance is full of vigour and Guest creates a proper sense of apotheosis in the work's closing section. The 1980 recording is full and vivid, and the CD transfer demonstrates the excellence of the original Argo sound-balance.

Vesperae solennes de confessore, K.339.
(M) *** Decca 430 157-2; *430 157-4* [id.]. Palmer, Cable, Langridge, Roberts, St John's College, Cambridge, Ch., Wren O, Guest – HAYDN: *Paukenmesse.****

Although Guest's version of Mozart's masterpiece does not always match the recording by Sir Colin Davis for Philips (412 873-2) – Felicity Palmer is a less poised soloist than Kiri Te Kanawa – the Decca account has the advantage of authenticity in the use of boys in the chorus. Moreover the CD transfer of the 1979 Argo recording is preferable to the less well-defined Philips sound: the Decca remastering is cleanly focused, yet has plenty of warmth and atmosphere.

OPERA

Bastien und Bastienne (complete). Concert arias: *Mentre ti lascio, o figlia, K.513; Misero! o sogno . . . Aura, che intorno spiri, K.431. Le nozze di Figaro: Giunse alfin il momento . . . Deh vieni; Un moto di gioia.*
*** Sony Dig. CD 45855; *40-45855* [id.]. Gruberová, Cole, Polgar, Liszt CO, Leppard.

Leppard, recently neglected by the record companies, here conducts a near-ideal performance of the eleven-year-old Mozart's charming little one-Acter, very well recorded. The trio of soloists is excellent. Edita Gruberová is delectably fresh and vivacious as the heroine, Vinson Cole is a sensitive and clean-voiced Bastien and Laszlo

Polgar is full of fun in the buffo role of Colas. The dialogue is excellently directed, and the Liszt Chamber Orchestra of Budapest plays with dazzling precision, bringing wit to the opening with its anticipation of Beethoven's *Eroica*. As a generous fill-up, the three soloists sing Mozart arias, including the big scena for tenor, *Misero! o sogno*, and a replacement aria for Susanna, especially written for the 1789 production of *Le nozze di Figaro*: *Un moto di gioia*.

La clemenza di Tito (opera): complete.
(M) ** Decca 430 105-2 (2) [id.]. Krenn, Berganza, Casula, Popp, Fassbaender, Franc, VPO Ch. & O, Kertész.

Kertész attacks Mozart's last opera with fine dramatic directness, but over the span of this formal *opera seria* one cannot help missing a more individual interpretative hand. He seems to have no idea about the grammar of the *apoggiatura*, for the endings of phrases requiring them are regularly left blunt. The recitative too is taken ponderously and one longs to have more pace and contrast in the story-telling. But with very vivid recording and production, generally excellent singing – particularly from Teresa Berganza as Sesto – and strong playing, this might be considered, although Boehm's mellower DG set in the same price-range (which also includes Teresa Berganza) is far more persuasive (429 878-2).

Così fan tutte (complete).
*** Ph. Dig. 422 381-2; *422 381-4* (3) [id.]. Mattila, Von Otter, Szmytka, Araiza, Allen, Van Dam, Amb. Op. Ch., ASMF, Marriner.
(M) (***) EMI mono CHS7 63864-2 (2). Souez, Helletsgruber, Nash, Domgraf-Fassbaender, Brownlee, Eisinger, Glyndebourne Festival Ch. & O, Fritz Busch.
(M) **(*) EMI CMS7 63845-2 (3). M. Price, Minton, Popp, Alva, Evans, Sotin, Alldis Ch., New Philh. O, Klemperer.
(M) ** Decca 430 101-2 (3) [id.]. Lorengar, Berganza, R. Davies, Krause, Bacquier, Berbié, ROHCG Ch., LPO, Solti.
(B) ** Naxos Dig. 8.660008/10 [id.]. Borowska, Yachmi, John Dickie, Martin, Coles, Mikulas, Slovak Philharmonic Ch., Capella Istropolitana, Johannes Wildner.
*(*) Erato/WEA Dig. 2292 45475-2 (3) [id.]. Cuberli, Bartoli, Rodgers, Furlanetto, Streit, Tomlinson, Berlin RIAS Chamber Ch., BPO, Barenboim.

Marriner directs a fresh and resilient performance, beautifully paced, often with speeds on the fast side, and with the crystalline recorded sound adding to the sparkle. Though the women principals (Karita Mattila a warm Fiordiligi, Anne Sofie von Otter a characterful Dorabella and Elzbieta Szmytka a light, charming Despina) make a strong team, the men are even finer: Francisco Araiza as Ferrando, Thomas Allen as Guglielmo and José van Dam as Alfonso all outstanding. Individual as they are, they work together superbly to produce the crispest possible ensembles so that, though the reading is lighter in weight than those of Boehm (EMI CMS7 69330-2), Karajan (EMI mono CHS7 69635-2), Haitink (EMI CDS7 47727-8) or Davis (Philips 416 633-2), it has more fun in it, bringing out the laughter in the score. For those wanting a modern digital recording this could well be a first choice; but the classic Boehm set and Karajan's sparkling mono version both remain indispensable, and both were given a Rosette in our main volume – see p. 715.

Available during the LP era only for a very brief period as an import from France, this legendary Glyndebourne performance, the first ever recording of *Così fan tutte*, is the finest of the three pioneering sets recorded on 78s in the mid-1930s with the newly founded Glyndebourne company. The sound in the CD transfer, though limited, is amazingly vivid, with voices very well focused and with a keener sense of presence than on many recordings of the 1990s. Busch at the time was a progressive Mozartian, preferring athletic treatment – occasionally to excess, as in the concluding ensemble of Act I – but this is as efferverscent as any more recent recording, and nowadays even the use of a piano for the recitatives instead of a harpsichord seems less outlandish with the emergence of the fortepiano. John Brownlee as Don Alfonso is very much the English aristocrat, with 'fruffly-fruffly' English vowels instead of Italianate ones, but he is a fine, stylish singer. Ina Souez and Luise Helletsgruber as the two sisters outshine all but the very finest of their successors on record, technically superb; and Heddle Nash and Willi Domgraf-Fassbaender as their lovers are at once stylish and characterful, with Irene Eisinger as a delightfully soubrettish Despina. Cuts are made in the recitatives according to the custom of the time and, more seriously, four numbers disappear – including, amazingly, Ferrando's *Tradito, schernito* and Dorabella's *E amore un ladroncello*. The bonus is that, with those cuts, the opera fits on to only two mid-price CDs.

Klemperer's last opera set was predictably idiosyncratic. When the record company jibbed at his suggestion of recording this sparkling comedy, he is alleged to have protested (aged eighty-six at the time), 'What do you want? A posthumous interpretation?' The result proved by no means as funereal as had been predicted, with fine rhythmic pointing to lighten the slow tempi. There is fine singing too from the whole cast (Alva alone at times disappointing) to make the whole a satisfying entertainment, a different view of Mozart to be heard at least once. It is a pity the recitatives are not more imaginatively done. An excellent transfer to CD.

Solti's set will please those who want high voltage at all costs even in this most genial of all Mozart comedies. There is little relaxation and little charm, which underlines the shortcomings of the singing cast, notably of Pilar Lorengar, whose grainy voice is not treated kindly by the microphone and who here in places conveys uncertainty. It is a pity that the crackling wit of Solti's Covent Garden performances was not more magically captured on record. Brilliant recording.

On three budget-price CDs (each costing slightly more than this super-bargain label's orchestral and instrumental repertory) the Naxos version comes out at a price comparable to the Glyndebourne two-disc set, yet provides a text without the omissions of the latter, and the modern digital recording is fresh and bright. But with the exception of Joanna Borowska as a strong, stylish Fiordiligi, the Czech cast is in a different league. After Borowska, Peter Mikulas is the most successful of the soloists, a forthright, clean-toned Don Alfonso. John Dickie, as recorded, sounds rather too throaty as Ferrando and Rohangiz Yachmi as Dorabella has too fruity a vibrato for Mozart. After a gabbled overture, Wildner directs a well-played, generally well-paced performance. It is worth remembering that for the price of these discs one would be well pleased to come across such a performance in the opera house, be it in Bratislava or elsewhere.

Barenboim, too, has a first-rate cast – with Joan Rodgers as Despina making a very welcome recording déut in a major operatic role – but some are well below their best. Ferruccio Furlanetto is miscast as Guglielmo, sounding far too venerable, and even Lella Cuberli, a fine Fiordiligi, has her powerful, agile singing in the big test of *Come scoglio* seriously undermined by limp accompaniment. Generally the Berlin Philharmonic sounds too thick and heavy, lacking resilience. The playing sounds breathless and unsprung when Barenboim, in his erratic choice of speeds, opts to take a number fast. Dull recording does not help.

Così fan tutte: highlights.
(M) **(*) DG Dig. 431 290-2; *431 290-4* [id.] (from recording with Te Kanawa, Murray, McLaughlin, Blochwitz, Hampson, Furlanetto, VPO, cond. Levine).

A generous selection (75 minutes) from Levine's brisk, rather unsmiling *Così*, especially useful for sampling Dame Kiri's Fiordiligi, one of her finest Mozartian performances on record, and Thomas Hampson's characterfully rich portrayal of Guglielmo. Marie McLaughlin is a splendid Despina, so there is much to enjoy here, although Ann Murray's Dorabella is a disappointment.

(i) *Così fan tutte*: highlights; (ii) *Le nozze di Figaro*: highlights.
(B) **(*) DG Compact Classics *427 712-4* [id.]. From complete sets with (i; ii) Janowitz; (i) Ludwig, Loose, Dermota, Kunz, Schoeffler, Vienna State Op. Ch., VPO; (ii) Mathis, Troyanos, Fischer-Dieskau, Prey, German Op. Ch. & O; Boehm.

This Compact Classics tape combines highlights from the 1977 Salzburg Festival recording of *Così* with an earlier, 1968 studio recording of *Figaro*. Boehm conducts both with his customary stylish warmth, and if in *Così*, understandably, the live performance is less than ideally polished, the sparkle of the singing projects splendidly, especially as the tape transfer is so lively, with the balance favouring the voices. The *Figaro* cast is very strong with Janowitz, common to both operas, in ravishing voice. An excellent tape for the car.

Don Giovanni (complete).
(M) (***) EMI mono CHS7 63860-2 (3) [Hunt CD 509]. Siepi, Schwarzkopf, Berger, Grümmer, Dermota, Edelmann, Berry, Ernster, V. State Op. Ch., VPO, Furtwängler.
**(*) O-L Dig. 425 943-2; *425 943-4* (3) [id.]. Hagegård, Cachemaille, Augér, Della Jones, Van der Meel, Bonney, Terfel, Sigmundsson, Drottningholm Court Theatre Ch. & O, Östman.
(M) **(*) EMI CMS7 63841-2 (3); *EX 763841-4*. Ghiaurov, Watson, Gedda, Ludwig, Berry, Freni, Montarsolo, Crass, New Philh. O & Ch., Klemperer.
(M) ** Decca 425 169-2 (3) [id.]. Weikl, M. Price, Burrows, Sass, Bacquier, Popp, Sramek, Moll, London Op. Ch., LPO, Solti.
*(*) Teldec/Warner Dig. 2292 44184-2 (3) [id.]. Hampson, Polgár, Gruberová, Alexander, Bonney, Blochwitz, Scharinger, Holl, Netherlands Op. Ch., Concg. O, Harnoncourt.

The historic Furtwängler performance was recorded live by Austrian Radio at the 1954 Salzburg Festival, barely three months before the conductor's death. Far from taking a weightily Germanic view, he consistently brings out the sparkle in this '*Dramma giocoso*', to use Mozart's term on the title-page. Though speeds are often slow by today's standards, his springing of rhythm never lets them sag. Even the very slow speed for Leporello's catalogue aria is made to seem charmingly individual. With the exception of a wobbly Commendatore, this is a classic Salzburg cast, with Cesare Siepi a fine, incisive Don, dark in tone, Elisabeth Schwarzkopf a dominant Elvira, Elisabeth Grümmer a vulnerable Anna, Anton Dermota a heady-toned Ottavio and Otto Edelmann a clear and direct Leporello. Stage noises often suggest herds of animals lumbering about, but both voices and orchestra are satisfyingly full-bodied in the CD transfer, and the sense of presence is astonishing.

Östman follows up his earlier recordings of *Così fan tutte* and *Le nozze di Figaro* with this period performance of *Don Giovanni*. This time, with a far darker score, he has modified his stance. Though speeds are still often fast, this time they rarely seem breathless. The tough sound of period instruments sharpens the drama, even if scrawny violins are at times a trouble. Exceptionally, some speeds are unusually slow – as for example the rustic ensembles – but rhythms are well sprung and the intimate scale of a Drottningholm production is well caught. Håkan Hagegård as Giovanni could be sweeter-toned, but his lightness and spontaneity, particularly in exchanges with the vividly alive Leporello of Gilles Cachemaille, are most winning, with recitative often barely vocalized. Arleen Augér is a radiant Donna Anna, while two Welsh singers also make fine contributions: Della Jones a full-toned Elvira and Bryn Terfel a resonant Masetto. Understandably, the original Prague text is used, which means that each of the two Acts can be fitted complete on to a single disc, an obvious advantage. Such essential additions as Ottavio's *Dalla sua pace* (beautifully sung by Nico van der Meel) and Elvira's *Mi tradi* are given in an appendix on the third disc.

The lumbering tempo of Leporello's opening music will alert the listener to the predictable Klemperer approach and at that point some may dismiss his performance as 'too heavy' – but the issue is far more complex than that. Most of the slow tempi which Klemperer regularly adopts, far from flagging, add a welcome breadth to the music, for they must be set against the unusually brisk and dramatic interpretation of the recitatives between numbers. Added to that, Ghiaurov as the Don and Berry as Leporello make a marvellously characterful pair. In this version, the male members of the cast are dominant and, with Klemperer's help, they make the dramatic experience a strongly masculine one. Nor is the ironic humour forgotten with Berry and Ghiaurov about, and the Klemperer spaciousness allows them extra time for pointing. Among the women, Ludwig is a strong and convincing Elvira, Freni a sweet-toned but rather unsmiling Zerlina; only Claire Watson seriously disappoints, with obvious nervousness marring the big climax of *Non mi dir*. It is a serious blemish but, with the usual reservations, for those not allergic to the Klemperer approach, this stands as a good recommendation – at the very least a commanding experience.

Solti directs a crisp, incisive performance, with generally fast tempi and very well-directed recitatives. If it shows no special signs of affection, it contains one glorious performance in Margaret Price's Anna, pure in tone and line but powerfully dramatic too, always beautiful. Next to her, Sylvia Sass as a somewhat gusty Elvira sounds rather miscast, characterful though her singing is. The two baritones, Bernd Weikl and Gabriel Bacquier, are clearly contrasted as Giovanni and Leporello respectively, though the microphone is not kind to either. The recording is brilliant in its realistic clarity.

Harnoncourt's version with the Concertgebouw rather falls between two stools. He persuades the orchestra's reduced strings to play with a lighter, more detached style than usual and with little vibrato, but the heavily over-reverberant recording removes any advantages; Harnoncourt's fast speeds, unlike Östman's, tend to sound perverse instead of helpful. Thomas Hampson as Don Giovanni is splendid, the archetypal seducer; and the others are generally good too, but Edita Gruberová is a surprisingly squally and often raw Donna Anna, no match for most rivals. Giulini's classic EMI set with Wachter, Schwarzkopf, Sutherland, Taddei and Cappuccilli, lovingly remastered, is a clear best buy for this work, even though it remains at full price (EMI CDS7 47260-8 [Angel CDCC 47260].

Don Giovanni: highlights.
(M) *** DG Dig. 431 289-2; *431 289-4* [id.] (from recording with Ramey, Tomowa-Sintow, Baltsa, Battle, Winbergh, Furlanetto, Malta, Burchuladze, BPO, cond. Karajan).
(B) ** Pickwick (DG) IMPX 9023 (from recording with Fischer-Dieskau, Arroyo, Nilsson, Grist, Schreier, Flagello, cond. Boehm).
(M) *(*) Decca 421 875-2; *421 875-4*. Siepi, Nilsson, L. Price, Ratti, Valletti, Corena, V. State Op. Ch., VPO, Leinsdorf.

A generous selection (66 minutes) from Karajan's digital set, most of the favourite items included and all the principals given a chance to sparkle, in solos, duets and ensembles. The selection opens with the Overture and closes with the powerful final scene.

A good sampler for Boehm's first Prague set, which is uneven but which has some fine, characterful performances and is worth hearing for Birgit Nilsson's unexpected casting as Donna Anna, represented here by *Or sai chi l'onore*. The selection is a little short on quantity (56 minutes), but the major participants are all given a chance to shine.

Although the selection is generous (70 minutes), there is little else to recommend in Leinsdorf's 1960 recording. It begins with a fierce, fast version of the *Overture* and elsewhere has drama without charm, for Leinsdorf's direction is largely uninspired. Nilsson again makes a gusty Donna Anna and Leontyne Price is equally poorly cast. Siepi and Corena are reliable but are better served in the Krips version. The sound is vivid but lacks bloom.

(i) *Don Giovanni:* highlights; (ii) *Die Entführung aus dem Serail:* highlights.
(B) *** DG Compact Classics *431 181-4* [id.]. (i) Milnes, Tomowa-Sintow, Zylis-Gara, Mathis, Schreier, Berry, V. State Op. Ch., VPO; (ii) Augér, Grist, Schreier, Neukirch, Moll, Leipzig R. Ch., Dresden State O, Boehm.

With sparkling sound, this is one of the finest operatic tape bargains in the DG Compact Classics catalogue. The *Don Giovanni* highlights were recorded live at the 1977 Salzburg Festival. The strong cast is dominated by a swaggering Don in Sherrill Milnes, and Anna Tomowa-Sintow proves a generally creamy-toned Donna Anna. Teresa Zylis-Gara and Edith Mathis are good too, and Walter Berry is a genial Leporello. The selection is well made and it is joined by an equally attractive set of excerpts from Boehm's superb *Entführung*, with Arleen Augér at her very finest in the rôle of Constanze, Kurl Moll relishing the characterization of Osmin, and the rest of the cast almost equally impressive. Again the transfer is vivid, and both overtures are included.

(i) *Die Entführung aus dem Serail* (complete). (ii) Arias from: *La clemenza di Tito; Die Entführung; Idomeneo.*
(M) **(*) EMI stereo/mono CHS7 63715-2 (2). (i) Lois Marshall, Hollweg, Simoneau, Unger, Frick, Beecham Ch. Soc., RPO, Beecham; (ii) Léopold Simoneau.

There is much to treasure in Beecham's vivid but idiosyncratic reading, not least the incomparable portrayal of Osmin by the great German bass, Gottlob Frick, thrillingly dark and firm, characterizing superbly. His aria, *O wie will ich triumphieren*, like the *Overture* and the *Chorus of Janissaries* in Act I, finds Beecham fizzing with energy, spine-tingling in intensity. Léopold Simoneau as Belmonte has rarely been matched on record for mellifluous beauty and flawless line, and Gerhard Unger is a charming Pedrillo, not least in the spoken dialogue. The two women soloists are more variable. Lois Marshall is technically fine as Constanze, but the voice has a hint of rawness, while Ilse Hollweg, bright and clear, could be more characterful too. The oddity of the set lies in the text. Beecham, dissatisfied with the heroine's two big arias following each other so closely, moved the second, heroic one, *Martern aller Arten,* to Act III and he also made an unwarranted cut in *Traurigkeit.* He also moved Belmonte's *Wenn der Freude* to the beginning of Act III, where it replaces *Ich baue ganz*, a curious decision. The transfer of early stereo sound is first rate. The four mono recordings of Mozart arias sung by Simoneau – including the missing *Ich baue ganz* – make an excellent bonus.

Idomeneo (complete).
*** DG Dig. 431 674-2 (3) [id.]. Rolfe Johnson, Von Otter, McNair, Martinpelto, Robson, Hauptmann, Monteverdi Choir, E. Bar. Soloists, Gardiner.

(M) **(*) Teldec/Warner 2292 42600-2 (3) [id.]. Hollweg, Schmidt, Yakar, Palmer, Zürich Op. O, Harnoncourt.
(M) (***) EMI mono CHS7 63685-2 (2) [Ang. CDHB 63685]. Richard Lewis, Simoneau, Jurinac, Glyndebourne Fest. Ch. & O, Pritchard.

Gardiner's revelatory recording, taken from live performances at Queen Elizabeth Hall in June 1990, is the first on period instruments. With its exhilarating vigour and fine singing it will please many more than period-performance devotees. Using period instruments 'played with gusto', Gardiner says, the result in this opera is 'earthier and emotionally raw'. He also suggests that this is 'the most orchestrally conceived of all Mozart's operas', and the recording substantiates both these claims. Gardiner's aim has been to include all the material Mozart wrote for the original 1781 production, whether it was finally used or not. It is astonishing to find that, with all the variants and amendments, the music for Act III alone lasts an hour and three-quarters, and he recommends the use of the CD programming device for listeners to select the version they prefer, with supplementary numbers put at the end of each disc. The abrasiveness is modified by Gardiner's Mozartian style, well sprung and subtly moulded rather than severe, and his choice of singers puts a premium on clarity and beauty of production rather than weight. Even Hillevi Martinpelto, the young soprano chosen to sing the dramatic role of Elettra, keeps a pure line in her final fury scene, avoiding explosiveness – a passage given in alternative versions. The other principals sing beautifully too, notably Anne Sofie von Otter as Idamante and Sylvia McNair as Ilia, while Anthony Rolfe Johnson, a tenor on the light side for the role of Idomeneo in a traditional performance, is well suited here, with words finely projected. The electrifying singing of the Monteverdi Choir adds to the dramatic bite, and the sound is excellent, remarkably fine for a live performance in a difficult venue.

Using a text very close to that of the Munich première of Mozart's great *opera seria*, and with the role of Idamante given to a soprano instead of being transposed down to tenor register, Harnoncourt presents a distinctive and refreshing view, one which in principle is preferable to general modern practice. The vocal cast is good, with Hollweg a clear-toned, strong Idomeneo, and with no weak link. Felicity Palmer finds the necessary contrasts of expression as Elettra. With remastering for CD, the sound is transformed and the edginess, present in the original LP format, smoothed without loss of presence. It is surprising that, in an account which aims at authenticity, appoggiature are so rarely used. This is hardly a performance to warm to, but it is refreshing and alive.

The very first 'complete' recording of the opera, recorded in 1955 with Glyndebourne forces under John Pritchard, makes a timely reappearance on CD. Though it uses a severely cut text and the orchestral sound is rather dry, it wears its years well. The voices still sound splendid, notably Sena Jurinac as a ravishing Ilia, Richard Lewis in the title-role, and Léopold Simoneau so delicate he almost reconciles one to the casting of Idamante as a tenor (from Mozart's compromised Vienna revision). The cuts mean that the whole opera is fitted on to two (mid-price) discs instead of three.

Lucio Silla (slightly abridged).
*** Teldec/WEA Dig. 2292 44928-2 (2). Schreier, Gruberová, Bartoli, Kenny, Upshaw, Schoenberg Ch., VCM, Harnoncourt.

The sixteen-year-old Mozart wrote his fifth opera, on the subject of the Roman dictator Sulla (Silla), in double quick time. The speed of composition brought inspiration of high voltage, with most arias urgently fast and with strong symphonic ideas often developed at surprising length. There are many pre-echoes of later Mozart operas, not just of the great *opera seria*, *Idomeneo*, but of *Entführung* and even of *Don Giovanni*. The snag in a complete performance is the length, some three and a half hours, with *secco* recitatives often outstaying their welcome, as Leopold Hager's earlier recording demonstrated. What Harnoncourt has done is to record a text which fits on to two generously filled CDs, not just trimming down the recitatives but omitting no fewer than four arias, all of them valuable. Yet his sparkling direction of an outstanding, characterful team of soloists brings an exhilarating demonstration of the boy Mozart's genius, with such marvels as the extended finale to Act I left intact. The Hager version of 1975 with its complete text is due for reissue in the Philips Complete Mozart Edition, with just as star-studded a cast as this, but anyone not over-concerned about completeness will find Harnoncourt's two CDs a vivid experience. As in the earlier set, Schreier is masterly in the title-role, still fresh in tone, while Dawn Upshaw is warm and sweet as Celia, and Cecilia Bartoli is full and rich as Cecilio. The singing of Edita Gruberová as Giunia and Yvonne Kenny as Cinna is not quite so immaculate, but still confident and stylish. The Concentus Musicus of Vienna has rarely given so bright and lightly sprung a performance on record. Excellent digital sound.

Le nozze di Figaro (complete)
❀ (B) *** CfP CD-CDPD 4724; *TC-CFPD 4724* (2). Sciutti, Jurinac, Stevens, Bruscantini, Calabrese, Cuenod, Wallace, Sinclair, Glyndebourne Ch. & Festival O, Gui.
(M) (**(*)) EMI mono CMS7 69639-2 (2) [Ang. CDMB 69639]. Schwarzkopf, Seefried, Jurinac, Kunz, Majkut, London, V. State Op. Ch., VPO, Karajan.
(M) **(*) EMI CMS7 63849-2 (3) [id.]. Grist, Söderström, Berganza, Evans, Bacquier, Hollweg, Alldis Ch., New Philh. O, Klemperer.
(M) ** EMI CMS7 63646-2 (3) [Ang. CDMC 63646]. Harper, Blegen, Berganza, Fischer-Dieskau, G. Evans, Alldis Ch., ECO, Barenboim.
** Erato/Warner 2292 45501-2 (3) [id.]. Cuberli, Rodgers, Bartoli, Tomlinson, Schmidt, Berlin RIAS Ch., BPO, Barenboim.

The most effervescent performance of *Figaro* on disc, brilliantly produced in early but well-separated stereo, the 1955 Glyndebourne recording makes a bargain without equal on only two CDs from CfP. The transfer on CD brings sound warmer, more naturally vivid and with more body than on many modern recordings. There is no added edginess, as occurs on so many CD transfers involving voices (in that respect it is far superior to the disappointing Decca CD transfer of the vintage Decca Kleiber set from the same period). The realistic projection instantly makes one forget any minimal tape-hiss, and the performance, recorded in the studio immediately after a vintage Glyndebourne season, offers not only unsurpassed teamwork, witty in its timing, but a consistently stylish and characterful cast. Just as Sesto Bruscantini is the archetypal Glyndebourne Figaro, Sena Jurinac is the perfect Countess, with Graziella Sciutti a delectable Susanna and Risë Stevens a well-contrasted Cherubino, vivacious in their scenes together. Franco Calabrese as the Count is firm and virile, if occasionally stressed on top; and the three character roles have never been more vividly cast, with Ian Wallace as Bartolo, Monica Sinclair as Marcellina and the incomparable Hugues Cuenod as Basilio. The only regret is that Cuenod's brilliant performance of Basilio's aria in Act IV has had to be omitted (as it so often is on stage) to keep the two discs each within the 80-minute limit. There is no libretto, but a detailed synopsis is provided with cueing points conveniently indicated.

Recorded in 1950, Karajan's first recording of *Figaro* offers one of the most distinguished casts ever assembled; but, curiously at that period, they decided to record the opera without the *secco* recitatives. That is a most regrettable omission when all these singers are not just vocally immaculate but vividly characterful – as for example Sena

Jurinac, later the greatest of Glyndebourne Countesses, here a vivacious Cherubino. The firmness of focus in Erich Kunz's singing of Figaro goes with a delightful twinkle in the word-pointing, and Irmgard Seefried makes a bewitching Susanna. Schwarzkopf's noble portrait of the Countess – not always helped by a slight backward balance of the microphone placing for her – culminates in the most poignant account of her second aria, *Dove sono*. Erich Majkut is a delightfully bright-eyed Basilio. Karajan at this early period was fresher as a Mozartian than later, sometimes hurrying his singers but keeping a necessary lightness. The sound, though obviously limited, presents the voices very vividly. Conveniently, each of the CDs contains two Acts.

Klemperer may seem to have been the most solemn of conductors but he had a great sense of humour. Here he shows very clearly how his humour fits in with the sterling characteristics we all recognize. Though the tempi are often slow, the pointing and shading are most delicate and the result, though hardly sparkling, is full of high spirits. A clue to the Klemperer approach comes near the beginning with Figaro's aria *Se vuol ballare*, which is not merely a servant's complaint about an individual master but a revolutionary call, with horns and pizzicato strings strongly defined, to apply to the whole world: 'I'll play the tune, sir!' Geraint Evans is masterly in matching Klemperer; though his normal interpretation of the role of Figaro is more effervescent than this, he is superb here, singing and acting with great power. Reri Grist makes a charming Susanna and Teresa Berganza is a rich-toned Cherubino. Gabriel Bacquier's Count is darker-toned and more formidable than usual, while Elisabeth Söderström's Countess, though it has its moments of strain, gives ample evidence of this artist's thoughtful intensity. Though this is not a version one would regularly laugh over, it represents a unique experience. The recording has transferred very well to CD.

For so lively a Mozartian, Barenboim takes a strangely staid view of *Figaro* in both his recordings. His EMI one, now reissued at mid-price, was recorded soon after live performances at the Edinburgh Festival and with substantially the same cast. Though recitatives are sharp enough, the result lacks sparkle, despite the characterful – if at times unsteady – Figaro of Sir Geraint Evans, in a classic characterization. The others too, on paper a fine, starry team, fail to project at full intensity, often thanks to slow speeds and unlifted rhythms. Those interested in individual singers might consider the set, but there are far finer versions than this.

In Barenboim's new Berlin recording for Erato he takes a similar approach, with speeds again on the slow side and rhythms stodgy. On the question of scale this new version loses out in relation to the EMI, when a relatively large orchestra is set in a big, boomy acoustic. Superbly as the Berlin Philharmonic plays, that seriously undermines the sparkle of the piece. These shortcomings are the more regrettable when the cast is a strong one. The singer who most completely overcomes the problems, to give an enchanting performance, is Joan Rodgers as Susanna. John Tomlinson as Figaro sings strongly too, but he makes a rather dour figure. Cecilia Bartoli is a characterful Cherubino, but the voice remains disconcertingly feminine in its richness, not at all boyish. There is less need for sparkle in the roles of Count and Countess, and Andreas Schmidt and Lella Cuberli both sing well, but even they suffer from the curious focus of the sound.

(i–v; viii) *Der Schauspieldirektor.* Concert arias: (ii; vii; ix) *Misera, dove son!, K.369; Un moto di gioia, K.579; Schon lacht der holde Frühling, K.580.* (i; vii; ix) *Vado, ma dove? oh Dei!, K.583; Bella mia fiamma, addio, K.529; Nehmt meinen Dank, ihr holden Gonner!* (iv; vi; x) *Die Entführung: Ha! Wie will ich triumpheren.* (v; viii) *Le nozze di Figaro: Overture.*

*** Decca Dig. 430 207-2 [id.]. (i) Te Kanawa, (ii) Gruberová, (iii) Heilmann, (iv)

Jungwirth; (v) VPO; (vi) Vienna Haydn O; (vii) Vienna CO; (viii) Pritchard; (ix) Fischer; (x) Kertész.

This recording of the four musical numbers from *Der Schauspieldirektor* (presented 'dry' with no German dialogue) was made only six months before Sir John Pritchard died, an apt last offering from him, a great Mozartian. Having two such well-contrasted star sopranos adds point to the contest, and the performances are a delight, though the recorded sound is not as well focused as usual from this source. The *Figaro overture*, also conducted by Pritchard, is another completely new item. The rest is reissue material, with three concert arias each from Gruberová and Dame Kiri, taken from Decca's 1981 boxed set of the collected arias. Manfred Jungwirth's bitingly dark account of Osmin's aria from *Entführung* dates from ten years before that, a welcome extra. The single disc is boxed with texts and notes.

Zaïde (complete).
** Orfeo Dig. C 055832 I (2) [id.]. Blegen, Hollweg, Schöne, Moser, Holl, Salzburg Mozarteum O, Hager.

Zaïde, written between 1779 and 1780 and never quite completed, was a trial run for *Entführung*, based on a comparable story of love, duty, escape and forgiveness in the seraglio. It has nothing like the same dramatic sharpness of focus, which may perhaps account for Mozart's failure to complete the piece when within sight of the end. For whatever reason, he left it minus an overture and a finale, but it is simple enough for both to be applied from other sources, as is done here: the *Symphony No. 32* makes an apt enough overture, and a *March* (K 335/1) rounds things off quickly and neatly. Much of the music is superb; melodramas at the beginning of each Act are strikingly effective and original, with the speaking voice of the tenor in the first heard over darkly dramatic writing in D minor. Zaïde's arias in both Acts are magnificent: the radiantly lyrical *Ruhe sanft* is hauntingly memorable, and the dramatic *Tiger aria* is like Constanze's *Martern aller Arten*, but briefer and more passionate. This Orfeo performance is generally well sung and well recorded. The CDs have presence and atmosphere. However, this version does not quite match the earlier, Philips set under Bernhard Klee, either in playing or in singing. The Sultan of the earlier version, Werner Hollweg, here becomes the hero, Gomatz, free-toned and stylish, if hardly passionate. Judith Blegen makes an appealing Zaïde, though the voice could be steadier, and Robert Holl is a fine, dark-toned Osmin. (We note from their introductory booklet that Philips are planning to re-introduce the Klee set as part of their Complete Mozart Edition.)

Die Zauberflöte (complete).
*** Ph. Dig. 426 276-2; *426 276-4* (2) [id.]. Te Kanawa, Studer, Lind, Araiza, Bär, Ramey, Van Dam, Amb. Op. Ch., ASMF, Marriner.
(M) ** Decca 414 362-2; *414 362-4* (2) [id.]. Lipp, Gueden, Loose, Simoneau, Berry, Böhme, V. State Op. Ch., VPO, Boehm.

Marriner directs a pointed and elegant reading of *Zauberflöte*, bringing out the fun of the piece. It lacks weight only in the overture and finale, and the cast is the finest in any modern recording. Dame Kiri – who could have sounded grand rather than girlish – lightens her voice delightfully, and consistently sings with fine control. Olaf Bär, vividly characterful, brings the Lieder-singer's art to the role of Papageno, as Gerhard Hüsch and Dietrich Fischer-Dieskau did in earlier vintage recordings. Araiza's voice has coarsened since he recorded the role of Tamino for Karajan, but this performance is subtler and conveys more feeling. Cheryl Studer's performance as Queen of the Night is easily the finest among modern recordings; and Samuel Ramey, not quite as rich and firm as usual, yet gives a generous and wise portrait of Sarastro. José van Dam, Karajan's Sarastro, is here a superb Speaker. With spoken dialogue directed by August Everding, this is now the finest digital version, superbly recorded, with the added advantage that it comes on only two discs instead of the three used for most other recent recordings.

The principal attraction of the Decca mid-price reissue is the conducting of Karl Boehm. With surprisingly good recording quality (vintage 1955), vivid, warm and full in the bass, that might well be counted enough recommendation, in spite of the absence of dialogue, particularly when the Tamino of Léopold Simoneau and the Papageno of Walter Berry are strongly and sensitively sung. But the rest of the singing is rather variable, with Hilde Gueden a pert, characterful Pamina unhappy in the florid divisions, Wilma Lipp an impressive Queen of the Night, but Kurt Böhme a gritty and ungracious Sarastro. Although, with such remarkably atmospheric sound, this is certainly enjoyable, there are far stronger recommendations available in the mid-price range, not least Karajan's outstanding 1950 mono set (EMI CHS7 69631-2), while Klemperer's inspired version is one of his outstanding achievements on record (EMI CMS7 69971-2). Both these sets are also without dialogue.

Die Zauberflöte: highlights.
(M) *** DG Dig. 431 291-2; *431 291-4* [id.] (from recording with Mathis, Ott, Perry, Araiza, Hornik, Van Dam, BPO, cond. Karajan).
(B) **(*) DG Compact Classics *427 713-4* [id.]. From complete set with Lear, Peters, Otto, Wunderlich, Fischer-Diesdkau, Hotter, Crass, Berlin RIAS Chamber Ch., BPO, Boehm – BEETHOVEN: *Fidelio* highlights.*(*)

The Karajan set of highlights is reasonably generous (61 minutes); it includes the Overture and most of the key numbers, including the Papageno/Papagena items, and it demonstrates the overall strength of a generally first-rate cast. At mid-price this is probably a best buy for a highlights disc from this opera, alongside the Klemperer selection (EMI CDM7 63451-2; *EG 763451-4*).

The Compact Classics *Magic flute* highlights are much more successful than the Beethoven coupling. The male soloists shine especially brightly, and it is a pity that the selection does not include very much of Fischer-Dieskau's engaging Papageno. The overture is included. The sound is pleasing but somewhat bass-orientated.

Arias: *Don Giovanni; Die Entführung aus dem Serail; Idomeneo; Le nozze di Figaro; Die Zauberflöte.*
(M) (***) EMI mono CDH7 63708-2 [id.]. Elisabeth Schwarzkopf (with various orchestras & conductors, including John Pritchard).

Just how fine a Mozartian Schwarzkopf already was early in her career comes out in these 12 items, recorded between 1946 and 1952. The earliest are Konstanze's two arias from *Entführung*, and one of the curiosities is a lovely account of Pamina's *Ach ich fuhls*, recorded in English in 1948. The majority, including those from *Figaro* – Susanna's and Cherubino's arias well as the Countess's – are taken from a long-unavailable recital disc conducted by John Pritchard. Excellent transfers.

ANNIVERSARY ANTHOLOGIES

The Mozart Almanac: The Early Years (Volumes 1–2); 1775–91 (Volumes 3–20) (recordings selected by H. C. Robbins Landon).
(M) *** Decca Dig./Analogue 430 111-2 (20). Various artists.

Devised by H. C. Robbins Landon, a musicologist who wears his scholarship more lightly than almost any rival, Decca's 'Mozart Almanac' is the most imaginative of the Mozart compilations issued to celebrate bicentenary year. Landon's shrewd eye and ear are evident on every one of the twenty discs. The first two cover the period from when the boy started composing in 1761, to 1774. Then the year of his death, 1791, has two whole discs devoted to it, with *Zauberflöte* and *Clemenza* represented alongside the *Clarinet concerto* and *Requiem*; each of the years in between is covered by a single disc. In his choice of works, as well as of specific recordings, Landon repeatedly gives magic to the idea, with essays in each volume to illustrate particular themes related to the period; Mozart is vividly brought to life against his background. So Landon inserts unexpected musical gems among the popular masterpieces, for example the interludes from *Thamos, King of Egypt* on the 1779 disc (offering the *Coronation Mass*, *Symphony No. 32* and wind *Sinfonia concertante*). Complete works are the rule, though operas are represented by individual items merely – not by popular arias as a rule, but often by the long, musically revolutionary finales to Acts. A high proportion of recordings are digital, and many period performances are included – generally overlooked in the other bicentenary series. With generous measure on each disc, all twenty make excellent and illuminating bargains at mid-price.

'The Complete Mozart Edition': highlights. Excerpts from: *Horn concerto No. 4, K.495; Piano concerto No. 5 in D, K. 175; Serenade No. 12 in C min., K.388; Symphony No. 29, K. 201; Flute quartet No. 1 in D, K.285; Piano trio No. 4 in E, K.542; Allegretto in B flat for string quartet, K.App.68* (completed by Erik Smith); *String quartet No. 22 in B flat, K.589; Violin sonata No. 25 in F, K.377; Piano sonata No. 8 in A min., K.310; Exsultate Jubilate, K.165. Die kleine Spinnerin*. Excerpts from: *Requiem Mass, K.626; La clemenza di Tito; Così fan tutte; Don Giovanni; Die Entführung aus dem Serail; Le nozze di Figaro; Die Zauberflöte.*
(B) *** Ph. Dig./Analogue 426 735 2 [id.]. Various artists.

Issued as a sampler for Philips' Complete Mozart Edition and designed to tempt purchasers to explore further, this is a thoroughly worthwhile anthology in its own right. Rather modestly, Erik Smith suggests in the introduction that his selection cannot claim to represent the Edition very seriously, as twenty other items might be 'just as valid'. But he goes on to explain that 'In general the pieces have been chosen for the delight they can give out of context with their charm and melodiousness', and he notes two exceptions to this: Don Giovanni's dramatic final scene with the Commendatore, and an excerpt from the *Requiem* which includes the opening of the *Lacrymosa*, the last music Mozart wrote. The major novelty, previously unrecorded, is the *Allegretto for string quartet* in polonaise rhythm, of which Mozart completed only the first eight bars but then continued with 68 bars for the first violin alone. Smith reconstructed this himself, and very worthwhile it proves. The rest of the programme fits together uncannily well and includes artists of the calibre of the Beaux Arts Trio, Brendel, Grumiaux, Marriner and Uchida, plus many famous vocal soloists, making a fine and certainly a tempting entertainment. The recording is consistently real and refined in the best Philips manner, and the CD offers some 76 minutes of marvellous music. To make this issue even more of a bargain, the accompanying 204-page booklet offers an excellent potted biography, directly related to Mozart's output, with much about the social background against which his works were composed. Of course it also includes details of the 180 CDs which comprise the 45 volumes of the Edition, all of which will have appeared by November 1991, and it provides pictures and information about the principal performing artists. Finally, the

Index gives a complete Köchel listing of Mozart's works, together with the volume number in which each appears.

'A Capella Mozart': Excerpts from: *Horn concerto No. 4: Rondo. Piano concerto No. 21: Andante. Serenade: Eine kleine Nachtmusik: Finale. Symphony No. 40 in G min., K.550. String quartet No. 14 in G, K.387: Andante. Fantasia in F min., K.608. Piano sonata No. 11 in A, K.331: Alla turca. Ave verum corpus. Requiem. Così fan tutte; Don Giovanni; Die Zauberflöte: Overture.*
(**) Virgin Dig. VC7 91208-2; *VC7 91208-4* [id.]. The Swingle Singers.

There is some pretty stunning vocalism here, but it won't be to all tastes, even though the matching and control of vocal colour is phenomenally polished and the treble line remarkably true. The opening excerpt, with the fugue of *Die Zauberflöte Overture*, is remarkable, and all four movements of the *G minor Symphony* are given entertainingly in chrysalis, with a total playing time of about about 11 minutes! The *Horn Concerto Rondo* (which evokes memories of Flanders and Swann) has a certain wit, in spite of its anachronistic cadenza, and the *Alla turca* from the *A major Piano sonata* is articulated with engagingly crisp precision. But elsewhere (notably in the famous *Andante* of the *C major Piano concerto*) the singing becomes indulgently romantic, and the original vocal music, including the soupy *Ave verum*, and the operatic excerpts are too often unacceptably flaccid, though the famous *Terzettino* Trio from *Così fan tutte* is indestructible.

'Fifty Years of Mozart singing on record': (i) *Concert arias;* Excerpts from: (ii) *Mass in C min., K.427;* (iii) *La clemenza di Tito;* (iv) *Così fan tutte;* (v) *Don Giovanni;* (vi) *Die Entführung aus dem Serail;* (vii) *La finta giardiniera;* (viii) *Idomeneo;* (ix) *Le nozze di Figaro;* (x) *Il re pastore;* (xi) *Zaïde;* (xii) *Die Zauberflöte.*
(M) (***) EMI mono CMS7 63350-2 (4) [id.]. (i) Rethberg, Ginster, Francillo-Kaufmann; (ii) Berger; (iii) Kirkby-Lunn; (iv) V. Schwarz, Noni, Grümmer, Hahn, Kiurina, Hüsch, Souez, H. Nash; (v) Vanni-Marcoux, Scotti, Farrar, Battistini, Corsi, Leider, Roswaenge, D'Andrade, Pinza, Patti, Maurel, Renaud, Pernet, McCormack, Gadski, Kemp, Callas; (vi) Slezak, L. Weber, Tauber, Lehmann, Nemeth, Perras, Ivogün, Von Pataky, Hesch; (vii) Dux; (viii) Jurinac, Jadlowker; (ix) Stabile, Helletsgruber, Santley, Gobbi, Lemnitz, Feraldy, Schumann, Seinemeyer, Vallin, Rautawaara, Mildmay, Jokl, Ritter-Ciampi; (x) Gerhart; (xi) Seefried; (xi) Fugère; Wittrisch; Schiøtz, Gedda, Kurz, Erb, Kipnis, Galvany, Hempel, Sibiriakov, Frick, Destinn, Norena, Schöne, Kunz.

This is an astonishing treasury of singing, recorded over the first half of the twentieth century. It begins with Mariano Stabile's resonant 1928 account of Figaro's *Se vuol ballare*, snail-like by today's standards, while Sir Charles Santley in *Non piu andrai* a few tracks later is both old-sounding and slow. The stylistic balance is then corrected in Tito Gobbi's magnificently characterful 1950 recording of that same aria. Astonishment lies less in early stylistic enormities than in the wonderful and consistent purity of vocal production, with wobbles – so prevalent today – virtually non-existent. That is partly the result of the shrewd and obviously loving choice of items, which includes not only celebrated marvels like John McCormack's 1916 account of Don Ottavio's *Il mio tesoro* (breaking all records for breath control, and stylistically surprising for including an appoggiatura), but many rarities. The short-lived Meta Seinemeyer, glorious in the Countess's first aria, Germaine Feraldy, virtually unknown, a charming Cherubino, Johanna Gadski formidably incisive in Donna Anna's *Mi tradi*, Frieda Hempel incomparable in the Queen of the Night's second aria – all these and many dozens of others make for compulsive listening, with transfers generally excellent. There are far more women singers represented than men, and a high proportion of early recordings are done in languages other than the original; but no lover of fine singing should miss this feast. The arias are gathered together under each opera, with items from non-operatic sources grouped at the end of each disc. Helpfully, duplicate versions of the same aria are put together irrespective of date of recording, and highly informative notes are provided on all the singers.

'The magic of Mozart': (i) *Horn concerto No. 4, K.495;* (ii) *Piano concerto No. 21 in C, K.467;* (iii) *Serenade: Eine kleine Nachtmusik. Così fan tutte:* (i) *Overture;* (iv) *Soave sia il vento; Come scoglio. Don Giovanni:* (v) *Là ci darem la mano; Batti, batti. Le nozze di Figaro:* (vi) *Non più andrai.*
(B) *** EMI Miles of Music *TC2-MOM 137* [id.]. (i) Tuckwell, ASMF, Marriner; (ii) Annie Fischer, Philh. O, Sawallisch; (iii) Philh. O or RPO, Sir Colin Davis; (iv) Schwarzkopf, Ludwig, Berry; (v) Waechter, Sciutti; (vi) Taddei.

For once the sobriquet here is correct: there is over 92 minutes of magic on this tape, admirably designed for motorway listening. The upper range is rather restricted, but the balance is good and the voices reproduce pleasingly. All three major works are complete, and Annie Fischer's 1959 account of the *C major Piano concerto* (with cadenzas by Busoni) is distinctive. The excerpts from the Giulini sets of *Don Giovanni* and *Nozze di Figaro* are delightful, but most ravishing of all is the glorious Trio from Boehm's 1963 *Così fan tutte*, followed by Schwarzkopf's superb *Come scoglio.*

'The world of Mozart': Excerpts from: *Clarinet concerto; Piano concerto No. 21, K.467. Masonic funeral music, K.477.* Excerpts from: *A Musical joke; Serenade: Eine kleine Nachtmusik; Symphonies Nos. 25 in G min., K.183; 40 in G min., K.550; Piano sonata No. 11, K.331 (Rondo alla turca). Ave verum corpus.* Excerpts from: *Requiem Mass; Così fan tutte; Le nozze di Figaro.*
(B) **(*) Decca 430 498-2; *430 498 4* [id.]. Various artists.

There are some fine performances here, notably Ashkenazy's lovely *Andante* from the *Piano concerto No. 21*, Solti's vivacious *Nozze di Figaro Overture*, followed by Kiri te Kanawa's *Dove sono.* Kertész's very characterful *Masonic funeral music* is given complete, and another highlight is András Schiff's *Alla turca*, which most effectively alternates delicate articulation with strong rhythmic feeling. But overall the collection is inclined to feel piecemeal and thus does not quite amount to the sum of its parts. Characteristically bright Decca transfers. However, with 75 minutes of music, the tape should prove useful in the car.

Mussorgsky, Modest (1839–81)

Night on the bare mountain (orch. Rimsky-Korsakov)
(M) *** Sony SBK 46329; *40-46329* [id.]. Phd. O, Ormandy – BERLIOZ: *Symphonie fantastique* **; DUKAS: *L'apprenti sorcier.****
(M) *** Mercury 432 004-2 [id.]. LSO, Dorati – PROKOFIEV: *Romeo and Juliet suites.****
*** Denon Dig. CO 77068 [id.]. Philh. O, Krivine – RIMSKY-KORSAKOV: *Scheherazade.***(*)
(M) **(*) Decca Dig. 430 700-2; *430 700-4* [id.]. Montreal SO, Dutoit – RIMSKY-KORSAKOV: *Capriccio espagnol*; TCHAIKOVSKY: *1812* etc.**(*)

With virtuoso playing from the Philadelphia Orchestra, Ormandy's 1967 recording has plenty of thrills, with its shrieking banshees and darkly sonorous brass. As in the coupled

Sorcerer's apprentice of Dukas, the potent imagery of Walt Disney's *Fantasia* springs readily to mind.

Dorati's fine 1960 account of *Night on the bare mountain* comes as an encore for Skrowaczewski's outstanding Prokofiev, and it is interesting at the end of *Romeo and Juliet* to note the subtle shift of acoustic from the Minneapolis auditorium to Wembley Town Hall.

The banshees certainly wail at the opening of the Krivine/Philharmonia performance and, helped by spectacular Denon recording, this makes a very powerful impact: dramatic, yet with the closing pages touchingly gentle.

Dutoit's *Night on the bare mountain* is strong and biting, but the adrenalin does not flow as grippingly as in, say, Ormandy's version. The brilliant, atmospheric recording is naturally balanced, with the bloom characteristic of the Montreal sound.

Night on the bare mountain (arr. Rimsky-Korsakov); *Pictures at an exhibition* (orch. Ravel).
*** DG Dig. 429 785-2; *429 785-4* [id.]. NYPO, Sinopoli – RAVEL: *Valses nobles et sentimentales.***(*)
(B) *** DG Compact Classics 413 153-2 (2); *413 153-4* [id.]. Boston Pops O, Fiedler; Chicago SO, Giulini – TCHAIKOVSKY: *1812* etc.**(*) (CD only: BORODIN: *In the Steppes of central Asia* **).
** Virgin Dig. VC7 91174-2; *VC7 91174-4* [id.]. Royal Liverpool PO, Mackerras – BORODIN: *Prince Igor.****

Sinopoli's electrifying New York recording of Mussorgsky's *Pictures at an exhibition* not only heads the list of modern digital versions but also it again displays the New York Philharmonic as one of the world's great orchestras, performing with a epic virtuosity and panache that recall the Bernstein era of the 1960s. The playing of violins and woodwind alike is full of sophisticated touches, so well demonstrated by their colourful, brilliant articulation in *Tuileries Gardens* and *Limoges*, the wittily piquant portrayal of the *Unhatched chicks*, and the firm, resonant line of the lower strings in *Samuel Goldenberg and Schmuyle*. But it is the brass that one rememembers most, from the richly sonorous opening *Promenade*, through the ferocious bite and subtle grotesquerie of *Gnomus*, the bleating trumpet of *Schmuyle*, the stabbing sforzandos at the opening of *Catacombs*, to the malignantly forceful rhythms of *The Hut on fowl's legs*, with the playing of the trombones and tuba often assuming an unusual yet obviously calculated dominance of the texture. The finale combines power with dignified splendour, and the bells toll out from their tower to emphasize the Byzantine character of Hartmann's picture of the *Kiev Gate*. *A Night on the bare mountain* is comparably vibrant, with the Rimskian fanfares particularly vivid and the closing pages full of Russian nostalgia. The splendid digital recording, made in New York's Manhattan Center, has breadth and weight, and its fullness comes with a believable overall perspective and excellent internal definition.

It is interesting that Giulini's very successful account of the *Pictures* should use the Chicago orchestra, thus repeating Reiner's success of the early days of stereo. The modern recording, however, is noticeably more refined and detailed, with brilliant percussive effects (a superb bass drum in *The Hut on fowl's legs*). With superlative orchestral playing and strong characterization, this is highly recommendable; the tape transfer is generally of excellent quality. It is here paired with an excitingly volatile account of *Night on the bare mountain*, directed by Fiedler. Both sound well on this bargain-price Compact Classics tape, generously coupled with Tchaikovsky. The pair of digitally remastered CDs also includes an acceptable performance of Borodin's *In the Steppes of Central Asia*, well played by the Dresden State Orchestra under Kurt Sanderling, but hardly representing a very generous bonus.

After Sinopoli, Mackerras surprisingly comes over at an altogether lower voltage. Although Mackerras's opening *Promenade* is fairly brisk, the first few pictures, though well played, are almost bland and, while *Bydlo* reaches a fairly massive climax, it is not until *Limoges* that the performance springs fully to life; then *The Hut on fowl's legs* is powerfully rhythmic, with an impressive tuba solo. *The Great Gate of Kiev* is not as consistently taut as in some versions, but it is properly expansive at the close, with the recording, always full-bodied, producing an impressive breadth of sound. Perhaps the tam-tam might ideally have been placed a fraction nearer (as it is in the famous Telarc/Cleveland recording: CD 80042). *Night on the bare mountain*, although vivid enough, lacks Satanic bite, and the closing pages fail to wring the heartstrings.

Pictures at an exhibition (orch. Ravel).
(B) *** EMI CDZ7 62860-2; *LZ7 62860-4* [id.]. Philh. O, Karajan – LISZT: *Hungarian rhapsody No. 2* etc.***
*** Sony Dig. SK 45935 [id.]; *40-45935*. BPO, Giulini – STRAVINSKY: *Firebird suite*.**(*)
(M) *** Decca Dig. 430 446-2; *430 446-4* [id.]. Chicago SO, Solti – PROKOFIEV: *Symphony No. 1* *(*); TCHAIKOVSKY: *1812*.**(*)
(*) Chan. Dig. CHAN 8849; *ABTD 1466* [id.]. Chicago SO, Järvi – SCRIABIN: *Poème de l'extase*.(*)
(M) ** Decca Dig. 430 709-2; *430 709-4* [id.]. Concg. O, Chailly – STRAVINSKY: *Rite of spring*.**(*)
** Ph. Dig. 426 437-2 [id.]. LPO, Gergiev – TCHAIKOVSKY: *Francesca da Rimini*.**

Karajan's Philharmonia recording of Mussorgsky's *Pictures* was made in the Kingsway Hall in 1955–6. The quality is astonishing, yet another tribute to the skill of Walter Legge as producer. There is extraordinary clarity and projection, yet no lack of body and ambience, and it is matched by the brilliantly polished detail of the orchestral playing – the Philharmonia offering breathtaking standards of ensemble and bite. The presentation of each picture is outstandingly strong, even if some other versions, including Karajan's own analogue Berlin Philharmonic recording (DG 429 162-2), are at times pictorially more vivid. But *The Great Gate of Kiev* brings a frisson-creating climax of great breadth and splendour, achieved as much by Karajan's dignified pacing as by the spread of the sound.

Giulini's newest account of Mussorgsky's *Pictures* can also be counted among the finest recent versions. Recorded in the Jesus-Christus Kirche, Berlin, the sound is rich and spacious, the orchestral playing superb. The reading has a pervading sense of nostalgia which haunts the delicate portrayal of *The old castle* and even makes the wheedling interchange between the two Polish Jews more sympathetic than usual. In the lighter pieces the scherzando element brings a sparkling contrast, with the unhatched chicks cheeping piquantly, and there is sonorous solemnity for the *Catacombs* sequence. A powerful and weighty *Baba Yaga*, yet with the bizarre element retained in the subtle rhythmic pointing of the middle section, leads naturally to a majestic finale, with the Berlin brass full-bloodedly resplendent, and the tam-tam flashing vividly at the climax.

Solti's virtuoso account is very brilliantly recorded, but it is also available coupled with a comparably exciting account of Bartók's *Concerto for orchestra* (Decca 417 754-2). The present couplings are less recommendable.

Järvi's Chandos version has the advantage of expansive Chicago acoustics and an extrovert response from the Chicago brass, strong and characterful at the opening and magnificently grandiloquent in the *Great Gate of Kiev* when Järvi, after a volatile quickening, then broadens the final peroration. The earlier pictures produce much virtuoso playing from all departments of the orchestra but are less individually drawn than in some accounts, although (like Mata on RCA) Järvi indulges in a little gentle rubato in *Tuileries*. The most striking moment of his reading comes in *Baba Yaga*, first pungently dramatic, then dropping to a weird *sotto voce* in the middle section.

Chailly's brilliant Concertgebouw recording – one of the first discs he made with them after being appointed their music director – takes an oddly metrical view of the score. This means that the *Promenade* links sound square and plodding while the final *Great Gate of Kiev*, at a very slow and steady speed, is shattering in the wrong way as well as in the right one. But the light, brilliant numbers are done delightfully; and the Decca recording has spectacular range.

Valéry Gergiev's reading brings vivid, picaresque detail, with rasping brass in *Gnomus* and deftly articulated LPO woodwind in *Tuileries* and the *Limoges market* sequence. *The old castle* is gently evocative, and the Jewish dialogue uses the gradation of dynamic more subtly than usual. Even though the finale is splendidly bold, overall this reading is not as memorable as the finest versions.

(i) *Pictures at an exhibition* (orch. Ravel); (ii) *Pictures at an exhibition* (original piano version).
(M) ** Ph. Dig. 432 051-2; *432 051-4* [id.]. (i) VPO, Previn; (ii) Alfred Brendel.

What looks to be a fascinating juxtaposition of the orchestral version under Previn with Brendel playing the piano original in the event proves a little disappointing, although it is easy for the listener to move backwards and forwards between piano and orchestra by using the cues provided on the liner leaflet at the back of the disc. Previn's performance was recorded during live performances in Vienna, and obviously the Philips engineers had problems with the acoustics of the Musikvereinsaal: the bass is noticeably resonant and inner definition could be sharper. The performance, though not lacking spontaneity, is not distinctive, and there is a lack of the grip which makes Karajan's readings so unforgettable.

Brendel's account of the original piano version has its own imaginative touches and some fine moments: *The Ballet of the unhatched chicks* is delightfully articulated, and both *Bydlo* and *Baba Yaga* are powerful, the latter coming after a darkly evocative *Catacombs/Cum mortuis* sequence. The closing pages, however, need to sound more unbuttoned. Brendel is weighty but fails to enthral the listener. The recording is admirably faithful; but those seeking this natural pairing will do better with an earlier, analogue, Philips disc which combines splendid accounts of these two scores by the Rotterdam Philharmonic Orchestra under Edo de Waart, and Misha Dichter, respectively (420 708-2).

Pictures at an exhibition (original piano version).
❀ *** Virgin Dig. VC7 91169-2; *VC7 91169-4* [id.]. Mikhail Pletnev – TCHAIKOVSKY: *Sleeping Beauty*: excerpts.*** ❀
(M) *** DG 431 170-2; *431 170-4* [id.]. Lazar Berman – PROKOFIEV: *Romeo and Juliet.****
(*) Collins Dig. 1276-2; *1276-4* [id.]. Vladimir Ovchinikov – SHOSTAKOVICH: *Piano concerto No. 1.**
(M) (**(*)) Decca mono 425 961-2 [id.]. Julius Katchen – BALAKIREV: *Islamey*; LISZT: *Funérailles* etc.(**(*))

Pictures at an exhibition (piano version, ed. Horowitz); *Sunless: By the water.*
(M) *** RCA GD 60449; *GK 60449.* Vladimir Horowitz – TCHAIKOVSKY: *Piano concerto No. 1.*(***)

Some of the finest artists play Mussorgsky's *Pictures* as you can only imagine them in your mind's ear; others, like Horowitz, Richter and Pletnev, play them as you could never imagine them! There are remarkable effects of colour and of pedalling in Pletnev's performance – easily the most commanding to have appeared since Richter and, one is tempted to say, a re-creation rather than a performance. Pletnev does not hesitate to modify the odd letter of the score in order to come closer to its spirit. *The Ballet of the unhatched chicks* has great wit and the *Great Gate of Kiev* is extraordinarily rich in colour. An altogether outstanding issue.

Horowitz's famous 1951 recording, made at a live performance at Carnegie Hall, is as thrilling as it is perceptive. Mussorgsky's darker colours are admirably caught (and this applies also in the pianist's own arrangement of the final song from the *Sunless* cycle, which is played as a sombre encore). The rhythmic angularity, forcefully accented, projects *Bydlo* potently and the lighter scherzando evocations are dazzlingly articulated. But it is the closing pictures which are especially powerful, the pungent *Baba Yaga*, and the spectacular *Great Gate of Kiev*, where Horowitz has embroidered the final climax to add to its pianistic resplendency. The piano image is bold and clear, somewhat hard but not lacking fullness.

Like Horowitz, Lazar Berman brings an uncompromisingly fast pacing to the opening *Promenade.* One can picture him striding brusquely round the exhibition, hands behind his back. But when he stops, he is strongly involved in each picture, and his playing makes a very direct communication with its arresting power and atmosphere, notably so in *Bydlo*, *Catacombs* and *Cum mortuis*, although the *Ballet of the unhatched chicks* finds him more concerned with articulation (the playing is superb) than with humorous evocation. The *Great Gate of Kiev* makes a riveting climax. It is rather less flamboyant than with Horowitz, but effective in its sparer way, using just the notes Mussorgsky wrote. Recorded in 1977, this is undoubtedly among the most compelling versions to have appeared in recent years, and the CD transfer brings an impressively realistic piano image.

Vladimir Ovchinikov proves to be a highly cultured guide to this exhibition, and he produces as fine a reading as almost any of the pianists listed in our main volume. The sound is always beautifully rounded and dynamic shadings are most subtle and well thought out. He is not a big barn-storming virtuoso player to put alongside Richter or Horowitz but his performance is most musicianly. Nor does his account have the character or originality of Pletnev's recent (and rather outsize) reading, but its merits are far from inconsiderable and the recording is altogether first class.

Decca have reissued their 1950 account as part of a tribute to Julius Katchen, whose masterly performance has not been available for many years. It is undeniably impressive, though it does not have quite the mystery and incandescence of Horowitz or Richter. The sound is good but not outstanding for its period; older collectors with fond memories of Katchen's artistry will want it.

Pictures at an exhibition (arr. for brass by Elgar Howarth).
(M) *** Decca 425 022-2; *425 022-4* [id.]. Philip Jones Brass Ens., Howarth – SAINT-SAENS: *Carnival of the animals.***

Pictures at an exhibition (arr. Howarth); *St John's Night on the bare mountain* (arr. Alan Wiltshire).

*** Collins Dig. 1227-2; *1227-4* [id.]. The Wallace Collection, John Wallace (with KHACHATURIAN: *Spartacus: Adagio of Spartacus and Phrygia* (arr. John Miller) **).

There is no reason why Mussorgsky's famous piano work should not be transcribed for brass as effectively as for a full symphony orchestra, and Elgar Howarth's imaginatively inspired arrangement fully justifies the experiment. There is never any suggestion of limited colour; indeed, in the pioneering 1977 Philip Jones recording (originally Argo), the pictures of the marketplace at Limoges and of the unhatched chicks have great pictorial vividness, and the evocation of the dead (in *Catacombs*) has an almost cinematic element of fantasy. The *Great Gate of Kiev* is as thrilling here as in many orchestral recordings, and the splendidly rich and sonorous Kingsway Hall recording remains in the demonstration bracket in its Decca CD format. If the Saint-Saëns coupling is rather less successful in transcription, that is no fault either of players or of engineers.

The Collins version by the John Wallace Collection brings more modern, digital recording, and the slightly drier acoustics of the Blackheath Concert Hall. Combined with the highly dramatic characterization of the playing, the effect is to increase the brilliance and pungency of the more grotesque portrayals; *Gnomus* and *The Hut on fowl's legs* are both given considerable malignant force, *Bydlo* approaches menacingly, and the *Catacombs* sequence is even more powerfully sinister than with Philip Jones. The cheeping chicks, too, are more piquantly vociferous than usual, and the *Great Gate of Kiev* has striking power and impact. What makes this record a collector's item is the inclusion of Alan Wiltshire's dazzling brass arrangement of Mussorgsky's own rather crude original version of what we know as *Night on the bare mountain*. Wiltshire and Wallace create weirdly barbarous climaxes and some ear-tickling pianissimo effects with muted brass and xylophone, so that the starkness of Mussorgsky's inspiration comes over compellingly. The performance brings much instrumental bravura, but it concentrates on drama and colouristic detail at the expense somewhat of structural cohesion. The famous *Spartacus Adagio*, which is placed between the two Mussorgsky works, has a thrilling climax, but here one misses the string textures, despite the eloquence of the performance.

Khovanshchina (complete).
*** DG Dig. 429 758-2 (3) [id.]. Lipovšek, Burchuladze, Atlantov, Haugland, Borowska, Kotscherga, Popov, V. State Op. Ch. & O, Abbado.
** Sony Dig. S3K 45831 (3) [id.]. Ghiaurov, Gadjev, Kaludov, Popov, Ghiuselev, Miltcheva, Popova, Sofia Nat. Op. Ch. & O, Tchakarov.
(**) Chant du Monde LDC 2781024-6 (3) [id.]. Arkhipova, Ognivtsev, Piavko, Krictchenia, Maslennikov, Bolshoi Op. Ch. & O, Khaikin.

Abbado's live recording brings the most vivid account of this epic Russian opera yet on disc, giving cohesion to a sequence of scenes even more episodic than those in *Boris Godunov*. With the text left incomplete and in a fragmentary state at the composer's death, there is no clear answer to the work's textual problems, but Abbado's solution is more satisfying than any other: he uses the Shostakovich orchestration (with some cuts), darker and harmonically far more faithful than the old Rimsky-Korsakov version, now regarded as a travesty by Mussorgskians. Yet Abbado rejects the triumphant ending of the Shostakovich edition and follows instead the orchestration that Stravinsky did for Diaghilev in 1913 of the original subdued ending as Mussorgsky himself conceived it. When the tragic fate of the Old Believers, immolating themselves for their faith, brings the deepest and most affecting emotions of the whole opera, that close, touching in its tenderness, is far more apt. One is left sharing the pain of their stoic self-sacrifice, instead of being brought back to automatic praise of Mother Russia. Lipovšek's glorious singing as Marfa, the Old Believer with whom one most closely identifies, sets the seal on the whole performance. Aage Haugland is a rock-like Ivan Khovansky and, though Burchuladze is no longer as steady of tone as he was, he makes a noble Dosifei. Stage noises sometimes intrude and voices are sometimes set back, but this remains a magnificent achievement.

The great merit of the Sony version, one of that company's series recorded in Sofia, is that it presents the text as Shostakovich restored and arranged it, absolutely complete. Unlike Abbado, Tchakarov accepts the triumphant ending with its reference back to the Moscow River theme; but his conducting is dull, not only in comparison with Abbado's but after his own colourful account of Borodin's *Prince Igor*. There is some fine singing, notably from Alexandrina Miltcheva as Marfa, Nicolai Ghiaurov as Ivan Khovansky and the characterful Nicolai Ghiuselev as Dosifei. The recording is first rate.

The old Bolshoi version, using the Rimsky-Korsakov text, is valuable for letting us hear the commanding Marfa of Irina Arkhipova, but the close balance undermines the subtleties in her singing. The Bolshoi basses are splendid, matching those on more recent versions; but the coarseness of the recorded sound is all the more obvious on CD.

Newman, Alfred (1901–70)

Film music: *20th Century-Fox Fanfare*. Excerpts from: *Airport; Anastasia; Best of Everything; The Bravados; Captain from Castile;* (i) *Conquest. Down to the Sea in Ships; How to Marry a Millionaire (Street scene).* (i; ii) *The Robe.* (ii) *The Song of Bernadette. Wuthering Heights.*
(M) *** BMG/RCA GD 80184; *GK 80184* [0184-2-RG; *0184-4-RG*]. National PO, (i) with Band of the Grenadier Guards; (ii) Amb. S.; Charles Gerhardt.

Alfred Newman was Hollywood's own man. Unlike his émigré colleagues, Korngold, Rózsa and Waxman, he was born in Connecticut, and Hollywoodian hyperbole was an intrinsic part of his musical nature. He was good at rumbustious, rather empty marches (as in *Captain from Castile*) and tended to overscore. The very first piece here (after the famous *Twentieth Century-Fox Fanfare*, which will ensure his immortality) is genuinely memorable. *Street scene*, a Gershwinesque evocation originally written in 1931 for a film of the same name but more recently made familiar by its re-use as an introduction for *How to Marry a Millionaire*, combines strong thematic interest with a real feeling for atmosphere. For the rest, there is sentimentality (*Cathy's theme* from *Wuthering Heights*), orchestral inflation, the occasional vivid evocation (the vision sequence in *The Song of Bernadette* very effective, even if essentially tasteless), and luscious religiosity (*The Robe*). Charles Gerhardt's committed advocacy and the splendid orchestral playing ensure maximum impact throughout and, if one accepts the noise, there is something almost endearing about such ingenuous vulgarity, when the end result was exactly what the directors and producers wanted to match the spectacular cinematography of the period. As usual in this series, there are good notes but not enough movie stills.

Nielsen, Carl (1865–1931)

(i) *Clarinet concerto, Op. 57;* (ii) *Flute concerto;* (iii) *Violin concerto, Op. 33.*
*** Chan. Dig. CHAN 8894; *ABTD 1505* [id.]. (i) Thomsen; (ii) Christiansen; (iii) Sjøgren; Danish RSO, Schønwandt.

This is the first CD to accommodate all three Nielsen concertos on one disc: together they take 80 minutes. Each performance can hold its own against even the most exalted rivals: the most impressive is Niels Thomsen's powerfully intense account of the late *Clarinet concerto* which is completely gripping. He is scrupulous in observing every dynamic and expressive marking, and penetrates its character as well as any rival and better than most. Michael Schønwandt gives sensitive and imaginative support, both here and in the two companion works. Toke Lund Christiansen is hardly less successful in the *Flute concerto* (1926), although he does not have the dazzling virtuosity and keen sensibility of Patrick Gallois and the Gothenburg orchestra on BIS. Kim Sjøgren and Schønwandt give a penetrating and thoughtful account of the *Violin concerto*; although in terms of purity of tone and impeccable technical address he is not in quite the same league as Cho-Liang Lin, there is real depth here, thanks in no small measure to Schønwandt, who is immeasurably superior to Salonen on Lin's record. This is a most useful issue which will save the collector needless duplication; the recording, made in collaboration with Danish Radio, is first class.

(i) *Violin concerto, Op. 33; Symphony No. 4 (Inextinguishable), Op. 29.*
** Virgin Dig. VC7 91111-2; *VC7 91111-4* [id.]. (i) Arve Tellefsen, RPO, Y. Menuhin.

This is the second time around for both artists. Menuhin recorded the Nielsen *Violin concerto* way back in 1952 with Mogens Wöldike (this is scheduled for reissue on CD soon), and Tellefsen did it with Blomstedt over two decades later. Their collaboration promises well, for Tellefsen has a strong feeling for this underrated work and is given sympathetic support from Menuhin. However, the latter is not on strong ground in the *Fourth Symphony*, which is sadly lacking in fire and momentum. Though it is well recorded, the *Symphony* is much less recommendable and, good though the *Concerto* is, it does not displace Cho-Liang Lin (Sony MK 44548, coupled with the Sibelius *Violin concerto* and discussed on pp. 735–6 of our main volume).

Symphonies Nos. (i) *1, Op. 7;* (ii) *2 (Four Temperaments);* (iii) *3 (Espansiva);* (ii) *4 (Inextinguishable); 5, Op. 50;* (i) *6 (Sinfonia Semplice);* (iv; ii) *Clarinet concerto;* (v; ii) *Flute concerto;* (i) *Helios overture; Maskarade: Overture; Prelude, Act II; Pan and Syrinx; Rhapsodic overture.*
(M) ** Sony SM4K 45989 (4) [id.]. (i) Phd. O, Ormandy; (ii) NYPO, Bernstein; (iii) Guldbaek, Møller, Royal Danish O, Bernstein; (iv) Drucker; (v) Baker.

The complete symphonies and much else besides on four mid-price CDs seems quite a bargain, though these performances are all from the period 1962–73 when CBS was going through a rough patch so far as recorded sound was concerned. The strings still retain their unpleasant edge (try the slow movement of the *Inextinguishable* or the opening of the *Second*). Ormandy's recordings of Nos. 1 and 6, made in 1966–7, are on the first CD and are marginally improved (No. 6 was rather good, technically, in its LP incarnation); even so, they still do not do justice to the sound this great partnership made – nor, to be fair, were the performances particularly outstanding. Well played though it was, No. 1 lacked the freshness and spontaneity of the Previn account that came out at about the same time. Bernstein's accounts of Nos. 2 and 4 come on the second CD, and again the improvement is marginal, though, for all their fire and intensity, neither performance really holds up against later versions (Blomstedt and Ole Schmidt). Oddly enough, the *Espansiva*, which Bernstein recorded in Copenhagen in 1965 with the Royal Danish Orchestra, sounds best, even if its finale is rather too deliberate in pace and self-conscious in phrasing. The slow movement is also just a shade too intense; at the time, we thought it missed the innocence and sense of rapture of Tuxen's old LP, and we still do. All the same, it has a lot going for it: vitality, enthusiasm and a certain freshness. In the 1970s many of these performances were competitive, and there are still some powerful insights in Bernstein's account of the *Fifth*, which he recorded first of all. This has many admirers and rightly so, as it is both a perceptive and a deeply felt performance, even if allowances have to be made for the sound. The last disc contains the two concertos with Bernstein conducting (the *Clarinet concerto* is particularly fine), and the *Helios overture, Pan and Syrinx* and the *Rhapsodic overture* (*An imaginary journey to the Faeroes*) under Ormandy. All in all, there are good things here, even if there are better modern (but full-price) alternatives. Those wanting a boxed set of the six symphonies could well be satisfied with the integral Unicorn reading (UKCD 2000/2) by the LSO under Schmidt, performances that are ablaze with life, warmth and a sense of discovery. They obviously represent good value and are better recorded than the Sony set. Blomstedt's coupling of Nos. 1 and 6 (Decca 425 607-2; *425 607-4*) is in a class of its own and is recorded superbly.

Symphonies Nos. 2 (The Four Temperaments), Op. 16 ; 3 (Espansiva), Op. 27.
*** Decca Dig. 430 280-2; *430 280-4* [id.]. (i) Kromm, McMillan; San Francisco SO, Blomstedt.

This coupling is possibly the finest of Blomstedt's cycle: he finds just the right tempo for each movement and nowhere is this more crucial than in the finale of the *Espansiva*. The two soloists are good and the orchestra play with all the freshness and enthusiasm one could ask for. The recording, though not quite in the demonstration bracket (the Davies Symphony Hall imparts a slight chill to the upper strings), is very fine indeed.

Symphony No. 3 (Espansiva), Op. 27; Overture, Maskarade.
**(*) Audiophon Dig. CD 72025 [id.]. Danish Nat. O, Sixten Ehrling.

The Audiophon sleeve-note seems not too sure about the provenance of these performances. In discussing radio orchestras in general, mention is made of the BBC Symphony as having been founded in 1930 by Sir John Barbirolli! For all that, it seems fairly certain that we are listening to a performance by Sixten Ehrling and the Danish Radio Orchestra, deriving from a live concert at the Kennedy Center for the Performing Arts in 1984, that was much hailed in America at the time. Rightly so – and particularly for the eloquence of its slow movement and the straightforward, no-nonsense approach of the first, and for the convincing tempo of the finale. All the same, the performance is not more illuminating nor the sound as clean nor the texture as well ventilated as the Blomstedt on Decca, which also offers a first-class account of the *Second Symphony*. Here the string sound is a bit opaque and wanting in brilliance. Ehrling's concert also included a spirited account of the *Maskarade Overture*, again very well played but not so special that, with just over 40 minutes' playing time, its claims displace the Blomstedt as a primary recommendation.

Symphony No. 4 (Inextinguishable), Op. 29.
(M) ** EMI Phoenixa CDM7 63775-2; *EG 763775-4*. Hallé O, Barbirolli – SIBELIUS: *Pohjola's Daughter; Scènes historiques*.**

Symphony No. 4 (Inextinguishable), Op. 29; An Imaginary journey to the Faroe Islands (Rhapsodic overture); Pan and Syrinx, Op. 49.
(M) **(*) Chan. CHAN 6524 [id.]. SNO, Gibson – SIBELIUS: *The Dryad* etc.***

Sir Alexander Gibson has well-judged tempi and an obvious sympathy for the *Inextinguishable*, and there is no want of commitment from the Scottish players. Perhaps the strings do not have quite the weight that is required, and one misses the last ounce of fire. Yet there is much to admire, including a well-balanced (1979) analogue sound-picture, truthfully transferred to CD. Both *Pan and Syrinx* and the much later *Rhapsodic overture* are given perceptive readings that realize much of the mystery these scores evoke, and the Sibelius couplings bring a similar sensitivity to atmosphere and colour. At mid-price this is worth considering.

Sir John Barbirolli's account of the symphony was the first to be made in stereo: it dates from 1958 and was well regarded in its day. The performance has plenty of fire and warmth; but the sound is far from ideal, even though it is now considerably cleaned up. The timpani in the finale are a bit clattery and some coarseness remains in climaxes. There is some fine playing, particularly from the woodwind in the second movement, and Sir John obviously had a strong feeling for the work.

Symphony Nos. 4 (Inextinguishable), Op. 29; 5, Op. 50; Maskarade: Overture.
**(*) Virgin Dig. VC7 91210-2; *VC7 91210-2* [id.]. BBC SO, Andrew Davis.

Andrew Davis and the BBC Symphony Orchestra give fine performances of both symphonies. There is plenty of spirit and enthusiasm here and in No. 4 something of the incandescent quality missing in the Menuhin, also on Virgin. The strings have a distinctive, full-bodied sound and there is a forceful vigour about the whole orchestra which is invigorating. The *Fifth* is powerfully shaped too, and there are none of the mannerisms that spoilt Salonen's Sony versions. Davis is completely inside the idiom and has a good feeling for the architecture of this music. The brass are a bit crude at times, but on the whole these are powerful accounts and well recorded, even if they in no way supersede Blomstedt on Decca, who offers the same coupling without the overture (421 524-2; *421 524-4*).

(i) *String quartets Nos. 1 in G min., Op. 13; 2 in F min., Op. 5; 3 in E flat, Op. 14; 4 in F, Op. 44;* (ii) *String quintet in G;* (iii) *Wind quintet, Op. 43.*
(M) *(*) DG 431 156-2 (2) [id.]. (i) Carl Nielsen Qt, (ii) with Børge Mortensen; (iii) Vestjysk Chamber Ens.

In his youth Nielsen was a violinist and he composed half a dozen string quartets, disowning the first two. However, like Sibelius after his *Voces intimae Quartet*, he abandoned the medium in mid-career. Of the four listed and recorded, the early *G minor Quartet*, although composed in 1887–8, was revised for delayed publication in 1900, hence the later opus number. The fourth (and last) quartet dates from 1906, and Nielsen made no further attempt to return to the medium. All four works are worth representing in any comprehensive collection, particularly Nos. 3 and 4; but they really need to be played much better than they are here in these DG recordings from the 1970s. The playing of the eponymous Carl Nielsen Quartet is all very unpolished and their tone distinctly wanting in lustre. Nor do these players sound very much better in the early *G major Quintet* of 1888, which is much indebted to Svendsen. In the *Wind quintet* of 1922 the West Jutland ensemble are a good deal better, but all the same there are much better versions on the market. This set can only serve as a stop-gap until something better comes along.

Wind quintet, Op. 43.
*** Sony Dig. CD 45996. Ens. Wien-Berlin – TAFFANEL: *Quintet.****
(M) ** Sony SMK 46250 [id.]. Members of the Marlboro Festival – BARBER: *Summer Music* **(*); HINDEMITH: *Octet.***

The Ensemble Wien-Berlin gives one of the best accounts of the Nielsen *Wind quintet* to have appeared in years. Their tonal blend and purity of intonation are beyond praise and there are too many felicities of characterization in the variation movement to enumerate. They are meticulous in observing expressive and dynamic shadings and have a good feel for the Nielsen idiom. They could perhaps have produced a more robust and rustic character at some places (at the opening of the *Praeludium* to the *Theme and variations*, for instance) but, for the most part, this account gives great pleasure. It is also beautifully recorded, and the only reservation must be that, at 50 minutes, this disc gives short measure. The Taffanel piece is urbane and civilized but inconsequential – however, there can be no grumbles at the distinction of the playing or the recording.

The Marlboro performance of the *Wind quintet* dates from 1971 and is a good one. If it is not a first choice, this is not because of any artistic reservations but rather because of the recording balance which places the listener just a little too close to the players. There are some perceptive things here, and these players penetrate the spirit of the poignant preamble that opens the *Theme and variations*.

CHORAL MUSIC

(i) *Hymnus amoris, Op. 12;* (ii) *3 Motets, Op. 55; The sleep, Op. 18;* (iii) *Springtime in Fünen, Op. 43.*
*** Chan. Dig. CHAN 8853; *ABTD 1470* [id.]. Soloists; (i) Copenhagen Boys' Ch.; (ii–iii) Danish Nat. R. Ch.; (iii) Skt. Annai Gymnasium Children's Ch., Danish Nat. RSO; (i; iii) Segerstam; (ii) Parkman.

A well-filled disc of some 75 minutes which collects four major Nielsen works, only one of which (*Springtime in Fünen*) is otherwise available. *Hymnus amoris* is an early work from the mid-1890s, full of glorious music whose polyphony has a naturalness and freshness that it is difficult to resist, and which is generally well sung. *Søvnen* (*The Sleep*) comes from 1903–4, between *Saul and David* and *Maskarade*, and just after Nielsen had evoked an interest in Reger's music. The harsh dissonances of the middle *Nightmare* section rather shocked Danish musical opinion at the time and still generate a powerful effect. Segerstam gets very good results both here and in the enchanting *Springtime in Fünen*, and the solo singing is good. The three motets, written in the last years of the composer's life for Mogens Woldike and his Palestrina Choir, actually contain a Palestrina quotation. Generally excellent performances and fine recorded sound make this an invaluable addition to Nielsen's representation on CD.

OPERA

Saul and David (opera; complete).
❀ *** Chan. Dig. CHAN 8911/12; *DBTD 2026* [id.]. Haugland, Lindroos, Kiberg, Westi, Ch. & Danish Nat. RSO, Järvi.

Nielsen's first opera comes from the same period as the *Second Symphony*; most collectors have known it in the English-language version, made in 1972, with Boris Christoff as Saul and with Jascha Horenstein conducting. This is in every way a vast improvement: the sound is glorious, it is sung in the original language, which is as important with Nielsen as it is with Janáček, and it has the merit of an outstanding Saul in Aage Haugland. The opera centres on Saul: his is the classic tragedy concerning the downfall of a heroic figure through some flaw of character. The remainder of the cast is very strong and the powerful choral writing is well served by the Danish Radio Chorus. The opera is abundant in wonderful and noble music, the ideas are fresh and abundant and full of originality. The opera convinces here in a way that it rarely has before, and the action is borne along on an almost symphonic current that disarms criticism. A marvellous set.

Offenbach, Jacques (1819–80)

Les Contes d'Hoffmann: highlights.
** DG Dig. 429 788-2; *429 788-4* [id.] (from complete recording with Gruberová, Domingo, Eder, Schmidt, Bacquier, Morris, Diaz, cond. Ozawa).

This is a slightly more generous selection than the Decca highlights disc (also starring Domingo, and including Sutherland – with Bacquier, like Sutherland, taking triple roles with great distinction). When put alongside that disc, however, Ozawa's performance has much less magnetism. Not only is the Decca selection offered at mid-price, it is one of the finest compilations of its kind from any opera, marvellously sung and edited most skilfully (421 866-2). The complete set from which this is drawn (417 363-2) was awarded a Rosette in our main volume.

Gaîté parisienne (ballet, arr. Rosenthal): complete.
(M) **(*) Decca Dig. 430 718-2; *430 718-4* [id.]. Montreal SO, Dutoit – GOUNOD: *Faust: ballet music.***(*)

Dutoit has the advantage of sound that is bright and has good projection, though the acoustic is resonant and detail is not especially clear; but the recording undoubtedly emerges from Decca's top drawer. He opens the music racily and there are many admirable touches, yet as the ballet proceeds there is a hint of blandness in the lyrical moments, and the *Barcarolle* is somewhat disappointing; however, some may like the extra feeling of breadth Dutoit generates. The disc has the advantage of including also the *Faust* ballet music, warmly and elegantly played, but here also Dutoit's touch is a shade heavy. The feeling in both works is redolent of the concert hall rather than of the ballet theatre, and this effect is enhanced on the excellent CD. The best buy for this delightful confection is Fiedler's bargain RCA version with the Boston Pops Orchestra which has spectacular sound (BMG/RCA VD 87734; *VK 87734* [7734-2-RV; *7734-4-RV*].

Orff, Carl (1895–1982)

Carmina Burana.
(B) **(*) DG Compact Classics *413 160-4* [id.]. Janowitz, Stolze, Fischer-Dieskau, Schöneberger Boys' Ch., German Op. Ch. & O, Jochum – STRAVINSKY: *Rite of spring.***(*)
** EMI Dig. CDC7 54054-2; *EL 754054-4* [id.]. Hendricks, Black, Chance, St Alban Abbey and Cathedral Ch., LPO Ch., LPO, Welser-Möst.

The DG performance under Jochum is highly distinguished, and some might well acquire it for Fischer-Dieskau's contribution. His singing is refined but not too much so, and his first solo, *Omnia sol temperat*, and later *Dies, nox et omnia* are both very beautiful, with the kind of tonal shading that a great Lieder singer can bring. Perhaps *Estuans interius* needs a heavier voice, but Fischer-Dieskau is suitably gruff in the Abbot's song – so much so that for the moment the voice is unrecognizable. Gerhard Stolze too is very stylsh in his falsetto *Song of the roast swan*. The soprano, Gundula Janowitz, finds a quiet dignity for her contribution, and this is finely done. The chorus are best when the music blazes, and the closing scene is moulded by Jochum with a wonderful control, almost Klemperian in its restrained power. The snag is that in the quieter music the choral contribution is less immediate. On this Compact Classics cassette the recording is well transferred on chrome stock. The Stravinsky coupling is rather less successful because of a resonant acoustic, but this remains good value, even if there is no supporting translation or detailed analysis.

Welser-Möst's account of Orff's hedonistic evocation is full of energy and fire, but the music's sensuous atmosphere is made less explicit. In the *Cours d'amour* section both men and boys are bursting with sexual vigour, and the double chorus, *Veni veni venias*, has tremendous urgency. But Barbara Hendricks as the submissive Girl in the red shift lacks sensuous charm, and the overall mood of Orff's hymn to physical love is bracingly athletic rather than seductive. Of the other soloists, the baritone Jeffrey Black is a characterfully solemn Abbot and elicits a strong choral response, and many will respond to the timbre of a counter-tenor in the song of the roasting swan. The spirited orchestral playing adds to the feeling of vivacity (particularly in the dance music on the village green), helped by the bright, clear EMI recording, but the brilliant sound underlines the missing element of voluptuousnesss. First digital choice of Orff's justly popular cantata is with Ozawa's freshly spontaneous Boston version, which is superbly recorded (Philips 422 363-2; *422 363-4*).

(i) *Die Kluge;* (ii) *Der Mond.*
(M) *** EMI CMS7 63712-2 (2) [Ang. CDMB 63712]. (i) Cordes, Frick, Schwarzkopf, Wieter, Christ, Kusche; (ii) Christ, Schmitt-Walker, Graml, Kuen, Lagger, Hotter; Philh. Ch. & O, Sawallisch.
(M) **(*) BMG/Eurodisc GD 69069 (2) [69069-2-RG]. (i) Stewart, Frick, Popp, Kogel, Schmidt, Nicolai, Gruber; (ii) Van Kesteren, Friedrich, Kogel, Gruber, Kusche, Grumbach, Buchta, Kiermeyer Kinderchor; Bavarian R. Ch., Munich R. O, Kurt Eichhorn.

Sawallisch's pioneering Orff recordings of the mid-1950s were regularly used as demonstration recordings in the early days of stereo; the sound, well balanced, is still vivid and immediate on CD, with such effects as the thunderbolt in *Der Mond* impressive still. The recording producer was Walter Legge, using all his art of presentation, and the casts he assembled would be hard to match. His wife, Elisabeth Schwarzkopf, is here just as inspired in repertory unusual for her as in Mozart, characterful and dominant as the clever young woman of the title in *Die Kluge*. It is good too to hear such vintage singers as Gottlob Frick and Hans Hotter in unexpected roles. Musically, these may not be at all searching works, but both short operas provide easy, colourful entertainment, with Sawallisch drawing superb playing from the Philharmonia. No texts are provided, but the discs are very generously banded.

Eichhorn's Eurodisc version of the early 1970s provides an excellent alternative, with casts equally consistent. *Der Mond* is given in Orff's revised, 1970 version, and the composer himself is credited with having supervised the production of the recordings. Certainly their great merit is the fun and jollity they convey, beautifully timed if not always quite as crisp of ensemble as the EMI versions. The sound as transferred is shriller and brighter than the 1950s EMI, rather wearingly so, with voices not quite so cleanly focused. German texts are given but no translation.

De temporum fine comoedia.
(M) (***) DG 429 859-2 [id.]. Ludwig, Schreier, Greindl, Boysen, Cologne R. Ch., RIAS Chamber Ch., Tölz Boys' Ch., Cologne RSO, Karajan.

There must be some merit in this tiresome, meretricious stuff. Musical invention is not its strong suit; the simplicity and melodic spontaneity that one encounters in *Carmina burana* are not to be found here. The performance offers the very highest standards and the recording is extremely lively and vivid, but musically this is a very thin brew, whatever impact it may have had as theatre.

Paganini, Niccolò (1782–1840)

Violin concerto No. 1 in D, Op. 6.
*** DG Dig. 429 786-2 [id.]. Gil Shaham, NYPO, Sinopoli – SAINT-SAËNS: *Concerto No. 3.****

Gil Shaham, the young American violinist, was just eighteen when he made this début recording, and very impressive it is. His technical ease in the histrionics of Paganini's stratospheric tessitura, harmonics and all, is breath-taking, and he can phrase an Italianate lyrical melody – and there are some good ones in this *Concerto* – with disarming charm and ravishing timbre. His dancing spiccato in the finale is a joy, with its light rhythmic touch, and, however high he ascends, there is never a hint of scratchiness. That is also a tribute to the DG engineers for, though he is forwardly balanced, it is against a vividly full-bodied orchestral backing, and the microphones do not intrude. Sinopoli's finely graduated and often dramatic accompaniment could hardly be more sympathetic. Perlman's famous recording of this work is currently out of the catalogue but, even so, Shaham's charismatic version compares very favourably with it. The Saint-Saëns coupling is pretty beguiling, too.

Violin concertos Nos. 1–2; Le Streghe (Witches' dance); 4 Caprices, Op. 1.
(B) *** DG Compact Classics *413 848-4* [id.]. Accardo, LPO, Dutoit.

Accardo, like Perlman, has a formidable technique, marvellously true intonation and impeccably good taste and style; it is a blend of all these which makes these performances so satisfying and enjoyable. These recordings are taken from the complete set he made in the mid-to-late 1960s. He is beautifully accompanied by the LPO under Dutoit and the sound is very good. The recording's resonance has meant that DG's tape transfer is rather lower than usual, but the image has not lost its immediacy. Apart from the witchery of *Le Streghe*, Accardo includes also four *Caprices*, including the most famous, on which the multitude of variations are based.

Panufnik, Andrzej (born 1914)

(i) *Bassoon concerto;* (ii) *Violin concerto;* (iii) *Hommage à Chopin.*
*** Conifer Dig. CDFC 182; *MCFC 182* [id.]. (i) Thompson; (ii) Smietana; (iii) K. Jones; L. Musici, Stephenson.

Along with the attractive *Sinfonia rustica*, this disc would make an excellent introduction to the music of Andrzej Panufnik, who has made his home in England since the 1950s. The *Violin concerto* comes from 1971 and was composed in response to a commission from Menuhin; it is a strongly atmospheric piece and, although some may feel it is let down by a rather thin finale, it is well worth a place in the repertory; it is beautifully played here by Krzysztof Smietana. The *Hommage à Chopin* is an earlier piece which also owes its origin to a commission, this time from Unesco, who asked a number of composers to pay tribute to Chopin at the time of the centenary of his death in 1949. Panufnik composed five vocalises for voice and piano, transcribing them for flute and orchestra in 1966. Highly evocative and sensitive pieces that make use of folk music from Masovia, the central part of Poland where Chopin was born, they could not have more persuasive advocacy than they do from Karen Jones and the London Musici. The

Bassoon concerto (1985), a darker piece dedicated to the memory of the Polish priest, Jerzy Popieluszko, who was murdered that year, was commissioned by the American player, Robert Thompson, who plays it with great sensitivity. Perhaps the strongest movement is the elegiac *Aria*. The London Musici under Mark Stephenson play with dedication throughout and, as the recording was made in the presence of the composer, it can be assumed to be authoritative. The Conifer sound, very well balanced at the Maltings, Snape, is in the first flight.

Parry, Hubert (1848–1918)

Symphonies Nos. 3 in C (English); 4 in E min.
*** Chan. Dig. CHAN 8896; *ABTD 1507* [id.]. LPO, Matthias Bamert.

The rehabilitation of Parry is long overdue, and this disc and its companion, both sponsored by the Vaughan Williams Trust, do more than any previous issues to achieve that. Bamert proves a masterly interpreter, bringing out the warmth and thrust of the writing, akin to that of Elgar but quite distinct. No. 3 is the most immediately approachable of the symphonies, with its bold melodies, often like sea-shanties, and its forthright structure. Yet it is No. 4 which proves even more rewarding, a larger-scale and more ambitious work which, amazingly, was never performed at all between the first performance of the revised version in 1910 and the present recording. The bold opening, in its dark E minor, echoes that of Brahms's *First Piano concerto*, leading to an ambitious movement lightened by thematic transformation that can take you in an instant into infectious waltz-time. The elegiac slow movement and jolly and spiky scherzo lead to a broad, noble finale in the major key. The sound is rich and full to match the outstanding playing.

Symphony No. 5 in B min.; Elegy for Brahms; From death to life.
*** Chan. Dig. CHAN 8955; *ABTD 1549* [id.]. LPO, Bamert.

The *Fifth* and last of Parry's symphonies, completed in 1912, is in four linked movements, terser in argument than the previous two in the series and often tougher, though still with Brahmsian echoes. Amazingly, Parry seems to have been influenced in his structure by the example of Schoenberg in his *Chamber Symphony No. 1*, a work which this generous, broad-minded musician greatly admired. Yet after the minor-key rigours of the first movement, *Stress*, there is little in the idiom to link this with the avant-garde writing of the time. The other three movements are comparably subtitled *Love*, *Play*, and *Now*, with the scherzo bringing echoes of Berlioz and the optimistic finale opening with a Wagnerian horn-call. The other two works make an apt and rewarding coupling. The *Elegy for Brahms* conveys grief, but its vigour rises above passive mourning into an expression of what might almost be anger. *From death to life* consists of two connected movements – hardly Lisztian, as the title implies – but exuberantly melodic, with a theme in the second which echoes Sibelius's *Karelia*. As with the companion disc, it would be hard to imagine finer, more committed performances or richer sound.

Violin sonata in D, Op. 103; Fantasia-sonata in B, Op. 75; 12 short pieces.
*** Hyp. CDA 66157 [id.]. Erich Gruenberg, Roger Vignoles.

Much of Parry's prolific output still lies buried; this attractive collection gives a fair sample of its distinguished quality. The *Fantasie sonata*, an early work written at high speed just after Parry had left his job at Lloyd's in the City to become a full-time composer, provides a fascinating example of cyclic sonata form, earlier than most but also echoing Schumann. The three-movement *Sonata in D* is another compact, meaty piece, again written fast, the strongest work on the disc. The *Twelve short pieces*, less demanding technically, are delightful miniatures dedicated to Parry's wife and daughters, some of them later providing material for larger-scale works. Gruenberg and Vignoles prove persuasive advocates, and the recording is first rate.

Pärt, Arvo (born 1935)

(i) *Arbos* (two performances); (ii) *Pari Intervallo;* (iii) *An den Wassern zu Babel; De Profundis;* (iv; v) *Es sang vor langen Jahren;* (iii) *Summa;* (iii; v; vi) *Stabat Mater.*
*** ECM Dig. 831 959-2 [id.]. (i) Brass Ens., Stuttgart State O, Davies; (ii) Bowers-Broadbent; (iii) Hilliard Ens., Hillier; (iv) Bickley; (v) Kremer, Mendelssohn; (vi) Demenga.

Arvo Pärt studied in Tallinn with Heino Eller, who also taught Tubin, after which he served for a time with Estonian Radio. He was the first Estonian composer to embrace serialism, but he has also taken on board other techniques, ranging from a kind of neo-medievalism to aleatoric practices. In 1980 he settled in the West, where his minimalist yet atmospheric scores have gained a certain following. All the music recorded here was composed in the period 1976–85 and gives a good picture of Pärt's musical make-up with all its strengths and limitations. *Arbos*, which is heard in two different versions, 'seeks to create the image of a tree or family tree'. It does not modulate and has no development, though pitch and tempi are in proportional relationships. Like the *Cantus in memory of Benjamin Britten*, the *Stabat Mater* (1985) for soprano, counter-tenor, tenor and string trio, commissioned by the Alban Berg Foundation, is distinguished by extreme simplicity of utterance and is almost totally static. This music relies for its effect on minimal means and invites one to succumb to a kind of mystical, hypnotic repetition rather than a musical argument. The artists performing here do so with total commitment and are excellently recorded. This is music that will either infuriate through its lack of perceptible movement or enchant the listener by its strong and austere atmosphere.

Passio Domini Nostrum Jesu Christi secundum Joannem.
*** ECM Dig. 837 109-2 [id.]. Michael George, John Potter, Hilliard Ens., Western Wind Chamber Ch. (Instrumental group), Paul Hillier.

Pärt's *Passion of our Lord Jesus Christ according to St John* was composed in 1982 in a bleak narrative style that reminds one of a mixture of Stravinsky and Schütz. It repeats the same scraps of ideas over and over again; it takes 70 minutes and never seems to leave the Aeolian mode, and it ought to be intolerable; yet in its way it is a strangely impressive experience, albeit not a wholly musical one. Impeccable recording and a dedicated performance.

Penderecki, Kryszstof (born 1933)

St Luke Passion.
**(*) Argo 430 328-2; *430 328-4* [id.]. Von Osten, Roberts, Rydl, Warsaw Philharmonic Ch., Polish RSO, composer.

The *St Luke Passion* was the work which first brought Penderecki international fame and popularity. With its bold choral effects, including widely spaced choirs uttering crowd noises, this was one of the very first avant-garde works to make a breakthrough into a wider public. This first CD version is welcome, beautifully recorded by British engineers in Poland; but Penderecki's own reading cannot quite match in intensity the earlier version made under Henryk Czyz in the 1960s. The composer's relatively detached approach exposes a dangerous thinness in the argument, though it remains a powerful and moving piece.

Pergolesi, Giovanni (1710–36)

Magnificat.
(M) **(*) Decca 425 724-2; *425 724-4* [id.]. Vaughan, J. Baker, Partridge, Keyte, King's College Ch., ASMF, Willcocks – VIVALDI: *Gloria; Magnificat.***(*)

This Pergolesi *Magnificat* – doubtfully attributed, like so much that goes under this composer's name – is a comparatively pale piece to go with the Vivaldi *Magnificat* and *Gloria.* But the King's Choir gives a beautiful performance and the recording matches it in intensity of atmosphere. The CD transfer is expertly managed.

Miserere II in C min.
(M) *** Decca 430 359-2; *430 359-4* [id.]. Wolf, James, Covey-Crump, Stuart, Magdalen College, Oxford, Ch., Wren O, Bernard Rose – A. and G. GABRIELI: *Motets.***(*)

Pergolesi's *Miserere* was long listed under doubtful or spurious works, but modern opinion seems to favour its probable authenticity. In the liner-note which accompanies this CD, Dr Rose argues its similarity to the *Stabat Mater*, where there are striking parallels in melodic lines, motifs and harmonic progressions. Whatever the case, this work is both ambitious and moving. It consists of fifteen numbers: seven solo arias, two trios and six choruses. The singers are all of quality, particularly Richard Stuart, and Bernard Rose secures expressive and persuasive results from the Magdalen College Choir and the Wren Orchestra. The (originally Argo) recording, made in Magdalen College Chapel in 1979, is warm and atmospheric and sounds magnificently real and vivid in its CD format.

Pettersson, Allan (1911–80)

(i) *Viola concerto; Symphony No. 5.*
*** BIS Dig. CD 480 [id.]. (i) Nobuko Imai; Malmö SO, Moshe Atzmon.

Allan Pettersson came to wider prominence in the 1960s with his one-movement *Seventh Symphony*. This frankly Mahlerian piece came as something of a relief to Swedish audiences who had tired of an unremitting diet of serial and post-serial offerings. His *Fifth* is also a one-movement work and begins well. However, invention flags and the brooding, expectant atmosphere and powerful ostinatos arouse more promise of development than fulfilment. The *Viola concerto* comes from the last year of Pettersson's life and is pretty amorphous, but has rather greater substance than the garrulous, self-pitying symphonies he composed in the 1970s. Both pieces lack the concentration and quality of Tubin or Holmboe. The three stars are for the performers and the recording team.

7 Sonatas for 2 violins.
** Caprice CAP 21401 [id.]. Josef Grünfarb, Karl-Ove Mannberg.

Pettersson composed these seven sonatas while he was studying in Paris with René Leibowitz, the apostle of serialism. They are not in any way dodecaphonic and, if anything, are closer to Bartók than to Schoenberg. They vary in length: the *Seventh* lasts just over three minutes and the longest (No. 1) is not much more than thirteen. They are played with considerable virtuosity and a kind of heroic stoicism by Josef Grünfarb and Karl-Ove Mannberg. Most collectors will find the music pretty rebarbative stuff, though it may well be of interest to violinists and admirers of this composer. The analogue recordings were made in the 1970s and are very good.

Pfitzner, Hans (1869–1949)

(i) *Duo for violin, cello and orchestra, Op. 43;* (ii) *Symphony in C, (An die Freunde), Op. 43;* (iii) Songs: *Abbitte; Die Einsame; Der Gärtner; Hast du von den Fischerkindern das alte Märchen vernommen?; Herbstgefühl; Hussens Kerker; In Danzig; Leuchtende Tage; Michaelskirchplatz; Nachts; Säerspruch; Zum Abschied meiner Tochter.*
(***) Preiser mono 90029. (i) Max Strub, Ludwig Hoelscher, Berlin Staatsoper O; (ii) Berlin PO, composer; (iii) Gerhard Hüsch, composer.

This CD collects recordings made by Hans Pfitzner, both as a conductor and as pianist, between 1938 and 1940, when the German record industry was celebrating his seventieth birthday. The most astonishing performances for the younger generation will be Gerhard Hüsch's remarkable accounts of the songs. (He recorded these at much the same time as he sang Papageno in Beecham's legendary *Magic Flute.*) What a voice and what diction! The Preiser CD does not run to the full texts of the songs, let alone a translation, but, sung like this, you don't need them. These Lieder inhabit much the same world as those of Brahms and Strauss and have moments of great poignancy. The simplicity of Pfitzner's setting of Eichendorff's *Der Gärtner* or the opening song on the disc, *Hast du von den Fischerkindern das alte Märchen vernommen?* have an eloquence all their own. Pfitzner was by this time a better conductor than pianist (he is inclined to overpedal) and his performances of both the *Duo* and the *Symphony in C* have splendid grip. German recording of this period was much admired at the time and, to judge from the quality of the orchestral sound, rightly so.

Piston, Walter (1894–1976)

Symphony No. 2.
(M) *** DG 429 860-2 [id.]. Boston SO, Tilson Thomas – RUGGLES: *Sun-treader;* SCHUMAN: *Violin concerto.****

Walter Piston is the most underrated of the generation of American symphonists to appear in the 1930s and '40s. He has suffered rather by comparison with Copland and Roy Harris, yet, at his finest, he is inferior to neither. All three studied with Nadia Boulanger, and Piston's fastidious craftsmanship and formidable technique owe much to her. He has greater reticence and refinement than Copland and is less a prisoner of his own mannerisms than Harris. His wartime *Second Symphony* (1943) makes a good entry point if you are starting to collect his music. It is more than finely crafted: it has a generosity of melodic invention and in the slow movement possesses a nobility that makes a strong impression. Michael Tilson Thomas and the Boston Symphony are very persuasive in its advocacy and the recording from the early 1970s is very good.

(i) *Piano quintet; Passacaglia; Piano sonata; Toccata.*
**(*) Northeastern/Koch Int. Dig. NR 232-CD [id.]. Leonard Hokanson; (i) Portland Qt.

The *Piano quintet* is a fine work – indeed, it must be numbered among the finest post-Second World War piano quintets. Its claims on the repertoire are every bit as strong as either of the Bloch quintets and, though it does not have as strong a profile or personality as the Shostakovich, it is a work of great vitality and integrity. These artists give a more than respectable account of it, and Leonard Hokanson proves no less convincing and responsive in the early *Piano sonata*. The recording is not three-star, but this should not seriously inhibit a recommendation to those with an interest in this fine composer.

String quartets Nos. 1–3.
** Northeastern/Koch Dig. NR 9001-CD [id.]. Portland Qt.

Piston's five string quartets embrace the period 1933–62 and are finely crafted pieces, sinewy and Hindemithian at times (the first movement of No. 1), thoughtful and inward-looking at others (the *Lento* opening of No. 2 and the slow movement of No. 3). His music never wears its heart on its sleeve, but if its emotional gestures are restrained there is no real lack of warmth. Some of the faster movements, such as the finale of No. 1, are a bit busy. The Portland Quartet play well, though there is some less than absolutely true intonation in the slow movement of No. 3. The recordings are clear but the acoustic is a little on the small side.

Porter, Cole (1891–1964)

Kiss me Kate (musical).
*** EMI Dig. CDS7 54033-2; *EX 754033-4* (2). Barstow, Hampson, Criswell, Dvorsky, Burns, Evans, Amb. Ch., L. Sinf., John McGlinn.

It may seem extravagant for a Cole Porter musical to stretch to two discs but, as in his previous recordings for EMI, McGlinn has delved into the archives and has rescued the originally neglected material, so providing a substantial and fascinating appendix, unearthing such lovely songs as the heroine's *We shall never be younger*. There is also a nicely judged sprinkling of dialogue between numbers. Having two opera-singers, Josephine Barstow and Thomas Hampson, in the principal roles of the ever-argumentative husband-and-wife team who play Kate and Petruchio in *The Taming of the Shrew* also works excellently, both strong and characterful. There is little of the inconsistency of style which made the choice of Dame Kiri Te Kanawa so controversial in *West Side Story*. Kim Criswell is delectable as Lois Lane, brassy but not strident in *Always true to you, darling, in my fashion*. Strong characterization too from George Dvorsky, Damon Evans and Karla Burns, with the London Sinfonietta – as in the prize-winning set of *Show Boat* – playing their hearts out. The recording is full and vivid with enough atmosphere to intensify the sense of presence.

Nymph Errant (musical).
*** EMI Dig. CDC7 54079-2; EL *754079-4* [id.]. Welch, McGovern, McKenna, Montevecchi, Munsel, Santell, Alexis Smith, Waring, Stephen Hill Singers, O, Pippin & Firman.

Unlike most other EMI sets of Broadway musicals, this one is a live recording of a charity concert, given at Drury Lane in May 1989, with the numbers shared between a wide range of soloists. Only two numbers have survived to become standards, *Entertainment* and *Solomon* – the latter inimitably done by the veteran, Elizabeth Welch, who rightly receives an ovation – but there is plenty of charm and point in the rest. There is also an appendix of five more numbers to add to the regular fifteen. The sound, though less sophisticated in balance than in EMI's studio recordings, is pleasantly atmospheric, and the single disc comes with an excellent booklet and libretto.

Poulenc, Francis (1899–1963)

PIANO MUSIC

Humoresque; Improvisations Nos. 4, 5, 9–11 & 14; 2 Intermezzi; Intermezzo in A flat; Nocturnes; Presto in B flat; Suite; Thème varié; Villageoises.
*** Decca Dig. 425 862-2; *425 862-4* [id.]. Pascal Rogé.

Pascal Rogé's second Poulenc recital is every bit as captivating as his earlier disc (Decca 417 438-2 – see our main volume, p. 762), whether in the beguiling *Bal fantôme*, the third of the *Nocturnes*, inspired by Julien Green's *Le Visionnaire* in which an invalid hears the distant strains of a ball from his sick-bed, or in its dazzling, Stravinsky-like successor, evoking the myriads of moths and other winged creatures of the night. As in Rogé's first recital, there is charm and character here. The acoustic is somewhat reverberant but not excessively so. Elegant playing, responsive to all the rapidly changing shifts of tone in Poulenc's music, and strongly recommended.

Humoresque; 15 Improvisations; Intermezzi Nos. 1 in C; 2 in D flat; Mélancolie; 3 Novelettes; Presto in B flat; Suite française d'après Claude Gervaise; Thème varié; Villageoises (Petites pièces enfantines).
*** Chan. Dig. CHAN 8847; *ABTD 1464* [id.]. Eric Parkin.

Eric Parkin is consistently underrated within these shores. He is an artist of instinctive taste and a refined musical intelligence who is completely inside this idiom. Readers who have begun collecting his cycle (the first collection, on CHAN 8637; *ABTD 1235*, is discussed on p. 762 of our main volume) need not hesitate: he has plenty of spirit and character and abundant sensitivity. Perhaps Rogé has the greater pianistic finesse plus a gamin-like charm, but Parkin too has charm and, in many of the pieces where they overlap, there is often little to choose between them. The Chandos recording is slightly closer than the Decca, but the sound is very present and natural.

Mélodies: *Allons plus vite; Banalités; Le bestiare; Calligrammes; Chansons galliardes; Dans le jardin d'Anna; Epitaphe; La Grenouillère; Montparnasse; Le Pont; Priez pour paix.*
**(*) Adès 14114-2 & 14115-2 [id.]. Pierre Bernac, composer.

Pierre Bernac and Francis Poulenc were among the most celebrated partnerships in the recital rooms and broadcasting studios of the 1950s. Like his pupil Gérard Souzay, Bernac had enormous charm and great feeling for characterization and, although Poulenc was not the greatest of pianists, he was a sympathetic accompanist. Poulenc's contribution to the literature of French song is second only to that of Debussy and this recital is an invaluable guide to it. These recordings were made in Paris in 1959, when Bernac's vibrato was a little wider than in earlier life but his powers of characterization were undimmed. What a singer he was! The sound is stereo, and very alive and fresh for its period. (An earlier recital, recorded in 1950, can also be found in the Vocal Recitals section, below.)

Figure humaine; Laudes de Saint Antoine de Padoue; 4 Motets pour le temps de Noël; 4 Motets pour un temps de pénitence; 4 Petites prières de Saint François d'Assise.
*** Virgin Dig. VC7 91075-2 [id.]. The Sixteen, Harry Christophers.

A lovely record which assembles the cantata for double choir, *Figure humaine*, with some of the composer's most celebrated *a cappella* motets. These performances can more than hold their own with much of Poulenc's choral music already listed in our main volume and is to be strongly recommended both on artistic grounds and for the excellence of the sound.

Mass in G; 4 petites prières de Saint François d'Assise; Salve regina.
*** Nimbus Dig. NI 5197 [id.]. Christ Church Cathedral Ch., Oxford, Stephen Darlington – MARTIN: *Mass for double choir.* **(*)

The *Mass in G* comes from 1937, not long after Poulenc's return to Catholicism, and has been described as combining the asceticism of Victoria with the brutality of Stravinsky. It is a work of strong appeal and greater dramatic fire than the *Salve regina* of 1941 or the more intimate *Quatre petites prières de Saint François d'Assise* (1948) for men's voices. The Choir of Christ Church Cathedral, Oxford, under Stephen Darlington sing with clean tone and excellent balance. The boys generally cope well with the demanding writing above the stave, and the Nimbus recording is very good indeed.

4 Motets pour un temps de pénitence.
(M) *** Decca 430 346-2 [id.]. Christ Church Cathedral, Oxford, Ch., L. Sinf., Simon Preston – STRAVINSKY: *Canticum sacrum* etc.***

These motets are of great beauty and they are vibrantly performed here; indeed Simon Preston's account of them with the Christ Church Catherdral Choir could hardly be improved on, and the 1973 (originally Argo) recording produces rich timbre and a clean focus within an ideal ambience.

Previn, André (born 1929)

(i) *Guitar concerto;* (ii) *Piano concerto.*
*** Decca Dig. 425 107-2; *425 107-4* [id.]. (i) Fernández; (ii) Ashkenazy, RPO, composer.

With echoes of Walton and Rachmaninov, the Previn *Piano concerto* of 1985 is lively, colourful and full of good tunes. It was written for Ashkenazy who, with the composer conducting, here gives a dazzling performance, making light of the formidable technical difficulties. There are not many recent piano concertos as warm and refreshing as this. The *Guitar concerto*, written for John Williams, in its eclectic way is an attractive piece too, with electric and bass guitar as well as drums providing a jazz commentary in the finale. As with so many works in this genre, there is too much stopping and starting, but Fernández, a superb player, minimizes the problems in another colourful and brilliant performance. The sound is full and rich to match.

Prokofiev, Serge (1891–1953)

Andante for strings, Op. 50 bis; Autumn (symphonic sketch), *Op. 8; Lieutenant Kijé: suite, Op. 60; The Stone flower: suite, Op. 118; Wedding suite, Op. 126.*
*** Chan. Dig. CHAN 8806; *ABTD 1434* [id.]. SNO, Järvi.

The suite from *Lieutenant Kijé* is the most familiar score here, and it is played with great flair and spirit; indeed, it is as good as any account now available. The *Andante* is a transcription for full strings of the slow movement of the *First String quartet*, made at the suggestion of Miaskovsky, and its eloquence is more telling in this form. *Autumn*, on the other hand, is an early piece, much influenced by Rachmaninov, in particular his symphonic poem, *The Isle of the dead*, and is full of imaginative touches. Järvi takes it at a fairly brisk tempo (it would have gained by a more spacious opening), but it remains appropriately atmospheric. The *Wedding suite* is drawn from *The Stone flower* and complements the Op. 118 suite from Prokofiev's last full-length ballet. Though not the equal of his other full-length ballets, *The Stone flower* has some engaging lyrical invention, and the music recorded here is still full of appeal. The performances and recording are in the best traditions of the house.

Chout (*The Buffoon;* ballet), *Op. 21: suite; Romeo and Juliet* (ballet), *Op. 64:* excerpts.
(M) *** Decca 425 027-2; *425 027-4* [id.]. LSO, Claudio Abbado.

It is difficult to see why a well-selected suite from *Chout* should not be as popular as any of Prokofiev's other ballet scores. It is marvellously inventive music which shows Prokofiev's harmonic resourcefulness at its most engaging. Abbado's version with the LSO offers a generous part of the score, including some of the loosely written connecting material, and he reveals a sensitive ear for balance of texture. The excerpts from *Romeo and Juliet* are also well chosen: they include some of the most delightful numbers, which are often omitted from selections, such as the *Dance with mandolins*, the *Aubade* and so on. The *Dance of the girls* is very sensuous and rather slow, far slower than Prokofiev's own 78s. But Abbado brings it off, and elsewhere there is admirable delicacy and a lightness of touch that are most engaging, while the wit of the humorous narrative is readily caught. The analogue recording, made in the Kingsway Hall in 1966, was a model of its kind, with a beautifully balanced perspective; the remastering has brought an added intensity of impact without losing the ambient warmth and colour. This was one of the prophetic records which helped to establish Abbado's international reputation, a quarter of a century before he acceded to the throne at the Berlin Philharmonie on the death of Karajan.

Cinderella (ballet): *suites Nos. 1 & 3.*
*** Chan. Dig. CHAN 8939; *ABTD 1535* [id.]. SNO, Järvi.

While there are no complaints about either the performances or the recordings, which mostly emanate from 1986–7 (four numbers were added for this issue), at 55 minutes and full price this is not the most generous of selections. All the same, Neeme Järvi and the Royal Scottish National Orchestra are thoroughly persuasive. Ashkenazy's complete Cleveland set, however, is an even better buy and involves only one more CD (Decca 410 162-2).

Cinderella: suite No. 1, Op. 107; Lieutenant Kijé (suite); *The Love for 3 Oranges: March; Scherzo; The Prince and Princess. Romeo and Juliet: Madrigal; Dance of the girls with lilies.*
(BB) *** Naxos Dig. 8.550381 [id.]. Slovak State PO, (Košice), Andrew Mogrelia.

An excellent Prokofievian ballet sampler, well chosen, vividly played and excellently recorded in a sympathetic acoustic. The calibre of this excellent Slovak orchestra is well demonstrated, and its perceptive conductor, Andrew Mogrelia (who studied at the Royal College of Music, London, with Norman Del Mar), is at his finest in his gently humorous portrait of *Lieutenant Kijé*, full of fantasy and gentle irony. The admirable selection of the three 'best bits' from *The Love for Three Oranges* brings out Prokofiev's Rimskian inheritance of Russian colour, rather than emphasizing the music's abrasive edge. The charming items from *Romeo and Juliet* are not duplicated in the fuller selection below.

(i) *Flute concerto* (orch. Palmer); (ii) *Humoresque scherzo, Op. 12 bis; Overture on Hebrew themes, Op. 34 bis; Sonata for unaccompanied violins, Op. 115; Symphony No. 1 in D (Classical), Op. 25.*

**(*) Conifer Dig. CDCF 173; *MCFC 173* [id.]. (i) Jonathan Snowden; (ii) Alexander, Gatt, Mackie, Orford; L. Musici, Mark Stephenson.

The *Flute concerto* is an arrangement of the *Sonata in D major*, which Prokofiev himself transcribed for violin and piano. It is expertly scored by Christopher Palmer but is in no sense a concerto, the orchestra's role being confined to that of accompaniment, for Prokofiev's piano writing was essentially small-scale and intimate. The *Humoresque scherzo* is one of the Op. 12 piano pieces in Prokofiev's own transcription for four bassoons, and the *Sonata*, Op. 115, so often heard for solo violin, was originally intended to be heard played by violins in unison, and sounds effective in this form. The *Overture on Hebrew themes* in its full orchestral form is well played and recorded, and so is the *Classical Symphony*, though it is rather on the slow side. Jonathan Snowden gives an excellent account of the arrangement of the *D major Sonata* and the recordings are well balanced, natural and realistic.

Piano concertos Nos. 1–5.
*** Chan. Dig. CHAN 8938; *DBTD 2027* (2) [id.]. Boris Berman (in *Nos. 1, 4 & 5*); Horacio Gutiérrez (in *Nos. 2 & 3*), Concg. O, Järvi.

The merits of the single discs are discussed below. As a package, its claims are strong, both artistically and in terms of recording quality, though the excellent mid-priced packages from Michel Béroff (EMI CMS7 62542-2) and Ashkenazy (Decca 425 570-2) should not be forgotten (although the Decca transfer to CD is very brightly lit). Both offer all five *Concertos* on two CDs, and the EMI set has the bonus of the *Overture on Hebrew themes* and *Visions fugitives*.

(i) *Piano concertos Nos. 1 in D flat, Op. 10; 3 in C, Op. 26. Piano sonata No. 3 in A min., Op. 28.*
(M) **(*) Sony MYK 44876 [id.]; *40-44876*. Gary Graffman; (i) Cleveland O, George Szell.

These are performances of great virtuosity and stunning brilliance. They have wit and humour too, and the orchestral playing is superb. (Try the ethereal opening, by the strings, of the *Andante* of No. 1, which comes second on the CD, or the perky woodwind at the beginning of the central movement of No. 3.) Just occasionally these artists emphasize the motoric, mechanistic side of Prokofiev, but the lyrical geniality comes over too. The playing has considerable thrust but is never unrelenting. The early-1960s recording has the advantage of the attractive Cleveland ambience and the piano balance is more realistic than in many CBS recordings from this period; moreover its upper range is smoother than Decca's remastered Ashkenazy recordings, which now sound rather too brightly lit (see our main volume, pp. 767/8).

Piano concertos Nos. 1 in D flat, Op. 10; 4 in B flat for the left hand, Op. 53; 5 in G, Op. 56.
*** Chan. Dig. CHAN 8791; ABTD 1424 [id.]. Boris Berman, Concg. O, Järvi.

On Chandos, very fine performances of all three *Concertos* which challenge but perhaps do not displace existing versions, except in terms of recorded quality. Detail is very sharply defined and the orchestral playing is very distinguished, as one would expect from this incomparable Dutch ensemble. Boris Berman has established an enviable reputation as interpreter of this composer, and he plays with great panache and (at times) dazzling virtuosity. He holds the music on a taut rein and has the nervous energy and ebullience this music needs. The superb recording quality will sway many collectors in his favour.

Piano concertos No. 2 in G min., Op. 16; 3 in C, Op. 26.
*** Chan. Dig. CHAN 8889; *ABTD 1500* [id.]. Horacio Gutiérrez, Concg. O, Neeme Järvi.

Horacio Gutiérrez gives a vital and brilliant account of the solo part of the *Second Piano concerto* and is keenly responsive to the shifting moods and extreme dynamics of Prokofiev's writing. If you think his fortissimo playing too unrelieved in the first-movement cadenza or elsewhere, it is because the composer marks it so. Gutiérrez has far more intensity and sense of involvement than Feltsman on Sony, though he will be a little too high-voltage for some tastes in the *Third*: he is not to be preferred to Argerich or Béroff here. The Concertgebouw Orchestra under Neeme Järvi play magnificently throughout, and though the Chandos recording favours the piano, it does not do so to excess. In terms of recording quality alone, this must rank high in the lists.

Piano concerto No. 3 in C, Op. 26.
(*) Elan Dig. CD 2220 [id.]. Rodriguez, Sofia PO, Tabakov – RACHMANINOV: *Piano concerto No. 3.**(*)

Santiago Rodriguez and the Sofia orchestra directed by Emil Tabakov offer very full-blooded playing on the Elan label. Prokofiev once described his *First Concerto* as 'footballish' but, by this token, Rodriguez offers rugger. The opening clarinets are alarmingly insensitive (nothing *piano* here), but with the soloist's entry there is a dramatic change. Rodriguez plays for all he is worth – there is a dazzling virtuosity and real excitement. The Sofia orchestra also contribute with enthusiasm and, though this account does not displace Béroff, and Argerich is far more aristocratic, it is well worth hearing. The recording is a bit two-dimensional, with an up-front soloist.

Piano concerto No. 4 in B flat for the left hand, Op. 53.
(M) (***) Sony MPK 46452 [id.]. Rudolph Serkin, Phd. O, Ormandy – REGER: *Piano concerto.***

Prokofiev's *Fourth Piano concerto* is still the least often played of the five (recordings of it usually come within complete sets). It was commissioned by the one-armed pianist and philosopher, Paul Wittgenstein, but was never played by him; he rejected it on the grounds that it was too aggressively modern (a curious reason, when the argument is as clear as crystal to us today) and it remained unperformed until 1956, well after the composer's death. Serkin's recording was made only two years later and the performance is not likely to be bettered. His mastery helps to disguise some of the work's defects, though even he cannot quite conceal the fact that the *vivace* finale is far too short to balance the rest properly. The mono recording is excellent, better balanced and with more agreeable sound than its Reger coupling, which nevertheless also has considerable documentary value.

Violin concertos Nos. 1 in D, Op. 49; 2 in G min., Op. 63.
*(*) Olympia OCD 178 [id.]. Valentin Zhuk, Moscow SO, Dmitri Kitaenko.

Valentin Zhuk is an accomplished enough player and is quite well supported by the Moscow orchestra under Dmitri Kitaenko. However, these accounts are best described as decent rather than distinguished, and the recordings similarly are adequate rather than outstanding. The performances will give some pleasure but, given the excellent alternatives (Mintz/Abbado (DG 410 524-2), Perlman/Rozhdestvensky (EMI CDC7 47025-2), Sitkovetzky and Colin Davis (Virgin VC7 90734-2; *VC7 90734-4*)) as well as the mid-price Chung/Previn disc which throws in the Stravinsky *Concerto* for good measure (Decca 425 003-2; *425 003-4*), this is not terribly competitive.

Lieutenant Kijé (incidental music): *suite, Op. 60.*
(M) *** EMI Dig. CD-EMX 2168; *TC-EMX 2168.* LPO, Takuo Yuasa – RIMSKY-KORSAKOV: *Scheherazade.****

There are many fine accounts of Prokofiev's *Lieutenant Kijé* currently available, but this ranks among the best, the performance beguiling in its affectionate geniality and sense of nostalgia, yet with the *Troika* strongly rhythmic but without heaviness. The full, warm recording helps in this impression, slightly softer in focus than in the vivid coupling.

Lieutenant Kijé (suite), *Op. 90; The Love for 3 Oranges* (suite); *Symphony No. 1 in D (Classical).*
(M) **(*) Sony Dig. MDK 46502 [id.]. O Nat. de France, Lorin Maazel.

After a brilliant account of the *Classical Symphony*, very well played and brightly lit, Maazel gives exceptionally dramatic and strongly characterized accounts of Prokofiev's two colourful suites. Though he does not miss the romantic allure in the portrait of *The Prince and Princess* from *The Love for three Oranges* or the nostalgia of *Kijé*, it is the Prokofievian sharpness of the rhythms and the crisp pointing of detail that register most strongly, helped by the resonant acoustic, which adds an effective pungency of colour to Prokofiev's bolder scoring. Inner detail registers vividly at all dynamic levels; while Maazel is clearly seeking a strongly presented projection rather than refinement and gentle irony, the committed orchestral response is certainly exhilarating.

(i) *Love of three oranges (suite);* (ii) *La pas d'acier: suite, Op. 41 bis;* (i) *Scythian suite, Op. 20.*
(M) (**) EMI mono CZS7 62647-2 (2) [Ang. CDMB 62647]. (i) French Nat. R. O; (ii) Philh. O, Markevitch – STRAVINSKY: *Le baiser de la fee* etc.(***)

Sharply characterized performances from Markevitch, brilliantly played. No apologies need be made for the mono sound, which is both brilliant and atmospheric and is transferred to CD without added edge or thinness. However, it is the Stravinsky coupling which makes this reissue distinctive.

Peter and the wolf, Op. 67.
(M) **(*) EMI Dig. CD-EMX 2165; *TC-EMX 2165.* William Rushton, LPO, Sian Edwards – BRITTEN: *Young person's guide* ***; RAVEL: *Ma Mère l'Oye.***

Although narrative and orchestral commentary were recorded separately, it is remarkable how well the two fit together. But the flair and professionalism of Sian Edwards meant that William Rushton was able to add his story-telling to a vividly colourful orchestral tapestry which had a momentum already established. He is a personable narrator, adding touches of his own like a 'vast' grey wolf and 'nothing to report' from the bird; but his delivery does not have the relish for the words that makes the versions by Sir John Gielgud and Sir Ralph Richardson so memorable. However, this remains a direct, sparkling presentation, brightly and realistically recorded, which cannot fail to entertain children of all ages.

(i) *Peter and the wolf, Op. 67. March in B flat, Op. 99; Overture on Hebrew themes, Op. 34b; Symphony No. 1 (Classical), Op. 25.*
**(*) DG Dig. 429 396-2; *429 396-4* [id.]. (i) Sting, COE, Abbado.

Before making his recording, Sting (otherwise Gordon Sumner) listened to other recordings, notably to our own special favourite among modern versions, with Sir John Gielgud benignly presiding over the events of the tale, relishing every word of the dialogue and colouring his voice with a great actor's feeling for their resonance (Virgin VC7 90786-2; *VC7 90786-4*). Sting provides instead what he calls a 'proletarian version', vociferous in its excited involvement and very free in its use of the original text. Abbado obviously enjoys working with such a vigorous narrator and provides an orchestral backing which is both vividly spontaneous-sounding and very polished. Children will undoubtedly respond to this. The account of the *Classical Symphony* is comparably elegant and stylish and it is beautifully played and recorded. But the other items here, though attractive enough, are curiously chosen and not particularly generous.

Romeo and Juliet (ballet): *suites Nos. 1 & 2, Op. 64.*
(M) *** Mercury 432 004-2 [id.]. Minneapolis SO, Skrowaczewski – MUSSORGSKY: *Night on the bare mountain.****

Skrowaczewski's recording of the two ballet suites was made in 1962. The playing of the Minneapolis orchestra is on a virtuoso level: the string ensemble is superbly assured, the horn playing spectacular, and the wind solos are at one with the special character of Prokofiev's orchestral palette. The crystal-clear acoustic of the hall in Edison High School, with its backing ambience, seems ideally suited to the angular melodic lines and pungent lyricism of this powerful score, to underline the sense of tragedy without losing the music's romantic sweep. There are many marvellous moments here, and the fidelity and spectacle of the Mercury engineering reach a zenith in the powerful closing sequence of *Romeo at Juliet's tomb.*

Romeo and Juliet (ballet): *suites Nos. 1, 2 & 3.*
*** Chan. Dig. CHAN 8940; *ABTD 1536* [id.]. SNO, Järvi.

These derive from various couplings which appeared between 1985 and 1988. At 78 minutes this is a generous selection of the ballet and eminently competitive. Not necessarily a first choice, but as good as many and better than some. It is unlikely to disappoint.

Romeo and Juliet (ballet), *Op. 64:* extended excerpts.
*** Decca Dig. 430 279-2; *430 279-4* [id.]. Montreal SO, Dutoit.
(BB) **(*) Naxos Dig. 8.550380 [id.]. Slovak State PO (Košice), Andrew Mogrelia.

As a recording, the Dutoit selection is in a class of its own. This is characteristic Decca Montreal sound, very much in the demonstration bracket, vivid in colour, translucent in its delicacy in presenting the pianissimo strings, and with plenty of power and spectacle at climaxes. The playing is polished, sensitive and very refined, yet warm; Dutoit's reading is full of perceptive and affectionate detail. This is greatly enjoyable – but what is missing is the tearing agony of the tragedy; the passionate ardour of the lovers becomes warmly expansive romanticism. If one turns to Scrowaczewski in Minneapolis, one finds that here the bite of the tragedy and the deep feelings of its participants come over the more pungently, and his recording is pretty impressive by any standard. Among modern digital selections, Yoel Levi in Cleveland (Telarc CD 80089) and Salonen in Berlin (Sony MK 42662) also offer magnificent orchestral playing and greater involvement with the passion of the narrative. But the Decca sound is the finest yet given to Prokofiev's marvellous score: the Montreal acoustic seems tailor-made for this music, and Dutoit offers 75 minutes (24 out of the total of 52 numbers), ideally arranged in narrative order.

The Naxos selection draws on the three suites and offers less music (55 minutes) but is very economically priced and vividly recorded. The Slovak orchestral playing has plenty of character and there is no lack of emotional bite, even if the strings have not the weight of their colleagues in Montreal, Cleveland or Berlin. Prokofiev's colours are given a strikingly individual tang by these excellent East European musicians, and this is both rewarding and excellent value for money.

Romeo and Juliet: suites Nos. 1 and 2: excerpts.
(B) *** DG Compact Classics *413 430-4* [id.]. San Francisco SO, Ozawa – TCHAIKOVSKY: *Sleeping Beauty; Swan Lake.**(*)*

This is one of Ozawa's finest recordings. He draws warmly committed playing from the San Francisco orchestra, helped by vividly rich recording, and this shorter selection from Prokofiev's ballet is well chosen. In his coupled excerpts from *Swan Lake* the music-making is at a lower voltage, but Rostropovich's companion suite from the *Sleeping Beauty* is marvellous. At bargain price, with excellent transfers, this is good value.

Romeo and Juliet: suite.
(M) *** DG 431 170-2; *431 170-4* [id.]. Lazar Berman – MUSSORGSKY: *Pictures.****

Prokofiev made these piano transcriptions of the *Romeo and Juliet* music and played them in public in 1937 before the ballet itself was staged at the Bolshoi. Berman characterizes each piece to excellent effect and is well served by the engineers, who produce bold and well-focused tone. The music's inspiration comes over remarkably well in pianistic colouring.

(i) *Sinfonia concertante for cello and orchestra, Op 125; Symphony No. 7, Op. 131.*
** Ph. Dig. 426 306-2 [id.]. (i) Heinrich Schiff, LAPO, Previn.

No grumbles about Heinrich Schiff's playing in the *Sinfonia concertante* (or *Symphony-concerto* as it is sometimes called), which Prokofiev composed for (and in consultation with) Rostropovich. The composer had originally planned to call it '*Cello concerto No. 2*', but it is so closely related to the thematic material of his pre-war *Cello concerto* as to be a re-working. Schiff's is an impassioned, red-blooded and eminently well-recorded account which will give pleasure. Previn gets better results from the orchestra here than he does in the *Seventh Symphony*, written at much the same time, which is curiously lacking in zest and vitality. The vivid recording does not make up for this and Neeme Järvi on Chandos (CHAN 8442, coupled with the *Sinfonietta*) or Malko on Classics for Pleasure (CD-CFP 4352, coupled with No. 1 and the *Love of three oranges* suite) are really much better.

Symphonies Nos. 1–7.
*** Chan. Dig. CHAN 8931/4 [id.]. SNO, Järvi.

These recordings all date from the mid-1980s and are of the highest quality. They have been shorn of their couplings in this box, the only important loss being the delightful *Sinfonietta*. Both versions of the *Fourth Symphony* are included: the 1947 revision appears with the *Classical* on the first disc, while the 1930 original is coupled with the *Third*. Nos. 2 and 6 are on the third disc, and 5 and 7 on the last, so that no side-breaks are involved. As performances, these are the equal of the best. In No. 5 Dutoit (Decca 421 813-2; *421 813-4*) and Previn (Philips 420 172-2) are finer as recordings, and of course the Karajan on DG at mid-price (423 216-2; *423 216-4*) is a classic. But in the Prokofiev centenary year you can't go far wrong with this Chandos set, and these recordings are all available separately – see our main volume.

Symphony No. 1 in D (Classical), Op. 25.
(M) *(*) Decca Dig. 430 446-2; *430 446-4* [id.]. Chicago SO, Solti – MUSSORGSKY: *Pictures* ***; TCHAIKOVSKY: *1812.***(*)

Symphony No. 1 in D (Classical); Romeo and Juliet: excerpts.
(M) *(*) Decca Dig. 430 731-2; *430 731-4* [id.]. Chicago SO, Solti.

The outer movements of Solti's performance of the *Classical Symphony* could do with more spontaneity and sparkle; the slow movement, however, has an occasional moment of charm. As far as the sound is concerned, there is spectacular presence and impact, a wide dynamic range and maximum detail. Alas, there is little distance to lend enchantment, and many collectors will find everything fiercely overlit. There are many other accounts of this work that are preferable. Alongside the new couplings, Decca have also restored the original pairing with *Romeo and Juliet*, also at mid-price. Here Solti compiles a suite of his own from the ballet. He is wholly unmannered and secures a brilliant response from the Chicago orchestra, but the sound is again very much up-front.

Symphony No. 5 in B flat, Op. 100; The Meeting of the Volga and the Don.
** Ph. Dig. 432 083-2; *432 083-4* [id.]. Phd. O, Muti.

Riccardo Muti's plush account of the *Fifth Symphony* is rather lower-voltage than one might expect – and no harm in that! If we are to believe the very good Philips recording, the strings of this wonderful orchestra have lost just a little of the sheen they had in the days of Ormandy. Muti gives a very straightforward account of the work, free from interpretative idiosyncrasy. The disc brings a rarity of his last years, *The Meeting of the Volga and the Don*, a platitudinous orchestral piece that occupies very nearly the same place in his output as *The Song of the forests* does in that of Shostakovich. Among modern recordings of the symphony, Dutoit (Decca 421 813-2; *421 813-4*, offering the finest sound), Karajan at mid-price (DG 423 216-2; *423 216-4*) and Previn (Philips 420 172-2), all coupled with the *Classical Symphony*, remain the ones to have.

CHAMBER MUSIC

Cello sonata in C, Op. 119.
*** Decca Dig. 421 774-2; *421 774-4* [id.]. Harrell, Ashkenazy – SHOSTAKOVICH: *Sonata* etc.***

Prokofiev's *Sonata* is the product of his last years and, like the *Sinfonia concertante*, was inspired by the playing of the young Rostropovich. This excellent new account displaces earlier recommendations: readers will find Harrell and Ashkenazy wholly satisfying on all counts.

String quartets Nos. 1 in B min., Op. 50; 2 in F, Op. 92.
*** Olympia Dig. OCD 340 [id.]. American Qt.
** Chan. Dig. CHAN 8929; *ABTD 1531* [id.]. Chilingirian Qt.

Although the wartime *Second Quartet* is played from time to time, the *First* is something of a rarity. It comes from 1930 and Prokofiev subsequently arranged its slow movement as an *Andante for string orchestra.* The American Quartet play it far more persuasively than any earlier version and reveal it to be a work of some appeal as well as substance. The *Second* incorporates folk ideas from Kabarda in the Caucasus, where Taneyev had also studied earlier in the century, but to highly characteristic ends. Although the performance does not have quite the bite and zest of the unforgettable pioneering disc by the Hollywood Quartet, it does not fall far short of it. Apart from one trifling blemish (the image recedes momentarily at one point), the recording is absolutely first class and can be recommended confidently. A rewarding issue.

The Chilingirians in an excellent Chandos recording give musicianly and carefully prepared accounts of both pieces that are perfectly recommendable. They take considerably less time (6½ minutes less to be exact), but paradoxically it is the American Quartet that seems more taut and concentrated – and ultimately more convincing. They have a stronger sense of line and at mid-price enjoy a price advantage too.

Piano sonata No. 5 in C, Op. 38/135; 4 Pieces, Op. 32; Love of three oranges: Scherzo and March; Romeo and Juliet: 10 Pieces, Op. 75.
*** Chan. Dig. CHAN 8851; *ABTD 1468* [id.]. Boris Berman.

State-of-the-art recording from Chandos: this is as good a piano sound as one is likely to find on any disc. Made at The Maltings, Snape, it has outstanding presence, naturalness and realism. Boris Berman is Israeli born and now heads the piano department at Yale. As those who have followed his concert and BBC performances over the last few years will know, he is a pianist of impeccable technique, concentration and intensity, and his temperament is ideally suited to this repertoire. He plays the post-war revision of the *Fifth Sonata*, and its crisp, brittle inner movement is heard to splendid advantage. The other works are presented with equal perception.

Piano sonata No. 7, Op. 83; Sarcasms, Op. 17; Tales of an old grandmother, Op. 31; Visions fugitives, Op. 22.
*** Chan. CHAN 8881; *ABTD 1494* [id.]. Boris Berman.

Boris Berman's account of the *Visions fugitives* is the best since Michel Béroff's of the 1970s. Berman is completely inside the astringent idiom and subtle character of these pieces, and his playing in the *Sarcasms* could scarcely be bettered. He gives altogether outstanding performances of all four works, and the superbly vivid recording greatly enhances the sheer musical satisfaction this disc gives.

Piano sonatas Nos. 7 in B flat, Op. 83; 8 in B flat, Op. 84; 9 in C, Op. 103.
*** ASV Dig. CDDCA 755; *ZCDCA 755* [id.]. John Lill.

This disc, coupling the last three *Sonatas*, offers exceptionally good value and makes a very acceptable alternative to Boris Berman on Chandos. Differences between the two artists are relatively slight and both can be recommended with reasonable confidence. In the slow movement of No. 7, Berman perhaps has the greater intensity and concentration, and the excellent ASV recording, made in Henry Wood Hall, yields to the outstandingly present sound Chandos achieved at The Maltings, Snape. Be that as it may, all three *Sonatas* are performances of high quality and John Lill is never less than a thoughtful and intelligent guide in this repertoire.

(i) *Alexander Nevsky* (cantata), *Op. 78;* (ii) *Romeo and Juliet, Op. 64:* excerpts.
(M) ** Sony/CBS CD 45557. (i) Lilli Chookasian, Westminster Ch., NYPO, Schippers; (ii) NYPO, Mitropoulos.

Schippers' mid-priced reissue dates from 1961, but the remastering is vividly managed and there is some brilliant brass playing from the NYPO. With slow tempi in the first and third movements, Schippers does not always avoid portentousness, and the singing of Lilli Chookasian in the lament for the dead does not have the weight of emotion of Anna Reynolds' account for Previn whose EMI CD makes the favoured mid-price choice (CDM7 63114-2). Previn offers the ideal coupling of Rachmaninov's *The Bells*. The CBS disc brings a generous selection from Mitropoulos's vibrant and distinguished set of excerpts from *Romeo and Juliet*, recorded in 1957 and still sounding very impressive.

OPERA

The Fiery angel (complete).
*** DG Dig. 431 669-2 (2) [id.]. Secunde, Lorenz, Zednik, Moll, Gothenburg SO, Järvi.

Like his even earlier one-Act opera, *Maddalena*, *The Fiery angel* centres on a neurotically obsessed woman, the tragic Renata, whose hysterical visions finally get her condemned as a witch. Though the story is largely distasteful, the score is masterly, containing passages as rich and warm as anything Prokofiev ever wrote before his return to Soviet Russia, as, for example, some of the duetting in Act III between Renata and her lover, the knight Ruprecht. What reinforces the impact of the work is its compactness, telling a complicated story in five crisply tailored Acts, with the first two Acts on the first CD, the remaining three on the second. Prokofiev's vivid orchestration adds colour and atmosphere, as when in Act IV Mephistopheles is conjured up, along with Faust, and proceeds to eat an offending serving lad – cue for horrific whoopings on the horns. After that the final scene with the Inquisitor (Kurt Moll ever sinister) and chattering nuns does not quite rise to the expected climax. This fine recording easily outshines the only previous version, which was recorded in 1957 with a cast singing in French. Nadine Secunde for Järvi sings passionately as Renata, well supported by Siegfried Lorenz as Ruprecht. With such warm advocacy one can fully appreciate the work's mastery, even if the reasons for its failure to get into the repertory remain very clear.

Maddalena (opera) complete.
**(*) Olympia Dig. OCD 215 [id.]. Ivanova, Martynov, Yakovenko, Koptanova, Rumyantsev, male group of State Chamber Ch., MoC SO, Rozhdestvensky.

Maddalena is an opera which Prokofiev wrote in 1911, two years after graduating, but he then failed to finish the scoring. It was left to the conductor, Edward Downes, to complete the orchestration over 60 years later, revealing a fascinating example of Russian *Grand Guignol.* Though Prokofiev orchestrated only the first and shortest of the four scenes, Downes's contribution has a true Prokofiev ring, with distinctive colouring. His edition is here adopted by these Russian performers for the first recording. Any disappointment with the work lies more in the relative lack of melodic distinction in the vocal writing which, for the most part, flows in an easy cantilena. Nevertheless, this 50-minute piece very ably tells the horrific story of the predatory Maddalena and her savage way with men. Rozhdestvensky, with his fine orchestra of young players, directs a persuasive performance, even if some of the singing is indifferent. Ivavova is a bright, precise soprano, with Martynov singing splendidly in the tenor role of her wronged husband, Genaro. By contrast, Yakovenko in the baritone role of Maddalena's lover is disappointingly wobbly. Full, forward sound, not always refined. The disc comes with libretto, translation and notes.

Puccini, Giacomo (1858–1924)

La Bohème (complete).
(M) (**) EMI mono CHS7 63335-2 (2) [Ang. CDHB 63335]. Albanese, Gigli, Poli, Baracchi, Baronti, La Scala, Milan, Ch. & O, Berrettoni.
(M) (**) RCA GD 60288; *GK 60288* (2) [60288-2-RG; *60288-4-RG*]. Albanese, Peerce, Valentino, McKnight, Moscona, Cehanovsky, NBC Ch., NBC SO, Toscanini.

(B) ** Naxos Dig. 8.66000-3/4 [id.]. Orgonasova, Welch, Gonzales, Previati, Senator, Slovak Philharmonic Ch., Slovak RSO (Bratislava), Will Humburg.
EMI Dig. CDS7 54124-2; *EX 754124-4* (2). Sabbatini, Antoniozzi, Zecchillo, Dessi, Gavanelli, Colombara, Piccolo Coro dell'Antoniano, Bologna Teatro Comunale Ch. & O, Gianluigi Gelmetti.

The pre-war EMI set conducted by Berrettoni is dominated – as was planned at the time of recording – by the great tenor, Beniamino Gigli, a superstar of his day. The way he spices the role of Rodolfo with little Gigli chuckles is consistently charming. From first to last his facial expression comes over vividly in his strongly characterized singing, and the pity is that he is not well served by the conducting (unimaginative) or the recording, which is markedly less vivid than in the parallel recording of *Tosca* with Gigli as Cavaradossi. Licia Albanese, later to sing the same role for Toscanini in his 1946 concert performance and recording, is tenderly affecting but, thanks to the recording, the voice is recessed. Afro Poli sings firmly, but proves a colourless Marcello, and Tatiana Menotti is an edgy, fluttery Musetta.

Toscanini's 1946 set is taken from the first of his concert performances of opera in New York, recorded in 1946. The sound is even drier than most from this source, but the voices are vivid in their forward placing, and fortunately the singers had been chosen for their clean focus. Albanese, though held in an expressive straitjacket by the conductor, sounds fuller and sweeter as Mimi than in her earlier recording with Gigli; indeed she is delightfully fresh, even though no pianissimos are possible in the NBC acoustic. Jan Peerce as Rodolfo and Francesco Valentino as Marcello are reliable rather than imaginative – not surprising with the conductor such a disciplinarian – and Anne McKnight makes a bright, clear Musetta. Toscanini is heavy-handed and often rigid in his direction, but his love of this score, which he knew from its earliest performances, shines out all through, not least in his loud and endearing vocal obbligatos during the big tunes.

With good digital recording and fresh, clear sopranos taking the roles of Mimi and Musetta, the Naxos set makes a viable bargain issue, despite prosaic conducting. Luba Orgonasova and Carmen Gonzales both sing with fine control of the soaring vocal lines, but Jonathan Welch as Rodolfo is coarse, his tenor throaty and at times unsteady. Fabio Previati is a firm if unimaginative Marcello.

Recorded live in Bologna in 1990, the most recent EMI set balances the voices behind the orchestra, which may be just as well when the singing is so indifferent. When Giuseppe Sabbatini sings above a cooing *mezza voce*, his tenor becomes strangulated, while Daniela Dessi makes a colourless Mimi, fluttery and effortful. Gelmetti's conducting brings rough and ready ensemble in the larking of the Bohemians, with the score alternately overdriven and languorously soupy. Add to that a vinegary Musetta and a Marcello who blurts like a foghorn, and one wonders how this set ever came to appear as a premium-price issue. The possible only excuse is that the revised Ricordi score is used, for the first time on record. First choice for *La Bohème* still rests with Beecham's uniquely magical performance with Victoria de los Angeles and Jussi Bjoerling challenged to their utmost in loving, expansive singing. However, the voices are treated far better by the CD remastering of the mono recording than the orchestra, which is rather thinner-sounding than it was on LP (EMI CDS7 47235-8). Those who understandably want a modern stereo recording can turn to Karajan on Decca whose reading is characteristically spacious but with an electric intensity which holds the whole score together as at a live performance. Pavarotti is an inspired Rodolfo, while Freni is a seductive Mimi and the Decca recording is superb (421 049-2; *421 049-4*). Tebaldi should not be forgotten; Joan Sutherland regards her Mimi as the finest of all, and she is well partnered by Carlo Bergonzi as Rodolfo (Decca 425 534-2). This makes a superb mid-price recommendation.

La Bohème: highlights.
(B) Pickwick (DG) IMPX 9024. Scotto, Poggi, Gobbi, Maneguzzer, Maggio Musicale Fiorentino Ch. & O, Votto.

This highlights disc comes from a singularly unsuccessful DG *Bohème*, recorded at the beginning of the 1960s; it might be considered a collector's item that Gianni Poggi's *Che gelida manina* easily wins the prize for the crudest performance on record! Even Tito Gobbi is less than a success as Marcello, and Scotto's voice is caught not at all well.

La Fanciulla del West.
(**) Nuova Era 2324/5 (2) [id.]. Olivero, Limarilli, Puglisi, Carlin, Susca, Trieste Teatro Verdi Ch. & O, Arturo Basile.

Recorded at a live performance in 1965, this historic recording offers the legendary Magda Olivero in a role for which she was ideally suited. In the command of her singing, she consistently gives life to the fire-eating, gun-toting Minnie who yet has the softest, most vulnerable heart. Sadly, the sound is depressingly thin and dry, and stage noises often submerge the music in the many crowd scenes. The tenor, Gastone Limarilli, matches Mario del Monaco in coarseness, without offering so thrilling a voice, but Lino Puglisi makes a firm, dark Jack Rance, and the conducting of Basile builds up to a moving climax in Act III, though Limarilli's milking of applause at the end of *Ch'ella mi creda* is hilarious. Capuana's Decca set, made as early as 1958 but sounding astonishingly realistic on CD, remains a clear primary recommendation for this opera, with Tebaldi giving one of her most warm-hearted and understanding performances on record (421 595-2). This was given a Rosette in our main volume.

Madama Butterfly (complete).
(M) **(*) EMI CMS7 63634-2 (2) [Ang. CDMB 63634]; *TC-CFPD 4446*. De los Angeles, Bjoerling, Pirazzini, Sereni, Rome Op. Ch. & O, Santini.

In the late 1950s and early 1960s, Victoria de los Angeles was memorable in the role of Butterfly, and her 1960 recording displays her art at its most endearing, her range of golden tone-colour lovingly exploited, with the voice well recorded for the period, though rather close. Opposite her, Jussi Bjoerling was making one of his last recordings, and, though he shows few special insights, he produces a flow of rich tone to compare with that of the heroine. Mario Sereni is a full-voiced Sharpless, but Miriam Pirazzini is a disappointingly wobbly Suzuki; Santini is a reliable, generally rather square and unimaginative conductor who rarely gets in the way. With recording quality freshened, this fine set is most welcome either on a pair of mid-priced CDs or, still sounding bright and clear, in its CfP cassette format (offered in a chunky box with a synopsis rather than a libretto). First choice lies with Ludwig and Pavarotti with Karajan inspiring singers and orchestra to a radiant performance which brings out all the beauty and intensity of Puccini's score (Decca 417 577-2; *417 577-4*), although Sinopoli's marvellous set, idiosyncratic though it is, should also be considered – see below for our further comments under the Compact Classics tape selection of highlights.

Madama Butterfly: highlights.
(M) ** Decca 421 873-2; *421 873-4* [id.] (from complete recording with Tebaldi, Bergonzi, Cossotto, Santa Cecilia Academy Ch. & O, Rome, Serafin).

The Tebaldi/Bergonzi Decca set dates from 1958 but the sound is rich in ambience, and the dated upper string sound is seldom distracting for the voices are vividly projected. The magnetism of the singing is very compelling, but the 51 minutes' selection is ungenerous and still omits the *Humming chorus.* Readers would be much better advised to invest in the complete set which is one of Tebaldi's major recording achievements and is now available at mid-price (Decca 425 531-2).

(i) *Madama Butterfly:* highlights; (ii) *Manon Lescaut:* highlights.
(B) *** DG Dig. Compact Classics *431 182-4* [id.]. (i; ii) Freni, (i) Carreras, Berganza, Pons, Amb. Op. Ch.; (ii) Domingo, Bruson, ROHCG Ch., Philh. O, Sinopoli.

This outstanding set of combined highlights from two of Sinopoli's finest opera sets marks a new level of sophistication in tape transfer for DG's market-leading bargain Compact Cassettes. Both these recordings are digital, and the sound here is remarkably clean, fresh and vivid. Mirella Freni sings ravishingly, whether as Mimi or Manon, and the supporting casts are admirable, with Domingo both stirring and providing subtle detail in his portrait of Manon's lover, Des Grieux. The finesse of the transfer ensures that the *Humming chorus*, from *Butterfly*, sung at a haunting pianissimo, registers magically.

Manon Lescaut (complete).
(M) **(*) Decca 430 253-2 (2) [id.]. Tebaldi, Del Monaco, Corena, St Cecilia Ac., Rome, Ch. & O, Molinari-Pradelli.
(M) (***) RCA mono GD 60573 (2) [60573-2-RG]. Albanese, Bjorling, Merrill, Rome Op. Ch. & O, Perlea.

At mid-price, the Decca set with Tebaldi, dating from the mid-1950s, is still well worth considering, even if the Sinopoli DG digital version with Freni and Domingo remains a clear first choice (DG 413 893-2). The Decca recording still sounds well, with good detail, and the direction of Molinari-Pradelli is warm and intense. While Tebaldi is not quite the little woman of Puccini's dreams, she still produces a flow of gorgeous, rich tone. Only the coarseness of Mario del Monaco as Des Grieux mars the set, but this is exciting, red-blooded singing and he does not overwhelm Tebaldi in the duet sequences.

Perlea's 1954 recording of *Manon Lescaut*, well paced, fresh and vigorous, makes a valauble addition to the excellent Victor Opera series at mid-price. The mono sound may be limited (with the orchestra in this transfer not given the body it originally had on LP), but no Puccinian should miss it, when Jussi Bjoerling gives the finest ever interpretation on record of the role of Des Grieux. This is one of Bjoerling's best recordings, passionately committed and gloriously sung; and Robert Merrill too is superb as Manon's brother, giving delightful irony to the closing scene of Act I which has rarely sounded so effervescent. The Manon of Licia Albanese is sensitively sung, but the voice is not at all girlish, even less so than in her two classic recordings as Mimi in *Bohème* – with Gigli in 1939 and in Toscanini's concert performance in 1946.

Tosca (complete).
(M) (***) EMI mono CHS7 63338-2 (2) [Ang. CDHB 63338]. Caniglia, Gigli, Borgioli, Dominici, Rome Op. Ch. & O, Fabritiis.
(M) ** Decca 411 871-2 (2) [id.]. Tebaldi, Del Monaco, London, St Cecilia Ac., Rome, Ch. & O, Molinari-Pradelli.
** Decca 414 036-2 (2) [id.]. Freni, Pavarotti, Milnes, Nat. PO, Rescigno.
(B) *(*) Naxos Dig. 8. 660001/2 [id.]. Miricioiu, Lamberti, Carroli, Slovak Philharmonic Ch., Slovak R. SO (Bratislava), Alexander Rahbari.
* Sony Dig. S2K 45847 (2) [id.]; *40-45847.* Marton, Carreras, Pons, Hungarian State R. & TV Ch. & State O, Tilson Thomas.

Collectors with long memories will be nostalgic about what inevitably, if illogically, must be described as 'the Gigli Tosca'; in the days of 78s, it was one of the glories of Puccini representation in the catalogue. The transfer brings astonishingly vivid sound, as in the rasping trombones on the opening Scarpia chords, along with a fine sense of presence. The great tenor dominates the whole performance, his facial expressiveness consistently beaming out through his voice, while Maria Caniglia, not characterful enough to be a memorable Tosca, sings with warmth and total commitment. Armando Borgioli is a young-sounding, virile Scarpia, forceful and upstanding rather than sinister. The conducting of Fabritiis brings far more natural and convincing timing than you find on many a more recent recording.

Tebaldi's early stereo *Tosca* is outclassed by most later versions, notably the 1963 Decca Vienna set with Leontyne Price, Di Stefano and Taddei, with Karajan at his most electrifying; this costs exactly the same but remains our first choice on all counts, irrespective of price (Decca 421 670-2). Yet Tebaldi is splendidly dramatic and often sings very affectingly. The set is well worth hearing for her classic assumption of the role, but unfortunately the other two principals do not match her.

The trio of principals in the 1978 Decca version was originally lined up for a Karajan recording, but in the event DG opted to record that maestro with quite a different cast. Rescigno is no substitute, hard and unsympathetic in his conducting even if, with vivid (analogue) sound, the drama comes over well, and the *Te Deum* scene is thrillingly caught at the end of Act I. Pavarotti, a bright-eyed Cavaradossi, lacks his usual bloom till the last Act, and Freni as Tosca sounds a little over-strained. Milnes makes a fresh, direct Scarpia. Though a reissue of analogue material, this comes at full price and seems expensive.

The Naxos version at budget price is worth hearing for the vibrant and strong performance of Nelly Miricioiu as Tosca, a soprano who deserves to be recorded far more. She is not helped by the principals around her and least of all by the conductor, Alexander Rahbari, whose preference for slow speeds undermines any tension the soprano builds up. Yet she both brings echoes of Maria Callas in her dramatic moments and gives a beautifully thoughtful and inward account of *Vissi d'arte*, finely controlled at a spacious speed. Giorgio Lamberti is a coarse-grained Cavaradossi, hammy in his underlining, and Silvano Carroli, despite a fine, weighty voice, is a rough-edged Scarpia, too often shouting rather than vocalizing. Good digital sound and refined playing.

Eva Marton makes a coarse and often unsteady Tosca on the Sony set. José Carreras sings well as Cavaraodossi, but not as well as on his two previous versions, for Karajan and Colin Davis. Juan Pons is a lightweight Scarpia, not sinister enough. Such vocal shortcomings undermine the thrust of Tilson Thomas's direction, making it a disappointing version all round.

Tosca: highlights.
(B) **(*) DG Compact Classics *427 719-4* [id.] (from complete set, with Vishnevskaya, Bonelli, Manuguerra, French R. Ch., O Nat. de France, Rostropovitch) – BIZET: *Carmen*: highlights.**

There is plenty of drama in Rostropovich's set of *Tosca* highlights, with all three principals at their best and Manuguerra a particularly compelling Scarpia. Vishnevskaya has her rough moments but is otherwise very compelling, and Bonelli sings with comparable ardour as Cavaradossi. The selection includes the complete final scene of the opera from *E lucevan le stelle onwards*. Good, vivid sound.

Il Trittico: Il Tabarro; Suor Angelica; Gianni Schicchi.
(M) ** Decca 411 665-2 (3). Tebaldi, Del Monaco, Simionato, Merrill, Corena, Maggio Musicale Fiorentino Ch. & O, Gardelli.

Puccini's three one-act operas show him musically and dramatically at the peak of his achievement. They are balanced like the movements of a concerto: *Il Tabarro*, sombre in its portrait of the cuckolded bargemaster, but made attractive by the vividness of the atmosphere and the sweetness of the love music; *Suor Angelica*, a lyrical slow movement with its picture of a nunnery, verging on the syrupy but never quite falling; and *Gianni Schicchi*, easily the most brilliant and witty one-act comedy in the whole field of opera. The return of the early Decca set, however, does not alter our current recommendations for this triptych. On grounds of recording it remains very impressive, but the performances are variable. Fernando Corena's Schicchi is too coarse-grained, both vocally and dramatically. This is buffo-bass style with too much parlando 'acting'. Nor is Tebaldi entirely at home in the open-eyed part of the young Lauretta, though she sings *O mio babbino caro* very sweetly. She is more at home in the role of Sister Angelica and gives a rich-voiced and affecting portrayal, only slightly troubled by the top notes at the end. Simionato makes a fine, firm Zia Principessa: one can really believe in her relentlessness, while Gardelli keeps the performance moving forward gently but firmly, and in a somewhat static piece this is most important. The scene of *Il Tabarro* is set on a barge on the banks of the Seine, in Paris, and though the Decca production team capture all of Puccini's background effects, the result has not so much a Parisian flavour as the acoustic of an empty opera-house. Merrill sings very strongly as the cuckolded bargemaster, and Tebaldi and del Monaco are good in a conventional, whole-hogging Italian way. The recording has been effectively remastered and sounds a shade drier than when first issued, but the voices are vividly projected on CD, and the sense of atmosphere remains.

Turandot complete.
*** Decca 414 274-2; *414 274-4* (2) [id.]. Sutherland, Pavarotti, Caballé, Pears, Ghiaurov, Alldis Ch., Wandsworth School Boys' Ch., LPO, Mehta.

Mehta directs a gloriously rich and dramatic performance, superlatively recorded, with Sutherland giving an intensely revealing and appealing interpretation of the icy princess. Pavarotti provides a performance equally imaginative and Caballé is a splendid Liù.

Purcell, Henry (1659–95)

(i) *Funeral music for Queen Mary;* (ii) Anthems and verse anthems: *Blessed are they that fear the Lord; Hear my prayer, O Lord; My beloved spake; Rejoice in the Lord alway; Remember not, Lord, our offences.*
(M) **(*) EMI CD-EMX 2172; *TC-EMX 2174*. Soloists, King's College Ch., Ledger; with (i) Philip Jones Brass Ens.; (ii) ASMF.

(i) *Funeral music for Queen Mary* (complete); *Jubilate Deo in D; Te Deum laudamus in D.* (ii) Verse anthems: *I was glad; O give thanks O Lord God of hosts.*
(M) **(*) Decca 430 263-2; *430 263-4* [id.]. (i) Bowman, Brett, Partridge, Forbes Robinson, Consort of Sackbuts, ECO; (ii) Esswood, Partridge, Anthony Dawson; (i; ii) St John's College, Cambridge, Ch., George Guest.

The *Funeral music for Queen Mary* consists of far more than the unforgettable *March* for lugrubious sackbuts with punctuating timpani (later repeated without timpani), which still sounds so modern to our ears. In the event, this brings the least effective performance on the 1972 Decca (originally Argo) collection, not as bitingly tragic as it might have been. The rest of the work is beautifully done, and so are the grand ceremonial settings of the *Te Deum* and *Jubilate*, although the solo contributions are a little uneven. The verse anthems – intended for Charles II's Chapel Royal – were recorded three years later.Though their direction could be more flamboyant, the singing is superb, with Paul Esswood and Ian Partridge especially fine among the soloists. The recording is vivid and atmospheric, though the focus on CD is not absolutely sharp.

Philip Ledger has the benefit of superbly expansive 1975 sound for his darkly memorable performance of the *March* with the Philip Jones Brass Ensemble, but the funeral anthems are given less alert performances than on the rival St John's reissue. However, the verse anthems are very impressively sung, and the remastered recording has much splendour on CD. The soloists are from the choir.

STAGE WORKS AND THEATRE MUSIC

Dido and Aeneas (complete).

❀ (M) *** Decca 425 720-2; *425 720-4* [id.]. Dame Janet Baker, Herincx, Clark, Sinclair, St Anthony Singers, ECO, Anthony Lewis.

*** Chan. Dig. CHAN 0521; *EBTD 0521* [id.]. Kirkby, Thomas, Nelson, Noorman, Rees, Taverner Ch. & Players, Parrott.

It was Janet Baker's 1962 recording of *Dido* for the Oiseau-Lyre label that established her as a recording star of the front rank: it is a truly great performance. The radiant beauty of the voice is obvious enough, but here she goes beyond that to show what stylishness and insight she can command. The emotion is implied, as it should be in this music, not injected in great uncontrolled gusts. Listen to the contrast between the angry, majestic words to Aeneas, *Away, away!* and the dark grief of the following *But death alas I cannot shun*, and note how Baker contrasts dramatic soprano tone-colour with darkened contralto tone. Even subtler is the contrast between the opening phrase of *When I am laid in earth* and its repeat a few bars later: it is a model of graduated *mezza voce*. Then with the words *Remember me!*, delivered in a monotone, she subdues the natural vibrato to produce a white tone of hushed, aching intensity. When this record was first issued, we suggested that it would be surprising if a more deeply satisfying interpretation were recorded within the foreseeable future, and so it has proved: three decades later, this reissue still occupies the top of the recommended list. Anthony Lewis chooses fast speeds, but they challenge the ECO (Thurston Dart a model continuo player) to produce the crispest and lightest of playing which never sounds rushed. The other soloists and chorus give very good support. Herincx is a rather gruff Aeneas, but the only serious blemish is Monica Sinclair's Sorceress. She overcharacterizes in a way that is quite out of keeping with the rest of the production. Generally, by concentrating on musical values, Lewis and his singers and instrumentalists make the clear, simple dramatic point of the opera all the more telling, and it proves a most moving experience. Like most vintage Oiseau-Lyre recordings, this was beautifully engineered: the remastering thins out the upper range a little, but the effect is to increase the feeling of authenticity, for the ambient bloom remains.

Parrott in one of his earliest recordings, before his EMI contract, re-creates the sort of intimate atmosphere that might have been found in Josias Priest's school for young ladies, where Purcell's masterpiece was first given. The voices enhance that impression, not least Emma Kirkby's fresh, bright soprano, here recorded without too much edge, but still very young-sounding. It is more questionable to have a soprano singing the tenor role of the Sailor in Act II; but anyone who fancies the idea of an authentic performance need not hesitate. The CD gives refined sound, well focused, with plenty of atmosphere.

Dioclesian; Timon of Athens.
*** Erato/Warner 2292 45327-2; *2292 45327-4* (2) [id.]. Dawson, Fisher, Covey-Crump, Elliot, George, Varcoe, Monteverdi Ch., E. Bar. Soloists, Gardiner.

On his two-disc Erato set John Eliot Gardiner rescues some of the most colourful and memorable of Purcell's theatre music. It is tragic that such inspired writing should by its very format have fallen out of the current repertory, when these pieces illustrate plays that are totally non-viable on the stage today. Like *The Fairy Queen*, *The Prophetess or the History of Dioclesian* is one of Purcell's semi-operas and presents similar problems in modern performance. Gardiner relies purely on musical quality in performing the copious amount of music Purcell wrote for the piece, hardly attempting to give any idea of the dramatic context which these disconnnected arias, ensembles and scenes illustrate. The martial music, shining with trumpets, is what stands out from *Dioclesian*, adapted from a Jacobean play first given in 1622. Gardiner is such a lively conductor, regularly drawing out the effervescence in Purcell's inspiration, that the result is delightfully refreshing, helped by an outstanding team of soloists. The incidental music for *Timon of Athens* offers more buried treasure, including such enchanting inventions as *Hark! how the songsters of the grove*, with its '*Symphony of pipes* imitating the chirping of birds', and a fine *Masque for Cupid and Bacchus*, beautifully sung by Lynne Dawson, Gillian Fisher and Stephen Varcoe. Excellent Erato sound.

The Indian Queen (incidental music; complete).
**(*) Erato/Warner 2292 45556-2; *2292 45556-4* [id.]. Hardy, Fischer, Harris, Smith, Stafford, Hill, Elwes, Varcoe, Thomas, Monteverdi Ch., E. Bar. Soloists, Eliot Gardiner.

The Indian Queen is one of the Purcellian entertainments that fit into no modern category, a semi-opera. The impossible plot matters little; Purcell's music contains many delights and, indeed, the score seems to get better as it proceeds. The reissued Erato version is fully cast and uses an authentic accompanying baroque instrumental group. The choral singing is especially fine, with the close of the work movingly expressive. John Eliot Gardiner's choice of tempi is apt and the soloists are all good, although the men are more strongly characterful than the ladies; nevertheless the lyical music comes off well. The recording is spacious and well balanced, and the performance has many individual felicities. Recommended alongside the Deller set on Harmonia Mundi (HMC 90243), which has fine individual contributions from Maurice Bevan, Honor Sheppard, Paul Elliott and, of course, Deller himself.

The Tempest (incidental music; complete).
*** Erato/Warner 2292 45555-2; *2292 45555-4* [id.]. Jennifer Smith, Hardy, Hall, Elwes, Varcoe, David Thomas, Earle, Monteverdi Ch. & O, Eliot Gardiner.

Whether or not Purcell himself wrote this music for Shakespeare's last play (the scholarly arguments are still unresolved), Gardiner demonstrates how delightful it is, a masterly collection, in performances both polished and stylish and with excellent solo and choral singing. At least the Overture is clearly Purcell's, and that sets the pattern for a very varied collection of numbers, including three *da capo* arias and a full-length masque celebrating Neptune for Act V. The recording, full and atmospheric, has transferred vividly to CD.

Theatre music (collection).

Disc 1: *Abdelazar: Overture & suite. Distressed Innocence: Overture & suite. The Gordian Knot Untied: Overture & suite; The Married Beau: Overture & suite. Sir Anthony Love: Overture & suite.*

Disc 2: *Bonduca: Overture and suite. Circe: suite. The Old Bachelor: Overture and suite. The Virtuous Wife: Overture and suite.*

Disc 3: *Amphitrion: Overture and suite; Overture in G min.; Don Quixote: suite.*

Disc 4: *Overture in G min. The Double Dealer: Overture and suite. Henry II, King of England: In vain, 'gainst love, in vain I strove. The Richmond Heiress: Behold the man. The Rival Sisters: Overture; 3 songs. Tyranic Love: Hark my Damilcar!* (duet); *Ah! how sweet it is to love. Theodosius*: excerpts. *The Wives' Excuse:* excerpts.

Disc 5: *Overture in D min.; Cleomenes, the Spartan Hero: No, no, poor suff'ring heart. A Dialogue between Thirsis and Daphne: Why, my Daphne, why complaining?. The English Lawyer: My wife has a tongue:* excerpts. *A Fool's Preferment:* excerpts. *The History of King Richard II: Retir'd from any mortal's sight. The Indian Emperor: I look'd and saw within. The Knight of Malta: At the close of the ev'ning. The Libertine:* excerpts. *The Marriage-hater Match'd: As soon as the chaos . . . How vile are the sordid intregues. The Massacre of Paris: The genius lo* (2 settings). *Oedipus:* excerpts. *Regulus: Ah me! to many deaths. Sir Barnaby Whigg: Blow, blow, Boreas, blow. Sophonisba: Beneath the poplar's shadow. The Wives' excuse:* excerpts.

Disc 6: *Chacony; Pavans Nos. 1–5; Trio sonata for violin, viola de gamba & organ. Aureng-Zebe: I see, she flies me. The Canterbury Guests: Good neighbours why?. Epsom Wells: Leave these useless arts. The Fatal Marriage: 2 songs. The Female Virtuosos: Love, thou art best. Love Triumphant: How happy's the husband. The Maid's Last Prayer:* excerpts. *The Mock Marriage: Oh! how you protest; Man is for the woman made. Oroonoko: Celemene, pray tell me. Pausanius: Song (Sweeter than roses) and duet. Rule a Wife and Have a Wife: There's not a swain. The Spanish Friar: Whilst I with grief.*

(M) *** O-L 425 893-2 (6) [id.]. Kirkby, Nelson, Lane, Roberts, Lloyd, Bowman, Hill, Covey-Crump, Elliott, Byers, Bamber, Pike, David Thomas, Keyte, Shaw, George, Taverner Ch., AAM, Hogwood.

This set of six CDs creates an anthology from the contents of a selective but wide-ranging series of LPs recorded between 1974 and 1983. Most of the music Purcell wrote for the theatre is relatively little heard, and one must remember that the 'suites' assembled here were not originally intended for continuous performance. If in the earlier discs they do not provide the variety and range one would expect from works conceived as a whole, much of the music comes up with striking freshness in these performances using authentic instruments. As well as the charming dances and more ambitious overtures, as the series proceeds we are offered more extended scenas with soloists and chorus, of which the nine excerpts from *Theodosius*, an early score (1680), are a particularly entertaining example. Before that, on Disc 3 we have already had the highly inventive Overture and incidental music for *Don Quixote*. Purcell was one of three contributors on this occasion (there were three plays to service, all by Thomas D'Urfey and based on Cervantes' famous novel). Though the music was written at high speed, much of it was attractively lively and it deserves to be resurrected in such stylish performances, with much enchanting singing from both the soprano soloists, Emma Kirkby and Judith Nelson. Disc 4 also includes a delightful duet from *The Richmond Heiress*, representing a flirtation in music. There are other attractive duets elsewhere, for instance the nautical *Blow, blow, Boreas, blow* from *Sir Barnaby Whigg*, which could fit admirably into *HMS Pinafore* (Rogers Covey-Crump and Davis Thomas) and the jovial *As soon as the chaos* from *The Marriage-hater Match'd.* In *Ah me! to many deaths* from *Regulus*, Judith Nelson is at her most eloquent while, earlier on Disc 5, she sings charmingly the familiar *Nymphs and shepherds*, which comes from *The Libertine*, a particularly fine score with imaginative use of the brass. The equally famous *Music for a while*, beautifully sung by James Bowman, derives from *Oedipus.* The last disc again shows Judith Nelson at her finest in a series of arias, but it also includes a splendidly boisterous Quartet from *The Canterbury Guests.* The collection is appropriately rounded off by members of the Academy giving first-class performances of some of Purcell's instrumental music, ending with the famous *Chacony.* The sharpness of inspiration comes over very compellingly on original instruments, though Hogwood tends to prefer tempi faster than one might expect. Throughout, the sound is admirably fresh, with clean transfers retaining the warmth and bite of the original analogue recordings, yet without adding any abrasive edge. The discs are comprehensively documented and with full texts included.

Rachmaninov, Sergei (1873–1943)

Piano concertos Nos. 1–4; Rhapsody on a theme of Paganini.
**(*) Chan. Dig. CHAN 8882/3; *DBTD 2025* (2) [id.]. Howard Shelley, SNO, Bryden Thomson.

Chandos, having had considerable success with their remastered Earl Wild recordings with Horenstein, which remain highly recommendable (CHAN 8521/2), were obviously hoping to repeat the trick with this new set from Howard Shelley and the Royal Scottish National Orchestra under Bryden Thomson. They set up their microphones to capture the warm acoustics of Caird Hall, Dundee, and the result is certainly sumptuous, almost overwhelmingly so at climaxes, with rich strings and powerfully resonant brass and a bold, truthful piano image projected way out in front. The performances do not lack adrenalin either, although their ebb and flow of tension is not consistent, and at times the music-making almost tends to run away with itself, notably in the *Third Concerto.* The first-movement climax of the *Second Concerto* is very powerful, and there is some lovely playing from the orchestra at the end of the slow movement. The finales have great dash and much charisma from Shelley, but Bryden Thomson at times seems less assured in the idiom. Just after the opening of the *Rhapsody on a theme of Paganini* he produces a curious echo effect (in which his soloist joins), while his *Eighteenth variation* could have more unbuttoned fervour. In the finale of the *First concerto* his caressing of the lyrical string-tune is too cosy. Moreover he fails to match exactly his soloist's ardour in the big statement of the great melody at the climax of the finale of the *Second Concerto.* The *Fourth Concerto* has some spectacular moments but lacks a really firm profile. Even so, there is much to enjoy here, and Howard Shelley's contribution is consistently distinguished.

Piano concertos Nos. 1 in F sharp min., Op. 1; 4 in G min., Op. 40; Rhapsody on a theme of Paganini, Op. 43.
(M) **(*) Sony SBK 46541 [id.]. Philippe Entremont, Phd. O, Ormandy.

Entremont gives a marvellously dashing account of both early and late concertos, rivalling the composer himself in the sheer effrontery of his bravura. By rights, no ten fingers could possibly play like this and, as with Rachmaninov himself, the speeds have one on the edge of one's seat. Where Entremont falls short – and he is not helped by the American recording (dating from 1963 and 1961 respectively) which boosts pianissimos – is in the gentler music, where he could be more affectionate. The recording quality could be sweeter too, and the piano tone is rather clattery. In the *Rhapsody on a theme of Paganini*, recorded in in 1958, Ormandy oversees a strongly directed performance, with Entremont rising excitingly to the challenge. Ormandy was one of the finest of all concerto conductors, and this work suits him admirably. The forward momentum becomes increasingly compulsive but does not prevent a full romantic blossoming, and the closing section of the work, after the eighteenth variation, is a blaze of excitement. The balance here is rather more natural, and if overall there have to be some reservations about the brightly lit, and larger-than-life sound-quality, this remains vividly compelling playing, and the coupling is very generous. However, Mikhail Pletnev's account of the *F sharp minor Concerto* is in a class of its own and the coupled *Paganini rhapsody* is distinguished by quite stunning virtuosity and also by great feeling. Pešek provides splendid accompaniments with the Philharmonia Orchestra and the sound is first class (Virgin VC7 90724-2; *VC7 90724-4*).

Piano concerto No. 2 in C min., Op. 18.
(M) *** EMI Dig. CDD7 63903-2 [id.]; *ET 763903-4.* Cécile Ousset, CBSO, Rattle – GRIEG: *Concerto.***(*)

Cécile Ousset gives a powerful, red-blooded performance in the grand manner, warmly supported by Simon Rattle and the CBSO. Her rubato may often be extreme but it never sounds studied, always convincingly spontaneous; and the EMI recording copes well with the range of the playing. Those wanting a coupling with the Grieg *Concerto* will find Ousset's account similarly strong.

(i) *Piano concerto No. 2 in C min.; Rhapsody on a theme of Paganini. Lilacs, Op. 21/5; Moment musical in E min., Op. 16/4; Preludes Nos. 16 in G, Op. 32/5; 21 in B min., Op. 32/10.* arr. of MENDELSSOHN: *Scherzo from A Midsummer Night's Dream.*
(M) **(*) EMI stereo/mono CDH7 63788-2 [id.]. Benno Moiseiwitsch; (i) Philh. O, Rignold.

Older readers will remember Moiseiwitsch's 'plum-label' 78-r.p.m. discs of Rachmaninov's *Second Piano concerto*, with Walter Goehr, which some collectors prized more highly than the composer's own recording on the more prestigious 'red label'. Moiseiwitsch plays pretty impressively, too, on this 1955 coupling of the *Concerto* and *Rhapsody* and, although Hugo Rignold does not exert an ideal grip over the readings and there is less dramatic intensity than before, there is no lack of brilliance or concentration in the solo contribution; with superb Philharmonia playing, the first-movement climax is expansive and exciting. The early stereo sound, made at the Abbey Road Studio, is astonishly full and vivid, with a very lifelike piano quality. The solo items, recorded much earlier in mono, include a brilliant account of Rachmaninov's Mendelssohn arrangement, which Moiseiwitsch regarded as the best recording he ever made.

(i) *Piano concerto No. 2 in C min.;* (ii) *Preludes Nos. 3 in B flat; 8 in C min., Op. 23/2 & 7; 13 in B flat min., Op. 32/2* (CD only: (i) *Piano concerto No. 1 in F sharp min., Op. 1*).
(B) ** DG Compact Classics 413 850-2 (2); *413 850-4.* (i) Vásáry, LSO, Ahronovitch; (ii) Sviatoslav Richter – LISZT: *Concertos Nos. 1–2* etc.**(*)

Vásáry and Ahronovitch make quite an effective partnership in the *C minor Concerto* and the performance of the first movement has a fine climax. But after that the voltage is lower, and the *Adagio* does not distil the degree of poetry which makes the finest versions so memorable. The DG recording is bold and colourful, but the piano timbre is drier for Richter's masterly performances of the three *Preludes*, used as a makeweight on this Compact Classics chrome cassette. On the equivalent pair of (digitally remastered) CDs, the *First Concerto* is added as a substantial bonus. Here Ahronovitch's direction is nothing if not impetuous and the reading is full of vigour and bursts of vivid romanticism. Vásáry's rather more introvert manner seems to fit rather well within this dashing framework and there is no doubt about the freshness of this performance.

Piano concertos Nos. 2 in C min., Op. 18; 3 in D min., Op. 30.
(M) *** Chan. CHAN 6507 [id.]. Earl Wild, RPO, Horenstein.

Earl Wild's performances derive from a complete set produced by Charles Gerhardt for RCA and recorded at the Kingsway Hall in 1965, to be issued subsequently in a subscription series through *Reader's Digest* magazine. It is curious that the coupling of Rachmaninov's two greatest concertos has not come about until now, but this mid-priced reissue must be counted a great success. The first movement of the *C minor Concerto* is faster than usual, but the expressive fervour is in no doubt; the *Adagio*, too, blossoms readily. The *Third Concerto* is among the very finest versions of this work on record and, in terms of bravura, is in the Horowitz class. The digital remastering is a great success, the overall balance is truthful and the hall ambience brings a rich orchestral image and plenty of brilliance.

Piano concerto No. 2; Rhapsody on a theme of Paganini, Op. 43.
(M) *(*) Sony MKY 44830 [id.]. Gary Graffman, NYPO, Bernstein.

Piano concerto No. 2; Rhapsody on a theme of Paganini; Vocalise, Op. 34/14 (arr. Kocsis).
(M) ** Ph. Dig. 432 044-2; *432 044-4* [id.]. Kocsis, San Francisco SO, Edo de Waart.

Zoltán Kocsis has fleet fingers and here combines dash with panache. But in No. 2 he gives the listener all too little time to savour incidental beauties or to surrender to the melancholy of the slow movement. He is just too carried away with his own virtuosity and, although this playing is thrilling enough, it is not the whole story.

Graffman and Bernstein are more convincing in the *Rhapsody*; the *Concerto*, romantically relaxed, could do with more concentration, although the first-movement climax is rhythmically purposeful. The mid-1960s recording is undistracting, but this version cannot compare with Ashkenazy and Previn in the same coupling (Decca 417 702-2; *417 702-4*), or indeed with the splendid, digital Naxos super-bargain CD (8.550117).

(i) *Piano concerto No. 2 in C min., Op. 18. Preludes Nos. 6 in G min., Op. 23/5; 16 in G, Op. 32/5; 23 in G sharp min., Op. 32/12.*
(M) ** EMI CDM7 63525-2 *EG 763525-4* [id.]. John Ogdon, (i) Philh. O, Pritchard – TCHAIKOVSKY: *Piano concerto No. 1.***

John Ogdon's 1962 performance of the *C minor Concerto* is sensitive and introspective, and it is easy to enjoy the relaxed, lyrical beauty of the first two movements. But the partnership with Pritchard did not strike any sparks, and there is a lack of impulse and romantic virility, especially in the finale. The recording still sounds excellent, both in the *Concerto* and in the *Preludes*, which are splendidly played: the *G major* is especially delectable.

Piano concerto No. 3 in D min., Op. 30.
(M) *(*) EMI Dig. CD-EMX 2171; *TC-EMX 2171.* Dimitris Sgouros, BPO, Simonov.

Dimitris Sgouros made this record in 1984 when he was fifteen. It was his first concerto recording and much of the playing is pretty dazzling as such. But, however remarkable it may be, the standards of the gramophone differ from those of the concert hall; much of the musical meaning of this concerto seems to escape him and the bravura passages are thus rendered relatively ineffective. Compare the main theme in the hands of a Rachmaninov or a Horowitz and it is evident that Sgouros is an artist of enormous facility and promise, rather than one of fulfilment. He plays the second cadenza, rather than the shorter one chosen by Rachmaninov. The digital recording itself is serviceable rather than distinguished: the Berlin Philharmonic does not produce its characteristic rich sonority for Yuri Simonov.

(i) *Piano concerto No. 3; Rhapsody on a theme of Paganini;* (ii) *The Isle of the dead, Op. 29.*
(B) **(*) DG Compact Classics *419 392-4* [id.]. (i) Vásáry, LSO, Ahronovitch; (ii) BPO, Maazel.

Vásáry's Compact Classics tape is excellent value, as it also includes Maazel's fine version of *The Isle of the dead.* In the *Concerto* Vásáry uses the longer version of the first-movement cadenza; his playing is highly musical, clean and often gentle in style. The impetuous Ahronovitch offers some extremes of tempi; taken as a whole, however, this performance has both poetry and excitement (especially in the finale). The conductor's chimerical style is more obviously suited to the *Rhapsody*, with its opening faster than usual and with strong contrasts of tempo and mood between brilliant and lyrical variations. The sound is very good.

Piano concerto No. 4 in G min., Op. 40.
❀ *** EMI CDC7 49326-2 [id.]. Michelangeli, Philh. O, Gracis (with RAVEL: *Piano concerto in G* *** ❀).

This is one of the most brilliant piano records ever made. It puts the composer's own recorded performance quite in the shade, and the Ravel coupling is equally illuminating. The recording does not quite match the superlative quality of the playing but still sounds pretty good.

Études-tableaux (orch. Respighi).
*** Collins Dig. 1175-2; *1175-4* [id.]. LPO, Rozhdestvensky – BRAHMS: *Piano quartet.****

Respighi was a master of the orchestra and his celebrated version of Rachmaninov's *Études-tableaux* sounds splendidly idiomatic. If one did not know them in their piano form, one could be entirely convinced that they were conceived for the orchestra. Rozhdestvensky gets excellent results from the LPO, and the Collins recording is absolutely first class.

The Isle of the dead, Op. 29; Symphonic dances, Op. 45.
(M) *** Decca Dig. 430 733-2; *430 733-4* [id.]. Concg. O, Ashkenazy.

Ashkenazy's is a superb coupling, rich and powerful in playing and interpretation. One here recognizes *The Isle of the dead* as among the very finest of Rachmaninov's orchestral works, relentless in its ominous build-up, while at generally fast speeds the *Symphonic dances* have extra darkness and intensity too, suggesting no relaxation whatever at the end of Rachmaninov's career. The splendid recording highlights both the passion and the fine precision of the playing. Previn's alternative, analogue EMI CD (from 1976) offers extra music (CDM7 69025-2; *EG 769025-4*, see our main volume) but the Decca remains a marginal first choice.

Symphonies Nos. 1–3; Youth Symphony (1891).
(M) *** Decca Dig. 421 065-2 (3) [id.]. Concg. O, Ashkenazy.

Ashkenazy's mid-price set still leads the field in this repertoire and can be given an unqualified recommendation, with the performances passionate and volatile, intensely Russian. However, Rozhdestvensky's splendid LSO version of No. 2 should not be forgotten, a remarkable bargain (Pickwick PCD 904; *CIMPC 904*).

Symphony No. 3 in A min., Op. 44; Symphonic dances, Op. 45.
(M) **(*) DG Dig. 429 981-2; *429 981-4* [id.]. BPO, Maazel.

Maazel takes a highly personal view of both these Rachmaninov masterpieces. The symphony is unusually fierce and intense, with refined, incisive playing spotlit by the overtly clear digital recording. The result is sharper and tougher than one expects, less obviously romantic, with the great second-subject melody sounding detached and rather chilly. The finale is made to sound like a Walton comedy overture at the start, brilliant and exciting, but at the end it lacks joyful exuberance. The reading of the *Symphonic dances* is crisp and light-textured. Brilliance there is in plenty, but full warmth of lyricism is lacking. Bright, spacious recording, made in the Philharmonie in 1983 and characteristic of the digital sound the DG engineers were achieving at the time. Previn remains first choice for the *A minor Symphony* and the LSO has rarely displayed its virtuosity more brilliantly in the recording studio. With its generous coupling of Shostakovich's *Sixth Symphony*, this is a bargain (EMI CDM7 69564-2; *EG 769564-4*).

MUSIC FOR TWO PIANOS

Suites Nos. 1–2, Opp. 5 & 17; Symphonic dances, Op. 45.
*** Hyp. Dig. CDA 66375 [id.]. Howard Shelley, Hilary Macnamara.

Two pianos are notoriously difficult to balance, and the present disc is not as triumphantly successful as, say, the Louis Lortie–Hélène Mercier Ravel recital on Chandos, though it is still pretty good. Howard Shelley and Hilary Macnamara give strong performances of both the *Suites* and the *Symphonic dances*. In the *Second suite* their responses are not quite as refined as those of Argerich and Freire (Philips 411 034-2), and there are moments in the middle movement of the *Symphonic dances* when more subtle and lighter rhythmic accents would not have come amiss. But there is plenty of dramatic fire in the outer movements, and some musicianly playing elsewhere in this generously filled disc.

VOCAL MUSIC

Vespers, Op. 37.
*** Hyp. Dig. CDA 66460; *KA 66460* [id.]. Corydon Singers, Matthew Best.

Rachmaninov's setting of the *Vespers* – more correctly the 'All-night vigil' – is among his supreme masterpieces, a beautiful and dedicated example of his writing in an idiom totally different from most of his work. Though this British choir lacks the dark timbres associated with Russian choruses and though the result could be weightier and more biting, this is a most beautiful performance, very well sung and recorded in an atmospheric, reverberant setting very apt for such church music.

Raff, Joachim (1822–82)

Octet in C for strings, Op. 176.
** Chan. Dig. CHAN 8790; *ABTD 1423* [id.]. ASMF Chamber Ens. – MENDELSSOHN: *Octet.***

Raff's *Octet for strings* is a late work and pleasant enough, but it is not a patch on Mendelssohn's juvenile masterpiece with which it is coupled on this record. It is well played and very well recorded, but the ASMF Chamber Ensemble do not make a special case for it.

Ravel, Maurice (1875–1937)

(i) *Alborada del gracioso;* (ii) *Une barque sur l'océan; Boléro;* (i; iii) *Piano concerto for the left hand;* (ii; iv) *Daphnis et Chloé* (complete ballet); (ii) *Fanfare pour L'Éventail de Jeanne; Menuet antique; Ma Mère l'Oye* (complete ballet); (i) *Pavane pour une infante défunte; Rapsodie espagnole;* (ii) *Shéhérazade: Ouverture de feerie. Le tombeau de Couperin; La valse; Valses nobles et sentimentales.*
(M) **(*) Sony SM3K 45842 (3) [id.]. (i) Cleveland O; (ii) NYPO; Boulez; (iii) with Entremont; (iv) Camerata Singers.

Boulez's distinguished Sony set unfortunately comes into direct competition with Dutoit's outstanding Montreal box of four CDs, also at mid-price. On grounds of recording alone, the latter takes precedence, for the superb Decca sound is in the demonstration bracket. Dutoit's performances are also remarkably fine, and this reissued compilation earned a Rosette in our main volume (421 458-2). However, CBS do offer very good value. Three CDs are used, yet only the *G major Piano concerto* is missing and instead we are offered a glitteringly iridescent account of the *Ouverture de feerie*, which is omitted by Dutoit. Entrement's account of the *Left-hand concerto* is strong and characterful and not lacking in poetic colour; but the rather forward CBS sound is a little fierce at the orchestral climax and does not altogether flatter the piano timbre. On the whole, however, the remastering makes the most of recordings which were originally among the best of their period (1972–5) from this source, even if they were at times balanced artificially in the interests of internal clarity and strong projection. Both orchestras respond with splendid virtuosity to Boulez's direction. The *Alborada* is quite brilliant and, throughout, Boulez allows all the music ample time to breathe; gentler textures have the transluscence for which this conductor is admired. *Une barque sur l'océan* has a genuine magic, while the complete *Daphnis et Chloé* has a sense of ecstasy and enchantment, and an ability to transport the listener into the enchanted landscape that this work inhabits, with its wonder, its vivid colours and innocence. The playing of the New York Philharmonic here is beyond praise: every detail is affectionately phrased, there is effortless virtuosity and brilliance and, despite some highlighting, the recording produces a warmly atmospheric quality, although again there is a touch of aggressiveness at climaxes. Boulez is also at his very best in *Ma Mère l'Oye*: the luminous textures of the gentle music are matched by the glitter and impact of the score's more dramatic moments. The *Menuet antique* has a pleasing directness of manner; the effect is most refreshing. Boulez's *Rapsodie espagnole* is equally distinctive: it is beautifully shaped and atmospheric in an entirely different way from Karajan's; the latter is heavy with exotic scents and sultry half-lights, whereas Boulez's Spain is brilliant, dry and well lit. The recording is more discreetly balanced and here, as in the *Valses nobles et sentimentales*, after a spectacular opening the delectably refined woodwind colours are kept in reasonable perspective. Both *Boléro* and *La valse* generate considerable tension and have powerful climaxes. There is no doubt that this music-making with its cleanly etched sound is immensely strong in character, and many listeners will respond to it very positively. There is excellent internal cueing, with even *Boléro* subdivided into individual entries, and the *Valses nobles et sentimentales* individually accessible.

Alborada del gracioso; Une barque sur l'océan; Boléro; Daphnis et Chloé (complete ballet); *L'Éventail de Jeanne; Fanfare; Menuet antique; Ma Mère l'Oye* (complete); *Pavane pour une infante défunte; Rapsodie espagnole; Shéhérazade: Ouverture de feerie; Le tombeau de Couperin; La valse; Valses nobles et sentimetales.*
*** DG Dig. 429 768-2 (3) LSO & Ch., Claudio Abbado.

Abbado's fastidiously polished and highly sensitive Ravel performances occupy three CDs as opposed to the four of Dutoit on Decca (421 458-2). The Decca includes the two *Piano concertos* with Pascal Rogé, but not the *Shéhérazade Overture*; neither include the song-cycle of that name though, to be fair, Margaret Price's recording of it (with Abbado) was not the unqualified success one might have expected. Abbado's complete *Daphnis* is not quite as vivdly recorded as the Dutoit (in fact the opening is barely audible unless the controls are adjusted to a high-level setting). But Abbado has impeccable taste in this repertoire and it goes without saying that the LSO play gloriously throughout. The mid-price Decca set has just that extra edge over the DG, though musically honours are pretty evenly divided.

(i) *Alborada del gracioso; Boléro;* (ii) *Pavane pour une infante defunte;* (i) *Rapsodie espagnole* (CD only: (i) *Le tombeau de Couperin; Valse nobles et sentimentales*).
(B) **(*) DG Compact Classics 413 154-2 (2); *413 154-4* [id.]. Boston SO, (i) Ozawa; (ii) Abbado – DEBUSSY: *Danses sacrée; La Mer* etc.***

Even though Ozawa's Ravel performances are somewhat faceless – *Boléro* moves to its climax steadily but in a curiously unmotivated way – the Boston orchestral playing is superb and the recording first class. *Rapsodie espagnole* has plenty of glitter and the sound has warmth and much beauty of texture. *Le tombeau de Couperin*, cool and poised, showing Ozawa at his best, and the *Valses nobles et sentimentales* are added to fill out the pair of digitally remastered CDs, but this music-making makes its strongest impression heard on tape in the car. Abbado's performance of the *Pavane* is characteristically refined, and the Debussy couplings are similarly distinguished.

Alborada del gracioso; Boléro; Rapsodie espagnole; Le tombeau de Couperin; La valse.
(B) *** RCA VD 60485; *VK 60485* [id.]. Dallas SO, Mata.

Mata and his excellent Dallas orchestra give impressive performances of the virtuoso showpieces and find both delicacy and grace for *Le tombeau de Couperin*. There are more individual accounts of several of these works in the lower price-range (one thinks of Reiner, Karajan and Paray) but, now that RCA have made this bargain reissue generous in playing time (68 minutes), it is very competitive, helped by digital recording of great range and the glowing, yet not over-resonant ambience of the Dallas Hall. This gives an advantage in the *Alborada*, compared with the Karajan/EMI version, while *Boléro* develops from a whisper of a pianissimo at the start to a formidably powerful climax, though the detailed balancing is not always consistent.

Alborada del gracioso; Boléro; Rapsodie espagnole; La valse.
(M) ** Sony Dig. MDK 46501. O Nat. de France, Lorin Maazel.

Maazel's 1981 collection is brilliantly played and his extrovert sentience in the *Rapsodie* is certainly involving. *La valse* is high-powered, with an indulgent treatment of the climax. The sound is resonant and brightly lit. Frankly, this is not in the same league as Dutoit, and it costs more than Mata's excellent Dallas collection, which is more enticingly recorded and includes also *Le tombeau de Couperin*.

Alborada del gracioso; Pavane pour une infante défunte; Rapsodie espagnole; Le tombeau de Couperin; La valse.
(M) *** Mercury 432 003-2 [id.]. Detroit SO, Paray – IBERT: *Escales*.**(*)

Paray's Ravel performances enjoyed a high reputation in the 1960s. His *Rapsodie espagnole* can be spoken of in the same breath as the Reiner/RCA and Karajan/EMI versions, with its languorous, shimmering textures and sparkling *Feria*. His *Alborada* glitters and the *Pavane* is glowingly elegiac. *La valse*, too, is impressively shaped and subtly controlled. *Le tombeau de Couperin* has great refinement and elegance: the solo oboist plays beautifully. This last item was recorded in the old Detroit Orchestral Hall, with its mellow acoustic; the rest of the programme was done at Cass Technical High School, and the sound is that bit brighter and more vivid. All have been excellently remastered.

Alborada del gracioso; Rapsodie espagnole; Le tombeau de Couperin; La valse.
(M) *** EMI CDM7 63526-2; *EG 763526-4* [id.]. O de Paris, Karajan.

These superb performances were recorded just a decade after Karajan's DG analogue *Daphnis et Chloé suite* (427 250-2 – coupled with *Boléro* and Debussy's *La Mer* plus the *Prélude à l'après-midi d'un faune*), one of the best things he ever did for the gramophone. The Orchestre de Paris, while not the Berlin Philharmonic – the horn vibrato, though unobtrusive, may not be appreciated by all ears – responds splendidly to Karajan's sensuous approach to these scores. The dynamic range is very wide and the acoustic somewhat too resonant. The *Alborada* is on the slow side, and doubtless the reverberation prompted this. But, even if the atmospheric quality of these performances is not wholly free from a trace of self-consciousness, there is no doubt about the mastery of *La valse*, which is extremely fine, or of the *Rapsodie espagnole*, the best performance since Reiner's. The remastering for CD is extremely successful.

Boléro; (i) *Daphnis et Chloé: suite No. 2; Pavane pour une infante défunte; La valse.*
(M) *** Decca Dig. 430 714-2; *430 714-4* [id.]. Montreal SO, Dutoit; (i) with chorus.

A further permutation of Dutoit's beautifully made Montreal recordings, warmly and translucently recorded at St Eustache, now reissued at mid-price. The *Daphnis et Chloé* suite is drawn from the highly praised complete set. If this programme is suitable, the performances and recordings cannot be bettered.

Boléro; Le tombeau de Couperin.
(M) *(*) Decca 430 444-2; *430 444-4* [id.]. Chicago SO, Solti – DEBUSSY: *La Mer* etc.**

Solti's metrically vigorous (analogue) *Boléro* builds to its climax relentlessly and the recording makes a most powerful effect. *Le tombeau de Couperin* is well played but sounds hard and brilliant rather than classically elegant. The recording is partly to blame, with close-up sound reducing the sense of ambience.

(i) *Piano concerto in G;* (ii) *Piano concerto in D for the left hand.*
(M) ** Sony SBK 46338; *40-46338* [id.]. Entremont, (i) Phd. O, Ormandy; (ii) Cleveland O, Boulez – GERSHWIN: *Concerto in F*.**

Entremont's account of the *G major Concerto* is not especially sensitive, nor is it helped by the crude recording. The *Left-hand concerto* fares much better, although the sound is still rather resonant. This is among the most highly characterized readings available; the partnership with Boulez produced the most vivid results. First choice for a coupling of Ravel's two *Piano concertos* probably rests with Jean-Philippe Collard, who gives a meticulous, sparkling and refined account of the *G major* and a marvellously brilliant and poetic performance of the *Left-hand concerto* (EMI CDC7 47386-2). However, Anne Queffélec should not be passed by; her accounts of both *Concertos* are thoughtful and imaginative. She also includes Debussy's rare *Fantasy for piano and orchestra* and her record is offered at mid-price (Erato/Warner 2292 45086-2; *2292 45086-4*). Michelangeli's account of the *G major Concerto*, coupled with the Rachmaninov No. 4, is special and is fully worthy of the Rosette we awarded it in our main volume (EMI CDC7 49326-2).

Daphnis et Chloé (ballet; complete).
**(*) Ph. Dig. 426 260-2 [id.]. Tanglewood Festival Ch., Boston SO, Bernard Haitink.
(M) ** DG Dig. 429 982-2; *429 982-4* [id.]. VPO, Levine.

(i) *Daphnis et Chloé* (ballet; complete); (ii) *Rapsodie espagnole.*
(M) *** EMI Dig. CDD7 63887-2 [id.]; *ET 763887-4*. (i) LSO Ch. & LSO; (ii) RPO, André Previn.

With rhythm more important than atmosphere, Previn directs a very dramatic performance of *Daphnis et Chloé*, clear-headed and fresh, an exciting mid-priced alternative to the superlative Dutoit version (Decca 400 055-2). It is certainly made vivid, full-bodied too, yet with with textures sharply defined. The original full-priced issue (like the Decca CD) had very few internal cues, and it is good to see that, for the reissue, EMI have now provided a total of eighteen. Previn's unashamedly sultry 1985 *Rapsodie espagnole* with the RPO has also been added for good measure. Both recordings were made at Abbey Road, but the balance gives a concert-hall effect, and the glowing ambience in the *Rapsodie* nicely offsets the glitter. (Excellent value: 73 minutes.)

Haitink's disc with Boston forces has an almost symphonic breadth and sense of space and is sumptuously recorded, though this is not evident except at a higher than usual level-setting, when reproducing the record. Otherwise, at the beginning of the *Nocturne*, for example (fig. 70), the strings are barely audible. However, Haitink's reading leaves one with much to think about and impresses one as 'a symphony in dance' rather than a ballet. The sopranos of the Tanglewood Festival Chorus are not absolutely in tune, but the performance as a whole has greater warmth than Abbado's, even if it does not displace such old favourites as Monteux, Martinon, Previn and Dutoit.

With ripe Viennese horns adding opulence to Ravel's rich textures and with recording that brings an uncomfortably wide dynamic range, Levine's reading could hardly be more high-powered, with superb playing from the Vienna Philharmonic. He has a natural feeling for Ravelian rubato, but what the reading consistently lacks is poetry, for in even the gentlest moments there is a want of evocative warmth. Despite the excessive contrasts between loud and soft and some hardness on violin tone, the recording is one of the most brilliant the DG engineers have made recently in Vienna.

Daphnis et Chloé: suite No. 2.
(*) EMI Dig. CDC7 49964-2 [id.]. Oslo PO, Mariss Jansons – DUKAS: *L'apprenti sorcier*; RESPIGHI: *Feste romane.**

(M) (***) DG mono 427 783-2 [id.]. BPO, Wilhelm Furtwängler – SIBELIUS: *En Saga*; R. STRAUSS: *Till Eulenspiegel*.(***)

Whether played complete or in the familiar second suite of symphonic fragments, Ravel's score for *Daphnis et Chloé* must have magic. Mariss Jansons and the superb Oslo Philharmonic have more magic than some but not quite enough to displace from memory such accounts as the 1965 Karajan – without taking into consideration newer recordings. The playing is marvellous and at times breathtaking, but there is the occasional moment of self-consciousness, in the *Pantomime* and elsewhere, that invites admiration rather than inspiring that heady intoxication which the greatest interpreters can create in this score.

A *Daphnis suite* from a most unlikely source – Furtwängler, with whom we hardly associate the French master, and the Berlin Philharmonic Orchestra, recorded in 1944. Sonic limitations are soon forgotten, for this has a sense of colour and an ecstasy that elude most modern interpreters. Everything seems just right and the texture glows in a way that quite transcends the physical sound.

Daphnis et Chloé: suite No. 2; Ma Mère l'Oye (ballet): *suite; La valse.*
(M) **(*) EMI/Phoenixa stereo/mono CDM7 63763-2; *EG 763763-4* [id.]. Hallé O, Barbirolli – DEBUSSY: *La Mer*.**(*)

Barbirolli's languorous shaping of Ravel's great yearning string phrase in *Daybreak* really tugs at the heartstrings, its sense of ecstasy is profound and unforgettable. He has the advantage of using a chorus, very well balanced into the texture; indeed the 1959 recording is astonishingly full and luminous, more immediate in focus than the Debussy coupling. The flute playing in the *Pantomime* is wonderfully brilliant and sensitive; the *Danse générale* sparkles, with the chorus (not credited in the performance details) contributing very vividly to the climax. *La valse* also has plenty of temperament and excitement, and *Ma Mère l'Oye* great delicacy and innocence; the Hallé textures are ravishing, and the ear could hardly guess that this later recording derives from a 1957 mono master, so transluscent is the sound.

Ma Mère l'Oye (ballet): *suite.*
(M) ** EMI Dig. CD-EMX 2165; *TC-EMX 2165*. LPO, Sian Edwards – BRITTEN: *Young person's guide* ***; PROKOFIEV: *Peter and the wolf*.**(*)

Warm and beautiful orchestral playing from the LPO under Sian Edwards, but Ravel's magical score does not yield all its secrets here; its sense of gentle, innocent ecstasy is missing. Sian Edwards will present this music more perceptively when she has lived with it a little longer. Excellent recording.

Rapsodie espagnole.
(M) **(*) EMI CDM7 63572-2; *EG 763572-4* [id.]. Phd. O, Muti – CHABRIER: *España*; FALLA: *Three-cornered hat*.**(*)

Muti directs a performance which is aptly refined in its orchestral detail and also strikingly vigorous in the sharp definition of the dance rhythms. With a brightly lit recording, drenching everything in mid-day sunlight, the work here sounds more Spanish music than French. The vividness of the sound is matched by the virtuosity – often suitably restrained – of the players. But the concert overall (at 44 minutes) is short measure.

Le tombeau de Couperin; Valses nobles et sentimentales.
*** Chan. Dig. CHAN 8756; *ABTD 1395* [id.]. Ulster O, Yan Pascal Tortelier – DEBUSSY: *Children's corner* etc.***

Yan Pascal Tortelier's accounts of *Le tombeau de Couperin* and the *Valses nobles* have plenty of appeal. They come in harness with two Debussy pieces, also originally composed for the piano though transcribed by other hands; whether you want these performances rather than the many alternatives now on the market will doubtless depend on the matter of coupling. The Ulster Orchestra certainly play very well for Tortelier and the recording is every bit as good as predecessors in this series.

Valses nobles et sentimentales.
(*) DG Dig. 429 785-2; *429 785-4* [id.]. NYPO, Sinopoli – MUSSORGSKY: *Night* etc.*

With Sinopoli Ravel's *Valses nobles et sentimentales* is perhaps a shade too idiosyncratic, even though it is played superbly by the New York Philharmonic. At the beginning Sinopoli is attractively genial in his rhythmic impetus, rather than seeking to overwhelm the listener; but in the last three sections he takes Ravel's markings to an extreme, with the music almost coming to a halt in the middle of the *Moins vif.* Nevertheless the delicacy of the playing and the sensuous radiance of the texture remind one of *Ma Mère l'Oye*, and it is all too easy to be seduced.

CHAMBER MUSIC

Introduction and allegro for harp, flute, clarinet and string quartet; Pavane pour une enfante défunte; Sonata for violin and cello.
** DG Dig. 429 738-2 [id.] Vienna/Berlin Ens. – DEBUSSY: *Sonata for flute, viola and harp* etc.**

There are more otherworldly and magical accounts of the *Introduction and allegro*, but this is still more than acceptable. The flautist, Wolfgang Schultz, produces a rather richer, creamier sound than is ideal and his account of Quinto Maganini's transcription for flute and harp of the *Pavane pour une enfante défunte* is too much of a good thing. The disc is valuable for including the rarely heard *Sonata for violin and cello* in a very rich and full-bodied performance by Gerhart Hetzel and Georg Faust.

Piano trio in A min.
(*) Decca Dig. 425 860-2; *425 860-4* [id.]. Thibaudet, Bell, Isserlis – CHAUSSON: *Concert.*(*)

(i) *Piano trio in A min.;* (ii) *Sonatine: Menuet.*
(M) (**) RCA mono GD 87871; *GK 87871* [7871-2-RG; *7871-4-RG*]. Heifetz; (i) Rubinstein, Piatigorsky; (ii) Bay – DEBUSSY: *Sonata* etc.(**); RESPIGHI: *Sonata* (***); MARTINŮ: *Duo.****

Joshua Bell, Jean-Yves Thibaudet and Steven Isserlis are not a permanent trio like the Beaux Arts (Philips), the Borodin (Chandos) or the Trio Zingara (Collins), but nevertheless they show keen responsiveness in their account of the Ravel. These gifted players are second to none in sensitivity, and both Bell and Isserlis play with great tonal finesse and artistry. They are recorded with great clarity and presence, and those wanting this particular coupling will find much to admire. All the same, their Chausson *Concert* is not a first choice, nor is their Ravel more satisfying than that of the Beaux Arts (coupled with the Chausson *Trio* on Philips 411 141-2).

It goes without saying that the million-dollar trio (Heifetz, Rubinstein and Piatigorsky), recorded in 1950, play the Ravel like a million dollars, yet its inspired opening is curiously lacking in magic and atmosphere. Peerless though the playing is, this is not a version to which one would often be tempted to return when the Beaux Arts is to hand.

Sonatine en Trio (arr. Salzedo).
(B) *** Van. VBD 25002. Orpheus Trio – with Recital.***

Carlos Salzedo's transcription of Ravel's *Sonatine* for piano into a *Sonatine en Trio*, for flute, viola and harp, is obviously inspired by Debussy's *Sonata* for the same combination of instruments. It is a great success; in some ways its atmosphere and texture make it even more enjoyable than the original and it is beautifully played and recorded here.

String quartet in F.
(*) Pickwick Dig. MCD 17; *MCC 17* [id.]. New World Qt – DEBUSSY: *Quartet* **(*); DUTILLEUX: *Ainsi la nuit.**

The Harvard-based New World Quartet give an admirable account of the Ravel, a shade overprojected at times, and the leader's expressive rubato and that of the violist may not be to all tastes. Well recorded though it is, it does not displace existing recommendations though it offers the inducement of a Dutilleux rarity. However, first choice for this coupling with the Debussy *Quartet* rests either with the outstanding Melos version (DG 419 750-2) or, at mid-price, with the thoroughly committed Chilingirian account (EMI CD-EMX 2156 [CDM7 63483-2]; *TC-EMX 2156*).

Tzigane.
(*) DG Dig. 429 729-2 [id.]. Gil Shaham, Gerhard Oppitz – FRANCK: *Sonata*; SAINT-SAËNS: *Violin sonata No. 1.*(*)

Gil Shaham gives an impressive account of Ravel's celebrated display piece, coupling it with the delightful Saint-Saëns *D minor Sonata* and a fine version of the Franck *Sonata*.

Violin sonata in G.
*** Collins Dig. 1112-2; *1112-4* [id.]. Lorraine McAslan, John Blakely – DEBUSSY; SAINT-SAËNS: *Sonatas.****

Lorraine McAslan is a gifted young player who made a strong impression with her recent record of the Britten *Violin concerto*. She possesses a strong musical personality as well as excellent technique and a wide command of colour and dynamics. She is splendidly partnered by John Blakely, and their account of the *Sonata* is as characterful as any in the catalogue.

PIANO DUET

Boléro; Introduction and allegro; Ma Mère l'Oye; Rapsodie espagnole; La valse.
❀ *** Chan. Dig. CHAN 8905; *ABTD 1514* [id.]. Louis Lortie and Helène Mercier.

Louis Lortie has already made a solo Ravel record for Chandos (see our main volume, p. 836) and has given an impressive account of himself in the two *Concertos*; but his recital for piano (four hands and two pianos) with his Canadian partner, Helène Mercier, is quite magical. As with his solo recital, the acoustic is that of The Maltings, Snape, and the result is quite outstanding sonically: you feel that you have only to stretch out and you can touch the instruments. The transcriptions are, of course, Ravel's own – he was an absolute master of this art – and, given the quality of the playing, one hardly misses the orchestra, whether it be in the *Feria* of the *Rapsodie espagnole* or the mysterious half-colours of the *Prélude á la nuit*; these artists command an exceptionally wide range of colour and dynamic nuance. Probably not all listeners will relish the idea of the *Introduction and allegro* on two pianos, yet Ravel's transcription, particularly in their hands, is stunningly effective, as – even more surprisingly – is *Boléro*, which is omitted in the much-admired disc of Stephen Coombs and Christopher Scott.

SOLO PIANO MUSIC

Jeux d'eau; Menuet sur le nom de Haydn; Miroirs; Pavane pour une infante défunte; Sonatine; Valses nobles et sentimentales.
** EMI Dig. CDC7 49942-2 [id.]. Cécile Ousset.

The distinguished French pianist offers almost 70 minutes of Ravel, and there are some fine things during the course of her recital. However, she can seem a little too steely-fingered in forte or fortissimo passages; though there are many felicities, this CD would not be the best starting point for a Ravel collection; readers should turn first to Lortie or any of the fine rivals listed in our main volume. Of course Cécile Ousset produces some moments of poetry, but there is more sensitive and imaginative Ravel playing to be heard on disc, though little which is better served by the engineers.

VOCAL MUSIC

Chansons madécasses; 3 Poèmes de Stéphane Mallarmé.
❀ (M) *** Decca 425 948-2 [id.]. Dame Janet Baker, Melos Ens. (with *Recital of French songs* *** ❀).

Superb singing from Dame Janet, her voice at its most radiant in 1966, and a wonderfully sympathetic accompaniment from members of the Melos group, matched by a recording which spins a lovely web of atmospheric sound.

Reger, Max (1873–1916)

Piano concerto in F min., Op. 114
(M) ** Sony MPK 46452 [id.]. Rudolf Serkin, Phd. O, Ormandy – PROKOFIEV: *Piano concerto No. 4.*(***)

Reger's *Piano concerto* is a remarkable and powerful composition. Its dark opening momentarily suggests Shostakovich! No one but Reger, however, could have conceived the rugged, Brahmsian piano writing. The slow movement is a contemplative, rapt piece that touches genuine depths. Less successful, perhaps, is the rhetorical finale. Serkin gives a magisterial performance and is well supported by the Philadelphia Orchestra under Ormandy; this record has considerable documentary value, even though the early-1960s sound is not very inviting and is even rather harsh in its CD transfer (the outstanding mono coupling is much more agreeable!).

Variations and fugue on a theme by Mozart, Op. 132.
❀ *** Ph. Dig. 422 347-2 [id.]. Bav. RSO, C. Davis – HINDEMITH: *Symphonic metamorphosis.****

It is little short of amazing that Reger's *Variations and fugue on a theme by Mozart* is so little heard in the concert hall, for it deserves great popularity. Sir Colin Davis's account with the Bavarian Radio Symphony Orchestra is the best since Karl Boehm's pioneering pre-war 78s. The playing has great subtlety and the strings produce a particularly cultured sound (though one could reasonably ask how it could be otherwise with this wonderful orchestra). The whole performance has a radiance and glow that does full justice to this masterpiece, which is not only scored with great delicacy but has wit and tenderness in equal measure. The Philips recording is state of the art. Recommended with enthusiasm.

8 Geistliche Gesänge, Op. 138.
*** Koch Bayer Dig. BR 100084. Frankfurt Vocal Ens., Ralf Otto – MARTIN: *Mass for double choir.****

These eight spiritual songs are simple homophonic settings of various sacred texts. Only one of them takes longer than three minutes, but all of them are of a substance that belies their length and have a gravely expressive beauty that is conveyed well by this excellent Frankfurt choir, who also offer an outstanding performance of Frank Martin's *Mass for double choir*. Excellent recording.

Reich, Steve (born 1936)

8 Lines.
*** Virgin Dig. VC7 91168-2; *VC7 91168-4* [id.]. LCO, Warren-Green – ADAMS: *Shaker loops* *** ❀; GLASS: *Company* etc.***; HEATH: *Frontier.****

Steve Reich's *8 Lines* (originally called an *Octet*) is minimalism in its most basic form, and, although the writing is full of good-humoured vitality, the listener without a score could be forgiven for sometimes thinking that 'the needle had got stuck in the groove'. The performance is expert and the recording seems admirable.

Music for 18 musicians.
(**) ECM 821 417-2; *821 417-4* [id.]. Ens., composer.

With only a single track to cover all 56 minutes-plus of this characteristic example of minimalism, this is for Reich devotees. The newcomer, without any help on identifying individual sections (Pulse – Sections I–X – Pulse) can only sit back in a hypnotic trance and perhaps from time to time relish a pretty timbre, or even a distant echo of *Petrushka*, against the unceasing beat. Better to try Reich in less expansive mood first.

Music for a large ensemble; Octet; Violin phase.
(**) ECM 827 287-2; *827 287-4* [id.]. Steve Reich & musicians.

Violin phase presents minimalism at its most relentless, with the violinist playing against one, then two and finally three pre-recorded tracks of himself, until the scrape of double-stopping drills itself into the mind beyond endurance. The other two works are much more considerate to the listener, with the *Music for a large ensemble* relying on gentle marimba and xylophone textures like a translation of gamelan music. *Octet*, marginally longer than the other two works, brings brighter textures just as ear-tickling.

Tehillim.
** ECM 827 411-2 [id.]. Steve Reich & musicians, George Manahan.

Steve Reich is listed among the percussion players in *Tehillim*, with Manahan conducting, a work completed in 1982. The central focus, in this Hebrew setting of Psalms 19 and 18 (in that order), is on the vocal ensemble of four voices, a high soprano, two lyric sopranos and an alto. The minimalist technique is the same as in the purely instrumental works, but the result – with clapping and drumming punctuating the singing – has an element of charm rare in minimalist music. With jazzy syncopations and Cuban rhythms, the first of the two movements in this half-hour-long work, setting verses from Psalm 18, sounds like Bernstein's *Chichester Psalms* caught in a groove. The second starts slowly but speeds up for the verses of praise to the Lord and the final *Hallelujahs*. Clear, forward, analogue recording.

Respighi, Ottorino (1879–1936)

(i) *Adagio with variations for cello and orchestra; The Birds (Gli Ucelli); 3 Botticelli pictures (Trittico Botticelliano);* (ii) *Il tramonto.*
*** Chan. Dig. CHAN 8913; *ABTD 1517* [id.]. Bournemouth Sinf., Tamás Vásáry, (i) with Raphael Wallfisch; (ii) Linda Finnie.

This is the Respighi record of the year. Respighi's only work for cello and orchestra dates from 1920 and began life as a duo for cello and piano eight years earlier. It is not great music but is well worth having in a performance as sympathetic as this. *The Birds* is most beautifully played, with the freshest detail and, fine though Dorati's Mercury version is, it is good to have a first-class, modern, digital recording. The Chandos sound is equally colourful and vivid in the *Botticelli pictures* and Vásáry makes a good case for this colourful triptych (*La Primavera*, with its trilling aviary of birdsong; *L'adorazione dei Magi*, with its quotation from the hymn, *O come, o come Emmanuel*; and the engagingly evocative *La nascita di Venere*). But what makes this collection especially appealing is the inclusion of *Il tramonto* ('The sunset'). It is a glorious work and is radiantly sung here by Linda Finnie, whose voice and warm Italianate line remind one a little of the young Tebaldi. This is an even finer account than Carol Madalin's on Hyperion (see our main volume, pp. 844–5) and it is also more sensibly coupled.

Ancient airs and dances: suite No. 3 for strings.
** Denon Dig. CO 77150 [id.] I Solisti Italiani – MALIPIERO: *String quartet No. 1* ***; WOLF: *Italian serenade.***

Respighi's third suite sounds appealingly delicate and transparent in texture on a small group of strings, as the opening *Italiana* readily demonstrates in this fine Denon recording. However, the performance itself, though well played, lacks spontaneity and charm; Marriner is much to be preferred (Philips 420 485-2 – see our main volume, p. 843).

(i) *The Birds* (suite); *Brazilian impressions;* (ii) *The Fountains of Rome; The Pines of Rome.*
(M) **(*) Mercury 432 007-2 [id.]. (i) LSO; (ii) Minneapolis SO, Antal Dorati

This Mercury reissue combines the contents of two analogue LPs, one of which had not previously been issued in the UK, probably because of the established and justly famous RCA/Reiner/Chicago coupling of the same music. This has reappeared on CD in the USA [RCA RCD1-5407] but is still awaited in the UK. The Minneapolis Northrop Auditorium – for all the skill of the Mercury engineers – never produced a web of sound with quite the magical glow which Orchestral Hall, Chicago, could provide in the late 1950s. Nevertheless, in Dorati's hands the opening and closing evocations of the *Fountains of Rome*, cleanly focused as they are by the use of Telefunken 201 microphones, have a unique, shimmering brightness which certainly suggests a sun-drenched landscape, although the turning of the Triton fountain brings a shrill burst of sound that almost assaults in the ears. The tingling detail in the companion *Pines of Rome* is again matched by Dorati's powerful sense of atmosphere, so that the sepulchral Catacombs sequence, with its haunting nightingale's song, has a disturbing melancholy, while the finale has an overwhelming juggernaut forcefulness. The coupling of *The Birds* and *Brazilian impressions* was made in the smoother, warmer acoustics of Watford Town Hall in 1957, and here the vividness of detail particularly suits Dorati's spirited account of *The Birds*, bringing pictorial piquancy of great charm and strongly projected dance-rhythms. The liveliness of the LSO playing is most appealing. Resphighi wrote *Brazilian impressions* while spending the summer of 1927 in Rio de Janeiro. The triptych recall's Debussy's *Ibéria*, though it is much less subtle. The second impression invokes the *Dies irae* in sinister fashion; it is named after Butantan, famous for its reptile institute, where poisonous snakes are bred in large numbers for the production of serum. The finale, *Canzone e danza*, certainly glitters in Dorati's hands even if overall this work does not represent Respighi at his finest.

Concerto Gregoriano; Poema autunnale.
**(*) Marco Polo Dig. 8.220152 [id.]. Nishizaki, Singapore SO, Choo Hoey.

The Roman trilogy has overshadowed Respighi's other music to such an extent that many music-lovers are unaware even of the existence of his *Piano* and *Violin concertos*. The *Concerto Gregoriano* (for violin) comes from 1921 and, as its name suggests, is strongly modal in character, though its scoring is fully characteristic and at times lush. The first two movements are linked together and are both slow and ruminative in feeling, while there is a longer and more vigorous finale. Takako Nishizaki and the Singapore orchestra under Choo Hoey give a thoroughly committed account of both this work and the slightly later *Poema autunnale*, though the rather subfusc recording inhibits a totally unqualified welcome.

(i) *Piano concerto in modo misolidio. 3 Preludes on Gregorian themes.*
** Marco Polo Dig. 8.220176 [id.]. Sonya Hanke, (i) with Sydney SO, Myer Fredman.

Respighi's *Piano concerto in modo misolidio* dates from 1925 and was first heard that same year in New York with Respighi himself as soloist and Mengelberg conducting. It is a far from ineffective piece, but the present recording falls short of the ideal: the piano is a bit close and the instrument does not sound in absolutely first-class condition (there are some tired notes). The *Three Preludes on Gregorian themes* for piano were written in 1919 and dedicated to Casella. They were subsequently scored and another movement added to become the more familiar *Vetrate di chiesa*. Good, but not particularly outstanding, playing from the Australian pianist, Sonya Hanke, with the Sydney orchestra.

Feste romane.
*** EMI Dig. CDC7 49964-2 [id.]. Oslo PO, Mariss Jansons – DUKAS: *L'apprenti sorcier* ***; RAVEL: *Daphnis.***(*)
(M) (*) BMG/RCA mono GD 60328; *GK 60328* (4) [60328-2-RG; *60328-4-RG*]. Phd. O, Toscanini – Concert.(**(*))

Feste romane; The Pines of Rome; The Fountains of Rome.
(B) **(*) RCA VD 60486; *VK 60486*. Phd. O, Ormandy.
(M) (**(*)) BMG/RCA mono GD 60262; *GK 60262* [60262-2-RG; *60262-4-RG*]. NBC SO, Toscanini.

In *Feste romane* Mariss Jansons gets playing of high voltage and no mean virtuosity from the Oslo Philharmonic. They may not be a first choice but they certainly rank high among the very finest versions, and anyone wanting this particular coupling need not hesitate. The recording is very clean and well detailed, though not wanting in atmosphere.

Ormandy plays all three works with enormous gusto and panache, and the orchestral virtuosity is thrilling, with the robust vulgarity of *Feste romane* breathtaking in its unbuttoned zest. The cascade at the turning on of the Triton fountain is like a dam bursting, and all the pictorial effects spring vividly to life. The 1973/4 recording is immensely spectacular. It is atmospheric too, but brightly lit to the point of garishness, and not all ears will respond to the tingling brilliance. But the performances make an unforgettable impact.

Toscanini's recordings of the Roman trilogy are in a class of their own; they (and Reiner in the *Pines* and the *Fountains*, still awaited on CD in the UK) are the yardstick by which all others are measured. This is electrifying playing, which comes over well in this transfer – though, to be fair, the old LPs (particularly the German RCA pressings of the *Feste romane*) had a rounder, fuller (less acidulated) tone on the strings above the stave.

Violin sonata in B min.
(M) (***) RCA mono GD 87871; *GK 87871* [7871-2-RG; *7871-4-RG*]. Heifetz, Bay – DEBUSSY: *Sonata* (**); RAVEL: *Trio* etc.(**); MARTINŮ: *Duo*.***

Heifetz and Emanuel Bay recorded this sonata in 1950 (on the day after the Debussy, with which this is coupled) and their performance has never been surpassed, not even by the superbly played and sumptuously recorded version by Kyung Wha Chung and Krystian Zimerman (DG 427 617-2). The latter remain the obvious recommendation, for it is difficult to summon up great enthusiasm for the Heifetz–Rubinstein–Piatigorsky Ravel *Trio*. All these performances, save the Martinů, are in mono.

La sensitiva.
*** Virgin VC7 91164-2; *VC7 91164-4* [id.]. J. Baker, City of L. Sinf., Hickox – BERLIOZ: Mélodies (including *Nuits d'été*).***

Tautly structured over its span of more than half an hour, Respighi's setting of Shelley's poem, *The sensitive plant* (in Italian translation), is a most beautiful piece, which Dame Janet and Richard Hickox treat to a glowing first recording. The vocal line, mainly declamatory, is sweetly sympathetic and the orchestration is both rich and subtle. An unexpected but very enjoyable and generous coupling for the Berlioz items.

Rimsky-Korsakov, Nikolay (1844–1908)

Capriccio espagnol, Op. 34.
(B) *** DG Compact Classics 413 422-2 (2); *413 422-4* [id.]. BPO, Maazel – BIZET: *L'Arlésienne; Carmen*; DUKAS: *L'apprenti sorcier*; CHABRIER: *España*.**(*) (CD only: FALLA: *Three-cornered hat:* dances **).
(M) **(*) Decca Dig. 430 700-2; *430 700-4* [id.]. Montreal SO, Dutoit – MUSSORGSKY: *Night*; TCHAIKOVSKY: *1812* etc.**(*)

Maazel's 1960 recording of the *Capriccio espagnol* remains one of the very finest of recorded performances. With gorgeous string and horn playing, and a debonair relaxed virtuosity in the *Scene e canto gitano* leading to breathtaking bravura in the closing section, every note in place, this is unforgettable. The remastering for the Compact Classics tape has smoothed the treble a little, but otherwise the sound remains vivid. With Claudio Abbado's splendid account of Bizet's *L'Arlésienne* and *Carmen* suites, this is worth acquiring for the car, even if some duplication may be involved with the other items. The pair of remastered CDs also includes excerpts from Falla's *Three-cornered hat* ballet.

Dutoit's *Capriccio espagnol* is given a genial performance though one not lacking in brilliance in terms of the orchestral playing. The recording is characteristic of the Montreal acoustic: full and warm, with luminous detail.

Scheherazade (symphonic suite), *Op. 35.*
(M) *** EMI Dig. CD-EMX 2168; *TC-EMX 2168.* LPO, Takuo Yuasa – PROKOFIEV: *Lieutenant Kijé.****
(B) **(*) DG Compact Classics *413 155-4* [id.]. Boston SO, Ozawa – STRAVINSKY: *Firebird suite*; KHACHATURIAN: *Gayaneh.***(*)
(*) Denon Dig. CO 77068 [id.]. Philh. O, Emmanuel Krivine – MUSSORGSKY: *Night on the bare mountain.**

Scheherazade, Op. 35; Capriccio espagnol, Op. 34.
❀ *** Telarc Dig. CD 80208 [id.]. LSO, Sir Charles Mackerras.

(i) *Scheherazade, Op. 35;* (ii) *Russian Easter festival overture, Op. 36;* (i) *Tsar Saltan, Op. 57: March; Flight of the bumble-bee.*
(B) **(*) RCA VD 60487; *VK 60487.* (i) LSO, Previn; (ii) Chicago SO, Stokowski.

Two new versions of Rimsky-Korsakov's glitteringly sensuous orchestral showpiece now take their places at the top of the list, both being readily comparable with Haitink's famous 1974 Philips version (420 898-2; *420 898-4*) which dominated the LP catalogue for over a decade. Each has the freshness of impact of the Haitink performance, although Mackerras is a more dynamic interpreter of this vividly Russian score and he has the advantage of a superb Telarc digital recording – produced by Jack Renner, who masterminded the famous Mussorgsky *Pictures at an exhibition* on the same label – which is very much in the demonstration class. Mackerras's reading combines gripping drama with romantic ardour, subtlety of colour with voluptuousness; he is helped, as is Haitink, by a wonderfully beguiling portrait of Scheherazade herself, provided by his orchestral leader, in this case Kees Hulsmann. The solo violin is naturally balanced within the overall orchestral picture, yet Hulsmann's gently alluring image dominates the narrative. Scheherazade's presence is felt at the very opening through the vivid kaleidoscoping colours of the second movement, blossoming in the ravishing slow movement, which recalls Beecham in its elegant sumptuousness. She returns in gentle triumph, at the end of the grippingly thrustful finale with its spectacular climax, to bring a magical closing meditation. The charming closing reverie, with the Sultan lying peacefully satiated in the arms of his young wife, their themes blissfully intermingled, is unforgettable. After an appropriate pause, Mackerras then delivers a thrilling bravura account of *Capriccio espagnol*, lushly opulent in the variations, glittering in the exotic *Scena e canta gitano*, and carrying all before it in the impetus of the closing *Fandango asturiano*.

On EMI's mid-priced label, Eminence, comes another romantically compulsive account of *Scheherazade*, very responsively played by the same orchestra which was so successful in the earlier, Haitink version. Again there is a freshness and an absence of routine in the music-making, and the sinuously supple contribution of the orchestral leader, Stephen Bryant, in the role of the heroine is believably placed in the orchestral texture. Takuo Yuasa's reading is more spacious, less urgent than Mackerras's, but his evocation of the sea in the first movement is very compelling, and the central movements are full of colour and warmth, with a burst of passion to climax the idyllic rapture of the slow movement. The finale brings grippingly animated orchestral virtuosity and a powerful climax, with the tam-tam flashing out at the moment of the shipwreck. The poetic close has a lustrous rapture, even if it is not quite as enchanting as on the Mackerras disc. At mid-price, with a splendid Prokofiev coupling, no one will be disappointed with this, for the sound is full-bodiedly brilliant, with an attractive ambient glow.

Previn's tempi are expansive, but the first movement is commandingly spacious. The inner movements are unexpectedly cool, the very opposite of vulgar, but, with rhythmic pointing which is characteristically crisp, the result grows attractive on repetition, while the finale brings one of the most dramatic and brilliant performances of that showpiece ever recorded. Previn's fill-ups provide a charming bonus, particularly the *Tsar Saltan march*. The recording is outstanding for its late-1960s vintage and it has been richly and vividly transferred to CD. With Stokowski's brilliant and colourful (1968) account of the *Russian Easter festival overture* added for good measure, this remains competitive in the bargain range.

Ozawa's version, available on a Compact Classics cassette, makes a fair bargain alternative if the couplings, Maazel's early stereo recording of the *Firebird suite* and Rozhdestvensky's *Gayaneh*, are suitable. It is an attractive performance, richly recorded. The first movement is strikingly spacious, building to a fine climax; if the last degree of vitality is missing from the central movements, the orchestral playing is warmly vivid. The finale is lively enough, if not earth-shaking in its excitement; the reading as a whole has plenty of colour and atmosphere, however, and it is certainly enjoyable. The chrome-tape transfer is sophisticated.

The Denon recording is undoubtedly in the demonstration class in terms of its full orchestral sound, with sonorously weighty brass and plenty of overall brilliance. The snag is that Jean-Jacques Kantorow's solo contribution is less flatteringly caught, and at times his sinuous timbre is in danger of sounding wiry. He plays sympathetically but fails to dominate the performance in the way of the soloists on both competing versions. Even so, the performance is easy to enjoy. Krivine's pacing is convincing: the slow movement is beautifully played and the finale is thrilling in its impetus and virtuosity, helped by the vivid sound. But the very close of the work is not as beguiling as on either the Telarc or EMI versions.

Symphony No. 2 (Antar), Op. 9.

(B) ** Van. VCD 72019 [id.]. Utah SO, Abravanel – IPPOLITOV-IVANOV: *Caucasian sketches.***

Antar is unevenly inspired, although its motto theme is memorable and the third-movement scherzo contains some of Rimsky-Korsakov's most attractive invention. The scoring too is full of felicitous touches. Abravanel's is a characteristically direct account, well played and recorded but without any striking individuality. Good value, if the couplings are required. (They include also Glière's *Russian sailor's dance* and two excerpts from Tchaikovsky's *Swan Lake*.)

Rodrigo, Joaquín (born 1902)

Concierto de Aranjuez.

❀ (M) *** Decca Dig. 430 703-2; *430 703-4* [id.]. Carlos Bonell, Montreal SO, Dutoit – FALLA: *El amor brujo* etc.*** ❀

(B) *** Sony MBK 45642 [id.]. John Williams, ECO, Barenboim – VILLA-LOBOS: *Concerto.****

(M) **(*) EMI Dig. CDD7 63886-2 [id.]; *ET 763886-4*. Alfonso Moreno, LSO, Bátiz – FALLA: *Nights*; TURINA: *Danzas fantásticas.***(*)

In our main volume (on p. 851) we neglected to indicate – in our listing, if not in our review – that the much-praised Bonell/Dutoit recording of the *Concierto* – still our first choice – remained coupled (on Decca 417 748-2) with the *Fantasia para un gentilhombre*. But Decca have reissued it a second time at mid-price (again on the Ovation label, as above) and now the *Fantasia* has disappeared and instead we are offered Alicia de Larrocha's splendid digital recording of Falla's *Nights in the gardens of Spain* plus Dutoit's outstanding complete *El amor brujo*. This is a very attractive pairing and the reasons for the success of the Rodrigo performance remain unaltered: an exceptionally clear, atmospheric and well-balanced digital recording plus Bonell's imaginative account of the solo part, and the strong characterization of the orchestral accompaniments by Charles Dutoit and his excellent Montreal orchestra. A feeling of freshness pervades every bar of the orchestral texture. De Larrocha's luminous account of *Nights in the gardens of Spain* is equally distinguished, and this makes one of the most desirable compilations of Spanish music in the catalogue.

John Williams's second analogue recording of the *Concierto*, with Barenboim, made in 1974, is superior to his earlier version with Ormandy. The playing has marvellous point and spontaneity; the *Adagio* had rarely before been played with this degree of poetic feeling. There is a hint of rhythmic over-emphasis in the finale, but in general the performance is first class; if the digital version (Sony CD 37848) is even finer, this remains fully satisfying. The CD transfer is first class and the orchestral sound very natural, although the guitar image is larger than life.

The Moreno/Bátiz partnership works well enough in this famous concerto, with the digital recording lending a bright-as-a-button effect to a performance which is thoroughly sympathetic without being really distinctive. However, the equally vivid couplings are well played, and altogether this makes quite an attractive Spanish triptych.

(i) *Concierto de Aranjuez; Fantasia para un gentilhombre;* (ii) *Concierto serenata for harp and orchestra.*
(B) ** DG Compact Classics 413 156-2 (2); *413 156-4* [id.]. (i) Yepes, Spanish R. & TV O, Alonso; (ii) Zabaleta, Berlin RSO, Marzendorfer – FALLA: *Nights in the gardens of Spain* **(*) (CD only: BACARISSE: *Guitar concertino* *(*); CASTELNUOVO-TEDESCO: *Guitar concerto* ***).

The DG Compact Classics reissue offers Yepes' disappointing, 1970 coupling of the two most famous Rodrigo concertante works, with Odon Alonso not the most imaginative conductor (he is rhythmically rather stiff in the finale of the *Concierto*). Yepes is at his finest in the *Adagio* and plays nobly in the *Fantasia* (which is generally more successful); but the dry, studio-ish recording sounds even drier on CD in its remastered format, while the *Concierto serenata*, played with much piquancy and charm by Zabaleta, is made to seem very sharply etched. As can be seen, these same recordings are also available on an equivalent tape, made from the original analogue master and sounding rather more atmospheric and without the brighter, sharper treble. However, the pair of CDs includes two extra concertos.

Rosenberg, Hilding (1892–1985)

String quartets Nos. (i) *1;* (ii) *6;* (iii) *12.*
** Caprice CAP 21352 [id.]. (i) Kyndel Qt; (ii) Gotland Qt; (iii) Copenhagen Qt.

Hilding Rosenberg, the leading Swedish composer after Stenhammar, was a powerful symphonist. Like his somewhat younger Danish contemporary, Holmboe, he has made an important contribution to the quartet medium. However, the *Quartets* are not the equal of his symphonies, the finest of which (No. 5) remains unrecorded, nor are they even in quality. The *First* comes from 1920 and is dedicated to his teacher, Stenhammar, but in 1956 the composer returned to the score and revised it. There are Bergian touches here and there, and in some ways this is musically the most interesting of the three. This CD offers the 1956 Swedish Radio recording, in passable sound, of its première, performed with great conviction by the Kyndel Quartet. The *Sixth* enjoyed cult status in Sweden in the mid-1950s and prompted a commission from Swedish Radio for a further six. (They were greatly amazed when the composer delivered them all within the year!) It is a well-wrought piece but not as fresh or lyrical as the *Fourth*. No. 12 is arid and manufactured. The performances come from the 1970s (No. 6 could do with more finesse) and the recordings are satisfactory rather than distinguished.

String quartets Nos. (i) *2;* (ii) *5; 8.*
** Caprice CAP 21354 [id.]. (i) Lysell Qt; (ii) Gotland Qt.

The *Second* is one of the shortest of Rosenberg's twelve *Quartets* and one of the best. There is a distinctly French flavour to some of its ideas. The quality of the invention both here and in the *Fifth*, dedicated to Sibelius, is high, though the latter is not as naturally lyrical as No. 4. The *Eighth Quartet* is an uninteresting, rather anonymous piece.

String quartets Nos. (i) *4;* (ii) *7;* (iii) *6 Moments musicaux.*
** Caprice CAP 21353 [id.]. (i) Fresk Qt; (ii) Berwald Qt; (iii) Gotland Qt.

The *Fourth Quartet* comes from the same period as the *Third Symphony* and *The Revelation of St John the Divine* and is arguably the finest of the series. The thematic material is fresh and memorable, and there is a strong atmosphere. The playing of the Fresk Quartet is eminently serviceable. In both the *Seventh* and the more recent *Moments musicaux* of 1972, inspiration is thin.

Rosetti, Antoni (1750–92)

Horn concertos: in E flat, K.3:39; in E, K.3:42; in E, K3:44.
(B) *** CfP Dig. CD-CFP 4578; *TC-CFP 4578*. Barry Tuckwell, ECO.

The Bohemian composer, born Franz Anton Rössler, who adopted an Italian version of his name, wrote prolifically for the horn; the present concertos are characteristic of the taxing melodic line he provides for the soloist, with high-ranging lyrical tessitura contrasting with very florid arpeggios. He was especially good at rondo finales and the *E major Concerto*, K.3:42, shows him at his melodically most exuberant. Tuckwell's style is agreeably robust and he is very well recorded. He directs his own accompaniments with polish and spirit. This EMI collection is well worth having for anyone who enjoys horn concertos, although the invention here is far more conventional than those of Mozart. The EMI CD has exceptional realism and presence.

Rossini, Gioacchino (1792–1868)

La boutique fantasque (ballet, arr. Respighi) complete.
❀ (M) *** Sony Dig. MDK 46508 [id.]. Toronto SO, Andrew Davis – BIZET: *L'Arlésienne: suite No. 2* etc.

At last comes a really outstanding complete CD of *La boutique fantasque*, one of the great popular triumphs of Diaghilev's Ballets Russes. Respighi created a fully integrated and wonderfully colourful score from tuneful Rossinian miniatures, enhancing the originals with sumptuously brilliant orchestration imbued with an Italianate feeling for atmosphere. In the sympathetic hands of Andrew Davis there is never a dull bar, for Respighi's linking passages (usually omitted) are ingeniously crafted and he leads the ear on affectionately. The Toronto orchestra is on peak form, playing with glittering bravura and warmth; the gentler second half of the ballet is particularly enticing. The digital recording has a spectacularly wide dynamic range; the magical opening (here taken faster than usual) with gentle pizzicato strings evoking gleaming horn chords, at first a mere whisper, then expands gloriously. The vividness of the CBS sound is balanced by a glowing underlying warmth, and this becomes a demonstration disc for the digital era which recalls Ansermet's famous Decca mono LP of the early 1950s (LXT 2555), made with the LSO in the Kingsway Hall, London.

La boutique fantasque (ballet, arr. Respighi): *suite.*
(M) **(*) Chan. CHAN 6503 [id.]. SNO, Gibson – DUKAS: *L'apprenti sorcier*; SAINT-SAENS: *Danse macabre.***(*)
(M) **(*) Sony SBK 46340 [id.]; *40-46340.* Phd. O, Ormandy – TCHAIKOVSKY: *Sleeping Beauty:* highlights.**

Gibson's version of the suite is strikingly atmospheric. Helped by the glowing acoustics of Glasgow's City Hall, his performance sounds for all the world as if the Scottish conductor had first listened to Ansermet's famous Decca mono LP. Tempi are similar and the opening has much of the evocation that the Swiss maestro created. The orchestra is on its toes and plays with warmth and zest, and the 1973 recording has transferred vividly to CD. The only snag is the short playing time (37 minutes).

Ormandy presents Respighi's glittering orchestration with much brilliance and dash, and the Philadelphia Orchestra has all the sumptuousness one could ask for. This is more extrovert music-making than Gibson's and it is undoubtedly exhilarating, even if the effect of the recording is less refined. The playing time of the Sony CD is much more generous too, but not everyone will want the rather inflated coupling.

Overtures: *Il Barbiere di Siviglia; La Cenerentola; La gazza ladra; L'Italiana in Algeri; La scala di seta; Semiramide; William Tell.*
** DG Dig. 431 653-2; *431 653-4* [id.]. COE, Claudio Abbado.

Abbado's newest disc of Rossini overtures is a disappointment. The tightly disciplined playing is too tense: the cellos at the opening of *William Tell* are charmless, and Abbado's occasional tiny agogic phrase distortions seem eccentric rather than conveying affection. The actual playing is brilliantly polished, especially in *La scala di seta*, but the music is not allowed to smile. Only in *La Cenerentola* does the spick-and-span playing bring an element of abrasive wit to remind us of Abbado's splendid earlier (now mid-priced) collection with the LSO (DG 419 869-2; *419 869-4*), sparkling, vibrant and with a flavour of dry champagne.

Overtures: *Il Barbiere di Siviglia; La gazza ladra; L'Italiana in Algeri; La scala di seta; Il Signor Bruschino; Semiramide; William Tell.*
❀ *** EMI Dig. CDC7 54091-2; *EL 754091-4* [id.]. L. Classical Players, Norrington.

It is the drums that take a star role in Norrington's Rossini collection. They make their presence felt at the beginning and end of an otherwise persuasively styled reading of *Il Barbiere*; at the introduction of *La gazza ladra*, where the snares rattle spectacularly and antiphonally; creating tension more distinctly than usual at the beginning of *Semiramide*, and bringing tumultuous thunder to the Storm sequence in *William Tell.* Of course the early wind instruments are very characterful too, with plenty of piquant touches: the oboe colouring is nicely spun in *L'Italiana in Algeri* and properly nimble in *La scala di seta*, a particularly engaging performance, mainly because of the woodwind chirpings. The brass also make their mark, with the stopped notes on the hand horns adding character to the solo quartet in *Semiramide*, and both horns and trumpets giving a brilliant edge to the announcement of the galop in *William Tell*. The strings play with relative amiability and a proper sense of line and are obviously determined to please the ear as well as to stimulate; altogether these performances offer a very refreshing new look over familiar repertoire. The recording is first class.

Overtures: *Il barbiere di Siviglia; La gazza ladra; L'Italiana in Algeri; La scala di seta; William Tell.*
(B) *** DG Compact Classics *431 185-4* [id.]. BPO, Karajan – VERDI: *Overtures.****

Karajan's virtuoso Rossini performances are superbly polished and vivid. *La scala di seta* abandons almost all decorum when played as brilliantly as here, but this music-making is nothing if not exhilarating. The 1971 recordings are crisply transferred with plenty of supporting weight and good ambience. With equally distinguished Verdi for coupling, this is one of the finest of the later Compact Classics tapes.

Cantata: *Giovanna d'Arco*. Songs: *L'âme délaissée; Ariette à l'ancienne; Beltà crudele; Canzonetta spagnuola (En medio a mis colores); La grande coquette (Ariette pompadour); La légende de Marguerite; Mi lagnerò tacendo* (5 settings including *Sorzico* and *Stabat Mater*); *Nizza; L'Orpheline du Tyrol (Ballade élégie); La pastorella; La regata veneziana* (3 songs in Venetian dialect); *Il risentimento; Il trovatore.*
*** Decca Dig. 430 518-2 [id.]. Cecilia Bartoli, Charles Spencer.

The songs of Rossini's old age were not all trivial, and this brilliantly characterized selection – with the pianist as imaginative as the singer – gives a delightful cross-section. The big solo cantata on the theme of Joan of Arc provides a culmination, but it is also fascinating to have five entirely different settings of the same text, *Mi lagnerò tacendo*, each representing a totally different but entirely apt mood. Bartoli's artistry readily encompasses such a challenge, a singer who, even at this early stage of her career, is totally in command both technically and artistically. The recording, too, has splendid presence.

OPERA

Il Barbiere di Siviglia: highlights.
(B) * Pickwick (DG) IMPX 9022. Gianna d'Angelo, Capecchi, Monti, Tadeo, Bav. RSO, Bartoletti.

The Pickwick/DG selection is reasonably generous (58 minutes) and includes most of the key numbers. Gianna d'Angelo sings very sweetly as Rosina, her coloratura is impressively clean, but there is little of the minx in her characterization. Capecchi's *Largo al factotum* is breezy, but elsewhere he gives a somewhat over-respectable account of the Barber. The recording emerges vividly enough on CD but, curiously, opens with a truncated account of the Overture, lasting 2 minutes 47 seconds! An easy first choice for a recording of *Il Barbiere* is the Philips set with Baltsa, Thomas Allen and Araiza. This was Sir Neville Marriner's first opera recording, and he finds a rare sense of fun in Rossini's witty score (411 058-2). There is also a fine highlights disc taken from Marriner's complete set (Philips 412 266-2).

Il Barbiere di Siviglia: highlights; *La Cenerentola:* highlights.
(B) **(*) DG Compact Clasics *427 714-4* [id.] (from complete recordings, with Berganza, Alva, Prey, Capecchi, Amb. Op. Ch. or Scottish Op. Ch., LSO, Abbado).

Abbado's 1972 recordings of two favourite Rossini operas have a pleasing freshness. Both overtures are included, and the lack of theatrical feeling matters less in highlights; certainly Teresa Berganza, with her agile coloratura, and the stylish Luigia Alva together lead a reliable cast, with Herman Prey as Figaro in *The Barber* and Renato Capecchi as Dandini in *Cenerentola* bringing plenty of sparkle to their performances. The tape transfer reproduces the voices most naturally.

La Cenerentola (complete).
** Sony/CBS S2K 46433 (2) [id.]; *40-46433*. Valentini-Terrani, Araiza, Dara, Trimarchi, Ravaglia, W. German R. (male) Ch., Cappella Coloniensis, Ferro.

Ferro, one of the ablest of Rossini scholars who earlier recorded *L'Italiana in Algeri* impressively, here conducts an easy-going, at times pedestrian account of *La Cenerentola*, well played and well sung but lacking some of the fizz essential in Rossini. Even the heroine's final brilliant aria hangs fire, and that in spite of warm, positive singing from Valentini-Terrani, whose stylish contribution is spoilt only by a high quota of intrusive aitches. The rest of the cast is strong and, apart from backward placing of the orchestra, the digital transfer is full and realistic; but the set cannot take precedence over the best earlier versions. Indeed Marriner's set of *Cenerentola*, following the pattern of *Il Barbiere* and with a similar cast, conveys Rossinian fun to the full (Philips 420 468-2).

La gazza ladra (complete).
(**) Sony Dig. S3T 45850 (3) [id.]; *40-45850*. Ricciarelli, Matteuzzi, Ramey, di Nissa, D'Intino, Furlanetto, Prague Philharmonic Ch., Turin RAI SO, Gelmetti.

Sadly, this live recording, made at the Rossini Festival in Pesaro in 1989, is too rough and unstylish to recommend with great enthusiasm, though it is valuable as a complete recording of a Rossini rarity, usually remembered for its overture alone. Often with distractingly slipshod ensemble from the singers, the whole work is coarsened. The sound too is dry and unflattering, and Gelmetti proves a vigorous but often rigid Rossinian, with a tendency to press too hard. Those shortcomings are the more frustrating when the cast is a strong one, with four excellent singers in the principal roles. The work itself is fascinating, an *opera semiseria*, with passages of romantic melodrama set against sparkling music such as one expects from the overture.

L'Italiana in Algeri: complete.
(M) *** Erato/Warner 2292 45404-2 (2) [id.]. Horne, Palacio, Ramey, Trimarchi, Battle, Zaccaria, Prague Ch., Sol. Ven., Scimone.

Scholarship as well as Rossinian zest have gone into Scimone's highly enjoyable version, beautifully played and recorded with as stylish a team of soloists as one can expect nowadays. The text is complete, the original orchestration has been restored (as in the comic duetting of piccolo and bassoon in the reprise in the overture) and alternative versions of certain arias are given as an appendix. Marilyn Horne makes a dazzling, positive Isabella, and Samuel Ramey is splendidly firm as Mustafa. Domenico Trimarchi is a delightful Taddeo and Ernesto Palacio an agile Lindoro, not coarse, though the recording does not always catch his tenor timbre well. Nevertheless the sound is generally very good indeed, and the fullness and atmosphere come out the more vividly on CD. In our main volume we gave a Rosette to Abbado's complete version of *L'Italiana in Algeri*, which also offers the restored complete text, and this remains our primary choice for the opera; however, the Erato two-CD set offers a splendid medium-price alternative.

L'Italiana in Algeri: highlights.
*** DG Dig. 429 414-2 [id.] (from complete set, with Baltsa, Raimondi, Dara, Lopardo, V. State Op. Konzertvereinigung, VPO, Abbado).

This 67-minute selection of highlights provides an admirable and sparkling sampler with well-chosen excepts; but this is surely a case where the complete recording would prove an even better investment (DG 427 331-2), and it involves only one more CD.

Roussel, Albert (1869–1937)

Bacchus et Ariane (ballet): *suite No. 2.*
(M) *** EMI CZS7 62669-2 (2) [Ang. CDMB 62647]. O de Paris, Serge Baudo (with Concert: *French music* ***).

Many collectors will rest content with a suite from Roussel's vivid ballet. Although Prêtre's digital version of the complete score can be strongly recommended (EMI CDC7 47376-2 – see our main volume), Serge Baudo achieves a performance of striking colour and intensity. The music's passion is projected as vehemently as its rhythmic feeling, and the Salle Wagram in Paris again provides an acoustic which brings out the rich colours as well as the evocation of the haunting introduction. The CD transfer of the 1969 recording is first class.

Symphonies Nos. 1 in D min. (Le Poème de la forêt), Op. 7; 3 in G min., Op. 42.
*** Erato/Warner Dig. 2292 45253-2; *2292 45253-4* [id.]. O Nat. de France, Dutoit.

The *First Symphony* belongs to the first decade of the present century, a particularly glorious one in French music which saw Debussy's *La Mer*, Ravel's *Shéhérazade* and d'Indy's *Jour d'été à la montagne*, though Roussel is closer to d'Indy than Debussy, even if plenty of Debussian echoes resonate in his pages. It is subtitled *Le Poème de la forêt* and, unlike its successors, it is relatively loosely held together. The first movement, *Forêt d'hiver*, is a kind of prelude, though the winter would be gentle and warm to northern ears, and the closing bars have some of the balminess of a Mediterranean night. The *Third* is both Roussel's most concentrated and his best-known symphony. Dutoit gets first-class playing from the Orchestre National and the recording is excellent. The delicate colourings of *Le Poème de la forêt* are heard to great advantage on CD and there is altogether admirable range, body and definition.

Symphonies Nos. 2 in B flat, Op. 23; 4 in A, Op. 53.
*** Erato/Warner Dig. 2292 45254-2; *2292 45254-4* [id.]. O Nat. de France, Dutoit.

The *Second Symphony* (1919–21) is the product of an abundantly resourceful musical mind and a richly stocked imagination, eminently well served by the finely developed feeling for craftsmanship Roussel had acquired from d'Indy. Indeed some of d'Indy's gravitas can be felt in the impressive, indeed thrilling, opening pages; this is a reading of great vitality. Dynamic and agogic markings are faithfully observed; however, it is not just the letter but also the spirit of the score that is well served. The Erato engineers do full justice to the dark and richly detailed textures. The scoring has some of the opulence of the first two Bax symphonies, particularly in the lower wind, and in some of the work's brooding, atmospheric slow sections. While recordings of the *Third* come and go, the *Fourth Symphony* of 1934 has been relatively neglected: it is a delightful score and has Roussel's most infectiously engaging Scherzo. Again, in this and the captivating finale, Dutoit and the French National Orchestra are in excellent form. CD does particular justice to the opulence of Roussel's scoring and is particularly imposing in the definition of the bottom end of the register.

Rubbra, Edmund (1901–86)

Symphonies Nos. 3, Op. 49; 4, Op. 53; Resurgam overture, Op. 149; A Tribute, Op. 56.
*** Lyrita Dig. SRCD 202 [id.]. Philh O, Norman Del Mar.

Neither symphony has been recorded before and both are strong works. Indeed the opening of the *Fourth* (1942) is of quite exceptional beauty and has a serenity and quietude that silence criticism. Although the scoring in climaxes is sometimes opaque, there is a consistent elevation of feeling and continuity of musical thought. Rubbra's music is steeped in English polyphony and, though his writing is resolutely diatonic and conservative in idiom, it could not come from any time other than our own. Unquestionably both symphonies have a nobility and spirituality that is rare in any age. The fine *Resurgam overture* is a late work.

Ruggles, Carl (1876–1971)

Sun-treader.
(M) *** DG 429 860-2 [id.]. Boston SO, Tilson Thomas – PISTON: *Symphony No. 2*; SCHUMAN: *Violin concerto.****

Carl Ruggles belongs to the same generation as Ives, whose exploratory outlook he shared, though not his carefree folksiness. Ruggles's music is expressionist and powerful, and he always structures finished works of art. *Sun-treader* was originally written in 1926 for a concert of contemporary music to be conducted by Edgard Varèse. It was finished only in 1931 and first heard in America in 1966. It takes its inspiration from Browning and, like so much of Ruggles's music, is uncompromising and makes tough but rewarding listening. Tilson Thomas and the Boston orchestra make out a very good case for it.

Saint-Saëns, Camille (1835–1921)

Carnival of the animals (arr. for brass by Peter Reeve).
(M) ** Decca 425 022-2; *425 022-4* [id.]. Philip Jones Brass Ens., Jones – MUSSORGSKY: *Pictures.****

A promising idea which proves disappointing in the execution, despite superb sound and plenty of colour – if very different from the original. But the pianists are sorely missed and a horn solo is no substitute for the cello in capturing the grace of Saint-Saëns' portrayal of *The Swan.* The wit, too, is coarsened, even if the geniality of the playing is evident. Fortunately there is an outstanding recording of the normal orchestral version with Anton Nel and Keith Snell comprising the witty piano duo, and Richard Stamp directing the Academy of London in a performance which is full of affectionate humour. Moeover this is coupled with Sir John Gielgud's unforgettable narration of Prokofiev's *Peter and the wolf* (Virgin VC7 90786-2; *VC7 90786-4*).

Cello concerto No. 1 in A min., Op. 33.
(B) *** DG 431 166-2; *431 166-4* [id.]. Heinrich Schiff, New Philh. O, Mackerras – FAURÉ: *Élégie*; LALO: *Cello concerto.****

Cello concerto in A min., Op. 33; Allegro appassionato, Op. 43.
(*) Ph. Dig. 432 084-2; *423 084-4* [id.]. Julian Lloyd Webber, ECO, Yan Pascal Tortelier – FAURÉ: *Élégie* **; D'INDY: *Lied* **(*); HONEGGER: *Concerto.*(*)

Schiff was very young at the time of this recording (1977), but there are no signs of immaturity here. He gives as eloquent an account of this concerto as any on record. He sparks off an enthusiastic response from Mackerras, and the recorded sound and balance are excellent. At bargain price, this deserves the strongest recommendation.

Julian Lloyd Webber plays both Saint-Saëns pieces with considerable virtuosity, though he does not command the range of sonority or colour possessed by some of his rivals listed in our main volume. He has the advantage of first-class accompaniment from Yan Pascal Tortelier and the ECO, impressively natural recorded sound and couplings of special interest.

(i) *Cello concerto No. 1 in A min., Op. 33;* (ii) *Piano concerto No. 2 in G min., Op. 22;* (iii) *Violin concerto No. 3, Op. 61.*
❀ (M) *** Sony/CBS Dig. MDK 46506 [id.]. (i) Yo-Yo Ma, O Nat. de France, Maazel; (ii) Cécile Licad, LPO, Previn; (iii) Cho-Liang Lin, Philh. O, Tilson Thomas.

Three outstanding performances from the early 1980s are admirably linked together in this highly desirable CBS mid-price reissue. Yo-Yo Ma's performance of the *Cello Concerto* is distinguished by fine sensitivity and beautiful tone. One is tempted to speak of him as being 'hypersensitive', so fine is his attention to light and shade, yet there is not a trace of posturing or affectation. The Orchestre National de France respond with playing of the highest quality throughout. Superb recorded sound which reflects great credit on the engineers, with added refinement and transparency of texture on CD.

Cécile Licad and the LPO under Previn turn in an eminently satisfactory reading of the *G minor Piano Concerto* that has the requisite delicacy in the Scherzo and seriousness elsewhere. It is a satisfying and persuasive performance of strong contrasts, with both power and thoughtfulness in the opening movement and a toccata-like brilliance of articulation in the finale. The recording is very realistic, with the acoustic of the London Henry Wood Hall pleasingly atmospheric, the orchestral focus a little diffuse, but attractively so, with the centrally placed piano dominating the proceedings, as much by the strength of Miss Licad's musical personality as by the actual balance.

Cho-Liang Lin's account of the *B minor Violin Concerto* with the Philharmonia Orchestra and Michael Tilson Thomas is exhilarating and thrilling; indeed, this is the kind of performance that prompts one to burst into applause. Bernard Shaw's famous remark about the Saint-Saëns *Concerto* as consisting of 'trivially pretty scraps of serenade music sandwiched between pages from the great masters' has always seemed almost on target, but Cho-Liang Lin manages to persuade one otherwise. He is given excellent recording from the CBS engineers and, in terms of both virtuosity and musicianship, his version is certainly second to none and is arguably the finest yet to have appeared. The CD format is admirably 'present'.

Piano concerto No. 2 in G min., Op. 22.
(**(*)) Olympia mono OCD 236 [id.]. Moura Lympany, LPO, Jean Martinon – KHACHATURIAN: *Piano concerto.*(***)

Moura Lympany's 1951 account of Saint-Saëns's *Second Piano concerto* is a delight from the ruminative opening to the coruscating brilliance of the finale, with the wonderfully nimble scherzo a central highlight. She is very well accompanied by Martinon, and it is a pity that the transfer of the (originally Decca) mono recording is so cavernous. Moreover there is a serious pitch fluctuation in the first movement (7 minutes 49 seconds).

Violin concerto No. 3 in B min., Op. 61.
*** DG Dig. 429 786-2 [id.]. Gil Shaham, NYPO, Sinopoli – PAGANINI: *Concerto No. 1.****

One only has to sample the delectable way Gil Shaham presents the enchanting *Barcarolle*, which forms the principal theme of Saint-Saëns's *Andante*, to discover the distinction of this performance. Sinopoli, who proves a splendid accompanist, is equally impressive when he introduces, very quietly and evocatively, the almost equally memorable chorale tune that plays such a major role in the finale and which, after Shaham has relished it with fine lyrical warmth, is to reappear, boldly resplendent on the brass. This is a performance which balances elegant *espressivo* with great dash and fire: the very opening bars of the *Concerto* are commanding indeed, and neither soloist nor conductor lets even the slightest suspicion of routine into a performance which dazzles and charms in equal measure. The recording is first class.

Danse macabre, Op. 40.
*** Denon Dig. DC 8097 [id.]. Tokyo Metropolitan SO, Jean Fournet – BERLIOZ: *Symphonie fantastique.****
(M) **(*) Chan. CHAN 6503 [id.]. SNO, Gibson – DUKAS: *L'apprenti sorcier*; ROSSINI/RESPIGHI: *La boutique fantasque.***(*)

Jean Fournet's 1987 performance of *Danse macabre* comes as a fill-up to a thoroughly recommendable account of the *Symphonie fantastique* and it is a very persuasive reading, well recorded.

Gibson's performance is well played and vividly recorded, but this CD offers rather short measure (37 minutes), even at mid-price.

Symphonies in A; in F (Urbs Roma); Symphonies Nos. 1–3.
(M) *** EMI CZS7 62643-2 (2) [Ang. CDMB 62643]. French Nat. R. O, Martinon (with Bernard Gavoty, organ de l'église Saint-Louis des Invalides in *No. 3*).

Martinon was the most persuasive advocate of Saint-Saëns, and this complete set of the five *Symphonies*, recorded in Paris between 1972 and 1975, is very welcome to the CD catalogue. The A and F major works were totally unknown and unpublished at the time of their recording and have never been dignified with numbers. Yet the A major, written when the composer was only fifteen, is a delight and may reasonably be compared with Bizet's youthful work in the same genre. Not surprisingly, it betrays the influence of Mozart as well as Mendelssohn (who is very 'present' in the first movement) and, consciously or not, Saint-Saëns uses a theme from the *Jupiter Symphony*. Scored for strings with flute and oboe, the charming scherzo survived the early ban as a separate piece and, with its delectable *moto perpetuo* finale, the whole work makes delightful gramophone listening. More obviously mature, the *Urbs Roma Symphony* came six years later, postdating the official No. 1. The writing is perhaps a shade more self-conscious, but more ambitious too, showing striking imagination in such movements as the darkly vigorous scherzo and the variation movement at the end.

The first of the numbered symphonies was written when Saint-Saëns was eighteen. It is a well-fashioned and genial piece, again much indebted to Mendelssohn, and to Schumann too, but with much delightfully fresh invention. The *Second*, written much later, in 1878, is more familiar and we already have two modern digital recordings of it (notably Yondani Butt's LSO recording on ASV CDDCA 599 – see our main volume, pp.

875–6). It is full of excellent ideas and makes a welcome change from the familir *Third*. Martinon directs splendid performances of the whole set, well prepared and lively; one can sense the pleasure of the French orchestral players in their discovery of the early works. The account of the *Third* ranks with the best: freshly spontaneous in the opening movement, then comes a spacious *Poco adagio*, a rumbustious scherzo and the threads are knitted powerfully together at the end of the finale. Here the recording could do with rather more sumptuousness, for the remastering has lost some of the original amplitude. Elsewhere the quality is bright and fresh, with no lack of body, and it suits the Saint-Saëns textures very well.

Symphony No. 3 in C min., Op. 78.
(B) ** CfP Dig. CD-CFP 4572; *TC-CFP 4572* [CDB7 62992-2]. Parker-Smith, LPO, Baudo (with WIDOR: *Organ symphony No. 5: Toccata. Organ symphony No. 6: Finale* **).

(i) *Symphony No. 3;* (ii) *Danse macabre, Op. 40.*
(B) *** Compact Classics *413 423-4* [id.]. (i) Chicago SO; (ii) O de Paris, Barenboim – FRANCK: *Symphony.**

Barenboim's inspirational 1976 performance of the *Symphony* glows with warmth from beginning to end. In the opening 6/8 section the galloping rhythms are irresistibly pointed, while the linked slow section has a poised stillness in its soaring lyricism which completely avoids any suspicion of sweetness or sentimentality. A brilliant account of the Scherzo leads into a magnificently energetic conclusion, with the Chicago orchestra excelling itself with radiant playing in every section. The Compact Classics tape offers the symphony uninterrupted in a transfer made from the original analogue master, and includes a fine account of *Danse macabre*; even if the coupled Franck *Symphony* is a much less attractive proposition, this is well worth considering for the car.

Baudo on Classics for Pleasure has the advantage of modern digital recording, made at Watford Town Hall. There is a hint of shrillness in the upper strings, but otherwise the quality is full and refined in detail. The recording has a wide dynamic range and uses the organ of Paisley Abbey, which is laminated on to the orchestra effectively. The performance is at its most vivacious in the opening movement. In the finale, the organ entry is very spacious and grandiloquent, but Baudo steadily increases his grip and pulls everything together in the coda. The Widor encores are analogue and were recorded a decade earlier in Westminster Cathedral. The effect is certainly spectacular – Jane Parker-Smith is at her most exciting in the famous *Toccata* – and the pedals resonate expansively, if without the sharpest focus. The primary digital choice for *Symphony No. 3* remains with Levine, with the Berlin Philharmonic in cracking form throughout and Simon Preston making a thunderous organ entry in the finale (DG 419 617-2; *419 617-4*).

Violin sonata No. 1 in D min., Op. 75.
*** Collins Dig. 1112-2; *1112-4* [id.]. Lorraine McAslan, John Blakely – DEBUSSY; RAVEL: *Sonatas.****
(*) DG Dig. 429 729-2 [id.]. Gil Shaham, Gerhard Oppitz – FRANCK: *Sonata*; RAVEL: *Tzigane.*(*)
** Audiofon Dig. CD 72026 [id.]. Aaron Rosand, Seymour Lipkin – GRIEG; STRAUSS: *Violin sonatas.***

Lorraine McAslan and her fine pianist give a good account of themselves in Saint-Saëns's entertaining *D minor Sonata*, and their reading can hold its head high in the current catalogue. Doubtless couplings will settle the matter, but this player has a wide range of colour and dynamics and has personality. Both the Debussy and Ravel are well played, and the latter is quite outstanding. The recording is very good indeed, well balanced and truthful.

The young American violinist Gil Shaham is twenty this year and was only eighteen when this record was made; he is still studying at the Juilliard with Dorothy DeLay. He produces a big and varied range of tone in the engaging *D minor Sonata* and has plenty of temperament. Gerhard Oppitz partners him with great dexterity but could perhaps have brought greater lightness of touch. Accardo and Canino play this with somewhat greater delicacy of colouring (see our main volume, p. 878). To judge by their concert performances in London some years ago, Amoyal and Rogé should record it for Decca.

Aaron Rosand is a good player who made some remarkably fine records in the 1960s, since when his vibrato has widened. However, there is no lack of character in this vigorous performance either from him or from his excellent partner, though the recording needs to put more space around the artists.

Samson et Dalila (opera): complete.
(M) **(*) DG 413 297-2 (2) [id.]. Obraztsova, Domingo, Bruson, Lloyd, Thau, Ch. & O de Paris, Barenboim.
**(*) Ph. Dig. 426 243-2; *426 243-4* (2) [id.]. Carreras, Baltsa, Estes, Burchuladze, Bav. R. Ch. & RSO, C. Davis.

Barenboim proves as passionately dedicated an interpreter of Saint-Saëns here as he did in the *Third Symphony*, sweeping away any Victorian cobwebs. It is important, too, that the choral passages, so vital in this work, be sung with this sort of freshness, and Domingo has rarely sounded happier in French music, the bite as well as the heroic richness of the voice well caught. Renato Bruson and Robert Lloyd are both admirable too; sadly, however, the key role of Dalila is given an unpersuasive, unsensuous performance by Obraztsova, with her vibrato often verging on a wobble. The recording is as ripe as the music deserves.

When the role of Samson is not one naturally suited to Carreras, it is amazing how strong and effective his performance is, even if top notes under stress grow uneven. Particularly after his near-fatal illness, the very strain seems to add to the intensity of communication, above all in the great aria of the last Act, when Samson, blinded, is turning the mill. Unevenness of production is more serious with Agnes Baltsa as Dalila. The microphone often brings out her vibrato, turning it into a disagreeable judder, and the changes of gear between registers are also underlined. She remains a powerful, characterful singer, but hers is hardly the seductive portrait required in this role, and it is a shortcoming that, like the rest of the cast, she is not a native French-speaker. Both Burchuladze as the Old Hebrew and Simon Estes as Abimelech equally seem intent on misusing once-fine voices, but Jonathan Summers as the High Priest of Dagon is far more persuasive. Despite all these reservations, the inspired conducting of Sir Colin Davis, coupled with refined, atmospheric recording, makes this preferable to the old EMI set conducted by Georges Prêtre, also seriously flawed. In particular the new recording gains from splendid choral singing, vital in this work.

Salieri, Antonio (1750–1825)

Les Danaïdes (complete).
*** EMI Dig. CDS7 54073-2 (2). Margaret Marshall, Gimenez, Kavrakos, Stuttgart RSO, Gelmetti.

This recording, the first ever of a tragic Salieri opera, offers a piece written for Paris in

1784 to a libretto originally intended for Gluck. The result is very Gluckian in the racy way it sets a classical subject, rejecting the formality of *opera seria* in favour of a much freer structure. This emerges as a direct successor to Gluck's two last Iphigénie operas, compact and fast-moving; and the musical invention, though hardly on a Mozartian level, is on balance livelier and more sharply memorable than in all but the greatest Gluck operas. Though the language is French and the composer Italian, there is a Germanic feel to much of the writing, in the often surprising 'symphonic' modulations and in the line of many of the arias, which at times are almost Schubertian. The five Acts last a mere hour and three-quarters, centring on the conflict of loyalty felt by the heroine, Hypermnestre, between her love for Lyncee and the command from her father, Danaus, that in line with her sisters she must slaughter her husband. The speed masks the enormity of the story, with brisk exchanges in accompanied recitative, brief set numbers – including some charming duets – and, above all, powerful comment from the chorus. Margaret Marshall as the heroine surpasses all she has done so far on record. She sings with superb attack and brilliant flexibility, as well as with tender intensity when Hypermnestre pleads with her father. Dimitri Kavrakos is not always adequately sinister-sounding as Danaus, but the voice is warmly focused. Raul Gimenez in the tenor role of Lyncee is first rate too, straining only occasionally, and so is Clarry Bartha as one of Danaus's younger daughters. Gelmetti secures a crisp, stylish performance from the Stuttgart Radio Orchestra and the excellent South German Radio Choir. The booklet contains notes in English but no translation of the French libretto.

Sallinen, Aulis (born 1935)

Ratsumies (The Horseman): opera; complete.
** Finlandia FACD 101 (2). Salminen, Valjakka, Erkkilä, Välkki, Wallén, Nieminen, Viitanen, Toivanen, Savonlinna Op. Festival Ch. & O, Söderblom.

Sallinen's first opera, *The Horseman* (1972–5), was a landmark in the recent renaissance of opera in Finland. It is both more atmospheric and musically more interesting than either of its immediate successors (though that is admittedly not difficult). The opera has something of the symbolism that distinguished *The King goes forth to France*, and its libretto by Paavo Haavikko has the same deep-seeming quality that afflicts the later opera. It is strong on atmosphere and holds the listener: at times it calls to mind Britten, but its sound-world, with constant recourse to the evocation of bells, is undoubtedly imaginative, and there are a few moments of real power. A good performance, though the rather dry acoustic environment and stage noises diminish its appeal. Sallinen's operas will not (one suspects) hold the stage in the future, but they are nevertheless better than most modern opera after Britten (and that wouldn't be very difficult either).

Salmanov, Vadim (1912–78)

Symphony No. 4 in B min.
** Olympia OCD 225 [id.]. Leningrad PO, Mravinsky – BEETHOVEN: *Symphony No. 4.***

Vadim Salmanov was born in St Petersburg and at first studied geology, turning to music in 1935 when he became a pupil of Gnessin. The war interrupted his career, but he attracted attention with a series of chamber works immediately afterwards and with an early symphony in 1952. Mravinsky's record of the *Fourth Symphony* of 1972 comes from a concert performance given in Leningrad in 1977. The symphony is an ambitious affair, playing for just over half an hour, with a long first movement. On first hearing it seems a bit misery-mongering, but it does leave the listener wanting to return to it. There is a genuine sense of movement and the idiom is tonal and completely accessible. There are strong whiffs of Shostakovich and fainter scents of Bartók. It is well worth hearing and is played with great dedication by the great Russian conductor and his wonderful orchestra. Although the sound-quality is less than first class, it is a good deal better than on the Beethoven, with which it is coupled. The upper strings are a bit acidulous and climaxes discolour. Excellent notes are included by the pianist, Murray McLachlan.

Sarasate, Pablo (1844–1908)

Carmen fantasy, Op. 25.
(B) *** CfP CD-CFP 4492; *TC-CFP 4492* [Ang. CDB 62988-2]. Perlman, RPO, Foster – *Concert.****

(i) *Carmen fantasy;* (ii) *Zigeunerweisen, Op. 20.*
(M) *** EMI CDM7 63533-2; *EG 763533-4* [id.]. Perlman, (i) as above; (ii) Pittsburg SO, Previn – *Concert.****

Perlman's superb 1972 account of the *Carmen fantasy* is one of his most dazzling recordings. It is now available in a choice of EMI couplings. On the mid-priced record, *Zigeunerweisen* (recorded with Previn five years later) is added for good measure, and again the playing is both virtuosic and idiomatic. Here the microphone balance is rather too close, but Perlman can survive any amount of scrutiny.

Satie, Erik (1866–1925)

PIANO MUSIC

Satie's piano music has been admirably served on compact disc, but the two Decca digital recitals by Pascal Rogé probably lead the field. The first (410 220-2; *410 220-4*) includes the famous *Gymnopédies*, and the second (421 731-2; *421 731-4*) is hardly less rewarding. Rogé's playing has a special elegance and charm that are altogether rather special, and the recorded sound is very good indeed, though not quite as full and realistic as that which Virgin provide for Anne Queffélec. Her collection overlaps with the Rogé recitals, although it includes some items not on either. Her playing has great tonal subtlety and character, and this record and tape (the latter almost as impressive as the disc) can also be highly recommended (Virgin VC7 90754-2; *VC7 90754-4*).

Saxton, Robert (born 1953)

Music to celebrate the resurrection of Christ.
*** Collins Dig. 1102-2; *1102-4* [id.]. ECO, Bedford – BRITTEN: *Piano concerto* etc.***

Positive and colourful, to reflect wonder in the subject, Saxton's piece makes an unusual but valuable fill-up to Bedford's disc of Britten rarities.

Scarlatti, Alessandro (1660–1725)

Il giardino di amore (*The garden of love:* cantata).
(M) *** DG 431 122-2; *431 122-4* [id.]. Gayer, Fassbaender, Munich CO, Stadlmair.

Scarlatti called this delightful work a '*serenata*', for there are only two characters and the orchestra is basically a string group with colourful obbligatos for recorder, violin and trumpet. The names of the two principal characters, Venus and Adonis, will recall the somewhat earlier work by Blow. Here the (originally castrato) role of Adonis is attractively sung by a soprano, Catherine Gayer, with Brigitte Fassbaender providing a foil in her portrayal of Venus. The two voices are well matched and the singing has both charm and character. Repeats are skilfully ornamented and the whole production has an engaging spontaneity to match its stylishness. There are some delightful pictorial touches in Scarlatti's word-settings and they are imaginatively realized. The nightingale song (with recorder obbligato) is especially memorable, as is the aria *Con battaglia die fiero tormento*, which has a trumpet obbligato worthy of Handel. The excellent 1964 recording has transferred vividly to CD, and the documentation includes a full translation.

Scarlatti, Domenico (1685–1757)

Keyboard sonatas (complete).
*** Erato/Warner 2292 45309-2 (34) [id.]. Scott Ross, Huggett, Coin, Henry, Vallon.

Scott Ross's highly distinguished survey of Scarlatti's keyboard music is welcome back to the catalogue. This project, sponsored by the Gulbenkian Foundation, was initiated by the tercentenary of Domenico Scarlatti's birth, prompting the production of an integral recording of Scarlatti's 555 *Keyboard sonatas*, including the three intended for organ, others for violin and continuo, and two for the unlikely combination of violin and oboe in unison. Scott Ross, who, with the participation of Monica Huggett (violin), Christophe Coin (cello), Michel Henry (oboe) and Marc Vallon (bassoon), is primarily responsible, plays five different harpsichords plus the organ, and he is very well recorded throughout in varying acoustics. Scarlatti's invention shows an inexhaustible resourcefulness, and Ross's playing is fully worthy: he is lively, technically assured, rhythmically resilient and, above all, he conveys his enjoyment of the music, without eccentricity. We cannot claim to have heard all thirty-four CDs, but all the evidence of sampling suggests that for the Scarlatti addict they will prove an endless source of satisfaction. The documentation is ample, providing a 200-page booklet about the composer, his music and the performers. The overall cost of this set is somewhere in the region of £200.

Keyboard sonatas, Kk. 28, 52, 132–3, 208–9, 490–92, 544–5.
(B) *** CfP CD-CFP 4538 [Ang. CDB 62989-2]; *TC-CFP 4538.* Valda Aveling (harpsichord).

Valda Aveling plays a Goff harpsichord, not an authentic period instrument or copy. Indeed there is little period flavour here, for this artist favours frequent changes of registration. However, she plays with superb panache and is splendidly vital; and the full and vivid recording is an additional attraction. The robust effect will not suit purists; but this recital may well win over listeners new to this repertoire. The 1975 recording has added life on CD.

Schmelzer, Johann (*c.* 1620–80)

Balletto di centauri ninfe e salvatici; Balletto di spiritelli; Sonata I à 8; Sonata à 7 flauti; Sonata con arie zu der kaiserlichen Serenada.
*** O-L Dig. 425 834-2 [id.]. New L. Cons., Pickett – BIBER: *Sonatas.****

Johann Schmelzer made his reputation initially as a virtuoso violinist ('the famous and nearly most distinguished in all Europe', suggested a contemporary accolade); as a climax to his career, he was apppointed Vice-Kapellmeister to the Viennese Imperial Court, and in 1679 he became Kapellmeister – almost too late, for he died of the plague a year later. One of his tasks was the provision of ballet music for use in pageants, and much of this survives. The two brief scores included here last for about five minutes each, with an average of a movement per minute, but these vignettes have considerable charm. The *Balletto di spiritelli* is scored for recorders and curtal (an ancester of the bassoon), violins and viols, and the *Balletto di centauri* uses cornetts and sackbuts, as well as recorders, strings and continuo. The even more robust *Sonata con arie zu der kaiserlichen Serenada* (with three trumpets, timpani plus a string ensemble and continuo) has six movements, including two *Arias* and a *Canario*, but still only lasts seven minutes. Philip Pickett himself leads the consort of recorders in the *Sonata à 7*, which is a fairly ambitious continuous piece, longer than either of the ballets, and the *Sonata à 8* highlights a trumpet duo against a group of violins and viols. This is agreeably inventive music, which is brought refreshingly to life by Pickett's instrumetal ensemble, using original instruments to persuasive effect. The recording is both clear and spacious.

Schmidt, Franz (1874–1939)

Symphony No. 4 in C.
(M) **(*) Decca 430 007-2 [id.]. VPO, Mehta – SCHOENBERG: *Chamber symphony No. 1.***(*)

Schmidt's noble *Fourth Symphony* is much loved in Vienna, as the playing of the VPO on this Decca recording readily testifies. The work is given the intensity of Mahler, without the hint of hysteria, and the breadth and spaciousness of Bruckner – though it is very different from either: Mehta finds also a dignity that reminds one a little of Elgar. The brightened recording gains in vividness in its CD transfer but loses a little of its fullness, though the Vienna ambience remains very telling.

Schnittke, Alfred (born 1934)

Violin concertos Nos. 1–2.
*** BIS Dig. CD 487 [id.]. Mark Lubotsky, Malmö SO, Eri Klas.

The *First Violin concerto* was composed in 1956, when Schnittke was still a student, but was revised in 1963. It inhabits a post-romantic era: in the composer's own words, its 'sound world is dominated by Tchaikovsky and Rachmaninov, overshadowed by Shostakovich and adorned with the orchestral conventions of the day'. Its lyricism is profoundly at variance with its successor of 1966, commissioned by Mark Lubotsky, the soloist on this record. Here the central concept is what Schnittke calls 'a certain drama of tone colours', and there is no doubt that much of it is vividly imagined and strongly individual. The double-bass is assigned a special role of a caricatured 'anti-soloist'. The 12-note series serves as the thematic foundation, but there is nevertheless a centre of gravity, a constantly recurring note which sometimes lends the music an illusion of tonality. There is recourse to the once fashionable aleotoric technique, but this is all within carefully controlled parameters. The Malmö orchestra under Eri Klas play with evident feeling in both works and are very well recorded. This is an altogether highly satisfactory coupling.

Schoeck, Othmar (1886–1957)

(i) *Violin concerto, Op. 21; Serenade, Op. 1; Suite in A flat, Op. 59.*
*** Novalis Dig. 150070-2; *150070-4.* (i) Ulf Hoelscher, ECO, Howard Griffiths.

Schoeck's *Violin concerto* comes from 1911–12 and was inspired, like Bartók's *First concerto* (1908) by Stefi Geyer, with whom both composers were in love. (She recorded it in Switzerland during the war on four 78-r.p.m. discs, but the performance was diminished by her obtrusively wide vibrato.) The *Concerto*'s neglect on record is really unaccountable: it has great warmth and enormous appeal and would doubtless enjoy wide popularity if only the public could find a way to it. There is a rich fund of melody here and, though imbued by the tradition of Brahms and Strauss, an individual profile is already emerging, not least in its sound-world. The ideas are fresh and memorable, and there is an autumnal melancholy about the slow movement almost reminiscent of Elgar. Ulf Hoelscher and the English Chamber Orchestra under Howard Griffiths play this movement – and, for that matter, the whole work – as if they were in love with it (as indeed they should be). The *Serenade* of 1907 has some of the charm of late Strauss, and the *Suite for strings* (1945) is a work of strong character: it has the same luminous quality and sad, gentle ambience as the pastoral intermezzo, *Summer night*, written the same year (see our main volume). Occasionally one feels the need for a richer string sonority, but the performance is dedicated and the recording is well balanced and has both clarity and warmth. Strongly recommended.

Schoenberg, Arnold (1874–1951)

(i) *Piano concerto in C, Op. 42;* (ii) *Violin concerto, Op. 36.*
(M) **(*) DG 431 740-2 [id.]. (i) Brendel; (ii) Zeitlin; Bav. RSO, Kubelik – BERG: *Violin concerto.****

Schoenberg devotees tend to suggest that both these works, consciously echoing the world of the romantic concerto in twelve-note serial terms, present the most approachable road to appreciating the master. For some that may be so, particularly in performances as sympathetic as these; but more than usual in these relatively late works the thick textures favoured by Schoenberg obscure the focus of the argument rather than making it sweeter on the ear. Brendel – who made a recording for Vox very early in his career – remains a committed Schoenbergian, and Zeitlin is impressive too. Though even the CD transfer does not manage to clarify the thorny textures completely, the sound, as transferred, is very good. With the Berg *Violin concerto* offered as coupling, this is excellent value in DG's 20th Century Classics series.

Chamber Symphony No. 1, Op. 9.
*** Teldec/WEA Dig. 2292 46019; *2292 46019-4* [id.]. COE, Holliger – BERG: *Chamber concerto.****
(M) **(*) Decca 430 007-2 [id.]. LAPO (members), Mehta – SCHMIDT: *Symphony No. 4.***(*)

Schoenberg's *Chamber Symphony No. 1* makes an apt coupling for the fine COE version of the Berg, played with equal warmth and thrust, with complex textural problems masterfully solved.

It was to Los Angeles that Schoenberg moved to live out his last years, and it would have gladdened him that his local philharmonic orchestra had achieved a degree of brilliance to match that of any other orchestra in America. The *First Chamber symphony* is given a rich performance under Mehta, arguably too fast at times but full of understanding for the romantic emotions which underlie much of the writing. The 1969 recording is appropriately brilliant, but the CD transfer is very brightly lit.

Violin concerto, Op. 36.
* Olympia OCD 135 [id.]. Ilana Isakadze, USSR Ac. SO, Lazarev – KHACHATURIAN: *Concerto.**

A weird coupling which juxtaposes one of the most difficult of modern concertos with perhaps the lightest and most immediately accessible example of the genre. Ilana Isakadze gives a far from negligible account of this unlikeable but nevertheless powerful work, and the USSR Academic Symphony Orchestra under Alexander Lazarev bring a certain freshness of approach to an idiom that must have still been pretty alien to them at the time of this recording (1980). The soloist is very up-front and the recording scarcely does justice to the sumptuous tone that this orchestra can (and probably does) make. The balance is synthetic and the overall aural picture is far from pleasing.

Pelleas and Melisande, Op. 5.
** Sony Dig. CD 45870 [id.]. Israel PO, Mehta – FAURÉ; SIBELIUS: *Pelléas.**(*)

The Israel Philharmonic is an infinitely finer body now for Mehta than it was some years ago, and it turns in a perfectly good account of Schoenberg's score. The Sony recording is eminently detailed and every strand in the orchestral tapestry is clearly audible. However, Mehta has strong competition from Karajan's masterly account on DG, which scores in atmosphere and subtlety (DG 423 132-2).

5 Pieces for orchestra, Op. 16.
(M) *** Mercury 432 006-2 [id.]. LSO, Dorati – BERG: *3 Pieces; Lulu suite*; WEBERN: *5 Pieces.****

Schoenberg put evocative titles on his *Five Pieces*, but it would be misleading to think of them as programmatic pieces. His titles were prompted by his publisher, and the arguments – colourful as they may be – had been established without them. Here for the first time he was writing 'abstract' instrumental music in his new role as atonalist, and even today it is amazing that such forward-looking music could have been written in 1909. Nowadays it is the combination of clarity and colour, with a big orchestra used in chamber style, that still seems intensely original and new. Dorati, in his pioneering coupling with other works written at the same period by Schoenberg's emergent pupils, used the version the composer made in 1949, with a slightly reduced orchestra. The performance is strong and vivid; the 1962 sound is admirably vivid and clear.

Variations, Op. 31.
(M) **(*) Decca 425 008-2 (2) [id.]. Chicago SO, Solti – BRUCKNER: *Symphony No. 5.***(*)

Solti's reading of the challenging Schoenberg *Variations* is characteristically strong and forceful, with the Chicago orchestra playing with virtuoso brilliance; but Karajan's recording (DG 415 326-2) has shown what extra depths this initially difficult music contains. The Decca sound is bright and clear, rather firmer than it was on LP.

Verklaerte Nacht (see also under CHAMBER MUSIC, below).
(M) **(*) Decca 430 002-2 [id.]. ASMF, Marriner – R. STRAUSS: *Metamorphosen* **(*); WEBERN: *5 Movements.****

Marriner's interpretation of Schoenberg's sensuous string work is relatively reticent until the culminating climaxes, when the final thrust is more powerful than almost any rival. The 1974 recording, still atmospheric, has lost some of its allure in the remastering, and the fortissimo violins become fierce.

(i) *The Book of the Hanging Gardens, Op. 15;* (ii) *Pierrot Lunaire, Op. 21.*
*** Nonesuch/Warner 7559 79237-2 [id.]. Jan DeGaetani; (i) Gilbert Kalish; (ii) Contemporary Chamber Ens., Arthur Weisberg.

The Nonesuch New York performance of *Pierrot Lunaire* has long been admired for steering a splendidly confident course among all the many problematic interpretative points. Now it comes coupled with another equally impressive recording of *The Book of the Hanging Gardens.* Jan DeGaetani is a superbly precise soloist, but there is no feeling whatever of pedantry in her performances which, more than most, allow a welcome degree of expressiveness, while keeping a sharp focus and projecting a strong sense of drama.

CHAMBER MUSIC

Verklaerte Nacht, Op. 4 (string sextet version).
*** Hyp. Dig. CDA 66425 [id.]. Raphael Ens. – KORNGOLD: *Sextet.****
* EMI Dig. CDH7 54140-2 [id.]. Vienna String Sextet – BRAHMS: *String sextet No. 2.**

The Raphael Ensemble have the advantage of very good recorded sound and give a fine account of Schoenberg's score. They convey its atmosphere without indulging in overstatement or its reverse. They have, too, the advantage of a rarity in their coupling, the youthful *Sextet* of Korngold.

The Vienna String Sextet gives a curiously pedestrian account of the opening and are generally under-vitalized. There is little real sense of forward movement and not much atmosphere. No challenge here to existing recommendations.

VOCAL MUSIC

Gurrelieder.
*** Decca Dig. 430 321-2; *430 321-4* (2) [id.]. Jerusalem, Dunn, Fassbaender, Brecht, Haage, Hotter, St Hedwig's Cathedral Ch., Berlin, Düsseldorf State Musikverein, Berlin RSO, Chailly.
** Denon Dig. CO 77066-67 (2) [id.]. Frey, Connell, Van Nes, Groonroos, Vogel, Franzen, NDR Choir, Bav. R. Ch., Frankfurt State Op. Ch., Frankfurst RSO, Inbal.

Chailly's magnificent recording of Schoenberg's massive *Gurrelieder* effectively supplants all existing versions, even Ozawa's impressive Boston set, recorded live. This Berlin recording not only brings richer, fuller, more detailed and better-balanced sound, but it conveys a natural dramatic tension not easy to find in studio conditions. Chailly has a finer team of soloists than on any rival set, with Siegfried Jerusalem as Waldemar not only warmer and firmer of tone than his rivals but more imaginative too. Susan Dunn makes a sweet, touchingly vulnerable Tove, while Brigitte Fassbaender gives darkly baleful intensity to the message of the Wood-dove. Hans Hotter is a characterful Speaker in the final section. The impact of the performance is the more telling with sound both atmospheric and immediate, bringing a fine sense of presence, not least in the final choral outburst.

Inbal directs a convincing, well-paced reading, but with Paul Frey strained and rough-toned as Waldemar and Elizabeth Connell as Tove less well focused than her rivals, this is no match for either Chailly or Ozawa (Philips 412 511-2 – see our main volume, pp. 931–2). Jard van Nes is effective in the Wood-dove's song, but tensions are lower than in the rival sets, not helped by slightly distanced recording.

Schubert, Franz (1797–1828)

Rondo in A for violin and strings, D.438.
(B) *** Ph. 426 977-2; *426 977-4* [id.]. Grumiaux, New Philh. O, Leppard – HAYDN: *Violin concertos*; MOZART: *Adagio; Rondo.****

Schubert's *Rondo* has never danced more engagingly than on Grumiaux's bow, and Leppard captures the music's rhythmic lilt equally pleasingly. Excellent 1967 sound. A bargain.

Rosamunde Overture (Die Zauberharfe, D.644) and incidental music, D. 797 (complete).
*** DG Dig. 431 655-2(id.]. Anne Sofie von Otter, Ernst Senff Ch., COE, Abbado.

As a superb supplement to their masterly set of the Schubert symphonies (DG 423 651-2), Abbado and COE give joyful performances of this magical incidental music. It is a revelation to hear the most popular of the entr'actes played so gently: it is like a whispered meditation. Even with a slow speed and affectionate phrasing, it yet avoids any feeling of being mannered. Glowing recording to match. Anne Sofie von Otter is an ideal soloist.

Symphonies Nos. 3 in D, D.200; 5 in B flat, D.485; 6 in C, D.589.
❀ (M) *** EMI CDM7 69750-2; *EG 769750-4*. RPO, Beecham.

Beecham's are magical performances in which every phrase breathes, and this record and tape equivalent is an absolute delight. This is an indispensable purchase for all collectors and a supreme bargain in the Schubert discography.

Symphony No. 5 in B flat, D.485.
(M) *** EMI CDM7 63869-2 [id.]; *EG 763869-4*. Philh. O, Klemperer – DVOŘÁK: *Symphony No. 9.***
(*) Linn CKD 003 [id.]. English Classical Players, Jonathan Brett – MOZART: *Symphony No. 40.(*)*

More charm here than one might have expected from Klemperer, but basically his conception is stronger than most, so that something like an ideal balance is kept between Schubert's natural lyricism and the firmness of sonata form. The Philharmonia Orchestra is on top form, and rarely has Klemperer recorded a more exhilarating performance than this 1963 version. Recording excellent.

As with his Mozart coupling, Jonathan Brett is generous with repeats, so the overall playing time of this Schubert performance by the excellent English Classical Players is 29 minutes. Brett moves the *Andante con moto* on nicely and, thoughout, the light orchestral touch is very pleasing, especially so in the engagingly Schubertian finale, which is the highlight of the performance, very spirited yet admirably graceful. The recording, made in the London Henry Wood Hall, is most naturally balanced.

Symphonies Nos. 5 in B flat, D.485; 8 in B min. (Unfinished), D.759.
(M) *** Decca Dig. 430 439-2; *430 439-4* [id.]. VPO, Solti.
(M) *** Sony MK 42048 [id.]. Columbia SO or NYPO, Bruno Walter.
(B) ** Hung. White Label HRC 152; *WLMC 152* [id.]. Hungarian State O, Ferencsik.

One of Solti's very best records, the performances fresh and concentrated, weightier, more dramatic than Walter's but equally beautifully played, and excellently recorded in the Sofiensaal (see our main volume, p. 896). It is most welcome at mid-price as part of the 'Solti Collection'.

Bruno Walter's famous coupling, recorded in 1960 and 1958, has now been reissued by Sony at mid-price, still with its earlier, premium-price catalogue number. Walter brings special qualities of warmth and lyricism to the *Unfinished.* Affection, gentleness and humanity are the keynotes of this performance; while the first movement of the *Fifth* is rather measured, there is much loving attention to detail in the *Andante.* The recording emerges fresh and glowing in its CD format and, like the rest of the Walter series, completely belies its age. The sound is still richly expansive as well as clear, and the CD is in every way satisfying.

Ferencsik's *Fifth* is graceful and strong, with the *Andante* flowing and the scherzo genial, yet with an attractive rhythmic feeling. The *Unfinished* is less individual, but has no lack of drama or momentum. The orchestral playing has character and polish in both works, and the Hungaroton recording is full and vivid.

Symphonies No. 5 in B flat, D.485; 8 in B min. (Unfinished) (completed and orch. Newbould).
(M) *** Ph. Dig. 432 045-2; *432 045-4* [id.]. ASMF, Marriner.

The balance in the *Fifth Symphony* is not quite ideal in the relationship between wind and strings, and the recording is not as clearly defined internally as one might expect. Nevertheless this remains a highly desirable performance, among the finest in Marriner's series. The *Unfinished* is here completed, with Schubert's Scherzo filled out and the *Rosamunde B minor Entr'acte* used as finale. Given a fresh, direct performance, the work becomes fully convincing in its own right.

Symphonies Nos. 5 in B flat, D.485; 9 in C (Great). Rosamunde: Ballet music No. 1, D.797.
(B) *** DG Compact Classics *419 389-4* [id.]. BPO, Boehm.

On the DG Compact Classics tape, Boehm's version of No. 5 makes a perfect coupling for his *Great C major*: the first movement is wonderfully light and relaxed; the slow movement, though also relaxed, never seems to outstay its welcome; and in the last two movements the Berlin playing makes for power as well as lightness. Boehm's Berlin *Ninth* stands in the lyrical Furtwängler tradition. His modification of tempo in the various sections of the first movement is masterly in its finesse, often so subtle that it requires close attention to be spotted. In the slow movement the rhythmic spring to the repeated quavers is delectable. Nor is there any lack of drama in the performance, although in the finale, taken rather fast, the playing is slightly less gripping; even so, there is excitement in plenty. The recording is full and resonant.

Symphony No. 8 in B min. (Unfinished), D.759.
(BB) ** Pickwick (Decca) PWK 1149. VPO, Münchinger – MENDELSSOHN: *Symphony No. 4.**(*)

At the beginning of his reading of the *Unfinished*, Münchinger achieves a degree of pianissimo rare even on CD – cellos and basses barely audible – and the exposition is slow, steady and rather withdrawn. Then in the development Münchinger suddenly comes out into the open. The orchestral sound is brighter and freer: it is as though the climax is the real argument of the work, with the sun suddenly appearing from behind the clouds. The moment of high drama is short-lived, for at the recapitulation we return to the withdrawn mood of the opening. The second movement is less idiosyncratic, thoughtful and again withdrawn. The reading is altogether refreshingly different, almost Byronic is its romanticism. The recording is early, 1959, but its wide dynamic range does not mean that the sound is not robust, and the CD medium with its background quiet adds to the sense of dramatic contrast. However, at mid-price Sinopoli's outstanding Philharmonia version, coupled with Schumann's *Symphony No. 3*, must take precedence. He secures the most ravishingly refined and beautiful playing; the orchestral blend, particularly of the woodwind and horns, is magical (DG 427 818-2; *427 818-4*).

Symphonies Nos. 8 in B min. (Unfinished), D.759; 9 in C (Great), D.944.
(M) **(*) EMI CDM7 63854-2 [id.]; *EG 763854-4*. Philh. O, Klemperer.

Klemperer's approach to the *Unfinished* is utterly individual. Gone is any attempt to charm; instead the work is seen as a massive symphonic structure. And massive it is if one regards the two movements in relation to the first halves of other symphonies. But Klemperer's approach is anything but stodgy, for his determination to play the score straight has inspired his players to keen, alert playing that never lets the attention wander. The opening is deliberately grim but, when the second subject finally arrives, there is no attempt to beautify the melody: it simply fends for itself and acquires an unusual purity thereby. So through the whole performance, recorded in 1963. This will hardly please everyone, but it remains an outstanding example of Klemperer's interpretative genius. In the *Great C Major*, recorded in 1960, Klemperer's view is certainly individual, with a measured performance, deliberately literal and rather heavy, particularly in the first movement. But once the speeds and the severe approach are accepted, the fascination of the reading becomes clear; there is some glorious playing from the Philharmonia: the oboe solo at the beginning of the slow movement is deliciously pointed. Like others in the Klemperer Edition, this coupling will appeal primarily to those interested in tracing the career of a great but individual conductor.

Symphony No. 9 in C (Great), D.944.
(M) **(*) DG Dig. 429 983-2; *429 983-4* [id.]. Chicago SO, Levine.
(M) (**) BMG/RCA GD 60328; *GK 60328* (4) [60328-2-RG; *60328-4-RG*]. Phd. O, Toscanini – Concert.(**(*))

Levine conducts a refined performance, beautifully played and excellently recorded, which is commendably free from mannerism, yet which may on that account seem under-characterized. He omits the exposition repeats in the outer movements (just as was universally done until recently). Conversely, all the repeats in the Scherzo are observed, which unbalances the structure.

Those who know Toscanini's NBC recording of the *Great C major* will be surprised how much more sympathetic – more lyrical and less rigid – his Philadelphia performance is. Speeds tend to be brisk, as in the second-movement *Andante*, but rhythms are well sprung. The 1941 recording has been refurbished well to give it fair body, though there is still some harshness.

In the first recording to use period instruments Mackerras and the Orchestra of the Age of Enlightenment give an entirely winning performance that will delight devotees of the new authenticity (Virgin VC7 90708-2; *VC7 90708-4*). Those who prefer a performance on modern instruments but on an authentic scale should choose Abbado with the COE (DG 423 656-2), while Solti provides a happily glowing, larger-scale version, spontaneous and fresh, and confirming the Vienna Sofiensaal as an ideal recording location for Schubert (Decca 400 082-2).

CHAMBER MUSIC

Fantaisie in C, D.934.
(M) ** RCA GD 87873; *GK 87873* [7873-2-RG; *7873-4-RG*]. Heifetz, Brooks Smith – BEETHOVEN: *String trio No. 3*; BRAHMS: *Piano quartet No. 3.***

Heifetz's account of the *C major Fantasy* was recorded in 1968, though the dry studio acoustic almost suggests an earlier provenance. Brooks Smith is a fine player but not quite as imaginative as Kentner who had recorded this with Menuhin a few years earlier (see our Recitals section). Heifetz is his incomparable self.

Octet in F, D.803.
❀ *** EMI Dig. CDC7 54118-2. Hausmusik.

Hausmusik's performance of Schubert's *Octet* on period instruments is so winning that it can be recommended warmly even to those who do not normally follow the authenticity cult. This talented ensemble even outshines its achievement in the earlier EMI recording of Mendelssohn's *Octet*. This time the group includes such imaginative wind-players as the clarinettist, Antony Pay – playing the opening solo of the *Adagio* slow movement with heavenly phrasing – and the horn-player, Anthony Halstead. Speeds are rarely extreme, allowing full, open expressiveness, as in that *Adagio*; and allegros are generally easy enough to allow a delectable rhythmic spring. The pointing is the more infectious when period string-playing allows textures to be so transparent. There are few Schubert records that so consistently convey the joys of spring.

(i) *Piano quintet in A (Trout);* (ii) *String quartet No. 14 in D min. (Death and the Maiden).*
(M) **(*) Sony SBK 46343 [id.]; *40-46343*. (i) Horszowski, Budapest Qt (members), Julius Levine; (ii) Juilliard Qt.

Horszowski's contribution to the *Trout* is undoubtedly distinguished and his clean, clear playing dominates the performance which, although full of imaginative detail, is a little on the cool side – though refreshingly so, for all that. The Juilliard Quartet are far from cool in the *Death and the Maiden Quartet*. They begin the famous slow movement with a rapt pianissimo, and the variations are played with great feeling and the widest range of expression and dynamic. The scherzo has a comparable *agitato* feeling, but the bite and crispness of ensemble bring a firm sense of control, and the middle section is beautifully contrasted. The finale is infectiously alert and vigorous, the unanimity of ensemble consistently impressive. A fine performance overall, among the best in the catalogue. In both works the sound is a little dry, but not confined. First choice for the *Trout* remains with the delectably fresh and youthful reading by András Schiff and the Hagen Quartet, beautifully recorded too (Decca 411 975-2). First choice for the *Death and the Maiden* quartet remains with the fine Lindsay version, coupled with the *Quartetsatz* (ASV CDDCA 560; *ZCDCA 560*).

String quartets Nos. 9 in G min., D.173; 13 in A min., D.804.
**(*) Teldec/Warner 2292 43205-2 [id.]. Alban Berg Qt.
** EMI Dig. CDC7 49900-2 [id.]. Cherubini Qt.

The Alban Berg recorded this account of the *A minor* in 1975 and – despite the more generous coupling (*Death and the Maiden*) offered in their more recent, EMI version – this is to be preferred. It matches the latter in tonal finesse and perfection of ensemble and surpasses it in terms of spontaneity. The *G minor Quartet* is fine; on balance, both are better played here than by the Melos Quartet of Stuttgart, whose complete set is now available on CD.

The Cherubini play both quartets with great technical finish and superb control. Their approach is perhaps a bit too sophisticated and they seem unwilling to let phrases unfold naturally, and much of the innocence of the slow movement of the early *G minor Quartet*, D.173, eludes them.

String quartet No. 15 in G, D.887.
* DG Dig. 429 224-2 [id.]. Emerson Qt – BEETHOVEN: *String quartet No. 16.**

The Emersons give an over-projected, sensationally virtuosic account of the Schubert which is overstated and brash. They are determined to astonish the listener with their stunning technique and attack. There is no sense of any private music-making here: dramatic outbursts are thunderously declamatory, and the pianissimo writing is exaggerated. Nor is there any sense of mystery or innocence. The recording is very bright and forward.

String quintet in C, D.956.
*** ASV Dig. CDDCA 537; *ZCDCA 537* [id.]. Lindsay Qt, with Douglas Cummings.

The Lindsay version of Schubert's miraculous *String quintet* gives the impression that one is eavesdropping on music-making in the intimacy of a private concert. They do the amazing first movement justice, as indeed they do the ethereal *Adagio*. Their reading must rank at the top of the list; it is very well recorded.

Impromptus Nos. 1–4, D.899; 5–8, D.935.
** DG Dig. 423 612-2; *423 612-4* [id.]. Krystian Zimerman.

Krystian Zimerman sees the first of the *Impromptus* in an almost symphonic light: in his hands it is massive and powerful. Accents in the second are over-emphatic and there are some agogic distortions. Throughout all eight pieces there is some wonderful pianism, but the artless innocence which pianists like Perahia (CBS CD 37291), Brendel (Philips 411 040-2) or Lupu (Decca 411 711-2) achieve is present only intermittently. The piano is rather more closely balanced than is desirable. Choice remains between the three artists mentioned above (see our main volume, p. 911).

PIANO SONATAS

We have not so far encountered any breathtaking new recordings of this repertoire during our current record year, so our overall recommendation remains with Alfred Brendel, who offers the *Sonatas 14–21* plus *German dances*, the *Impromptus*, *Moments musicaux* and *Wanderer fantasia* on seven discs (Philips 426 128-2). Generally speaking, these are warm performances, strongly delineated and powerfully characterized, which occupy a commanding place in the catalogue. The discs are all available separately. We must also mention Radu Lupu's searching and poetic coupling of the *A minor Sonata*, D.845, with the *G major*, D.894, to which we gave a Rosette in our main volume (Decca 417 640-2).

VOCAL MUSIC

Lieder Vol. 8: *Abendlied der Fürstin; An Chloen; An den Mond; An den Mond in einer Herbstnacht; Berthas Lied in der Nacht; Erlkönig; Die frühen Gräber; Hochzeitslied; In der Mitternacht; Die Mondnacht; Die Nonne; Die Perle; Romanze; Die Sommernacht; Ständchen; Stimme der Liebe; Trauer der Liebe; Wiegenlied.*
*** Hyp. Dig. CDJ 33008; *KJ 33008* [id.]. Sarah Walker, Graham Johnson.

Volumes 1 to 7 of Graham Johnson's great Schubert project (Hyperion CDJ 330.1/7; *KJ 330.1/7*), featuring artists of the calibre of Dame Janet Baker, Stephen Varcoe, Anthony Rolfe Johnson and Elly Ameling, have all been given an enthusiastic, three-star welcome in our main volume. In designing each recital, it is Graham Johnson's gift not only to choose songs for every contributor which illustrate an apt theme but also to select those which draw out the fullest beauties of each voice. Sarah Walker, always a most characterful artist, has never made a more beautiful record than this, with her perfectly controlled mezzo at its most sensuous. The theme is 'Schubert and the Nocturne', leading from the first, lesser-known version of the Goethe poem, *An den Mond*, to two of the best-loved of all Schubert's songs, the delectable *Wiegenlied*, 'Cradle-song', and the great drama of *Erlkönig*, normally sung by a man, but here at least as vividly characterized by a woman's voice.

Lieder Vol. 9: *Blanka; 4 Canzonen, D.688; Daphne am Bach; Delphine; Didone abbandonata; Gott! höre meine Stimme; Der gute Hirte; Hin und wieder Fliegen Pfeile*; (i) *Der Hirt auf dem Felsen. Ich schleiche bang und still (Romanze). Lambertine; Liebe Schwärmt auf allen Wegen; Lilla an die Morgenröte; Misero pargoletto; La pastorella al prato; Der Sänger am Felsen; Thelka; Der Vollmond strahlt (Romanze).*
*** Hyp. Dig. CDJ 33009; *KJ 33009* [id.]. Arleen Augér, Graham Johnson; (i) with Thea King.

'Schubert and the theatre' is the theme of Arleen Augér's contribution to the great Hyperion project, leading up to the glories of his very last song, the headily beautiful *Shepherd on the rock*, with its clarinet obbligato. That solo is all the more atmospheric for being played here with gentle reticence by Thea King, with Augér firm as a rock over the widest leaps. The *Romanze, Ich schleiche bang* – adapted from an opera aria – also has a clarinet obbligato. As ever in illustrating a theme, Graham Johnson has chosen a delightfully wide range of items, most of them little-known. Notable are the lightweight Italian songs that the young Schubert wrote for his master, Salieri, and a lovely setting, *Der gute Hirt*, ('The good shepherd') in which the religious subject prompts a melody which anticipates the great staircase theme in Strauss's *Arabella.*

Lieder Vol. 10: *Adelwold und Emma, Am Flusse; An die Apfelbäume, wo ich Julien erblickte; An die Geliebte; An Mignon; Auf den Tod einer Nachtigall; Auf einen Kirchhof; Harfenspieler I; Labetrank der Liebe; Die Laube; Der Liebende; Der Sänger; Seufzer; Der Traum; Vergebliche Liebe; Der Weiberfreund.*
*** Hyp. Dig. CDJ 33010; *KJ 33010* [id.]. Martyn Hill, Graham Johnson.

Graham Johnson's themes in the Hyperion Edition never fail to illuminate Schubert in new ways. Here he correlates the year 1815, an *annus mirabilis* for the teenage composer in his exuberant song-writing, with what has been documented of his life over those twelve months, which is remarkably little. So the songs here form a kind of diary, outlined in Johnson's revealing liner-notes. The big item, overtopping everything else, is the astonishing 38-stanza narrative song, *Adalwold and Emma.* It was an item that Fischer-Dieskau refused to consider in his great recorded cycle for DG; with Hill ranging wide in his expression, it proves a fascinating piece here. It is almost half an hour long, from the bold march-like opening to the final happy resolution.

Lieder Vol. 11: *An den Tod; Auf dem Wasser zu singen; Auflösung; Aus 'Heliopolis' I & II; Dithyrambe; Elysium; Der Geistertanz; Der König in Thule; Lied des Orpheus; Nachtstück; Schwanengesang; Seligkeit; So lasst mich scheinen; Der Tod und das Mädchen; Verklärung; Vollendung; Das Zügenglöcklein.*

*** Hyp. Dig. CDJ 33011; *KJ 33011* [id.]. Brigitte Fassbaender, Graham Johnson.

There is no more vibrantly characterful Lieder-singer today, man or woman, than Brigitte Fassbaender, and her disc in the Hyperion Schubert Edition is electrifying. Starting with a chilling account of *Death and the maiden*, the theme of the disc is Death and the composer. Fassbaender's ability precisely to control her vibrato brings baleful tone-colours, made the more ominous by the rather reverberant, almost churchy, acoustic. Yet the selection imaginatively ranges wide in mood, illustrating Johnson's argument in his brilliant essay that, with the average life-span often shorter, death in Schubert's time was ever-present, and not just a matter for gloom. So in *Auf dem Wasser zu singen* the lightly fanciful rippling-water motif presents the soul gliding gently 'like a boat' up to heaven, and the selection ends astonishingly with what generally seems one of the lightest of Schubert songs, *Seligkeit*. This, as Johnson suggests, returns the listener from heaven back to earth, when the last stanza dismisses the idea of staying in heaven so as to go on enjoying the smiles of the beloved Laura. In this, as elsewhere, Fassbaender sings with thrilling intensity, with Johnson's accompaniment comparably inspired.

Lieder: *Am Bach in Frühling; An den Mond II; An die Nachtigall; Auf der Donau; Ave Maria; Berthas Lied in der Nacht; Dass sie hier gewesen; Frühlingsglaube; Gretchen am Spinnrade; Im Abendrot; Die junge Nonne; Kennst du das Land; Klärchens Lied; Der König in Thule; Lachen und Weinen; Lied der Anna Lyle; Lilla an die Morgenröte; Das Mädchen; Des Mädchens Klage; Mignon Lied I–III; Mignon Romanze; Sehnsucht;* (i) *Ständchen; Der Tod und das Mädchen; Wehmut; Der Zwerg.*
(M) *(*) DG 431 476-2 (2) [id.]. Christa Ludwig, Irwin Gage, (i) with women's voices of Fr. R. Ch.

This reissue combines two collections by Christa Ludwig, made in 1974 and 1975 (each CD contains a complete recital). Neither shows her at her finest. She is most effective in the dramatic songs on the first disc; *Auf der Donau* and *Der Tod und das Mädchen* are both strikingly done, and the *Mignon Romanze* is beautiful. But *Ave Maria* is not relaxed enough and the simpler songs are lacking in charm. This applies even more to the second group, a challenging sequence of songs which fails to live up to the detailed imagination of her earlier Schubert performances on record. The results are often disappointingly lacking in charisma. Moreover, the microphones were evidently placed very near the singer, and the digital remastering, while giving striking projection of the dramatic songs, at times adds a hint of edge to the vocal timbre. However, Irwin Gage's sympathetic accompaniments are well in the picture.

Lieder: *Ave Maria; Jäger, ruhe von der Jagd; Raste Krieger!; Schwestergruss; Der Zwerg.*
(M) **(*) Ph. 426 642-2; *426 642-4* [id.]. Jessye Norman, Irwin Gage – MAHLER: *Des Knaben Wunderhorn* etc.**(*)

These five Schubert songs come as fill-ups to Jessye Norman's early (1971) recordings of songs from Mahler's *Des Knaben Wunderhorn*, plus two *Rückert Lieder*, all sensitively done, if with less detail than she would later have provided. Good recording for its period, well transferred.

Song-cycles: *Die schöne Müllerin, D.795; Schwanengesang, D.957; Winterreise, D.911.* Lieder: *Du bist die Ruh. Erlkönig; Nacht und Träume.*
(M) (***) EMI mono CMS7 63559-2 (3) [Ang. CDMC 63559]. Dietrich Fischer-Dieskau, Gerald Moore.

Fischer-Dieskau's early mono versions may not match his later recordings in depth of insight, but already the young singer was a searching interpreter of these supreme cycles, and the voice was at its freshest and most beautiful, so that one misses stereo remarkably little. Gerald Moore was, as ever, the most sympathetic partner.

Die Schöne Müllerin (song-cycle), *D.795*.
*** Decca Dig. 430 414-2; *430 414-4* [id.]. Peter Schreier, András Schiff.

Not since Benjamin Britten accompanied Peter Pears has a pianist played Schubert accompaniments with such individuality as András Schiff. He brings new illumination in almost every phrase, to match the brightly detailed singing of Schreier, here challenged to produce his most glowing tone. So in *Wohin?* Schiff transforms the accompaniment into an impressionistic fantasy on the flowing stream, and his rhythmic pointing regularly leads the ear on, completely avoiding any sense of sameness in strophic songs. Schreier, matching his partner as he did in their earlier, prize-winning recording of *Schwanengesang* (Decca 425 612-2), transcends even his earlier versions of this favourite cycle, always conveying his response so vividly that one clearly registers his changes of facial expression from line to line. At times the voice develops a throaty snarl, purposely so for dramatic reasons. Outstandingly warm and well-balanced recording.

Die Winterreise (song-cycle), *D.911*.
❀ (M) *** Decca 417 473-2 [id.]. Peter Pears, Benjamin Britten.

Winterreise (song-cycle), *D.911;* Lieder: *Erlkönig; Ganymed; Im Abendrot; Nachtgesang; Wanderers Nachtlied.*
(B) *** DG Compact Classics *427 724-4* [id.]. Dietrich Fischer-Dieskau, Gerald Moore.

Schubert's darkest song-cycle was in fact originally written for high voice, not low; quite apart from the intensity and subtlety of the Pears/Britten version, it gains enormously from being at the right pitch throughout. When the message of the poems is so gloomy, a dark voice tends to underline the sombre aspect too oppressively, whereas the lightness of a tenor is even more affecting. That is particularly so in those songs where the wandering poet in his despair observes triviality – as in the picture of the hurdy-gurdy man in the last song of all. What is so striking about the Pears performance is its intensity. One continually has the sense of a live occasion and, next to it, even Fischer-Dieskau's beautifully wrought singing sounds too easy. As for Britten, he recreates the music, sometimes with a fair freedom from Schubert's markings, but always with scrupulous concern for the overall musical shaping and sense of atmosphere. The sprung rhythm of *Gefror'ne Tränen* is magical in creating the impression of frozen teardrops falling, and almost every song brings similar magic. The recording, produced by John Culshaw, was made in the Kingsway Hall in 1963, and the CD transfer is exceptionally successful in bringing a sense of presence and realism.

In the early 1970s Fischer-Dieskau's voice was still at its freshest, yet the singer had deepened and intensified his understanding of the greatest of song-cycles to a degree where his finely detailed and thoughtful interpretation sounded totally spontaneous. Moore exactly matches the hushed concentration of the singer, consistently imaginative. It might be argued that this 1972 account is the finest of all Fischer-Dieskau's recorded performances of the cycle. This Compact Classics tape is very smoothly transferred and adds five other favourite Lieder for good measure, to make a genuine bargain.

OPERA

Fierrabras (complete).

*** DG Dig. 427 341-2 (2) [id.]. Protschka, Mattila, Studer, Gambill, Hampson, Holl, Polgár, Schoenberg Ch., COE, Abbado.

Few operas by a great composer have ever had quite so devastatingly bad a press as *Fierrabras*. However, in Vienna in 1988 Claudio Abbado conducted for a staging which, against all the odds, proved a great success; and the present recording was taken live from that. As with so many operas, the libretto is the main problem, absurd and cumbersome even by operatic standards. Yet the relationships between the central characters are clear enough, in this story from the days of chivalry. Schubert may often let his musical imagination blossom without considering the dramatic effect, so that there are jewels in plenty in this score; for example, the tenor *Romance* for Eginhard, the second hero, at the start of the Act I finale magically turns from minor to major when his beloved, Emma, takes over the tune. Later in Act II the other heroine, Florinda, transforms an already lovely melody by adding a mezzo-soprano descant. Many solos and duets develop into delightful ensembles, and the influence of Beethoven's *Fidelio* is very striking, with spoken melodrama and offstage fanfares bringing obvious echoes. By the standards of 1823 this was an adventurous opera, and it is sad that Schubert never saw it staged, so that he might have learnt to time the drama more effectively. A recording is the ideal medium for such buried treasure, and Abbado directs a performance as electrifying as his earlier one of Rossini's *Viaggio a Reims*, also with the Chamber Orchestra of Europe. Both tenors, Robert Gambill and Josef Protschka, are on the strenuous side, but have a fine feeling for Schubertian melody. Cheryl Studer and Karita Mattila sing ravishingly, and Thomas Hampson gives a noble performance as the knight, Roland, who finally wins Florinda. Only Robert Holl as King Karl (Charlemagne) is unsteady at times. The sound is comfortably atmospheric, outstanding for a live recording.

Schuman, William (born 1910)

Violin concerto.

(M) *** DG 429 860-2 [id.]. Zukofsky, Boston SO, Tilson Thomas – PISTON: *Symphony No. 2*; RUGGLES: *Sun-treader.****

William Schuman's *Violin concerto* was commissioned by Samuel Dushkin, who had partnered Stravinsky in the 1930s. It was revised twice and was championed by Isaac Stern, who played both versions in 1950 and 1956 respectively; but this later reworking dates from 1959. It is a tough but thoughtful piece with moments of characteristic dramatic intensity and poignant lyricism. Paul Zukofsky rises to its considerable technical demands with imposing virtuosity.

Symphony No. 4; Prayer in time of war.

** Albany TROY 027-2 [id.]. Louisville O, Jorge Mester – BECKER: *Symphonia Brevis*; HARRIS: *Epilogue to profiles in courage* etc.**

The *Fourth* is perhaps just a bit of a disappointment after the vital and exhilarating *Third* or the marvellous *Symphony for strings* (No. 5). By far the best (and most characteristic) sections are the eloquent and thoughtful central movement and the exhilarating finale. The work opens promisingly, with a powerful ground bass, but lapses into something very close to note-spinning. All the same, the more inspired passages leave a stronger impression in the memory than the passages of manufactured writing. *Prayer in time of war* comes from 1942, the period of the *Third Symphony*. It is a deeply felt piece, well played here by the Louisville forces. The recordings date from 1968 and 1972 respectively but have come up well.

Schumann, Robert (1810–56)

Piano concerto in A min., Op. 54.
(BB) **(*) Pickwick PWK 1148. Friedrich Gulda, VPO, Andrae – TCHAIKOVSKY: *Piano concerto No. 1.****
(M) **(*) Sony/CBS CD 44849; *40-44849.* Fleisher, Cleveland O, Szell – GRIEG: *Concerto.***(*)
(M) *(*) Decca Dig. 430 719-2; *430 719-4* [id.]. Jorge Bolet, Berlin RSO, Chailly – GRIEG: *Concerto.**
(B) * EMI CDZ7 62859-2; *LZ 762859-4.* John Ogdon, New Philh. O, Berglund – FRANCK: *Symphonic variations*; GRIEG: *Concerto.**
(M) (*) Decca mono 425 968-2 [id.]. Lipatti, SRO, Ansermet – BEETHOVEN: *Concerto No. 4.*(*)

Piano concerto in A min.; Konzertstück for piano and orchestra in G, Op. 92.
(M) * Sony SBK 46543 [id.]. Rudolf Serkin, Phd. O, Ormandy – GRIEG: *Concerto.***(*)

(i) *Piano concerto in A min. Arabeske in C, Op. 18.*
(M) *** Mercury 432 011-2 [id.]. Byron Janis, Minneapolis SO, Skrowaczewski – TCHAIKOVSKY: *Piano concerto No. 1.***(*)

Byron Janis's Schumann *Concerto* is a lovely performance, and the 1962 recording sounds amzingly improved over its previous incarnations, especially in regard to the orchestra. The piano is full and firm, if forward, and the orchestral sound has body as well as range. Janis's reading finds an almost perfect balance between the need for romantic ardour and intimacy in the *Concerto* – the exchanges between the piano and the woodwind soloists in the first movement are most engagingly done. Skrowaczewski provides admirable support throughout, and this is highly recommendable.

Gulda's performance is refreshingly direct with a brisk basic tempo in the first movement (the tempo in the coda is really nippy) yet, with light and crisp playing, the movement never sounds rushed. Similarly, the *Intermezzo* is moved along, but remains delicate in feeling, with nicely pointed pianism. The finale is just right, with an enjoyable rhythmic lilt. The Decca recording, from the beginning of the 1960s, is full and vivid, with excellent piano-tone.

Fleischer's 1960 account with Szell is also distinguished, the reading combining strength and poetry in a most satisfying way, yet with a finale that sparkles. In the first movement Szell relaxes the tempo for the famous piano and woodwind dialogues, and the effect is beguilingly intimate, in spite of a very bold, upfront orchestral recording, which tends to sound a little fierce. If the piano timbre is shallower than we would expect in a European recording, the effect remains warm and this makes a vivid listening experience.

Jorge Bolet's Schumann is rather more successful than the Grieg with which it is coupled, but he does not show any true feeling for this repertoire. The performance is agreeably relaxed – the short central movement comes off best – but the interplay between wind soloists and pianist in the first movement seems disappointingly matter-of-fact and the finale tends towards heaviness. The recording is admirable.

John Ogdon, as in the other works on this well-transferred CD, is unexpectedly below form in what should be one of the most poetic of piano concertos. Clearly the partnership with Berglund did not work well. The interchanges with the orchestral wind soloists in the first movement are lucklustre and the performance overall refuses to catch fire.

Serkin's harshly overdriven reading of Schumann's ever-fresh *Concerto* misses the spirit of the music altogether. Surprisingly, the performance of the *Konzertstück*, which follows on afterwards, is much more sympathetic, in spite of garish recorded quality.

Dinu Lipatti's Schumann comes from the archives of Radio Suisse Romande and was a public performance in Victoria Hall in February 1950. To be frank, the recorded sound is quite execrable. Lipatti has a small memory-lapse (at bar 66), which is not in itself important when ranged against his many poetic insights, some of which differ from his commercial recording with Karajan; but the sonic limitations here make this recommendable only for those studying the work rather than the general collector.

Violin concerto in D min., Op. posth.
(M) **(*) EMI Dig. CDD7 63898494-2 [id.]; *ET 763894*. Gidon Kremer, Philh. O, Muti – SIBELIUS: *Violin concerto*.**(*)

The Schumann *Violin concerto*, with its vein of introspection, seems to suit Gidon Kremer, who gives a generally sympathetic account of it and has very good support from the Philharmonia Orchestra under Riccardo Muti. It is not Schumann at his most consistently inspired, but there are good things in it, including a memorable second subject and a characteristic slow movement. The recording is full-bodied and vivid, balanced in favour of the soloist. It is good to have this recording reissued at mid-price, as it may tempt collectors to try the work.

Overture, Scherzo and Finale in E, Op. 52.
(B) *** DG 431 161-2; *431 161-4* [id.]. BPO, Karajan – BRAHMS: *Symphony No. 1*.***

This serves merely as a bonus for Karajan's fine 1964 recording of the Brahms *First Symphony*. He and his great orchestra are equally at home in the music of Schumann, and this performance is second to none. One could make the criticism that the CD transfer has lost some of the original weight and resonance in the bass, but the result is undoubtedly fresh and there is no suggestion here of the supposed thickness of Schumann's orchestration.

Symphonies Nos. 1–4.
(M) **(*) EMI CZS7 67319-2 (2). Philh. or New Philh. O, Muti.

Symphonies Nos. 1–4; Manfred overture, Op. 115.
(M) ** Sony/CBS M2YK 45680 (2) [id.]. Bav. RSO, Kubelik.

Symphony Nos. 1 in B flat (Spring), Op. 38; 3 in E flat (Rhenish), Op. 97.
(M) ** Sony/CBS MYK 42603 [id.]. Bav. RSO, Kubelik.

Reissued to celebrate Muti's fiftieth birthday, this Schumann cycle is not quite as successful as his Philharmonia set of the Tchaikovsky symphonies. But Muti is a spirited and warm-hearted interpreter of Schumann, and all four symphonies are most enjoyable. The very opening of No. 1 brings what is probably the most controversial speed in the whole set, so hectic that the spring-like lightness is rather missed. But it is is a purposeful reading, and Muti brings out the reserve of the *Second Symphony*; the dark inward quality of No. 3 is given a noble reading, and No. 4 (recorded first) an exhilarating, glowing one. Though the Philharmonia strings are not always as polished as they have since become, both playing and recording are warm and ripe, though the CD transfer has brightened the sound and given it rather more edge.

In his CBS/Sony set from the end of the 1970s Kubelik was recording the complete Schumann symphonies for the second time. The readings display the same bright and alert sensitivity to Schumann's style as does his set for DG, but the playing is less polished than that of the Berlin Philharmonic. Even so, it has plenty of life and vitality and the brass is impressive in the *Rhenish Symphony*. The recording is wide-ranging and emerges vividly on CD. It has rather more body and depth than the remastered DG sound but also has an element of coarseness in music which ideally needs refined textures. However, the performances have undoubted spontaneity and conviction and are enjoyable despite the above reservations. In many ways Karajan's versions of the four Schumann symphonies, now offered together in a box at medium price (DG 429 672-2), stand above all other modern versions. However, the digital remastering has brought leaner textures, while in tuttis the violins above the stave may approach shrillness; so our first choice in this repertoire at mid-price must move to Sawallisch and the Dresden State Orchestra on EMI. These performances are as deeply musical as they are carefully considered; the orchestral playing combines superb discipline with refreshing naturalness and spontaneity. Here the digital remastering has been entirely advantageous; the sound-picture has the essential fullness which the Karajan transfers lack, and the upper range is much firmer than it was on LP. Nos. 1 and 4 plus the *Overture, scherzo and finale* are on EMI CDM7 69471-2; *EG 769471-4*; Nos. 2 and 3 are on CDM7 69472-2; *EG 769472-4*.

Symphonies Nos. 1 in B flat min. (Spring), Op 38; 4 in D min., Op. 120.
(M) **(*) Ph. Dig. 432 059-2; *432 059-4* [id.]. Concg. O, Haitink.

Haitink conducts thoughtful and unexaggerated readings of these symphonies, beautifully paced and with refined playing from the Concertgebouw Orchestra. His chosen speeds are never controversial, and the playing is both polished and committed, to make these consistently satisfying performances. The only snag is the recording quality which, with works that from the start are thick in their orchestration, is too reverberant. It is an ample, pleasing sound, but something sharper would have helped more to rebut criticism of Schumann's orchestration.

Symphonies Nos. 3 in E flat (Rhenish); 4 in D min., Op. 120.
*** EMI CDC7 54025-2 [id.]; *EL 754025-4*. L. Classical Players, Norrington.

With Schumann's orchestration usually accused of being too thick, there is much to be said for period performances like this. Norrington not only clarifies textures, with natural horns in particular standing out dramatically, but, at unexaggerated speeds for the outer movements – even a little too slow for the first movement of No. 3 – the results are often almost Mendelssohnian. Middle movements in both symphonies are unusually brisk, turning slow movements into lyrical interludes. Warm, atmospheric recording.

Symphony No. 4 in D min., Op. 120.
** DG Dig. 431 095-2; *431 095-4* [id.]. VPO, Karajan – DVOŘÁK: *Symphony No. 8.***

Like the coupled Dvořák symphony, Karajan's last (1987) recording of Schumann's *Fourth* follows the pattern of his earlier interpretation, and is very well played; but the performance lacks spontaneity, particularly in the finale, which has much less grip than the earlier version. The recording too is thick, even approaching congestion at times.

CHAMBER MUSIC

Piano quintet in E flat, Op. 44.
(BB) *** Naxos Dig. 8.550406 [id.]. Jenö Jandó, Kodály Qt – BRAHMS: *Piano quintet.****

A strongly characterized performance of Schumann's fine *Quintet* from Jenö Jandó and the Kodály Quartet, bringing out the sombre character of the March of the second movement without being too doleful and finding plenty of energy for the scherzo and finale. Jandó has the right kind of personality for this work and he forms a genuine partnership with his colleagues. One notices the warm tone of the cellist in the first movement's secondary theme. This is robust music-making, romantic in spirit, and its spontaneity is well projected by a vivid recording, made in an attractively resonant acoustic. With its comparable Brahms coupling, this makes an excellent bargain.

Piano trios Nos. 1 in D min., Op. 63; 2 in F, Op. 80; 3 in G min., Op. 110; Fantasiestücke in A min., Op. 88.
** Chan. Dig. CHAN 8832/3; *DBTD 2020* (2) [id.]. Borodin Trio.

It is good to have all three of Schumann's *Piano trios* in one two-CD set with the *Fantasiestücke*, Op. 88, thrown in for good measure. These are full-hearted performances that give undoubted pleasure – and would give more, were it not for some swoons from Rostislav Dubinsky who, at the opening of the *D minor Trio*, phrases with a rather ugly scoop. While too much should not be made of this, greater reticence would have been more telling throughout. There are excellent notes by Joan Chissell and the Chandos recording is vivid and faithful.

String quartet No. 3 in A, Op. 41/3.
** EMI Dig. CDC7 54036-2 [id.]. Cherubini Qt – MENDELSSOHN: *String quartet No. 2.***
* DG Dig. 431 650-2 [id.]. Emerson Qt – BRAHMS: *String quartet No. 1.***

The Cherubini are a highly accomplished quartet who, alas, leave no phrase to speak for itself. Every gesture is carefully worked out and self-conscious; dynamic markings are exaggerated and phrasing is studied. The somewhat plainer two-star account by the Voces Intimae Quartet listed in our main volume (BIS CD 10, coupled, unexpectedly, with Sibelius), though not digital, is probably to be preferred.

The Emersons play superbly – incomparably even – but they are not wholly attuned to Schumann's sensibility. At no time does one sense Schumann's vulnerability; this is all too high-powered, with overnourished sonority and glossy surfaces. This is the world of Concorde and the jet era in which there is no real repose.

PIANO MUSIC

Carnaval; Faschingsschwank aus Wien, Op. 26; Kinderszenen, Op. 15.
(B) *** DG 431 167-2; *431 167-4* [id.]. Daniel Barenboim.

Barenboim's 1979 reading of *Carnaval* is one of his finest recording achievements in his role as pianist rather than as conductor. His lively imagination lights on the fantasy in this quirkily spontaneous sequence of pieces and makes them sparkle anew. It is as if he were in the process of improvising the music, yet his liberties of expression are never too great. He may allow himself free rubato in such a piece as *Valse noble*, but the result remains noble, not sentimental. The 'Masked ball' piece (*Carnival jest from Vienna*) is more problematic, but the challenge inspires Barenboim, and here too he is at his most imaginative and persuasive, bringing out the warmth and tenderness as well as the brilliance. The recital opens with a tender and charismatic reading of *Kinderszenen*, sensitive yet unmannered, and with the gentle opening bringing the lightest touch and the closing *Der Dichter sprich* wonderfully serene. The 1979 recording is bold and truthful, but the CD transfer has lost a little of the fullness in the bass that made the *Marche des Davidsbündler contre les Philistins* at the end of *Carnaval* so resonantly expansive on LP. Even so, this reissue offers a genuine bargain.

Fantasia in C, Op. 17; Fantasiestücke, Op. 12.
(M) **(*) EMI CDM7 63576-2 [id.]. Martha Argerich.

A rather exaggerated beginning to the *Fantasia* from Martha Argerich, with wide dynamic range and slightly mannered rubato, but with fabulous tone-production. She is always a fascinating artist; here, however, there are too many agogic distortions and touches of impetuosity to make one feel entirely happy with it as the only version for one's collection. There are many beautiful moments throughout this record, but her view of the *Fantasiestücke* is also too personal to be recommended without reservation. The recording is good but rather close.

Gesänge der Frühe, Op. 133; Nachtstuke, Op. 23; Waldszenen, Op. 82.
*(*) Nimbus Dig. NI 5250 [id.]. Daniel Levy.

Daniel Levy is currently engaged on a project to record all of Schumann's piano music and he has obvious feeling for the composer – indeed at times a little too much, for he lingers rather lovingly over some or other detail in some of the *Waldszenen*, such as *Einsame Blumen* and *Verrufene Stelle*. On the whole he is a sensitive (if almost too ruminative) artist. In such a competitive field, however, he needs better-focused sound than he gets here; there is far too much resonance, and some of the notes on his piano merit the attention of a technician. Dipping into other records in the series has not yielded significantly improved results.

Scriabin, Alexander (1872–1915)

(i) *Piano concerto; Symphony No. 3 in C min. (Le divin poème).*
*(**) BIS Dig. CD 475 [id.]. (i) Roland Pöntinen, Stockholm PO, Leif Segerstam.

Roland Pöntinen has a particularly strong affinity for Scriabin, as his concert appearances have shown, and his playing here in the *Piano concerto* strikes the right blend of musing intimacy and display. He rarely puts a foot (or perhaps one should say finger) wrong and is given sensitive support from Leif Segerstam and the Stockholm Philharmonic. Indeed, he is in some ways more totally attuned to this composer's sensibility than any of his current rivals. Perhaps Segerstam overdoes things in the opening of the second movement, where the string pianissimos are just a little self-conscious, but both here and in the *Third Symphony* he shows great finesse in matters of phrasing and tonal colour. Unfortunately these players are badly handicapped by the excessive reverberation of the hall; this muddies the texture and limits the pleasure these performances should give.

Le Poème de l'extase, Op. 54.
*** EMI Dig. CDC7 54061-2 [id.]; *EL 754061-4*. Phd. O, Muti – TCHAIKOVSKY: *Symphony No. 6.**
(*) Chan. Dig. CHAN 8849; *ABTD 1466* [id.]. Chicago SO, Järvi – MUSSORGSKY: *Pictures.*(*)
(M) ** Ph. (Everest) 422 306-2 [id.]. Houston SO, Stokowski – SHOSTAKOVICH: *Symphony No. 5.***(*)

Coupled with Muti's disappointing new version of Tchaikovsky's *Pathétique*, this Scriabin coupling brings a performance white-hot with passionate intensity, yet masterfully controlled, with each section following inevitably in one great span. One hopes that so fine a performance will soon be issued with a Scriabin coupling instead; meanwhile it is also available in the boxed set of the symphonies, see below.

Järvi's reading is powerfully extrovert, with the vibrant trumpet solo erotically dominating a boldly textured opulence. The reading does not look for subtlety, but it makes a powerful impression when the recording is so vivid in its primary colours.

Stokowski was surely born to conduct Scriabin's *Poème de l'extase*, but he needed a more sumptuous acoustic than was afforded him in this somewhat shallow 1960 recording, made at Houston. The result is a performance full of extrovert ardour but which lacks a sultry sentience. The excess of vividness borders on the vulgar.

Prometheus (Poem of fire), Op. 60.
*** EMI Dig. CDC7 54112-2 [id.]; *EL 754112-4*. Dmitri Alexeev, Phd. O, Muti – TCHAIKOVSKY: *Symphony No. 4*.**(*)

This Philadelphia version of *Prometheus* cannot quite match the vintage analogue rival, with Maazel conducting and Ashkenazy as soloist (Decca 417 252-2). Yet with Alexeev a brilliant soloist and the reading warm and sensuous, in line with Muti's previous recordings of Scriabin, anyone wanting this particular coupling can safely go ahead.

Symphonies Nos. 1–3; Poème de l'extase; (i) *Prometheus.*
*** CDS7 54251-2 (3) [id.]. Toczyska, Myers, Westminster Ch. (in *No. 1*), Phd. O, Muti, (i) with Alexeev.

Muti's complete set of the Scriabin *Symphonies* can be recommended almost without reservation. True, in No. 3 the recording could be more refined, but overall the sound is as vivid and richly coloured as the performances. With the two additional symphonic poems (discussed above) now added, in the place of the original, less appropriate Tchaikovsky couplings, this is an impressive achievement.

Symphony No. 2 in C min., Op. 29.
*** EMI Dig. CDC7 49859-2 [id.]; *EL 749859-4*. Phd. O, Muti – TCHAIKOVSKY: *Hamlet*.***

Muti's account of the *First Symphony* (on EMI CDC7 47349-2 – see our main volume, p. 939) was impressive, with its refinement of dynamic nuance, sumptuous tone and beautifully shaped phrasing. The *Second* fares no worse and must assume pride of place among modern recordings. Fine though Neeme Järvi's recent disc with the Royal Scottish National Orchestra is, the superbly responsive playing of the Philadelphia Orchestra puts this EMI CD in a rather special category. It would be invidious to single out any individual department of the orchestra, though some of the wind solos are particularly sensitive. The slow movement, with its strong atmosphere and art-nouveau wind decoration, has never sounded more convincing. Undoubtedly this is by far the finest account of the work yet to appear on disc – not forgetting the pioneering LP accounts from Svetlanov and Semkow. The recording too is good, though the climaxes sound opaque (yet this is due in no small measure to Scriabin's scoring). As with Muti's account of the *Third Symphony*, there is a Tchaikovsky coupling.

Piano sonatas Nos. 1–10; Piano sonata in E flat min. (1887–9); Sonata fantaisie in G sharp min.
(M) **(*) DG 431 747-2 (3) [id.]. Roberto Szidon.

Roberto Szidon recorded all ten sonatas as well as the two early sonatas and the Op. 28 *Fantasy* in 1971, and this reissue offers the whole set. This comes into direct competition with Ashkenazy's mid-price set on Decca (425 579-2). The Decca set accommodates sonatas Nos. 1–10 on two discs; Ashkenazy is at his finest in the early sonatas, whereas Szidon seems especially at home in the later works. His version of the *Black Mass sonata* (No. 9) fares best and conveys real excitement. At medium price this is an attractive reissue and can be considered alongside Ashkenazy's series. The DG recording is good but not ideal and the tone tends to harden at climaxes.

Serly, Tibor (1901–78)

Viola concerto; Rhapsody for viola and orchestra.
** Conifer Dig. CDCF 189; *MCFC 189* [id.]. Rivka Golani, Budapest SO, András Ligeti – BARTÓK: *Viola concerto* etc.*

Tibor Serly emigrated to the United States in early childhood, returning to Hungary to study with Hubay and Kodály. His *Viola concerto* dates from his late twenties and is written in a general-purpose post-nationalist style that owes much to the latter and to Bartók. Serly was the friend and colleague who completed the *Viola concerto* which Bartók was in the course of writing for William Primrose at the end of his life; that makes it very apt to have two of his concertante works for viola as coupling for the Bartók *Concerto*. With the best will in the world, neither the rather anonymous *Concerto* nor the later *Rhapsody* (1947–8), based on folksong harmonizations by Bartók, reveals any great distinction or personality. Rivka Golani, a disappointing soloist in the Bartók *Concerto*, is less taxed by the Serly works, with the orchestra providing colourful support, well recorded.

Servais, Adrien-François (1807–66)

Caprice sur des motifs de l'opéra, Le Comte Ory; Caprices, Op. 11/2 & 4; Grand duo de concert sur deux airs nationaux anglais; Grand fantaisie, Op. 20; Souvenir de Bade; Souvenir de Spa, Op. 2.
*** HM/BMG Dig. GD 77108; [77108-2-RG]. Bylsma, Smithsonian Chamber Players.

The names of Anner Bylsma and the Smithsonian Chamber Players on the label, noted as they are for performances of baroque music, might prompt the irreverent thought that Servais is a contemporary of Marais, Couperin or Leclair; but he was in fact a virtuoso who arrived on the scene rather later in musical history, and was hailed by Berlioz as 'the Paganini of the cello'. He made several extensive tours of Russia, where he played not only in St Petersburg and Moscow but in small villages, amazing all his listeners by the sheer size and magnificence of his tone and the effortlessness of his virtuosity. He composed two concertos and a number of *Souvenirs* and *Caprices*, which are presented here on Servais' own instrument, a Stradivarius from 1701 which, so rumour goes, had been presented to him by the Princess Youssopoff (or alternatively promised to him and prised out of her estate only after he threatened her heirs to publish some compromising letters). His music is entertaining stuff, particularly the *Grand duo de concert sur deux airs nationaux anglais*, written in collaboration with his colleague, Hubert Léonard. Somewhat unexpectly the the second '*air anglais*' turns out to be *Yankee doodle dandy*! The Servais cello is currently in use at the Smithsonian Institute, and so it is appropriate that six expert string-players of the Smithsonian group, plus harmonium, perform this music for us, providing a delightful entertainment – best not heard all at once, for the music is of spectacular triviality. But it is great fun, and very well recorded too.

Shostakovich, Dmitri (1906–75)

Cello concertos Nos. 1 in E flat, Op. 107; 2, Op. 126.
**(*) BMG/RCA Dig. RD 87918 [7918-2-RC]. Natalia Gutman, RPO, Temirkanov.

Natalia Gutman enjoys an almost legendary reputation in the Soviet Union and the Scandinavian countries, though she has made relatively few appearances in the UK and her representation in the CD catalogue is slender. Her thoughtful account of the two Shostakovich *Concertos* with the RPO and Yuri Temirkanov should satisfy collectors on most counts: the recording itself is first class and the playing has both eloquence and refinement. All the same, given the competition – Schiff, for instance, in the same coupling on Philips 412 526-2 and the newly restored DG version of the *Second Concerto* with Rostropovich, it is probably not a first choice.

Cello concerto No. 2, Op. 126.
(M) *** DG 431 475-2; *431 475-4* [id.]. Rostropovich, Boston SO, Ozawa – GLAZUNOV: *Chant du ménestrel*; TCHAIKOVSKY: *Andante cantabile.****

Shostakovich's *Second Cello concerto* first appeared in the mid-1960s; whereas Rostropovich recorded the *First* almost immediately, this concerto languished, unrepresented in the catalogue for a decade. The *Second* is completely different from its predecessor: its first movement is closer to the ruminative *Nocturne* of the *First Violin concerto* than to the taut, concentrated *Allegro* of the *First Cello concerto*. At first it appears to lack density of musical incident and seems deceptively rhapsodic, but closer acquaintance reveals its strength. Indeed it is an evocative and haunting work and the rhapsodic opening *Largo* seems curiously dreamlike until one realizes how purposeful is the soloist's course through its shadowy landscape. There is a short but succinct scherzo (in some ways, musically the least substantial of the three movements) and a haunting, lyrical finale, gently discursive, sadly whimsical at times and tinged with a smiling melancholy that suggests deeper sorrows. At first this finale, too, seems insubstantial, but it possesses concentration of mood rather than of musical content and lingers in the listener's mind long after the performance is over. Rostropovich plays with beautifully controlled feeling, and Seiji Ozawa brings sympathy and fine discipline to the accompaniment, securing admirably expressive playing from the Boston orchestra. The analogue recording is first class; if Rostropovich is forward in the aural spectrum, the balance is otherwise impeccably judged and the most is made of the spacious and warm acoustic, although in the CD transfer the snares of the side drum in the closing *Allegretto* are not absolutely sharply in focus.

Piano concerto No. 1 in C min., Op. 35.
*** Collins Dig. 1276-2; *1276-4* [id.]. Vladimir Ovchinikov, John Wallace (trumpet), Philh. O, Maxim Shostakovich – MUSSORGSKY: *Pictures.***(*)

Vladimir Ovchinikov's record of the *Concerto for piano, trumpet and strings* is cultivated and musical and has the advantage of some excellent playing from John Wallace and the Philharmonia Orchestra under Maxim Shostakovich. It is rather softer-edged and perhaps more thoughtful than some earlier readings on record, and some may feel that these artists over-beautify the slow movement. There is, however, no want of bite or wit in the finale. The recorded balance between the two soloists and orchestra is altogether excellent.

(i) *Piano concerto No. 2 in F, Op. 102;* (ii) *Violin concerto No. 1 in A min., Op. 77.*
*** Decca Dig. 425 793-2; *425 793-4* [id.]. (i) Ortiz; (ii) Belkin; RPO, Ashkenazy.

Though there are finer versions of both concertos, there are none better recorded, and anyone who wants this unusual coupling can safely invest in this unexpected instalment in the Ashkenazy Shostakovich series. Cristina Ortiz gives a sparkling account of the jaunty first movement of the *Piano concerto No. 2*, and she also brings out the fun and wit of the finale with fluent, finely pointed playing, not least in the delicious interpolated bars of 7/8. The central *Andante*, taken rather more slowly than usual, is both warm and refined, avoiding sentimentality in the haunting main theme, which here more than ever is like Rachmaninov slimmed down to the bare bones.

Boris Belkin in the first and more popular of the violin concertos plays immaculately and with consistently sweet, pure tone, but he misses some of the work's darker, deeper undertones, whether in the meditative *Nocturne* of the first movement or in the solo leading into the cadenza in the third movement. Decca sound is full and well balanced, not as distanced as other recordings in Ashkenazy's series. Those looking for a coupling of both *Piano concertos* can turn with confidence to Alexeev's superb Classics for Pleasure coupling with the ECO under Maksymiuk (CD-CFP 4547; *TC-CFP 4547*). Given the quality of both the performances and the sound, this record and tape should make new friends for the two concertos, particularly at such an attractive price.

Violin concertos Nos. 1 in A min., Op. 77; 2 in C sharp min., Op. 129.
*** Virgin Dig. VC7 91143-2; *VC7 91143-4* [id.]. Sitkovetsky, BBC SO, Andrew Davis.

No sooner had Lydia Mordkovitch's Chandos account been released to much acclaim (including our main volume) than Virgin followed it with another, from Dmitri Sitkovetsky and the BBC Symphony Orchestra under Andrew Davis. This is hardly less impressive and, in some ways, is more intense. Those who acquired the Mordkovitch/Järvi set need not (and will not) feel they should have waited, but there is no doubt as to the excellence of the newcomer, which has tremendous bite. It is also splendidly recorded, and takes its place at the top of the list.

Film music: *The Fall of Berlin, Op. 82; The Golden Mountains, Op. 30a; Michurin, Op. 78.*
** BMG/RCA Dig. RD 60226 [60226-2-RC]. Belgian RSO, Serebrier.

Shostakovich spent some of his youth playing in cinemas in the days of the silent films and before he came to international attention with the première of his *First Symphony*. He wrote copiously for the cinema in later life, and scores such as *Hamlet* are highly effective. José Serebrier's series with the Belgian Radio-TV Symphony Orchestra is filling in some of the gaps and his discs will inevitably be noted by those with a specialized interest in the composer. *Michurin* comes from 1948, a fateful year for him, and recycles some material he had already used in the 1930s. Both it and the music for *The Fall of Berlin* come from a particularly sterile period when Stalinist philistinism was at its height. Muted enthusiasm, then, for the music, but the performances are welcome in letting us judge this music away from its source.

SYMPHONIES

Among available versions of the Shostakovich symphonies, recordings by Haitink and Rozhdestvensky stand out. Our readers will need to turn to our main volume for a considered view of their merits. Haitink's readings of Nos. 1 and 9 (Decca 414 677-2), 2 and 3 (Decca 421 131-2), 13 (Decca 417 261-2), 14 (Decca 417 514-2) and 15 – see below – stand out for their directness, weight and architectural feeling. Rozhdestvensky is rather more volatile and incisive, and his couplings of Nos. 5 and 9 (Olympia OCD 113) and 6 and 12 (Olympia OCD 111) are both well worth having, as are his versions of No. 11 (Olympia OCD 152), 14 (Olympia OCD 182) and 15, where his gift of tapping the music's irony comes especially to the fore (Olympia OCD 179). Among individual records of distinction come Järvi's superb account of No. 4 (Chandos CHAN 8640; *ABTD 1328*) and 7, the *Leningrad* (Chandos CHAN 8623; *ABTD 1312*) with the SNO;

and Mravinsky's undoubtedly great performance of No. 8, admirably recorded at a live performance with the Leningrad PO in 1982 (Philips 422 442-2).

Symphony No. 5 in D min., Op. 47.
(M) **(*) Ph. (Everest) 422 306-2 [id.]. NY Stadium O, Stokowski – SCRIABIN: *Poème de l'extase.***
(M) *(**) Sony MYK 44770 [id.]. NYPO, Leonard Bernstein.
(M) *(*) EMI CD-EMX 2163. Chicago SO, Previn.

Stokowski gave us the first recording of this symphony in the era of 78s: it was one of the very finest of his many outstanding achievements with the Philadelphia Orchestra. He recorded it again in 1958 with the New York Stadium Orchestra, which drew its players mainly from the New York Philharmonic. It was neither as flexible nor as virtuoso an ensemble as the superb instrument Stokowski created in Philadelphia during the first decade of electric recording. Nevertheless the Stokowski electricity is at its highest voltage throughout this performance and especially in the slow movement, which is comparable with Previn's early LSO version (BMG/RCA GD 86801; *GK 86801* [6801-2-RG; *6801-4-RG*]). There is perhaps less subtlety in the individual wind solos than in the old 78 set, but the intensity of the playing more than compensates. The strings again create that 'drenched' radiance of texture in the upper register that Stokowski made his own and which makes the lyrical climaxes of the first and third movements so memorable, while the central episode of the brashly gripping finale is no less telling. This is a thrilling performance, and the late-1950s sound remains fully acceptable; its tendency to shrillness on top at fortissimo levels is easily controllable when there is plenty of spacious atmosphere and supporting weight. The master recording was made on 35-mm magnetic film, which is probably why there has been virtually no degradation over the intervening years.

Bernstein's analogue version comes from the end of the 1950s; his reading displays great emotional power and a driving force of great intensity. The New York players clearly feel the music the way Bernstein does, and the continual tension in the playing makes the very fast speed for the finale sound perfectly in accord with the reading as a whole. The composer was known to admire this performance, and it has undoubted greatness; however, the very brightly lit recording grows harsh at fortissimos, and the imbalance is more of a problem as the bass is relatively dry.

Previn's second recording, made in Chicago in 1977, does not match his earlier, RCA version (BMG/RCA GD 86801 [6801-2-RG]) in intensity. His view of the work does not seem to have changed in the intervening years; although the playing of the Chicago orchestra is of the highest quality, there is little sense of freshness or urgency. The first movement is a good deal slower than usual, so much so that one feels the want of momentum. The scherzo is played impressively, but the climax of the slow movement, so powerful in the earlier version, lacks real urgency. The remastered sound is very vivid; but this is a non-starter.

(i) *Symphony No. 9 in E flat;* (ii) *Symphony No. 10 in E min.*
(M) (***) Sony mono CD 45698. NYPO, (i) Efrem Kurtz; (ii) Dmitri Mitropoulos.

Dmitri Mitropoulos's pioneering account of the *Tenth Symphony* with the New York Philharmonic was for many years the yardstick by which later versions were judged. It still is. In spite of the inevitable sonic limitations, it penetrates more deeply into the heart of this score than any of the recent newcomers; only Karajan's mid-1960s version can be put alongside it. It comes with Efrem Kurtz's 1949 version of the *Ninth* (not quite pioneering, since Koussevitzky had beaten him to it) with the same orchestra, playing with great virtuosity. The sound is remarkably good for its period (an edit has removed one note from the opening phrase of the scherzo), but apart from that hiccup this is a stunning performance. Two great performances on one disc must represent one of the bargains of the year.

Symphony No. 10 in E min., Op. 93.
*** Telarc Dig. CD 80241 [id.]. Atlanta SO, Levi.
** Collins Dig. 1106-2; *1106-4* [id.]. LSO, Maxim Shostakovich.

Neither of the new CDs of the *Tenth Symphony* mounts a real challenge to either the digital Karajan recording (DG 413 361-2) or his earlier, 1967 account (at mid-price: DG 429 716-2; *429 716-4*) listed in our main volume, let alone Mitropoulos's inspired account listed above. Yoel Levi's developing experience and confidence are producing some fine performances in Atlanta, however, and he and his orchestra have the advantage of very good recording.

Collins also provide excellent sound for Maxim Shostakovich and the LSO. But Maxim's account is at lower voltage than one would expect and tension is not always maintained. Levi has greater intensity and his performance is recommendable, albeit not in preference to Järvi's Chandos alternative, which includes also the *Ballet suite No. 4* (CHAN 8630; *ABTD 1319*). James DePreist has recorded both this and the *Eleventh Symphony* with Finnish forces; they have been highly spoken of, but we have not yet been able to hear them.

Symphony No. 11 (The Year 1905).
**(*) DG Dig. 429 405-2 [id.]. Gothenburg SO, Järvi.

Neeme Järvi's account of the *Eleventh Symphony* has much to recommend it, including good orchestral playing and very fine recorded sound. Good though it is, the performance misses the last ounce of intensity that made the old LP accounts of Mravinsky and Stokowski so extraordinarily powerful. Neither Bychkov with the Berlin Philharmonic (Philips 420 935-2) nor Rozhdestvensky (Olympia OCD 152) really bowl one over, and for the moment the Chandos is the best recommendation for this work, *faute de mieux.*

Symphony No. 15 in A, Op. 141; The Gadfly, Op. 97a.
** Collins Dig. 1206-2; *1205-4* [id.]. LSO, Maxim Shostakovich.

Symphony No. 15 in A, Op. 141; October, Op. 131; Overture on Russian Kirghiz folk tunes, Op. 115.
**(*) DG Dig. 427 616-2 [id.]. Gothenburg SO, Neeme Järvi.

Neeme Järvi has a good feeling for the composer and, of the two digital new accounts of the *Fifteenth Symphony*, his should certainly be considered; it has personality and is played characterfully by the Gothenburg orchestra. *October* is a powerful work, written for the fiftieth anniversary of the Revolution in 1967, at about the same time as the *Second Violin concerto*. Very good sound, better than that on Rozhdestvensky's Olympia version (see our main volume). Rozhdestvensky, however, brings out the vein of dry humour in the music more than other interpreters, and his coupling is an exciting performance of the *First Piano concerto*, Yevgeny Kissin's brilliant début recording (OCD 179).

Maxim Shostakovich conducted the première recording of the *Fifteenth Symphony* with the Moscow Radio Orchestra, as well as its first performance. His splendidly recorded Collins version is a little wanting in tension by comparison (it certainly sags in the slow movement, which is much more measured). It is a thoughtful reading but, for all its sonic excellence, does not displace Mravinsky (Olympia OCD 224) or Rozhdestvensky. The suite from *The Gadfly* is not vintage Shostakovich and, though it is well played, would not sway matters. First analogue choice for this work still rests with Haitink, who couples it with the superb song-cycle, *From Jewish folk poetry* (Söderström, Wenkel, Karcykowski). This received a Rosette in our main volume (Decca 417 581-2).

CHAMBER MUSIC

Cello sonata, Op. 40; Moderato.
*** Decca Dig. 421 774-2; *421 774-4* [id.]. Harrell, Ashkenazy – PROKOFIEV: *Sonata.****

Lynn Harrell and Vladimir Ashkenazy give a convincing account of the *Sonata*, though they slow down rather a lot for the second group of the first movement. All their same, their brisk tempo and their freedom from affectation are refreshing (Yo-Yo Ma and Emanuel Ax take almost three minutes longer – Sony MK 44664). Harrell and Ashkenazy also include a short *Moderato* for cello and piano that came to light only five years ago in the Moscow State Archives and which could at some stage have been intended for the *Sonata* itself, though its brevity and its quality both make one doubtful.

24 Preludes and fugues, Op. 87.
❀ *** Hyp. Dig. CDA 66441/3 [id.]. Tatiana Nikolaieva.
** Kingdom Dig. KCLCD 2923 & 2924/5; *CKCL 2023 & 2024/5* [id.]. Marios Papadopoulos.

In this repertoire, the first choice must inevitably be Tatiana Nikolaieva, 'the onlie begetter', as it were, of the *Preludes and fugues*. It was when he heard her playing Bach in Leipzig in 1950 that Shostakovich conceived the idea of composing his cycle and, during the process of gestation, he telephoned Nikolaieva almost every day to discuss its progress. If Nikolaieva served as both its inspiration and midwife, her association with the work has been lifelong, and this shows. Her reading has enormous concentration and a natural authority that is majestic. There is wisdom and humanity here, and she finds depths in this music that have eluded most other pianists who have offered samples. When heard in its entirety over a couple of evenings, the whole cycle has a cumulative effect much greater than its individual parts. No grumbles about the Hyperion recording, which is very natural.

Marios Papadopoulos is a highly gifted player whose enterprise in recording the *Preludes and fugues* deserves the highest praise for, until Nikolaieva recorded them, there was no complete set in the UK, since her 1987 Melodiya recording was never issued here. Papadopoulos is both sensitive and intelligent, and is generally well recorded. The sound is slightly drier than that which Hyperion provide for Nikolaieva and, unlike Hyperion who accommodate all three discs in one box, the set is packaged in rather cumbersome fashion: the first twelve fit on to a single CD (KCLCD 2023); the remainder, which last 87 minutes, take two CDs which are boxed – the only advantage being that collectors can buy them in two instalments.

The Execution of Stepan Razin, Op. 119.
(*) Koch Dig. 3-7017-2 [id.]. Vassilev, Bulgarian R. & TV Ch. & O, Andreev – SVIRIDOV: *Oratorio patheique.*(*)

The Execution of Stepan Razin comes from 1964, the period of the *Thirteenth Symphony* and the *Ninth* and *Tenth Quartets*. It has been in and out of the catalogue over the years and in a strong performance can make a powerful impression. This version offers some fine singing from the bass, Assen Vassilev, who is very up-front in this balance, but otherwise both the performance and recording fall very far short of distinction.

Sibelius, Jean (1865–1957)

Violin concerto in D min. (1903–4 version); *Violin concerto in D min., Op. 47* (1905; published version).
*** BIS Dig. CD 500 [id.]. Leonidas Kavakos, Lahti SO, Osmo Vänskä.

Although the main ideas for the *Violin concerto* came to him much earlier, the work occupied Sibelius for much of 1903–4. Its first performance left him dissatisfied and he immediately withdrew it for revision. This CD presents Sibelius's initial thoughts so that for the first time we can see the familiar final version struggling to emerge from the chrysalis. The differences are considerable (though not by any means as extensive as those in the 1915 and 1919 versions of the *Fifth Symphony*, of which paired recordings are planned by this company). Comparison of the two concertos makes a fascinating study: the middle movement is the least affected by change, but the outer movements are both longer in the original score, and the whole piece takes almost 40 minutes. Very early on one is brought up with a start by an assertive rhythmic figure in the orchestra which Sibelius subsequently removed; and there is some solo writing of enormous difficulty, including a complete and demanding cadenza. Sibelius purified the concerto's form, deleting unnecessary ornament. A rather lovely idea which looks forward to the lighter palette of the *Humoresques* was also removed: the ability to sacrifice good ideas in the interests of structural coherence is one of the hallmarks of a great composer. But though there is some regret at the losses, the overall gain leaves one in no doubt as to the correctness of Sibelius's judgement. The Greek violinist, Leonidis Kavakos, proves more than capable of handling the hair-raising difficulties of the 1904 version and is an idiomatic exponent of the definitive concerto. The Lahti orchestra under Osmo Vänskä give excellent support and the balance is natural and realistic, with the soloist occupying the kind of aural space you would expect in the concert hall. An issue of exceptional interest and value.

Violin concerto in D min., Op. 47.
(BB) *** Naxos Dig. 8.550329 [id.]. Dong-Suk Kang, Slovak (Bratislava) RSO, Adrian Leaper – HALVORSEN: *Air Norvégien* etc.; SINDING: *Légende*; SVENDSEN: *Romance.****
(M) **(*) EMI Dig. CDD7 63894-2 [id.]; *ET 763894-4* [id.]. Gidon Kremer, Philh. O, Muti – SCHUMANN: *Concerto.***(*)

Dong-Suk Kang gave a commanding performance of the Sibelius *Violin concerto* at a 1990 (televised) BBC Prom. and is familiar to both concert and radio audiences on both sides of the Atlantic. He has already recorded the Nielsen *Concerto* (see our main volume, p. 736) and the six *Humoresques*, Opp. 87 and 89, and the *Serenades* (see above) and so chooses some popular Scandinavian repertoire pieces, such as the charming Svendsen *Romance in G*, as makeweights. Although Cho-Liang Lin's version on Sony, coupled with the Nielsen, is rather special, this newcomer is also very fine. He is perhaps a little wanting – albeit only a little – in tenderness as opposed to passion in the slow movement, but there is splendid virtuosity in the outer movements. The orchestral playing is decent rather than distinguished. In the bargain basement, this enjoys a strong competitive advantage, but even if it were at full price it would feature quite high in the current lists.

Kremer presents the *Concerto* essentially as a bravura showpiece and his is a vibrantly extrovert reading. While the recording balance places the soloist well forward, the orchestral texture has plenty of impact and good detail, and the fortissimo brass blaze out excitingly. There is undoubted poetry in the slow movement, and throughout Muti gives his soloist splendid support. This is hardly a first choice, with Cho-Liang Lin, Heifetz, Mullova and Accardo available (see our main volume pp. 959–60), but it is now much more competitive at mid-price, and it has an interesting and unique coupling.

(i) *Violin concerto; Symphony No. 5 in E flat, Op. 82; Tapiola.*
(B) **(*) DG Compact Classics *415 619-4* [id.]. (i) Ferras; BPO, Karajan.

Christian Ferras's account of the *Violin concerto* is a very good one and is well recorded. Although he begins the work with a winningly golden tone, when he is under stress, at the end of the first movement and in the finale, his intonation and general security are less than impeccable. However, there is still much to enjoy, and Ferras again develops a rich romantic tone for the main tune of the slow movement. Karajan's 1964 recording of the *Fifth Symphony* is undoubtedly a great performance. The orchestral playing throughout is glorious and the effect is spacious and atmospheric. Karajan finds an engrossing sense of mystery in the development section of the first movement, and there is jubilation in the finale. The only snag is that the Compact Classics tape is transferred at the highest level and there is a degree of harshness in the climaxes of the symphony, but this tape remains a formidable bargain.

The Dryad, Op. 45/1; En Saga, Op. 9.
(M) *** Chan. CHAN 6524 [id.]. SNO, Gibson – NIELSEN: *Symphony No. 4* etc.**(*)

Sir Alexander Gibson's analogue recordings of the Sibelius tone-poems date from the late 1970s and were originally issued by RCA. The recordings have been digitally remastered with great success; the slightly distant sound-balance is admirably suited to the music, with the spacious acoustic of Glasgow City Hall generally flattering the orchestra and creating a suitable ambient atmosphere. Gibson's affinity with the Sibelius idiom is at its most convincing here, particularly in an elusive piece like *The Dryad*, although *En Saga*, which opens the collection, is also evocative and shows an impressive overall grasp. The fine playing and natural perspectives of the recording contribute a great deal to the music-making. Although both ends of the sound spectrum are less sharply focused than in a digital recording (most noticeable in *En Saga*) climaxes are made excitingly expansive, with the brass superbly sonorous. At mid-price and offered coupled with the Nielsen *Fourth*, these versions make rewarding listening.

En Saga.
(M) (***) DG mono 427 783-2 [id.]. BPO, Wilhelm Furtwängler – RAVEL: *Daphnis et Chloé*; R. STRAUSS: *Till Eulenspiegel.*(***)

Furtwängler's account of *En Saga* has the right air of narrative and magic, and its sense of atmosphere and space completely transcends the sonic limitations inevitable in a 1944 recording.

En Saga; Finlandia; Karelia suite, Op. 11; Legend: The Swan of Tuonela; (i) *Pohjola's daughter.*
(M) *** EMI CDM7 63367-2 [id.]; *EG 763367-4*. VPO or (i) BBC SO, Sir Malcolm Sargent.

Sargent's collection is highly successful and a fine reminder of his affinity with this repertoire. Each performance has conviction and character, and the five pieces complement one another, making a thoroughly enjoyable CD programme. The Vienna

Philharmonic bring a distinctive freshness to their playing of music which must have been unfamiliar to them and Sir Malcolm Sargent imparts his usual confidence. The brass is especially full-blooded in *En Saga*, a performance full of adrenalin (as is *Pohjola's daughter*, the one item featuring the BBC Symphony Orchestra). *Finlandia* sounds unhackneyed and, with brisk tempi, *Karelia* has fine impetus and flair. The recordings, made in the Musikverein in 1961 and Kingsway Hall in 1958, are remarkably full and vivid; one would never suspect their age from these vibrant CD transfers, of EMI's best vintage.

(i) *Finlandia, Op. 26;* (ii) *Karelia suite, Op. 11;* (i) *Kuolema: Valse triste, Op. 44* (CD only: (ii) *En Saga, Op. 9; Legend: The Swan of Tuonela, Op. 22/2*).
(B) *** DG Compact Classics 413 158-2 (2); *413 158-4* [id.]. (i) BPO, Karajan; (ii) Helsinki R. O, Kamu – GRIEG: *Piano concerto; Peer Gynt.***

The bargain Compact Classics tape includes, alongside the fine Karajan performances of *Finlandia* and *Valse triste*, Kamu's splendid *Karelia suite*, as fine as almost any available, the outer movements atmospheric and exciting and the *Ballade* eloquently played, without idiosyncrasy. The pair of digitally remastered CDs further adds Kamu's admirable versions of *En Saga* and *The Swan of Tuonela.* The sound is very good throughout; Karajan's *Finlandia* has slightly more body on tape than than on compact disc. If the couplings are suitable (and Géza Anda's account of the Grieg *Piano concerto*, if not among the finest available, is certainly enjoyable), this is excellent value.

Finlandia, Op. 16; Legend: The Swan of Tuonela, Op. 22/2; The Oceanides, Op. 73; Pohjola's daughter, Op. 49; Tapiola, Op. 112.
(M) **(*) Chan. CHAN 6508; *MBTD 6508* [id.]. SNO, Gibson.

Gibson has a real feeling for Sibelius, and these very well-played performances are given an atmospheric and convincingly balanced analogue recording which makes a very realistic impression. *The Oceanides* is particularly successful and, if Karajan finds even greater intensity in *Tapiola*, Gibson's account certainly captures the icy desolation of the northern forests. He is at his most persuasive in an elusive piece like *The Dryad*, although *En Saga* is also evocative, showing an impressive overall grasp. The SNO are at the peak of their form throughout these performances.

(i) *6 Humoresques, Opp. 87 & 89; 2 Serenades, Op. 69; 2 Serious melodies, Op. 79. Ballet scene* (1891); *Overture in E* (1891).
*** BIS Dig. CD 472 (i) Dong-Suk Kang, Gothenburg SO, Neeme Järvi.

The *Humoresques* are among Sibelius's most inspired smaller pieces. They come from the same period as the *Fifth Symphony*, and some of the ideas may well have had their origin in a second violin concerto that we know was being planned in 1915. (One of the main themes of the *Sixth Symphony* was originally destined for it.) The *Humoresques* are poignant as well as virtuosic and have a lightness of touch, a freshness and a sparkle that make one wonder why they are not in the repertoire of every violinist of standing. Only Accardo, Aaron Rosand and one or two others have recorded them complete. The two *Serenades* are earlier (1912–13) and have great poetic feeling and a keen Nordic melancholy. They are wonderfully played by this distinguished Korean artist, who has impeccable technical address and is beautifully accompanied. The two orchestral works are juvenilia which predate the *Kullervo Symphony*. There are some characteristic touches (the second group of the *Overture* is very much in the *Karelia* idiom), but Sibelius himself did not think well enough of them to permit their publication. All the violin pieces, however, are to be treasured, and the recording is top class. A rewarding and indeed indispensable disc in its way, and not only for Sibelians.

Pelléas et Mélisande: suite, Op. 46.
*(*) Sony Dig. CD 45870 [id.]. Israel PO, Mehta – FAURÉ: *Pelléas* *(*); SCHOENBERG: *Pelléas.***

There is nothing very special to recommend Mehta's account of Sibelius's atmospheric score for *Pelléas et Mélisande.* It is certainly no match for Beecham or Karajan – or, for that matter, the more recent account by Neeme Järvi on BIS. It is of course a good idea to bring together three such disparate works inspired by Maeterlinck's play, but the best thing on this disc is the Schoenberg, where Mehta seems more completely attuned to the composer's sensibility.

Pohjola's daughter, Op. 49; Scènes historiques: All'overtura; Scena, Op. 25/1–2; The Hunt, Op. 66/1.
(M) ** EMI Phoenixa CDM7 63775-2 [id.]; *EG 763775-4.* Hallé O, Barbirolli – NIELSEN: *Symphony No. 4.***

This version of *Pohjola's daughter* is not to be confused with the later recording Sir John made with the Hallé for EMI in the 1960s. This comes from 1958 and is not its equal either as a performance or as a recording. The three *Scènes historiques* he includes here come from the mid-1960s and are much better in every respect.

Symphonies Nos. 1 in E min., Op. 39; 5 in E flat, Op. 82.
**(*) Telarc Dig. CD 80246 [id.]. Atlanta SO, Yoel Levi.

Both symphonies are well played by the Atlanta orchestra under Yoel Levi, and very well recorded. Though neither would be a first choice, both have many good qualities. The *First* has some sensitive orchestral playing and is strongly characterized. Perhaps the slow movement suffers from some expressive exaggeration (dynamic markings are exaggerated and the brass sforzandos at the movement's climax are certainly a bit larger-than-life) but the performance as a whole is very fresh and has plenty of feeling. The *Fifth* is very good without being exceptional, save in one respect: the handling of the difficult transition between the two sections of the first movement, which is quite masterly.

Symphonies Nos. 1 in E min, Op. 39; 6 in D min., Op. 104.
(M) *** EMI Dig. CDD7 63896-2 [id.]; *ET 763896.* BPO, Karajan.

In the *First Symphony* Karajan, a great Tchaikovsky interpreter, identifies with the work's inheritance. But there is a sense of grandeur and vision here, and the opulence and virtuosity of the Berliners helps to project the heroic dimensions of Karajan's performance. The early digital recording (1981) is not top-drawer: the bass is overweighted, but the full upper strings sing out gloriously with the richest amplitude in the finale, which has an electrifying climax; the brass is comparably rich and resonant.

The *Sixth* was the first of Sibelius's symphonies that Karajan conducted half a century ago when it was still new music and, as a young conductor at Aachen, he was invited to Stockholm for concerts with the Swedish Radio Orchestra in the mid-1930s. He has recorded it twice before, with the Philharmonia in the 1950s and with the Berlin Philharmonic a decade later. This version was made in 1981 and brings to life the other-worldly quality of this score: the long white nights of the northern summer and their 'fragile melancholy', that the slow movement (or, for that matter, the opening polyphony) conjures up. Even though this is a spacious account, we are never unaware of the sense of forward movement. Although this performance seems more spacious and more unhurried than the DG account recorded in 1967, each movement is in fact marginally quicker. In short, this is Karajan at his finest: not even Beecham made the closing pages sound more magical. This recording is better than its predecessor, and the EMI team have achieved a more spacious acoustic ambience. The French critic, Marc Vignal, spoke of Sibelius as 'the aristocrat of symphonists', and this, surely, is the aristocrat of performances.

Symphonies Nos. 1 in E min., Op. 39; 7 in C, Op. 105.
(M) *** Decca Dig. 425 028-2; *425 028-4* [id.]. Philh. O, Ashkenazy.

Ashkenazy's digital coupling of the *First* and *Seventh Symphonies*, recorded in 1982 and 1984 respectively, is outstandingly successful; at mid-price, it will become a ready first choice for most collectors. The performance of the *First* is held together well and is finely shaped. Ashkenazy is exactly on target in the Scherzo. The resultant sense of momentum is exhilarating and here, as when echoing the main theme of the first movement, the timpani make a riveting effect. Throughout, the sheer physical excitement that this score engenders is tempered by admirable control. Only at the end of the slow movement does one feel that Ashkenazy could perhaps have afforded greater emotional restraint, but the big tune of the finale is superbly handled. The recording has splendid detail and clarity of texture, and there is all the presence and body one could ask for, with the bass-drum rolls particularly realistic. The *Seventh Symphony* is also very fine. Ashkenazy does not build up this work quite as powerfully as some others do, but he has the measure of its nobility and there is much to admire – indeed, much that is thrilling in his interpretation. As in the *First Symphony*, the playing of the Philharmonia Orchestra, like the recording, is of the very first order.

Symphony No. 2 in D, Op. 43.
**(*) Chesky/New Note CD-3 [id.]. RPO, Barbirolli.
(M) (*(*)) EMI mono CDH7 63307-2 [id.]. BBC SO, Toscanini.

Symphony No. 2 in D.; Finlandia, Op. 26.
*(*) Teldec/WEA Dig. 2292 46317 [id.]. NYPO, Mehta.

Symphony No. 2 in D.; Karelia Suite, Op. 11.
** Collins Classics Dig. 1105-2; *1105-4*. RPO, Gibson.

Symphony No. 2 in D; Kuolema: Valse triste; Legend: The Swan of Tuonela; Pohjola's daughter.
(B) **(*) RCA VD 60489; *VK 60489*. Phd. O, Ormandy.

Barbirolli's version with the RPO is a performance of stature and is by far the finest of the four versions he committed to disc. There is a thrilling sense of live music-making here and a powerful sense of momentum. A high-voltage account, then, and very well recorded, though the upper strings are slightly drier than they were in the LP version on RCA. It retails at full price, which reduces its competitiveness, particularly as it comes without a fill-up. The sleeve has some howlers: Rapallo, where Sibelius started working on it, is not 'an art-laden town south of Benice' but on the other side of Italy, to the east of Genoa; and the work's dedicatee, Axel Carpelan, was far from 'wealthy'. All the same, this performance is powerful and must rank among the best currently before the public.

There is no doubt that Ormandy offers a thrilling performance of the *Second Symphony*, and the Philadelphia strings play with great fervour. This would bring the house down at a concert, but on record one needs a shade more subtlety. Nevertheless, with its fine bonus items, this is highly competitive in the bargain range.

The Collins Classic account of the *Second Symphony*, well played by Sir Alexander

Gibson and the Royal Philharmonic and impressively recorded, is not a great improvement on his Chandos version (the string-tone sounds better-nourished) though he remains an artist of strong Sibelian instinct. He never interposes himself between the music and the listener, but the reading has just a touch of the routine about it.

Toscanini's BBC recording was made during his 1938 visit to London, but it is not quite as electrifying as his Wagner and Debussy of 1935. He tends to press ahead, as indeed he does in his two subsequent performances. The BBC Symphony Orchestra was a splendidly responsive instrument at this time but, high voltage though it is, there is not the sense of atmosphere or conviction as in the Koussevitzky and Beecham issues. The ends of each movement are barbarously cut off without any atmosphere.

Zubin Mehta and the New York Philharmonic are well recorded on Teldec and there is no great cause for complaint on any grounds. They give a perfectly acceptable account of the work. But judged alongside the versions listed in our main volume this is a little wanting in real character and personality.

Symphony No. 4 in A min., Op. 63; The Bard, Op. 64; The Oceanides, Op. 73; Pohjola's Daughter, Op. 49.
*** RCA Dig. RD 60401 [60401-2-RC]. Finnish RSO, Saraste.

Saraste's *Fourth* is a useful addition to the catalogue. His disc offers three other essential Sibelius works in very good performances. The *Symphony* too is well played and has plenty of atmosphere and power; though not all details are perfect (sufficient attention is not paid to dynamics at the opening of the finale), his is basically a convincingly shaped reading which penetrates well inside this dark, elusive world. He rightly uses the glockenspiel in the *Symphony* and follows Sibelius's instructions (in a letter to Leslie Heward) recommending tubular bells for *The Oceanides*, the only conductor to do so. Quite apart from that, his reading is very fine indeed, and there is nothing much wrong with *The Bard* or *Pohjola's daughter* either – and a lot that is right. The Finnish Radio Orchestra plays well for him and the recording is both present and full-bodied.

Symphony No. 4 in A min., Op. 63; The Tempest: suite No. 1, Op. 109 bis.
**(*) Chan. Dig. CHAN 8943; *ABTD 1539* [id.]. Danish Nat. RSO, Leif Segerstam.

Leif Segerstam's reading is powerfully conceived. Like Maazel, Segerstam takes a broadly expansive view of the score but, unlike Maazel, he takes the finale at a proper allegro, though he slows down rather more than he should in the final bars. There are some expressive exaggerations (he more or less halves speed at the *Tranquillo* marking in the scherzo), but there is much more to admire than to cavil at. He gives us a powerfully atmospheric account of the first of the two suites from Sibelius's music to *The Tempest* which, while it is not always as concentrated in feeling or as beautifully paced as the Beecham recording listed in our main volume (EMI CDM7 63397-2; *EG 763397-4*), is still the best to have appeared for some time. Very good recorded sound.

Symphonies Nos. 4 in A min, Op. 63; 5 in E flat, Op. 82.
*** Decca Dig. 425 858-2; *425 858-4* [id.]. San Francisco SO, Herbert Blomstedt.
** Sony Dig. SK 46499 [id.]. Pittsburgh SO, Maazel.

Blomstedt's accounts of the *Fourth* and *Fifth Symphonies* are the finest to have appeared for some years. He allows the music to unfold naturally and conveys a real sense of space. At no point is one ever aware of the barline. The *Fourth Symphony*, some of whose ideas began life as a quartet, has the intimacy of chamber music and yet communicates a strong feeling of the Nordic landscape. Blomstedt is particularly attentive to dynamic shading and gets playing of great tonal refinement from the San Francisco orchestra. He uses tubular bells in the finale of the *Fourth* (Sibelius asked for glockenspiel, and for tubular bells in *The Oceanides*) but no one makes the closing bars of the finale sound more affecting. The *Fifth Symphony* is also wonderfully spacious. Some may find the accellerando between the two sections of the first movement a shade steep, but there is a powerful sense of mystery in the development section.

The *Fourth Symphony* is very different from Maazel's 1968 recording with the Vienna Philharmonic (still available on Decca at mid-price and coupled with the *First* – 417 789-2; *417 789-4*). This new reading is much more expansive and takes the best part of 40 minutes, as opposed to 32! Yet it doesn't seem all that much slower and is obviously very well thought out. The Pittsburgh produce a sumptuous sound in all departments and have obvious enthusiasm for the piece. There is a particularly strong feeling for nature evident throughout and, although ultimately Blomstedt and Karajan (DG 415 108-2) have more to say about the work, Maazel's is a most thoughtful reading and, save for the very spacious finale, a generally convincing one. The *Fifth* was one of the least successful of his Vienna cycle, nor does it wholly succeed here. There are impressive things. The transition into the second section of the first movement is very well managed, but elsewhere Maazel is self-conscious, and the finale is too rushed.

Symphony No. 5 in E flat; Pohjola's daughter, Op. 49.
(M) **(*) Sony CD 44720 [MYK 38474]; *40-44720.* NYPO, Bernstein.

Bernstein's earlier NYPO *Fifth* is splendidly played and totally unmannered. It is a reading of genuine stature, among the very finest on record. Although the recording is not ideal – it could have more richness of texture and less brilliance – the quality of this performance earns it the strongest recommendation. The coupling is a finely proportioned reading of *Pohjola's daughter*, again lacking amplitude in the sound, but certainly a thrilling performance.

Symphony No. 6 in D min., Op. 104; Scènes historiques, Op. 25 & Op. 66.
* RCA Dig. RD 60157; *RK 60157* [60157-2-RC]. Finnish RSO, Jukka-Pekka Saraste.

Saraste's sense of direction in the *Sixth Symphony* flags and his tempi tend to be too slow for any sense of line to be sustained effectively. He is splendidly recorded, and both sets of the *Scènes Historiques* fare rather better but are not sufficiently outstanding to give this record more than a very qualified welcome.

String quartet in D min. (Voces intimae), Op. 56.
** Ph. Dig. 426 286-2 [id.]. Guarneri Qt – GRIEG: *Quartet.***

The Guarneri play Sibelius's only mature *Quartet* with great brilliance and some insight, though the finale is dreadfully rushed. The performance has a high gloss – though, to be fair, these players manage the slow movement well, and the celebrated hushed chords that give the piece its title are suitably withdrawn. The high finish of their playing excites admiration, but this music requires more than polish.

Simpson, Robert (born 1921)

Energy; Introduction & allegro on a theme by Max Reger; The Four Temperaments; Volcano; Vortex.
*** Hyp. Dig. CDA 66449 [id.]. Desford Colliery Caterpillar Band, James Watson.

There is some extraordinary music here, including one masterpiece, *The Four*

Temperaments (1983), which packs quite a punch. This is a four-movement, 22-minute symphony of great imaginative power, and ingeniously laid out for the band. Simpson played in brass bands as a boy and this is doubtless where he acquired some of his expertise in writing for them. Yet he did not write his first mature band piece until he was fifty: this was *Energy* (1971) which came in response to a commission from the World Brass Band Championships. The *Introduction and allegro on a theme by Max Reger* (1987) is based on a figure that occurs in Reger's *Fantasia and fugue in D minor*, Op. 135b, for organ and is every bit as awesome and impressive as the annotator claims. Together with *Volcano* and his most recent piece, *Vortex*, this makes up his entire output in this medium. The Desford Colliery Caterpillar Band under James Watson play with all the expertise and virtuosity one expects, and the recording has admirable clarity and body, though the acoustic is on the dry side. All the same, this is not to be missed, particularly by those who imagine that they don't like the medium.

String quartets Nos. 1; 4.
*** Hyp. Dig. CDA 66419; *KA 66419* [id.]. Delmé Qt.

The *First Quartet* comes from 1951, the same year as Simpson's *First Symphony*, and is a remarkable piece. This is not its first appearance on record but is decidedly the best. It opens in as innocent a fashion as the Haydn *Lark Quartet* or Nielsen's *E flat* but, the better one comes to know it, the more it is obvious that Simpson is already his own man. The second movement is a palindrome (most modern composers do not know how to write forwards, let alone backwards as well) but its ingenuity is worn lightly. The *Fourth* (1973) is part of the trilogy which Simpson conceived as a kind of commentary on Beethoven's *Rasumovsky quartets* (Simpson suggests that 'if these works enhance the understanding of the genius of Beethoven at their own expense, their purpose will be served'.) Yet they live very much in their own right. Excellent performances from the Delmé, and fine recording too.

Sinding, Christian (1856–1941)

Légende, Op. 46.
(BB) *** Naxos Dig. 8.550329 [id.]. Dong-Suk Kang, Slovak (Bratislava) RSO, Adrian Leaper – HALVORSEN: *Air Norvégien* etc.; SIBELIUS: *Violin concerto*; SVENDSEN: *Romance.****

Dong-Suk Kang plays Sinding's *Légende* with great conviction and an effortless, songful virtuosity. It is by no means as appealing as the Halvorsen and Svendsen pieces but makes a good makeweight for an excellent collection in the lowest price range.

Smetana, Bedřich (1824–84)

Má Vlast (complete).
*** DG Dig. 431 652-2 [id.]. VPO, James Levine.
**(*) Denon Dig. DC 8095 [id.]. Czech PO, Václav Neumann.

At long last DG have remastered James Levine's outstanding complete *Má Vlast* on to a single CD (76 minutes). The recording, made in the Grosser Saal of the Vienna Musikverein in 1986, is admirably spacious, with a fine sweep to the strings and resonant brass. Levine's reading of Smetana's cycle of six symphonic poems is both imaginative and full of romantic flair; the VPO are admirably responsive and, while Pešek's fine Liverpool version brings its own insights and a certain Czech idiomatic feeling (Virgin

VC7 91100-2; *VC7 91100-4*), the greater polish of the VPO playing and the attractive Viennese ambience mean that the DG version now becomes the primary recommendation.

We are familiar with Neumann's reading of *Má Vlast*, heard at its best in a 1968 Teldec recording with the Leipzig Gewandhaus Orchestra (not at present available on CD). Here, with the advantage of live music-making and with the Czech Philharmonic in good form, one expected something rather more gripping. Certainly the playing has its exciting moments, as when the Vltava River approaches the St John's Rapids, and it is never dull. Moreover there is much delightful wind-playing (in the central section of *Blaník*, for instance) and the violins bring a gossamer transparency to their pianissimo entry in *From Bohemia's woods and fields*. Neumann undoubtedly has a special feeling for the music's lyrical flow but, even so, this performance remains obstinately unmemorable. The recording, made in Tokyo's Bunka Kaikan (Public Hall), is not especially flattering: the Japanese engineers have chosen to go for brilliance and clear detail rather than evocation and sumptuous warmth.

Má Vlast: Vltava.
(M) (**) BMG/RCA GD 60279; *GK 60279* [60279-2-RG; *60279-4-RG*]. NBC SO, Toscanini – DVOŘÁK: *Symphony No. 9*; KODÁLY: *Háry János suite.*(***)

Recorded several years earlier than the other two items on the disc, *Vltava* has painfully dry and close sound; but the intensity of Toscanini's performance still makes it a valuable document, along with the searing accounts of Dvořák and Kodály.

Má Vlast: Vltava; Vyšehrad.
(B) *** DG Compact Classics *413 159-4* [id.]. Bav. RSO, Kubelik – DVOŘÁK: *Slavonic dances*; LISZT: *Hungarian rhapsodies; Les Préludes.****

Part of a generally attractive collection of Slavonic music. Kubelik's excellent performances come from his complete set and are splendidly played and very well recorded, although the acoustic is slightly dry.

String quartet No. 1 in E min. (From my life).
**(*) Virgin Dig. VC7 90807-2; *VC7 90807-4* [id.]. Endellion Qt – DVOŘÁK: *Quartet No. 12* **(*)
** DG Dig. 429 723-2 [id.]. Emerson Qt – DVOŘÁK: *Quartet No. 12.***

The Endellions give a spirited account of the Smetana *Quartet*, one of the best to have appeared in the last year. It is more strongly characterized than the Medici (on Nimbus) though it does not always speak with wholly idiomatic accents. But their playing is always vitally musical, rich in sonority and strongly passionate. They are very well recorded indeed and are competitive, though their leader spoils the Dvořák coupling by pulling the second theme of the first movement out of shape.

The Emerson Quartet are nothing if not high-powered, and Smetana is dispatched with record precision and attack. They sound at times almost like a small orchestra, and words like tenderness, respose and intimacy appear only on the farmost horizons of their vocabulary. Their playing is phenomenonal but slick.

Smyth, Ethel (1858–1944)

Mass in D; March of the Women; Boatswain's mate: Mrs Water's aria.
*** Virgin Dig. VC7 91188-2; *VC7 91188-4* [id.]. Harrhy, Hardy, Dressen, Bohn, Ch. & O of Plymouth Music Series, Minnesota, Philip Brunelle.

Written in the early 1890s in devotion to a young woman friend who was a Catholic, Ethel Smyth's *Mass in D* is one of her most ambitious works, a piece that boldly seeks to echo Beethoven's great *Missa solemnis* in its moods and idiom. Though Smyth's invention is less memorable than Beethoven's, the drive and the vehemence of her writing make this a warmly rewarding piece, with Brahms's *Requiem* another, if less marked, influence. Daringly, Smyth makes the *Christe eleison* into a bitingly insistent sequence, an urgent plea to Christ, which leads to a fortissimo return of the *Kyrie* on an idea originally presented in meditative counterpoint. The composer herself counted the *Gloria*, the longest and most energetic movement, as the finest and prescribed that it should be performed, not in the usual liturgical sequence, but last, as a happy ending, as is done here. Brunelle, first heard in the Virgin set of Britten's *Paul Bunyan*, here comparably resurrects a forgotten British work with great success, drawing fine playing and singing from the members of the Plymouth Music Series. Smyth's once-celebrated suffragette march is done with polish rather than feminist fervour, and Eiddwen Harrhy makes a characterful soloist in the extended aria from Smyth's best-known opera. First-rate sound.

Soler, Vicente Martín y (1754–1806)

Keyboard sonatas Nos. 18 in C min.; 19 in C min.; 41 in E flat; 72 in F min.; 78 in F sharp min.; 84 in D; 85 in F sharp min.; 86 in D; 87 in G min.; 88 in D flat; 90 in F sharp; Fandango.

*** Virgin Dig. VC7 91172-2; *VC7 91172-4* [id.]. Maggie Cole (harpsichord or fortepiano).

Maggie Cole plays a dozen Soler pieces, eleven *Sonatas* and the celebrated *Fandango*, half of them on the harpsichord and the remainder on the fortepiano; she gives altogether dashing performances on both. The fortepiano is a Derek Adlam copy of a Viennese instrument of the 1790s by Anton Walther and the harpsichord is a Goble. Good pieces to sample are *No. 87 in G minor* (track 5) and, on the harpsichord, *No. 86 in D major* (track 9) or the *Fandango* itself. The playing is all very exhilarating and inspiriting. Played at a normal level-setting, both instruments sound a bit thunderous but, played at a lower level, the results are very satisfactory.

Spohr, Ludwig (1784–1859)

(i) *Violin concerto No. 8 in A min. (In modo d'una scena cantate), Op. 47;* (ii) *Double quartet in D min., Op. 65.*

(M) (***) RCA mono GD 87870; *GK 87870* [7870-2-RG; *7870-4-RG*]. Heifetz, with (i) RCA Victor O, Izler Solomon; (ii) Baker, Thomas, Piatigorsky, Amoyal, Rosenthal, Harshman, Lesser – BEETHOVEN: *Serenade.***

Spohr's *Gesangszenekonsert* is in mono and dates from 1954. A dazzling performance which, in sheer beauty and refinement of tone, remains unsurpassed. Although the recording acoustic could with advantage have been more ample, this is still very good sound for its period and in some ways is more appealing than the dryish, 1968 stereo recording of the *D minor Double quartet*, Op. 65, made with various artists including the young Pierre Amoyal, then his pupil, who leads the second (and more subservient) quartet. The first violin dominates the texture, a reminder both of Spohr's prowess as a violinist and – certainly – of Heifetz's. His distinctive timbre and glorious tone shine through. Incomparable playing, without doubt, though they do not exactly produce a homogeneous quartet-blend. But, given Heifetz's sound, who cares!

String quartets Nos. 27 in D min.; 28 in A flat, Op. 84/1–2.
**(*) Marco Polo Dig. 8.223251 [id.]. New Budapest Qt.

These two works, written in 1831–2, exemplify Spohr's smooth, finely integrated quartet-writing at its most characteristic. The slow movement, sustaining a mood of serene simplicity, is the most memorable in each case, although the lyrical finale of the *A flat major Quartet* is also rather appealing. Good performances, lively enough, but capturing the suaveness of the idiom. The recording is truthful.

String quartets Nos. 29 in B min., Op. 84/3; 30 (Quatuor brillant) in A, Op. 93.
**(*) Marco Polo Dig. 8.223252 [id.]. New Budapest Qt.

In many ways *No. 29 in B minor* is the finest of the Op. 84 set, with its touch of melancholy in the first movement, a lively minuet and a pensive slow movement. Op. 93, written in 1835, is more extrovert in atmosphere in the first movement (after a sombre introduction), but it offers another thoughtfully intense slow movement and a very jolly finale. It brings out the best in these players – and there is plenty of bravura for the first violin – and, again, good tonal matching plus a smooth, warm recording combine effectively for this slightly suave music.

Steiner, Max (1888–1971)

Film scores: *The Big Sleep* (suite). *The Charge of the Light Brigade: The charge; The Fountainhead* (suite). (i) *Four Wives: Symphonie moderne.* (ii) *The Informer* (excerpts). *Johnny Belinda* (suite); *King Kong* (excerpts); *Now Voyager* (excerpts); *Saratoga Trunk: As long as I live. Since you went away:* Title sequence.
(M) *** BMG/RCA GD 80136; *GK 80136* [0136-2-RG; *0136-4-RG*]. National PO, Charles Gerhardt, with (i) Earl Wild; (ii) Amb. S.

Max Steiner, Viennese born, emigrated to the USA in 1914 and, after working as a conductor–arranger–pianist on the East Coast, was lured out West with the coming of the talkies in 1929. He worked first for RKO (providing music for some 135 pictures), then moved to the Selznick studio and on to Warner Brothers, where he wrote scores for 155 more films. Selznick borrowed him back for *Gone with the Wind.* Steiner would wait until a film was completed and edited before producing his ideas; he would then develop the finished work quickly and spontaneously, but would leave the orchestration to others. He understood that music could slow up as well as enhance a scene, and his professionalism was justly admired. His style is unashamedly eclectic, but his writing never sounds thin in ideas. He could produce a good tune on demand, with the luscious themes for *Now Voyager* and *As long as I live* from *Saratoga Trunk* almost approaching the famous *Gone with the Wind* melody in memorability; and a dulcet touch was available for the wistful portrayal of *Johnny Belinda. King Kong* and *The Big Sleep* introduce appropriate elements of menace, and in *The Informer* the Ambrosian Singers provide a characteristic outpouring of Hollywood religiosity at the final climax (the death of the principal character). Charles Gerhardt is a master of the grand orchestral gesture and presents all this music with enormous conviction and with care for atmospheric detail. The orchestra (92 strong) are obviously enjoying themselves hugely, and the recording offers a fine blend of spaciousness and spectacle. There are excellent notes, but one would have welcomed more movie stills – only *Now Voyager*, *King Kong* and Erroll Flynn leading *The Charge of the Light Brigade* are represented pictorially.

Film scores: *The Big Sleep: Love theme; The Caine Mutiny: March; Casablanca* (suite); *Key Largo* (suite); *Passage to Marseilles: Rescue at sea; The Treasure of the Sierra Madre* (suite); *Virginia City* (excerpts). (Also includes music by WAXMAN: *To Have and Have Not; The Two Mrs Carrolls.* HOLLANDER: *Sabrina.* YOUNG: *The Left Hand of God.* ROZSA: *Sahara.*)
(M) ** BMG/RCA GD 80422; *GK 80422* [0422-2-RG; *0422-4-RG*]. National PO, Gerhardt.

This collection concentrates on the key Humphrey Bogart movies and certainly shows Steiner's versatility. The changes of mood in the five brief sequences from *The Treasure of the Sierra Madre* are mirrored most imaginatively. However, the evocative piano solo, so famous in *Casablanca*, is not very successful here, although there is some touchingly romantic lyrical writing in *Key Largo*. Among the items by other composers, the Waxman excerpts and the eloquent Victor Young melody for *The Left Hand of God* stand out. This is one of the least repeatable of the Gerhardt compilations, although performances, recording and CD transfers are all well up to standard. Again good notes, but only three movies are represented pictorially.

Gone with the Wind (film score).
(M) *** BMG/RCA GD 80452; *GK 80452* [0452-2-RG; *0452-4-RG*]. National PO, Charles Gerhardt.

It was sensible of Steiner not to associate his most potent musical idea in *Gone with the Wind* with one or more of the principal characters, but instead to centre it on Tara, the home of the heroine. Thus he could work it as a leitmotif and have it return again and again through a complex score of some two and a half hours to remind the audience nostalgically that Tara represented permanence and continuity against a foreground of changing human destinies. It says something for the quality of Steiner's tune that its ability to haunt the memory is not diminished by its many reappearances. The rest of the music is professionally tailored to the narrative and makes agreeable listening, although the quality of the lyrical invention inevitably becomes more sentimental as the film nears its close. As ever, Charles Gerhardt is a splendid advocate and he secures fine playing and obvious involvement from his orchestra. The recording, too, is both full and brilliant.

Stenhammar, Wilhelm (1871–1927)

Serenade in F, Op. 31; Chitra (incidental music), *Op. 43;* (i) *Midwinter, Op. 24.*
** Caprice/Musica Sveciae Dig. MSCD 626 [id.]. Swedish RSO, (i) with Ch.; Salonen.

The *Serenade* is Stenhammar's masterpiece and Salonen plays it for all it is worth – and more! There are some moments of exaggeration and he dawdles over and sentimentalizes the glorious *Romanza*. The orchestral playing is highly polished and there is great refinement of colour. The recording balance is good though not in the demonstration class: the orchestral textures could be more transparent. The incidental music to Tagore's play, *Chitra*, is a late work, which Hilding Rosenberg arranged for concert use. It is full of atmosphere and indeed is quite magical at times. Salonen gives a robust and intelligent account of *Midwinter*. In the *Serenade* Järvi remains a first choice and is better recorded (BIS CD 310). He also adds the *Reverenza* movement that Stenhammar suppressed.

Lodolezzi sings: suite, Op. 39; (i) *Midwinter, Op. 24;* (ii) *Snöfrid, Op. 5; The Song* (interlude).
*** BIS Dig. CD 438 [id.]. (i; ii) Gothenburg Concert Hall Ch., (ii) with Åhlén, Nilsson, Zackrisson, Enoksson; Gothenburg SO, Järvi.

Snöfrid is an early cantata from 1891, based on a celebrated poem of Viktor Rydberg, which Sibelius also set. The young composer was completely under the spell of Wagner at this time and, like *Florez och Blanzeflor* (*Flower and whiteflower*), offers only occasional glimpses of the mature Stenhammar. *Midwinter* comes from 1907 when the composer was working in Florence on the *Second Piano concerto* and the *Fourth Quartet*. It is a kind of folk-music fantasy or pot-pourri on the lines of Alfvén's *Midsummer vigil*, though not quite so appealing. *Lodolezzi sings* is a play by Hjalmar Bergman, for which Stenhammar provided incidental music in 1919. He had a particularly soft spot for it – as well he might, for it has much innocent charm. None of this is great Stenhammar but it is well worth hearing; the performances under Neeme Järvi are very sympathetic, and the recording is natural and present.

Sterndale Bennett, William (1816–75)

Piano concertos Nos. 1 in D min., Op. 1; 3 in C min., Op. 9.
❀ *** Lyrita Dig. SRCD 204 [id.]. Malcolm Binns, LPO, Nicholas Braithwaite.

Sterndale Bennett earned the admiration of both Mendelssohn and Schumann and was briefly the white hope of English music. Perhaps it was hearing Mendelssohn play his *G minor Concerto* in 1832 that prompted the young sixteen-year-old, who had just embarked on his studies with Cipriano Potter, to write his Opus 1, a concerto in D minor and a work of extraordinary fluency and accomplishment. David Byers, who has edited the concertos, speaks of Bennett's 'gentle lyricism, the strength and energy of the orchestral tuttis, and the appropriateness and economy of the scoring', and they are in ample evidence, both here and in the *Third Piano concerto*, composed when he was eighteen. No praise can be too high for the playing of Malcolm Binns whose fleetness of finger and poetic sensibility are a constant source of delight, and for the admirable support he receives from Nicholas Braithwaite and the LPO. If the Danes can revive all the symphonies of Gade, there is no reason why the British should be shy in advancing the claims of Sterndale Bennett's concertos. The engineers produce sound of the highest quality. A most enjoyable disc.

Piano concertos Nos. 2 in E flat, Op. 4; 5 in F min.; Adagio.
*** Lyrita Dig. SRCD 205 [id.]. Malcolm Binns, Philh. O, Nicholas Braithwaite.

This coupling is hardly less successful than its companion, reviewed above. Sterndale Bennett made his Philharmonic Society début when he was in his seventeenth year with the *Second concerto* (1833). It was dedicated to his teacher, Cipriano Potter, and it proves to be a work of great facility and charm. It takes as its model the concertos of Mozart and Mendelssohn, and the brilliance and delicacy of the keyboard writing make one understand why the composer was so highly regarded by his contemporaries. As was the case with both Chopin and Beethoven, there is some confusion in the numbering of the *F minor concerto* of 1836, which was composed before No. 4, and is also in F minor. It, too, is eminently civilized music with lots of charm; the *Adagio*, which completes the disc, is thought to be an alternative slow movement for Bennett's *Third Concerto* (1837). Whether or not this is the case, it is certainly a lovely piece. Malcolm Binns, surely this country's most underrated pianist – his masterly playing really is worth the hype expended on lesser talents – plays with great artistry, and the accompaniment by the Philharmonia Orchestra and Nicholas Braithwaite is equally sensitive. First-class recording.

Strauss, Johann Jnr (1825–99)

New Year's Day concert (1979): Polkas: *Auf der Jagd* (with encore); *Bitte schön! Leichtes Blut; Pizzicato* (with Josef); *Tik-Tak.* Waltzes: *An der schönen Blauen Donau; Bei uns z'Haus; Wein, Weib und Gesang.* Josef STRAUSS: *Moulinet polka; Sphärenklänge waltz.* Johann STRAUSS, Snr: *Radetzky march.*
(M) **(*) Decca Dig. 430 715-2; *430 715-4* [id.]. VPO, Boskovsky.

Decca chose to record Boskovsky's 1979 New Year's Day concert in Vienna for one of their very first digital issues on LP. The clarity, immediacy and natural separation of detail are very striking throughout, although the upper strings of the Vienna Philharmonic are very brightly lit indeed and there is some lack of bloom at the top. The CD does not include the whole concert, and one notices that there is not the degree of ambient glow that Decca were to achieve in digital recordings made only a year or so after this. The music-making itself is another matter. It gains much from the spontaneity of the occasion, and the electricity is very apparent; it reaches its peak when the side-drum thunders out the introduction to the closing *Radetzky March*, a frisson-creating moment which, with the audience participation, is quite electrifying.

'1989 New Year Concert in Vienna': Overture: *Die Fledermaus.* Csárdás: *Ritter Pasman.* Polkas: *Bauern; Eljen a Magyar!; Im Krapfenwald'l; Pizzicato* (with Josef). Waltzes: *Accelerationen; An der schönen blauen Donau; Frühlingsstimmen; Künstlerleben.* Josef STRAUSS: Polkas: *Jockey; Die Libelle; Moulinet; Plappermäulchen.* Johann STRAUSS, Snr: *Radetzky march.*
**(*) Sony/CBS CD 45938 [id.]. VPO, Carlos Kleiber.

Originally issued very uneconomically spread over two CDs, Kleiber's 1989 New Year concert now reappears on a single disc, playing for 76 minutes and omitting just one waltz, *Bei uns zu Haus.* Not everyone responds positively to Kleiber's rather precise style with Viennese rhythms, but this is still an enjoyably spontaneous concert, made the more attractive by the warm, full recording.

'The world of Johann Strauss': Egyptischer Marsch; Perpetuum mobile; Polkas: *Auf de Jagd; Pizzicato* (with Josef); Waltzes: *An den schönen Blauen Donau; Frühhlingstimmen; Geschichten aus dem Wienerwald; Rosen aus dem Süden; 1001 Nacht; Wiener Blut.*
(B) *** Decca 430 501-2; *430 501-4* [id.]. VPO, Boskovsky.

A further generous and inexpensive Decca permutation of the justly famous Boskovsky/VPO recordings, which still dominate the Strauss family listings. If the programme suits, this is excellent value; but readers might first care to look at pp. 989–90 of our main volume, where virtually all the Boskovsky repertoire is listed, assembled on five separate mid-priced CDs under the collective title 'Strauss Gala' (Decca 425 425/6/7/8/9-2; *425 425/6/7/8/9-4*).

Egyptischer Marsch. Overtures: *Die Fledermaus. Der Zigeunerbaron; Perpetuum mobile.* Polkas: *Annen; Auf der Jagd; Pizzicato; Tritsch-Tratsch* (CD only: *Eljen a Magyar; Unter Donner und Blitz*). Waltzes: *An der schönen blauen Donau; Geschichten aus dem Wiener Wald; Kaiser; Rosen aus dem Süden; Wiener Blut* (CD only: *Morgenblätter*).

(B) **(*) DG Compact Classics 413 432-2 (2); *413 432-4* [id.]. Berlin R. O, Fricsay; BPO, Karajan; VPO, Boehm.

This Compact Classics compilation juxtaposes the contrasting personalities of Ferenc Fricsay, Boehm and Karajan – all effective Johann Strauss exponents – in a fairly generous collection of favourites. Fricsay's volatile temperament brings individuality to the *Blue Danube* and *Emperor* waltzes, and he is at his most charismatic in *Tales from the Vienna Woods* and in registering the changing moods of the *Fledermaus overture.* Boehm and Karajan are at their most exuberant in *Roses from the South* and *Vienna blood* respectively, while the *Egyptian march* has striking panache in Karajan's hands. The recordings come from the 1960s, the earliest 1961; while the sound is variable, it does not seem obviously dated. For the digitally remastered pair of CDs, two extra polkas and one waltz have been added, as indicated in the listing.

Egyptischer Marsch; Kaiser Franz Josef Marsch; Banditen-Galopp. Polkas: *Eljen a Magyar!; Furioso; Tritsch-Tratsch; Unter Donner und Blitz.* Waltzes: *An der schönen blauen Donau; Rosen aus dem Süden; 1001 Nacht; Wiener Blut; Wiener Bonbons.* Josef STRAUSS: *Die Libelle polka; Perlen der Liebe waltz.*
(M) ** Chan. Dig. CHAN 6528 [id.]. Johann Strauss O, leader Jack Rothstein (violin).

This reshuffling for Chandos's mid-priced Collect series brings fairly generous measure (69 minutes) and many will be attracted by the bright digital recording, which has plenty of bloom. The polkas go with an infectious swing and there is no lack of lilt in the waltzes, although Josef's *Perlen der Liebe* is a shade disappointing. Otherwise there is no lack of spontaneity here; good though Rothstein is, however, he does not equal Boskovsky or Karajan in this repertoire.

Waltzes: (ii) *Accelerationen;* (i) *An der schönen blauen Donau; Frühlingsstimmen;* (ii) *Geschichten aus dem Wienerwald;* (i) *Kaiser;* (i) *Künsterleben;* (ii) *Morgenblätter;* (i) *Rosen aus dem Suden; Wein, Weib und Gesang;* (ii) *Wiener Blut.*
(M) ** Ph. 422 277-2; *422 277-4* [id.]. VSO, (i) Sawallisch; (ii) Paul Walter.

There are 72 minutes of music here and so virtually all the favourite Johann Strauss waltzes are offered on a single disc. Sawallisch conducts with élan and no lack of rhythmic nuance: his *Blue Danube, Emperor* and *Roses from the South* are very enjoyable. The VSO is not the VPO and their string patina is less sumptuous, but the warmly resonant hall ambience is flattering. The snag is that some of the waltzes, including all four conducted, very ably, by Paul Walter, are truncated and this applies, alas, to *Tales from the Vienna Woods.* But if you just want all the famous Strauss melodies and are not worried about the composer's artistically tailored introductions and postludes, then the present selection should meet the bill.

Waltzes: *An der schönen blauen Donau; Geschichtem aus dem Wienerwald; Kaiser; Künsterleben; Morgenblätter; Schatz; Wiener Blut; Wo zie Zitronen blüh'n.*
(B) ** RCA VD 60490; *VK 60490.* Phd. O, Ormandy.

Vividly recorded in the late 1960s, these performances have plenty of zest and panache, with the Philadelphia string section making the very most of the sumptuous melodies. Ormandy is clearly enjoying himself and, although there are a few eccentricities of pulse and phrasing and these are obviously not Viennese performances, they are enjoyable for their ready vitality.

Strauss, Richard (1864–1949)

Also sprach Zarathustra, Op. 30; Death and transfiguration, Op. 24.
*** Decca Dig. 425 942-2; *425 942-4* [id.]. Cleveland O, Ashkenazy.
** DG Dig. 423 576-2 [id.]. NYPO, Sinopoli.

Glorious Decca Cleveland sound for this latest in Ashkenazy's Strauss series, and marvellously responsive playing from the orchestra. As sound, this is in a special class, but Previn's Telarc record is also in the demonstration bracket, the VPO play magnificently, and his are even more characterful readings. Of course Karajan has something very special to offer in this repertoire, but his coupling is with *Don Juan* (on DG 410 959-2). The DG sound is pretty impressive too, but not quite as sumptuous as the Decca and Telarc CDs.

Sinopoli is at his most warmly persuasive in these two symphonic poems but, sadly, his special relationship with the often difficult New York Philharmonic is let down by the recording, too harsh and with too little bloom for this music. In this coupling, Previn's Telarc disc and Ashkenazy's Decca are both preferable.

Also sprach Zarathustra, Op. 30; Don Juan, Op. 20; Macbeth, 23.
(M) **(*) Decca Dig. 430 708-2; *430 708-4* [id.]. Detroit SO, Dorati.

Dorati's *Zarathustra* is well played but not so firmly held together as with Karajan and Kempe. *Macbeth* is a good rather than a distinctive account. It is an early work whose first version appeared in 1887 when Strauss was barely twenty-three; but the composer revised it at the instigation of von Bülow and it was completed in its definitive form after *Don Juan* – hence the later opus number. Dorati's view of *Don Juan* is heroic, the sensuality played down by the sound-balance, brilliant rather than sumptuous. After a central love scene which is tenderly delicate, there is satiety and disillusion at the end. The recording has remarkable clarity of inner detail throughout.

Also sprach Zarathustra, Op. 30; Don Juan, Op. 20; Till Eulenspiegel, Op. 30.
(M) **(*) Decca 430 445-2; *430 445-4* [id.]. Chicago SO, Solti.

Solti's performances come from analogue originals of the mid-1970s, and the coupling is apt and generous. Solti is ripely expansive in *Also sprach Zarathustra* and throughout there is glorious playing from the Chicago orchestra in peak form. This is Solti at his strongest, with this most Germanic of American orchestras responding as to the manner born. The transfer to CD is impressive, even if the finest digital versions aerate the textures more.

Burleske for piano and orchestra in D min., Op. 11.
(M) ** Sony MK 42261 [id.]. Rudolf Serkin, Phd. O, Ormandy – BRAHMS: *Piano concerto No. 1.***(*)

This is a generally excellent performance of what is still a comparative rarity on disc. Serkin plays with great brilliance and Ormandy makes a good partner, but unfortunately the piano tone is dry and the recording overall is shallow.

Death and transfiguration, Op. 24.
(M) (***) BMG/RCA mono GD 60328; *GK 60328* (4) [60328-2-RG; *60328-4-RG*]]. Phd. O, Toscanini – Concert.(**(*))

Toscanini's characteristically taut control of tension goes with what was for him a more warmly expressive style than usual, thanks to the influence of the Philadelphia Orchestra.

With the transfer giving good body to the limited sound, it is comparable with his equally intense reading of Tchaikovsky's *Pathétique* from the same period.

Death and transfiguration, Op. 24; Don Juan, Op. 20; Till Eulenspiegel, Op. 28.
(BB) ** Naxos Dig. 8.550250 [id.]. Slovak PO, Zdeněk Košler.

Anyone impulsively picking up Košler's record of Strauss's three favourite symphonic poems may be surprised at how enjoyable it it. The Slovak Philharmonic Orchestra cannot match the Berlin Philharmonic under Karajan (DG 423 222-2; *423 222-4*) in polish and impulse, nor Abbado and the LSO (DG 429 492-2; *429 492-4*) in dash and brilliance, but their voluptuously relaxed, sentient feeling in *Don Juan* and the powerful atmosphere at the close of *Death and transfiguration* give the readings plenty of character, even if Košler's structural grip is rather loose. Similarly, the Bratislava solo horn opens *Till* most personably, and the work's picaresque detail is observed with pleasing geniality, but the powerful execution scene at the close is prepared rather too broadly. The digital recording makes a fine impact here, and the warm acoustic ambience of the Reduta Hall, Bratislava, gives a pleasing opulence to the Straussian textures. Haitink's outstanding Philips record of these three masterpieces should be returning to the catalogue at mid-price soon; when it does, it will constitute a clear first recommendation.

Ein Heldenleben, Op. 40.
(M) *** Ph. 432 276-2; *432 276-4* [id.]. Concg. O, Haitink – ELGAR: *Enigma variations.***

Haitink's 1970 version of *Ein Heldenleben* is one of his finest records. He gives just the sort of performance, brilliant and swaggering but utterly without bombast, which will delight those who normally resist this rich and expansive work. With a direct and fresh manner that yet conveys consistent urgency, he gives a performance that makes even such fine rival versions as Karajan's 1959 recording sound just a little lightweight. In the culminating fulfilment theme, a gentle, lyrical 6/8, Haitink finds a raptness in restraint, a hint of agony within joy, that links the passage directly with the great Trio from *Der Rosenkavalier*. The Philips sound, admirably faithful and skilfully remastered, cannot match, for instance, Blomstedt and the Dresden Staatskapelle (Denon C37 7561) in its combination of homogeneity and detail, but that is a modern digital recording at full price. By any standards, the Haitink reissue is a splendid record, even if its Elgar coupling has less concentration and dynamism.

Metamorphosen for 23 solo strings.
(M) **(*) Decca 430 002-2 [id.]. ASMF, Marriner – SCHOENBERG: *Verklaerte Nacht* **(*); WEBERN: *5 Movements.****

Marriner's version is not as strongly characterized as Karajan's (DG 410 892-2 – see our main volume, p. 1004) but it is finely played, although the CD transfer brings a touch of shrillness to the upper range of the otherwise excellent and certainly clear 1968 recording.

Till Eulenspiegel.
(M) (***) DG mono 427 783-2 [id.]. BPO, Wilhelm Furtwängler – RAVEL: *Daphnis et Chloé*; SIBELIUS: *En Saga.*(***)

Furtwängler's excellence as a Strauss conductor is well known, and this wartime performance is well worth hearing. It comes with quite magical accounts of Ravel's *Daphnis et Chloé suite* and Sibelius's *En Saga*.

Violin sonata in E flat, Op. 18.
** Audiofon Dig. CD 72026 [id.]. Aaron Rosand, Seymour Lipkin – GRIEG; SAINT-SAËNS: *Violin sonatas.***

Aaron Rosand's virtuosity was exhibited to excellent effect in his LPs of the 1960s and it is pretty impressive here in this 1990 recording. However, his youthful purity of tone has given way to a wider vibrato than some collectors may like. A vigorous and powerful account nevertheless, though the recording balance needs to put more space round the artists. Kyung Wha Chung and Krystian Zimerman (DG 427 617-2) remain unchallenged in this work.

VOCAL MUSIC

Richard Strauss's Lieder are well represented in our main volume, but a recommendation for the *Four Last songs* would seem essential, and this is shared between Elisabeth Schwarzkopf with Szell (EMI CDC7 47276-2) and Jessye Norman with Masur (Philips 411 052-2). Both of these records, which include also other Lieder, were awarded a Rosette in our main volume, and the balance of advantage between them is impossible to resolve.

OPERA

The operas of Strauss are well served by the CD catalogue and readers must turn to our main volume for an extended discussion of the main recordings. It seems unlikely that any Straussian would be unaware of the glory of Karajan's 1956 version of *Der Rosenkavalier*, one of the greatest operatic recordings ever made; with an ideal cast led by Elisabeth Schwarzkopf and Christa Ludwig, this has earned its Rosette over and over again through the various editions of our *Guide* (EMI CDS7 49354-8; *EX 749354-4*).

Die Frau ohne Schatten (complete).
(M) ** Decca 425 981-2 (3) [id.]. Rysanek, Loose, Hopf, Terkal, Höngen, Böhme, V. State Op. Ch., VPO, Boehm.

This 1955 recording is reissued in Decca's Historical series, but it is an example of very early stereo, thanks to a rescue attempt from the original master-tape made by the recording manager, Christopher Raeburn. Since then Karl Boehm has re-recorded the opera live for DG, with the co-operation of Austrian Radio and that version (415 472-2) must take precedence, although of course it is at full price. Leonie Rysanek as the Empress is common to both sets; otherwise the singing on the Decca set is variable, with a high proportion of wobblers among the soloists, and Hans Hopf often producing coarse tone as the Emperor. However, once one accepts the strange symbolism of Hofmannsthal's libretto, one can go on to appreciate the richness of Strauss's inspiration, a score utterly different from anything else he ever did, in many ways more ambitious. It is a work that deserves the closest attention of Straussians and many may feel tempted to try this version, in spite of its vocal limitations, for it is above all Boehm's set, and his direction is masterly. The recording is remarkably good for its period.

Elektra (complete).
**(*) EMI Dig. CDS7 54067-2 (2) [Ang. CDCB 54067]; *EX 754067-4*. Eva Marton, Studer, Lipovšek, Weikl, Winkler, Moll, Bav. R. Ch. & SO, Sawallisch.

Sawallisch may miss the full violence of Strauss's score, which the fierce Solti so brilliantly captured in his vintage Decca version (417 345-2) but, with its warm, wide-ranging sound, the EMI set conveys more light and shade, more mystery. Eva Marton in her characterization of the tormented heroine similarly finds more light and shade than Birgit Nilsson did for Solti, but the voice spreads distressingly under pressure. Notably disappointing is the failure of both singer and conductor to convey the full emotional thrust of Elektra's radiant solo after the great moment of recognition between her and her brother, Orest (Bernd Weikl in fine, incisive voice). Lipovšek's Klytemnestra is the finest yet on record, and Cheryl Studer as Chrysothemis, well contrasted in bright clarity, has wonderful moments, notably in her solo after the murders. This hardly replaces the Solti set but it far outshines other modern versions, like the Philips live recording of Ozawa and the Boston orchestra with Hildegard Behrens a touchingly vulnerable heroine.

Salome: Dance of the seven veils; Closing scene. Lieder: *Cäcilie; Ich liebe dich; Morgen; Wiegenlied; Zueignung.*
(M) **(*) DG 431 171-2; *431 171-4* [id.]. Caballé, Fr. Nat. O, Bernstein – BOITO: *Mefistofele.***(*)

One of Caballé's earliest and most refreshingly imaginative opera sets was Strauss's *Salome* with Leinsdorf conducting. This version of the final scene, recorded over a decade later with a very different conductor, has much of the same imagination, the sweet innocent girl still observable next to the bloodthirsty fiend. The remainder of the recital is less recommendable, partly because Caballé underlines the expressiveness of works that remain Lieder even with the orchestral accompaniment. Bernstein too directs an over-weighted account of the *Dance of the seven veils.* The recording is warm and full.

Stravinsky, Igor (1882–1971)

The Stravinsky edition: Volume 1, Ballets, etc.: (i) *The Firebird;* (i) *Fireworks;* (iii) *Histoire du soldat;* (i) *Pétrushka;* (iv, iii) *Renard the fox;* (i) *The Rite of spring;* (i) *Scherzo à la russe;* (ii) *Scherzo fantastique;* (v) *The Wedding (Les Noces).*

Volume 2, Ballets etc.: (vi) *Agon;* (i) *Apollo;* (i) *Le baiser de la fée;* (i) *Bluebird (pas de deux);* (vii) *Jeux de cartes;* (viii) *Orphée;* (ix, i) *Pulchinella;* (ii) *Scènes de ballet.*

Volume 3, Ballet suites: (i) *Firebird; Pétrouchka; Pulchinella.*

Volume 4, Symphonies: (i) *Symphony in E;* (ii) *Symphony in C;* (i) *Symphony in 3 movements;* (x, ii) *Symphony of Psalms;* (i) Stravinsky in rehearsal: *Apollo, Piano concerto; Pulchinella; Sleeping beauty; Symphony in C; 3 Souvenirs.*

Volume 5, Concertos: (xi, i) *Capriccio for piano and orchestra* (with Robert Craft); *Concerto for piano and wind;* (xii, i) *Movements for piano and orchestra;* (xiii, i) *Violin concerto in D.*

Volume 6, Miniatures: (i) *Circus polka; Concerto in D for string orchestra; Concerto in E flat for chamber orchestra;* (ii) *4 Études for orchestra;* (i) *Greeting prelude;* (ii) *8 Instrumental miniatures; 4 Norwegian moods; Suites Nos. 1–2 for small orchestra.*

Volume 7, Chamber music and historical recordings: (iii) *Concertino for 12 instruments;* (xiv, xv) *Concerto for 2 solo pianos;* (xv, xvi) *Duo concertant for violin and piano;* (xvii, xviii) *Ebony Concerto (for clarinet and big band);* (iii) *Octet for wind;* (xix, iii) *Pastorale for violin and wind quartet;* (xv) *Piano rag music;* (xviii) *Preludium;* (xx, iii) *Ragtime* (for 11 instruments); (xv) *Serenade in A;* (iii) *Septet;* (xii) *Sonata for piano;* (xxi) *Sonata for 2 pianos;* (xviii) *Tango;* (xxii) *Wind symphonies.*

Volume 8, Operas and songs: (xxiii, iii) *Cat's cradle songs;* (xxiii, xxiv) *Elegy for J. F. K.;* (xxv, ii) *Faun and shepherdess;* (xxvi,iii) *In memoriam Dylan Thomas;* (xxvii, iii) *3 Japanese Lyrics* (with Robert Craft)*;* (xxvii, xxix) *The owl and the pussycat;* (xxvii, iii) *2 poems by K. Bal'mont;* (xxx, i) *2 poems of Paul Verlaine;* (xxiii,i) *Pribaoutki (peasant songs);* (xxiii, i) *Recollections of my childhood;* (xxviii, xxxi) *4 Russian songs;* (xxxvii) *4 Russian peasant songs;* (xxiii, iii) *3 songs from William Shakespeare;* (xxvii, i) *Tilim-Bom (3 stories for children);* (xxxii) *Mavra;* (xxxiii) *The Nightingale.*

Volume 9: (xxxiv) *The Rake's progress.*

Volume 10, Oratorio and melodrama: (xxxv, i) *The Flood* (with Robert Craft); (i) *Monumentum pro Gesualdo di Venosa (3 madrigals recomposed for instruments);* (vii) *Ode;* (xxxvi) *Oedipus Rex;* (xxxvii, xxxviii, i) *Perséphone.*

Volume 11, Sacred works: (x) *Anthem (the dove descending breaks the air);* (x) *Ave Maria;* (xxxix, x, i) *Babel;* (xxviii, xxvi, x, iii) *Cantata;* (xl) *Canticum sacrum;* (x, ii) *Credo;* (x, iii) *Introitus (T. S. Eliot in Memoriam);* (xli) *Mass;* (x, i) *Pater noster;* (xlii, i) *A Sermon, a narrative & a prayer;* (xliii, i) *Threni;* (x, i) *Chorale: Variations on: Vom Himmel hoch, da komm ich her* (arr.); *Zvezdoliki.*

Volume 12, Robert Craft conducts: (xliv, i) *Abraham and Isaac;* (iii) *Danses concertantes;* (xlv) *Double canon: Raoul Dufy in memoriam;* (xlvi) *Epitaphium;* (i) *Le chant du rossignol* (symphonic poem); (i) *Orchestral variations: Aldous Huxley in memoriam;* (xlvii) *Requiem canticles;* (i) *Song of the nightingale (symphonic poem).*

(M) *** Sony SX 22K 46290 (22) [id.]. (i) Columbia SO; (ii) CBC SO; (iii) Columbia CO; (iv) Shirley, Driscoll, Gramm, Koves; (v) Allen, Sarfaty, Driscoll, Samuel Barber, Aaron Copland, Lukas Foss, Roger Sessions, American Chamber Ch., Hills, Columbia Percussion Ens.; (vi) Los Angeles Festival SO; (vii) Cleveland O; (viii) Chicago SO; (ix) Jordan, Shirley, Gramm; (x) Festival Singers of Toronto, Iseler; (xi) Philippe Entremont; (xii) Charles Rosen; (xiii) Isaac Stern; (xiv) Soulima Stravinsky; (xv) Igor Stravinsky; (xvi) Szigeti; (xvii) Benny Goodman; (xviii) Columbia Jazz Ens.; (xix) Israel Baker; (xx) Tony Koves; (xxi) Arthur Gold, Robert Fizdale; (xxii) N. W. German RSO; (xxiii) Cathy Berberian; (xxiv) Howland, Kreiselman, Russo; (xxv) Mary Simmons; (xxvi) Alexander Young; (xxvii) Evelyn Lear; (xxviii) Adrienne Albert; (xxix) Robert Craft; (xxx) Donald Gramm; (xxxi) Di Tullio, Remsen, Almeida; (xxxii) Belinck, Simmons, Rideout, Kolk; (xxxiii) Driscoll, Grist, Picassi, Smith, Beattie, Gramm, Kolk, Murphy, Kaiser, Bonazzi, Washington, D. C., Op. Society Ch. & O; (xxxiv) Young, Raskin, Reardon, Sarfaty, Miller, Manning, Garrard, Tracey, Colin Tilney, Sadler's Wells Op. Ch., John Baker, RPO; (xxxv) Laurence Harvey, Sebastian Cabot, Elsa Lanchester, John Reardon, Robert Oliver, Paul Tripp, Richard Robinson, Columbia SO Ch., Gregg Smith; (xxxvi) Westbrook (nar.), Shirley, Verrett, Gramm, Reardon, Driscoll, Chester Watson Ch., Washington, D. C., Op. Society O; (xxxvii) Gregg Smith Singers, Gregg Smith; (xxxviii) Zorina, Molese, Ithaca College Concert Ch., Fort Worth Texas Boys' Ch.; (xxxix) John Calicos (nar.); (xl) Robinson, Chitjian, Los Angeles Festival Ch. & SO; (xli) Baxter, Albert, Gregg Smith Singers, Columbia Symphony Winds & Brass; (xlii) Verrett, Driscoll, Hornton (nar.); (xliii) Beardslee, Krebs, Lewis, Wainner, Morgan, Oliver, Schola Cantorum, Ross; all cond. composer. (xliv) Richard Frisch; (xlv) Baker, Igleman, Schonbach, Neikrug; (xlvi) Anderson, Bonazzi, Bressler, Gramm, Ithaca College Concert Ch., Gregg Smith; cond. Robert Craft.

On these 22 discs, a revised and remastered version of the 1982 CBS set originally issued on LP, you have the unique archive of recordings which Stravinsky left of his own music. Presented in a sturdy plastic display box that enhances the desirability of the set, almost all the performances are conducted by the composer, with a few at the very end of his career – like the magnificent *Requiem canticles* – left to Robert Craft to conduct, with the composer supervising. In addition there is a handful of recordings of works otherwise not covered, mainly chamber pieces. With some recordings of Stravinsky talking and in rehearsal (included in the box devoted to the symphonies) it makes a vivid portrait.

Stravinsky may not have been a brilliant conductor, but in the recording studio he knew how to draw out alert, vigorous performances of his own music, and every one of these items illuminates facets of his inspiration which other interpreters often fail to notice. There are few if any rival versions of the *Rite of spring* – nowadays, astonishingly, his most frequently recorded work – to match his own recording of 1960 in its compelling intensity and inexorable sense of line.

Nonetheless, there are some disappointments in the set. It is a pity that Stravinsky's earlier, mono version of *Oedipus Rex* (with Jean Cocteau as narrator and Peter Pears in the title-role) was not preferred to his much less taut, stereo remake, and sadly the spoken items fail to include his intensely memorable talk, *Apropos le sacre*, originally issued with his 1960 recording of *The Rite*. It ends unforgettably with the thought: 'I was the vessel through which *Le sacre* passed.' But transfers have been done very well, clarifying and refining the original analogue sound.

Of the major ballets, *Petrushka* and *The Firebird* are valuable, but *The Rite* is required listening: it has real savagery and astonishing electricity. The link between *Jeu de cartes* from the mid-1930s and Stravinsky's post-war opera, *The Rake's progress*, is striking and Stravinsky's sharp-edged conducting style underlines it, while the curiously anonymous-sounding *Scènes de ballet* certainly have their attractive moments. *Orpheus* is a post-war score, written for Balanchine, and has a powerful atmosphere, although one of Stravinsky's most classically restrained works. A good performance, with the composer's own authority lending it special interest. However, its invention is less memorable and distinguished than *Apollo*, one of Stravinsky's most gravely beautiful scores. *Agon* is one of the most stimulating of Stravinsky's later works. Again composed for Balanchine, all the pieces are modelled on a French dance manual of the mid-seventeenth century. The sonorities are as individual and astringent as one expects, and the performance and recording are both of a high order. The orchestra respond with tremendous alertness and enthusiasm to Stravinsky's direction. The recording of *Le baiser de la fée* is a typical CBS balance with forward woodwind. However, if the recorded quality does not inspire too much enthusiasm, the performance of this enchanting score, based on themes by Tchaikovsky, certainly does. There is a ruthlessness in the composer's own reading of *Les Noces* which exactly matches the primitive robustness in this last flowering of Russian nationalism in Stravinsky. It must be a long time since four distinguished composers paid such a tribute as this in playing the work of a fifth. The earlier parts are perhaps too rigid, but as the performance goes on so one senses the added alertness and enthusiasm of the performers. The recording is good, but the balance favours the voices. *Renard* is a curious work, a sophisticated fable which here receives too unrelenting a performance. The voices are very forward and tend to drown the instrumentalists. Stravinsky began *Le chant du rossignol* in 1909, but when Diaghilev commissioned *The Firebird* he put it aside and did not take it up again until after *Petrushka* and *The Rite of spring*. Much has been made of the stylistic discrepancy which resulted, but one doubts if many listeners would object if they did not already know the history of the work's composition. It is unashamedly exotic in a way that sets it aside from almost every other work Stravinsky has ever written, even

The Firebird. It is perhaps surprising that Stravinsky wanted to record it, but his handling shows that what can seem over-exotic acquires an almost barbaric strength in his hands.

In the early *Symphony in E flat,* Op. 1, the young Stravinsky's material may be comparatively conventional and the treatment much too bound to the academic procedures taught to him by his master, Rimsky-Korsakov, but at least in this performance the music springs alive. Each movement has its special delights to outweigh any shortcomings. The performance is obviously as near definitive as it could be. The composer's account of the *Symphony in three movements* is an object lesson for every conductor who has tried to perform this work. Stravinsky shows how, by vigorous, forthright treatment of the notes, the emotion implicit is made all the more compelling. The Columbia Symphony plays superbly and the recording is full and brilliant. Stravinsky never quite equalled the intensity of the pre-war 78-r.p.m. performance of the *Symphony of Psalms.* That had many more technical faults than his later, stereo version, and it is only fair to say that this new account is still impressive. It is just that, with so vivid a work, it is a shade disappointing to find Stravinsky as interpreter at less than maximum voltage.

The iron-fingered touch of Philippe Entremont has something to be said for it in the *Capriccio for piano and wind,* with the bright echoes of cake-walk and early jazz, and even in the Bach-like florid writing in the slow movement, but this performance conveys too little of the music's charm. The *Movements for piano and orchestra* are far more formidable. Here serial technique is strictly applied, and even Stravinsky admitted that the work's harmony is more complex than anything he had previously attempted. Despite the fearsome idiom, however, one really *wants* to understand the argument, and the composer's conducting could hardly be more compelling. Stravinsky wrote the *Concerto for piano and wind* to play himself on his concert tours. A strange work which at first seems brittle and arid, this performance reveals a steely strength. Sometimes conductor and soloist are over-dramatic – but then Stravinsky himself is – and firmness and vitality are the main essentials. The recording is excellent. Stern's account of the *Violin concerto in D* adds a romantic perspective to the framework, and at one time, no doubt, Stravinsky would have objected. But an expressive approach to Stravinsky is permissible in a soloist, when the composer is there to provide the bedrock under the expressive cantilena. Plainly this has the forthright spontaneity of a live performance.

The collection of Stravinsky's shorter pieces begins with the very brief prelude on 'Happy birthday to you' which Stravinsky wrote for Pierre Monteux. Most of the suites were adapted from piano-duet works written for children. The *Circus polka* was written for a Barnum & Bailey elephant and erupts magnificently into a distortion of Schubert's *Marche militaire.* The *Dumbarton Oaks concerto* with its obvious echoes of Bach's *Brandenburgs* is one of the most warmly attractive of Stravinsky's neo-classical works, all beautifully played and acceptably recorded. The *Octet for wind* of 1924 comes out with surprising freshness and, throughout, the unexpected combination of neo-Bach and neo-Pop is most refreshing, The *Ragtime* dates from the end of Stravinsky's Russian period, when he was beginning to dabble in the exotic sounds of Western music. The performance could be more lighthearted, but Stravinsky gives the impression of knowing what he wants. The *Ebony concerto,* in this version conducted by the composer, may have little of 'swung' rhythm, but it is completely faithful to Stravinsky's deadpan approach to jazz.

Of the piano music, the *Concerto for two pianos* was written for the composer and his son to play, yet it presents formidable technical difficulties. It is a taut, four-movement work that deserves to be better known. The *Sonata* is much easier, musically and technically, and the *Eight easy pieces* are better known in their later transformation into the two *Suites for orchestra.*

The songs represent a fascinating collection of trifles, chips from the master's workbench dating from the earliest years. There are many incidental delights, not least those in which the magnetic Cathy Berberian is featured.

In Stravinsky's opera, *The Rake's progress*, The Rake of Alexander Young is a marvellous achievement, sweet-toned and accurate and well characterized. In the choice of other principals, too, it is noticeable what store Stravinsky set by vocal precision. Judith Raskin makes an appealing Anne Trulove, sweetly sung if not particularly well projected dramatically. John Reardon too is remarkable more for vocal accuracy than for striking characterization, but Regina Sarfaty's Baba is marvellous on both counts. The Sadler's Wells Chorus sings with even greater drive under the composer than in the theatre, and the Royal Philharmonic plays with a warmth and a fittingly Mozartian sense of style to match Stravinsky's surprisingly lyrical approach to his score.

The *Mass* is a work of the greatest concentration, a quality that comes out strongly if one plays this performance immediately after *The Flood*, with its inevitably slack passages. In 1951 when it first appeared, the *Mass* was criticized by some for its perfunctory treatment of the words of the service. What this performance under the composer shows conclusively is that there is a difference between unseemly haste and genuine concentration. As with other Stravinsky works – the *Wind symphonies* and *Movements for piano and orchestra* – the argument is so concentrated that it is almost a musical shorthand. This is a microcosm of a *Mass*. As directed in the score, trebles are used here, and it is a pity that the engineers have not brought them further forward: their sweet, clear tone is sometimes lost among the lower strands. Otherwise the quality is up to the standard of CBS's other Stravinsky recordings. In *The Flood*, originally written for television, it is difficult to take the bald narrations seriously, particularly when Laurence Harvey sanctimoniously keeps talking of the will of 'Gud'. The Disneyland hill-billy style of narration quite destroys enjoyment and it is difficult to know what its dramatic aim was, fascinating though the work is. *Perséphone* is full of that cool lyricism that marks much of Stravinsky's music inspired by classical myths. As with many of these vocal recordings, the balance is too close, and various orchestral solos are highlighted.

The *Cantata* of 1952 is a transitional piece between Stravinsky's tonal and serial periods. However, of the two soloists, Alexander Young is much more impressive than Adrienne Albert, for her voice is entirely unsuitable, with an unformed choirboy sound somehow married to wide vibrato. For the sake of Stravinsky one endures her. The *Canticum sacrum* dates from the mid-1950s and includes music that some listeners might find tough (the strictly serial choral section). But the performance is a fine one and the tenor solo from Richard Robinson is very moving. The Bach *Chorale variations* has a synthetic modernity that recalls the espresso bar, though one which still reveals underlying mastery. The *Epitaphium* and the *Double canon* are miniatures, dating from the composer's serial period. but the *Canon* is deliberately euphonious.

Of the items recorded by Robert Craft, the *Requiem canticles* stands out, the one incontrovertible masterpiece among the composer's very last serial works and one of the most deeply moving works ever written in the serial idiom. Even more strikingly than in the *Mass* of 1948, Stravinsky conveys his religious feelings with a searing intensity. The *Aldous Huxley variations* are more difficult to comprehend but have similar intensity. Valuable too, are the ballad *Abraham and Isaac* and the brief *Introitus for T. S. Eliot*.

Apollo (Apollon Musagète): complete; *The Rite of spring* (complete).
**(*) EMI Dig. CDC7 49636-2 [id.]; *EL 749636-4*. CBSO, Rattle.

Rattle gives a relaxed reading of *Apollo*, at once refined and easy-going, but lacking something of the bite one expects with Stravinsky (and with Rattle) even in this amiably neo-classical work. That goes with a reading of *The Rite of spring* which has more joy in it than barbarism. The EMI sound is full and rich against a warm acoustic, not ideally sharp enough but with plenty of body and with good detail. Speeds are often broad, at times diminishing the bite of the performance in favour of warmth and high spirits. This is not quite the supreme version one might have expected after Rattle's youthful recording with the National Youth Orchestra, made in the late 1970s (well worth having at bargain price on ASV CDQS 6031; *ZCQS 6031*, coupled with Dorati's complete *Firebird* with the RPO).

Le baiser de la fee (Divertimento); The Firebird: suite (1919 version); *Pulcinella: suite.*
**(*) BMG/RCA Dig. RD 60394 [60394-2-RC]. RPO, Yuri Temirkanov.

An enjoyable and generous (73 minutes) triptych. The RPO are on top form, and Yuri Temirkanov has a feel for balletic nuance and a fine ear for orchestral detail. The performance of *Le baiser de la fee* is particularly attractive, with the lightest touch in the *Scherzo* and *Pas de deux* reminding us that this delectably scored music is as much Tchaikovsky as Stravinsky. The Rimskian colours in the *Firebird* emerge vividly, yet King Kastchei and his entourage are as malignantly pungent as anyone could wish, and the finale expands gloriously. Perhaps in *Pulcinella* the warm acoustics of Watford Town Hall are a little too amiable for the dances of Pergolesi focused through Stravinsky's harmonic and rhythmic distorting lens, but otherwise the recording is first class.

(i) *Le baiser de la fee (Divertimento);* (ii) *Petrushka: excerpts: (Danse russe; Chez Petrushka; La fête populaire);* (i) *Pulcinella: suite;* (ii) *The Rite of spring* (complete ballet).
(M) (***) EMI mono CZS7 62647-2 (2) [Ang. CDMB 62647]. (i) French Nat. R. O; (ii) Philh. O, Markevitch – PROKOFIEV: *Love of three oranges* etc.(**)

Markevitch's electrifying 1959 mono recording of *The Rite of spring* has long been famous. The Philharmonia playing is superbly exciting, and the conductor's rhythmic vitality and ruthless thrust are matched by an amazingly spectacular recording which hardly sounds dated even now. One of the highlights of the performance is the dramatic use of the tam-tam, and in Part 2 the drums are thrillingly crisp and make a powerful impact. The elegant *Divertimento*, which Stravinsky culled from his Tchaikovskian ballet *Le baiser de la fee*, was made famous by Ansermet's mono recording, but the French orchestral playing here has rather more finesse: the horns in their attractive ostinato (taken from a Tchaikovsky piano piece) articulate buoyantly, and the whole performance has flair. The three excerpts from *Petrushka* are similarly lively and colourful, and only *Pulcinella* is slightly disappointing: the trombones blow rasberries in their famous *Vivo* duet with the doubles basses, and elsewhere Markevitch dilutes the music's charm by his forcefulness.

Le Chant du rossignol (symphonic poem).
*** Erato/WEA 2292 45382-2; *2292 45382-4* [id.]. French Nat. O, Boulez – *Pulcinella.***(*)

The Boulez performance is masterly; the French National Orchestra on Erato capture detail vividly and have the advantage of a first-class 1982 recording.

Violin concerto in D.
*** Denon Dig. CO 73325 [id.]. Kantorow, LPO, Bryden Thomson – TCHAIKOVSKY: *Concerto.***(*)

Kantorow gives a clean and classical account of the *Violin concerto*, crisply accompanied and very well recorded. It can be highly recommended for anyone wanting the Tchaikovsky coupling.

The Firebird (ballet; complete); *Le chant du rossignol; Fireworks; Scherzo à la russe.*
❀ (M) *** Mercury 432 012-2 [id.]. LSO, Dorati.

Many collectors have been eagerly awaiting the return of Dorati's electrifying, 1960 Mercury version of *The Firebird* with the LSO. The CD transfer makes the recording sound as fresh and vivid as the day it was made; the brilliantly transparent detail and enormous impact suggest a modern digital source, rather than an analogue master made over 30 years ago. The stereo has remarkable atmosphere too, and the balance is very natural. The performance sounds completely spontaneous and the LSO wind playing is especially sensitive. Only the sound of the massed upper strings reveals the age of the original master, although this does not spoil the ravishing final climax; the bite of the brass and the transient edge of the percussion are thrilling. The recording of Stravinsky's glittering symphonic poem, *The song of the nightingale*, is hardly less compelling, with sparkle in the upper range and an impressive bass drum. Dorati's reading is urgent and finely pointed yet is strong, too, on atmosphere. The other, shorter pieces also come up vividly, but it was a mistake to programme the rather abrasively recorded *Fireworks* before the main work, which should have opened the disc, leaving *Fireworks* as a final strident *bonne bouche* after *The song of the nightingale.* Fortunately on CD one can re-order the programme to taste, and this remains one of the most stimulating Stravinsky compilations in the catalogue.

The Firebird: suite (1919 version).
(B) **(*) DG Compact Classics *413 155-4* [id.]. Berlin RSO, Maazel – KHACHATURIAN: *Gayaneh*; RIMSKY-KORSAKOV: *Scheherazade.***(*)
(*) Sony SK 45935 [id.]; *40-45935*. Concg. O, Giulini – MUSSORGSKY: *Pictures.**

Maazel's reading of the *Firebird suite* has an enjoyable éclat and he has the advantage of the most beautiful woodwind playing; indeed the Berlin Radio Orchestra is consistently on top form. The recording dates from 1960 and tended to betray its age by the sound of the massed upper strings. However, in the present transfer the DG engineers have smoothed off the upper partials and in consequence the recording, although still impressive, has lost some of its bite.

The Concertgebouw acoustic – as anyone who has experienced live music-making there will know – is less than ideal for fast-moving, sharply dissonant twentieth-century music. Its wide reverberation tends to blur the transients, as here in *Kashchei's dance* which, however, does not lack malignancy. It also brings a voluptuous weight to the richly scored finale, perhaps unmatched on record. Giulini secures wonderfully refined playing in the gentler music, but the lack of rhythmic bite minimizes the balletic feeling and makes the suite seem more symphonic than usual.

Petrushka (1947 score; complete).
(M) ** Decca 425 026-2; *425 026-4* [id.]. VPO, Dohnányi – BARTÓK: *Miraculous Mandarin.***

Dohnányi directs a genial and well-paced reading, slightly lacking in sparkle and imagination but revealing the Vienna Philharmonic as a band surprisingly sympathetic to repertory not normally associated with it. Though the piano and trumpet might have been placed closer with advantage, the CD transfer of refined analogue sound is impressive, though detail is not sharply etched.

Pulcinella (ballet) complete.
(*) Erato/WEA 2292 45382-2 [id.]. Murray, Rolfe Johnson, Estes, Ens. InterContemporain, Boulez – *Le Chant du rossignol*.*

Boulez secures superb playing from the Ensemble InterContemporain, and his singers are first class in every way. His is a fine performance, but his pacing is more extreme than some versions, with contrasts between movements almost overcharacterized. However, some may like the periodic added edge, and the Erato recording has been excellently transferred to CD.

The Rite of spring (complete ballet).
(M) **(*) Decca Dig. 430 709-2; *430 709-4* [id.]. Cleveland O, Chailly – MUSSORGSKY: *Pictures*.**
(B) **(*) DG Compact Classics *413 160-4* [id.]. Boston SO, Tilson Thomas – ORFF: *Carmina Burana*.**(*)

With speeds faster than usual – markedly so in Part Two – Chailly's taut and urgent reading brings one of Decca's sound spectaculars. The bass-drum, so important in this work, leaps out with a power, precision and resonance to startle the listener. It may not be the easiest version to live with, and the fast speeds in Part Two provide less contrast than usual before the onslaught of the final *Sacrificial dance*; but anyone wanting the Mussorgsky coupling – or, for that matter, to startle friends with the *Rite* – will be well pleased.

Michael Tilson Thomas's reading is dramatic enough but warmly expressive too, missing some of the music's bite. The amply reverberant acoustic emphasizes his approach but, with fine playing from the Boston orchestra and the advantage of continuity, this Compact Classics tape is well worth considering, as it also contains Jochum's outstanding account of Orff's *Carmina Burana*, which has the composer's imprimatur.

The Rite of spring (orchestral & pianola versions).
*** Pickwick Dig. MCD 25; *MCC 25*. Boston PO, Zander.

The Rite of spring; 4 Études; Scherzo à la russe.
*(*) Teldec/Warner Dig. 2292 44938-2; *2292 44938-4* [id.]. Philh. O, Inbal.

(i) *The Rite of spring;* (ii) *Pulcinella* (ballet): *suite.*
(M) *(**) Sony MK 44709 [id.]. (i) LSO; (ii) NYPO; Bernstein.

The Rite of spring; Symphony in 3 movments.
** Sony Dig. SK 45796 [id.]; *40-45796*. Philh. O, Esa-Pekka Salonen.

The most fascinating of the new recordings of Stravinsky's *Rite of spring* is Benjamin Zander's live recording with the Boston Philharmonic, full and vivid if slightly confined in sound. It brings a hard-hitting, colourful performance, directly related to the pianola version with which it is coupled. Stravinsky himself in the 1920s supervised the original Pleyela piano roll recording, which Rex Lawson 'plays' very effectively on a resonant Bösendorfer Imperial. With this pianola system (unlike the reproducing rolls which captured the actual playing of a concert pianist) the piano roll represented a form of transcription of the printed score, accurate in note lengths and time values. The pianolist playing the score back uses pedals to create dynamic levels and accents, and levers to phrase and sustain and bring the music back to life. The speeds at which everything is presented remain predetermined and unalterable; and here the most striking point on speed is the very fast tempo for the opening of the final *Sacrificial dance*, markedly faster even than Stravinsky's own on the last – and finest – of his three recordings. With tracks correlated between the two performances, it is very easy to make illuminating comparisons. Zander suggests (and he offers additional documentary evidence from Marie Rambert, the Russian ballerina, quoting comments made by the composer at the original dance rehearsals of the ballet) that Stravinsky intended a faster pacing for the ballet's finale and that he modified the tempo only when he discovered that orchestras could not cope with the music at his intended speed (even his own 1960 recording contains inaccuracies). There is no doubt that, played up to this faster tempo, the *Danse sacrale* is electrifying and, once experienced, the slower speed to which we are all accustomed seems comparatively restrained. It is a final irony that the first recording of the suggested intended 'original' tempo made since Pierre Monteux's somewhat chaotic attempt with a Paris orchestra in 1929 is presented on CD by a semi-professional group (of considerable excellence) which now projects rhythms with biting confidence that defeated professionals 70 years earlier! This CD costs a little over medium price.

Bernstein's LSO version dates from 1972 at the time of quadraphonic experiments. The problems of conducting in the round led Bernstein finally to suggest at the sessions that he should simply conduct a straight performance. That is substantially what appears on the record, a larger-than-life, colourfully romantic view with tremendous impact. As transferred to CD, the sound is full and spacious, less aggressive than it originally was on LP. Bernstein's New York account of the *Pulcinella suite*, recorded in 1960, brings rather edgy sound, making the performance seem over-heavy for Stravinsky's wittily neo-classical inspirations.

Salonen couples his colourful but idiosyncratic reading of the *Rite* with an involvingly larger-than-life account of the *Symphony in three movements*. The playing in the *Symphony* is vivid and intense, with the jazz rhythms of the outer movements bitingly effective and with the central *Andante* moulded at an unusually slow speed. But, quite apart from the interpretative quirks, the *Rite* is given a softer-grained performance, partly a question of the playing, partly of the recording.

Inbal takes a very metrical view of the *Rite* which, in principle, may be totally valid but which in practice here makes the music sound too safe, lacking excitement. The sound too is full and smooth rather than brilliant, and the coupling is ungenerous.

VOCAL MUSIC

(i) *Canticum sacrum;* (ii) *Mass;* (iii) *Symphony of Psalms.*
(M) *** Decca 430 346-2 [id.]. Christ Church Cathedral, Oxford, Ch., Simon Preston; with (i) Morton, Creed; (i; iii) Philip Jones Ensemble; (iii) N. Jones, Giles, Cave, Lindley, Herron, L. Sinf. – POULENC: *Motets.****

It is fascinating to hear Stravinsky's rapt and masterly *Symphony of Psalms* in a performance with boys' voices, as the composer said he had in mind. The freshness of the choral sound and its ethereal clarity make this a most moving performance, as though sung by an angel choir. The *Canticum sacrum*, more taxing still in its serial austerity, brings another superb example of the artistry of these youngsters. Here again Stravinsky's markings suggest that he may have had such a tone-colour in mind, though in normal circumstances it would seem all but impossible to achieve. The *Symphony* lacks some of the weight and bite of larger-scale performances but, with atmospheric, resonant yet well focused sound, the effect is most moving. The comparably spare but very beautiful *Mass* for voices and instruments, given a direct, classical reading, is hardly less impressive, and is equally well transferred to CD. The recordings (originally Argo) date from 1973/4.

Oedipus Rex (opera-oratorio).
(M) **(*) Decca 430 001-2 [id.]. McCowen (narrator), Pears, Meyer, McIntyre, Dean, Ryland Davies, Luxon, John Alldis Ch., LPO, Solti.

Solti's view of this highly stylized work is less sharp-edged than one would expect, and the dominant factor in the performance is not so much the conductor's direction as the heartfelt singing of Peter Pears in the title-role. It was he who sang the part in the composer's first LP recording, twenty years earlier, and here the crispness and clarity of his delivery go with an ability to point the key moments of deep emotion with extraordinary intensity. The rest of the vocal team is good, if not outstanding, and the narration (in English) of Alec McCowen is apt and undistracting. The transfer to CD is outstandingly vivid and brilliant.

Suk, Josef (1874–1935)

Asrael Symphony, Op. 27.
❀ *** Virgin VC7 91221-2; *VC7 91221-4* [id.]. Royal Liverpool PO, Pešek.

As we commented in our main volume, it is astonishing that a work of this stature should have been cold-shouldered for so long outside Czechoslovakia. This is only its third recording ever, and its first in Britain. It displaces the Neumann account on Supraphon, which we were glad to see and to which we accorded three stars. But there is altogether much greater sensitivity and imagination from Libor Pešek, who seems to have won the sympathy of his players; though the Czech Philharmonic is rather special, the Liverpool orchestra shows itself very responsive indeed. It is very different from Vačláv Talich's pioneering mono disc, but no less powerful. Asrael is the Angel of Death (Suk wrote the work under the burden of a double grief: the death of his 27-year-old wife and of his father-in-law and teacher, Dvořák). Even if you have Neumann's eminently serviceable record, you should lose no time in investigating this. Let us hope its success will encourange Vigin Classics to record more of Suk with Pešek. We know he is keen that his compatriot's music should be better known outside Czechoslovakia.

Fantastic Scherzo, Op. 25.
*** Chan. Dig. CHAN 8897; *ABTD 1508* [id.]. Czech PO, Bělohlávek – MARTINŮ: *Symphony No. 6*; JANÁČEK: *Sinfonietta.****

This captivating piece has invariably turned up as a fill-up for other Suk works, and this may have limited its dissemination. The playing of the Czech Philharmonic under Bělohávek is even finer than any of the earlier performances and it cannot be too strongly recommended, particularly in view of the excellence of the coupling.

Serenade for strings, Op. 6.
*** Virgin Dig. VC7 91165-2; *VC 791165-4* [id.]. LCO, Warren-Green – DVOŘÁK; TCHAIKOVSKY: *Serenades.***(*)

Warren-Green and his LCO give a wonderfully persuasive account of Suk's *Serenade*, easily the finest on record, making obvious that its inspiration is every bit as vivid as in the comparable works of Dvořák and Tchaikovsky. One readily feels the added intensity, which this group's leader and conductor believes comes from performing (even in the recording studio) standing up. The gleaming radiance of tone in the opening *Andante* is matched by the sparkle of the following *Allegro ma non troppo e grazioso* which has much charm, the haunting nostalgia of the *Adagio* and the spirited joy of the closing *Allegro giocoso*. The recording, made in All Saints', Petersham, is well up to the standard of previous records from this group, fresh, full and natural without blurring from the ecclesiastical acoustic.

Sullivan, Arthur (1842–1900)

(i) *Pineapple Poll: ballet music* (arr. Mackerras); (ii) *Savoy dances* (arr. Robinson); (i) *Overtures: Iolanthe; Mikado.*
(M) **(*) EMI CDM7 63961-2 [id.]; *EG 763961-4*. Pro Arte O, (i) John Hollingsworth; (ii) Stanford Robinson.

Hollingsworth offers a lively reading of *Pinapple Poll*, supported by good orchestral playing, and the slightly brash recorded quality quite suits the ebullience of the score. The upper register is over-bright but can be smoothed out. With its tuneful bonuses more smoothly done, this is enjoyable and quite good value for money.

Overtures: *Cox and Box; The Gondoliers; HMS Pinafore; Iolanthe; The Mikado; Patience; The Pirates of Penzance; Princess Ida; Ruddigore; The Sorcerer; The Yeomen of the Guard.*
(B) ** CfP CD-CFP 4529; *TC-CFP 4529* [id.]. Pro Arte O, Sir Malcolm Sargent.

Overtures: (i; ii) *Di Ballo;* (i; iii) *The Gondoliers;* (iv; v) *HMS Pinafore;* (i; iii) *Iolanthe; The Mikado;* (iv; iii) *The Pirates of Penzance;* (iv; vi) *The Yeomen of the Guard.*
(B) ** Pickwick IMPX 9014. (i) New SO of L; (ii) Collins; (iii) Godfrey; (iv) RPO; (v) Walker; (vi) Sargent.

Among bargain collections, Sargent's collection must be the best buy. It includes eleven overtures and the performances are characteristically bright and polished, although they do not always have quite the flair Godfrey brought to this music. The recordings date from between 1957 and 1961 (which brings less than ample strings) and have been brightly transferred to CD.

The Decca performances (on Pickwick) reflect the unfailing sparkle and lyrical feeling (witness the quotation of *Leave me not to pine alone* in *The Pirates of Penzance*) which Godfrey brought to his performances. *HMS Pinafore* is directed by James Walker, a Decca recording producer, who conducted the D'Oyly Carte Company briefly when Godfrey died, while *The Yeomen of the Guard* shows Sargent at his very best. The recordings have more colour and ambience than the EMI versions. As a bonus we are offered a vivacious account of *Di Ballo* admirably presented by Anthony Collins (better known for his Sibelius!). This must date from the mid-1950s yet still provides stereo of excellent quality. The transfers to CD are very well managed but, with only seven items included, one wonders why a more complete anthology was not assembled from the Decca/D'Oyly Carte archives for this reissue.

'The Best of Gilbert and Sullivan': excerpts from: *The Gondoliers; HMS Pinafore; The Mikado; The Pirates of Penzance.*
(B) *** EMI Miles of Music *TC2-MOM 106*. Morison, Sinclair, Graham, Thomas, Lewis, Young, Baker, Cameron, Brannigan, Evans, Milligan, Wallace, Glyndebourne Festival Ch., Pro Arte O, Sargent.

'Gilbert and Sullivan favourites': excerpts from: *The Gondoliers; HMS Pinafore; Iolanthe; The Mikado; Patience; The Pirates of Penzance; Ruddigore; The Yeomen of the Guard.*
(B) *** EMI Miles of Music *TC2-MOM 114*. (artists as above, plus) Anthony, Harwood, Bowden, Rouleau; Glyndebourne Festival Ch., Pro Arte O, Sargent.

Sargent's vintage studio recordings of the Savoy Operas were recorded between 1957 and 1963, with a wholly admirable cast. They blew a fresh breeze through the D'Oyly Carte performing tradition (of which Sargent himself had theatrical experience) and set very high musical standards. The complete sets are currently awaiting reissue at mid-price; meanwhile these two admirable cassette compilations, each offering over 80 minutes of music, should prove stimulating motorway entertainment. The first offers more extensive selections from four favourite operas, while the second ranges more widely; however, as nothing is duplicated, they are complementary. The lollipops are fairly evenly divided: Owen Brannigan's immortal account of the *Policeman's song* from *Pirates* is on *TC2-MOM 114* (which is a marginal first choice), while the longer groups of numbers from that same opera, *Iolanthe* and *Pinafore* on *TC2-MOM 106* contain much that is very engaging indeed. Excellent, fresh transfers with the words coming through clearly.

'The world of Gilbert and Sullivan': excerpts from: (i) *The Gondoliers; HMS Pinafore; Iolanthe;* (ii) *The Mikado;* (i) *The Pirates of Penzance;* (iii) *The Yeomen of the Guard.*
(B) *** Decca 430 095-2; *430 095-4* [id.]. Soloists, D'Oyly Carte Op. Co., New SO or RPO, (i) Godfrey; (ii) Nash; (iii) Sargent.

A quite admirable selection from the vintage series of Decca D'Oyly Carte recordings made between 1959 (*HMS Pinafore* – still the finest of the whole series) and 1973 (Royston Nash's *Mikado*). This was the right choice, as it is much more strongly cast than the earlier, Godfrey set, with John Reed shining brightly as Koko. His 'Little list' song is wonderfully relaxed, and *Tit willow* is charming. He is equally good as Sir Joseph Porter, KCB, in *Pinafore*, where his splendid *I am the monarch of the sea* is preceded by some highly atmospheric stage business. Owen Brannigan's unforgettable portrayal of the Sergeant of Police is demonstrated in the excerpts from *The Pirates of Penzance* (as is Valerie Masterson's charming Mabel), and two of the most delectable items are the Second Act trios from *Pinafore* and *Iolanthe*, both liltingly infectious. Sargent's fine *Yeomen of the Guard* is only briefly represented, so we must hope that further selections are to follow. The recording has fine atmosphere and presence throughout; *The Gondoliers*, however, betrays the same slightly degraded treble response of the complete recording. But overall, with 62 minutes of music offered, this is a real bargain which will give much delight. The catalogue numbers of the complete sets from which these come, almost all of which are three-star recommendations, are as follows. *Cox and Box* and *Ruddigore* are currently available only on cassette (Decca 417 355-4); *The Gondoliers* is available only on CD (Decca 417 254-2), and here there are reservations about the sound: the treble is fierce, making the strings edgy and the female voices peaky. *HMS Pinafore*, perhaps the finest recording of any Gilbert and Sullivan opera ever made and carrying its Rosette with honour, is available on both CD and tape (Decca 414 283-2; *414 283-4*), as is *Iolanthe* (Decca 414 145-2; *414 145-4*). *The Mikado* – the preferable 1973 re-recording conducted by Royston Nash (Decca 425 190-2), *Patience* (Decca 425 193-2) and *The Pirates of Penzance* (Decca 425 196-2), with Owen Brannigan again playing the Sergeant of Police, are all available on CD only; but Sargent's *Yeomen of the Guard* in harness with Godfrey's stylish *Trial by Jury*, with John Reed in the two roles of Jack Point and the Judge, is again available in both formats (Decca 417 358-2; *417 358-4*).

Suppé, Franz von (1819–95)

Overtures: *Die Frau Meisterin; Die Irrfahrt um's Glück; Light cavalry; Morning, noon and night in Vienna; Pique Dame; Poet and Peasant; Tantalusqualen; Wiener-Jubel (Viennese Jubilee).*
❀ *** EMI Dig. CDC7 54056-2 [id.]; *EL 754056-4.* ASMF, Marriner.

Marriner's new collection of Suppé *Overtures* goes straight to the top of the list. It is expansively recorded in EMI's No. 1 Studio and, played up to concert volume on big speakers, it produces the most spectacular demonstration quality. The sound has bloom, a wide amplitude, plenty of sparkle and a natural presence. This is just the disc to confound those who decry digital recording – there is all the opulence of the best analogue sound, with more realistic definition. The performances have tremendous exuberance and style: this is one of Marriner's very best records. The established warhorses come up splendidly: the introductions are given plenty of breadth and dignity, *Poet and Peasant* especially. *Pique Dame* has fine, gutsy excitement, while in the similarly lively *Light cavalry*, Marriner halves the tempo at the end to bring the fanfare tune back very broadly. The novelties are delightful. *Die Irrfahrt um's Glück* – concerned with magical goings-on – has a massively portentous opening, superbly realized here; *Die Frau Meisterin* produces a deliciously jiggy waltz tune, and *Wiener-Jubel*, after opening with resplendent fanfares, is as racy as you could wish. Not to be missed.

Svendsen, Johan Severin (1840–1911)

Romance in G, Op. 26.
(BB) *** Naxos Dig. 8.550329 [id.]. Dong-Suk Kang, Slovak (Bratislava) RSO, Adrian Leaper – HALVORSEN: *Air Norvégien* etc.; SIBELIUS: *Violin concerto*; SINDING: *Légende.****

Svendsen's once-popular *Romance in G* is otherwise available only in Grumiaux's version from the 1960s. Dong-Suk Kang plays it without sentimentality but with full-hearted lyricism. The balance places him a little too forward, but the recording is very satisfactory.

Sviridov, Yuri (born 1915)

Oratorio pathétique.
(*) Koch Dig. 3-7017-2 [id.]. Vassilev, Bulgarian R. & TV Ch. & O, Andreev – SHOSTAKOVICH: *Execution of Stepan Razin.*(*)

Yuri (or Georgy) Sviridov was a favourite pupil of Shostakovich and his uneventful *Oratorio pathétique* (1959), to words of Mayakovsky, enjoyed some success in the Soviet Union in the 1960s and was recorded on LP. It disappointed then, and the passage of time has not improved it. Very thin and insubstantial stuff, which is neither performed nor recorded particularly persuasively.

Sweelinck, Jan (1562–1621)

Chorale variations: Da pacem, Domine, in diebus nostris; Puer nobis nascitur; Echo fantasia No. 12 in A min.; Fantasia No. 4 in D min; Hexachord fantasia; Toccata No. 17 in A.

(M) ** HM/BMG GD 77148 [77148-2-RG]. Gustav Leonhardt (organ of Grote of St Jakobswerk, The Hague).

It is good to have an authoritative introduction to Sweelinck's organ music played on a splendid Dutch organ, but the recording, though faithful, is less than ideal in its close balance which – together with Gustav Leonhardt's playing – seems too often to project the music on an unvarying dynamic level. Leonhardt's registrations are often attractive, and he clearly has the measure of the composer's often complex contrupuntal devices (as in the *Hexachord fantasia*), but one feels more could have been made with the imitation in the *Echo fantasia*, achieved by the repetition of a phrase on a different manual, or played an octave lower. We hope Peter Hurford may turn his attention to this repertoire.

Szymanowski, Karol (1882–1937)

Violin concerto No. 1, Op. 35.
** Thorofon Capella CTH 2057 [id.]. Edinger, Katowice RSO, Penderecki – HARTMANN: *Concerto funèbre.***

Szymanowski's glorious *First Violin concerto* is conducted by his fellow-composer and countryman, Krzysztof Penderecki, coupled with a rarity by Karl Amadeus Hartmann. Christiane Edinger is an accomplished player, but the performance does not carry the conviction of Wanda Wilkomirska (see our main volume, pp. 1042–3). Penderecki often breaks up the seamless flow of the line and even inserts tiny pauses where there should be none. A decent recording but not a first choice.

Mythes, Op. 30; Kurpian folk song; King Roger: Roxana's aria (both arr. Kochanski).
❀ (M) *** DG 431 469-2; *431 469-4* [id.]. Kaja Danczowska, Krystian Zimerman – FRANCK: *Violin sonata.****

The violinist Kaja Danczowska, a pupil of Eugenia Uminska and David Oistrakh, brings vision and poetry to the ecstatic, soaring lines of the opening movement of *Mythes, The Fountains of Arethusa.* Her intonation is impeccable, and she has the measure of these other-worldly, intoxicating scores. There is a sense of rapture here that is totally persuasive, and Krystian Zimerman plays with a virtuosity and imagination that silence criticsm. An indispensable issue, the more so as the CD transfer of this 1980 analogue recording is so vividly realistic.

Études, Op. 4; Fantasy, Op. 14; Masques, Op. 34; Métopes, Op. 29.
*** Hyp. Dig. CDA 66409; *KA 66409* [id.]. Dennis Lee.

Dennis Lee is a Malaysian-born pianist who has not enjoyed the exposure to which his talents entitle him. His Hyperion CD is the finest record of Szymanowski's piano music to have appeared to date. He is totally in sympathy with this repertoire and has a real feeling for the exoticism and hothouse atmosphere of *Masques* and the *Métopes.* He has all the refinement of colour and sensitivity to dynamic nuance that this repertoire calls for; he handles the early Chopinesque Op. 4 *Études* and the Op. 14 *Fantasy* with much the same feeling for characterization and artistry that distinguishes his readings of the mature pieces. The recording is very good indeed.

STAGE WORKS

(i) *King Roger* (opera; complete); (ii) *Harnasie (The Highland Robbers)* (ballet pantomime), *Op. 55.*
*** Olympia OCD 303A/B [id.]. (i) Hiolski, Rumowska, Nikodem, Pustelak, Dabrowski,

Malewicz-Madey, Polish Pathfinders' Union Children's Ch.; (ii) Bachleda; (i; ii) Warsaw Nat. Op. House Ch. & O; (i) Mierzejewski; (ii) Wodiczko.

These two CDs accommodate Szymanowski's masterpiece, the opera *King Roger*, and his last stage-work, the ballet *Harnasie*. Both recordings date from the mid-1960s; they first appeared here, on the Muza label, in very inferior LPs which sounded as if they were made from dog biscuits. The present transfer has made a magnificent job of the originals, which sound strikingly detailed and rich. *King Roger* is the product of Szymanowski's fascination with eastern mysticism and Arab culture. It is set in twelfth-century Sicily and its opening scene, at Mass in the Cathedral of Palermo, is music of awesome beauty. The sense of ecstasy he evokes is intoxicating, and the complex textures and unparalleled wealth of colour he has at his command are impressive by any standards. The Dionysiac atmosphere will be familiar to those who know *The Song of the night* and the *First Violin concerto*. Andrzej Hiolski is a more than adequate Roger and Hanna Rumowska an excellent Roxane. The whole cast is dedicated and the extensive forces involved, including a children's choir and a large orchestra and chorus, respond to the direction of Mieczyslaw Mierzejewski with fervour. It is a pity that Rowicki's later account of *Harnasie*, made in the mid-1970s, could not have been chosen in preference to this earlier version, which runs to about 25 minutes, whereas the whole ballet takes about 34. Not that there are any serious inadequacies here, for the playing and singing are totally committed and do justice to its hedonistic nationalism. An indispensable set for all lovers of this composer.

Taffanel, (Claude) Paul (1844–1908)

Wind quintet in G min.
*** Sony Dig. CD 45996. Ens. Wien-Berlin – NIELSEN: *Wind quintet.****

Taffanel played an important part in the rehabilitation of the flute in late nineteenth-century French music; he composed a good deal of polished music for wind instruments. This quintet is an urbane, expertly fashioned piece by a musician of obvious culture who knows how to pace the flow of his ideas. The Ensemble Wien-Berlin play it with the utmost persuasion and charm, but this is a very lightweight companion to the Nielsen masterpiece.

Tallis, Thomas (*c.* 1505–85)

The Lamentations of Jeremiah; Absterge Domine; Mass for four voices, O sacrum convivium, Salvator mundi.
** ECM Dig. 833308-2 [id.]. Hilliard Ensemble, Paul Hillier.

The Hilliard couple the *Lamentations of Jeremiah* with the four-part *Mass* which is of much greater simplicity than most of his other music. The singing itself is impeccable, though the reverberant acoustic of All Hallows Church, Hampstead, serves to produce a rather dark, thick texture and this might tempt some listeners to look elsewhere.

Missa Salve intemerata Virgo.
(M) *** EMI Dig. CD-EMX 2155; *TC-EMX 2155*. St John's College, Cambridge, Ch., Guest – TAVERNER: *Western wynde.****

Taverner's Mass, *The Western wynde*, with which this is coupled, is based on the celebrated popular tune of the day, while the Tallis derives from an earlier motet of the same name. But the *Missa Salve intemerata Virgo* does in fact rework more of the original than is customary in parody Masses; only about a quarter is completely new. The Choir of St John's College, Cambridge, under George Guest is very well recorded and give a very spirited account of themselves, very different from the small, chamber-like performances which are prevalent nowadays, but musically no less satisfying. At this price, a splendid bargain.

Taneyev, Sergei (1856–1915)

Symphonies Nos. 2 in B flat min.; 4 in C min., Op. 12.
** Marco Polo 8.223196 [id.]. Polish State PO (Katozice), Stephen Gunzenhauser.

Neither of these symphonies is a masterpiece, and the unfinished *Second* is too long for its material. There is already a similar coupling available on Chant du Monde (LDC 278 931 – see our main volume, pp. 1046–7) in which Fedoseyev does his best for No. 2 and Rozhdestvensky makes as fervent a case as is possible for the uneven, but more coherent No. 4. The playing of the USSR Radio Orchestra is very committed indeed, even if the orchestral sounds are unrefined and the recording overlit, with moments of coarseness. Gunzenhauser has the advantage of 1988 digital sound, although the Marco Polo balance is in no way outstanding. His performance too is committed, but the orchestral playing here is not outstandingly sophisticated, and the Russians prove more convincing advocates of these scores.

Tartini, Giuseppe (1692–1770)

Violin concertos: in E min., D.56; in A, D.96; in A min., D.113.
(M) *** Erato/Warner Dig. 2292 45380-2 [id.]. Uto Ughi, Sol. Ven., Scimone.

Tartini is a composer of unfailing originality, and the three violin concertos on this record are all rewarding. Uto Ughi's performances are distinguished by excellent taste and refinement of tone, and I Solisti Veneti are hardly less polished. The harpsichord continuo is somewhat reticent but otherwise the recording is exemplary.

Taverner, John (*c.* 1495–1545)

Mass: The Western wynde; Song: The Western wynde.
(M) *** EMI Dig. CD-EMX 2155; *TC-EMX 2155.* St John's Coll., Cambridge, Ch., Guest – TALLIS: *Missa Salve intemerata Virgo.****

This St John's performance of John Taverner's mass, *The Western wynd*, is prefaced by the song on which both it and the motet of the same name are based. It also attracted both Tye and Sheppard. The Mass is basically a sequence of 36 variations of much subtlety and ingenuity on the theme and is one of the key works of the period. This spirited and robust performance by the Choir of St John's College, Cambridge, under George Guest is very well recorded; it is very different in style from the small chamber-like, vibrato-free performances to which we are becoming accustomed (and beguiled) but is every bit as valid. An admirable and, at this price, economical introduction to the composer.

Missa Mater Christi; Motets: *Mater Christi; O Wilhelme, pastor bone.*
*** Nimbus Dig. NI 5218 [id.]. Christ Church Cathedral Ch., Stephen Darlington.

This is a liturgical reconstruction by Andrew Carwood for the Feast of the

Annunciation of Our Lady, at Eastertide, which intersperses Tallis's *Missa Mater Christi* with the appropriate chant. The disc also includes the Motet *Mater Christi*, on which the Mass itself is built, and the antiphon, *O Wilhelme, pastor bone*, composed in honour of St William of York (Wolsey's archbishopric). It was Wolsey who founded Cardinal (later Christ Church) College, at which Taverner was Master of the Choristers. The singing under Stephen Darlington is first class, and the recording made, not at Christ Church, but at Dorchester Abbey, Oxfordshire, is difficult to fault: it is well focused and excellently balanced with a firm image. There are helpful and scholarly notes by John Caldwell.

Missa Corona Spinea; Votive antiphon: O Wilhelme pastor bone.
**(*) ASV Dig. CDGAU 115; *ZCGAU 115* [id.]. Christ Church Cathedral Ch., Francis Grier.

Francis Grier's pursuit of authenticity leads him to having his choir – as finely disciplined as it was under his predecessor, Simon Preston – singing this superb setting of the Mass a third higher than modern concert pitch. The result is a strain, both on the boy trebles and on listeners' ears. A degree of abrasiveness seems a necessary ingredient of authentic performances, but greater ease in those high mellifluous lines would be more in character. The digital recording is admirably clear as well as atmospheric, but one still has lingering doubts about the correctness of Grier's pitching of the melodic line.

Tchaikovsky, Peter (1840–93)

Andante cantabile for cello and orchestra, Op. posth.
(M) *** DG 431 475-2; *431 475-4* [id.]. Rostropovich, BPO – GLAZUNOV: *Chant du ménestrel*; SHOSTAKOVICH: *Cello concerto No. 2.****

Andante cantabile, Op. 11; Nocturne, Op. 19/4 (both arr. for cello & orchestra); *Pezzo capriccioso, Op. 62; Variations on a rococo theme, Op. 33* (original versions).
(*) Virgin Dig. VC7 91134-2; *VC7 91134-4* [id.]. Isserlis, COE, Gardiner (with GLAZUNOV: *2 Pieces, Op. 20, Chant du ménestrel, Op. 71.* RIMSKY-KORSAKOV: *Serenade, Op. 37.* CUI: *2 Morceaux, Op. 36**).

The composer himself arranged the *Andante cantabile* for cello and orchestra from his *D major String quartet*, transposing it from B flat to B major, but it was not published until after his death. Rostropovich indulges himself affectionately in the work, and the balance – all cello with a discreet orchestral backing – reflects his approach. The sound is warm and pleasing.

It was Rafael Wallfisch on Chandos (CHAN 8347, *ABTD 1080*) who first recorded the original version of Tchaikovsky's *Rococo variations*. The published score (as presented so unforgettably by Rostropovich and Karajan on DG 413 819-2, coupled with the Dvořák *Cello concerto*) omits the short scherzando, Variation No. 8, and alters the order of the others. There is evidence that the composer accepted the revision without exactly approving it and, while the differences are not fundamental, most collectors will want to hear the composer's original intentions; indeed one hopes that the original version will eventually become standard. On the whole, Wallfisch's performance is riper in romantic feeling than that of Isserlis, though neither can match Rostropovich. The Chandos CD includes all Tchaikovsky's concertante music for cello and orchestra, as listed above, but also features the original score of the *Pezzo capriccioso* and includes two song arrangements (*Legend* and *Was I not a little blade of grass?*).

The Virgin collection omits the song arrangements, offering instead an attractive bonus recital of Russian concertante lollipops, all of considerable charm. Isserlis's playing has slight reserve but also an elegant delicacy which is appealing, although it suits Glazunov and Cui rather better than it does Tchaikovsky's *Andante cantabile*. John Eliot Gardiner provides gracefully lightweight accompaniments and the Virgin recording is faithfully balanced, fresh in texture and warm in ambience. Some listeners may find this music-making lacking in extrovert feeling; others may feel that its lightness of touch makes a special appeal.

Capriccio italien, Op. 45; Nutcracker suite, Op. 71a; Sleeping Beauty (ballet) *suite, Op. 66a.*
(M) *** DG 431 610-2; *431 610-4* [id.]. BPO, Rostropovich.

We have given the highest praise (and a Rosette) to the Rostropovich triptych combining the three Tchaikovsky ballet suites, which added *Swan Lake* to the two listed here (DG 429 097-2; *429 097-4*), and that still seems the most appropriate coupling; but anyone whose collection has room for *Capriccio italien* rather than *Swan Lake* will find the present reissue hardly less rewarding. Here the vulgarity inherent in the principal theme (which Tchaikovsky thought was a folksong but which proved to be a local Italian 'pop' tune of the time) evaporates, so decoratively elegant is the playing of the Berlin Philharmonic, especially the violins. The finale, too, has an attractive burst of exuberance, and the bright CD transfer lightens any hint of rhythmic heaviness in the fully scored reprise of the main tune. These were among the finest recordings the DG engineers made in the Philharmonie in the late 1970s.

Piano concertos Nos. 1–3; Concert fantasia (for piano and orchestra), *Op. 56.*
(M) **(*) EMI Dig. CMS7 63658-2 (2) [id.]; *EX 763658-4*. Peter Donohoe, Bournemouth SO, Rudolf Barshai.

Piano concerto No. 1 in B flat min.; Concert fantasia, Op. 56.
**(*) EMI Dig. CDC7 49939-2 [id.]; *EL 749939-4*. Peter Donohoe, Bournemouth SO, Barshai.

If only Peter Donohoe could have repeated the success of his recording of the *Second Piano concerto* (which won the *Gramophone* magazine's Concerto Award in 1988 and a Rosette from us – see below) when he returned to the Poole Arts Centre to record these other Tchaikovsky works, this mid-priced box would have been a very attractive proposition. But the account of the *B flat minor Concerto*, although thoroughly sympathetic and spaciously conceived, lacks the thrust and indeed the electricity of the finest versions. The *Third Piano concerto* is altogether more successful, dramatic and lyrically persuasive, and well held together by Barshai; this is now available sensibly coupled with the *Second* – see below. The *Concert fantasia* is even more in need of interpretative cohesion. It is laid out in two balancing movements, lasting about half an hour. The first opens with charming *Nutcracker* overtones yet develops a powerful central cadenza, which Donohoe plays grandly and rumbustiously. The second movement brings a series of chimerical changes of mood and tempo, which both pianist and conductor negotiate with zestful, spontaneous abandon. The lyrical interludes have a pleasing Russian folksiness, and the rhetoric of the allegros brings an exhilarating dash which almost carries the performers away with it. A little more poise would have been welcome, but there is no denying the spontaneous combustion of the music-making, and the recording – but for a little too much resonance for the solo cadenza in the opening movement – is effectively spectacular.

Piano concerto No. 1 in B flat min., Op. 23.
*** Chesky CD-13 [id.]. Earl Wild, RPO, Fistoulari – DOHNÁNYI: *Variations on a nursery tune* etc.***

(M) (***) RCA mono GD 60449; *GK 60449*. Horowitz, NBC SO, Toscanini – MUSSORGSKY: *Pictures*.***
(BB) *** Pickwick PWK 1148. Peter Katin, LSO, Eric Kundell – SCHUMANN: *Concerto*.**(*)
(M) **(*) Mercury 432 011-2 [id.]. Byron Janis, LSO Menges – SCHUMANN: *Piano concerto*.***
(M) ** EMI CDC7 63525-2; *EG 763525-4* [id.]. John Ogdon, Philh. O, Barbirolli – RACHMANINOV: *Concerto No. 2* etc.**

Even in the shadow of Horowitz, the spectacular reissue by Earl Wild with the RPO under Fistoulari stands as one of the finest accounts ever of this much-recorded work. The recording was originally made for Reader's Digest by RCA engineers in the early 1960s and has had a chequered career, lying in the RCA vaults for many years. Now it re-emerges on the enterprising Chesky label, and one's only complaint is the premium price. However, it is certainly a premium performance and needs no apology for its sound, which is vintage quality of that period, although the violins have become a little drier with the digital remastering for CD. But this compares favourably with many modern recordings and the piano tone is bold and natural. From the first sweep of the opening the reading is distinguished by its feeling of directness and power, yet the lyrical side of the music (the first movement's second subject, the outer sections of the *Andantino*) brings a comparable sensitivity. In the first movement there are some wholly spontaneous bursts of bravura from the soloist which are quite electrifying; and in the big cadenza one is equally reminded of Horowitz when Wild, by impetuous tempo changes in the imitative passages, makes himself sound almost like a piano duo. The finale too, taken with crackling bravura, again recalls the famous Horowitz/Toscanini live Carnegie Hall recording. Fistoulari, splendidly assured throughout, produces a vivid orchestral response (the flute and piccolo interjections in the finale are as dashing as the solo playing) and makes a superb final climax.

Horowitz's earlier version was made in Carnegie Hall, in 1941, under studio conditions. The recording is altogether better balanced than the famous live performance by the same artists two years later, and the orchestral sound is much fuller; indeed the quality brooks no real criticism. The performance has all the thrills and electricity of the 1943 version and the playing is prodigious in its bravura. But throughout one feels that Toscanini – with his soloist responding readily – is forcing the pace, creating enormous urgency in the first movement, which here is nearly a minute and a half shorter. The finale, too, has even more dazzling *fuoco*. This is an exhilarating listening experience; but the sense of occasion of the live performance created a really great performance which is undoubtedly more satisfying, in spite of its sonic limitations. It is coupled with an impressive account of Beethoven's *Emperor concerto* (RCA GD 87992 [7792-2-RG]).

Peter Katin's performance from the beginning of the 1970s is alive and direct, the opening big tune taken fast but with a fine sweep which continues through the first movement. The *Andantino* is played very stylishly, and the finale has plenty of bravura. With vintage Decca sound this is an enjoyable bargain, and the coupled Schumann *Concerto* is equally characterful.

Byron Janis's account is in many ways as dazzling as his Rachmaninov recordings (still awaited on CD). Menges is not as strong an accompanist as Dorati, most noticeably so in the finale. But this remains a memorable performance, with much dash and power from the soloist in the outer movements and the *Andantino* agreeably delicate. There are plenty of thrills, not least Janis's final stormy octaves before the bold restatement of the great tune in the finale. The Mercury sound is excellent, full and resonant, with a big piano image up front. There will be many who will enjoy this reading for its warmth of response in the lyrical material of the first movement, taking it nearer the (coupled) Schumann *Concerto* in romantic feeling.

The Ogdon/Barbirolli performance brings many highly musical touches, especially in its lyrical moments – the *Andantino*, with its natural simplicity, is most successful. But the barnstorming element is missing, and the finale seems underpowered. The 1962 recording still sounds very good.

Piano concertos Nos. 1 in B flat min.; 3 in E flat.
** Sony Dig. SK 45756 [id.]. Vladimir Feltsman, Nat. SO of Washington, DC, Rostropovich.

On the Sony coupling there is some highly musical if ultimately cool playing from Vladimir Feltsman in both *Concertos*. He has excellent taste and no lack of technique, and Rostropovich gets a refined and at times fastidious response from the Washington orchestra. The Sony recording is eminently satisfactory and the disc has much going for it, but in a field which includes such luminaries as Gilels, Richter, Argerich, Wild and Pletnev, it is not quite spontaneous enough to be among the first choices.

(i) *Piano concerto No. 1 in B flat min., Op. 23;* (ii) *Violin concerto in D, Op. 35.*
(B) *** BMG/RCA VD 60491; *VK 60491* [60491-2-RV; *60491-4-RV*]. (i) John Browning; (ii) Erick Friedman, LSO, Ozawa.
(M) **(*) Sony Dig./Analogue SBK 46339 [id.]; *40-46339.* (i) Gilels, NYPO, Mehta; (ii) D. Oistrakh, Phd. O, Ormandy.
(M) **(*) DG Analogue/Dig. 431 609-2; *431 609-4* [id.]. (i) Argerich, RPO, Dutoit; (ii) Kremer, BPO, Maazel.

The BMG/RCA coupling is an outstanding reissue, combining performances recorded in the mid-1960s. Browning's interpretation of the solo role in the *Piano concerto* is remarkable, not only for power and bravura but for wit and point in the many *scherzando* passages. His slow movement has an attractively cool simplicity, and in the finale he adopts a fast and furious tempo to compare with Horowitz. Erick Friedman, Heifetz's pupil, is a thoughtful violinist who gives a keenly intelligent performance of the companion work, imbued with a glowing lyricism and with a particularly poetic and beautiful account of the slow movement. There is plenty of dash and fire in the finale, and Ozawa gives first-rate support to both soloists. The recording was always excellent but now seems even firmer with the digital remastering, which gives the soloists excellent presence and the orchestra a more arresting impact at the opening of the *Piano concerto*. Two performances to match those of almost any rival: for this coupling they are unsurpassed. Incidentally, Heifetz's magical 78-r.p.m. recording of the *Violin concerto* with Barbirolli, which he never surpassed and which is recalled to the memory by Friedman's performance, is now available on CD (Biddulph LAB 026).

Having already offered Gilels's 1980 digital recording of the *Piano concerto* (in which the solo playing is more impressive than either the accompaniment or the sound-balance), together with Zukerman's version of the *Violin concerto* (MDK 44643 – see our main volume, p. 1054), Sony now try again, choosing an alternative pairing with David Oistrakh's performance, recorded with Ormandy a decade earlier. It is, not surprisingly, an excellent performance but, perhaps because of the close microphones, Oistrakh's tone sounds thinner than usual. Such moments as the recapitulation of the second subject high among the ledger lines are beautifully done, but elsewhere the effect is not always as ravishing as one might expect. As usual, Ormandy provides a sympathetic accompaniment, although the imagery of the recording is slightly overblown, with the solo image made larger than life-size.

Argerich's 1971 version of the *Piano concerto* with Dutoit remains among the finest ever made, and the recording still sounds marvellous, bold and full and with striking presence. It is still available at full price, coupled with an equally distinguished account of Prokofiev's *Third Concerto* (see our main volume, pp. 1051–2 and 768). This new pairing is offered at mid-price. Kremer's was the first digital recording of the *Violin concerto.* This artist blends keen nervous energy with controlled lyrical feeling; it goes without saying that his virtuosity is impressive. Self-regarding agogic distortions are few (bars 50–58 and the first-movement cadenza are instances) and there is no lack of warmth – yet there is something missing. An outstanding performance of this work refreshes the spirit and resonates in the mind (Campoli's version – see below – does just this). With Kremer, although both the playing of the Berlin Philharmonic under Maazel and the 1979 recording are excellent, there is not the humanity and perception of a special kind which are needed if a newcomer is to take pride of place in a collection.

(i) *Piano concerto No. 1;* (ii) *Violin concerto in D, Op. 35;* (iii) *Serenade for strings: Waltz* (CD only: *Serenade for strings:* complete). (iv or v) *Variations on a rococo theme, Op. 33.*
❀ (B) *** DG Compact Classics 413 161-2 (2); *413 161-4.* (i) Argerich, RPO, Dutoit; (ii) Milstein, VPO, Abbado; (iii) BPO, Karajan (cassette only: (iv) Rostropovich, Leningrad PO, Rozhdestvensky; CD only: (v) Rostropovich, BPO, Karajan).

This extended-length chrome tape was the jewel in the crown of DG's Walkman series (now renamed Compact Classics), always generous but here exceptionally so, both in quality of performances and recording, as well as in the amount of music offered. We awarded it a Rosette as the outstanding Tchaikovsky bargain compilation. Now for their digitally remastered 2-CD equivalent, DG have gone one better by replacing Karajan's elegant and polished *Waltz* from the *String serenade* (which remains on the tape) with the complete analogue performance of the work from which it was drawn. Moreover, on CD Rostropovich's later recording of the *Rococo variations,* with Karajan, is substituted for his earlier version with Rozhdestvensky. He and Karajan find a splendid symbiosis, and this performance is superb in every way, and very well recorded. Yet tape collectors need not feel deprived, for Rostropovich's earlier (1961) version *also* offers playing with just the right amount of jaunty elegance as regards the theme and the first few variations; and when the virtuoso fireworks are let off, they are brilliant, effortless and breathtaking in their éclat. Indeed, Rostropovich needs no superlatives and his accompanist shows a mastery all his own. Argerich's account of the *B flat minor Piano concerto* is second to none; Milstein's (1973) performance of the *Violin concerto* is equally impressive, undoubtedly one of the finest available, while Abbado secures playing of genuine sensitivity and scale from the Vienna Philharmonic. The only slight drawback on the cassette is that the turnover comes between the first and second movements of the *Piano concerto.* But it is difficult to see how this could have been avoided within the chosen format. The sound is excellent.

Piano concertos Nos. 2 in G; 3 in E flat.
❀ *** EMI Dig. CDC7 49940-2 [id.]; EL 749940. Donohoe, Bournemouth SO, Barshai.
**(*) Virgin Dig. VC7 91202-2; *VC7 91202-4* [id.]. Mikhail Pletnev, Phil. O, Vladimir Fedoseyev.

Donohoe's much-praised recording of Tchaikovsky's *Second Piano concerto* now returns to the catalogue, coupled with his excellent account of the *Third.* This latter is almost equally distinctive, with its volatile qualities well recognized. This superb recording of the full, original score of the *Second* in every way justifies the work's length and the unusual format of the slow movement, where the piece temporarily becomes a triple concerto, with its extended solos for violin and cello; these are played with beguiling warmth by Nigel Kennedy and Steven Isserlis. Barshai's pacing is not only perfectly calculated but he gives the opening tune an engaging rhythmic lift. The whole movement goes with a splendid impetus, yet the central orchestral episode is broadened effectively. The slow movement has one of Tchaikovsky's very best tunes, and the performance is a delight from beginning to end. Peter Donohoe plays marvellously in the first two movements – he is quite melting in the *Andante* – and in the finale he is inspired to bravura which recalls Horowitz in the *B flat minor Concerto*. The main theme, shooting off with the velocity of the ball in a pinball machine, is exhilarating, and the orchestral response has a matching excitement. The coda, with its cascading octaves, is a *tour de force* and brings one to the edge of one's seat in admiration. The recording has a fine, spacious ambience and is admirably realistic and very well balanced. Tchaikovsky's work has never before received such convincing advocacy on record.

Commanding playing from Mikhail Pletnev, whose exceptional affinity for the composer is much in evidence. In the *Second Piano concerto* his handling of the second group of the first movement has great tenderness, and his seemingly effortless virtuosity is little short of breathtaking. He also has the advantage of totally idiomatic string soloists in the slow movement where, unfortunately, a few bars are cut. (Why do artists detract from a recording in this way?) It would be difficult to improve on the *Third*, which is strongly and interestingly characterized. Not only is the pianism of the highest voltage but the orchestral playing is highly charged too. The recording is very good but performs rather better on high-grade and sophisticated equipment than it does on more modest machines, where climaxes can give the impression of discoloration.

Violin concerto in D, Op. 35.
(*) Denon Dig. CO 73325 [id.]. Kantorow, LPO, Thomson – STRAVINSKY: *Concerto.**
(BB) **(*) Pickwick PWK 1145. Campoli, LSO, Argenta.

(i; ii) *Violin concerto in D;* (ii) *Capriccio italien*; (iii) *Francesca da Rimini.*
(M) **(*) EMI Dig. CDD7 63890-2 [id.]; *ET 763890-4.* (i) Vladimir Spivakov; (ii) Philh. O; (iii) BPO; Ozawa.

Violin concerto in D; Sérénade mélancholique, Op. 26; Souvenir d'un lieu cher, Op. 42/3: Mélodie. Valse-scherzo, Op. 34.
*** ASV Dig. CDDCA 713; *ZCDCA 713* [id.]. Xue-Wei, Philh. O, Accardo.

(i) *Violin concerto in D; Sleeping Beauty* (ballet): *suite.*
** Collins Dig. 1046-2; *1046-4* [id.]. (i) Igor Oistrakh, LSO, Frühbeck de Burgos.

(i) *Violin concerto in D;* (ii) *Andante cantabile, Op. 11.*
(*) EMI Dig. CDC7 54108-2 [id.]; *EL 754108-4.* Perlman, (i) Israel PO, Mehta; (ii) Janet Goodman (with TARTINI: *Devil's Trill Sonata.* KREISLER: *Liebeslied.* PROKOFIEV: *Love for 3 oranges: March.* BLOCH: *Nigun.* WIENIAWSKI: *Caprice in A min.* BAZZINI: *Ronde des Lutins* *).

Xue-Wei gives a warmly expressive reading of this lovely concerto, lacking some of the fantasy and mystery that Kyung Wha Chung for one finds; but, with rich, full tone, he brings out the sensuousness of the work, while displaying commanding virtuosity. With the central *Canzonetta* turned into a simple song without words, not over-romanticized, this is a performance that confirms all the qualities displayed in Xue-Wei's first concerto disc for ASV of Bruch and Saint-Saëns. The coupling will be ideal for many, consisting of violin concertante pieces by Tchaikovsky, not just the *Sérénade mélancolique*, but the

Valse-scherzo in a dazzling performance, and *Mélodie*, the third of the three pieces that Tchaikovsky grouped as *Souvenir d'un lieu cher*, freely and expressively done. The orchestral playing under another great violin virtuoso is warmly sympathetic but could be crisper, not helped for detail in tuttis by the lively acoustic of St Barnabas Church, Mitcham. However, this makes a very enjoyable collection.

Perlman's new recording of the Tchaikovsky *Violin concerto* is first and foremost a memento of his first visit to Russia, together with Zubin Mehta and the Israel Philharmonic Orchestra. The concerto performance here is hardly a direct rival to Perlman's earlier, Philadelphia version (EMI CDC7 47106-2). The live recording, made in the Philharmonic Hall in Leningrad on 2 May 1989, is rather dehydrated and edgy, with a heavy background, but the performance ends in an account of the finale that, at breakneck speed and with dazzlingly clean articulation, rightly brings the house down. The first two movements are too heavily underlined, and even the opening of the finale sounds a little perfunctory, but this is an amazing document of supreme violin virtuosity. The recital was recorded in the Tchaikovsky Hall in Moscow during the same trip, and the sound, though still harsh, has more bloom on it. Such points must be put in perspective, when the recording brings some of the most amazing violin wizardry ever heard on disc. Perlman's adrenalin flows, as – after announcing each item in a loud, clear voice – he tackles one formidable encore after another. A rather old-fashioned atmosphere is established in the Tartini, done in the Kreisler edition with his cadenza; and that leads to a delicious account of Kreisler's *Liebeslied*. Though Perlman's announcement of the Wieniawski brings no ripple of applause – as his other announcements do – this little squib, let off with dazzling lightness, brings bigger cheers than ever. For his final item, the Bazzini, he keeps the biggest excitement of all: it is most moving to hear the Moscow audience audibly gasping with astonishment, not once but many times over.

At brisk speeds Kantorow gives a crisply classical reading of the first movement, with little lingering on the second subject, but that makes the Stravinsky coupling seem more appropriate. In the slow movement of the Tchaikovsky by contrast, Kantorow is extremely romantic at a very expansive speed, using extreme rubato. His classical manners return in the finale which, very fast and light, verges on the perfunctory, not sounding as exciting as it should. There are more powerful versions of both works; but anyone who specially wants this coupling is unlikely to be seriously disappointed, when the sound is full and well balanced. Significantly, Denon put the Stravinsky concerto first. Kantorow's account of the third movement, *Aria II*, brings the most poised, moving playing on the disc.

Campoli's performance of Tchaikovsky's *Violin concerto* has a lyrical simplicity and a natural warmth and spontaneity that are very appealing. Ataulfo Argenta accompanies with much sensitivity and shows his feeling for Tchaikovsky's orchestral colouring – especially in the *Canzonetta*, which has much wistful charm – as well as creating plenty of excitement and contrast in the tuttis – the polacca treatment of the main theme in the first movement is infectiously joyous. The finale brings fireworks from all concerned. The 1958 Decca recording, outstanding in its day, hardly shows its age, although a little judicious smoothing at the top is useful, for the sound has plenty of bloom. In today's marketplace a CD of this work, playing for 34 minutes and offering no coupling, can hardly be considered competitive, but anyone buying this super-bargain disc on impulse could well be surprised at the pleasure which it offers.

Spivakov takes a relatively heavyweight view of the *Concerto*, rich and warm, helped by strikingly full (even if early – 1981) digital recording, made at EMI's Abbey Road Studio. With Ozawa directing the Philharmonia in a most persuasive accompaniment, this is simultaneously a reading which brings out the almost Mozartian elegance of much of the writing, emphasizing the happiness of the inspiration. A joyful performance, too, of the *Capriccio italien*, the original fill-up; only the additional Berlin Philharmonic *Francesca da Rimini* (made in the Philharmonie in 1984) brings disappointment. Its essential neurosis means that at the end of the middle section Ozawa begins his accelerando much too early (at the cor anglais scalic figure) and, while what follows is undoubtedly thrilling, it turns Tchaikovsky's construction into melodrama.

In the Igor Oistrakh version of the *Concerto*, the playing of the LSO is disappointingly routine, as it is in the pedestrian *Sleeping Beauty* coupling. Tension is on the low side; but it is good to hear a master like Igor Oistrakh giving such a warm, relaxed account of a work with which he has long been associated. Very expansive, sometimes he is wilful but is always spontaneous-sounding. The rather distant recording balance tends to damp down the work's excitement. Kyung Wha Chung, engagingly volatile as a performer, responding to the inspiration of the moment, has made herself a special niche with this concerto. Her digital recording with Dutoit (Decca 410 011-2), coupled with the Mendelssohn *Concerto*, is one of the finest recordings of this work ever made, although the difference between this and her earlier version with Previn is marginal and readers preferring a coupling with the Bruch *G minor* and the Saint-Saëns *Havanaise* can be well satisfied with this at mid-price (Decca 417 707-2; *417 707-4*).

1812 Overture, Op. 49.
(M) **(*) Decca Dig. 430 446-2; *430 446-4* [id.]. Chicago SO, Solti – MUSSORGSKY: *Pictures* ***; PROKOFIEV: *Symphony No. 1.**(*)

1812 Overture; Francesca da Rimini, Op. 32.
(M) **(*) Decca Dig. 430 700-2; *430 700-4* [id.]. Montreal SO, Dutoit – MUSSORGSKY: *Night*; RIMSKY-KORSAKOV: *Capriccio espagnol.***(*)

1812 Overture; Francesca da Rimini, Op. 32; Marche slave, Op. 31.
(M) ** DG 431 608-2; *431 608-4* [id.]. Chicago SO, Barenboim.

(i) *1812 Overture;* (ii) *Marche slave;* (iii) *Romeo and Juliet.*
(B) **(*) DG Compact Classics 413 153-2 (2); *413 153-4*. (i) Boston Pops O, Fiedler; (ii) BPO, Karajan; (iii) San Francisco SO, Ozawa – MUSSORGSKY: *Pictures* etc.***

Fiedler's account of *1812* has plenty of adrenalin and is brilliantly recorded, with the effective display of pyrotechnics at the end adding spectacle without drowning the music. The direct manner of the performance does all Tchaikovsky asks, if with no special individuality. Nevertheless, with Karajan's *Marche slave* plus Ozawa's excellent *Romeo and Juliet*, and first-class sound throughout, this Compact Classics chrome tape, coupled with Mussorgsky, is certainly good value. The pair of digitally remastered CDs ungenerously add only one short piece, Kurt Sanderling's idiomatic version of Borodin's *In the Steppes of Central Asia.*

Dutoit's performances are individually characterized and by no means conventional in approach. *1812*, complete with cannon provided by the 22nd Regiment of Quebec, is exciting without making one sit on the edge of one's seat. The sound is refined and luminous but lacks the sumptuous weight which is needed to give Tchaikovsky's climaxes a physical thrill. *Francesca da Rimini* has both weight and strength, backed up by a recording of spectacular range, but with less variation of tension than in the very finest versions.

Solti's *1812*, like the coupled Mussorgsky, is exciting and spectacular, and the engineering is impressively brilliant, apart from a rather inexact focus for the carillon that accompanies the very precise cannonade at the end. This performance is also available at full price, coupled with *Romeo and Juliet* and the *Nutcracker suite*, both showing Solti at his best (Decca 417 400-2).

Barenboim's are enjoyable performances, but he is too ready to let the tension relax to be entirely convincing throughout this programme, although his affection for the music is never in doubt. In *1812*, the lyrical string-melody is appealingly expansive; but by the finest Chicago standards the playing, although not without excitement, has less than the usual grip. *Marche slave* is slow and solemn, while the middle section of *Francesca da Rimini* yields some beguilingly languorous wind playing and its passionate string climax has ardour. Yet in the outer sections the frenzied nervous tension of the whirlwinds is partly subdued by the conductor's partiality for breadth, although the coda is exciting enough. The digital recording is vivid but could expand more.

Francesca da Rimini, Op. 32.
** Ph. Dig. 426 437-2 [id.]. LPO, Valéry Gergiev – MUSSORGSKY: *Pictures.***

After the sepulchral opening chords, Gergiev's frenzied pacing of the main allegro approaches that of hysteria; then he slows right down for the central episode and, understandably, lingers over Tchaikovsky's glowing woodwind colours, drawing a seductive response from the LPO. The demonic closing section almost surpasses the delirium of the opening, and the discords of the coda bring a shatteringly resonant culmination.

Hamlet (fantasy overture), Op. 67a.
*** EMI Dig. CDC7 49859-2 [id.]; *EL 749859-4*. Phd. O, Muti – SCRIABIN: *Symphony No. 2.****

Muti's performance of *Hamlet* is hardly less impressive than his reading of the Scriabin *Second Symphony*, with which it is coupled. It is taut, powerful and dramatic and, in terms of both virtuosity and feeling, can hold its own with any modern recording now on offer, although Stokowski's famous Everest version (Dell'Arte CDDA 9006) is in a very special class.

Manfred Symphony, Op. 58.
❀ *** Chan. Dig. CHAN 8535; *ABTD 1245* [id.]. Oslo PO, Jansons.

Jansons' performance of *Manfred* with the Oslo Philharmonic crowned his outstanding series of Tchaikovsky symphonies in an electrifying account of this difficult, unconventionally structured work. The performance culminates in a thrilling account of the finale, leading up to the entry of the organ, gloriously resonant and supported by luxuriant string-sound. With superb recording, this is an easy first choice.

The Nutcracker (ballet), *Op. 71* (complete).
(BB) ** Naxos Dig. 8.550324/5 [id.]. Slovak RSO (Bratislava), Lenárd – CHOPIN/GLAZUNOV: *Chopinina.***

The Naxos super-bargain *Nutcracker* is played with great zest in Bratislava, and there is no lack of polish either. There is never a dull moment here, and the famous 'characteristic dances' of the Act II *Divertissement* emerge vividly. The digital recording has the brightest colouring and the effect overall could never be described as dull. But there are snags: there is a relative absence of charm and the *Waltz of the snowflakes* is minus its children's chorus. The Bolshoi Ballet did it that way at a London performance, but on a record the omission of a highly engaging and appealingly innocent effect is not easy to forgive. The *Waltz of the flowers*, too, lilts much more persuasively in Ormandy's hands –

see below – even though he takes liberties with it. The break between the two Naxos CDs is at an awkward spot, just before the arrival of the Spanish dancers in the *Divertissement*, and the listener is left 'in mid-air' until the second disc continues the music. Either Previn's version on EMI (CDS7 47267-8 [CDCB 47267]; *EX 270457-5*) or the superbly recorded Mackerras Telarc reading (CD 8137) is to be preferred.

Nutcracker suite, Op. 71a.
(M) **(*) Sony SBK 46550 [id.]. Phd. O, Ormandy – CHOPIN: *Les Sylphides*; DELIBES: *Coppélia; Sylvia:* suites.***

Ormandy's 1963 recording of the suite is obviously derived from a more complete version, for the *Sugar Plum Fairy* is given her extended exit music as in the ballet, rather than the coda which Tchaikovsky provided for the concert suite. The Philadelphia Orchestra made this wonderful music universally famous in Walt Disney's *Fantasia* and they know how to play it just as well under Ormandy as they did under Stokowski. Perhaps there is less individuality in the characteristic dances, but the music-making has suitable moments of reticence (as in the neat *Ouverture miniature*) as well as plenty of flair. In the *Waltz of the flowers* Ormandy blots his copybook, by taking the soaring violin tune an octave up on its second appearance, both at the beginning and in the reprise, but the Philadelphia violins make such a brilliant effect that one can almost forgive the excess.

Nutcracker suite, Op. 71a; Romeo and Juliet (fantasy overture); Swan Lake suite, Op. 20.
(M) *** Decca Dig. 430 707-2; *430 707-4* [id.]. Chicago SO, Solti.

Solti's digital recording of the *Swan Lake suite* was originally coupled with the *Fifth Symphony*. Now it comes in what is an attractive triptych, given Decca's best standard Chicago recording. *Romeo and Juliet* has an unexpected element of restraint and the love-theme, very tender and gentle when it first appears on the cor anglais, finds a yearning passion without histrionics; the battle sequences have plenty of bite in the strings, and at the climax the trumpets ring out resplendently. The *Nutcracker suite* produces marvellously characterful solo playing and much subtle detail.

(i) *Nutcracker suite;* (ii) *Sleeping Beauty: suite;* (iii) *Swan Lake: excerpts.*
(B) ** Ph. 426 975-2; *426 975-4* [id.]. LSO, (i) Dorati; (ii) Fistoulari; (iii) Monteux.

There is some fine music-making here, especially under Fistoulari and Monteux. Dorati is lively but his *Waltz of the flowers*, though rhythmically neat, lacks something in glamour. However, apart from the *Nutcracker*, the selections are arbitrary and not particularly generous. To have a *Swan Lake* 'suite' without *the* oboe tune seems extraordinarily bad planning. On DG, costing only a little more, Rostropovich offers nine more minutes of music and secures superlative playing from the Berlin Philharmonic, while the DG engineers enhance his very special music-making with recording that is both lustrous and spectacular (DG 429 097-2 – awarded a Rosette in our main volume).

Serenade for strings in C, Op. 48 (see also below, under *Symphonies Nos. 3 and 5*).
(*) RCA Dig. RD 60368; *RK 60368* [60368-2-RC; *60368-4-RC*]. Moscow Soloists, Yuri Bashmet – GRIEG: *Holberg suite* etc.(*)
(*) Virgin Dig. VC7 91165-2; *VC7 91165-4*. LCO, Warren-Green – DVOŘÁK: *Serenade* **(*); SUK: *Serenade.**

Serenade for strings; Suite No. 4 (Mozartiana), Op. 61; Andante cantabile, from Op. 11.
*** ASV Novalis Dig. 150 057-2; *150 057-4* [id.]. ECO, James Judd.

Serenade for strings; Suite No. 4 (Mozartiana); Elegy in G (in remembrance of Ivan Samarin); Andante cantabile (arr. Serebrier); *The Sleeping Beauty: Variations of the Lilac Fairy; Entr'acte* (both orch. Stravinsky).
**(*) ASV Dig. CDDCA 719; *ZCDCA 719* [id.]. SCO, José Serebrier.

In considering new versions of the *Serenade*, readers should bear in mind that Karajan's 1980 digital recording, with marvellously polished playing from the Berlin Philharmonic on their finest form, has been reissued at mid-price. If the coupling, with an equally impressive account of the *Third Symphony*, is suitable, this makes an obvious first choice.

James Judd's performances have a natural flow and an appealing directness and spontaneity. Tempi are never pressed too hard; if, in the *Serenade*, the *Waltz* is a little lacking in romantic ripeness, its simplicity fits in well with the overall conception. The slow movement has pleasing ardour and the finale, nicely prepared, brings plenty of energetic bustle. The *Mozartiana suite* sounds equally fresh: the vividness of Tchaikovsky's scoring is well caught by the excellent recording, the nineteenth-century feeling in the central movements is tastefully handled, and an elegant spirit pervades the music-making throughout. The *Andante cantabile* has a comparable sensibility and is most stylishly presented, while retaining its warmth.

Serebrier offers much more music (77 minutes, against 64 from Judd) and the Scottish Chamber Orchestra play warmly for him. He opens the *Serenade* spaciously and provides an enjoyably easy going reading, with neat if not sharply focused detail and with no lack of elegance; the *Waltz* here has more seductive feeling than with either Judd or Bashmet. The finale is buoyant and light-hearted. Serebrier also presents the *Mozartiana suite* very winningly, but before that comes the valedictory *Elegy* with its bitter-sweet melancholy. The SCO play it tenderly, with wistful *espressivo*, and are equally sympathetic in Serebrier's arrangement of the *Andante cantabile.* His concert ends with two attractive novelties, orchestrations of two numbers from *The Sleeping Beauty*, made by Stravinsky from the piano score and commissioned by Diaghilev when the ballet was staged in London in 1921. Serebrier's programme is certainly generous and all the music is easy to enjoy, for the recording is full and pleasing; but other versions of the *Serenade* have a stronger profile.

Certainly Bashmet's version has. His performance with the Moscow Soloists has enormous energy and fire. Their bravura brings very precise articulation in the busy secondary theme of the first movement, taken briskly after the strongly contoured introduction, and enormous finesse in the matter of light and shade. The *Waltz* is neat and airy, the tenutos observed without voluptuous feeling. The slow movement opens gently and delicately but develops a volatile, passionate ardour at its climax; and the finale is also highly animated, its dance-rhythms bursting with energy. The virtuosity of the playing is emphasized by the brightly lit recording, which has plenty of ambience and a very wide dynamic range.

Not surprisingly, Christopher Warren-Green's reading with his excellent LCO players is full of individuality. The first movement's secondary idea has an appealing feathery lightness, and when the striding opening theme reappears at the end of the movement it brings a spontaneous-sounding burst of expressive intensity characteristic of this group. The *Waltz* lilts gently, with the tenutos nicely observed, the *Élègie* has delicacy as well as fervour, and the finale has plenty of energy. This may not be quite as polished or as romantically powerful as Karajan's outstanding version (now an amazing bargain in its pairing with the *Polish Symphony*) but, with an outstanding coupling of the Suk, and enjoyable Dvořák too, this Virgin Classics triptych, very naturally recorded, will give pleasure for its freshness and natural impetus.

Serenade for strings, Op. 48; Souvenir de Florence, Op. 70.
(BB) **(*) Naxos Dig. 8.550404 [id.]. Vienna CO, Philippe Entremont.

Souvenir de Florence, Op. 70.
** Chan. Dig. CHAN 8547; *ABTD 1255* [id.]. I Musici di Montreal, Turovsky (with SCHUBERT: *5 Minuets & 6 Trios, D.89.***)

Entremont's performances of Tchaikovsky's two major string works communicate above all a feeling of passionate thrust and energy. The first movement of the *Serenade* opens strongly, the pointedly rhythmic secondary theme is crisply accented, and the running passages which follow are imaginatively detailed. The *Waltz*, with its neatly managed tenutos, has a nice touch of romantic feeling and, after the ardour of the *Élégie*, the finale steals in persuasively, again producing an unflagging impetus, with dance-rhythms bracing and strong. The unaccountably neglected *Souvenir de Florence* has comparable momentum and eagerness. The dashing main theme of the first movement swings along infectiously, while the wistful secondary idea also takes wing. The finale has yet another indelible tune which responds to the impulsive energy generated by these Viennese players. The two central movements are hardly less memorable in their melodic inspiration, the *Adagio* opening delicately, then, after a quickening of tempo, producing a characteristically Tchaikovskian solo violin and cello duet. Entremont brings out the charm and responds easily to the variety of mood, both here and in the *Allegretto*, permeated with a flavour of Russian folksong. Throughout, the commitment and ensemble of the VCO bring the most persuasive advocacy and make one wonder why the *Souvenir* does not have a more central place in the string repertoire.

Any lack of refinement, compared with the old analogue Argo LP version by the ASMF under Marriner, is more than offset by the conviction of Entremont's reading; by its side, the competing CD performance from I Musici di Montreal – although well played and at times bringing rather more subtlety of detail – seems much more of a routine affair which certainly fails to produce any real feeling of incandescence, and the Canadian recording is much less flattering. The Chandos Schubert coupling offers some attractive music but seems inappropriate as well as ungenerous. The Naxos digital sound is brightly lit and immediate, yet has plenty of body and ambience.

Sleeping Beauty (ballet): highlights.
(M) ** Sony SBK 46340 [id.]; *40-46340*. Phd. O, Ormandy – ROSSINI: *Boutique fantasque.***(*)

Ormandy provides a sumptuously glossy selection, with nearly an hour's music (the CD plays for 76 minutes overall). Superbly polished and often exciting playing but, with a forward balance, the effect is somewhat overwhelming. The sound is opulently brilliant rather than refined.

Sleeping Beauty (excerpts) arr. Pletnev.
❀ *** Virgin Dig. VC7 91169-2; *VC7 91169-4* [id.]. Mikhail Pletnev – MUSSORGSKY: *Pictures at an exhibition.**** ❀

When he was twenty-one and had just won the Tchaikovsky prize, Pletnev made transcriptions of the *Nutcracker suite* and of scenes from Shchedrin's ballet, *Anna Karenina*, which were of such extraordinary pianistic colour and virtuosity that one barely noticed the absence of the orchestra. In the present transcription he gives us about

30 minutes of *The Sleeping Beauty* in an equally dazzling transcription. In sheer clarity of articulation and virtuosity this is pretty remarkable – also in poetry and depth of feeling. Let us hope that the *Nutcracker* transcription is restored to circulation soon. An altogether outstanding issue and in every way a *tour de force*. (It is reported that, concerning the *Nutcracker*, Horowitz told Pletnev in Moscow, 'There are only two people who can play this – you and me!' But we don't think he can have heard Kissin! – see our Recitals section, below.)

Sleeping Beauty: suite; Swan Lake: suite.
(M) *** EMI CD-EMX 2067; *TC-EMX 2067*. Philh. O, Karajan (with MUSSORGSKY: *Khovanshchina: Dance of the Persian slaves* ***).

Karajan has recorded this Tchaikovsky coupling three times in stereo and this, the first, with the Philharmonia Orchestra on peak form, shows Walter Legge's balancing skills at their most striking, for the recording is still impressive three decades after it was made. There is a rich ambient bloom and a resonant bass; the very slight lack of upper range means that the violin tone remains quite full-bodied while still retaining a brilliant sheen in the remastering, although the sound in *Sleeping Beauty* is a little less ample than in *Swan Lake*. Even so, the effect is amazingly vivid and full for a recording from the late 1950s. The orchestral playing in such items as the violin/cello duet and the dapper *Dance of the little swans* in *Swan Lake* or the lustrous *Rose Adagio* and seductive *Panorama* of *Sleeping Beauty* makes this issue especially desirable. The sinuous *Dance of the Persian slaves* from Mussorgsky's *Khovanshchina* proves a welcome bonus.

(i) *Sleeping Beauty: suite;* (ii) *Swan Lake, Op. 20:* excerpts.
(B) **(*) DG Compact Classics *413 430-4* [id.]. (i) BPO, Rostropovich; (ii) Boston SO, Ozawa – PROKOFIEV: *Romeo and Juliet*.***

Rostropovich's *Sleeping Beauty suite* is highly distinguished, as fine as any in the catalogue. The recording is wonderfully expansive and the performances admirably combine Slavonic intensity with colour. The whimsical portrait of the cats contrasts with the glorious *Panorama* melody, floated over its gently rocking bass with magical delicacy. The collection of *Swan Lake* excerpts from Ozawa is generous. Here the sophistication of playing and recording, within the warm Boston acoustic, is impressive; while the individual items have less individuality of approach than with Rostropovich, the orchestral response is first class and the final climax expands magnificently. Combined with an excellent selection from Prokofiev's *Romeo and Juliet*, this Compact Classics tape is very good value.

(i) *Suites Nos. 2 in C, Op. 53; 4 in G (Mozartiana), Op. 61;* (ii) *Sérénade mélancolique, Op. 26; Mélodie, Op. 42/3.*
(M) **(*) Sony/CBS Dig. MDK 46503 [id.]. (i) Philh. O, Tilson Thomas; (ii) Zukerman, Israel PO, Mehta.

Michael Tilson Thomas makes a very good case for Tchaikovsky's *Mozartiana suite*, finding both sparkle and elegance in the music and effectively balancing the personalities of both the composers represented. The Philharmonia's response is first class, and the *Second Suite* is also played with great vitality. The bright, slightly dry, early digital recording (made in EMI's No. 1 Studio at Abbey Road), which suits *Mozartiana* rather well, makes the more extrovert, fully scored first movement of the *Second*, *Jeu de sons*, seem a little aggressive in its brilliance, although the sharp focus is just right for the *Scherzo burlesque*, bustling with its accordions. Tilson Thomas finds elegance in the *Valse* and a wistful charm in the *Rêves d'enfant*; he directs the closing *Danse baroque* most stylishly. The fill-ups, if brief, are scarcely apt but are tenderly played and very appealing. Zukerman is closely balanced and his G string tone in the *Sérénade mélancolique* is ravishing without being too schmalzy. This is a very good disc, and reservations about the recording are not serious; there is no lack of basic ambience.

Swan Lake (ballet), *Op. 20:* complete.
(BB) ** Naxos Dig. 8.550246/7 [id.]. Slovak RSO (Bratislava), Ondrej Lenárd.

Recorded in the Concert Hall of the Slovak Radio (Bratislava) in 1989, Lenárd's complete *Swan Lake* is both exhilarating and full-blooded and does not lack refinement or colour either. The sound is wide-ranging and full, and the very quality of racy excitement which makes his complete *Nutcracker* seem too hard-driven, here, more appropriately adds zest, although at times tempi are very fast indeed. This emphasizes the lyrical contrasts (as does the very wide dynamic range of the recording) and the famous oboe tune is always presented gracefully. Wind and brass playing is vivid, and altogether this makes a lively entertainment and, with the whole ballet complete on two discs, very economic too. Mark Ermler's fine Covent Garden performance (ROH 301/3) is much more spacious and, although the playing of the Covent Garden Orchestra is superb, this means his version stretches to three full-price discs. His broad speeds consistently convey the feeling of an accompaniment for dancing, and many will enjoy the more relaxed, more voluptuous experience that it provides, but at a far greater cost than the Naxos set.

Swan Lake (ballet): *highlights.*
(M) **(*) DG 431 607-2; *431 607-4* [id.]. Boston SO, Ozawa.
(M) ** Sony SBK 46341 [id.]; *40-46341.* Phd. O, Ormandy – ADAM: *Giselle*; MEYERBEER: *Les Patineurs.***

The DG disc offers some 59 minutes from the complete 1978 Boston/Ozawa set. The sophistication of the playing here, especially of the strings, is impressive, and Ozawa has a genuine rhythmic feeling for the world of ballet. Yet there is at times a lack of individuality in the score's lyrical moments. The CD transfer has made the analogue sound brighter and more vivid, if somewhat less refined, but the final climax expands spectacularly.

Ormandy's *Swan Lake* has much the same characteristics as his *Sleeping Beauty* selection, highly polished playing and sumptuously resonant sound which tends to detract from a sense of musical refinement. Yet the ebullient spirit of the music-making and the superb orchestral response cannot fail to make an effect in such a vividly coloured selection, with impeccable contributions from all the orchestral soloists.

Symphonies Nos. 1–6.
(B) *** Ph. 426 848-2 (4) [id.]. LSO, Markevitch.

This admirable Philips set represents the least expensive way to acquire first-class versions of the six Tchaikovsky *Symphonies.* They were recorded between 1962 and 1966 and at the time had to compete with distinguished sets from Karajan, Haitink and Muti. Now they come into their own as a genuine bargain alternative. The recording is resonant and full-bodied; the CDs retain the ambient bloom on the strings and provide a fine weight and sonority for the brass. The layout on four CDs means that *Symphonies Nos. 2* and *5* are centrally divided between movements, but the other four works are uninterrupted. Markevitch is a genuine Tchaikovskian and his readings have fine momentum and plenty of ardour. In the *First Symphony* he finds the Mendelssohnian lightness in his fast pacing of the opening movement, while there is real evocation in the *Adagio*, and a sense of desolation at the reprise of the *Andante lugubre*, before the final rousing peroration. In the *Little Russian Symphony* the opening horn solo is full of character and the allegro tautly rhythmic. The *marziale* marking of the *Andantino* is taken literally, but its precise rhythmic beat is well lifted. The finale is striking for its bustling energy rather than its charm. The *Polish Symphony* has a comparably dynamic first movement, but the central movements are expansively warm, the ballet-music associations not missed. The finale is strongly full-blooded. No. 4 is as exciting as almost any available. It has a superb, thrusting first movement and, although Markevitch allows himself a lilting degree of rubato in the rocking crescendo passage, he then produces an exhilarating stringendo and relaxes naturally for the second subject. The close of the movement, like the coda of the finale, brings the highest degree of tension and a real sense of triumph over adversity. The central movements are no less striking, with a vigorous dotted climax to the *Andante* contrasting with the repose of the outer sections, and a swift scherzo, where the duple rhythms of the woodwind in the Trio are emphasized, to bring out the peasant imagery. No. 5 has a less flexible first movement, and some might feel that here the forward momentum is too hard pressed to let the secondary material really blossom. The slow movement has plenty of passion, but the other controversial point is that the final statement of the big tune in the finale is slow and rather stolid. But Markevitch is fully back on form in the *Pathétique*. He takes the first-movement allegro at a brisk pace, then produces a stringendo which further tautens the climax at the reprise of the second subject. The second movement has both warmth and elegance and the scherzo/march is treated broadly, providing suitable contrast before a deeply felt performance of the finale, where the second subject is introduced with great tenderness. The close of the symphony has an elegiac quality to complete a reading which has a wide emotional range and is gripping from first to last.

Symphonies Nos. 1–6; Romeo and Juliet (fantasy overture).
(M) *** EMI CZS7 67314-2 (4) [Ang. CDMB 67314]. Philh. O, Muti.

Muti recorded his Tchaikovsky cycle over a period of six years in the late 1970s, during which time the New Philharmonia, thanks to its principal conductor, was restored both to its original name and to its earlier quality. The set of *Symphonies* is now appropriately reissued to celebrate the conductor's fiftieth birthday. It represented not only the high point of his recording partnership with that orchestra but also the peak of his interpretative career. The performances are as fine as any ever made, full of a kind of thrustful spontaneity he now finds less easy to achieve. It is a measure of Muti's success that even the first of the series to be recorded, No. 1, brings a performance as refined and persuasive as it is exciting, and the three early symphonies all bring orchestral playing which is both sophisticated and colourful. Throughout the cycle, and especially in the strong, urgent No. 4, Muti's view is brisk and dramatically direct, yet never lacking in feeling or imagination. In No. 5 he underlines the symphonic strength of the first movement rather than the immediate excitement. The Waltz may lack a little in charm but the slow movement is beautifully shaped, at first noble in feeling, with the passion held back for the climax. The finale then presents a sharp contrast, with its fast tempo and controlled excitement. In the *Pathétique* tempi are again characteristically fast, yet the result is fresh and youthful, with the flowing first-movement second subject given an easy expressiveness, The March, for all its urgency, never sounds brutal and the finale has satisfying depth and power. The recording here does not quite match the fullness of the others in the series, but generally the sound is well up to EMI's best analogue standard of this period, and it has been transferred to CD very impressively, with the focus firm and no lack of body and weight. The layout involves just one break between discs in the middle of a symphony. Nos. 1 and 2 are on the first disc; The *Polish* and the first three movements of No. 4 are on the second; the finale of No. 4 and all of No. 5 are together on the third disc; and the final CD offers the *Pathétique* plus Muti's superb analogue *Romeo and Juliet*, one of the finest available, and full of imaginative touches. However, the Jansons set with the Oslo Philharmonic Orchestra on Chandos, which includes *Manfred* (CHAN 8672/8; *DBTD 7001*), is self-recommending. The full romantic power of the music is consistently conveyed, and the seven separate CDs are packaged in a box, priced as for five discs.

Symphony No. 1 in G min. (Winter daydreams), Op. 13; (i) *Variations on a rococo theme for cello and orchestra, Op. 33.*
(M) *** DG 431 606-2; *431 606-4* [id.]. BPO, Karajan; (i) with Rostropovich.

Karajan's performance of the *Winter daydreams symphony* is second to none and the playing of the Berlin Philharmonic is quite marvellous. Although he takes the opening *Allegro tranquillo* of the first movement quite fast, there is no feeling of breathlessness: it is genuinely *tranquillo*, though the rhythmic bite of the syncopated passages, so important in these early symphonies, could hardly be sharper. If the folk element is underplayed, the beautiful *Andante cantabile* has genuine Russian melancholy, while the fugato in the last movement is given classical strength and the final peroration has regality and splendour. Rostropovich's account of the published score of the *Rococo variations* is hardly less distinguished, and Karajan accompanies him warmly. Both analogue recordings are among DG's best, the *Symphony* dating from 1979 and the *Variations* from a decade earlier. Neither is lacking in brilliance or fullness, and both have a realistic ambience.

Symphonies Nos.1 (Winter Daydreams); 2 (Little Russian).
*** Virgin Dig. VC7 91119-2; *VC7 91119-4* [id.]. Bournemouth SO, Andrew Litton.
**(*) Capriccio Dig. 10 355 [id.]. ASMF, Marriner.

In their Tchaikovsky series for Virgin, Litton and the Bournemouth orchestra here come up with a clear winner, giving urgently spontaneous performances of both symphonies. Not only is this ideal coupling of the first two symphonies exceptionally generous (a few seconds under 80 minutes), but the performances in every way rival any in the catalogue. With warm and full recording, less distanced than many on this label, the disc earns the strongest recommendation. A relaxed, atmospheric view of the opening introduction of No. 1 leads into an exhilarating account of the main first-movement allegro. In this movement and elsewhere Litton reveals himself as a volatile Tchaikovskian, free with accelerandos and slowings, yet never sounding self-conscious or too free. The hushed pianissimos of the Bournemouth strings in the slow movement of No. 1 are ravishing, and the *Second Symphony* too brings a beautifully sprung reading which allows plenty of rhythmic elbow-room in the jaunty account of the syncopated second subject in the finale.

On Capriccio, beautifully played by the Academy and very well recorded, both works are given fine, sensitive readings. Some of the speeds are on the fast side, as for example the rather breathless allegro for the first movement of No. 2; but Marriner and the Academy are at their very peak in the scherzo movements of each symphony, wonderfully crisp and lightly pointed, and there are few accounts of the *Andantino marziale* of No. 2 as delicately rhythmic as this. But what emerges from direct comparisons is that the polish of the Academy's playing goes with a degree of emotional restraint, as though these players would really feel more at home back in the eighteenth-century repertory. Litton, in readings which are freer and more volatile, repeatedly finds a degree more panache, as well as Tchaikovskian passion, and the risk of vulgarity only adds to the intensity of communication. Though the Capriccio sound is firmer and more forward, preference remains with that Virgin issue.

Symphony No. 2 in C min. (Little Russian); Romeo and Juliet (fantasy overture).
**(*) Teldec Dig. 2292 44943-2 [id.]. Leipzig GO, Masur.

The Masur disc has a relatively ungenerous coupling for No. 2, but it is that coupling, a most refreshing account of *Romeo and Juliet*, passionate and direct without a hint of vulgarity, which sets the seal on an issue that gets better and better as it goes along. Unexpectedly, a squarely symphonic view such as Masur's works rather well in the first movement of the symphony, even if the *Andantino* is charmless. But then Masur begins to lift rhythms in a way generally missing earlier. The end of the finale – with the coda taken very fast, and with an extra accelerando – is as exciting as any, flouting good manners and skirting vulgarity. The sound is among the finest from this source, clearer, more forward and less bass-heavy than usual.

Symphonies Nos. (i) *2 (Little Russian), Op. 17;* (ii) *4 in F min.*
❀ (M) *** DG 431 604-2; *431 604-4* [id.]. (i) New Philh. O; (ii) VPO, Claudio Abbado.

Abbado's coupling of Tchaikovsky's *Second* and *Fourth Symphonies* is one of the supreme bargains of the current catalogue. It is listed in our main volume (on p. 1075) in its previous incarnation on DG's Privilege bargain label (429 527-2; *429 527-4*), and at the time of going to press this is still available. Should it disappear, however, the new listing above is more than worth its slightly higher price, although the insert leaflet still includes nothing about the music! The *Fourth Symphony* is unforgettable in its passionate Russian feeling. The VPO playing has enormous grip and complete spontaneity, and the 1975 recording, made in the Musikverein, still sounds very good. The *Little Russian* is pretty impressive too, with much charm in the *Andantino marziale* and a dazzling finale. It was recorded in Wembley Town Hall, and again the 1968 sound has emerged impressively on CD.

Symphony No. 3 in D (Polish), Op. 29; Serenade for strings in C, Op. 48.
❀ (M) *** DG Analogue/Dig. 431 605-2; *431 605-4* [id.]. BPO, Karajan.

Karajan's version of the *Polish Symphony* ranks with the finest, and no other version offers more polished orchestral playing. The first movement is full of flair, and in the central movements Karajan is ever conscious of the variety of Tchaikovsky's colouring. He even finds an affinity with Brahms in the second movement, and yet the climax of the *Andante* is full of Tchaikovskian fervour. In the finale the articulation of the *Polacca* is both vigorous and joyful and it brings a sense of symphonic strength often lacking in other versions. The 1979 analogue recording is bold, brilliant and clear, with the ambience of the Philharmonie well conveyed. The *String Serenade* is equally compelling, with taut, alert and superbly articulated playing in the first movement, a passionately intense *Élégie* and a bustling, immensely spirited finale. And no group plays the *Waltz* with more panache and elegance than the Berlin Philharmonic. The digital recording is early (1980) but satisfyingly well balanced, with a firm, resonant bass-line to balance the bright upper range.

Symphonies Nos. 4–6 (Pathétique).
(M) ** EMI CMS7 63838-2 (2) [Ang. CDMB 63838]. Philh. O, Klemperer.

Klemperer was not a conductor who took naturally to Tchaikovsky, but nothing he recorded was without certain insights, and these recordings are no exception. Klemperer's view of the first movement in the *Fourth* is weighty yet relaxed. The basic dotted rhythm sometimes recalls Beethoven's *Seventh*, and many listeners will feel that coasting along in the first movement – even with the feeling of real power inherent underneath – does not really catch the almost barbaric Russian spirit that other interpreters find in the movement. There are no complaints elsewhere and, throughout, the Philharmonia solo playing is highly pleasing, especially in the very attractive Scherzo. The bright, vivid yet full-bodied 1963 recording ensures that the finale makes a suitable impact. The reading of the *Fifth*, however, is surprisingly successful in a way one would not perhaps expect. There is an expanding emotional warmth in the treatment of the opening movement, with the second subject blossoming in a ripely romantic way. The slow movement too, if not completely uninhibited, is played richly, with a fine horn solo from Alan Civil. The Waltz is perhaps marginally disappointing, but the finale has splendid dignity and the recording (again from 1963) has transferred impressively to CD. Klemperer's *Pathétique*, however, is surely a record to be heard rather than lived with. The outer movements are best, although the finale is not entirely convincing. The opening of the first movement goes well; it has great poise and dignity, and the beginning of the allegro is well managed. Later the climaxes are restrained without losing too much intensity and the coda is nicely moulded. The *Allegro con grazia* is heavy and without grace, and the March forgets that it is a Scherzo too; it has little cumulative excitement. The recording is spacious and full, with a good brass (and a notable bass-drum).

Symphony No. 4 in F min., Op. 36.
(M) *** Decca Dig. 425 972-2 [id.]. LSO, Szell – BEETHOVEN: *Egmont.****
(*) EMI Dig. CDC7 54112-2 [id.]; *EL 754112-4*. Phd. O, Muti – SCRIABIN: *Prometheus.**

Symphony No. 4 in F min.; Andante cantabile; Marche slave, Op. 31.
(M) *** EMI CDM7 63960-2 [id.]; *EG 763960-4*. Hallé O, Barbirolli (with rehearsal sequence).

Symphony No. 4 in F min.; Fatum (symphonic ballad), *Op. 77; The Voyevoda* (symphonic ballad), *Op. 78.*
** BMG/RCA Dig. RD 60432 [60432-RC-2]. St Louis SO, Slatkin.

Symphony No. 4 in F min.; Francesca da Rimini.
*** DG Dig. 429 778-2; *429 778-4* [id.]. NYPO, Bernstein.

Symphony No. 4 in F min.; (i) *Overture 1812. Marche slave.*
(M) ** Sony SBK 46334 [id.]; *40-46334*. Phd. O, Ormandy; (i) with Mormon Tabernacle Ch., Valley Forge Military Ac. Band.

Symphony No. 4 in F min.; Romeo and Juliet (fantasy overture).
* Telarc Dig. CD 80228 [id.]. Baltimore SO, Zinman.

Szell's white-hot performance is one of the very finest ever put on disc. At the sessions in 1962 the irascible conductor was in an angry mood, and John Culshaw deliberately prodded him still further by having the first playback in dull sound. Szell then unleashed a force in the subsequent takes that has to be heard to be believed. It was a recording that was not released until after his death – he would not allow it – but it was one of his very finest. It now sounds superb on CD, clean, forward and full, with thrillingly immediate brass. Tape-hiss is audible but undistracting, and the interpretation at ideally chosen speeds has a freshness rarely matched. The *Egmont* fill-up is odd but attractive, and is very well recorded in the Sofiensaal.

As with others in EMI's Phoenixa series of Barbirolli's recordings from the end of the

1950s and early 1960s, the sound has been immeasurably improved, and one can appreciate the sheer power and drive of the performance which, as with the *Fifth*, has much in common with Szell's version in its highly charged romanticism. The outer movements are electrifying in their excitement, and the elegantly structured *Andantino* has many characteristic touches of individuality, so that the performance overall can be spoken of in the same breath as Abbado's reading in its feeling for Tchaikovskian ebb and flow. After the *Symphony* comes a complete contrast in a refined and delicate account of the *Andante cantabile*; then comes a thrilling *March slave*, although here the recording is somewhat shrill. The disc ends with a rehearsal sequence, made during the preparation of the *Symphony*, not especially illuminating but valuable in letting us hear the way Barbirolli communcated with his orchestra who so often approached greatness under his baton.

The third of Leonard Bernstein's recordings of the late Tchaikovsky symphonies for DG brings eccentric speeds in the first two movements comparable to those in the *Fifth* and the *Pathétique*, but the electricity is of a quite different order. This is not a performance to compare with any other: it is one that came from an interpreter of genius at a particular moment, white-hot and compelling. The fanfare motto theme at the opening is very grand indeed, with big rallentandos and big pauses. Most surprisingly, in a live recording from Avery Fisher Hall in New York, one of the most difficult for engineers, the sound is aptly big and fruity. The recording may not match what we have on the finest versions, thick rather than clean, but it certainly allows the power and warmth of Bernstein's reading to be fully appreciated. The last two movements are taken at speeds that no one would regard as unconventional. The pizzicato scherzo is not ideally precise of ensemble but it is infectiously sprung and, in Bernstein's big, bold account of the finale, his slowing for the second subject (the *Birch tree* theme) is extreme but persuasive. The close is predictably exciting, with an unashamed accelerando in the closing bars, though without applause and obviously recorded at an editing session. The fill-up, *Francesca da Rimini*, brings a comparably spacious and big-scale performance.

With both Muti and Slatkin, the fill-ups, valuable and unexpected, are a prime consideration. For all Muti's electric qualities and the refinement of the Philadelphia Orchestra's playing, the EMI issue does not quite match the finest existing versions, whether in sound or as an interpretation, though speeds are well chosen and there is none of the lassitude which afflicts Muti's Philadelphia recording of the *Pathétique*. As for Scriabin's *Prometheus*, this is very successful and, if the coupling is suitable, this EMI disc might well be considered.

Slatkin's performance of the *Symphony* lacks tautness. Ensemble is good and the playing refined but, with the recorded sound lacking bite, the result is relatively uninvolving and short on tension. That is particularly so in the first movement, where Slatkin opts for surprisingly slow speeds. The value of the disc lies in the fill-ups. There is no current rival listed of *Fatum* and only one of *Voyevoda*, richly enjoyable works which Tchaikovsky thought he had destroyed but which have been reconstructed from orchestral parts. Notably in *Voyevoda*, Slatkin finds a tension largely missing in the *Symphony*.

Ormandy's account of the *Fourth* comes from the early 1960s and is a flamboyant reading, with moments of physical excitement but with specific mannerisms too, as in the broadened coda of the first movement or the rather heavy phrasing of the string theme which answers the oboe solo in the *Andantino*. The 'balalaika' scherzo shows the orchestra at its finest, but the resonant recording brings a degree of crudeness to the fortissimos of the outer movements. Ormandy's famous recording of *1812* comes from a decade later and in it the Mormon Tabernacle choir make a spectacular contribution to the work's opening section. Heard in quadraphony, their crescendo near the opening was thrilling, and the closing pages, with cannon shots all around, were equally impressive. Now the upper strings sound fierce and the climax has brilliance without a matching depth of sonority. *Marche slave* is exciting too, but again the sound has an element of harshness.

David Zinman's version brings impressive evidence of the quality of the Baltimore orchestra, but it is a low-key performance, sounding a little cautious – even sluggish at times. The Telarc recording is very good, without being spectacular. *Romeo and Juliet* as fill-up is similarly clean and direct, with the battle music less exciting than it might be and the love-theme well-behaved rather than passionate.

Symphony No. 5 in E min., Op. 64.
(B) *** Sony MBK 45643 [id.]. Cleveland O, George Szell.

Symphony No. 5 in E min.; Romeo and Juliet (fantasy overture).
(M) ** DG 431 603-2; *431 603-4* [id.]. (i) Boston SO, (ii) San Francisco SO, Ozawa.
* DG Dig. 429 234-2; *429 234-4* [id.]. NYPO, Bernstein.

(i) *Symphony No. 5 in E min., Op. 64;* (ii) *Serenade for strings in C, Op. 48.*
(M) *** EMI CDM7 63962-2 [id.]. (i) Hallé O; (ii) LSO, Barbirolli.

Symphony No. 5 in E min.; The Tempest, Op. 18.
**(*) Virgin Dig. VC7 91140-2; *VC7 91140-4* [id.]. Bournemouth SO, Andrew Litton.
** BMG/RCA Dig. RD 60425; *RK 60425* [id.]. St Louis SO, Slatkin.

Szell's *Fifth* is undoubtedly a great performance, to match his electrifying version of the *Fourth*, which he recorded for Decca in London three years later. The sense of romantic urgency in the *Fifth* is irresistible: the reading moves forward in a single sweep, and the ebb and flow of tempo and tension springs from the very essence of the music. The broad style of the horn solo in the slow movement may not suit every taste, but the passion of the climax is unforgettable; following a beautifully elegant third-movement Waltz, the finale is gloriously satisfying, from the opening statement of the big tune, through an allegro of great power, to the final peroration and coda which has enormous confidence. The recording is far from ideal: it is not shallow but has an element of harshness; but Szell's performance has an intensity of spirit to make one forget such matters.

As with the *Fourth*, Barbirolli's urgent, thrustfully romantic reading of the *Fifth* has much in common with Szell, particularly in the way its irresistible forward momentum springs from the very essence of the music. Tempi are unerrringly apt, not only in themselves but also in the way they interrelate. The reading has passion and drama (the entries of the motto theme in the *Andante* are almost cataclysmic), and the energy of the finale is matched by the nobility with which Barbirolli invests the great main tune when it is introduced in the strings; yet, at its final appearance in the coda, the blazing trumpets have no inhibition whatsoever. The orchestra are galvanized into playing of remarkable emotional tension and, as the final hammered chords die away at the end, the listener is left to take a deep breath and recover from the adrenalin flow. EMI have recoupled this Pye reissue with one of their own recordings of the *Serenade for strings* (made in 1964), characteristically ripe and romantic, especially in the *Élégie*. In the first movement Barbirolli is surprisingly metrical when the second subject arrives, but the effect is not in the least heavy. He is naturally expressive in the Waltz and prepares the bustling finale with subtle, loving anticipation. A suberb disc: any lack of refinement in the recording is forgotten when the playing is so consistently involving.

Litton is surprisingly slow and steady in the first movement of the *Fifth*. There is a case – as Klemperer and Boehm both showed in their diffent ways – for taking a squarely symphonic view, but Litton's reading lacks the high voltage of his finest Tchaikovsky performances. The other three movements are first rate. The slow movement brings a beautiful horn solo, with the sound exquisitely distanced and with Litton sustaining his slow *Andante* well. At a well-judged speed, the Waltz third movement is then delightfully fresh and delicate in a simple way, and the finale, again on the broad side, is warm rather than ominous, with very clean articulation in the playing and fine detail. Atmospherically recorded with slightly distanced sound in the Virgin manner, and transferred at a lower level than the rival issues, this version certainly has its attractions, despite that first movement, particularly when it has so rare and generous a fill-up. The Shakespearean symphonic fantasy, *The Tempest* – not to be confused with the much less ambitious overture of the same name, written for Ostrovsky's play – is given a glowing performance, passionately committed yet refined, to suggest a forgotten masterpiece.

Slatkin's performance of the symphony is one which never quite captures the biting intensity needed in this highly charged work. It does not help that the speed for the slow movement is exaggeratedly slow, square and lacking in tension. The impact of the playing is further undermined by a rather dry acoustic – not kind to high violins – and a transfer at rather a low level. The Virgin recording is far warmer, with a keen sense of presence, though, curiously, the contrast of sound is quite different between the two versions of *The Tempest*. There the St Louis recording is brighter and fuller than the Virgin. The St Louis cellos are richer than those of the Bournemouth orchestra, but otherwise the evocative colourings and drama of this fine symphonic fantasy, inspired by Shakespeare, are more compellingly brought out by Litton.

Ozawa has the advantage of excellent DG sound. In the finale the brass is superb: this is undoubtedly the finest movement; the music-making springs vividly to life and the listener is swept along by the impact and projection of the Boston orchestra. But the first three movements are disappointing, and until the finale the performance is a routine one. In the *Romeo and Juliet* overture, however Ozawa is at his best, drawing warmly committed playing from the San Francisco orchestra.

The wilful inconsistencies and the very variable playing of the New York Philharmonic under Bernstein, along with sound which grows rough and confused in tuttis, get in the way of any serious recommendation, even with the sort of reservations required with his earlier account of the *Pathétique*. A ponderously slow reading of the introduction leads to an attack on the *Allegro con anima* so hectic that ensemble is totally undermined, while there is no lift to rhythms, just a scramble. Other sections find Bernstein drawing the music out exaggeratedly in the opposite direction. The overture follows a similar pattern, and even Bernstein's shaping of the great love-theme is oddly stiff rhythmically.

Symphonies Nos. 5–6 (Pathétique).
(B) **(*) DG Compact Classics *413 429-4* [id.]. LSO, VPO, Abbado.

The Compact Classics chrome cassette couples Abbado's lightweight but refreshingly individual DG accounts of Tchaikovsky's two most popular symphonies. The performance of the *Fifth* is both sophisticated and sparkling: there is lyrical intensity and the outer movements have plenty of vigour; the finale is genuinely exciting, yet with no sense of rhetoric. There are more powerful accounts available but none more spontaneously volatile. The *Pathétique* is also slightly underpowered but may have many attractions for those who prefer a reading that is not too intense. There is a strong impulse throughout, with the third movement essentially a Scherzo, the march-rhythms never becoming weighty and pontifical. The recordings have transferred well to tape, that of the *Fifth* richer than the *Sixth*, which is slightly dry.

Symphony No. 6 in B min. (Pathétique), Op. 74.
(M) (***) BMG/RCA mono GD 60328; *GK 60328* (4) [60328-2-RG; *60328-4-RG*]. NBC SO, Toscanini – Concert.(**(*))
(M) ** DG Dig. 431 602-2; *431 602-4* [id.]. LAPO, Giulini.
* EMI Dig. CDC7 54061-2 [id.]; *EL 754061-4*. Phd. O, Muti – SCRIABIN: *Poème de l'extase.****

Symphony No. 6 in B min. (Pathétique); Romeo and Juliet (fantasy overture).
**(*) DG Dig. 429 740-2; *429 740-4* [id.]. Philh. O, Sinopoli.
(M) ** EMI stereo/mono CDM7 63776-2 [id.]; *EG 763776-4*. Hallé O, Barbirolli.
(M) *(*) Decca Analogue/Dig. 430 442-2; *430 442-4* [id.]. Chicago SO, Solti.

Toscanini's Philadelphia version of the *Pathétique* glows with the special magic that developed between him and the orchestra over the winter season of 1941–2. Though far more disciplined than most readings, it is altogether warmer than his NBC recording, with the great second-subject melody of the first movement tender in its emotions, not rigid in its easy rubato. He even eases the tempo sympathetically for the fortissimo entries of the march in the third movement. Alongside a magnificent account of the Strauss – an apt link, with death the theme – it makes a superb historic document.

If one divides interpreters of this *Symphony* into those who tend to press ahead in stringendo and those who hold back in ritenuto, Sinopoli – perhaps surprisingly after his Elgar *Second* – is firmly in the former group. What is similar to that Elgar performance is the passion of the playing of the Philharmonia, recorded with the most satisfying opulence. Sinopoli is not always as electric as Jansons in his fine Oslo reading (Chandos CHAN 8446; *ABTD 1158*) which remains first choice, adopting slow basic speeds for the middle two movements but sustaining them well, with the 5/8 rhythm of the second brought even closer than is common to the feeling of a waltz. In the march of the third movement, many will prefer Sinopoli's broader view, with a slight easing on the big swaggering fortissimo entries. The big advantage Sinopoli has over Jansons is that it is generously coupled with *Romeo and Juliet*. There Sinopoli's reading is not quite so spontaneous-sounding, with a hint of self-consciousness at the first entry of the big love-theme, though with plenty of uninhibited passion on the later repeats.

Giulini's digital *Pathétique* is curiously lightweight, the mood set with the almost *scherzando* quality of the opening Allegro. The 5/4 movement is relatively unlilting and, though the march is impressive, it is no match for the Ashkenazy version. The finale does not lack eloquence, but Giulini's Philharmonia version of two decades earlier had more individuality than this. The digital recording is impressive, if slightly dry. The CD tends to emphasize rather than disguise the recording's faults, especially the close balance.

The 1958 Barbirolli version brings a characteristically gutsy performance, at once firm in purpose and passionate. Inevitably the recording has a high tape-hiss and is limited in range, with violins often rough-sounding, but the EMI transfer has transformed it, so that the sense of presence is vivid, and the sound is full and satisfying enough to let one enjoy the central strength of the interpretation, although there is a degree of fierceness at climaxes. Barbirolli's reading begins rather coolly, but the secondary theme is beautifully phrased and the slight restraint adds to the contrast of the development, which opens with a dramatic fortissimo; the Hallé strings, however, ideally need to be able to produce a greater body of tone at the climax, though it does not lack fervour. The second movement is light and gracious and the third is a genuine scherzo, with Sir John holding back the big guns until the final peroration. The most powerful playing comes in the finale, which is passionately impulsive though not lacking dignity. The (mono) *Romeo and Juliet*, recorded in 1957, is notable for Barbirolli's delicacy of feeling at the introduction of the great love-theme, yet the performance is exciting enough.

Solti's *Pathétique* – reissued in the 'Solti Collection' – brings dangerously fast tempi throughout the first and third movements, and the feeling of hysteria is never far away. The element of nobility, so necessary to provide emotional balance, is missing. The March/scherzo loses all charm at this hectic pace; indeed the march element almost disappears altogether. The finale is more under control but does not resolve the performance in any satisfactory way. Brilliantly clear recording to match the playing. *Romeo and Juliet* – digitally recorded – has greater restraint and is altogether more successful as a performance; but it is better acquired in its original compilation with *1812* and the *Nutcracker suite* (see our main volume, pp. 1059–60).

Muti's Philadelphia version does not begin to match his much earlier, Philharmonia recording. This one is uncharacteristically slack and lacking in dramatic tension, and the digital recording is poorly focused. The coupling is generous, but hardly allows a recommendation.

Symphony No. 7 in E flat (reconstructed Bogatyryev); (i) *Variations on a rococo theme for cello and orchestra, Op. 33.*
(M) ** Sony MPK 46453 [id.]. Phd. O, Ormandy; (i) with Leonard Rose.

In 1892 Tchaikovsky began a new symphony, but he was not satisfied with the way his ideas were working out and decided that the material was more suitable for a piano concerto – and, if one listens to the one-movement *Third Concerto*, one might well feel that the composer was right, even though the work has never gained a place in the repertoire. Tchaikovsky discarded the rest of his material, but the sketches for the symphony as originally planned were not destroyed and it was to these that the Soviet musicologist, Bogatyryev, turned. As there was no scherzo, one was provided from a set of piano pieces written in 1893. Skilfully scored, it recalls the scherzo from *Manfred*, with its middle section introduced by oboe and harp and then taken up by the strings. The finale, however, is bizarre and here sounds rumbustious, blatant, even vulgar, with the reprise of the main theme against a side-drum in no way characteristic of Tchaikovsky's symphonic writing. Ormandy's performance has great fervour and is superbly played; but the recording, although spectacular, also has the harshness one associates with this source. Leonard Rose's warm and elegant account of the *Rococo variations* comes like balm to the ears after the noisy finale of the symphony. However, this CD does have distinct curiosity value.

Variations on a rococo theme for cello and orchestra, Op. 33.
(M) *** Decca 425 020-2; *425 020-4* [id.]. Harrell, Cleveland O, Maazel – BRUCH: *Kol Nidrei* ***; DVOŘÁK: *Cello concerto.****
(M) ** Mercury 432 001-2 [id.]. Starker, LSO, Dorati – BRUCH: *Kol Nidrei*; DVOŘÁK: *Cello concerto.***

An assured, vividly characterized set of *Variations* from Lynn Harrell, with plenty of matching colour from the Cleveland woodwind. Harrell begins a little briskly, but there is no lack of poise here. Expressive feeling and sparkle are nicely matched, as is shown by the elegant account of the *Andante* (Variation 6) which acts as an interlude before the exhilarating finale. The analogue recording is bright and colourful, with the Cleveland ambience adding warmth and the cellist given a spotlight.

Starker's performance is elegant, and his precise, clean playing brings out the music's elegance, if not always its full charm. Dorati accompanies sympathetically and the 1964 recording is very believable.

OPERA

Eugene Onegin (complete).
* Sony Dig. CD 45539; *40-45539* [id.]. Tomowa-Sintow, Mazurok, Gedda, Ghiuselev, Sofia Nat. Op. Ch., Sofia Festival O, Emil Tchakarov.

After some of Tchakarov's other Russian opera recordings for Sony, this is a disappointment, despite a rather more starry cast than most in the series. The recording is full and immediate, with the sound brightly caught. But there is little attempt to capture the subtlety of atmosphere, so vital in this work, above all in the haunting off-stage effects, as in the duetting of Tatiana and Olga at the start. They both sound raw and not very steady. Tomowa-Sintow, who has made so many fine recordings for DG and others, is caught unflatteringly all through, with unevenness in the voice brought out. That is particularly damaging in the first Act, including the *Letter scene*, when there is little that is girlish in the sound. Gedda characterizes splendidly as Lensky, but the voice now sounds too old; and Masurok, impressive as Onegin, is relatively rough in timbre. Tchakarov takes a literal, rather pedestrian view of the score, failing to convey excitement in the great dance movements. Both the Levine set on DG (423 959-2) with Thomas Allen as Onegin and Solti's vintage Decca set (417 413-2) in fine analogue sound are preferable, and all in all the Solti is our prime recommendation.

Eugene Onegin: highlights.
(M) **(*) DG 431 611-2; *431 611-4* [id.] (from recording with Freni, Thomas Allen, Schicoff, Von Otter, Burchuladze, cond. Levine).

Even though the Levine set is not our first choice for the complete opera (that rests with Teresa Kubiak, Bernd Weikl and Solti on Decca 417 413-2), this 68-minute selection makes an admirable entertainment. It includes the *Letter scene* (with Freni a freshly charming Tatiana), the *Waltz* and *Polonaise* scenes (with the excellent Leipzig Radio Chorus), other key arias, all strongly characterized, and the entire closing scene (11 minutes). The recording, made in the Dresden Lukaskirche, is too closely balanced and surprisingly unexpansive; but this still makes an impressive sampler.

Pique Dame (complete).
**(*) Sony Dig. S3K 45720 [id.]. Dilova, Evstatieva, Toczyska, Konsulov, Ochman, Masurok, Bulgarian Nat. Ch., Sofia Festival O, Tchakarov.

Tchakarov in his Sony series of Russian operas conducts a fresh, expressive and alert account of *Queen of Spades*, very well recorded. Wieslaw Ochman makes an impressive Herman, amply powerful and only occasionally rough. Yuri Masurok is a superb Yeletsky, and the duet of Lisa and her companion, Pauline, is beautifully done by Stefka Evstatieva and Stefania Toczyska, one of Tchaikovsky's most magical inspirations. As the old Countess, Penka Dilova has a characteristically fruity Slavonic mezzo, very much in character, if with a heavy vibrato. The Countess's famous solo is taken very slowly indeed but is superbly sustained. Ensembles and chorus work are excellent, timed with theatrical point. Conveniently, each Act is fitted on a single CD. When DG issues its Paris version conducted by Rostropovich, on CD, that will outshine this one in the solo singing, but the Bulgarian performance is the more idiomatic.

Arias from: *The Enchantress; Eugene Onegin; Iolantha; Mazeppa; Queen of Spades.*
*** Ph. Dig. 426 740-2; *426 740-4* [id.]. Dmitri Hvorostovsky, Rotterdam PO, Gergiev – VERDI: *Arias.****

Hvorostovsky, a golden boy among young baritones, here makes his recording début in the West with Tchaikovsky arias which ideally exhibit both the magnificent dark voice which won him the title of 'Cardiff Singer of the World' and also his way with Russian words. He presents an eager, volatile Onegin, a passionate Yeletski in *Queen of Spades* and an exuberant Robert in *Iolantha.* One can only hope that he will be guided well, to develop such a glorious instrument naturally, without strain.

Telemann, Georg Philipp (1681–1767)

Oboe d'amore concerto No. 2 in A.
(M) *** DG 431 120-2; *431 120-4* [id.]. Holliger, Camerata Bern, Füri – GRAUN: *Concerto* ***; KREBS: *Double concerto.***(*)

Telemann's *Oboe d'amore concerto* is in four engaging movements, opening with a lovely Siciliana which Holliger plays beautifully. It is a highly inventive work throughout, and this excellent performance and recording make the very most of it.

(i) *Viola concerto in G. Don Quichotte: suite; Overture in C (Hamburger Ebb und Flut); Overture in D.*
(M) **(*) Decca 430 265-2; *430 265-4* [id.]. (i) Stephen Shingles; ASMF, Marriner.

Anyone daunted by the sheer volume of Telemann's instrumental music could not do better than investigate this ASMF collection from the late 1970s which presents a nicely varied group of works, not just the relatively well-known *Viola concerto* (with Stephen Shingles a stylish soloist) but also the colourful and endearing *Don Quichotte suite*, a vivid example of early programme music. The *Hamburg Ebb and Flow* also has programmatic implications in the manner of Vivaldi; but the musical descriptions are never too literal and the titular associations with the figures of classical mythology serve only to fire the composer's imagination. Finally we are given the *Overture* (Suite) *in D*, written in 1765 when Telemann was well into his eighties but still retained all his creative flair. Each movement is intensely individual and the work climaxes with a graceful *Carillon* for oboes and pizzicato strings and a rumbustious *Tintamare.* The only reason for our reservation bracket is that the digital remastering has brought a brighter, tighter sound to the upper range and a drier bass response. On the original Argo LPs the strings were gloriously resonant, as rich and refined as any on record, but now some of this amplitude has been lost, although the transparency of detail and most of the ambient bloom remain.

Tafelmusik (Productions 1–3) complete.
*** Teldec/Warner Dig. 2292 44688-2 (4). VCM, Harnoncourt.
*** DG Dig. 427 619-2 (4) [id.]. Col. Mus. Ant., Reinhard Goebel.

When it first appeared in the 1960s, the complete *Tafelmusik* (or 'Banqueting music') filled six LPs, and two eminently recommendable sets dominated the catalogue (August Wenzinger with the Schola Cantorum Basiliensis, and Frans Brüggen's Concerto Amsterdam). With the arrival of the present recordings we are faced with much the same dilemma, though the work now requires four CDs. Harnoncourt's Vienna Concentus Musicus and Goebel's Musiqua Antiqua, Köln, each have a devoted following for whom choice will be a foregone conclusion: at present the Musiqua Antiqua enjoys cult status in Early Music circles. For collectors with allegiance to neither group, choice will be more difficult. Moving from one to the other, it is tempting to think it is a matter of swings and roundabouts: the playing of the Musiqua Antiqua is distinguished by the highest order of virtuosity and unanimity of ensemble and musical thinking. They also have the advantage of very vivid and fresh recording quality; the balance is close and present without being too forward and there is a pleasing acoustic ambience.

Harnoncourt has a slightly more distant, less analytical balance, and his recording has the added poignancy of offering the last performances by the oboists, Jürg Schaeftlein and David Reichenberg (the set bears a dedication to their memory). It also offers distinguished playing, perhaps less virtuosic than the Cologne ensemble but no less sensitive. However, the greater breadth of the Harnoncourt set tells in its favour: Reinhard Goebel and his Cologne players opt for breathlessly quick tempi in which liveliness becomes headlong and there are some self-conscious dynamic exaggerations and expressive bulges. At times one's attention momentarily strays to their polish rather than staying with Telemann's unfailingly inventive resource. All the same, there is much to relish and few coming to this music afresh will be disappointed by either set. Incidentally for older collectors the two LP sets hold up rather well against these newcomers and, were they to be reissued on a bargain label, they would still be quite competitive.

Tafelmusik, Production 3: *Overture in B flat; Quartet in E min.;* Production 2: *Concerto in F; Trio sonata in E flat; Solo (Violin) sonata in A; Conclusion in B flat.*
*** DG Dig. 429 774-2 [id.] (from above set, directed Goebel).

For those not wanting a complete set, this arbitrary but well-chosen 75-minute selection may prove useful. Goebel (quoting from writings of Telemann's time) suggests that the 'unforced merriment' of the French pastoral idyll, represented by the descriptive dance movements from the *Overture*, contrasts with the learning, the 'German diligence' of the following *Quartet*. Then after the *Concerto*, where the opening movement has something of the melodic and rhythmic zest of Handel's *Arrival of the Queen of Sheba*, comes 'something gratifying' from Italy in the four-movement *Trio sonata*, followed by the *Solo sonata for violin and continuo*. The recording is faithful, though the edginess of Goebel's violin timbre will not suit all tastes.

VOCAL MUSIC

(i) *Ino (cantata); Ouvertüre in D (suite).*
*** DG Dig. 429 772-2 [id.]. (i) Barbara Schlick, Col. Mus. Ant., Reinhard Goebel.

Both the cantata *Ino* and the delightful seven-movement *Ouvertüre* or *Suite in D* were written in 1765 during what Peter Czornyi's excellent essay calls Telemann's Indian Summer. *Ino* has been out of the catalogue for some years; rediscovering it serves as a reminder that Telemann is still underrated, even following the pioneering work of the DG-Archiv label in the 1950s and 1960s. Listening to the effortless flow of remarkable invention, one can almost understand the disappointment of the Leipzig burghers that they could not entice Telemann into their service. Barbara Schlick is a delightful soloist, just a little lacking in fire and colour, but certainly lacking nothing in charm; and the wind players of the Musica Antiqua, Köln, have a delicacy and virtuosity that are irresistible. The *Rêjouissance* in the *Overture* is – as so often with this ensemble – uncomfortably rushed (the internal-combustion engine had not been invented in the 1760s, let alone Concorde!), but there is so much that is right and thought-provoking about their playing, both here and in this remarkable cantata, that criticism must be muted. The balance captures just the right perspective between soloist and players, and there is a pleasingly warm acoustic.

(i) *Der Tag des Gerichts (The Day of Judgement;* oratorio): complete; (ii) *Pimpinone* (opera): complete; (iii) *Paris quartets Nos. 1 & 6.*
(M) **(*) Teldec/Warner 2292 42722-2 (3) [id.]. (i) Landwehr-Herrmann, Canne-Meijer,

Equiluz, Van Egmond, soloists from Vienna Boys' Ch., Hamburg Monteverdi Ch., VCM, Harnoncourt; (ii) Spreckelsen, Nimsgern, Tachezi, Florilegium Musicum Ens., Hirsch; (iii) Amsterdam Qt.

Although these discs are offered at mid-price, the layout seems extravagant, since *Pimpinone* fits on to a single CD and could have been offered separately. This charming chamber opera anticipates *La Serva padrona* and offers music of great tunefulness and vivacity. The opera, here given uncut at 70 minutes, has only two characters, no chorus whatever, and a small orchestra. Yet its music is as witty as its libretto, and from the very opening one can sense that Telemann is enjoying every moment of this absurd comedy about a serving maid (Vespetta) who battens on a wealthy but stupid gentleman (Pimpinone), eventually persuading him not only to marry her but to give her the freedom of his purse and at the same time to do her bidding. Uta Spreckelsen and Sigmund Nimsgern are perfectly cast, and there is both charm and sparkle, while Hirsch accompanies in suitably spirited fashion. Excellent (1975) recording, with the voices given good presence. *The Day of Judgement* – the last of Telemann's great oratorios, coming from 1761–2 – is less convincing. Although there are moments of considerable inspiration in a work subtitled 'a poem for singing in four contemplations', one feels that Telemann was far too urbane a master to measure himself fully against so cosmic a theme. But the work is well worth sampling, particularly as the performers give it so persuasive and musical an advocacy and are, moreover, given the advantage of well-balanced recording. Nevertheless this is not a work that would figure high on the list of priorities for most Telemann admirers. The 1966 sound has been effectively remastered and, although the choral focus is not always completely clean, the overall effect is vivid. Since it runs to some 84 minutes' length, the last contemplation is placed on a separate CD, and two of the highly inventive *Paris quartets* are used as the fill-up; with the personnel of the Amsterdam group consisting of Frans Brüggen, Jaap Schröder, Anner Bylsma and Gustav Leonhardt, one can expect a high order of virtuosity put at the service of the composer. The only snag is the close recording, vivid enough but with dynamic contrast relatively limited. The other drawback to this set is the absence of translations – only the German words are given.

Die Tageszeiten.
*** HM/BMG RD 77092 [77092-RC-2]. Bach, Georg, Blochwitz, Mannov, Freiburg Vocal Ens. & Coll. Mus., Wolfgang Schäfer.

Telemann's cantata, *Die Tageszeiten* (1759), is a work of great freshness and inventive resource. Its four sections portray the various times of day (*Morning, Midday, Evening* and *Night*) and are full of imaginative ideas. Yet, fairly soon after its first appearance on LP in the early 1960s in an excellent performance from Helmut Koch and the Berlin Chamber Orchestra (DG), it returned to obscurity. This new version, recorded with period instruments and four excellent soloists, makes a different but almost equally strong impression. The strings prompt a fleeting nostalgia for the more robust timbre of modern forces, and the playing under Wolfgang Schäfer could afford to be more full-bodied. But there is some excellent singing, and the recording is clean and well balanced. An enjoyable disc.

Tippett, Michael (born 1905)

(i) *Concerto for double string orchestra;* (ii) *Fantasia concertante on a theme of Corelli;* (iii; iv) *Piano concerto;* (v) *String quartet No. 1;* (iii) *Piano sonatas Nos. 1–2.*

(M) *(**) EMI CMS7 63522-2 (2). (i) Moscow CO & Bath Festival O, Barshai; (ii) Y. Menuhin, Masters, Simpson, Bath Festival O, composer; (iii) John Ogdon; (iv) Philh. O, Sir Colin Davis; (v) Edinburgh Qt.

This is a useful and interesting compilation (provided with the composer's own notes on the music), and it is a pity that reservations have to be expressed concerning the sound of the CD transfers. Tippett's eloquent *Concerto for double string orchestra* is well served by Barshai's performance, which has both warmth and vitality. The recording is lively but a shade dry in the upper range. The string textures are clear but not ideally expansive. The *Fantasia concertante*, written for the 1953 Edinburgh Festival, is not as immediately striking as its predecessor but, with the composer in charge and Menuhin as principal soloist, its inventiveness and expressive feeling are never in doubt. The only snag is that the music by Corelli, with which it opens, is more obviously memorable than anything which follows. Again, the sound is clear and vivid but could be more sumptuous. The *Piano concerto* dates from around the same period – it was first performed in 1956 – and again represents Tippett's complex-textured and starkly conceived earlier style. None of the themes is specially memorable, and one gets the impression of too many notes chasing too few ideas. Ogdon gives it a fine performance, although he does not rescue it from waywardness, while the recording, if not ideal, now sounds clearer than originally. The *First String quartet* is an early work (1934–5) which the composer rewrote, changing it from a four-movement structure to a unitary piece in three sections (banded here, but played without a break). The piece is not difficult to come to grips with, although it is the outer movements which are most characteristic, and the *Molto lento e tranquillo* seems less striking. It is played rather slackly here and is more effective in a tauter performance; the sound is on the thin side. The difference between the style of the two *Piano sonatas* is the more striking for having them juxtaposed, particularly as Ogdon plays them both well and is especially convincing in the *First*. This is undeniably a work of power and originality, even though its relentless diatonicism may strike some listeners as limiting. The first movement is a set of variations and the *Andante* is a brief rondo using the Scottish folksong, *Ca' the yowes*, as its main idea. The finale is also a rondo with a hint of jazz in its principal theme. The work has a vitality of invention that it is easy to admire, even if as piano writing it is not as effective in the traditional sense as Tippett's later essay in this form. This is much more compressed in its argument, by way of kaleidoscopic reshuffling of tiny motifs rather than by conventional development, and though a more uninhibited approach can bring out the point of Tippett's scheme better, Ogdon displays his usual integrity, as well as virtuosity. The recording is faithful but a shade hard.

Turina, Joaquín (1882–1949)

Danzas fantásticas.

(M) **(*) EMI Dig. CDD7 63886-2 [id.]; *ET 763886-4*. LPO, Bátiz – FALLA: *Nights*; RODRIGO: *Concierto de Aranjuez*.**(*)

Bátiz certainly evokes a Mediterranean feeling in these three famous *Danzas* and he persuades the LPO to bring out the Latin colours and atmosphere. He is particularly beguiling in the gentle yet sultry charms of the central *Ensueño* ('Dream fantasy'), with a sensuous response from the LPO strings. The *Orgia* has plenty of energy and fire. The 1982 recording, made in – of all unlikely places – St Peter's Church, Morden, in Surrey – has an agreeably warm ambience, but fortissimos are very bright, in the way of early digital recordings; at times the ear craves rather more voluptuousness, although the effect is partly the result of Turina's brilliantly sunlit scoring.

Vaughan Williams, Ralph (1872–1958)

(i) *Piano concerto; Symphony No. 9 in E min.*
*** Chan. Dig. CHAN 8941; *ABTD 1537* [id.]. (i) Howard Shelley, LPO, Bryden Thomson.

Bryden Thomson's survey of the Vaughan Williams symphonies has been one of Chandos's many successes; each has been paired with a concerto or another major work. Whether or not you are collecting the whole series, this is a particularly valuable issue since it couples the little-known *Piano concerto* with the dark and much underrated *Ninth Symphony*. The *Concerto* had a long period of gestation: the first two movements were written in 1926, before *Job*, and the finale in 1931–2, although this was revised after the first performance in 1933. Perhaps the most strikingly original of the three movements is the imaginative and inward-looking *Romanza*, which has some of the angularity of line one finds in *Flos campi*, while the finale presages the *Fourth Symphony*. The work's neglect may be due to the absence of big themes; if the overt display to which the public is accustomed in bravura concertos is not obvious here, the piece abounds in difficulties of the most demanding nature, which Howard Shelley addresses with flair and brilliance. He makes light of the disconcerting cragginess of the piano writing and consistently brings out both the wit and the underlying emotional power.

Bryden Thomson conducts a powerful performance of the last of Vaughan Williams's symphonies, written when the composer was in his mid-eighties. Though the playing may not be as crisply incisive as that on Previn's 1971 version with the LSO, it brings out an extra warmth of expression, confirming that this is far more than the playful and noisy outburst of an old man. Both performances are greatly helped by the richness and weight of the Chandos sound, warmly atmospheric but with ample detail and a fine sense of presence.

(i) *Violin concerto in D min.;* (ii) *Flos campi.*
(M) (***) EMI mono CDH7 63828-2 [id.]. (i) Yehudi Menuhin, LPO; (ii) William Primrose (viola), Philh. O; Boult – WALTON: *Viola concerto* etc.(***)

Though the 1946 mono sound inevitably limits the atmospheric beauty of *Flos campi*, this première recording of a masterpiece brings revelatory playing from Primrose, as well as deeply understanding conducting from Boult. The soloist's degree of classical detachment adds to the intensity of emotion conveyed. It is almost the opposite with Menuhin's reading of what in its neo-classical figuration can seem a chilly work. Though there have been more immaculate performances on record since, none matches this in its heartfelt intensity, whether in the thrust and vigour of the outer movements or, most of all, in the yearning lyricism of the central *Adagio*, here revealed as among the composer's most tenderly beautiful slow movements. The recording, made in 1952 but never issued at the time, is also limited; but with excellent CD transfers and equally valuable Walton works as a generous coupling, this is a historic CD to cherish.

(i) *Fantasia on Greensleeves;* (ii) *Fantasia on a theme of Thomas Tallis;* (i) *Overture: The Wasps;* (i; iii; iv) *Serenade to music;* (iv) *Towards the Unknown Region.*
(M) *** EMI CDM7 63382-2; *EG 763382-4*. (i) LSO, (ii) Philh. O, with (iii) Elsie Morison, Marjorie Thomas, Duncan Robertson, Trevor Anthony, (iv) Chorus; Sargent.

Here is a splendid reminder of the art of Sir Malcolm Sargent, or 'Flash Harry' as he was none too affectionately known by orchestral players, to whom he could be inordinately rude. He was not a modest man, but he knew how to woo the amateur choristers who sang at his many annual *Messiahs*, and he was a great favourite with the wider musical public, becoming the first musician radio celebrity, through his broadcasts on the wartime 'Brains Trust'. His orchestral command was considerable and he did much to proselytize British music overseas, especially the works of Vaughan Williams. *The Wasps overture* was one of his favourite showpieces, and his reading is delightfully spick and span. When he played it once at a concert in Carnegie Hall, a local review described it engagingly as 'a pleasant trifle that sounds like Rimsky-Korsakov with bowler, mackintosh and umbrella'. But he could find an unexpected depth and sense of infinity as well as strength in the *Tallis fantasia* (which is why he performed Elgar's *Dream of Gerontius* so intuitively). Vaughan Williams's great string work is superbly played here by the 1959 Philharmonia strings. The recording producer was Walter Legge, and the sound is wonderfully full, yet clear, with a lovely ethereal effect from the solo group. In the *Serenade to music* Sargent chose the first of the composer's performing alternatives. Rather than using sixteen solo singers, he divided their music up between four, and expanded to a chorus where the sixteen voices unite. Moreover he chose two of his favourite soloists, Elsie Morison and Majorie Thomas, for the recording, and the work's closing section sounds particularly beautiful. *Towards the Unknown Region* further demonstrates Sargent's choral skills in a reading of considerable eloquence. All the LSO recordings here were made in the Abbey Road No. 1 Studio in 1957, with Peter Andry in charge, and they sound remarkably good.

The Pilgrim's progress (incidental music, ed. Palmer).
*** Hyp. CDA 66511; *KA 66511* [id.]. Sir John Gielgud, Richard Pasco, Ursula Howells, Corydon Singers, City of L. Sinfonia, Best.

Vaughan Williams had a lifelong devotion to Bunyan's great allegory, which fired his inspiration for at least five major musical projects. The last was the full-scale opera of 1951. Before that, in 1942 when he was completing the *Fifth Symphony* – another Bunyan inspiration – he wrote incidental music for a BBC radio adaptation of the complete *Pilgrim's Progress*. Much of the material, but not all, then found a place in the opera. Christopher Palmer, who, with equal flair, adapted Walton's *Henry V* film score into a similar mixture of speech and music, has here devised a sequence of twelve movements, which – overlapping with the opera and the symphony – throws up long-buried treasure. Matthew Best draws warmly sympathetic performances from his singers and players, in support of the masterly contributions of Sir John Gielgud, taking the role of Pilgrim as he did on radio in 1942, and Richard Pasco as the Evangelist.

A Sea Symphony (No. 1).
(M) *** EMI CDM7 64016-2 [id.]; *EG 764016-4*. Armstrong, Carol Case, LPO Ch., LPO, Boult.

Boult's is a warm, relaxed reading of Vaughan Williams's expansive symphony. If the ensemble is sometimes less perfect than one would like, the flow of the music consistently holds the listener, and this is matched by warmly atmospheric recorded sound. Boult, often thought of as a 'straight' interpreter, here demonstrates his affectionate style, drawing consistently expressive but never sentimental phrasing from his singers and players. John Carol Case's baritone does not sound well on disc with his rather plaintive tone-colour, but his style is right, and Sheila Armstrong sings most beautifully. The set has been remastered and freshened, and it is good to have this back in the catalogue on EMI's mid-priced CD label. There is no finer version.

A London symphony (No. 2): Fantasia on a theme of Thomas Tallis.
(M) *** EMI CDM7 64017-2 [id.]; *EG 764017-4.* LPO, Boult.

Though detail is sharper and the sound remains spacious on Boult's 1970 version, the upper strings sound less rich after remastering than they did before. The orchestral playing is outstandingly fine. The outer movements are expansive, less taut than in his much earlier mono version for Decca. The central *tranquillo* episode of the first movement, for instance, is very relaxed; but here, as in the slow movement, the orchestra produces lovely sounds, the playing deeply committed; and criticism is disarmed. The Scherzo is as light as thistledown and the gentle melancholy which underlies the solemn pageantry of the finale is coloured with great subtlety. With Boult's noble, gravely intense account of the *Tallis fantasia* offered as a coupling, this remains an attractive alternative to Previn. The CD impressively refines textures (especially in *Tallis*), but lightens the bass. First choice for this work, however, remains with Previn's exceptionally spacious Telarc version, coupled with *The Lark ascending* (CD 80158).

(i) *A Pastoral Symphony (No. 3);* (ii) *Symphony No. 5 in D.*
(M) *** EMI CDM7 64018-2 [id.]; *EG 764018-4.* (i) Margaret Price, New Philh. O; (ii) LPO, Boult.
(M) (***) Decca 430 060-2; *430 060-4* [id.]. (i) Margaret Ritchie; LPO, Boult.

On EMI, in the *Pastoral Symphony* Boult is not entirely successful in controlling the tension of the short but elusive first movement, although it is beautifully played. The opening of the *Lento moderato*, however, is very fine, and its close is sustained with a perfect blend of restraint and intensity. After the jovial third movement, the orchestra is joined by Margaret Price, whose wordless contribution is blended into the texture most skilfully. Boult gives a loving performance of the *Fifth Symphony*, one which links it directly with the great opera *The Pilgrim's Progress*, from which (in its unfinished state) the composer drew much of the material. It is a gentle performance, easier and more flowing than some rivals', and some may prefer it for that reason, but the emotional involvement is a degree less intense, particularly in the slow movement. Both recordings have been successfully remastered, retaining the fullness and atmosphere (while refining detail) to help the tranquil mood which is striking in both works.

It is good to have the earlier Kingsway Hall recordings back in the catalogue. They were made in 1952/3 with the composer present; although allowances have to be made for the pinched sound of the upper string climaxes, the recording is basically full and luminous. The transluscent textures Boult creates in the *Pastoral Symphony* (the opening is hauntingly ethereal) and his essential delicacy of approach are balanced by his intensity in the *Fifth*, where the climax of the first movement has wonderful breadth and passion. The LPO play with great sympathy and warmth in music that was still new, the *Fifth* only a decade old, at the time this record was made. However, Previn's outstandingly beautiful and refined LSO version of the *Pastoral Symphony* (coupled at mid-price with No. 4 on BMG/RCA GD 90503 [60583-2-RG]) would be first choice among modern recordings of this symphony.

Symphony No. 4 in F min.
(**) Koch mono 3-7018-2; *2-7018-4* [id.]. BBC SO, composer – HOLST: *Planets.*(**)

Vaughan Williams made his recording of the *Fourth Symphony* in 1937, not long after the ink had dried on the score. It is a performance of blazing intensity in which he made no attempt to smooth over any rough edges, while the BBC Symphony Orchestra played as if their very lives depended on it. Theirs is a reading which is intent on capturing the spirit rather than the letter of the work and, although there have been more impressive recordings from Sir Adrian Boult and others, this performance carries a unique and powerful charge. It remains thrilling and makes a stronger impression than almost any modern recording because of its high voltage and despite the handicap of rather dry recorded sound. The transfer is less full-bodied than the LP version which appeared in the 1970s (the upper strings are lacking in timbre), but this should not deter collectors from acquiring it, particularly in view of the interest of the coupling.

Symphonies Nos. 5 in D; 6 in E min.
*(*) Collins Dig. 1202-2; *1202-4* [id.]. ASMF, Marriner.

This coupling of what many would count the composer's two finest symphonies, both from the 1940s, is both generous and welcome. Sadly, Marriner's strong and sympathetic readings, well paced and beautifully played, are undermined by the recorded sound. Set rather distantly – as many Collins recordings are – the balance disconcertingly has the strings placed behind the other instruments. Particularly in No. 5, that is a serious flaw when the surging climaxes of the first and third movements so depend on the weight of string tone. Previn's mid-priced LSO recording (BMG/RCA GD 90506 [60586-2-RG]), dedicated and intense, is a recommendable choice for the *Fifth* while Vernon Handley's EMI version is finest of all (Eminence CD-EMX 9512; *TC-EMX 2122*).

(i) *Symphony No. 6* (includes original and revised Scherzo); (ii) *The Lark ascending;* (iii) *Song of thanksgiving.*
(M) (***) EMI mono CDH7 63308-2 [id.]. (i) LSO; (ii) Pougnet, LPO; (iii) Dolemore, Speight (nar.), Luton Ch. Soc. & Girls' Ch., LPO, Boult.

This is a valuable compilation of Sir Adrian Boult's early post-war recordings of Vaughan Williams's music, sounding surprisingly well in excellent transfers. One adjusts almost immediately to the flatter mono effect in the recording of the *Sixth Symphony*, made very soon after the first performance in 1948, so soon in fact that it was originally done with the unrevised version of the scherzo. As soon as the revision was written, Sir Adrian re-recorded that movement alone, and this disc includes both. On CD one can programme the player to include whichever of the two one chooses. Jean Pougnet, leader of the LPO at the time, is a natural soloist for *The Lark ascending* with his exceptionally pure tone, while the *Song of thanksgiving*, originally entitled 'Thanksgiving for victory', is an attractive period piece designed for victory celebrations after the Second World War. It proved rather more than an occasional piece but has never been recorded since. One has to make no apology for either of these recordings, and in the latter work the chorus sounds strikingly firm and clear. For a modern version of the *Sixth* one can turn to Previn and the LSO on BMG/RCA (GD 90508; *GK 90507* [60588-2-RG]). The CD, but not the cassette, is coupled with a fine account of the *Ninth Symphony*.

(i) *Sinfonia Antartica (No. 7); Serenade to music.*
(M) *** EMI Dig. CD-EMX 2173; *TC-EMX 2173*. (i) Alison Hargan; Royal Liverpool PO and Ch., Vernon Handley.

Vernon Handley in his Vaughan Williams series for EMI Eminence directs a warmly atmospheric reading of the *Antartica*. He is neither as rugged as Haitink in his highly individual account on full-price EMI nor so spectacularly recorded, but this is still a most satisfyingly symphonic view of a work that can seem merely illustrative. As in his other Vaughan Williams recordings, Handley shows a natural feeling for expressive rubato and draws refined playing from the Liverpool orchestra. At the end of the epilogue Alison Hargan makes a notable first appearance on disc, a soprano with an exceptionally sweet and pure voice. At mid-price in well-balanced digital sound it makes an outstanding bargain, particularly when it offers an excellent fill-up. Handley directs a warmly understanding reading of the *Serenade to music*, though in this lovely score a chorus never sounds as characterful as a group of well-chosen soloists.

(i) *Fantasia on Christmas carols;* (ii) *Flos Campi;* (i) *5 Mystical songs;* (iii) *Serenade to music.*
*** Hyp. Dig. CDA 66420; *KA 66420* [id.]. (i) Thomas Allen, (ii) Imai & Corydon Singers; (iii) 16 soloists; ECO, Best.

This radiant record was designed to celebrate the tenth anniversary of the foundation of the Hyperion label by Ted Perry, one of the best loved and most admired figures in the record world. It centres round the *Serenade to music*, one of the great celebratory works of the century, specially composed for the jubilee of Sir Henry Wood in 1938. As in the original performance, sixteen star soloists are here lined up and, though the team of women does not quite match the stars of 1938 – who included Dame Eva Turner and Dame Isobel Baillie – the men are generally fresher and clearer. Above all, thanks largely to fuller, modern recording, the result is much more sensuous than the original, with ensemble better matched and with Matthew Best drawing glowing sounds from the English Chamber Orchestra. The other items are superbly done too, with Nobuko Imai a powerful viola soloist in the mystical cantata, *Flos campi*, another Vaughan Williams masterpiece. Thomas Allen is the characterful soloist in the five *Mystical songs*. Warmly atmospheric sound to match the performances.

Fantasia on Christmas carols; Hodie.
**(*) EMI Dig. CDC7 54128-2 [id.]; *EL 754128-4*. Gale, Tear, Roberts, LSO Ch. & O, Hickox.

Though the three soloists cannot match the original trio in Sir David Willcocks's pioneering version (on EMI CDM7 69872-2), Hickox directs a more urgent and more freely expressive reading of the big Christmas cantata, *Hodie*, helped by more refined and incisive choral singing. As on the earlier disc, the *Christmas carol fantasia* proves an ideal coupling, also warmly done.

'The world of Vaughan Williams': (i) *English folksongs suite;* (ii) *Fantasia on Greensleeves;* (ii; iii) *The Lark ascending;* (iv; v) *Fantasia on Christmas carols;* (vi) *Linden Lea;* (vii; viii) *O clap your hands;* (vii) *O taste and see;* (v) *3 Shakespeare songs;* (vi) *Silent noon; The vagabond.*
(B) **(*) Decca 430 093-2; *430 093-4* [id.]. (i) Boston Pops O, Fiedler; (ii) ASMF, Marriner; (iii) with Iona Brown; (iv) Hervey Alan & LSO; (v) King's College Ch., Willcocks; (vi) Tear, Ledger; (vii) Canterbury Cathedral Ch., Allan Wicks; (viii) Philip Jones Brass Ens; David Flood.

Many collectors will feel that any single-disc summation of Vaughan Williams's art without the symphonies must include the great *Tallis fantasia*. It would certainly have been a welcome substitute for the *Folksongs suite*, breezily done though that is. Otherwise the selection is quite well made, as long as there is no objection to having songs with piano sandwiched between *Greensleeves* and Iona Brown's Elysian performance of *The Lark ascending*. *O clap your hands* is most welcome, a splendid, spectacular miniature, and so is the fine *Fantasia on Christmas carols*, a surprisingly rare work, presented here with much spirit.

Verdi, Giuseppe (1813–1901)

Ballet music, Overtures and Preludes: *Aida* (prelude and ballet); *Un ballo in maschera* (prelude); *La forza del destino* (overture); *Macbeth* (ballet); *Nabucco* (overture); *La Traviata* (Preludes to Acts I & III); *I vespri siciliani* (overture).
*** Collins Dig. 1072-2; *1072-4* [id.]. Philh. O, Jacek Kaspszyk.

The competition in this repertoire is considerable. Apart from Karajan's older, analogue recordings which have tremendous panache and virtuosity (DG 419 622-2 – see our main volume, p. 1111), there are outstanding digital collections by both Sinopoli (DG 411 469-2) and Chailly (Decca 410 141-2), both of which include the four finest of the overtures.

Jacek Kaspszyk omits *Luisa Miller* but, like Sinopoli, includes *Un ballo in maschera* and the *La Traviata Preludes* which, alongside the delicate introduction to *Aida*, are admirably refined in phrasing and beautifully played. Indeed all the performances here are first class and have an exhilarating spontaneity. There is drama – *Nabucco* is particularly successful in this respect – and the ballet music has an engaging rhythmic sparkle. What makes this Collins disc especially enjoyable is the full, resonant sound and the realistic balance within the pleasing acoustics of London's Henry Wood Hall.

Overtures or Preludes: *Aida; Il Corsaro; Luisa Miller; Macbeth; Rigoletto; La Traviata* (Act I); *I vespri siciliani*.
(B) *** DG Compact Classics *431 185-4* [id.]. BPO, Karajan – ROSSINI: *Overtures*.***

Not a predictable collection on this excellently transferred Compact Classics cassette. Karajan is in his element, with the polished BPO players producing both elegance (in the *Traviata Prelude*) and plenty of high drama. Most enjoyable!

4 Sacred pieces; Pater noster.
*(*) Argo Dig. 425 480-2; *425 480-4* [id.]. King's Coll. Ch., Cambridge University Music Soc. Ch., LPO, Cleobury.

A modern digital recording of the last music Verdi wrote is welcome, but Cleobury's performances are not quite powerful enough. With musical invention more thinly spread than in Verdi's earlier masterpieces, these works demand keener intensity, though the recording beautifully contrasts the chapel choir against the full Cambridge University Music Chorus.

Requiem Mass.
(M) (**(*)) EMI mono CDH7 63341-2 [id.]. Caniglia, Stignani, Gigli, Pinza, Rome Op. Ch. & O, Serafin.

Serafin's classic 1939 recording brings a glowing performance, beautifully shaped, warm and dramatic without drawing attention to itself. Maria Caniglia was not the most sensitive of Italian sopranos, but she ends here with a powerful *Libera me*, while the others could not be more characterful. Ebe Stignani and Ezio Pinza have never been surpassed in this music and Gigli, for all his stylistic peccadillos – with the vocal line often punctuated by aspirates and little sobs – is unique in his persuasiveness and honeyed tone. The choral singing is strong and dramatic, but the CD transfer requires some knob-twiddling if it is not to sound dull compared with the original 78s.

(i; ii) *Requiem Mass;* (iii; iv) *Inno delle nazione;* (ii) *Te Deum;* (iii) *Luisa Miller: Quando le sere al placido.* (iv) *Nabucco: Va pensiero.*

(M) (***) BMG/RCA mono GD 60299; *GK 60299* (2) [60299-RG-2; *60299-RG-4*]. (i) Nelli, Barbieri, Di Stefano, Siepi; (ii) Robert Shaw Ch.; (iii) Jan Peerce; (iv) Westminster Ch.; NBC SO, Toscanini.

Toscanini's account of the *Requiem* brings a supreme performance, searingly intense. The opening of the *Dies irae* has never sounded more hair-raising, with the bass-drum thrillingly caught, despite the limitation of dry mono recording. And rarely has the chorus shone so brightly in this work on record, with the Robert Shaw Chorale balanced well forward in sharp focus. Nelli sings well with clear, Italianate purity, while the others are near-ideal, a vintage team – Fedora Barbieri, the young Giuseppe di Stefano and Cesare Siepi. The other works make fascinating listening, too. The *Te Deum* was one of Toscanini's very last recordings, a performance more intense than usual with this work, and it is good to have the extraordinary wartime recording of the potboiling *Hymn of the Nations*. The *Internationale* is added to Verdi's original catalogue of national anthems, to represent the ally, Soviet Russia. It is fascinating that Robert Shaw, who made his name in the recording world as the chorus-master for some of Toscanini's finest records, was later to make an outstandingly successful recording of the Verdi *Requiem*, reflecting directly what he learned from the great maestro. With sound of spectacular quality, the many felicities of the performance, not least the electricity of the choral singing, add up to an exceptionally satisfying reading, which remains a clear first choice for this work on CD and carries a Rosette in our main volume (Telarc CD 80152).

OPERA

Aida (complete).

** Sony Dig. S3K 45973 (3) [id.]; *40-45973*. Millo, Zajick, Domingo, Morris, Metropolitan Op. Ch. & O, Levine.

(M) (**) BMG/RCA mono GD 60300; *GK 60300* (3/2) [60300-RG-2, *60300-RG-4*]. Nelli, Gustavson, Tucker, Valdengo, Robert Shaw Ch., NBC SO, Toscanini.

Levine's recording, made with Met. forces in the limited acoustic of the Manhattan Center, has the advantage of using a cast and company already well rehearsed in a stage production, but the result is often heavy-handed. The television relay of this same production, with three of the same principals, was rather more convincing than this. Placido Domingo still makes a commanding, imaginative Radames; but, on record and without the help of vision, both Aprile Millo in the title-role and Dolora Zajick as Amneris are disappointing, when the recording exaggerates unevenness of vocal production. Millo has lovely moments (as in *O patria mia*) but too much is squally, and Zajick's tangily characterful Amneris is often made to sound very raw. James Morris as Amonasro proves a gruff Verdian, but Samuel Ramey is a formidable Ramfis. In this of all operas you need a more spacious recording than is provided here, to allow for the grandeur of the big crowd-scenes to be fully appreciated.

Toscanini's 1949 performance of *Aida* is the least satisfying of his New York opera recordings. Richard Tucker sings well but makes a relatively colourless Radames, and Herva Nelli lacks weight as Aida, neatly though she sings and with some touching moments. Nancy Gustavson's Amneris lacks all menace, and Valdengo as Amonasro is the only fully satisfying principal. Yet Toscanini is so electrifying from first to last that his admirers will accept the limited, painfully dry recording. Karajan's EMI performance of *Aida* is cast from strength with Freni, Carreras, Raimondi and Cappuccilli. Moreover it is a performance that carries splendour and pageantry to the point of exaltation (EMI CMS7 69300-2 [Angel CMDC 69300]; *EX 290808-5*).

(i) *Aida:* highlights; (ii) *Don Carlos:* highlights.
(B) **(*) DG Compact Classics *427 715-4* [id.]. From complete sets with (i; ii) Ricciarelli, Domingo, Nucci, Raimondi, Ghiaurov; (i) Obraztsova; (ii) Valentini-Terrani; La Scala, Milan, Ch. & O, Abbado.

Four of the principals are common to both these fine Abbado sets, neither of which is a first choice in its complete format but both of which offer some superb singing, although in *Aida* Ricciarelli's contribution is flawed. Abbado's *Don Carlos* was the first recording to use French, the language of the original. Well-balanced if not brilliant tape transfers. First choice for a complete *Don Carlos* lies with Giulini (with Domingo, Caballé, Raimondi and Verrett) who uses the full, five-Act text, sung in Italian (EMI CDS7 47701-8 [Ang. CDCC 47701]).

Un ballo in maschera (complete).
(M) **(*) Ph. 426 560-2 (2) [id.]. Caballé, Carreras, Wixell, Payne, Ghazarian, ROHCG Ch. & O, Colin Davis.

Davis's version, based on a Covent Garden production, is particularly good in the way it brings out the ironic humour in Verdi's score. Caballé and Carreras match Davis's lightness, but the dramatic power is diminished. Despite fine recording this is less satisfying than most of the recordings listed in our main volume, and those seeking a recommendable mid-priced version should turn to Leinsdorf on RCA, with Leontyne Price, Bergonzi and Merrill all in splendid voice (GD 86645 [6645-2-RG]).

Un ballo in maschera: highlights.
*** DG Dig. 429 415-2 [id.] (from complete recording, with Domingo, Barstow, Nucci, Obraztsov, Gruberová, Raimondi, La Scala, Milan, Ch. & O, Karajan).
(M) ** Decca 421 874-2; *421 874-4* [id.] (from complete set with Tebaldi, Pavarotti, Milnes, Donath, Resnik, St Cecilia Academy, Rome, Ch. & O, Bartoletti).

This DG highlights disc is drawn from Karajan's last opera recording, made in 1989, and it is a fitting memorial. Josephine Barstow's contribution may be vocally flawed, but her singing is full of charisma; yet it is Domingo who dominates, singing superbly throughout. The selection is generous (71 minutes), following through the opera's narrative with both Acts well represented.

The complete Decca set from which the alternative, quite generous (64 minutes) and well-chosen excerpts are taken is seriously flawed, but the selection can be recommended to those who want to sample the singing of Tebaldi, obviously past her prime but still strong and distinctive. With Pavarotti as Riccardo and Milnes as Renato also well featured, there is much to enjoy here. The 1970 Decca sound is certainly vivid, but the remastering brings a drier, brighter effect than the original LPs.

(i) *Un ballo in maschera:* highlights; (ii) *Macbeth:* highlights.
(B) *** DG Compact Classics *431 184-4* [id.]. Ricciarelli, Domingo, Bruson, Obraztsova, Gruberová, Raimondi; (ii) Cappuccilli, Verrett, Ghiaurov, Domingo, La Scala, Milan, Ch. & O, Abbado.

Another fine Abbado pairing in DG's bargain Compact Classics tape series, offering 90 minutes of music drawn from two outstanding sets, *Un ballo in machera*, dating from 1976, and *Macbeth*, made five years earlier. Both are highly compelling performances and strongly cast, *Macbeth* notable for fine teamwork from all the principals, and *Un ballo* for memorable individual characterizations. Ricciarelli is at her finest and most individual, Domingo in freshest voice, and Bruson superb as the wronged husband, Renato. The La

Scala Chorus makes a strong contribution in *Macbeth* and the sound is vividly focused in both operas.

I Due Foscari (complete).
(*) Nuova Era Dig. 692/22 [id.]. Bruson, Martinucci, Canera, Caforio, Comacchio, Onesti, Faedda, Marangoni, Ch. & O del Teatro Regio di Torino, Maurizio Arena.

Apart from Renato Bruson in the role of the Doge, Francesco Foscari, the Nuova Era set, recorded live in 1984 in Turin with plentiful noise on stage, has little to offer in competition with the fine Philips set under Gardelli. Not even Bruson matches his opposite number, Piero Cappuccilli; and most of the others, including the conductor, fall lamentably short of their Philips rivals. Lorenza Canera as Lucrezia in particular is a terrible wobbler, not sounding like a young heroine at all. The advantage of digital sound is nil when balances are so faulty, with the chorus dimly caught. Libretto and translation are provided.

Falstaff (complete).
(M) (***) BMG/RCA mono GD 60251; *GK 60251* (2) [60251-RG-2; *60251-RG-4*]. Valdengo, Nelli, Merriman, Elmo, Guarrera, Stich-Randall, Robert Shaw Ch., NBC SO, Toscanini.

Toscanini's fizzing account of Verdi's last masterpiece has never been matched on record, the most high-spirited performance ever, beautifully paced for comedy. Even without stereo, and recorded with typical dryness, the clarity and sense of presence in this live concert performance set the story in relief. The cast is excellent, led by the ripe, firm baritone, Giuseppe Valdengo. Such singers as Nan Merriman as Mistress Page, Cloe Elmo as a wonderfully fruity Mistress Quickly and Frank Guarrera as Ford match or outshine any more recent interpreters. Toscanini's favourite soprano in his last years, Herva Nelli, is less characterful as Mistress Ford, rather over-parted but still fresh and reliable. For a modern digital recording of *Falstaff* one naturally turns to Giulini, whose reading combines the tensions and atmosphere of live performance with a precision normally achieved only in the studio. The impressive cast includes Bruson, Ricciarelli and Barbara Hendricks, charming as Nanetta (DG 410 503-2).

(i) *La forza del destino:* highlights; (ii) *Nabucco:* highlights.
(B) *** DG Compact Classics *431 183-4* [id.].(i) Plowright, Carreras, Bruson, Burchuladze, Baltsa, Amb. Op. Ch., Philh. O; (ii) Cappuccilli, Dimitrova, Nesterenko, Domingo, German Op. Ch. & O, Sinopoli.

Sinopoli's Compact Classics cassette, pairing selections from *Forza del destino* and *Nabucco*, generously offers 92 minutes of music and in *Nabucco* includes the three most famous choruses, including a memorable *Va pensiero*, with its hushed opening pianissimo. *La forza del destino* is very much a spacious reading, but Rosalind Plowright's *Pace, pace, mio Dio* is gloriously sustained, while Agnes Baltsa's *Rataplan* makes a lively contrast. The complete set from which these highlights are drawn makes a clear first choice for this opera (DG 419 203-2). *Nabucco* brings strong performances all round and this tape can be recommended also for the vividness of the transfer. Dimitrova is superb, noble in her evil, as is Cappucilli as Nabucco, and, with Domingo in a relatively small role and Nestorenko very impressive as the High Priest, Zaccaria, this brightly recorded set remains our first choice also in its complete form (DG 410 512-2).

(i) *I Lombardi, Act III: Trio.* (ii) *Rigoletto, Act IV* (complete).
(M) (**) BMG/RCA mono GD 60276; *GK 60276* (2); [60276-2-RG; *60276-4-RG*].

(i) Della Chiesa, Peerce, Moscona; (ii) Warren, Milanov, Peerce, Moscona, Merriman, All City Highschool Ch. & Glee Clubs, NBC SO, Toscanini – BOITO: *Mefistofele: Prologue.*(***)

These two fascinating Verdi items are wartime recordings, even more limited in sound than most of Toscanini's in his last years. The *Lombardi Trio* finds the acoustic of the notorious Studio 8H in Radio City at its driest, but the conductor's love for the music still dominates. It is interesting to find a little-known singer, Vivian della Chiesa, emerging strongly alongside Jan Peerce and Nicola Moscona. Equally impressive is the dazzling performance of the NBC Orchestra's concert-master, Mischa Mischakoff, in the virtuoso violin solo of the introduction. The last Act of *Rigoletto* was given in a wartime fund-raising concert in Madison Square Garden and, though the brittleness of sound is at times almost comic and the tautness of Toscanini's control was unrelenting, the performances of the principals are formidable, with Zinka Milanov at her most radiant. With Toscanini's searing account of the *Mefistofele Prologue*, this makes a generous compilation.

Nabucco: highlights.
(M) *** Decca 421 867-2; *421 867-4* [id.] (from complete recording, with Gobbi, Suliotis, Cava, Previdi, V. State Op. Ch. & O, Gardelli).

Suliotis's impressive contribution is well represented on this Decca highlights disc, and there are fine contributions too from Gobbi. Needless to say, the chorus *Va piensiero* is given its place of honour (the performance rhythmically a little mannered but eloquent enough), and *Gli arredi festivi* opens the selection, which runs for 58 minutes. The 1965 recording sounds splendid.

Otello (highlights; in English).
(M) **(*) EMI Dig. CDM7 63723-2; *EG 763723-4* (from complete recording, with Charles Craig, Plowright, Howlett, Bottone, E. Nat. Op. Ch. & O, Mark Elder).

A good hour-long sampler of the ENO's *Otello*, recorded live in 1983, will suit those who want the complete opera sung in the original language. The recording makes the words vividly clear – and also the stage noises. There are other flaws, but the spontaneous drama of the occasion is well conveyed and the power of Charles Craig's memorable portrayal of Otello is well balanced by Rosalind Plowright's moving Desdemona, beautifully sung. A translation is included. For those who want a complete set, sung in Italian, Levine's set has the best cast and is superbly conducted as well as magnificently sung (BMG/RCA RD 82951 [RCD-2-2951]).

Rigoletto (highlights; in English).
(M) **(*) EMI Dig. CDM7 63726-2; *EG 736726-4* (from complete recording, with John Rawnsley, Helen Field, Arthur Davies, Tomlinson, Rigby, E. Nat. Op. Ch. & O, Mark Elder).

Unlike the ENO *Otello*, *Rigoletto* was recorded in the studio (also in 1983), but there is no lack of intensity and, even if you normally resist opera in English, this 63 minutes of excerpts is well worth trying. The standard of singing is high, especially the appealing portrayal of the Duke by Arthur Davies, though Helen Field's *Caro nome* would not disgrace any operatic stage in the world. Excellent, vivid sound and a libretto, although the words are admirably clear. The finest version of *Rigoletto* sung in Italian is Sinopoli's Rome recording with Bruson, Gruberová and Fassbaender, with Neil Shicoff as the Duke more than a match for his most distinguished rivals (Philips 412 592-2).

La Traviata (complete).
*** Decca Dig. 430 491-2; *430 491-4* (2) [id.]. Sutherland, Pavarotti, Manuguerra, L. Op. Ch., Nat. PO, Bonynge.
(M) (*(**)) EMI mono CMS7 63628-2 (2) [Ang. CDMB 63628]. Callas, Di Stefano, Bastianini, La Scala Ch. & O, Giulini.
(M) * Decca 430 250-2 (2) [id.]. Tebaldi, Poggi, Protti, St Celia Ac., Rome, Ch. & O, Molinari-Pradelli.

Readers will note that the Bonynge *Traviata*, Sutherland's second recording of the role of Violetta for Decca, with Pavarotti singing with splendid panache as Alfredo, has now been reissued on two premium-priced CDs and cassettes. This is our first recommendation for this opera.

Callas's version with Giulini comes into rivalry with another live recording of her in this role, also from EMI but recorded in Lisbon and conducted by Ghione (CDS7 49187-8 – see our main volume, pp. 1134–5). This La Scala performance was recorded in 1955, three years before the other, when the voice was fresher. In the presence of a great conductor, one who often challenged her with unusually slow speeds, Callas responded with even greater depth of expression. There is no more vividly dramatic a performance on record than this, unmatchable in conveying Violetta's agony; sadly, the sound, always limited, grows crumbly towards the end. It is sad too that Bastianini sings so lumpishly as Germont père, even in the great duet of Act II, while di Stefano also fails to match his partner in the supreme test of the final scene. The transfer is fair, though in places it sounds as though an echo-chamber has been used.

Recorded in 1954, the Tebaldi version of *La Traviata* emerges on CD with the benefit of stereo, a very early example and one which certainly helps to give body to the voices. Though Violetta was not Tebaldi's ideal role – the coloratura of Act I is negotiated accurately rather than with joy – there is much superb singing from her here. The delicacy of her phrasing is a delight, bringing a most tender portrait, though the *Addio del passato* brings a suspicion of intrusive aitches. Her refinement contrasts with the coarseness of Gianni Poggi as Alfredo and the lack of imagination of Aldo Protti as Germont. Yet this is well worth hearing for Tebaldi in her early prime.

Il Trovatore (complete).
(M) ** EMI CMS7 63640-2 (2) [Ang. CDMB 63640]. Corelli, Tucci, Simionato, Merrill, Rome Op. Ch. & O, Schippers.

The EMI set of *Il Trovatore* is a long way short of the ideal, but Merrill's Conte di Luna is characterful and firmly sung, if sometimes ungainly. Simionato is an excellent Azucena; Tucci, though less assured than her colleagues, sings very beautifully. Corelli is at his powerful best as Manrico, a really heroic, if not always subtle, tenor. His *Di quella pira* displays rather crude histrionics, but its gutsiness is welcome when Schippers' conducting is inclined to be rigid, somewhat preventing the temperature from rising; otherwise Schippers' incisiveness is compelling in an atmospheric recording that is characteristic of the Rome Opera House. Choice for this opera lies between Mehta's immensely red-blooded version with Leontyne Price, Domingo, Milnes and Cossotto as an electrifying Azucena (BMG/RCA RD 86194 [6194-2-RC]) and Giulini's DG version which flouts convention at every point, transforming meldrama into a deeper experience. Rosalind Plowright is superb, Domingo matches his RCA performance and Fassbaender finds great intensity and detail as Azucena with Zancanaro a glorious Count di Luna, this an intensely revelatory performance (423 858-2).

I vespri siciliani (complete).
** EMI CDS7 54043-2 (3) [Ang. CDCC 54043]; *EX 754043-4.* Merritt, Studer, Zancanaro, Furlanetto, Ch. & O of La Scala, Milan, Muti.

This opera has been sadly neglected on record; it is a cumbersome, five-Act piece, written for Paris, and, for all the rousing ensembles and elaborate spectacle, not to mention the big half-hour ballet in Act III, it generally lacks the melodic individuality which marks even the lesser-known Verdi operas. Yet it contains many riches over its span of nearly three and a half hours, and it is good to have a modern recording. This is the most successful yet of the live recordings made by Muti at La Scala, Milan, plagued by a difficult acoustic which is dispiritingly dry for the engineers. The atmosphere is well caught and, though Muti can be too tautly urgent a Verdian, his pacing here is well geared to bring out the high drama. Outstanding in the cast is Cheryl Studer as the heroine, Elena, singing radiantly; while the tenor Chris Merritt as Arrigo sounds less coarse and strained than he has in the past. Giorgio Zancanaro also responds to the role of Monforte – the governor of Sicily, discovered to be Arrigo's father – with new sensitivity, and though Ferruccio Furlanetto as Procida lacks the full weight to bring out the beauty of line in the great aria, *O tu Palermo*, his is a warm performance too. Yet the 1974 RCA recording, made in London under James Levine, remains a preferred choice. Though Martina Arroyo is less responsive than Studer, Placido Domingo, Sherrill Milnes and the young Ruggero Raimondi are all preferable to the La Scala singers, and the sharpness of focus in both performance and recording exposes the relative fuzziness of Muti's live account (RD 80370 [0370-2-RC]).

COLLECTIONS

Arias: *Don Carlo: Son io, mio Carlo . . . Per me giunto . . . O Carlo, ascolta. Luisa Miller: Sacra la scelta. Macbeth: Perfidi! All'anglo contra me v'unite . . . Pietà, rispetto, amore. La Traviata: Di Provenza il mar. Il Trovatore: Tutto è deserto . . . Il balen.*
*** Ph. Dig. 426 740-2; *426 740-4* [id.]. Dmitri Hvorostovsky, Rotterdam PO, Gergiev – TCHAIKOVSKY: *Arias.****

With a glorious voice, dark and characterful, and with natural musical imagination and film-star good looks, Dmitri Hvorostovsky, 'Cardiff Singer of the World' in 1989, on this disc made his recording début in the West not just in Tchaikovsky arias, but here in Verdi, stylishly sung. With a voice of such youthful virility, he hardly sounds like the father-figure of the *Traviata* and *Luisa Miller* items, but the legato in Macbeth's Act IV aria is most beautiful. He also brings the keenest intensity to Posa's death-scene aria from *Don Carlo.*

Choruses from: *Aida; Un ballo in maschera; Don Carlo; I Lombardi; Macbeth; I Masnadieri; Nabucco; Otello; Rigoletto; La Traviata; Il Trovatore. Requiem Mass: Sanctus.*
*** Decca Dig. 430 226-2; *430 226-4* [id.]. Chicago Symphony Ch. & SO, Solti.

Choruses from: *Aida; La battaglia di Legnano; Don Carlo; Ernani; La forza del destino; Macbeth; Nabucco; Otello; La Traviata; Il Trovatore.*
(BB) *** Naxos Dig. 8.550241 [id.]. Slovak Philharmonic Ch. & RSO, Oliver Dohnányi.

The Solti collection is not drawn from the maestro's previous complete opera sets but is a first-class studio production, recorded in Orchestra Hall, Chicago, with Decca's most resplendent digital sound. The choral balance is forward, but there is plenty of depth too, and the wide dynamic range emphasizes, for instance, the dramatic contrast at the repeated cries of '*Gerusalem!*' from *I Lombardi* (a thrilling moment), while the gentle opening of *Va pensiero* from *Nabucco* (which was sung spontaneously by the crowds in the streets of Milan as Verdi's funeral cortège passed by) is beautifully focused. Solti is on top form. Besides the many exciting histrionic moments there are many refined touches too, notably in the stylish *La Traviata* excerpt, with soloists from the chorus, and the flashing fantasy of *Fuoco di gioia* from *Otello*. The Brigands in *I Masnadieri* sing of 'plunder, rape and arson' with great good humour, and the concert closes with the joyous *Sanctus* from the *Requiem* which, like the rest of the 70-minute programme, demonstrates the refined excellence of the Chicago Chorus, so splendidly prepared by their founder and director, Margaret Hillis. Full translations are included.

Although the super-bargain Naxos collection by the excellent Slovak Philharmonic Choir, trained by Marian Vach, is not as spectacularly recorded as the Decca Solti disc, the sound is very realistic, and in some ways the slightly recessed choral balance in the Bratislava Radio Concert Hall is more natural: it certainly does not lack impact and, in the *Fire chorus* from Otello, detail registers admirably. Under Oliver Dohnányi's lively direction the chorus sings with admirable fervour. *Patria oppressa* from *Macbeth* is particularly stirring, and *Va pensiero*, with a well-shaped line, is movingly projected. The *Soldiers' chorus* from *Il Trovatore* has a jaunty rhythmic feeling that is, if anything, more attractive than Solti's bolder approach. The two novelties from *La battaglia di Legnano* were well worth including, and the second, *Giuramento*, includes four impressive male soloists. The collection ends resplendently with the *Triumphal scene* from *Aida*, omitting the ballet, (which Solti includes) but with the fanfare trumpets blazing out on either side most tellingly. With a playing time of 56 minutes this is excellent value in every respect.

Villa-Lobos, Heitor (1887–1959)

Guitar concerto.
(B) *** Sony MBK 45642 [id.]. John Williams, ECO, Barenboim – RODRIGO: *Concierto de Aranjuez.****

John Williams makes the most of the finer points of this small-scale concerto, especially the rhapsodic quality of the *Andantino*, and the CBS recording is lively, full and immediate.

Magdalena.
*** Sony Dig. SK 44945 [id.]. Kaye, Rose, Esham, Gray, Hadley, O, Evans Haile.

Until this disc appeared, not many remembered that Villa-Lobos had written a Broadway musical. The promoters of *Song of Norway*, the musical based on Grieg's music, wanted to follow it up with a comparable one on South America, as being 'as far from the fjords of Norway as an author could possibly get'. They thought to use the music of Villa-Lobos, but the composer, much to everyone's surprise, took control of the project, to make it his own, rather than anyone else's, score. It is a colourful, vigorous piece, alas lacking the big tunes you really need in a musical, but full of delightful ideas. It tells the sort of story that Lehár might have chosen, only translated to South America. Sadly, in spite of an enthusiastic response from everyone, it closed on Broadway in 1948 after only eleven weeks. The present recording was prompted by a concert performance to celebrate the Villa-Lobos centenary, a splendid, well-sung account of what is aptly described as 'a musical adventure'.

Vivaldi, Antonio (1675–1741)

L'Estro armonico (12 Concertos), Op. 3.
(M) *** Ph. 426 932-2 (2) [id.]. Michelucci, Gallozzi, Cotogni, Vicari, Colandrea, Altobelli, Garatti, I Musici.

La Stravaganza (12 Concertos), Op. 4.
(M) *** Ph. 426 935-2 (2) [id.]. Ayo, Gallozzi, Altobelli, Garatti, I Musici.

Volumes 3 and 4 of the Philips Vivaldi Edition draw on recordings made (mostly in the highy suitable acoustics of La Chaux-de-Fonds, Switzerland) in 1962/3. The transfers are admirable and these CDs wear their years lightly. These are fresh and lively performances; melodies are finely drawn and there is little hint of the routine which occasionally surfaces in I Musici – and, for that matter, in Vivaldi himself. When originally issued, these two sets came into direct competition with Argo versions by the Academy of St Martin-in-the-Fields under Marriner or Iona Brown; the latter sets have crisper textures and greater imaginative enthusiasm, but these have yet to resurface on CD and, in their absence (and even alongside them), I Musici remain a good choice and are certainly thoroughly recommendable to collectors of this Edition. Maria Teresa Garatti's continuo features a chamber organ as well as harpsichord in Op. 4, to excellent effect.

6 Violin concertos, Op. 6.
(M) **(*) Ph. 426 939-2 [id.]. Pina Carmirelli, I Musici.

These concertos are not otherwise available and, while their invention is more uneven than in the named sets, their rarity will undoubtedly tempt keen Vivaldians. The 1977 performances, with Pina Carmirelli a stylish and responsive soloist, are polished and with well-judged tempi, if with no special imaginative flair. Excellent sound.

12 Concertos (for violin or oboe), Op. 7.
(M) *** Ph. 426 940-2 (2) [id.]. Accardo or Holliger (Opp. 7/1 & 7), I Musici.

The Op. 7 set is relatively unfamiliar and is certainly rewarding – indeed, much of the invention is vital and appealing. The playing of Accardo and Holliger is altogether masterly, and they have fine rapport with their fellow musicians in I Musici. The 1975 sound-balance is first class (the acoustically sympathetic venue is La Chaux-de-Fonds, Switzerland) and the two CDs are economically priced. This is among the most desirable of the boxes in the Philips Vivaldi Edition.

The Trial between harmony and invention (12 Concertos), Op. 8.
(M) **(*) Ph. 426 943-2 (2) [id.]. Felix Ayo, Garatti, I Musici.
(M) **(*) Sony M2YK 46465 (2) [id.]. Pinchas Zuckerman, Neil Black, ECO, Philip Ledger.

Op. 8 is available in comparative abundance, and Ayo's *Four Seasons* (which are the first four concertos of the set) date from as early as 1959. The recording still sounds well, though, with the warm, resonant sound disguising its age. Ayo produces lovely tone throughout and he plays as stylishly as ever, but the accompaniment is short on imaginative detail. At times the ensemble is a shade heavy-handed in the remaining concertos; but Ayo's contribution has both polish and vitality, and there is still a great deal to enjoy in these performances. The later concertos were recorded in 1961/2 and are transferred vividly.

Zuckerman's solo playing is distinguished throughout, and the ECO provide unfailingly alert and resilient accompaniments. In *Concerto No. 9 in D min.* oboist Neil Black takes the solo position and provides a welcome contrast of timbre – Vivaldi designed this concerto as optionally for violin or oboe, but it probably sounds more effective on the wind instrument. The recording throughout is lively, with a close balance for the soloists. The sound is attractive on CD and does not lack fullness.

The Four Seasons, Op. 8/1–4.
(M) *** DG 431 479-2; *431 479-4* [id.]. Schneiderhan, Lucerne Festival Strings, Baumgartner (with ALBINONI: *Adagio*; PACHELBEL: *Canon & Gigue*; PURCELL: *Chacony*; BACH: *Suite No. 3, BWV 1068: Air* ***).
(M) *** DG 431 172-2; *431 172-4* [id.]. Gidon Kremer, LSO, Abbado.
**(*) EMI Dig. CDC7 49767-2; *EL 749767-4* [id.]. Nadja Salerno-Sonnenberg, O of St Lukes.
(M) **(*) EMI CD-EMX 2009. Krzysztof Jakowicz, Polish CO, Jerzy Maksymiuk.
(M) ** Chan. CHAN 6510; *MBTD 6510* [id.]. Ronald Thomas, Bournemouth Sinf.

The Four seasons, Op. 8/1–4; Violin concertos: in E min., RV 278; in A min., RV 357 (from *La Stravazanza*), *Op. 4/4.*
*** BMG/RCA Dig. RD 60369; *RK 60369* [60369-2-RC; *60369-4-RC*]. Vladimir Spivakov, Moscow Virtuosi.

(i) *The Four Seasons, Op. 8/1–4;* (ii) *Double violin concerto in C min., RV 510; Triple concerto for 2 violins & cello in D min., Op. 3/11; Quadruple violin concerto in D, Op. 3/1.*
(M) ** EMI Dig. CDD7 63888-2 [id.]; *ET 763888-4.* Y. Menuhin, (i) with Hu Kun, Mi-Kyung Lee, Eduardo Vassallo; Camerata Lysy Gstaad, Alberto Lysy.

(i; ii) *The Four Seasons;* (iii) *Recorder concerto in C, RV 443;* (ii) *Double violin concerto in A (Echo), RV 552* (CD only: (ii) *L'Estro armonico: Concerto No. 1 in D min., Op. 3/1, RV 549;* (iii) *Cello concerto in C min., RV 401*).
(B) **(*) DG Compact Classics 413 142-2 (2); *413 142-4* [id.]. (i) Schneiderhan; (ii) Lucerne Festival Strings, Baumgartner; (iii) Linde, Emil Seiler CO, Hofmann (with: ALBINONI: *Adagio* (arr. Giazotto). CORELLI: *Concerto grosso in G min. (Christmas), Op. 6/8.* PACHELBEL: *Canon and Gigue in D* ***).

Vladimir Spivakov's highly enjoyable account of Vivaldi's *Four seasons* comes high on the list of current recommendations which include Accardo (on Philips 422 065-2; *422 065-4*), which gained a Rosette in our main volume, and the charismatic Christopher Warren-Green on Virgin Classics who offers the Albinoni *Adagio* and Pachelbel's *Canon* as encores – VCy7 91081-2; *VCy7 91081-4*). This BMG/RCA disc is made the more attractive by opening with two of Vivaldi's most imaginative concertos. The *E minor* begins with swirling strings, yet there is an immediately tender response, to make a movement of striking contrasts, while the *Largo*, with its plangent orchestral ritornello, delays the entry of the soloist until almost half-way through. The *A minor* (from *La Stravaganza*) brings a delectable central movement, where the soloist is accompanied very simply by a wistful texture of violins and violas. Both are very well played indeed by soloist and orchestra alike, as is the more famous main work, given an essentially chamber-style account, yet one not lacking its robust moments. Characterization is strong, and Spivakov's sweet, classically focused timbre is particularly melting in the sleepy sentience of the gentle episode of the first movement of *Autumn* and in the beguiling somnabulance of the central *Adagio. Winter* opens in a suitably frosty style, and the rain falls in the *Largo* with a gentle, soft quality that any Irishman would recognize.

There is plenty of vigour for the summer storms and *Spring* is tinglingly fresh, with its central movement played with contrasting gentle delicacy. Altogether this is highly successful, with the vivid, well-balanced recording achieving excellent presence against the background ambience of L'Église du Liban, Paris.

Schneiderhan's 1959 version of *The Four Seasons* re-emerges, as fresh as paint, on DG's Archiv Galleria label, now well buttressed by an excellent supporting list of Baroque ephemera. Pachelbel's *Canon*, Purcell's *Chacony* and the famous Bach *Air* all sound serenely spacious, while the Albinoni/Giazotto *Adagio* also has a certain refined dignity. These recordings are later (1966/67) and are pleasingly warm and full yet not too opulent. The *Seasons*, too, have a firmer focus than before, and Schneiderhan's timbre, pure and sweetly classical, suits Vivaldi very well indeed. The aptly chamber-scaled performance, with brisk tempi and alert orchestral playing, is full of life, with the pictorial detail emerging naturally (*Winter* as cold as you like, and the springtime shepherd's dog very much in the picture, but not too gruff) but without being overcharacterized.

On the Compact Classics tape the couplings are even more generous and include Vivaldi's ingenious *Echo concerto*, where the echo effects are not just confined to the soloists but feature the ripieno too; plus the engaging *Concerto for sopranino recorder*, RV 443, and Corelli's *Christmas concerto*. The pair of digitally remastered CDs also offer two other Vivaldi string concertos. Performances are of high quality throughout and the transfer is consistently vivid.

Kremer's version of *The Four Seasons* with Abbado is an enormously vital one, full of pictorial drama. The summer storms have never raged with more fury than here, yet the delicacy of the gentle zephyrs is matched by the sensuous somnolence of the slow movement of *Autumn*. The brilliant recording suits the music-making, and this version (see our main volume, p. 1151) now becomes competitive again at mid-price, even though it has no fill-up.

The EMI alternative from the dashing Nadja Salerno-Sonnenberg is nothing if not exciting, with dazzling, extrovert virtuosity throughout all the allegros. This does not imply a lack of repose in *Adagios* and *Largos*, while the shepherd's dog really makes its presence felt in the accompaniment of *Spring*. The summer gales rage furiously, as in the Kremer/Abbado version; like that DG record, this new EMI issue has no coupling – which, for all its strength of profile and vivid recording, makes it essentially uncompetitive in an already almost saturated market.

The performance by Krzysztof Jakowicz and the Polish Chamber Orchestra, although on a slightly smaller scale, also is not unlike the Kremer/Abbado version. It bustles with vigour, with strong dynamic contrasts and a similar balance between the fast, energetic allegros – rhythms crisp and incisive – and the gentle sostenuto of the lyrical music. However, the fast tempi bring the feeling that at times the music is driven very hard. The solo playing offers arresting bravura but is also sensitive, so that the gentle breezes and summer languor are as readily communicated as the violent storms and the icy briskness of what is plainly seen as a harsh Polish winter. The 1980 recording is bright, not edgy, but somewhat dry in timbre.

Menuhin's early (1979) digital recording of *The Four Seasons* was designed as much to provide a framework for the youthful Camerata Lysy as for its illustrious soloist, whose timbre is without much bloom above the stave and whose rhythmic control is not always stable (notably in the opening movement of *Autumn*). It is a characteristically extrovert account, robust and exuberant rather than refined. The continuo is insignificant and, while Menuhin's directness communicates readily, this hardly rates a strong recommendation in such a competitive marketplace; even if the sound has brilliant clarity, detail is not registered very subtly. Three multiple string concertos, recorded six years later, make an attractive bonus. Menuhin is a persuasive leader here, and the performances are all fresh and understanding, lively if not immaculate. The recording is rather dry and studio-ish, but not disagreeably so.

Ronald Thomas's approach on Chandos emphasizes the music's breadth and lyricism rather than its colourful scene-painting, so that the shepherd's dog barks gently and the winds blow amiably, certainly never reaching gale force. In its way this is pleasing, but there is distinct undercharacterization here, in spite of vivid recording.

La Cetra (12 Violin concertos), Op. 9.
(M) **(*) Ph. 426 946-2 (2) [id.]. Ayo, Cotogni (in Op. 9/9), Altobelli, Garatti, I Musici.

I Musici's *La Cetra* dates from 1964 and is again recorded at La Chaux-de-Fonds, which ensures a realistic and pleasing sound-balance. With Felix Ayo the principal soloist, the playing is spirited, characterful and expressively rich, though the overall effect is less individual than in the finest versions from the past. One drawback is that solo passages are given no continuo support, though Maria Teresa Garatti provides an organ continuo for the ripieno. Overall this is good value at mid-price.

6 Flute concertos, Op. 10.
(M) *** Ph. 426 949-2 [id.]. Severino Gazzelloni, I Musici.

Gazzelloni's version of the six concertos, Op. 10, was recorded in Switzerland in 1968 and the set has been in fairly continuous circulation since then. Its merits are well established, and it remains a safe recommendation for the general collector who does not seek the use of an early solo instrument. The sound is immediate and full.

6 Violin concertos, Op. 11.
(M) *** Ph. 426 950-2 [id.]. Salvatore Accardo, I Musici.

6 Violin concertos, Op. 12.
(M) *** Ph. 426 951-2 [id.]. Salvatore Accardo, I Musici.

More rare repertoire here. The Opp. 11 and 12 concertos are perhaps of uneven quality, but the best of them are very rewarding indeed and, played so superlatively by Salvatore Accardo, they are likely to beguile the most unwilling listener. Recorded in 1974/5, these two individual CDs are among the most desirable of the Philips Vivaldi Edition, and their CD transfers are among the best in the series.

(i) *Violin concertos: in A min., Op. 9/5, RV 358; in E min. (Il favorito), Op. 11/2, RV 277; in G min., Op. 12/1, RV 317; in E min. (L'amoroso), RV 271. Orchestral concertos (con molti stromenti) in C, RV 558; in G min., RV 576.*
(M) *** Ph. 432 281-2; *431 281-4* [id.]. (i) Arthur Grumiaux; Dresden State O (members), Vittorio Negri.

Arthur Grumiaux never disappoints, and this is one of the most attractive collections of Vivaldi's *Violin concertos* in the catalogue. The *G minor*, RV 317, is a particularly fine work and brings a highly imaginative response; and his playing is hardly less engaging in *L'amoroso*, full of lightness and grace. Negri accompanies sympathetically, and the 1973 sound is excellent though fuller in texture than we would expect today. But the solo playing offers endless pleasure. What makes this reissue doubly attractive is the inclusion of the orchestral concertos *con molti stromenti*. The *G minor* work was dedicated to its Dresden performers, though not the present group! Its piquant textures bring oboe and violin soloists, with a ripieno including 2 flutes, 2 oboes, bassoon and strings. RV 558 is aurally even more fascinating, with its delicacy of scoring for flutes, theorbos, mandolins, salmò, 2 violins *in tromba marina*, cello and strings. The performances are full of life and colour, and the 1970 recording is excellent.

Violin concertos: in D min. (Senza cantin), RV 243; in E (Il Riposo), RV 270; in E min. (Il Favorito), RV 277; in F (Per la solennità di San Lorenzo), RV 286.
(B) **(*) CfP Dig. CD-CFP 4536; *TC-CFP 4536.* Accardo, I Solisti delle Settimane Musicali Internazionali di Napoli.

Salvatore Accardo plays each of the four concertos on this record on a different instrument from the collection of the Palazzo Communale, Cremona. He plays the *E major, Il Riposo*, on the Niccolo Amati, *Il Favorito* on the Cremonose of 1715, the darker-hued *Concerto senza cantin* ('without using the E string') on the Guarnieri del Gesù, and the *Concerto per la solennità di San Lorenzo* on the Andrea Amati of Charles IX of France. But this is more than a record for violin specialists: it offers playing of the highest order by one of the finest violinists of our time. Accardo himself directs the excellent ensemble, and the EMI recording is very vivid and clear but also rather dry in the manner of some early digital recordings. We would expect a warmer, more ample string sound today. These are distinguished performances, but not all ears will respond to the relative lack of bloom.

MISCELLANEOUS CONCERTO COLLECTIONS

Bassoon concerto in B flat, RV 502; Cello concerto in C min., RV 401; Oboe concerto in C, RV 447; Double trumpet concerto in C, RV 537. L'Estro armonico: Double violin concerto in A min., RV 522; Quadruple violin concerto in B min., RV 580; Op. 3/8 & 10. Triple violin concerto in F, RV 551.
*** Virgin Dig. VC7 91167-2; *VC7 91167-4* [id.]. Soloists, LCO, Christopher Warren-Green.

Christopher Warren-Green and his LCO seldom disappoint and this generous (75 minutes) collection, offering seven of Vivaldi's most appealing concertos, is another fine example of their vividly spontaneous music-making. The record opens brightly with the *Double trumpet concerto* and, in the works for oboe and bassoon, both soloists (Gordon Hunt and Merrick Alexander respectively) play with much character and elegance and, in the case of the latter, also a touch of humour. The lovely slow movement of the *C minor Cello concerto* is warmly sympathic on Andrew Schulman's bow. For some reason a continuo is used only in the two woodwind concertos. The harpsichord swirls are rather effective in the first movement of the *Oboe concerto* and in the *Largo* of the *Bassoon concerto* a chamber organ piquantly introduces the solo entry. The excerpts from *L'Estro armonico* are gleamingly strong and expressive, and again one senses an added energy, possibly deriving from the musicians standing while they play. Excellent recording, made in All Saints', Petersham, yet with the resonance never becoming oppressive.

L'Estro armonico: Quadruple violin concerto in D; Double violin concerto in D min., Op. 3/1 & 11. Bassoon concerto in E min., RV 484; Flute concerto in G min. (La notte), Op. 10/2; Double mandolin concerto in G, RV 532; Oboe concerto in B flat, RV 548; Orchestral concerto (con molti stromenti) in C, RV 558; Concerto for strings in G (Alla rustica), RV 151.
(M) *** DG Dig. 431 710-2; *431 710-4* [id.]. Soloists, E. Concert, Trevor Pinnock.

This DG Archiv digital reissue is impressive for quantity as well as quality: eight concertos and 70 minutes must be some kind of record for a single Vivaldi disc! The collection of very varied works shows Pinnock and the English Concert at their liveliest and most refreshing, although not always so strong on charm. (The account of the *Bassoon concerto* is perhaps an unintentional exception, for the solo timbre has a certain bovine character.) The *Concerto for four Violins* is very lithe, and throughout the concert the solo playing is predictably expert. The *Orchestral concerto* involves an astonishing array of instruments; it is also available as listed above, played on modern instruments by the Dresden orchestra, but authenticists will prefer the spicier timbres displayed here. Excellent recording, giving a most realistic impression on CD.

L'Estro armonico: Quadruple violin concerto in D, Op. 3/1, RV 549; Flute concerto in D (Il gardellino), Op. 10/3, RV 428; Oboe concerto in C, RV 446; Double concerto in G for oboe & bassooon, RV 545; Concerto for strings in B flat, RV 166; Viola d'amore concerto in D, RV 392; Double concerto in F for violin, organ and strings, RV 542.
(M) *** Ph. Dig. 432 059-2; *432 059-4* [id.]. Carmirelli, Nicolet, Holliger, Thunemann, Paris, Perez, Garatti, I Musici.

A generous and well-planned collection, drawn from different sources but given a convincing overall relationship by all being digitally recorded in the excellent acoustics of La Chaux-de-Fonds, Switzerland. With distinguished names among the soloists the performances are predictably fresh, and they all show Vivaldi's amazing fecundity of invention appealingly, not least the miniature *Concerto for strings and continuo*. The work for four violins is also very successful, and Holliger and Thunemann are as expressively appealing as they are nimble. The only slight reservation is about Aurèle Nicolet's bird imitations in *Il gardellino*, engaging enough, but stylistically somewhat over the top.

L'Estro armonico: Quadruple violin concerto in B min., Op. 3/10, RV 580; La Stravaganza: Violin concerto in B flat, Op. 4/1; Cello concerto in C min., RV 401; Double horn concerto in F, RV 539; Concerto in F for 2 oboes, bassoon, 2 horns and violin, RV 569; Double trumpet concerto in C, RV 537.
(M) *** Decca 425 721-2; *425 721-4* [id.]. ASMF, Marriner.

Another excellent collection from the considerable array of Vivaldi concertos recorded by Marriner and his ASMF (on modern instruments) between 1965 and 1977. The soloists are all distinguished, offering playing that is constantly alert, finely articulated and full of life and imagination. The special interest here is that Neville Marriner himself is the first of four equals in the concerto from *L'Estro armonico*. Accompaniments are predictably stylish, and the recordings still sound admirably fresh in their CD transfers, with only a touch of shrillness on the *Double trumpet concerto*.

(i) *The Trial between harmony and invention: Violin concertos Nos. 5 in E flat (La tempesta di mare), RV 253; 6 in C (Il piacere), RV 180, Op. 8/5–6;* (ii) *Bassoon concertos: in C, RV 472; in C min., RV 480; in A min., RV 498; in B flat, RV 504.*
(M) *** Chan. CHAN 6529 [id.]. (i) Ronald Thomas, Bournemouth Sinf.; (ii) Robert Thompson, L. Mozart Players, Ledger.

The two concertos included here from *The Trial between harmony and invention* were among the best of the complete set recorded by Ronald Thomas in 1980. The use of modern instruments does not preclude a keen sense of style, and the balance is convincing. The bassoonist Robert Thompson turns a genial eye on his four concertos. He is rather forwardly projected but the performances are direct and personable and, like the sound, agreeably fresh, among the most attractive accounts of Vivaldi's bassoon concertos available on CD. An enjoyable collection.

Concerto for strings in D min., RV 129; Double violin concerto in A (Echo), RV 522; Double concerto in B flat for violin and cello, RV 547; Concerto for 2 violins and 2 cellos in D, RV 564; Sonata a quattro in E flat, RV 130.
(B) ** Ph. 432 678-2 [id.]. Soloists, I Musici.

This not particularly generous bargain collection (49 minutes) is intended as a sampler for the Philips Vivaldi Edition. In the event, it is not a very tempting collection. By far the most attractive item is the *Concerto in A major con violino principale con altro violino per eco in lontana*, where Vivaldi's ingeniously devised echo effects are pleasingly brought off. Elsewhere, however, although all the performances are polished, there is at times an element of routine.

CHAMBER MUSIC

12 Sonatas for 2 violins & continuo, Op. 1.
(M) *** Ph. 426 926-2 (2) [id.]. Accardo, Gulli, Canino, De Saram.

12 Violin sonatas, Op. 2.
(M) *** Ph. 426 929-2 (2) [id.]. Accardo, Canino, De Saram.

Besides offering an almost overwhelming commemoration of the bicentennial of Mozart's death, Philips now remind us that 1991 also marks 250 years since the death of Vivaldi. Drawing on a distinguished series of analogue recordings, originally published in 1978 to commemorate the 300th anniversary of the Italian composer's birth, this company now offers a mid-priced Vivaldi Edition, containing everything published from Op. 1 to Op. 12. These 19 CDs are available complete in a sturdy slip-case (426 925-2) or in a dozen separate issues. For the collector satiated by too many recordings of *The Four Seasons*, the two boxes offering the *Violin sonatas* should provide an admirable place to start. These sonatas are not otherwise obtainable – and in any case it is unlikely that Salvatore Accardo's performances, so ably supported by Bruno Canino and Rohan de Saram (and in Op. 1 by Franco Gulli), could be surpassed in terms of sympathetic fluency, musicianship and sheer beauty of tone. Textures are fuller and warmer than would be the case with original instruments, yet the recording balance brings admirable transparency, with the harpsichord coming through naturally. The shadow of Corelli still hangs over the earlier set, yet slow movements often have those specially memorable Vivaldian harmonic inflexions (sample the *Adagio* third movement of Op. 1/1, the *Grave* introduction of Op. 1/2 or the Adagio of the last of the set, Op. 1/6. The dance movements are genially vigorous and the invention is remarkable pleasing and fresh. Most of the sonatas in Op. 1 have four or five quite short movements, whereas in Op. 2 there are three or four, usually treating the material more ambitiously, over a longer span. Collectors will find unexpected rewards in both sets, and the CD transfer of recordings made in 1977 are completely natural yet vivid in Philips's best manner.

6 Violin sonatas, Op. 5.
(M) **(*) Ph. 426 938-2 [id.]. Accardo, Gazeau (in Op. 5/5–6), Canino, De Saram.

Warm, mellifluous playing from Salvatore Accardo in the Op. 5 *Sonatas* of 1716–17, four being solo works with continuo and the remainder *Trio sonatas*. The music is not quite as interesting or inventive as Opp. 1 and 2, but those collecting this Edition will still find much that is rewarding. The 1977 sound is well up to the excellent standard of this series.

VOCAL MUSIC

Gloria in D, RV 589; Kyrie in G min., RV 587.
(M) *** DG 427 142-2 [id.]. Regensburg Cathedral Ch., V. Capella Academica, Schneidt – BACH: *Motets.****

In the superb setting of the *Kyrie*, and the well-known *Gloria*, Schneidt with his fresh-toned Regensburg Choir (the celebrated Domspatzen, 'cathedral sparrows') brings out what may seem a surprising weight for an 'authentic' performance. Alongside the brilliant numbers in both these works, one can find music of Bach-like intensity. The use of semi-chorus for solo numbers is more questionable, but no one hearing these performances is likely to dismiss the music as trivial. The excellent 1977 recordings have been transferred to CD most effectively, with three favourite Bach motets now added as a bonus.

(i) *Gloria in D, RV 589;* (ii) *Magnificat, RV 610.*
(M) **(*) Decca 425 724-2; *425 724-4* [id.]. (i) Vaughan, J. Baker; (ii) Castle, Cockerham, King; King's College Ch., ASMF; (i) Willcocks; (ii) Ledger – PERGOLESI: *Magnificat.***(*)

The Willcocks version of the *Gloria* uses comparatively small forces and, save for the occasional trace of preciosity, it is very stylish. It has excellent soloists and is very well recorded, though some might feel that the exaggerated consonants are tiresome. Ledger also offers the small-scale setting of the *Magnificat* and opts for boys' voices in the solos such as the beautiful duet, *Esurientes*; though the singers are taxed by ornamentation, the result has all the accustomed beauty of this choir's recordings. Excellent transfers.

Juditha triumphans (oratorio) complete.
(M) *** Ph. 426 955-2 (2) [id.]. Finnilä, Springer, Hamari, Ameling, Burmeister, Berlin Radio Soloists Ch. & CO, Negri.

Issued as an adjunct to the Philips Vivaldi Edition, this excellent 1974 recording re-emerges vividly in its CD format. Described as a 'military' oratorio, *Juditha triumphans* demonstrates its martial bravado at the very start, as exhilarating a passage as you will find in the whole of Vivaldi. The vigorous choruses stand as cornerstones of commentary in a structure which, following convention, comes close to operatic form, with recitatives providing the narrative between formal *da capo* arias. Though Vivaldi fell into routine invention at times, the wonder is that so much of this music is so vividly alive, telling the story from the Apocrypha of Judith cutting off the head of the enemy general, Holofernes. As the cast-list will suggest, this Philips version rightly gives the castrato roles to women, with a generally stylish line-up of singers. It is a pity that the role of Judith is taken by one of the less interesting singers, Birgit Finnilä, and that Elly Ameling takes only a servant's role, though that is one which demands more brilliant technique than any. Overall, however, this is a considerable success.

Wagner, Richard (1813–83)

Siegfried idyll.
(M) *** Decca 430 247-2 (2) [id.]. VPO, Solti – MAHLER: *Symphony No. 9.***

So full is the sound, recorded by John Culshaw in the Sofiensaal in 1965, that in Solti's performance of the *Siegfried idyll* in its original chamber scoring one is never conscious of any asceticism. The playing is similarly warm and committed; only in the central climax does one sense the need for a larger body of strings, yet the reading as a whole is so compelling as to confound criticism.

(i) *Siegfried idyll;* (ii) *Der fliegende Holländer: Overture; Lohengrin:* (i) *Prelude to Act I;* (iii) *Bridal Chorus;* (i) *Die Meistersinger: Prelude;* (iv) *Tannhäuser: Overture;* (i) *Tristan und Isolde: Prelude and Liebestod;* (v) *Die Walküre: Ride of the Valkyries* (CD only: (vi) *Parsifal: Prelude and Good Friday music*).
(B) **(*) DG Compact Classics 413 849-2 (2); *413 849-4* [id.]. (i) BPO, Kubelik; (ii) Bayreuth Festival O, Boehm; (iii) Bayreuth Festival Ch., Pitz; (iv) cond. Gerdes; (v) cond. Karajan.

This Wagner Compact Classics concert centres on some fine performances made in 1963 by Kubelik and the Berlin Philharmonic, including the *Siegfried idyll.* Karajan contributes a lively *Ride of the Valkyries* (taken from his complete *Die Walküre*); Gerdes's *Tannhäuser overture* also comes from his (deleted) complete set; while the *Bridal chorus* from *Lohengrin* has a Bayreuth hallmark although in fact recorded in the studio. The sound is generally very good; only the opening *Flying Dutchman overture*, actually made at Bayreuth under Boehm, sounds slightly less refined than the rest of the concert. To fill out the pair of digitally remastered CDs, DG have added Jochum's inspirational account of the *Parsifal Good Friday* music, which was a famous early highlight of the stereo LP catalogue. The recording dates from 1958 but still sounds spacious and full in the present transfer.

Der fliegende Holländer: Overture; Lohengrin: Prelude to Act I; Die Meistersinger: Prelude to Act I; Tannhäuser: Overture; Tristan und Isolde: Prelude and Liebestod.
** Ph. Dig. 426 271-2 [id.]. BPO, Seiji Ozawa.

The Berlin Philharmonic are completely at home in this repertoire, but Ozawa obviously is not, and his control is uneven. The opening of the *Lohengrin Prelude* is texturally beautiful but relatively tensionless, and the adrenalin suddenly begins to flow just before the climax. Similarly the central section of *Die Meistersinger* is without much grip. The actual orchestral playing is first class, of course, and the *Prelude* to *Tristan and Isolde* cannot fail to make an effect on the listener when the recording is expansive and rich-textured. But there are many more powerful versions of this music listed in our main volume.

Der fliegende Holländer: Overture. Lohengrin: Prelude to Act III. Die Meistersinger: Preludes to Acts I & III. Tannhäuser: Overture and Venusberg music. Die Walküre: Ride of the Valkyries.
(M) ** EMI Dig. CD-EMX 2167; *TC-EMX 2167.* LPO, Mark Elder.

Direct, well-played but unmemorable performances, brightly but not particularly richly recorded. The *Ride of the Valkyries* comes off best, but it seems curious to include the *Venusberg music* from *Tannhäuser* without the chorus.

Overtures: Der fliegende Holländer; Die Meistersinger; Tannhäuser (original version). *Tristan und Isolde: Prelude and Liebestod.*
(M) **(*) Decca 430 448-2; *430 448-4* [id.]. Chicago SO, Solti.

A quite attractive collection of Wagner overtures, very well played. Except for the *Flying Dutchman overture*, these are newly made recordings, not taken from Solti's complete opera sets. So this is the self-contained *Tannhäuser overture* from the Dresden version, and the *Liebestod* comes in the purely orchestral version. Perhaps surprisingly, comparison between Solti in Chicago and Solti in Vienna shows him warmer in America. The CD has been digitally remastered and emphasizes the different recording balances: *Fliegende Holländer* very brightly lit, *Die Meistersinger* (recorded in Illinois) richer and mellower. The Medinah Temple, Chicago, where the other items were recorded, seems here to produce somewhat variable results.

OPERA

Most of the finest Wagner recordings are not recent, with Solti's unsurpassed account of *The Ring* going back to the earliest days of stereo, yet continuing to astonish by the sheer vividness of its sound. One can now buy the complete Solti *Ring* on 15 mid-priced Decca CDs (414 100-2) and, if you want this Rosetted set – one of the great achievements of the gramophone – there is no more economical way of obtaining it. It is discussed, alongside all the other major Wagner recordings, in our main volume, and we now detail our other primary recommendations for the remaining operas. Nelsson's outstanding version of *Der fliegende Holländer*, with a cast more consistent than any, derives from the 1985 Bayreuth Festival (Philips 416 300-2); Solti's version of *Lohengrin* is another of the crowning glories of his long recording career, with Jessye Norman and Domingo giving splendid support, while the Vienna Philharmonic Orchestra play radiantly (Decca 421 053-2). For *Parsifal* we turn to Karajan and his intensely beautiful Berlin recording which balances the opera's musical and spiritual elements with the greatest imaginative refinement. Kurt Moll and José van Dam both make distinguished contributions, and Dunja Vejzovic is a vibrant, sensuous Kundry. Only Peter Hofmann leaves a small measure of disappointment as Parsifal, but his natural tone is admirably suited to the part. Like Solti's *Lohengrin*, this has a justly deserved Rosette (DG 413 347-2). On balance, Sinopoli is first choice for *Tannhäuser*, using the Paris score and making it his most passionately committed opera recording yet, warmer and more flexible than Solti's Decca version. Placido Domingo produces sounds of great power as well as much beauty, Agnes Baltsa is a seductive Venus, while Cheryl Studer gives a most sensitive portrayal of Elisabeth; Andras Schmidt is a noble Wolfram and Matti Salminen a superb Landgrave, to make this a fine entertainment (DG 427 625-2). We return to Karajan for *Tristan und Isolde*, an essentially sensual performance of Wagner's masterpiece, with Dernesch a seductively feminine Isolde. Jon Vickers matches her in what is arguably his finest performance on record. This is on four CDs (against three for Boehm's competing 1966 Bayreuth performance) but they are offered at medium price (EMI CMS7 69319-2 [Angel CDMD 69319]).

Die Meistersinger von Nürnberg (complete).

(M) **(*) Ph. 432 573-2 (4) [id.]. Ridderbusch, Bode, Sotin, Hirte, Cox, Stricker, (1974) Bayreuth Festival Ch. & O, Varviso.

Die Meistersinger is an opera which presents serious problems for an engineer intent on recording it at a live performance. Not only do the big crowd scenes, with their plentiful movement, bring obtrusive stage noises; the sheer length of the work means that, by Act III, even the most stalwart singer is flagging. It follows that the Bayreuth performance, recorded during the Festival of 1974, is flawed; but the Swiss conductor Silvio Varviso still proves the most persuasive Wagnerian, one who inspires the authentic ebb and flow of tension, who builds up Wagner's scenes concentratedly over the longest span, and who revels in the lyricism and textural beauty of the score. It is not a lightweight reading and, with one exception, the singing is very enjoyable indeed, with Karl Ridderbusch a firmly resonant Sachs and the other Masters, headed by Klaus Hirte as Beckmesser and Hans Sotin as Pogner, really singing their parts. Jean Cox is a strenuous Walther, understandably falling short towards the end; Hannelore Bode as Eva brings the one serious disappointment but she is firmer here than on Solti's later set. For all the variability, the recording, retaining its atmosphere in the CD transfer, gives enjoyment, even if the stage noises are the more noticeable. First choice for this opera remains with Jochum, a performance which, more than any, captures the light and shade of Wagner's most warmly approachable score, its humour and tenderness as well as its strength. The cast is the most consistent yet assembled on record. Though Caterina Ligendza's big soprano is a little ungainly for Eva, it is an appealing performance and the choice of Domingo for Walther is inspired. However, the key to the set is the searching and highly individual Sachs of Fischer-Dieskau. On CD there is a lovely bloom on the whole sound (DG 415 278-2).

Der Ring des Nibelungen (complete).
(M) (***) EMI mono CZS7 67123-2 (13) [Ang. CDZM 67123]. Suthaus, Mödl, Frantz, Patzak, Neidlinger, Windgassen, Konetzni, Streich, Jurinac, Frick, RAI Ch. & Rome SO, Furtwängler.

When in 1972 EMI first transferred the Italian Radio tapes of Furtwängler's studio performances of 1953, the sound was disagreeably harsh, making sustained listening unpleasant. In this digital transfer, the boxiness of the studio sound and the closeness of the voices still take away some of the unique Furtwängler glow in Wagner, but the sound is acceptable and actually benefits in some ways from extra clarity. Each Act was performed on a separate day, giving the advantage of continuous performance but with closer preparation than would otherwise have been possible. Furtwängler gives each opera a commanding sense of unity, musically and dramatically, with hand-picked casts including Martha Mödl as a formidable Brünnhilde, Ferdinand Frantz a firm-voiced Wotan and Ludwig Suthaus (Tristan in Furtwängler's recording) a reliable Siegfried. In smaller roles you have stars like Wolfgang Windgassen, Julius Patzak, Rita Streich, Sena Jurinac and Gottlob Frick.

Siegfried (complete, in English).
(M) *** EMI CMS7 63595-2 (4). Remedios, Hunter, Bailey, Dempsey, Hammond-Stroud, Grant, Collins, London, Sadler's Wells Op. O, Goodall.

Compounded from three live performances at the Coliseum, this magnificent set gives a superb sense of dramatic realism. More tellingly than in almost any other Wagner opera recording, Goodall's spacious direction here conveys the genuine dramatic crunch that gives the experience of hearing Wagner in the opera house its unique power, its overwhelming force. In the *Prelude* there are intrusive audience noises, and towards the end the Sadler's Wells violins have one or two shaky moments, but this is unmistakably a great interpretation caught on the wing. Remedios, more than any rival on record, conveys not only heroic strength but clear-ringing youthfulness, caressing the ear as well as exciting it. Norman Bailey makes a magnificently noble Wanderer, steady of tone, and Gregory Dempsey is a characterful Mime, even if his deliberate whining tone is not well caught on record. The sound is superbly realistic, even making no allowances for the conditions. Lovers of opera in English should grasp the opportunity of hearing this unique set. The transfer is remarkably vivid and detailed, kind to the voices and with a natural presence so that the words are clear, yet there is no edge or exaggeration of consonants. This is the first of Goodall's *Ring* cycle to be transferred to CD and the orchestral recording is drier than in the others of the series: the brass sound brassier, less rounded than in *The Twilight of the Gods* for instance, but not less effective. The strings, however, have plenty of body and bloom.

Tannhäuser (Paris version): highlights.
*** DG Dig. 429 789-2 [id.] (from recording with Domingo, Studer, Baltsa, Salminen, Schmidt, cond. Sinopoli).

Those requiring highlights from *Tannhäuser* could hardly do better than this. The selection (which includes the *Overture* and *Venusberg scene*) plays for 76 minutes and makes an excellent sampler of our first choice among available complete recordings. Domingo is in noble voice in the title-role, well supported by Cheryl Studer (Elisabeth), Andras Schmidt as Wolfram, and Matti Salminen as a superb Landgrave. Sinopoli directs with passionate commitment, and the studio sound is first class.

The Valkyrie (complete; in English).
(M) *** EMI CMS7 63918-2 (4). Hunter, Remedios, Curphey, Bailey, Grant, Howard, E. Nat. Op. Ch. & O, Goodall.

Like *Siegfried*, this was recorded live at the Coliseum and, with minor reservations, it fills the bill splendidly for those who want to enjoy the *Ring* cycle in English. With the voices balanced a little more closely than in *Siegfried*, the words of Andrew Porter's translation are a degree clearer but the atmosphere is less vivid. The glory of the performance lies not just in Goodall's spacious direction but in the magnificent Wotan of Norman Bailey, noble in the broadest span but very human in his illumination of detail. Rita Hunter sings nobly too, and though she is not as commanding as Nilsson in the Solti cycle she is often more lyrically tender. Alberto Remedios as Siegmund is more taxed than he was as Siegfried in the later opera (lower tessituras are not quite so comfortable for him) but his sweetly ringing top register is superb. If others, such as Ann Howard as Fricka, are not always treated kindly by the microphone, the total dramatic compulsion is irresistible. The CD transfer increases the sense of presence and at the same time confirms the relative lack of sumptuousness

Die Walküre: Act III (complete).
(M) *** Decca 425 986-2 [id.]. Flagstad, Edelmann, Schech, VPO, Solti.

This recording was made in 1957. Flagstad came out of retirement to make it, and Decca put us eternally in their debt for urging her to do so. She sings radiantly. This great artist seemed to have acquired an extra wisdom and an extra maturity in interpretation in her period away from the stage. The meticulousness needed in the recording studio obviously brought out all her finest qualities, and there is no more than a touch of hardness on some of the top notes to show that the voice was no longer as young as it had been. Edelmann is not the ideal Wotan but he has a particularly well focused voice, and when he sings straight, without sliding up or sitting under the note, the result is superb and he is never wobbly. But it is Solti's conducting that prevents any slight blemishes from mattering. His rethinking of the score means that time and time again, at particularly dramatic points, one finds that the increased excitement engendered is merely the result of a literal following of all Wagner's markings. Not surprisingly, the recording too is remarkably vivid, anticipating the excellence of the great *Ring* project which was to follow.

Die Walküre: Act III: *Wotan's farewell.*
(M) **(*) EMI CMS7 63835-2 (2). Norman Bailey, New Philh. O, Klemperer – BRUCKNER: *Symphony No. 8* **; HINDEMITH: *Nobilissima visione*: suite.(**)

In places in *Wotan's farewell* there is almost a hint of self-parody in Klemperer's reading with its measured tempi and gruff manner, despite superb singing from Norman

Bailey. Nevertheless, with thrilling orchestral playing and splendid 1970 recording, this remains very dramatic indeed.

'Wagner gala': Lohengrin: Prelude to Act III. Rienzi: Overture. Excerpts from: *Der fliegende Holländer; Lohengrin; Die Meistersinger; Rienzi; Tannhäuser; Tristan und Isolde; Die Walküre.*
(M) **(*) Decca 421 877-2; *421 877-4* [id.]. London; G. Jones; J. King; Flagstad; Krause; Nilsson; VPO, Solti or Stein.

A generous and vivid concert (74 minutes) but hardly a gala occasion. It was a happy idea to open the programme with James King's appealing account of Rienzi's *Prayer*, based on the gorgeous lyrical tune which makes us all remember the *Overture*. He also sings Walther's *Prize song* from *Die Meistersinger* nobly. Other highlights include Kirsten Flagstad in *Die Männer Sippe* from *Die Walküre* and *Elsa's dream* from *Lohengrin*, and Birgit Nilsson's comparatively restrained, early 1960s account of the *Tristan Liebestod*, spaciously recorded with Knappertsbusch, before she undertook the complete set.

Walton, William (1902–83)

(i; ii) *Cello concerto;* (ii) *Improvisations on an impromptu of Benjamin Britten; Partita for orchestra;* (i) *Passacaglia for solo cello.*
*** Chan. Dig. CHAN 8959; *ABTD 1551* [id.]. (i) Rafael Wallfisch; (ii) LPO, Bryden Thomson.

Rafael Wallfisch was a pupil of Piatigorsky when the great Russian cellist was originally studying the concerto Walton wrote for him. Though Wallfisch's reading is individual, not in any way an imitation of Piatigorsky's, that experience plainly gave him an early insight. He may not be as powerful as Yo-Yo Ma (Sony MK 39541) or Tortelier (EMI CDM7 63020-2) on rival discs, and he is more clearly stretched than Yo-Yo Ma in the jagged central scherzo; but his playing is just as searching and passionate, with the finale even bringing echoes of Bloch's *Schelomo*. With its all-Walton coupling, this is plainly the version to recommend to those primarily concerned with the composer rather than with the cello. With his rich, even tone, Wallfisch is just as warm and purposeful in the solo *Passacaglia* Walton wrote at the end of his life for Rostropovich, while Thomson relishes the vivid orchestral colours in both the *Improvisations*, here wider-ranging in expression than usual, and the brilliant *Partita*. Excellent Chandos sound.

Film music: *The Battle of Britain (suite); Escape me never (suite); The First of the Few: Spitfire prelude and fugue; Three Sisters; A Wartime sketchbook.*
*** Chan. Dig. CHAN 8870; *ABTD 1485* [id.]. ASMF, Marriner.

This heartwarming record gathers together many of the fragments of film music that constituted what Walton regarded as his 'war work'. It occupied him so completely at the time that he produced no major concert piece over that period. *The Spitfire prelude and fugue*, from *The First of the Few*, was immediately turned into a highly successful concert-piece, but we owe it to Christopher Palmer that there is the 'Wartime Sketchbook', drawing material from three of the wartime films, plus scraps that Colin Matthews did not use in the suite from the much later *Battle of Britain* film music. On this showing Walton was at least the equal of Elgar in writing patriotic march tunes, repeatedly matching the achievement of the two well-known coronation marches, not least in the stirring theme from the credits of the film, *Went the day well.* The brief suite from the music for Olivier's film of Chekhov's *The Three Sisters*, from much later, brings more than one setting of the *Tsar's Hymn* and a charming imitation of *Swan Lake*. Earliest on the disc is *Escape me never*, the first of Walton's film-scores, written in 1935 in a more popular idiom; but the war-inspired music is what this delightful disc is really about. Marriner and the Academy give richly idiomatic performances, full of panache, of pieces ripe for performance at the Last Night of the Proms. Aptly opulent recording.

(i) *Viola concerto;* (ii) *Sinfonia concertante.*
(M) (***) EMI mono CDH7 63828-2 [id.]. (i) William Primrose, Philh. O; (ii) Phyllis Sellick, CBSO; composer – VAUGHAN WILLIAMS: *Violin concerto* etc.(***)

In the inter-war period William Primrose set new standards of virtuosity on the viola and here gives a formidable account of the greatest of viola concertos, with the composer conducting. Recorded in 1946, within weeks of the other viola work on the disc, Vaughan Williams's *Flos campi*, the mono sound fails to capture a genuine pianissimo, but otherwise the combination of romantic warmth tempered by classical restraint provides a lesson to some more recent interpreters. Unlike them, Primrose adopts an aptly flowing speed for the opening *Andante comodo*, refusing to sentimentalize it. The scherzo is phenomenally fast, sometimes sounding breathless, but the virtuosity is astonishing; and the spiky humour of the finale is delightfully pointed, leading to a yearning account of the epilogue. The *Sinfonia concertante* is another historic recording well deserving study, made in 1945, the first ever of this work. It is also a superb memento of a great pianist too little heard on record. Phyllis Sellick, in piano writing that is often ungrateful to the player, readily matches the composer-conductor in the thrusting urgency and romantic power of the performance. More than any more recent account it reveals the piece, Walton's first big symphonic work (completed in 1927), as a clear, warm-hearted precursor of the much better-known *Viola concerto* of two years later. The brilliant young *enfant terrible* who had written *Façade* was already a romantic. Excellent transfers of both concertos, generously coupled with the two Vaughan Williams works.

Crown Imperial (concert band version).
(M) *** Mercury 432 009-2 [id.]. Eastman Wind Ens., Fennell – BENNETT: *Symphonic songs*; HOLST: *Hammersmith*; JACOB: *William Byrd suite.*

Paced with dignity, yet with joyously crisp articulation, and with an organ added at the end to give an extra touch of grandiloquence, Fennell's performance is part of a highly recommendable collection of music for concert band. The Mercury sound, from the late 1950s, remains in the demonstration bracket.

Façade (complete, including *Façade 2*).
**(*) Chan. Dig. CHAN 8869; *ABTD 1484* [id.]. Lady Susana Walton, Richard Baker, City of L. Sinfonia (members), Richard Hickox.

Susana Walton, widow of the composer, makes a bitingly characterful reciter, matching with her distinctive accent – she was born in Argentina – the exoticry of many numbers. Richard Baker, phenomenally precise and agile in enunciating the Sitwell poems, makes the perfect foil, and Hickox secures colourful and lively playing from members of the City of London Sinfonia, who relish in particular the jazzy inflexions. *Façade 2* consists of a number of poems, beyond the definitive series of 21, which for various reasons, at different stages of the work's emergence in the 1920s, were omitted. Some of them were early inspirations and others overlapped with those in the *Façade* entertainment as we know it. All of them are fun and make an apt if not very generous coupling for the regular sequence. Warm sound, rather too reverberant for so intimate a work.

Façade: suites 1 & 2.
*** Hyp. Dig. CDA 66436; *KA 66436* [id.]. E. N. Philh. O, Lloyd-Jones – BLISS: *Checkmate* ***; LAMBERT: *Horoscope.**** ❀

Brilliantly witty and humorous performances of the two orchestral suites which Walton himself fashioned from his 'Entertainment'. This is music which, with its outrageous quotations, can make one chuckle out loud. Moreover it offers, to quote Constant Lambert, 'one good tune after another', all scored with wonderful felicity. The playing here could hardly be bettered, and the recording is in the demonstration bracket with its natural presence and bloom.

Henry V (film music): *A Shakespeare scenario* (arr. Christopher Palmer).
*** Chan. Dig. CHAN 8892; *ABTD 1503* [id.]. Christopher Plummer (nar.), Westminster Cathedral Ch., ASMF, Marriner.

Few film-scores can match Walton's for the Olivier film of *Henry V* in its range and imagination. Christopher Palmer has here managed to include over 90 per cent of the music Walton wrote for the film, omitting little more than disconnected fragments. What he has devised is a sequence of eight substantial sections, a 'Shakespeare scenario' with speeches and narrations interpolated, using discreetly edited texts, the whole lasting just over an hour. The most controversial change is to 'borrow' the first section of the march which Walton wrote much later for a projected television series on Churchill's *History of the English-Speaking Peoples*; otherwise, the chorus's call to arms, *Now all the youth of England is on fire*, would have had no music to introduce it. On textual points, such as the sources of some of the themes, Palmer's notes are a model of scholarship; as an appendix, three short pieces are included which Walton quoted in his score. Sir Neville Marriner caps even his previous recordings in this series, with the Academy producing heartfelt playing and singing in sumptuous sound. The only reservation is over the very slow speed for the *Passacaglia*, illustrating Falstaff's death. Christopher Plummer makes an excellent substitute for Olivier, unselfconsciously adopting a comparably grand style.

Film music: *Macbeth: Fanfare & march. Major Barbara (suite); Richard III (Shakespeare scenario).*
*** Chan. Dig. CHAN 8841; *ABTD 1460* [id.]. Sir John Gielgud (nar.), ASMF, Marriner.

The music for *Richard III* remains well enough known, thanks to the currency both of the film and of a video version; but this *Shakespeare scenario* in ten movements provides a different perspective. It may not quite rival *Henry V* in its scope and imagination – with Bosworth Field hardly a match for Agincourt – but this is a much meatier offering than the music for the other Olivier/Shakespeare film, *Hamlet*. Disappointingly, Sir John Gielgud underplays Richard III's great 'Now is the winter of our discontent' speech, but working to the underlying music – much of it eliminated in the film – may have cramped his style. The performance generally has all the panache one could wish for, leading up to the return of the grand Henry Tudor theme at the end. The six-minute piece, based on Walton's music for Gielgud's wartime production of *Macbeth*, is much rarer and very valuable too, anticipating in its Elizabethan dance-music the *Henry V* film-score. *Major Barbara* (dating from a year earlier, 1941) also brings vintage Walton material. The brazen opening sequence has hints of *Onward, Christian soldiers* and, as in *Belshazzar's Feast*, an anvil is prominent in the factory sequence, leading to carefree variations on *Boys and girls come out to play*. A love scene leads to a grand finale. Marriner and the Academy give performances just as ripely committed as in their previous discs in the series, helped by sonorous Chandos sound.

The Quest (ballet): complete; *The Wise Virgins* (ballet): suite.
*** Chan. Dig. CHAN 8871; *ABTD 1486* [id.]. LPO, Bryden Thomson.

Walton's two wartime ballet-scores make an attractive coupling, particularly when the greater part of *The Quest*, based on Spenser's *Faerie Queene*, remained unheard for almost half a century. Walton wrote the score, 42 minutes long, in under five weeks in 1943 for performances by the Sadler's Wells Ballet. Though John Piper did a memorable neo-romantic set, the ballet was not a success. Since then, only the four-movement suite arranged by Vilem Tausky in 1961 has been heard. Walton had little sympathy for the subject, but what this excellent performance and full, brilliant recording demonstrates is that his own disparaging comments on the score are totally unjustified. Far more than what is contained in the suite deserves to be preserved, with anticipations of Walton's film music and the *Second Symphony*, as well as echoes of *Scapino*. Walton, even in a hurry, could not help creating memorable ideas and, with the help of Constant Lambert – not to mention Christopher Palmer, who has expanded the instrumentation in line with the suite – the orchestral writing is often dazzling. As in most ballets, there are substantial sequences of purely illustrative music, but the *Variations on the Seven Deadly Sins* form a strong, substantial movement, and the final *Passacaglia* is the more magnificent for being almost twice as long as in the suite. The start brings an effective crib from the slow movement of Vaughan Williams's *Fourth Symphony*, bitonal in a similarly eerie way. Quite apart from the dramatic power of the performance, the recording is superb, among the fullest and clearest from Chandos. The sound for *The Wise Virgins* is more reverberant and the performance has less electricity, though Walton's distinctive arrangements of Bach cantata movements – including *Sheep may safely graze* – remain as fresh as ever. The sharp use of brass and woodwind brings a bite far closer to the new authenticity than you find in more traditional arrangements. The score of the full ballet had nine movements instead of the six in this suite but, sadly, the others were lost.

Symphony No. 1 in B flat min.
** Collins Dig. 1031-2; *1031-4* [id.]. Philh. O, Frémaux – BRITTEN: *Mont Juic* (suite).**(*)

Symphony No. 1; Varii Capricci.
*** Chan. Dig. CHAN 8862; *ABTD 1477* [id.]. LPO, Bryden Thomson.

Any fear that Thomson – who takes a rather relaxed and expansive view of the *Second Symphony* – would not convey the full bite of the *First*, the searingly intense inspiration of Walton's pre-war years, proves totally unfounded. His is a warmly committed, understandingly idiomatic account of the work, weighty and rhythmically persuasive, which brings out the full emotional thrust. In the slow movement his tender expressiveness goes with a flowing speed, well judged to avoid exaggeration. This is a work which builds tensions relentlessly, regularly working towards climaxes which are then dramatically resolved. In that process the extra impact at the moment of thrust, brought about by an agogic hesitation or a slight pressing forward, can be crucial, notably in the hammered repetitions so characteristic of Walton, and Thomson is masterly in judging that. If the scherzo is a degree less demonic than it might be, at a speed fractionally slower than usual, it is infectiously sprung. Previn's famous RCA version of the *Symphony* (GD 87830 [7830-2-RG]) has a unique, biting intensity, but Thomson's performance, helped by the splendid modern sound, is very satisfying in its own right, and leads all the modern digital recordings. The Chandos coupling is not as generous as some but is very welcome when it brings the first recording of *Varii capricci*, the orchestral suite in five compact movements which Walton developed from his set of guitar *Bagatelles*, written for Julian Bream. The outer movements are typically spiky, with guitar textures turned into ripe orchestral sound. The three middle movements are relaxed and relatively slow, the third a sensuously scored *Alla cubana*, with haunting tango rhythms, while the fourth with its tremolos *sul ponticello* might be subtitled 'Nights in the gardens of Ischia'. With a brilliant performance and sumptuous sound, it makes a fine supplement.

Frémaux, an understanding Waltonian, conducts a beautifully paced, well-played account of the *First Symphony*, which consistently reveals his natural feeling for the ebb-and-flow of tension as well as of rubato needed in this of all Walton's works. That it fails to make the impact it deserves is due to the recording, with sound so distanced that the edge of the performance is blunted, impairing the weight of expression. Only the brass comes over with the necessary sharpness and, with the CD transfer at rather low level, it is essential to listen at high volume. Only the slow movement gains from the distanced sound, with an extra chill and a sense of desolation. The distancing is a help too in the trumpet solo in the coda of the finale, but the scherzo in particular loses impact and clarity, despite crisp, well-sprung ensemble. The Britten coupling is odd, and – at only 12 minutes – far less generous than those on the Mackerras (EMI CD-EMX 2151) and Handley (EMI CDC7 49671-2) versions, both preferable in every way.

Symphony No. 2.
*** ASV Dig. CDRPO 8023; *ZCRPO 8023* [id.]. RPO, Ashkenazy – BRITTEN: *Serenade*; KNUSSEN: *Symphony No. 3.****

In the concerts that Vladimir Ashkenazy gave with the RPO on his return to Russia in 1989 after 26 years in exile, he included two outstanding British symphonies, the fine Knussen work and this, the more neglected of Walton's two symphonies. In this live recording, ensemble is inevitably less crisp than in most studio performances – as in the fugato of the finale – but the power and passion of Ashkenazy's reading amply compensate. He is somewhat brisker and more urgent than either Previn or Mackerras in the outer movements, bringing out the scherzando element in the finale even more effectively. He then most tellingly draws out the lyrical warmth of the central slow movement at a marginally slower speed. It could hardly be more sensuous, helped by sound that is amazingly good, considering the problems of live recording, atmospheric with plenty of detail and, on the whole, a natural balance.

Symphony No. 2; Partita for orchestra; Variations on a theme by Hindemith.
❀ (M) *** Sony MPK 46732 [id.]. Cleveland O, Szell.

In a letter to the conductor, Walton expressed himself greatly pleased with this performance of the *Second Symphony*: 'It is a quite fantastic and stupendous performance from every point of view. Firstly it is absolutely right musically speaking, and the virtuosity is quite staggering, especially the Fugato; but everything is phrased and balanced in an unbelievable way.' Listening to the splendidly remastered CD of this 1961 recording, one cannot but join the composer in responding to the wonderfully luminous detail in the orchestra, while the *Lento assai* is very moving, with richly sombre brass playing. In his recent book on Walton, Michael Kennedy suggests that this movement is a portrait of Cressida from Walton's opera, *Troilus and Cressida*. In the first-movement allegro, the violins above the stave are miraculously firm and radiant, and the orchestral playing has an exhilarating flair and impulse, to recall the mood of *Scapino*. Szell's performance of the *Hindemith variations* (recorded three years later), which opens the record most beguilingly, is no less praiseworthy. Again the music-making is technically immaculate, and under Szell there is not only a pervading warmth, but each fragment is perfectly set in place. What a colourful and imaginative work this is in his hands! Finally comes the earlier (1959) recording of the *Partita*, which was commissioned by the Cleveland Orchestra and given its première a year before the recording was made. The infectious writing is typical of the composer's earlier style, the opening *Toccata* having something of the hurly-burly of *Portsmouth Point* and, like the finale, again also reminds us of *Scapino*. The central *Pastorale* (*Siciliana*) is the slightest movement, but here the lambent Cleveland detail makes this seem like a soft-focus image of the lyrical writing in *Façade*. The recordings are bright, in the CBS manner, but the ambience of Severance Hall brings a backing warmth and depth, and these are technically among the finest of Szell's recordings in this venue. Even if pianissimos do not register as markedly as we would expect today, the dynamic range is by no means compressed, and at *piano* and *mezzoforte* levels the orchestral textures are given an appealing bloom. Mackerras's splendid digital mid-priced EMI coupling of both symphonies should not be forgotten (CD-EMX 2151; *TC-EMX 2151*), and he too makes a particularly strong case for No. 2, but this Cleveland disc occupies a very special place in the Walton discography.

String quartet in A min.
*** Virgin Dig. VC7 91196-2 [id.]. Endellion Qt – BRIDGE: *String quartet No. 3*.***

The contrast between haunting melancholy and spiky wit in this *Quartet* of 1947, Walton's first major work after a long gap during the Second World War, exactly suits the Endellion players. The warmth of their understanding culminates in an outstanding performance of the *Lento* slow movement, superbly sustained at a very measured speed. The marked difference of style and mood here between this work and the other fine quartet on the disc is beautifully brought out, the Walton resigned, the Bridge angry in a way that Walton had rather left behind in his pre-war work. Excellent, warm sound.

(i) *Christopher Columbus (suite of incidental music);* (ii) *Anon in love;* (iii) *4 Songs after Edith Sitwell: Daphne; Through gilded trellises; Long steel grass; Old Sir Faulk; A Song for the Lord Mayor's table. The Twelve (an anthem for the Feast of any Apostle).*
*** Chan. Dig. CHAN 8824; *ABTD 1449* [id.]. (i) Linda Finnie, Arthur Davies; (ii) Martyn Hill, (iii) Jill Gomez; Westminster Singers, City of L. Sinfonia, Hickox.

The composer's own orchestral versions of his song-cycles *Anon in love* (for tenor) and *A Song for the Lord Mayor's table* (for soprano) are so beautifully judged that they transcend the originals, which had, respectively, guitar and piano accompaniments. The strength and beauty of these strongly characterized songs is enormously enhanced, particularly in performances as positive as these by Martyn Hill and Jill Gomez. The anthem, *The Twelve*, which Walton wrote for his old college, Christ Church, Oxford, to words by W. H. Auden, also emerges far more powerfully with orchestral instead of organ accompaniment. The four Sitwell songs were orchestrated by Christopher Palmer, who also devised the suite from Walton's incidental music to Louis MacNeice's wartime radio play, *Christopher Columbus*, buried for half a century. It is a rich score which brings more happy anticipations of the *Henry V* film-music in the choral writing, and even of the opera *Troilus and Cressida*, as well as overtones of *Belshazzar's Feast*. Warmly committed performances, opulently recorded.

Ward, Robert (born 1917)

(i) *Symphony No. 6;* (ii) *Appalachian ditties and dances;* (iii) *Dialogues;* (iv) *Lamentation and Scherzo.*
** Bay Cities BCD 1015 [id.]. (i) St Stephen's CO, Lorenzo Muti; (ii) Stephen Shipps; (ii; iv) Eric Larsen; (iii) Amadeus Trio.

Now in his mid-seventies, Robert Ward studied at the Eastman School with Howard Hanson and Bernard Rogers and went on to a distinguished academic career at the Juilliard School and, later, the University of North Carolina. His idiom is tonal and unproblematic and his music is impeccably crafted. Having heard (and been impressed by) one of his earlier symphonies, the prospect of hearing some of his more recent works such as the *Symphony No. 6* (1989) for chamber orchestra, and the *Appalachian ditties and dances* (1988) or the slightly earlier *Dialogues* (1984) seemed promising. However, this disc is a disappointment: the *Symphony* is pretty anonymous, with none of the freshness one recalls from his earlier music, and there are few strong or individual ideas in the remaining pieces. Generally goodish performances and recording.

Warlock, Peter (1894–1930)

Capriol suite (orchestral version); *Serenade for strings (for the sixtieth birthday of Delius).*
*** Chan. Dig. CHAN 8808; *ABTD 1436* [id.]. Ulster O, Vernon Handley – MOERAN: *Serenade* etc.***

The *Capriol suite* exists in piano-duet form, a very familiar version for strings (both from 1926), and the present full orchestral score, which followed in 1928. The effect is to rob the music of some of its astringency. A dryish wine is replaced with one with the fullest bouquet, for the wind instruments make the textures more rococo in feeling as well as increasing the colour. There are losses as well as gains, but it is good to have Handley's fine performance, made to sound opulent by the acoustics of Ulster Hall, Belfast. The lovely *Serenade*, for strings alone, is also played and recorded very beautifully.

Wassenaer, Unico (1692–1766)

6 Concerti armonici.
(M) **(*) Decca 425 728-2; *425 728-4* [id.]. Stuttgart CO, Munchinger.

Munchinger gave us the first satisfactory stereo recordings of the *Concerti armonici* at a time when they were still being attributed to Pergolesi. His performances, although a little understated, nevertheless have much to commend them, especially for those who fight shy of original instruments: his degree of expressiveness keeps the phrasing supple and there is no hint of sentimentality. The string-playing is very fine and the recording wears its years lightly.

Weber, Carl Maria von (1786–1826)

Piano sonata No. 2 in A flat, Op. 39.
*** Ph. Dig. 426 439-2; *426 439-4* [id.]. Alfred Brendel – BRAHMS: *4 Ballades.****

Masterly playing from Alfred Brendel, who makes out a strong case for the Weber *Sonata* which in his hands has seriousness and strength as well as charm. Everything is thoroughly thought out, and one feels that the slightest hesitation is carefully calculated. If there is a certain want of spontaneity, there is no want of mastery. Brendel is recorded in sound of marvellous presence and clarity.

Oberon (complete).
(M) *** DG 419 038-2 (2) [id.]. Grobe, Nilsson, Domingo, Prey, Hamari, Schiml, Bav. R. Ch. & SO, Kubelik.

Rarely has operatic inspiration been squandered so cruelly on impossible material as in Weber's *Oberon.* We owe it to Covent Garden's strange ideas in the mid-1820s as to what English opera should be that Weber's delicately conceived score is a sequence of illogical arias, scenas and ensembles strung together by an absurd pantomime plot. Though, even on record, the result is slacker because of that loose construction, one can appreciate the contribution of Weber, in a performance as stylish and refined as this. The original issue included dialogue and a narrative spoken by one of Oberon's fairy characters. In the reissue this is omitted, cutting the number of discs from three to two, yet leaving the music untouched. With Birgit Nilsson commanding in *Ocean, thou mighty monster,* and excellent singing from the other principals, helped by Kubelik's ethereally light handling of the orchestra, the set can be be recommended without reservation, for the recording remains of excellent quality.

Webern, Anton (1883–1945)

(i) *Concerto for nine instruments, Op. 24; 5 Movements for string quartet* (orchestral version), *Op. 5; Passacaglia, Op. 1; 6 Pieces for large orchestra, Op. 6; 5 Pieces for orchestra, Op. 10; Symphony, Op. 21; Variations for orchestra, Op. 30.* Arrangements of: BACH: *Musical offering: Fugue* (1935). (ii) SCHUBERT: *German dances* (for small orchestra), *Op. posth.* Chamber music: (iii) *6 Bagatelles for string quartet, Op. 9; 5 Movements for string quartet, Op. 5*; (iv; v) *4 Pieces for violin and piano, Op. 7;* (v; vi) *3 Small pieces for cello and piano, Op. 11;* (v; vii) *Quartet, Op. 22* (for piano, violin, clarinet & saxophone); (iii) *String quartet, Op. 28; String trio, Op. 20;* (v) *Variations for piano, Op. 27.* (Vocal) (viii; i) *Das Augenlicht, Op. 26;* (ix; x) *3 Canons on Latin texts, Op. 16;* (viii; ix; i) *Cantata No. 1, Op. 29;* (viii; ix; xi; i) *Cantata No. 2, Op. 31;* (viii) *Entflieht auf leichten Kähnen, Op. 2;* (ix; x) *5 Sacred songs, Op. 15;* (xii; v) *5 Songs, Op. 3; 5 Songs, Op. 4;* (xii; x) *2 Songs, Op. 8;* (xii; v) *4 Songs, Op. 12;* (xii; x) *4 Songs, Op. 13; 6 Songs, Op. 14;* (ix; x; xiii) *3 Songs, Op. 18;* (viii; i) *2 Songs, Op. 19;* (xii; v) *3 Songs, Op. 23;* (ix; v) *3 Songs, Op. 25;* (ix; x) *3 Traditional rhymes, Op. 17.*
(M) *** Sony SM3K 45845 (3) [id.]. (i) LSO (or members), Pierre Boulez; (ii) Frankfurt R. O, composer (recorded December 1932); (iii) Juilliard Qt (or members); (iv) Stern; (v) Rosen; (vi) Piatigorsky; (vii) Majeske, Marcellus, Weinstein; (viii) John Alldis Ch.; (ix) Lukomska; (x) with Ens., Boulez; (xi) McDaniel; (xii) Harper; (xiiii) with John Williams. Overall musical direction: Boulez.

These three CDs contain all Webern's works with opus numbers, as well as the string orchestra arrangements of Op. 5 and the orchestration of the *Fugue* from Bach's *Musical offering.* A rare recording of Webern himself conducting his arrangement of Schubert dances is also included. Though the recording quality varies somewhat, the CD transfers are remarkably consistent, considering that the items included were made over a period of eleven years. The orchestral music was done in the sympathetic acoustics of what is described in the notes as Banking (Barking) Town Hall in 1969 and has atmosphere as well as vivid clarity, while the chamber music, recorded mostly in New York over the following three years, brings both immediacy and clean, realistic textures, even if the balance is close. The quality of the music-making is very high and, more importantly, all these performances convey the commitment without which such spare writing can sound merely chill. What Pierre Boulez above all demonstrates in the orchestral works (including those with chorus) is that, for all his seeming asceticism, Webern was working on human emotions. The spareness of the writing lets us appreciate how atonality can communicate tenderly, evocatively, movingly, not by any imitation of romantic models (as Schoenberg's and Berg's music often does) but by reducing the notes to the minimum. The Juilliard Quartet and the John Alldis Choir convey comparable commitment; though neither Heather Harper nor Halina Lukomska is ideally cast in the solo vocal music, Boulez brings out the best in both of them in the works with orchestra. Rarely can a major composer's whole *oeuvre* be appreciated in so compact a span. There are excellent notes, every item is cued, and perhaps it is carping to regret that the *Passacaglia* and *Variations for orchestra* were not indexed. With such consistently successful transfers and a realistic price, this set can be recommended to anyone who wants to come to grips with one of the key figures of the twentieth century.

Im Sommerwind.
*** Decca Dig. 430 324-2; *430 324-4* [id.]. Concg. O, Chailly – BRAHMS: *Symphony No. 2.****

Im Sommerwind, written by Webern when he was only twenty, is an evocative 'idyll for large orchestra', inspired by a poem of Bruno Wille. It is a vividly atmospheric musical picture of a summer day in woods and fields. In idiom it recalls Delius more than anyone else, and it is given a warmly understanding performance, refined in its textures, by the Concertgebouw under Chailly. It makes an unexpected but very attractive coupling for Chailly's Brahms, superbly recorded.

5 Movements, Op. 5.
(M) *** Decca 430 002-2 [id.]. ASMF, Marriner – SCHOENBERG: *Verklaerte Nacht*; R. STRAUSS: *Metamorphosen.***(*)

The CD remastering of Marriner's 1974 recording brings a more sharply etched sound, almost to match the original string quartet medium in clarity and bite. With dedicated playing, the result is very satisfying, even if the music is inevitably made more romantic.

5 Pieces for orchestra, Op. 10.
(M) *** Mercury 432 006-2 [id.]. LSO, Dorati – BERG: *3 Pieces; Lulu suite*; SCHOENBERG: *5 Pieces.****

Webern's *Five pieces*, Op. 10, written between 1911 and 1913, mark a radical point in his early development. Their compression is extreme, and their play with almost inaudible fragments may make the unsympathetic listener lose patience too quickly. What we have now gradually come to appreciate, thanks to such performances as this, is that, like so much of Berg and Schoenberg, they have their emotional point to make. The couplings could hardly be more fitting, and the whole record can be strongly recommended to anyone wanting to explore the early work of Schoenberg and his followers before they formalized their ideas in twelve-note technique. Bright, clear, 1962 recording to match the precision of the writing.

Weill, Kurt (1900–1950)

Happy End (play by Brecht with songs); *Das Sieben Todsunden (The Seven deadly sins).*
(M) *** Sony mono/stereo MPK 45886 [id.]. Lotte Lenya, male quartet & O, Ch. & O, Brückner-Rüggeberg.

An outstandingly valuable and generous coupling offering some 73 minutes of music. Originally recorded in mono in the mid-1950s, the CBS performance of *The Seven deadly sins,* with the composer's widow as principal singer, underlines the status of this distinctive mixture of ballet and song-cycle as one of Weill's most concentrated inspirations. The rhythmic verve is irresistible and, though Lenya had to have the music transposed down, her understanding of the idiom is unique. The recording is forward and slightly harsh, though Lenya's voice is not hardened, and the effect is undoubtedly vivid. *Happy end,* intended as the work's successor and yet more savagely cynical, took far longer to be appreciated. The present recording was made in Hamburg-Harburg in 1960. Lenya turned the songs into a kind of cycle (following a hint from her husband), again transposing where necessary, and her renderings in her individual brand of vocalizing are so compelling they make the scalp tingle. Many of these numbers are among the finest that Weill ever wrote. The excellent notes by David Drew are preserved with the CD, but the texts are printed out in German without any translations. The sound is again forwardly balanced, but the CD transfer still provides a backing ambience.

Die Dreigroschenoper (The Threepenny Opera) complete.
(M) ** Ph. 426 668-2; *426 668-4* [id.]. Teichmann, Korta, Huebner, Mey, Kutschera, Brammer, Frankfurt Op. Ch. & O, Wolfgang Rennert.

A mid-priced version of *The Threepenny Opera* is welcome, and the 1966 performance here has plenty of bite, even if some of the women's voices have little of the snarling character that one really wants in this 'black' music. However, for anyone except the most fluent German-speaker, a full text is essential; instead, here one has only an essay on how the Weill work relates to the *Beggar's Opera,* plus a very compressed synopsis of the story. The numbers are all separately cued, with the titles translated; but one sometimes needs to do a detective job to discover which characters are singing what. Without the right information, a work which relies far more than most operas on its words (by Brecht) can only be partially appreciated, even though the recording is lively, with the voices given a vivid presence. First choice still rests with the outstanding Decca Mauceri version, with Kollo, Milva and the vibrant and provocative Ute Lemper (430 075-2).

Wirén, Dag (1905–86)

(i) *Violin concerto, Op. 23;* (ii) *String quartet No. 5, Op. 41;* (iii) *Triptych, Op. 33;* (iv) *Wind quintet, Op. 42.*
** Caprice Dig./Analogue CAP 21326. (i) Nils-Erik Sparf, Stockholm PO, Comissiona; (ii) Saulesco Qt; (iii) Stockholm Sinf., Wedin; (iv) Stockholm Wind Quintet.

This release offers a cross-section of Dag Wirén's music not previously available on CD. Wirén is a 'one-work composer', and little of his music is widely known or shares the celebrity of the *Serenade for strings.* The best piece here is probably the post-war *Violin concerto* (1946) whose first two movements are often imaginative and inventive; it is very well played by Nils-Erik Sparf and the Stockholm Philharmonic under Sergiu Comissiona. Only the finale is a let-down. The other three pieces, the *Triptych* (1958), the

Fifth String quartet (1970) and the *Wind quintet* (1971), are all disappointingly thin and scrappy. The motivic ideas are short-breathed and rarely take creative flight: it is as if Wirén were constantly running out of steam; the adagio of the *Quintet* is based on the opening motive of the *Fourth Symphony*, not in itself a strong idea. A pity that this sympathetic composer is not represented by stronger works, like the *Divertimento for orchestra* and the *Sinfonietta*. The *Quartet* and the *Triptych* are analogue recordings, the other two come from the mid-1980s and are digital. Excellent performances and recordings all the same.

Wolf, Hugo (1860–1903)

Italian serenade (arr. for string orchestra).
** Denon Dig. CO 77150 [id.]. I Solisti Italiani – MALIPIERO: *Quartet No. 1* ***; RESPIGHI: *Ancient airs and dances: suite No. 3*.**

Wolf's *Italian serenade* transcribes effectively for a string orchestra of this size (6:2:2:1) and the performance is lively and polished and very well recorded. Yet one expects more charm from an Italian group than one finds here.

Italianisches Liederbuch (Italian Song Book, Parts 1 and 2): complete.
(M) *** EMI CDM7 63732-2 [id.]. Elisabeth Schwarzkopf, Dietrich Fischer-Dieskau, Gerald Moore.

The 46 songs of Wolf's *Italienisches Liederbuch* were published in two parts, in 1892 and 1896. All of them are here, on a CD playing for two seconds over 79 minutes, generous measure indeed at mid-price. These songs show the composer at his most captivatingly individual. Many of them are very brief fragments of fantasy, which call for the most intense artistry if their point is to be fully made. No one today can match the searching perception of these two great singers in this music, with Fischer-Dieskau using his sweetest tones and Schwarzkopf ranging through all the many emotions inspired by love. Note particularly the little vignette, *Wer rief dich denn?*, the song Schwarzkopf was rehearsing when she first met her husband-to-be, Walter Legge, and which she interprets more vividly than anyone else: scorn mingling with hidden heartbreak. Gerald Moore is at his finest, and Walter Legge's translations will help bring the magic of these unique songs even to the newcomer. The well-balanced 1969 recording has been admirably transferred, giving the artists a fine presence.

6 Lieder für eine Frauenstimme. Goethe-Lieder: Die Bekehrte; Ganymed; Kennst du das Land; Mignon I, II & III; Philine; Die Spröde. Lieder: *An eine Aeolsharfe; Auf einer Wanderung; Begegnung; Denk es, o Seele; Elfenlied; Im Frühling; Sonne der Schlummerlosen; Wenn du zu den Blumen gehst; Wie glänzt der helle Mond; Die Zigeunerin.*
(M) **(*) EMI CDM7 63653-2 [id.]. Elisabeth Schwarzkopf, Gerald Moore or Geoffrey Parsons.

This is a superb collection, issued as part of Schwarzkopf's 75th birthday edition, representing the peak of her achievement as a Lieder singer. It is disgraceful that no texts or translations are provided as this will seriously reduce its appeal for some collectors; but the selection of items could hardly be better, including many songs inseparably associated with Schwarzkopf's voice like *Mausfallen spruchlein* and, above all, *Kennst du das Land.* That supreme Lied may not be quite as intensely moving in this studio recording as in

Schwarzkopf's two live recordings, also issued by EMI, but it is commanding in its perfection.

Wood, Hugh (born 1932)

(i) *Cello concerto;* (ii) *Violin concerto.*
(M) *** Unicorn UKCD 2043 [id.]. (i) Parikian; (ii) Welsh; Royal Liverpool PO, Atherton.

Hugh Wood has so far been represented on record only by his chamber music. For his CD début Unicorn have reissued this excellent 1978 coupling of two of his most important bigger pieces: the *Cello concerto* of 1969 and the *Violin concerto*, first heard two years later. Wood is a composer of integrity who has steeped himself in the music of Schoenberg and Webern, yet emerged richer for the experience – in contrast to many post-serial composers. His music is beautifully crafted and far from inaccessible. Here he is given the benefit of good recording, and the performances are thoroughly committed. Those who like and respond to the Bartók concertos or even to the Walton should try this. Excellently balanced recording, well transferred to CD.

Wordsworth, William (1908–88)

Symphonies Nos. 2 in D, Op. 34; 3 in C, Op. 48.
*** Lyrita Dig. SRCD 207 [id.]. LPO, Nicholas Braithwaite.

William Wordsworth was a direct descendant of the poet's brother, Christopher; on the evidence of this disc, he was a real symphonist: he composed eight in all, the most recent in 1986, two years before his death. The *Third* enjoyed some measure of exposure in the 1950s (Barbirolli conducted it no fewer than eight times in its first year), but the encouragement its composer received from the BBC in the 1950s was not continued into the 1960s, and his music was relegated to the outermost fringes of the repertoire, while the somewhat embittered composer migrated to the solitude of the Scottish Highlands. The *Second*, dedicated to Tovey, has a real sense of space; it is distinctly Nordic in atmosphere and there is an unhurried sense of growth. It is serious, thoughtful music, both well crafted and well laid out for the orchestra. At times it almost suggests Sibelius or Walter Piston in the way it moves, though not in its accents, and the writing is both powerful and imaginative. The long first movement in particular is sustained impressively. The *Third* is less concentrated and less personal in utterance, but all the same this is music of integrity, and readers who enjoy, say, the symphonies of Edmund Rubbra should sample the *Second Symphony*. Nicholas Braithwaite gives a carefully prepared and dedicated account of it, and the recording is up to the usual high standard one expects from this label.

Zelenka, Jan (1679–1745)

Missa dei Filii; Litaniae Laurentanae.
*** HM/BMG Dig. RD 77922 [7922-2-RC]. Argenta, Chance, Prégardien, Gordon Jones, Stuttgart Chamber Ch., Tafelmusik, Bernius.

This fine set offers not only one of Zelenka's late Masses, but also a splendid *Litany* too, confirming him – for all the obscurity he suffered in his lifetime – as one of the most inspired composers of his generation. The *Missa dei Filii* (Mass for the Son of God), is a 'short' mass, consisting of *Kyrie* and *Gloria* only. Some of the movements into which the sections are divided are brief to the point of being perfunctory, but the splendid soprano solo of the *Christe eleison* points forward to the magnificent setting of the *Gloria*, in which the first two sections and the last are wonderfully cxpansive, ending with a sustainedly ingenious fugue. It seems that Zelenka never heard that Mass, but his *Litany*, another refreshing piece, was specifically written when the Electress of Saxony was ill. Zelenka, like Bach, happily mixes fugal writing with newer-fangled concertato movements. Bernius provides well-sprung support with his period-instrument group, Tafelmusik, and his excellent soloists and choir.

Zemlinsky, Alexander von (1871–1942)

6 Maeterlinck Lieder, Op. 3.

*** Decca Dig. 430 165-2; *430 165-4* (2) [id.]. Jard van Nes, Concg. O, Chailly – MAHLER: *Symphony No. 6.****

Beautifully sung by Jard van Nes in her finest recording to date, these ripely romantic settings of Maeterlinck make an unusual but valuable fill-up for Chailly's rugged and purposeful reading of the Mahler symphony. This is very much the world of medieval chivalry which inspired *Pelleas and Melisande*, and Zemlinsky responds wholeheartedly. The rich, vivid recording captures van Nes's full-throated singing with new firmness.

Collections

A selective list – we have included only the outstanding compilations from the many which are available

---

Concerts of Orchestral and Concertante Music

Academy of St Martin-in-the-Fields, Sir Neville Marriner

'English music for strings': HOLST: *St Paul's suite.* DELIUS (arr. Fenby): *2 Aquarelles.* PURCELL: *Chacony.* VAUGHAN WILLIAMS: *Rhosymedre: Prelude.* WALTON: *Henry V* (film music): *Death of Falstaff; Touch her soft lips and part.* BRITTEN: *Simple Symphony, Op. 4.*
(M) *** EMI CD-EMX 2170; *TC-EMX 2170.*

The ASMF's success with Marriner in a wide range of repertory stemmed from the earliest days, not only from the conductor's careful marking of parts but also from having players who understand one another. This attractively varied concert brings playing at once refined and resilient, delicately strong and warmly expressive by turns. Britten's *Simple Symphony* seems to be on a more impressive scale than usual in the fast movements, more openly romantic in the *Sentimental sarabande.* Holst's *St Paul's suite* brings wonderfully pointed rhythms in all four movements, while the Vaughan Williams (an arrangement of a haunting organ solo) and the Walton are finely atmospheric, against the sympathetic acoustic of EMI's Abbey Road Studio. The Delius too, atmospheric music *par excellence*, prepares the way for the bold and comparative astringency of the magnificent Purcell *Chacony*, which has never sounded more convincing on modern instruments. The remastered (1972) recording, while bringing string textures which are a little sparer than on the original analogue LP (most noticeably so in the Britten slow movement, which sounds less opulent), has refined detail and provides a somewhat firmer focus.

Anderson, John (oboe), Philharmonia Orchestra, Simon Wright

Venetian oboe concertos: ALBINONI: *Concertos in B flat and D, Op. 7/3 & 6.* MARCELLO: *Concerto in D min.* VIVALDI: *Concertos: in F, RV 455; in A min., RV 461.* CIMAROSA: *Concerto in C min.* (arr. Benjamin).
**(*) Nimbus Dig. NI 5188 [id.].

There are several top favourites here, and John Anderson plays the whole programme with warmth and elegance; despite his finesse in the engaging Cimarosa/Benjamin work, other versions do have more charm. The drawback to this concert is that the Philharmonia Orchestra (recorded in St Jude-on-the-Hill, Hampstead) bring rather too sumptuous textures for the accompaniments. Such an effect seems inflated for this kind of baroque programme, although the balance is good and the sound is agreeably full and real.

André, Maurice (trumpet)

'Classical trumpet concertos' (with Zurich CO, Stoutz): MOZART: *Concerto in A flat.* HAYDN: *Concerto in G.* BELLINI: *Concerto in E flat.* HUMMEL: *Introduction, theme and variations.*
** EMI Dig. CDC7 54086-2 [id.].

All these works were conceived for oboe, and none comes off particularly well on the trumpet. That by Mozart sounds particularly inept, losing much of its grace. This is not entirely the fault of André, who plays with good style; but even he cannot prevent a flavour of the bandstand creeping into the very operatic Bellini concerto. The finale of the piece attributed to Haydn comes off best, and the racier passages in the Hummel *Variations* readily demonstrate the soloist's easy bravura. Excellent accompaniments and good recording.

Trumpet concertos (with (i) ECO, Mackerras; (ii) Munich Bach O, Karl Richter; (iii) Munich CO, Stadlmair): (i) VIVIANI: *Sonata for trumpet & organ in C* (with Hedwig Bilgram). VIVALDI: *Double trumpet concerto in C, RV 537.* TELEMANN: *Concerto-Sonata in D.* (ii) HANDEL: *Concerto in G min.* (arr. from *Oboe concerto No. 3*). (iii) M. HAYDN: *Trumpet concerto in D.* J. HAYDN: *Trumpet concerto in E flat.*
(M) *** DG 419 874-2; *419 874-4* [id.].

This mid-priced DG collection (well recorded in the late 1960s and late 1970s) represents Maurice André's art far more impressively than the EMI CD, above. The only transcription included is from a Handel *Oboe concerto*, and that is reasonably effective. Michael Haydn's *Concerto*, a concertante section of a seven-movement *Serenade*, has incredibly high tessitura, with the D trumpet taken up to high A (the fourth ledger-line above the treble stave), the highest note in any classical trumpet concerto. It is just a peep but, characteristically, Maurice André reaches up for it with consummate ease. He is completely at home in all this repertoire: his version of the Joseph Haydn *Concerto* is stylish and elegant, with a memorably eloquent account of the slow movement, the line gracious and warmly serene. The *Sonata for trumpet and organ* by Giovanni Buonaventura Viviani (1638–*c.* 1692) is also an attractive piece, comprising five brief but striking miniatures, each only a minute or so in length. In the Vivaldi *Double concerto* André plays both solo parts.

Ballet

'Nights at the ballet' (with (i) RPO, Weldon; (ii) Philh. O; (iii) Kurtz; (iv) Irving; (v) RPO, Fistoulari; (vi) CBSO, Frémaux; (vii) New Philh. O, Mackerras): excerpts from: (i) TCHAIKOVSKY: *Nutcracker; Swan Lake.* (ii; iii) PROKOFIEV: *Romeo and Juliet.* (ii; iv) ADAM: *Giselle.* (v) LUIGINI: *Ballet Égyptien* (suite). (vi) SATIE: *Gymnopédies Nos 1 and 3.* (vii) DELIBES: *Coppélia.* GOUNOD: *Faust* (suite).
(B) *** EMI TC2-MOM 111.

Here (on tape only) is nearly an hour and a half of the most tuneful and colourful ballet music ever written. Kurtz's three excerpts from *Romeo and Juliet* are distinguished, if a little sombre, the inclusion of the Fistoulari recording of *Ballet Égyptien* is most welcome, and Mackerras is at his sparkling best in the *Coppélia* and *Faust* selections. Weldon's Tchaikovsky performances lack the last degree of flair, but they are alert and well played. The sound is admirable both for home listening and in the car.

Baroque Classics

'Baroque classics: Vivace!' (with (i) Cantilena, Shepherd; (ii) SCO, Gibson; (iii) Soloists of Australia, Thomas): (i) HANDEL: *Solomon: Arrival of the Queen of Sheba.* (ii) *Water music: Overture; Alla hornpipe.* (iii) BACH: *Violin concerto No. 2 in E, BWV 1042.* (i) *Suite No. 3: Air.* PACHELBEL: *Canon.* VIVALDI: *Concerto for strings in A, RV 159.* (iii) *L'Estro armonico: Quadruple violin concerto in B min., Op. 3/10.* (i) CORELLI: *Concerto grosso in G min. (Christmas), Op. 6/8.*
(M) **(*) Chan. Dig. CHAN 6527.

A rather agreeable late-evening concert. Pachelbel's *Canon* is serene but rather bland; otherwise the selection does not lack vitality, and the contributions from Ronald Thomas (especially the Bach *Violin concerto*) and Sir Alexander Gibson make one wish they had a greater share of the programme. However, the Corelli *Concerto grosso* is very pleasing, and the sound is excellent throughout.

Baroque music

'The sound of baroque' (with (i) Royal Liverpool PO, Groves; (ii) Scottish CO, Tortelier; (iii) LPO, Boult; (iv) Menuhin, Ferras, Bath Fest. O; (v) Bournemouth Sinf., Montgomery; (vi) Reginald Kilbey and Strings; (vii) RPO, Weldon, (viii) ASMF, Marriner): (i) ALBINONI: *Adagio for strings and organ* (arr. Giazotto). (ii) BACH: *Suite No. 3 in D, BWV 1068: Air.* (iii) *Brandenburg concerto No. 3 in G, BWV 1048.* (iv) *Double violin concerto in D, BWV 1043.* (i) GLUCK: *Orfeo: Dance of the Blessed Spirits.* (v) HANDEL: *Messiah: Pastoral symphony. Berenice: overture.* (v) *Solomon: Arrival of the Queen of Sheba.* (vi) *Serse: Largo.* (vii) *Water music: suite* (arr. Harty). (viii) PACHELBEL: *Canon.*
(B) *** EMI TC2-MOM 103.

One of the first of EMI's 'Miles of Music' tapes, planned for motorway listening as well as at home, and offering about 80 minutes of favourite baroquerie, this is recommendable in every way. The sound is full and lively, the performances are first class, with Bach's *Double violin concerto* and *Brandenburg No. 3* (Boult) bringing substance among the lollipops.

Bavarian State Orchestra, Wolfgang Sawallisch

Russian orchestral music: KABALEVSKY: *The Comedians* (suite), *Op. 26.* RIMSKY-KORSAKOV: *Capriccio espagnole, Op. 34.* GLINKA: *Overture: Russlan and Ludmilla.* BORODIN: *In the steppes of Central Asia.* MUSSORGSKY (arr. Rimsky-Korsakov): *Night on the bare mountain.* PROKOFIEV: *The Love for 3 Oranges, Op. 33: March & Scherzo.*
(M) *** EMI Dig. CDD7 63893-2 [id.]; *ET 763893-4.*

This splendid concert of Russian music was included in EMI's first reissued release of mid-priced digital repertoire, although it had not appeared before in the UK. It was made in the Herkulessaal, Munich, in 1987. The sound is splendid, resonantly full, coloured by the attractive ambient bloom characteristic of this famous hall, yet vivid and lively too. Apart from offering the best-ever version of the winning Kabalevsky suite, the Rimsky-Korsakov performance is comparably memorable for its sophisticated and brilliant orchestral playing and for sustaining warmth and excitement throughout without ever going over the top. The Glinka and Mussorgsky pieces are similarly distinctive and *In the steppes of Central Asia* is particularly appealing, not overtly romantic but refreshingly direct. The programme ends with Prokofiev, sparkling and witty, but not too abrasive, like the Kabalevsky at the opening.

Berlin Philharmonic Orchestra, Karajan

'Karajan à Paris': RAVEL: *Boléro.* BIZET: *L'Arlésienne: suite No. 2.* CHABRIER: *España.* GOUNOD: *Faust: ballet suite.* BERLIOZ: *La Damnation de Faust: Hungarian march.*
(M) **(*) EMI CDM7 63527-2 [id.]; *EG 763527-4.*

The original LP was short measure, so EMI have added *Boléro*, which is exciting enough but does not match Karajan's DG analogue version. The climax, too, is fierce. The rest of the programme finds the conductor in Beecham territory, but his approach is less incandescent, and his phrasing sometimes seems heavy for a volatile French concert. His view is broad (some might say rhythmically sluggish) in the Bizet, taut in the Chabrier, while nevertheless presenting this colourful music with brilliance and flair; indeed *España* has an infectious, tingling zest. The *Faust* ballet music is very attractive too, the playing full of warmth and elegance; but the Berlioz march, although exciting, does not sound very French. This is partly the fault of the recording which is very well upholstered although brightened by the CD transfer. The result is extremely vivid but lacks something in refinement at climaxes.

'Karajan Festival': BRAHMS: *Hungarian dances Nos. 1, 3, 5, 6, 17–20.* BORODIN: *Prince Igor: Polvtsian dances.* TCHAIKOVSKY: *Eugene Onegin: Polonaise & Waltz.* SMETANA: *The Bartered Bride: Polka; Furiant; Dance of the Comedians.* GRIEG: *Peer Gynt suites 1 & 2.* SIBELIUS: *Finlandia, Op. 26. Kuolema: Valse triste. Tapiola, Op.112.* RAVEL: *Boléro; Daphnis et Chloé: suite No. 2.* DEBUSSY: *La Mer; Prélude à l'après-midi d'un faune.* ROSSINI: *Overtures: Il barbiere di Siviglia; L'Italiana in Algeri; La gazza ladra; La scala di seta.* VERDI: *Overtures & Preludes: Nabucco; La Traviata; I vespri siciliani; Un ballo in maschera; La forza del destino; Aida.* SMETANA: *Má Vlast: Vltava; Vyšehrad.* DVOŘÁK: *Scherzo capriccioso.* LISZT: *Les Préludes; Hungarian rhapsody No. 4.*
(B) **(*) DG 429 436-2 (5).

There are many favourite Karajan warhorses here, played with finesse and brilliance. Everything sounds alive, but the CD transfers are often very brightly lit, notably the Brahms and Tchaikovsky items and the Rossini overtures. However, this is fair value at bargain price, and the Smetana, Grieg and Sibelius performance show Karajan at his finest, while the Ravel and Debussy coupling represents one of the conductor's indispensable recording achievements.

Bournemouth Sinfonietta, or (i) Arioso Chamber Orchestra, Carolann Martin

'Journeys': orchestral works by American women: VAN DE VATE: *Journeys.* GARDNER: *Rainforest.* LARSEN: *Overture: Parachute dancing.* Marga RICHTER: *Lament for string orchestra.* HOOVER: *Summer night.* MAMLOK: *Elegy.* BROCKMAN: *Perihelion II.*
** Leonarda Dig. LE 327 [id.].

One would like to give a more positive welcome to this enterprising collection of music by American women composers, but on this evidence they seem a cheerless lot and not strong on melodic resource. Nancy Van de Vate's various *Journeys* included Bali, and this produces a certain exoticism of texture, but the piece fails to sustain its quarter of an hour's evocation very convincingly. Kay Gardner's minimalist *Rainforest* has a good deal more charm and at 6½ minutes does not outstay its welcome; but Libby Larsen's *Parachute dancing* (inspired by a Renaissance court dance with umbrellas in which the participants finally jumped off a high wall and, it was to be hoped, floated safely down to earth) has more energy than substance. Marga Richter's restless *Lament*, however, is pungently eloquent and generates considerable expressive power; while Katherine Hoover's *Summer night*, with its flute and horn obbligati, brings an imaginative suggestion of fireflies at dusk. Yet one wonders how often the collector who invest in this concert would want to return to many of these pieces. They are all very well played, in committed performances under Carolann Martin, and the sound is spacious and realistic.

Capella Istropolitana, Adrian Leaper

'English string festival': DOWLAND: *Galliard a 5.* ELGAR: *Elegy, Op. 58; Introduction and allegro, Op. 47; Serenade, Op. 20.* BRIDGE: *Lament.* PARRY: *An English suite; Lady Radnor's suite.*
(BB) **(*) Naxos Dig. 8.550331 [id.].

It is fascinating and rewarding to hear these excellent Slovak players turn their attention to essentially English repertoire, and with a considerable degree of success. The brief Dowland *Galliard* makes a strong introduction, and the attractive pair of neo-Baroque Parry suites of dance movements, played with warmth, finesse and spirit, are given bright and lively sound. In the Elgar *Introduction and allegro* the violins above the stave have their upper partials over-brilliantly lit by the digital recording, the focus not quite sharp; but otherwise the sound is full, with plenty of resonant ambience. The playing is strongly felt, but the fugue is a bit too measured, and the great striding theme, played in unison on the G string, could also do with more pace, especially when it returns. Otherwise this is persuasive, and the *Serenade* is presented simply, combining warmth and finish. At super-bargain price, this is worth exploring.

Chicago Symphony Orchestra

'Centennial collection' (cond. Stock, Defauw, Rodzinski, Kubelik, Reiner, Martinon, Solti, Stokowski, Gould, Ozawa, Levine, Giulini, Leinsdorf, Hendl; with Rubinstein, Sviatoslav Richter and Heifetz): Complete performances or excerpts from: SCHUMANN: *Symphony No. 1 (Spring); Piano concerto in A min.* FRANCK: *Redemption.* WAGNER: *Tristan: Liebestod.* SMETANA: *Má Vlast: Vltava.* R. STRAUSS: *Don Juan.* BARTÓK: *Hungarian sketches.* MARTIN: *Concerto for 7 wind instruments and percussion.* VERDI: *Requiem: Dies irae* (with Price, Baker, Luchetti, Van Dam & Chicago Symphony Ch.). RIMSKY-KORSAKOV: *Russian Easter festival overture.* IVES: *Variations on America.* MUSSORGSKY: *Night on the bare mountain.* TCHAIKOVSKY: *Symphony No. 6 (Pathétique).* BRAHMS: *Piano concerto No. 2 in B flat.* SIBELIUS: *Violin concerto in D.*
(M) (**) BMG/RCA mono/stereo GD 60206 (3) [60206-2-RG].

Issued to mark the centenary celebrations of the Chicago Symphony Orchestra, this is not a wholly satisfactory compilation, since it offers complete performances of some works and only bits and pieces of others. The bits and pieces are from the Verdi *Requiem*, Heifetz's celebrated version of the Sibelius *Violin concerto* with Walter Hendl conducting (finale only), the Brahms *B flat Concerto* with Richter (first movement), the Schumann *Concerto* with Giulini and Rubinstein (finale), and so on. However, there are also treasures here: Frank Martin's *Concerto for seven wind instruments*, really rather superior to (and generally better played than) the Ansermet on Decca, Stokowski's thrilling 1968 account of the Rimsky-Korsakov *Russian Easter festival overture*, Reiner conducting Bartók's *Hungarian sketches* marvellously in 1958 and *Don Juan* in 1954, the latter perhaps not quite as splendid as his slightly later version with the Vienna Philharmonic. Désiré Defauw is represented by his Franck *Rédemption* (a rarity not previously transferred) rather than his electrifying Prokofiev *Scythian suite*, but the Franck is well worth having. However, it is a pity that this omission was made, when room was found for the 5/4 movement from a not particularly special *Symphonie Pathétique* under Levine and an eminently forgettable *Night on the bare mountain* from Ozawa. For many people the big surprise of the compilation will be Frederick Stock's 1929 version of the Schumann *Spring Symphony*, which sounds amazingly good in every respect. It is a very well-shaped performance and the recording is way ahead of its years!

Cleveland Orchestra, Lorin Maazel

Overtures: VERDI: *La forza del destino.* BEETHOVEN: *Creatures of Prometheus.* BERLIOZ: *Le carnaval romain.* GLINKA: *Russlan and Ludmilla.* BRAHMS: *Academic festival overture.* ROSSINI: *La gazza ladra.*
(B) *** Pickwick IMPX 9027.

A most enjoyable collection of overtures, very well recorded by Decca in 1976 and enjoying the splendid acoustics of the Cleveland Hall. Maazel's charisma is especially well demonstrated by the opening *Forza del destino* and there is no more effective modern recording of *Le carnaval romain*, in which the hall ambience makes an impressive effect with the brass. The orchestral response is as spontaneous as it is polished throughout a vivid programme. The timing is only 47 minutes 40 seconds, but this is fair value in the bargain range.

'Country gardens'

English music (various artists, including Bournemouth SO, Silvestri; Hallé O, Barbirolli; Royal Liverpool PO, Groves; E. Sinfonia, Dilkes): VAUGHAN WILLIAMS: *The Wasps: Overture. Rhosymedre.* WARLOCK: *Capriol suite.* DELIUS: *Summer night on the river. A Song before sunset.* GRAINGER: *Country gardens. Mock Morris; Shepherd's Hey.* arr. BRIDGE: *Cherry Ripe.* COLERIDGE TAYLOR: *Petite suite de concert* (excerpts). GERMAN: *Nell Gwyn: 3 Dances.* COATES: *Meadow to Mayfair: In the country. Summer Days: At the dance. Wood Nymphs.* ELGAR: *Chanson de matin. Salut d'amour.*
(B) **(*) EMI TC2-MOM 123.

A recommendable tape-only collection, essentially lightweight but never trivial. Barbirolli's Delius and Neville Dilkes's *Capriol suite* are among the highlights, and certainly it makes a most entertaining concert for use on a long journey, with the lively Grainger, Coates and German pastoral dances providing an excellent foil for the lyrical music. On domestic equipment the quality is slightly variable, with side two noticeably brighter than side one. Thus the opening *Wasps overture* is a little bass-heavy and the attractive *Capriol suite* has a more restricted upper range here than when it appears on EMI's companion tape collection '*Serenade*' (see below). But the rest of the programme sounds well.

Detroit Symphony Orchestra, Paul Paray

'French opera highlights': HÉROLD: *Overture: Zampa.* AUBER: *Overture: The Crown diamonds.* GOUNOD: *Faust: ballet suite; Waltz* (from Act II). SAINT-SAENS: *Samson et Dalila: Bacchanale.* BIZET: *Carmen: Danse bohème.* BERLIOZ: *Les Troyens: Royal hunt and storm.* MASSENET: *Phèdre overture.* THOMAS: *Mignon: Gavotte.*
(M) *** Mercury 432 014-2 [id.].

Paul Paray's reign at Detroit tempted the Mercury engineers to record a good deal of French music under his baton, and here is a good example of the Gallic verve and sparkle that were achieved. The two overtures combine colour and flair with high spirits, while the highly animated *Faust ballet music* has much elegance, with the famous *Waltz* joyfully following at the end, with superb rhythmic lift. The *Danse bohème* from *Carmen* has comparable dash. The only disappointment is the unslurred horn phrasing at the magical opening and close of the *Royal hunt and storm.* This may be authentic, but, under Beecham and Munch, the gently moulded effect is much more evocative. However, this piece does not lack excitement, and one's only other complaint is that the deliciously polished account of the very Parisian *Gavotte* from *Mignon,* which acts as a bonne-bouche at the end, makes one wish for the whole overture instead.

English Concert Orchestra, Richard Bonynge

'Ballet gala': MINKUS: *Paquita: Grand pas; Don Quixote: Pas de deux.* PUGNI: *Pas de quatre* (all arr. P. March). OFFENBACH: *Le Papillon.* DRIGO: *Le Corsaire: Pas de deux* (arr. Lanchbery). *Diane et Actéon: Pas de deux* (arr. P. March). AUBER: *Pas classique.* AUBER/LAMBERT: *Les Rendez-vous.* D. SCARLATTI/TOMMASINI: *The Good-humoured ladies.* THOMAS: *Françoise de Rimini.*
**(*) Decca Dig. 421 818-2 (2).

Richard Bonynge is a master of this repertoire, but the music by Minkus, Pugni and Drigo on the first disc is conventional pre-Delibes stuff and will be of more interest to balletomanes than to the average collector. The highlight is undoubtedly a suite from Offenbach's charming *Le Papillon,* which Bonynge has recorded complete (Decca 425 450-2, coupled with Tchaikovsky's *Nutcracker*). The second disc deserves a separate issue, for it includes not only Auber's jolly *Pas classique* (with some fine horn playing) but also Lambert's arrangement of more Auber tunes (mainly drawing on *L'enfant prodigue*), with witty, plangent scoring in the manner of his Meyerbeer ballet, *Les Patineurs.* It was compiled in 1933 for Markova and choreographed by Frederick Ashton for the young Vic-Wells Ballet. Also included is the charming *Good-humoured ladies,* a Diaghilev ballet. It was the great impresario himself who suggested drawing on Domenico Scarlatti's keyboard sonatas and he helped to choose the 23 movements, which were then felicitously transcribed by Vincenzo Tommasini. The suite from Thomas's opera *Françoise de Rimini* is also attractive and well worth having on disc. Lively, alert orchestral playing throughout, typically bright Decca sound, vividly recorded in London's Henry Wood Hall; at times, however, the ear craves a more voluptuous effect in the Kingsway Hall mannner.

English String Orchestra or English Symphony Orchestra, William Boughton

'The spirit of England': ELGAR: *Overture Cockaigne; Introduction and allegro, Op. 47; Sospiri, Op. 70.* DELIUS: *Summer evening.* BUTTERWORTH: *The banks of green willow; A Shropshire lad.* FINZI: *Suite from Love's Labour's Lost*; *Clarinet concerto* (with Alan Hacker). VAUGHAN WILLIAMS: *The lark ascending* (with Michael Bochmann); *Oboe concerto* (with Maurice Bourgue); *Fantasia on a theme of Thomas Tallis; Fantasia on Greensleeves.* PARRY: *Lady Radnor's suite.* BRIDGE: *Suite for string orchestra.* HOLST: *St Paul's suite.* WARLOCK: *Capriol suite.* BRITTEN: *Variations on a theme of Frank Bridge, Op. 10.*
❀ (B) *** Nimbus Dig. NI 5210/3 [id.].

From 1984 onwards Nimbus have been carefully building a catalogue of English orchestral works, much of it drawn from our great legacy of string music, played by the Birmingham-based English String and Symphony Orchestras under William Boughton. He is completely at home in this repertoire and also has the gift of making a studio recording sound like live music-making. One has only to sample his excitingly animated account of Holst's *St Paul's suite* (which also has much delicacy of feeling), the ideally paced Warlock *Capriol suite*, or the vibrant account of Britten's *Frank Bridge variations*, to discover the calibre of this music-making. The recordings were made in the Great Hall of Birmingham University which, with its warm reverberation, gives the strings a gloriously rich body of tone, supported by sumptuous cello and bass sonorities. At the very opening of the Britten *Variations* one might feel a certain excess of resonance at the bottom end but, when the great *Funeral march* arrives, one revels in its amplitude and physical impact. The Elgar *Introduction and allegro* expands wonderfully at its climax (yet the fugue is not blurred) and in Vaughan Williams's *Lark ascending*, where the violin solo is exquisitely played with wonderful purity of tone by Michael Bochmann, the closing pianissimo seems to float in the still air. The work most suited to such an expansive acoustic is Vaughan Williams's *Tallis fantasia*, a deeply expressive performance which gives the listener the impression of sitting in a cathedral, with the solo string group, perfectly matched and blended in timbre, evoking a distant, ethereal organ. The lovely Butterworth pieces are tenderly sympathetic, and Alan Hacker's rhapsodically improvisatory account of Finzi's *Clarinet concerto* is full of colour and warmth. Perhaps Maurice Bourgue's oboe is balanced a little too closely in Vaughan Williams's *Oboe concerto* but the ear adjusts. On the other hand, the flutes melt magically into the strings in the famous *Greensleeves fantasia*. Delius's *Summer evening*, an early work, is quite memorable, and the suites of Parry and Finzi are full of colourful invention. The Bridge *Suite for strings* brings a lively response, with sumptuous textures. Because of the consistency of the acoustic illusion given to the listener, it is easy to sit back and be enveloped by this very involving music-making, which is made more rather than less communicative by its distancing. Only the opening *Cockaigne overture* of Elgar is a little lacking in profile and drama – and even here Boughton's relaxed lyrical approach is enjoyable, for he broadens the final climax very satisfyingly. Very reasonably priced, this box makes an outstanding bargain.

Galway, James (flute)

'The Concerto collection' (with various orchestras & conductors): BACH: *Concertos in A min., BWV 1056; in E min., BWV 1059.* VIVALDI: *Concertos, Op. 10/1–3.* Karl STAMITZ: *Concerto in G.* MOZART: *Concertos Nos. 1–2, K.313/4.* MERCADANTE: *Concerto in E min.* REINECKE: *Concerto in D, Op. 283.* MAYER: *Concerto (Mandala ki Raga Sangeet: A circle of Raga music).* RODRIGO: *Concierto pastoral.* KHACHATURIAN: *Concerto* (arr. from *Violin concerto* by Rampal/Galway). IBERT: *Concerto.* NIELSEN: *Concerto.*
*** BMG/RCA Analogue/Dig. RD 60450 (4) [60450-2-RC].

Four CDs of flute concertos may seem indigestible, but with James Galway's consistent artistry, remarkable bravura and distinct charisma always put at the service of the music – which covers a remarkably wide stylistic range – these records will give much pleasure. Most of the recordings are analogue (the Khachaturian, Mayer, Mercadante, Nielsen and Vivaldi are digital) but nearly all the transfers bring first-class sound. The Mozart concertos (among Galway's earliest recordings) are a bit fierce in the orchestra; they have recently been available on Pickwick CD at bargain price, and their inclusion makes one reflect that this box is expensive, even though its excellence is undeniable and it includes much fascinating repertoire that is not otherwise available. Some might feel that in Bach, Mozart and Vivaldi Galway's vibrato is stylistically inappropriate; yet his ability to charm is irresistible: he plays the famous slow-movement cantilena of Bach's BWV 1056 (the *F minor Harpsichord concerto*) as beautifully as one would expect, and his virtuosity in Vivaldi allegros is dazzling. His accounts of the charmingly spiky Rodrigo *Concierto pastoral* (which he commissioned) with its lovely contrasting central *Adagio*, and the delectably high-spirited Ibert piece (with its cool *Andante*) are unlikely to be bettered. When the Mayer *Concerto* was first issued on LP, we gave Galway's record a Rosette. Musical collusions between the cultures of East and West can easily become collisions, but not so here. John Mayer, Calcutta born, spices his five-movement concertante piece with Indian idioms, albeit westernized, and in Galway's hands the result is refreshingly spontaneous. There are perhaps finer versions of the Nielsen *Concerto* available, but Galway's is still a considerable one. Throughout the lesser works the star quality of his presentation makes second-rate music seem much better than it is. The Stamitz (Karl, not Johann), Reinecke and Mercadante are all most winning here. The Mercadante is quite dramatic, and in its *Largo* the orchestra ushers in the plaintive flute cantilena with a distinctly operatic flourish, while the Rondo has a catchy Russian theme. The slow movement of the Reinecke is also portentous at the opening but yields a rhapsodic melody that soars easily on Galway's silver flute, followed by a Weberian finale. The Stamitz is quite an ambitious piece, and Galway makes its elegance sound almost Mozartian. Throughout these discs he is given expert accompaniments; if the solo balance is usually rather forward, the orchestra is always well in the picture. There are fully adequate notes.

Gothenburg Symphony Orchestra, Neeme Järvi

Russian music (with (i) Gothenburg Symphony Ch.; (ii) Gothenburg Symphony Brass Band): BORODIN: *In the Steppes of Central Asia.* (i) *Prince Igor: Polovtsian dances.* RIMSKY-KORSAKOV: *Capriccio espagnol, Op. 34; Russian Easter festival overture, Op. 36.* TCHAIKOVSKY: (i; ii) *Overture 1812, Op. 49; Marche slave, Op. 31.*
*** DG Dig. 429 984-2; *429 984-4* [id.].

Järvi's Russian programme is generous in content (76 minutes); it is splendidly recorded and brings performances of all these favourite showpieces which are as fine as any available. Järvi finds both romance and poetry in Borodin's evocation of the Russian steppes and is equally impressive in the *Polovtsian dances* from *Prince Igor*, with lovely lyrical singing from the Gothenburg Chorus and a spirited conclusion. It is a pity that the percussion-led opening *Dance of the Polovtsi maidens* is omitted, but in the *General dance* (the one with the strenuous whacks on the bass drum) Torgny Sporsen makes a brief but effective contribution as the Khan. Both Rimsky-Korsakov pieces are brilliantly played: the close of the *Capriccio espagnol* is exhilarating in its unbuttoned exuberance, and the changing moods of the *Russian Easter festival overture*, whether solemn, ecstatic or bursting with energy, are combined impressively in an account which is unsurpassed in the current catalogue. *1812* is exciting too, and not just for the added Gothenburg brass and artillery, and for the fervour of the chorus at the opening. Järvi clearly knows how to structure the piece, and he obviously enjoys the histrionics, and so do we. *Marche slave* has a comparable Slavonic grandeur, its touch of melancholy offset by the quirky rhythmic feeling in the middle section with its nicely placed horn obbligato, and an exultant surge of adrenalin at the close. One might complain that the balance at the climax of *1812*, with carillon and chorus interpolated, is less than perfect, but the cannon make their contribution tellingly; the orchestral texture underpins brilliance and fullness in the upper strings with a fine brass sonority and plenty of weight in the bass, so that overall this is very successful indeed.

'Greensleeves'

English music (with (i) Sinfonia of L. or Hallé O, Barbirolli; (ii) New Philh. O, LPO or LSO, Boult; (iii) Williams, Bournemouth SO, Berglund; (iv) E. Sinfonia, Dilkes): (i) VAUGHAN WILLIAMS: *Fantasia on Greensleeves.* (ii) *The Lark ascending* (with Hugh Bean). (iii) *Oboe concerto in A min.* (ii) *English folksongs suite.* (i) DELIUS: *A Village Romeo and Juliet: Walk to the Paradise Garden. On hearing the first cuckoo in spring.* (iv) BUTTERWORTH: *The Banks of green willow.* (ii) ELGAR: *Serenade for strings, Op. 20.* (iii) MOERAN: *Lonely waters.*
(B) *** EMI TC2-MOM 104.

Looking at the programme and artists' roster, the reader will hardly need the confirmation that this is a very attractive tape anthology. Performances never disappoint, the layout is excellent, and for the car this is ideal. On domestic equipment the sound is a little variable, although the tape has been remastered since its first issue and now sounds pleasantly smooth on top. Often the quality is both vivid and rich, as in the title-piece and the Elgar *Serenade*. Vaughan Williams's *Oboe concerto*, stylishly played by John Williams, is admirably fresh. This is excellent value.

Hardenberger, Håkan (trumpet)

Twentieth-century trumpet concertos (with BBC PO, Elgar Howarth): HARRISON BIRTWISTLE: *Endless parade.* MAXWELL DAVIES: *Trumpet concerto.* BLAKE WATKINS: *Trumpet concerto.*
*** Ph. 432 075-2 [id.].

All three works here offer considerable difficulties for the ordinary music-lover to approach, but the performances are of a superlative standard, and a record of this calibre gives one the chance to explore their musical intricacies at leisure. Hardenberger commented on the high concentration at the recording sessions for Harrison Birtwistle's aptly named *Endless parade*, where textures and ideas, dynamics and colour all continually vary, as in a kaleidoscope. The trumpet leads throughout, often playing within the aura of a solo vibraphone. Maxwell Davies's *Concerto* (at 31 minutes) is even more ambitious, and the music moves through a series of changing patterns and tempi, using a plainsong, *Franciscus pauper et humilis*, as a basis, centrally evoking the idea of St Francis preaching to the birds. There is no question as to the evocative power of this work, in spite of its cryptic format. Michael Blake Watkins's *Concerto* may have an apparently more conventional layout, but its argument is complex; at one point the soloist has a heated dialogue with the three orchestral trumpets. The recording is outstandingly vivid.

Hardenberger, Håkan (trumpet), LPO, Elgar Howarth

Trumpet concertos: M. HAYDN: *Concerto No. 2 in C.* HERTEL: *Concerto No. 1 in E flat.* MOLTER: *Concerto No. 1 in D.* L. MOZART: *Concerto in D.* F. RICHTER: *Concerto in D.*
*** Ph. Dig. 426 311-2; *426 311-4* [id.].

Edward Tarr's excellent note begins by saying that the works recorded here 'testify to the high level of trumpet-playing after the death of Bach' – which might well be modified to read the astonishing level of trumpet-playing attained by Håkan Hardenberger. This young Swedish virtuoso makes everything sound completely effortless and, although none of these pieces is an imperishable masterpiece, he plays them all as if they were. Hugely enjoyable and beautifully recorded, with just the right amount of resonance, presence and bloom. Strongly recommended.

Haskil, Clara (piano)

Concertos (with various orchestras & conductors): MOZART: *Piano concertos Nos. 9 in E flat, K.271; 20 in D min., K.466; 23 in A, K.488; 24 in C min., K.491.* CHOPIN: *Piano concerto No. 2 in F min., Op. 21.* FALLA: *Nights in the gardens of Spain.* SCHUMANN: *Piano concerto in A min., Op. 54.* (Solo piano) *Kinderszenen, Op. 15; Waldszenen, Op. 82.*
(B) *** Ph. 426 964-2 (4) [id.].

These celebrated performances have come up well: they made their first reappearance in a 5-LP box and the recording quality largely belies their years – even the Mozart *A major*, K.488, made in Vienna with Sacher in 1954, sounds more than acceptable. The *D minor* (K.466) and *C minor* (K.491) *Concertos*, with Markevich and the Lamoureux Orchestra, are remarkably fresh for 1960 and offer beautifully rounded quality. Haskil rarely puts a foot wrong here, and though she does no more than hint at the darker dramatic fires of the *D minor*, K.466, she never beautifies the piano writing or reaches for the Dresden china. The Chopin and Falla, again both with Markevich, come from 1960, the last year of her life, and they serve as a reminder that she had a stronger temperament and a wider command of keyboard than her reputation as a Mozartian showed. Her Schumann *Concerto*, recorded in The Hague in 1951 under Willem van Otterloo, is particularly sympathetic, though the piano sound is not quite so fresh on this last disc. The solo Schumann pieces, recorded in the early 1950s, are entirely inside the composer's sensibility and, though again allowances must be made for the engineering, they are fewer than one might have expected. Not only is this set a welcome tribute to an artist of vision and gentleness that her admirers will want to collect, it is one that will give much quiet musical satisfaction.

Heifetz, Jascha (violin)

'The Acoustic recordings 1917–1924' (with André Benoist; Samuel Chotzinoff; O, Pasternak): SCHUBERT: *Ave Maria.* DRIGO: *Valse bluette.* ELGAR: *La Capricieuse, Op. 17.* SARASATE: *Malagueña, Habanera, Op. 21/1 & 2; Introduction and tarantelle, Op. 43; Zapateado, Op. 23/2; Zigeunerweisen, Op. 20/1; Carmen fantasy, Op. 25.* BAZZINI: *La ronde des lutins.* BEETHOVEN: *Ruins of Athens: Chorus of Dervishes; Turkish march.* WIENIAWSKI: *Scherzo-Tarantelle, Op. 16; Concerto No. 2, Op. 22: Romance.* ACHRON: *Hebrew melody, Op. 33; Hebrew lullaby, Hebrew dance, Op. 35; Stimmung, Op. 32.* PAGANINI: *Moto perpetuo; Caprices, Nos. 13 & 20.* KREISLER: *Minuet; Sicilienne et Rigaudon.* GLAZUNOV: *Meditation; Valse.* MOSZKOWSKI: *Guitarre, Op. 45/2.* CHOPIN: *Nocturnes, Op. 9/2; Op. 27/2.* TCHAIKOVSKY: *Souvenir d'un lieu cher: Scherzo, Op. 42/2. Serenade: Valse, Op. 48/2. Concerto, Op. 35: Canzonetta. Sérénade mélancolique, Op. 26.* MENDELSSOHN: *On wings of song, Op. 34/2; Concerto in E min.: finale.* DVOŘÁK: *Slavonic dances, Op. 46/2; Op. 72/2 & 8.* SCHUMANN: *Myrthen: Widmung, Op. 25/1.* LALO: *Symphonie espagnole, Op. 21: Andante.* MOZART: *Divertimento No. 17, K.334: Minuet. Haffner Serenade, K.250: Rondo.* D'AMBROSIO: *Serenade, Op. 4.* JUON: *Berceuse, Op. 28/3.* GOLDMARK: *Concerto in A min., Op. 28: Andante.* GODOWSKY: *Waltz in D.* BRAHMS: *Hungarian dance No. 1 in G min.* HAYDN: *Quartet (Lark), Op. 64/5: Vivace.* GRANADOS: *Danzas españolas, Op. 37/5; Andaluza.* BOULANGER: *Nocturne in F; Cortège.* SCOTT: *The gentle maiden.* SAINT-SAËNS: *Havanaise, Op. 83.*
(M) (***) BMG/RCA mono GD 80942 [0942-2-RG] (3).

These recordings first appeared on LP during the mid-1970s and their reissue on CD serves as a salutary reminder of Heifetz's extraordinary powers. The earliest records come from the year of the Russian Revolution, when Heifetz was still sixteen and only five years after he had made his début in St Petersburg. As always with Heifetz, even the highest expectations are surpassed: his effortless technical mastery is dazzling, the golden tone strong and pure, the accuracy of his intonation almost beyond belief and his taste impeccable. The collector will also be agreeably surprised by the quality of sound; the earliest was made only two weeks after his Carnegie Hall début, when the art of recording was still relatively primitive, and the original 78-r.p.m. disc was single-sided. One critic, writing in 1918, said of the then seventeen-year-old boy, 'Kreisler is king, Heifetz the prophet, and all the rest violinsts.' Seventy or more years later, his brilliance remains undimmed. The recordings are arranged in chronological order, though the differences during the period are relatively small. This set is a mandatory purchase for all who care about the art of violin playing.

Hess, Myra (piano)

'A vignette': (i) MOZART: *Piano concerto No. 21 in C, K.467.* HAYDN: *Sonata No. 37 in D, Hob XVI/37.* SCHUBERT: (ii) *Piano trio No. 1 in B flat, D.898. Rosamunde: No. 9: ballet in G; Sonata in A, D.664.* (iii) BRAHMS: *Piano trio No. 2 in C, Op. 87.*
(**) APR mono CDAPR 7012 (2) [id.]; with (i) Hallé O, Leslie Heward; (ii; iii) Jelly d'Arányi (violin); (ii) Felix Salmond (cello); (iii) Gaspar Cassadó (cello).

The first CD brings to light a recording of the Mozart *C major concerto*, K.467, made with the Hallé Orchestra and Leslie Heward in 1942, and never before published. Bryan Crimp's excellent notes explain that pitch fluctuations in the records caused by erratic electricity supplies troubled the sessions and in the end the project was abandoned and the masters were destroyed. However, shellac test-pressings of seven of the eight sides were discovered in 1970 and, quite accidentally, a tape transfer of the whole set surfaced. Quality is remarkably good, and what strikes one about the performance is the measured, urbane humanity of it all. In this day and age when the outer movements are taken so briskly, this seems almost demure. This is lovely Mozart playing and it is good to have Denis Matthews' cadenzas. What a superbly musical accompanist Leslie Heward was! The Schubert *Sonata*, recorded in 1928, also sounds as if it comes from a more leisurely age, but there is a great deal of surface noise. The chamber-music recordings call for much more tolerance: the Schubert *B flat Trio* was recorded in America in 1927, with Jelly d'Arányi and Felix Salmond, and issued on the light-blue L label, and the Brahms, with Cassadó as cellist, in 1935 on four LX discs. The sound is not very good in either and surfaces are heavy.

Holliger, Heinz (oboe)

Concertos (with (i) Frankfurt RSO, Inbal; (ii) ECO, Leppard): (i) BELLINI: *Oboe concerto in E flat.* MOLIQUE: *Oboe concertino in G min.* MOSCHELLES: *Concertante in F for flute and oboe* (with Aurèle Nicolet). RIETZ: *Konzertstück in F min., Op. 33.* (ii) FIALA: *Cor anglais concerto in E flat.* HUMMEL: *Adagio, theme and variations in F.*
(B) **(*) Ph. 426 972-2; *426 972-4* [id.].

The playing here is of high quality and the measure generous: six concertante works with a playing time of 76 minutes. The recording is very good too, if rather resonantly inflated orchestrally, and the cost is modest. So perhaps this collection (mostly recorded in the mid-1970s) may be acquired for the two-movement Bellini concerto which is delightful, and the Moschelles double concerto is attractively inventive too, with a very fetching tune in the Rondo finale. The other works are more conventional and rather anonymous; although the Fiala is agreeable enough, the main theme of the Hummel sounds a trifle faded in its intended charm. But Holliger makes the most of all his many opportunities for stylish bravura throughout this disc, and he is well accompanied too.

Hollywood Bowl Symphony Orchestra, Carmen Dragon

'Fiesta': MASSENET: *Le Cid: Aragonaise.* BIZET: *Carmen: Chanson bohème.* arr. DRAGON: *La Paloma.* GLINKA: *Jota aragonesa.* MONTERDE: *La Virgen de la Macarena.* DE CAMPO: *La Chiapanecas.* DELIBES: *Maids of Cadiz.* GRANADOS: *Andaluza; Goyescas: Intermezzo.* BENJAMIN: *Jamaican rumba.* SERRADELL: *La Golandrina.* LARA: *Granada.* CHABRIER: *España.* LECUONA: *Andalucia.* PONCE: *Estrelita.* LECUONA: *Malagueña.*
(M) **(*) EMI stereo/mono CDM7 63734-2 [id.].

This was the best of a series of recordings, originally issued on LP on the Capitol label at the very beginning of the 1960s. Carmen Dragon proved to be a master of this popular Latin repertoire and produced orchestral playing that was both brilliant and seductive, and always polished. The recording acoustic is rather dry and the CD transfer tends to emphasize this effect. But the performances of pieces like *La Golandrina*, Dragon's own enticing arrangement of *La Paloma*, and Arthur Benjamin's catchy *Jamaican rumba* are very appealing when the presentation is so sympathetic and sparkling. Chabrier's *España* is also highly successful; though this, like the last three pieces listed and the Granados *Goyescas Intermezzo*, is a mono recording, the sound remains full and immediate.

Hollywood Bowl Symphony Orchestra, Felix Slatkin

'Symphonic dances': TCHAIKOVSKY: *Sleeping Beauty: Waltz.* KABALEVSKY: *The Comedians: Galop.* GRIEG: *Norwegian dance No. 2.* WEINBERGER: *Schwanda the Bagpiper: Polka.* GLIÈRE: *The Red Poppy: Russian sailors' dance.* BIZET: *L'Arlésienne: Farandole.* DELIBES: *Sylvia: Pizzicato.* KHACHATURIAN: *Gayaneh: Sabre dance.* SAINT-SAENS: *Samson et Dalila: Bacchanale.* MENDELSSOHN: *Midsummer Night's Dream: Scherzo.* OFFENBACH, arr. ROSENTHAL: *Gaîté parisienne* (ballet; complete).
(M) ** EMI CDM7 63737-2 [id.].

The original collection issued under this title on analogue LP was a great success, offering a stream of good tunes, brilliantly played and recorded, and producing a fair degree of variety. For the reissue EMI have added the complete score of Offenbach's *Gaîté parisienne* (38 minutes), racily played but with sound that is very bright and somewhat two-dimensional, and with the studio acoustic the more noticeable.

'Boléro': RAVEL: *Boléro; Pavane pour une infante défunte.* ALBÉNIZ: *Iberia: Triana.* RIMSKY-KORSAKOV: *Capriccio espagnol.* MASSENET: *Le Cid: Navarraise.* WALDTEUFEL: *España waltz.* GOULD: *Latin-American symphonette.*
(M) ** EMI CDM7 63738-2 [id.].

The star item here is Gould's engaging *Latin-American Symphonette,* written in 1940; all the movements are based on dance themes, with the *Scherzo-Guaracha* particularly witty. The performance is as fine as any available and the vividly forward balance suits the music, although in Ravel's *Boléro* it reduces the overall dynamic range somewhat. The other short pieces are all brightly done, with the gentle melancholy of Ravel's *Pavane* caught well; but the account of Rimsky's *Capriccio espagnol* is not distinctive, and the climax of *Triana* is rather brittle and overlit.

(Philip) Jones Brass Ensemble

'Baroque brass': BIBER: *Sonata a 7.* ANON.: *Sonata from Die Bankelsangerlieder.* M. FRANCK: *Intrata.* HASSLER: *Intrada V.* SPEER: *Sonata for trumpet & 3 trombones; Sonata for 3 trombones; Sonata for 4 trombones; Sonata for 2 trumpets and 3 trombones.* SCHEIDT: *Canzona a 10.* BACH: *Chorale: Nun danket alle Gott. Capriccio on the departure of a beloved brother, BWV 992: Aria & fugue in imitation of the postillion's horn (arr. Breuer). Cello suite No. 1: Menuetto & Courante* (arr. Fletcher for solo tuba). D. SCARLATTI: *Keyboard sonatas, Kk.380; Kk.430; Kk.443* (arr. Dodgson). C. P. E. BACH: *March.*
(M) *** Decca 425 727-2; *425 727-4* [id.].

An imaginative and highly rewarding programme, among the best of the Philip Jones anthologies. The music of Daniel Speer is strikingly inventive and the Bach and Scarlatti arrangements are highly engaging – the latter with no attempt at miniaturization. The C. P. E. Bach *March* makes a superbly vigorous coda. If the baroque idiom and the sound of modern brass instruments combine easily in your aural consciousness, this can be recommended, though not to be taken all at once. The recording is first class.

Kaufman, Louis (violin)

'Louis Kaufman plays' ((i) with LSO, Bernard Herrmann): (i) PISTON: *Violin concerto No. 1.* COPLAND: *Violin sonata.* RUSSELL BENNETT: *Hexapoda.* MCBRIDE: *Aria and toccata in swing.* STILL: *Blues from Lennox Avenue Suite.* KERN: *The song is you; Smoke gets in your eyes.*
(***) Bay Cities mono BCD 1019 [id.].

Louis Kaufman has had a long and distinguished career, both as a soloist in the concert hall and in Hollywood, and has been an eloquent champion of American music. The *First Violin concerto* (1939) is typical Piston, fertile in invention and finely crafted. Its sole representation so far has been an American LP (on the Mace label) by Hugo Kohlberg, but Kaufman's eloquent and fervent performance makes out an even stronger case for it. The ideas are memorable, beautifully fashioned and with a strong lyric impulse and a keen sense of momentum. This version comes from a concert given by the LSO and Bernard Herrmann, broadcast in 1956 from the BBC's Maida Vale Studios. The Copland *Violin sonata*, with the composer at the piano, is an even earlier recording, from 1948, originally on the Concert Hall label. The *Sonata* is vintage Copland, with some reflective and tender slow music. The other pieces, by Richard Russell Bennett, William Grant Still and Jerome Kern, all testify to the nervous energy and strong personality of this fine player. The recordings are naturally of variable quality (there is some occasional surface noise in the Copland and Piston pieces), but lovers of American music and of the violin should not be put off by this.

Lipatti, Dinu (piano)

(with Nadia Boulanger; Philh. O, Zürich Tonhalle O, Lucerne Festival O; Galliera, Ackermann, Karajan): BACH: *Chorale, Jesu, joy of man's desiring* (arr. Hess, from BWV 147); *Chorale preludes, BWV 599 & 639* (both arr. Busoni); *Partita No. 1, BWV 825; Siciliana* (arr. Kempff, from BWV 1031). D. SCARLATTI: *Sonatas, Kk. 9 & 380.* MOZART: *Piano concerto No. 21 in C, K.467; Piano sonata No. 8 in A min., K.310.* SCHUBERT: *Impromptus Nos. 2–3, D.899/2 & 3.* SCHUMANN: *Piano concerto in A min., Op. 54.* GRIEG: *Piano concerto in A min., Op. 16.* CHOPIN: *Piano concerto No. 1 in E min., Op. 11; Barcarolle, Op. 60; Études, Op. 10/5 & 25/5; Mazurka No. 32, Op. 50/3; Nocturne No. 8, Op. 27/2; Piano sonata No. 3 in B min., Op. 58; Waltzes Nos. 1–14.* LISZT: *Années de pèlerinage, 2nd Year: Sonnetto 104 del Petrarca.* RAVEL: *Alborada del gracioso.* BRAHMS: *Waltzes* (4 hands), *Op. 39/1–2, 5–6, 10, 14–15.* ENESCU: *Piano sonata No. 3 in D, Op. 25.*
❀ (M) (***) EMI CZS7 67163-2 (5) [id.].

This set represents Lipatti's major recording achievements. Whether in Bach (*Jesu, joy of man's desiring* is unforgettable) or Chopin – his *Waltzes* seem to have grown in wisdom and subtlety over the years – Scarlatti or Mozart, these performances are very special indeed. The remastering is done well, and this is a must for anyone with an interest in the piano.

London Classical Players, Roger Norrington

'Early Romantic overtures': WEBER: *Oberon.* MENDELSSOHN: *The Hebrides (Fingal's Cave), Op. 26.* BERLIOZ: *Les Francs-juges, Op. 3.* SCHUMANN: *Genoveva, Op. 81/5.* SCHUBERT: *Rosamunde (Die Zauberharfe).* WAGNER: *Der fliegende Holländer.*
**(*) EMI Dig. CDC7 49889-2; *EL 749889-4* [id.].

In these performances of six high-Romantic overtures, Norrington and his orchestra of period instrumentalists bring out the same tangy qualities as in earlier music. Even if Mendelssohn's *Hebrides* lacks atmospheric magic, there are many compensations, and Wagner's *Flying Dutchman* is the most ear-catching item of all, with its braying horns, using the 1841 text. One reservation is that Norrington, having once chosen a speed, is reluctant to modify it. This is not for everyone but is fascinating nevertheless. Sound that is characteristic of EMI engineers working at Abbey Road.

London Philharmonic Orchestra Brass, Jorge Mester

'Fanfares for the common man': COPLAND: *Fanfare for the common man; Ceremonial fanfare; Inaugural fanfare.* HANSON: *Chorale & fanfare; Fanfare for the Royal Signal Corps.* HARRIS: *Fanfare for the forces.* COWELL: *Fanfare for Latin allies.* WAGENAAR: *Fanfare for airmen.* GOULD: *Fanfare for freedom; Columbian fanfares.* DEEMS TAYLOR: *Fanfare for Russia.* BERNSTEIN: *Fanfares 1–2; Shivaree.* FULEIHAN: *Fanfare for the Medical Corps.* Virgil THOMSON: *Fanfare for France.* PISTON: *Ceremonial fanfare; Fanfare for the Fighting French.* CRESTON: *Fanfare for paratroopers.* E. GOOSSENS: *Fanfare for the Merchant Marine.*
*** Koch Dig. 37012-2; *27012-4* [id.].

This collection – although not to be taken at a single sitting – offers more musical variety than might be expected. It is centred on a series of commissions made by the late Sir Eugene Goossens between 1931 and 1946. At that time he was Musical Director of the Cincinnati Symphony Orchestra and also a particular devotee of fanfares. A dozen of the items included here were among the nineteen he brought into being, including his own which genially interpolates famous traditional melodies like *The roast beef of Old England* and a rather grand version of *Heart of oak.* The most famous of the other commissions is the title-piece by Copland (here played majestically), and the other two contributions by this composer are only marginally less popular in appeal. Walter Piston, however, offers the toughest brass polyphony; Morton Gould unashamedly increases the range of colour possible by introducing woodwind, while Bernstein's mood is uninhibited, especially in his Ivesian *Shivaree.* Hanson's ambitious three-part *Chorale and Fanfare* expands to a thrilling climax which will appeal to all who enjoy his *Romantic Symphony.* Virgil Thomson combines the style of a classic French military march with witty quotations of *Frère Jacques* and *Yankee doodle dandy*, and Deems Taylor draws on a Russian folksong (*Dubinushka*). The LSO brass playing is polished and spectacular, and the recording, made in St John's, Smith Square, is well balaced and sonorously brilliant.

Menuhin, Yehudi (violin)

'75th Birthday Edition' (with various artists): BARTÓK: *Violin concerto No. 1; Viola concerto; Rhapsodies 1–2.* RAVEL: *Piano trio in A min.* DEBUSSY: *Violin sonata; Sonata for flute, viola & harp.* FAURÉ: *Andante in B flat, Op. 75; Berceuse in D, Op. 16.* SIBELIUS:

Violin concerto, Op. 47. NIELSEN: *Violin concerto, Op. 33.* SCHUBERT: *Fantasia in C, D.934.* MENDELSSOHN: *Sonata in F.* BRAHMS: *Horn trio in E flat, Op. 40.* BERG: *Violin concerto.* BLOCH: *Violin concerto.*
(M) *** EMI mono/stereo CMS7 63984-2 (5).

This mid-price CD compilation restores a number of valuable Menuhin performances to the catalogue, most of them from the mid-1960s. Not all of them show this great artist on top form, but nothing he touches is without musical insights, and it is good to have this fascinating retrospective, warts and all. The first disc is devoted to the Bartók *Concertos* (with Dorati and the New Philharmonia) and the two *Rhapsodies* (with Boulez and the BBC Symphony Orchestra). (Readers will note that the *Second Violin concerto* is not included. Menuhin recorded it three times, twice with Dorati, in 1946 and again in 1967; of the three, the 1953 mono account with Furtwängler is surely the one to have – see our main volume, p. 74.) Less well known is his Ravel *Piano trio* with Cassadó and Louis Kentner, dating from 1961, beautifully played by all concerned, but with the balance placing the cello too far back and allowing Menuhin to dominate rather more than he might perhaps have intended. The Debussy *Violin sonata*, with Jacques Février, and the other-worldly *Sonata for flute, viola and harp*, with Michel Debost and the legendary Lili Laskine, were both recorded in the mid-1970s (and not issued in the UK). It must be conceded that there are more subtle and better-integrated accounts of both. Menuhin conveys much of the innocence of the Schubert *C major Fantasy*, again with Kentner making a distinguished contribution. It is also good to have the Mendelssohn *F major Sonata* (with Gerald Moore) – though the 1953 mono recording sounds its age – and even better to have the Brahms *Horn trio* with Alan Civil and Hephzibah Menuhin. Despite some felicities, neither the Nielsen *Concerto*, recorded with Mogens Wöldike and the Danish State Radio Orchestra in 1952, nor the Sibelius with Sir Adrian Boult and the LPO (1956) shows Menuhin at his very best, but his classic 1964 account of the Bloch *Concerto*, made with Paul Kletzki and the Philharmonia, is an altogether different matter. For a considerable period Szigeti's pioneering account with Charles Münch and the Paris Conservatoire had an intimidating effect upon other performers, including (as he told us at the time) Menuhin himself. His was only the second recording of this powerful work, and this deeply felt and finely balanced account is a worthy successor to the Szigeti, which so far has not been transferred to CD in the UK. Menuhin's thus remains the only current CD version of this intense and evocative score. His account of the Berg, with Boulez conducting the BBC Orchestra, also comes up well.

Mexican State Symphony Orchestra, Enrique Bátiz

'Music of Spain': TURINA: *La procession du Rocio; La oración del Torero.* GRANADOS: *Danzas españolas: Oriental; Andalouse; Rondalla, Op. 37. Goyescas: Intermezzo.* ALBÉNIZ: *Catalonia.* FALLA: *La vida breve: Danza No. 1. El amor brujo:* excerpts.
** ASV Dig. CDDCA 735; *CDCA 735* [id.].

Bátiz and his orchestra have the full measure of this repertoire, but the recording lacks a sultry glamour to offset its brash brightness. The most effective pieces are the three Granados *Dances*, and it was a pity that *El amor brujo* was not given complete, since there is plenty of room left on the CD.

Moiseiwitsch, Benno (piano)

BEETHOVEN: *Piano concerto No. 5 in E flat, Op. 73* (with LPO, Szell). GODOWSKY: *Concert paraphrase on 'Die Fledermaus'*. LISZT: *Hungarian fantasia* (with LPO, Constant Lambert). MEDTNER: *Fairy Tale in E min., Op. 34/2*. PROKOFIEV: *Suggestion diabolique, Op. 4/4*.
(**) Koch mono 3-7035-2 [id.].

Moiseiwitsch gives a commanding and magisterial account of the *Emperor*, with Szell and the LPO, recorded in 1938, and a pretty dazzling account of the Liszt *Hungarian fantasia* with Lambert the following year. As a pupil of Leschetitzky, who had studied with Czerny (who had in his turn studied with Beethoven), Moiseiwitsch was a renowned interpreter of this Beethoven *Concerto* (it was among the last things he played in public) and he gives a noble reading of great eloquence. As an example of virtuosity, his *Suggestion diabolique* can hold its own with most newcomers. The Medtner and Prokofiev date from 1928 and actually sound better than later recordings. In the otherwise satisfactory transfer of the *Emperor* there is an acidulated sound on the upper strings which we do not recall from the original plum-label 78s.

Moscow Virtuosi, Vladimir Spivakov

'Modern portraits': HARTMANN: *Concerto funèbre*. STRAVINSKY: *Concerto in D for strings*. PENDERECKI: *Capriccio for oboe and 11 strings*. SCHNITTKE: *Suite in the old style* (with E. Kissin). PROKOFIEV: *Overture on Hebrew themes, Op. 34*.
**(*) RCA Dig. RD 60370 [60370-2-RC].

The most haunting work on this record is the *Concerto funèbre* that Karl-Amadeus Hartmann composed in 1939 after Hitler annexed Czechoslovakia, a work of bleak pessimism which quotes the celebrated Hussite theme used by Smetana in *Má Vlast*. A powerful and thoughtful piece, very different in character from the bright neo-classical Stravinsky *Concerto in D*, which is played with great spirit and expertise. Otherwise it is a fairly rum anthology: it is difficult to envisage the kind of collector whose taste would necessarily embrace all these pieces. Schnittke's *Suite* is indifferent pastiche, and the Prokofiev *Overture* seems curiously out of place. No grumbles about either the performances or recordings.

Murphy, Maurice (trumpet), **Consort of London, Robert Haydon Clark**

'Favourite trumpet concertos': ARUTIUNIAN: *Concerto*. CLARKE: *Prince of Denmark's march*. HAYDN: *Concerto in E flat*. HUMMEL: *Concerto in E flat*. PURCELL: *Trumpet tune and air*.
**(*) Collins Dig. 1073-2; *1073-4* [id.].

Maurice Murphy is a first-class soloist; anyone wanting the Haydn and Hummel concertos, plus the piece we used to know as the '*Trumpet voluntary*', on a single disc or tape should be well satisfied. The solo timbre is gleamingly bright and there is bravura and sparkle and warm phrasing in slow movements. There is not quite the stylistic distinction of Hardenberger here, but the music-making is enjoyable and well recorded.

However, few collectors will want to return to the Arutiunian work very often: it is colourful and fluent but not much else.

I Musici

BARTÓK: *Rumanian folk dances* (with R. Michelucci). BRITTEN: *Simple Symphony, Op. 4*. HINDEMITH: *Trauermusik for viola and strings* (with Cino Ghedin). MARTIN: *Études*. NIELSEN: *Little Suite, Op. 1*. ROUSSEL: *Sinfonietta, Op. 52*.
(M) **(*) Ph. 426 669-2; *426 669-4* [id.].

A valuable anthology, particularly at mid-price. The Britten *Simple Symphony*, recorded in 1962, is perhaps the least convincing and needs more tonal bloom, but otherwise few qualifications need be made. The Frank Martin *Studies* are played marvellously: tone is always in focus and everyone is in the middle of the note, so that the timbre is particularly rich and full. I Musici play these and most of the other pieces with tremendous virtuosity; the Hindemith *Funeral music*, written in a few hours on the death of King George V, is given with real feeling. The first movement of the Nielsen is a bit on the fast side, but otherwise this record gives much pleasure; at the time of writing, no other CD version of the Roussel *Sinfonietta* is available. The recordings are mostly from 1968 and come up very well indeed.

NBC Symphony Orchestra, Arturo Toscanini

'The Toscanini collection': BEETHOVEN: *Leonora overture No. 3*. VERDI: *Nabucco: Va pensiero* (with Westminster Ch.). SMETANA: *Má Vlast: Vltava*. BERLIOZ: *Roméo et Juliette: Queen Mab scherzo*. BRAHMS: *Academic festival overture*. WAGNER: *Die Walküre: Ride of the Valkyries*. PUCCINI: *La Bohème: Ehi! Rodolfo!; O soave fanciulla* (with Albanese, Peerce, Cehanovsky, Moscona, Valentino). ROSSINI: *William Tell: Overture*.
(B) (**(*)) BMG/RCA VD 60340; *VK 60340* [60340-2-RV; *60340-4-RV*].

This generous limited-edition bargain sampler for the BMG/RCA Toscanini Edition offers 68 minutes of Toscanini recordings, warts and all. It is one of the tragedies of recording history that the great Italian maestro did not have a producer with the strength of personality of a Walter Legge to supervise his recordings. (Indeed, Elisabeth Schwarzkopf has recounted the occasion when her husband and Toscanini eventually met and – to her dismay – Legge fearlessly criticized the Toscanini recorded legacy. Toscanini's response was surprisingly positive, and he agreed, almost ruefully, that perhaps he had needed someone of Legge's calibre as his producer.) However, we have to accept what there is and that includes the excrably dry sounds afforded by the notorious Studio 8-H, which is used for the Beethoven and Brahms Overtures and the *La Bohème* excerpt, totally without atmosphere. Verdi's *Va pensiero*, with its clear chorus, and Smetana's *Vltava* sound rather better, although the latter has some distortion. The Carnegie Hall recordings are more attractive, notably the marvellously played *Queen Mab scherzo* and the brilliantly charismatic *William Tell overture*.

French music: FRANCK: *Symphony in D min*. DEBUSSY: *Marche écossaise*. MEYERBEER: *Prologue Dinorah*. ROUSSEL: *Le festin de l'araignée, Op. 17*.
(***) Dell'Arte mono CD DA 9021 [id.].

The recording of the Franck *Symphony* comes from 1946; an earlier account in the Franklyn Mint Toscanini LP edition gave two movements from a 1940 performance, but the present version is making its first appearance, at least on this side of the Atlantic. The Roussel comes from the same year; the Meyerbeer and Debussy are earlier, from 1938 and 1940 respectively, and we are offered the *Prologue* to the Meyerbeer rather than a straightforward overture, as it includes extensive passages for chorus. The playing is pretty dazzling throughout, though the Roussel is rather spoilt by too hurried a tempo for the first animated section (the *Entry of the Ants*) and then again at the *Funeral of the Day-Fly*. The Franck is a marvellously strong performance. As always with these dry NBC recordings, the sound calls for a tolerance that is well worth extending for the sake of music-making which has much charisma.

Northern Sinfonia of England, Richard Hickox

'English miniatures': BALFOUR GARDINER: *Overture to a comedy.* QUILTER: *3 English dances; Where the rainbow ends: suite.* WALTON: *Siesta.* GOOSSENS: *By the tarn.* BAX: *Mediterranean.* WARLOCK: *An old song.* GERMAN: *Henry VIII: 3 dances.*
**(*) EMI Dig. CDC7 49933-2 [id.]; *EL 749933-4.*

An extremely lightweight programme, given polished and sympathetic performances, brightly recorded. Only the German *Henry VIII Dances* and the charming *Rosamund* from Quilter's *Where the rainbow ends* incidental music are at all well known, but the rest is agreeably tuneful and nicely scored. Warlock's *Old song* has flavours of both Delius and Butterworth. What a pity the opportunity was not taken to include Quilter's delightful *Children's overture.*

Orchestre de Paris, (i) Sir John Barbirolli or (ii) Serge Baudo

'French music': (i) DEBUSSY: *La Mer; Nocturnes* (with female chorus). (ii) RAVEL: *Ma Mère l'Oye: suite.* FAURÉ: *Dolly, Op. 56. Masques et bergamasques; Pelléas et Mélisande: suite.* ROUSSEL: *Bacchus et Ariane: suite.* MESSIAEN: *Les offrandes oubliées.*
(M) *** EMI CZS7 62669-2 (2) [Ang. CDMB 62669].

As can be seen, Serge Baudo has the lion's share of this highly recommendable collection, recorded in the Paris Salle Wagram in 1968–9 and admirably transferred to CD. His performances are perceptive and sensitive and the Orchestre de Paris plays beautifully. Barbirolli's music-making has plenty of sensuous warmth too, but his earlier, Hallé version of *La Mer* has more grip. Nevetheless the Fauré, Messiaen and Roussel items (all discussed separately under their individual composers) make this concert well worth having. Incidentally, the French documentation by Jean Roy is worth taking the trouble to translate: it is more colourful and often has more of interest to say about the music than the English notes by Barry Millington.

Osipov State Russian Folk Orchestra, Vitaly Gnutov

'Balalaika favourites': BUDASHIN: *Fantasy on two folk songs.* arr. GORODOVSKAYA: *At sunrise.* KULIKOV: *The Linden tree.* OSIPOV: *Kamarinskaya.* MIKHAILOV/SHALAYEV: *Fantasy on Volga melodies.* ANDREYEV: *In the moonlight; Under the apple tree; Waltz of the faun.* SOLOVIEV/SEDOY: *Midnight in Moscow.* TCHAIKOVSKY: *Dance of the comedians.* SHISHAKOV: *The living room.* arr. MOSSOLOV: *Evening bells.* arr. POPONOV: *My dear friend, please visit me.* RIMSKY-KORSAKOV: *Flight of the bumble-bee.*
❀ (M) *** Mercury 432 000-2 [id.].

The Mercury recording team visited Moscow in 1962 in order to make the first recordings produced in the Soviet Union by Western engineers since the Revolution. Wilma Cozart Fine, the Recording Director, recalls that every morning, more in hope than expectation, they would set up their equipment (although they lacked official permission from the bureaucracy, because of arguments over royalty rights), and every morning the musicians would appear, arriving in all kinds of conveyances and carrying balalaikas plus other instruments; and, full of enthusiasm, the sessions would begin. The spirit of that unique occasion is captured wonderfully here – analogue atmosphere at its best. The rippling waves of balalaika sound, the accordion solos, the exhilarating accelerandos and crescendos that mark the style of this music-making: all are recorded with wonderful immediacy. Whether in the shimmering web of sound of *The Linden tree* or *Evening bells*, the sparkle of the folksongs or the sheer bravura of items like *In the moonlight*, which gets steadily faster and louder, or in Rimsky's famous piece (sounding like a hive full of bumble-bees), this is irresistible, and the recording is superbly real in its CD format.

Perlman, Itzhak (violin)

'Popular violin repertoire': SARASATE: *Carmen fantasy* (with RPO, Foster). TARTINI/KREISLER: *Variations on a theme by Corelli.* NOVÁČEK: *Perpetuum mobile.* JOPLIN: *The Entertainer.* BACH: *Violin concerto No. 2 in E, BWV 1042* (with ECO, Barenboim). PAGANINI: *Caprices, Op. 1/9 & 24.*
(B) *** CfP CD-CFP 4492; *TC-CFP 4492.*

Spanish music: SARASATE: *Carmen fantasy* (with RPO, Foster); *Zigeunerweisen* (with Pittsburgh SO, Previn). *Danzas españolas: Malagueña; Habanera, Op. 21/1–2; Playera and Zapateado, Op. 23; Spanish dance, Op. 26/8. Caprice basque, Op. 24; Romanza andaluza, Op. 22.* FALLA, arr. KOCHANSKI: *Suite populaire espagnole.* GRANADOS: *Spanish dance.* HALFFTER: *Danza de la gitana.* ALBENIZ: *Malagueña, Op. 165/5* (all with Samuel Sanders, piano).
(M) *** EMI CDM7 63533-2; *EG 763533-4.*

Perlman's dazzling account of Sarasate's *Carmen fantasy* is offered here with a choice of couplings. The collection of popular Spanish pieces demonstrates a delight in virtuosity in the most joyful way; but some may feel that the balance is a shade too close, and this effect is emphasized somewhat on CD. The miscellaneous collection is less expensive and would be our first choice. It includes not only a delectable account of Scott Joplin's most popular rag and Paganini's best-known *Caprice* (the source of all those variations) but also a fine account of Bach's *E major Violin concerto.*

Philadelphia Orchestra, Arturo Toscanini

'The Philadelphia recordings, 1941–2': DEBUSSY: *La Mer; Images: Ibéria.* RESPIGHI: *Feste romane.* TCHAIKOVSKY: *Symphony No. 6 in B min. (Pathétique), Op. 74.* R. STRAUSS: *Death and transfiguration, Op. 24.* MENDELSSOHN: *A Midsummer Night's Dream: Overture, Op. 21, & incidental music, Op. 61.* BERLIOZ: *Romeo et Juliette: Queen Mab scherzo.* SCHUBERT: *Symphony No. 9 in C (Great), D.644.*
(M) (**(*)) BMG/RCA GD 60328; *GK 60328* (4) [60328-2-RG; *60328-4-RG*]. Phd. O, Toscanini.

During the winter season of 1941/2 Toscanini was resident maestro in Philadelphia, and he made a series of recordings with the orchestra, at the peak of its form, many of which – though not all – bring a more relaxed style of performance than he often achieved in New York at that time. Most successful are the performances of Schubert's *Great C major Symphony* and Tchaikovsky's *Pathétique*, although the *Midsummer night's dream* selection brings a pleasing lightness of touch to match his Berlioz *Queen Mab scherzo*. The Strauss tone-poem, too, has the right kind of tension. The disappointments are the Debussy and Respighi, which he recorded more successfully elsewhere; the recording too is much less satisfactory in these works.

Richter, Sviatoslav (piano)

'Sviatoslav Richter plays': GRIEG: *Concerto in A min., Op. 16.* SCHUMANN: *Concerto in A min., Op. 54* (with Monte Carlo Opera O, Matačić). MOZART: *Concerto No. 22 in E flat, K.482.* BEETHOVEN: *Piano concerto No. 3 in C min., Op. 37* (with Philh. O, Muti). *Sonatas Nos. 1 in F min., Op. 2/1; 7 in D, Op. 10/3; 17 in D min. (Tempest), Op. 31/2.* SCHUBERT: *Wanderer fantasy, D.760; Sonata No. 13 in A, D.664.* SCHUMANN: *Faschingsschwank aus Wien, Op. 26.*
(M) **(*) EMI CZS7 67197-2 (4).

Some reservations have to be expressed here, of course: the performances of the Grieg and Schumann *Concertos* are very wilful, but the commanding mastery of this playing is truly remarkable. The standard of the recorded sound, too, is often very realistic, particularly the solo recordings Peter André made of Schubert and Schumann from recitals in Paris and Italy. They need to be reproduced at a high volume level; then the artist's presence is uncanny, while the playing here shows Richter at his most poetically charismatic: the slow movement of the Schubert *A major* is unforgettable. The Beethoven *Sonatas* are pretty impressive too, and can be ranked alongside the versions of Gilels. In the concertos Richter is never less than illuminating; and overall this box has many insights to offer and much musical stimulation.

'Romantic Overtures'

'Romantic Overtures' (played by: (i) LPO, Inbal; (ii) Spanish R. & TV O, Markevitch; (iii) BBC SO, C. Davis; (iv) LPO, Leppard): (i) WEBER: *Overtures: Oberon; Euryanthe;* (ii) *Preciosa.* (iii) BEETHOVEN: *Overture Leonora No. 1.* WAGNER: *Prelude: Die Meistersinger.* MENDELSSOHN: *The Hebrides (Fingal's Cave).* (iv) SCHUBERT: *Overtures: in E min., D.648; in B flat, D.470.*
(B) **(*) Ph. 426 978-2; *426 978-4* [id.].

A useful bargain collection and well recorded throughout (mostly during the early 1970s). The LPO play beautifully at the opening of *Oberon*, to get the concert off to an atmospheric start and, if otherwise the two Inbal performances have no special charisma, they are enjoyably polished and fluent. There is plenty of vitality and sparkle in Markevitch's *Preciosa*, and Sir Colin Davis brings breadth to Beethoven and Wagner and evokes Mendelssohn's seascapes with dramatic effect. The two Schubert novelties are not otherwise available: not great music, but agreeable when Leppard's touch is affectionate.

'Serenade for strings'

Serenades (with (i) Philh. O, C. Davis; (ii) LSO, Barbirolli; (iii) N. Sinfonia, Tortelier; (iv) RPO, Sargent; (v) E. Sinfonia, Dilkes; (vi) Bournemouth Sinf., Montgomery; (vii) LPO, Boult): (i) MOZART: *Serenade No. 13 in G (Eine kleine Nachtmusik), K.525.* (ii) TCHAIKOVSKY: *String serenade, Op. 48: Waltz.* (iii) GRIEG: *Holberg suite, Op. 40.*

Elegiac melody: Heart's wounds, Op. 34/1. (iv) DVOŘÁK: *String serenade, Op. 11: March.* (vii) ELGAR: *Introduction and allegro for strings, Op. 47.*
(B) *** EMI TC2-MOM 108.

This was the finest of EMI's first release of 'Miles of Music' tapes with an attractive programme, good (and sometimes distinguished) performances and consistent sound-quality, slightly restricted in the upper range, but warm, full and clear. Tortelier's Grieg and Boult's complete version of Elgar's *Introduction and allegro* are obvious highlights, and this certainly makes an attractive background for a car journey, yet can be enjoyed at home too.

I Solisti Veneti, Claudio Scimone

Baroque mandolin concertos (with Ugo Orlandi): PAISIELLO: *Concertos: in E flat; in C.* LECCE: *Concerto in G.* ANTONIO MARIA GIULIANI: *Concerto in E for 2 mandolins and viola* (with D. Frati and J. Levitz).
(M) **(*) Erato/Warner Dig. 2292 45239-2 [id.].

The Giuliani on this record is not Mauro but Antonio Maria; neither he nor Francesco Lecce are exactly household names and they are not liberally documented in the accompanying liner-notes. However, whatever their stature, the music is appealing and its invention far from pale. Pleasant out-of-the-way repertoire, nicely played and recorded.

Solomon (piano)

'Great recordings of the century': (i) BLISS: *Piano concerto.* (ii) SCRIABIN: *Piano concerto in F sharp min., Op. 20.* (iii) LISZT: *Hungarian fantasia.*
(M) (***) EMI mono CDH7 63821-2 [id.] (with (i) Liverpool PO, Boult; (ii; iii) Philh. O; (ii) Dobrowen; (iii) Susskind).

Solomon's pioneering account of the Bliss *Piano concerto* was made during the war. Neither the music nor the recorded sound wear their years lightly, though the slow movement has more to recommend it than its more flamboyant neighbours. (It must be said, however, that some listeners find the ambitiously grand overstatement of the first movement rather endearing.) Solomon, of course, plays marvellously and the disc is important in offering us what would have been the first recording to be issued of the Scriabin *Piano concerto in F sharp minor* had Solomon and Dobrowen passed it for release. It is a lovely reading, every bit as poetic and polished as one would expect, and the sound is not bad for its period. It was made in 1949, at the same time as Solomon recorded the Tchaikovsky, which EMI must surely reissue soon. The Liszt *Hungarian fantasia* accompanied the Bliss when it came out on LP, and it is a pretty dazzling performance. The sonic limitations cannot diminish the sheer aristocratic finesse of this great pianist.

Stinton, Jennifer (flute)

'20th-century flute concertos' ((i) with Geoffrey Browne; SCO, Steuart Bedford): HONEGGER: (i) *Concerto da camera for flute, cor anglais and strings.* IBERT: *Flute concerto.* NIELSEN: *Flute concerto.* POULENC, arr. Berkeley: *Flute sonata.*
*** Collins Dig. 1210-2; *1210-4.*

Jennifer Stinton's record is called '20th-century flute concertos' – which, strictly speaking, it is not; only two works here can accurately be so described. Honegger's *Concerto da camera for flute, cor anglais and strings* is a duo concertante piece, and the Poulenc is a transcription by Lennox Berkeley of the *Sonata for flute and piano* (1957). Not that this matters, given the quality of the solo playing. The Nielsen is not quite as dazzling as Patrick Gallois's account (BIS CD 454) nor, for that matter, as the Danish performance by Toke Lund Christiensen (Chandos CHAN 8894), and its contrasts could be more strongly made. But Ibert's charming and effervescent piece (also offered by James Galway, above) comes off very well, though the orchestral playing is not particularly subtle. Honegger's *Concerto da camera* comes from the same period as the *Fourth Symphony* and the slow movement is strongly reminscent of it. It is very nicely played, as is the Poulenc, and beautifully recorded; though the orchestral contribution falls short of real distinction, this remains a very enjoyable recital, which deserves its third star.

Stuttgart Chamber Orchestra, Karl Münchinger

Baroque concert: PACHELBEL: *Canon*. ALBINONI: *Adagio in G min*. (arr. Giazotto). BACH: *Orchestral suites Nos. 2–3, BWV 1067/8*. HANDEL: *Organ concerto in F (Cuckoo and the nightingale* (with M. Haselböck).
(M) *(*) Decca Dig. 430 706-2; *430 706-4* [id.].

Münchinger is a little heavy-handed in the famous *Canon*, but the strongly expressive account of Albinoni's *Adagio* is convincing. The *Cuckoo and the nightingale organ concerto* (with Martin Haselböck an excellent soloist) also comes off well, but the Bach *Suites* are not an asset, unattractively heavy, with rhythms unlifted. Very good sound.

Ulster Orchestra, Vernon Handley or Bryden Thomson

'An Irish rhapsody': HARTY: *The Londonderry air. Irish Symphony: The fair day (scherzo). In the Antrim Hills*. STANFORD: *Irish rhapsody No. 4 (The Fisherman of Loch Neagh and what he saw), Op. 141; Symphony No. 3 (Irish): Scherzo*. MOERAN: *In the mountain country (symphonic impressions)*. BAX: *In the faery hills; Roscatha*.
(M) *** Chan. Dig. CHAN 6525 [id.].

It was a happy idea for Chandos to create this Irish anthology from a catalogue rich in music influenced by that country. It is especially good to have the *Scherzo* from Harty's *Irish Symphony* (a real lollipop), together with the skippity jig from the similar work by Stanford. His *Irish rhapsody No. 4* is also very colourful, and the two Bax pieces offer a strong contrast: one atmospheric, the other more dramatic and lively. Excellent performances throughout; all the recordings except the obligatory (and analogue) *Londonderry air* are of Chandos's best digital quality.

Williams, John (guitar)

Guitar concertos (with ECO, (i) Sir Charles Groves; (ii) Daniel Barenboim): (i) GIULIANI: *Concerto No. 1 in A, Op. 30*. VIVALDI: *Concertos in A and D*. RODRIGO: *Fantasia para un gentilhombre;* (ii) *Concierto de Aranjuez*. VILLA-LOBOS: *Concerto*. (i) CASTELNUOVO-TEDESCO: *Concerto No. 1 in D, Op. 99*.
(M) *** Sony M2YK 45610 (2) [id.].

Like the James Galway collection, above, this bouquet of seven concertante works for guitar from John Williams could hardly be better chosen, and the performances are comparably appealing. Moreover the set is offered at mid-price and the transfers are very well managed. Only the Vivaldi concertos (unidentified but attractive, especially the *D major* with its striking central *Largo*) bring quality which sounds in the least dated. Elsewhere the orchestral texture is full and pleasing and, if the guitar is very forward and larger than life, the playing is so expert and spontaneous that one hardly objects. All these performances are among the finest ever recorded, and Groves and Barenboim provide admirably polished accompaniments, matching the eager spontaneity of their soloist. The Rodrigo works seem as fresh as the day when they were written, the Castelnuovo-Tedesco has no want of charm (although John Williams's earlier account with Ormandy and the Philadelphia Orchestra had rather more pace), and the account of the Villa-Lobos makes it seem a stronger work than usual. (This is also available separately, coupled with the Rodrigo *Concierto* – see above under the relevant composers.)

Instrumental Recitals

Amato, Donna (piano)

'A piano portrait': LISZT: *Hungarian rhapsody No. 2* (cadenza by Rachmaninov); *Consolation No. 3; Liebestraum No. 3.* DEBUSSY: *Arabesque No. 1; Suite bergamasque: Clair de lune. Préludes: La fille aux cheveux de lin; La cathédrale engloutie.* RAVEL: *Pavane pour une infante défunte.* GERSHWIN: *3 Preludes; Rhapsody in blue* (solo piano version). Song transcriptions: *The man I love; Swanee; Oh, lady be good; I'll build a stairway to paradise; 'S wonderful; I got rhythm.*
*** Olympia OCD 352; Altarus *AIR-TC 9007* [id.].

The young American pianist Donna Amato has already made a considerable impression with her recordings of the MacDowell *Concertos* and the Balakirev and Dutilleux *Sonatas.* Here she proves her mettle in standard repertoire and, more importantly, confirms her ability to create 'live' performances in the recording studio. None of the readings is routine or conventional: the Liszt *Consolation* has an attractive simplicity and the famous *Liebestraum,* while not lacking romantic impulse, has an agreeable lack of gush. Her Debussy is particularly impressive: the *Arabesque* has a lightly chimerical variety of touch and colour and the two most famous pieces are made to seem refreshingly unhackneyed. The highlight, however, is *La cathédrale engloutie,* an unforgettably powerful evocation, played quite superbly. She is, not surprisingly, completely at home with Gershwin. The song transcriptions are splendidly stylish and sparkling and her solo account of the *Rhapsody in blue* is highly idiomatic. In its strong, natural impulse and rhythmic freedom it can be spoken of in the same breath as Bernstein's version, although it has completely its own character. Donna Amato's style is not that of a Horowitz, and so it was perhaps a pity she chose to open with the Liszt *Hungarian rhapsody,* which would have been better placed later on in the programme, while the Ravel *Pavane* is a little too sober; but as a whole this 76-minute recital, recorded very realistically indeed in Salen Church Hall, Ski, Norway, is most enjoyable.

Barere, Simon (piano)

'The complete HMV recordings, 1934–6': LISZT: *Étude de concert, G.144/2. Années de pèlerinage, 2nd Year (Italy): Sonnetto 104 del Petrarca, G.161/5. Gnomenreigen, G.145/2; Réminiscences de Don Juan, G.418* (2 versions); *Rapsodie espagnole, G.254; Valse oubliée No. 1, G.215.* CHOPIN: *Scherzo No. 3 in C sharp min., Op. 39; Mazurka No. 38 in F sharp min., Op. 59/3; Waltz No. 5 in A flat, Op. 42.* BALAKIREV: *Islamey* (2 versions). BLUMENFELD: *Étude for the left hand.* GLAZUNOV: *Étude in C, Op. 31/1.* SCRIABIN: *Études: in C sharp min., Op. 2/1; in D sharp min., Op. 8/12* (2 versions). LULLY/GODOWSKI: *Gigue in E.* RAMEAU/GODOWSKI: *Tambourin in E min.* SCHUMANN: *Toccata in C, Op. 7* (2 versions).
❀ (***) Appian mono CDAPR 7001 (2) [id.].

We have had to wait nearly a decade for the new medium to get round to Simon Barere, but now at last he is adequately represented by Carnegie Hall recitals of the music of Chopin, Liszt and Rachmaninov. This two-CD set offers all of Barere's HMV recordings, made in the mid-1930s, including the alternative takes he made in the studio. In several cases, including Balakirev's *Islamey* and Liszt's *Réminiscences de Don Juan,* Barere became dissatisfied with the performances after publication and re-recorded them, and this set includes a generous appendix of alternative published takes, and two rejected takes that were not included in the original LP compilation, the Chopin *Mazurka* and the Schumann *Toccata*. What can one say of his playing without exhausting one's stock of superlatives? His fingerwork is quite astonishing and his virtuosity almost in a class on its own. The set contains an absolutely stunning account of the *Réminiscences de Don Juan*, and his *Islamey* knocks spots off any successor in sheer virtuosity and excitement; it is altogether breathtaking, and much the same might be said of his *Rapsodie espagnole*. Nor is there any want of poetry – witness the delicacy of the Scriabin *C sharp minor Étude* or Liszt's *La leggierezza*. Bryan Crimp's excellent booklet is not only full of interesting discographical material but also details Barere's extraordinary childhood development and subsequent career. Readers wanting to investigate this legendary artist should start here, for this is the most desirable of all the Barere sets listed in this volume. One of the most important functions of the gramophone is to chart performance traditions that would otherwise disappear from view, and this set is one to celebrate.

'Simon Barere at the Carnegie Hall, Vol. 3': BEETHOVEN: *Piano sonata No. 27 in E min., Op. 90.* LISZT: *Études de concert Nos. 2, La leggierezza; 3, Un sospiro, S.144.* WEBER: *Piano sonata No. 1 in C: Presto, J.138.* SCHUMANN: *Carnaval, Op. 9.* CHOPIN: *Andante spianato and Grande polonaise brillante in E flat, Op. 22; Ballade No. 1 in G min., Op. 23; Études: in C sharp min.; in G flat; in F; Op. 10/4, 5 & 8; Fantaisie in F min., Op. 49; Impromptu No. 1 in A flat, Op. 29; Nocturne No. 8 in D flat, Op. 27/2; Scherzo No. 3 in C sharp min., Op. 39; Waltz No. 5 in A flat, Op. 42.*
(*(**)) APR mono CDAPR 7009 (2) [id.].

All these recordings were made at Carnegie Hall recitals at various times between 1946 and 1949 and are of varying quality. The Beethoven *Sonata*, Op. 90, is splendidly played but is disfigured by heavy surfaces and some distortion. The Liszt items, which were made two years earlier, are better. The playing of *La leggierezza* is pretty breathtaking and, for that matter, so is his hair-raising account of the Weber *Perpetuum mobile*. Schumann's *Carnaval* is artistically more controversial, with some scrambled passages (the end of the *Préamble* is a case in point), and it suffers from particularly shallow recording quality. Barere must have been an impressive Chopin interpreter if some of the performances on the second CD are anything to go by. The variety and quality of touch in the *D flat Nocturne*, Op. 27/2, are to be marvelled at, and one is reminded of Harold Schonberg's phrase, 'miracles of light-fingered dexterity' quoted on the sleeve. Some of the performances suffer from rough – not to say execrable – recording quality (the *F minor Fantasy* has obtrusive surfaces) but they all serve as evidence of Barere's stature. All the same, this set is for the converted; collectors are better advised to set out on their investigation of this extraordinary artist with the 1934–6 HMV recordings.

Bate, Jennifer (organ)

'Virtuoso French organ music' (organ of Beauvais Cathedral): BOELLMANN: *Suite gothique.* GUILMANT: *Cantilène pastorale; March on 'Lift up your heads'.* SAINT-SAENS: *Improvisation No. 7.* GIGOUT: *Toccata in B min.; Scherzo; Grand choeur dialogué.*
(M) **(*) Unicorn Dig.UKCD 2045 [id.].

The playing here has enormous flair and thrilling bravura. Jennifer Bate's imaginative touch makes Boëllmann's *Suite gothique* sound far better music than it is. In the closing *Toccata*, as in the spectacular Guilmant march based on Handel's famous chorus, the panache and excitement of the playing grip the listener firmly, and the clouding of the St Beauvais acoustic is forgotten. But in the swirling Saint-Saëns *Improvisation* and the

Gigout *Scherzo* detail is masked. In the massive *Grand choeur dialogué*, the clever timing makes the firm articulation register, but, although the Unicorn engineers achieve a splendidly sumptuous sound-image, elsewhere there is blurring caused by the wide reverberation of the empty cathedral.

Brendel, Alfred (piano)

'For Amnesty International': BACH: *Italian concerto in F, BWV 971.* HAYDN: *Andante with variations in F min., Hob XVII/6.* BEETHOVEN: *Piano sonata No. 14 in C sharp min. (Moonlight).* LISZT: *Harmonies poétiques et religieuses: Funérailles.* BERG: *Sonata, Op. 1.* BUSONI: *Preludio – Fantasia – Ciaccona.*
*** Ph. Analogue/Dig. 426 814-2 [id.].

This compilation derives both from studio recordings and from recitals given in the Vienna Grosser Konserthaussaal in 1972 and 1981, and thus the recordings included have come from both analogue and digital sources, and the latter are not always superior. Among the finest is the Bach *Italian concerto*, meticulously articulated in a warm but clean acoustic and in excellent analogue sound, recorded in 1976, and the marvellous Busoni *Toccata*, recorded live in 1972 and superbly played and thoroughly exhilarating (in spite of one or two tired notes inevitable on a live occasion). The Haydn, also included in the four-CD set of the *Sonatas*, is digital but made in a slightly drier studio than the 1972 Beethoven *Moonlight sonata*, which it immediately precedes. The Alban Berg *Sonata*, a studio recording from 1982, is also commanding and powerful, and Liszt's *Funérailles*, a 1981 Viennese occasion, is very distinguished indeed. Some of Brendel's best performances and designed to make a contribution to one of the world's best causes. Strongly recommended on both counts.

Cambridge Buskers

'Classic Busking'.
(B) *** DG Compact Classics *415 337-4.*

This highly diverting collection is ideal entertainment for a long car journey – though, for all its effervescence and wit, it is best taken a side at a time. The Cambridge Buskers are a duo, Michael Copley (who plays the flute, piccolo and various recorders, with often astonishing bravura) and Dag Ingram, the hardly less fluent accordionist. They met at Cambridge, and these recordings date from the end of the 1970s. There are 34 items here, including a remarkably wide range of classical lollipops. The recital immediately establishes the stylistic credentials of the players by opening with an engaging account of the *Rondo* from Mozart's *Eine kleine Nachtmusik.* The programme ranges from Chopin and Praetorius to Bach and Vivaldi, with ear-tickling operatic excerpts by Bizet, Gluck, Rossini, Mozart and Verdi. With tongue-in-cheek irreverence, they manage to include not only the *Quartet* from *Rigoletto*, but even the *Ride of the Valkyries* – which sounds a good deal more enticing than some over-enthusiastic orchestral versions. The players clearly delight in their more outrageous transcriptions, and they are such natural musicians that good taste comes easily. With crisp, clean recording and 83 minutes of music, this is certainly value for money.

Curley, Carlo (organ of Girard College Chapel, Philadelphia)

'The Emperor's Fanfare': SOLER: *Emperor's fanfare* (arr. Biggs). WAGNER: *Tristan und Isolde: Liebestod.* JONGEN: *Choral.* BACH: *Toccata and fugue in D min., BWV 565.* ALBINONI: *Adagio* (arr. Giazotto). ALAIN: *Litanies.* SCHUBERT: *Ave Maria.* KARG-ELERT: *Nun danket alle Gott, Op. 65/9.* GRIEG: *Sigurd Jorsalfar: Homage march.* GUILMANT: *March upon Handel's 'Lift up your heads', Op. 15.*
*** Argo Dig. 430 200-2; *430 200-4* [id.].

The flamboyant Carlo Curley describes with engaging enthusiasm the organ he plays here: 'Nearly one hundred feet from the [Girard] Chapel's marble floor and above the vast, coffered ceiling, entirely covered incidentally with real gold leaf, the organ, all thirty-five metric tonnes, and with 6,587 hand-made pipes, is miraculously suspended. In a chapel so cavernous, and with such remarkable reverberation, it is well nigh impossible to identify the source of the sound.' Yet the Argo engineers manage to provide an excellent focus and capture the extremely wide dynamic range of Curley's playing with precision at both ends of the spectrum. The performances are full of drama and temperament, unashamedly romantic yet very compelling. The title-piece by Soler is an anachronistic but irresistible arrangement by E. Power Biggs which provides an opportunity for great splashes of throaty timbre and uses – as does the Alain *Litanies* – the powerful *Tuba mirabilis* stop. 'Its pipes', Curley tells us, 'lie horizontally or *en chamade*, and this stop speaks with an unrivalled speed and clarity on twenty-five inches of wind pressure, a veritable hurricane when compared to the two to four inches common to modern instruments.' The sheer verve and panache of Curley's playing, matching the eloquence of his prose and the depth and spectacle of the reproduced sound – the pedals are stunningly caught – cannot fail to entertain any organ fancier.

Gilbert, Kenneth (harpsichord)

Pièces de clavecin: CLÉRAMBAULT: *Suites Nos. 1 in C; 2 in C min.* D'ANGELBERT: *Gailliarde et Double; Chaconne du vieux gautier.* L. COUPERIN: *Pavane in F sharp min.* GASPARD LE ROUX: *Suite No. 5 in F.* MARAIS: *Polonaise in D min.* LEBÈGUE: *Les cloches in F.*
(M) *** DG Dig. 431 709-2 [id.].

The two Clérambault suites recorded here represent only a fraction of this composer's output for the harpsichord, but they are all that survive. Both suites were published during the composer's lifetime, in 1702 or 1704. They have splendid improvisatory preludes, rather in the style of Louis Couperin, and are notated without bar-lines; they also have a genuine vein of lyricism, not inappropriate in a composer of so much vocal music. Gaspard Le Roux's *Suite* also dates from the same period (1705) and is attractively inventive, especially its impressive fifth movement, *Chaconne*. There is also much of appeal in the rest of the progamme here, not least the engaging piece by Lebègue, *Les cloches*, which is something of a find. Kenneth Gilbert plays persuasively and authoritatively; most appropriately he uses a modern copy, by David Rubio, of the 1680 Vaudry harpsichord from the Victoria and Albert Museum. The 1981 recording, made in the Henry Wood Hall in London, is vividly real.

Horowitz, Vladimir (piano)

'Encores': BIZET/HOROWITZ: *Variations on a theme from Carmen.* SAINT-SAENS/LISZT/HOROWITZ: *Danse macabre.* MOZART: *Sonata No. 11, K.331: Rondo alla turca.* MENDELSSOHN/LISZT/HOROWITZ: *Wedding march and variations.* MENDELSSOHN: *Élégie, Op. 85/4; Spring song, Op. 62/6; The shepherd's complaint, Op. 67/5; Scherzo a capriccio: Presto.* DEBUSSY: *Children's corner: Serenade of a doll.* MOSZKOWSKI: *Études, Op. 72/6 & 11; Étincelles, Op. 36/6.* CHOPIN: *Polonaise in A flat, Op. 53.* SCHUMANN: *Kinderszenen: Träumerei.* LISZT: *Hungarian rhapsody No. 15; Valse oubliée No. 1.* RACHMANINOV: *Prelude in G min., Op. 23/5.* SOUSA/HOROWITZ: *The Stars and stripes forever.*
(M) (***) RCA mono GD 87755; *GK 87755* [7755-2-RG; *7755-4-RG*].

These encore pieces have been around for some time and, apart from the Rachmaninov *Prelude* and the Mendelssohn, derive from the days of the 78-r.p.m. record and the mono LP. Allowances have to be made for the quality which, as one would expect in this kind of compilation, is variable. So in its different way is the playing, which varies from dazzling to stunning!

'A Tribute': SCARLATTI: *Sonatas, Kk.55; Kk.380.* CHOPIN: *Ballade No. 1 in G min., Op. 23; Mazurkas: in C sharp min., Op. 30/4; B min., Op. 33/4; Étude in F, Op. 10/8.* SCRIABIN: *Sonata No. 9 (Black mass), Op. 68; Étude in D sharp min., Op. 8/12.* LISZT: *Années de pèlerinages, 1st Year: Vallée d'Obermann.* SCHUMANN: *Arabeske in C, Op. 18; Kinderszenen: Träumerei.* DEBUSSY: *L'isle joyeuse.* MOSZKOWSKI: *Étude in A flat, Op. 72/11.* HOROWITZ: *Variations on a theme from Bizet's Carmen.*
**(*) Sony MK 45829 [id.]; *40-45829*.

These celebrated performances come from the 1960s, last appearing as part of a three-CD compilation, '*Horowitz Live at Carnegie Hall*', containing concert performances from 1965, 1966 and 1968; they have been discussed at length in past issues of the Penguin *Guide*. Suffice it to say that few of these performances have lost their magic and some, such as the Scriabin *Ninth Sonata* (*The Black Mass*) have never been surpassed. The recordings are not quite of the very highest quality but serve to convey much of the electricity of the occasion.

'The last recording': HAYDN: *Piano sonata in E flat, Hob XVI/20.* CHOPIN: *Mazurka in C min., Op. 56/3. Nocturnes: in E flat, Op. 55/2; in B, Op. 62/1. Fantaisie impromptu, Op. 66; Études: in A flat; E min., Op. 25/1 & 5.* LISZT: *Prelude: Weinen, Klagen, Sorgen, Zagen; Concert paraphrase on Isoldens Liebestod.*
*** Sony Dig. SK 45818 [id.].

Rarely did Horowitz betray his advanced years, and the Haydn for the most part has great delicacy and elegance: it is far less tense and taut than either of his previous accounts of this big, late *E flat Sonata.* Only once (the fortissimo left-hand octaves in the slow movement) does one feel a lapse in his concentration and perspective. The Chopin pieces offer some fresh insights and display a command of tone gradation that is still pretty remarkable, except perhaps for an unexceptionable account of the *Fantaisie-impromptu.* Ah, if only the piano sound the CBS engineers produce here could have been lavished on his earlier recitals from the 1960s! There is a fine written tribute to Horowitz from Murray Perahia.

Johnson, Emma (clarinet)

'A Clarinet celebration' (with Gordon Back): WEBER: *Grand duo concertante; Variations concertantes.* BURGMÜLLER: *Duo.* GIAMPIERI: *Carnival of Venice.* SCHUMANN: *Fantasy pieces, Op. 73.* LOVREGLIO: *Fantasia de concerto, La Traviata.*
*** ASV Dig. CDDCA 732; *ZCDCA 732* [id.].

These are party pieces rather than encores, all of them drawing electric sparks of inspiration from this winning young soloist. Even in such virtuoso nonsense as the Giampieri *Carnival of Venice* and the Lovreglio *Fantasia*, Johnson draws out musical magic, while the expressiveness of Weber and Schumann brings heartfelt playing, with phrasing creatively individual. Gordon Back accompanies brilliantly, and the sound is first rate.

Kissin, Yevgeni (piano)

'Carnegie Hall Début' (30 September 1990): CHOPIN: *Waltz, Op. 64/2.* LISZT: *Étude d'exécution transcendante No. 10; Liebestraum No. 3; Rhapsodie espagnole.* PROKOFIEV: *Sonata No. 6 in A, Op. 82; Étude, Op. 2/3.* SCHUMANN: *Abegg Variations, Op. 1; Études symphoniques, Op. 13; Widmung* (arr. Liszt).
*** BMG/RCA Dig. RD 60443 (2) [60443-2-RC].

Yevgeni Kissin caused something of a sensation in 1984 when he played both the Chopin *Concertos* in the Great Hall of the Moscow Conservatoire while still only twelve years of age (see our main volume, p. 277). The present recording of his Carnegie Hall début was made a few days before his nineteenth birthday. He has phenomenal pianistic powers; not only is this a *tour de force* in terms of technical prowess but also in sheer artistry. Both sets of Schumann *Variations* are remarkable: Op. 13 is infinitely more impressive and natural than Pogorelich's rendition, and is full of poetic insights. Similarly, the Prokofiev *Sonata* is stunningly played, with greater control and less abandon, but with hardly less sustained concentration than in his earlier recording. The Liszt *Rhapsodie espagnole* is played with superb bravura and the Prokofiev *Study* brings the house down – and rightly so. Kissin's range of colour and keyboard command throughout is dazzling. The Carnegie Hall was packed and the recording balance, while a bit close, is perfectly acceptable. The excitement of the occasion is conveyed vividly.

'In Tokyo' (12 May 1987): CHOPIN: *Nocturne in A flat, Op. 32/2; Polonaise in F sharp min., Op. 44.* LISZT: *Concert studies Nos. 1 in D flat (Waldesrauschen); 2 in F min. (La Leggierezza).* PROKOFIEV: *Sonata No. 6 in A, Op. 82.* RACHMANINOV: *Études tableaux, Op. 39/1 & 5; Lilacs.* SCRIABIN: *Étude in C sharp min., Op. 42/5; Mazurka in E min., Op. 25/3.*
*** Sony Dig. SK 45931 [id.].

Kissin was only fifteen at the time of his Tokyo début, but he sounds fully mature throughout this recital. He plays Prokofiev's *Sixth Sonata* for all it is worth with no holds barred, and the effect is altogether electrifying. Moreover, this is not merely an exhibition of brilliant technique but a display of remarkable artistic understanding – one finds oneself on the edge of one's chair. He is no less at home in the Rachmaninov *Études tableaux* and the Liszt *La Leggierezza*, which he delivers with marvellous assurance and poetic feeling. His Scriabin, too, is pretty impressive, and the only unremarkable part of his concert is the group of Japanese encores. The microphone placing is too close – but no matter, this is breathtaking piano playing.

Lack, Fredell (violin)

Sonatas (with Albert Hirsh or Barry Snyder (piano)): CORIGLIANO: *Sonata for violin and piano.* DIAMOND: *Sonata No. 2 for violin and piano.* LEES: *Sonata No. 2 for violin and piano.* MENNIN: *Sonata concertante for violin and piano.*
** Bay Cities Dig. BCD 1018 [id.].

Fredell Lack was a frequent broadcaster in the UK in the days of the Third Programme, playing mostly enterprising repertoire. She now teaches in the United States and is Professor of Music and Artist-in-Residence in Houston, Texas. John Corigliano's *Sonata* (1963) is spiky, very Stravinskyish but lively and inventive; it is not as spiky or rebarbative though as the *Sonata No. 2* of Benjamin Lees, composed in 1973. David Diamond's *Sonata No. 2* (1981) is a thoughtful, well-wrought piece and, along with Peter Mennin's *Sonata concertante* (1956), forms the strongest part of the recital. These artists are decently recorded.

Lawson, Peter (piano)

'The American piano sonata, Vol. 1': COPLAND: *Piano sonata.* IVES: *Three page sonata.* CARTER: *Piano sonata.* BARBER: *Piano sonata, Op. 26.*
*** Virgin Dig. VC7 91163-2 [id.].

An indispensable collection for anyone interested in American piano music. Considering its excellence, the Copland *Sonata* (1939–41) has been uncommonly neglected since Andor Foldes's mono LP of the 1950s. Peter Lawson plays it with an understanding that is persuasive and an enthusiasm that is refreshing. Elliott Carter's *Sonata* (1946, revised 1982) owes much to the Copland. Its idiom is thoroughly accessible (far more so than some of Carter's more impenetrable later music) as well as convincing. Lawson can hold his own with such earlier recordings as the Charles Rosen, and he certainly has the advantage of fresher recording quality. In the 1950s and 1960s, the Barber *Sonata*, Op. 26, like that of Ginastera, had a far stronger profile than any other American sonata, and the catalogue has recently been enriched by the return of Horowitz's and Van Cliburn's recordings. Lawson comfortably takes its various hurdles in his stride, and he also gives us the Charles Ives *Three page Sonata.* A generous and valuable recital.

McLachlan, Murray (piano)

Piano music from Scotland: SCOTT: *8 Songs* (trans. Stevenson): *Since all thy vows, false maid; Wha is that at my bower-door?; O were my love yon lilac fare; Wee Willie Gray; Milkwort and bog-cotton; Crowdieknowe; Ay waukin, O; There's news, lasses, news.* CENTER: *Piano sonata; 6 Bagatelles, Op. 3.; Children at play.* MACMIL4SON: *Beltane bonfire. 2 Scottish ballads: The Dowie Dens O Yarrow; Newhaven fishwife's cry.*
❀ *** Olympia Dig. OCD 264 [id.].

An important, fascinating and rewarding recital. For most collectors, Scottish music comprises dozens of wonderful folk-songs and a single orchestral piece, Hamish MacCunn's overture *The Land of the mountain and the flood.* Francis George Scott (1880–1958) was a prolific and striking composer of songs and we obviously need a major Scottish artist to record a representative selection of his work. Meanwhile Ronald Stevenson's very free transcriptions, somewhat after the fashion of Liszt's concert paraphrases, are imaginatively creative in their own right, with the witty, scherzando grotesquerie of *Wee Willie Gray* surpassed by the even more complex *Crowdieknowe*, with its quotations from the *Requiems* of Verdi and Berlioz included in the endpiece. Ronald Center's *Piano sonata* is restless and mercurial, lacking much in the way of repose, but the joyous syncopations of the first movement are infectious and the work is a major contribution to the repertory and not in the least difficult to approach. The *Six Bagatelles* are even more strikingly diverse in mood. The second introduces an engaging wooden-legged waltz, the third, *Mesto*, has a whiff of Satie and the fifth, *Andantino*, a flavour of Poulenc, yet both retain their Scottish individuality. *Children at play* is an enchanting piece, with a musical-box miniaturism of texture at times, yet the writing is by no means inconsequential. All this music is played with commitment and considerable bravura by Murray McLachlan, who is clearly a sympathetic exponent, and the recording is extremely vivid and real. Our Rosette is awarded not just for enterprise, but equally from admiration and pleasure.

Menuhin, Sir Yehudi and **Stéphane Grappelli** (violins)

'Menuhin & Grappelli play Gershwin, Kern, Porter, Rodgers and Hart, "Jealousy" and other great standards'.
(M) **(*) EMI Analogue/Dig. CMS7 63939-2; *EX 763939-4* (3).

Menuhin and Grappelli fans will want this three-disc collection representing their fruitful collaboration between 1973 and 1985, even if the digital remastering of the analogue recordings included has at times added a hint of edginess to the violin timbre. The general collector will perhaps be satisfied with one of the individual issues while they remain available. Perhaps the Gershwin recital is most attractive of all (CDM 7 69218-2 see p. 415 of our main volume). The other two (Berlin, Kern, etc. on CDM 7 69219-2, and *Jealousy* on CDM7 69220-2) are listed out and discussed on pp. 1274–5).

Moiseiwitsch, Benno (piano)

1938–1950 recordings: MUSSORGSKY: *Pictures at an exhibition*. BEETHOVEN: *Andanti favori, WoO 57; Rondo in C, Op. 51/1*. WEBER: *Sonata No. 1: Presto; Invitation to the dance* (arr. Tausig). MENDELSSOHN: *Scherzo in E min., Op. 16*. SCHUMANN: *Romanzen: No. 2, Op. 28/2*. CHOPIN: *Nocturne in E flat, Op. 9/2; Polonaise in B flat, Op. 71/2; Barcarolle, Op. 60*. LISZT: *Liebestraume No. 3; Étude de concert: La leggierezza. Hungarian rhapsody No. 2 in C sharp min. Concert paraphrase of Wagner's Tannhäuser overture*. DEBUSSY: *Pour le piano: Toccata. Suite bergamasque: Clair de lune. Estampes: Jardins sous la pluie*. RAVEL: *Le tombeau de Couperin: Toccata*.
(**) APR mono CDAPR 7005 (2) [id.].

Moiseiwitsch never enjoyed quite the exposure on records to which his gifts entitled him, though in the earlier part of his career he made a great many. Later, in the electrical era he was a 'plum-label' artist and was not issued on the more prestigious and expensive 'red-label'. In this he was in pretty good company, for Solomon and Myra Hess were similarly relegated. This anthology gives a good picture of the great pianist in a wide variety of repertory: his *Pictures at an exhibition*, made in 1945, was for some time the only piano version; and those who identify him solely with the Russians will find his

Chopin *Barcarolle* and Debussy *Jardins sous la pluie* totally idiomatic. The transfers are variable – all are made from commercial copies, some in better condition than others.

Orpheus Trio

French music: RAVEL: *Sonatine en Trio* (arr. Salzedo). FAURÉ: *Impromptu for harp, Op. 86.* DEBUSSY: *Sonata for flute, viola & harp. Syrinx for solo flute.* DEVIENNE: *Duo No. 3 for flute & viola.*
(B) *** Van. VBD 25002.

The novelty here is Carlos Salzedo's enchanting realization of Ravel's (Piano) *Sonatine en Trio* for the same combination as Debussy's *Sonata.* All the works here are beautifully played, and these artists, Paula Robinson (flute), Scott Nickrenz (viola) and Heidi Lehwalder (harp), show themselves at one with the special delicacy of atmosphere which pervades all this music. The analogue sound is naturally balanced and real, and this bargain collection can be strongly recommended.

Perahia, Murray (piano)

'Aldeburgh Recital': BEETHOVEN: *32 Variations in C min., WoO 80.* SCHUMANN: *Carnival jest from Vienna, Op. 26.* LISZT: *Hungarian rhapsody No. 12.* RACHMANINOV: *Études-tableaux in C, Op. 33/2; in E flat min., A min., D, Op. 39/5, 6 & 9.*
*** Sony Dig. SK 46437; *40-46437* [id.].

This concert is misleadingly called 'The Aldeburgh Recital', giving the impression that it is a recording of a public event, rather than the repertoire which he actually played during the festival. Not that this matters too much, for Murray Perahia plays with all the spontaneity and freshness that distinguish his concert appearances. Listening to his Rachmaninov serves as a reminder that the Russians have no monopoly on this repertoire; there is a depth and sense of pain that eludes even such artists as Ovchinnikov and Kissin. Perahia produces an extraordinary range of colour and tone; though one knows him to be a great Schumann interpreter, it is good to hear him in such barnstorming repertoire as the *Hungarian rhapsody No. 12* and the *Études-tableaux*, with which we do not normally associate him. This is one of the finest recitals to have appeared in a year not exactly lacking in remarkable piano CDs.

'Piano pops'

'Piano Pops' (played by: (i) Garrick Ohlsson; (ii) Ronald Smith; (iii) Moura Lympany; (iv) Cyril Smith and Phyllis Sellick; (v) Daniel Adni; (vi) John Ogdon): (i) CHOPIN: *Polonaise No. 5 in F sharp min., Op. 55;* (ii) *Mazurka Nos. 1 in F sharp min.; 2 in C sharp min.; 4 in E flat min., Op. 6/1, 2 & 4; 34 in C, Op. 56/2; 47 in A min., Op. 67/4;* (iii) *Nocturnes Nos. 2 in E flat, Op. 9/2; 5 in F sharp, Op. 15/2.* (iv) DEBUSSY: *Petite suite:* 4th movement. RACHMANINOV: *Lilacs.* BENJAMIN: *Mattie rag; Jamaican rumba.* SCOTT: *Water wagtail.* BIZET: *Jeux d'enfants: La bal.* FAURÉ: *Dolly: Berceuse.* WALTON: *Façade: Popular song.* MILHAUD: *Scaramouche: Brazileira.* (v) MENDELSSOHN: *Song without words: Venetian gondola song, Op. 19/6;* (i) *Midsummer night's dream: Scherzo* (trans. Rachmaninov). (vi) BEETHOVEN: *5 Variations on Rule Brittania.* (i) TCHAIKOVSKY: *Lullaby.* RIMSKY-KORSAKOV: *Flight of the bumble-bee* (both trans. Rachmaninov). (v) GRIEG: *Lyric pieces: Melody; Norwegian dance (Halling), Op. 47/3–4; Nocturne; Scherzo, Op. 54/4–5.* GRAINGER: *Irish tune from County Derry; Molly on the shore; Shepherd's hey.*

(B) *** EMI Miles of Music *TC2-MOM 130*.

It is difficult to imagine a more attractively varied collection of piano genre pieces than this. Moreover, with a fine roster of artists to draw on, the performances are consistently distinguished. Highlights include Moura Lympany's Chopin *Nocturnes*, meltingly played; Daniel Adni sympathetic in Grieg and sprightly in Percy Grainger; Garrick Ohlsson bringing prodigious bravura to the Rachmaninov transcriptions, and John Ogdon showing Beethoven in a spontaneously light-hearted mood. But the undoubted pearl of the collection is the set of nine pieces played with consistent charm and sparkle by Cyril Smith and Phyllis Sellick (piano duo, three hands). Excellent, fresh transfers: this sounds splendid in the car.

Preston, Simon (organ)

'The world of the organ' (organ of Westminster Abbey): WIDOR: *Symphony No. 5: Toccata.* BACH: *Chorale prelude, Wachet auf, BWV 645.* MOZART: *Fantasia in F min., K.608.* WALTON: *Crown imperial* (arr. Murrill). CLARKE: *Prince of Denmark's march* (arr. Preston). HANDEL: *Saul: Dead march.* PURCELL: *Trumpet tune* (arr. Trevor). ELGAR: *Imperial march* (arr. Martin). VIERNE: *Symphony No. 1: Finale.* WAGNER: *Tannhäuser: Pilgrims' chorus.* GUILMANT: *March on a theme of Handel.* SCHUMANN: *Study No. 5* (arr. West). KARG-ELERT: *Marche triomphale (Now thank we all our God).*
(B) *** Decca 430 091-2; *430 091-4* [id.].

A splendid bargain compilation from the Argo catalogue of the early to mid-1960s, spectacularly recorded, which offers 69 minutes of music and is in every sense a resounding success. Simon Preston's account of the Widor *Toccata* is second to none, and both the Vierne *Finale* and the Karg-Elert *March triomphale* lend themselves admirably to Preston's unashamed flamboyance and the tonal splendour afforded by the Westminster acoustics. Walton's *Crown imperial*, too, brings a panoply of sound which compares very favourably with an orchestral recording. The organ has a splendid trumpet stop which makes both the Purcell piece and Clarke's *Prince of Denmark's march*, better known as the '*Trumpet voluntary*', sound crisply regal.

'Variations on America' (Organ of Methuen Memorial Music Hall): SOUSA: *Stars and Stripes.* SAINT-SAËNS: *Danse macabre.* IVES: *Variations on 'America'.* BUCK: *Variations on 'The last rose of summer'.* BOSSI: *Étude symphonique, Op. 78.* LEMARE: *Andantino in D flat.* GUILMANT: *Sonata No. 1 in D min., Op. 42.*
*** Argo Dig. 421 731-2; *421 731-4* [id.].

Here we are introduced to another fascinating American organ, the second in the relaunched Argo label's series of specialist recitals of more than specialist interest. The instrument in question originated in Boston Music Hall. After a delayed Atlantic crossing it was installed in 1863, and for two decades it anteceded the Boston Symphony Orchestra as the prime focus of Boston music-making. When the orchestra was inaugurated, the organ was moved to the Methuen Memorial Hall, which was built specially to house it, and the instrument we now hear was rebuilt to modern specifications in the 1940s. Simon Preston is perhaps not as flamboyant a musical personality as Carlo Curley, but he gives a dazzling display of the instrument's capabilities, from the flashily registered opening Sousa march through to the dashing passage-work of Guilmant's finale. On the way we encounter Charles Ives's gleefully disrespectful treatment of a solemn national tune, equally famous on both sides of the Atlantic, more variations by Donald Buck, who was resident organist in Boston in the 1970s, a sentimental *Andantino* by Lemare, which is perhaps better known as a setting of the words, *Moonlight and roses*, plus more rhetorical bravura from Bossi and transcribed orchestral spectacle from Saint-Saëns. One can appreciate here not only the skill of the Argo engineers but also that of the architect, Henry Vaughan, who designed the hall in Methuen, Massachusetts, which so effectively displays the colour and range of this remarkable instrument.

Rogé, Pascal (piano) and **Wind Ensemble**

French chamber music: SAINT-SAENS: *Caprice sur des airs danois et russes.* D'INDY: *Sarabande et menuet.* ROUSSEL: *Divertissement.* TANSMAN: *Danse de la sorcière.* FRANÇAIX: *L'heure du berger.* POULENC: *Élégie.* MILHAUD: *Sonata, Op. 47.*
❀ *** Decca Dig. 425 861-2 [id.].

A well-chosen and varied recital of French chamber music, performed with elegance and charm by these fine wind players and by Pascal Rogé at the piano. The Saint-Saëns *Caprice sur des airs danois et russes* was written for a visit the composer made to Russia in 1887 with three wind players. It is great fun, as is most of the music on the disc, notably the delightful minuet of Vincent d'Indy's *Sarabande et menuet*, the early Roussel *Divertissement* and Alexandre Tansman's *Danse de la sorcière*. Perhaps the humour of Françaix's *L'heure du berger* may strike some as a bit arch but, played with such flair, such thoughts are instantly banished. Poulenc's *Élégie* for horn and piano, composed on the death of Dennis Brain, is eloquently played by André Cazalet. It is invidious to mention him alone, as the flautist, Catherine Cantin, and those stalwarts of French wind music, Maurice Bourgue, Michel Portal, and Amaury Wallez, are equally splendid. Milhaud's *Sonata*, Op. 47, for flute, oboe, clarinet and piano (from 1918) has the fresh, easy-going zest of this composer at his best. The recording is very well balanced and should give unqualified delight to all who are sensible enough to buy it.

Snowden, Jonathan (flute), **Andrew Litton** (piano)

'Danse de la chèvre' (music for flute and piano): WIDOR: *Suite.* FAURÉ: *Fantaisie, Morceau de concours.* DEBUSSY: *Syrinx.* HONEGGER: *Danse de la chèvre.* ROUSSEL: *Joueurs de flûte.* MESSIAEN: *Le merle noir.* POULENC: *Flute sonata.*
*** Virgin Dig. VC7 90846-2; *VC7 90846-4* [id.].

The brilliant first flute of the LPO, deftly accompanied by the conductor, Andrew Litton, a formidable pianist, here gathers a vintage collection of French works for flute. The Poulenc *Sonata* is dazzlingly done, and so are the other virtuoso pieces, all strongly characterized. The surprise is the opening item by Widor, delicate and pointed, charmingly lyrical, a *Suite* by a composer now remembered only for his heavyweight organ works. Good, though slightly recessed recording.

Tan, Melvyn (fortepiano)

'Salonkonzert': BEETHOVEN: *Horn sonata in F, Op. 17* (with M. Garcin-Marrou). MENDELSSOHN: *6 Songs without words; Rondo capriccioso, Op. 14.* SCHUBERT: *Introduction and variations on 'Trockne Blumen' for flute & piano, D.802* (with K. Hünteler). WEBER: *Grand duo concertante for clarinet & piano, Op. 48* (with E. Hoeprich).
*** EMI Dig. CDC7 54021-2 [id.].

This so-called *'Salonkonzert'* is a thoroughly enjoyable affair. The Beethoven *Horn sonata*, played on period instruments, is a very different musical experience from the familiar modern performance; the uneven horn-tone with its strong bottom notes makes a striking contrast with the fortepiano. It is played with great expertise and musicianship by Michel Garcin-Marrou. He is partnered with style and fluency by Melvyn Tan, who also captures the spirit of the six Mendelssohn *Songs without words*, Op. 14, as well as the familiar *Rondo capriccioso*, to perfection. Listening to Schubert's *Introduction and variations on 'Trockne Blumen'*, even in such a sympathetic account as that of Konrad Hünteler, makes one understand Mozart's aversion to the early flute, with its pale, watery tone and occasional flatness. The Weber *Grand duo concertante* is much more enjoyable and finds expert advocacy from Eric Hoeprich. The balance is thoroughly natural and realistic, with the fortepiano observed at just the right distance.

Williams, John (guitar)

'Spanish guitar music': Isaac ALBÉNIZ: *Asturias; Tango; Cordoba; Sevilla.* SANZ: *Canarios.* TORROBA: *Nocturno; Madroños.* SAGRERAS: *El Colibri.* Mateo ALBÉNIZ: *Sonata in D.* FALLA: *Homenaje; Three-cornered hat: Corregidor's dance; Miller's dance. El amor brujo: Fisherman's song.* CATALAN FOLKSONGS: *La Nit de Nadal; El noy de la mare; El testamen de Amelia.* GRANADOS: *La maja de Goya. Spanish dance No. 5.* TARREGA: *Recuerdos de la Alhambra.* VILLA-LOBOS: *Prelude No. 4 in E min.* MUDARRA: *Fantasia.* TURINA: *Fandanguillo, Op. 36.*
(M) *** Sony SBK 46347 [id.].

This generous (74 minutes) recital is drawn from two LPs, recorded in the mid-1970s and highly praised by us at the time. John Williams has the full measure of this repertoire. He can show strong Latin feeling, as in the vibrant *Farruca* of the *Miller's dance* from Falla's *Three-cornered hat*, or create a magically atmospheric mood, as in the hauntingly registered transcription of the *Fisherman's song* from *El amor brujo*. He can play with thoughtful improvisatory freedom, as in the Villa-Lobos *Prelude*, with its pianissimo evocation, or be dramatically spontaneous, as in the memorable performance of Turina's *Fandanguillo*, which ends the recital magnetically. He does not create quite the degree of tension that Julian Bream achieves in the central section of the Granados *Spanish dance No. 5* or in the Albéniz *Cordoba*, but these pieces bring imaginative rubato and are full of colour. The instinctive control of atmosphere and dynamic is constantly rewarding throughout a varied programme, and the technique is phenomenal, yet never flashy, always at the service of the music. The remastering brings a clean and truthful, if very immediate, image. Background is minimal and never intrusive.

Xue-Wei (violin)

'Virtuoso' (with Pamela Nicholson, piano): BRAHMS: *Hungarian dance No. 17.* CASTELNUOVO-TEDESCO: *Sea murmurs.* DINICU: *Hora staccato.* ELGAR: *La capricieuse, Op. 17.* GERSHWIN: *Porgy and Bess: Summertime; Bess, you is my woman; It ain't necessarily so.* GLUCK: *Orfeo: Dance of the Blessed Spirits.* HEUBERGER: *Der Opernball: Midnight bells.* MENDELSSOHN: *Song without words, Op. 62/1.* PROKOFIEV: *Love for 3 oranges: March.* RACHMANINOV: *Daisies; Lilacs.* SARASATE: *Spanish dance: Playera.* TCHAIKOVSKY: *Souvenir d'un lieu cher, Op. 42: Mélodie.* arr. HEIFETZ: *Deep river.* WIENIAWSKI: *Capriccio-valse, Op. 7.*
** ASV Dig. CDDCA 698; *ZCDCA 698* [id.].

This is an unashamedly old-fashioned virtuoso's collection, presented with such fervour that you even accept the very nineteenth-century treatment of the Gluck *Dance of the Blessed Spirits.* Xue-Wei plays with assurance, flair and warmth, but he is not well served by the engineers, who present his violin very close in a dry acoustic, so giving his tone an edge and exaggerating even the slightest unevenness. The recording of the piano, by contrast, is bass-heavy.

Yamash'ta, Stomu (percusssion)

20th-Century music: HENZE: *Prison song.* TAKEMITSU: *Seasons.* MAXWELL DAVIES: *Turis campanarum sonantium.*
(M) *** Decca 430 005-2 [id.].

Henze's remarkable *Prison song* was written especially for Yamash'ta; whether or not it is a masterpiece, the performance here is totally compelling. The words of the poem (from the *Prison Diary of Ho Chi Minh*) are mixed in with a prerecorded *musique concrète* tape, and to this the percussionist adds his own rhythmic commentary. Yamash'ta both recites (if that is the word – the vocal delivery is quite different from anything one might expect) and plays, and the result is an artistic *tour de force.* Toru Takemitsu's *Seasons* is strong in atmosphere but does not quite match the imaginative quality of Peter Maxwell Davies's *Turis campanarum sonantium.* In this work, perhaps the most ambitious of the three here recorded, Yamash'ta creates and holds the strongest possible tension and builds a climax of tremendous power. The Decca recording is truly spectacular, and this is a reissue not to be missed by those interested in twentieth-century avant-garde writing.

Yepes, Narciso (guitar)

Spanish guitar music: TÁRREGA: *Recuerdos de la Alhambra; Capricho arabe; Serenata; Tango; Alborada; Marieta mazurka.* SOR: *Theme and variations, Op. 9; Minuet in G, Op. 11/1. Variations on Marlborough, Op. 28.* SANZ: *Spanish suite.* RODRIGO: *En los trigales.* GRANADOS: *Spanish Dance No. 4.* ALBÉNIZ: *Rumores de la Caleta; Malagueña, Op. 165. Suite española: Asturias (Leyenda).* Arr. LLOBET: *La canço del lladre; La filla del marxant* (Catalan folksongs). SEGOVIA: *El noi de la mare.* YEPES: *Forbidden games* (film score): *Romance.* VILLA-LOBOS: *Prelude No. 1.* RUIZ PIPÓ: *Canción and Danza No. 1* (CD only: ALBÉNIZ: *Piezas caracteristicas No. 12.* MOMPOU: *Canco i danca.* ASENCIO: *Collectici itim*).
❀ (B) *** DG Compact Classics 413 434-2 (2); *413 434-4.*

This cassette can be recommended with the utmost enthusiasm to anyone wanting an inexpensive, generous (88 minutes) and representative programme of Spanish guitar music. Narciso Yepes is not only an outstanding exponent of this repertoire, he also has the rare gift of consistently creating electricity in the recording studio, and all this music springs vividly to life. In popular favourites like the famous opening *Recuerdos de la Alhambra* of Tárrega, the exciting transcription of Falla's *Miller's dance*, the earlier Baroque repertoire (the *Suite* of Sanz is particularly appealing), and in the communicative twentieth-century items by Rodrigo and Ruiz Pipó, Yepes' assured and always stylish advocacy brings consistent pleasure. The tape transfer level is quite high and the attendant hiss is not a problem. There are three extra items on the digitally remastered pair of CDs, but this is surely a case where the tape is the best buy. It costs much less and can be used both domestically and in the car.

Vocal Recitals and Choral Collections

Angeles, Victoria de los (soprano)

Opera arias from: VERDI: *Ernani; Otello.* PUCCINI: *La Bohème.* BOITO: *Mefistofele.* ROSSINI: *La Cenerentola.* MASCAGNI: *Cavalleria Rusticana.* CATALANI: *La Wally.* MOZART: *Le nozze di Figaro.* WAGNER: *Tannhäuser; Lohengrin.* MASSENET: *Manon.* GOUNOD: *Faust.*
(M) (***) EMI mono CDH7 63495-2 [id.].

Most of the items here are taken from an early LP recital by de los Angeles that has rarely been matched in its glowing beauty and range of expression. The *Willow song* and *Ave Maria* from *Otello* have never been sung with more aching intensity than here, and the same goes for the Mascagni and Catalani arias. The final cabaletta from *Cenerentola* sparkles deliciously with de los Angeles, as so often, conveying the purest of smiles in the voice. The CD reissue is augmented by the valuable Mozart, Massenet, Gounod and Wagner items, all recorded in the days of 78s.

Baker, Dame Janet (mezzo-soprano)

French song recital (with the Melos Ensemble): RAVEL: *3 Poèmes de Stéphane Mallarmé; Chansons madécasses.* CHAUSSON: *Chanson perpétuelle, Op. 37.* DELAGE: *4 Poèmes hindous.*
❀ (M) *** Decca 425 948-2 [id.].

This is a very beautiful record. Chausson's extended cantilena about a deserted lover has a direct communication which Janet Baker contrasts with the subtler beauties of the Ravel songs. She shows great depth of feeling for the poetry here and an equally evocative sensitivity to the songs about India, written in 1912 by Ravel's pupil, Maurice Delage, which are by no means inferior to the mélodies by his more famous contemporaries. With superbly atmospheric playing from the Melos group and an outstanding 1966 (originally Oiseau-Lyre) recording, this is a ravishing collection which must be placed among Dame Janet's most outstanding records.

Barstow, Josephine (soprano)

Final scenes (with Scottish Op. Ch. & O, Mauceri) from: R. STRAUSS: *Salome.* CHERUBINI: *Medée.* JANÁČEK: *The Mukropoulos case.* PUCCINI: *Turandot* (with L. Bartolini).
**(*) Decca Dig. 430 203-2 [id.].

Josephine Barstow's recital disc is particularly valuable for offering the first ever recording of Alfano's completion of Puccini's *Turandot* in its original full form, substantially longer than the abridged version which resulted when Toscanini took a hand. In the opera house it might well make the final Act too long, but on its own it certainly provides a more fully rounded and convincing view of the heroine's surprising volte-face over Prince Calaf. The return of the *Nessun dorma* theme is also more satisfying in the expanded form here. Barstow's abrasive voice may not be ideally suited to the role, but her singing conveys total involvement, as it does in the other varied items representing some of her most notable roles. First-rate recording.

Battle, Kathleen (soprano), **Jessye Norman** (soprano)

'Spirituals in concert' (with Ch. and O, James Levine): *Ride on, King Jesus; Swing low, sweet chariot; Gospel train; He's got the whole world in his hand; Great day;* etc.
*** DG Dig. 429 790-2; *429 790-4* [id.].

The American critic, Will Crutchfield, writes of the recital recorded here: 'In the hands of artists like these, the Spiritual is not only alive and flourishing but enjoying a kind of Golden Age'. Also seen on television, this was a larger-than-life event, with some items made too glossy. But with two such dynamic, characterful artists giving heartfelt performances, the result is consistently compelling, the more so when most items are relative rarities. There is fun in the mixture too, typified by the most surprising and memorable of the items, *Scandalize my name*, an overtly comic duet on a serious theme, with piano accompaniment alone, very like a cabaret number. The singers' timing in it is delicious, pointing their witty attempts to upstage each other. The live recording, not ideally balanced, has plenty of presence.

Berganza, Teresa (mezzo-soprano)

Spanish and Italian songs (with Felix Lavilla, piano): CHERUBINI: *Ahi! che forse ai miei di.* CESTI: *Intorno all'idol mio.* PERGOLESI: *Confusa, smarrita.* A. SCARLATTI: *Qual mia colpa . . . Se delitto è l'adorati; Chi vuol innamorarsi; La Rosaura (Un cor da voi ferito); Elitropio d'amor.* GURIDI: *Canzones castellanas: Cómo quieres que adivine; Mañanita de San Juan.* LAVILLA: *4 canciones vascas.* TURINA: *Saeta en forma de Salve a la Virgen de la Esperanza, Op. 60.* GRANADOS: *El tra la la y el Punteado; El majo timido; La maja dolorosa.* TURINA: *Está tu imagen, que admiro (Farruca).*
(M) *** Decca 425 947-2 [id.].

This 1962 recital was made when Teresa Berganza's voice was at its freshest and most appealing. If anyone in the world could approach Victoria de los Angeles in Spanish song at that time it was Berganza, and her singing here is very nearly as spontaneous-sounding and imaginative. The second of the two Guridi songs included is especially beautiful with a movingly tender melody. The arias by Cherubini, Scarlatti and others would have gained from having more than just a piano accompaniment, but the classical quality of the singing is most beguiling. The recording was made in Decca's West Hampstead studio and is vivid and well balanced.

Bernac, Pierre (baritone), **Francis Poulenc** (piano)

Mélodies: POULENC: *Banalités; Calligrammes (Guillaume Apollinaire); Chansons villageoises; Main dominée par le coeur; 4 Poèmes de Guillaume Apollinaire; Tu vois le feu du soir.* DEBUSSY: *Beau soir; L'échelonnement des haies; Le promenoir de deux amants.* RAVEL: *Histoires naturelles; Mélodies hébraïques.* SATIE: *Le Chapelier; Daphénéo; La statue de bronze.*
(M) (***) Sony mono MPK 46731 [id.].

This famous partnership recorded widely for HMV in the late 1940s, but these performances were made for Columbia Records in New York in 1950 and appeared on two LPs in America in the 1970s. Bernac's voice is fresher than ever and his powers of characterization remarkable. In addition to the two-dozen Poulenc songs, there are another fourteen by Ravel and a handful by Debussy and Satie. They sound very well indeed and should not be missed. Thirty-eight songs by a great interpreter in very acceptable recorded sound at mid-price is a real bargain.

'Birthday concert'

'A birthday concert for my grandmother' (with Rostropovich, Garcia, Mary McLaughlin, Tallis Chamber Ch., ECO, Leppard): arr. LEPPARD: *National anthem.* J. STRAUSS, jnr: *Albion polka.* MATTHEWS: *Romanza for cello and small orchestra, Op. 49.* ELGAR: *Nursery suite: The wagon passes.* GOWERS: *Suite for solo violin and chamber orchestra.* COATES: *Three Elizabeths: Elizabeth of Glamis.* DOYLE: *The thistle and the rose.*
*** EMI Dig. CDC7 54164-2 [id.].; *EL 754164-4.*

HRH the Prince of Wales hit on the happy idea of commissioning a birthday concert for the Queen Mother, to include three newly written works, with the requirements that the music be 'happy and nostalgic; that it should have recognizable melodies and themes; that it should be memorable and, hopefully, enjoyed by a much wider audience than just a few of the musical cognoscenti'. Long before this occasion Elgar had met these specifications unprompted with the charming patrol, *The wagon passes,* which readily caught the fancy of the then Duchess of York when she attended the composer's first recording session of the piece at the Kingsway Hall in 1931. During the war years, Eric Coates penned his own delightful tribute to *Elizabeth of Glamis,* as the second movement of his *Three Elizabeths suite.* Whether the new works by David Matthews, Patrick Gowers or Patrick Doyle's four ebullient song-settings will similarly stand the test of time one can only hazard a guess. The last two are certainly agreeable, although Matthews' *Romanza,* written for Rostropovich, is lyrically a little wan. But the performances here are all persuasive, especially Marie McLaughlin's solo contribution (in Scottish dialect) with the admirable Tallis Chamber Choir; and the excellent recordings demonstrate the flattering acoustics of the ballroom of Buckingham Palace.

Burrows, Stuart (tenor), John Constable (piano)

'The world of favourite ballads': TOURS: *Mother o' mine.* RAY: *The sunshine of your smile.* FOSTER: *I dream of Jeannie.* HAYDN-WOOD: *Roses of Picardy.* MARSHALL: *I hear you calling me.* BALFE: *Come into the garden, Maud.* ADAMS: *The star of Bethlehem; Thora.* SANDERSON: *As I sit here.* JOHNSON: *When you and I were young, Maggie.* DANKS: *Silver threads among the gold.* LINTON: *I give thanks for you.* WEATHERBY: *Danny Boy.* HANDEL: *Silent worship.* AITKEN: *Maire my girl.* E. PURCELL: *Passing by.* DE KOVEN: *Oh, promise me.* GREEN: *Gortnamona.* COATES: *I hear you singing.* MOLLOY: *The Kerry dance.* DEL RIEGO: *O dry those tears.*
(B) *** Decca 430 090-2; *430 090-4* [id.].

With his headily beautiful voice at its freshest – the recordings were made in 1978 – and much simple charm, Burrows makes an excellent interpreter of popular ballads like these. The engineers, recording in a London chapel, placed the microphones rather close, but the effect on CD is to give a most vivid presence. John Constable accompanies strongly.

Cambridge Singers, John Rutter

'Christmas with the Cambridge Singers': MASON: *Joy to the world.* SWEELINCK: *Hodie Christus natus est.* RUTTER: *Shepherd's carol; What sweeter music.* Arr. WOOD: *Ding*

dong! merrily on high. TRAD., arr. RUTTER: *'Twas in the moon of winter time; Personent hodie; Somerset wassail; Still, still; Coventry carol; What child is this?; Quem pastores laudavere.* TRAD., arr. WILLCOCKS: *Sussex carol; The Infant King.* SCHEIDT: *In dulci jubilo.* HANDEL: *Messiah: For unto us a child is born.* ADAM: *O holy night.* VICTORIA: *O magnum mysterium.* BERLIOZ: *L'enfance du Christ: Shepherds' farewell.* BRITTEN: *New year carol.* GRUBER: *Silent night.*
**(*) Collegium Dig./Analogue COLCD 111; *COLC 111* [id.].

Another atmospheric Christmas collection from Rutter. Although *Joy to the World* and Scheidt's setting of *In dulci jubilo* effectively feature trumpets, most of the programme is serene. Indeed the famous *Messiah* chorus could do with a shade more exuberance. The Berlioz excerpt is pleasing, yet it would have had more character sung in French, and Adam's *O holy night* is unashamedly romantic. But there are the usual felicitous arrangements here, and this is a pleasing record for late evening: Rutter's own carols are always enticing. The recording, made in the glowing ambience of the Great Hall of University College School, London, is very naturally balanced.

Carreras, José (tenor)

'The essential José Carreras': Arias from: PUCCINI: *La Bohème; Manon Lescaut; Turandot; Tosca.* LEONCAVALLO: *I Pagliacci.* DONIZETTI: *L'elisir d'amore; Lucia di Lammermoor.* VERDI: *Il Trovatore; Luisa Miller.* BERNSTEIN: *West Side story.* Neapolitan songs. FRANCK: *Panis angelicus.*
*** Ph. 432 692-2; *432 692-4* [id.].

José Carreras has a less flamboyant personality than Pavarotti and less vocal presence than Domingo – but he is a very pleasing singer in his own right and his style is entirely without vulgarity. In the famous Puccini warhorses some might prefer more robust fervour, but one can believe in Mimi being attracted to a Rodolfo who sings as winningly as this, and the Donizetti arias also suit the voice well. If *Di quella pira* from *Trovatore* was a less suitable choice, Carreras makes up for it in the Neapolitan songs, which are sung with a refined lyrical fervour that is refreshing, even if sometimes listeners may seek a more gutsy, peasant style. Accompaniments are always sympathetic, the sound is first class, and the recital plays for 70 minutes; even so, this should have been offered at mid-price.

(i) Carreras, José, (ii) Placido Domingo and (iii) Luciano Pavarotti (tenors)

'In concert at the Baths of Caracalla, Rome, 7 July 1990' (with Maggio Musicale Fiorentino O & Rome Opera O, Mehta): Arias from: (i) CILEA: *L'Arlesiana.* (ii) MEYERBEER: *L'Africaine.* (iii; ii) PUCCINI: *Tosca;* (ii) *Turandot.* (iii) LEHÁR: *Das Land des Lächelns.* (i) GIORDANO: *Andrea Chénier.* (i–iii) Songs by DE CRESCENDO; CARDILLO; DE CURTIS; LARA; SOROZÁBAL. Medley including excerpts from BERNSTEIN: *West Side story.* LLOYD WEBBER: *Memory. La vie en rose; Mattinata; 'O sole mio; Amapola.* Encores.
*** Decca 430 433-2; *430 433-4* [id.].

Planned years in advance to coincide with the football World Cup in Rome in 1990, this unmatchable extravaganza relied on the devotion of all three great tenors to that game. The success of the resulting record with the wider musical public (it temporarily ousted Nigel Kennedy's *Four Seasons* from the top place in the 'Charts') means that our comments are of no real consequence. A series of purple patches – even the orchestra goes over the top – vividly recorded and with the voices close-miked inevitably brings a feeling of coarseness, although there are undoubted physical thrills if you enjoy loud, straining, tenor *fortissimos*. There are a few, rarer moments of quiet singing. José Carreras was not in his best voice, yet he is still impressive in *L'Improvviso* from *Andrea Chénier*, as is Domingo in the Lehár and the excerpt from the Spanish zarzuela. Pavarotti's Puccini makes the usual strong impact but can be heard with more finesse on his studio recordings. However, there is certainly a sense of occasion here, with the rivalry between the three superstars in the culminating trio a special delight: a far cry from the animosity that comparable tenors of the past often showed towards one another.

Collegeum Aureum or Collegium Terpsichore

'Dances from Terpsichore' (with Siegfried Behrend; Siegfried Fink).
(B) *** Pickwick IMPX 9026 [id.].

An unexpectedly successful and rewarding collection of early dance music, some of it sounding quite primitive, but with the later items, collected by Praetorius, more sophisticated; yet all full of vitality and presented here with the most piquant instrumental effects. The performances by the Collegium Terpsichore are especially spontaneous, but the whole programme of 36 items encourages dipping into.

Divas

'Prima Voce': Divas Volume 2, 1909–40 (Hempel, Galli-Curci, Farrar, Kurz, Garrison, Gluck, Ivogün, Onegin, Schoene, Norena, Ponselle, Leider, Vallin, Teyte, Koshetz, Flagstad, Favero): Arias from: BELLINI: *I Puritani*. MOZART: *Le nozze di Figaro; Die Entführung aus dem Serail*. PUCCINI: *Tosca*. VERDI: *Rigoletto; La forza del destino*. OFFENBACH: *Les contes d'Hoffmann; La Périchole*. GODARD: *Jocelyn*. BIZET: *Carmen*. J. STRAUSS, Jnr: *Die Fledermaus*. THOMAS: *Hamlet*. WAGNER: *Tristan und Isolde; Die Walküre*. MASSENET: *Werther*. PONCE: *Estrellita*. MASCAGNI: *Lodoletta*.
(M) (***) Nimbus mono NI 7818 [id.].

As in the previous *Divas* volume, the choice of items will delight any lover of fine singing, a most discriminating choice. Maria Ivogün, the teacher of Schwarzkopf, contributes a wonderfully pure and incisive *Martern aller Arten* (*Entführung*) dating from 1923, and Lotte Schoene is unusually and characterfully represented by Adele's *Mein Herr Marquis* from *Fledermaus*. Frida Leider's *Liebestod* is nobly sung but is surprisingly fast by latterday standards. Maggie Teyte sings delectably in an aria from *La Périchole*; and though some of the pre-electric items in Nimbus's resonant transfers suggest an echo-chamber, the voices are warm and full.

Domingo, Placido (tenor)

Arias from: VERDI: *Rigoletto; Aida; Il Trovatore; La Traviata; Ernani; Macbeth*. DONIZETTI: *L'Elisir d'amore; Lucia di Lammermoor*. BIZET: *Carmen; Les Pêcheurs de perles*. MEYERBEER: *L'Africaine*. PUCCINI: *La Fanciulla del West*. LEHÁR: *Land des Lächelns*. Songs: LEONCAVALLO: *Mattinata*. LARA: *Granada*. CURTIS: *Nonti scorda*. GREVER: *Mucho*. CARDILLO: *Catari, catari*.
(B) *** DG Compact Classics *419 091-4* [id.].

A self-recommending Compact Classcs tape, offering nearly an hour and a half of Domingo in excellent operatic form. The programme includes obvious favourites but some less-expected items too, and the songs are welcome in showing the great tenor in lighter mood. A bargain, very useful for a long journey if you like to turn your car into La Scala Motorway.

Early Music Consort of London, David Munrow

'Music of the Crusades': Anonymous thirteenth-century French music and music by: MARCABRU; CUIOT DE DIJON; WALTER VON DER VOGEL-WEIDE; FAIDIT; CONON DE BETHUNE; RICHARD COEUR-DE-LION; THIBAUT DE CHAMPAGNE.
(M) *** Decca 430 264-2; *430 264-4*.

Of all the Early Music groups, the Early Music Consort under the late David Munrow can be relied on best to entertain and titillate the ear without ever descending into vulgarity. Not all the music in this collection can be associated directly with the Crusades themselves but, in his scholarly and informative note, James Tyler does not make particular claims that it can. The characteristic combination of familiarity with their repertoire and imaginative flair which characterizes the work of this group informs the whole programme. Most of the accompaniments are purely speculative (only the melodic line survives in some cases) so that listeners should be prepared to approach these lively performances for what they are, resourceful and stimulating reconstructions rather than exact reproductions of what was heard in the thirteenth century. The performances, like the realizations, are brilliantly effective and the presentation deserves the highest praise for its blend of scholarship and inventiveness. The 1970 (Argo) recording sounds as fresh here as the day it was made.

Ewing, Maria (mezzo-soprano)

'From this moment on' (with RPO, Neil Henderson; Richard Rodney Bennett (piano): PORTER: *Medley*. YOUMANS: *More than you know*. KERN: *All the things you are; Yesterdays*. BURKE: *But beautiful*. HUPFIELD: *As time goes by*. WEILL: *It never was you*. ARLEN: *Come rain or come shine; When the sun comes out; One for my baby*. GERSHWIN: *The man that got away; Medley*. RODGERS: *Spring is here*.
**(*) Pickwick Dig. MCD 18; *MCC 18* [id.].

The RPO here attempt a crossover collection, not an easy area for success, but, with sophisticated orchestral backing, Maria Ewing's smoky mezzo is heard at its most seductive in Kern's *All the things you are* and *Yesterdays* (the latter with a sinuous violin solo from David Towse). In five songs, *More than you know, But beautiful, It never was you, When the sun comes out* and the gently expressive Rogers and Hart number, *Spring is here*, Richard Rodney Bennett provides intimately understanding piano accompaniments to give a sultry, night-club ambience. Ewing's dark timbre suits Arlen's *When the sun comes out* rather well; before that, in the livelier *Come rain or come shine*, the accompaniment needs the extra uninhibited bite an American group could provide. But clearly the London players are enjoying themselves, and both singer and orchestra are at their most vibrant and silkily sentient in the closing Gershwin medley. This is a string of five famous standards, to which the piano also contributes, and if *Our love is here to stay* is a shade drawn out, the following *S'Wonderful*, with a superb sally from the horns, comes off infectiously, and *Someone to watch over me* ends the recital in beguilingly gentle evocation, with its interweaving violin obbligati.

Ferrier, Kathleen (contralto)

BBC Recitals (with (i) Frederick Stone; (ii) Ernest Lush): (i) STANFORD: *The fairy lough; A soft day.* PARRY: *Love is a bable.* VAUGHAN WILLIAMS: *Silent noon.* BRIDGE: *Go not, happy day.* WARLOCK: *Sleep; Pretty ring-time.* arr. BRITTEN: *O waly, waly; Come you not from Newcastle.* arr. HUGHES: *Kitty my love.* (ii) FERGUSON: *Discovery.* WORDSWORTH: *Red skies; The wind; Clouds.* RUBBRA: *Psalms 6, 23 & 150.*
(M) (***) Decca mono 430 061-2 [id.].

These recordings come from two BBC broadcasts, made on 5 June 1952 and 12 January 1953, in the last two years of Kathleen Ferrier's life. Her vocal line is immediately at its most ravishing in the opening Stanford song; throughout, the warm personality and wonderful sense of timing illuminate repertoire in which she was completely at home. No one has presented arranged folksongs so endearingly – just sample the ravishing pianissimo at the end of *O waly waly.* Most valuable are the rare William Wordsworth songs, of which *Clouds* is totally memorable, and the very characteristic Rubbra Psalm settings, *O Lord rebuke me not, The Lord is my Shepherd* and *Praise ye the Lord.* The recordings are of excellent quality and have a natural presence, so that the occasional click from the acetate disc original is, alas, the more noticeable.

'The world of Kathleen Ferrier': TRAD.: *Blow the wind southerly; The Keel Row; Ma bonny lad; Kitty my love.* arr. BRITTEN: *Come you not from Newcastle.* HANDEL: *Rodelinda: Art thou troubled? Serse: Ombra mai fu.* GLUCK: *Orfeo: What is life?* MENDELSSOHN: *Elijah: Woe unto them; O rest in the Lord.* BACH: *St Matthew Passion: Have mercy, Lord, on me.* SCHUBERT: *An die Musik; Gretchen am Spinnrade; Die junge Nonne; Der Musensohn.* BRAHMS: *Sapphische Ode; Botschaft.* MAHLER: *Rückert Lieder: Um Mitternacht.*
⊛ (B) (***) Decca mono 430 096-2; *430 096-4* [id.].

This selection, revised and expanded from the original LP issue, admirably displays Kathleen Ferrier's range, from the delightfully fresh folksongs to Mahler's *Um Mitternacht* in her celebrated recording with Bruno Walter and the VPO. The noble account of *O rest in the Lord* is one of the essential items now added, together with an expansion of the Schubert items (*Die junge Nonne* and *An die Musik* are especially moving). Her spoken introduction, together with the Jensen *Altar* (taken from a BBC broadcast) are now omitted, perhaps for copyright reasons. The CD transfers are remarkably trouble-free and the opening unaccompanied *Blow the wind southerly* has uncanny presence. The recital plays for 65 minutes and fortunately there are few if any technical reservations to be made here about the sound quality.

Ghiaurov, Nicolai (bass)

Operatic arias from: GOUNOD: *Faust.* MEYERBEER: *Les Huguenots.* BIZET: *La jolie fille de Perth.* VERDI: *Don Carlo; Macbeth.* PUCCINI: *La Bohème.* BOITO: *Mefistofele.* TCHAIKOVSKY: *Eugene Onegin.* BORODIN: *Prince Igor.* MUSSORGSKY: *Boris Godunov.*
(M) *** Decca 421 872-2 [id.].

The first five items here were studio (recital) recordings made in the early 1960s, with the LSO under Edward Downes, and if the singing has to yield to Ghiaurov's fellow Bulgarian, Boris Christoff, in detailed artistry, there is no doubt about its panache, nor indeed the vocal richness. As Mephistofeles from Gounod's *Faust,* Ghiaurov lacks something in biting humour but not in gusto (and he is equally good in the same role as set by Boito). The other items, apart from the extremely lively Galitzky's aria from *Prince Igor*, again with Downes, come from his various complete sets, ending appropriately with Boris's Monologue and the moving *Death of Boris* (with Karajan). Given Decca's consistently vivid projection of a magnificent voice, the whole programme is worth investigating.

Gigli, Beniamino (tenor)

'Prima Voce': Volume 2 (1925–40). Arias from: DONIZETTI: *L'elisir d'amore; Lucia di Lammermoor.* PUCCINI: *Manon Lescaut; La Bohème; Tosca.* VERDI: *La forza del destino; La Traviata; Rigoletto.* THOMAS: *Mignon.* BIZET: *I pescatori di perle.* PONCIELLI: *La Gioconda.* MASSENET: *Manon.* GOUNOD: *Faust.* RIMSKY-KORSAKOV: *Sadko.* GLUCK: *Paride ed Elena.* CILEA: *L'Arlesiana.* CACCINI: Song: *Amarilli.*
(M) (***) Nimbus mono NI 7817 [id.].

Issued to celebrate the Gigli centenary in 1990, the Nimbus selection concentrates on recordings he made in the very early years of electrical recording up to 1931, when his voice was at its very peak, the most golden instrument, ideally suited to recording. The items are very well chosen and are by no means the obvious choices, though it is good to have such favourites as the *Pearlfishers duet* with de Luca and the 1931 version of Rodolfo's *Che gelida manina.* The Nimbus transfers are at their best, with relatively little reverberation.

Arias and excerpts from: GIORDANO: *Andrea Chénier.* DONIZETTI: *La Favorita; L'elisir d'amore; Lucia di Lammermoor.* GOUNOD: *Faust; Roméo et Juliette.* LALO: *Le roi d'Ys.* PUCCINI: *Tosca.* PONCHIELLI: *La Gioconda.* BIZET: *Les pêcheurs de perles.* VERDI: *Attila; I Lombardi.* GOMES: *Lo schiavo; Il Guarany.*
(M) (***) BMG/RCA mono GD 87811.

This RCA compilation with its bright, forward CD transfers of the original 78s underlines the astonishing consistency of Gigli's golden tenor over the whole of his long recording career, whether in heroic outbursts or in gentle *bel canto.* The selection ranges wide, from pre-electrics like Chénier's big aria, always a favourite with him, to ten items from the early electric period – 1925–30 – and with two little songs by Gomes from 1951 as a postscript. Specially notable from these American recordings are the duets and trios with his great contemporaries at the Met. in New York, Ezio Pinza, Titta Ruffo and Elisabeth Rethberg. The voice is consistently close and immediate, with an astonishing sense of presence, yet with none of the histrionic harshness one can expect from other tenors.

Hubbard, Bruce (baritone)

'For you, for me' (with St Lukes O, Russell Davies): COPLAND: *Old American songs.* BERLIN: *Always.* BERNSTEIN: *Mass: Simple song. 1600 Pennsylvania Ave: Seena.* GERSHWIN: *Girl Crazy: Bidin' my time. Porgy and Bess: Bess, you is my woman* (with Marvis Martin); *A woman is a sometime thing. The Shocking Miss Pilgrim: For you, for me. Show Girl: Home blues. Centennial Summer: All through the day. Swing time: The way you look tonight. Very warm for May: All the things you are.* SONDHEIM: *Anyone can whistle: Everybody says don't. A Little Night Music: In praise of women.* TRAD.: *Shenandoah.*
*** EMI Dig. CDC7 49928-2; *EL 749928-4* [id.].

Hubbard, the rich-toned and characterful black baritone who had such striking success in the EMI set of *Show Boat*, both on record and on stage, here offers an unusual and most attractive crossover collection. It starts with all ten of Aaron Copland's *Old American songs*, not just the popular favourites like *Simple gifts* but delightful rarities like *The golden willow tree*. Some of the others too are surprisingly little known, but all of them are warmly characterized, with pointed accompaniment from the Orchestra of St Luke's under Dennis Russell Davies. Excellent, vivid recording.

Kanawa, Kiri Te (soprano)

'The young Kiri': Arias and excerpts from: PUCCINI: *La Bohème; Tosca; Madama Butterfly; Turandot.* GOUNOD: *Faust.* ROSSINI: *Il barbiere di Siviglia.* J. STRAUSS, Jnr: *Die Fledermaus; Casanova.* WEBER: *Der Freischütz.* BERNSTEIN: *West Side story.* BIZET: *Carmen.* RODGERS: *The Sound of Music.* GERSHWIN: *Porgy and Bess.* KERN: *Showboat.* Songs: BACH/GOUNOD: *Ave Maria.* MALOTTE: *The Lord's prayer.* SIBELIUS: *The tryst.* LECUONA: *Malagueña.* LARA: *Granada.* TRAD.: *Havah nagilah; My lady Greensleeves; Geordie; Soldier soldier; False love; Hokihoki tonu mai; Hine e hine; Tahi nei taru kino.* LENNON/MCCARTNEY: *Yesterday.* Popular songs.
(**) Decca stereo/mono 430 325-2 (2) [id.].

Though with hindsight one can readily detect signs of the star who was soon to develop, these recordings, made in New Zealand before Dame Kiri began studying in London, are more valuable for the devotee than for the general collector. The very gaucheness is often attractive, and it is good to hear the young singer at this early stage tackling the popular repertory she was devoted to at the time. Yet many allowances have to be made, both in performance and in the limited sound-quality, with a fair proportion of the recordings in mono only. With so little help from the engineering, it is a wonder the voice sounds as beautiful as it does.

King's College, Cambridge, Choir, Philip Ledger

'Festival of lessons and carols' (1979) includes: TRAD.: *Once in Royal David's city; Sussex carol; Joseph and Mary; A maiden most gentle; Chester carol; Angels, from the realms of glory.* HANDEL: *Resonet in laudibus.* ORD: *Adam lay ybounden.* GRÜBER: *Stille Nacht.* MATHIAS: *A babe is born.* WADE: *O come all ye faithful.* MENDELSSOHN: *Hark! the herald angels sing.*
(M) *** EMI CDM7 63180-2 [id.].

'Procession with carols on Advent Sunday' includes: PALESTRINA (arr. from): *I look from afar; Judah and Jerusalem, fear not.* PRAETORIUS: *Come, thou Redeemer of the earth.* TRAD.: *O come, o come, Emmanuel!; Up, awake and away!; 'Twas in the year; Cherry tree carol; King Jesus hath a garden; On Jordan's bank the Baptist's cry; Gabriel's message; I wonder as I wander; My dancing day; Lo! he comes with clouds descending.* BYRT: *All and some.* P. NICOLAI, arr. BACH: *Wake, o wake! with tidings thrilling.* BACH: *Nun komm' der Heiden Heiland.*
(M) *** EMI CDM7 63181-2 [id.].

Readers will be glad to see that these two CDs, discussed in our main volume, are now available at mid-price.

King's College, Cambridge, Choir, Sir David Willcocks

'The world of King's': HANDEL: *Coronation anthem: Zadok the Priest* (with ECO). ALLEGRI: *Miserere.* PALESTRINA: *Hodie Beata Virgo.* TALLIS: *Sancte Deus.* VIVALDI: *Gloria in D, RV 589: Gloria; Et in terra pax* (with ASMF). BYRD: *Ave verum corpus.* CROFT: *Burial service.* GIBBONS: *This is the record of John* (with Jacobean Consort of Viols). BACH: *O Jesu so meek.* HANDEL: *Chandos anthem No. 9: O Praise the Lord with one consent* (with ASMF).
(B) *** Decca 430 092-2; *430 092-4* [id.].

A fine demonstration of the creative excellence of Sir David Willcocks's regime at King's, recorded for Argo between 1958 and 1966. The programme is well made, opening and closing brightly and colourfully with extrovert Handel, and including the famous performance of Allegri's *Miserere* with the ethereal treble solo of the young Roy Goodman, now better known – nearly thirty years later – for his music-making with the Hanover Band. The soaring lines of Tallis and the serenity of Byrd are to be heard alongside the most famous of Gibbons's verse-anthems (with accompanying viols) and William Croft's nobly austere *Funeral service* (given complete). The excellence of the sound throughout, bright and fresh, with the King's acoustics always an atmospheric asset, is a tribute to the orignal Argo engineering.

Luca, Giuseppe de (baritone)

'Prima voce': Arias from: VERDI: *Don Carlos, Ernani, Il Trovatore, La Traviata, Rigoletto.* ROSSINI: *Il Barbiere di Siviglia.* DONIZETTI: *L'elisir d'amore.* BELLINI: *I Puritani.* DIAZ: *Benvenuto Cellini.* PUCCINI: *La Bohème.* PONCHIELLI: *La Gioconda.* WOLF-FERRARI: *I gioielli della madonna.* Songs: DE LEVA: *Pastorale.* ROMILLI: *Marietta.*
(M) (***) Nimbus mono NI 7815 [id.].

There has never been a more involving account on record of the Act IV Marcello–Rodolfo duet than the one here with de Luca and Gigli, a model of characterization and vocal art. The baritone's mastery emerges vividly in item after item, whether in the power and wit of his pre-electric version of *Largo al factotum* (1917) or the five superb items (including the *Bohème* duet and the *Rigoletto* numbers, flawlessly controlled) which were recorded in the vintage year of 1927. Warm Nimbus transfers.

McCormack, John (tenor)

'Prima voce': Arias and excerpts from: DONIZETTI: *Lucia di Lammermoor; L'elisir d'amore; La figlia del reggimento.* VERDI: *La Traviata; Rigoletto.* PUCCINI: *La Bohème.* BIZET. *Carmen; I pescatore di perle.* DELIBES: *Lakmé.* GOUNOD: *Faust.* PONCHIELLI: *La gioconda.* BOITO: *Mefistofele.* MASSENET: *Manon.* MOZART: *Don Giovanni.* WAGNER: *Die Meistersinger.* HERBERT: *Natomah.* HANDEL: *Semele; Atalanta.*
(M) (***) Nimbus mono NI 7820 [id.].

With the operas represented ranging from Handel's *Atalanta* and *Semele* to *Natomah*, by Victor Herbert, the heady beauty of McCormack's voice, his ease of production and perfect control are amply illustrated in these 21 items. His now legendary 1916 account of *Il mio tesoro* from *Don Giovanni*, with its astonishing breath control, is an essential item; but there are many others less celebrated which help to explain his special niche, even in a generation that included Caruso and Schipa. Characteristic Nimbus transfers.

'The art of John McCormack' (with Gerald Moore; O, cond. Walter Goehr; Fritz Kreisler): MARTINI: *Plaisir d'amour.* HANDEL: *Semele: Where'er you walk. Il pastor fido: Caro amor. Atalanta: Come, my beloved.* MOZART: *Oh what bitter grief is mine; Ridente la calma.* SCHUBERT: *Who is Sylvia?.* BRAHMS: *Die Mainacht; Feldeinsamkeit.* R. STRAUSS: *Allerseelen; Morgen; Du meines Herzen Krönelein.* WOLF: *Auch kleine Dinge; Herr was trägt der Boden hier; Schlafendes Jesuskind; Wo find ich Trost; Anakreons Grab.* RACHMANINOV: *Before my window; How fair this spot; To the children.* FRANCK: *La procession.* FAURÉ: *L'Automne.* DONAUDY: *O del mio amato ben; Luoghi sereni.* ELGAR: *Is she not passing fair?.* QUILTER: *Now sleeps the crimson petal.*
(M) (***) EMI mono CDH7 63306-2 [id.].

Even though it opens – winningly – with Martini's *Plaisir d'amour*, this McCormack anthology centres on his classical 78-r.p.m. discs, from finely spun Handelian lyricism through German Lieder and songs by Rachmaninov (with Fritz Kreisler ready at hand to provide violin obbligatos) to French Mélodie and songs of Elgar and Quilter. His French pronunciation was hardly colloquial, nor was he ever entirely at home in German, yet his contributions to the Wolf Society recordings celebrated a unique feeling for this composer, readily shown here. Overall, the recordings span a long time-period and include a batch of pre-electrics from 1924. But transfers are exemplary. Desmond Shaw Taylor's notes are indispensable too.

Melchior, Lauritz (tenor)

'Prima voce': Arias from: WAGNER: *Siegfried: Tannhäuser; Tristan und Isolde; Die Walküre; Die Meistersinger; Götterdämmerung.* LEONCAVALLO: *Pagliacci.* MEYERBEER: *L'Africana.* VERDI: *Otello.*
(M) (***) Nimbus mono NI 7816 [id.].

The Nimbus disc of Melchior, issued to celebrate his centenary in 1990, demonstrates above all the total consistency of the voice between the pre-electric recordings of *Siegfried* and *Tannhäuser*, made for Polydor in 1924, and the *Meistersinger* and *Götterdämmerung* extracts, recorded in 1939. Of those, the Siegfried–Brünnhilde duet from the *Prologue* of *Götterdämmerung* is particularly valuable. It is fascinating too to hear the four recordings that Melchior made with Barbirolli and the LSO in 1930–31: arias by Verdi, Leoncavallo and Meyerbeer translated into German. As a character, Otello is made to sound far more prickly. Characteristic Nimbus transfers.

Muzio, Claudia (soprano)

'Prima voce': Arias from: MASCAGNI: *Cavalleria Rusticana.* VERDI: *La forza del destino; Otello, Il Trovatore; La Traviata.* PUCCINI: *Tosca; La Bohème.* GIORDANO: *Andrea Chénier.* BOITO: *Mefistofele.* CILEA: *Adriana Lecouvreur; L'Arlesiana.* BELLINI: *La Sonnambula.* Songs by BUZZI-PECCIA; PERGOLESI; REGER; DELIBES; REFICE.
(M) (***) Nimbus mono NI 7814 [id.].

This Nimbus collection of recordings by the sadly short-lived Claudia Muzio duplicates much that is contained on the EMI Références CD of her. The main addition here is the Act III duet from *Otello* with Francesco Merli, but some cherishable items are omitted. The Nimbus acoustic transfer process sets the voice more distantly as well as more reverberantly than the EMI, with its distinctive tang less sharply conveyed.

L'Opéra français

'L'Opéra français' (sung by Corelli; Crespin; Ghiaurov; Horne; Krause; Pavarotti; Resnik; Di Stefano; Sutherland): excerpts from: BIZET: *Carmen; Les pêcheurs de perles.* DELIBES: *Lakmé.* GOUNOD: *Faust; Sapho.* SAINT-SAENS: *Samson et Dalila.* MASSENET: *Werther.*
(M) ** Decca 421 876-2; *421 876-4.*

This is another generous (73 minutes) collection that looks enticing but which fails to add up to the sum of its parts. It opens with Marilyn Horne's vibrant account of the *Habanera* from *Carmen*, taken from her highlights disc (see under Bizet in the composer index); but not everything else here is quite so riveting. The highlights are two of Régine Crespin's contributions, the enchanting *Air des lettres* from *Werther* and the no less engaging *O ma lyre immortelle* from *Sapho*, and her performance of the key aria from *Samson et Dalila* is pretty impressive too. Sutherland contributes a sparkling *Bell song* from *Lakmé*, and she is joined by Jane Berbié in the charming *Flower duet* from the same opera. But the other famous French duet, from Bizet's *Pearl fishers*, is represented, curiously, by a forthright mono recording by Libero de Luca and Jean Borthayre. There are some enjoyable excerpts from *Faust*, and everything sounds vivid, but this is a recital to pick and choose from rather than to listen to right through.

Pavarotti, Luciano (tenor)

'Gala concert at the Royal Albert Hall' (with RPO, Kurt Adler): Arias from: PUCCINI: *Tosca; Turandot.* VERDI: *Macbeth; I Lombardi; Luisa Miller. Un giorno di regno: Overture.* DONIZETTI: *Lucia di Lammermoor.* CILEA: *L'Arlesiana.* DE CURTIS: Song: *Torna a Surriento.* BERLIOZ: *Les Troyens: Royal hunt and storm.*
(M) **(*) Decca 430 716-2; *430 716-4* [id.].

This disc celebrates a much-hyped appearance by Pavarotti at the Royal Albert Hall in 1982, in the days when one tenor alone was enough! It would be unfair to expect much subtlety before such an eager audience, but the live recording conveys the fever well. There are bold accounts of the two most famous arias from *Tosca*, and the celebrated *Nessun dorma* from *Turandot*, and even simple recitatives as intimate as Macduff's in *Macbeth* are proclaimed grandly. The bright digital recording shows up some unevenness in the voice, but no one will miss the genuine excitement, with the electricity of the occasion conveyed equally effectively on disc or tape.

Pavarotti, Luciano (tenor) and Mirella Freni (soprano)

Arias and duets from: PUCCINI: *Tosca; La Bohème.* ROSSINI: *Guglielmo Tell.* BOITO: *Mefistofele.*
(M) *** Decca 421 878-2; *421 878-4* [id.].

Both artists come from the same small town in Italy, Modena, where they were born in 1935; less surprisingly, they studied under the same singing teacher. Their artistic partnership on record has always been a happy one, and perhaps reached its zenith in their 1972 *Bohème* with Karajan (unexpectedly, recorded in the Jesus-Christus Kirche, Berlin). Their great introductory love-duet as Mimi and Rodolfo, perhaps the most ravishing in all opera (from *Che gelida manina*, through *Sì, mi chiamano Mimì* to the soaring *O soave fanciulla*) is an obvious highlight here, but the much less familiar *Lontano, lontano* from *Mefistofele* shows no less memorably that the voices were made for each other. It was a very good idea to include a substantial selection from their 1978–9 *Tosca* (recorded in the Kingsway Hall), not a first choice as a complete set, but with some marvellous singing in Act III, of which some 17 minutes is offered (including *E lucevan le stelle* and the dramatic finale of the opera). The recital opens very spontaneously with 13 minutes from Act I (*Mario! Mario!*), the engagingly temperamental interplay between the lovers, in the Church of Sant'Andrea della Valle. The only slight disappointment is Freni's *Vissi d'arte*; otherwise this is 70 minutes of vintage material, given Decca's top drawer sound.

Partridge, Ian (tenor), **Stephen Roberts** (baritone)

'Songs by Finzi and his friends' (with Benson, piano): FINZI: *To a poet; Oh fair to see, Op. 13/a–b* (song collections). GURNEY: *Sleep; Down by the Salley Gardens; Hawk and buckle.* MILFORD: *If it's ever spring again; The colour; So sweet love seemed.* GILL: *In memoriam.* FERRAR: *O mistress mine.*
**(*) Hyp. CDA 66015 [id.].

Finzi's sensitive response to word-meanings inspires a style of setting that is often not unlike an operatic recitative. His individuality and poetic originality are not always matched by memorability, but the songs of his contemporaries and friends – even where the names are unknown – make immediate communication even on a first hearing. An imaginative collection, well sung, worth exploring by those interested in the repertoire. The recording is somewhat over-resonant.

Royal Opera House, Covent Garden

Royal Opera House Covent Garden (An early history on record). Singers included are: Melba, Caruso, Tetrazzini, McCormack, Destin, Gadski, Schorr, Turner, Zanelli, Lehmann, Schumann, Olczewska, Chaliapin, Gigli, Supervia, Tibbett, Tauber, Flagstad, Melchior. Arias from: GOUNOD: *Faust.* VERDI: *Rigoletto, Otello.* DONIZETTI: *Lucia di Lammermoor.* VERDI: *La Traviata.* PUCCINI: *Madama Butterfly; Tosca.* WAGNER: *Götterdämmerung; Die Meistersinger; Tristan und Isolde.* R. STRAUSS: *Der Rosenkavalier.* MUSSORGSKY: *Boris Godunov.* GIORDANO: *Andrea Chénier.* BIZET: *Carmen.* MOZART: *Don Giovanni.*
(M) (***) Nimbus mono NI 7819 [id.].

Nimbus's survey of great singers at Covent Garden ranges from Caruso's 1904 recording of *Questa o quella* from *Rigoletto* to the recording of the second half of the *Tristan* love duet, which Kirsten Flagstad and Lauritz Melchior made in San Francisco in November 1939, a magnificent recording never issued in Britain and little known which repeated the partnership initiated during the 1937 Coronation season at Covent Garden. The Vienna recording of the *Rosenkavalier* trio with Lehmann, Schumann and Olczewska similarly reproduces a classic partnership at Covent Garden, while Chaliapin's 1928 recording of the *Prayer* and *Death of Boris* was actually recorded live at Covent Garden, with the transfer giving an amazingly vivid sense of presence. Those who like Nimbus's acoustic method of transfer will enjoy the whole disc, though the reverberation round some of the early offerings – like the very first, Melba's *Jewel song* from *Faust* – is cavernous. Particularly interesting is the 1909 recording of part of Brünnhilde's immolation scene, with Johanna Gadski commandingly strong.

Schipa, Tito (tenor)

'Prima voce': Arias from: MASCAGNI: *Cavalleria Rusticana. L'amico Fritz.* VERDI: *Rigoletto; Luisa Miller.* DONIZETTI: *Lucia di Lammermoor; Don Pasquale; L'elisir d'amore.* LEONCAVALLO: *Pagliacci.* MASSENET: *Manon; Werther.* ROSSINI: *Il barbiere di Siviglia.* THOMAS: *Mignon.* FLOTOW: *Martha.* CILEA: *L'Arlesiana.*
(M) (***) Nimbus mono NI 7813 [id.].

The first nine items on this well-chosen selection of Schipa's recordings date from the pre-electric era. The voice is totally consistent, heady and light and perfectly controlled, between the *Siciliana* from Mascagni's *Cavalleria*, recorded with piano in 1913, to the incomparable account of more Mascagni, the *Cherry duet* from *L'amico Fritz*, made with Mafalda Favero in 1937. It says much for his art that Schipa's career continued at full strength for decades after that. The Nimbus transfers put the voice at a slight distance, with the electrical recordings made to sound the more natural.

Schumann-Heink, Ernestine (contralto)

'Prima voce': Arias from: DONIZETTI: *Lucrezia Borgia.* MEYERBEER: *Le Prophète.* WAGNER: *Das Rheingold; Rienzi; Götterdämmerung.* HANDEL: *Rinaldo.* Songs by: ARDITTI; BECKER; SCHUBERT; WAGNER; REIMANN; MOLLOY; BRAHMS; BOEHM & TRAD.
(M) (***) Nimbus mono NI 7811 [id.].

Ernestine Schumann-Heink was a formidable personality in the musical life of her time, notably in New York, as well as a great singer. 'I am looking for my successor,' she is reported as saying well before she retired, adding, 'She must be *the* contralto.' Schumann-Heink combines to an astonishing degree a full contralto weight and richness with the most delicate flexibility, as in the *Brindisi* from Donizetti's *Lucrezia Borgia.* This wide-ranging collection, resonantly transferred by the Nimbus acoustic method, presents a vivid portrait of a very great singer.

Heinrich Schütz Choir, Roger Norrington

'A Baroque Christmas' (with London String Players, Philip Jones Brass Ensemble; Camden Wind Ensemble; Charles Spinks): SCHÜTZ: *Hodie Christus natus est; Ach Herr, du Schöpfer aller Ding.* PURCELL: *Behold I bring you glad tidings.* ANON.: *Soberana Maria.* HAMMERTSCHMIDT: *Alleluja! Freuet euch, ihr Christen alle.* BOUZIGNAC: *Noé! Pastores, cantate Dominum.* G. GABRIELI: *O magnum mysterium.* MONTEVERDI: *Christe Redemptor.* PRAETORIUS: *Singt, ihr lieben Christen all.* HASSLER: *Angeles as pastores ait.*
❀ (M) *** Decca Dig. 430 065-2; *430 065-4* [id.].

A superlative collection which celebrates the joyful Renaissance approach to Christmas. The glorious opening number is matched in memorability by the engaging lullaby, *Soberana Maria*, and *Noé! Pastores* has a delightful interplay between Gabriel (Hazel Holt) and the Shepherds. Giovanni Gabrieli's *O magnum mysterium* is justly famous and sounds superbly sonorous here, while the Michael Praetorius carol has a tune most will readily recognize. The performances are splendid and the recording in the demonstration bracket. There are few more unusual or more rewarding Christmas celebrations than this.

Schwarzkopf, Elisabeth (soprano)

75th Birthday Edition: WOLF: 24 Lieder and Lieder by: SCHUBERT; SCHUMANN; R. STRAUSS. Arias from: MOZART: *Le nozze di Figaro; Così fan tutte; Don Giovanni.* HUMPERDINCK: *Hänsel und Gretel.* NICOLAI: *Die lustige Witwe.* J. STRAUSS, Jnr: *Die Fledermaus.* PUCCINI: *Turandot.* R. STRAUSS: *Ariadne auf Naxos; Der Rosenkavalier; Capriccio.* VERDI: *Requiem.* Various encores by BACH; BEETHOVEN; MARTINI; TCHAIKOVSKY; DEBUSSY; ARNE etc.
(M) *** EMI stereo/mono CMS7 63790-2 (5).

The five discs of the Birthday Edition, available in a box, provide a comprehensive survey of Schwarzkopf's astonishing achievement on record, not least in the early years of her career in the days before stereo was universally adopted. The individual discs – the Wolf Lieder collection as well as the four recitals listed below – are available separately. With excellent transfers, all can be warmly recommended.

Recital: BACH: *Cantatas Nos. 51, 68 and 208.* HANDEL: *Sweet bird.* MOZART: *Exsultate jubilate, K.165.* BEETHOVEN: *Ah! perfido, Op. 65. Fidelio: Abscheulicher!*
(M) (***) EMI mono CDH7 63201-2 [id.].

This collection, one of the five discs issued to celebrate Schwarzkopf's 75th birthday, brings together some ravishing examples of her very early recordings, with the voice exceptionally fresh and flexible. Most fascinating of all are the two Beethoven items, originally recorded as fill-ups for Karajan's Philharmonia recordings of the symphonies. The role of Leonore in *Fidelio* was not one that Schwarzkopf would ever have taken on stage, but the vehemence of her *Abscheulicher!* has never been surpassed on record, a searingly intense reading.

'Encores' (with Gerald Moore or Geoffrey Parsons): BACH: *Bist du bei mir.* GLUCK: *Einem Bach der fliesst.* BEETHOVEN: *Wonne der Wehmut.* LOEWE: *Kleiner Haushalt.* WAGNER: *Träume.* BRAHMS: *Ständchen; 3 Deutsche Volkslieder.* MAHLER: *Um schlimme Kinder artig zu machen; Ich atmet' einen linden Duft; Des Antonius von Padua Fischpredigt.* TCHAIKOVSKY: *Pimpernella.* arr. WOLF-FERRARI: *7 Italian songs.* MARTINI: *Plaisir d'amour.* HAHN: *Si mes vers avaient des ailes.* DEBUSSY: *Mandoline.* arr. QUILTER: *Drink to me only with thine eyes.* ARNE: *When daisies pied; Where the bee sucks.* arr. GUND: *3 Swiss folk songs.* arr. WEATHERLY: *Danny Boy.* J. STRAUSS, Jnr: *Frühlingsstimmen* (with VPO, Joseph Krips).
(M) *** EMI stereo/mono CDM7 63654-2 [id.].

Schwarzkopf herself has on occasion nominated this charming account of *Danny Boy* as her own favourite recording of her singing, but it is only one of a whole sequence of lightweight songs which vividly capture the charm and intensity that made her recitals so memorable, particularly in the extra items at the end. As a rule she would announce and explain each beforehand, adding to the magic. The range here is wide, from Bach's heavenly *Bist du bei mir* to the innocent lilt of the Swiss folksong, *Gsätzli*, and Strauss's *Voices of spring.*

Lieder (with Gerald Moore or Geoffrey Parsons): SCHUBERT: *Die Vögel; Liebhaber in allen Gestalten; Heidenröslein; Die Forelle; Der Einsame; Der Jüngling an der Quelle; An mein Klavier; Erlkönig, Was bedeutet die Bewegung & Ach, um deine feuchten Schwingen (Suleika I & II); Hänflings Liebeswerbung; Meeres Stille; Gretchen am Spinnrade.* SCHUMANN: *Der Nussbaum; Aufträge; 2 Venetian Lieder; Die Kartenlegerin; Wie mit*

innigstem Behagen (Suleika). R. STRAUSS: *Hat gesagt, bleibt's nicht dabei; SchlechtesWetter; Wiegenliedchen; Meinem Kinde; Wiegenlied; 3 Ophelia Lieder; Die Nacht.*
(M) (***) EMI stereo/mono CDM7 63656-2 [id.].

With the Schubert selection including a high proportion of favourites, this compilation provides a fine survey of Schwarzkopf's unique achievement as a Lieder-singer outside the specialist area of Hugo Wolf. The earliest recordings, made in 1948, are of two Schubert songs, *Die Vögel* and a Goethe setting, *Liebhaber in allen Gestalten*, and the latest, Schumann's *Der Nussbaum*, from 25 years on in her career, all beautifully transferred.

Opera arias: MOZART: *Le nozze di Figaro; Così fan tuti; Don Giovanni.* HUMPERDINCK: *Hänsel und Gretel.* LEHÁR: *Die lustige Witwe*; J. STRAUSS, Jnr: *Die Fledermaus.* PUCCINI: *Turandot.* R. STRAUSS: *Ariadne auf Naxos; Der Rosenkavalier; Capriccio.* VERDI: *Messa da requiem.*
(M) (***) EMI stereo/mono CDM7 63657-2 [id.].

This fine collection of arias is taken from various sets Schwarzkopf contributed to in the 1950s. They range from Mozart operas, conducted by Karajan and Furtwängler, to the glories of her supreme recordings of Strauss operas, Ariadne's lament, the Marschallin's final solo in Act I of *Rosenkavalier* and the Countess's final aria in *Capriccio.* Also featured is the *Recordare* from de Sabata's early recording of the Verdi *Requiem.*

'Unpublished recordings' (with (i) Philh. O, Thurston Dart; (ii) Kathleen Ferrier, VPO, Karajan; (iii) Philh. O, Galliera; (iv) Walter Gieseking, Philh. O, Karajan): J. S. BACH: (i) *Cantata No. 199: Mein Herze schwimmt im Blut: Auf diese Schmerzens Reu; Doch Gott muss mir genädig sein; Mein Herze schwimmt im Blut.* (ii) *Mass in B min.: Christe eleison; Et in unum Dominum; Laudamus te.* (iii) MOZART: *Nehmt meinen Dank, K.383.* (iv) GIESEKING: *Kinderlieder.* R. STRAUSS: *4 Last songs.*
(M) (**(*)) EMI CDM7 63655-2 [id.].

Long-buried treasure here includes Bach duets with Kathleen Ferrier conducted by Karajan, a collection of charming children's songs by Gieseking, recorded almost impromptu, and, best of all, a live performance of Strauss's *Four Last songs* given under Karajan at the Festival Hall in 1956, a vintage year for Schwarzkopf. Sound quality varies, but the voice is gloriously caught.

'To my friends' (with Parsons, piano): WOLF: *Mörike Lieder: Storchenbotschaft; Fussreise; Elfenlied; Bei einer Trauung; Jägerlied; Selbstgeständnis; Heimweh; Nixe Binsefuss; Mausfallen Sprüchlein; Nimmersatte Liebe; Lebe Wohl; Das verlassene Mägdlein; Auf eines altes Bild.* LOEWE: *Die wandelnde Glocke.* GRIEG: *Ein Schwan.* BRAHMS: *Mädchenlied; Am jüngsten Tag; Therese; Blinde Kuh.*
(M) *** Decca 430 000-2 [id.].

This glowing collection of Lieder was Schwarzkopf's last record and also the last recording supervised by her husband, Walter Legge. With excellent Decca sound, the charm and presence of Schwarzkopf, which in a recital conveyed extraordinary intensity right to the very end of her career, comes over vividly. Most cherishable of all are the lighter, quicker songs like *Mausfallen Sprüchlein* ('My St Trinians reading', as she herself says) and *Blinde Kuh* ('Blind man's bluff'). Superbly balanced, bringing the artists right into one's room.

The Sixteen, Harry Christophers

Music from The Eton Choirbook: BROWNE: *Salve Regina; Stabat Mater.* LAMBE: *Nesciens mater* (with Plainsong); *Stella caeli.* CORNYSHE: *Ave Maria.* WYLKYNSON: *Salve Regina.* DAVY: *Stabat Mater.*
**(*) Mer. CDE 84175; *KE 77175* [id.].

The current catalogue is not exactly overflowing with this repertoire, and these performances usefully fill a gap. They are more than a stop-gap, however, for the singing has plenty of character and a fine sense of line. Those unfamiliar with this repertoire will find these performances, which come from the early 1980s, eminently persuasive, though the sound-quality is not of consistent excellence.

Souzay, Gérard (baritone)

Mélodies (with Jacqueline Bonneau): FAURÉ: *Tristesse; Au bord de l'eau; Après un rêve; Clair de lune; Arpège; En sourdine; L'Horizon chimérique; Spleen; C'est l'extase; Prison; Mandoline.* CHAUSSON: *Nanny; Le charme; Sérénade italienne; Le Colibri; Cantique à l'épouse; Les papillons; Le temps de lilas.* Airs: BOESSET: *Me veux-tu voir mourir?.* ANON.: *Tambourin.* BATAILLE: *Cachez, beaux yeux; Ma bergère non légère.* CANTELOUBE: *Brezairola; Malurous qu'o uno fenno.*
❀ (M) (***) Decca mono 425 975-2 [id.].

The great French baritone made these recordings for Decca when he was at the very peak of his form and they have been much sought after by many collectors (and much treasured by those fortunate enough to have bought them at the time). The Fauré were recorded in 1950 and the glorious Chausson songs in 1953. Lotte Lehmann is quoted as saying that she would travel miles to hear him, and one is tempted to say that this 70-minute recital offers the best singing of the year. Souzay was endowed with the intelligence of Bernac as well as his powers of characterization, the vocal purity of Panzera and a wonderful feeling for line. The Decca transfer does complete justice to the original sound, and it is good to have these performances without the surface distractions of LP. Full texts and translations are provided. A marvellous record worth as many rosettes as stars!

Sutherland, Joan (soprano)

Russian music (with LSO, Richard Bonynge, (i) Osian Ellis; or (ii) Josef Sivo, SRO, Horst Stein): GLIÈRE: *Coloratura concerto*; (i) *Harp concerto.* STRAVINSKY: *Pastorale.* CUI: *Ici-bas.* GRETCHANINOV: *Lullaby.* (ii) GLAZUNOV: *Violin concerto.*
(M) **(*) Decca 430 006-2 [id.].

The two highly engaging concertos are discussed in the composer index. Dreamy beauty perhaps goes a little far in Sutherland's account of Stravinsky's early *Pastorale* (there is too much vocal sliding), while the Cui and Gretchaninov songs are accompanied by Richard Bonynge at the piano. The addition of Sivo's account of the Glazunov *Violin concerto* for the CD reissue is no great advantage. There is some less than ideal intonation, and the performance, though well recorded, is not distinctive.

Tebaldi, Renata (soprano)

'La Tebaldi': (arias recorded between 1955 & 1968): PUCCINI: *Madama Butterfly; La Bohème; Tosca; Gianni Schicchi; Suor Angelica; Turandot; La rondine.* BOITO: *Mefistofele.* VERDI: *Aida; Otello; Il Trovatore; La forza del destino; Don Carlo; Un ballo in maschera; Giovanna d'Arco.* ROSSINI: *Guglielmo Tell.* CILEA: *Adriana Lecouvreur; L'arlesiana.* GIORDANO: *Andrea Chénier.* CATALANI: *La Wally.* PONCHIELLI: *La Gioconda.* MASCAGNI: *Cavalleria rusticana.* REFICE: *Cecilia.*
❀ (B) *** Decca 430 481-2 (2) [id.].

This two-disc collection superbly celebrates one of the sopranos with a special place in the history of recording, the prima donna who in the early days of LP most clearly reflected a great period of operatic expansion. Unlike her great rival, Callas, thrilling, dynamic, unpredictable, often edgy and uneven on record, Tebaldi was above all reliable, with her creamy-toned voice, exceptionally even from top to bottom, and with its natural warmth ideally suited to recording. The 24 items here, entirely devoted to the Italian opera, cover the full range of her repertory from her justly famous assumption of the role of Butterfly to her personification of Leonora in *La forza del destino*, while she was an unforgettably moving Mimì in *La Bohème*. Many of the items are taken from the complete sets she recorded for Decca, generally more freely expressive than those originally issued on recital discs. The actual interpretations are totally consistent, though over the years the detail grew ever more refined. Excellent transfers. An indispensable set for all those who respond to this lovely voice, bringing a magical feeling of vulnerability to her personifications, when she creates a gentle, glowing pianissimo.

'The Early Recordings': VERDI: *Aida: Act I, Ritorna vincitor!; Act III* (complete; with Stignani, Caselli, Protti, del Monaco, Ac. di Santa Cecilia Ch. & O, Erede); *Il Trovatore: Tacea la notte placida.* Arias from: GOUNOD: *Faust.* PUCCINI: *Madama Butterfly; Manon Lescaut; Tosca; La Bohème.*
(M) (***) Decca mono 425 989-2 [id.].

This fascinating collection includes the very first records Tebaldi made for Decca in November 1949, in effect the start of a new era in operatic recording. More recital recordings were made in 1951. (I. M. remembers the great impact her initial mono LP made on him at the time, with the ravishing bloom of her lyrical line bringing a frisson of excitement and sentient pleasure which he has never forgotten). This led to her early version of *Aida* of 1952, here represented by Act III, opposite two of her regular partners, neither showing anything like her finesse: the coarse Mario del Monaco and the colourless Aldo Protti, firmer here than he was to become. Though her later recordings are more refined in expressive detail, the freshness of these performances is a delight and, with the reservations noted concerning the mixed blessings of the *Aida* cast, our Rosette for her two-disc set, above, could be extended to cover many of the earlier items included here. Good transfers.

Tibbett, Lawrence (baritone)

'Tibbett in opera': excerpts from: LEONCAVALLO: *Pagliacci.* BIZET: *Carmen.* PUCCINI: *Tosca.* VERDI: *Un ballo in maschera; Simon Boccanegra; Rigoletto; Otello.* ROSSINI: *Il barbiere di Siviglia.* GOUNOD: *Faust.* WAGNER: *Tannhäuser, Die Walküre.*
(M) (***) Nimbus mono NI 7825 [id.].

The scale and resonance of Lawrence Tibbett's voice come over vividly in this fine selection of his recordings made between 1926 and 1939. The Nimbus process allows the rapid vibrato in his voice to emerge naturally, giving the sound a thrilling richness in all these varied items. Particularly interesting is the longest, the whole of *Wotan's farewell*, with Stokowski conducting the Philadelphia Orchestra in 1934. It is an over-the-top performance that carries total conviction, even if the sheer volume produces some clangorous resonances in the Nimbus transfer. Also memorable is the celebrated *Boccanegra* Council chamber sequence, recorded in 1939 with Martinelli and Rose Bampton in the ensemble.

A CHOICE OF PENGUINS

Brian Epstein: The Man Who Made the Beatles Ray Coleman

'An excellent biography of Brian Epstein, the lonely, gifted man whose artistic faith and bond with the Beatles never wavered – and whose recognition of genius created a cultural era, even though it destroyed him' – *Mail on Sunday*

A Thief in the Night John Cornwell

A veil of suspicion and secrecy surrounds the last hours of Pope John Paul I, whose thirty-three day reign ended in a reported heart attack on the night of 28 September 1978. Award-winning crime writer John Cornwell was invited by the Vatican to investigate. 'The best detective story you will ever read' – *Daily Mail*

Among the Russians Colin Thubron

One man's solitary journey by car across Russia provides an enthralling and revealing account of the habits and idiosyncrasies of a fascinating people. 'He sees things with the freshness of an innocent and the erudition of a scholar' – *Daily Telegraph*

Higher than Hope Fatima Meer

The authorized biography of Nelson Mandela. 'An astonishing read ... the most complete, authoritative and moving tribute thus far' – *Time Out*

Stones of Aran: Pilgrimage Tim Robinson

Arainn is the largest of the three Aran Islands, and one of the world's oldest landscapes. This 'wholly irresistible' (*Observer*) and uncategorizable book charts a sunwise journey around its coast – and explores an open secret, teasing out the paradoxes of a terrain at once bare and densely inscribed.

Bernard Shaw Michael Holroyd
Volume I 1856–1898: The Search for Love

'In every sense, a spectacular piece of work ... A feat of style as much as of research, which will surely make it a flamboyant new landmark in modern English life-writing' – Richard Holmes in *The Times*

THE PENGUIN GUIDE TO COMPACT DISCS

Edward Greenfield, Robert Layton and Ivan March

***The Penguin Guide to Compact Discs* is the biggest and most comprehensive survey of classical music on CD ever published: an indispensable guide designed to help you make an informed choice from the vast and bewildering range of recordings currently on sale.**

Listing the major recordings of each work alphabetically by composer, the book evaluates the interpretation and performance of each work, assesses which is the most realistic recording and – with many new mid-price and bargain CDs available – offers advice on the best value for money.

Replacing *The New Penguin Guide to Compact Discs and Cassettes*, this fully revised and updated guide includes:

•ALL THE LATEST IMPORTANT CD RELEASES
•THE BEST OF THE OLD CATALOGUE
•BEST BUYS
•BARGAIN AND MID-PRICED CDs
•THE NEW 'SUPER BARGAIN' CDs
•IMPORTANT COLLECTIONS AND RECITALS ON CD

'The authors' scope and zeal are stunning, their standards of judgement and accuracy high' – *Sunday Times*

'A magnificent achievement' – Edward Heath

'To anyone concerned with serious music it will be absolutely invaluable' – Sir Ian Trethowan

'The authors have set high standards of accuracy, "user-friendliness" and critical acumen in their previous books, and they have again lived up to them' – *Gramophone*